Helen Dawson.

Love's Redeeming Work

Love's Redeeming Work

The Anglican Quest for Holiness

COMPILED BY

GEOFFREY ROWELL, KENNETH STEVENSON

AND

ROWAN WILLIAMS

OXFORD

UNIVERSITY PRESS

OXFORD
UNIVERSITY PRESS

Great Clarendon Street, Oxford, OX2 6DP,
United Kingdom

Oxford University Press is a department of the University of Oxford.
It furthers the University's objective of excellence in research, scholarship,
and education by publishing worldwide. Oxford is a registered trade mark of
Oxford University Press in the UK and in certain other countries

Published in the United States of America by Oxford University Press
198 Madison Avenue, New York, NY 10016, United States of America

British Library Cataloguing in Publication Data

Data available

ISBN 978-0-19-107058-7

Contents

PART 2 · 1650–1830

PART 3 · 1830–2001

Preface

BOTH inside and outside the Anglican Communion, the question is often heard about where the centre of Anglican identity really lies. Anglicans have never defined themselves in terms of any confession of faith other than allegiance to Scripture and the ancient creeds, and that has been seen as both strength and weakness over the centuries. But it is not accurate to say that beyond these basic criteria there is no distinctive Anglican theological and devotional style. Even leaving out of consideration the Prayer Book and the Thirty-Nine Articles, there are themes and emphases that help to define a very distinctive way of being a Catholic and Reformed Christian; and this anthology seeks to present some of these with as much breadth of range as possible.

The hope of the editors is that this book will be not only a tool of study but what earlier Christian generations called an *encheiridion*—a handbook for faithful living, a resource for wisdom in leading an intelligent, humble, and grateful life of discipleship. It has already found enthusiastic readers throughout the Anglican Communion and has been a significant interpreter of the Anglican heritage more widely. I trust that it will play its part in a renaissance of Anglican theology, equipped to meet the challenges of the new millennium by learning to draw on the deepest sources of Anglican witness to the word and works of God.

✠ ROWAN CANTUAR:

We owe a debt of gratitude to many people. Among those who helped us with researching extracts or answering queries we would like to thank in particular the following: Canon Donald Allchin, the Very Revd Peter Barrett, the Revd Gregory Cameron, Dr Elizabeth Clarke, Canon Dr Christopher Cocksworth, the Revd Professor Timothy Gorringe, the Revd Professor Stuart Hall, Dr Douglas Hedley, Dr Bruce Hindmarsh, Ms Denise Inge, the Rt Revd Colin James, the Rt Revd Noel Jones, the Revd Fergus King, Canon Graham Kings, the Revd Brian Macdonald–Milne, Mr Calum MacFarlane, Mrs Jean Marshall, Canon Arthur Middleton, the Revd Dr Charles Miller, Dr Peter Nockles, the Rt Revd Peter Nott, the Revd Dr Daniel O'Connor, Dr Muriel Porter, the Rt Revd Paul Richardson, the Revd Mother Rosemary, SLG., Dr Julia Smith, Miss Elisabeth Stevenson, the Revd Canon Dr Patrick Thomas, Mr Ian Thompson, the late Revd Dr Gordon Wakefield, Dr John Walsh, the Revd Professor Louis Weil, and the Revd Canon Dr Alan Wilkinson, together with the Principal and Librarians of Pusey House, Oxford, and the Warden and staff of St Deiniol's Library, Hawarden.

Particular thanks are also due to those who gave considerable assistance with a host of practical tasks, amongst whom special mention must be made of the Revd Andrew Tremlett, chaplain to the Bishop of Portsmouth, Miss Vicky Wilson, secretary to the Bishop of Basingstoke, and Mrs Jean Maslin and Ms Julie Anderson, secretaries to the Bishop of Portsmouth, together with Mr Adam Watkinson, head of religious studies at Hutton Grammar School, Lancashire, who was of sterling service during a week's intensive sifting of texts at St Deiniol's Library.

GEOFFREY ROWELL
KENNETH STEVENSON
ROWAN WILLIAMS

Michaelmas, 2000

Acknowledgements

The Publishers and Compilers are grateful for permission to reprint from the following:

Eric Symes Abbott: extracts reprinted from *Invitation to Prayer* (Forward Movement Publications, 1989), by permission of the publisher.

Aiyadurai Jesudasen Appasamy: extracts reprinted from *The Johannine Doctrine of Life: A Study of Christian and Indian Thought* (SPCK, 1934), by permission of the publishers.

George Kennedy Allen Bell: extract reprinted from *The Church and Humanity* (Longman, 1946), by permission of Pearson Education Ltd.

R F C Browne: extracts reprinted from *The Ministry of the Word* (SCM Press, 1958), by permission of the publishers.

Christopher Rex Bryant, SSJE: extract reprinted from *The River Within: The Search for God in Depth* (Darton Longman & Todd Ltd, 1978), copyright © Darton Longman & Todd Ltd 1978, by permission of the publishers.

Ernest H. Burgmann: extract reprinted from *The Education of an Australian* (1991), reprinted by permission of the publisher, St Marks National Theological Centre, Australia.

Owen Chadwick: extract reprinted from *Michael Ramsey: A Life* (Clarendon Press, 1990), by permission of the author.

Mother Mary Clare, SLG: extracts reprinted from *Encountering the Depths* edited by Ralph Townsend (Darton Longman & Todd Ltd, 1981), copyright © Darton Longman & Todd Ltd 1981, by permission of the publishers.

Frederick Donald Coggan: extracts reprinted from *The Servant Son: Jesus Then and Now* (SPCK, 1995) and from *Meet Paul* (SPCK, 1998), by permission of the publishers.

John MacLeod Campbell Crum: 'O Lord Jesus, I Adore Thee' translated from the original by John Mauburn, reprinted from *Hymns Ancient and Modern Revised* (1972), by permission of Hymns Ancient and Modern, Norwich.

Joan de Mel: extract reprinted from *Lakdasa de Mel—God's Servant—World Citizen—Lanka's Son* (ISPCK, 1980), by permission of the publisher.

Father Denis, SSF: extract reprinted from *Father Algy* (1964), by permission of the publishers, Hodder & Stoughton Ltd.

F. W. Dillistone: extract reprinted from *Charles Raven: Naturalist, Historian, Theologian* (1975), by permission of the publishers, Hodder & Stoughton Ltd.

George Eglington Alson (Dom Gregory) Dix: extract reprinted from *The Shape of the Liturgy* (Dacre, 1945/Continuum 2001), by permission of The Continuum International Publishing Group Ltd.

Alan Ecclestone: extracts reprinted from *Yes to God* (Darton Longman & Todd Ltd, 1975), copyright © Darton Longman & Todd Ltd 1975, and from *Staircase for Silence* (Darton Longman & Todd Ltd, 1977), copyright © Darton Longman & Todd Ltd 1977, by permission of the publishers.

T. S. Eliot: lines from 'Choruses from *The Rock*' (1934), copyright 1936 by Harcourt, Inc, copyright © 1964, 1963 by T. S. Eliot, lines from 'The Dry Salvages', copyright 1941 by T. S. Eliot and renewed 1969 by Esme Valerie Eliot, and lines from 'Little Gidding', copyright 1942 by T. S. Eliot and renewed 1970 by Esme Valerie Eliot, both from *Four*

Quartets, all reprinted from *Collected Poems 1909–1962* (1963); and extract reprinted from *Murder in the Cathedral* (1934), copyright 1935 by Harcourt, Inc and renewed 1963 by T. S. Eliot, all by permission of the publishers, Faber & Faber Ltd and Harcourt, Inc.

Austin Marsden Farrer: extract reprinted from 'Engaging the will of God' in *God and the Universe: A course of sermons preached in the Chapel of Pusey House, Oxford* (Mowbray, 1960), by permission of The Continuum International Publishing Group Ltd; extracts reprinted from *Interpretation and Belief* edited by Charles Conti (SPCK, 1976) and from *Words for Life* edited by Charles Conti and Leslie Houlden (SPCK, 1993), by permission of the publishers.

Charles Gore: extracts reprinted from *St Paul's Epistle to the Ephesians* (John Murray, 1902), and from *The Incarnation of the Son of God* (John Murray, 1891), by permission of John Murray (Publishers) Ltd.

Adrian Hastings: extract reprinted from *Robert Runcie* (Mowbray, 1991), by permission of The Continuum International Publishing Group Ltd.

Henry Ernest (Father Andrew, sdc) Hardy: extracts reprinted from *The Life and Letters of Father Andrew* sdc edited by Kathleen E. Burne (1948), by permission of The Continuum International Publishing Group Ltd.

Gwen Harwood: 'Revival Rally' reprinted from *Collected Poems* (OUP, Oxford 1991) and 'Death Has No Features of His Own' reprinted from *The Lion's Bride* (Angus & Robertson, Sydney, 1981), by permission of the Estate of Gwen Harwood.

Arthur Cayley Headlam: extract reprinted from *The Building of the Church of Christ: University and other sermons* (John Murray, 1928), by permission of John Murray (Publishers) Ltd.

Herbert Hensley Henson: extract reprinted from *The Creed in the Pulpit* (1908), by permission of the publishers, Hodder & Stoughton Ltd.

Herbert Arthur Hodges: extract reprinted from *The Pattern of Atonement* (SCM Press, 1955), by permission of the publishers; extract reprinted from 'The self disclosure of God' in *God and the Universe: A course of sermons preached in the Chapel of Pusey House, Oxford* (Mowbray, 1960), by permission of The Continuum International Publishing Group Ltd.

Roger Hardman Hooker: extract reprinted from *Uncharted Journeys* (CMS, 1973, by permission of the Church Mission Society as copyright holders.

Edwyn Clement Hoskyns: extracts reprinted from *Cambridge Sermons* (SPCK, 1938), by permission of the publishers.

Shirley Carter Hughson: extracts reprinted from *The Spiritual Letters of Father Hughson* (Mowbray, 1953), by permission of The Continuum International Publishing Group Ltd.

William Ralph Inge: extract reprinted from *Faith and Knowledge: Sermons* (T. & T. Clark Ltd, 1905) by permission of the publishers; extracts reprinted from *Goodness and Truth* (Mowbray, 1958), by permission of The Continuum International Publishing Group Ltd; and extract reprinted from *The Gate of Life* (Longmans, Green & Co, 1958), by permission of Pearson Education Ltd.

Eric James: extracts reprinted from *A Life of Bishop John A. T. Robinson: Scholar, Pastor, Prophet* (Collins, 1987), by permission of HarperCollins Publishers Ltd.

Herbert H. Kelly, ssm: extracts reprinted from *The Gospel of God* (SCM Press, 1959), and from *Catholicity* (SCM Press, 1932), by permission of the publishers.

Graham Kings: Letter 31, 19 October 1965, reprinted from *Christianity Connected: Hindus, Muslims and the World in the Letters of Max Warren and Roger Hooker* (Boekencentrum, 2001), by permission of the author.

C. S. Lewis: extract from *Mere Christianity* (G. Bles, 1952), copyright © C. S. Lewis Pte. Ltd. 1942, 1943, 1944, 1952, and extract from *The Weight of Glory and Other Addresses* (Wm B.

Eerdmans, 1965), copyright © C. S. Lewis Pte. Ltd. 1949, both reprinted by permission of The C. S. Lewis Company; extract from *A Grief Observed* (rev. ed. 1966), copyright © C. S. Lewis Pte. Ltd. 1961, reprinted by permission of The C. S. Lewis Company and the publishers, Faber & Faber Ltd. 'Prayer', 'No Beauty We Could Desire', and 'Footnote to Prayers' from *Poems* (G. Bles, 1964), copyright © The Executors of the Estate of C. S. Lewis 1994 and renewed 1992 by C. S. Lewis Pte. Ltd; and extracts from *Letters to Malcolm: Chiefly on Prayer* (G. Bles, 1964), copyright © C. S. Lewis Pte. Ltd. 1963, 1964, and renewed 1991, 1992 by Arthur Owen Barfield; all reprinted by permission of The C. S. Lewis Company and Harcourt, Inc.

Margaret Lycett: extract reprinted from *Brothers: The story of the Nature Brotherhood of Melanesia* (SPCK, 1935), by permission of the publishers.

Henry Robert McAdoo: extracts reprinted from *Anglican Heritage: Theology and Spirituality* (Canterbury Press, 1991), by permission of the Estate of Archbishop McAdoo, c/o Orpen Franks, Solicitors, Dublin.

Eric Milner-White: extracts reprinted from *My God, My Glory: Aspirations, Acts and Prayers on the Desire for God* (SPCK, 1954), by kind permission of the Friends of York Minster.

David Freestone (Dom Augustine, OSB) Morris: extract reprinted from *Straight Course to God* (Nashdom Abbey, 1949), by permission of the Abbot of Elmore Abbey.

Stephen C. Neill: extracts reprinted from *Christian Holiness* (The Lutterworth Press, 1960), by permission of the publisher.

Hubert Northcott, CR: extracts reprinted from *The Venture of Prayer* (SPCK, 1954), by permission of the publishers.

William Braithwaite O'Brien, SSJE: extracts reprinted from *A Cowley Father's Letters: selected from the letters of W. B. O'Brien* SSJE (Darton Longman & Todd Ltd, 1962), copyright © Darton Longman & Todd Ltd 1962, by permission of the publishers.

Richard Godfrey Parsons: 'We Hail Thy Presence Glorious' reprinted from *New English Hymnal* (1986), by permission of Hymns Ancient and Modern, Norwich.

David Penman: extract reprinted from *A Garden of Many Colours: The report of the Archbishop's Commission on multicultural ministry and mission* presented to the synod of the Anglican Diocese of Melbourne, March 1985, by permission of the Anglican Diocese of Melbourne.

William Gostwyck Charles (Dom Denys, OSB) Prideaux: extracts reprinted from *Laudate*, June 1929 and December 1944, by permission of the Abbot of Elmore Abbey.

Michael Ramsey: extracts reprinted from *The Christian Priest Today* (SPCK, 1972) and extract reprinted from *Canterbury Pilgrim* (SPCK, 1974), by permission of the publishers; extract reprinted from *Be Still and Know: A Study in the Life of Prayer* (Collins Fount, 1982 in association with Faith Press) copyright © Michael Ramsey 1982, by permission of The Zondervon Corporation, a division of HarperCollins Publishers.

Timothy Rees: 'Thirsting for God' reprinted from *Edward Keble Talbot: His Community and His Friends* compiled by G. P. H. Pawson CR (SPCK, 1954) by permission of the publishers.

R. E. Roberts: extract reprinted from *H. R. L. Sheppard, Life and Letters* (John Murray, 1942), by permission of John Murray (Publishers) Ltd.

Emani Sambayya: extract reprinted from 'The Genius of the Anglican Communion'; in E. R. Morgan and Roger Lloyd (eds): *The Mission of the Anglican Communion* (SPCK, 1948), by permission of the publishers.

Teddy Saunders and Hugh Sansom: extract reprinted from *David Watson: A Biography* (1992), by permission of the publishers, Hodder & Stoughton Ltd.

Dorothy Leigh Sayers: extract reprinted from *The Mind of the Maker* (Mowbray, 1994), by permission of The Continuum International Publishing Group Ltd.

Gilbert Shaw: extracts reprinted from 'The Service of Love' and 'A Last Homily', copyright © SLG Charitable Trust Ltd, by permission of Mother Rosemary SLG.

Edward Keble Talbot: extracts reprinted from *Retreat Addresses of Edward Keble Talbot* edited by Lucy Menzies (SPCK, 1954), by permission of the publishers.

John V. Taylor: 'Siesta' and 'Love's Self-Opening', Prayer for the blessing of a Parish Priest, extracts reprinted from *A Matter of Life and Death* (SCM, 1986) including Prayer of Daily Dedication, and extracts from a letter published in *The Church Mission Society and World Christianity 1799–1999* edited by Kevin Ward and Brian Stanley (Cambridge University Press, 2000), all by permission of the literary executor of the Estate of John Taylor.

William Temple: extracts reprinted from *Christian Faith and the Life: Being eight addresses delivered in The University Church at Oxford* (SCM Press, 1931), by permission of the publishers; extracts reprinted from *Personal Religion and the Life of Fellowship* (Longmans, Green & Co, 1926), by permission of Pearson Education Ltd.

Ronald Stuart Thomas: 'Crucifixion' reprinted from *Counterpoint* (Bloodaxe Books, 1990), and 'Bleak Liturgies' reprinted from *Mass for Hard Times* (Bloodaxe Books, 1992), by permission of the publishers; 'Via Negativa' reprinted from *H'm* (Macmillan, 1972); and 'Poste Restante' and 'The Bright Field' reprinted from *Laboratories of the Spirit* (Macmillan, 1975), by permission of the Estate of R. S. Thomas.

William Turton: 'O Thou, Who at Thy Eucharist Didst Pray' reprinted from *New English Hymnal* (1986), by permission of Hymns Ancient and Modern, Norwich.

Evelyn Underhill: extracts reprinted from *The Letters of Evelyn Underhill* edited by Charles Williams (Longmans, Green & Co, 1943); from *Abba: Meditations Based on the Lord's Prayer* (Longmans, Green & Co, 1945); and from *The Mount of Purification (with Meditations and Prayers, 1949, and Collected Papers 1946* (Longmans, 1960), by permission of Pearson Education Ltd; extracts reprinted from *Fragments from an Inner Life: The Notebooks of Evelyn Underhill* edited by Dana Greene (1993), copyright © 1993 Dana Greene, by permission of The Underhill Estate.

William Hubert Vanstone: extracts reprinted from *Love Endeavour, Love's Expense: The Response of Being to the Love of God* (Darton Longman & Todd Ltd, 1977), copyright © Darton Longman & Todd Ltd 1977, by permission of the publishers.

Alexander Roper Vidler: extracts reprinted from *Essays in Liberality* (SCM Press, 1957), and from *Windsor Sermons* (SCM Press, 1958), by permission of the publishers.

Reginald Somerset Ward: extracts reprinted from *To Jerusalem: Devotional Studies in Mystical Religion* (Mowbray/Morehouse 1994), from *Reginald Somerset Ward 1991–1962: His Life and Letters* edited by Edmund R. Morgan (Mowbray, 1963), and from *The Mind of the Maker* (Mowbray, 1994), by permission of The Continuum International Publishing Group Ltd.

Charles Walter Stanesby Williams: extracts reprinted from *The Descent of the Dove: A Short History of the Holy Spirit in the Church* (Wm Eerdmans, 1939), and from *The Image of the City and other Essays* selected by Anne Ridler (OUP, 1958), by permission of David Higham Associates.

J. M. Winter and D. M. Joslin (Eds): extracts reprinted from *R. H. Tawney's Commonplace Book* (Cambridge University Press, 1972), by permission of the publisher.

Sir Frank Woods: extracts reprinted from *Sermons and Addresses: Forward in Depth* edited by Brian Porter (JBCE, 1987), by permission of Uniting Education, PO Box 1245, Collingwood 3066, Australia.

Although every effort has been made to trace and contact copyright holders prior to publication, this has not been possible in every case. If notified the publishers will be pleased to rectify any errors or omissions at the earliest opportunity.

General Introduction
The Anglican Quest for Holiness

NOTORIOUSLY, different groups within Anglicanism like to claim that they are the *real* heirs of the classical tradition established in the first century and a half of independent Anglican life. Those in the evangelical corner emphasize that the English Reformation was an affirmation of the absolute supremacy of scripture in all matters affecting the Church; some would—like their predecessors in the sixteenth century—add that the Reformation was therefore an unfinished process, and that the purifying of the Church according to biblical principles must be taken further in each generation. Those from the catholic wing will stress the concern of sixteenth– and seventeenth–century Anglicans to preserve the forms of ministry handed down from the earliest days of the Church, and their sense of spiritual and sacramental continuity with the early Fathers and the faith of the 'undivided Church'; quite often, *they* will add that the feverish intensity of the period distorted the proper character and calling of the Anglican Church by allying it to various Protestant principles that were really extraneous to the central business of creating a reformed, non–papal Catholicism, based on a renewed sacramental life. Liberals point out the way in which early Anglicans had to live with diversity and never bound themselves too tightly to a single confessional formula focused on specific theological principles, in contrast to the Reformed Churches of the continent of Europe; and they would probably add (like the evangelicals, but with a different agenda) that the process of reformation continues, and that the doctrinal formulae still taken for granted at the beginnings of Anglicanism are open for reinterpretation. They might also say that, since Anglicanism has never taken the line that scripture alone is the source of true doctrine, they have the advantage of being able to use the results of biblical criticism without anxiety, and to move away from the literal injunctions of the Bible without feeling that the essence of their Christian identity has been betrayed.

It is interesting that all three groups can sometimes have the same heroes. Archbishop Cranmer, Richard Hooker and George Herbert, for example, have been venerated and appealed to by a remarkable spectrum of Anglicans; and this is perhaps not irrelevant to the question of where the heart of Anglicanism lies. Each of these three figures was in fact deeply embroiled in controversy, each had firm theological convictions; but each came to stand for a style of Christian language available to people of rather varied perspectives. Their achievement was to give English–speaking Christians a way of talking about God and about the Christian life that was not confined to those who shared their particular theological concerns within the controversies of their day. How did they manage this? One plausible answer is that they all did their theology less by the systematic examining of doctrinal structures than by reflecting on the shape of Christian life. They did this, of course, in widely differing ways—Cranmer by liturgical composition (his works of theological controversy were far less vividly remembered, even in the sixteenth century), Hooker by relating his theological concerns to the overarching principle of 'law', understood as the transmission of God's wisdom as a pattern for human wholeness and justice, and Herbert by a very specially intense and concentrated expression of how human struggle and questioning are both received and transformed by God—a God who unmistakably speaks to his human creatures, but often speaks in the most unexpected words.

This should not be taken to suggest that the doctrinal structures were of no importance to them, let alone that their language for Christian living and understanding could be preserved unchanged if the fundamental doctrines were different or absent. That is a very typically modern misreading. But it is true that the coherence of their Christian worldviews depends less on system than on a sense of what a human life looks like when it is in the process of being transformed by God in Christ. To call this approach 'pragmatic' in the usual sense is not helpful if it implies that their only concern was what works in practice; but it is pragmatic to the extent that they all sought to answer the question, 'What should I do and say as someone brought into the communion of Christ's faithful people?' For them, thinking about God was closely bound up with thinking about how human beings became holy, came to show in their lives the grace and the glory of God. And that is part of the background to the present collection of texts. We have begun by asking how Anglican holiness has been defined and imagined over the last three and a half centuries or so, in the conviction that an answer to that will tell us more about what is distinctive—and valuable—in Anglicanism than a good deal of past and current discussion of Anglican attitudes to authority or ministry or the sacraments. If holy lives are recognizable, there is a prima facie case for believing that some kind of unity in doctrine is being taken for granted; and the job of theology will be to draw out what that might be, rather than to clear up all possible controversies before anyone is allowed to recognize holiness.

But there is of course an element of circularity in this. If we begin from the common language of holy lives, we shall probably develop a degree of hesitancy about just how final and exhaustive we think some theological formulations to be. George Herbert's poem (unpublished until the modern period), below, pp. 171–2, on the eucharistic controversies of his day is a good example: he sets out with clarity and feeling why Christians might equally believe in an 'objective' presence in the eucharistic bread and in a direct spiritual communication with the soul through the elements of Holy Communion. He dismisses transubstantiation as a misconceived technicality that shifts the emphasis of the sacrament away from where it belongs, away from the process of *our* transformation and assurance. But he will not commit himself finally to a single theological model as capturing everything that matters about the sacrament. Likewise, Hooker's objection to Puritan appeals for further and more radical reformation of Church and ministry has a lot to do with his wariness about imagining that there is a finally satisfactory pattern for church order established straightforwardly by Christ and revealed in scripture: history and experience have their place in the unfolding of God's wisdom. Even Cranmer, who was not at all indifferent about theological language, works through nuance and echo, through a mixture of almost invisible precision and very deliberate ambiguity, in his formation of a vocabulary for public prayer. And this hesitancy about exact and exclusive verbal formulation in turn allows some latitude in the recognition of holiness even across the boundaries of controversy.

What needs stressing, especially in the contemporary climate, is that the touch of scepticism evident here is not at all a laissez–faire approach to basic theological data and dogma. It would be more accurate to say that the great doctrinal themes are a steady backdrop, sensed and believed but not to be pulled centre–stage for debate and explanation; an inhabited landscape rather than an Ordnance Survey map. We need to understand the difference between two kinds of scepticism, in fact. There is a natural scepticism that has to do with self–protection against being made a fool of: how do I know anything for sure? I am always likely to be deceived, so I do better to reserve my options and commit myself to as little as possible. But there is also a reflective and theological scepticism: I am always ready to deceive *myself*, because my passions distort clear judgement. I am a fallen being whose mind is readily swayed by selfish concern and idleness or cowardice. The former kind of scepticism is usually revolutionary: let us rise up and destroy the systems that have deceived us, the authorities that have falsely claimed to be able to tell us the truth. The latter is conservative: if I so often deceive myself, I need the presence of history and community to check my self–obsessions. I can only move by tracing analogies and probabilities, by a very patient listening and looking and not being afraid of depending on others. And this second form of scepticism is very characteristic of much of the Anglican style over the centuries.

Where does this come from in Anglican history? The answer is quite complex. For a start, it has a lot to do with two distinct themes in Reformation thinking. There is, first, the conviction of most Reformed Christians that humanity has travelled a long way from where it ought to be, and that this journey from home has radical effects upon our innate human capacities for learning and knowing. But there is also a conviction, more evident perhaps in the English Reformation than in the continental movements, that the system of medieval Catholicism had made the faith something bound to earthly and material objects administered by a priestly caste who formed a kind of society alongside 'ordinary' human community (nation, family). The hidden and mysterious world of faith had been reduced to a tangible realm on earth; grace was doled out as if it were a commodity, and the realm of God had been distorted into a human system of power competing—sometimes violently and savagely—with others. Reformed faith refused to identify the sphere of faith with a visibly separate order here on earth, with (as the Reformers saw it) the 'pseudo–state' of the medieval Church. Faith transformed the relations of human beings as they concretely existed in family and society; it worked from within—not in a way that excluded the necessity of external change (a bizarre misunderstanding of this conviction), but by transfiguring the whole of our motivation, so that there is no longer any question of good being done only in order to discharge an external obligation and win a specific reward.

This concern with interiority meant that Anglicans, like other Reformed Christians, were alert to the importance of *hiddenness* in Christian life. Appearances were not to be relied upon; externals were at best ambiguous signs. The works of God were not simply to be read off from visible phenomena. Some scholars have noted the way in which Reformation thought in general underlined the importance of hearing rather than seeing as the main metaphor for receiving revealed truth, since hearing is more obviously *passive* or receptive than seeing. Thus there are further theological grounds for a sort of scepticism, in addition to the overall mistrust of the fallen intellect. The tangible, visible showings of Christian truth are pointers at best, not objects in which faith may find certainty to be possessed. Even hearing is not wholly secure, for the words spoken of God in theology and preaching need to be chastened and interrupted by God. Herbert, in his advice for the parish priest in the pulpit, recommends that the preacher sometimes pause and ask God to interpret for those listeners what has been said and reinforce its message. God is invited to 'interrupt' the sermon in the prayer, uttered or silent, which the preacher addresses to him. In Herbert's poetry, the meditative expression of belief or of devout feeling is regularly broken into by the stark and usually monosyllabic words of God: 'Your suit is granted', 'Child', 'You must sit down'. The best language for God is one that draws back to leave God room to speak in his own right.

The modern reader will probably react with mixed feelings. Surely, we may say, the stress on the inner life as opposed to the outward sign, the encouragement of a certain detachment with regard to the material world, and the denial of 'independent' life to the Church is exactly what has been so wrong with so much of Christianity across the centuries. But we have to read all this very carefully against the background of what the English Reformers were consciously opposing. They were chiefly concerned to deny that grace could be locked up in objects or guaranteed by the Church's management, and that the Church was a kind of extra 'nation', with its own government and officers and citizens existing alongside the political orders of the world. At best, the theology which was built upon this suspicion was a way of affirming the presence of grace in the ordinary associations of human life—but grace considered as God in *action* towards us rather than as solidified lumps of divine benevolence; and it is very characteristic of Anglican sacramental theology (as in the poem of Herbert's already referred to) to emphasize the presence of God as action rather than object in the sacrament: God is truly *there*, objectively present in a way that certainly doesn't depend on the believer's mental processes; but God is not there as the product of a human performance or as a passive object to be contemplated from outside.

Of course, this general approach explains why Anglicans, up to the beginning of the nineteenth century, commended as one of the loftiest virtues the ideal of 'passive obedience'. The natural order of society was by no means guaranteed to be just; this is, after all, a deeply fallen world. But if it is unjust, our task is not to resist but to suffer—to 'obey' by taking the consequences of non–compliance with the state, rather than calling for revolution. Hence the language, at first sight rather strange, of Lancelot Andrewes, early in the seventeenth century, about the essentially non–violent character of Christianity—strange because of the un-doubted violence of the way political power was exercised by Anglicans, including Anglican prelates, at the time. But there is no insincerity here: there is a genuine appeal to the spiritual priority of self–doubt in public matters. We are liable to deceit here as elsewhere; we can disguise our selfish passion and ambition as zeal for the public good, and so produce the sort of division in society that poisons the whole social world. The 'Prayer for Unity' included in the 1662 Prayer Book's order of thanksgiving for the anniversary of the monarch's accession is often used these days as a prayer for unity between Christians. But when it speaks of 'the great dangers we are in by our unhappy divisions' and prays that 'we may henceforth be all of one heart, and of one soul, united in one holy bond of Truth and Peace, of Faith and Charity', its primary focus is social conflict rather than theological. It is directed against acts that would fracture the good order and mutual charity of the commonwealth as a whole.

This could be and often was both an oppressive scheme of thought and a recipe for personal moralism combined with indifference about public injustice. But it also took for granted a strong doctrine of the obligations that power brought. Anyone studying the sixteenth–century texts that lay out the duties of different orders of persons in the commonwealth will realize that the last thing they want to commend is tyrannical power: and up to the mid–nineteenth century injunctions continued to be uttered that fathers, employers, gentry and monarchs should use their power strictly for the welfare and advancement of those they ruled. It is one of many areas in which Anglican piety carried a strong echo of Augustine's teachings. Beyond dispute, it was a highly ambiguous aspect of the Anglican spiritual heritage, but it should not be assumed that it was a covert way of defending brutal absolutism. It was often Tory Anglicans in the nineteenth century who protested most vigorously against the effects of industrialism and the inhumanity of supposedly efficient methods of dealing with the poor and destitute—even though they were increasingly confused about what practical political solutions could be offered.

The deeper dimensions of this sceptical and interior spirit can be seen in numerous writers. We have noted Herbert's subversive silences and interruptions in his language about God; his junior contemporary and admirer, Henry Vaughan, celebrated the divine darkness in terms that owe a great deal to the

Eastern Christian and Platonic tradition of speaking about God in paradoxes where light and dark, knowledge and ignorance, are brought together. Vaughan's imagery, like that of John of the Cross, freely combines the themes of night, escape, loss, and erotic yearning. Hooker will say of God that our best eloquence is silence; and his reluctance to use the Bible as a sole authority to clinch every debate reflects his sense that the Bible is a book always *being read* by a historical community, whose corporate sense of what scripture says and skills in 'translating' scriptural doctrine into new situations must equally be taken with theological seriousness. Bishop Butler in the eighteenth century sought to establish that the way we learned about God's revealed purpose was not wholly alien to the way we learned about the world we inhabited—by analogy, probability, the gradual development of trust in the common life of humanity. In natural as in supernatural learning, clear evidence would take us only so far; there always remained the intuitive connection that would bind us to a conclusion or a commitment. Newman, in the next century, developed this still further in both his Anglican and his Roman Catholic days. It is not an exaggeration to say that his characteristic appeals to probability and intuition were among the gifts he brought to his new communion from the old.

But the mention of Newman reminds us of how far Anglican thought had moved by the late nineteenth century. The loosening of traditional social bonds by industrialization, the new Poor Laws, new levels of social mobility and diversity—and of course the growing move towards toleration for Protestant Dissenters and Roman Catholics, culminating in the 1820s and early 1830s with Catholic Emancipation and the First Reform Act—all contributed to the dissolution of much of what had been thought of as near the heart of Anglican piety. While the Evangelical movement of the early nineteenth century was more than anything a renewal and intensification of an earlier age's concern with the inner life, distinguished by a greater emphasis on authentic feeling and a fuller vision of how this might 'cash out' in the morality of public life, the Tractarians, drawing on earlier theologies of the divine authority of the ordained ministry and on the historic continuities between Reformed English Christianity and medieval Catholicism, took a new and radical path.

They appealed against the way that the historic Anglican consensus had developed to a clearer theology of the Church's essential independence, to the direct spiritual authority of the ordained ministry working fully and effectively without any mediation from the political order. They encouraged the reintroduction into Anglicanism of monastic life, which for the English Reformers had been a major example of how medieval Catholicism had set up artificial communities alongside 'natural' ones. Increasingly, they fostered a spiritual climate in which serious attention to the processes of interior growth was normative, as it had become in Counter–Reformation piety—though they often underrated the extent to which the English Reformers had fostered a deep seriousness about regular prayer. In a very paradoxical way, they represented a profoundly *modern* reaction to the collapse of the old Anglican state. They recognized that the organic Christian commonwealth assumed by earlier Anglicans had practically faded away, and saw more clearly than many of their contemporaries that the events of the 1820s and 1830s had been a death blow to much of what had been thought of as Anglican identity. Tractarianism faced and countered some of the shadows of the English Reformation, the slippage towards private piety, moralism and sombre passivity about public life. The Oxford Movement, acknowledging that the authority of the British state could no longer be theologically grounded in any simple way, increasingly demanded the right for the Church to determine its own discipline and doctrine. Without this, it would have been harder for the Anglican Church to develop as it did outside the United Kingdom—and harder for it to move as it did in the early years of the twentieth century towards having institutions of self–government.

In the midst of all this, though, many Tractarians and the more overtly ritualist clergy of the next generation retained the underlying 'classical' sense of Anglican suspicion, reserve, pragmatism, and humility. The best minds in the Catholic movement resisted the temptation, always strong for this party, of simply identifying the authoritative pattern of church government and piety with modern Roman Catholic models; their achievement was to translate their heritage into a political and social world utterly different from the age that had been the matrix of early Anglican writing. Father Benson, Dr Pusey, Canon Liddon all spoke a language that might have sounded familiar to Hooker and Herbert. And in the next generation, Gore, Figgis, and others in the same circles, many associated, as they were, with the new religious communities as well as the universities and parishes, developed this further, with a far sharper sense of the need for the Church to take up a critical stance in British society. Their relatively relaxed views about the scholarly criticism of the Bible distanced them rather from the older Tractarians. Like them, they still kept largely to a spirituality that was reticent and freighted with a sense of the tragic, the ever–present possibilities of falsity and betrayal; but this could not now be automatically associated with a passive attitude to the social environment. What is more, Evangelicals in this period, though more limited in their public influence than they had been in their Victorian heyday, were likewise moved to a more overt and theologically sophisticated vision of the Christian life in society, building on their roots at the beginning of the nineteenth century; despite the dismissive attitudes of some Anglo–Catholics, it was not true that they stood for an uncritical support for or appeal to the state and the status quo. And in the field of the Anglican Church's overseas development, especially in Africa, Evangelical and Catholic missions shared more assumptions than they realized about how the Church was to grow and function outside the (nominally) confessional state.

In short, nineteenth–century holiness had moved on from the reserved but often profound conformity of the eighteenth century (so wonderfully summed up in Addison and Dr Johnson); it had been obliged to define itself afresh and to become more 'visible'. Two consequences of this, however, foreshadowed new and serious problems. First, it was no longer true that the questions of the

Church of England were the questions of the realm, and this meant that the influential voices in the Church were always in danger of letting purely ecclesiastical problems dominate the horizon. The impatience of people like Arnold and Maurice with both Evangelicals and Tractarians had much to do with this sense that a narrower agenda was taking over; but it often proved difficult for such writers to match the depth and sophistication of more partisan souls in exploring the struggles of mind and heart in prayer, and the patterns of spiritual growth. Second, the Tractarians had unwittingly given immense impetus to a trend they would have deplored: once they had claimed the right to redefine Anglican identity from within, they opened the floodgates to an attitude of mind that assumed it was acceptable to debate the nature of this identity with practically no boundaries set in advance, and to opt for a version that you found suitable.

In other words, the Tractarians had been 'liberals' without realizing it; and while they and many others maintained the basic theological seriousness that grounded Anglican reticence in a clear doctrinal vision of human dignity and human disaster, something was introduced into the Anglican mind that was more like the first kind of scepticism sketched above, a scepticism focused on how I am liable to be deceived by history and community. This was an attitude of mind more liable to collude with a reluctance to believe anything that does not make sense in primarily individual and experiential terms. Much of the twentieth–century history of Anglicanism, in Britain and elsewhere, turns on the tension this generates—especially when allied, as it has long been, with the effects of Enlightenment historical and literary scholarship on biblical and doctrinal sources. The ghosts of eighteenth–century 'latitudinarianism' walked again, in the shape of a new and fashionable moralism allied to a growing haziness about the integral theological vision within which the Church as a whole, never mind Anglicanism in particular, operated.

Yet twentieth–century liberalism in theology often retained a strong groundedness in disciplined piety—in personal devotion, sacramental reverence and respect for the mystical dimension. Perhaps the two greatest figures of Anglican liberalism in the latter part of the twentieth century, John Robinson and Geoffrey Lampe, may be taken as illustrations of this, though Robinson preferred to be thought a 'radical' (in the sense of someone returning to the roots of belief), and was fundamentally Catholic in his concerns, while Lampe represented the legacy of a liberal Evangelicalism that was generally in retreat in the Church of England. Both had a real understanding of the centrality of contemplative witness in Christianity, and in this at least spoke the same language as those who identified more straightforwardly with the Catholic tradition, like Michael Ramsey, Austin Farrer, and Gregory Dix. All of these, with the many whose thinking they helped to shape, declined to be theological specialists, despite their varied and formidable scholarly gifts, and preferred to focus upon the comprehensive rhythms and patterns of doctrine. Of twentieth–century writers, they are probably the ones who most clearly anchor theology in the discernment of holiness, and spirituality in the context of doctrine.

Evangelicalism revived dramatically and unexpectedly in the later twentieth century, often, but not by any means exclusively, in connection with the experience of charismatic renewal. Some 'classical' Evangelicals gradually discovered that the renewal movement was a stimulus to beginning afresh the exploration of Christological and Trinitarian themes in theology; and the growing presence of scholarly Evangelicals in Anglican commissions on liturgy and doctrine made its mark. As these theological developments gathered momentum, the demand in Evangelical circles for a doctrinally sophisticated spirituality grew; the tribalism that would once have prevented Evangelicals from learning anything from Catholics—or Catholics from Evangelicals—broke down more and more. Catholics concentrated more on the Bible; icons and candles began to appear in Evangelical churches and theological colleges.

It has been said that the typical Anglican of the twenty–first century will be an African under thirty; statistically, this seems unchallengeable. What has the history of Anglican devotion and holiness to offer this new model Anglican? The classical voices of the sixteenth and seventeenth centuries will seem very remote, unattractively allied to a politics that no–one could now endorse. Nineteenth–century Evangelicalism is a long way from the vibrant enthusiasms of the younger churches today; and nineteenth–century Tractarianism likewise seems preoccupied with issues that have little to do with the priorities of mission. The liberal explorations of the twentieth century evidently look like an idle and corrupt luxury to believers facing stark life and death choices, persecution, famine, nakedness, and poverty. There is a widespread perception that the Anglican Communion needs to grow beyond its historic ethos into a more consistently biblical and evangelistic identity; though there are other voices in the Communion that argue for a new reformation infinitely more radical, a revitalizing of the entire doctrinal tradition, perhaps even of the conventional language of belief in a God independent of the universe or of the thinking mind. There seems no obvious way of bringing two such diverse perspectives together.

The texts here presented are not being offered in such a cause. Rather, they may suggest to the contemporary reader that some of our modern tensions arise from failing to see where the integrity of doctrine and holiness lies. Talking about spirituality simply in terms of an undefined intensity or 'authenticity' of human life has little to do with talking of holiness, because holiness presupposes a transcendent source and measure for itself. To speak at all about Christian holiness is to seek for the criteria by which a life can be recognized as communicating the holiness of God as made known in Jesus. A doctrine–free spirituality risks descending into sentimentality, to the level of what makes us feel generally better about ourselves or reminds us in a wholly unsystematic way of the mystery around us; it is a weak support for resistance to the political and cultural tyrannies of our day. Without the structures of both discipline and doctrine, 'spirituality' can be vacuous and indulgent. Equally, doctrine that loses sight of its own roots in the painful and gradual re–formation of how holiness is experienced and understood becomes idle, even idolatrous. Christian language began its distinctive life as the speech the community developed for new, shared senses of what was possible for God and humanity. So, if some area of doctrinal language has become apparently arid, the question demanding to be asked is not *first* whether it makes sense before some imaginary tribunal of disengaged intellect or contemporary relevance, but what possibilities for Christian life and discipleship it was meant to 'encode' and whether the problem lies in a shrinking of our imagination in respect of this discipleship.

It is in this context that the texts presented here are meant to work. They do not represent an appeal to some golden age of Anglican divinity, whether early seventeenth century or mid–twentieth—though, if we are wise, we shall not be ashamed of acknowledging the decisive role of certain periods in establishing the register of Anglican thought and prayer. They are meant to suggest a method and style of Christian reflection that has been typical of Anglican writing and which—the editors believe—remains lively and available in the multi–cultural environment of the Anglican Communion today. What has been called the 'sceptical' dimension of Anglican spirituality is still (perhaps more than ever) a necessary contribution to the Christian spectrum. It is the spirit that begins in humility, in the confession that what I see is limited because of my fallen and selfish habits of perception. It is the doctrinal vision itself that teaches this reticence and self–questioning; in other words, the Christian theological world-view is one that, in its very abundance and comprehensiveness, challenges anyone who thinks they have compassed and possessed it in excessively tight formula-tions. I am first called not to pass judgement on my neighbour's holiness or orthodoxy, but to stand before the revealed mystery of the triune God, God in the flesh, God in the common life of prayer and sacrament, holding myself under scrutiny. Confidence and gratitude in the gift bestowed allow me to bear this without fear and to sustain it without the scepticism becoming agnosticism. External forms are not—as the Reformers quite rightly said—the objects or guarantors of faith. But, while this may often have assisted a passivity in public matters that few would now want to own, it may also allow an element of conversational patience to pervade doctrinal discussion and speculation and to give to each baptized person the expectation that visible systems of authority will not always be beyond questioning. How to maintain this without the corrosion of our first style of scepticism and without an individualist outcome is a perennial challenge; it can only really be met according to how seriously the believer takes the priority of the mood of humility and self–questioning.

A last thought on this: the Anglican note of sobriety and penitence, of realism interwoven with a reticence and indirectness born of gratitude or wonder, has been a note struck remarkably often by Anglican laypeople, from Elizabeth I to Fulke Greville to Thomas Browne, Dr Johnson, W. E. Gladstone, Evelyn Underhill, T. S. Eliot and the contemporary Anglican poet, Geoffrey Hill. It sits well with the recognition by the lay Christian that discipleship rarely follows textbook models, that tragedy is never far away because of our fallibility, and that the doctrinal deposit should not lend itself quite as easily as it sometimes seems to in the clerical mind to competitive, overconfident partisanship and the use of revelation as a weapon of war.

It is not a matter of national style or national genius—as if Anglicanism's gift to the Christian world were indistinguishable from a purely cultural and local way of talking and doing things. As has been said, there are reasons in the history and culture of Britain that produced this kind of style at a particular moment, at the Reformation period; but it would be dangerous to ally it with any sort of national peculiarity—English talent for compromise, English reticence or whatever. No one is claiming or should claim that the strengths of the classical Anglican idiom for exploring and recognizing holiness are unique to Anglicanism; only that Anglicanism's evolution and position have allowed it to develop and to nurture these strengths in ways in principle available to other cultures and other confessions. Anglicanism shares with Orthodoxy a legacy of literature impossible to divide up between 'theology' and 'spirituality'. It shares with classical European Protestantism a concern with fallibility and self–deceit. It shares with the Western Catholic world a conviction that the hidden givenness of sacramental life takes precedence over short–term assessments of success and satisfaction. But by various historical accidents (or providences) these have been woven together inextricably in the Anglican tradition, woven often in the medium of a language that, for all its concern with our weakness and infidelity, can flower into a sort of concentrated but unhurried delight. Think of Herbert again, of the Wesleys, of Bishop King, or Gregory Dix, or David Watson. If these texts suggest that Anglicans in the twenty–first century, including Anglicans very far from the historic heartlands of the Communion, can still learn to speak such a language and to stand with their predecessors in the same questioning but grateful and contemplative attitude, they will have done what the editors hope and pray they will do.

PART 1

1530 – 1650

Introduction

In some ways, it is misleading to talk about 'Anglican' identity in the sixteenth and early seventeenth centuries. No one was conscious of being an Anglican, as opposed to a Lutheran or a Calvinist; there was no system to which a person's adherence was sought, no attempt to develop a deliberately distinctive style of theology. What we are faced with in this period is primarily the records of English-speaking (and, as the sixteenth century advances, Welsh-speaking) Christians who were broadly loyal to the notion that the realm of England had authority to determine how the Church in England should be reformed. As elsewhere in Europe, one of the most pressing questions in the Reformation era was that of who had the right—and, pragmatically, the power—to effect change in the Church. If the established authorities of the Church were not able or willing to do this, they had evidently forfeited their claim on the Christian's obedience; they were themselves disobedient to the Gospel. And to the early generations of Reformed Christians, it was clear that the civil authority, the 'prince', was the obvious place to look. The Bible commanded loyalty and obedience to rulers; so, if rulers could be persuaded to follow the Gospel's directives, their authority obviously overrode that of the Church's own administration. The experience of medieval conflicts between monarchs and prelates, demands for legal exemptions for clergy, papal attempts to undermine the authority of local rulers and so on prompted many in the sixteenth century to attack the whole idea that the Church could be seen as a community visibly and institutionally separate from the realm, with its own laws and conventions. And in the realm of England, already enjoying a higher level of political centralization than most continental states, the role of the king seemed especially significant.

In the reign of Henry VIII, it is especially hard to say who was an 'Anglican' in any sense we might readily recognize. Those retrospectively identified as martyrs for the Reformed faith as given to the English Church lost their lives at the hands of Henry's administration, after all, even if Protestant historians did their best to blame the authorities of the church rather than the state for this. The great William Tyndale, theologian and translator of the Bible, is a hugely significant figure for later generations of English Reformed Christians, yet he spent most of his later life as a refugee from Henry's England. He is included here, however, (along with the less well-known but irresistible figure of Anne Askewe, another victim of Henry's policy) because he not only shapes both the language and the agenda of a lot of later reflection and piety in the English Church, but also represents the first coherent plea for a reformation in England carried through by royal authority according to New Testament principle, a reformation that would be severe and thorough but not completely discontinuous with the shape and order of the Church as it had been (he wants godly bishops rather than the abolition of episcopacy).

With the accession of Edward VI, we have slightly clearer criteria, if only because there is now an officially sanctioned liturgy for the Reformed Church which acts as a test of conformity—though the pressures for greater discontinuity with medieval practice are growing in some quarters. Those who fled the country in Mary's reign often acquired more radical ideas in their European refuges; rather paradoxically, some who stayed and were martyred—notably the prolific and very original John Bradford—had a better understanding of some of the weaknesses of Edwardine radicalism. Bradford is clearly unhappy, for example, with some attitudes to the Eucharist prevalent in extreme Reformed circles. With Elizabeth, we see emerging a sharp political disjunction between those who thought reformation had gone far enough and those who pressed for more drastic measures (especially those who looked for a different system of church government, by presbyters only). The reign of James I saw a continuation of government attacks on the radicals, with some taking refuge in the new territories across the Atlantic; and, while the early years of Charles I witnessed some of the most impressive consolidation of a theological and spiritual identity for the Reformed Church in England, harsh policies against dissidents pushed the situation towards more and more open confrontation. As the country drifted towards civil war, the fact that the interests of monarchy and bishops were almost indistinguishable, politically and theologically, posed new problems for the self-understanding of the Church of England.

Some passages in the literature of this whole period reflect in interesting ways how the Reformed perspective offered, for many, a clearer doctrine of the nature and the priorities of the ordained ministry than that which prevailed (so it was thought) in 'Catholic' practice. If the monarch has the responsibility for social order and indeed the ultimate responsibility for doctrinal purity (in consultation with his learned Christian advisers), the clergy can concentrate on their real job, which is the preaching of the true faith, the nurturing of mature believers, and the rebuking of evildoers. The Prayer Book Collect for St John Baptist's Day, might well be taken as a summary of the prophetic office of the ordained minister in this connection—'that we may . . . after his example constantly speak the truth, boldly rebuke vice, and patiently suffer for the truth's sake'. In contrast, so writers like Jewel and Andrewes claim, the confusion of roles in the Roman Church between pastoral office and political power, the insistence of the Pope and his theologians (especially the much-demonized Jesuits) on the Church's freedom to challenge or resist local political authority, leaves the clergy distracted from their true office and makes the Church itself potentially complicit with violence and coercion. The political setting of this is complicated, and attitudes were very much hardened in the wake of Pope Pius V's excommunication of Queen Elizabeth in 1570. But behind it is a more straightforward and sympathetic concern that the clergy should be free for their pastoral and educative task rather than being treated as a 'power bloc' in the state.

There were of course some potential problems in focusing on the authoritative role of the monarch in the governance of the Church. If the monarch and the monarch's ministers were themselves consistently disobedient to the Gospel, was there not a duty to resist them just as the Pope had been resisted? This is a problem that becomes more and more acute in the period covered in this first section. What became the specifically 'Anglican' response to the question, as it developed especially under Elizabeth, assumed that loyalty to the given structures of social order was always essential (even when this meant suffering under a bad administration): the case of obedience to ecclesiastical authority is not comparable to that of obedience to the prince, because the latter is so clearly commanded in the Bible. Once set that aside and anarchy follows. By the end of the reign of Elizabeth I, the battle lines had been drawn on this issue, with Roman Catholics and Protestant radicals alike defined as enemies to good order in society because of their refusal to abide by the Queen's determination of doctrine and practice.

But it would be a great mistake to read all this as illustrating any kind of retreat by the Church, to see it in terms of the Church's 'subordination' to the state or the failure of the Church to resist tyranny, let alone a weakening of the stringency of the call to holiness. Central to the enterprise of Reformed Christianity in England and Wales during the century or so after the first stirrings of the Reformation is the conviction that, if there are no 'special' duties prescribed by the Church over and above the demands of the Gospel and no 'special' sector of the population (clergy in general and those in religious vows in particular) charged with fulfilling the requirements of holiness in an exceptional way, then the whole population is faced with the same fundamental vocation to holy living. Differences of calling are related not to the old monastic structures but to the different social locations and relationships in which the Christian may find himself or herself. Bishop Latimer preaching on the Lord's Prayer tells the story of how St Antony of Egypt discovered that his monastic sanctity was no greater than that of a pious layman in Alexandria; and the theme recurs (in Becon, Sandys and many others) of society itself now being the 'religious community' in which Gospel imperatives are carried out. Everyone is under monastic discipline, you might say; there is no vicarious holiness. William Perkins, towards the end of Elizabeth's reign, a theologian of radical Calvinist views, is eloquent on the priority to be given to the household as a school of sanctity and Christian education. Furthermore, a good deal is made, first by Tyndale, later by others, again including Sandys, of the idea that we are bound in 'debt' to one another in the Christian commonwealth. Tyndale is especially radical in his insistence that all financial surplus is owed to the poor—even, he daringly suggests, the non-Christian poor in distant lands—and that the diversion of practical almsgiving to benefactions bestowed on cultic purposes (requiem masses, memorials, monastic endowments) is a notable example of how medieval piety distracted Christians from the real work of building up the living Body of Christ through economic justice.

Hence, from Tyndale onwards, one of the most characteristic literary genres of

Reformed English Christianity is the catalogue of duties belonging to one's station in society. Tyndale's own *Obedience of a Christian Man* is the progenitor of a vast amount of similar material; the passages in *The Book of Common Prayer*'s catechism about duties to God and the neighbour represent the tip of an iceberg. Cranmer himself, exhorting his flock to Bible reading, commends Scripture precisely for giving concrete direction to all in their distinctive callings in a hierarchical and, as we should now say, patriarchal society. John Woolton's *Christian Manual* of 1576 was a popular digest of much of this conventional wisdom, and it draws very carefully the distinction between the vocation shared by all human beings and the need to be precise as to what holiness means in the different circumstances of family and social relations. Reformed Christians of this era would have been a good deal surprised at the common modern idea that medieval civilization represented a universal sacralizing of everyday experience; on the contrary, they would have said, the Catholic piety against which they were rebelling refused to treat the ordinary relations of home and work, kinship and social obligation (to superiors and inferiors) as the stuff of holy living. It undermined these solid bonds by fragmenting people's loyalties, suggesting that the Pope was a higher authority than the prince, that the body of the clergy was a separate enclave within the realm, and that vows, whether marital or monastic, taken against the will of parents and kindred were acceptable to God. These issues recur frequently in literature about states of life, and in polemic against the Roman Church; uncongenial as they may sound to the contemporary reader, it is essential to see them as part of a campaign to bring 'ordinary' experience under the rule of the Gospel, so that the entire fabric of common life might speak of God.

Hence, too, the repeated discussion of and provision for prayer throughout the day for lay people. Cranmer's chaplain, Becon, has a great deal to say on this, looking back to the primitive understanding of 'perpetual prayer' (again, a transferring of monastic ideals to the whole body of the laity); but he is only one example of the almost universal insistence on regular and earnest turning of the mind to God throughout the day's occupation. Tyndale sees prayer as a constant yearning for what we lack—wholeness, strength, and assurance; Sandys offers a coherent breakdown of the components of prayer and again commends constant inner reference to and awareness of God. Early Reformed writers like the martyred Bradford are eager to provide examples of formulae to be used from waking to sleeping, and prayers for various mundane situations and against regular temptation were officially promulgated during Elizabeth's reign. The works of John Woolton and Richard and John Day were in the hands of a large number of literate people (including the Queen) in the last decades of the sixteenth century, and Bishop Bayly's *Practice of Piety* performed the same job for a new generation.

Bayly typifies a trend towards more and more intensive preparation for Holy Communion. One of the great aims of the Reformed Church of England was to restore the primitive sense of the Eucharist as visibly the sacramental meal of the baptized rather than a mystery performed by the priest on behalf of the people; and this went hand in hand with an emphasis upon the Eucharist as an 'interior' matter. Bishop Jewel writes of the sacraments as a kind of language: an illiterate person may scan the visible signs but without any inner assent, any intelligent response; so with the sacraments, in that the visible sign has to be received, 'read', with the eyes of the mind and soul. This needs education, since we must, in the sacraments, learn to see one reality through the medium of another that is totally different. And specifically in the Eucharist, as Jewel writes in a particularly eloquent and moving passage reproduced in the composite *Treatise of the Sacraments* drawn from his sermons in Salisbury Cathedral, we must see in the bread and wine the force and effect of Christ's death: 'we see . . . the earth to quake, the stones to cleave asunder, the graves to open and the dead to rise'. Thus to receive the body and blood of the Lord in Holy Communion is inseparable from the conscious apprehension of what Christ has done and is doing; receiving Christ is deliberately letting him act now upon your inmost self. This is often polemically expressed in contrast to what was thought to be the medieval teaching that Christ's presence was invariably guaranteed in the physical presence of the consecrated elements. It is not fair to the Reformed theologians, though, to suggest that the presence of Christ in the sacrament depends upon what's going on in the believer's mind. The sacrament is delivered to us *as* sacrament, as an effectual sign, by the word of Christ himself; it is as truly a communication from Christ as the written word is a communication from the writer. But for the present activity of Christ to reach to the moral and spiritual centre of the believer, for the believer actually to receive or 'feed upon' the work of Christ, is something else. Certainly the Reformed thinkers here represented did not regard the bread and wine of the Eucharist as no more than visual aids to faith; they were, however, passionately determined to exclude any suggestion that Christ's presence was localized and passive. Christ is present in the Eucharist as one who is acting consistently and intently towards the believer. For the unbeliever or unworthy recipient, great danger is involved, not because of any possible profanation of the material sacramental stuff, but because unworthy receiving is a refusal to be open to the action of Christ. It becomes the conscious refusal of a manifest invitation to receive grace, and so is, as St Paul taught in 1 Corinthians, a matter of mortal peril to the soul.

It was natural, then, that a stress upon holy reception of the sacrament became more marked. Obviously, the medieval Catholic was concerned about unworthy reception; the whole confessional system pivoted about this issue. But whereas the medieval Catholic could abstain from the sacrament, yet adore the presence of Christ, the Reformed Christian believed that adoration of the divine presence could not be separated from spiritual openness, receiving the living and active Christ moving from heaven to earth to enter the soul of the believer (Herbert's poem on the Holy Communion expresses this in memorable fashion). There can be no 'isolated' adoration of a static Christ somehow contained within the bread and wine. So there develops in Reformed devotion a detailed and sophisticated system of self-examination and of prayer for help and strength which must be gone through before the sacrament is received, a system that continues to be elaborated throughout the seventeenth and eighteenth centuries. Its result is, ironically, that the sacrament comes to be celebrated with less frequency as the seventeenth century proceeds; extended preparation is still recommended and material for it provided, but the infrequency of celebration tends eventually not so much to intensify the solemnity of the occasion as to detach it from the regular routine of church life, and to impart to it a somewhat sombre colouring. This is indeed not alien to the thinking of someone like Jewel, nor to the sober rhetoric of *The Book of Common Prayer*; but it is important to note also that Herbert can still write about the Eucharist in terms of joyful festivity (and can use patently eucharistic imagery at the climax of several of his greatest poems, above all the conclusion of *Love III*—'So I did sit and eat').

By the end of the sixteenth century, the concern with inner experience had generated some rather intractable problems. Those who dissented from the political–religious 'settlement' of Elizabeth I's regime tended to be adherents of a rigorous and radical variety of Calvinism for which the conscious assurance of being in God's favour was a necessary mark of belonging with God's elect. Against this, you find Richard Hooker arguing that, while faith may be the sole medium for apprehending justification, it cannot, humanly speaking, spring to life in its totality in an instant; it grows as the human self grows, and it may persist even at a level below consciousness when the conscious mind is filled with depression or despair. Other opponents of radical Calvinism such as Field and Forbes echo his concerns. The *subjective* sense of being in God's favour is not a test of whether in truth God has accepted you; Hooker is painfully aware of the pastorally disastrous effects of nurturing self-tormenting doubts as to whether you are having the 'right' experiences in prayer and the Christian life. Herbert again—like Donne, in a quite different mode—reinforces the same message: real dependence on God's grace, real apprehension of God's free action to make us righteous in his eyes, is more evident in the unconsoled endurance of inner turmoil and darkness than in bland confidence that all has been achieved, since the sense of inner darkness turns our attention away from what our minds can register, contain, and be confident of, towards the utterly mysterious love of God. There are echoes here of Tyndale's stress on prayer as yearning and lack, and a foretaste of what was to be in the nineteenth and twentieth centuries a strong emphasis in Anglican spirituality upon the virtues of persistence through emotional and imaginative dryness or worse. Herbert's little-known poem on *Perseverance* is an intense and stark example of this idiom.

One of the effects of the turn to the inner life was to unite Reformed Christianity in England to the contemporary explosion of interest (the language is not too strong) in the byways and corners of human self-understanding as shown in the poetry and drama of the age. Shakespeare is not likely to have been a very reliable member of the Reformed Church of England (he certainly had connections and sympathies with Roman Catholics, though he seems to have been committed to the political settlement and hostile to papal power), but he clearly inhabits the same mental world as his theological contemporaries, and is capable of some striking echoes, parodies, and enlargements of biblical and theological language. Gradually, the Reformed faith came to be expressed and explored by numerous unusually gifted poets—Spenser and Greville in the sixteenth century, then the astonishing flowering of poetic genius in the early seventeenth century—Donne, Herbert, Vaughan, and others. Preaching in English was equally a vehicle for intense reflection on the self and its inner shadows. Donne pursued this not only in his sermons and poems, but in his varied essays in prose devotional writing; plenty of people wrote prose meditations, but Donne brought the genre to unprecedented heights of imaginative eloquence. He draws on a vast resource of classical and early Christian literature in his evocations of the ruined dignity of the human self, but his fascinated absorption with the recognition of mortality and the art of dying, for all its echoes of late medieval spiritual exercises, is very much of its own period.

The early seventeenth century has often been seen as a sort of Anglican golden age, abounding in writers of outstanding beauty and saintly characters, who somehow transcended the confessional squabbles of their day, harmonizing all that was best in patristic and medieval devotion with the clarity and simplicity of Reformed religion. Lancelot Andrewes would, for many, be among the supreme exponents of this triumphant synthesis. His private devotions certainly represent an exceptionally hospitable spirit, decisively shaped by the heritage of the Greek Fathers; the recurring themes of his sermons—amazing tours de force of exuberant imagery, blending verbal playfulness with theological depth—are those of the central texts of the early Church, divine mystery, humanity in the image of God restored in Christ, the transfiguring gift of the Spirit in the sacramental fellowship of the Church. It has more than once been noted that a great number of his sermons include passages on the Eucharist as the focal act and sign of Christian identity, and as a real communication to the believer of the divine life. When he preaches for Christmas, Easter, and Pentecost, he returns again and again to his favourite theme, so familiar from patristic theology: the divine Son becomes human so that we may become divine, and in the sacrament this communion of divine and human nature in Christ is shared with us. For all that he can be a fierce polemicist against Roman Catholicism, it is true enough that there is little in his preaching that seems (in seventeenth-century terms at least) distinctively or exclusively Protestant; and he is at times outspokenly critical of the extreme Calvinist thesis that Christ died only for those predestined to salvation.

Andrewes's spirituality at first sight seems to move far more easily at the level of *achieved* reconciliation and transfiguration than in the world of struggle and intermittent darkness found in Herbert (as in a good many pages of Hooker, though this is less widely recognized). Herbert should remind us that the great synthesis of the early Stuart period, the supposed golden age, was not simply a matter of celebratory and contemplative peace, such as a hasty reading of Andrewes's sermons and devotions might seem to indicate: indeed, something of Andrewes's own concern and anxiety comes through increasingly in later sermons. The civil strife of the sixteen-forties cast a shadow before it; and the typical tone (which we might by now begin to call 'Anglican') of sombre and penitent self-awareness is discernible, even close to the heart of the religious establishment; it is there in Archbishop Laud, even as he presses home his dangerous triumphs in ecclesiastical policy. It is there in a more domestic and prosaic setting in the world of Little Gidding, the lay community founded by Nicholas Ferrar and his family in 1625, a community known and valued by Herbert—and by Charles I. Here the sixteenth-century language that attempted to transfer the aura of the monastery to the Christian home is fleshed out in a particularly full way, through the discipline of daily prayer and study and a rigorous requirement of self-scrutiny and penitence. Although it was (predictably) stigmatized by some as 'popish', the truth is that it represents one of the most distinctive elements in English Reformed spirituality, and its inspiration has been long-lived in the Anglican world.

It may be that this penitential sobriety was one of the things that gave the Church of England resources for facing and surviving the trauma of the Commonwealth period. Although his work might be thought to belong strictly in the next section of this anthology, Henry Vaughan's poetry speaks eloquently, though often very indirectly, about the graces of darkness and the opportunities or liberations that come with loss. If Andrewes represents one pole of seventeenth-century 'Anglican' identity, resolutely moving beyond controversy and gathering up the fragments of a broken Christian world in intense imaginative unity, it is as well to remember that the Reformation's more austere recognition of self-deceit and alienation were never wholly muted in the Church of England, even in its most aggressive and confident days.

And of course *The Book of Common Prayer* remained through most of this period as the touchstone of the Church's identity and integrity. Its evolution is remarkable. Beginning in piecemeal translations and adaptations of liturgical material, it was already, by the time of its second (1552) version, providing a consistent style of reflection and public prayer that consciously set out to mould an entire religious sensibility. Cranmer, architect though not exclusive author of the 1549 and 1552 books, can be credited with the extraordinary achievement of expressing a fairly radical Protestant doctrine of dependence upon grace at all points in a language not only weighty and authoritative in itself but also evocative of ancient and medieval piety. Protestant theology is made to speak a dialect deeply rooted in Greek and Latin liturgy, and so acquires an added depth and seriousness; *this*, it seems to say, is what the true tradition of the Church has been saying all along. Cranmer is not likely to have relished the thought that by working in this way he left doors open to the reintroduction of theological themes he had hoped to remove; but that was one of the results of his strategy, a result that has affected practically all Anglican liturgy up to the present. The relatively small changes introduced in 1559 already show the resourcefulness of Anglicans in shifting theological emphases while retaining the same literary tenor and spiritual sensibility. The textual tradition survives changes in interpretation with few visible marks of change in itself (so that, for example, the popularity in the seventeenth century of a baptismal theology centred upon the idea of covenant leaves no trace in the Prayer Book revisions of 1662). If the devotion of the Church of England has throughout this period something of the feeling of sober and sceptical humility already outlined, it has much to do with the Prayer Book. By the beginning of the seventeenth century, it is already the object of both deep affection and awed veneration in regions and communities of the most diverse kinds.

The availability of English Bibles must equally be noted as a crucial factor in Reformed English devotion; appeal to scriptural example becomes wider in reference than in the Middle Ages, and the images and idioms of scripture penetrate devotional writing and, of course, preaching (you can see one simple effect of all this in the quantity of plain expository sermons by someone like Jewel, for instance). But we should beware of ascribing to people of this era the uncritical reverence for authorized translations that made the 1611 King James Bible something of a fetish for English-speaking Protestants of the nineteenth century and later. Several translations were current, and preachers might offer their own versions of a text—as Andrewes regularly does. If you add to this consideration the question of how many homes, even literate ones, actually possessed a Bible before 1650, you may hesitate to overrate the influence of any one biblical version on the English soul. But there can be no doubt that the quantity of reference and use in church did indeed establish a kind of biblical literacy as the basis for the devotion of most. And it is worth noticing in passing that in Wales, where one 'standard' translation was dominant from its publication in 1588, the impact of the biblical text on the stabilizing of the language itself was far greater than in England.

One last major influence to note, though it is not a text that can easily be adapted for the purposes of a volume like this, is the work commonly known as Foxe's *Book of Martyrs* (in the first English edition of 1563, *Acts and Monuments of these later and perilous dayes touching matters of the Church*, revised and reprinted in 1570 as *The Ecclesiastical History*—in clear allusion to the 'ecclesiastical histories' of Eusebius in the early Church and, probably, Bede at the beginnings of the English Church). Parish churches were expected to make copies available; at Little Gidding, it was treated almost in the same way as an official 'martyrology' in a Catholic community. It gave a full narrative rationale for the English Reformation up to the triumph of the Reformed faith under Elizabeth. It provided full accounts of the lives and heroic deaths not only of the familiar giants of the Reformation but of ordinary, stubborn, honest laypeople, resisting the tyranny of the Pope or the unenlightened monarch. As modern research has underlined, it suggested a picture of the English nation itself as a sort of chosen people, as the realm where the true religion of the Gospel was most firmly established by God's grace through the terrible history of trial and suffering played out in the days of Henry and Mary Tudor. And John Foxe deliberately extended his story back to the earlier days of the Church so as to make it clear that the English Reformation was a real 'apostolic succession' of costly witness.

The events of Elizabeth's reign—especially the debacle of the Armada's defeat in 1588—reinforced the image of England persecuted but faithful and triumphant; the uncovering of the Gunpowder Plot in 1605 again confirmed the model. The annual commemoration of this deliverance, before it degenerated into 'Guy Fawkes' Night', was a serious occasion for reaffirming God's providential care for this 'holy nation' (and for reawakening hostile suspicion towards the Pope and his servants). This strand in Tudor and Stuart devotion is another of those elements not easy for the modern reader to come to terms with; but it is an inescapable part of the world of Donne, Andrewes, and Herbert, as authentic to them as their absorption of Augustine, or Gregory of Nazianzus, or (as in Herbert's case) radical European humanist and Catholic thinking like that of Juan Valdés, the Spanish moralist and aphorist whom Ferrar translated and Herbert annotated.

'Anglicanism' as a designation may well be an anachronism in this period. What we see, though, is the steady accumulation of materials not for a system but for a language, a style, and an imaginative frame of reference. If the writers of the first century or so of the independent life of the Reformed English (and Irish and Welsh and—with some added complications—Scottish) Church give us a 'classical' deposit of thought and image, it is not just a matter of chronological priority. There really were themes that gave coherence to the Reformed enterprise in Britain; and they issued in a style of holy life that certainly remained recognizable for the two and a half centuries following—rather reticent, perhaps rather passive in the eye of an unsympathetic observer, not afraid to quarry other traditions, even across the gulfs of serious theological disagreement, very reluctant (for good and ill) to draw firm lines between ecclesiastical and social service and obligation; at best, in a Hooker or a Herbert, combining a clear-eyed and unconsoled awareness of the fragility of human thinking and motivation with an equally clear-eyed and deeply charged awareness of the terrible mysteriousness of God's grace, an awareness at once sweet and joyful and strange and frightening. A dazzling darkness.

Hugh Latimer

1485–1555

The son of a farmer in Leicestershire, Hugh Latimer was educated in Cambridge and became a Fellow of Clare Hall (1510). He was commissioned by Cambridge University with a Licence to preach anywhere in England, but his positive inclination to the doctrines of the Reformers necessitated him having to explain himself before Wolsey. Upon Cranmer's succession as Archbishop of Canterbury (1533) Latimer became a Royal Chaplain to Henry VIII and thereafter Bishop of Worcester (1535). However, his tenure did not last long and in 1539 he resigned his bishopric because of his opposition to the Act of Six Articles (imposed by Henry VIII to prevent the spread of Reformation doctrines and practices). He regained position and influence in Edward VI's reign. He was a powerful and popular preacher, colloquial, garrulous, and brilliantly vivid, one of the best propagandists for the Reformed faith. When Mary came to the throne in 1553 Latimer was committed to the Tower of London and in the following year, together with Cranmer and Ridley, was sent to Oxford to defend his views before University theologians. His refusal to recant led to his excommunication and, following his re-examination in 1555, he was condemned as a heretic and burnt with Ridley at Oxford on 16 October. His extant writings were collected for the Parker Society in 1844–45.

Enemies Within

These evil-disposed affections and sensualities in us are always contrary to the rule of our salvation. What shall we do now or imagine, to thrust down these Turks and to subdue them? It is a great ignominy and shame for a christian man to be bond and subject unto a Turk: nay, it shall not be so; we will first cast a trump in their way, and play with them at cards, who shall have the better. Let us play therefore on this fashion with this card. Whensoever it shall happen the foul passions and Turks to rise in our stomachs against our brother or neighbour, either for unkind words, injuries, or wrongs, which they have done unto us, contrary unto our mind; straightways let us call unto our remembrance, and speak this question unto ourselves, 'Who art thou?' The answer is, 'I am a christian man.' Then further we must say to ourselves, 'What requireth Christ of a christian man?' Now turn up your trump, your heart (hearts is trump, as I said before), and cast your trump, your heart, on this card; and upon this card you shall learn what Christ requireth of a christian man,—not to be angry, ne moved to ire against his neighbour, in mind, countenance, nor other ways, by word or deed. Then take up this card with your heart, and lay them together: that done, you have won the game of the Turk, whereby you have defaced and overcome him by true and lawful play. But, alas for pity! the Rhodes are won[1] and overcome by these false Turks; the strong castle Faith is decayed, so that I fear it is almost impossible to win it again.

The great occasion of the loss of this Rhodes is by reason that christian men do so daily kill their own nation, that the very true number of Christianity is

[1] Alluding to the capture of the island of Rhodes by the Turks, 1523.

decayed; which murder and killing one of another is increased specially two ways, to the utter undoing of Christendom, that is to say, by example and silence. By example, as thus: when the father, the mother, the lord, the lady, the master, the dame, be themselves overcome with these Turks, they be continual swearers, avouterers, disposers to malice, never in patience, and so forth in all other vices: think you not, when the father, the mother, the master, the dame, be disposed unto vice or impatience, but that their children and servants shall incline and be disposed to the same? No doubt, as the child shall take disposition natural of the father and mother, so shall the servants apply unto the vices of their masters and dames: if the heads be false in their faculties and crafts, it is no marvel if the children, servants and apprentices do joy therein. This is a great and shameful manner of killing christian men, that the fathers, the mothers, the masters, and the dames, shall not alonely kill themselves, but all theirs, and all that belongeth unto them: and so this way is a great number of christian lineage murdered and spoiled.

The second manner of killing is silence. By silence also is a great number of christian men slain; which is on this fashion: although that the father and mother, master and dame, of themselves be well disposed to live according to the law of God, yet they may kill their children and servants in suffering them to do evil before their own faces, and do not use due correction according unto their offences. The master seeth his servant or apprentice take more of his neighbour than the king's laws, or the order of his faculty, doth admit him; or that he suffereth him to take more of his neighbour than he himself would be content to pay, if he were in like condition: thus doing, I say, such men kill willingly their children and servants, and shall go to hell for so doing; but also their fathers and mothers, masters and dames, shall bear them company for so suffering them.

Wherefore I exhort all true christian men and women to give good example unto your children and servants, and suffer not them by silence to offend. Every man must be in his own house, according to St Augustine's mind, a bishop, not alonely giving good ensample, but teaching according to it, rebuking and punishing vice; not suffering your children and servants to forget the laws of God. You ought to see them have their belief, to know the commandments of God, to keep their holy-days, not to lose their time in idleness: if they do so, you shall all suffer pain for it, if God be true of his saying, as there is no doubt thereof. And so you may perceive that there be many a one that breaketh this card, 'Thou shalt not kill,' and playeth therewith oftentime at the blind trump, whereby they be no winners, but great losers. (1)

Finding Faith

Faith, faith, faith; we are undone for lack of faith. Christ nameth faith here, faith is all together: 'When the Son of man shall come, shall he find faith on the earth?' Why speaketh he so much of faith? Because it is hard to find a true faith. He speaketh not of a political faith, a faith set up for a time; but a constant, a permanent, a durable faith, as durable as God's word.

He came many times: first in the time of Noe when he preached, but he found little faith. He came also when Lot preached, when he destroyed Sodome and Gomora, but he found no faith. And to be short, he shall come at the latter day, but he shall find a little faith. And I ween the day be not far off. When he was here carnally, did he find any faith? Many speak of faith, but few there be that hath it. Christ mourneth the lack of it: he complaineth that when he came, he found no faith.

This Faith is a great state, a lady, a duchess, a great woman; and she hath ever a great company and train about her, as a noble estate ought to have. First, she hath a gentleman-usher that goeth before her, and where he is not there is not lady Faith. This gentleman-usher is called *Agnitio peccatorum*, knowledge of sin; when we enter into our heart, and acknowledge our faults, and stand not about to defend them. He is none of these winkers; he kicks not when he hears his fault. Now, as the gentleman-usher goeth before her, so she hath a train that cometh behind her; and yet, though they come behind, they be all of Faith's company, they are all with her: as Christ, when he counterfeited a state going to Jerusalem, some went before him, and some after, yet all were of his company. So all these wait upon Faith, she hath a great train after her, besides her gentleman-usher, her whole household; and those be the works of our vocation, when every man considereth what vocation he is in, what calling he is in, and doth the works of the same; as, to be good to his neighbour, to obey God, etc. This is the train that followeth lady Faith: as for an example; a faithful judge hath first an heavy reckoning of his fault, repenting himself of his wickedness, and then forsaketh his iniquity, his impiety, feareth no man, walks upright; and he that doth not thus hath not lady Faith, but rather a boldness of sin and abusing of Christ's passion. Lady Faith is never without her gentleman-usher, nor without her train: she is no anchoress[1], she dwells not alone, she is never a private woman, she is never alone. And yet many there be that boast themselves that they have faith, and that when Christ shall come they shall do well enough. Nay, nay, those that be faithful shall be so few, that Christ shall scarce see them. 'Many there be that runneth,' saith St Paul, 'but there is but one that receiveth the reward.' It shall be with the multitude, when Christ shall come, as it was in the time of Noe, and as it was in the time of Lot. In the time of Noe, 'they were eating and drinking, building and planting, and suddenly the water came upon them, and drowned them.' In the time of Lot also, 'they were eating and drinking, etc., and suddenly the fire came upon them, and devoured them.' And now we are eating and drinking: there was never such building then as is now, planting, nor marrying. And thus it shall be, even when Christ shall come at judgment.

Is eating, and drinking, and marrying, reproved in scripture? Is it not? Nay, he reproveth not all kind of eating and drinking, he must be otherwise under-standed. If the scripture be not truly expounded, what is more erroneous? And though there be complainings of some eating and drinking in the scripture, yet he speaketh not as though all were naught. They may be well ordered, they are God's allowance: but to eat and drink as they did in Noe's time, and as they did in Loth's time, this eating, and drinking, and marrying, is spoken against. To eat and drink in the forgetfulness of God's commandment, voluptuously, in excess and gluttony, this kind of eating and drinking is naught; when it is not done moderately, soberly, and with all circumspection. (2)

---

[1] A female hermit.

Preaching

For preaching of the gospel is one of God's plough-works, and the preacher is one
of God's ploughmen. Ye may not be offended with my similitude, in that I
compare preaching to the labour and work of ploughing, and the preacher to a
ploughman: ye may not be offended with this my similitude; for I have been
slandered of some persons for such things. It hath been said of me, 'Oh, Latimer!
nay, as for him, I will never believe him while I live, nor never trust him; for he
likened our blessed lady to a saffron-bag[1]:' where indeed I never used that
similitude. But it was, as I have said unto you before now, according to that which
Peter saw before in the spirit of prophecy, and said, that there should come after
men *per quos via veritatis maledictis afficeretur*; there should come fellows 'by
whom the way of truth should be evil spoken of, and slandered.' But in case I had
used this similitude, it had not been to be reproved, but might have been without
reproach. For I might have said thus: as the saffron-bag that hath been full of
saffron, or hath had saffron in it, doth ever after savour and smell of the sweet
saffron that it contained; so our blessed lady, which conceived and bare Christ in
her womb, did ever after resemble the manners and virtues of that precious babe
that she bare. And what had our blessed lady been the worse for this? or what
dishonour was this to our blessed lady? But as preachers must be wary and
circumspect, that they give not any just occasion to be slandered and ill spoken of
by the hearers, so must not the auditors be offended without cause. For heaven is
in the gospel likened to a mustard-seed: it is compared also to a piece of leaven;
and as Christ saith, that at the last day he will come like a thief: and what
dishonour is this to God? or what derogation is this to heaven? Ye may not then,
I say, be offended with my similitude, for because I liken preaching to a
ploughman's labour, and a prelate to a ploughman. But now you will ask me,
whom I call a prelate? A prelate is that man, whatsoever he be, that hath a flock to
be taught of him; whosoever hath any spiritual charge in the faithful congregation, and whosoever he be that hath cure of souls. And well may the preacher and
the ploughman be likened together: first, for their labour of all seasons of the year;
for there is no time of the year in which the ploughman hath not some special
work to do: as in my country in Leicestershire, the ploughman hath a time to set
forth, and to assay his plough, and other times for other necessary works to be
done. And then they also may be likened together for the diversity of works and
variety of offices that they have to do. For as the ploughman first setteth forth his
plough, and then tilleth his land, and breaketh it in furrows, and sometimes
ridgeth it up again; and at another time harroweth it and clotteth it, and
sometime dungeth it and hedgeth it, diggeth it and weedeth it, purgeth and
maketh it clean: so the prelate, the preacher, hath many diverse offices to do. He
hath first a busy work to bring his parishioners to a right faith, as Paul calleth it,
and not a swerving faith; but to a faith that embraceth Christ, and trusteth to his
merits; a lively faith, a justifying faith; a faith that maketh a man righteous,
without respect of works: as ye have it very well declared and set forth in the

---

[1] Among the 'erroneous opinions complained of in convocation', 1536, was 'that our lady was no
better than another woman, and like a bag of pepper or saffron when the spice is out.' Wilkins, Concil.
III, p. 806.

Homily[1]. He hath then a busy work, I say, to bring his flock to a right faith, and then to confirm them in the same faith: now casting them down with the law, and with threatenings of God for sin; now ridging them up again with the gospel, and with the promises of God's favour: now weeding them, by telling them their faults, and making them forsake sin; now clotting them, by breaking their stony hearts, and by making them supplehearted, and making them to have hearts of flesh. (3)

Prayer and the Common Good

To whom will he give the Holy Ghost? To lords and ladies, to gentlemen or gentlewomen? No, not so. He is not ruled by affections: he hath not respect unto personages. *Poscentibus*, saith he, 'unto those which call upon him,' being rich or poor, lords or knights, beggars or rich; he is ready to give unto them when they come to him. And this is a great comfort unto those which be poor and miserable in this world; for they may be assured of the help of God, yea, and as boldly go unto him, and desire his help, as the greatest king in earth. But we must ask, we must inquire for it; he would have us to be importunate, to be earnest and diligent in desiring; then we shall receive when we come with a good faith and confidence. To whom shall we call? Not unto the saints. *Poscentibus illum*, saith he. Those that call upon him shall be heard. Therefore we ought to come to him only, and not unto his saints.

But one word is left, which we must needs consider; *Noster*, 'our.' He saith not 'my,' but 'our.' Wherefore saith he 'our?' This word 'our' teacheth us to consider that the Father of heaven is a common Father; as well my neighbour's Father as mine; as well the poor man's Father as the rich: so that he is not a peculiar Father, but a Father to the whole church and congregation, to all the faithful. Be they never so poor, so vile, so foul and despised, yet he is their Father as well as mine: and therefore I should not despise them, but consider that God is their Father as well as mine. Here may we perceive what communion is between us; so that when I pray, I pray not for myself alone, but for all the rest: again, when they pray, they pray not for themselves only, but for me: for Christ hath so framed this prayer, that I must needs include my neighbour in it. Therefore all those which pray this prayer, they pray as well for me as for themselves; which is a great comfort to every faithful heart, when he considereth that all the church prayeth for him. For amongst such a great number there be some which be good, and whose prayer God will hear: as it appeared by Abraham's prayer (Gen. xviii.), which prayer was so effectuous, that God would have pardoned Sodome and Gomorre, if he might have found but ten good persons therein. Likewise St Paul in shipwreck preserved his company by his prayer (Acts xxvii.). So that it is a great comfort unto us to know that all good and faithful persons pray for us.

There be some learned men which gather out of scripture (Acts vii.), that the prayer of St Stephen was the occasion of the conversion of St Paul. St Chrysostom saith, that that prayer that I make for myself is the best, and is of more efficacy than that which is made in common. Which saying I like not very well. For our Saviour was better learned than St Chrysostom. He taught us to pray in common

---

[1] 'Of a true and lively faith'.

for all; therefore we ought to follow him, and to be glad to pray one for another: for we have a common saying among us, 'Whosoever loveth me, loveth my hound.' So, whosoever loveth God, will love his neighbour, which is made after the image of God.

And here is to be noted, that prayer hath one property before all other good works: for with my alms I help but one or two at once, but with my faithful prayer I help all. I desire God to comfort all men living, but specially *domesticos fidei*, 'those which be of the household of faith.' Yet we ought to pray with all our hearts for the other, which believe not, that God will turn their hearts and renew them with his Spirit; yea, our prayers reach so far, that our very capital enemy ought not to be omitted. Here you see what an excellent thing prayer is, when it proceedeth from a faithful heart; it doth far pass all the good works that men can do.

Now to make an end: we are monished here of charity, and taught that God is not only a private Father, but a common Father unto the whole world, unto all faithful; be they never so poor and miserable in this world, yet he is their Father. Where we may learn humility and lowliness: specially great and rich men shall learn here not to be lofty or to despise the poor. For when ye despise the poor miserable man, whom despise ye? Ye despise him which calleth God his Father as well as you; and peradventure more acceptable and more regarded in his sight than you be. Those proud persons may learn here to leave their stubbornness and loftiness. But there be a great many which little regard this: they think themselves better than other men be, and so despise and contemn the poor; insomuch that they will not hear poor men's causes, nor defend them from wrong and oppression of the rich and mighty. Such proud men despise the Lord's prayer: they should be as careful for their brethren as for themselves. And such humility, such love and carefulness towards our neighbours, we learn by this word 'Our.' (4)

Uncloistered Virtue

I read once a story of a holy man, (some say it was St Anthony,) which had been a long season in the wilderness, neither eating nor drinking any thing but bread and water: at the length he thought himself so holy, that there should be nobody like unto him. Therefore he desired of God to know who should be his fellow in heaven. God made him answer, and commanded him to go to Alexandria; there he should find a cobler which should be his fellow in heaven. Now he went thither and sought him out, and fell in acquaintance with him, and tarried with him three or four days to see his conversation. In the morning his wife and he prayed together; then they went to their business, he in his shop, and she about her housewifery. At dinner time they had bread and cheese, wherewith they were well content, and took it thankfully. Their children were well taught to fear God, and to say their *Pater-noster*, and the Creed, and the Ten Commandments; and so he spent his time in doing his duty truly. I warrant you, he did not so many false stitches as coblers do now-a-days. St Anthony perceiving that, came to knowledge of himself, and laid away all pride and presumption. By this ensample you may learn, that honest conversation and godly living is much regarded before God; insomuch that this poor cobler, doing his duty diligently, was made

St Anthony's fellow. So it appeareth that we be not destituted of religious houses: those which apply their business uprightly and hear God's word, they shall be St Anthony's fellows; that is to say, they shall be numbered amongst the children of God. (5)

Varieties of Temptation

Now peradventure there be some amongst the ignorant unlearned sort, which will say unto me, 'You speak much of temptations; I pray you tell us, how shall we know when we be tempted?' Answer: When you feel in yourselves, in your hearts, some concupiscence or lust towards any thing that is against the law of God rise up in your hearts, that same is a tempting: for all manner of ill motions to wickedness are temptations. And we be tempted most commonly two manner of ways, *a dextris et a sinistris*, 'on the right hand, and on the left hand.' Whensoever we be in honours, wealth, and prosperities, then we be tempted on the right hand: but when we be in open shame, out-laws, or in great extreme poverty and penuries, then that is on the left hand. There hath been many, that when they have been tempted *a sinistris*, 'on the left hand,' that is, with adversities and all kind of miseries, they have been hardy and most godly; have suffered such calamities, giving God thanks amidst all their troubles: and there hath been many which have written most godly books in the time of their temptations and miseries. Some also there were which stood heartily, and godlily suffered temptations, as long as they were in trouble: but afterward, when they came to rest, they could not stand so well as before in their trouble: yea, the most part go and take out a new lesson of discretion, to flatter themselves and the world withal; and so they verify that saying, *Honores mutant mores*, 'Honours change manners.' For they can find in their hearts to approve that thing now, which before time they reproved. Aforetime they sought the honour of God, now they seek their own pleasure. Like as the rich man did, saying, *Anima, nunc ede, bibe*, etc., 'Soul, now eat, drink,' etc. But it followeth, *Stulte*, 'Thou fool.' Therefore, let men beware of the right hand; for they are gone by and by, except God with his Spirit illuminate their hearts. I would such men would begin to say with David, *Proba me, Domine*, 'Lord, prove me: spur me forward; send me somewhat, that I forget not thee!' So it appeareth that a christian man's life is a strife, a warfare: but we shall overcome all our enemies; yet not by our own power, but through God which is able to defend us.

Truth it is that God tempteth. Almighty God tempteth to our commodities, to do us good withal; the devil tempteth to our everlasting destruction. God tempteth us for exercise' sake, that we should not be slothful; therefore he proveth us diversely. We had need often to say this prayer, 'Lord, lead us not into temptation.' When we rise up in a morning, or whatsoever we do, when we feel the devil busy about us, we should call upon God. The diligence of the devil should make us watchful, when we consider with what earnest mind he applieth his business: for he sleepeth not, he slumbereth not; he mindeth his own business, he is careful, and hath mind of his matters.

Seeing then that we have such an enemy, resist; for so it is needful. For I think that now in this hall, amongst this audience, there be many thousand devils, which go about to let us of the hearing of the word of God; to make hardness in our hearts, and to stir up such like mischief within us. But what remedy? *Resistite*, 'Withstand;' withstand his motions. And this must be done at the first. For, as strong as he is, when he is resisted at the first, he is the weakest; but if we suffer him to come into our hearts, then he cannot be driven out without great labour and travail. As for an ensample: I see a fair woman, I like her very well, I wish in my heart to have her. Now withstand; this is a temptation. Shall I follow my affections? No, no: call to remembrance what the devil is; call God to remembrance and his laws; consider what he hath commanded thee: say unto God, 'Lord, lead us not into temptation, but deliver us from evil.' For I tell thee, when he is entered once, it will be hard to get him out again. Therefore suffer him not too long: give him no mansion in thy heart, but strike him with the word of God, and he is gone; he will not abide. Another ensample: There is a man that hath done me wrong; taken away my living, or hurt me of my good name: the devil stirreth me against him, to requite him, to do him another foul turn, to avenge myself upon him. Now, when there riseth up such motions in my heart, I must resist; I must strive. I must consider that God saith, *Mihi vindicta*, 'Let me have the vengeance:' *Ego retribuam*, 'I will punish him for his ill doings.' (6)

NOTES / SOURCES

1. Hugh Latimer, Sermon 1 on the Card, in *The Works of Hugh Latimer*, ed. G. E. Corrie, Cambridge (Parker Society), 1844, pp. 12–14
2. Fourth Sermon Preached Before King Edward the Sixth, ibid., pp. 168–9
3. Sermon of the Plough, ibid., pp. 60–1
4. First Sermon on the Lord's Prayer, ibid., pp. 337–9
5. Fifth Sermon on the Lord's Prayer, ibid., pp. 392–3
6. Seventh Sermon on the Lord's Prayer, ibid., pp. 437–9

Myles Coverdale   1488–1568

Coverdale was ordained in 1514, as a member (like Luther) of the Augustinian friars, but was an early enthusiast for Reformed theology and pursued his work and studies on the Continent during the early years of religious change in England. In 1535 he published at Zurich the first complete English Bible, and, having returned to Britain as the climate became more favourable to reform, was involved with the production of the 'Great Bible' in 1539, the first English Bible formally authorized by monarch and Parliament for public reading in church. In 1551 he became Bishop of Exeter; he spent Mary's reign on the Continent, and resumed his office in 1559. A dedicated pastoral bishop, he continued to produce theological and devotional literature. His English adaptation of Erasmus's *Enchiridion* illustrates the close connection of some Reformed theologians with European humanist ideals, but the bulk of his original work is more directly biblical in its focus and inspiration.

Patience

Among all other virtues, in adversity patience is most necessary; not such a patience as to suffer all things to pass, whether they be good or bad, right or wrong, setting all on six and seven; but when we are in trouble and adversity, and can avoid it by no lawful mean, whereas after the desire and lust of our flesh we would murmur, forsake, and give over both God and all manner of righteousness; then to resist and strive against our afflictions and sorrowful thoughts, and, as a man would say, to spear up and to captivate and subdue our natural eyes, wit, and reason under and unto the obedience of God, yielding and submitting ourselves unto him, suffering whatsoever it be with a good and ready will, even though it were most bitter and cruel death, rather than we would swerve from the word of God (Luke ix. 62); yea, and moreover to praise God, and to give him thanks, that he will vouchsafe so fatherly to visit us, and that he hath not forgotten us.

This is called a right christian patience. For it is God's precept and commandment, that we should not murmur or grudge against him, when he chasteneth us; but that we should submit ourselves most humbly unto his holy will, and after a certain manner to wish, that is to say, willingly to suffer and bear such punishment and correction, whereby we remain and continue obedient unto his godly righteousness. 'Murmur not, as certain murmured, and were destroyed of the destroyer.' (Numb. xxi. 6, 1 Cor. x. 10)

Wherefore we ought to shew patience in all things, as a point of our duty; and it is a grievous sin to murmur and grudge against the judgment of God, and to resist and strive against God's will. And God doth not only command patience, but also is himself patient and long-suffering; which destroyeth not at once the whoremonger, the extortioner, and other such like wicked and damnable people with a lightning or thunderbolt, although his holy and strait righteousness requireth no less. (Deut. xxxii. 36) He giveth time and space sufficient for the man to repent, and to return to grace again.

Hence Paul saith: 'Dost thou despise the abundant riches of his goodness, his patience, and long-suffering? Knowest thou not that the goodness and gentleness of God calleth thee to repentence?' (Rom. ii. 4) According unto this godly example, though it be so that we must suffer somewhat against our will, and contrary to our minds and affections, yet should we not murmur and grudge, but amend our lives, and patiently look and wait for better.

And specially the unspeakable fidelity and love of God towards us ought lawfully to move and persuade us, to suffer God to work with us even according to his will and pleasure: for by this means we give God this honour, that he doth us no wrong nor injury, but disposeth all things most wisely, and will direct them to a good end.

On the contrary part, the unpatient man murmureth and grudgeth against God, and is angry with him, as though his judgments and works were not just and right, forasmuch as the wicked and ungodly live in pomp, pleasure, and all dissoluteness, and the virtuous and godly in poverty, sorrow, and misery. He may peradventure fancy and imagine with himself, that God overchargeth his faithful children, and will suffer them to remain in peril, necessity, and danger, and will not hear them. (Psalm xxxvii. 7)

And thus he is so poisoned with bitterness and obstinacy, that he beginneth to hate and to blaspheme God in heaven, and seeketh unlawful means to help and remedy himself: like as Saul did, running after witches and soothsayers. (1 Sam. xxviii. 7) Wherefore let every christian man take heed, that no such raving fierceness and bitterness come upon him, or at least that it remain not long by him; but in such temptation let him fight manfully, as in the face and sight of the heavenly Captain, which both seeth and knoweth all things, and also most faithfully rescueth his soldiers, and is, as it were, a fellow and one among them, and will recompense all their labour and travail a thousand-fold in the life everlasting.

Moreover, we have an evident and perfect image and spectacle of all patience in our Lord Jesus Christ, as he himself pointed us unto himself, saying: 'Whosoever will follow me, let him forsake himself, and take his cross upon his back, and follow me.' (Matt. xvi. 24) When his unspeakable martyrdom and passion began, he prayed: 'O Father, if it be possible, take this cup from me; but thy will, and not mine, be done.' Where did he ever once murmur or grudge, or cast out so much as one untoward and unpatient word, when he was mocked and scorned, scourged and beaten, and most cruelly misordered and dealt withal? (Matt. xxvi. Mark xiv. Luke xxii. John xviii. Isa. liii.)

Print this well and surely in thy mind, that he did pray upon the cross for his greatest enemies, and said: 'Father, forgive them, for they know not what they do.' (Luke xxiii. 34, Acts vii. 60) If he through his heavenly and divine might and power had rid himself of all his pain, sorrow, and danger, and that we in our sorrow, anguish, and necessity had not felt any heavenly strength nor power from God, then could we not have comforted ourselves at all with our Saviour Jesus Christ. But he would not put off his bitter passion through his almighty power, but rather overcome it through weakness.

Now then if he, whom all angels and creatures in heaven and earth do behold and look upon, (Psalm xcvii. 9, Heb. i.) yea, whom they all must serve and fear, doth suffer innocently undeserved with all patience and meekness more than ever any christian man was attempted with; it ought lawfully to make even an heart of stone or iron to yearn and melt, and to take these small afflictions well deserved most patiently and willingly, and to suffer and bear them most meekly. (1)

Spiritual Worship

It seemeth that Mary, with the ointment which she brought with her, thought to anoint the body of Christ, as she did afore in his life-time, and to reverence him, and to deal with him as with a mortal man; which thing Christ forbad her to do. Hereafter shall we hear, how he offereth unto his disciples his hands, feet, and side, willing them to touch him. But with this inhibition, and that commandment, he hath respect to only one thing; namely, to deliver Mary and the disciples from unbelief, from weak faith and doubting. Unto Mary he will say: 'Touch me not of a carnal devotion, as though thou wouldst anoint me. I need it no more. As for such corporal service, it is not necessary to do it unto my body any more. The cause why I became man was not that ye should alway hang upon my corporal flesh, and honour me with bodily service. Thou shalt now shortly understand, that I have like power with the Father. I am in thy heart not yet ascended up unto the Father: that is, thou hast as yet no right knowledge of my Godhead; therefore canst thou not now rightly touch me.'

Thus learn we also to know and honour Christ now no more after the flesh, and to shew no corporal outward service unto his person. In spirit will he be worshipped, with the faith and love of the inward mind. If any thing bodily be done of us, the same should be done unto the poor, and to the neighbour that hath need thereof. Thus may faith and love well use some outward things, not to do service therewith unto God, but unto ourselves or to our neighbour. As when we take and minister bread and wine about in the supper, distributing and eating it, the same is not done principally to the intent to declare a service unto God; but somewhat to provoke our outward senses and flesh by the exterior signs, that we may the better consider and ponder the grace of God declared unto us in the death of Jesus Christ, and that we may lift up our minds unto Christ, the heavenly food and living bread, which inwardly feedeth us with his flesh, and nourisheth us with his blood.

Thereto also hath Christ our Saviour instituted the figurative tokens and sacraments of his grace, to help our infirmity. For sacraments are gracious evidences of the faith that men have, or should have, to God; in the which they comfortably exercise and practise themselves towards God's promises; wherein also they declare the obedience of their inward faith, and that they faithfully believe the words and promises of Almighty God. For the token without belief is nothing profitable, but rather hurtful. All bodily service that the flesh imagineth, pleaseth not God. He sitteth at the right hand of God: there ought we to touch him with the lifting up of a faithful heart, and with the worship which he through his Spirit worketh and directeth into us: for therefore he died, rose again, and ascended up into heaven, that he might fulfil all things, and reign truly and spiritually in our hearts. Our hearts must we lift up there, as Christ sitteth at the right hand of God, and our conversation ought to be in heaven. (Col. iii. Phil. iii.)

Whereas the Lord willed his disciples to touch him, it was done to banish their doubtfulness, and to strengthen their weak faith. Which touching was not required of them as a worship, but that their flesh through the outward handling of his body might be quieted and stilled: and so is it a proof and testimony, that he verily rose with the former body, rather than a worshipping or service. Christ did not therefore take upon him his flesh, that we should always hang and depend thereon; but that we by his humanity should ascend up to his Godhead. For when we know the high and holy mystery of his passion and resurrection, with the which he hath served our turn, we ought to stir up our minds to know the Godhead, wherein he is like unto the Father. (2)

Hidden Glory

Forasmuch then as he became man, to make us God's and children of godly grace, he took upon him that which is ours, to give us and to part with us that which is his. Therefore calleth he us brethren, and maketh his own Father common unto us; so that he is also our Father and our God: that same which he hath of nature, doth he of grace give unto us. 'For his Spirit beareth record unto our spirit, that we are the children of God: for we have not received the spirit of bondage to fear, but the spirit of adoption, in the which we cry, Father, Father.'

Christ also calleth those that be his, not servants, but friends and brethren: he will be our God, and we his people; our Father, we his children: and his covenant which he hath made with us shall be everlasting: for it is sealed and confirmed with the blood of his only-begotten Son. Now have we fellowship and company with God the Father, the Son, and the Holy Ghost.

But such grace and glory is inwardly seen with the eyes of faith, and felt in the spirit, being hid here in time under the shape of the cross. For Christ doth not straightway by and by declare himself openly unto Mary Magdalene, as he is in his glory; but standeth there as a gardener, and speaketh unto her, by the which voice she knoweth him: he long deferreth the comfort, permitting her a good while to weep and lament, that the joy and consolation afterward may be the greater. But the cause why he so long delayeth his help and comfort from these that be his own, is, that their inward desires may be the more fervent and earnest, and that he may stir up and kindle their faith. Now when the fire is kindled enough, then cometh he with his comfort, as it is evident here in Mary Magdalene, and in the woman of Cananee. (Matthew xv.) (3)

Penitence and Unity

Furthermore, it is to be noted, that we cannot desire Christ, unless we do aspire to the justice of God, which consisteth in the denial of ourself, and the obedience that ought to be given unto him. For it can by no means agree, that we should be of the body of Christ, living in the mean time filthily, voluptuously, and without rule. Seeing that in Christ is nought else but all purity, continence, gentleness, sobriety, verity, humbleness, and all other like virtues; it behoveth us, if we will be members of his body, to be clear from all voluptuousness and riot, from arrogancy, intemperance, vanity, pride, and other vices; for we cannot mingle those with him, without great shame and reproach. It behoveth us alway to remember, that there is no more concord between him and iniquity, than is between light and darkness. Lo, by what means we may come to perfect repentance; by appointing our journey so, that our life be fashioned after the example of Christ. But although this thing be common to all parts of the life, yet take they place chiefly in charity, which in this sacrament is singularly commended unto us; by reason whereof it is also called the bond thereof. For as the bread, which for the use of all men is there sanctified, is made of many grains so compact together, that one cannot be separate and discerned from the other; even after the same rate ought we to be joined together with the indissoluble bond of friendship. And so do we all receive one body of Christ, to the end we may be his members. But if we be full of discords and dissensions, we do, as much as in us lieth, tear Christ, and pull him in sunder; neither shall we be guilty of smaller sacrilege than if we had done the thing in deed. Let us not therefore be bold to come thither, if any hatred or evil will towards any man, and chiefly a Christian, and joined to the unity of the church, do remain in us. We must also, for the keeping and following of the order of the Lord, bring with us another affection, that is to say, that we confess with mouth, and declare in very deed, how much we are bound to our Saviour, and that we may give thanks unto him; not only that we may give glory to his name, but that we may also instruct one another, and that our neighbours may through our example learn what they ought to do. (4)

Frequent Communion

In all congregations well ordered ought to be such custom, that the supper be celebrate so oft as may be, and so much as the people shall be able to receive. And every private person ought, so much as in him lieth, to be ready to receive it so often, as it shall be celebrate in a common assembly, unless he be by very urgent causes constrained to abstain. For albeit that the time is not assigned, nor the day expressed by any precept or commandment; yet ought this thing to suffice, that we know it to be the Lord's will we should use this sacrament oftentimes. Otherwise we know not the profit that cometh unto us thereby. The excuses that some men lay are void and vain. Some say, they are not worthy; and by that pretext they abstain all the year. Others do not only consider how unworthy they be; but they do also lay for them, that they cannot communicate with such as they see come thither unprepared. Also, other suppose, that the oft use of it is superfluous; neither do they think that it ought to be so often iterated and repeated, after that we have once received Christ.

I ask of those first, which lay for themselves their own unworthiness, how their conscience can sustain so great misery more than an year, and dare not call upon the Lord accordingly? For they will grant it to be a point of rashness to call upon God as a Father, unless we be the members of Christ; which thing cannot be done, unless the substance and verity of the supper be fulfilled in us: and if we have the verity itself, we are, with much better reason, meet to receive the same. Whereby we perceive, that they which would exempt themselves from the supper as unworthy, do rob themselves of that great commodity of invocating and praying to God. But I would not compel them, whose consciences be troubled and feared by any religion, to the intent they should intermingle themselves rashly. But rather I counsel them to tarry for a season, until the Lord shall vouchsafe to deliver them from that anxiety. In like manner, if there by any other cause, I do not deny but it is lawful to defer. I do only purpose to declare, that no man ought to continue long in this thing, that he may abstain for his unworthiness. For so is the congregation robbed of the communication, wherein all our health consisteth. Let him rather endeavour to fight against all the impediments which the devil casteth against him, lest he be excluded from so great a good thing, and consequently robbed of all the benefits together. (5)

Wisdom and Learning

Now though prayer be more excellent, because she talketh familiarly with Almighty God, yet is knowledge no less necessary: which as it ought not to be imperfect, so ought not prayer to be faint, slack, or without quickness; neither can we well perform the great journey that we have to go, without the aid and help of these two means. The use of prayer is not to mumble and babble much, as they do that are not ripe in God's Spirit. For five words spoken in knowledge are better than ten thousand babbled with the mouth. Neither is it the noise of our lips, but the fervent desire of the mind, that God alloweth. Which fervent prayer, with like study or meditation of the holy scripture, is able as well to put aback the great violence of our enemies, as to make easy our grievous adversity. If we with this heavenly manna and food of God be refreshed in the furtherance of our journey, it shall make us bold and strong to buckle with our enemies. For the doctrine of God, as it only is pure and undefiled, contrary to the nature of men's doctrines; even so to them that, spiritually understanding it, may abide the hearing thereof, there is nothing sweeter nor more pleasant, and therefore the more worthy to be searched and well pondered. This is the river of comfort, the fountain of ease, the well that refresheth the weary, the water of Siloe, where the blind receive their sight: to the study whereof if we apply ourselves wholly, that is, if we exercise our minds continually in the law of God, we shall be so armed, that we need not to fear any assault of our enemies.

Touching the heathen poets and philosophers, if we taste of them measurably, so that we wear not old nor die in them, they are not utterly to be disallowed. Yea, whatsoever they teach well, ought no more to be despised, than was the counsel of Jethro, whom Moses followed. As for such as write uncleanly, we ought either not to touch them, or else not to look too far in them. To be short, all manner of learning should be tasted in due season and measure, with good judgment and discretion, under the correction of Christ's doctrine; so that the wisdom of God be above all other, our best beloved, our dove, our sweetheart: which may not be touched, but with clean and washen hands, namely, with high pureness of mind and due reverence. For so coming unto it, we shall see the pleasures, delicacies, and dainties of our blessed spouse, the precious jewels of rich Solomon, even the secret treasure of eternal wisdom. Wherefore, considering the verity of God neither deceiveth, nor is deceived, we ought to give more credit thereunto, than to anything that we do bodily either see or hear.

As considering the interpreters of the holy scripture, we ought not to choose them that teach to brawl and contend, but such as go farthest from the letter; whose godliness and holy life is known, whose learning is more plenteous, and whose exposition is most agreeable to God's word. Now as we ought to grow unto perfectness and strength in the knowledge thereof, and not still to be children; even so, if we will have it to be savoury unto us and to nourish us, we must not read without understanding, as cloisters do, but break the rod, and taste of the sweetness therein; specially considering, that as it is the spirit and not the flesh that quickeneth, so will the Father of heaven be worshipped in the spirit, and not in the bark of the letter. Wherefore though we should not despise the weak, yet ought we to make speed unto more secret mysteries, and to stir up ourselves thereunto by often prayer, till it please God through his Son Jesus Christ to open it that yet is shut unto us. (6)

Simplicity of Life and Heart

The fourth rule is, that we have none other mark and ensample of living, save only Christ: who is nothing else save charity, simplicity, innocency, patience, cleanness, and whatsoever himself taught; to whom we direct our journey, if we be so given only unto virtue, that we love and desire nothing but either Christ, or else for Christ; hating, abhorring, flying, and avoiding nothing but only sin, or else for sin's sake. And thus if our eye be pure, all our body shall be bright; for that whatsoever honest or indifferent thing we take in hand, it shall turn to our wealth. As for filthy things, neither advantage; nor punishment should make us to commit them. Mean things, verily, and indifferent ought no further to be desired than they are profitable to a christian living. As for example, conning or learning must be loved for Christ's sake; so that when we know him and the secrets of his scripture, we love him in such sort, that opening him unto other, we both take fruit of him ourselves; and if we have knowledge of other sciences, we use them all to his honour. For better is it to have less knowledge and more love, than much to know, and not to love. Thus every thing, so far forth as it helpeth most unto virtue, ought chiefly to be applied. But rather ought we to lack them, than that they should hold us back from Christ; unto whom we ought to haste so fervently, that we should have no leisure to care for other things, whether they be given us, or taken away from us; but even to use the world as though we used it not. After this rule if we examine all our studies and acts, then like as having a craft or occupation, we will not labour to defraud our neighbours, but to find our households and to win them unto Christ; even so, when we fast, pray, or use any such like, we shall not do it for any carnal purpose, but proceed on still, till we come unto Christ, neither going out of the way, nor hoping or suffering any thing that shall not minister unto us some occasion of godliness. (7)

Respect for Others

This excellent learning then of Christ must be established in us, that we think us not to be born unto ourselves, but to the honour of God and wealth of all men: so that, loving him again which bestowed himself on us altogether for our redemption, we also for his sake love other men, and abhor their vices; having not only respect to their need, and what we are able to do for them, but also remembering the manifold causes, that by reason should move us to love them, to tender them, to be at one with them, and not to account them as strangers, or to hate them for any alteration of vesture, or of any such trifle; yea, in no wise to despise them, but esteeming their hurt our own; to consider that, whatsoever we have received, it is given us to bestow upon them, and to increase in edifying of them in charity. This learning will induce men to desire no vengeance, but to be the sons of their Father in heaven, to overcome evil with good, to suffer hurt rather than to do it, to forgive other men's offences, to be gentle in manners; if they be cunning, to forbear and amend the ignorance of the unlearned; if they be rich, to be circumspect in distributing the goods that God hath given them; in poverty, to be as well content as other men; in office, to be more careful and diligent in considering their charge, in noting the manners of evil persons, yet not to despise the profession of virtue; in labouring for a common office, or in executing of the same, to do it alway for the profit of the common, and not for their own singular wealth, being ready, even with the loss of their own life and goods, to defend that which is right; being loth to have pre-eminence, which if it chance unto them, yet to think that they also have a Lord and Master in heaven, even Jesus Christ, and that no man is bound to follow his doctrine more straitly than they; that he will of no man ask more strait accounts than of them; that they lean not to their own wills; that they flatter not themselves in evil; that their manners be such as deserve riches, honour, reverence, dignity, favour, and authority; that they themselves be not guilty in the offences which they do punish in others; that they despise no man in comparison of themselves; that in bearing rule they would not so much to excel as to profit all men; that they turn not to their own profit the things which are common, but bestow that they have, yea, and themselves also, upon the commonwealth; that in their titles of honour they refer all such things unto God; that in ministering their office they fetch not example of their predecessors or of flatterers, but only of Christ; that they be ready rather to lose their dominions than Christ, who hath a far better thing to give them. For nothing is so comely, so excellent, so glorious to kings, princes, and rulers, as in similitude to draw nigh unto the highest, greatest, and best king, even Jesus Christ; instead of violence to exercise charity, and to be minister unto all men. In conclusion, we must so cleave unto the learning of Christ, and be so circumspect therein, that we cloak not our own vices with other men's faults. For though holy men have sometime done anything not to be followed, (as David, when he committed adultery and murder; Solomon, when he had so many queens and concubines; Noe, when he was drunken; Lot, when he lay with his own daughters; Mary Magdalene, when she sinned so sore; Peter, when he denied the Lord; Paul, when he persecuted the Church of God;) yet ought we to do nothing that varieth from Christ; but as we have been like other men in sin, so should we be companions and partners also with them that repent and turn unto God. And as for other men's deeds, we ought not churlishly so much to bark against them, neither with cruelness to fear them, as with softness and apt means to amend them, and allure them unto Christ. (8)

NOTES / SOURCES

1. 'A Spiritual and Most Precious Pearl', in *Writings and Translations of Myles Coverdale*, ed. G. Pearson, Cambridge (Parker Society), 1844, pp. 169–71
2. 'Fruitful Lessons: Of the Resurrection of Christ', ibid., pp. 330–1
3. Ibid., pp. 332–3
4. 'A Treatise on the Sacrament of the Body and Blood of Christ', ibid., pp. 445–6
5. Ibid., pp. 448–9
6. 'Abridgement of Erasmus's Enchiridion, or, The Means to be Used in Christian Warfare', ibid., pp. 498–9
7. Ibid., pp. 509–10
8. Ibid., pp. 514–15

Thomas Cranmer   1489–1556

Born at Aslockton, Nottinghamshire, Thomas Cranmer was educated at Jesus College, Cambridge, where he became a Fellow in 1523. From an early stage Cranmer was concerned with the issue of Papal Authority over English concerns and played a major role in trying to justify Henry VIII's divorce from Katherine of Aragon. Soon after his accession as Archbishop of Canterbury in 1533, he annulled Katherine's marriage to Henry, as he also did with Anne Boleyn and Anne of Cleves. Whilst he was active in defending the use of the Bible in English, he did not take part in the Dissolution of the Monasteries and opposed the 'Six Articles' of 1539 (under which he was forced to send his wife to Germany). Upon the succession of Edward VI, Cranmer supervised the introduction of the First Prayer Book of 1549 and also that of 1552, both of which promoted the Reformation cause. However, when Katherine of Aragon's daughter, Mary Tudor, came to the throne (1553) Cranmer was accused of high treason and eventually tried for heresy. Under relentless pressure, lonely and uncertain, he signed documents acknowledging the supremacy of the Pope and the truth of Roman Catholic doctrine (apart from transubstantiation). He was burnt at the stake at Oxford on 21 March 1556, renouncing his recantations, famously holding his hand into the flames, saying 'this hand hath offended'.

Why read the Bible?

Wherefore, in few words to comprehend the largeness and utility of the scripture, how it containeth fruitful instruction and erudition for every man; if any things be necessary to be learned, of the holy scripture we may learn it. If falsehood shall be reproved, thereof we may gather wherewithal. If any thing be to be corrected and amended, if there need any exhortation or consolation, of the scripture we may well learn. In the scriptures be the fat pastures of the soul; therein is no venomous meat, no unwholesome thing; they be the very dainty and pure feeding. He that is ignorant, shall find there what he should learn. He that is a perverse sinner, shall there find his damnation to make him to tremble for fear. He that laboureth to serve God, shall find there his glory, and the promissions of eternal life, exhorting him more diligently to labour. Herein may princes learn how to govern their subjects; subjects obedience, love and dread to their princes: husbands, how they should behave them unto their wives; how to educate their children and servants: and contrary the wives, children, and servants may know their duty to their husbands, parents and masters. Here may all manner of persons, men, women, young, old, learned, unlearned, rich, poor, priests, laymen, lords, ladies, officers, tenants, and mean men, virgins, wives, widows, lawyers, merchants, artificers, husbandmen, and all manner of persons, of what estate or condition soever they be, may in this book learn all things what they ought to believe, what they ought to do, and what they should not do, as well concerning Almighty God, as also concerning themselves and all other. Briefly, to the reading of the scripture none can be enemy, but that either be so sick that they love not to hear of any medicine, or else that be so ignorant that they know not scripture to be the most healthful medicine. (1)

Faith and Works

A true faith cannot be kept secret but, when occasion is offered it will break out and shew itself by good works. And as the living body of a man ever exerciseth such things as belongeth to a natural and living body, for nourishment and preservation of the same, as it hath need, opportunity, and occasion; even so the soul, that hath a lively faith in it, will be doing alway some good work, which shall declare that it is living, and will not be unoccupied. Therefore, when men hear in the scriptures so high commendations of faith, that it maketh us to please God, to live with God, and to be the children of God; if then they phantasy that they be set at liberty from doing all good works, and may live as they list, they trifle with God, and deceive themselves. And it is a manifest token that they be far from having the true and lively faith, and also far from knowledge what true faith meaneth. For the very sure and lively christian faith is, not only to believe all things of God which are contained in holy scripture; but also is an earnest trust and confidence in God, that he doth regard us, and hath cure of us, as the father of the child whom he doth love, and that he will be merciful unto us for his only Son's sake, and that we have our Saviour Christ our perpetual advocate and priest, in whose only merits, oblation, and suffering, we do trust that our offences be continually washed and purged, whensoever we, repenting truly, do return to him with our whole heart, steadfastly determining with ourselves, through his grace, to obey and serve him in keeping his commandments, and never to turn back again to sin. Such is the true faith that the scripture doth so much commend; the which, when it seeth and considereth what God hath done for us, is also moved, through continual assistance of the Spirit of God, to serve and please him, to keep his favour, to fear his displeasure, to continue his obedient children, shewing thankfulness again by observing his commandments, and that freely, for true love chiefly, and not for dread of punishment or love of temporal reward; considering how clearly, without our deservings, we have received his mercy and pardon freely.

This true faith will shew forth itself, and cannot long be idle: for, as it is written, 'The just man doth live by his faith.' He neither sleepeth, nor is idle, when he should wake and be well occupied. And God by his prophet Jeremy saith, that 'he is a happy and blessed man which hath faith and confidence in God. For he is like a tree set by the water-side, that spreadeth his roots abroad toward the moisture, and feareth not heat when it cometh; his leaf will be green, and will not cease to bring forth his fruit:' even so faithful men, putting away all fear of adversity, will shew forth the fruit of their good works, as occasion is offered to do them. (2)

The Purpose of Sacraments

Although our carnal generation and our carnal nourishment be known to all men by daily experience, and by our common senses; yet this our spiritual generation and our spiritual nutrition be so obscure and hid unto us, that we cannot attain to the true and perfect knowledge and feeling of them, but only by faith, which must be grounded upon God's most holy word and sacraments.

And for this consideration our Saviour Christ hath not only set forth these things most plainly in his holy word, that we may hear them with our ears, but he hath also ordained one visible sacrament of spiritual regeneration in water, and another visible sacrament of spiritual nourishment in bread and wine, to the intent, that as much as is possible for man, we may see Christ with our eyes, smell him at our nose, taste him with our mouths, grope him with our hands, and perceive him with all our senses. For as the word of God preached putteth Christ into our ears, so likewise these elements of water, bread, and wine, joined to God's word, do after a sacramental manner put Christ into our eyes, mouths, hands, and all our senses.

And for this cause Christ ordained baptism in water, that as surely as we see, feel, and touch water with our bodies, and be washed with water, so assuredly ought we to believe, when we be baptized, that Christ is verily present with us and that by him we be newly born again spiritually, and washed from our sins, and grafted in the stock of Christ's own body, and be apparelled, clothed, and harnessed with him, in such wise, that as the devil hath no power against Christ, so hath he none against us, so long as we remain grafted in that stock, and be clothed with that apparel, and harnessed with that armour. So that the washing in water of baptism is, as it were, shewing of Christ before our eyes, and a sensible touching, feeling, and groping of him, to the confirmation of the inward faith, which we have in him.

And in like manner Christ ordained the sacrament of his body and blood in bread and wine, to preach unto us, that as our bodies be fed, nourished, and preserved with meat and drink, so as touching our spiritual life towards God we be fed, nourished, and preserved by the body and blood of our Saviour Christ; and also that he is such a preservation unto us, that neither the devils of hell, nor eternal death, nor sin, can be able to prevail against us, so long as by true and constant faith we be fed and nourished with that meat and drink. And for this cause Christ ordained this sacrament in bread and wine (which we eat and drink, and be chief nutriments of our body), to the intent that as surely as we see the bread and wine with our eyes, smell them with our noses, touch them with our hands, and taste them with our mouths, so assuredly ought we to believe that Christ is a spiritual life and sustenance of our souls, like as the said bread and wine is the food and sustenance of our bodies. (3)

The Symbolism of Holy Communion

Although there be many kinds of meats and drinks which feed the body, yet our Saviour Christ (as many ancient authors write) ordained this sacrament of our spiritual feeding in bread and wine, rather than in other meats and drinks, because that bread and wine do most lively represent unto us the spiritual union and knot of all faithful people, as well unto Christ, as also among themselves. For like as bread is made of a great number of grains of corn, ground, baken, and so joined together, that thereof is made one loaf; and an infinite number of grapes be pressed together in one vessel, and thereof is made wine; likewise is the whole multitude of true christian people spiritually joined, first to Christ, and then among themselves together in one faith, one baptism, one Holy Spirit one knot and bond of love.

As the bread and wine which we do eat be turned into our flesh and blood, and be made our very flesh and very blood, and so be joined and mixed with our flesh and blood, that they be made one whole body together; even so be all faithful Christians spiritually turned into the body of Christ, and so be joined unto Christ, and also together among themselves, that they do make but one mystical body of Christ, as St Paul saith: (1 Cor. x.) 'We be one bread and one body, as many as be partakers of one bread and one cup.' And as one loaf is given among many men, so that every one is partaker of the same loaf; and likewise one cup of wine is distributed unto many persons, whereof every one is partaker; even so our Saviour Christ (whose flesh and blood be represented by the mystical bread and wine in the Lord's supper) doth give himself unto all his true members, spiritually to feed them, nourish them, and to give them continual life by him. And as the branches of a tree, or member of a body, if they be dead, or cut off, they neither live, nor receive any nourishment or sustenance of the body or tree; so likewise ungodly and wicked people, which be cut off from Christ's mystical body, or be dead members of the same, do not spiritually feed upon Christ's body and blood, nor have any life, strength, or sustentation thereby. (4)

Spiritual Communion

If we receive no bread nor wine in the holy communion, then all these lessons and comforts be gone, which we should learn and receive by eating of the bread, and drinking of the wine: and that fantastical imagination giveth an occasion utterly to subvert our whole faith in Christ. For seeing that this sacrament was ordained in bread and wine (which be foods for the body) to signify and declare unto us our spiritual food by Christ; then if our corporal feeding upon the bread and wine be but fantastical, (so that there is no bread nor wine there indeed to feed upon, although they appear there to be,) then it doth us to understand, that our spiritual feeding in Christ is also fantastical, and that indeed we feed not of him: which sophistry is so devilish and wicked, and so much injurious to Christ, that it could not come from any other person, but only from the devil himself, and from his special minister antichrist.

This spiritual meat of Christ's body and blood is not received in the mouth, and digested in the stomach, (as corporal meats and drinks commonly be,) but it is received with a pure heart and a sincere faith. And the true eating and drinking of the said body and blood of Christ is, with a constant and lively faith to believe, that Christ gave his body, and shed his blood upon the cross for us, and that he doth so join and incorporate himself to us, that he is our head, and we his members, and flesh of his flesh, and bone of his bones, having him dwelling in us, and we in him. And herein standeth the whole effect and strength of this sacrament. And this faith God worketh inwardly in our hearts by his holy Spirit, and confirmeth the same outwardly to our ears by hearing of his word, and to our other senses by eating and drinking of the sacramental bread and wine in his holy supper.

What thing then can be more comfortable to us, than to eat this meat, and drink this drink? whereby Christ certifieth us, that we be spiritually, and truly, fed and nourished by him, and that we dwell in him, and he in us. Can this be shewed unto us more plainly, than when he saith himself, 'He that eateth me shall live by me?' (John vi.) (5)

Assurance through Communion

All men desire to have God's favour, and when they know the contrary, that they be in his indignation and cast out of his favour, what thing can comfort them? How be their minds vexed! What trouble is in their consciences! All God's creatures seem to be against them, and do make them afraid, as things being ministers of God's wrath and indignation towards them, and rest or comfort can they find none, neither within them, nor without them. And in this case they do hate as well God, as the devil; God, as an unmerciful and extreme judge, and the devil as a most malicious and cruel tormentor.

And in this sorrowful heaviness, holy scripture teacheth them, that our heavenly Father can by no means be pleased with them again, but by the sacrifice and death of his only-begotten Son, whereby God hath made a perpetual amity and peace with us, doth pardon the sins of them that believe in him, maketh them his children, and giveth them to his first-begotten Son Christ, to be incorporate into him, to be saved by him, and to be made heirs of heaven with him. And in the receiving of the holy supper of our Lord, we be put in remembrance of this his death, and of the whole mystery of our redemption. In the which supper is made mention of his testament, and of the aforesaid communion of us with Christ, and of the remission of our sins by his sacrifice upon the cross.

Wherefore in this sacrament, (if it be rightly received with a true faith,) we be assured that our sins be forgiven, and the league of peace and the testament of God is confirmed between him and us, so that whosoever by a true faith doth eat Christ's flesh, and drink his blood, hath everlasting life by him. Which thing when we feel in our hearts at the receiving of the Lord's supper, what thing can be more joyful, more pleasant, or more comfortable unto us? (6)

NOTES / SOURCES

1. Thomas Cranmer 'Preface to the Bible', *The Works of Thomas Cranmer*, ed. J. E. Cox, Cambridge (Parker Society), 1846, p. 121
2. 'Homily on Faith', ibid., p. 136
3. Thomas Cranmer 'The First Book of the Sacrament', *The Works of Thomas Cranmer*, ed. J. E. Cox, Cambridge (Parker Society), 1844, p. 41
4. Ibid., p. 42
5. Ibid., p. 43
6. Ibid., p. 44

William Tyndale   1494?–1536

Originally from Gloucestershire, William Tyndale studied at Magdalen Hall, Oxford, and subsequently at Cambridge. By 1522 Tyndale had decided to translate the Bible into English but, when the Bishop of London refused to support him, he left for Hamburg in Germany (1524). Having visited Luther at Wittenberg he started printing his first translation of the New Testament at Cologne in 1525, but was forced to complete the project at Worms later that year. When the work was published in England, it was denounced by both Archbishop Wareham and Thomas More. His writings, for example, *The Parable of the Wicked Mammon*, (1528) and *The Obedience of a Christian Man*, (1528) reveal his closeness to Luther in his insistence on the authority of scripture and the primacy of faith, but also a gradual move to a rather more radical theology. His denunciation of Henry VIII's divorce proceedings cost him the King's indulgence and he was betrayed, arrested, and tried for heresy at Vilvoorde near Brussels, (1535) where he was strangled and burnt at the stake. His biblical translations, noted for their pithy and memorable use of language, became the foundation for later English versions, including the King James Bible of 1611.

A Summary of Scripture

The Old Testament is a book, wherein is written the law of God, and the deeds of them which fulfil them, and of them also which fulfil them not.

The New Testament is a book, wherein are contained the promises of God; and the deeds of them which believe them, or believe them not.

Evangelion (that we call the gospel) is a Greek word; and signifieth good, merry, glad and joyful tidings, that maketh a man's heart glad, and maketh him sing, dance, and leap for joy: as when David had killed Goliah the giant, came glad tidings unto the Jews, that their fearful and cruel enemy was slain, and they delivered out of all danger: for gladness whereof, they sung, danced, and were joyful. In like manner is the Evangelion of God (which we call gospel, and the New Testament) joyful tidings; and, as some say, a good hearing published by the apostles throughout all the world, of Christ the right David; how that he hath fought with sin, with death, and the devil, and overcome them: whereby all men that were in bondage to sin, wounded with death, overcome of the devil, are, without their own merits or deservings, loosed, justified, restored to life and saved, brought to liberty and reconciled unto the favour of God, and set at one with him again: which tidings as many as believe laud, praise, and thank God; are glad, sing and dance for joy.

This Evangelion or gospel (that is to say, such joyful tidings) is called the New Testament; because that as a man, when he shall die, appointeth his goods to be dealt and distributed after his death among them which he nameth to be his heirs; even so Christ before his death commanded and appointed that such Evangelion, gospel, or tidings should be declared throughout all the world, and therewith to give unto all that [repent, and] believe, all his goods: that is to say, his life, wherewith he swallowed and devoured up death; his righteousness, wherewith he banished sin; his salvation, wherewith he overcame eternal damnation. Now can the wretched man (that [knoweth himself to be wrapped] in sin, and in danger to death and hell) hear no more joyous a thing, than such glad and comfortable tidings of Christ; so that he cannot but be glad, and laugh from the low bottom of his heart, if he believe that the tidings are true. (1)

Doing Good Freely

By faith we receive of God, and by love we shed out again. And that must we do freely, after the example of Christ, without any other respect, save our neighbour's wealth[1] only; and neither look for reward in the earth, nor yet in heaven, for the deserving and merits of our deeds, as friars preach; though we know that good deeds are rewarded, both in this life and in the life to come. But of pure love must we bestow ourselves, all that we have, and all that we are able to do, even on our enemies, to bring them to God, considering nothing but their wealth, as Christ did ours. Christ did not his deeds to obtain heaven thereby, (that had been a madness;) heaven was his already, he was heir thereof, it was his by inheritance; but did them freely for our sakes, considering nothing but our wealth, and to bring the favour of God to us again, and us to God. And no natural son, that is his father's heir, doth his father's will because he would be heir; that he is already by birth; his father gave him that ere he was born, and is loather that he should go without it, than he himself hath wit to be; but of pure love doth he that he doth. And ask him, Why he doth any thing that he doth? he answereth, My father bade; it is my father's will; it pleaseth my father. Bond-servants work for hire, children for love: for their father, with all he hath, is theirs already. So doth a Christian man freely all that he doth; considereth nothing but the will of God, and his neighbour's wealth only. If I live chaste, I do it not to obtain heaven thereby; for then should I do wrong to the blood of Christ; Christ's blood hath obtained me that; Christ's merits have made me heir thereof; he is both door and way thitherwards: neither that I look for an higher room[2] in heaven, than they

<hr>
[1] Wealth: welfare.   [2] Room: place.

shall have which live in wedlock, other than a whore of the stews (if she repent); for that were the pride of Lucifer: but freely to wait on the evangelion; and to avoid the trouble of the world, and occasions that might pluck me therefrom, and to serve my brother withal; even as one hand helpeth another, or one member another, because one feeleth another's grief, and the pain of the one is the pain of the other. Whatsoever is done to the least of us (whether it be good or bad), it is done to Christ; and whatsoever is done to my brother (if I be a Christian man), that same is done to me. Neither doth my brother's pain grieve me less than mine own: neither rejoice I less at his wealth than at mine own, if I love him as well and as much as myself, as the law commandeth me. If it were not so, how saith Paul? 'Let him that rejoiceth, rejoice in the Lord,' that is to say, Christ, which is Lord over all creatures. If my merits obtained me heaven, or a higher place there, then had I wherein I might rejoice besides the Lord. (2)

The Nature of Prayer

Prayer is a mourning, a longing, and a desire of the spirit to God-ward, for that which she lacketh; as a sick man mourneth and sorroweth in his heart, longing for health. Faith ever prayeth. For after that by faith we are reconciled to God, and have received mercy and forgiveness of God, the spirit longeth and thirsteth for strength to do the will of God, and that God may be honoured, his name hallowed, and his pleasure and will fulfilled. The spirit waiteth and watcheth on the will of God, and ever hath her own fragility and weakness before her eyes; and when she seeth temptation and peril draw nigh, she turneth to God, and to the testament that God hath made to all that believe and trust in Christ's blood; and desireth God for his mercy and truth, and for the love he hath to Christ, that he will fulfil his promise, and that he will succour, and help, and give us strength, and that he will sanctify his name in us, and fulfil his godly will in us, and that he will not look on our sin and iniquity, but on his mercy, on his truth, and on the love that he oweth to his Son Christ; and for his sake to keep us from temptation, that we be not overcome; and that he deliver us from evil, and whatsoever moveth us contrary to his godly will.

Moreover, of his own experience he feeleth other men's need, and no less commendeth to God the infirmities of other than his own, knowing that there is no strength, no help, no succour, but of God only. And as merciful as he feeleth God in his heart to himself-ward, so merciful is he to other; and as greatly as he feeleth his own misery, so great compassion hath he on other. His neighbour is no less care to him than himself: he feeleth his neighbour's grief no less than his own. (3)

Love of Neighbour and Stranger

The order of love or charity, which some dream, the gospel of Christ knoweth not of, that a man should begin at himself, and serve himself first, and then descend, I wot not by what steps. Love seeketh not her own profit, 2 Cor. xii.; but maketh a man to forget himself, and to turn his profit to another man, as Christ sought not himself, nor his own profit, but ours. This term, myself, is not in the gospel; neither yet father, mother, sister, brother, kinsman, that one should be preferred in love above another. But Christ is all in all things. Every Christian man to another is Christ himself; and thy neighbour's need hath as good right in thy goods, as hath Christ himself, which is heir and lord over all. And look, what thou owest to Christ, that thou owest to thy neighbour's need. To thy neighbour owest thou thine heart, thyself, and all that thou hast and canst do. The love that springeth out of Christ excludeth no man, neither putteth difference between one and another. In Christ we are all of one degree, without respect of persons. Notwithstanding, though a Christian man's heart be open to all men, and receiveth all men, yet, because that his ability of goods extendeth not so far, this provision is made, that every man shall care for his own household, as father and mother, and thine elders that have holpen thee, wife, children, and servants. If thou shouldest not care and provide for thine household, then were thou an infidel; seeing thou hast taken on thee so to do, and forasmuch as that is thy part committed to thee of the congregation. When thou hast done thy duty to thine household, and yet hast further abundance of the blessing of God, that owest thou to the poor that cannot labour, or would labour and can get no work, and are destitute of friends; to the poor, I mean, which thou knowest, to them of thine own parish. For that provision ought to be had in the congregation, that every parish care for their poor. If thy neighbours which thou knowest be served, and thou yet have superfluity, and hearest necessity to be among the brethren a thousand miles off, to them art thou debtor. Yea, to the very infidels we be debtors, if they need, as far forth as we maintain them not against Christ, or to blaspheme Christ. Thus is every man, that needeth thy help, thy father, mother, sister, and brother in Christ; even as every man, that doth the will of the Father, is father, mother, sister, and brother unto Christ.

Moreover, if any be an infidel and a false Christian, and forsake his household, his wife, children, and such as cannot help themselves, then art thou bound, and[1] thou have wherewith, even as much as to thine own household. And they have as good right in thy goods as thou thyself: and if thou withdraw mercy from them, and hast wherewith to help them, then art thou a thief. If thou shew mercy, so doest thou thy duty, and art a faithful minister in the household of Christ; and of Christ shalt thou have thy reward and thanks. If the whole world were thine, yet hath every brother his right in thy goods; and is heir with thee, as we are all heirs with Christ. Moreover the rich, and they that have wisdom with them, must see the poor set a-work, that as many as are able may feed themselves with the labour of their own hands, according to the scripture and commandment of God. (4)

Love Begins with God

The scripture speaketh as a father doth to his young son, Do this or that, and then will I love thee: yet the father loveth his son first, and studieth with all his power and wit to overcome his child with love and with kindness, to make him do that which is comely, honest, and good for itself. A kind father and mother love their children even when they are evil, that they would shed their blood to make them better, and to bring them into the right way. And a natural child studieth not to obtain his father's love with works; but considereth with what love his father

---

[1] And: if.

loveth him withal, and therefore loveth again, is glad to do his father's will, and studieth to be thankful.

The spirit of the world understandeth not the speaking of God; neither the spirit of the wise of this world, neither the spirit of philosophers, neither the spirit of Socrates, of Plato, or of Aristotle's ethics, as thou mayest see in the first and second chapter of the first to the Corinthians. Though that many are not ashamed to rail and blaspheme, saying, How should he understand the scripture, seeing he is no philosopher, neither hath seen his metaphysic? moreover they blaspheme, saying, How can he be a divine, and wotteth not what is *subjectum in theologia*[1]? nevertheless as a man, without the spirit of Aristotle or philosophy, may by the Spirit of God understand scripture; even so, by the Spirit of God, understandeth he that God is to be sought in all the scripture, and in all things; and yet wotteth not what meaneth *subjectum in theologia*, because it is a term of their own making. If thou shouldest say to him that hath the Spirit of God, the love of God is the keeping of the commandments, and to love a man's neighbour is to shew mercy; he would, without arguing or disputing, understand how that of the love of God springeth the keeping of his commandments, and of the love to thy neighbour springeth mercy. Now would Aristotle deny such speaking; and a Duns' man would make twenty distinctions[2]. If thou shouldest say (as saith John, the fourth chapter of his epistle), 'How can he that loveth not his neighbour whom he seeth, love God whom he seeth not?' Aristotle would say, Lo, a man must first love his neighbour and then God; and out of the love to thy neighbour springeth the love to God. But he that feeleth the working of the Spirit of God, and also from what vengeance the blood of Christ hath delivered him, understandeth how that it is impossible to love either father or mother, sister, brother, neighbour, or his own self aright, except it spring out of the love to God; and perceiveth that the love to a man's neighbour is a sign of the love to God, as good fruit declareth a good tree; and that the love to a man's neighbour accompanieth and followeth the love of God, as heat accompanieth and followeth fire. (5)

NOTES / SOURCES

1. William Tyndale 'A Pathway into the Holy Scripture', *Doctrinal Treatises . . . by William Tyndale*, ed. Henry Walter, Cambridge (Parker Society), 1848, pp. 8–9
2. Ibid., pp. 20–1
3. 'The Parable of the Wicked Mammon', ibid., p. 93
4. Ibid., pp. 98–9
5. Ibid., pp. 107–8

Thomas Becon 1512–1567

Born in Norfolk, Thomas Becon studied at St John's College, Cambridge, came under the influence of Hugh Latimer, and was ordained priest in 1538. Under Henry VIII he was compelled to recant his Protestant sympathies and for a time lived as a layman in Kent, earning his living by teaching. On the accession of Edward VI in 1547 he became

[1] After discussing the question in some sentences, Aquinas comes to the conclusion, that as theology is the science which treats of God, he can allow that its subject is God. Summ. Theolog. Quæst. 1. Art. vii.
[2] Duns' man: a follower of Duns Scotus.

Chaplain to Archbishop Cranmer and Vicar of St Stephen, Walbrook. However, when Mary came to throne in 1553, he was sent to the Tower as a 'seditious preacher' and removed from his living, being a married priest. On his release he taught in Germany, but returned to England in 1559 under Elizabeth I. Becon was a hugely prolific writer, with a vivid style. His *Potation for Lent* is a dramatized conversation (like several other of his works) between 'Philemon', 'Theophile', 'Eusebe' and 'Christopher'. He provides one of the first systematic Protestant treatises on prayer in English.

Confession

Theo. But we hear nothing all this while of auricular confession, which is chiefly used among us at this time. *Eus.* Of this we would be glad to hear. *Chris.* I pray you, express your mind concerning this kind of confession also: for some approve it, some again condemn it. *Phil.* Why auricular confession should be condemned and exiled from the bounds of christianity, I see no cause; but that it should be approved, retained, maintained, and used, I find causes many, yea, and those right urgent and necessary. *Chris.* Much absurdity and wickedness hath both been conspired, learned, practised, and done in this auricular confession, as histories make mention, neither want we experience of this thing. *Phil.* I cannot deny these things to be true. There is nothing so good and of so great excellency, but it may be abused. The abuse thereof is to be taken away, and not the thing itself. That confession hath been greatly abused it cannot be denied, as many other things in the church have been also; yet ought it not therefore to be rejected and cast away, but rather restored to the old purity, and to the use for the which it was first instituted. And so shall it not only not hurt, but also profit very highly, and bring much utility and profit to the christian congregation.

   Theo. This thing shall never come to pass, except they that sit on confession be men of gravity, sagacity, wisdom, discretion, sobriety, integrity, and able to teach, to instruct, and inform with all godly doctrine. *Eus.* Methink it an extreme point of madness for a man, if his body be diseased, to hunt, inquire, and seek about for a sober, wise, prudent, and cunning physician, that may cure and heal it, and to be so negligent in those things that pertain to his soul. For many care not to what priest they go unto, be he learned or unlearned, wise or foolish, modest or light, of good conversation or of naughty living, so that to satisfy the custom they come to one and receive their absolution, and go away never the better instructed, nor with the more penitent hearts. *Chris.* This is a great abuse. *Phil.* Ye say truth. Therefore were it convenient that they which should be appointed to be curates and overseers of the christian people, into whose hands the whole life and care of Christ's flock is committed, should be of such sort as St Paul describeth in his epistles to Timothy (1 Tim. iii.) and Titus (Titus i.), that is to say, irreprehensible, faultless, sober, discreet, righteous, holy, temperate, apt to teach, and such one as cleaveth unto the true word of doctrine, that he may be able to exhort with wholesome learning, and to improve them that speak against it. For this cause did God command in the old testament (Lev. xxi.), that they should not be chosen to be priests for to minister to him which had any blemish on them, whether they were blind, lame, with an evil-favoured nose, with any misshapen member, or that have a broken foot or hand, crookbacked, or any blemish in their eyes, etc.

What meant God by this perfection of the priests' members, but only to shew that he which should serve him, and give attendance on his flock, should be whole and sound in all kind of virtue and godliness; not corrupt nor deformed with any iniquity or uncleanness? A priest ought to have no blemish on him; that is to say, he ought to be pure both in his doctrine and conversation. *Chris.* God grant us once such curates, that may rule among us with such integrity of life and sincerity of doctrine, as is required of them in the holy scriptures! *Eus.* If this might be brought to pass, then should the gospel of Christ flourish, and the flock of Christ, whom he purchased with his most precious blood, be better looked upon and fed than they are now-a-days (Acts xx.28.). *Phil.* Truth it is. But, I pray you, mark what I shall now say unto you concerning this auricular confession. That auricular confession is a thing of much weight and grave importance, it appeareth well, inasmuch as it bringeth to men divers ample commodities and large profits. *Theo.* I pray you, what are those?

Phil. First, it engraffeth in us a certain humility, submission, and lowliness of mind, and depresseth all arrogancy and pride, while we humbly are contented to confess to our ghostly fathers such offences as wherewith we have offended God. Secondly, it incuteth and beateth into our hearts a shamefacedness, whereby we are so ashamed of our faults heretofore committed, that we utterly abhor them, and are wholly inflamed with the love of virtue. Thirdly, it bringeth us to the knowledge of ourselves, while we hear those things of the priest that are necessary to be known of every christian man. Fourthly, in confession we do not only learn to know how heinous and detestable a thing sin is before God, but also means and ways to eschew it. How many, think you, are there, which, if this auricular confession were taken away, would not care how they lived, neither would they regard any part of Christ's doctrine, but live like brute beasts, without any fear of God at all, or study of innocency, wallowing and tumbling themselves daily in sin, not once having a respect unto the correction of their old and wicked manners? Fifthly, if we be in doubt of any thing, in confession we may learn the assurance and certainty of it. Sixthly, in confession the ignorant is brought unto knowledge, the blind unto sight, the desperate unto salvation, the presumptuous unto humility, the troubled unto quietness, the sorrowful unto joy, the sick unto health, the dead to life. What need I make many words? Confession bringeth high tranquillity to the troubled conscience of a christian man, while the most comfortable words of absolution are rehearsed unto him by the priest.

Eus. I pray you, what is that absolution? *Phil.* Verily, a preaching of the free deliverance from all our sins through Christ's blood. How say you, is here any thing to be condemned in auricular confession thus used? *Chris.* No, verily, all things that you have rehearsed are rather worthy high praise and commendation. *Phil.* It is attributed and given us even of nature to communicate unto other the secrets of our hearts concerning temporal and worldly things, whether they be of joy or sadness; and till we have so done, we are never in rest. *Eus.* Ye say truth. *Phil.* Why should we then not be ready to do so likewise in spiritual affairs and things pertaining unto the salvation of our souls, except peradventure we be enemies of our own health? 'What is sweeter and more pleasant,' saith Cicero, 'than to have such one with whom thou darest be bold so to speak all things as with thyself?' A man having a learned, wise, discreet, silent, close, and faithful ghostly father, which loveth the penitent no less than a natural father doth his child, why should he fear to declare unto him the secrets of his heart, which is ready to comfort, to instruct, to counsel, to teach, and to do all things that should make unto his consolation and health? The prophet Malachy saith: 'The lips of a priest keep knowledge; and men shall seek the law at his mouth: for he is a messenger of the Lord of hosts.' (Mal. ii.) If this ought to be done at all times, when have we a more convenient and fit time to do it than in the time of confession, when we may freely talk to our spiritual fathers whatsoever pleaseth us? *Eus.* It is truth that ye say. But what if such a ghostly father doth not chance as ye have described heretofore? *Phil.* Verily, ye ought alway to resort to the best learned men, and to seek for such ghostly fathers as both will and can instruct and teach you the law of God. But let it so be, that your curate be not of the greatest learned men; yet is he too much simple if he can bring 'out of his treasure-house things neither new nor old,' seeing that the holy scriptures are so plenteously set forth in our English tongue, that even the very idiot may now become learned in the kingdom of God. Therefore, to make few words concerning this matter, disdain ye not to go to confession at the times appointed, according to the act of our most excellent king, yea, and that with all humble reverence. Declare the diseases of your souls unfeignedly, that ye may be healed with the most sweet and comfortable salve of God's word. Follow the godly and wholesome admonitions of your ghostly father. Go unto him with such an hatred and detestation of sin, that ye may return from him with hearts altogether inflamed with the perfect love of virtue, innocency, and true godliness, being full fixed never to return unto your old vomit and wallowing in the mire (2 Pet. ii.). And when he shall rehearse unto you the most sweet and comfortable words of absolution, give earnest faith unto them, being undoubtedly persuaded that your sins at that time be assuredly forgiven you, as though God himself had spoken them, etc. according to this saying of Christ, 'He that heareth you heareth me:' again, 'Whose sins ye forgive are forgiven them.' This have I spoken concerning auricular confession. *Theo.* Very godly, forsooth. *Eus.* What remaineth now? *Chris.* Ye promised consequently to entreat of satisfaction or amendment of life. *Phil.* Ye say truth. Of that matter therefore will I now entreat. (1)

True Fasting

If ye will fast aright, after the mind of St John Chrysostom, ye must first anoint your head, that is to say, comfort the poor people with such goods as God hath committed to you. For the riches that ye have be not yours only but they be God's also, as he saith by the prophet: 'Gold is mine, silver is mine. God hath put them in your hands, that ye should distribute part of them to the poor people.' (Hag. ii.) Ye are the stewards of God and the dispensators of his treasures, that you living of them, should also comfort the poor members of Christ. If ye spend then otherwise than God hath appointed you in his word, ye shall render an accompts for it. Ye have nothing at all but that ye shall be called to an accompts for it, even to the uttermost farthing. If ye be not found to have used your talent well, and unto the profit of other, ye shall with that unprofitable servant of the gospel be cast into outward darkness, where weeping and gnashing of teeth shall be (Matt. xxv.). If ye be proved unmerciful and negligent in the distribution of the worldly goods, surely, surely, ye shall be carried away with the rich man, of whom St Luke speaketh in the gospel (Luke. xvi.), unto hell, and there burn in such cruel and bitter flames, as 'the fire whereof shall never be quenched neither shall the worm of them that shall be there die at any time,' as the prophet saith (Isai. lxvi.). Thus see you that ye have no great cause to boast and glory of worldly goods nor yet to avance yourselves above other men for your possessions' sake, no more than a great man's servant hath, to whom his lord and master hath committed his goods for a certain space to keep, the servant looking at every hour when his master will require them again. 'He is a very thief and robber,' saith Basilius Magnus, 'which maketh that thing his own, that he hath received to distribute and give abroad. For the bread,' saith he, 'that thou retainest and keepest, is the bread of the hungry: the garment, which thou keepest in thy chest, is the garment of the naked: the shoe, that is mould with thee, is the shoe of him that is unshod; and the money, which thou hidest in the ground, is the money of the needy. Moreover, thou doest injury and plain wrong to so many as thou forsakest, when thou art able to help them.' Hitherto pertaineth the saying of the wise man: 'The bread of the needy is the life of the poor: he that defraudeth him of it is a manslayer.' (Ecclus. xxxiv.) Thus see you in how great jeopardy the rich men are that be unmerciful unto the poor people, and how little their fast pleaseth God in their unmercifulness, seeing they do not anoint their head, that is, shew no mercy to the poor members of Christ. God, teaching the true manner of fasting by his prophet, among all other things, saith: 'Break thy bread to the hungry.' (Isai. lviii.) Mark that he saith, break thy bread to the hungry. Certain doctors write on this text and say, that thou breakest thy bread then to the hungry, when thou so fastest that thou sparest from thine own belly to give it to the poor hungry man. For a christian man ought to be no less careful for the poor than for himself, so that, provision once made for his family, he must also shew mercy to the needy. Thou therefore dost break thy bread unto the hungry, when thou givest him that which thou thyself necessarily shouldest have eaten. And this is to anoint thy head aright, verily even to break thy bread to the hungry. *Theo.* Would God that all rich men did know thus much, and would follow it! For many think that they do God an high sacrifice, yea, and that they be good almsmen, if, when they have once pampered their own bellies with all kinds of dainties, they then at the last give or send to the hungry a few scraps which they will scarcely vouchsafe to give unto their dogs. *Phil.* I pray God give us all grace to do our duty. Now have ye heard what it is to anoint your head. I will also speak somewhat of washing your face, although I may seem abundantly to have spoken of the very effect of it in the definition of fasting.

If we will fast aright, we are not only commanded to anoint our head, that is to say, to shew mercy to the poor people, but also to wash our face, that is, to make our hearts clean from all sin, that we may have a pure conscience. For it is not enough to be beneficial to other, except we also be beneficial to ourselves. This shall come to pass, if we labour with all main to have a mind pure and clean from all carnal affects, and a body void of wicked deeds. What was the cause that God did cast away the fasts and solemn feasts which the Jews celebrated and kept holy in his name, but only that they washed not their face, that is, they went not about to put off their old conversation, and to become new men? 'I hate and abhor,' saith God, 'your sacrifices, your solemn feasts, your fasts.' (Isia. i.) Why so? For 'your hands' saith he, 'are full of blood.' Your hearts are full of vengeance, your consciences are spotted and defiled with all kind of sins; ye have no fear of God before your eyes. What is then to be done? 'Be ye washed,' saith he, 'be ye clean, take away the evil of your thoughts from mine eyes. Cease to do evil, learn to do well, seek judgment, help the poor oppressed, be favourable to the comfortless, defend the widow, etc.' God hateth those prayers, those fasts, those good deeds, as they call them, which come from a defiled body, a corrupt heart, a filthy mind, a bloody conscience, a spotted and pocky soul; as a certain man saith: 'It profit a man nothing at all to fast and pray, and to do other good things of devotion, except the mind be refrained from ungodliness, and the tongue from back-bitings.' For God hath ever a principal respect to the heart of the doer of the work. If the heart be pure, clean, and faithful, then doth God approve that work: but if it be spotted with sin, God casteth it away, appear it never so glistering and excellent in the sight of the world. 'Offer not,' saith the wise man, 'wicked gifts; for God will not receive them.' (Ecclus. xxxv.) *Chris.* It is evident then, that so many as change not their wicked life, cast away their hypocrisy, make clean their hearts, put out of their minds all rancour, malice, envy, grudge, etc., and study above all things to lead a pure and innocent life, can by no means please God. *Phil.* No, forsooth. Therefore if ye intend to fast aright, and to make your fast acceptable to God, provide earnestly that your fast proceed from a pure and clean heart, void of all carnal affects, stuffed full of faith and charity, and altogether studious of true innocency and unfeigned godliness. So shall it come to pass, that not only your fast, but all that ever ye do besides according to God's word, shall very greatly please God. *Theo.* I beseech God give us grace to do all things according to his most godly will and pleasure. *Phil.* Labour, and God will help. I have declared two things that are necessary to the true use of fasting. There remaineth now the third to be brought forth, which is so expedient and necessary for that purpose also, that the other two without this profiteth nothing. *Eus.* I pray you, let us hear it. *Phil.* We are not only commanded in our fasting to anoint our head and to wash our face, but also to fast in secret. *Theo.* What is it, I pray you, to fast in secret?

Phil. Verily, to fast in secret is not to keep you close from the sight of men, and so to abstain from your meats in privy corners; but not to hunt and hawk after vain glory nor praise of men for your fasting, nor to seek to be seen of men while ye fast, that they may commend and praise you. We are counted before God then to fast in secret, when we fast with such a mind, that we would fast in deed, though no man living did see us, and when we regard more the accomplishment of God's will, and the subjection and taming of our body, than all the human glory that can be attributed unto us. *Eus.* It is lawful then to fast even before men. *Phil.* Yea verily, or to do any other good work, so that the desire of worldly praise be not in your minds; for Christ saith: 'Let your light so shine before men, that they may see your good works, and glorify your Father which is in heaven.' (Matt. v.) But if we seek any praise of men, and desire to be magnified for our good deeds, verily then have we our reward, not of God, but of the world. For there is no more pestiferous infection to poison any good work, that it should lose the reward before God, than the desire of vain-glory and worldly praise. (Isai. xiv.) What did deject and cast down Lucifer from heaven into hell-pit, but vain-glory? (2 Pet. ii.) Again, what did exalt and lift up from the earth unto heaven the most blessed and glorious virgin Mary, the mother of our Saviour Jesus Christ, but humility? as she herself testifieth (Luke i.): 'My soul,' saith she, 'magnifieth the Lord; and my spirit rejoiceth in God my Saviour. For he hath looked upon the humility of his handmaid: behold, because of this shall all kindreds call me blessed.' 'God resisteth the proud, but to the humble he giveth grace and sheweth favour.' (1 Pet. v.) 'Unto whom shall I look,' saith God by his prophet (Isai. lxvi.), 'but unto him that is poor and contrite in spirit, and feareth my words?' 'Blessed are the poor in spirit; for to them belongeth the kingdom of heaven.' (Matt. v.) Therefore all your works that ye do, do them with a simple mind, and with such an heart as, being nothing desirous of vain-glory, seeketh only the honour of God, and the accomplishment of his most divine will.—Thus have I taught you, neighbours, both what the true and christian fast is, and also how ye ought to fast. (2)

Prayer and Charity

But some man will say peradventure, Is it enough if I pray with my mind, the heart being semoted from mundane affairs and worldly businesses? I answer: Our definition teacheth us not only to pray with the mind, but also with a pure mind. For 'prayer is the lifting up of a pure mind.' So see we that it is not enough to pray with the mind, except it be pure. It will be objected, Then shall we never pray: for 'who can say, My heart is clean, and I am pure from sin?' (Prov. xx.) I answer: 'If ye say, we have no sin, we deceive ourselves, and the truth is not in us. But if we confess our sins, God is faithful and righteous to forgive us our sins, and make us clean from all unrighteousness.' (1 John i.) The scripture saith: 'Blessed are they whose iniquities are forgiven, and whose sins are covered. Blessed is that man to whom the Lord hath imputed no sin.' (Psal. xxxii. Rom. iv.) It saith not: Blessed are they which have no iniquities, or which have no sin. For St James saith: 'In many things we sin all.' (James iii.) So long as we are in this mortal flesh, we can never be pure and clean from the dregs of sin, if from the sin itself. We can never in this life aspire unto so great perfection of innocency, that we may appear pure and guiltless in the sight of God, in whose eyes the very stars and angels be not clean. (Job xxv.)

How then may we pray with a pure mind? Verily, if our mind be faithful to God and charitable to our neighbour, God doth dissemble all our faults; and inasmuch as we are faithful unto him, and loving to our christian brothers, he counteth us all pure, as St John saith (1 John iii.): 'He that is born of God sinneth not,' that is to say, he that believeth in God, his sin is not imputed unto him, inasmuch as he consenteth not to the sin, but hungereth and thirsteth after the perfection of true innocency. Our hearts be purified by faith, saith the scripture (Acts xv.); so that whosoever prayeth with a faithful and charitable mind, he is counted before God to pray with a pure mind. For God judgeth not as the world doth. The world thinketh him to be a good, devout man, that goeth up and down with a cogging pair of beads in his hands, or kneeleth down in his stool solemnly with a great mattins-book in his hand, making such a noise with his lips and tongue, that all the whole church ringeth of it, although his heart be far from God and his mind occupied about worldly business. But God beholdeth the mind, the heart, the inward man, and looketh whether he prayeth in purity and cleanness or not. If the heart be stuffed with faith and charity, then is God well pleased, and accepteth the prayer for an high and pleasant sacrifice. Who being in the temple, hearing the proud pharisee and the poor publican praying together, would not have esteemed the pharisee to be more righteous and pure in the sight of God than the wretched publican? (Luke xviii.) For the pharisee confessed no sin, but virtues many. He gave God thanks that he was not like other men which are extortioners, unrighteous, adulterers, and as the publican was. He fasted twice in the week, and gave the tenths of all things that he possessed. O angelic righteousness and seraphical perfection.! Who would not have thought this holy religious father worthy to be canonized and related[1] into the number of saints? Yet saith Christ plainly, that the poor publican, which brought forth no good deeds, but stood afar off and durst not lift up his eyes to heaven, but humbly knocked his breast, saying, 'O God, be thou merciful unto me a sinner,' went home more righteous in God's sight than the pharisee. Why so? For the pharisee had no true faith in him, but an arrogant presumption, boasting and cracking of his good deeds, as though God were in his debt, and he not in God's. And that he had no christian charity in him it is evident, seeing that he despised his neighbour. For 'charity,' saith the scripture, 'covereth the multitude of sins.' (Prov. x. 1 Pet. iv.) (3)

Contemplating the Promises of God

Thirdly, when he hath on this manner pondered the commandment of God, wherewith he is provoked to pray, then doth convenient time require that he also considereth the most loving, gentle, and bounteous promises of God, in the which he promiseth for to hear us and to grant us our petitions. For what doth it profit for to ask and not to obtain? If God had only commanded us to pray, and not also promised for to hear us, and gently to give us our desires, what great pleasure had he done for us? what had he done for the which we had need once to say, Lord God a mercy? What singular benefit had we received of him? But although the commandment to pray putteth us in good comfort, yet when we are promised also graciously to be heard, this maketh us unfeignedly to rejoice and seriously to triumph. This maketh us to put out of our heart all dolour and sadness, and to be replete with all mirth and gladness. The promises of God bring quietness to the conscience, cheerfulness to the heart, tranquillity and peace to the soul. No man is able to express, how much and how great joy lieth buried up in the divine promises, and how fervent consolation the sinner taketh by the hearing of them. What joy, think ye, was this unto Adam for to hear after his offence, that the Son of God should be born of a pure maid, and tread down the serpent's head, that is, subdue Satan, and deliver Adam with all his posterity from his tyranny, bring them again into the favour of God, and make them heirs of eternal glory! What comfort, I pray you, was this to faithful Abraham for to hear that in his seed all nations of the earth should be blessed! (Gen. xxii.) What a great pleasure was this to the Israelites, when they were grievously stinged and slain of the fiery serpents for their disobedience, to hear this promise of God, 'Make a brasen serpent, and set it up for a sign: He that is stricken and looketh upon it shall live'! (Num. xxi.) What exceeding comfort received Josue by this promise of God unto him, 'I will not leave thee, neither will I forsake thee: be therefore strong, and take a good heart unto thee!' (Josh. i.) As I may come nearer to our matter, how much joy, consolation, and pleasure have the faithful felt of this one promise of God, 'Every one that calleth on the name of the Lord shall be saved!' (Joel ii. Acts ii. Rom. x.)

Therefore in this behalf the promises of God must be earnestly weighed,

---

[1] Related: referred, enrolled.

pondered, and considered. In them must we rest daily, as in a most pleasant harbour. In them must we repose ourselves. In them must be all our delight, pleasure, and felicity.

The chief promises concerning prayer are these: 'Delight thou in the Lord, and he shall give thee the petitions of thy heart.' (Psal. xxxvii.) 'Call on me,' saith God, 'in the day of thy trouble, and I will deliver thee, and thou shalt honour me.' (Psal. l.) Again he saith (Psal. xci.): 'Seeing that he hath put his trust in me, I will deliver him, and I will defend him, inasmuch as he hath known my name. He cried unto me, and I will graciously hear him. I am with him in tribulation, I will deliver him and glorify him. With the length of days will I replenish him, and shew him my saving health.' Christ also saith: 'Come unto me, all ye that labour and are laden, and I shall refresh you.' (Matt. xi.) 'Every one that is athirst, let him come to me and drink.' (John vii.) Again: 'Ask, and it shall be given you: seek, and ye shall find: knock, and it shall be opened unto you. For every one that asketh receiveth, and he that seeketh findeth, and to him that knocketh it shall be opened. (Matt. vii. Luke xi.) If the son asketh bread of any of you which is his father, will ye proffer him a stone? or if he asketh fish, will ye give him a serpent? or if he ask an egg, will ye proffer him a scorpion? If ye then, which are evil, know how to give good gifts to your children, how much more shall your heavenly Father give the Holy Ghost to them that desire it of him!' These, and such like promises of God, must he that intendeth to pray set before his eyes, that he, comforted with the remembrance of them, may with the more frank courage give himself to godly and devout prayer at all times. (4)

Where to Pray

'Let us not excuse ourselves, saying that it is no easy thing for a man being entangled with worldly business to pray, seeing that he hath no oratory nor house fit for prayer nigh unto him. For wheresoever thou be, thou mayest make and appoint thine altar. For the place hindereth nothing, neither doth the time let; but though thou dost not bow thy knees, nor knock thy breast, nor stretch out thy hands to heaven, yet mayest thou pray aright, and make thy prayer perfect, so that thou only shewest and bringest forth a fervent mind. For thou mayest, when thou goest unto market, and walkest by thyself alone, make long prayers. Thou mayest also, sitting in thy shop, and sewing skins, dedicate thy soul unto the Lord. The servant also that buyeth, or goeth up and down, and the cook doing his office, when he cannot go to church, may make a prayer long and discreet. For God disdaineth not the place, but requireth one thing, that is to say, a fervent mind and a pure soul. For Paul also, not in an oratory, but in the prison, lying wide open, nor standing right up, nor bowing his knees, (for the clog wherewith his feet were bound did not suffer him,) yet, seeing that he lying prayed fervently, he shaked the prison, unloosened the foundation, and did bind the keeper of the prison, and afterward brought him unto holy religion. And Ezechias, not standing right up, nor bowing his knees, but lying wide open in his bed because of his sickness, when he turned himself unto the wall, inasmuch as he called upon God fervently and with a pure soul, he both called again the sentence pronounced, obtained much bene-volence, and was restored to his old health. And the thief, being stretched out upon the cross, with few words purchased the heavenly kingdom. And Jeremy in the mire and lake, and Daniel in the prison and among the wild beasts, and Jonas in the belly of a whale, praying unto God, did both dissolve all manner of evils wherewith they were besieged, compassed, and set about, and also found favour at the hand of God. What then oughtest thou to say when thou prayest? Verily, even the same thing that the woman of Canaan did. For even as she said, "Have mercy on me, my daughter is grievously vexed of a devil;" so say thou likewise, Have mercy upon my, my soul is very grievously vexed of a devil. For sin is a great devil. She that had the devil did find mercy, and yet was she hated when she did sin. "Have mercy on me," is but a short saying; yet doth it contain an whole sea of mercy. For wheresoever mercy is, there are all good things. Though thou be without the church, cry, saying, Have mercy on me,—though thou dost not move thy lips, but only cry in thy mind: for God also heareth them that hold their peace. There is no place to be sought, but a beginning of a place. Jeremy was in the mire, and he made God bounteous unto him by prayer. Job was on the dunghill, and he made God merciful unto him. Jonas was in the whale's belly, and he had God gentle to him. Though thou be in a barn, pray. Wheresoever thou be, pray. Thou art the temple; seek no place. The sea was before the Jews, and the Egyptians behind at their backs, and Moses in the midst speaking nothing, for he was greatly troubled in his prayer; yet said God unto him, "What criest thou to me?" In like manner thou therefore, whensoever temptation shall come unto thee, fly unto God, and call on the Lord. Is he a man, that thou shouldest seek after a place? God is ever at hand. For thou yet speaking, he will say, Behold, here I am present. Thou hast not yet made thy prayer, and he bringeth help. For if thou hast a mind pure from unclean motions, though thou be in the market, or in the way, or in the consistory, or in the sea, or in the inn, or in the ship, or in any other place of the world, look, wheresoever thou callest on God, there mayest thou obtain thy petition.'

Hitherto have I rehearsed the words of St Chrysostom. Like unto this writeth St Austin, saying: 'Why dost thou seek for a fit and holy place, when thou shouldest make thy supplication to God? make clean thy inward parts, and, all evil lusts expulsed from thence, prepare thyself a secret place in the peace of thy heart. Thou willing to pray in the temple, pray in thyself, and so behave thyself alway, that thou mayest be the temple of God. For God heareth there, where he dwelleth.'

Thus see we, both by the authority of the holy scriptures, and the ancient fathers, that a faithful and christian man may pray lawfully in every place, inasmuch as he is the temple of God, as St Paul saith: 'Do ye not know that ye are the temple of God, and the Spirit of God dwelleth in you?' (1 Cor. iii. vi.) 'The temple of God is holy, which you are.' (2 Cor. vi.) And this is that Christ saith: 'When thou shalt pray, enter into thy closet, and, the door speared, pray to thy Father which is in secret.' (Matt. vi.) Therefore let him that shall pray nothing fear to pray unto God in every place boldly, with this persuasion that God will hear him, and grant him his heart's desire, in whatsoever place he be. (5)

Pray without Ceasing

Whereas some man will say, peradventure, that it is not possible for men to pray at all times, seeing that divers other affairs and businesses must also be done of them so long as they live in this world, as eating, drinking, sleeping, etc. and men must also labour for their living, every man according to his vocation and calling, which things all must needs be an impediment and let to the continual exercise of prayer; I will in few words declare how a christian man may pray without ceasing at all times, according to the precept of Christ and the apostle St Paul.

Some expositors of the holy scripture write, that to pray alway and without ceasing is nothing else than to pray seriously, earnestly, and diligently, after the example of the widow, which would never leave crying and calling upon the unrighteous judge until he had heard her request, that she might be revenged of her adversary (Luke xviii.). They say it is a trope called hyperbole, so that he is counted to pray alway and without ceasing, which pray usually, oftentimes, seriously, and instantly, and doth not cease from prayers until he hath obtained that which he asketh. After that manner is this spoken: 'Cry, cease not, lift up thy voice as a trump.' (Isai. lviii.)

Some say that to pray alway and not to cease is, throughout all our life fervently to desire that high goodness which is promised us in the world to come. After this sort, say they, whatsoever men do in this life, whether they eat, drink, sleep, work, talk, bargain, study, meditate, etc. so long as this celestial desire remain in them, all their whole life is a certain perpetual prayer. 'The perpetual study of living godly,' saith Erasmus, 'is a continual prayer.' And Beda saith: 'He prayeth alway that doeth good things alway, neither doth he cease to pray but when he ceaseth to be righteous.'

Other affirm that to pray without ceasing is, fervently and with an ardent mind to pray at certain hours destinated and appointed unto prayer. Verily all these expositions, inasmuch as they be godly, are not to be rejected nor cast away. Therefore seeing that we cannot for our imbecility, weakness, and imperfection, alway and without ceasing pray unto God, yet, besides the godly meditation of celestial things in our mind, and the perpetual desire of living innocently, which ought never to depart from a christian breast that hath the fear of God before her eyes, we ought to prescribe and appoint unto ourselves certain peculiar hours every day, which should not pass away without prayer, and which should have the whole affects of the mind utterly occupied in this behalf. And when those hours shall come, then ought we to lay aside all mundane affairs and worldly businesses, and wholly to give ourselves to devout meditation and divine contemplation of celestial things. Then ought we fervently to pray with the heart and mind, and so with all humility to behave ourselves, as though God were there present, and we spake unto him face to face, yea, then ought we to watch, as the scripture admonisheth, (Matt. xxvi.) that is, so take heed and cast all perils, that our 'adversary the devil, which goeth about like a roaring lion, seeking whom he may devour,' (1 Pet. v.) do not once draw away our minds from talking with God, but that quietly and attentively we may be occupied in offering up our petitions unto God at that time of prayer.

And because no man should be offended with the observance and appointment of certain hours unto prayer, as a thing superstitious and repugnant to the christian liberty, I will shew that divers holy men had their certain hours also, wherein they used customably to pray. We read that David did pray and give thanks unto God seven times in a day. His words are these: 'Seven times in a day have I given praise unto thee for the judgments of thy righteousness.' (Psal. cxix.) What seven times in a day these were, all are not manifest in the holy scripture, but some are, which I will here rehearse.

As touching the morning he saith: 'O Lord, early shalt thou hear my voice, betimes in the morning shall I make my prayer unto thee, and I shall see that I have obtained my prayer.' (Psal. v.) Now for the time of his repast he saith: 'As ashes did I eat my bread, and my drink did I mingle with weeping.' (Psal. cii.) Though here he make the none evident mention of prayer, yet it is not to be doubted but that in this his great sorrow he also used at that present prayers unto God. As for his prayer at night, we read on this manner: 'Let my prayer,' saith he, 'be directed unto thee as frankincence in thy sight, the lifting up of my hands as an evening sacrifice.' (Psal. cxli.) Again he saith: 'I shall wash every night my bed, yea, even with my tears will I water my bed.' (Psal. vi.) That he prayed to God at midnight also, it is manifest by these words: 'At midnight,' saith he, 'did I rise to give praise unto thee.' (Psal. cxix.)

Of these scriptures aforesaid it is evident, that David prayed unto God customably these four times besides other, that is, in the morning, at his dinner, in the evening, and at midnight; which all be very convenient times for a christian man to pray. As he prayed at these times, so did he undoubtedly at other, though they be not expressed in the scripture. (6)

Adoption

Father. If Christ be the only Son of God, how cometh it then to pass, that the faithful are also called the sons of God in so many places of the holy scripture? *Son.* Christ Jesus is the true and natural Son of God, begotten of his Father from everlasting, before all worlds, of the same substance, majesty, might, and power, with his Father. The elect and faithful people are also the sons of God, not by nature, but by adoption.

Father. What meanest thou by this word adoption? *Son.* I call adoption when one doth take a child, which is not his own proper child, begotten of his own body, for his own proper and legitimate child, giving unto him all rights and titles, as though he were truly and naturally his child, not as though he were bound unto it, but doeth it of his own free goodness, and of the very love that he beareth toward him. Even so be we the sons of God by Jesus Christ, in whom and for whose sake God doth love us, adopt, choose, and receive us for his children, and maketh us inheritors of his everlasting and glorious kingdom, as St Paul saith (Eph. i.): 'Blessed be God the Father of our Lord Jesus Christ, which hath blessed us with all manner of spiritual blessings in heavenly things by Christ, according as he had chosen us in him before the foundation of the world was laid, that we should be holy and without blame before him through love, and ordained us before through Jesus Christ to be sons and heirs unto himself, according to the good pleasure of his will, to the praise of the glory of his grace, wherewith he hath made us accepted in his well-beloved Son, by whom we have redemption through his blood, even the forgiveness of sins, according to the riches of his grace,' etc. Again: (Tit. iii.) 'Not of the deeds of righteousness which we wrought, but of his mercy hath God saved us, by the fountain of the new birth and the renewing of the Holy Ghost, which he shed on us abundantly through Jesus Christ our Saviour, that we, being justified by his grace, should be heirs of everlasting life through hope.'

Therefore, when the scripture calleth Christ the Son of God, it is to be understand that he is the Son of God by nature and by the divine substance. But when it nameth the faithful to be the sons or children of God, it is meant by grace and adoption. And so are these sentences to be understand: (John i.) 'So many as received him (Christ), to them he gave power to be the sons of God,' etc. (Rom. viii.) 'As many as are led by the Spirit of God, they are the sons of God. For ye have not received the spirit of bondage to fear any more, but ye have received the Spirit of adoption, whereby we cry, Abba, dear Father. The same Spirit certifieth our spirit that we are the sons of God. If we be sons, we are also heirs, the heirs, I mean, of God, and fellow-heirs with Christ.' 'Ye are all the sons of God, because ye have believed in Christ Jesu.' (Gal. iii.) 'Behold, what love the Father hath shewed on us, that we should be called the sons of God.' (1 John iii.)

Father. What learnest thou of this, that Christ is the only-begotten Son of God? *Son.* By this I am fully and most certainly persuaded, that Jesus Christ, the second Person in the Deity (in whom I do believe as in the Father), is true, perfect, immortal, and everlasting God, begotten of God the Father before all worlds, of the same majesty, nature, substance, might, and power with the Father. For even as of the substance of a true man there is none born but a true man, so likewise of the substance of the true God there is none born but true God. Every thing begetteth the thing that is like unto itself in nature and substance.

Father. What doth it profit thee, that Christ is the Son of God, yea, God himself? *Son.* Very much. For in that he is God, or the Son of God, he is able to forgive me my sins, to beget me of new by his Holy Spirit, to defend me from mine enemies, to save me, to give me all good things necessary both for body and soul, to make me the son of God and heir of everlasting glory. (7)

The One True Church

Father. Why dost thou rather say and confess, that there is one holy catholic or universal church, than many churches; seeing there are in the world so many companies, fellowships, or congregations of the faithful, that call on the name of the Lord? *Son.* As there is but one head of this holy catholic or universal church, which is the Lord Christ Jesus alone, so likewise is there but one holy church, as it is written (Cant. vi.) 'One is my dove and my darling. She is the only beloved of her mother, and dear unto her that bare her. When the daughters saw her, they said she was blessed.' And, although this holy church in her members be dispersed and scattered abroad throughout the world, so that there be in divers countries divers companies, that profess and confess Christ and his holy gospel; yet, forasmuch as they are gathered and linked together in one faith and one doctrine, under one head Christ, into whose name alone they are consecrate and sworn, all those so great and so many multitudes are counted and called but one church, which church 'is the house of the living God, the pillar and ground of truth,' (1 Tim. iii.) so stedfastly founded on the rock Christ, that 'the very gates of hell shall never be able to prevail against her;' (Matt. xvi.) so surely 'built upon the foundation of the apostles and prophets,' (Eph. ii.) that though abundance of rain descend, and the winds blow, yet can they not move her; (Matt. vii.) yea, though Satan goeth never so much about to sift her, yet shall her faith never fail, but remain perfect, whole, and sound (Luke xxii.). For this church is that holy congregation or fellowship of God's elect (Matt. xxiv. John x.), which cannot err, nor be brought into error, much less perish and be damned.

Father. There is at this present day great contention concerning the church, every sect sweating to prove that they are the church of God, and that all other, which dissent from them, are synagogues of Satan: come off, tell me therefore, how the true church of Christ may be known from the malignant and wicked churches, which are led with the spirit, not of God, but of the devil. *Son.* Albeit many signs, tokens, and marks might here be rehearsed, whereby we may easily discern the church of Christ from the synagogue of antichrist, the people of God from the bond-slaves of Satan, the vessels of mercy from the vessels of wrath; yet will I recite at this present only four tokens, or marks, whereby we may truly and undeceivably know the true catholic and apostolic church.

Father. Which are those four? *Son.* The first is, the sincere, true, and uncorrupt preaching of God's word, without the intermixtion or mingling of man's doctrine, in the which God, that mighty Lord, hath opened himself, his will, his mercy, and favour to his faithful congregation, as it is written: 'He that is of God heareth the words of God.' (John viii.) Again: 'My sheep hear my voice;' (John x.) 'as for a stranger, they follow him not, but fly from him; for they know not the voice of strangers.'

The second is, the true administration of the sacraments according to the institution and ordinance of Christ, as we read of St Paul entreating of the supper of the Lord: (1 Cor. xi.) 'That which I delivered unto you received I of the Lord. For the Lord Jesus, the same night in the which he was betrayed, took the bread,' etc.

The third is, fervent prayer and the diligent invocation of God in the name of our alone Mediator Jesus Christ, with continual thanksgiving for his benefits.

The fourth is, ecclesiastical discipline according to the prescript and appointment of God's word.

Although many other signs, notes, tokens, and marks, might here be rehearsed, whereby also the church of Christ may easily be discerned from the synagogue of antichrist, yet these be the principal and chief; so that, in whatsoever congregation these aforesaid signs be found, there may we well affirm and say the true church of Christ to be, and the faithful people of God.

Father. But what dost thou mean by calling the holy universal church 'the company or fellowship of saints'? *Son.* These words, 'The company or fellowship of saints' or holy men, do nothing else in a manner than declare what the holy universal church is; verily, a company of saints or of holy and godly-disposed persons knit together by one Spirit, in one faith, in one hope, in one love, in one baptism, in one doctrine, having one head, which is Christ Jesus, and serving one God, which is the Father of our Lord Jesus Christ, 'in holiness and righteousness all the days of their life.' (Luke i.) For this fellowship of saints, although they be dispersed never so far abroad, yea, in all quarters under the sun, not only in Europa, but also in India, Persia, etc., be they Jews or gentiles, barbarous or Scythians, have, hold, and maintain one baptism, one faith, one God and Lord, one doctrine, and are led with one Spirit, and make one flock, whereof Christ Jesus is the pastor and shepherd. And in this company or fellowship of saints all things appertaining unto everlasting salvation are common, as the favour of God, remission of sins, quietness of conscience, the gift of the Holy Ghost, and everlasting life; yea, in this holy fellowship there is such a love and hearty good will one toward another (for they are members all of one body, and therefore like affected and minded), that there is also, as I may so speak, a certain community of temporal things among them, as we read in the Apostles' Acts of Christ's church at the beginning (Acts iv.); so that the rich have not too much, nor the poor too little, but a certain equality is among them, no man wanting, that is of that holy fellowship, but having sufficient to satisfy his necessity; such and so great care one for another reigneth in them, provoked thereunto by the Holy Ghost, which ruleth and governeth that holy congregation and fellowship of saints.

Father. I cannot disallow that thou speakest. But as concerning this word 'saint,' methink it ought rather to be appropriated unto the saints departed and reigning in glory with Christ, than unto us, which live in this world and are subject to many infirmities. *Son.* The holy scriptures, both of the old and new testaments, do rather ascribe this word 'saint' unto us in this world, which believe in Christ, than unto the godly, which are now in glory with their head Christ. And we are termed saints by the Holy Ghost in the divine scriptures, first, to put us in remembrance that we are made saints, that is to say, holy, pure, and blameless, by the free grace of God through faith for Christ's sake, and so recounted just and righteous before God for the righteousness not of ourselves, but of our Mediator Christ Jesus: secondly, that we should endeavour ourselves unto the uttermost of our power in all our manners, life, and conversation, to answer to our name, that is to say, to be saints, I mean holy, pure, blameless, good, righteous, merciful, gentle, liberal, and altogether virtuous, 'putting on that new man which is shapen after the image of God in true righteousness and holiness,' as it is written: 'Even as he which hath called you is holy, even so be ye holy also in your conversation; for it is written, Be ye holy, for I am holy.'

Father. What doth it profit thee to believe that there is an holy universal church, which is the company or fellowship of saints, that is to say, of godly and virtuous persons? *Son.* Very much. For in believing that there is such an holy church, I am well ascertained and fully persuaded, that I also am a member of the same church, and partaker of all the goods of the church, having Christ my head, my bridegroom, and, most loving friend, and with him all that ever he hath. (8)

NOTES / SOURCES

1. Thomas Becon *The Potation for Lent*, in The Early Works of Thomas Becon, ed. John Ayre, Cambridge, Parker Society, 1843, pp. 100–2
2. Ibid., pp. 108–10
3. *The Pathway Unto Prayer*, ibid., pp. 136–7
4. Ibid., pp. 146–7
5. Ibid., pp. 157–9
6. Ibid., pp. 170–1
7. *The Catechism of Thomas Becon*, ed. John Ayre, Cambridge, Parker Society, 1844, p. 25
8. Ibid., pp. 42–3

Nicholas Ridley   1500?–1555

Following studies at Cambridge, the Sorbonne, and Louvain Universities, Nicholas Ridley became a Fellow and later Master of Pembroke Hall, Cambridge. From 1535 he began to promote Reformation doctrines and was an influence on Thomas Cranmer's eucharistic theology; he assisted in the production of *The Book of Common Prayer* of 1549. On Edward VI's death in 1553, he supported Lady Jane Grey in her claim to the throne, and on Mary's accession was forced to relinquish the Bishopric of London. With Latimer and Cranmer he was sent to Oxford to defend his views, where he was condemned and burnt at the stake on 16 October 1555. He was noted for preaching on social justice, and his call to improve the condition of the poor was one of the reasons for the foundation of Christ's Hospital and St Thomas's Hospital.

Facing Death

Why should we Christians fear death? Can death deprive us of Christ, which is all our comfort, our joy, and our life? Nay, forsooth. But contrary, death shall deliver us from this mortal body, which loadeth and beareth down the spirit, that it cannot so well perceive heavenly things (2 Cor. v.); in the which so long as we dwell, we are absent from God.

Wherefore, understanding our state in that we be Christians (2 Cor. v.), 'that if our mortal body, which is our earthly house, were destroyed, we have a building, a house not made with hands, but everlasting in heaven, etc., therefore we are of good cheer, and know that when we are in the body, we are absent from God; for we walk by faith, and not by clear sight. Nevertheless we are bold, and had rather be absent from the body, and present with God. Wherefore we strive, whether we be present at home or absent abroad, that we may always please him.'

And who that hath true faith in our Saviour Christ, whereby he knoweth somewhat truly what Christ our Saviour is, that he is the eternal Son of God, life, light, the wisdom of the Father, all goodness, all righteousness, and whatsoever is good that heart can desire, yea, infinite plenty of all these, above that that man's heart can either conceive or think, (for in him dwelleth the fulness of the Godhead corporally,) and also that he is given us of the Father (1 Cor. i.), 'and made of God to be our wisdom, our righteousness, our holiness, and our redemption;'—who (I say) is he, that believeth this indeed, that would not gladly be with his master Christ? Paul for this knowledge coveted to have been loosed from the body, and to have been with Christ, for that he counted it much better for himself, and had rather to be loosed than to live. Therefore these words of Christ to the thief on the cross, that asked of him mercy, were full of comfort and solace: 'This day thou shalt be with me in paradise,' (Luke xxiii.). To die in the defence of Christ's Gospel, it is our bounden duty to Christ, and also to our neighbour. To Christ, (Rom. ix.) 'for he died for us, and rose again, that he might be Lord over all.' And seeing he died for us, 'we also (saith St John) should jeopard, yea give, our life for our brethren' (1 John iii.). And this kind of giving and losing is getting and winning indeed; for he that giveth or loseth his life thus, getteth and winneth it for evermore. 'Blessed are they therefore, that die in the Lord' (Rev. xiv.); and if they die in the Lord's cause, they are most happy of all.

Let us not then fear death, which can do us no harm, otherwise than for a moment to make the flesh to smart; for that our faith, which is surely fastened and fixed unto the word of God, telleth us that we shall be anon after death in peace, in the hands of God, in joy, in solace, and that from death we shall go straight unto life. For St John saith, 'He that liveth and believeth in me, shall never die' (John xi.). And in another, place 'He shall depart from death unto life' (John v.). And therefore this death of the Christian is not to be called death, but rather a gate or entrance into everlasting life. Therefore Paul calleth it but a dissolution and resolution; and both Peter (2 Pet. i.) and Paul (2 Cor. v.), a putting off of this tabernacle or dwell-house, meaning thereby the mortal body, as wherein the soul or spirit doth dwell here in this world for a small time. Yea, this death may be called, to the Christian, an end of all miseries. For so long as we live here, 'we must pass through many tribulations, before we can enter into the kingdom of heaven' (Acts iv.). And now, after that death hath shot his bolt, all the Christian man's enemies have done what they can, and after that they have no more to do. What could hurt or harm poor 'Lazarus, that lay at the rich man's gate' (Luke xvi.)? his former penury and poverty, his miserable beggary, and horrible sores and sickness? For so soon as death had stricken him with his dart, so soon came the angels, and carried him straight up into Abraham's bosom. What lost he by death, who, from misery and pain, is set by the ministry of angels in a place both of joy and solace?

NOTES / SOURCES

1. Nicholas Ridley, Letter 33, in *The Works of Bishop Ridley*, ed. H. Christmas, Cambridge (Parker Society), 1841, pp. 425–6

Richard Davies 1501?–1581

A priest's son, both of whose parents came from well-connected North Welsh families (his uncle was a distinguished literary figure), Davies was educated at Oxford, where he first developed his sympathies with the Reformed religion. After a brief period as a parish priest in England under Edward, he fled to Frankfurt in Mary's reign, where he made influential contacts with prominent Reforming figures. This assisted his promotion, on return to Britain, as Bishop of St Asaph (1559) and then of St Davids (1561). He was a tirelessly active bishop, collaborating with William Salesbury on the translation of the New Testament into Welsh (as well as collaborating with Archbishop Matthew Parker in the production of the English 'Bishops' Bible' in 1568). His preface to the Welsh Testament of 1567 set out not only guidelines for reading the Bible, but also a theory close to that of Archbishop Parker about the antiquity of the British Church prior to any Roman missions. He wrote a lucid and powerful Welsh prose and uses both Welsh colloquial expressions and literary allusions to reinforce his conviction that the ancient Celtic Church was effectively 'Protestant'.

Returning to Christian Origins

. . . The Old Testament was what God ordained for a certain time and for one nation only, the Jews; the New Testament has reached all the peoples of the world, with no distinction between one nation and another. So now you have some idea why the one is called 'Old' and the other 'New': 'old' because it teaches the eternal will of God, the true belief and Christian faith of the ancient people that lived before Christ's birth; 'new' because it teaches the same thing to the people who live after Christ's birth. 'Old' because it teaches one nation only, the Jews; 'new' because it teaches all the nations of the world without distinction. 'Old' because it teaches through the medium of signs drawn from the elements of the world and corporeal ceremonies; 'new' because it teaches in unconcealed light through inspiration and truth, in its own proper form.

Take it in your hand, brother, and read: here you may see where you once stood, here you may recognise your own ancient faith, the laudable Christian religion that once was yours. Here you have the faith that once you defended to the point of risking fire and sword, the faith in whose cause your co-religionists and learned teachers were martyred. Perhaps it is strange for you to hear that your ancient faith should have been the history of the Testament and the Word of God; for you have never seen a Bible or Testament in Welsh, written or printed. Truth to tell, I have never succeeded in having sight of a Bible in Welsh, except that I remember seeing as a boy a copy of the five books of Moses in Welsh in the house of an uncle who was a learned man. But no one understood the book or valued it. It is doubtful, as far as I know, that you would be able to find in the whole of Wales one ancient Bible in Welsh, since the Welsh lost or destroyed all their books, as I have already said. Yet I have no doubt at all that the Bible was once commonly available enough in Welsh. The perfection of the faith of the martyrs, the clerics and the laity that I have already spoken of above is a strong proof that you once had the Holy Scriptures in your own tongue. For nothing is able to secure faith in a man to the point of suffering death in its cause than the Word of God when a man knows it and understands it for himself. . . .

. . . In Welsh we have a number of sayings and proverbs still in use that are taken from the heart of Holy Scripture, and from the very centre of the Gospel of Christ . . . I have noted and remembered some of these. It is often said, *A Duw a digon: heb Dduw, heb ddim* ('With God, enough; without God, nothing'). Where does this teaching come from, where is its root and its warrant? Is not this the thrust and the purpose of the whole of Holy Scripture? Is it not this that the prophets, the psalms and the New Testament all the way through teach the Christian man? No need here to search for precise evidence: the need is rather—because the evidence is so abundant—to see which instances should be chosen and which left out so as to shorten the treatment of the matter.

The prophet David says,

> The Lord is my shepherd: therefore can I lack nothing.
> He shall feed me in a green pasture: and lead me forth beside the waters of comfort.

He shall convert my soul: and bring me forth in the paths of righteousness
for his name's sake.
Yea, though I walk through the valley of the shadow of death, I will fear no
evil: for thou art with me; thy rod and thy staff comfort me.

You see here in this psalm one of the roots of our proverb, and you hear the
same point in this psalm as in the words, *A Duw a digon*, etc. And read the last
part of the fifth chapter of the Gospel of Matthew, where the Lord Christ tells us
not to be anxious about what we eat and drink and wear; and tells us to take
example from the birds of the air and the lilies of the field which God satisfies
with food and clothes with beauty. . . .

. . . No need to labour further to make you understand whence grows the
Welshman's proverb, *A Duw a digon: heb Dduw, heb ddim*. Its root, its history, its
origin, are in Holy Scripture. But (alas) although the proverb is still current
among the Welsh and the words are familiar, it has completely lost its effect. Look
at how the world goes and you have proof enough. There is so much greed in the
world today, for land and property, gold and silver and wealth; only infrequently
do you find someone who trusts God and his promises . . . What is public office
in Wales today but a hook on which to hang your neighbour's fleece and harvest?
. . . Forgive me these unwelcome truths: for speaking unwelcome truths is the
preacher's charge. . . .

Next I am going to take this saying, *A gair Duw yn ucha* ('With the Word of
God above me'): it is a familiar saying in my own region; when a man intends to
say something, make something or go somewhere, he says, 'I shall do this or say
this,' or, 'I shall go to this or that place *with the Word of God above me*' . . . When
a man says, 'With the Word of God above me', it is as much as to say, 'So long as
it is not against the Word of God', or 'If the Word of God permits'; or 'So long as
it accords with the Word of God, I shall do it', or 'I shall say this or that'. In the
light of this, we can believe that in those days [of ancient faith], people did not
think it right to do or say anything against God's Word. . . . Whoever takes these
words like a candle in his hand, they will accuse and unmask many of the
defilements and vanities of the Roman creed. . . .

. . . The third common expression among the Welsh that is taken from Holy
Scripture is this, *Y mab rhad* ('The freeborn son')—only three short words of
one syllable each, yet they contain so much meaning and spiritual teaching, the
teaching that the third and fourth chapters of Paul's letter to the Romans in
particular expound, and many other places in Scripture besides. Jesus Christ is
called the freeborn son because, through the ransom he paid for us on the tree
of the cross, he purchased for us the father's mercy from heaven, to forgive our
sins freely, without any deserving on our part, with no price or payment, but
freely. We are not justified before God because of our deeds, but as a free gift
through that mercy of God which the freeborn Son purchased for us. Because
of this, it is faith that brings us before God; for it is faith that grasps and
receives that mercy which the freeborn Son purchased for us. On this, Paul the
Apostle says, 'Therefore we conclude that a man is justified by faith without the
deeds of the law' [Rom. 3.28]. . . . Works are the fruit of faith. Just as there is
no fire without warmth, so there is no faith without good works. But for all
this, you will be completely deluded if you think your works will suffice to

justify you before God: stand back from your deeds, recognise your impurity, and give yourself over in your weakness and incapacity to God's mercy. Confess in your heart and believe firmly, fruitfully and without doubt: this is the target and the conclusion of Holy Scripture throughout its pages—Christ's purchase for you of free forgiveness for your sins. That is why the Welshman's expression, drawn long since from Holy Scripture, is true, when he calls Christ 'the freeborn Son'.

NOTES / SOURCES

The preface to the New Testament is reprinted in full in *Rhagymadroddion*, 1547–1659, ed. G. H. Hughes, Cardiff 1951, 1976. The extracts here are from pp. 29–36 (tr. R.D.W.)

John Bradford   1510?–1555

Upon hearing the sermons of Hugh Latimer, John Bradford was prompted by a guilty conscience over some doubtful financial dealings to study theology at Cambridge where he was elected Fellow of Pembroke Hall. Ordained Deacon in 1550 by Nicholas Ridley, Bishop of London, he became a Prebendary of St Paul's and a King's Chaplain. On the accession of Mary in 1553, he was charged with sedition and imprisoned in the Tower. He was tried for his Protestant beliefs and burnt at Smithfield on 1 July 1555. His meditations on the Creed and the sacraments, and his systematic provision of prayers and reflections for daily use by laypeople made him particularly admired and influential among Reformed Christians in England.

What is the True Church?

This church is nothing else but a communion and society of saints; that is, not only a society of all such as be, have been, or shall be thy people, but also a society or partaking of Christ Jesus, which is 'the head' of the same; yea, by him of thee, O blessed Father which art 'the head of Christ,' and of thee, O Holy Ghost which now shadowest and sittest upon the same, to hatch and cherish it, as the hen her chickens, by the extending of thy wings; not only to defend them from their enemies, but also to cover their sins, and to remit them in this life; beginning also here the resurrection of the flesh and everlasting life, the which thou wilt in the end of the world consummate, so that they shall not need to be covered for sin; for then shall they be pure, and have glorious bodies, immortal and spiritual (Phil. iii), the which shall have the fruition of eternal joy, life everlasting, and glory, such as 'the eye hath not seen, the ear hath not heard' (1 Cor. ii.), nor the heart of man can conceive. For then Christ Jesus shall give up his kingdom to God the Father (1 Cor. xv.), that God may be 'all in all' concerning the governance of it by the ministration of his word, and other means whereby now he governeth it, that it may be his Father's kingdom, we being become 'like unto him' (1 John iii.): that is, as to the manhood of Christ the Godhead is united, and is 'all in all' without any other means; even so God shall be in us, assuming then not only in the person of Christ the human nature, but also all the human nature of his church which be members of Christ; the wicked and reprobate being separate then from this communion, and cast into eternal perdition with Satan and antichrist, there to be in torments and horror for ever.

By reason of this their faith they are thankful to thee, O Holy Spirit, which hast taught them this, and given them to believe it. By reason of this faith they singularly pray, love, and help thy church here militant, and labour to be holy, etc. By reason of this faith they confess themselves sinners, they desire and believe pardon of their sins, they are risen and rise daily concerning the inward man, and do feel the life eternal begun in them; more and more labouring, praying, wishing, and desiring for the same wholly and perfectly. (1)

A Sweet Contemplation of Heaven and Heavenly Things

O my soul, lift up thyself above thyself; fly away in the contemplation of heaven and heavenly things; make not thy further abode in this inferior region, where is nothing but travail and trials, and sorrow, and woe, and wretchedness, and sin, and trouble, and fear, and all deceiving and destroying vanities. Bend all thine affections upward unto the superior places where thy Redeemer liveth and reigneth, and where thy joys are laid up in the treasury of his merits which shall be made thy merits, his perfection thy perfection, and his death thy life eternal, and his resurrection thy salvation. Esteem not the trifling pleasures of this life to be the way to this wealth, nor thy ignominious estate here to be any bar to prevent thee from the full use and joyful fruition of the glory there prepared for thee.

I am assured that though I want here, I have riches there; though I hunger here, I shall have fulness there; though I faint here, I shall be refreshed there; and though I be accounted here as a dead man, I shall there live in perpetual glory.

That is the city promised to the captives whom Christ shall make free; that is the kingdom assured to them whom Christ shall crown; there are the joys prepared for them that mourn; there is the light that never shall go out; there is the health that shall never be impaired; there is the glory that shall never be defaced; there is the life that shall taste no death; and there is the portion that passeth all the world's preferment. There is the world that never shall wax worse; there is every want supplied freely without money; there is no danger, but happiness, and honour, and singing, and praise, and thanksgiving unto the heavenly Jehovah, 'to him that sitteth on the throne,' 'to the Lamb' that here was led to the slaughter, that now 'reigneth;' with whom I 'shall reign' after I have run this comfortless race through this miserable earthly vale. (2)

Meditation on the Lord's Supper

Jesus Immanuel

This heavenly banquet (wherewithin thou dost witness thyself, O sweet Saviour, to be 'the bread of life' wherewith our souls are fed unto true and eternal life and immortality) grant me grace so now to receive, as may be to my singular joy and comfort.

The signs and symbols be bread and wine, which are sanctified in thy body and blood, to represent the invisible communion and fellowship of the same. For, as in baptism thou, O God, dost regenerate us, and as it were engraft us into the fellowship of thy church, and by adoption make us thy children; so, as a good householder and Father, thou dost afterwards minister meat to nourish and continue us in that life whereunto thou 'by thy word hast begotten us.' And truly, O Christ, thou art the food of the soul: and therefore our heavenly father giveth thee unto us, that we being refreshed in communicating of thee might be received into immortality.

Now, because this mystery is of itself incomprehensible, thou dost exhibit and give unto us a figure and image hereof in visible signs: yea, as though thou paidest down present earnest, thou makest us so certain hereof, as if with our eyes we saw it. And this is the end wherefore thou didst institute this thy supper and banquet, namely, that it might confirm us, as of thy body once so offered for us that we may feed on it, and in feeding feel in us the efficacy and strength of thy one alone sacrifice; so of thy blood once so shed for us that it is unto us a continual potion and drink, according to the words of thy promise added there, 'Take, eat, this is my body which is given for you.' So that the body which was once offered for our salvation we are commanded to 'take and eat,' that, whiles we are partakers thereof, we might be most assured the virtue of thy lively death is of force in us: whereof it cometh that thou callest the cup 'the testament (or covenant) in thy blood;' for the covenant which thou once hast stricken with us in thy blood, thou dost as it were renew the same as concerning the confirmation of our faith, so often as thou reach unto us this holy cup to drink of.

O wonderful consolation which cometh to the godly hearts by reason of this sacrament! For here we have assured witness that thou Christ art so coupled unto us, and we so engrafted in thee, that we are 'one body' with thee; and whatsoever thou hast we may call it our own. Boldly therefore we may boast that 'everlasting life,' thine inheritance, is ours; that 'the kingdom of heaven,' whereinto thou art entered, can no more be taken away from us or we from it, than from thee or thou from it. Again, our sins can no more condemn us than thee; for thou would they should be laid to thy charge as though they were thine.

This is a wonderful change which thou makest with us of thy unspeakable mercy. Thou wast made 'the Son of man' with us, that we with thee might be made 'the sons of God:' thou camest down from heaven unto earth, to bring us from the earth into heaven: thou tookest upon thee our mortality, that thou mightest give us thy immortality: thou tookest upon thee our weakness, that thou mightest make us strong with thy strength: thou tookest upon thee our poverty, to pour upon us thy plenty: thou tookest upon thee our unrighteousness, that thou mightest cloak us with thy righteousness. (3)

The Effects of the Sacrament

We teach these benefits to be had by the worthy receiving of the sacrament, namely, that we abide in Christ, and Christ in us; again that we attain by it a celestial life, or a life with God; moreover that by faith and in spirit we receive not only Christ's body and blood, but also whole Christ, God and man. Besides these we grant, that by the worthy receiving of this sacrament we receive remission of our sins and confirmation of the new Testament. Last of all by worthy receiving we get by faith an increase of incorporation with Christ and amongst ourselves which be his members: than which things what more can be desired? Alas! that men consider nothing at all, how that the coupling of Christ's body and blood to the sacrament is a spiritual thing; and therefore there needs no such carnal presence as the papists imagine. Who will deny a man's wife to be with her husband one body and flesh, although he be at London and she at York? But the papists are animal men, guided by carnal reason only: or else would they know how that the Holy Ghost because of our infirmity useth metaphorically the words of abiding, dwelling, eating, and drinking of Christ, that the unspeakable conjunction of Christ with us might something be known. God open their eyes to see it! And thus much for this.

Now to that part of the objection with saith, that we teach Christ to be none otherwise present in the sacrament than in his word. I would that the objectors would well consider, what a presence of Christ is in his word. I remember that St Austin writeth how that Christ's body is received sometime 'visibly,' and sometime 'invisibly:' the 'visible' receipt he calleth that which is by the sacraments; the 'invisible' receipt he calleth that which by the exercise of our faith with ourselves we receive. And St Jerome, in the third book upon Ecclesiastes, affirmeth that 'we are fed with the body of Christ, and we drink his blood, not only in mystery, but also in knowledge of holy scripture:' where he plainly sheweth that the same meat is offered in the words of the scriptures, which is offered in the sacraments; so that no less is Christ's body and blood offered by the scriptures, than by the sacraments. Upon the hundred and forty-seventh Psalm he writeth also, that 'though these words, "he that eateth my flesh, and drinketh my blood," may be understand in mystery, yet,' saith he, 'it is more true to take Christ's body and his blood for the word of the scriptures and the doctrine of God.' Yea, upon the same Psalm he saith plainly, that 'Christ's flesh and blood is poured into our ears by hearing the word, and therefore great is the peril if we yield to other cogitations while we hear it.' And therefore, I trow, St Austin saith that 'it is no less peril to hear God's word negligently than so to use the sacrament.' But hereout may no man gather that therefore it needeth not to receive the sacrament; or to affirm that a man may as much by himself meditating the word in the field receive Christ's body, as in the church in the right use of the sacraments: for Christ ordaineth nothing in vain or superfluously; he ordaineth nothing whereof we have not need; although his authority is such that without any questioning his ordinances are to be obeyed.

Again, though in the field a man may receive Christ's body by faith, in the meditation of his word; yet deny I that a man doth ordinarily receive Christ's body, by the only meditation of Christ's death or hearing of his word, with so much light and by such sensible assurance (whereof, God knoweth, our infirmity hath no small need), as by the receipt of the sacrament. Not that Christ is not so much present in his word preached, as he is in or with his sacrament; but because there are in the perception of the sacrament more windows open for Christ to enter into us, than by his word preached or heard. For there (I mean in the word) he hath an entrance into our hearts, but only by the ears through the voice and sound of the words; but here in the sacrament he hath an entrance by all our senses, by our eyes, by our nose, by our taste, and by our handling also: and therefore the sacrament full well may be called seeable, sensible, tasteable, and touchable words. As therefore when many windows are opened in a house, the more light may come in than when there is but one opened; even so by the perception of the sacraments a christian man's conscience hath more help to receive Christ, than simply by the word preached, heard, or meditated. And therefore, methinks, the apostle full well calleth the sacraments obsignations or 'sealings' of God's promise. Read Romans the fourth, of circumcision.

And thus much for the answer to the objection aforesaid. (4)

Trials and Weaknesses

To his Mother[1]

[TOWER OF LONDON, *February 24, 1554*]

Good mother and right dear to me in the Lord, I wish to you for ever God's peace in Christ. But this cannot be had or kept without war with ourselves, with the world, and with the devil: therefore accordingly prepare yourself, though you be a woman, to take unto you a man's heart, that valiantly you may 'fight a good fight,' and receive a crown of victory, which none shall have but he that fighteth lawfully. If in yourself you feel weakness, let the same be so far from making you faint-hearted, that thereby you rather gather matter of courage and comfort, because God's power is never so much seen and known as to them and by them which see and lament their weakness: as Paul testifieth, who said he would 'gladly rejoice in his infirmities,' that God's virtue and power might dwell in him; thereby teaching, none to be so fit for God to choose as his instruments to work by and set forth his power, as those which be most weak, that all power and glory might be ascribed to the Lord, and 'he that rejoiceth might rejoice in him' which 'triumpheth by the weak against the mighty of the world.'

Therefore, my good mother, of your infirmities and weakness gather rather matter to comfort you and to cause you to be courageous, than to discomfort you, and to make you faint-hearted. That you may have hereof more experience, do as I know you do in your trouble and temptations, 'call upon the Lord,' upon whose back you are commanded to 'cast your burthen' (for he will bear it), and, as Peter teacheth, 'all your care:' 'Cast all your care on him,' saith he: and then doubtless you shall find it true that he is 'with you in trouble, will deliver you, and glorify you.' Call therefore, I say, on him in your trouble and terror, for so he commandeth you to do; and doubtless, according to his promise, he will so help you that you shall glorify and praise him at the length. For oftentimes at the first he maketh as though he heard us not: whereas of truth it is otherwise, according to this, 'Before they call on me I hear them, whilst they are in speaking I grant them their petitions.'

But he doth so put off, and as it were dissemble, as though he heard not, for three causes. First, thereby to try our faith, that is, that we might thereby better see our faith, the which, the more it is tried, the more it shall be found praiseworthy, as gold, the oftener and more it is cast into the fire, the more it is pure and to be esteemed. Secondly he lingereth to grant our requests, to make us to call more earnestly, and that we might acknowledge his gifts with more

---

[1] It is possible that this letter might have been intended for Mistress Wilkinson, of whom Bradford speaks, at the close of the last letter, as 'my good mother', and whom he addresses in a letter probably written in February 1555, as 'good mother and dear mistress in the Lord', 'right dear mother'.

gratitude and thankfulness when we shall obtain the same. Last of all he doth put off our prayers, that he might recompense it with abundance, that is, that he might more plentifully pour upon us the effect of our petitions.

Whensoever therefore we pray, and be not forthwith heard as we think, let us remember these three things; and then, as we shall persevere in prayer, so we shall indeed have lively experiment of that which I spake—I mean, how that God careth for our weakness in such sort, that the weaker we be the dearer we should think ourselves to be unto God; as we commonly see parents have a great deal more care for their children that be sickly and weak, than they have for the others that be whole enough, that be in good plight and liking. (5)

NOTES / SOURCES

1. John Bradford 'Meditation on the Belief', in *Writings of John Bradford I*, ed. A. Townsend, Cambridge (Parker Society), 1848, pp. 146–7
2. 'A Sweet Contemplation of Heaven and Heavenly Things', ibid., pp. 266–7
3. 'Meditation on the Lord's Supper', ibid., pp. 260–1
4. 'Sermon on the Lord's Supper', ibid., pp. 99–101
5. 'To his Mother', *Writings of John Bradford II*, ed. A. Townsend, Cambridge (Parker Society), 1853, pp. 72–3

Edwin Sandys   1516?–1588

Having studied at St John's College, Cambridge, Edwin Sandys became Master of St Catherine's Hall in 1547 and Vice Chancellor of Cambridge University in 1553. A supporter of Lady Jane Grey's cause, he was imprisoned in the Tower when Mary came to the throne, but escaped for a time to the Continent. On Elizabeth I's accession, Sandys became Bishop of Worcester (1559), London (1570), and York (1577). He was one of the translators of the Bishops' Bible (published 1568), and took part in its revision in 1572. He was a thoughtful and sober preacher, inclining to a more strongly Protestant theology than the Queen and Archbishop Parker.

Defining Prayer

Prayer is a lifting up of the mind unto God, or a friendly talking with the Lord, from an high and a kindled affection of the heart. In the word God speaketh unto us, in prayer we speak unto him. Prayer is the pouring out of a contrite heart, with a sure persuasion that God will grant our requests, and give ear to the suits which we make unto him. This prayer must be only unto God. It is prayer unto God that only hath promise, that only hath example in the scriptures (Psal. 1. 15). 'Call upon me,' saith God (John xvi. 23, 24); 'Ask the Father in my name,' saith our Saviour, 'ask, and ye shall have' (Matt. vi. 9). 'When ye shall pray,' saith Christ, 'pray thus, Our Father which art in heaven.' So and none otherwise prayed all the patriarchs, prophets, apostles, and Christ himself, and all true Christians in all ages. In prayer no creature may be joined with God. 'God and our Lady help us,' is no allowable prayer.

This prayer, which must be made only to God, our apostle divideth into his parts, 'requests,' 'supplications,' 'intercessions,' thanksgivings.' Requests or petitions are when we pray for the increase of God's good gifts in us, and that of his mercy and favour he would give us whatsoever is necessary for body or soul; and, forasmuch as we cannot obtain any thing for our own merits, that he would grant us all things for his Son our Saviour's sake.

Supplications, when we pray to be delivered from evil; as when we pray that the wrath of God, which we have deserved, may through his mercy be removed from us as far as the east is from the west, that our sin may be remitted and blotted out of God's books.

Intercessions are when we pray for such as do afflict and wrong us, for our enemies which persecute us; that God would forgive them, turn their hearts, and better them. Or when we pray for others; either for removing of evil from them, or for God's favour and blessing towards them.

Thanksgivings are when we praise and thank God for the great mercies, graces, and gifts which we have received at his hands. For we must acknowledge that 'every good and perfect gift cometh down from above, from the Father of lights' (James i. 17), and is by his mercy freely given. Prayer generally may be divided into two parts, petition and thanksgiving: in the one we ask of God; in the other we offer unto God: both are accepted as sweet-smelling sacrifices; pure, and through the merit of his Son pleasant in his sight. I shall not need to put you in remembrance, that we must pray both for ourselves and others; that there is a private, and a public prayer; that we must pray for things pertaining to salvation absolutely, and for things that pertain to this life conditionally. These are matters wherewith ye are throughly acquainted.

The next thing to be considered in prayer, is when, where, and how to pray. When? Always, 'without ceasing' (1 Thess. v. 17). Where? In all places, especially that place which, being sanctified to this use, is therefore called the house of prayer. How? From the heart (1 Tim. ii. 8), 'lifting up pure and clean hands;' that is to say, in faith, and in love. Our prayer, feathered with these two wings, flieth straight into heaven. (1)

Feeding on Christ

In this sacrament there are two things, a visible sign, and an invisible grace: there is a visible sacramental sign of bread and wine, and there is the thing and matter signified, namely, the body and blood of Christ: there is an earthly matter, and an heavenly matter. The outward sacramental sign is common to all; as well the bad, as the good. Judas received the Lord's bread; but not that bread, which is the Lord to the faithful receiver. The spiritual part, that which feedeth the soul, only the faithful do receive. For he cannot be partaker of the body of Christ, which is no member of Christ's body. This food offered us at the Lord's table is to feed our souls withal: it is meat for the mind, and not for the belly. Our souls, being spiritual, can neither receive nor digest that which is corporal; they feed only upon spiritual food. It is the spiritual eating that giveth life (John vi. 63). 'The flesh,' saith Christ, 'doth nothing profit.' We must lift up ourselves from these external and earthly signs, and like eagles fly up and soar aloft, there to feed on Christ, which sitteth on the right hand of his Father, whom the heavens shall keep until the latter day. From thence and from no other altar shall he come, in his natural body, to judge both quick and dead. His natural body is local, for else it were not a natural body: his body is there, therefore not here: for a natural body doth not occupy sundry places at once. Here we have a sacrament, a sign, a memorial, a commemoration, a representation, a figure effectual, of the body and blood of Christ. These terms the ancient fathers, Irenæus, Tertullian, St Augustine, St Jerome, St Chrysostom, do use. Seeing then that Christ in his natural body is absent from hence; seeing he is risen, and is not here; seeing he hath left the world, and is gone to his Father; 'how shall I,' saith St Augustine, 'lay hold on him which is absent? how shall I put my hand into heaven? Send up thy faith, and thou hast taken hold.' 'Why preparest thou thy teeth? Believe, and thou hast eaten.' Thy teeth shall not do him violence, neither thy stomach contain his glorious body. Thy faith must reach up into heaven. By faith he is seen, by faith he is touched, by faith he is digested. Spiritually by faith we feed upon Christ, when we stedfastly believe that his body was broken, and his blood shed for us, upon the cross; by which sacrifice, offered once for all, as sufficient for all, our sins were freely remitted, blotted out, and washed away. This is our heavenly bread, our spiritual food. This doth strengthen our souls and cheer our hearts. Sweeter it is unto us than honey, when we are certified by this outward sacrament of the inward grace given unto us through his death, when in him we are assured of remission of sins and eternal life. Better food than this thy soul can never feed upon. This is the bread of everlasting life. They which truly eat it shall live by it. (2)

Humility

Every man hath the mind of a king in himself. Goliah thought bigly of himself, but of David how basely! This self-liking hath infected and possessed all flesh.

The way to redress it is to look upon ourselves and upon others, but not upon both with the same eyes; upon ourselves with the eyes of strait judgment, upon our neighbours with a favourable and a charitable eye. Whosoever therefore thou art that depisest another, consider in thyself these two things. First, whatsoever thou hast that good is, it is of God, the author of all goodness; and as all that thou hast is from him, so to him thou dost stand accountable for it. Thou art but a steward of his goods, which will call thee to a strict and a hard reckoning for every mite. If thou consider this, thou shalt find small cause to boast and glory of thyself, but shalt give all glory to the King of glory. But open thine other eye, and look down to thy sins; there shalt thou see an ugly sight: thou shalt be forced to leave off glorying, and to cry with the prophet David, 'Mine iniquities are gone over my head, and as a weighty burthen they are too heavy for me' (Psal. xxxviii. 4). Yea, if thou rightly look upon thy sins, thou shalt see in that glass God's face turned away from thee, and his ears shut up against thy prayers: 'Your iniquities,' saith God, 'have made a division between you and me' (Isai. lix. 2). If thou truly enter into thyself, and consider of thy sin, thou shalt say with the prodigal child, 'Lord, I am not worthy to be called thy son' (Luke xv. 21); and with Peter, 'Depart from me, for I am a sinner' (Luke v. 8); and with David, 'It is I that have sinned; as for these sheep, what have they done?' (2 Sam. xxiv. 17) Thou wilt think of others, as Saul did say of David, 'Thou art more righteous than I' (1 Sam. xxiv. 17). But the prince of darkness hath dimmed, or rather put out both these eyes: we can neither see our gifts that be good to be of God, nor our sin, as we should, to be of ourselves; and therefore we esteem most highly of ourselves, and most vilely of

others. Which we would not do, if we did lovingly and charitably behold with
reverence the graces and gifts of God which are in them. For who is there in
whom some commendable thing doth not appear? Lazarus seemed a contempt-
ible thing in the eyes of that rich glutton; yet was his patience to be preferred
before the other's riches. The publican seemed ugly and odious to the Pharisee;
yet his humbleness was much more worthy praise, than the other's supposed
purity and holiness of life. There is no man so base, but a charitable eye may find
out in him some good and precious thing. And no man may be despised, in
whom there is any appearance at all of that which is good. At the least this we may
see in all men, that they shew the workmanship of him which made them, they
carry the image of him by whom they were created. (3)

Fear and Love

Him we must serve 'without fear.' In the psalm it is said, 'Serve the Lord with fear,
and rejoice unto him with reverence' (Psal. ii. 11). And here we are taught to serve
him without fear. As there is but one God, so the scripture is always one. There is
a fear which children have towards their parents, and a fear of servants towards
their masters. God will be feared of us as children, but not as servants; or if as
servants, not as slaves. The believing Christian, the regenerate child of God, who
through faith in Christ is certain of his deliverance from the devil and from hell,
assured of remission of sins and of life everlasting in the death and resurrection of
Jesus Christ our Saviour, he serveth in the reverent fear of love, and not in that
dreadful fear of death and everlasting damnation, wherewith the reprobate mind
is daunted. He feareth not death, for he is sure of life: he feareth not damnation,
for he is assured of salvation: he believeth that which Christ hath promised, and
doubteth nothing of the obtaining of that which Christ hath procured for him.
He is surely persuaded with St Paul, that 'neither death, nor life, nor tribulation,
nor affliction, nor any thing present, or to come, shall separate him from the love
of God, which is in Christ Jesus' (Rom. viii. 38). He feareth therefore neither the
sting of death, nor the power of Satan (1 Cor. xv. 55). But this certainty of God's
love towards him in Christ, and the testimony of his love towards God again,
casteth out all fear of eternal punishment. 'For ye have not,' saith the apostle,
'received again the spirit of bondage unto fear; but ye have received the Spirit of
adoption, by which we cry Abba, Father' (Rom. viii. 15). The Spirit testifieth with
our spirit, that God is our gracious Father; and if he our Father, we his children;
and if his children, heirs of his glorious kingdom. The preaching of the law letteth
us see our sin, but no remedy against the sting thereof; so that it maketh us fear,
and with trembling look for the reward of sin, which is everlasting death. But the
Spirit of adoption by the preaching of the gospel telleth us that in Christ we have
remission of sins; we are reconciled unto God, and adopted by him; we are his
chosen children, and may boldly and joyfully call him Father. And this certainty
of our salvation the Spirit of God testifieth to our spirit, whereby we put away all
servile fear of punishment, being assured of God's constant favour and eternal
love towards us; who never leaveth unfinished that which he hath begun, nor
forsaketh him whom he hath chosen. (4)

The Debt of Service

The minister is also a debtor to the people committed to his charge. 'I am a debtor,' saith the apostle (Rom. i. 14), 'both to Greeks and barbarians, to learned and unlearned.' The pastor is a debtor unto his flock (1 Pet. v. 2), to feed it so much as in him lieth, to feed it both spiritually and corporally; spiritually by life and doctrine, corporally with hospitality according to his ability. Woe be to that pastor that payeth not this debt! For if the flock perish for want of food, all that perishing blood shall be required at his hands. A hand reckoning for him to answer, and a sharp punishment to sustain for not answering.

The flock is indebted to their pastor, to honour and to reverence him as their father, to hear him as their schoolmaster, to obey and submit themselves unto him as to one whom God hath set over them for to rule them, to observe his wholesome precepts, to follow him in life as he followeth Christ, to love him, and to minister necessaries unto him for his convenient sustentation. All this debt is set down in the scriptures; and God requireth payment of it.

The husband doth owe unto his wife due benevolence, tender and faithful love, provision for things needful and honest, wise government, good instruction, protection, custody, and honour: the wife is indebted unto her husband to honour him, to love him, to obey him, to learn of him, to be governed by him, to live under him in silence with all subjection, to ease him in the orderly nurturing of his children and the wise governing of his house, to be not only an help, but a credit unto him, by her keeping home, by her industry and painfulness, by her sober, holy, and discreet behaviour. The master oweth to his servant meat, wages, correction, instruction: the servant to his master honour, obedience, faithful service, and whatsoever he is able by labour to perform.

Every man is to his neighbour a debtor, not only of that which himself borroweth, but of whatsoever his neighbour needeth; a debtor not only to pay that he oweth, but also to lend that he hath and may conveniently spare; to lend, I say, according to the rule of Christ, 'Lend, looking for nothing thereby: and your reward shall be much: you shall be the sons of the Most High.' So that these over-payments, the usury which hath spoiled and eaten up many, the canker of the commonwealth, is utterly both forbidden to man, and abhorred of God. To bargain for lead, grain, or leases, with such as have neither lead, grain, nor lease to pay, neither any such matter meant, but only unlawful gain of money, the party to forfeit his obligation, because he neither can nor meaneth such payment, and the lender not content to receive less advantage than thirty at the hundred; this is but a patched cloak to cover this vile sin withal. Whatsoever thou receivest upon condition, or by what means soever thou receivest more than was lent, thou art an usurer towards thy brother, and God will be a revenger against thee. He whom thou shouldest obey, if thou wilt be saved, doth in express words command thee not to lend thy money for usury. (5)

The Debt of Love

The debt of love is natural and continual. We all owe it, and we owe it unto all. And unto whom we owe it we never pay it, except we acknowledge that we owe it still. In this debt of love we must consider why we must love, whom we must love, and lastly, how we must love.

To omit the reasons drawn from nature, this one taken from the God of nature shall suffice. We must love because God hath so commanded, and because it is the fulfilling of all his commandments. 'I give you a new commandment,' saith Christ, 'that ye love one another' (John xiii. 34). In our new birth or regeneration we are made brethren and fellow-heirs with Christ of God's kingdom. As God therefore for ever loveth us in Christ, so we ought to love our brethren for God, and in Christ, for ever. If ye will be known to be his servants, by this men shall know you. If ye will be counted not hearers only, but also doers of the law, the law is love. He that loveth another fulfilleth the law. Which the apostle proveth thus. The law saith: 'Thou shalt not kill, thou shalt not steal, thou shalt not bear false witness, thou shalt not covet:' that is to say, Thou shalt no way harm thy brother. Love doth no evil or hurt to any: he that loveth his neighbour will not take away his life, will not defile his bed, will not steal or rob him of his goods, will not witness untruly against him, will not in his heart covet any thing that is his; and he that doth any of these things against him beareth not indeed hearty and true love towards him. 'Therefore is love the fulfilling of the law.' So that you see great cause why we should enter into this holy and christian band of love.

But whom must we love? 'Thou shalt love thy neighbour. And who is our neighbour?' Not he only to whom we are joined by familiar acquaintance, by alliance, or nearness of dwelling; but whosoever doth need our help, he is our neighbour, be he Jew or gentile, Christian or infidel, yea, friend or enemy, he is our neighbour. To him we ought to be near to do him good. It is frivolous for thee to object, He is mine enemy, he hath many ways wronged me, he hath raised slanderous reports of me, he hath practised against me, spoiled and robbed me: how can I love him? If Christ had loved his friends only, he had never loved thee, whosoever thou art. Look upon him, whose hands were stretched out upon the cross for his enemies, and for thee when thou wast his foe. No man proposeth him as a pattern to be followed, whom in his heart he doth mislike. Thou mislikest thine enemy because he hateth thee: if thou hate him, then dost thou imitate the very thing which thou hatest. Love thy neighbour therefore without exception, and love him as thyself. (6)

NOTES / SOURCES

1. Edwin Sandys 'The Fourth Sermon ('I exhort therefore . . .')', in *The Sermons of Edwin Sandys*, ed. J. Ayre, Cambridge (Parker Society), 1842, pp. 76–7
2. Ibid., pp. 88–9
3. 'The Fifth Sermon ('Be like-minded . . .')', ibid., pp. 104–5
4. 'The Tenth Sermon ('That being delivered . . .')', ibid., pp. 184–5
5. 'The Eleventh Sermon ('Owe nothing to any man . . .')', ibid., pp. 202–3
6. Ibid., pp. 204–5

Anne Askewe   1521–1546

Born in Lincolnshire of a well-to-do family, Anne Askewe was married to Thomas Kyme, who seems to have abandoned her in order to seek a divorce. By 1545 she had settled in London and was heavily involved in reforming circles. She was arrested and tried for heresy and burned in 1546. In prison she set down a full record of her examinations and also wrote the lyric here reproduced. Her writings were published and circulated by the prominent Reformed publicist, Bishop John Bale.

The ballad which Anne Askewe made and sang when she was in Newgate

Like as the armed knight,
  Appointed to the field,
With this world will I fight,
  And Christ[1] shall be my shield.

Faith is that weapon strong,
  Which will not fail at need:
My foes, therefore, among
  Therewith will I proceed.

As it is had in strength
  And force of Christe's way,
It will prevail at length,
  Though all the devils say nay.

Faith in the fathers old
  Obtained righteousness;
Which make me very bold
  To fear no world's distress.

I now rejoice in heart,
  And hope bid me do so;
For Christ will take my part,
  And ease me of my woe.

Thou say'st, Lord, whoso knock,
  To them wilt thou attend;
Undo therefore the lock,
  And thy strong power send.

More enemies now I have
  Than hairs upon my head:
Let them not me deprave,
  But fight thou in my stead.

[1] 'Faith', Mr Offor's copy.

On thee my care I cast,
　　For all their cruel spite:
I set not by their haste;
　　For thou art my delight.

I am not she that list
　　My anchor to let fall
For every drizzling mist,
　　My ship substantial.

Not oft use I to write,
　　In prose, nor yet in rhyme;
Yet will I shew one sight
　　That I saw in my time.

I saw a royal throne,
　　Where justice should have sit,
But in her stead was one
　　Of moody, cruel wit.

Absorbed was righteousness,
　　As of the raging flood:
Satan, in his excess,
　　Sucked up the guiltless blood.

Then thought I, Jesus Lord,
　　When thou shall judge us all,
Hard is it to record
　　On these men what will fall.

Yet, Lord, I thee desire,
　　For that they do to me,
Let them not taste the hire
　　Of their iniquity.

NOTES / SOURCES

Selected Works of John Bale, ed. H. Christmas, Cambridge (Parker Society), 1849, pp. 238–40

John Jewel   1522–1571

A Devonian by origin, Jewel studied at Oxford, where he became a Fellow of Corpus Christi College in 1542. Influenced by the thinking of Peter Martyr Vermigli, the Italian reformer who held the Regius chair of Divinity at Oxford, he became increasingly involved in the reforming movement. After some initial compromise with the revival of the old religion under Queen Mary, he left Britain in 1555 for Frankfurt, returning on Elizabeth's accession. In 1560, he became Bishop of Salisbury. His *Apologia* for the Church of England (1562) and subsequent controversy with the Jesuit Harding established him as the major theological defender of the new settlement. He was a stern suppressor of unreformed practices, but handled patristic and medieval theology with sympathy and insight. His sermons in Salisbury Cathedral were a major teaching tool for him, and the posthumous *Treatise of the Sacraments* (1583) is in fact a digest of some of his sermons. He was a patron and mentor to the young Richard Hooker.

The Purpose of the Sacraments

But why were sacraments ordained? He telleth you: *In nullum . . . nomen religionis, ceu verum etc.*: 'Men cannot be gathered together to the profession of any religion, whether it be true or false, unless they be bound in the fellowship of visible signs or sacraments.' The first cause why they were ordained is, that thereby one should acknowledge another, as fellows of one household, and members of one body. So was all Israel reckoned the children of Abraham, because of their circumcision; and all such as were uncircumcised were cut off from the people, and had no part in the commonwealth of Israel, because they were uncircumcised: even as we take them that are not baptized to be none of our brethren, to be no children of God, nor members of his church, because they will not take the sacrament of baptism.

Another cause is, to move, instruct, and teach our dull and heavy hearts by sensible creatures; that so our negligence in not heeding or marking the word of God spoken unto us might be amended. For, if any man have the outward seal, and have not the faith thereof sealed within his heart, it availeth him not: he is but an hypocrite and dissembler. So the circumcision of the foreskin of the flesh taught them to mortify their fleshly affections, and to cut off the thoughts and devices of their wicked hearts. Therefore said Stephen to the Jews: 'Ye stiff-necked and of uncircumcised hearts and ears, you have always resisted the Holy Ghost' (Acts vii.).

So, when in baptism our bodies are washed with water, we are taught that our souls are washed in the blood of Christ. The outward washing or sprinkling doth represent the sprinkling and washing which is wrought within us: the water doth signify the blood of Christ. If we were nothing else but soul, he would give us his grace barely and alone, without joining it to any creature, as he doth to his angels: but, seeing our spirit is drowned in our body, and our flesh doth make our understanding dull, therefore we receive his grace by sensible things.

Chrysostom saith: *Aliter ego, et aliter incredulus disponitur. Ille cum, etc.*: 'I am otherwise affected than is he which believeth not. . . . When he heareth of the water of baptism, he thinketh it is nothing else but water; but I see' not the creature only, which mine eyes do see, but also 'the cleansing of my soul by the Holy Ghost. He thinketh that my body only is washed: I believe that my soul is thereby made pure and holy; and withal I consider Christ's burial, his resurrection, our sanctification, righteousness, redemption, adoption, our inheritance, the kingdom of heaven, and the fulness of the Spirit. For I judge not of the things I see by my bodily eyes, but by the eyes of my mind.'

When one that is unlearned, and cannot read, looketh upon a book, be the book never so true, never so well written, yet, because he knoweth not the letters, and cannot read, he looketh upon it in vain. He may turn over all the leaves, and look upon all, and see nothing; but another that can read, and hath judgment to understand, considereth the whole story, the doughty deeds, grave counsels, discreet answers, examples, promises, threatenings, the very drift and meaning of him that wrote it. So do the faithful receive the fruit and comfort by the sacraments, which the wicked and ungodly neither consider nor receive. Thus do the sacraments lead us and instruct us to behold the secret and unknown mercies of God, and to carry ourselves to the obedience of his will. And this is the other cause why sacraments were ordained.

Thirdly, they are seals and confirmations of God's promise. St Paul saith: 'Abraham received the sign of circumcision, as the seal of the righteousness of the faith, which he had when he was uncircumcised' (Rom. iv.). By these we stop the mouth of heretics. For, if they deny that our Lord Jesus Christ was delivered to death for our sins, and is risen again for our justification; we shew them our sacraments, that they were ordained to put us in remembrance of Christ, and that by the use of them we shew the Lord's death till he come. We tell them these are proofs and signs that Christ suffered death for us on the cross. As Chrysostom saith: 'Laying out these mysteries, we stop their mouths.'

What? Are they nothing else but bare and naked signs? God forbid. They are the seals of God, heavenly tokens, and signs of the grace, and righteousness, and mercy given and imputed to us. (1)

Feeding Spiritually on Christ

The body then which we eat is in heaven, above all angels, and archangels, and powers, and principalities. Our meat is in heaven on high; and we are here below on the earth. How may it be that we may reach it, or taste, or eat it? Here let us imagine that there are two men in every man, and that every man is flesh and spirit, body and soul. This man thus doubled must be furnished with double senses; bodily, to serve the body; and spiritual, to serve the soul. He must have eyes of the body, and eyes of the soul; ears of the body, and ears of the soul. Spiritual senses are quick, sharp, and lively: they pierce any thing, be it never so thick: they reach any thing, be it never so far off. Christ saith of Abraham: 'Abraham rejoiced to see my day: he saw it, and was glad' (John viii.). He saw it, not with his bodily eyes, but with the inner eyes of the soul.

When we speak of the mystery of Christ, and of eating his body, we must shut up and abandon all our bodily senses. And, as we cannot say that we see him with our bodily eyes, or hear him with our bodily ears, or touch him with bodily feeling; so likewise can we not, and therefore may we not, say we taste him or eat him with our bodily mouth. In this work we must open all the inner and spiritual senses of our soul: so shall we not only see his body, but hear him, and feel him, and taste him, and eat him. This is the mouth and the feeling of faith. By the hand of faith we reach unto him, and by the mouth of faith we receive his body.

Touching the eating of Christ's body St Augustine taught the people on this wise: *Crede, et manducasti. Credere in Christum, hoc est, manducare panem vivum*: 'Believe in Christ, and thou hast eaten Christ.' 'For believing in Christ is the eating of the bread of life.' Believe that he is that 'Lamb of God that taketh away the sins of the world.' Believe that there is no other name given unto men wherein we shall be saved, but the name of Jesus Christ. Believe that he hath paid the ransom for the sins of the whole world. Believe that he hath made peace between God and man. Believe that it is he which hath reconciled all things by his blood. Here is nothing to be done by the mouth of the body. Whosoever thus believeth, he eateth, he drinketh him.

Clemens saith: '*Hoc est bibere sanguinem Jesu, participem esse incorruptionis ejus*: 'This is the drinking of the blood of Jesus, to be made partaker of his immortality.' Tertullian saith: 'He must be received in cause of life: he must be devoured by hearing: he must be chewed by understanding: he must be digested by faith.' Thus did Christ himself teach his disciples to understand him: 'The words which I speak are spirit and life' (John vi.). St Hierome therefore saith: *Quando audimus sermonem Domini, . . . caro Christi et sanguis ejus in aures nostras infunditur.* 'When we hear the word of God, the flesh of Christ and his blood is poured into our ears.'

The patriarchs and prophets and people of God, which lived before the birth of Christ, did by faith eat his flesh and drink his blood. St Paul saith: 'They did all eat the same spiritual meat, and did all drink of the same spiritual drink' (1 Cor. x.). Whosoever believed in Christ, they were nourished by him then, as we are now. They did not see Christ: he was not yet born: he had not yet a natural body; yet did they eat his body: he had not yet any blood; yet did they drink his blood. They believed that it was he in whom the promises should be fulfilled, that he should be that blessed Seed in whom all nations should be blessed. Thus they believed, thus they received and did eat his body. (2)

The Effects of Christ's Passion

What were the effects of his death? What followed? 'God hath highly exalted him, and given him a name above every name, that at the name of Jesus should every knee bow; and that every tongue should confess that Jesus Christ is the Lord, to the glory of God the Father' (Phil. ii.). God spake out of the heavens, and said: 'This is my beloved Son, in whom I am well pleased.' He crowned him with glory and honour: he hath not only advanced Christ, but us also together with him; 'and made us sit together in heavenly places in Christ Jesus;' 'he hath made us like to the image of his Son' (Eph. ii.). Thus hath he made us an acceptable people, and hath renewed the face of the earth: so that now he saith not, as he did to Adam, Thou art earth, and shalt return to earth; but he saith, Thou art heaven: an immortal and undefiled inheritance, that fadeth not away, is reserved in heaven for thee. This is the effect and value of the death of Christ.

All these things are laid before us in the holy table, if we have eyes to see and behold them. There may we see the crucifying of his body, and the shedding of his blood, as it were in a glass. Therefore Christ saith: 'Do this in remembrance of me;' in remembrance of my benefit wrought for you; in remembrance of your salvation purchased by me. St Paul saith: 'As often as ye shall eat this bread, and drink this cup, ye shew the Lord's death till he come' (1 Cor. xi.).

In this supper lieth a hidden mystery. There is the horror of sin, there is the death of our Lord for our sin represented, how he was wounded for our sins, and tormented for our iniquities, and led as a lamb to the slaughter. There may we see the shame of the cross, the darkness over the world, the earth to quake, the stones to cleave asunder, the graves to open, and the dead to rise. These things may we see in the supper: this is the meaning of these holy mysteries.

Therefore 'let every one examine himself,' and search and weigh his own heart, whether he be the child of God, and a member of the body of Christ; 'and so let him eat of this bread and drink of this cup.' The sacrament of the Lord's supper is a holy food, the seal of our faith, the assurance of God's promises, and a covenant between God and man. He, that doth unworthily thrust himself to this table, eateth and drinketh his own damnation. When a sick man, of a weak and feeble stomach, sitteth down to eat with them that are whole, whatsoever he eateth or drinketh, it doth increase his sickness. To them that perish the word of God is a savour of death unto death. 'Whoso disagreeth from Christ, neither eateth his bread nor drinketh his blood,' as saith St Augustine.

If any of us come to the sacrament of the body of Christ, and yet make ourselves the members of the devil, we tread Christ under our feet, we regard not his body crucified nor his blood shed for us, we regard not the price of our salvation, we are guilty of his death, we betray the innocent blood, we are fallen from grace; and Christ hath died in vain for us. (3)

Holy Communion and Heavenly Worship

Let us die with Christ, let us be crucified unto the world. Let us be holy eagles, and soar above. Let us go up into the great parlour, and receive of our Lord the cup of the new testament. There let us behold the body that was crucified for us, and the blood which was shed for us. There let us say, This is the ransom of the world: this was once offered, and hath made perfect for ever all them that believe: this entered once into the holy place, and obtained everlasting redemption for us: this standeth always in the presence of God, and maketh intercession for us: this is 'the Lamb of God that taketh away the sins of the world:' by this body I am now no more earth and ashes: by this I am now not a bondman, but made free. This body hath broken the gates of hell, and hath opened heaven. In this are all the treasures of God's mercy: by this the prince of darkness is cast forth: in this body shall he come again to judge the quick and the dead. (4)

Confession

We are taught to lay open and acknowledge our sins, not to hide them, but to make confession of them. This is one two ways; either in the secret thought of thy heart before God, or else in the hearing and presence of men.

David made confession of his sins before God. 'I acknowledged my sin before thee, neither hid I mine iniquity. I said, I will confess against myself my wickedness unto the Lord; and thou forgavest the punishment of my sin' (Psal. xxxii.). And again: 'I know mine iniquities; and my sin is ever before me. Against thee, against thee only have I sinned, and done evil in thy sight' (Psal. li.). Such a confession made Daniel (Dan. ix.): 'We have sinned, and have committed iniquity, and have done wickedly: yea, we have rebelled, and have departed from thy precepts, and from thy judgments. For we would not obey thy servants the prophets; which spake in thy name to our kings, to our princes, and to our fathers, and to all the people of the land.' Even so the prophet Esay (Isai. lxiv.):

'Behold, thou art angry; for we have sinned. . . . We have all been as an unclean thing; and all our righteousness is as filthy clouts; and we all do fade like a leaf; and our iniquities, like the wind, have taken us away. . . . But now, O Lord, thou art our Father: we are the clay, and thou art our potter; and we all are the work of thy hands.' This is true and christian confession. We are required after this sort to examine ourselves, and confess our sins before God: who doth not so, he shall not find mercy and forgiveness of his sins.

The other sort of confession, made unto men, I do not condemn. It may do much good, if it be well used. St James commendeth it among the faithful: 'Acknowledge your faults one to another, and pray one for another, that ye may be healed' (James v.). He speaketh not of priest or minister, but of every one of the faithful. Every Christian may do this help unto another, to take knowledge of the secret and inner grief of the heart, to look upon the wound which sin and wickedness hath made, and, by godly advice and earnest prayer for him, to recover his brother. This is a private exhortation, and as it were a catechizing or instructing in the faith, and a means to lead us by familiar and special conference to examine our conscience, and to espy wherein we have offended God. The use and practice hereof is not only to be allowed, but most needful and requisite, if so the superstition, and necessity, and conscience, which many have fondly used and put therein, be taken away. (5)

Deathbed Counsel

In this case the good father calleth his son unto him, and exhorteth him in this manner: My son, hearken unto me: these be the last words which I shall speak unto thee. Thou seest in me the weakness and decay of flesh: thou shalt be as I am now. One passeth before another: the world and the beauty thereof fade away and come to an end. Trust not the world; it will deceive thee: walk advisedly, know that thou shalt give an account of thy doings. 'For we must all appear before the judgment-seat of Christ; that every man may receive the things which are done in his body, according to that he hath done, whether it be good or evil' (2 Cor. v.). Deceive no man by wrongful dealing: increase not thy goods by extortion nor by usury: he that giveth his money unto usury shall not enter into the tabernacle of the Lord. He that taketh usury of his neighbour killeth him without a sword. The Lord will avenge it: he will not bless ill-gotten goods: they cannot prosper: they will never continue, nor remain unto the third heir. My son, in all thy doings fear the Lord. If thou fear the Lord, thou shalt prosper; and in the day of thine end thou shalt be blessed. Meddle not much with other men's business, lest thou be entangled with controversies: abhor the slanderer and double-tongued. Let my doings, which am thy father, be ever before thine eyes. Those few goods which I have were truly gotten. I have not gathered them of the tears, and heaviness, and undoing, or hindering of any. Be faithful to thy wife; and besides her know none other. Help thy neighbour according to thy power; and turn not thy face from the poor and needy. 'Be merciful after thy power. If thou hast much, give plenteously: if thou hast little, do thy diligence gladly to give of that little.' Be not slow to visit the sick: whatsoever thou takest in hand, remember the end, and thou shalt never do amiss. As for me, I have passed the vanities and miseries of this world. 'The Lord hath given, and the Lord taketh away: blessed be the name of the Lord.' He

is the Lord my God; let him do with me as it seemeth good unto him. I know that
this shall hasten my salvation; and that Christ shall be magnified in my body,
whether it be by life or by death. I have not so lived that I am ashamed to live:
neither am I afraid to die, for we have a gracious Lord. I know that, if my earthly
house of this tabernacle be destroyed, I have a building given of God, that is, an
house not made with hands, but eternal in the heavens. They that die in the Lord
are blessed; they shall rest from their labours. 'Christ is unto me both in life and
in death advantage.'

In such sort do the godly prepare themselves to their journey out of this life.

Then the minister prayeth that he may be constant in this faith; he strength-
eneth him, and confirmeth him in it. He exhorteth the sick to commend himself
unto God: he prayeth unto God, that he will give his angels charge over him to
keep him and defend him, that he fall not into temptation. He teacheth him to
say: 'O Lord, in thee have I trusted; let me never be confounded.' Come, Lord
Jesus, come, and take me unto thee: 'Lord, let thy servant depart in peace:' 'thy
kingdom come.' I am thy son: 'thine am I, O save me:' 'into thine hands, O Lord,
I commend my spirit: thou hast redeemed me, O Lord God of truth.' In this state
he dieth, and hath his eyes always fastened upon God and so seeth how indeed
'the dead are blessed which die in the Lord.' (6)

NOTES / SOURCES

1. John Jewel, 'A Treatise of the Sacraments', *Works of Bishop Jewel*, ed. J. Ayre, Cambridge (Parker
   Society), 1847, pp. 1100–1
2. Ibid., pp. 1118–19
3. Ibid., pp. 1123
4. Ibid., pp. 1124
5. Ibid., pp. 1133
6. Ibid., pp. 1138

Henry Bull   ? before 1530–1575

No details are known of Bull's early life, but he was a Fellow of Magdalen College,
Oxford, in the reign of King Edward. *Christian Prayers and Meditations* was published
in 1566, including a quite lengthy treatise on the theology of prayer and a number of
prayers for daily use drawn, for the most part, from other writers. It illustrates very well
the style of prayer commended to educated laypeople in Elizabeth's reign—usually
rather penitential in tone, and saturated with biblical allusions.

Reverence and Distraction

And here let us call to mind how unreverently we abuse the great goodness of
God in calling us into familiar talk with him, when we have not that reverent fear
of his sacred majesty that we would have of an earthly creature or a worldly
prince; but suffering our hearts to be carried away with wandering thoughts and
worldly imaginations, are otherwise occupied, and forsake him in the midst of
our prayer. Let us know therefore, that none prepare themselves rightly to prayer,
but such as have a reverent fear of God's majesty, which they cannot have that
come not to it unburdened of earthly cares and affections: for nothing is more

contrary unto the reverence of God than such lightness and vanity. And this is it that is meant by the lifting up of hands, that we should remember that we be far distant from God unless we lift up our hearts and minds also on high[. . .] And though it be hard to be so bent to prayer, but that we shall find that many by-thoughts will creep upon us to hinder our prayer; yet the more hard it is, the more earnestly we must wrestle to overcome all lets and hinderances, and labour with inward groanings unto the Lord, that he will link our hearts fast unto him (Ps. lxxxvi.), and not suffer us to be led away from him by the vain suggestions of Satan, who, at all times compassing us about, is never more busy than when we address and bend ourselves to prayer, secretly and subtilly creeping into our breasts, calling us back from God, and causing us to forget what we have to do: so that oftentimes, when we with all reverence should speak to God, we find our hearts talking with the vanities of the world, or with the foolish imaginations of our own hearts.

Finally, we must be in christian charity, love, and concord with all men, seeking unfeigned, hearty, and brotherly reconciliation, if we have offended any man, before we enter into prayer, or else God will not hear our prayers; yea, they are otherwise execrable, and full of damnable hypocrisy in God's sight. And this that is spoken of prayer may be said also of the hearing of God's word, or any other service of God. We must therefore lay aside all malice, envy, wrath, grudge, contention, wrangling, dissimulation, all guileful, crafty, and subtle dealing; and with a single heart do to other as we would they should do unto us. Therefore St Peter willeth that such as have once tasted how good and bounteous the Lord is (1 Pet. ii.), and are become new creatures, new-born babes, by the heavenly regeneration through the doctrine of the gospel, should, like holy and innocent babes, lay aside all such works of the flesh (Gal. v.), as St Paul calleth them, which do deprive a man of the kingdom of God. (1)

Right Dispositions for Prayer

Although we know that it is the only work of the Holy Ghost, thus to move and incline our hearts to prayer, we may not be negligent and slothful to dispose and stir up ourselves thereunto; but rather contrariwise, so often as we feel ourselves cold and not disposed to prayer as we ought to be, we must make our supplication unto the Lord, that it would please him to inflame us with his holy Spirit, whereby we may be framed to pray with such affection of mind as we ought to be.

When we are cast down with true humility by the feeling of our own infirmity, sin, and misery, we must nevertheless be encouraged to pray with a sure and stedfast hope to obtain our requests. These be things indeed contrary in shew, to join with the feeling of the just vengeance of God sure affiance of favour: which things do yet very well agree, in that it is the goodness of God only that raiseth us up being oppressed with our own evils, from the which of ourselves we cannot rise. For as repentance and faith are knit as companions together (albeit the one driveth us down with fear, and the other lifteth us up again with comfort), so in prayer they must needs meet together. (2)

Asking and Thanking

Of Prayer there be two parts, Petition and Thanksgiving. By petition, we pour forth our desires before God, requiring first those things that may set forth his glory, and then such benefits as are profitable for our use. By giving of thanks, we praise and magnify his benefits bestowed upon us, acknowledging that whatsoever good things we enjoy, we have received them of his free goodness and liberality. Therefore David joineth these two parts together in one verse, when he saith, Call upon me in the day of necessity: I will deliver thee, and thou shalt glorify me (Psalm. l.). The scripture commandeth us to use both, and that continually. For our necessity is so great, our life is so full of troubles and calamities, and so many dangers hang over our heads every moment, that we have all cause enough, yea, even the most holy, with sighs and groanings continually to fly unto God, and to call upon him in most humble wise. But this we may better perceive in things pertaining to the soul. For when shall so many great sins, whereof we know ourselves guilty, suffer us to sit still without care, and not to crave pardon of God for the same? when will Satan give us rest and quietness? when will he cease to range about seeking whom he may destroy? when shall our temptations give us truce, so that we shall not need to hasten unto God for help? Finally, the desire of the kingdom and glory of God ought so to draw us wholly unto it, not by fits, but continually, that it should be alway fit and convenient time for us to pray. Wherefore, not without cause, we are so often commanded to pray continually. (3)

Daily Bread

Give us this day our daily bread

By *Bread*, the food of the body, are understood all things necessary for this corporal life, as meat, drink, health, success in our vocation, etc. By this word *give*, we should understand that not only spiritual things but also corporal benefits are God's free gifts, and come not for our worthiness or travail taken about the same, although our travails be oftentimes means by the which God doth give corporal things.

By *daily*, we understand that contented minds of thy children with that which is sufficient for the present time, as having hope in thee that they shall not want, but daily shall receive at thy hands plenty and enough of all things.

By this word *our*, are as well understood public benefits, as peace on the commonweal, good magistrates, seasonable weather, good laws etc., as particular benefits, namely, children, health, success in the works of our vocation, etc. And besides this, by it we should see the care even for corporal things, which thy children have for others as well as for themselves. So that here I may learn how far I am from that I should be, and that I see thy children are come unto. I see my ignorance also, how that as spiritual things do come from thee, so do temporal things, and as they come from thee, so are they conserved and kept of thee; and therefore thy children are thankful, and look for them as thy mere gifts, notwithstanding the means which they use, if they have them: howbeit they use them but as means; for except thou work therewith, all is in vain (Ps. cxxvii.).

Again, here I am taught to be content with that which is sufficient for the present time, as thy children be which have the shortness of this life always before their eyes; and therefore they ask but for daily sustenance, knowing this life to be compared to a day, yea, a watch, a sound, a shadow, etc. Moreover, I may learn to see the compassion and brotherly care which thy children have one for another. Last of all, here I may see thy goodness, which as thou wilt give me all things necessary for this life, (or else thou wouldest not bid me ask, etc.), so thou commandest all men to pray and care for me, and that bodily; much more then, if they be able, they are commanded to help me both in body and soul.

By reason whereof I have great cause to lament and rejoice. To lament, because I am not so affected as thy children be; because of my ignorance, my ingratitude, my perversity and contempt of thy goodness, and of the necessity of thy people, which (alas!) be in great misery; some in exile, some in prison, some in poverty, sickness, etc. To rejoice I have great cause, because of thy goodness in teaching me these things, in commanding me to ask whatsoever I want, in giving me so many things unasked, in keeping the benefits given me, in commanding men to care for me, to pray for me, to help me, etc. But, alas! how far I am either from true lamentation or rejoicing, Lord, thou knowest. Oh, be merciful unto me, and help me; forgive me, and grant me thy holy Spirit to reveal to me my need, ignorance, great ingratitude, and contempt of thy mercies and thy people; and that in such sort, that I might heartily lament and bewail my misery, and through thy goodness be altered with thy people, to mourn for the miseries of thy children as for mine own.

Again, reveal to me thy goodness, dear Father, even in corporal things, that I may see thy mercy, thy presence, power, wisdom and righteousness in every creature and corporal benefit, and that in such sort, that I may be throughly affected truly to reverence, fear, love, obey thee, hang upon thee, to be thankful to thee, and in all my need to come unto thee, not only when I have ordinary means by the which thou commonly workest, but also when I have none, yea, when all means and helps are clean against me.

[Here remember the state of your children and family, also your parents, neighbours, kinsfolks; also your friends, country, and magistrates, etc., as you shall have time thereto, and by God's good Spirit shall be provoked.] (4)

Meditation upon the Lord's Prayer

Our Father which art in Heaven

We, being gloriously formed unto the image of thy divine Majesty, and created by thy gracious goodness to most high honour, howbeit through sin disfigured with vileness deserving damnation, and yet by Christ's death redeemed and restored unto grace to be citizens with saints, of the family of God, now altogether in christian unity, as members of one body: we pray, desire, and trust to obtain of thee our heavenly Father, according unto thy gracious goodness, mighty power, and faithful promise unto us that ask abundance of thy grace:

That thy Name may be hallowed

That thy divine power and glorious majesty may be certainly known and reverently honoured. That the hearts of us men, by thy word and prayer, may be sanctified from all sin and vanity, so that we, with all that we have, serving thee in holiness and righteousness, may so shine afore men upon earth, that they thereby may be occasioned to honour thee, our Father which art in heaven.

Thy kingdom come

That thy word may be so fruitfully preached amongst us thy people, that we may be throughly instructed and taught to bridle our sensual appetites by natural reason, and to submit our wits and reasons unto a godly spirit, and to try our spirits by the true scriptures: so that within us may reign the kingdom of God, which is neither meat nor drink; which is neither superstitious ceremonies, voluptuous pleasures, nor vain glory, but righteousness, peace, and comfort in the Holy Ghost, by the which we now tasting of thy heavenly joys, may be made from henceforth weary of all worldly vanities, continually looking and praying for the appearance and coming of thy eternal and everlasting kingdom.

Thy will be done in earth as it is in heaven

In heaven the angels of reverent love do thy will and commandment with comfortable courage and joyful pleasure. In hell the wicked spirits through malice and envy, repining and grudging, do torment and vex themselves whatsoever they be doing: and upon earth men, being subject unto sin, do think it a labour and pain to be occupied in any thing that is good and godly. Wherefore we pray that the grace of thy heavenly Spirit may so work in our earthly bodies, that we, being delivered from sin and vanity, may freely delight and take pleasure to do thy will and commandment here on earth, as thy glorious angels do in heaven.

Give us this day our daily bread

We having great need, and not able of ourselves to deserve any thing, beseech thee of thy fatherly goodness, to give freely unto us all (so that none be hurt nor hindered this day when we cry unto thee, constrained by present need, not craftily craving through vain care against tomorrow) our daily bread, our daily and necessary food and relief, both bodily and ghostly: and especially so, that the spiritual food of Christ's flesh and his blood, by daily preaching of the Gospel and ministration of the sacraments, may replenish our hearts and minds with continual remembrance of his death and passion, daily to be used for our necessary and spiritual consolation.

Forgive us our trespasses, as we forgive them that trespass against us

We feeling and knowing our own sinfulness, do desire thy merciful forgiveness of our faults and trespasses, which we have committed against thee, so that we, freely forgiving all other that have offended us in any thing, whatsoever it be, may be sure that mercy springing in thee hath proceeded unto us, and being graciously offered of thee, hath been thankfully received of us, and being charitably used of us towards other, shall most certainly be confirmed and enlarged of thee towards us; so that by free mercy, springing and proceeding from thee, all faults may be freely forgiven, even as those which other have committed against us, so likewise those which we have done against thee.

And lead us not into temptation

Suffer not the devil by the abuse of thy benefits to lead us captives into deceitful and damnable temptation; drawing us by dainty meats unto greedy gluttony, by money and riches unto unsatiable covetousness, and by wealth and prosperity unto pride and vain glory, and by all thy godly and gracious gifts unto every devilish and abominable sin.

But deliver us from evil

Deliver our goods from abuse, our bodies from corruption, our souls from damnation. Deliver us by Christ Jesu, from the bondage of sin, unto the liberty of the gospel; so that from all danger of devilish temptation, training and enticing men towards damnation, we may be delivered to serve thee in holiness and righteousness all the days of our life, with most certain and sure hope of everlasting salvation, through Christ Jesu, in whom our hope and thy promise is most certain, that is to say, Amen.

[Your time is short; your dangers be great; you are well warned by God's word written. Mark. xiii. *Take heed, watch, and pray.*

Take heed that your hearts and minds be not made heavy, hard, and dull, with meats and drinks, vain pleasures, or worldly cares.

Watch with diligence to do your own duties, in desirous looking for Christ's coming.

Pray, that ye may escape all dangers, and stand in grace and favour afore the face of Christ at his coming.]

REV. XXII.
Behold, I come soon. (5)

Sundry Prayers

A prayer to be said before meat

All things depend upon thy providence, O Lord, to receive at thy hands due sustenance in time convenient. Thou givest to them, and they gather it: thou openest thy hand, and they are satisfied with all good things (Ps. clv.).

O heavenly Father, which art the fountain and full treasure of all goodness, we beseech thee to shew thy mercies upon us thy children, and sanctify these gifts which we receive of thy merciful liberality[1], granting us grace to use them soberly and purely, according to thy blessed will[2]: so that hereby we may acknowledge thee to be the author and giver of all good things, and above all that we may remember continually to seek the spiritual food of thy word, wherewith our souls

---

[1] 1 Tim. iv.   [2] Tit. ii.

may be nourished everlastingly, through our Saviour Christ, who is the true bread of life, which came down from heaven, of whom whosoever eateth shall live for ever, and reign with Him in glory world without end[1]. So be it.

A thanksgiving after meals

Let all nations magnify the Lord: let all people rejoice in praising and extolling his great mercies: for his fatherly kindness is plentifully shewed forth upon us, and the truth of his promise endureth for ever[2].

We render thanks unto thee, O Lord God, for the manifold benefits which we continually receive at thy bountiful hand; not only for that it hath pleased thee to feed us in this present life, giving unto us all things necessary for the same, but specially because thou hast of thy free mercy fashioned us anew[3], into an assured hope of a far better life, the which thou hast declared unto us by thy holy gospel[4]. Therefore we humbly beseech thee, O heavenly Father, that thou wilt not suffer our affections to be so entangled or rooted in these earthly and corruptible things, but that we may always have our minds directed to thee on high[5], continually watching for the coming of our Lord and Saviour Christ[6], what time He shall appear for our full redemption[7]. To whom, with thee and the Holy Ghost, be all honour and glory, for ever and ever. So be it. (6)

A prayer to be said before the receiving of the communion

O Father of mercy, and God of all consolation, seeing all creatures do acknowledge and confess thee to be their Governor and Lord, it becometh us, the workmanship of thine own hands, at all times to reverence and magnify thy godly Majesty. First, for that thou hast created us to thine own image and similitude[8], but chiefly because thou hast delivered us from that everlasting death and damnation into the which Satan drew mankind by the means of sin[9]; from the bondage whereof neither man nor angel was able to make us free; but thou, O Lord, rich in mercy, and infinite in goodness, hast provided our redemption to stand in thine only and well-beloved Son, whom of very love thou didst give to be made man like unto us in all things, sin excepted, that in his body He might receive the punishment of our transgression, by his death to make satisfaction to thy justice, and by his resurrection to destroy him that was author of death, and so to bring again life to the world, from which the whole offspring of Adam was most justly exiled[10].

O Lord, we acknowledge that no creature was able to comprehend the length and breadth, the deepness and height, of that thy most excellent love, which moved thee to shew mercy where none was deserved, to promise and give life where death had gotten victory, to receive us into thy grace when we could do nothing but rebel against thy majesty. O Lord, the blind dulness of our corrupt nature will not suffer us sufficiently to weigh these thy most ample benefits: yet, nevertheless, at the commandment of Jesus Christ our Lord, we present ourselves

[1] John vi. [2] Ps. cxvii. [3] Coloss. iii. [4] 2 Tim. i. [5] 1 John ii. [6] Tit. ii., 1 Cor.i.
[7] Rom. viii. [8] Gen. i. [9] Ephes. ii., Gal. i., Gen. iii.
[10] Acts iv., Hebr. i., Rev. v., John iii., Hebr. viii. iv., 1 Peter ii., Isai. xliii., liii., Matt. iii. xvii., Jerem. xxxi., Hebr. viii., Rom. v., Hebr. ii., John vi., Gen. iii., Rom. v., Ephes. iii.

to this his table, which He hath left to be used in remembrance of his death until his coming again, to declare and witness before the world, that by Him alone we have received liberty and life; that by Him alone thou dost acknowledge us to be thy children and heirs; that by Him alone we have entrance to the throne of thy grace; that by Him alone we are possessed in our spiritual kingdom, to eat and drink at his table, with whom we have our conversation presently in heaven, and by whom our bodies shall be raised up again from the dust, and shall be placed with Him in that endless joy, which thou, O Father of mercy, hast prepared for thine elect, before the foundation of the world was laid[1]. And these most inestimable benefits we acknowledge and confess to have received of thy free mercy and grace, by thine only beloved Son Jesus Christ[2]. For the which, therefore, we thy congregation, moved by thy holy Spirit, render to thee all thanks, praise, and glory, for ever and ever[3]. (7)

A prayer to be said before the preaching and hearing of God's word

Almighty God and most merciful Father, whose word is a lantern to our feet and a light unto our steps; we most humbly beseech thee to illuminate our minds, that we may understand the mysteries contained in thy holy law, and into the selfsame thing that we godly understand we may be virtuously transformed, so that of no part we offend thy divine majesty; through our Saviour Jesus Christ. (8)

NOTES / SOURCES

1. Henry Bull, *Christian Prayers and Meditations*, reprinted Cambridge (Parker Society), 1842, pp. xv–xvi
2. Ibid., pp. xix
3. Ibid., pp. xxix–xxx
4. Ibid., pp. 28–31
5. Ibid., pp. 41–4
6. Ibid., pp. 54–6
7. Ibid., pp. 90–1
8. Ibid., pp. 125

John Woolton   1535–1593/4

A native of Wigan, Woolton studied at Brasenose College in Oxford and spent the reign of Queen Mary in exile on the Continent. After his return, he served in various ecclesiastical offices, becoming Bishop of Exeter in 1579. His *Christian Manual* was an influential summary of practical instruction and theological orientation, drawing on patristic and classical as well as biblical sources.

---

[1] Ephes. ii., John vi. xvii., Ephes. ii., Gen. vi., Rom. iii., Isai. lxiv., Ps. v. xii., Rom. vii., Matt. xvi., 1 Cor. ii., Luke xi., Mark x., Matt. xxvi., Luke xxii., 1 Cor. xi., John viii., Galat. v., Rom. viii., 1 Peter i., Ephes. v. ii., Heb. iv., Rom. iii., Matt. xxv., John xiv., Luke xii., xxii., Rev. ii., Phil. iii., Ephes. ii. i., Rev. xiii.
[2] Rom. iii., Ephes. ii., Titus iii.
[3] Rom. viii.

Faith and Works

For although we are justified before God freely, without works, either going before or coming after, through and for the merits of Jesus Christ only our mediator, which we apprehend by faith; yet the immutable will of our God is, that all justified men should walk in a new obedience, doing those works that are acceptable to God, beautifying their profession with a virtuous conversation. But because in these latter days charity waxeth cold, and iniquity every aboundeth; those preachers and writers cannot choose but lightly please God and good men, that press the world to wear their badges, and to shew forth as it were their passport in this their peregrination, in eschewing vice and following virtue, albeit neither merit nor justification or salvation came thereby.

For, as St Paul writeth (2 Tim. iii.), these are 'the days which are perilous, and men love themselves; having a shew of godliness, but have denied the power thereof.' Wherefore, to the end that the effectual causes may be known which may stir men to piety[1], virtue, and innocency of life, I have thought good to comprehend in this treaty the duties of every vocation and calling, and as[2] virtues, which as ornaments and precious stones do beautify and garnish the same. But before I come particularly to every estate and condition, I judge it most convenient to put down in few words the causes and commodities of good works, so much the rather, for that I said before, that works do not deserve neither merit justification nor salvation: whereby my readers may haply be discouraged from that whereunto I bend all my study, to move and inflame them, or at the least to leave [no] occasion to the papists to cry out with open mouths, that our doctrine is a doctrine of licentiousness and liberty. (1)

The Ground of Confidence

Whereas many take offence with this proposition, which we preach and teach, That men are justified by faith only in Christ; it is because they do not understand our doctrine in that behalf. For we mean nothing less than to reject or take away good works and honest actions; but we only exclude confidence and trust in men's works, which have no place at all in justification. And that dignity is ascribed to faith, because it is as it were an instrument to apprehend Christ; and is much like a conduit-pipe, whereby, as by a mean, the water of life, that is, justice in Christ, is conveyed and communicated unto us: by whose merits we have remission and forgiveness of sins, and are adopted and made the children of God. Faith by her own dignity and worthiness doth not demerit justice and right-eousness; but receiveth and embraceth the same offered unto us in the gospel: so that in the free mercy of God, and merits of Christ, who in shedding of his precious blood, hath made satisfaction for the sins of the whole world, we ought to repose all our trust and confidence. (2)

---

[1] Pity, 1576.   [2] Perhaps *all*.

Children of God

To conclude this matter of merit and reward: the merciful and gracious Lord rewardeth his loving children for their good works, not for the perfection and dignity of the said works, but because the doers of those good works are sons and children. They are made sons and heirs by adoption in Christ; and therefore their works are acceptable to God, not in respect of themselves, but for Christ's sake, in whom they are engraffed, and of whose moisture (as it were of heavenly dew) they are partakers: so that all their rewards are of necessity referred to the grace and mercy of God. (3)

Caring for Mind and Body

I will therefore speak first of man's duty being alone in his study and bedchamber, as he is sequestered from all fellowship and company of men.

And because man consisteth of soul and body, I will say somewhat briefly of both those parts. The mind of man is to be garnished and informed with the science and knowledge of many excellent matters; but especially with those which are available to a blessed life, to correct and frame manners to true religion and sincere worshipping of God: for unto this end ought we to refer all our studies and endeavours. And without these things no man can rightly have the name of a Christian, nor enjoy assured hope of eternal salvation, nor yet a quiet and peaceable conscience. Let our minds differ very much from the purposes and intents of the infidels, who neither seek nor do these things perfectly or sincerely, not led with the love and fear of God; but are kindled to virtue either with desire of vainglory, or are stayed from vice for fear of punishment; and respect nothing less than the glory of God, the profit of their brethren, or the salvation of their own souls. But we that profess Christ ought most ardently to embrace virtues, inflamed with an earnest desire to enlarge and set out God's glory: neither ought we to respect external discipline only; but to do well with a single eye in the sight of the living God, and to be fruitful in good works before men, having always the assistance of God's Spirit, to lighten our reason, and to guide our will. So it shall come to pass that, faith shining and burning like a bright lamp before our actions, we shall not be puffed up with a vain conceit and opinion of ourselves, but shall acknowledge our own corruption, and behave ourselves humbly before God and man; daily desiring mercy and remission of sins, and reposing all our confidence and hope of salvation in the mercy of God through his Son Christ. The solace and comfort, which ariseth of actions and virtues thus done in christian men's breasts is so great, that no tongue or pen can counterpoise the same, albeit I have endeavoured before to shadow (as it were) and give a gleamish[1] thereof. And thus much I thought good to speak of the mind: now I will come to man's body also.

Let every man so diet and govern his body, that he may conserve the same safe and sound, so far as he possibly may. For we ought to have a care of our health, to the end that we may be more ready to do our duty in our vocations and callings. It behoveth us to regard, that we neither corrupt our bodies with riot and surfeiting, (for we ought to eat and drink so much that our power and strength

[1] Gleamish: glimpse.

may be refreshed and not oppressed,) nor yet that we do not enervate and weaken the same with over much abstinence and famine; for in both these there is sin and offence. Therefore, as in all other things, so in this also, mediocrity is a commendable and necessary virtue: although besides a certain perpetual sobriety and temperancy in diet, which we ought to observe, we must sometime, as occasion offereth, compress and subdue the wanton looseness of our flesh with fasting, abstinence, and spare diet; because most commonly lust is a companion of gluttony. The body must be chastened therefore, and brought into subjection; neither may we lawfully 'take care for the flesh, to satisfy the lusts of it.'

And as those that impair and decay their health with riot and surfeiting, breeding diseases, and hastening their own end, are murderers of themselves; even so they that weaken and utterly destroy their bodies with immoderate abstinence and other austerity of life, are in no less fault, whiles they make their bodies unable to execute anything, unto whom the Apostle chargeth us to give honour; and therefore did write unto his scholar Timothy, that he should 'drink no more water, but to use a little wine for the weakness of his stomach:' albeit I shall not need to speak many words in this behalf; for few there are found now-a-days, that offend in that part. Every man therefore must guide his body with skill and discretion; and beware that he destroy not that which God hath given unto him to cherish and conserve. All the order of our diet, motion, and exercise, together with all trimming and dressing of the body, ought to respect sanity and good health; but without delicacy and nice pleasure. (4)

Excess

And why are the rich men cursed, who have their consolation, who are full, who laugh, who sleep in ivory beds, who join land to land, whose banquets are full of harmony and music? (Luke vi. Amos vi. Isai. v.) Doubtless, ivory, gold, meats, and music, are the good gifts of God, appointed by his providence for the use and comfort of man, and there is no sin in their natures. But when God hath blessed us with these his good gifts, if we use them with excess, filthy pleasure, vain jactation; and, being never satisfied, do still groan and gape after more; we abuse God's good gifts, and pollute our bodies and consciences. Let men cut off then, in the use of these things, immoderate lust, prodigality, vanity, and arrogancy, and frame their natures to sobriety; and the use of God's creatures shall be both lawful and holy. And this my counsel I offer as well to the poor husbandman, as to the gentleman: for they in their callings, so far as their ability will stretch, exceed in prodigality and riot; and if they keep a better stay herein than others, it is rather for want of power than of will. And that vulgar speech is commonly verified, 'Under a frieze coat oftentimes there lurketh a purple mind;' and again, 'Under purple and silk an humble and gentle nature.' This is the best then, for every man to live according to his calling and order, either homely or worshipfully. (5)

Duties and Callings

The office and duty of a Christian, as he liveth publicly, and hath to do in the world, is of two sorts, to wit, either particular in respect of some state and vocation in the which he liveth, being either a master or a servant, a father or a child, a husband or a wife, etc.; or else general in that he is a man and a christian man, whereby he is linked to others with that fast knot of humanity and pity, wherein he excelleth all other earthly creatures. (6).

Virtue and Holiness

Herein may we easily perceive what difference there is between divine and philosophical precepts touching manners. For wheresoever the scripture exhorteth men to good works, it adjoineth by and by something out of the first table of the ten commandments: as for example, of the fear of God, of faith, of charity, of obedience toward God, of his promises and threats, of Christ's benefits toward his servants, and of his punishments toward the obstinate and rebellious: which thing profane writers do not touch, when they entreat of civil duties. They speak not a word in their precepts of the will of God, of the worshipping of God, neither of faith, which is the mother of all christian virtues. Neither do they teach men to do well for God's honour and glory, which thing is chiefly inculcate in the scriptures. neither do they refer all things to one God, neither make him the end of their actions, neither yet do they look for rewards at his hands. So that briefly and by these few words we may see an apparent difference between the philosophical and apostolical precepts concerning virtue. (7)

Fasting

I would have men to use often fasting, which is not a choice of some certain sorts of meats, but a perpetual sobriety and temperance of life, to the end they may the rather bridle and keep under carnal lusts and concupiscences. Our Saviour Christ therefore biddeth us beware that our hearts not be oppressed with surfeiting (Luke xxi.). And his Apostle: 'Oppress not yourself with wine, wherein is riot.' Fasting is commended unto us in the examples of Moses, Elias, Daniel, Christ, and his Apostles. Let us never forget that woe of the prophet (Isai. v.): 'Woe be unto those that rise early in the morning to follow drunkenness!' And that of Ambrose is worthy remembrance: 'Use a little wine to avoid infirmity, not to augment pleasure: wine and youth kindle a flame. But fasting doth bridle young years; and a spare diet doth keep under lust and carnality.' And St Chrysostom: 'He that coupleth fasting and prayer hath two wings, which will make him able to pass the winds in swiftness.'

Thirdly, alms-deeds are commendable and needful: and it is to be observed, that of these three virtues, prayer is properly referred unto God, fasting to ourselves, and alms to our neighbour. And for that many now-a-days do err and are deceived in the name of alms, thinking that to be only when a piece of money, meat, or cloth, is given unto the poor; I think it not amiss to put down Augustine's mind touching this matter; who doth not account only those vulgar matters to be alms, which I rehearsed before, but these also, 'to forgive the offender, to amend others with reprehension and correction: for many alms are given to those that are unwilling to receive them, when we rather respect men's welfare than wilfulness'. (8)

NOTES / SOURCES

1. John Woolton, *A Christian Manual, or, The Life and Manners of True Christians*, reprinted Cambridge (Parker Society), 1851, pp. 30–1
2. Ibid., pp. 32–3
3. Ibid., p. 77
4. Ibid., pp. 86–9
5. Ibid., p. 91
6. Ibid., p. 115
7. Ibid., pp. 121–2
8. Ibid., pp. 135–7

Material from the Reign of Edward VI   1547–1553

The first full English Prayer Book was issued in 1549, authorized by the Act of Uniformity, with an Ordinal added in 1550. A fair amount of traditional ceremonial was left intact at this point, but supplemented by exhortation and exposition. 1552 saw the Second Prayer Book published, a far more radical revision, and in 1553 appeared a 'Primer' of daily prayers for the laity, again supplemented by a full exposition of the nature and purpose of Christian prayer. The educational campaign of the Reformers was also furthered by both a shorter and a longer catechism in 1553, the longer version providing a quite extensive summary of basic doctrine. In 1559, on the accession of Elizabeth, the 1552 Prayer Book was reissued with a few minor changes in a somewhat more conservative direction.

An Exhortation to Communion

Dear friends, and you especially upon whose souls I have cure and charge, on ——— next, I do intend by God's grace, to offer to all such as shall be godly disposed, the most comfortable Sacrament of the body and blood of Christ, to be taken of them in the remembrance of his most fruitful and glorious Passion: by the which passion we have obtained remission of our sins, and be made partakers of the kingdom of heaven, whereof we be assured and ascertained, if we come to the said Sacrament with hearty repentance for our offences, stedfast faith in God's mercy, and earnest mind to obey God's will, and to offend no more. Wherefore our duty is to come to these holy mysteries, with most hearty thanks to be given to Almighty GOD for his infinite mercy and benefits given and bestowed upon us his unworthy servants, for whom he hath not only given his body to death, and shed his blood, but also doth vouchsafe in a Sacrament and mystery to give us his said body and blood to feed upon spiritually. The which Sacrament being so divine and holy a thing, and so comfortable to them which receive it worthily, and so dangerous to them that will presume to take the same unworthily: My duty is to exhort you in the mean season, to consider the greatness of the thing, and to search and examine your own consciences, and that not lightly nor after the manner of dissimulers with GOD: but as they which should come to a most Godly and heavenly banquet, not to come but in the marriage garment required of God in scripture; that you may (so much as lieth in you) be found worthy to come to such a table. The ways and means thereto is,

First, that you be truly repentant of your former evil life, and that you confess with an unfeigned heart to Almighty God your sins and unkindness towards his Majesty committed, either by will, word, or deed, infirmity or ignorance: and that with inward sorrow and tears you bewail your offences, and require of Almighty God mercy and pardon, promising to him (from the bottom of your hearts) the amendment of your former life. And amongst all others, I am commanded of God, especially to move and exhort you to reconcile yourselves to your neighbours, whom you have offended, or who hath offended you, putting out of your hearts all hatred and malice against them, and to be in love and charity with all the world, and to forgive other as you would that God should forgive you. And if any man have done wrong to any other, let him make satisfaction, and due restitution of all lands and goods, wrongfully taken away or withholden, before he come to God's board, or at the least be in full mind and purpose so to do, as soon as he is able; or else let him not come to this holy table, thinking to deceive God, who seeth all men's hearts. For neither the absolution of the priest can any thing avail them, nor the receiving of this holy sacrament doth any thing but increase their damnation. And if there be any of you, whose conscience is troubled and grieved in any thing, lacking comfort or counsel, let him come to me, or to some other discreet and learned priest, taught in the law of God, and confess and open his sin and grief secretly, that he may receive such ghostly counsel, advice, and comfort, that his conscience may be relieved, and that of us (as of the ministers of GOD and of the church) he may receive comfort and absolution, to the satisfaction of his mind, and avoiding of all scruple and doubtfulness: requiring such as shall be satisfied with a general confession, not to be offended with them that do use, to their further satisfying, the auricular and secret confession to the priest; nor those also which think needful or convenient, for the quietness of their own consciences, particularly to open their sins to the priest, to be offended with them that are satisfied with their humble confession to GOD, and the general confession to the church. But in all things to follow and keep the rule of charity, and every man to be satisfied with his own conscience, not judging other men's minds or consciences; where as he hath no warrant of God's word to the same. (1)

A Summary of Why and How to Pray

Pray because
1. Thou hast need.
2. God commands thee.
3. Of God's promises.
4. Pray in faith of God's promise.
5. Ask all things in Christ's name.
6. Ask worldly and temporal things conditionally.
7. Appoint God no time but abide his pleasure.
8. In any wise pray in charity.
9. Ask things pertaining to thy salvation, remission of sin and life everlasting, without condition.

¶ For these hath God certainly promised to all them that with a true faithful and obedient heart doth come unto him in earnest and continual prayer. (Ps. lxxxvii) (2)

Fall and Redemption

Master. Why dost thou call God Father?

Scholar. For two causes: the one, for that he made us all at the beginning, and gave life unto us all: the other is more weighty, for that by his Holy Spirit and by faith he hath begotten us again: making us his children: giving us his kingdom and the inheritance of life everlasting, with Jesu Christ his own, true, and natural Son.

Master. Seeing then God hath created all other things to serve man: and made man to obey, honour, and glorify him: what canst thou say more of the beginning and making of man?

Scholar. Even that which Moses wrote: that God shaped the first man of clay: and put into him soul and life: then, that he cast Adam in a dead sleep, and brought forth a woman, whom he drew out of his side, to make her a companion with him of all his life and wealth. And therefore was man called Adam, because he took his beginning of the earth; and the woman called Eve, because she was appointed to be the mother of all living.

Master. What image is that, after the likeness whereof thou sayest that man was made?

Scholar. That is most absolute righteousness and perfect holiness: which most nearly belongeth to the very nature of God: and most clearly appeared in Christ, our new Adam. Of the which in us there scant are to be seen any sparkles.

Master. What? are there scant to be seen?

Scholar. It is true forsooth: for they do not now so shine, as they did in the beginning, before man's fall: forasmuch as man by the darkness of sins, and mist of errors, hath corrupted the brightness of this image. In such sort hath God in his wrath wreaked him upon the sinful man.

Master. But I pray thee tell me, wherefore came it thus to pass?

Scholar. I will shew you. When the Lord God had made the frame of this world, he himself planted a garden, full of delight and pleasure, in a certain place eastward, and called it Eden: wherein, beside other passing fair trees, not far from the midst of the garden was there one specially called the tree of life, and another called the tree of knowledge of good and evil. Herein the Lord of his singular love placed man: and committed unto him the garden to dress, and look unto: giving him liberty to eat of the fruits of all the trees of paradise, except the fruit of the tree of knowledge of good and evil. The fruit of this tree if ever he tasted, he should without fail die for it. But Eve, deceived by the devil counterfeiting the shape of a serpent, gathered of the forbidden fruit: which was for the fairness to the eye to be desired: for the sweetness in taste to be reached at: and pleasant for the knowledge of good and evil: and she eat thereof, and gave unto her husband to eat of the same. For which doing they both immediately died; that is to say, were not only subject to the death of the body, but also lost the life of the soul, which is righteousness. And forthwith the image of God was defaced in them: and the most beautiful proportion of righteousness, holiness, truth, and knowledge of God, was confounded and in a manner utterly blotted out. There remained the earthly image, joined with unrighteousness, guile, fleshly mind, and deep ignorance of godly and heavenly things. Hereof grew the weakness of our flesh:

hereof came this corruption, and disorder of lusts and affections: hereof came that pestilence: hereof came that seed and nourishment of sins wherewith mankind is infected, and it is called sin original. Moreover thereby nature was so corrupted and overthrown, that unless the goodness and mercy of almighty God had holpen us by the medicine of grace, even as in body we are thrust down into all wretchedness of death, so must it needs have been, that all men of all sorts should be thrown into everlasting punishment and fire unquenchable.

Master. Oh the unthankfulness of men! But what hope had our first parents, and from thenceforth the rest, whereby they were relieved?

Scholar. When the Lord God had both with words and deeds chastized Adam and Eve (for he thrust them both out of the garden with a most grievous reproach), he then cursed the serpent, threatening him, that the time should one day come, when the Seed of the woman should break his head. Afterward the Lord God stablished that same glorious and most bountiful promise: first with a covenant made between him and Abraham, by circumcision, and in Isaac his son: then again by Moses: last of all by the oracles of the noble prophets.

Master. What meaneth the serpent's head, and that Seed that God speaketh of?

Scholar. In the serpent's head lieth all his venom, and the whole pith of his life and force. Therefore do I take the serpent's head to betoken the whole power and kingdom, or more truly the tyranny, of the old serpent the devil. The Seed (as saint Paul doth plainly teach) is Jesus Christ, the Son of God, very God and very man: conceived of the Holy Ghost: engendered of the womb and substance of Mary, the blessed pure and undefiled maid: and was so born and fostered by her as other babes be, saving that he was most far from all infection of sin. (3)

NOTES / SOURCES

1. 'Order for Holy Communion' in the *First Prayer Book of King Edward VI*, in *Liturgies of Edward VI*, ed. J. Ketley, Cambridge (Parker Society), 1844, pp. 81–2
2. 'The Primer', ibid., p. 377
3. 'The Catechism', ibid., pp. 501–3

Edmund Spenser   1552?–1599

Born in East Smithfield, London, Spenser's family originated from Burnley in Lancashire. Edmund Spenser studied Latin, Greek, French, and Italian at Pembroke Hall, Cambridge, where he began his writing career. In 1578 he took up residence in the Earl of Leicester's household and began his friendship with Sir Philip Sidney. His early work, *The Shepheards' Calendar*, reflected his connection with Lancashire and was published as twelve eclogues in 1579. Its enthusiastic reception prompted him to start the work for which he is best known, *The Faerie Queene*, which was published in 1589 to immediate acclaim. Much of his life was spent in Ireland, but in 1598 he was forced to flee in the face of the rebellion against English rule.

An Hymne of Heavenly Love

Before this world's great frame, in which al things
Are now contained, found any being-place,

Ere flitting Time could wag his eyas wings
About that mightie bound which doth embrace
The rolling spheres, and parts their houres by space,
That High Eternall Powre, which now doth move
In all these things, mov'd in its selfe by love.

It lov'd it selfe, because it selfe was faire;
(For fair is lov'd;) and of it self begot
Like to it selfe his eldest Sonne and Heire,
Eternall, pure, and voide of sinfull blot,
The firstling of His ioy, in whom no iot
Of love's dislike or pride was to be found,
Whom He therefore with equall honour crown'd.

With Him he raign'd, before all time prescribed,
In endlesse glorie and immortall might,
Together with that Third of them derived,
Most wise, most holy, most almightie Spright!
Whose kingdome's throne no thoughts of earthly wight
Can comprehend, much lesse my trembling verse
With equall words can hope it to reherse.

Yet, O most blessed Spright! pure lampe of light,
Eternall spring of grace and wisedom trew,
Vouchsafe to shed into my barren spright
Some little drop of thy celestiall dew,
That may my rymes with sweet infuse embrew,
And give me words equall unto my thought,
To tell the marveiles by thy mercie wrought.

Yet being pregnant still with powrefull grace,
And full of fruitfull Love, that loves to get
Things like himselfe, and to enlarge his race,
His second brood, though not of powre so great,
Yet full of beautie, next He did beget
And infinite increase of angels bright,
All glistring glorious in their Maker's light.

To them the heaven's illimitable hight
(Not this round heaven, which we from hence behold,
Adorn'd with thousand lamps of burning light,
And with ten thousand gemmes of shyning gold,)
He gave as their inheritance to hold,
That they might serve Him in eternall blis,
And be partakers of these ioyes of His.

There they in their trinall triplicities
About Him wait, and on His will depend,

Either with nimble wings to cut the skies,
When He them on His messages doth send,
Or on His owne dread presence to attend,
Where they behold the glorie of His light,
And caroll hymnes of love both day and night.

Both day and night is unto them all one;
For He His beames doth unto them extend,
That darknesse there appeareth never none;
Ne hath their day, ne hath their blisse, an end,
But there their termelesse time in pleasure spend:
Ne ever should their hapinesse decay,
Had not they dar'd their Lord to disobay.

So that next off-spring of the Maker's love,
Next to Himselfe in glorious degree,
Degendering to hate, fell from above
Through pride, (for pride and love may ill agree,)
And now of sinne to all ensample bee:
How then can sinnful flesh it selfe assure,
Sith purist angels fell to be impure?

But that Eternall Fount of love and grace,
Still flowing forth His goodnesse unto all,
Now seeing left a waste and emptie place
In His wyde pallace, through those angels' fall,
Cast to supply the same, and to enstall
A new unknowen colony therein,
Whose root from earth's base groundworke should begin.

Therefore of clay, base, vile, and next to nought,
Yet form'd by wondrous skill, and by His might
According to an heavenly patterne wrought,
Which He had fashioned in his wise foresight,
He man did make, and breath'd a living spright
Into his face, most beautiful and fayre,
Endewd with wisedome's riches, heavenly, rare.

Such He him made, that he resemble might
Himselfe, as mortall thing immortall could;
Him to be lord of every living wight
He made by love out of his owne like mould,
In whom He might His mightie selfe behould:
For Love doth love the thing belov'd to see,
That like it selfe in lovely shape may bee.

But man, forgetfull of his Maker's grace
No lesse than Angels, whom he did ensew,

Fell from the hope of promist heavenly place
Into the mouth of Death, to sinners dew,
And all his offspring into thraldome threw,
Where they for ever should in bonds remaine
Of never-dead ye ever-dying paine:

Till that great Lord of Love, which him at first
Made of meere love, and after liked well,
Seeing him lie like creature long accurst
In that deep horror of despeyred hell,
Him, wretch, in doole would let no longer dwell,
But cast out of that bondage to redeeme,
And pay the price, all were his debt extreeme.

Out of the bosome of eternall blisse,
In which He reigned with His glorious Syre,
He downe descended, like a most demisse
And abject thrall, in fleshes fraile attyre,
That He for him might pay sinne's deadly hyre,
And him restore unto that happie state
In which he stood before his haplesse fate.

In flesh at first the guilt committed was,
Therefore in flesh it must be satisfyde;
Nor spirit, nor angel, though they man surpas,
Could make amends to God for man's misguyde,
But onely man himselfe, who selfe did slyde:
So, taking flesh of sacred virgin's wombe,
For man's deare sake He did a man become.

O blessed Well of Love! O Floure of Grace!
O glorious Morning-Starre! O Lampe of Light!
Most lively image of thy Father's face,
Eternal King of Glorie, Lord of Might,
Meeke Lambe of God, before all worlds behight,
How can we Thee requite for all this good?
Or what can prize that Thy most precious blood?

Yet nought Thou ask'st in lieu of all this love,
But love of us, for guerdon of thy paine:
Ay me! what can us lesse than that behove?
Had He required life for us againe,
Had it beene wrong to ask His owne with gaine?
He gave us life, He it restored lost;
Then life were least, that us so little cost.

But He our life hath left unto us free;
Free that was thrall, and blessed that was band;

Ne ought demaunds but that we loving bee,
As He Himselfe hath lov'd us afore-hand,
And bound therto with an eternall band,
Him first to love that was so dearely bought,
And next our brethren, to his image wrought. (1)

From a Hymn of Heavenly Beauty

Faire is the heaven where happy soules have place
In full enioyment of felicitie,
Whence they doe still behold the glorious face
Of the Divine Eternall Maiestie:
More faire is that, where those Idees on hie
Enraunged be, which Plato so admyred,
And pure Intelligences from God inspyred.

Yet fairer is that heaven, in which do raine
The soveraigne Powres, and mightie Potentates,
Which in their high protections doe containe
All mortall princes and imperiall states;
And fayrer yet, where as the royall Seates
And heavenly Dominations are set,
From whom all earthly governance is fet.

Yet farre more faire be those bright Cherubins,
Which all with golden wings are overdight,
And those eternall burning Seraphins,
Which from their faces dart out fierie light:
Yet fairer then they both, and much more bright,
Be th' Angels and Archangels, which attend
On God's owne person without rest or end.

These thus in faire each other farre excelling,
As to the Highest they approach more near,
Yet is that Highest farre beyond all telling
Fairer then all the rest which there appeare,
Though all their beauties ioyned together were:
How then can mortall tongue hope to expresse
The image of such endlesse perfectnesse?

Humbled with feare and awfull reverence,
Before the footestoole of His Maiestie
Throwe thy selfe downe, with trembling innocence,
Ne dare looke up with córruptible eye
On the dred face of that great Deity,
For feare, lest if He chaunce to look on thee,
Thou turne to nought, and quite confounded be.

But lowly fall before His mercie seate,
Close covered with the Lambes integrity
From the iust wrath of His avengefull threate,
That sits upon the righteous throne on hy:
His throne is built upon Eternity,
More firme and durable then steele or brasse,
Or the hard diamond, which them both doth passe.

His scepter is the rod of Righteousnesse,
With which He bruseth all His foes to dust,
And the great Dragon strongly doth represse
Under the rigour of His iudgment iust:
His seate is Truth, to which the faithfull trust,
From whence proceed her beames so pure and bright,
That all about Him sheddeth glorious light. (2)

A Sonnet

Most glorious Lord of lyfe! that, on this day,
Didst make thy triumph over death and sin;
And, having harrow'd hell, didst bring away
Captivity thence captive, us to win:
This ioyous day, deare Lord, with ioy begin;
And grant that we, for whom thou diddest dy,
Being with thy deare blood clene washt from sin,
May live for ever in felicity!
And that thy love we weighing worthily
May likewise love thee for the same againe
And for thy sake, that all lyke deare didst buy,
With love may one another entertayne!
So let us love, deare Love, lyke as we ought:
Love is the lesson which the Lord us taught. (3)

NOTES / SOURCES

1. Edmund Spenser, selections from 'An Hymne of Heavenly Love'
2. Edmund Spenser, selections from 'An Hymn of Heavenly Beauty', in the *Penguin Book of English Christian Verse*, ed. Peter Levi, (1984)
3. Edmund Spenser, 'A Sonnet: Most glorious Lord of Life', in *The New Oxford Book of Sixteenth Century Verse*, ed. Emrys Jones, (1991) Oxford
   See also other standard editions.

Sir Philip Sidney   1554–1586

Educated at Shrewsbury School and Christ Church, Oxford, Philip Sidney spent much of the 1570s travelling throughout Europe. With Edmund Spenser he formed the Areopagus Club in 1579 with the aim of promoting the use of classical metres in English poetry. Sidney became Member of Parliament for Kent in 1581 and thereafter undertook a number of diplomatic and military tasks, including joining in 1586 an attack on a Spanish convoy attempting to relieve the Dutch town of Zutphen. He was wounded in this action and died shortly afterwards at Arnhem. He poetic works, including *Archadia, Astrophel and Stella,* and the *Apologie for Poetrie*, were all published posthumously. He was one of the most prominent of those English Reformed Christians who saw themselves as part of an international network of Protestant humanists.

Psalme LXII

Nonne Deo

Yet shall my soule in silence still
    On God, my help, attentive stay:
Yet he my fort, my health, my hill,
    Remove I may not, move I may.
How long then shall your fruitlesse will
    An enemy soe fair from thrall
With weake endevor strive to kill,
    You rotten hedge, you broken wall?

Forsooth, that hee no more may rise
    Advaunced oft to throne and crown,
To headlong him their thoughtes devise,
    And past reliefe to tread him down.
Their love is only love of lies:
    Their wordes and deeds dissenting soe,
When from their lippes most blessing flyes,
    Then deepest curse in hart doth grow.

Yet shall my soule in silence still
    On God, my hope, attentive stay:
Yet hee my fort, my health, my hill,
    Remove I may not, move I may.
My God doth me with glory fill,
    Not only shield me safe from harme:
To shun distresse, to conquer ill,
    To him I clime, in him I arme.

O then on God, our certaine stay,
    All people in all times rely:
Your hartes before him naked lay;
    To Adam's sonnes tis vain to fly.
Soe vain, soe false, soe fraile are they,
    Ev'n he that seemeth most of might,
With lightnesse self if him you weigh,
    Then lightnesse self will weigh more light.

In fraud and force noe true repose:
    Such idle hopes from thought expell,
And take good heed, when riches growes,
    Let not your hart on riches dwell.
All powre is God's, his own word showes,
    Once said by him, twice heard by mee:
Yet from thee, Lord, all mercy flowes,
    And each man's work is paid by thee. (1)

Psalme CXVII

Laudate Dominum

P raise him that aye
R emaines the same:
A ll tongues display
I   ehova's fame.
S ing all that share
T his earthly ball;
H is mercies are
E xpos'd to all:
L ike as the word
O nce he doth give,
R old in record,
D oth tyme outlyve.

Psalme CXXV

Qui confidunt

As Sion standeth, very firmly stedfast,
Never once shaking; soe on high Jehova
Who his hope buildeth, very firmly stedfast
                Ever abideth.

As Salem braveth with her hilly bullwarkes
Roundly enforted; soe the greate Jehova
Closeth his servantes, as a hilly bullward
                Ever abiding.

Though tirantes' hard yoke with a heavy pressure
Wring the just shoulders, but a while it holdeth,
Lest the best minded by too hard abusing
                Bend to abuses.

As the well-workers, soe the right beleevers,
Lord, favour further: but a vaine deceiver,
Whose wryed footing not aright directed
                Wandreth in error;

Lord, hym abjected set among the number,
Whose doings lawlesse study bent to mischiefe
Mischief expecteth; but upon thy chosen
                              Peace be for ever. (2)

NOTES / SOURCES

1. Sir Philip Sidney, Psalme LXII, Nonne Deo
2. Sir Philip Sidney, Psalme CXVII, Laudate Dominum
3. Sir Philip Sidney, Psalme CXXV, Qui Confidunt

Fulke Greville   1554–1628

A school friend of Philip Sidney, Fulke Greville studied at Jesus College, Cambridge, and became a favourite at the Court of Elizabeth I. His long political career included being secretary for the Principality of Wales (1583–1628), Member of Parliament and Chancellor of the Exchequer (1614–1621). Created a peer (Baron Brook) by James I in 1621, he was murdered by a servant. His written works, dating from *His Youth* were printed posthumously and included tragedies, sonnets, and a *Life of Sidney*. His religious verse combines humanist learning and elegance with sombre Calvinist themes.

Self-Deceit

The Manicheans did no idolls make
Without themselues, nor worship gods of wood;
Yet idolls did in their ideas take,
And figur'd Christ as on the cross he stood:
    Thus did they when they earnestly did pray,
    Till clearer faith this idoll tooke away.

We seeme more inwardly to knowe the Sonne,
And see our owne saluation in his blood:
When this is said, we thinke the worke is done,
And with the Father hold our portion good:
    As if true life within these words were laid
    For him that in life neuer words obey'd.

If this be safe, it is a pleasant way;
The crosse of Christ is very easily borne:
But six dayes' labour makes the Sabboth-day;
The flesh is dead before grace can be borne:
    The heart must first beare witnesse with the booke,
    The earth must burne, ere we for Christ can looke. (1)

Descent into Hell

Downe in the depth of mine iniquity,
That vgly center of infernall spirits,
Where each sinne feeles her own deformity,
In those peculiar torments she inherits—
   Depriu'd of human graces and diuine,
   Euen there appeares this sauing God of mine.

And in this fatall mirrour of transgression,
Shewes man, as fruit of his degeneration,
The errours vgly infinite impression,
Which beares the faithlesse down to desperation—
   Depriu'd of human graces and diuine,
   Euen there appeares this sauing God of mine.

In power and birth, Almighty and Eternall,
Which on the sinne reflects strange desolation,
With glory scourging all the spirits infernall,
And vncreated hell with vnpriuation,
   Depriu'd of human graces and diuine,
   Euen there appeares this sauing God of mine.

For on this spirituall Crosse, condemned, lying,
To paines infernall by eternal doome,
I see my Sauiour for the same sinnes dying,
And from that hell I fear'd to free me come;
   Depriu'd of human graces, *not* diuine,
   Thus hath his death rais'd vp this soule of mine. (2)

NOTES / SOURCES

1. Fulke Greville 'The Manicheans did no idolls make'
2. Fulke Greville, from 'Caelica', in *The New Oxford Book of Sixteenth-Century Verse*, ed. Emrys Jones, Oxford (1991)

Minor Poets

George Gascoigne (1542–1577) is best known as a lyricist, but wrote several meditative pieces, of which the one reproduced here is a good sample. Sir Walter Ralegh (?1552–1618) was celebrated as a courtier, wit, and explorer; the poem printed here was written when he was under sentence of death, and shows an unexpected depth of religious feeling. Sir John Davies (1569–1626) wrote a substantial work, *Orchestra* (1596), on dance as a mirror of cosmic order, and a number of lyrical pieces of a philosophical or contemplative character.

George Gascoigne

Good Nighte

When thou hast spent the lingring daye
In pleasure and delight,
Or after toyle and wearie waye
Dost seeke to rest at nighte:
Unto thy paynes or pleasures past
Adde thys one labor yet,
Ere sleepe close vp thyne eie too fast,
Doo not thy God forget.

But searche within thy secret thought,
What deeds did thee befall;
And if thou find amisse in ought,
To God for mercie call.
Yea, though thou find nothing amisse,
Which thou canst call to mind,
Yet euermore remember this,
There is the more behind.

And thinke, how well so euer it be
That thou hast spent the daye,
It came of God, and not of thee,
So to direct thy waye.
Thus if thou trie thy dayly deedes,
And pleasure in thys payne,
Thy life shall clense thy corne from weeds,
And thine shal be the gaine.

But if thy sinfull sluggishe eye
Will venter for to winke,
Before thy wading will maye trye
How far thy soule maye sinke;
Beware and wake, for else thy bed,
Which soft and smoth is made,
May heape more harm vpon thy head,
Than blowes of enmies' blade.

Thus if this paine procure thine ease
In bed as thou doost lye,
Perhaps it shall not God displease
To sing thus soberly—
I see that sleepe is lent me here
To ease my wearie bones,
As death at laste shall eeke appeere,
To ease my greeuous grones. (1)

Sir Walter Ralegh

The Passionate Man's Pilgrimage
Supposed to be written by One at the Point of Death

Give me my scallop-shell of quiet,
My staff of faith to walk upon,
My scrip of joy, immortal diet,
My bottle of salvation,
My gown of glory, hope's true gage,
And thus I'll take my pilgrimage.

Blood must be my body's balmer,
No other balm will there be given,
Whilst my soul like a white palmer
Travels to the land of heaven,
Over the silver mountains,
Where spring the nectar fountains;
And there I'll kiss
The bowl of bliss,
And drink my eternal fill
On every milken hill.
My soul will be a-dry before,
But after it will ne'er thirst more.

And by the happy blissful way
More peaceful pilgrims I shall see,
That have shook off their gowns of clay
And go apparelled fresh like me.
I'll bring them first
To slake their thirst,
And then to taste those nectar suckets,
At the clear wells
Where sweetness dwells,
Drawn up by saints in crystal buckets.

And when our bottles and all we
Are filled with immortality,
Then the holy paths we'll travel,
Strewed with rubies thick as gravel,
Ceilings of diamonds, sapphire floors,
High walls of coral and pearl bowers.

From thence to heaven's bribeless hall
Where no corrupted voices brawl,
No conscience molten into gold,
Nor forged accusers bought and sold,

No cause deferred, nor vain-spent journey,
For there Christ is the King's Attorney,
Who pleads for all without degrees,
And he hath angels, but no fees.

When the grand twelve million jury
Of our sins with sinful fury
'Gainst our souls black verdicts give,
Christ pleads his death, and then we live.
Be thou my speaker, taintless pleader,
Unblotted lawyer, true proceeder;
Thou movest salvation even for alms,
Not with a bribed lawyer's palms.

And this is my eternal plea
To him that made heaven, earth and sea:
Seeing my flesh must die so soon,
And want a head to dine next noon,
Just at the stroke when my veins start and spread,
Set on my soul an everlasting head.
Then am I ready, like a palmer fit,
To tread those blest paths which before I writ. (2)

Sir John Davies

False and True Knowledge

Why did my parents send me to the schooles,
    That I with knowledge might enrich my mind,
Since the desire to know first made men fooles,
    And did corrupt the roote of all mankind?

For when God's hand had written in the harts
    Of the first parents all the rules of good,
So that their skill enfusd did passe all arts
    That euer were, before or since the flood;

And when their reason's eye was sharpe and cleere,
    And, as an eagle can behold the sunne,
Could haue approch't th' eternall light as neere
    As the intellectual angels could haue done;

Euen then to them the spirit of lies suggests,
    That they were blind, because they saw not ill,
And breathes into their incorrupted breasts
    A curious wish, which did corrupt their will.

For that same ill they straight desir'd to know;
   Which ill, being nought but a defect of good,
In all God's works the diuell could not shew,
   While man, their lord, in his perfection stood;

So that themselues were first to do the ill,
   Ere they thereof the knowledge could attaine;
Like him that knew not poison's power to kill,
   Vntill, by tasting it, himselfe was slaine.

Euen so, by tasting of that fruite forbid,
   Where they sought *knowledge*, they did *error* find;
Ill they desir'd to know, and ill they did;
   And, to giue *Passion* eyes, made *Reason* blind:

For then their minds did first in Passion see
   Those wretched shapes of miserie and woe,
Of nakednesse, of shame, of pouertie,
   Which then their owne experience made them know.

But then grew Reason darke, that she no more
   Could the faire formes of *Good* and *Truth* discerne:
Battes they became, who eagles were before;
   And this they got by their desire to learne.

But we, their wretched offspring, what do we?
   Doe not wee still tast of the fruite forbid,
Whiles, with fond fruitlesse curiositie,
   In bookes prophane we seeke for knowledge hid?

What is this knowledge but the skie-stolne fire,
   For which the thiefe[1] still chain'd in ice doth sit,
And which the poore rude satyre[2] did admire,
   And needs would kisse, but burnt his lips with it? (3)

The Soul and the Body

But how shall we this union well express?
   Nought ties the soul; her subtlety is such,
She moves the body, which she doth possess,
   Yet no part toucheth, but by virtue's touch.

Then dwells she not therein as in a tent;
   Nor as a pilot in his ship doth sit;
Nor as the spider in his web is pent;
   Nor as the wax retains the print in it;

---

[1] Prometheus.   [2] See Æsop's Fables.

Nor as a vessel water doth contain;
   Nor as one liquor in another shed;
Nor as the heat doth in the fire remain;
   Nor as a voice throughout the air is spread.

But as the fair and cheerful morning light
   Doth here and there her silver beams impart,
And in an instant doth herself unite
   To the transparent air, in all and part;

Still resting whole, when blows the air divide,
   Abiding pure, when the air is most corrupted,
Throughout the air her beams dispersing wide,
   And when the air is tossed, not interrupted:

So doth the piercing soul the body fill,
   Being all in all, and all in part diffused,
Indivisible, incorruptible still,
   Not forced, encountered, troubled or confused.

And as the sun above the light doth bring,
   Though we behold it in the air below,
So from the eternal Light the soul doth spring,
   Though in the body she her powers do show. (4)

NOTES / SOURCES

1. George Gascoigne 'Good Nighte', in *Elizabethan Devotional Poetry* Vol. 1, pp. 38–9, ed. E. Farr, the Parker Society, Cambridge 1845. Also included in *The New Oxford Book of Sixteenth-Century Verse*, ed. Emrys Jones, Oxford, 1991
2. Sir Walter Ralegh, *The Passionate Man's Pilgrimage*, ibid.
3. Sir John Davies, from *Nosce Teipsum*, 1599, printed in *Chapters into Verse*, Vol. 1: Genesis to Malachi, eds. Robert Atwan and Laurance Wieder, Oxford, 1993
4. Sir John Davies, from *Nosce Teipsum*, 1599, included in *The New Oxford Book of Sixteenth-Century Verse*, ed. Emrys Jones, Oxford, 1991

Richard Hooker   1554?–1600

Born at Heavitree, near Exeter, Richard Hooker studied at Corpus Christi College, Oxford, where he was elected a Fellow in 1577 and became Deputy Professor of Hebrew in 1579. Upon his marriage to Joan Churchman he became Rector of Drayton Beauchamp (1584), Master of the Temple (1585), Rector of Boscombe (1591) and lastly of Bishopsbourne near Canterbury (1595). Hooker is renowned as the supreme apologist of the Elizabethan Settlement of 1559 which he promoted eloquently in his treatise *The Lawes of Ecclesiasticall Politie*, the first five books of which were published in his lifetime. In these he opposed Puritan inflexibility in the interpretation of scripture and asserted that natural law undergirded both ecclesiastical and civil government. He stressed the continuity of the Church of England with its medieval predecessor, but nonetheless advocated the doctrines of the Reformers. His writings were widely influential for later political theorists. His sermons are less well known than the *Lawes*, but represent an equally profound and sustained response to extreme Calvinism.

The Law of God and the Will of God

God therefore is a law both to himself, and to all other things besides. To himself he is a law in all those things, whereof our Saviour speaketh, saying, 'My Father worketh as yet, so I.' God worketh nothing without cause. All those things which are done by him have some end for which they are done; and the end for which they are done is a reason of his will to do them. His will had not inclined to create woman, but that he saw it could not be well if she were not created. *Non est bonum*, 'It is not good man should be alone; therefore let us make a helper for him.' That and nothing else is done by God, which to leave undone were not so good.

If therefore it be demanded, why God having power and ability infinite, the effects notwithstanding of that power are all so limited as we see they are: the reason hereof is the end which he hath proposed, and the law whereby his wisdom hath stinted the effects of his power in such sort, that it doth not work infinitely, but correspondently unto that end for which it worketh, even 'all things χρηστῶς, 'in most decent and comely sort,' all things in Measure, Number, and Weight.

The general end of God's external working is the exercise of his most glorious and most abundant virtue. Which abundance doth shew itself in variety, and for that cause this variety is oftentimes in Scripture exprest by the name of *riches*. 'The Lord hath made all things for his own sake.' Not that any thing is made to be beneficial unto him, but all things for him to shew beneficence and grace in them. (1)

Scripture, Nature, Custom

The main drift of the whole New Testament is that which St John setteth down as the purpose of his own history; 'These things are written, that ye might believe that Jesus is Christ the Son of God, and that in believing ye might have life through his name.' The drift of the Old that which the Apostle mentioneth to Timothy, 'The Holy Scriptures are able to make thee wise unto Salvation.' So that the general end both of Old and New is one; the difference between them consisting in this, that the Old did make wise by teaching salvation through Christ that should come, the New by teaching that Christ the Saviour is come, and that Jesus whom the Jews did crucify, and whom God did raise again from the dead, is he. When the Apostle therefore affirmeth unto Timothy, that the Old was able to make him wise to salvation, it was not his meaning that the Old alone can do this unto us which live sithence the publication of the New. For he speaketh with presupposal of the doctrine of Christ known also unto Timothy; and therefore first it is said, 'Continue thou in those things which thou hast learned and art persuaded, knowing of whom thou hast been taught them.' Again, those Scriptures he granteth were able to make him wise to salvation; but he addeth, 'through the faith which is in Christ.' Wherefore without the doctrine of the New Testament teaching that Christ hath wrought the redemption of the world, which redemption the Old did foreshew he should work, it is not the former alone which can on our behalf perform so much as the Apostle doth avouch, who presupposeth this when he magnifieth that so highly. And as his words concerning the books of ancient Scripture do not take place but with presupposal of the Gospel of Christ embraced; so our own words also, when we extol the complete sufficiency of the whole entire body of the Scripture, must in like sort be understood with this caution, that the benefit of nature's light be not thought excluded as unnecessary, because the necessity of a diviner light is magnified.

There is in Scripture therefore no defect, but that any man, what place or calling soever he hold in the Church of God, may have thereby the light of his natural understanding so perfected, that the one being relieved by the other, there can want no part of needful instruction unto any good work which God himself requireth, be it natural or supernatural, belonging simply unto men as men, or unto men as they are united in whatsoever kind of society. It sufficeth therefore that Nature and Scripture do serve in such full sort, that they both jointly and not severally either of them be so complete, that unto everlasting felicity we need not the knowledge of any thing more than these two may easily furnish our minds with on all sides; and therefore they which add traditions, as a part of supernatural necessary truth, have not the truth, but are in error. For they only plead, that whatsoever God revealeth as necessary for all Christian men to do or believe, the same we ought to embrace, whether we have received it by writing or otherwise; which no man denieth: when that which they should confirm, who claim so great reverence unto traditions, is, that the same traditions are necessarily to be acknowledged divine and holy. For we do not reject them only because they are not in the Scripture, but because they are neither in Scripture, nor can otherwise sufficiently by any reason be proved to be of God. That which is of God, and may be evidently proved to be so, we deny not but it hath in his kind, although unwritten, yet the selfsame force and authority with the written laws of God. It is by ours acknowledged, 'that the Apostles did in every church institute and ordain some rites and customs serving for the seemliness of church-regiment, which rites and customs they have not committed unto writing.' Those rites and customs being known to be apostolical, and having the nature of things changeable, were no less to be accounted of in the Church than other things of the like degree; that is to say, capable in like sort of alteration, although set down in the Apostles' writings. For both being known to be apostolical, it is not the manner of delivering them unto the Church, but the author from whom they proceed, which doth give them their force and credit.

Laws being imposed either by each man upon himself, or by a public society upon the particulars thereof, or by all the nations of men upon every several society, or by the Lord himself upon any or every of these; there is not amongst these four kinds any one but containeth sundry both natural and positive laws. Impossible it is but that they should fall into a number of gross errors, who only take such laws for positive as have been made or invented of men, and holding this position hold also, that all positive and none but positive laws are mutable. Laws natural do always bind; laws positive not so, but only after they have been expressly and wittingly imposed. Laws positive there are in every of those kinds before mentioned. As in the first kind the promises which we have passed unto men, and the vows we have made unto God; for these are laws which we tie ourselves unto, and till we have so tied ourselves they bind us not. Laws positive in the second kind are such as the civil constitutions peculiar unto each particular commonweal. In the third kind the law of heraldry in war is positive: and in the last all the judicials which God gave unto the people of Israel to observe. And although no laws but positive be mutable, yet all are not mutable which be positive. Positive laws are either permanent or else changeable, according as the matter itself is concerning which they were first made. Whether God or man be the maker of them, alteration they so far forth admit, as the matter doth exact.

Laws that concern supernatural duties are all positive, and either concern men supernaturally as men, or else as parts of a supernatural society, which society we call the Church. To concern men as men supernaturally is to concern them as duties which belong of necessity to all, and yet could not have been known by any to belong unto them, unless God had opened them himself, inasmuch as they do not depend upon any natural ground at all out of which they may be deduced, but are appointed of God to supply the defect of those natural ways of salvation, by which we are not now able to attain thereunto. The Church being a supernatural society doth differ from natural societies in this, that the persons unto whom we associate ourselves, in the one are men simply considered as men, but they to whom we be joined in the other, are God, Angels, and holy men. Again the Church being both a society and a society supernatural, although as it is a society it have the selfsame original grounds which other politic societies have, namely, the natural inclination which all men have unto sociable life, and consent to some certain bond of association, which bond is the law that appointeth what kind of order they shall be associated in: yet unto the Church as it is a society supernatural this is peculiar, that part of the bond of their association which belong to the Church of God must be a law supernatural, which God himself hath revealed concerning that kind of worship which his people shall do unto him. The substance of the service of God therefore, so far forth as it hath in it any thing more than the Law of Reason doth teach, may not be invented of men, as it is amongst the heathens, but must be received from God himself, as always it hath been in the Church, saving only when the Church hath been forgetful of her duty.

Wherefore to end with a general rule concerning all the laws which God hath tied men unto: those laws divine that belong, whether naturally or supernaturally, either to men as men, or to men as they live in politic society, or to men as they are of that politic society which is the Church, without any further respect had unto any such variable accident as the state of men and of societies of men and of the Church itself in this world is subject unto; all laws that so belong unto men, they belong for ever, yea although they be Positive Laws, unless being positive God himself which made them alter them. The reason is, because the subject or matter of laws in general is thus far forth constant: which matter is that for the ordering whereof laws were instituted, and being instituted are not changeable without cause, neither can they have cause of change, when that which gave them their first institution remaineth for ever one and the same. On the other side, laws that were made for men or societies or churches, in regard of their being such as they do not always continue, but may perhaps be clean otherwise a while after, and so may require to the otherwise ordered than before; the laws of God himself which are of this nature, no man endued with common sense will ever deny to be of a different constitution from the former, in respect of the one's constancy and the mutability of the other. And this doth seem to have been the very cause why St John doth so peculiarly term the doctrine that teacheth salvation by Jesus Christ, *Evangelium œternum*, 'an eternal Gospel;' because there can be no reason wherefore the publishing thereof should be taken away, and any other instead of it proclaimed, as long as the world doth continue: whereas the whole law of rites and ceremonies, although delivered with so great solemnity, is notwithstanding clean abrogated, inasmuch as it had but temporary cause of God's ordaining it. (2)

Our Prayer and Christ's Prayer

To think we may pray unto God for nothing but what he hath promised in Holy Scripture we shall obtain, is perhaps an error. For of prayer there are two uses. It serveth as a mean to procure those things which God hath promised to grant when we ask; and it serveth as a mean to express our lawful desires also towards that, which whether we shall have or no we know not till we see the event. Things in themselves unholy or unseemly we may not ask; we may whatsoever being not forbidden either nature or grace shall reasonably move us to wish as importing the good of men, albeit God himself have nowhere by promise assured us of that particular which our prayer craveth. To pray for that which is in itself and of its own nature apparently a thing impossible, were not convenient. Wherefore though men do without offence wish daily that the affairs which with evil success are past might have fallen out much better, yet to pray that they may have been any other than they are, this being a manifest impossibility in itself, the rules of religion do not permit. Whereas contrariwise when things of their own nature contingent and mutable are by the secret determination of God appointed one way, though we the other way make our prayers, and consequently ask those things of God which are *by this supposition* impossible, we notwithstanding do not hereby in prayer transgress our lawful bounds.

That Christ, as the only begotten Son of God, having no superior, and therefore owing honour unto none, neither standing in any need, should either give thanks, or make petition unto God, were most absurd. As man what could beseem him better, whether we respect his affection to Godward, or his own necessity, or his charity and love towards men? Some things he knew should come to pass and notwithstanding prayed for them, because he also knew that the necessary means to effect them were his prayers. As in the Psalm it is said, 'Ask of me and I will give thee the heathen for thine inheritance and the ends of the earth for thy possession.' Wherefore that which here God promiseth his Son, the same in the seventeenth of John he prayeth for: 'Father, the hour is now come, glorify thy Son, that thy Son also may glorify thee according as thou hast given him power over all flesh.'

But had Christ the like promise concerning the effect of every particular for which he prayed? That which was not effected could not be promised. And we know in what sort he prayed for removal of that bitter cup, which cup he tasted, notwithstanding his prayer.

To shift off this example they answer first, 'That as other children of God, so Christ had a promise of deliverance *as far* as the glory of God in the accomplishment of his vocation would suffer.'

And if we ourselves have not also in that sort the promise of God to be evermore delivered from all adversity, what meaneth the sacred Scripture to speak in so large terms, 'Be obedient, and the Lord thy God will make thee plenteous in every work of thy hand, in the fruit of thy body, and in the fruit of thy cattle, and in the fruit of the land for thy wealth.' Again, 'Keep his laws, and thou shalt be blest above all people, the Lord shall take from thee all infirmities.' 'The man whose delight is in the Law of God, *whatsoever he doeth it shall prosper.*' 'For the ungodly there are *great plagues* remaining; but whosoever putteth his trust in the Lord mercy embraceth him *on every side.*' Not only that mercy which keepeth from being *overlaid* or *oppressed*, but mercy which saveth from being *touched* with grievous miseries, mercy which turneth away the course of 'the great water-floods,' and permitteth them not to 'come near.'

Nevertheless, because the prayer of Christ did concern but one calamity, they are still bold to deny the lawfulness of our prayer for deliverance out of all, yea though we pray with the same exception that he did, 'If such deliverance may stand with the pleasure of Almighty God and not otherwise.' For they have secondly found out a rule that prayer ought only to be made for deliverance 'from this or that particular adversity, whereof we know not but upon the event what the pleasure of God is.' Which quite overthroweth that other principle wherein they require unto every prayer which is of faith an assurance to obtain the thing we pray for. At the first to pray against all adversity was unlawful, because we cannot assure ourselves that this will be granted. Now we have license to pray against any particular adversity, and the reason given because we know not but upon the event what God will do. If we know not what God will do, it followeth that for any assurance we have he may do otherwise than we pray, and we may faithfully pray for that which we cannot assuredly presume that God will grant.

Seeing therefore neither of these two answers will serve the turn, they have a third, which is, that to pray in such sort is but idly mispent labour, because God already hath revealed his will touching this request, and we know that the suit is denied before we make it. Which neither is true, and if it were, was Christ ignorant what God had determined touching those things which himself should suffer? To say, 'He knew not what weight of sufferances his heavenly Father had measured unto him,' is somewhat hard; harder that although 'he knew them' notwithstanding for the present time they were 'forgotten through the force of those unspeakable pangs which he then was in.' The one against the plain express words of the holy Evangelist, 'he knew all things that should come upon him;' the other less credible if any thing may be of less credit than what the Scripture itself gainsayeth. (3)

Praying for the Salvation of All

There is in the knowledge both of God and man this certainty, that life and death have divided between them the whole body of mankind. What portion either of the two hath, God himself knoweth; for us he hath left no sufficient means to comprehend, and for that cause neither given any leave to search in particular who are infallibly the heirs of the kingdom of God, who castaways. Howbeit concerning the state of all men with whom we live (for only of them our prayers are meant) we may till the world's end, *for the present,* always presume, that *as far as in us there is power to discern* what others are, and as far as any duty of ours dependeth upon the notice of their condition in respect of God, the safest axioms for charity to rest itself upon are these: 'He which believeth already is;' and 'he which believeth not as yet may be the child of God.' It becometh not us 'during life altogether to condemn any man, seeing that' (for any thing we know) 'there is hope of every man's forgiveness, the possibility of whose repentance is not yet cut off by death.' And therefore Charity which 'hopeth all things,' prayeth also for all men.

Wherefore to let go personal knowledge touching vessels of wrath and mercy, what they are inwardly in the sight of God it skilleth not, for us there is cause sufficient in all men whereupon to ground our prayers unto God in their behalf. For whatsoever the mind of man apprehendeth as good, the will of charity and love is to have it enlarged in the very uttermost extent, that all may enjoy it to whom it can any way add perfection. Because therefore the farther a good thing doth reach the nobler and worthier we reckon it, our prayers for all men's good no less than for our own the Apostle with very fit terms commendeth as being καλὸν, a work commendable for the largeness of the affection from whence it springeth, even as theirs, which have requested at God's hands the salvation of many with the loss of their own souls, drowning as it were and overwhelming themselves in the abundance of their love towards others, is proposed as being in regard of the rareness of such affections ὑπέρκαλου, more than excellent. But this extraordinary height of desire after other men's salvation is no common mark. The other is a duty which belongeth unto all and prevaileth with God daily. For as it is in itself good, so God accepteth and taketh it in very good part at the hands of faithful men. (4)

Spiritual Self-Doubt

St Paul wishing well to the Church of Rome prayeth for them after this sort: 'The God of hope fill you with all joy of believing' (Rom. xv. 13). Hence an error groweth, when men in heaviness of spirit suppose they lack faith, because they find not the sugared joy and delight which indeed doth accompany faith, but so as a separable accident, as a thing that may be removed from it; yea there is a cause why it should be removed. The light would never be so acceptable, were it not for that usual intercourse of darkness. Too much honey doth turn to gall; and too much joy even spiritually would make us wantons. Happier a great deal is that man's case, whose soul by inward desolation is humbled, than he whose heart is through abundance of spiritual delight lifted up and exalted above measure. Better it is sometimes to go down into the pit with him, who, beholding darkness, and bewailing the loss of inward joy and consolation, crieth from the bottom of the lowest hell, 'My God, my God, why hast thou forsaken me?' (Psal. xxii. 1) than continually to walk arm in arm with angels, to sit as it were in Abraham's bosom, and to have no thought, no cogitation, but 'I thank my God it is not with me as it is with other men' (Luke xviii. 11). No, God will have them that shall walk in light to feel now and then what it is to sit in the shadow of death. A grieved spirit therefore is no argument of a faithless mind.

A third occasion of men's misjudging themselves, as if they were faithless when they are not, is, they fasten their cogitation upon the distrustful suggestions of the flesh, whereof finding great abundance in themselves, they gather thereby, Surely unbelief hath full dominion, it hath taken plenary possession of me; if I were faithful, it could not be thus: not marking the motions of the Spirit and of faith, because they lie buried and overwhelmed with the contrary: when notwithstanding as the blessed Apostle doth acknowledge (Rom. viii. 26, 27), that 'the Spirit groaneth,' and that God heareth when we do not; so there is no doubt, but that our faith may have and hath her privy operations secret to us, in whom, yet known to him by whom they are.

Tell this to a man that hath a mind deceived by too hard an opinion of himself, and it doth but augment his grief: he hath his answer ready, Will you make me think otherwise than I find, than I feel in myself? I have thoroughly considered and exquisitely sifted all the corners of my heart, and I see what there is; never seek to persuade me against my knowledge; 'I do not, I know I do not believe.'

Well, to favour them a little in their weakness; let that be granted which they do imagine; be it that they are faithless and without belief. But are they not grieved for their unbelief? They are. Do they not wish it might, and also strive that it may, be otherwise? We know they do. Whence cometh this, but from a secret love and liking which they have of those things that are believed? No man can love things which in his own opinion are not. And if they think those things to be, which they shew that they love when they desire to believe them; then must it needs be, that by desiring to believe they prove themselves true believers. For without faith, no man thinketh that things believed are. Which argument all the subtilty of infernal powers will never be able to dissolve.

The faith therefore of true believers, though it have many and grievous downfalls, yet doth it still continue invincible; it conquereth and recovereth itself in the end. The dangerous conflicts whereunto it is subject are not able to prevail against it. The Prophet Habakkuk remained faithful in weakness, though weak in faith. (5)

Dark Faith

Of us who is here which cannot very soberly advise his brother? Sir, you must learn to strengthen your faith by that experience which heretofore you have had of God's great goodness towards you: 'Per ea quæ agnoscas præstita, discas sperare promissa;' 'By those things which you have known performed, learn to hope for those things which are promised.' Do you acknowledge to have received much? Let that make you certain to receive more: 'Habenti dabitur;' 'To him that hath more shall be given.' When you doubt what you shall have, search what you have had at God's hands. Make this reckoning, that the benefits, which he hath bestowed, are bills obligatory and sufficient sureties that he will bestow further. His present mercy is still a warrant of his future love, because, 'whom he loveth, he loveth unto the end' (John xiii. 1). Is it not thus?

Yet if we could reckon up as many evident, clear, undoubted signs of God's reconciled love towards us as there are years, yea days, yea hours, past over our heads; all these set together have not such force to confirm our faith, as the loss, and sometimes the only fear of losing a little transitory goods, credit, honour, or favour of men,—a small calamity, a matter of nothing,—to breed a conceit, and such a conceit as is not easily again removed, that we are clean crost out of God's book, that he regards us not, that he looketh upon others, but passeth by us like a stranger to whom we are not known. Then we think, looking upon others, and comparing them with ourselves, Their tables are furnished day by day; earth and ashes are our bread: they sing to the lute, and they see their children dance before them; our hearts are heavy in our bodies as lead, our sighs beat as thick as a swift pulse, our tears do wash the beds wherein we lie: the sun shineth fair upon their foreheads; we are hanged up like bottles in the smoke, cast into corners like the sherds of a broken pot: tell not us of the promises of God's favour, tell such as do reap the fruit of them; they belong not to us, they are made to others. The Lord be merciful to our weakness, but thus it is.

Well, let the frailty of our nature, the subtilty of Satan, the force of our deceivable imaginations be, as we cannot deny but they are, things that threaten every moment the utter subversion of our faith; faith notwithstanding is not hazarded by these things. (6)

NOTES / SOURCES

1. Richard Hooker, *Of the Lawes of Ecclesiasticall Politie*, I.ii.3, ed. John Keble, Oxford, 1841, vol. I, pp. 202–3
2. Ibid., I.xiv.4–xv.3, pp. 270–5
3. Ibid., V.xlviii.4–8, vol. II, pp. 202–5
4. Ibid., V.xlix.2–3, vol. II, pp. 214–5
5. Sermon I, 'Of the Certainty and Perpetuity of Faith in the Elect', ibid., vol. III, pp. 474–6
6. Ibid., pp. 479–81

Lancelot Andrewes 1555–1626

Born in Barking, London, Lancelot Andrewes was a gifted student of languages who became Fellow and later Master of Pembroke Hall, Cambridge. Under Elizabeth I he was offered the Bishoprics of Salisbury and Ely, which he declined, but after the accession of James I in 1603 he became Bishop of Chichester (1605), Ely (1609), and, lastly, Winchester (1619). He attended the Hampton Court Conference and was one of the leading translators of the Authorized Version of the Bible (1611). In his own lifetime, his reputation was chiefly derived from his frequent appearances at Court as a preacher, and his *Ninety-Six Sermons* were published posthumously in 1629. His *Preces Privatae* became famous as a collection of devotions for personal use, and English translations became available after his death in 1626. His theology is much marked by patristic and Eastern Christian themes, and his preaching shows a particularly 'high' sacramental doctrine.

An Act of Charity

Thyself, o my God, Thyself for thine own sake, above all things else I love. Thyself I desire. Thyself as my last end I long for. Thyself for thine own sake, not aught else whatsoever, alway and in all things I seek, with all my heart and marrow, with groaning and weeping, with unbroken toil and grief. What wilt Thou render me therefore for my last end? If Thou render me not Thyself, Thou renderest nought: if Thou give me not Thyself, Thou givest nought: if I find not Thyself, I find nought. To no purpose Thou rewardest me, but dost wring me sore. For, or ever I sought Thee, I hoped to find Thee at the last and to keep Thee: and with this honied hope in all my toils was I sweetly comforted. But now, if Thou have denied me Thyself, what else soever Thou give me, frustrate of so high an hope, and that not for a little space but for ever, shall I not alway languish with love, mourn with languishing, grieve with mourning, bewail with grief, and weep for that alway I shall abide empty and void? Shall I not sorrow inconsolably, complain unceasingly, be wrung unendingly? This is not thy property, o best, most gracious, most loving God: in no sort is it congruous, no wise it sorteth. Make me therefore, o best my God, in the life present alway to love Thyself for Thyself before all things, to seek Thee in all things, and at the last in the life to come to find and to keep Thee for ever. (1)

(Translated and adapted from Archbishop Bradwardine)

A Commendation

I commend unto Thee, o Lord,

impulses,	my soul and my body,
occasions,	my mind and my thoughts,
purposes,	my vows and prayers,
endeavours,	my senses and my members,
going out and coming in,	my words and my deeds,
downsitting and uprising:	my life and my death:

my brothers and sisters
  their children
my benefactors
  wellwishers
    household
    neighbours
    country
    all Christian folk. (2)

Prayer at the End of the Day

Comprecation

Blessed art Thou, o Lord,
who givest thy beloved pleasant sleep,
  and to them that fear Thee to lie down safely.
Lighten our eyes,
  that we sleep not in death:
deliver us from the terror by night,
  from the pestilence that walketh in darkness.
Behold He that keepeth Israel
  shall neither slumber nor sleep:

the Lord preserve us from all evil,
    yea the Lord keep our souls.
Lord, I will sleep,
    but my heart shall be awake.
Visit me, o Lord, with the visitation of the saints,
    and discover mine ear in visions of night.
Let my sleep be a respite,
    as from toil, so from sin:
let me not in dreams think aught
    to offend Thee or pollute me.
Grant me, Lord, to remember that with Thee
    night is no night
    and darkness is like the noonday light.
Grant me, o Lord, when sleep flieth from mine eyes,
    to remember thy Name in the night season,
    that so I may keep thy law.
Grant me to commune in the night with my heart,
    and to be sore exercised and to search out my spirits
    and not to neglect the instruction of my reins—
        what I may do rightly, what more rightly,
        how to be more acceptable to Thee,
        how to be more pleasing unto men:
        that Thou art about my paths
            and about my bed:
        that my ways are thine:
    when my lamp is alight to see Thee,
    when my lamp is quenched to see Thee.
Grant me, o Lord, to think
    of the long sleep,
        the sleep of death,
        the bed of the grave,
        the mattrass of worms,
        the coverlet of dust.

Commendation

I will lay me down in peace
    and take my rest:
for it is Thou Lord only
    that makest me dwell in safety.
Into thy hands, o Lord,
    I commend my spirit,
        for Thou hast redeemed me,
            o Lord Thou God of truth. (3)

Participating in Christ

It is very agreeable to reason, saith the Apostle, that we endeavour and make a proffer, if we may by any means, to 'apprehend' Him in His, by Whom we are thus in our nature 'apprehended,' or, as He termeth it, 'comprehended,' even Christ Jesus; and be united to Him this day, as He was to us this day, by a mutual and reciprocal 'apprehension.' We may so, and we are bound so; *vere dignum et justum est.* And we do so, so oft as we do with St James lay hold of, 'apprehend,' or receive *insitum verbum,* the 'word which is daily grafted into us' (Jam. 1. 21). For 'the Word' He is, and in the word He is received by us. But that is not the proper of this day, unless there be another joined unto it. This day *Verbum caro factum est* (John 1. 14), and so must be 'apprehended' in both. But specially in His flesh as this day giveth it, as this day would have us. Now 'the bread which we break, is it not the partaking of the body, of the flesh, of Jesus Christ?' (1 Cor. 10. 16) It is surely, and by it and by nothing more are we made partakers of this blessed union (Heb. 2. 14). A little before He said, 'Because the children were partakers of flesh and blood, He also would take part with them'—may not we say the same? Because He hath so done, taken ours of us, we also ensuing His steps will participate with Him and with His flesh which He hath taken of us. It is most kindly to take part with Him in that which He took part in with us, and that, to no other end, but that He might make the receiving of it by us a means whereby He might 'dwell in us, and we in Him;' He taking our flesh, and we receiving His Spirit; by His flesh which He took of us receiving His Spirit which He imparteth to us; that, as He by ours became *consors humanæ naturæ,* so we by His might become *consortes Divinæ naturæ,* 'partakers of the Divine nature' (2 Pet. 1. 4). Verily, it is the most straight and perfect 'taking hold' that is. No union so knitteth as it. Not consanguinity; brethren fall out (Gen. 45. 24). Not marriage; man and wife are severed. But that which is nourished, and the nourishment wherewith—they never are, never can be severed, but remain one for ever. (4)

The House of Bread

It may be said and said truly, the Church in this sense is very Bethlehem no less than the town itself. For that the town itself never had the name rightly all the while there was but bread made there, bread (*panis hominum*) 'the bread of men.' Not till this Bread was born there, which is *Panis Angelorum,* as the Psalm calleth it, 'and man did eat Angels' Food.' Then, and never till then, was it Bethlehem; and that is in the Church, as truly as ever in it. And accordingly the Church takes order we shall never fail of it. There shall ever be this day a Bethlehem to go to—a house wherein there is bread, and this bread. And shall there be Bethlehem, and so near us, and shall we not go to it? Or, shall we go to it, to the House of Bread, this Bread, and come away without it? Shall we forsake our Guide leading us to a place so much for our benefit? (5)

Cradle and Altar

Christ in the Sacrament is not altogether unlike Christ in the cratch [crib]. To the cratch we may well liken the husk or outward symbols of it. Outwardly it seems little worth but it is rich of contents, as was the crib this day with Christ in it. For what are they, but *infirma et egena elementa*, 'weak and poor elements' of themselves? yet in them find we Christ. Even as they did this day *in præsepi jumentorum panem Angelorum*, 'in the beasts' crib the food of Angels;' which very food our signs both represent, and present unto us.

Let me say this farther; it is the last word in the Sacrament, 'this is a sacrifice of praise and thanksgiving,' and the whole text resolves into *laudantium Deum*, 'to praise God;' and not to praise Him alone, but to praise Him with this hymn of the Angels. Now being to praise Him with the Angels' hymn, it behoves to be in or as near the state of Angels as we can; of very congruity to be in our very best state, when they and we to make but one choir. And when are we so? If at any time, at that time when we have newly taken the holy Sacrament of His blessed Body and most precious Blood—when we come fresh from it. And as if there were some near alliance between this song of the Angels and these signs, to shew that the signs or Sacrament have a special interest in this hymn; therefore is it, that even then upon the administration of it hath the Church ordered this very hymn ever to be sung or said, whatever day it fall in the whole year. For then sure of all other times are we on earth most near to Angelic perfection, then meetest to give glory unto God, then at peace with the whole earth, then a goodwill and purpose in us if ever. (6)

The Power of the Resurrection

Enable us He will, and can, as not only having passed the resurrection, but being the Resurrection itself; not only had the effect of it in Himself, but being the cause of it to us. So He saith Himself (Joh. 11. 25): 'I am the Resurrection and the Life;' the Resurrection to them that are dead in sin, to raise them from it; and the Life to them that live unto God, to preserve them in it.

Where, besides the two former, 1. the article of the Resurrection, which we are to know; 2. and the example of the Resurrection, which we are to be like; we come to the notice of a third thing, even a virtue or power flowing from Christ's resurrection, whereby we are made able to express our *similiter et vos*, and to pass this our account of 'dying to sin,' and 'living to God.' It is in plain words called by the Apostle himself, *virtus resurrectionis*, 'the virtue of Christ's resurrection,' issuing from it to us (Phil. 3. 10); and he prayeth that as he had a faith of the former, so he may have a feeling of this; and as of them he had a contemplative, so he may of this have an experimental knowledge. This enabling virtue proceedeth from Christ's resurrection. For never let us think, if in the days of His flesh there 'went virtue out' from even the very edge of His garment to do great cures, as in the case of the woman with the bloody issue we read (Lu. 8. 46), but that from His Ownself, and from those two most principal and powerful actions of His Ownself, His 1. death and 2. resurrection, there issueth a divine power; from His death a power working on the old man or flesh to mortify it; from His resurrection a power working on the new man, the spirit, to quicken it. A power able to roll back any stone of an evil custom, lie it never so heavy on us; a power able to dry up any issue, though it have run upon us twelve years long.

And this power is nothing else but that divine quality of grace, which we receive from Him. Receive it from Him we do certainly: only let us pray, and endeavour ourselves, that we 'receive it not in vain' (2 Cor. 6. 1), the Holy Ghost by ways to flesh and blood unknown inspiring it as a breath, distilling it as a dew, deriving it as a secret influence into the soul. For if philosophy grant an invisible operation in us to the celestial bodies, much better may we yield it to His eternal Spirit, whereby such a virtue or breath may proceed from it, and be received of us.

Which breath, or spirit, is drawn in by prayer, and such other exercises of devotion on our parts; and, on God's part, breathed in, by, and with, the word, well therefore termed by the Apostle, 'the word of grace' (Acts 20. 32). And I may safely say it with good warrant, from those words especially and chiefly; which, as He Himself saith of them, are 'spirit and life' (Joh. 6. 63), even those words, which joined to the element make the blessed Sacrament.

There was good proof made of it this day. All the way did He preach to them, even till they came to Emmaus, and their hearts were hot within them, which was a good sign; but their eyes were not opened but 'at the breaking of bread,' and then they were (Lu. 24. 31). That is the best and surest sense we know, and therefore most to be accounted of. There we taste, and there we see (Ps. 34. 8); 'taste and see how gracious the Lord is.' There we are made to 'drink of the Spirit' (1 Cor. 12. 13), there our 'hearts are strengthened and stablished with grace' (Heb. 13. 9). There is the blood which shall 'purge our consciences from dead works,' whereby we may 'die to sin' (Heb. 9. 14). There the Bread of God, which shall endue our souls with much strength; yea, multiply strength in them, to live unto God; yea, to live to Him continually; for he that 'eateth His flesh and drinketh His blood, dwelleth in Christ, and Christ in him' (Joh. 6. 33, 56); not inneth, or sojourneth for a time, but dwelleth continually. And, never can we more truly, or properly say, *in Christo Jesu Domino nostro*, as when we come new from that holy action, for then He is in us, and we in Him, indeed. And so we to make full account of this service, as a special means to further us to make up our Easter-day's account, and to set off a good part of our charge. In Christ, dropping upon us the anointing of His grace. In Jesus, Who will be ready as our Saviour to succour and support us with His *auxilium speciale*, 'His special help.' (7)

Resurrection and New Birth

. . . But where is Easter-day, what is become of it all this while? For methinks, all the time we are thus about Father and Son, and taking our nature and becoming one of us, it should be Christmas by this, and not Easter as it is; that this a meeter text one would think for that feast, and that now it comes out of season.

Not a whit. It is Christ That speaketh, and He never speaketh but in season; never but to the purpose, never but on the right day.

A brotherhood, we grant, was begun then at Christmas by His birth, as upon that day, for 'lo then was He born.' But so was He now also at Easter; born then too, and after a better manner born. His resurrection was a second birth, Easter a second Christmas. *Hodie genui Te*, as true of this day as of that. The Church appointeth for the first Psalm this day the second Psalm, the Psalm of *hodie genui Te*. The Apostle saith expressly, when He rose from the dead, then was *hodie genui Te* fulfilled in Him, verified of Him (Acts 13. 33). Then He was *primogenitus a mortuis*, 'God's first-begotten from the dead' (Col. 1. 18). And upon this latter birth doth the brotherhood of this day depend.

There was then a new begetting this day. And if a new begetting, a new paternity, and fraternity both. By the *hodie genui Te* of Christmas, how soon He was born of the Virgin's womb He became our brother, sin except, subject to all our infirmities; so to mortality, and even to death itself. And by death that brotherhood had been dissolved, but for this day's rising. By the *hodie genui Te* of Easter, as soon as He was born again of the womb of the grave, He begins a new brotherhood, founds a new fraternity straight; adopts us we see anew again by His *fratres Meos*, and thereby He That was *primogenitus a mortuis* becomes *primogenitus inter multos fratres*; when 'the first-begotten from the dead' (Rom. 8. 29), then 'the first-begotten' in this respect 'among many brethren' (Rev. 1. 5). Before He was ours, now we are His. That was by the mother's side; so, He ours. This is by *Patrem vestrum*, the Father's side;—so, we His. But half-brothers before, never of whole blood till now. Now by Father and mother both, *fratres germani, fratres fraterrimi*, we cannot be more.

To shut all up in a word, that of Christmas was the fraternity rising out of *Deum Meum, Deum vestrum* [My God and your God]; so then brethren. This of Easter, adopting us to His Father, was the fraternity of *Patrem Meum, Patrem vestrum* [My Father and your Father]; so brethren now.

This day's is the better birth, the better brotherhood by far; the fore-wheels are the less, the hinder the larger ever. For first, that of ours was when He was mortal; but His adoption He deferred, He would not make it while He was mortal; reserved it till He was risen again, and was even upon His ascending, and then He made it. So mortal He was, when He ours; but now when we His, He is immortal, and we brethren to Him in that state, the state of immortality. Brethren before, but not to *ascendo*; now to *ascendo* and all. Death was in danger to have dissolved that, but death hath now no power on Him, or on this; this shall never be in danger of being dissolved any more. That without this is nothing.

But we shall not need to stand in terms of comparison, since then it was but one of these; now it is both. His Father is now become our Father, to make us joint-heirs with Him of His Heavenly Kingdom; His God likewise become our God, to make us 'partakers' with them both 'of the Divine nature.' *Patrem Meum* and *Patrem vestrum, Deum Meum* and *Deum vestrum*, run both merrily together, and *ascendo* upon them both.

Whereof, I mean of the partaking of His divine nature, to give us full and perfect assurance, as He took our flesh and became our Brother, flesh of our flesh then, so He gives us His flesh, that we may become His brethren, flesh of His flesh, now; and gives it us now upon this day, the very day of our adoption into this fraternity. (8)

The Spirit of Peace

The Holy Ghost is a Dove, and He makes Christ's Spouse, the Church, a Dove; a term so oft iterate in the Canticles, and so much stood on by Saint Augustine and the Fathers, as they make no question, No Dove, no Church. Yea, let me add this: St Peter, when the keys were promised, never but then, but then I know not how, he is called by a new name, and never but there, 'Bar-jona,' that is *Filius columbæ* (Mat. 16. 17). But so he must be, if ever he will have them. And his successors, if they claim by any other fowl, painted keys they may have, true keys they have none. For sure I am, *extra Columbam*, out of that Church, that is, such and so qualified, *non est Columba*, there is no Holy Ghost, and so no remission of sins. For they go together, 'Receive the Holy Ghost, whose sins ye remit, they are remitted.'

And what shall we say then to them that will be Christians, that they will, and yet have *nihil columbæ*, nothing in them of the dove; quit these qualities quite, neither bill, nor eye, nor voice, no colour; what shall we say? This, that Jesuits they may be, but Christians, sure, they are none. No dove's eye, fox-eyed they; not silver-white feathers, but party-coloured; no *gemitus columbæ*, but *rugitus ursi*; not the bill or foot of a dove, but the beak and claws of a vulture; no spirit of the olive-branch, but the spirit of the bramble, from whose root went out fire to set all the forest on a flame.

Ye may see what they are, they even seek and do all that in them lies to chase away this Dove, the Holy Ghost. The Dove, they tell us, that was for the baby-Church, for them to be humble and meek, suffer and mourn like a dove. Now, as if with Montanus they had yet *Paracletum alium*, 'another Holy Ghost' to look for, in another shape, of another fashion quite, with other qualities, they hold these be no qualities for Christians now. Were indeed, they grant, for the baby-Christians, for the 'three thousand' first Christians, this day; poor men they did all *in simplicitate cordis*. And so too in Pliny's time: harmless people they were, the Christians, as he writes, did nobody hurt. And so to Tertullian's, who tells plainly what hurt they could have done, and yet would do none. And so all along the primitive Churches, even down to Gregory, who in any wise would have no hand in any man's blood. But the date of these meek and patient Christians is worn out, long since expired; and now we must have Christians of a new edition, of another, a new-fashioned Holy Ghost's making. [. . .]

For do they not begin to tell us in good earnest, and speak it in such assemblies and places as we must take it for their tenet, that they are simple men that think Christians were to continue so still; they were to be so but for a time, till their beaks and talons were grown, till their strength was come to them, and they able to make their party good; and then this dove here might take her wings, fly whither she would, 'and take her ease;' then a new Holy Ghost to come down upon them that would not take it as the other did, but take arms, depose, deprive, blow up; instead of an olive-branch, have a match-light in her beak or a bloody knife.

Methinks, if this world go on, it will grow a question problematic, in what shape it was most convenient for the Holy Ghost to have come down? Whether as He did, in the meek shape of a dove? or whether, it had not been much better He had come in some other shape, in the shape of the Roman eagle, or of some other fierce fowl *de vulturino genere*?

Sure, one of the two they must do; either call us down a new-fashioned Holy Ghost, and institute a new baptism—and if both these new, I see not why not a new Christ too—or else, make a strange metamorphosis of the old; clap Him on a crooked beak, and stick Him full of eagle's feathers, and force Him to do contrary to that He was wont, and to that His nature is.

But lying men may change—may, and do; but the Holy Ghost is *unus idemque Spiritus*, saith the Apostle, changes not, casts not His bill, moults not His feathers. His qualities at the first do last still, and still shall last to the end, and no other notes of a true Christian, but they. (9)

NOTES / SOURCES

1. The *Preces Privatae of Lancelot Andrewes*, ed. and translated F. E. Brightman, London 1903, p. 192
2. Ibid., p. 277
3. Ibid., pp. 114–5
4. 'Sermon I of the Nativity' in *Ninety-Six Sermons*, Oxford and London 1874, vol. I, pp. 16–17
5. 'Sermon X of the Nativity', ibid., p. 174
6. 'Sermon XII of the Nativity', ibid., p. 214
7. 'Sermon I of the Resurrection', ibid., vol. II, pp. 206–7
8. 'Sermon XVI of the Resurrection', ibid., vol. III, pp. 58–9
9. 'Sermon VIII of the Sending of the Holy Ghost', ibid., pp. 258–9

William Perkins   1558–1602

William Perkins was a Fellow of Christ's College, Cambridge, from 1584 to 1595, where his preaching and writings earned him a great reputation. His works range widely over devotional and ethical issues as well as controversial theological matters, and he is perhaps the most learned and sophisticated spokesman for a full-bloodied Calvinism in the later Elizabethan Church, arguing for a disciplined spiritual and sacramental practice, with extensive reference to the Fathers and even the Scholastics.

Of the Lord's Supper

The Lord's Supper is a sacrament wherewith in the signs of bread and wine such as are engrafted into Christ are in him daily, in a spiritual manner, nourished to eternal life. The proportion of the parts of the Lord's Supper is on this wise. The elements of bread and wine are signs and seals of the body and blood of Christ. The action of the minister is a note of God's action. The minister's action is fourfold. The first is his taking of the bread and the wine in his own hands. This doth seal the action of God the Father by which he, from all eternity, did separate and elect his Son to perform the duty of a mediator betwixt God and man. The second is his blessing of it, whereby he, by the recital of the promises and prayers conceived to that end, doth actually separate the bread and wine received from their common unto a holy use. This doth seal that action of God by which he did in the fulness of time send Christ to perform the office of a mediator unto the which he was foreordained. The third is the breaking of the bread and pouring out of the wine. This doth seal the passion of Christ by which he, verily upon the cross, was both in soul and body bruised for our transgressions. The fourth is his distributing of the bread and wine into the hands of the communicants. This sealeth the action of God offering Christ unto all, yea, to the hypocrites, but giving him indeed to the faithful for the daily increase of their faith and repentance.

The action of the receiver is double. The first is his taking of the bread and wine in his hand. This sealeth a spiritual action of the receiver, namely his apprehension of Christ by the hand of faith. The second is his eating of the bread and drinking the wine to the nourishment of his body. This sealeth the application of Christ by faith, that the feeling of his true union and communion with Christ may daily be increased . . .

Such as will in an holy sort prepare themselves to celebrate the Lord's Supper must have first, a knowledge of God and man's fall and of the promised restoration into the covenant by Christ. Secondly, true faith in Christ, for every man receiveth so much as he believeth he receiveth: furthermore true repentance of their sins. Thirdly, renewed faith and repentance for daily and new sins committed upon infirmity, because every new sin requireth a new act both of repentance and faith: and this renovation must be seen by our reconciliation of ourselves to our neighbours for injuries and wrongs. If thou canst come furnished with these things, abstain not from the Lord's table by reason of thy many infirmities. (1)

What is Holiness?

Vivification is the second part of sanctification, whereby inherent holiness being begun is still augmented and enlarged. First, we receive the first-fruits of the Spirit, then a continual increase of them. The means of vivification is a virtue derived from Christ's resurrection to those that are quickened, which maketh them rise up to newness of life. The power of Christ's resurrection is that whereby he first did in his own flesh, as conqueror over death and sin, begin to live with God and to be exalted above every name: and then in his members, sin being dead and buried, he causeth in them an endeavour and purpose to live according to the will of God. The efficient cause of them both is the Holy Ghost who doth by his divine power convey himself into the believers' hearts and in them, by applying the power of Christ his death and resurrection, createth holiness.

Furthermore, this inherent holiness is to be distinguished into parts, according to the several faculties of the body and soul of man.

I. The holiness or renewing of the mind, which is the illumination thereof to the knowledge of the will of God. Illumination is either spiritual understanding or spiritual wisdom. Spiritual understanding is an illumination of the mind whereby it acknowledgeth the known truth of the word of God. Spiritual wisdom is an illumination of the mind whereby the same truth is applied to the good ordering of particular both things and actions, as person, place and time require. These two have the effects which follow: to discern between good and evil; to discern of spirits; to meditate upon the words and works of God; to discern and acknowledge man's own inward blindness.

II. The sanctity of the memory is an ability to keep a good thing when it is offered to the mind, and as need serveth to remember it.

III. The sanctity of conscience is a grace of God whereby a man's conscience excuseth him for all his sins after they are [for]given him in Christ, as also of his upright walking in the whole course of his life. Hence in all godly men ariseth the inward peace of God and the outward alacrity in the countenance.

IV. Sanctity of will, whereby man beginneth to will that which is good and to refuse the contrary. Therefore in this estate the will is partly freed from bondage, partly in bondage to sin.

V. Sanctity of affections is the right moving of them. Affections of most special note are these: hope whereby men with sighing look for the accomplishment of their redemption; this hope when it is once strong and lively hath also her *plerophorian*, that is full assurance, as faith hath; fear of offending God because of his mercy; a base account of worldly things in respect of Christ Jesus; the love of God in Christ which is like unto death and as a fire that cannot be quenched; a fervent zeal to God's glory; anguish of mind for our own sins and others also; exceeding great joy in the Holy Ghost; sanctity of body whereby it is a fit instrument for the soul to accomplish that which is good. (2)

The Christian Household

Christian œconomy is a doctrine of the right ordering of a family. The only rule of ordering the family is the written word of God (Psa. 101. 2; Prov. 24. 3). A family is a natural and simple society of certain persons having mutual relations one to another under the private government of one. These persons must be at least three, because two cannot make a society. And above three under the same head, there may be a thousand in one family, as it is in the households of princes and men of state in the world.

Of the household service of God

A family for the good estate of itself is bound to the performance of two duties: one to God and the other to itself. The duty unto God is the private worship and service of God, which must be established and settled in every family. And the reasons hereof are these. First, because this duty standeth by the express commandment of God (1 Tim. 2. 8). Again, it is confirmed by the custom and practice of holy men in their times (Gen. 18. 19; Josh. 24. 15; Acts 10. 2). Thirdly, common reason and equity showeth it to be a necessary duty, for the happy and prosperous estate of the family (which consisteth in the mutual love and agreement of the man and wife, the dutiful obedience of children to their parents and in the faithful service of servants to their masters), wholly dependeth upon the grace and blessing of God: and this blessing is annexed to his worship (1 Tim. 4. 8; Psa. 127. 1–2, 13; Psa. 128. 1–3, 6; 1 Sam. 1. 27).

The household service of God hath two parts. The first is a conference upon the word of God for the edification of all the members thereof to eternal life. The second is invocation of the name of God, with giving of thanks for his benefits: both of these are commanded in the scriptures (Deut. 6. 6–7, 20–24; Psa. 14. 1–4). The times of this service are these. The morning, in which the family coming together in one place is to call upon the name of the Lord, before they begin the works of their callings. The evening also is another time to be used in prayer, because the family hath seen the blessing of God upon their labours the day before: and now the time of rest draweth on, in which every one is to commend his body and soul into the protection of the Lord. For no man knoweth what shall befall him before he rise again, neither knoweth any whether he shall rise again or not. It is therefore a desperate boldness without praying to go to rest. (3)

Daily Discipline

When thou first openeth thine eyes in a morning, pray to God and give him thanks heartily. God then shall have his honour and thy heart shall be the better for it the whole day following. For we see in experience, that vessels keep long the taste of that liquor with which they were first seasoned. And when thou liest down, let that be the last also, for thou knowest not whether fallen asleep, thou shalt ever rise again alive. Good therefore it is that thou shouldest give up thyself into the hands of God, whilst thou art waking.

Labour to see and feel thy spiritual poverty, that is to see the want of grace in thyself, specially those inward corruptions of unbelief, pride, self-love, etc. Labour to be displeased with thyself: and labour to feel that by reason of them thou standest in need of every drop of the blood of Christ to heal and cleanse thee from these wants. And let this practice take such place with thee, that if thou be demanded what in thine estimation is the vilest of the creatures upon earth, thine heart and conscience may answer with a loud voice, I, even I, by reason of mine own sins: and again, if thou be demanded what is the best thing in the world for thee, thy heart and conscience may answer with a loud and strong cry, One drop of the blood of Christ to wash away my sins.

Shew thyself to be a member of Christ and a servant of God, not only in the general calling of a Christian, but also in the particular calling in which thou art placed. It is not enough for a magistrate to be a Christian man, but he must also be a Christian magistrate. It is not enough for a master of a family to be a Christian man, but he must also be a Christian in his family and in the trade which he followeth daily. Not everyone that is a common hearer of the word and a frequenter of the Lord's table is therefore a good Christian, unless his conversation in his private house, and in his private affairs and dealings be suitable. There is a man to be seen what he is.

Search the scriptures to see what is sin and what is not sin in every action. This done, carry in thy heart a constant and resolute purpose not to sin in anything, for faith and the purpose of sinning can never stand together.

Let thine endeavour be suitable to thy purpose and therefore do nothing at any time against thy conscience, rightly informed by the word. Exercise thyself to eschew every sin and to obey God in every one of his commandments that pertain either to the general calling of a Christian, or to thy particular calling. This did good Josiah, who turned unto God with all his heart, according to all the law of Moses and thus did Zechariah and Elizabeth, that walked in all the commandments of God without reproof (2 Kings 23. 25; Luke 1. 6).

If at any time, against thy purpose and resolution, thou be overtaken with any sin little or great, lie not in it, but speedily recover thyself, confessing thine offence and by prayer intreat the Lord to pardon the same, and that earnestly; till such time as thou findest thy conscience truly pacified and thy care to eschew the same sin increased.

Consider often of the right and proper end of thy life in this world, which is not to seek profit, honour, pleasure, but that in serving of men we might serve God in our callings. God could, if it so pleased him, preserve man without the ministry of man, but his pleasure is to fulfil his work and will, in the preservation of our bodies and the salvation of our souls, by the employment of men in his service, every one according to his vocation. Neither is there so much as a bondslave, but he must in and by his faithful service to his master, serve the Lord. Men therefore do commonly profane their labours and their lives by aiming at a wrong end, when all their care consisteth only in getting sufficient maintenance for them and theirs, for the obtaining of credit, riches and carnal commodities. For thus men serve themselves, and not God or men, much less do they serve God in serving of men.

Give all thy diligence to make thy election sure and to gather manifold tokens thereof. For this observe the works of God's providence, love and mercy, both in thee and upon thee, from time to time; for the serious consideration of them and the laying of them together when they are many and several, minister much direction, assurance of God's favour and comfort. This was the practice of David (1 Sam. 17. 34, 36; Psa. 23).

Think evermore thy present estate, whatsoever it be, to be the best estate for thee, because whatsoever befalls thee, though it be sickness, or any other affliction or death, befalls thee of the good providence of God. That this may be better done, labour to see and acknowledge a providence of God as well in property as in abundance, as well in disgrace as in good report, as well in sickness as in health, as well in life as in death.

Pray continually, I mean not by solemn and set prayer, but by secret and inward ejaculations of the heart; that is by a continual elevation of mind unto Christ sitting at the right hand of God the Father, and that either by prayer or giving of thanks, so often as any occasion shall be offered. (4)

Social Charity

Despise not civil honesty: good conscience and good manners go together. Therefore remember to make conscience of lying and customable swearing in common talk. Contend not either in deed or word with any man, be courteous and gentle to all, good and bad. Bear with men's wants and frailties, hastiness, forwardness, self-liking, curiousness, etc., passing them by as being not perceived. Return not evil for evil, but rather good for evil. Use meat, drink and apparel in that manner and measure that they may further godliness and may be, as it were, signs in which thou mayest express the hidden grace of thy heart. Strive not to go beyond any, unless it be in good things. Go before thine equals in the giving of honour, rather than in taking of it, making conscience of thy word, and let it be as a bond. Profess no more outwardly than thou hast inwardly in heart, oppress or defraud no man in bargaining, in all companies either do good, or take good.

Cleave not by inordinate affection to any creature, but above all things quiet and rest thy mind in Christ; above all dignity and honour, above all cunning and policy, above all glory and honour, above all health and beauty, above all joy and delight, above all fame and praise, above all mirth and consolation that man's heart can feel or devise beside Christ. (5)

NOTES / SOURCES

1. William Perkins 'A Golden Chain, or, the Description of Theology', in *The Works of William Perkins*, ed. J. Breward, Appleford, Berks., 1970, pp. 222–3
2. Ibid., pp. 235–6
3. 'A Christian Oeconomy', ibid., pp. 416–17
4. 'A Graine of Mustard-Seede', ibid., pp. 406–9
5. Ibid., pp. 409–10

John Norden

Nothing is known for certain about Norden, except that he was almost certainly a layman, who published in 1591 an essay on holy living and the necessary dispositions for prayer, including some model prayers (and some fervent thanksgivings for Queen Elizabeth's rule). The book was reprinted in 1596, but does not seem to have had wide circulation thereafter.

Prayer and Knowledge

We know that the tongue and lips are the instruments of the body, to utter the intent and meaning of the heart of man to man in private conference or speech: and they are also the members by whose aid the minister poureth forth the meaning of the spirit to the understanding of the hearers in public or common prayers. And although they be indeed the instruments whereby that is outwardly uttered which is inwardly desired; yet are the words (be they never so godly in themselves) of no value, and bring neither profit nor comfort to him that prayeth, unless the heart within be touched with the feeling and taste of many particular virtues, which are required in every one that will pray unto God aright: by which virtues we must prepare ourselves to approach before our God in the name of his Son.

And first there is to be sought for, obtained, and embraced, knowledge; and a necessity is laid upon us, that we know and be acquainted with God himself, who hath laid himself open and made himself apparent unto us in his word; and unless we know him, we can never call upon him aright. 'God is a spirit, and he that will worship him aright, must worship him in spirit and truth' (John iv. 24, 2 Cor. iii. 17). God is not as man, who only seeth, seeketh, and knoweth outwardly: but he seeth and searcheth the hearts, and our very thoughts are not hid from him (Acts i. 24. xv. 8). 'He knoweth what we need before we ask,' and what the spirit meaneth which groaneth within us: which spirit, and not the outward words, 'maketh request' with sighs which cannot be outwardly discerned.

This spiritual worship therefore is altogether acceptable unto our God; and, all carnal consideration exempted, we must only seek him as he is, namely, in spirit, who by his divine working revealeth unto us his will, whereupon all our petitions are to be grounded, and without the same knowledge we cannot observe the things requisite in this so high function and progress.

The principal and absolute hand, whereby we apprehend and take hold of the power, love, justice, judgment, purpose, wisdom, will, and providence of God, is faith; which faith cometh by knowledge and understanding of the word of God; for 'faith cometh by hearing, and hearing by the word of God.' And without faith our prayers are but as wind passing by and from our lips, and by reverberation of the air makes a sound, but to no profit, and (as the Holy Ghost saith) it turneth unto sin. (1)

Faith, Hope, and Love in Prayer

Being endued with this faith, it cannot be but it will break forth into this excellent work of prayer; whereunto also is adjoined hope, the unseparable companion of faith: for when by faith there is conceived an assurance of the obtaining of our requests, there must be an attendance for and waiting on the Lord's performing; as Abraham waited and was attending the time when the Lord would send the seed which he promised should be borne by Sarah his wife, faith having first conceived the truth of God, that what he had said should come to pass, but in a time when the Lord had decreed it. And this and such like attendance, waiting, and patience, is a hope to receive that hereafter which we see not, whereby the faithful are as it were fed with patient abiding the Lord's leisure in all things: for 'hope that is seen' (that is, the thing that we look for being in possession) 'is no hope; for how can a man hope for that which he hath? But if we hope for that we see not, we do with patience abide for it.' In this is great consolation offered unto the faithful, for that, having prayed for the things which they would either avoid or receive, they abide patiently the burden of the one, and the want of the other, until at last they receive their expectation fully answered to their notable comfort. And in this we learn, that in no case we may indent with God for the thing we ask, the manner how, or the time when we shall obtain the same; for in so doing we should shew ourselves over malapert and bold (being as indeed we are of ourselves beggars) to appoint the Lord when or how he should work for us, or give us his benevolence: and especially, for that we of ourselves be so gross of conceit, that we often ask amiss. Many times we would have the performance of things after such a sort, and in such a time, as God seeth it not necessary for us: and therefore the Lord, considering our infirmities and bearing with our weakness, giveth us hope whereby we receive comfort, and faint not under the burden of whatsoever affliction. Ask therefore in faith, and wait in hope.

Faith having gotten this acceptable and inseparable companion hope, then is there another fellow-virtue which must attend this faith and hope, without the which there is no absolute preparation to this notable exercise of prayer; and that is love, which is more acceptable unto the Lord than faith or hope: insomuch as faith and hope extend but unto a man's own private good, and hath an end, and is not seen; but love extendeth itself to wish well unto all, and abideth for ever, and sheweth itself apparently. It is the badge and cognisance of a true Christian indeed; and therefore saith Christ, 'By this shall men know that ye are my disciples, if ye love one another.' The commendation of this singular virtue is great, and largely set forth by the Spirit of God in the scriptures; for it is 'the fruit of the Spirit of God,' it 'is the bond of perfection,' without which there is no union between us, but a continual striving, contention, and hatred, which poisoneth all other affections, be they never so good in our own eyes. And where there is no love, there is no assurance whether a man stand in the favour of God or no; and without that assurance faith is dead, without which there is no salvation. And therefore, it was 'a message and commandment which we have heard from the beginning, that we should love one another.' Again, 'we are translated from death unto life, because we love one another.' But on the contrary, 'He that loveth not his brother abideth in death.' We must 'forgive, if we have any thing against any man, that God may forgive us.' 'Love is the fulfilling of the law.' It is a most high and sacred virtue, 'covering the multitude of sins.'

Such is the integrity of this virtue, that it bewrayeth not the imperfections of other men, but rather charitably deemeth of all, wishing well unto all, and doing good unto all; not as the world useth, to love only in words, and in smiling countenance, as to have honey in our lips and gall in our hearts, as Judas had; but to have a perfect love, an affection seasoned with the spirit of meekness, of patience, and inward desire of the wealth of all, mortifying all hateful and malicious affections, all desire of revenge, lest that we deceive ourselves with a persuasion that we please God in prayer, when we hate our brother whom indeed we should absolutely forgive. But how? not as some use to forgive and not forget; but we must both forgive and forget, and thirst only in love to do good for evil. For a man that beareth hatred against his brother, how dare he ask forgiveness of God? We must therefore forgive one another before we take our journey in this progress, and be so far possessed with love that we pray one for another. 'Love must be without dissimulation,' that our faith may be thereby approved, and that knowledge may be joined with faith, with knowledge temperance, with temperance patience, with patience' (which is hope) 'godliness, with godliness brotherly kindness, and with brotherly kindness love.' Having thus sealed up the assurance of our calling, let us proceed unto humility, a singular virtue, and the next step to come unto our heavenly heart's ease.

Humility is a casting down of ourselves in our own conceits, and an inward abasing of ourselves before God, acknowledging ourselves unworthy of his favour, and disclaiming our own deserts, attributing all things that we receive to proceed only of his mercy; wherein we must carry a very short hand over our affections, lest that through the pride of nature we counterfeit this humiliation, and frame unto ourselves a humility not only not necessary, but merely offensive: and such humility Paul condemneth; for whiles we labour to subject ourselves under the power of angels and saints, by whose mediation and intercession we covet to approach unto God, under colour of lowliness of mind, we do not only miss the way, which is Christ, but betake us to a way which cannot lead us to God: for none cometh to the Father but by Christ; and we have free warrant to come immediately unto him who calleth us, 'Come unto me,' etc. And this kind of humiliation doth diminish his love towards us, wherein he hath finished all things for us, and resteth himself ready to hear us, to accept us, and to relieve us; and therefore we must fly unto him in all meekness of heart and soul, assuming unto ourselves nothing but the merits of Christ to join us to God through faith. (2)

Where and When to Pray

We need not to stand scrupulous of the place where to pray (1 Tim. ii. 8); 'for it must be everywhere, lifting up pure hands without wrath or doubting' (Acts xxii. 17). Paul prayed in the temple. Christ willeth us to enter into our chamber (Matt. vi. 6). David and Ezekias prayed in their beds; Elisha in the house, the door being shut, and in the fields. Peter prayed in the upper part of his house; Daniel in the lions' den; Moses in the wilderness; Christ in the fields, and Jonas in the whale's belly. So that it appeareth by these examples, that the place doth neither sanctify or pollute our prayers.

But wheresoever the Spirit moveth us thereunto, we may find the Lord; yea, seven times a day with David, or three times a day with Daniel; yea, as often as we feel ourselves apt to call upon him. And therefore at all times, and in all places, let us prepare ourselves to this holy exercise: going, riding, working, writing, or whatsoever we do, or wheresoever we be, let us always be inwardly meditating of the goodness, mercy, and power of our good God: so shall we find him always ready and willing to answer our desires with good and comfortable success in all our proceedings. (3)

Wealth as an Enemy to Prayer

The greatest impediment or let is the abundance of worldly things, as riches, health, authority, mighty and many friends, whereby we grow into a conceit of a secure estate of ourselves; insomuch as we imagine that we have no need of the aid of God. It casteth us into a slumber, which procureth many drowsy dreams of self-ability to wade through all adverse things of the world, and to need nothing, when as indeed we stand weak, poor, miserable, naked, and in need of all things. And therefore it often falleth out, that the poor, miserable, and afflicted men of the world are more exercised in prayer than the rich and secure men of the world. For what driveth a man to God but want? What moveth us to seek him but misery, trouble, enemies, sickness, and the crosses of this life? And therefore David, finding that dulness bred security, security idleness, and idleness negligence of this divine exercise, whereby he fell into sin, and being touched with the hand of God and roused out of that slumber, acknowledged that 'it was good for him that the Lord humbled him with his cross:' and then he began to seek the Lord in prayer. So if we men be not in some sort humbled with the cross of Christ, we shall, in security, forget our duty towards our God in this behalf. Wherefore it is good for every man to call to mind his estate: if he be poor, miserable, and afflicted, let him pray unto God, who applieth medicines to all our miseries, and giveth issue to all our crosses, and maketh them comfortable unto us. Let him that is rich examine from whom his abundance of wealth, rest, and tranquillity cometh, and he shall find that it is from God; even that God that can give and take away, set aloft and pull down: he can alter estates at his pleasure. And therefore, I say, let all degrees bow unto him, and watch in prayer, lest that, his divine honour being neglected, his blessings be denied and turned to our confusion. (4)

A Motion to Prayer

That God by his Spirit will teach us how to pray

Let us consider how willing and ready our good God is to hearken unto the desires of all such as hunger and thirst for the riches of his grace, without which such is our poverty, that 'we know not what to ask as we ought: but the Spirit helpeth our infirmities, and maketh request for us with sighs which cannot be expressed.' And although that flesh and blood be so corrupt that it always grovelleth on the puddle of worldly cares, and the better part, namely, the inner man, in the mean time is forgotten, and standeth endangered to fall into many evils; yet, having the 'earnest of this Spirit,' we may boldly come unto our God, who hath promised to send the same: if we ask it at his hands, he will give it in such abundance and full measure, that by the virtue thereof we shall be 'able to pray according to the will of God.' This is the Comforter which Christ promised to send unto us, even 'the Holy Ghost, which should teach us all things.' And without it we know nothing. And, alas! what were it for us to fall down before God in most reverent outward manner, pouring forth a huge heap of words from the lips, not having this inward director? Surely it were but to spend time to no purpose: it is the Spirit that crieth in our hearts, Abba, Father: 'the spirit of a man knoweth only the things that are of man; but the Spirit of God knoweth and desireth the things that are of God. And the natural man perceiveth not the things of the Spirit of God, for they are foolishness unto him: but he that hath the Spirit of God, he discerneth all things.' Let us, therefore, 'pray in the Holy Ghost: let us pray always with all manner prayer and supplications in the Spirit' (Jude, 20. Eph. vi. 18).

And let us pray continually for the aid of this sacred guide, the Holy Spirit of God, which will both move us unto, and direct us in all things that are requisite to the due performance of this godly exercise.

THE PRAYER FOR THE AID OF GOD'S SPIRIT

Forasmuch, dear Father, as every man living is of himself before thee as a beast, neither knowing thee nor the things concerning their own duties unto thee; I, as one of the most perverse, filthy, and corrupt, do here humble myself before thee, begging at thy hands that which thou hast promised to give unto as many as ask it of thee, thine Holy Spirit, that sacred Comforter, which revealeth thee and thy will to the simple and ignorant: which also stirreth up the minds and inward affections of thy children to call upon thee: it prepareth the hearts, and openeth the mouths of thy children to celebrate thy name. Bestow it therefore, good Father, bestow it upon me, thy poor creature, and upon all thy children. And grant that, although all of us are of corrupt affections and of polluted lips, yet we may be besprinkled with that heavenly hyssop, that we thereby may have our hearts cleansed from the corrupt affections of the world, and the eyes of our understandings opened, that we may see the good things that we should ask; that our feet, which are fettered with the cares of vain things, may be set at liberty, that we may walk the right way unto the kingdom of heaven; that the hands of our souls may apprehend and take hold of the riches and righteousness of thy Son, Christ Jesus; and that, by the aid of the same Spirit, we may cast off all impediments, lets, and incumbrances that detain us from coming unto thee. Sanctify me within and without: wash me, and I shall be whiter than snow. Let thy truth and thy Spirit meet together in my soul, that my prayer may enter into thy presence; and that thine ears may incline unto my humble petitions: so shall I declare thy loving kindness in the morning, and thy truth in the night.

Thou knowest whereof we be made; thou forgettest not that we are but dust, and unprofitable people; not fit, apt, or able of ourselves to pray unto thee, or praise thy name.

Wherefore, good Father, enlighten us, and teach our hearts rightly to conceive, and our tongues freely to speak, what may be to thy glory and our comfort: allure us to seek thee, and grant that our hearts may rejoice in thee, and that we may live and die in thee. Amen.

'Let us now seek the Lord; let us seek his strength: yea, let us seek his face continually.' Psal. cv. 4.

O Lord, increase our faith. (5)

A Prayer of Trust

When have I come unto thee, and have been rejected? Never hath my complaint been put back, but lovingly heard, and my petitions granted, so that I rest assured of thy continual help. I am forced, good Father, to see thee daily, and thou offerest thyself daily to be found: whensoever I seek, I find thee, in my house, in the fields, in the temple, and in the highway. Whatsoever I do, thou art with me, whether I eat or drink, whether I write or work, go or ride, read, meditate or pray, thou art ever with me; wheresoever I am, or whatsoever I do, I feel some measure of thy mercies and love. If I be oppressed, thou defendest me; if I be envied, thou guardest me; if I hunger, thou feedest me; whatsoever I want thou givest me. O continue this thy loving kindness towards me for ever, that all the world may see thy power, thy mercy, and thy love, wherein thou hast not failed me, and even my enemies shall see that thy mercies endure for ever.

Lord, increase my faith. (6)

NOTES / SOURCES

1. John Norden, *A Progress of Piety*, reprinted Cambridge (Parker Society), 1847, pp. 15–16
2. Ibid., pp. 18–22
3. Ibid., pp. 25–6
4. Ibid., pp. 27–9
5. Ibid., pp. 34–7
6. Ibid., pp. 148–9

Material from the Reign of Queen Elizabeth I   1558–1603

Despite the Queen's lukewarm attitude to the more outspoken representatives of Reformed piety and theology, above all those who had spent Mary's reign in exile on the Continent, she authorized the continuation of a programme of popular religious publishing designed to reinforce the Protestant loyalties of the nation. A primer was issued in 1559, similar in character and content to the Edwardian primer of 1553, and books of devotion continued to appear throughout the reign. The London printer John

Day (1522–1584) was especially important in this programme, and, with his son Richard (1552–?1607), he oversaw the production of the *Book of Christian Prayers* in 1578. Richard's introduction shows what a competent theologian he was; the material contained in the book represents a wide range of sources, but is marked by extensive biblical quotation and reference. These prayers were meant to inculcate not only biblical knowledge, but also the sense of living a life directly comparable to the lives of biblical saints and heroes. They also emphasize the importance of social charity and harmony.

Prayers against Sin

A PRAYER AGAINST WORLDLY CAREFULNESS

O most dear and tender Father, our defender and nourisher, endue us with thy grace, that we may cast off the great blindness of our minds, and carefulness of worldly things, and may put our whole study and care in keeping of thy holy law; and that we may labour and travail for our necessities in this life, like the birds of the air and the lilies of the field, without care. For thou hast promised to be careful for us, and hast commanded, that upon thee we should cast all our care, which livest and reignest world without end. Amen.

A PRAYER AGAINST PRIDE AND UNCHASTENESS

O thou Lord, Father, and God of my life, let me not use proudly to look, but turn away from me all filthy desires. Take from me the lust of the body, let not the desires of uncleanness take hold upon me, and give me not over into an unshamefaced and obstinate mind. Amen.

ANOTHER PRAYER AGAINST PRIDE

O Lord Christ, in most mighty power most meek, and in greatest excellency most lowly, yea, of thine own will most humble; give unto me thy mind and spirit, that I may knowledge my weakness, leavened and infected with maliciousness, that through thine example I may be humble and meek, which have no cause to boast myself. Things of the world be uncertain, left to a short use. The body is fading, frail and filthy, the mind is blind and froward; whatsoever I have of mine own, it is naught: if I have any goodness, it is of God, and not of me. Knowing this feebleness of myself, why should I magnify myself? And specially, sith thou, Lord of heaven and earth, being of such wonderful excellency, didst humble thyself to the lowest state of men, grant me true humility, that I may be exalted to the everlasting glory: which livest and reignest with the Father and the Holy Ghost for ever. Amen.

A PRAYER AGAINST ENVY

Lord, the inventor and maker of all things, and the disposer of thy gifts, which thou bestowest of thy bounteous liberality, giving to each man more than he deserveth, unto each man sufficiently, so that we have no cause of grudge or envy, sith thou givest unto all men of thine own, and unto such as deserve it not, and to each man sufficiently toward the heavenly blessedness: grant us, that we be not envious, but quietly content with thy judgment, and the disposing of thy gifts and benefits. Grant us to be thankful for that we receive, and not to murmur secretly with our selves against thy judgment and blessed will in bestowing thy free benefits; but rather, that we love and praise thy bounteous liberality, as well in others, as in our life, and always magnify thee, O Lord, the well of all gifts and goodness. To thee be glory for ever. Amen. (1)

Prayers and the Promises of God

But yet here remaineth a farther question, how it may stand with God's immutable will and decree, that our prayers should be of such strength and force to alter the threatenings which are decreed, and therefore of force must come to pass. I answer, God never promised anything in scripture, for the most part, (except it were the absolute promises concerning *Messias*, and such like,) but it hath a condition annexed unto it, either expressly, or to be understood. Likewise, he never threateneth (for the most part) but a condition is added thereunto. As for example. Adam was created of God, that he should have lived continually in blessed estate, if he would so remain: this was the condition and the decree. Destruction was preached to the Ninevites, if they repented not: this was the condition and the decree. Nineve repented, and was not destroyed, but saved: was, therefore, God's decree altered? No. For he decreed their destruction, but upon this condition, if they repented not. Pray, therefore, if thou be godly, that he would give thee the grace to continue: and if thou be sinful, pray that he give thee the grace to repent. And thus very well our prayers have strength to stay God's wrath, his decree remaining immutable, because it is threatened but upon a condition, if we repent not.

But whence hath prayer this strength? of itself? No. For we, being justified through faith, have peace toward God (that is, the favour of God) through our Lord Jesus Christ (Rom. 5). So that Christ is our mouth, whereby we speak to the Father; our eyes, by which we see the Father; our right hand, by which we offer to the Father: which Christ except he be our advocate, neither we, nor all the saints, can have anything to do with God. For no man cometh to the Father, but by him (John 14). Why then are not our prayers always heard, having continually such a spokesman, who hath all power both in heaven and earth? Truly, because either we ask amiss, not according to God's will, and that which is not for us to receive, or it pleaseth the Lord to defer our requests for trial of our faith and patience. Hereupon it was, that David said: *Expectans expectavi Dominum.* With long waiting I waited for the Lord, and he inclined unto me, and heard my calling (Psal. 40). Pray, therefore, continually with faith, love, and understanding, in the name of Jesus Christ: pray for all men, at all times, in all places, and for all things according to God's will. Though thou be a sinner, though God foreknoweth the heart, though his decree be immutable, yet pray unto him in Jesus Christ, and he will refresh thee. (2)

A PRAYER TO BE SAID AT THE LIGHTING UP OF CANDLES

Great and thick darkness overwhelmeth our hearts, O Lord, until thy light do chase it away. Thy day-sun, O most wise Workmaster, is as the cresset of this bodily world: and unto the spiritual world the cresset is thy wisdom, from whence springeth the light, both of our bodies and of our souls. At the coming of the night upon the day thou hast given us candles for a remedy of the darkness: and for a remedy of our ignorance after sin, thou hast given us thy doctrine, which thy Son (who loveth us most dearly) hath brought down unto us.

Wherefore, thou fountain and teacher of all truth, make us thorough both those lights to see such things, as may drive away the dimness of our minds. The light of thy countenance is sealed upon us, O Lord: thou hast put lightsomeness into our hearts. Thy word is a lantern to my feet, and a light to my paths. (3)

A PRAYER TO GOD FOR HIS SPIRIT, AND GRACE TO PRAY EFFECTUALLY

Eternal and most merciful Father, we know not ourselves, neither can easily understand, what, or how we should pray as we ought.

But thou art able to do exceeding abundantly above all that we ask or think.

Give us the Spirit, O Lord, to help our infirmities, which maketh request for us unto thee with sighs which cannot be expressed.

I lift up mine eyes to thee, that dwellest in the heavens.

Stir up my heart and mind, O Lord: come into me, O Spirit of God, that I may come unto thee with heart and soul, not with mouth and lips only.

Give us thy grace, that we may call upon thee, as true worshippers in spirit and truth, with the inward attention, without hypocrisy and ambition.

Grant, that I ask nothing of thee, but that which may agree to thy holy will, to thy praise and glory, and to the health of my soul.

Inspire me also with an assured hope to obtain these things, when I shall ask of thy merciful goodness with a strong and sure faith.

Neither let my prayers, O Lord, prescribe the time, when, and how, they should be fulfilled. (4)

PRAYERS FOR THE CHURCH

O singular lover of us, Christ Jesu, O bridegroom, to whom thy church is most dear, and which hast promised, that thou wilt never fail her; increase her, and multiply her, with good issue like the father, that is to wit, like thyself. Make us to be all of one mind both in thee, and in the things that concern thee, so as we may verily be that body, whereof thou art the head, being (as it were) glued and fastened together with mutual charity, kindled with that everlasting fire of thine, which hast so loved us, that thou hast spent thy blood and thy life for us.

O Christ, the author and persuader of peace, love, and good-will, soften our hard and steelly hearts, warm our icy and frozen hearts, that we may wish well one to another, so as all men may perceive us to be thy true disciples. And give us grace even now to begin to shew forth that heavenly life, wherein there is no disagreement nor hatred, but peace and love on all hands, one towards another. Amen.

The church is one body, derived from thee, O Christ, the head thereof, into divers members, knit to thee, and together among themselves, with the knot of mutual love, a great mystery of God's goodness. Now look, how great a benefit love, unity, and peace are; so great a mischief is dissension, the mother of hatred. The author of the former is God, and the author of this other is the devil. And like as nothing can be devised more blessed, than to have the earthly church to imitate the concord of the heavenly church, so nothing is more wretched than the contrary, which is the image of hell.

O head and Father of ours, thou only art of power to perform what thou listest. Therefore, gather thou us together dispersed: and knit us together now jarring, and rent asunder with opinions: unite us together, whom hatred and enmity hath set as far at odds as can be. Grant, that all of us, which are regenerated, and renewed by baptism in thy name, may close together in one body, meet for such a head as thou art, than the which none can be imagined either better or greater.

Let us be all of one mind, let us set our hearts all upon one thing, namely, upon thee, the only almighty God, and singular lover of us: which art also a most meek man, and wast nailed to the cross for our sins, and art the redeemer of mankind, and the setter up again of the whole world. Lord, asswage the great number of waves, wherewith this ship of thine is assaulted and shaken. Awake, Christ Jesu, and save us, or else we are like to suffer sore and horrible shipwreck. No strength, no wisdom, no riches of men can now help us, there remaineth no hope of remedy. Only thy merciful look can save us from this cruel storm, and make it calm again. Therefore, put to thy helping hand, that we, being preserved by thy power, may glory in thy name. Amen. (5)

NOTES / SOURCES

1. From the Primer of 1559, *Private Prayers Put Forth by Authority During the Reign of Queen Elizabeth*, ed. W. K. Clay, Cambridge (Parker Society), 1851, pp. 104–5
2. Richard Day, Preface to *The Book of Christian Prayers* (1578), ibid., pp. 436–7
3. Ibid., p. 445
4. Ibid., p. 457
5. Ibid., pp. 468–9

Richard Field   1561–1616

One of the foremost theologians of his day, Richard Field found favour under both Elizabeth I and James I, both of whom he served as Chaplain. He participated in the Hampton Court Conference in 1604 and became Dean of Gloucester (1609). He is principally known for his *Of the Church Five Bookes*, published 1606–1610. This work was an apology for the Church of England based on a number of marks of historical as well as doctrinal continuity with the Early Church, and may stand alongside Hooker's *Lawes* as a statement of the more 'Catholic' (although strongly anti-Roman) conception of the Reformed English Church.

Original Bliss

Every thing attaineth nature's perfection, by nature's force and guidance; but that other, which is divine and supernatural, consisting in the vision and fruition of God, they that attain unto it, must impute it to the sweet motions and happy directions of divine grace.

This grace God vouchsafed both men and angels in the day of their creation, thereby calling them to the participation of eternal happiness, and giving them power that they might attain to the perfection of all happy and desired good if they would, and everlastingly continue in the joyful possession of the same. But such was the infelicity of these most excellent creatures, that knowing all the different degrees of goodness found in things, and having power to make choice of what they would, joined with that mutability of nature which they were subject unto, in that they were made of nothing; they fell from the love of that which is the chief and greatest good to those of meaner quality, and thereby deprived themselves of that sweet and happy contentment they should have found in God; and denying to be subject to their great sovereign, and to perform that duty they owed unto him, were justly dispossessed of all that good, which from Him they received, and under Him should have enjoyed; yea, all other things which were made to do them service, lost their native beauty and original perfection, and became feeble, weak, unpleasant, and intractable, that in them they might find as little contentment as in themselves. For, seeing nothing can prevail or resist against the laws of the omnipotent Creator; no creature is suffered to deny the yielding of that, which from it is due to God. For either it shall be forced to yield it, by right using of that which from Him it received, or by loosing that which it would not use well; and so, consequently, if it yield not that by duty it should, by doing and working righteousness, it shall by feeling smart and misery. This then was the fall of men and angels from their first estate, in that by turning from the greater to the lesser good, they deprived themselves of that blessedness, which, though they had not of themselves, yet they were capable of, and might have attained unto, by adhering to the chief and immutable good, and so by their fault fell into those grievous evils they are now subject unto; yet in a very different sort and manner. (1)

Mercy and Discipline

The true Church admitteth and receiveth all, that with sorrowful repentance return and seek reconciliation, how great soever their offences have been; not forgetting to use due severity, which yet she sometime remitteth, either upon due consideration, or of negligence. The due and just consideration moving the Church to remit something of her wonted severity, is either private, or public peril. Private, as when the party being of a tender, timorous, and relenting disposition, if he be proceeded with rigorously, is in danger to fall into despair, or to be swallowed up with overmuch sorrow. In this case the Apostle, having excommunicated the incestuous Corinthian, writeth to the Church of Corinth speedily to receive him again, lest he should be swallowed up with overmuch grief: and in this sort the ancient bishops were wont to cut off great parts of enjoined penance; which remission and relaxation was called an indulgence. Out of the not understanding whereof, grew the Popish pardons, and indulgences. Public peril is then, when the multitude, authority, and prevailing of the offenders is so great, as that if they be cut off, and separated from the rest, a schism may justly be feared, without hope of any good to be effected thereby; in this case there is just cause why the Church forbeareth to proceed to excommunication. For whereas the end of excommunication is, that evil-doers being put from the company of right-believing Christians, and forsaken of all, may be made ashamed of their evil doing, and so brought to repentance, this cannot be looked for, when the multitude of offenders hath taken away all shame.

These are the due and just motives which cause the Church sometimes to forbear to punish with that extremity, which the quality and condition of the offender's fault may seem to require. But sometimes, of negligence, not led by any of these considerations, she omitteth the due correction of such as have offended God and scandalized his people. So the Corinthians, before the Apostle's letter written unto them, suffered an incestuous person, and seemed not much to be moved with so vile a scandal. And the like negligence is often found in the Churches of God, which notwithstanding their fault in this behalf, continue the true Churches of God still; and private men may communicate with them, that, through the Church's negligence, are thus tolerated and suffered, and that both in public acts of religion, and private conversation, without being partakers of their sins, if they neither do the same things, nor approve, like, and applaud them that do, and if they neglect not by all good means to seek their correction and amendment. (2)

The Church of Saints and Sinners

There are, and have been always some, who, possessed with a false opinion of absolute sanctity, and spotless righteousness, reject the societies and companies of them in whom any imperfection may be found; which was the furious zeal of the Pelagians in old time, and the Anabaptists in our time. Others there are, which, though they proceed not so far, yet deny those societies of Christians to be the true Churches of God, wherein the severity of discipline is so far neglected, that wicked men are suffered and tolerated without due and condign punishment. These, while they seem to hate the wicked, and fly from their company for fear of contagion, do schismatically rent, and inconsiderately divide themselves from the body of God's Church, and forsake the fellowship of the good, through immoderate hate of the wicked. But these do dangerously and damnably err; the first in that they dream of heavenly perfection to be found amongst men on earth, when as contrariwise the prophet Isaiah pronounceth, that 'all our righteousness is like the polluted and filthy rags of a menstruous woman.' And David desireth of Almighty God, that he will 'not enter into judgment with him, for that in his sight no flesh shall be justified:' and Augustine denounceth a woe against our greatest perfections, if God do straitly look upon them. The latter, though they do not require absolute and spotless perfection in them that are in and of the Church, yet think it not possible that any wicked ones should be found in so happy and blessed a society: not remembering that the Church of God is compared to 'a net, that gathereth into it all sorts of fishes, great and small, good and bad,' which are not separated one from another, till they be cast out upon the shore; that it is like 'a field sown with good seed wherein the envious man soweth tares'; like 'a floor, wherein wheat and chaff are mingled together;' like the 'ark of Noah, wherein cursed Cham was as well preserved from drowning as blessed Sem.'

But they will say, there may be hypocrites, who, for that their wickedness is not known, cannot be separated from them, who in sincerity serve and worship God; but if their wickedness break forth, that men may take notice of it, either they are presently reformed, or by the censures of the Church cut off from the rest; which course, if it be not so holden, but that wicked ones without due punishment be suffered in the midst of God's people, those societies wherein so great negligence is found, cease to be the true Churches of God, and we may, and must divide ourselves from them. This was the error of the Donatists in former times, and is the error of certain proud and arrogant sectaries in our time. But if the Church of God remained in Corinth, where there were 'divisions, sects, emulations, contentions, and quarrels;' 'and going to law one with another for every trifle, and that under the infidels;' where that 'wickedness was tolerated and winked at, which is execrable to the very heathens;' where 'Paul's name and credit was despitefully called in question, whom they should have honoured as a father;' where 'the resurrection of the dead (which is the life of Christianity) was with great scorn denied;' who dare deny those societies to be the Churches of God, wherein the tenth part of these horrible evils and abuses is not to be found? We see then the difference between the turbulent disposition of these men, and the mild affection of the Apostles of Christ, who writing to the Corinthians, and well knowing to how many evils and faults they were subject, yet doth not thunder out against them the dreadful sentence of anathema, exclude them from the kingdom of Christ, or make a division and separation from them, but calleth them the Church of Christ and society of saints. What would these men have done, if they had lived amongst the Galatians, who so far adulterated the Gospel of Christ, that the apostle pronounceth, that 'they were bewitched;' and if they still persisted in circumcision, and the works of the law with Christ, they 'were fallen from grace, and Christ could profit them nothing;' whom yet the apostle acknowledgeth to be the Church of God, writing 'to the Church which is at Galatia?' (3)

NOTES / SOURCES

1. Richard Field, *Of the Church Five Bookes*, Cambridge, 1847, pp. 10–11
2. Ibid., pp. 54–5
3. Ibid., pp. 55–8

William Shakespeare   1564–1616

The son of a well-to-do farmer, William Shakespeare was born at Stratford-upon-Avon and was educated at the Free Grammar School at Stratford from 1571 to 1577. He moved to London in 1586 and soon joined the Earl of Leicester's company of actors through which he performed at the Rose, the Curtain, and the Globe Theatres. It is thought that his early literary ventures were the revision or re-writing of plays others had written, probably for performance at Court, of which *Love's Labour's Lost* (1593–1594?) is thought to be the first. Having performed at Court during the Christmas of 1594, Shakespeare was thereafter particularly favoured by Elizabeth I. His writing career continued until 1611 or possibly 1614, *The Tempest* being thought to be his last surviving composition. In the latter part of his life he returned to Stratford where he took a prominent part in civic life and where he was buried on 25 April 1616.

Argument continues as to whether Shakespeare had direct links with Catholic recusants (though his father seems to have retained sympathies with the old religion); but by the time of his maturity as an artist, he is likely to have severed any links with such dissidents, and nothing suggests that he failed to conform to the established Church. He seldom addresses religious issues directly in his poetry or drama; but he

was clearly interested in the dangers and contradictions of the human exercise of
authority and judgement, and touches on these matters in language redolent of the
English Bible and The Book of Common Prayer. Older Catholic and even Platonic
themes surface regularly, along with the standard reflections of the age on mortality.

Mercy and Justice

ISABELLA.   Alas, alas!
   Why, all the souls that were were forfeit once;
   And He that might the vantage best have took
   Found out the remedy. How would you be,
   If He, which is the top of judgement, should
   But judge you as you are? O, think on that;
   And mercy then will breathe within your lips,
   Like man new made. (1)

Self-deceit

ISABELLA.
          . . . Man, proud man,
   Drest in a little brief authority,
   Most ignorant of what he's most assured,
   His glassy essence, like an angry ape,
   Plays such fantastic tricks before high heaven
   As make the angels weep; who, with our spleens,
   Would all themselves laugh mortal. (2)

Solidarity in Weakness

ANGELO.
   Why do you put these sayings upon me?
ISABELLA.
   Because authority, though it err like others,
   Hath yet a kind of medicine in itself,
   That skins the vice o' the top. Go to your bosom;
   Knock there, and ask your heart what it doth know
   That's like my brother's fault: if it confess
   A natural guiltiness such as is his,
   Let it not sound a thought upon your tongue
   Against my brother's life. (3)

Power and Mercy

PORTIA.
   The quality of mercy is not strain'd,
   It droppeth as the gentle rain from heaven
   Upon the place beneath: it is twice blest;

It blesseth him that gives, and him that takes:
'Tis mightiest in the mightiest: it becomes
The throned monarch better than his crown;
His sceptre shows the force of temporal power,
The attribute to awe and majesty,
Wherein doth sit the dread and fear of kings;
But mercy is above this sceptred sway;
It is enthroned in the hearts of kings,
It is an attribute to God himself;
And earthly power doth then show likest God's
When mercy seasons justice. (4)

Natural Theology

LORENZO.
Sit, Jessica. Look how the floor of heaven
Is thick inlaid with patines of bright gold:
There's not the smallest orb which thou behold'st
But in his motion like an angel sings,
Still quiring to the young-eyed cherubins;
Such harmony is in immortal souls;
But whilst this muddy vesture of decay
Doth grossly close it in, we cannot hear it. (5)

Mortal Wisdom

Poor soul, the centre of my sinful earth,
    My sinful earth these rebel powers array,
Why dost thou pine within and suffer dearth,
    Painting thy outward walls so costly gay?
Why so large cost, having so short a lease,
    Dost thou upon thy fading mansion spend?
Shall worms, inheritors of this excess
    Eat up thy charge? Is this thy body's end?
Then, soul, live thou upon thy servant's loss,
    And let that pine to aggravate thy store;
Buy terms divine in selling hours of dross;
    Within be fed, without be rich no more:
        So shalt thou feed on Death, that feeds on men,
        And Death once dead, there's no more dying then. (6)

NOTES / SOURCES

1. William Shakespeare, *Measure for Measure*, Act II, sc. ii
2. Ibid.
3. Ibid.
4. William Shakespeare, *The Merchant of Venice*, Act IV, sc. i
5. Ibid., Act V, sc. i
6. Sonnet 146

Lewis Bayly   1565–1631

Possibly a native of Carmarthen and educated at Oxford, Lewis Bayly was appointed Chaplain to Henry, Prince of Wales (son of James I), who died of typhoid fever in 1612. Although his Puritan beliefs brought him into some disfavour, he nonetheless became Chaplain to James I and in the same year (1616) was made Bishop of Bangor. He is best known for his *Practice of Piety* (1611) which won great acclaim especially among the Puritans and is known to have been an influence on John Bunyan.

Behaviour in Church

When prayers begin, lay aside thy own private meditations, and let thy heart join with the minister and the whole church, as being one body of Christ (1 Cor. xii. 12) and because that God is the God of order, he will have all things to be done in the church with one heart and accord (Acts ii. 46) and the exercises of the church are common and public (chap. iv. 32). It is therefore an ignorant pride, for a man to think his own private prayers more effectual than the public prayers of the whole church. Solomon therefore advises a man not to be rash to utter a thing in the church before God. Pray, therefore, when the church prayeth, sing when they sing; and in the action of kneeling, standing, sitting, and such indifferent ceremonies (for the avoiding of scandal, the continuance of charity, and in testimony of thine obedience), conform thyself to the manner of the church wherein thou livest (Ezek. xlvi. 10; Psal. cx. 3).

Whilst the preacher is expounding and applying the word of the Lord, look upon him; for it is a great help to stir up thine attention, and to keep thee from wandering thoughts: so the eyes of all that were in the synagogue are said to have been fastened on Christ whilst he preached, and that all the people hanged upon him when they heard him. Remember that thou art there as one of Christ's disciples, to learn the knowledge of salvation, by the remission of sins, through the tender mercy of God (Luke i. 77).

Be not, therefore, in the school of Christ, like an idle boy in a grammar-school, that often hears, but never learns his lesson; and still goes to school, but profiteth nothing. Thou hatest it in a child—Christ detesteth it in thee. To the end, therefore, that thou mayest the better profit by hearing, mark—

1. The coherence and explication of the text.
2. The chief sum or scope of the Holy Ghost in that text.
3. The division or parts of the text.
4. The doctrines; and in every doctrine, the proofs, the reasons, and the uses thereof.

A method, of all others, easiest for the people (being accustomed to it), to help them to remember the sermon; and therefore all faithful pastors, who desire to edify their people in the knowledge of God, and in his true religion, much wish it to be put in practice.

If the preacher's method be too curious or confused, then labour to remember—

1. How many things he taught which thou knewest not before; and be thankful.
2. What sins he reproved, whereof thy conscience tells thee that thou art guilty; and therefore must be amended.
3. What virtues he exhorted unto, which are not so perfect in thee; and therefore endeavour to practise them with more zeal and diligence.

But in hearing, apply every speech as spoken to thyself, rather by God than by man (Isa. ii. 3; Acts x. 33; Gal. iv. 14; 1 Thess. ii. 13); and labour not so much to hear the words of the preacher sounding in thine ear, as to feel the operation of the Spirit working in thy heart. Therefore it is said so often, 'Let him that hath an ear hear what the Spirit speaks to the church,' (Rev. ii. 7); and, 'Did not our hearts burn within us whilst he opened unto us the Scriptures?' (Luke xxiv. 32). And thus to hear the word, hath a blessing promised to it (Luke xi. 28). It is the most acceptable sacrificing of ourselves unto God (Rom. xv. 16). It is the surest note of Christ's saints (Deut. xxxiii. 3); the truest mark of Christ's sheep (John x. 4); the most apparent sign of God's elect (John viii. 47; xviii. 37); the very blood, as it were, which unites us to be the spiritual kindred, brethren and sisters of the Son of God (Luke i. 21; Mark iii. 35). This is the best art of memory for a good hearer.

When the sermon is ended—

1. Beware thou depart not like the nine lepers, till, for thine instruction to saving health, thou hast returned thanks and praise to God by an after prayer, and singing of a psalm. And when the blessing is pronounced, stand up to receive thy part therein, and hear it as if Christ himself (whose minister he is) did pronounce the same unto thee: For in this case it is true, 'He that heareth you heareth me,' (Luke x. 16); and the Sabbath day is blessed, because God hath appointed it to be the day wherein by the mouth of his ministers he will bless his people which hear his word and glorify his name (Num. vi. 23, 27). For though the Sabbath day in itself be no more blessed than the other six days, yet, because the Lord hath appointed it to holy uses above others, it as far excels the other days of the week as the consecrated bread which we receive at the Lord's table does the common bread which we eat at our own table.
2. If it be a communion-day, draw near to the Lord's table in the wedding garment of a faithful and penitent heart, to be partaker of so holy a banquet.

And when baptism[1] is to be administered, stay and behold it with all reverent attention, that so thou mayest—First, Shew thy reverence to God's ordinance; Secondly, That thou mayest the better consider thine own ingrafting into the visible

---

[1] I cannot refrain from remarking the careless and indifferent manner in which too often this divine ordinance is administered, as well as witnessed. And it is a fact, evident to the most common observer, that, generally, the minister who lays the greatest stress upon the *regenerating* efficacy of the mere rite itself, is the most remarkable for the indevout and regardless manner in which he performs the sacred service; so that spectators who knew no better might well suppose that he was hurrying over some unmeaning and distasteful ceremony, destitute of divine sanction, which had been imposed upon him, instead of dispensing a holy ordinance, necessary to salvation, commanded by Christ himself.

body of Christ's church, and how thou performest the vows of thy new covenant; Thirdly, That thou mayest repay thy debts, in praying for the infant which is to be baptized (as other Christians did in the like case for thee), that God would give him the inward effects of baptism, by his blood and Spirit; Fourthly, That thou mayest assist the church in praising God for grafting another member into his mystical body; Fifthly, That thou mayest prove whether the effects of Christ's death killeth sin in thee, and whether thou be raised to newness of life by the virtue of his resurrection; and so to be humbled for thy wants, and to be thankful for his graces; Sixthly, To shew thyself to be a freeman of Christ's corporation, having a voice or consent in the admission of others into that holy society.

If there be any collection for the poor, freely without grudging bestow thine alms, as God hath blessed thee with ability (1 Cor. xvi. 1; 2 Cor. ix. 5, 6, 7, &c).

And thus far of the duties to be performed in the holy assembly.

NOTES / SOURCES

Lewis Bayly, *The Practice of Piety*, London, 1820, pp. 197–200

John Donne   1572–1631

John Donne was brought up a Roman Catholic (his mother being the sister of a Jesuit) and his early adulthood was marked by a struggle over his religious affiliation. By 1598 he had conformed to the Church of England but was not ordained until 1615. As Dean of St Paul's (1621), he became well known as a preacher and was a favourite both of James I and Charles I. Donne's secular poetry belongs mainly to his youth, whilst his middle years (when he was earning a living from writing) produced his religious poetry. After ordination his creative skills turned to his preaching, for which he gained repute. His writings fell from favour after the Restoration; but he has long been acknowledged as one of the foremost 'metaphysical' poets of the seventeenth century, and his modern reputation is unchallenged (he was a definitively important figure for T. S. Eliot.).

I am a Little World

I am a little world made cunningly
Of Elements, and an Angelike spright,
But black sinne hath betraid to endlesse night
My worlds both parts, and (oh) both parts must die.
You which beyond that heaven which was most high
Have found new sphears, and of new lands can write,
Powre new seas in mine eyes, that so I might
Drowne my world with my weeping earnestly,
Or wash it, if it must be drown'd no more:
But oh it must be burnt! alas the fire
Of lust and envie have burnt it heretofore,
And made it fouler; Let their flames retire,
And burn me ô Lord, with a fiery zeale
Of thee and thy house, which doth in eating heale. (1)

A Hymne to Christ, at the Author's last going into Germany[1]

In what torne ship soever I embarke,
That ship shall be my embleme of thy Arke;
What sea soever swallow mee, that flood
Shall be to mee an embleme of thy blood;
Though thou with clouds of anger do disguise
Thy face; yet through that maske I know those eyes,
     Which, though they turne away sometimes, they never will despise.

I sacrifice this Iland unto thee,
And all whom I lov'd there, and who lov'd mee;
When I have put our seas twixt them and mee,
Put thou thy sea betwixt my sinnes and thee.
As the trees sap doth seeke the root below
In winter, in my winter now I goe,
     Where none but thee, th'Eternall root of true Love I may know.

Nor thou nor thy religion dost controule,
The amorousnesse of an harmonious Soule,
But thou would'st have that love thy selfe: As thou
Art jealous, Lord, so I am jealous now,
Thou lov'st not, till from loving more, thou free
My soule: Who ever gives, takes libertie:
     O, if thou car'st not whom I love alas, thou lov'st not mee.

Seale then this bill of my Divorce to All,
On whom those fainter beames of love did fall;
Marry those loves, which in youth scatter'd bee
On Fame, Wit, Hopes (false mistresses) to thee.
Churches are best for Prayer, that have least light:
To see God only, I goe out of sight:
     And to scape stormy dayes, I chuse an Everlasting night. (2)

A Hymne to God the Father

I

Wilt thou forgive that sinne where I begunne,
   Which is my sin, though it were done before?
Wilt thou forgive those sinnes through which I runne,
   And do run still: though still I do deplore?
     When thou hast done, thou hast not done,
          For, I have more.

---

[1] The title refers to Donne's journey to the Continent with Lord Doncaster on 12 May 1619.

II

Wilt thou forgive that sinne by which I'have wonne
　　Others to sinne? and, made my sinne their doore?
Wilt thou forgive that sinne which I did shunne
　　A yeare, or two: but wallow'd in, a score?
　　　　When thou hast done, thou hast not done,
　　　　　　　For I have more.

III

I have a sinne of feare, that when I have spunne
　　My last thred, I shall perish on the shore;
But sweare by thy selfe, that at my death thy sonne
　　Shall shine as he shines now, and heretofore;
　　　　And, having done that, Thou hast done,
　　　　　　　I have no more. (3)

Reading the Bible in Community

One opinion makes not catholic doctrine, one man makes not a Church. For this knowledge of God, the Church is our academy; there we must be bred and there we may be bred all our lives and yet learn nothing. Therefore, as we must be there, so there we must use the means, and the means in the Church are the Ordinances, and institutions of the Church.

The most powerful means is the Scripture, but the Scripture in the Church. Not that we are discouraged from reading the Scripture at home: God forbid we should think any Christian family to be out of the Church. At home the Holy Ghost is with thee in the reading of the Scriptures, but there he is with thee as a remembrancer ('The Holy Ghost shall bring to your remembrance whatsoever I have said unto you,' says our Savior (John 14. 26)). Here in the Church he is with thee as a Doctor to teach thee. First learn at Church and then meditate at home. Receive the seed by hearing the Scriptures interpreted here and water it by returning to those places at home. When Christ bids you 'Search the Scriptures' (John 5. 39), he means you should go to them, who have a warrant to search, a warrant in their calling. To know which are Scriptures, to know what the Holy Ghost says in the Scriptures, apply thyself to the Church. Not that the Church is a judge above the Scriptures (for the power and the commission which the Church hath, it hath from the Scriptures), but the Church is a judge above thee, which are the Scriptures and what is the sense of the Holy Ghost in them.

So then thy means are the Scriptures. That is thy evidence. But then this evidence must be sealed to thee in the Sacraments and delivered to thee in preaching, and so sealed and delivered to thee in the presence of competent witnesses, the congregation. When St Paul was carried up . . . in an ecstasy 'into Paradise' (2 Cor. 12. 4), that which he gained by this powerful way of teaching is not expressed in a '*Vidit*,' but an '*Audivit*.' It is not said that he saw, but that he heard unspeakable things. The eye is the devil's door, before the ear, for, though he do enter at the ear by wanton discourse, yet he was at the eye before. We see before we talk dangerously. But the ear is the Holy Ghost's first door. He assists us with ritual and ceremonial things which we see in the Church, but ceremonies have their right use when their right use hath first been taught by preaching. Therefore to hearing does the Apostle apply faith. And, as the Church is our academy and our medium the Ordinances of the Church, so the light by which we see this, that is know God so as to make him our God, is faith; and that is our other consideration in this part. (4)

The Vision of Glory

The light of glory is such a light as that our Schoolmen dare not say confidently that every beam of it is not all of it. When some of them say that some souls see some things in God and others, others, because all have not the same measure of the light of glory, the rest cry down that opinion and say that as the essence of God is indivisible and he that sees any of it sees all of it, so is the light of glory communicated entirely to every blessed soul. God made light first, and three days after that light became a sun, a more glorious light. God gave me the light of nature when I quickened in my mother's womb by receiving a reasonable soul. And God gave me the light of faith when I quickened in my second mother's womb, the Church, by receiving my baptism. But in my third day, when my mortality shall put on immortality, he shall give me the light of glory, by which I shall see himself. To this light of glory the light of honor is but a glow-worm; the majesty itself but a twilight; the cherubims and seraphims are but candles; and that Gospel itself, which the Apostle calls the glorious Gospel, but a star of the least magnitude. And if I cannot tell what to call this light by which I shall see it, what shall I call that which I shall see by it, the essence of God himself? And yet there is something else than this sight of God intended in that which remains. I shall not only 'see God face to face,' but I shall 'know' him (which, as you have seen all the way, is above sight) and 'know him, even as also I am known.'

   In this consideration, God alone is all. In all the former there was a place, and a means, and a light; here, for this perfect knowledge of God, God is all those. 'Then,' says the Apostle, 'God shall be all in all' (1 Cor. 15. 28). . . . Says St. Jerome, here God does all in all; but here he does all by instruments; even in the infusing of faith he works by the ministry of the Gospel; but there he shall be all in all, do all in all, immediately by himself; for Christ shall deliver up the kingdom to God, even the Father (1 Cor. 15. 24). His kingdom is the administration of his Church by his Ordinances in the Church. At the resurrection there shall be an end of that kingdom; no more Church; no more working upon men by preaching, but God himself shall be all in all. '*Ministri quasi larvæ Dei*,' says Luther. It may be somewhat too familiarly, too vulgarly said, but usefully, 'The ministry of the Gospel is but as God's vizor,' for by such a liberty the Apostle here calls it *ænigma*, a riddle, or (as Luther says too) God's picture; but in the resurrection God shall put off that vizor and turn away that picture and show us his own face. Therefore is it said, 'That in heaven there is no temple, but God himself is the temple' (Rev. 21. 22). God is service, and music, and psalm, and sermon, and sacrament, and all *Erit vita de verbo sine verbo*. 'We shall live upon the word and hear never a word;' live upon him, who being the word, was made flesh, the eternal Son of God. *Hic non est omnia in omnibus, sed pars in singulis*. 'Here God is not all in all; where he is at all in any man, that man is well.' *In Solomone sapientia*, says that father: it was well with Solomon, because God was wisdom with him, and patience in Job, and faith in Peter, and zeal in Paul but there was something in all these, which God was not. But in heaven he shall be so all in all . . . that every soul shall have every perfection in itself; and the perfection of these perfections shall be that their sight shall be 'face to face,' and their knowledge 'as they are known.' (5)

Knowledge in Heaven

And there we shall 'see him face to face,' by the light of his countenance, which is the light of glory. What shall we see, by seeing him so, 'face to face?' . . . We shall see whatsoever we can be the better for seeing. First of all, all things that they believed here, they shall see there; and therefore . . . let us meditate upon no other things on earth then we would be glad to think on in heaven. And this consideration would put many frivolous and many fond thoughts out of our mind, if men and women would love another but so, as that love might last in heaven.

This then we shall get concerning ourselves, by seeing God 'face to face;' but what concerning God? Nothing but the sight of the humanity of Christ, which only is visible to the eye. So Theodoret, so some others have thought, but that answers not the *sicuti est*. And we know we shall see God (not only the body of Christ) as he is in his essence. Why? Did all that are said 'to have seen God face to face' see his essence? No. In earth God assumed some material things to appear in and is said 'to have been seen face to face' when he was seen in those assumed forms. But in heaven there is no material thing to be assumed, and if God be seen face to face there, he is seen in his essence. St. Augustine sums it up fully, upon these words, '*In lumine tuo*, In thy light we shall see light, *Te scilicet in te*,' we shall see thee in thee; that is, says he, 'face to face.'

And then, what is it 'to know him, as we are known?' First, is that it which is intended here, 'That we shall know God as we are known'? It is not expressed in the text so. It is only 'that we shall know so;' not 'that we shall know God so.' But the frame and context of the place hath drawn that unanimous exposition from all that it is meant of our knowledge of God then. A comprehensive knowledge of God it cannot be. To comprehend is to know a thing as well as that thing can be known; and we can never know God so, but that he will know himself better. Our knowledge cannot be so dilated, nor God condensed and contracted so, as that we can know him that way, comprehensively. It cannot be such a knowledge of God as God hath of himself, nor as God hath of us; for God comprehends us and all this world and all the worlds that he could have made, and himself. But it is, *nota similitudinis, non æqualitatis*. As God knows me, so I shall know God; but I shall not know God so as God knows me. It is not *quantum*, but *sicut*; not as much, but as truly; as the fire does as truly shine as the sun shines, though it shine not out so far, nor to so many purposes. So then I shall know God so as that there shall be nothing in me to hinder me from knowing God; which cannot be said of the nature of man, though regenerate, upon earth, no, nor of the nature of an angel in heaven, left to itself, till both have received a super-illustration from the light of glory.

And so it shall be a knowledge so like his knowledge, as it shall produce a love like his love, and we shall love him as he loves us. For, as St. Chrysostom and the rest of the fathers whom Oecumenius hath compacted interpret it, '*Cognoscam practicè, id est, accurendo.*' I shall know him, that is embrace him, adhere to him. *Qualis sine fine festivitas!* What a Holyday shall this be, which no working day shall ever follow! By knowing and loving the unchangeable, the immutable God, '*mutabimur in immutabilitatem,*' we shall be changed into an unchangeableness, says that father that never said anything but extraordinarily. He says more, '*Dei præsentia si in inferno appareret.*' If God could be seen and known in hell, hell in an instant would be heaven.

How many heavens are there in heaven? How is heaven multiplied to every soul in heaven, where infinite other happinesses are crowned with this, this sight and this knowledge of God there? And how shall all those heavens be renewed to us every day, '*qui non mirabimur hodiè,*' that shall be as glad to see and to know God, millions of ages after every day's seeing and knowing, as the first hour of looking upon his face. And as this seeing and this knowing of God crowns all other joys and glories, even in heaven, so this very crown is crowned. There grows from this a higher glory, which is *participes erimus Divinæ naturæ* (1 Peter 1. 4 words, of which Luther says, that both testaments afford none equal to them), 'That we shall be made partakers of the Divine nature'—immortal as the Father, righteous as the Son, and full of all comfort as the Holy Ghost.

Let me dismiss you with an easy request of St. Augustine. '*Fieri non potest ut seipsum non diligat, qui Deum diligit*; that man does not love God, that loves not himself.' Do but love yourselves. '*Imo solus se diligere novit, qui Deum diligit*; only that man that loves God, hath the art of love to himself.' Do but love yourselves. For if he love God, he would live eternally with him, and if he desire that, and endeavor it earnestly, he does truly love himself, and not otherwise. And he loves himself, who by seeing God in the theater of the world, and in the glass of the creature, by the light of reason, and knowing God in the academy of the Church, by the Ordinances thereof, through the light of faith, endeavors to see God in heaven, by the manifestation of himself, through the light of glory, and to know God himself, in himself, and by himself as he is all in all; contemplatively by knowing as he is known, practically by loving as he is loved. (6)

The Weight of Affliction

Let me wither and wear out my age in a discomfortable, in an unwholesome, in a penurious prison, and so pay my debts with my bones and recompense the wastefulness of my youth with the beggary of my age. Let me wither under sharp and foul and infamous diseases, and so recompense the wantonness of my youth with that loathesomeness in my age. Yet if God withdraw not his spiritual blessings, his grace, his patience; if I can call my suffering his doing, my passion his action, all this that is temporal is but a caterpillar got into one corner of my garden, but a mildew fallen upon one acre of my corn. The body of all, the substance of all, is safe as long as the soul is safe.

But when I shall trust to that which we call a good spirit, and God shall deject, and impoverish, and evacuate that spirit; when I shall rely upon a moral constancy and God shall shake, and enfeeble, and enervate, destroy and demolish that constancy; when I shall think to refresh myself in the serenity and sweet air of a good conscience and God shall call up the damps and vapors of hell itself and spread a cloud of diffidence and an impenetrable crust of desperation upon my conscience; when health shall fly from me, and I shall lay hold upon riches to succor me and comfort me in my sickness, and riches shall fly from me and I shall snatch after favor and good opinion to comfort me in my poverty; when even this good opinion shall leave me and calumnies and misinformation shall prevail against me; when I shall need peace because there is none but thou, O Lord, that should stand for me, and then shall find that all the wounds have come from thy hand, all the arrows that stick in me from thy quiver; when I shall see that because I have given myself to my corrupt nature, thou hast changed thine; and because I am all evil towards thee, therefore thou hast given over being good towards me; when it comes to this height, that the fever is not in the humors but in the spirits, that mine enemy is not an imaginary enemy (fortune) nor a transitory enemy (malice in great persons), but a real, and an irresistible, and an inexorable, and an everlasting enemy, the Lord of Hosts himself, the Almighty God himself—the Almighty God himself only knows the weight of this affliction. And except he put in that *pondus gloriæ*, exceeding weight of an eternal glory, with his own hand, into the other scale, we are weighed down, we are swallowed up, irreparably, irrevocably, irrecoverably, irremediably.

This is the fearful depth, this is spiritual misery, to be thus fallen from God. But was this David's case? Was he fallen thus far into a diffidence in God? No. But the danger, the precipice, the slippery sliding into that bottomless depth, is to be excluded from the means of coming to God, or staying with God. And this is what David laments here, that by being banished and driven into the wilderness of Judah, he had not access to the sanctuary of the Lord, to sacrifice his part in the praise and to receive his part in the prayers of the congregation. For Angels pass not to ends but by ways and means, nor men to the glory of the Triumphant Church but by participation of the Communion of the Militant. (7)

Longing and Satisfaction

There is a spiritual fulness in this life, of which St. Jerome speaks, . . . 'A happy excess and a wholesome surfet . . . in which the more we eat the more temperate we are, and the more we drink, the more sober.' In which (as St. Bernard also expresses it, in his mellifluence) . . . 'By a mutual and reciprocal, by an undeterminable and unexpressible generation of one another . . . the desire of spiritual graces begets satiety,' if I would be, I am full of them. And then this satiety begets a farther desire, still we have a new appetite to those spiritual graces. This is a holy ambition, a sacred covetousness, and a wholesome dropsy. Napthali's blessing, 'O Napthali satisfied with favor and full with the blessing of the Lord' (Deut. 33. 23); St. Stephen's blessing, 'Full of faith and of the Holy Ghost' (Acts 6. 5); the blessed Virgin's blessing, 'Full of grace' (Luke 1. 28); Dorcas' blessing, 'Full of good works and of almsdeeds' (Acts 9. 36); the blessing of him, who is blessed above all, and who blesseth all, Christ Jesus, 'Full of wisdom' (Luke 2. 40), 'Full of the Holy Ghost' (Luke 4. 1), 'Full of grace and truth' (John 1. 14). But so far are all temporal things from giving this fulness or satisfaction, as that even in spiritual things, there may be, there is often an error or mistaking.

Even in spiritual things there may be a fulness and no satisfaction. And there may be satisfaction and no fulness. I may have as much knowledge as is presently necessary for my salvation, and yet have a restless and unsatisfied desire to search into unprofitable curiosities, unrevealed mysteries, and inextricable perplexities. And, on the other side, a man may be satisfied and think he knows all when, God knows, he knows nothing at all. For I know nothing if I know not Christ crucified, and I know not that if I know not how to apply him to myself. Nor do I know that if I embrace him not in those means which he hath afforded me in his church, in his Word and Sacraments. If I neglect this means, this place, these exercises, howsoever I may satisfy myself with an over-valuing mine own knowledge at home, I am so far from fulness as that vanity itself is not more empty.

In the wilderness every man had one and the same measure of manna, the same gomer went through all, for manna was a meat that would melt in their mouths, and of easy digestion. But then for their quails, birds of a higher flight, meat of a stronger digestion, it is not said, that every man had an equal number. Some might have more, some less, and yet all their fulness. Catechistical divinity, and instructions in fundamental things, is our manna. Every man is bound to take his gomer, his explicit knowledge or articles necessary to salvation. The simplest man, as well as the greatest doctor, is bound to know that there is one God in three persons, that the second of those, the Son of God, took our nature and died for mankind. And that there is a Holy Ghost, which in the Communion of Saints, the church established by Christ, applies to every particular soul the benefit of Christ's universal redemption. But then for our quails, birds of a higher pitch, meat of a stronger digestion, which is the knowledge how to rectify every straying conscience, how to extricate every entangled and scrupulous and perplexed soul, in all emergent doubts, how to defend our church and our religion from all the mines and all the batteries of our adversaries, and to deliver her from all imputations of heresy and schism which they impute to us, this knowledge is not equally necessary in all. In many cases a master of servants and a father of children is bound to know more than those children and servants, and the pastor of the parish more than parishioners. They may have their fulness, though he have more, but he hath not his except he be able to give them satisfaction.

This fulness then is not an equality in the measure; our fulness in heaven shall not be so . . . In a word, the fulness that is inquired after, and required by this prayer, carry it upon temporal, carry it upon spiritual things, is such a proportion of either, as is fit for that calling in which God hath put us. (8)

Microcosm

It is too little to call man a little world; except God, man is a diminutive to nothing. Man consists of more pieces, more parts, than the world; than the world doth, nay, than the world is. And if those pieces were extended, and stretched out in man as they are in the world, man would be the giant, and the world the dwarf; the world but the map, and the man the world. If all the veins in our bodies were extended to rivers, and all the sinews to veins of mines, and all the muscles that lie upon one another, to hills, and all the bones to quarries of stones, and all the other pieces to the proportion of those which correspond to them in the world, the air would be too little for this orb of man to move in, the firmament would be but enough for this star; for, as the whole world hath nothing, to which something in man doth not answer, so hath man many pieces of which the whole world hath no representation. Enlarge this meditation upon this great world, man, so far as to consider the immensity of the creatures this world produces; our creatures are our thoughts, creatures that are born giants; that reach from east to west, from earth to heaven; that do not only bestride all the sea and land, but span the sun and firmament at once; my thoughts reach all, comprehend all. Inexplicable mystery; I their creator am in a close prison, in a sick bed, any where, and any one of my creatures, my thoughts, is with the sun, and beyond the sun, overtakes the sun, and overgoes the sun in one pace, one step, everywhere. (9)

Prayer in Sickness

O eternal and most gracious God, who hast made little things to signify great, and conveyed the infinite merits of thy Son in the water of baptism, and in the bread and wine of thy other sacrament, unto us, receive the sacrifice of my humble thanks, that thou hast not only afforded me the ability to rise out of this bed of weariness and discomfort, but hast also made this bodily rising, by thy grace, an earnest of a second resurrection from sin, and of a third, to everlasting glory. Thy Son himself, always infinite in himself, and incapable of addition, was yet pleased to grow in the Virgin's womb, and to grow in stature in the sight of men. Thy good purposes upon me, I know, have their determination and perfection in thy holy will upon me; there thy grace is, and there I am altogether; but manifest them so unto me, in thy seasons, and in thy measures and degrees, that I may not only have that comfort of knowing thee to be infinitely good, but that also of finding thee to be every day better and better to me; and that as thou gavest Saint Paul the messenger of Satan, to humble him so for my humiliation, thou mayst give me thyself in this knowledge, that what grace soever thou afford me today, yet I should perish tomorrow if I had not had tomorrow's grace too. Therefore I beg of thee my daily bread; and as thou gavest me the bread of sorrow for many days, and since the bread of hope for some, and this day the bread of possessing, in rising by that strength, which thou the God of all strength hast infused into me, so, O Lord, continue to me the bread of life: the spiritual bread of life, in a faithful assurance in thee; the sacramental bread of life, in a worthy receiving of thee; and the more real bread of life in an everlasting union to thee. (10)

Prayer and Praise

If we compare these two incomparable duties, prayer and praise, it will stand thus: Our prayers besiege God (as Tertullian speaks, especially of public prayer in the congregation . . .) but our praises prescribe in God, we urge him, and press him, with his ancient mercies, his mercies of old. By prayer we incline him, we bend him, but by praise we bind him; our thanks for former benefits, is a producing of a specialty, by which he hath contracted with us for more. In prayer we sue to him, but in praise we sue him himself. Prayer is our petition, but praise is as our evidence. In that we beg, in this we plead. God hath no law upon himself, but yet God himself proceeds by precedent, and whensoever we present to him with thanksgiving what he hath done, he does the same, and more again. Neither certainly can the church institute any prayers more effectual for the preservation of religion, or of the state, then the collects for our deliverances, in the like cases before. And when he hears them, though they have the nature of praise only, yet he translates them into prayers. And when we ourselves know not how much we stand in need of new deliverances, he delivers us from dangers which we never suspected, from armies and navies which we never knew were prepared, and from plots and machinations which we never knew were brought into consultation, and diverts their forces and dissipates their counsels with an untimely abortion. And farther I extend not this first part of prayer in general, in which, to that which you may have heard often and usefully of the duty and dignity of prayer, I have only added this of the method and elements thereof, that prayer consists as much of praise for the past, as of supplication for the future. (11)

NOTES / SOURCES

Standard editions are readily available. The texts are reproduced here from *John Donne: Selections from Divine Poems, Sermons, Devotions*, and *Prayers*, ed. J. Booty, New York/Mahwah (Classics of Western Spirituality), 1990

1. John Donne, *Divine Poems*, 14, ed. cit., p. 83
2. Ed. cit., p. 104
3. Ibid., p. 106
4. From a sermon for Easter Day, 1628, on 1 Cor. 13. 12; ibid., pp. 143–4
5. Ibid., pp. 148–9
6. Ibid., pp. 150–2
7. From a pre-Lent sermon of 1625 on Ps. 63. 7; ibid., pp. 174–5
8. From a sermon of 1621 or 1622 on Ps. 90. 14; ibid., pp. 204–5
9. From *Devotions*, ibid., p. 257
10. Ibid., p. 285
11. From the sermon cited in n. 8; ibid., p. 201

William Laud   1573–1645

Born at Reading, William Laud was a student of St John's College, Oxford, where he became a Fellow (1593) and later President (1611). A noted opponent of Calvinist theology, Laud found favour under Charles I and became Chancellor of the University of Oxford (1630) and, after holding several increasingly important bishoprics, Archbishop of Canterbury (1633). He attempted to impose liturgical uniformity, a policy which was opposed by the Puritans and failed disastrously in Scotland (1637). His introduction at the Sitting of Convocation in 1640 of a new canon upholding the Divine Right of Kings and the imposition of the 'Etcetera Oath' made him deeply unpopular and led to his impeachment by the Long Parliament. Following his imprisonment in the Tower (1641) he was executed on Tower Hill, London, on 10 January 1645. He collaborated in the publication of Andrewes's *Ninety-Six Sermons* in 1629, and was also involved in anti-Roman controversy.

God's Cause

The cause of the Church, in what kind soever it be,—be it in the cause of truth, or in the cause of unity, or in the cause of right and means,—it is God's cause too: and it must needs be so; for Christ and His Church are 'head and body' (Eph. i.

22, 23): and, therefore, they must needs have one common cause. One cause; and you cannot corrupt the Church in her truth, or persecute her for it, nor distract her from her unity, nor impoverish and abuse her in her means, but God suffers in the oppression. Nay more, no man can wilfully corrupt the Church in her doctrine, but he would have a false God; nor persecute the profession of the Church, but he would have no God; nor rent the Church into sects, but he would have many gods; nor make the Church base, but he would pluck God as low, were God as much in his power as the Church is; and, therefore, the Church's cause is God's cause. And as Eusebius tells us, when by Stephen, Bishop of Laodicea, the state of that Church was much hazarded; it, and the means of it, were mightily upheld by God Himself. And Elias Cretensis goes full upon it in the general. It is 'God's cause,' any controversy that He debates against His 'enemies.'

Now this ever holds true, in whatsoever the Church suffers for the name of God and Christ. And therefore if either State or Church will have their 'cause' God's, the State must look their proceedings be just, and the Church must look their devotions and actions be pious. Else, if the State be all in wormwood and injustice; if the Church savour of impurity and irreligion; if either of these threaten either body, neither can call upon God then. For sin is their own and the devil's 'cause,' no 'cause' of God's, who punishes sin ever, but never 'causes' it. (1)

Unity, Political and Spiritual

The 'unity,' then, 'of the Spirit,' to which the apostle exhorts, includes both; both concord in mind and affections, and love of charitable unity, which comes from the Spirit of God, and returns to it. And, indeed, the grace of God's Spirit is that alone which makes men truly at peace and unity one with another. *Ei tribuendum non nobis*; to Him it is to be attributed, not to us, saith Saint Augustine. It is 'He that makes men to be of one mind in an house.' Now one mind in the Church, and one mind in the State, come from the same fountain with 'one mind in an house;' all from 'the Spirit.' And so the Apostle clearly, 'one body, and one Spirit,' that is, 'one body,' by 'one Spirit.' For it is 'the Spirit' that joins all the members of the Church into 'one body.' And it is the Church that blesses the State, not simply with 'unity,' but with that unity with which itself is blessed of God. A State not Christian may have 'unity' in it. Yes; and so may a State that hath lost all Christianity, save the name. But 'unity of the Spirit' nor Church nor State can longer hold, than they do in some measure obey the 'Spirit,' and love the 'unity.'

This 'unity of the Spirit' is closer than any corporal union can be; for spirits meet where bodies cannot, and nearer than bodies can. The reason is given by Saint Chrysostom: because the soul or spirit of man is more simple, and of one form. And the soul apter in itself to union is made more apt by the Spirit of God which is 'one,' and loves nothing but as it tends to one. Nay, as the Spirit of God is one, and cannot dissent from itself, no more ought they whom the Spirit hath joined in one; and the Spirit hath joined the Church in one; therefore he that divides the unity of the Church, practises against the 'unity of the Spirit.'

Now this 'unity of the Spirit,' so called because it proceeds from the Spirit of grace, continues in obedience to it, and in the end brings us to the Spirit that gave it, is the cause of all other 'unity' that is good; and the want of it, the cause of all defects in 'unity.' The presence of it is the cause of all 'unity' that is good; of all within the Church, no man doubts. But it is of all without the Church too. For no heathen men or states did ever agree in any good thing whatsoever, but their 'unity' proceeded from this 'Spirit,' and was so far forth at least 'a unity of the Spirit.' And for States that are Christian, and have mutual relations to the Church that is in them, Saint Gregory's rule is true: the unity of the State depends much upon the peace and unity of the Church; therefore upon the guidance of the same 'Spirit.'

And as the presence of 'the unity of the Spirit' is the cause of all 'unity' that is good; so the want of it is the cause of all defects in 'unity.' For as in the body of a man the spirit holds the members together, but if the soul depart, the members fall asunder; so it is in the Church, saith Theophylact, and so in the State. So little 'unity,' then, in Christendom as is, is a great argument that 'the Spirit is grieved,' and hath justly withdrawn much of His influence. And how is the Spirit grieved? How? why, sure by our neglect, if not contempt, of Him as He is 'one.' For as He is the 'Spirit of fortitude,' there we will have Him,—He shall defend us in war. And as He is 'the Spirit of wisdom,' there we will have Him too,—He shall govern us in peace. But as He is 'one Spirit,' and requires that we keep His 'unity,' there we will none of Him; though we know right well, that without 'unity' peace cannot continue, nor war prosper.

One unity there is—take heed of it—it is a great enemy to the 'unity of the Spirit,' both in Church and commonwealth. Saint Basil calls it *concors odium*, unity in hatred to persecute the Church. And to this work there is 'unity' enough; 'men take counsel together.' Saint Augustine calls it *unitatem contra unitatem*, a unity against unity; when pagans, Jews, and heretics, or any profane crew whatsoever, make a league against the Church's 'unity.' And about that work, 'that the name of Israel may be no more in remembrance,' that there may be no Church, or no reformed Church, 'Gebal, and Ammon, and Amalek, the Philistines, and they that dwell at Tyre, are confederates together.' Saint Hilary will not vouchsafe to call such union 'unity;' indeed it deserves not the name, it is not unity, saith he, be it in Church, or be it in State; but it is a combination. And he gives this reason: for unity is in faith and obedience; but combination is *consortium factionis*, no other, no better, the consenting in a faction. And all faction is a fraction too, and an enemy to 'unity,' even while it combines in one. For while it combines but a part, it destroys the unity of the whole.

Is 'the Spirit in this?' Out of question, No. For a faction to compass its end, I will not say, 'when it sees a thief it consents to him;' or that it is always 'partaker with the adulterers;' but this it doth, 'it speaks against its own brother, and slanders its own mother's son.' Can any man call this 'the unity of the Spirit?' or is this the way to 'unity?'

And now I cannot but wonder what words Saint Paul, were he now alive, would use, to call back 'unity' into dismembered Christendom. For my part, death were easier to me, than it is to see and consider the face of the Church of Christ scratched and torn, till it bleeds in every part, as it doth this day. (2)

NOTES / SOURCES

1. William Laud, 'Sermon on the Fast Day', *The Works of William Laud*, ed. W. Scott, Vol. 1, Oxford (Library of Anglo-Catholic Theology), 1847, pp. 132–3
2. William Laud, *Sermons Before King Charles's Third Parliament*, ibid., pp. 162–5

Rhys Prichard   1579–1644

Prichard was born at Llanymddyfri (Llandovery) and educated at Jesus College, Oxford, returning to his native town as vicar in 1602. In 1614, he became chaplain to the Earl of Essex and a Prebendary of the collegiate foundation of Christ College, Brecon; in 1626 he was appointed Chancellor of St Davids. Despite his Puritan leanings, he did not approve of the Parliamentary rebellion. He wrote a considerable quantity of simple religious verse, whose purpose was to teach his rural parishioners the elements of Christian ethics and Reformed theology. The collection of these verses, published as a whole in 1681 and entitled *Canwyll y Cymro*, 'The Welshman's Candle', was one of the most influential religious books in the Welsh language for many generations.

Christ is All in All

Christ himself is all in all,
Keeping man from being lost,
No one, nothing but Christ himself
Suffices to keep the soul of man . . .

Christ alone and Christ himself,
Christ with no one taking any part or share,
Christ with none but Christ himself,
The only Saviour of man's soul.

Christ our ransom, Christ our sacrifice,
Christ our offering, Christ our strength;
Christ our treasure, Christ our light,
Christ, with all this, our true redeemer . . .

Christ himself is our righteousness,
Our sanctification, our true wisdom,
Our deliverance, our full price,
Christ is our comfort, Christ our Saviour . . .

Christ, with no help from any saint,
Christ with no aid from man or woman,
Christ with none but Christ himself,
The only Saviour of man's soul.

No one but Christ himself bears
The weight and burden of our stain and sin:
No one has ploughed the field in blood and tears
But God's own Son, weighed down by our faults . . .

God wanted no angel's help,
No saint's mediation, or effort or travail;
Martyr's blood or human work,
Only Christ's work to save the Christian . . .

Jesus' blood, the blood of the covenant,
Is the blood that cleanses from sin:
Not the blood of all the martyrs is able
To wash away the least of our defilement.

It is not the work of saints or angels
That preserves the soul of the Christian:
It is the work of our Redeemer, Christ alone,
That saves lost man.

The work of two natures in one person
Keeps the soul of the Christian:
Our Redeemer, God and man, must
Work his work before even one can be saved . . . (1)

Let us go to Bethlehem

Let us all go to Bethlehem, singing,
Leaping, dancing and rejoicing,
To see our dear Redeemer
Born today, Christmas Day.

He has been born in Bethlehem,
In the stable, behind the inn;
Let us all, all Christians go to present ourselves
And turn our gaze on him . . .

Let us go to see the freeborn Son,
Older than his mother, the same age as his Father;
Son and Father of the mother and daughter [maid]:
The less we say, the more we love . . .

Let us go to see the conqueror of death
Bound in swaddling cloths;
The Son who tears apart Satan's kingdom
In the crib, unable even to scratch himself.

Let us go to see the Messiah,
The Redeemer our faith speaks of, our peace, our order;
The only Saviour of our souls
On Mary's arm, sucking her breasts . . .

Let us go to see the daughter [maid] who is a mother,
The mother who is a maid [daughter], peaceful and spotless:
The daughter [maid] nursing her Father in his wrappings,
The Father sucking the child's breasts.

Let us go to see the master-builder
Who made the sun and all the planets,
The great heavens with so royal a rule,
Lying here in the stable . . . (2)

NOTES / SOURCES

1. Rhys Prichard no. 82, 'Crist sydd oll yn oll', in *Gogoneddus Arglwydd, Henffych Well! Detholiad o ryddiaeth a barddoniaeth Gristnogol Gymraeg drwy'r Canrifoedd*, ed. Gwynn ap Gwilym, Churches Together in Wales 1999, pp. 151–2; tr. R. D. W.

2. Rhys Prichard no. 83, 'Awn I Fethlem,' ibid., pp. 153–4 (extracts); tr. R. D. W.

James Ussher   1581–1656

The son of a Dublin lawyer, James Ussher was a scholar of the newly founded Trinity College, Dublin (1594), where he became a Fellow (1599) and later the first Professor of Divinity (1607–1621). Appointed Bishop of Meath (1621) and Archbishop of Armagh (1625), Ussher was known both for his encyclopaedic scholarship as well as his tolerance in matters of doctrine. A Calvinist in theology, he rejected the 1604 Anglican canons in favour of the Irish ones of 1634. Such was his standing that he was afforded a state funeral in Westminster Abbey by Oliver Cromwell.

Union with Christ

Yet was it fit also, that this head should be of the same nature with the body which is knit unto it: and therefore that he should so be God, as that he might partake of our flesh likewise. 'For we are members of his body,' saith the same apostle, 'of his flesh, and of his bones.' And, 'except ye eat the flesh of the Son of man,' saith our Saviour himself, 'and drink his blood, ye have no life in you.' 'He that eateth my flesh, and drinketh my blood, dwelleth in me, and I in him.' Declaring thereby, first, that by his mystical and supernatural union, we are as truly conjoined with him, as the meat and drink we take is with us, when by the ordinary work of nature, it is converted into our own substance. Secondly, that this conjunction is immediately made with his human nature. Thirdly, that the 'Lamb slain,' that is, 'Christ crucified,' hath by that death of his, made his flesh broken, and his blood poured out for us upon the cross, to be fit food for the spiritual nourishment of our souls, and the very well-spring from whence, by the power of his Godhead, all life and grace is derived unto us.

Upon this ground it is, that the apostle telleth us, that we 'have boldness to enter into the Holiest by the blood of Jesus, by a new and living way which he hath consecrated for us, through the vail, that is to say, his flesh.' That as in the tabernacle, there was no passing from the Holy to the most Holy place, but by the vail; so now there is no passage to be looked for from the Church militant to the Church triumphant, but by the flesh of him, who hath said of himself, 'I am the way, the truth and the life; no man cometh unto the Father but by me.' Jacob in his dream beheld 'a ladder set upon the earth, the top whereof reached to heaven, and the angels of God ascending and descending on it, the Lord himself standing above it.' Of which vision none can give a better interpretation than he who was prefigured therein, gave unto Nathanael: 'Hereafter you shall see heaven opened, and the angels of God ascending and descending upon the Son of man.' Whence we may well collect, that the only means whereby God standing above, and his Israel lying here below are conjoined together, and the only ladder whereby heaven may be scaled by us, is the Son of man; the type of whose flesh, the vail, was therefore commanded to be made with cherubims, to shew that we come 'to an innumerable company of angels,' when we come to 'Jesus, the Mediator of the New Testament:' who as the head of the Church hath power to 'send forth all those ministering spirits, to minister for them who shall be heirs of salvation.' (1)

Righteousness

Q. What are the parts of repentance?

A. Two. A true grief wrought in the heart of the believer, for offending so gracious a God by his former transgressions. And a conversion unto God again, with full purpose of heart ever after to cleave unto him, and to refrain from that which shall be displeasing in his sight.

Q. What is the direction of that obedience which God requireth of man?

A. The moral law: whereof the ten commandments are an abridgement.

Q. What is the sum of the law?

A. Love.

Q. What be the parts thereof?

A. The love which we owe unto God, commanded in the first; and the love which we owe unto our neighbour, commanded in the second table.

Q. How do you distinguish the four commandments which belong unto the first table?

A. They do either respect the conforming of the inward powers of the soul to the acknowledgment of the true God, as the first commandment; or the holy use of the outward means of God's worship, as the three following.

Q. What are the duties which concern the outward means of God's worship?

A. They are either such as are to be performed every day, as occasion shall require; or such as are appointed for a certain day.

Q. What commandments do belong unto the first kind?

A. The second, concerning the solemn worship of religion; and the third, concerning that respect which we are to have of God's honour in the common carriage of our life.

Q. What commandment belongeth to the second kind?

A. The fourth; enjoining the special sanctification of the Sabbath day.

Q. How do you distinguish the six commandments, belonging to the second table?

A. The first five do order such actions as are joined with consent of the mind at least: the last respecteth the first motions that arise in the heart, before any consent is given.

Q. What are the duties appertaining to the first kind?

A. They are either due unto certain persons in regard of some special bond; or unto all men in general, by a common right, the first sort is set down in the fifth commandment: the other in the four next.

Q. What is the outward means whereby the Gospel is offered unto mankind?

A. The ministry of the Gospel; which is exercised in the visible Church of Christ.

Q. Of whom doth the visible Church consist?

A. Of public officers, ordained to be ministers of Christ, and disposers of heavenly things, according to the prescript of the Lord: and the rest of the saints, who with obedience are to subject themselves unto the ordinances of God.

Q. What are the parts of the outward ministry?

A. The administration of the Word, and of the ordinances annexed thereunto; which are especially sacraments and censures.

Q. What is the Word?

A. That part of the outward ministry, which consisteth in the delivery of doctrine: and this is the ordinary instrument which God useth in begetting faith. (2)

Enduring Injustice

'The Lord knoweth,' saith St. Peter, 'how to deliver the godly out of temptations; and to reserve the unjust unto the day of judgment to be punished.' And although 'the wrath of man worketh not the righteousness of God:' yet doth God so order the matter, that 'The wrath of man shall praise him, and the remainder of wrath shall be restrained by him.' Whereupon St. Augustine when he had declared, that 'The power even of hurtful kings is from none but God;' for the justifying of his proceeding therein he addeth, that 'It is not unjust that naughty men receiving power to hurt, both the patience of the good should be tried, and the iniquity of the wicked persecutors should be punished.' For, as he elsewhere also noteth: 'When emperors do make evil laws for falsehood and against the truth, the right believers are tried, and such as persevere are crowned.' And again: 'The terror of the temporal powers, when it doth oppose the truth, is to the just and strong a glorious trial, but to the weak a dangerous temptation: but when it proposeth the truth to such as err, and are at discord; to men of understanding it proveth a profitable admonition, and to such as are not sensible thereof an unprofitable affliction. And yet there is no power but of God; and he that resisteth the power, resisteth the ordinance of God: for rulers are not a terror to good works, but to the evil. Wilt thou then not be afraid of the power? do that which is good, and thou shalt have praise for the same. For whether power favouring the truth, doth correct any man, he that is amended hath praise thereby; or being enemy to the truth, doth use cruelty against any, he that receiveth the crown for obtaining the victory hath praise for the same.' And therefore, saith he: 'If thy governor be good, he is thy nourisher: if he be evil, he is thy tempter. Receive thy nourishment willingly, and approve thyself in temptation. Be thou gold: consider this world as the furnace of the workman. In one narrow place there are three things: gold, chaff, and fire. The fire is put unto the other two: the chaff is burned, the gold is purged. To which kind of 'fiery trial' those passages of Scripture are to be referred: 'When he hath tried me, I shall come forth as gold.' 'That the trial of your faith being much more precious than of gold that perisheth, though it be tried with fire, might be so found unto praise, and honour, and glory, at the appearing of Jesus Christ.' 'Many shall be purified and made white and tried.'

'Blessed is the man that endureth temptation: for when he is tried, he shall receive the crown of life, which the Lord hath promised to them that love him.'

To draw them to a conclusion of this point. 'Either thou dost justly, and the just power will praise thee; or thus doing justly, although the unjust power should condemn thee, the just God will crown thee;' is the saying of Primasius. (3)

Christian Joy

Now, when he saith, Rejoice ye righteous in the Lord, one might object and think, that these words were an abridgment to God's children. What, may some say, may they not rejoice in anything, but in the Lord? May they not rejoice in seeing their friends, their children, or their blessings, but only in God? I answer, you must understand that this is no restraint to God's children from their joy, but it is added for a direction for them to moderate their joys. Thou mayest rejoice in thy friends and children, which God hath given thee; but also remember that that which setteth thine heart on work by thy joy in God. I rejoice in my children, my friends, my wealth, yet always I must have an eye unto God, as these are gifts coming from him. And of this there is good reason, because it is the power of God which maketh the joy to be; from him is the life of all: good reason then that in all things we should have respect unto the giver. This should moderate all joy in this life, that always God be the founder of them, that he accompany us in our merry feasts, that he be the founder of them. And this I mark as a special point, because there are many who think this to be the utter destruction of joy; if a man at a merry meeting maketh mention of God, then they think all the sport is spoiled. And if the children of God be at a feast, cannot they rejoice as well as the wicked? I defy that wicked man, which should take any such comfort in these outward things, as the children of God can: they are their's and belong unto them; they are the owners of them, and have them under God's seal; whereas the wicked are but usurpers, and shall one day answer for abusing them.

But here is the point, if in a feast a righteous man talk of God, this puts his heart on work, this is the tune and string of the feast; there is no true joy so long as his tongue is out of tune. It is otherwise with the wicked, who may be censured as the wife was who loured always in her husband's presence, being joyful in his absence. What should we, I pray you, think of such a woman, but that she were not a good wife, and that all were not well betwixt her husband and she? So may we judge of these men, who think there can be no joy when God standeth by; talk of God, and then all mirth is destroyed: he is counted an indifferent man who, when we come to be merry, is always talking of God; which showeth their joy to be unsound, when the talk of God marreth the feast. It is a wicked thing when he who is our joy, procureth all our joy, without whom we cannot rejoice, should be he who marreth all our joy. Therefore we may so far only rejoice in earthly things as God is amongst us, one eye being always towards the giver. But if otherwise we rejoice with consideration of God's mercy, if we have an eye to God as well in our mirth as otherwise, this is a true sign that our joy is true. (4)

Renewing Mercy

There is difference between an act done, and an act continued; when the world was made by God, God had finished that work. And when Christ took our flesh upon him, the act was done; but the forgiveness of sin is a continued act, which holds to-day and to-morrow, and world without end. God is pleased not to impute thy sins, but cover them; now this covering is no constant act, but upon a supposition of constant indulgence, which ought to be solicited by constant prayer. I may cover a thing now, and uncover it again; now forgiveness of sin being an act not complete, but continued, and continued world without end, and therefore we say the saints in heaven are justified by imputative righteousness, God's continuance of his act of mercy. The point then is this; as long as we continue in the world, and by contrary acts of disobedience continue to provoke God to discontinue his former acts of mercy, and our sins being but covered, therefore so long must we pray for forgiveness. (5)

NOTES / SOURCES

1. James Ussher, *The Incarnation of the Son of God*, The Works of Archbishop Ussher, ed. C. R. Elrington, Dublin, 1864, Vol. IV, pp. 608–9
2. James Ussher, *The Method of Christian Religion*, ibid., Vol. XI, pp. 214–5
3. James Ussher, *The Power of the Prince*, ibid., pp. 374–6
4. James Ussher, *Sermons*, ibid., Vol. XIII, pp. 466–7
5. Ibid., p. 253

William Forbes   1585–1634

Forbes was a native of Aberdeen, where he taught Logic for a few years after graduating. From 1606 to 1611 he studied in Europe and then spent some time in Oxford before returning to Scotland to be ordained. He was a minister in Aberdeen from 1616 to 1621, and, after a brief and not very happy interlude in Edinburgh, resumed his work in Aberdeen, where he enjoyed a good deal of popularity. In 1633, impressed by his reputation as a preacher and scholar, Charles I created the new see of Edinburgh for him, but he did not long survive his assumption of office in 1634, and was spared the final and bloody stages of the savage controversies about episcopacy that racked Scotland at this period. Forbes's 'Considerationes modestae', a monumental essay on the doctrine of justification, arguing a strong case against many aspects of orthodox Calvinism, was assembled from his notes and published in 1658.

Faith and Forgiveness

Justifying faith is the instrument or medium by which we obtain forgiveness of sins, and therefore it is the cause of it, and must be prior to it in the order of nature at least. Secondly, whether we say that by justifying faith we believe that our sins have been already forgiven, or that they are forgiven at the present moment, yet forgiveness is, in either case, considered as the object of faith, and therefore in nature it would precede faith; for the object is not created by that act of which it is the object; because the act of the intellect or will (at least of that which is created) does not make its object, but always presupposes it, as vision does not make the visible object, but supposes it. I therefore regret that Daniel Chamier (to name no others), a man in other respects not void of learning or eloquence, should have on these grounds so inconsiderately affirmed that 'justifying faith, if not in time, yet in reason at least follows justification;' and that 'faith is not the cause of justification.' Therefore he says that 'faith justifies, not because it effects justification, but because it is effected in and required from a justified person.' These are most absurd statements, nor will any sane and sober Protestant deny that faith is an efficient cause of justification; not indeed the principal nor the meritorious, but the instrumental cause, as the words 'by' and 'through' signify, (as Romanists rightly urge from St. Paul); and that therefore it is always prior to justification in the order of nature. Thirdly, those who contend that justifying faith is the assurance of the forgiveness of sins, as accomplished whether at some previous time or now at this present, do not, as they suppose, comfort those who are troubled in mind, but rather from most persons they altogether take away every consolation, and all but plunge them into the abyss of despair. For how many pious souls firmly and from the heart believe and assent to the gospel promises, and even recline solely on Christ alone, who nevertheless are not certain, much less persuaded by a divine faith, that their sins have been forgiven, although they desire this above all things. God forbid that we should say that these are destitute of saving faith, and therefore incapable of salvation. (1)

Faith and Assurance

Justifying faith (to speak accurately and theologically) is nothing else than a firm and sure assent of the mind, produced by the Holy Ghost from the word, by which we acknowledge all things revealed by God in the Scriptures, and especially those concerning the mystery of our redemption and salvation, wrought by Christ, to be most true, by reason of the authority of God who has revealed them.

Therefore, considered in itself and in its essence, it is nothing else than Catholic faith, which itself doubtless justifies a man, if all the other things which are necessary to justification accompany it.

And its subject is the intellect, and not the will, although belief is ruled by the will; for 'faith is a willing assent of the soul;' 'Other things a man can do though unwilling; but he can believe only when he is willing;' and when the act of belief is in Scripture attributed to the heart, we must thereby understand the mind; since to believe, properly speaking, is nothing else than to assent to what is said, and to account it true; for thus far we have shown, by many proofs, that assurance is no part of faith, nor indeed does it properly belong to hope either; for assurance is an assurance not only of what is future, but also of what is present, as when any one confides in his strength when carrying a burden, or in his swiftness when he runs; yet it approaches nearer to the nature of hope than to that of faith, whence it is said to be 'hope strengthened.' (2)

Continuing Struggle and Continuing Growth

We willingly therefore grant, that in the regenerate, the flesh, (to wit, its concupiscence,) is often moved against the spirit, in some more often, in others less often, according to their greater or lesser advance in grace; but we deny that it moreover struggles against the spirit always, and necessarily, and that in every one. For it cannot be denied that some acts are done without any grief and sorrow of soul, nay with great joy, by those at least whom the Scripture, in comparison of those who are more imperfect, calls grown up and perfect. For the Scripture protests in many passages against the contrary assertion, as does the experience of many among the faithful also. (3)

Continuing Forgiveness

Justification certainly is a continuous act, which is and lasts so long as the acts of living faith endure; but is broken off always, and as often as they cease, contrary to the duty of Christian piety. (4)

Unity and the Sacrament

There is nothing more to be lamented in this sad religious dissension than that whereas this all-holy sacrament of the Eucharist was specially instituted by our Lord Christ, that by it we might be more closely incorporated into Him, and receive continuous supplies of life from Him, and by a mutual love be more firmly joined among ourselves under Christ our one head; yet Satan, that most dire enemy of the human race, by his wickedness and audacity, and very many doctors and ministers of the Church, from their love of contending and lust of rule, have now for many centuries past, and most especially in this present age abused it, and still abuse it day by day, to the purpose of supplying food for strife and factiousness. May the merciful God grant in Christ with the Holy Ghost, that, all contention being done away, all Christians may again, on this matter as in all others, return to unity with concord in their hearts, without the loss of any verity necessary to be believed. (5)

NOTES / SOURCES

1. William Forbes, 'Considerationes Modestae (. . . On Justification)', in *The Works of William Forbes*, ed. G. H. Forbes, Oxford (Library of Anglo-Catholic Theology), Vol. I, 1850, pp. 11–13
2. Ibid., p. 17
3. Ibid., p. 397
4. Ibid., p. 409
5. William Forbes, 'Consideratio Aequa (A Moderate and Peaceful Consideration . . . of the Eucharist),' ed. cit., vol. II, Oxford, 1856, pp. 379–81

Francis Quarles

1592–1644

Born at Romford, Francis Quarles was educated at Christ's College, Cambridge, and Lincoln's Inn. In 1620 he began to publish a series of biblical paraphrases including Jonah and Job. He became Private Secretary to Ussher, Archbishop of Armagh (1629), during which time he published his famous 'Emblems' (1635). Appointed Chronologer to the City of London (1640), his latter years were spent writing devotional literature, though his defence of Charles I led to the destruction of his manuscripts by Parliamentary soldiers. His works were widely reprinted in the century following his death in 1644.

My Beloved is Mine and I am His

Even like two little bank-dividing brooks,
　　That wash the pebbles with their wanton streams,
And having ranged and searched a thousand nooks,
　　Meet both at length in silver-breasted Thames
　　　Where in a greater current they conjoin:
So I my Best-Beloved's am, so he is mine.

Even so we met; and after long pursuit
　　Even so we joined; we both became entire;
No need for either to renew a suit,
　　For I was flax and he was flames of fire:
　　　Our firm united souls did more than twine,
So I my Best-Beloved's am, so he is mine.

If all those glittering monarchs that command
　　The servile quarters of this earthly ball
Should tender in exchange their shares of land,
　　I would not change my fortunes for them all;
　　　Their wealth is but a counter to my coin;
The world's but theirs, but my Beloved's mine.

Nay, more: if the fair Thespian ladies all
　　Should heap together their diviner treasure,
That treasure should be deemed a price too small
　　To buy a minute's lease of half my pleasure.
　　　'Tis not the sacred wealth of all the Nine
Can buy my heart from him, or his from being mine.

Nor time, nor place, nor chance, nor death can bow
　　My least desires unto the least remove;
He's firmly mine by oath, I his by vow;
　　He's mine by faith, and I am his by love;
　　　He's mine by water, I am his by wine;
Thus I my Best-Beloved's am, thus he is mine.

He is my altar, I his holy place;
　　I am his guest, and he my living food;
I'm his by penitence, he mine by grace;
　　I'm his by purchase, he is mine by blood;

He's my supporting elm, and I his vine:
Thus I my Best-Beloved's am, thus he is mine.

He gives me wealth, I give him all my vows;
 I give him songs, he gives me length of days;
With wreaths of grace he crowns my conquering brows;
 And I his temples with a crown of praise,
  Which he accepts as an everlasting sign,
That I my Best-Beloved's am; that he is mine.

Nicholas Ferrar and the Little Gidding Community   1592–1637

A brilliant student at Clare Hall, Cambridge, Nicholas Ferrar was forced to leave the University because of ill health and spent some five years travelling on the Continent. He worked for the Virginia Company and became a Member of Parliament (1624) but the political outlook and his own religious vocation took him in a new direction. In 1625 he established a community at Little Gidding, near Huntingdon, where he brought together his brother's and brothers-in-law's families to live a community life under the disciplines of the Church of England. William Laud ordained him deacon in 1626 and the community was visited by Charles I (1633), who was said to be greatly impressed. After Ferrar's death (1637) the community fell foul of the Puritans who destroyed most of his manuscripts and eventually caused his 'Arminian Nunnery' to be disbanded by Parliament (1647).

Welcoming Words

[I.H.S.]

He who by reproof of our errors and remonstrance of that which is more perfect seeks to make us better is welcome as an angel of God.

but

He who in any way goes about to disturb us in that which is or ought to be among Christians, tho' it be not usual in the world, is a burden whilst he stays, and shall bear his judgment whoever he be.

and

He who by a cheerful participation and approbation of that which is good, confirms us in the same, is welcome as a Christian friend.

but

and

He who censures us in absence for that which in presence he made a show to approve of, doth by a double guilt of flattery and slander violate both the bands of friendship and Christianity. (1)

A Vow of Celibacy

[I.H.S.]

[IN THE NAME OF GOD. AMEN]

'Mine honoured parents and dearest friends that I may not be wanting in what I am able to perform, I beseech you accept of my humblest thanks which I tender to you, for that it hath pleased you freely to give me your consent to that which I so much desired both from God and from you—that is, that I may end my days in a Virgin's Estate. And this desire, I hope, hath been of and from God, although mixed with much corruption of my own, for which I crave pardon; and further beseech that none would judge it to proceed either of persuasion by anyone to it, or that I contemn the estate of marriage, or think it inferior to that which I choose. For I here profess in the sight of Heaven that the choice be freely my own, not any other's further than their leave; not out of contempt for that of Marriage, for I truly honour it, but have not the heart . . . mine own choice.[1] Wherefore, as I have had your consents to be freed from it, so I humbly oblige your prayer that I may continue so in my desires and that your blessings may rest on me. (2)

Humility

There were two brethren, the one of a great Age and long exercised, the other younger and but a Novice in true and pure Religion, who being late together one Night at their Devotion, the Lampe which hung between them went out suddenly. Whereupon the younger rose and lighted it againe, but in vaine. He was scarce well settled in his place when it went out again, and a third time; at which the elder, being much troubled for the interruption of his better thoughts, gave his Brother not only sharp words but by a sore Blow that chastisement which, he told him, was due for his negligent or unskilful trimming of the Lampe. The younger, though he knew the Imputation wrong, and knew not how to mend the fault, yet seeing plainly a fault, was content to take it upon himselfe; and now finding the immediate Cause, either in himselfe or in the Lampe, not only began to think but to say that it was guilt of his former errors that now without cause made the light fail and bred disturbance in those holy Exercizes, whereof (sayth he, turning to his brother and kissing the hand that strook him) by how much I am unworthy to partake, by so much I beseech your fervent prayers may bee the more intended for mee, that the light and fire of grace which God has kindled in my heart may never be quenched by mine own sinnes or any devises of the evil one. The remembrance of my grievous Crimes would persuade mee so to interpret this strange accident, but God's mercy assures me the contrary, and that hee will never fail to give new illumination to my soule whenever darkness overshadows it, as I will still supply fresh light to this extinguished Lampe. Having so said, and stepping to the fire to do what he had said, the Lampe burst out of itself with an unusual Flame and brightness. At which, whilst they both stood amazed, and the old Man began a little to swell in the Conceit of his

[1] The manuscript is torn here and several words are missing.

Holiness, to which the spirit of vain glory persuaded him to attribute this admirable effect, they heard a voice, which was of greater Majesty of sound than can proceed from Man's Brest, told the elder that as the Lighting, so the putting out of the Lampe was miraculous. This last by the Devill's Malice to cause diversion in their good Imployment, and to raise Contention between them; but the lighting of it again was by God's appointment, and the Ministry of an Angell. Not in regard of thy holiness (sayd the Voice) which both by Error and Impatiency hath manifested itselfe to be much more imperfect than thou perhaps esteemdst it, but in approbation of thy Brother's Patience and Humility, which in God's account is of farre greater worth than all thine Innocency with the least taint of self conceit thereunto annexed. Not he that doth most, but he that thinks least of himselfe gains the Prize in well doing; and he that in suffering Evil lays the blame on himselfe getts the soonest cleare. He that meekely condemns himself as worthy of what he undergoes makes God to plead his Cause, and getts certaine pardon, though he be in fault. But if innocent, the wrong that he thus takes and beares turnes to a Crown both of Glory and Content.

[. . .]

There's no sin so inconpetible with God's grace as Pride; there's no kind of pride so evil as that which perswades itselfe to deserve God's grace.

Let a man search well (says the Cheife) and he shall find that there's no entanglement of the soul in any sin whatsoever, but the fastening of the corde is always in some kind of Pride or other. (3)

Patience

I thought the exercise of Patience a burden that would tyre out my strength, a block that encombred the way and made me stumble, and made me fall, and therefore thought even Impatience itselfe in removing that which was offensive to have been a piece of wisedome, a practize of goodness. That nobody should crosse mee, that nothing should be contrary to my mind, was that which I supposed most just to desire, most profitable to endeavour. I see my errour, I feele my losse. (4)

Ferrar's Deathbed

'Oh what a blessed change is here! What do I see? Oh, let us come and sing unto the Lord and magnify His holy name together! I have been at a great feast.'

'At a feast, dear father?' asked Mary Collet.

'Aye,' he replied, 'at a great feast, the great King's feast.' (5)

A Thanksgiving Prayer

Thou has given us a freedom from all other affairs that we may without distraction attend Thy service. That Holy Gospel which came down from heaven, with things the angels desire to look into, is by Thy goodness continually open to our view; the sweet music thereof is continually sounding in our ears; heavenly songs are by Thy mercy put into our mouths, and our tongues and our lips made daily instruments of pouring forth Thy praise. This, Lord, is the work of, and this the pleasure of, angels in heaven; and dost Thou vouchsafe to make us partakers of so high a happiness? The knowledge of Thee and of Thy Son is everlasting life. Thy service is perfect freedom; how happy are we that thou dost constantly retain us in the daily exercises thereof! (6)

NOTES / SOURCES

Material is scattered and not easily accessible; see particularly E. C. Sharland, ed., *The Story Books of Little Gidding*, London, 1899, and *The Ferrar Papers*, Cambridge, 1938. Texts here are mostly quoted from Margaret Cropper, *Flame Touches Flame*, London, 1949

1. Inscription on the parlour wall at Little Gidding; Cropper, p. 50
2. Vow of celibacy by Anna Collett (Ferrar's niece), from A. L. Maycock, *Nicholas Ferrar of Little Gidding*, London, 1938, p. 184
3. From the Storybooks; Cropper, pp. 64–6
4. Ibid., p. 66
5. Ibid., p. 71
6. Ibid., pp. 71–2

Henry King   1592–1669

The son of John King, Bishop of London (1611–21), Henry King became Archdeacon of Colchester (1617) and Canon of Christ Church, Oxford (1624), before being appointed Bishop of Chichester (1642). A friend of John Donne, the poet, and of Izaak Walton, the biographer and author of *The Compleat Angler*, King published secular as well as religious poetry, and a substantial number of sermons.

Praying Christ's Prayer

In this short Prayer, as in a little Orbe, the Sonne of righteousnesse moves. From hence doth every Starre, every faithfull servant and Confessor of Christ (for they are Incarnate Starres), borrow a ray of light, to illuminate and sanctifie the body of his meditations—The Church in her Liturgie, and the Preacher both enjoyn'd to use it. A small quantity of this Leven seasons a great lumpe of Devotion, and a few spirits give taste & quicknesse to much liquor. This Prayer is a *Quintessence* extracted by the greatest Chymist that ever was, from Him that brought Nature out of Chaos, Separated Light from Darknesse, and extracted the foure Elements out of Nothing. All parts of it are spirits: *Quæ enim spiritualior oratio.*[1] And the mixture of a few graines therof with our prayers proves the strongest and best Christian Antidote. Let us gladly *use that forme of Prayer which Christ our Lord hath taught us* ('tis Cyprian's inference), and give unto God what the Sonne of God gave unto us. *It is a familiar and friendly tribute to present God with his owne.* A petition *cloth'd in Christ's words* will finde the ready way to heaven, and *a speedy accesse into the eares of God.*

And when the Father acknowledges his Sonne's words in our Prayers, hee will acknowledge and ratifie that promise, which through him he made unto us, that *whatsoever we should aske him in his sonne's name should not be denied.* (1)

[1] For what prayer is more spiritual?

The Language of Prayer

'Tis most requisite when we speake to God, we should use a decent Method, an orderly proceeding, since he is the *God of Order*. 'Twere a rude presumption for any to sue unto him in that fashion which they would not use unto men, if their superiours. When wee make any request unto them, we hold it manners to prefix some modest introduction before the suit, wee doe not bluntly discover it at first. If thou begin a Petition with this homely phrase, and in this peremptory manner, *Give mee what I require*, can it avoid the censure of rudenesse?—As if thou cam'st to command, not intreat, and to challenge or lay a claime to a favour, not to sue for it. And canst thou hold it fit to petition Almighty God without some preface, as well to confesse his power as to declare thine owne modesty?

Humblenesse becomes the person of a suitour. *To beseech* is a terme that confounds an ingenious man, dejects and casts downe his looks, as asham'd that his eye should follow the suit which his tongue preferres. Which bashfull recognition of his wants finds an easie way to pitty: whereas he that begs in arrogant termes or impudent behaviour shuts up the hand of bounty, and destroyes the good intention of the giver. The dejected *Publican* in the Gospell stood fairer and better justified in our Saviour's estimation than the *Pharisee*, insolently bragging of his worth (Luke 18. 14).

You shall finde in the Scripture that Prophets and holy men, whensoever they spake or prayed unto God, used some Preface, to prepare his eare and to make way for their words. When Abraham besought God concerning Sodome (Gen. 18. 27), he begins, *Let not my Lord bee angry if I speake that am but dust and ashes.* And Moses, pleading for the people (Exodus 34. 9), begins, *If I have found favour in thy sight.* And when David prayes unto God to forget *the sinnes of his youth*, he makes a commemoration of the goodnes and mercy of God, *Remember, O Lord, thy tender mercies, etc. even for thy goodnesse' sake* (Psal. 25. 6, 7). It gives life and hope to our Petitions when before wee aske, we urge God with the precedents of his owne goodnesse. This kinde of acknowledgement is *Ad plus dandum invitatio*, a fit preparing of his favour; and wee invite him to grant againe when we revive what already he hath done. Good cause then had our Saviour to lay the ground of our Petitions on God's *fatherly* care and love to us, by bidding us cry *Our Father*. That as Orators, before they plead, use some *Exordium or Preface* to make the Judge favourable to their causes, so wee, being to speake unto the Judge of Heaven and Earth, might by this beginning make him propitious to our Prayers.

Whereby let mee note unto you, formes of Oratory and Rhetoricke are allowed in our Devotions: *Eloquentiam non pugnare cum simplicitate religionis.*[1] Nor doth Christ dislike an elegant Prayer.

And let mee tell those men who have such an unlearned conceit of God's service, that they think it a trespasse of high nature to staine their Discourses with a Latine sentence, or authority of Fathers quoted in their owne dialect; or that make it a nice case of Conscience to present God with a set studied Prayer, or any other forme of speech than *Quod in buccam venerit*: what comes into their heads whilest they are speaking, when the tongue strives with the Invention for precedence or at least both goe together—that if they please they may bee more

---

[1] Eloquence does not war with simplicity in religion.

elaborate, take more paines and time for what they speake then an extemporary minute or an instant, unlesse they finde it more for their ease to keepe unto that naturall vaine of theirs, unstudied or unlaboured; and hold it a better protection and excuse, for those that know little, to condemne Learning and all that know more then themselves.

I confesse that *Pia rusticitas*, Devotion clothed in the rudest phrase that can be, is to bee preferred before eloquent hypocrisie, and an holy Ignorance is better than learned irreligion. I would advice all men to use more Religion than Rhetoricke in their Prayers; yet none can deny but that an eloquent Meditation, so it be not affected, and so it doe not *Exercendæ linguæ magis operam dare quam menti mundandæ*,[1] is acceptable both to God and Men.

View the Scripture, the Dictate and worke of the Holy Ghost: you shall finde that for the elegance of the phrase and weight of the words, it passes all the weake shallow Oratory of Man's tongue. Therefore Saint Augustine calls it *the venerable stile of the Holy Ghost*. And in the Gospell, the Jewes acknowledged our Saviour for the best Rhetorician that ever was: *He spake as never man spake* (Joh. 7. 46). The practick perfection of which Eloquence he hath declar'd in nothing more then in this Prayer, which in a narrow compasse comprehends the summe of all Oratory, Brevity, and Elegance and Perspicuity.

In the beginning, it was the Trinity which fathered all mankinde: *Faciamus hominem*, which originall title of Son to that Father Man might still have preserv'd, had he not by his wilfull disobedience made a forfeiture of it. For though God had setled an estate upon Adam, it was not so firmly intailed but that it might bee, and was, quickly cut off. His sinne did dis-inherit him, and us in him, dispossest him of the Garden, his first Mansion and Patrimony, and devested him of the title of a Sonne: For hee was then no more *filius Dei*, the Sonne of God, but *servus peccati*, sinne's bondslave. Nay (saith Saint Augustine), *before Christ's mercy, the Devill only had title to him*, and in that bondage was he concluded till that time; by whose mediation God was reconceil'd to Man, and the lost Sonne acknowledged by the right Father (Gal. 4. 7): *Iam non servus est sed filius; quod si filius hæres*. So that Christ, having now by grace restor'd to Man what originally hee lost, purchased the title of Sonne by Adoption. Since that we tooke from Creation was extinct, he held it meetest that, as God now tooke us for his children, wee should also in our Prayers claime him for *Our Father*. Since we had received *Spiritum Adoptionis filiorum Dei*, the spirit of Adoption should crie *Abba, Father* (Rom. 8. 15): So beginning where Adam left, and directing our supplications to that Father which first made us, the *Blessed Trinity*.

Which though it be here meant, yet is not the Essentiall name, as *Deus or Dominus*, God or Lord, used, but a Personall *Father—Voca me patrem* (as 'tis in the Prophet (Jerem. 3. 19)): *Call me not Lord, but Father*.

Saint Chrysostome gives the reason. God (saith he) would be called *Father*, and not *Lord*, that hee might give us more confidence of obtaining what wee sue for. Servants doe not always finde an easinesse in their Lords to grant what they aske, but Sonnes presume it. (2)

---

[1] Serve rather to exercise the tongue than adorn the mind.

NOTES / SOURCES

1. Henry King, *An Exposition Upon the Lord's Prayer*, London, 1634, p. 39
2. Ibid., pp. 43–50

George Herbert   1593–1633

Educated at Westminster School and Trinity College, Cambridge, George Herbert's skills in composition and performance were acknowledged through his appointment as Public Orator of Cambridge University in 1620. Under the influence of Nicholas Ferrar, Herbert studied theology and was ordained priest in 1630, becoming Rector of Fugglestone with Bemerton where he remained until his death (1633). His works, published posthumously, include *The Priest to the Temple; or The Countrey Parson* (1652) and a collection of poems entitled *The Temple*, which was entrusted to Nicholas Ferrar. His work influenced writers as diverse as Henry Vaughan, Charles Wesley, and Gerard Manley Hopkins, and several of his poems have become popular as hymns.

Affliction

My heart did heave, and there came forth, *O God!*
By that I knew that thou wast in the grief,
To guide and govern it to my relief,
    Making a scepter of the rod:
      Hadst thou not had thy part,
Sure the unruly sigh had broke my heart.

But since thy breath gave me both life and shape,
Thou knowst my tallies; and when there's assign'd
So much breath to a sigh, what's then behinde?
    Or if some yeares with it escape,
      The sigh then onely is
A gale to bring me sooner to my blisse.

Thy life on earth was grief, and thou art still
Constant unto it, making it to be
A point of honour, now to grieve in me,
    And in thy members suffer ill.
      They who lament one crosse,
Thou dying dayly, praise thee to thy losse. (1)

Prayer

  Of what an easie quick accesse,
My blessed Lord, art thou! how suddenly
  May our requests thine eare invade!
To shew that state dislikes not easinesse,
If I but lift mine eyes, my suit is made:
Thou canst no more not heare, then thou canst die.

Of what supreme almightie power
Is thy great arm, which spans the east and west,
    And tacks the centre to the sphere!
By it do all things live their measur'd houre:
We cannot ask the thing, which is not there,
Blaming the shallownesse of our request.

Of what unmeasurable love
Art thou possest, who, when thou couldst not die,
    Wert fain to take our flesh and curse,
And for our sakes in person sinne reprove,
That by destroying that which ty'd thy purse,
Thou mightst make way for liberalitie!

Since then these three wait on thy throne,
Ease, Power, and *Love*; I value prayer so,
    That were I to leave all but one,
Wealth, fame, endowments, vertues, all should go;
I and deare prayer would together dwell,
And quickly gain, for each inch lost, an ell. (2)

Aaron

Holinesse on the head,
    Light and perfections on the breast,
Harmonious bells below, raising the dead
    To leade them unto life and rest:
        Thus are true Aarons drest.

Profanenesse in my head,
    Defects and darknesse in my breast,
A noise of passions ringing me for dead
    Unto a place where is no rest:
        Poore priest thus am I drest.

Onely another head
    I have, another heart and breast,
Another musick, making live not dead,
    Without whom I could have no rest:
        In him I am well drest.

Christ is my onely head,
    My alone onely heart and breast,
My onely musick, striking me ev'n dead;
    That to the old man I may rest,
        And be in him new drest.

So holy in my head,
  Perfect and light in my deare breast,
My doctrine tun'd by Christ, (who is not dead,
  But lives in me while I do rest)
    Come people, Aaron's drest. (3)

The Holy Communion

O gratious Lord, how shall I know
Whether in these gifts thou bee so
    As thou art evry-where;
Or rather so, as thou alone
Tak'st all the Lodging, leaving none
    ffor thy poore creature there?

ffirst I am sure, whether bread stay
Or whether Bread doe fly away
    Concerneth bread, not mee.
But that both thou and all thy traine
Bee there, to thy truth, and my gaine,
    Concerneth mee and Thee.

And if in comming to thy foes
Thou dost come first to them, that showes
    The hast of thy good will.
Or if that thou two stations makest
In Bread and mee, the way thou takest
    Is more, but for mee still.

Then of this also I am sure
That thou didst all those pains endure
    To' abolish Sinn, not Wheat.
Creatures are good, and have their place;
Sinn onely, which did all deface,
    Thou drivest from his seat.

I could beleeue an Impanation
At the rate of an Incarnation,
    If thou hadst dyde for Bread.
But that which made my soule to dye,
My flesh, and fleshly villany,
    That allso made thee dead.

That fflesh is there, mine eyes deny:
And what shold flesh but flesh discry,
    The noblest sence of five?
If glorious bodies pass the sight,
Shall they be food and strength and might
    Euen there, where they deceiue?

Into my soule this cannot pass;
fflesh (though exalted) keeps his grass
   And cannot turn to soule.
Bodyes and Minds are different Spheres,
Nor can they change their bounds and meres,
   But keep a constant Pole.

This gift of all gifts is the best,
Thy flesh the least that I request.
   Thou took'st that pledg from mee:
Give me not that I had before,
Or give mee that, so I have more;
   My God, give mee all Thee. (4)

Perseverance

My God, the poore expressions of my Love
Which warme these lines and serve them vp to thee
Are so, as for the present I did moue,
   Or rather as thou mouedst mee.

But what shall issue, whither these my words
Shal help another, but my iudgment bee,
As a burst fouling-peece doth saue the birds
   But kill the man, is seald with thee.

ffor who can tell, though thou hast dyde to winn
And wedd my soule in glorious paradise,
Whither my many crymes and vse of sinn
   May yet forbid the banes and bliss?

Onely my soule hangs on thy promisses
With face and hands clinging vnto thy brest,
Clinging and crying, crying without cease,
   Thou art my rock, thou art my rest. (5)

Love

Love bade me welcome: yet my soul drew back,
     Guiltie of dust and sinne.
But quick-ey'd Love, observing me grow slack
     From my first entrance in,
Drew nearer to me, sweetly questioning,
     If I lack'd any thing.

A guest, I answer'd, worthy to be here:
     Love said, You shall be he.
I the unkinde, ungratefull? Ah my deare,
     I cannot look on thee.

Love took my hand, and smiling did reply,
        Who made the eyes but I?

Truth Lord, but I have marr'd them: let my shame
        Go where it doth deserve.
And know you not, sayes Love, who bore the blame?
        My deare, then I will serve.
You must sit down, sayes Love, and taste my meat:
        So I did sit and eat. (6)

The Parson Praying

The Countrey Parson, when he is to read divine services, composeth himselfe to all possible reverence; lifting up his heart and hands, and eyes, and using all other gestures which may expresse a hearty, and unfeyned devotion. This he doth, first, as being truly touched and amazed with the Majesty of God, before whom he then presents himself; yet not as himself alone, but as presenting with himself the whole Congregation, whose sins he then beares, and brings with his own to the heavenly altar to be bathed, and washed in the sacred Laver of Christ's blood. Secondly, as this is the true reason of his inward feare, so he is content to expresse this outwardly to the utmost of his power; that being first affected himself, hee may affect also his people, knowing that no Sermon moves them so much to a reverence, which they forget againe, when they come to pray, as a devout behaviour in the very act of praying. Accordingly his voyce is humble, his words treatable, and slow; yet not so slow neither, as to let the fervency of the supplicant hang and dy between speaking, but with a grave livelinesse, between fear and zeal, pausing yet pressing, he performes his duty. Besides his example, he having often instructed his people how to carry themselves in divine service, exacts of them all possible reverence, by no means enduring either talking, or sleeping, or gazing, or leaning, or halfe-kneeling, or any undutifull behaviour in them, but causing them, when they sit, or stand, or kneel, to do all in a strait, and steady posture, as attending to what is done in the Church, and every one, man, and child, answering aloud both Amen, and all other answers, which are on the Clerks and peoples part to answer; which answers also are to be done not in the hudling, or slubbering fashion, gaping, or scratching the head, or spitting even in the midst of their answer, but gently and pausably, thinking what they say; so that while they answer, *As it was in the beginning,* etc. they meditate as they speak, that God hath ever had his people, that have glorified him as wel as now, and that he shall have so for ever. And the like in other answers. This is that which the Apostle calls a reasonable service, *Rom.* 12. when we speak not as Parrats, without reason, or offer up such sacrifices as they did of old, which was of beasts devoyd of reason; but when we use our reason, and apply our powers to the service of him, that gives them. (7)

The Parson Preaching

. . . He often tels them, that Sermons are dangerous things, that none goes out of Church as he came in, but either better, or worse; that none is careless before his Judg, and that the word of God shal judge us. By these and other means the

Parson procures attention; but the character of his Sermon is Holiness; he is not witty, or learned, or eloquent, but Holy. A Character, that *Hermogenes* never dream'd of, and therefore he could give no precepts thereof. But it is gained, first, by choosing texts of Devotion, not Controversie, moving and ravishing texts, whereof the Scriptures are full. Secondly, by dipping, and seasoning all our words and sentences in our hearts, before they come into our mouths, truly affecting, and cordially expressing all that we say; so that the auditors may plainly perceive that every word is hart-deep. Thirdly, by turning often, and making many Apostrophes to God, as, Oh Lord blesse my people, and teach them this point; or, Oh my Master, on whose errand I come, let me hold my peace, and doe thou speak thy selfe; for thou art Love, and when thou teachest, all are Scholers. (8)

Spiritual Certainty

[NOTES ON THE *CONSIDERATIONS* OF VALDESSO]

> *That in the motions to pray the Spirit doth certifie a man, that he shall obtaine that which he demands.*

Upon these words:

'The proper countersigne, whereby they may be able to judge between these motions, is the *Inward certainty, or uncertainty with which they shall finde themselves in prayer.* Finding themselves uncertain that they should obtain of God that which they demand, they shall judge, that the motion is of *humane spirit*; And finding themselves certain to obtain it, they shall judge that the motion is of the *holy spirit.* . . . With this *assurance* I see, that Christ *prayed*, raising up *Lazarus*, and *praying* for the conservation of his Disciples. And with *doubtfulnesse* I see he prayed in the *Garden*; and because he felt, whence this motion did arise in praying, he remitted himselfe unto the will of God.'

To say our Saviour prayed with doubtfulnesse, is more then I can or dare say; But with condition, or conditionally he prayed as man, though as God he knew the event. Feare is given to Christ, but not doubt, and upon good ground.

[. . .]

> *That humane wisdome hath no more iurisdiction in the judgement of their workes, who are the sonnes of God, then in the iudgement of the proper works of God.*

'That rashnesse of men is not lesse, which follow the iudgement of humane wisdome, when they sett themselves to iudge evill of *Moses* for the Hebrews whom he slew when they worshipped the Calfe; and when they sett themselves to judge evill of *Abraham*, because he commanded his wife *Sarah*, that she should lye, saying that she was his sister, and not his wife: And because *S. Paul* cursed *Ananias* standing at iudgement in his presence. And because hee excused his cursing, saying, he did not know him. . . . Humane wisdome hath no more iurisdiction in the iudgement of the works of pious men, then in the iudgement of the works of God. . . . Men should not haue had more reason to haue chastised *Abraham*, if he had killed his sonne *Isaac*, then to condemne God, because he slaies many men by suddain death.'

This Chapter is considerable. The intent of it, that the world *pierceth* not godly mens actions no more then Gods, is in some sort true because they are spiritually discerned, 1 *Cor.* 2. 14. So likewise are the godly in some sort exempt from Lawes, for *Lex iusto non est posita*: But when he enlargeth he goes too farre. For first concerning *Abraham* and *Sara*, I ever tooke that for a weaknesse in the great Patriark: And that the best of Gods Servants should have weaknesses is no way repugnant to the way of Gods Spirit in them, or to the Scriptures, or to themselves being still men, though godly men. Nay they are purposely recorded in holy Writ. Wherefore as *David's* Adultery cannot be excused, so need not *Abraham's* Equivocation, nor *Paul's* neither, when he professed himselfe a Pharisee, which strictly he was not, though in the point of Resurrection he agreed with them, and they with him. The reviling also of *Ananias* seemes, by his owne recalling, an oversight; yet I remember the Fathers forbid us to judge of the doubtfull actions of Saints in the Scriptures; which is a modest admonition. But it is one thing not to judge, another to defend them. Secondly, when he useth the word Iurisdiction, allowing no Iurisdiction over the godly, this cannot stand, and it is ill Doctrine in a common-wealth. The godly are punishable as others, when they doe amisse, and they are to be judged according to the outward fact, unlesse it be evident to others, as well as to themselves, that God moved them. For otherwise any Malefactor may pretend motions, which is unsufferable in a Common-wealth. Neither doe I doubt but if *Abraham* had lived in our Kingdome under government, and had killed his sonne *Isaac*, but he might have been justly put to death for it by the Magistrate, unlesse he could have made it appeare, that it was done by Gods immediate precept. He had done justly, and yet he had been punished justly, that is *in humano foro & secundum praesumptionem legalem*. So may a warre be just on both sides, and was just in the Canaanites and Israelites both. How the godly are exempt from Laws is a known point among Divines, but when he sayes they are equally exempt with God, that is dangerous and too farre. (9)

NOTES / SOURCES

1. *The Works of George Herbert*, ed. F. E. Hutchinson, Oxford, 1945 (second, revised edition), p. 73
2. Ibid., p. 103
3. Ibid., p. 174
4. Ibid., pp. 200–1
5. Ibid., pp. 204–5
6. Ibid., pp. 188–9
7. From *A Priest to the Temple, or, The Countrey Parson*, ibid., pp. 231–2
8. Ibid., p. 233
9. From *Briefe Notes on Valdesso's* Considerations, ibid., pp. 314–6

Thomas Browne   1605–1682

Browne came from a Cheshire family, but was actually born in London, and educated at Winchester and at Broadgate Hall in Oxford. He completed his medical studies at Leiden around 1633, and on his return to England worked briefly in Halifax before settling in 1637 at Norwich, where he spent the rest of his life. *Religio Medici* ('The religion of a physician') was written in the mid 1630s and published in a 'pirated' edition in 1642, followed rapidly by an authorized edition. It proved hugely popular as a compendium of tolerant and educated lay piety, and was translated into many European languages in the seventeenth century. The *Pseudodoxia Epidemica* of 1646 was a survey of popular beliefs and superstitions on a large scale, but it never fully shared the acclaim of the earlier work. Browne became an Honorary Fellow of the Royal College of Physicians in 1664 and was knighted in 1671.

Tolerance

We have reformed from them [the Roman Church] not against them; for (omitting those Improperations and Terms of Scurrility betwixt us, which only difference our Affections, and not our Cause,) there is between us one common Name and Appellation, one Faith and necessary body of Principles common to us both; and therefore I am not scrupulous to converse and live with them, to enter their Churches in defect of ours, and either pray with them, or for them. I could never perceive any rational Consequence from those many Texts which prohibit the Children of Israel to pollute themselves with the Temples of the Heathens; we being all Christians, and not divided by such detested impieties as might prophane our Prayers, or the place wherein we make them; or that a resolved Conscience may not adore her Creator any where, especially in places devoted to His Service; where, if *their* Devotions offend Him, mine may please Him; if theirs prophane it, mine may hallow it. Holy-water and Crucifix (dangerous to the common people,) deceive not my judgment, nor abuse my devotion at all. I am, I confess, naturally inclined to that which misguided Zeal terms *Superstition*. My common conversation I do acknowledge austere, my behaviour full of rigour, sometimes not without morosity; yet at my Devotion I love to use the civility of my knee, my hat, and hand, with all those outward and sensible motions which may express or promote my invisible Devotion. I should violate my own arm rather than a Church; nor willingly deface the name of Saint or Martyr. At the sight of a Cross or Crucifix I can dispense with my hat, but scarce with the thought or memory of my Saviour. I cannot laugh at, but rather pity, the fruitless journeys of Pilgrims, or contemn the miserable condition of Fryars; for, though misplaced in Circumstances, there is something in it of Devotion. I could never hear the Ave-Mary Bell without an elevation; or think it a sufficient warrant, because *they* erred in one circumstance, for me to err in all, that is, in silence and dumb contempt. Whilst, therefore, they directed their Devotions to *Her*, I offered mine to GOD, and rectified the Errors of their Prayers by rightly ordering mine own. (1)

The Book of Nature

Thus there are two Books from whence I collect my Divinity; besides that written one of GOD, another of His servant Nature, that universal and publick Manuscript, that lies expans'd unto the Eyes of all: those that never saw Him in the one, have discovered Him in the other. This was the Scripture and Theology of the Heathens: the natural motion of the Sun made *them* more admire Him than its supernatural station did the Children of Israel; the ordinary effects of Nature wrought more admiration in *them* than in the other all His Miracles. Surely the Heathens knew better how to joyn and read these mystical Letters than we Christians, who cast a more careless Eye on these common Hieroglyphicks, and disdain to suck Divinity from the flowers of Nature. Nor do I so forget GOD as to adore the name of Nature; which I define not, with the Schools, to be the principle of motion and rest, but that streight and regular line, that settled and constant course the Wisdom of GOD hath ordained the actions of His creatures, according to their several kinds. To make a revolution every day is the Nature of the Sun, because of that necessary course which GOD hath ordained it, from which it cannot swerve but by a faculty from that voice which first did give it motion. Now this course of Nature GOD seldome alters or perverts, but, like an excellent Artist, hath so contrived His work, that with the self same instrument, without a new creation, He may effect His obscurest designs. Thus He sweetneth the Water with a Wood, preserveth the Creatures in the Ark, which the blast of His mouth might have as easily created; for GOD is like a skilful Geometrician, who, when more easily and with one stroak of his Compass he might describe or divide a right line, had yet rather do this in a circle or longer way, according to the constituted and fore-laid principles of his Art. Yet this rule of His He doth sometimes pervert, to acquaint the World with His Prerogative, lest the arrogancy of our reason should question His power, and conclude He could not. And thus I call the effects of Nature the works of GOD, Whose hand and instrument she only is; and therefore to ascribe His actions unto her, is to devolve the honour of the principal agent upon the instrument; which if with reason we may do, then let our hammers rise up and boast they have built our houses, and our pens receive the honour of our writings. (2)

Friendship and Charity

There are wonders in true affection: it is a body of *Enigma*'s, mysteries, and riddles; wherein two so become one, as they both become two. I love my friend before my self, and yet methinks I do not love him enough: some few months hence my multiplied affection will make me believe I have not loved him at all. When I am from him, I am dead till I be with him; when I am with him, I am not satisfied, but would still be nearer him. United souls are not satisfied with imbraces, but desire to be truly each other; which being impossible, their desires are infinite, and must proceed without a possibility of satisfaction. Another misery there is in affection, that whom we truly love like our own selves, we forget their looks, nor can our memory retain the Idea of their faces; and it is no wonder, for they are our selves, and our affection makes their looks our own. This noble affection falls not on vulgar and common constitutions, but on such as are mark'd for virtue: he that can love his friend with this noble ardour, will in a competent degree affect all. Now, if we can bring our affections to look beyond the body, and cast an eye upon the soul, we have found out the true object, not only of friendship, but Charity; and the greatest happiness that we can bequeath the soul, is that wherein we all do place our last felicity, Salvation; which though it be not in our power to bestow, it is in our charity and pious invocations to desire, if not procure and further. I cannot contentedly frame a prayer for my self in particular, without a catalogue for my friends; nor request a happiness, wherein my sociable disposition doth not desire the fellowship of my neighbour. I never hear the Toll of a passing Bell, though in my mirth, without my prayers and best wishes for the departing spirit; I cannot go to cure the body of my patient, but I forget my profession, and call unto GOD for his soul; I cannot see one say his prayers, but, in stead of imitating him, I fall into a supplication for him, who perhaps is no more to me than a common nature: and if GOD hath vouchsafed an ear to my supplications, there are surely many happy that never saw me, and enjoy the blessing of mine unknown devotions. To pray for Enemies, that is, for their salvation, is no harsh precept, but the practice of our daily and ordinary devotions. (3)

Conscience

There is another man within me, that's angry with me, rebukes, commands, and dastards me. I have no Conscience of Marble to resist the hammer of more heavy offences; nor yet so soft and waxen, as to take the impression of each single peccadillo or scape of infirmity. I am of a strange belief, that it is as easie to be forgiven some sins, as to commit some others. For my Original sin, I hold it to be washed away in my Baptism: for my actual transgressions, I compute and reckon with GOD but from my last repentance, Sacrament, or general absolution; and therefore am not terrified with the sins or madness of my youth. I thank the goodness of GOD, I have no sins that want a name; I am not singular in offences; my transgressions are Epidemical, and from the common breath of our corruption. (4)

NOTES / SOURCES

1. Thomas Browne, *Religio Medici: Letter to a Friend etc. and Christian Morals*, ed. W. A. Greenhill, London, 1881, pp. 8–10
2. Ibid., pp. 27–8
3. Ibid., pp. 104–5
4. Ibid., pp. 106–7

Henry Vaughan   1621–1696

Born at Scethrog in the vale of Usk and educated at Jesus College, Oxford, Vaughan went on to study law in London, but returned to Wales at the outbreak of the Civil War, and (with his twin brother, Thomas) served in the Royalist army. In 1648, he underwent a profound religious conversion. Already a poet of some skill and reputation, he produced a remarkable body of meditative, sometimes even mystical verse, published in two collections, *Silex Scintillans I* and *II* (1650 and 1655). By the fifties, he was practising as a physician; but he was also working intensively at translations of early Christian, medieval, and more recent works on contemplation and the ascetical life, as well as prose meditations of his own. Although *Silex Scintillans* belongs partly to the period covered by the next section, it is in its tone and concerns closer to Herbert than to any Restoration poet.

The Brittish Church

Ah! he is fled!
And while these here their *mists* and *shadows* hatch,
   My glorious Head
Doth on those hills of Myrrhe and Incense watch.
    Haste, haste, my dear!
    The Souldiers here
  Cast in their lots againe.
    That seamlesse coat,
    The Jewes touch'd not,
These dare divide and stain.

2

   O get thee wings!
Or if as yet, until these clouds depart,
   And the day springs,
Thou think'st it good to tarry where thou art,
    Write in thy bookes,
    My ravish'd looks,
  Slain flock, and pillag'd fleeces;
    And haste thee so,
    As a young Roe
Upon the mounts of spices.

O Rosa Campi! O Lilium Convallium! quomodo nunc facta es pabulum Aprorum! (1)

The Lampe

'Tis dead night round about: Horrour doth creepe
And move on with the shades; stars nod and sleepe,
And through the dark aire spin a firie thread,
Such as doth gild the lazie glow-worm's bed.
  Yet burn'st thou here a full day, while I spend
My rest in cares, and to the dark world lend
These flames, as thou dost thine to me; I watch
That houre, which must thy life and mine dispatch,
But still thou doest out-goe me, I can see
Met in thy flames all acts of piety;
Thy light, is *Charity*; Thy heat, is *Zeale*;
And thy aspiring, active fires reveale
Devotion still on wing; Then, thou dost weepe
Still as thou burn'st, and the warme droppings creepe
To measure out thy length, as if thou'dst know
What stock, and how much time were left thee now;

Nor dost thou spend one teare in vain, for still
As thou dissolv'st to them, and they distill,
They're stor'd up in the socket, where they lye,
When all is spent, thy last and sure supply:
And such is true repentance; ev'ry breath
Wee spend in sighes is treasure after death.
Only one point escapes thee; That thy Oile
Is still out with thy flame, and so both faile;
But whensoe're I'm out, both shal be in,
And where thou mad'st an end, there I'll begin.

Mark, cap. 13. ver. 35

*Watch you therefore, for you know not when the master of the house cometh, at
Even, or at Midnight, or at the Cock-crowing, or in the Morning.* (2)

Dressing

O thou that lovest a pure and whiten'd soul!
That feedst among the Lillies, 'till the day
Break, and the shadows flee! touch with one coal
My frozen heart! and with thy secret key

Open my desolate rooms; my gloomie brest
With thy cleer fire refine, burning to dust
These dark confusions that within me nest,
And soyl thy Temple with a sinful rust.

Thou holy, harmless, undefil'd High-priest!
The perfect, full oblation for all sin,
Whose glorious conquest nothing can resist,
But even in babes doest triumph still and win;

    Give to thy wretched one
  Thy mysticall Communion,
      That, absent, he may see,
      Live, die, and rise with thee;
Let him so follow here, that in the end
He may take thee, as thou dost him intend.

    Give him thy private seal,
  Earnest, and sign. Thy gifts so deal
      That these forerunners here
      May make the future cleer.
Whatever thou dost bid let faith make good,
Bread for thy body, and Wine for thy blood.

Give him, with pitty, love,
Two flowres that grew with thee above;
Love than shall not admit
Anger for one short fit;
And pitty of such a divine extent,
That may thy members, more than mine, resent.

Give me, my God! thy grace,
The beams and brightness of thy face;
That never like a beast
I take thy sacred feast,
Or the dread mysteries of thy blest bloud
Use, with like custome, as my kitchin food.

Some sit to thee, and eat
Thy body as their common meat;
O let me not do so!
Poor dust should ly still low;
Then kneel, my soul, and body, kneel, and bow;
If Saints and Angels fall down, much more thou. (3)

The Nighte

. . . Dear night! this world's defeat;
The stop to busie fools; care's check and curb;
The day of spirits; my soul's calm retreat
Which none disturb!
Christ's progress, and his prayer time;
The hours to which high Heaven doth chime.

God's silent, searching flight;
When my Lord's head is filled with dew, and all
His locks are wet with the clear drops of night;
His still, soft call;
His knocking time; the soul's dumb watch,
When spirits their fair kinred catch.

Were all my loud, evil days
Calm and unhaunted as is thy dark tent,
Whose peace but by some *Angel*'s wing or voice
Is seldom rent;
Then I in Heaven all the long year
Would keep, and never wander here.

But living where the sun
Doth all things wake, and where all mix and tyre
Themselves and others, I consent and run
To ev'ry myre;

And by this world's ill guiding light,
Erre more than I can do by night.

　　There is in God, some say,
A deep, but dazzling darkness; as men here
Say it is late and dusky, because they
　　　　See not all clear.
　　O for that night! where I in him
　　Might live invisible and dim! (4)

NOTES / SOURCES

Standard editions available. Texts are quoted here from Henry Vaughan, 'Silurist', *Sacred Poems*, London, 1914

1. Ed. cit., pp. 40–1
2. Ibid., pp. 41–2
3. Ibid., pp. 108–10
4. Ibid., pp. 212–13

PART 2

1650 − 1830

Introduction

THE period that stretches from 1649 to 1830 is one of paradoxes and surprises. When King Charles I was beheaded outside Whitehall Palace on 31 January 1649, *The Book of Common Prayer* was already proscribed, and the *Westminster Directory*, reflecting a Presbyterian approach to Church government and worship, held official sway in England, Wales, Scotland, and Ireland as well. By 1830, on the other hand, *The Book of Common Prayer* of 1662 was long supreme in the Church of England, and Wales, and Ireland, but there were independent Episcopal Churches in Scotland and the United States of America; these had their own liturgies, which were produced in 1764 and 1789 respectively. And, while no more Anglican provinces were formed before 1830, there were new dioceses in Canada (from 1786), and one in India (Calcutta, 1814). At the death of King Charles I, theological, liturgical, and political tensions exploded which had been building up since the start of the Reformation in England. What the Restoration of 1660 achieved was to put an Anglican (i.e. Prayer Book) settlement in place, with the re-establishment of the monarchy. But, by 1830, we begin to look forward to the burgeoning of new Anglican provinces overseas, initially in the British colonies, developments which in time produced the need for the first Lambeth Conference in 1867 and the distinctive liturgical traditions that became much more apparent in the twentieth century. To travel from 1649 to 1830, whether one is a devout layperson in an English country church pew, a Scots Episcopalian pastor in Aberdeen caring for his scattered flock, a frontier community in West Virginia, or a member of a colonial chapel in Calcutta, is thus a rich and varied journey, enhanced by many different pressures and opportunities.

First, the Prayer Book of 1662 lies in the background of much of the devotional material written during this time. Opinions vary as to the extent of 'persecution' of those who doggedly—and usually clandestinely—used the Prayer Book in the time of the Commonwealth in England. The diarist, John Evelyn, gives an account of a eucharist which was forcibly interrupted by Parliamentary troops on Christmas Day 1657. Jeremy Taylor's little book of devotional prayers, *Golden Grove* (1655), opens on a mournful note, decrying the state of the Church. But there were more pragmatic figures, like Simon Patrick, who as a parish priest in Battersea gently prepared his people for the reintroduction of *The Book of Common Prayer* early in 1660 before King Charles II's return. It was only a matter of time before a fresh edition of the Prayer Book was issued. There were significant additions, including the General Thanksgiving, and alterations, such as the explicit blessing of the water in the baptism service. Not everyone would have been aware of the full significance of these changes. Indeed, in every age, the liturgical innovator needs to walk with a certain circumspection about how changes are perceived and digested by the ordinary worshipper.

The 1662 Prayer Book, however, stands as a landmark in the development of Anglicanism, its theology, ethos, and piety. There was little or no enthusiasm for bringing out any revisions in subsequent years. *The Book of Comprehension* of 1689, an attempt to woo parts of Dissent into the Establishment by adapting 1662, was an ill-fated project from the start. But some of its contents, for example the verbose collects drafted by Simon Patrick, reflect two significant features. First of all, mid-sixteenth-century English, in which the bulk of the Prayer Book was written, was more reticent than the later seventeenth. Secondly, a flowing and repetitive style of devotional prayer had emerged, which can be seen in the writings of Jeremy Taylor.

The official prayers of the Church and the devotional writings that accompanied them were diverging from one another, a process already seen in the work of Lancelot Andrewes in the early seventeenth century. When, for example, in 1764 the Duke of Newcastle asked his friend John Hume, Bishop of Oxford, to write some prayers for his personal use for receiving the Sacrament, one of his reasons was that some of the Prayer Book language was not always clear to him. The context of his request suggests that this was more a literary than a theological difficulty; as it happens, this is paralleled in the pressure—mainly from outside the Church of England, and unsuccessful in the event—for a revision of the Authorized Version of the Bible into plainer English. In other words, devotional prayers can move beyond the Prayer Book, in theological nuance just as much as in literary style. This poses the critical question as to how far the Prayer Book 'text' as given could continue to carry the weight of devotional 'context' as perceived and prayed by the ordinary worshipper. When Robert Nelson wrote his highly popular *Companion to the Festivals and Fasts of the Church of England* (1704), he gave to a wide readership new and hitherto largely unknown ways of appreciating the liturgical year, and he was able to make more explicit what was only implicit in the Prayer Book through his knowledge and application of ancient sources. It was an example taken up a century later by John Henry Hobart in relation to the American Prayer Book, using the same title.

What of the boundaries between private and public prayer? The supreme example is the Lord's Prayer, which is a biblical prayer, and arguably the only 'canonical' prayer in the Christian repertoire. It is used throughout public worship but it is also the backbone of much private devotion. Writers return again and again to this prayer—in the best traditions of the early and medieval Church—in order to locate the Christian gospel within its remarkably narrow confines. There are no fewer than nine series of meditations on the Lord's Prayer in Thomas Wilson's *Sacra Privata*, compiled during his long years as Bishop of Sodor and Man in the first part of the eighteenth century. Jeremy Taylor wrote eloquently about it in *The Great Exemplar* (1649). Robert Leighton expounded it in his series of lectures, as did Thomas Secker in the following century. Susanna Hopton provided her own devotional paraphrase, which is more expansive in style than the version which appears near the end of *The Whole Duty of Man* (1657), one of the key manuals of piety in this era.

But the tension between private and public comes to a head in a particularly poignant form with William Law's *Serious Call* (1728). Law began by asserting that there is no essential difference between the two. His agenda was twofold: to bring some depth into the formality of public worship and to provide a way of encouraging people to see prayer as part of daily life. His work was among the most influential of the time—and time is the key word, for it is clear that the contexts of *The Whole Duty* and Law's *Serious Call* differed considerably. *The Whole Duty* was written for a public in search of a simple guide to the life of faith and prayer at a time when people were tiring of religious controversy. Law's *Serious Call*, on the other hand, was compiled in order to bring some spiritual colour into religion, which was—in many places—in danger of settling down a mite too comfortably. And *The Whole Duty* was deemed inadequate for those of a more Evangelical approach, spurring Henry Venn on to write *The Complete Duty of Man* (1763).

The place of the two dominical sacraments, Baptism and Holy Communion, is central throughout the period. Around the time of the Restoration, there was a drive to bring the eucharist into more frequent and reverent celebration. Jeremy Taylor's popular classic *Holy Living* (1650) ended with a lengthy preparation for reception of the Sacrament, supported by devotional prayers. He followed this up with the more focused and doctrinal *Worthy Communicant* (1660), in the same year as Simon Patrick's *Mensa Mystica*. Patrick himself was to go on to write about the eucharist for different audiences, which included the ordinary layperson, as well as children and young people, an example followed by Edmund Gibson in 1705. Taylor and Patrick, like other Restoration divines, saw the eucharist as a renewal of the baptismal covenant, thus linking the two sacraments closely.

The tenor of this era's eucharistic theology and piety, instanced in *A Week's Preparation* (1679), is built on the tradition of Hooker and Andrewes. It had a strong view of eucharistic presence and memorial, as the sacrifice of praise, made in union with the heavenly offering of Christ himself. The eucharist was above all the action of the Saviour Lord in the Church. But the following century provided its own counterbalances. Benjamin Hoadly's *Plain Account* (1735) was in tune with the more Protestant strand of Anglicanism, and it also met the calls for accessibility which were in vogue at the time. Less controversial and gentler in style was *The New Week's Preparation* (1747), which continued to be popular right into the following century. These in turn provoked their own reaction. Thomas Haweis' *Communicant's Spiritual Companion* (1763) demonstrated an Evangelical fervour that found *The New Week*'s language and approach insufficiently demanding, and too reliant on the sacrament—rather than the cross—as the vehicle of sanctifying grace. Nearly all these writers, however, presupposed the Prayer Book rite as the locus of corporate faith and practice. The reader of today may be put off by their emphasis on preparation, but this was an

age in which the eucharist was held by many to have an importance requiring
quarterly or monthly celebration only. The emphasis on baptism, however, has
for us a strongly contemporary resonance; the close connection between baptism
and eucharist in some of these manuals must have made an impact on many
communicants. Thomas Wilson went so far as to provide a form of private re-
affirmation of the credal confession of faith before Communion (1734). Jeremy
Taylor followed John Cosin in writing a prayer for the anniversary of baptism. S.
T. Coleridge's poem on his baptismal anniversary, 28 October 1834, with its
gentle allusions to rebirth and forgiveness, a year before the poet's death, suggests
a profound sacramental piety.

The importance of catechesis is never far from the surface in many of our
writers. Regular use of the Prayer Book Catechism in connection with Evening
Prayer must have had its own effect, which in turn engendered a climate of
reflective teaching. There were many explanations of the Christian faith written
in the question and answer form of the Catechism, which are based on its overall
shape. William Wake's *Principles of the Christian Religion* (1700) and Samuel
Walker's *Familiar Catechism* (1759) are particularly popular examples. Mention
has already been made of expositions of the Lord's Prayer. The same is true of the
Apostles' Creed and the Ten Commandments, exemplified in many church
sanctuaries by decorative texts. And in comparing the kind of audiences, for
example, of Robert Leighton in seventeenth-century Scotland and of Thomas
Secker in mid-eighteenth-century England, one is struck by the needs of their
different contexts. Leighton was a man whose diplomatic temperament enabled
him to be admired by both Presbyterian and Episcopalian in his own day and
since. There is almost a sublime atmosphere to his writing, as if he were trying to
provide, apparently effortlessly, a unitive approach to the Christian life which
would transcend the unhappy divisions of the time. Secker, by contrast, openly
lamented the lack of courage on the part of the Church to expound the wholeness
of tradition, doctrines and all, and he went on to provide accessible explanations
of Christian teaching for an age that showed signs of impatience with tradition.
Sometimes we come across writers whose purpose is to explain the meaning of
the faith in terms of the Prayer Book services, their composition and structure, a
good example of which is Samuel Seabury in North America in the eighteenth
century.

It is perhaps worth observing at this stage a gradual shift in the way in which
the 'long century' (the eighteenth) has been perceived. There was a time when the
Hanoverian Church was written off as hopelessly in the bonds of Enlightenment
fashion, preaching a God of truth and beauty, neglecting uncomfortable apparel
in the Christian wardrobe like the forgiveness of sins, and celebrating the
sacraments as infrequently as possible. Fortunately, and as many of the writings
selected for our period show, the eighteenth century was far more of a mixed
scene. Much of the finest teaching of the preceding century lingered on; Jeremy
Taylor, Simon Patrick, and *The Whole Duty of Man* continued to be reprinted,
suggesting an enduring lay market. Charles Wheatly's *Rational Illustration of the*

Book of Common Prayer (first edition 1710), was constantly reprinted and read well into the nineteenth century. Important writers, such as George Horne, Samuel Horsley, and William Jones ('Jones of Nayland') provide a continuum with the tradition and also an openness to the questing spirit of their time. Jones wrote on every aspect of Christian doctrine, and had the time and interest to deal with how humans and monkeys are different beings. When the considerable body of Evangelical preachers and hymn writers is taken into account, the eighteenth century emerges as one in which different strands of Anglican life coexisted.

The sermon continues to be an essential part of the Christian life, and its impact and style can be observed in a number of ways. In the Prayer Book, it is appointed to be preached after the Creed in the Communion service. Most Sunday morning services consisted of Mattins and Litany, followed by the first part of the Eucharist, the full celebration taking place only quarterly or monthly. This meant that the sermon usually came towards the end of the service. Some of our writers comment on the actual occasions when sermons are preached. John Evelyn, at the receiving end, often noted in his diary preacher and text, frequently supplying a brief summary of the sermon. Augustus Toplady, on the other hand, who wrote few hymns, but whose 'Rock of Ages, cleft for me' has had an enduring popularity, provided observations on the atmosphere of the Church as he preached, the impact he hoped to have had, as well as the main theological truth that he tried to communicate. Different fashions and schools of thought produced their own results. Jeremy Taylor's sermons were devotional and ethical, and written in a florid style. John Tillotson, on the other hand, was briefer, more practical in approach, and keen to apply the text directly to the congregation. John Berridge was more consciously gospel-centred, recalling his hearers repeatedly to the need for salvation. Sydney Smith was distinctive in approach: precise, direct, challenging, at times sharp and witty. For all that one can try to categorize preaching, sermons remain bound by the occasion, the community addressed, and the preacher. But they were frequently published. Lancelot Andrewes's sermons were still being read in the second part of the seventeenth century, even though in style long out of date. Simon Patrick wooed his wife, Penelope Jepson, by sending her a bound copy of some of his sermons, with some prayers! Those of John Tillotson and Joseph Butler, for example, were published for a wider audience within their lifetime. To what end? The edification of the laity, who often had parts of them read aloud at family prayers.

Lay piety almost takes on a life of its own. The poets occupy an important place, whether we are considering Sir Matthew Hale's 'Christmas Day' or Joseph Addison's 'The spacious firmament on high'. It is a mark of a Church tradition forged alongside the lay supremacy of the monarch, in which the laity are fully part of the public conversation of the Christian faith, a mark of what has sometimes been described as a baptismal ecclesiology. John Evelyn's *Devotionarie Book*, only discovered and published in 1935, reveals another side to the seventeenth-century diarist's literary skills. It bears witness to the fact that those who occupy the pews are in every way the people of God, nourished by the reading and preaching of the Word, and the faithful administration of the Sacraments. But as Evelyn's prayers show, the Prayer Book ethos can be blended through biblical imagery into a different genre. His friendship with Jeremy Taylor—who was his spiritual director—may account for the existence of such a book in the first place. But that is a further indication of the importance of such a collection, and one is left wondering how many others there were in existence, and what were their sources and influences. Perhaps the finest examples of 'lay theologians' were William Wilberforce, abolitionist and author of *The Practical View* (1797), and Alexander Knox, as well as Dr Samuel Johnson, whose prayers are noted for their repeated emphasis on heavenly grace. Domestic prayer, too, was a feature of many a household, as one sees in Edmund Gibson's *Family Prayers* (1705), a book which was constantly reprinted, and was not unique, with its deft adaptation of Prayer Book material. The eighteenth-century Evangelicals, like Thomas Scott, one of the founders of the Church Missionary Society, aimed their published biblical expositions at a lay audience, in the best traditions of early Puritans, like William Perkins.

Attention needs to be drawn to three women writers, each of them of considerable importance. Mary Astell's *The Christian Religion as Professed by a Daughter of the Church of England* (1705), written anonymously, covered every aspect of Christian teaching. Astell, an enthusiast for the reintroduction of female religious communities, defends a woman's right to use her reason in religious matters. She also gives us what is so far the earliest treatment of the meaning of the Eucharist by an Anglican woman, in a style that combines Restoration piety with the plainer language of her time. Susanna Hopton's *Collection of Meditations and Devotions* (1717) stands in the tradition of the older books of daily prayers, such as the Primers. But it is less liturgical in style and tends to meditate in beauty and at length on events in Christ's life; in this respect, it harks back to the obsecrations in the Prayer Book Litany ('By the mystery of thy holy Incarna- tion . . .'), and the 'devotio moderna' of the late Middle Ages. Hannah More, originally part of the literary circle around Dr Samuel Johnson, associated with William Cowper and John Newton, and argued with conviction and feeling for a religion of the heart as well as the brain in her several works, including *Practical Piety* (1811). Together with Margaret Godolphin, whose exemplary piety John Evelyn describes in his *Life*, these writers all point the way towards a fuller feminine heritage, and are a harbinger of things to come.

The period in question sees the gradual shift from poetry written as poetry to poetry written to be sung as hymnody. Just as Lancelot Andrewes provided part of the background to the flowering of devotional writing, so George Herbert gave us some of the same for religious poetry. Herbert's poems were not originally intended to be sung as hymns; but a selection were adapted into common metre for singing by Dissenting congregations in the later seventeenth century. But hymnody as opposed to the singing of metrical psalms was not a feature of Prayer Book worship until the eighteenth century, when it developed under Evangelical and Methodist influences. Among the poetry subsequently sung as hymns is Samuel Crossman's 'My song is love unknown' (1664); first used in an abbreviated and slightly edited form as a hymn in 1868, it came into its own as part of mainstream twentieth-century sacred song in many Christian Churches, considerably aided by the tune written for it by John Ireland.

The eighteenth century sees hymnody take off, with such writers as Charles Wesley, John Newton, and William Cowper. The process continued in the next century with Reginald Heber (who also edited the works of Jeremy Taylor). He was keen to enliven Prayer Book worship by encouraging congregations to sing. Such hymns, like the texts of the Prayer Book, were written as vehicles of Christian teaching. John Newton's 'Glorious things of thee are spoken', a classic for its time, contains a fourth stanza on election, beginning 'Blest inhabitants of Zion', which has not proved to the taste of more inclusive approaches to the nature of Christian community, and it has therefore been regularly omitted since. There are signs, too, of different influences on hymnody. John and Charles Wesley prefixed their *Hymns on the Lord's Supper* (1745) with a shortened version of Daniel Brevint's *The Christian Sacrament and Sacrifice* (1673), and when Charles came to write his *Hymns on the Trinity* (1767), it is clear from his use of scripture texts that he had read carefully William Jones's *Catholic Doctrine of the Trinity*, whose third edition appeared in the same year. That is a strong enough statement of the need to re-express in the language of piety the historic faith of the Church at a time when there were those, like the influential Samuel Clarke, whose Arian tendencies wanted to dispense with the doctrine altogether. The genius of Charles Wesley's hymns on the Trinity—like all his hymns, rich in biblical imagery—is that they stress both the majesty and incomprehensibility of the triune God, and at the same time the intrinsic participation of the believer in the divine life.

Finally, one may well ask what are the principal theological 'strains' in this period, a period in which the good and humble country priest, like Parson Woodforde, simply got on with the job of visiting his flock, taking the Sunday services, visiting the sick, burying the dead, and much else besides. Woodforde compiled his diary in an ordinary fashion, down to the details of what food he provides for the poor at his gate. Theological controversy is part of the Christian story. But it must not be allowed to mask the devotional backdrop in which the Church carries on its life, whoever hits the headlines. By and large, Anglicanism emerges from this period a stronger animal because it is coming to terms with how and where to draw boundaries, which had already been experienced in various ways, negatively and positively, including with the Non-Juror schisms at the accession of King William III and Queen Mary II in 1689 and King George I in 1714, as well as with the Wesleyan Movement later that century. Chief of these is the ethos of the Prayer Book itself, whether altered officially (as in Scotland and America), unofficially (as with some Evangelicals, who wanted to simplify it), or (perhaps most often) left well alone. Anglicanism by 1830 is already an inter-national influence, for in this period alone translations into other languages appeared which included Welsh (1664, replacing that of 1567), Dutch (1645) and Mohawk (1715), the latter for the use of the native Americans of Nova Scotia. 'Indigenous' colouring is inevitable when different languages and cultures are involved. The Welsh tongue is indeed older and richer, as witness the prose of William Thomas, the only Welsh-speaking Bishop of St Davids in the seventeenth century. And the Scottish–American revisions of the eucharistic prayer echoed and at the same time developed a more comprehensive approach to eucharistic theology than was common in England.

But what of the sources for our writers? Apart from the Post-Restoration divines—Daniel Waterland will quote Hooker with approval—there is a steady trickle of ecumenism. For example, Patrick quotes the Puritan, Richard Baxter, when he needs to. Thomas Ken had a copy of the French Roman Catholic Francis De Sales' *Introduction to the Devout Life* (1609) in his library. And Taylor—like John Wesley—used the late medieval Thomas à Kempis' *Imitation of Christ*, by the occasional citation, but also in the very principle of the new kind of book he was writing. A devotional life of Christ like *The Great Exemplar* was a novelty, but it relied in part on the tradition of Christian spirituality represented by à Kempis himself, in which our lives and Christ's life are seen to be intertwined through prayer, self-examination, and reflection. This is what is sometimes called the 'moral-ascetic theology' of the seventeenth-century divines, in which the life of prayer and the way of right living form a unity, and are not to be locked away into separate compartments.

All in all, the quest for holiness which lies behind the use of the Prayer Book, backed up by interpretative material, supplementary prayers, devotional treatises, sermons, and hymnody, is one which may be summarized by a number of tendencies, which often coexisted in particular people or in different schools of thought. For example Charles Simeon, the noted Evangelical, had a life-changing experience in preparing for Communion as an undergraduate at Cambridge by reading the High Churchman, Thomas Wilson, on the Lord's Supper. This kind of observation may explain why we are reluctant to present these writers exclusively by label, preferring instead to concentrate on the genre and context of the writings themselves. Then there is the love of continuity, which views history as a process, in which the present is more likely to be continuous than discontinuous with the past. Here one thinks of figures like Mary Astell and Thomas Ken, and the Nonjurors, or those who consorted with them like Nelson and Spinckes. But it also leads to the rewriting of the eucharistic prayer in Scotland, thanks to a growing awareness of the wider tradition, including the Eastern Churches, in a renewed emphasis on the work of the Holy Spirit in the celebration of the sacrament. The desire for accessibility is already shared in different ways both by Enlightenment writers like Hoadly, Evangelicals like Newton, and High Churchmen like Robert Horsley. Nearly all our authors were at pains to show that prayer is an activity in which everyone can fully share, no matter what their calling, and which requires occasional defence, as witness the contributions of John Bramhall and Joseph Butler against the rationalism of Thomas Hobbes, the philosopher. There is also the Augustinian–Platonist strain, which sees the physical world as an imperfect copy of the heavenly. Jeremy Taylor and Thomas Traherne are perhaps the supreme examples of this. For them, and writers like Simon Patrick and George Bull, reason is as much an imaginative as a deductive faculty, in devotion and in eucharistic theology as well as the other areas of theological enterprise. Some of these ideas resurface in S. T. Coleridge, and in the Romantic tradition which followed in the nineteenth century.

There is, nonetheless, an underlying tension over the role of sanctification in the process of growth in holiness. Many Evangelicals, like John Berridge, held fast to the justifying work of Christ alone, though some, like Charles Simeon, distinguished between justification as the eternal event, and sanctification as the historical outworking of salvation in the life of discipleship, including prayer and sacraments. This may be described as distinguishing between Christ's work *for* us, on the cross, and his work *in* us, through the Holy Spirit. Such a view was, in fact, fed by the Prayer Book itself, which locates worship within the broad context of the pilgrimage of faith, and sees the sacraments as arising out of and at the same time feeding that pilgrimage. But for all these differences of emphasis, the quest for an experiential and imaginative dimension to Christianity can always be discerned, where the heart has to be as much part of the scene as the head, where the inward and the outward are continually drawn together, and the work of grace celebrated and explored by and for the whole people of God.

Thomas Pestell

1584?–1659?

After studying at Queens' College, Cambridge, Thomas Pestell became Vicar of Packington in Leicestershire (1613), and then Chaplain to Robert Devereux, Third Earl of Essex. He was later appointed Royal Chaplain and preached before the King, as well as before Council at York (1640). In the early part of the Civil War he resigned the living of Packington in favour of his son (also Thomas) and complained that he was robbed a number of times. As well as a publisher of sermons, he also contributed two poems to *Lachrymae Musarum* (1650) in memory of Henry, Lord Hastings. In 1659 some of his sacred verse and sermons preached before the Civil War were collected and published in *Sermons and Devotions Old and New*, in which appears 'Fairest of morning Lights', which has become a Christmas hymn, starting at stanza 5, 'Behold the great Creator makes'.

Poems on Various Occasions

On the Sacrament

Lord to thy flesh and blood when I repair,
When dreadful joys and pleasing tremblings are,
Then most I relish, most it does me good,
When my soul faints and pines and dies for food:
Did my sins murder thee? To make that plain
Thy pierced dead–living body bleeds again.
Flow sad sweet drops; what differing things you do
Reveal my sins; and seal my pardon too. (1)

The Relief on Easter Eve

Like an Hart, the live-long day
That in thorns and thickets lay,
Rouse thee soul, thy flesh forsake,
Got to relief from thy brake;
Shuddering I would have thee part,
And at every motion start.
Look behind thee still to see,
If thy frailties follow thee.
Deep in silence of the night,
Take a sweet and stolen delight.
Graze on Clover by this calm,
Precious spring of bleeding Balm,
Thou rememb'rest how it ran
From his side, that's God and man.
Taste the pleasures of this stream,
Thou wilt think thy flesh a dream.
Nightly this Repast go take,
Got to Relief from thy brake. (2)

A Psalm for Christmass Day morning

Fairest of morning Lights appear,
    Thou blest and gaudy day,
On whom was born our Saviour dear,
    Make haste and c[o]me away.

See, See, our pensive breasts do pant,
    Like gasping Land we lie,
Thy holy Dews our souls do want.
    We faint, we pine, we die.

Let from the skies a joyfull Rain
    Like Mel or Manna fall.
Whose searching drops our sins may drain,
    And quench our sorrows all.

This day prevents his day of Doom,
    His mercy now is nigh.
The mighty God of love is come;
    The day-spring from on high.

Behold the great Creator makes
    Himself an house of clay.
A Robe of Virgin flesh he takes
    Which he will wear for ay.

Heark, heark, the wise Eternal Word,
    Like a weak Infant cries,
In form of servant is the Lord;
    And God in Cradle lies.

This wonder struck the world amaz'd;
    It shook the stary frame.
Squadrons of spirits stood and gaz'd.
    Then down in Troops they came.

Glad Shepherds ran to view this sight,
    A quire of Angels sings,
And Eastern Sages with delight
    Adore this King of Kings.

Joyn then all hearts that are not stone,
    And all our voices prove
To celebrate this holy One,
    The God of Peace and Love. (3)

NOTES / SOURCES
1. *The Poems of Thomas Pestell*, Oxford, 1940, p. 6
2. Ibid., pp. 63–4
3. Ibid., pp. 66–7

John Bramhall   1594–1663

After study in Cambridge and ordination in 1616, John Bramhall went to Ireland and in 1634 became Bishop of Derry. Because of his rigorous opposition to the Covenanters he was forced to retire first to England and then to the Continent, where he met Thomas Hobbes. At the Restoration he returned permanently as Archbishop of Armagh in 1661 and Speaker of the Irish House of Lords. His religious writings were largely directed against the extreme Puritans, the philosophy of Hobbes, and Roman Catholics, and were collected and published posthumously (1677).

God's Actions in Humanity Show His Absolute Freedom

How shall a man praise God for His goodness, who believes Him to be a greater tyrant than ever was in the world. Who creates millions to burn eternally without their fault, to express His power? How shall a man hear the word of God with that reverence and devotion and faith which is requisite, who believeth, that God causeth His Gospel to be preached to the much greater part of Christians, not with any intention that they should be converted and saved, but merely to harden their hearts, and to make them inexcusable? How shall a man receive the blessed Sacrament with comfort and confidence, as a seal of God's love in Christ, who believeth, that so many millions are positively excluded from all fruit and benefit of the Passions of Christ, before they had done either good or evil? How shall he prepare himself with care and conscience, who apprehendeth, that 'eating and drinking unworthily'(1 Cor. xi. 29) is not the cause of damnation, but because God would damn a man, therefore He necessitates him to 'eat and drink unworthily?' How shall a man make a free vow to God, without gross ridiculous hypocrisy, who thinks he is able to perform nothing but as he is extrinsecally necessitated? For repentance, how shall a man condemn and accuse himself for his sins, who thinks himself to be like a watch which is wound up by God, and that he can go neither longer nor shorter, faster nor slower, truer nor falser, than he is ordered by God? If God sets him right, he goes right. If God set him wrong, he goes wrong. How can a man be said to 'return into the right way,' who never was in any other way but that which God Himself had chalked out for him? What is his purpose to amend, who is destitute of all power, but as if a man should purpose to fly without wings, or a beggar who hath not a groat in his purse purpose to build hospitals? We use to say, 'Admit one absurdity, and a thousand will follow.' To maintain this unreasonable opinion of absolute necessity, he is necessitated (but it is hypothetically,—he might change his opinion if he would) to deal with all ancient writers, as the Goths did with the Romans; who destroyed all their magnificent works, that there might remain no monument of their greatness upon the face of the earth. Therefore he will not leave so much as one of their opinions, nor one of their definitions, nay, not one of their terms of art standing. Observe what a description he hath given us here of repentance:—'It is a glad returning into the right way after the grief of being out of the way.' It amazed me to find 'gladness' to be the first word in the description of repentance. His repentance is not that repentance, nor his piety that piety, nor his prayer that kind of prayer, which the Church of God in all ages hath acknowledged. Fasting, and sackcloth, and ashes, and tears, and humicubations, used to be companions of repentance. Joy may be a consequent of it, not a part of it. It is a 'returning,' but whose act is this returning? Is it God's alone, or doth the penitent person concur also freely with the grace of God? If it be God's alone, then it is His repentance, not man's repentance. What need the penitent person trouble himself about it? God will take care of His own work. The Scriptures teach us otherwise,—that God expects our concurrence (Rev. iii. 19, [20.]):—'Be zealous and repent; behold, I stand at the door, and knock; if any man hear My voice, and open the door, I will come in to him.' It is 'a glad returning into the right way;'—who dare any more call that a wrong way, which God Himself hath determined? He that willeth and doth that which God would have him to will and to do, is never out of his 'right way.' It follows in his description,—'after the grief,' etc. It is true, a man may grieve for that which is necessarily imposed upon him; but he cannot grieve for it as a fault of his own, if it never was in his power to shun it. Suppose a writing-master shall hold his scholar's hand in his, and write with it: the scholar's part is only to hold still his hand, whether the master write well or ill; the scholar hath no ground, either of joy or sorrow, as for himself; no man will interpret it to be his act, but his master's. It is no fault to be out of the 'right way,' if a man had not liberty to have kept himself in the way.

NOTES / SOURCES

John Bramhall 'Discourse I: A Defence of True Liberty, being an Answer to a Late Book of Mr Thomas Hobbes', in *The Works of John Bramhall*, Vol. IV, Oxford, 1844, pp. 105–7

Herbert Thorndike   1598–1672

After studying theology, oriental languages, and rabbinical literature, Herbert Thorndike became Hebrew Lecturer at Trinity College, Cambridge (1640), and Rector of Barley in Herts (1642), but was deposed from both these offices in the Civil War. He was appointed Prebendary of Westminster at the Restoration. He advocated what he saw as a return to the primitive Church through a moderate form of episcopacy and a high doctrine of baptism, in both of which he was well ahead of his time. He was a voluminous writer.

The Sacraments of Baptism and Eucharist

The necessity of the Sacraments of Baptism and of the Eucharist unto salvation consisteth in the Covenant of Grace, in which our salvation consisteth; and which the one of them setteth and enacteth, the other reneweth and replenisheth . . .

But he that eateth and drinketh the Sacrament of the Eucharist with a conscience of a Christian, resolving to stand to what he undertaketh; he, discerning the body and blood of Our Lord in the elements thereof, receiveth thereby a supply of his Spirit, making him to perform the same. (1)

The Importance of Ceremonies

God hath made Christians, though governed by the Spirit of His grace, as gross in their bodily senses and faculties of their minds, as other men of like education are: and it is a debt which the guides of the Church owe to the wise and unwise of God's people, to conduct them in the way of godliness by means proportionable to their faculties. The outward form of public service availeth much, even with them whose minds are best in tune, to corroborate their reverence and devotion at the service of God, by the exercise of it: but speaking of them whose minds are less withdrawn from their senses, how great impression shall the example of the world, practising the service of God in an orderly and reverent form, make in the minds of men that cannot receive it from their reason, but from their senses? This effect in things of slight consequence in particular, which nevertheless altogether amount to a considerable sum, is better seen by the gross in practice, than convinced by retail in dispute: yet since the importunities of men have caused false reasons to prevail with weak people, it is requisite the true reasons be pleaded, lest it be thought there are none such, because not so fit to be pleaded.

The circumstances and ceremonies of public service are indeed a kind of discipline and pædagogy, whereby men subject to sense are guided in the exercise of godliness: it is, as it were, the apparel of religion at the heart; which some think, like the sun, most beautiful when it is most naked; and so it were indeed, did men consist of minds alone without bodies, but as long as our bodily senses are manageable to our soul's advantage, the heat within will starve without this apparel without. And therefore, under better judgment, I hold it requisite that the observance of rites and ceremonies in the public service of God, should increase and become more solemn after the world was come into the Church, than under the persecuting times of it. Persecution was like antiperistasis in nature, in preserving order and reverence in the public offices of the Church, with the respect of those guides that ruled it.

But since the net of the gospel hath been cast in the ocean, and caught good and bad, it is more requisite that all should pass, as under rule and observance, so in the most reverent form, that the coldness and indifference of the worser part appear not to debauch the good disposition of others. Though from the beginning, as early as the records of the Church are able to inform us, we are sure it was never without such outward observances as, according to the state of the time, tended to maintain, to witness the disposition of the heart answerable. (2)

NOTES / SOURCES

1. Herbert Thorndike, Unpublished discourse, Westminster Abbey, Muniment Room, Thorndike MS 2/1/4
2. 'The Service of God at Religious Assemblies' (1642) in the *Theological Works of Herbert Thorndike* (Vol. I, Pt. I, Library of Anglo-Catholic Theology), Oxford, 1844, pp. 301–2

Matthew Hale

1609–1676

Sir Matthew Hale was a prominent judge for more than three decades being counsel for, among others, Archbishop Laud (1643), and is said to have offered his services to Charles I. Although he took the Oath to the Commonwealth and was active through the period, he was keen to promote tolerance, and was a friend of a number of leading bishops, becoming Lord Chief Justice in 1671. He wrote no fewer than seventeen poems on Christmas, a festival outlawed during the Commonwealth, and died on 25 December 1676.

Christmas Day (1659)

But art Thou come, dear Saviour? Hath Thy love
Thus made Thee stoop, and leave Thy throne above
The lofty Heavens, and thus Thyself to dress
In dust to visit mortals? Could no less
A condescension serve? And after all,
The mean reception of a cratch and stall?
Dear Lord, I'll fetch Thee thence; I have a room
'Tis poor, but 'tis my best, if Thou wilt come
Within so small a cell, where I would fain
Mine and the world's Redeemer entertain;
I mean my heart; 'tis sluttish, I confess,
And will not mend Thy lodging, Lord, unless
Thou send before Thy harbinger, I mean
Thy pure and purging grace, to make it clean,
And sweep its nasty corners; then I'll try
To wash it also with a weeping eye;
And when 'tis swept and washed, I then will go,
And, with Thy leave, I'll fetch some flowers that grow
In Thine own garden, faith, and love to Thee;
With those I'll dress it up; and these shall be
My rosemary and bays; yet when my best
Is done, the room's not fit for such a Guest.
   But here's the cure; Thy presence, Lord, alone
   Will make a stall a court, a cratch a throne.

NOTES / SOURCES

Matthew Hale, in *The Works, Moral and Religious, of Sir Matthew Hale*, Vol. II, London, 1805, p. 613

Robert Leighton

1611–1684

After travelling on the Continent Leighton was ordained in 1641 and became Principal of Edinburgh University (1653), Bishop of Dunblane (1661), and subsequently Archbishop of Glasgow (1670). Despite his own Calvinist views, he accepted the bishoprics in order to resolve the continuing conflict between Presbyterians and Episcopalians in Scotland. His position eventually became untenable, and he retired to England in 1674. An outstanding preacher, he was a rare mixture of academic learning and devotional spirituality, whose influence embraced the poet, S.T. Coleridge (q.v.).

The Duty, Dignity and Utility of Prayer

Although the Lord knows well our wants, and doth according to His own good pleasure, yet there is for prayer: 1. *Duty.* 2. *Dignity.* 3. *Utility.*

1. *Duty.* We owe this homage to GOD, not only to worship Him, but particularly to offer up our supplications, and to acknowledge Him our king and ruler of the whole world, and to testify our dependence upon Him, as the giver of every good gift. It is not because He is unwilling and loth to give, for *He gives liberally, and upbraids none,* St James 1.5; yet, says the Apostle there, *If any man lack wisdom, let him ask it*; and so of all wants. That which thanksgiving doth acknowledge after receipt, supplication doth beforehand, viz. His power, and truth, and goodness, etc. This is His name still, The GOD that *heareth prayer,* and therefore, this homage is due to Him, *To Him shall all flesh come,* Psal. lxv. 2.

2. *Dignity.* This is the honour of the saints, that they are admitted to so near and frequent converse with the great GOD, that they do not only expect from Him, but may so freely speak to Him of their desires and wants, and may pour out their complaints into His bosom. Abraham is sensible of the greatness of this privilege, by reflecting upon the greatness of his distance, Gen. xviii. 27: *Behold, I have taken upon me to speak unto the LORD, who am but dust and ashes.* It is an unspeakable honour for dust and ashes to be received into such familiarity with the LORD of heaven and earth.

3. *Utility.* [1.] It quiets and eases the heart, when it is troubled, to vent itself to GOD. As there is some natural ease in sighs and tears (for otherwise nature would not have been furnished with them, nor teach us to use them), they discharge some part of grief, though addressed no whither, but only let out; but more when it is in the presence of some entire friend; so they must be most of all easing, when they are directed to GOD in prayer. *Cor serenat et purgat oratio, capaciusque efficit ad accipienda divina munera* : Prayer, says St Augustine, calms and purifies the heart, and renders it more capable of the Divine benefits. *Mine eye poureth forth tears unto GOD,* says Job, Job xvi. 20; and David, *My sighing is not hid from Thee,* Psal. xxxviii. 9. *Cast thy burden on the Lord,* says the Psalmist, Psal. lv. 22. The Lord calls for our burdens, would not have us wrestle with them ourselves, but *roll* them over on Him. Now, the desires that are breathed forth in prayer are, as it were, the very unloading of the heart: each request that goes forth carries out somewhat of the burden with it, and lays it on GOD. *Be careful in nothing,* says the Apostle, Phil. iv. 6. That were a pleasant life indeed, if it might be; but how shall that be attained? Why, this is the only way, says he, *In all things make your requests known unto GOD.* Tell Him what are your desires, and leave them there with Him, and so you are sure to be rid of all further disquieting care of them. Try as many ways as you will, there is no other will free you, in difficulties, of all perplexing thoughts, but this, and this will do it.

[2.] In it the graces of the Spirit are exercised, and they gain by that, as all habits do; they are strengthened and increased by acting. Faith is exercised in believing the promises; and that is the very basis of prayer: it cannot subsist without the support of faith. And Hope is raised up and set on tiptoe, ὑποκαραδοκεῖν, to look out for accomplishment. And Love, it is that which delights it, to impart its mind to Him on whom it is set, and thus to entertain converse and conference with Him, and all hours seem short to it that are thus spent; and by this it still rises to a higher flame, it is blown and stirred by prayer. The more the soul converses with GOD, doubtless the more it loves Him.

And this speaking your desires to GOD in prayer makes the heart still more holy, invites it to entertain new desires, but such as it may confidently acquaint GOD withal.

[3.] In relation to the particular things desired, it not only fits and disposes the heart for receiving them as blessings, but withal, it is a real means of obtainment, by reason of GOD's own appointment, and of His promise. He hath bound Himself by His promises not to disregard the prayers of His people. *His ear is open to their cry*, says the Psalmist, Psal. xxxiv. 15. And the many instances in Scripture, and the experience of the Church in all ages, bear witness to the truth of these promises. Imminent judgments have been averted, great armies conquered, and the very course of nature countermanded, the sun arrested, by the power of prayer. Moses' hands, only held up to heaven, routed the Amalekites more than all the swords that were drawn against them.

The goodness of GOD is expressed in His promises; and these promises encourage prayer; and prayer is answered with performance; and thanksgiving returns the performance in praise to GOD, Psal. l. 15. So all ends where it began, in Him who is *the Alpha and the Omega*, the Beginning and the End of all things.

If you would be rich in all grace, be much in prayer. Conversing with GOD assimilates the soul to Him, beautifies it with the beams of His holiness, as Moses' face shined when he returned from the mount. It is prayer that brings all our supplies from Heaven; as the virtuous woman is said, Prov. xxxi. 14, to be *like the merchant's ships, she bringeth her food from afar*. Prayer draws more grace out of GOD's hand, and subdues sin and the powers of darkness; it entertains and augments our friendship with GOD, raiseth the soul from earth, and purifies it wonderfully. Their experience, that have any of this kind, teacheth them that, as they abate in prayer, all their graces do sensibly weaken. Therefore, when the Apostle hath suited a Christian with his *whole Armour*, he adds this to all, *Praying always with all prayer and supplication in the Spirit*, Eph. vi. 18. (1)

Brevity of Prayer

This, then, briefly, is the fault here: when the long continuance and much repetition in prayer is affected as a thing of itself available; when heaping on words and beating often over the same words, though the heart bear them not company, is judged to be prayer; and generally, whensoever the tongue outruns the affection, then is prayer turned into babbling. Yea, though a man use this very short form here prescribed, yet he may commit this very fault against which it was provided, he may babble in saying it; and it is to be feared the greatest part do so. Men judge, and that rightly, a speech to be long or short, not so much by the quantity of words, as by the sense; so that a very short speech that is empty of sense, may be called long, and a long one that is full, and hath nothing impertinent, is truly short: thus, as men judge by the sense of speech, GOD judgeth by the affection of prayer, which is the true sense of it; so the quality is the rule of the quantity with Him. There is no prayer too long to Him, provided it be all enlivened with affection: no idle repetition, where the heart says every word over again as often, and more often than the tongue. Therefore, those repetitions in the Psalms, *Lord, hear, Lord, incline Thine ear, Lord attend*, etc., were not idle on this account; GOD's own Spirit did dictate them, there was not one of them empty, but they came from the heart of the holy penmen, full fraught with the vehemency of their affections. And it is reported of St Augustine, that he prayed over for a whole night, *Noverim te, Domine, noverim me* [1]: because his heart still followed the suit, all of it was prayer. So that in truth, where the matter is new, and the words still diverse and very rich in sense, yet, with GOD, it may be idle multiplying of words, because the heart stays behind; and where the same words are repeated, so that a man seems poor and mean in the gift of prayer to others, yet if it be not defect of affection but the abundance of it, as it may be, that moves often the same request, it is not empty, but full of that sense that the Searcher of hearts alone can read. I had rather share with that *publican* in his own words, and say it often over, as if I had nothing else to say, *GOD be merciful to me a sinner*, saying it with such a heart, than the most excellent prayer where the outside is the better half. (2)

Amen

In this word concentre all the requests and are put up together: *so be it*. And there is in it withal, as all observe, a profession of confidence that it shall be so. It is from one root with those words which signify *believing* and *truth*. The truth of GOD's promises persuades belief; and *it* persuades to hope for a gracious answer of prayer. And this is the excellent advantage of the Prayer of Faith, that it quiets and establishes the heart in GOD. Whatsoever be its estate and desire, when once the believer hath put his petition in GOD's hand, he rests content in holy security and assurance concerning the answer; refers it to the wisdom and love of GOD, how and when He will answer; not doubting that whatsoever it be, and whenso-ever, it shall both be gracious and seasonable. But the reason why so few of us find that sweetness and comfort that are in Prayer is because the true nature and use of it is so little known. (3)

NOTES / SOURCES

1. Robert Leighton 'Exposition of The Lord's Prayer' in *The Whole Works of Robert Leighton*, Vol. V, London, 1870, pp. 243–5
2. Ibid., pp. 250–1
3. Ibid., p. 305

Jeremy Taylor   1613–1667

Scholar and Fellow of Gonville and Caius College, Cambridge, Jeremy Taylor was nominated by Archbishop Laud to a Fellowship at All Souls, Oxford, in 1635. He was

---

[1] Lord, let me know thee, let me know me.

appointed Chaplain to Charles I and later became a Chaplain in the Royalist Army, for which he was imprisoned at Chepstow in 1655. Later he lived in seclusion at Golden Grove, Carmarthenshire, writing devotional and theological works, including *The Rule and Exercise of Holy Living* (1650) and *The Rule and Exercise of Holy Dying* (1651). He was made Bishop (1661) of Down and Connor where he was involved in disputes with both Presbyterian and Roman Catholic clergy.

The First General Instrument of Holy Living: Care of our Time

He that is choice of his time will also be choice of his company, and choice of his actions, lest the first ingage him in vanity and losse, and the latter by being criminal be a throwing his time and himself away, and a going back in the accounts of eternity.

God hath given to man a short time here upon earth, and yet upon this short time eternity depends: but so, that for every hour of our life (after we are persons capable of laws, and know good from evil) we must give account to the great Judge of Men and Angels. And this is it which our blessed Saviour told us, that we must account for *every idle word*; not meaning, that every word which is not designed to edification, or is less prudent, shall be reckoned for a sin, but that besides our sinful and hurtful, our tempting or malicious language, even the time which we spend in our idle talking and unprofitable discoursings, that time which might and ought to have been imployed to spiritual and useful purposes, that is to be accounted for.

For we must remember, that we have a great work to do, many enemies to conquer, many evils to prevent, much danger to run through, many difficulties to be mastered, many necessities to serve, and much good to do, many children to provide for, or many friends to support, or many poor to relieve, or many diseases to cure, besides the needs of nature, and of relation, our private and our publick cares, and duties of the world, which necessity and the Providence of God hath adopted into the family of *Religion.*

And that we need not fear this instrument to be a snare to us, or that the duty must end in scruple, vexation, and eternal fears, we must remember, that the life of every man may be so ordered (and indeed must,) that it may be a perpetual serving of God: The greatest trouble and most busy trade, and worldly incombrances, when they are necessary or charitable, or profitable in order to any of those ends, which we are bound to serve whether publick or private, being a doing Gods work. For God provides the good things of the world to serve the needs of nature, by the labours of the Plowman, the skill and pains of the Artisan, and the dangers and traffick of the Merchant: These men are in their callings the Ministers of the Divine providence, and the stewards of the creation, and servants of the great family of God, *the World*, in the imployment of procuring necessaries for food and clothing, ornament and Physick. In their proportions also, a King and a Priest, and a Prophet, a Judge and an Advocate, doing the works of their imployment according to their proper rules, are doing the work of God, because they serve those necessities which God hath made, and yet made no provisions for them but by their Ministery. So that no man can complain, that his calling takes him off from religion, his calling itself and his very worldly imployment, in honest trades and offices, is a serving of God, and if it be moderately pursued, and according to the rules of Christian prudence, will leave void spaces enough for prayers and retirements of a more spiritual religion.

God hath given every man work enough to do, that there shall be no room for idlenesse, and yet hath so ordered the world, that there shall be space for devotion. He that hath the fewest businesses of the world, is called upon to spend more time in the dressing of his soul, and he that hath the most affairs, may so order them, that they shall be a service of God; whilst at certain periods they are blessed with prayers and actions of religion, and all day long are hallowed by a holy intention.

However, so long as Idlenesse is quite shut out from our lives, all the sins of wantonnesse, softnesse and effeminacy are prevented, and there is but little room left for temptation: and therefore to a busie man temptation is fain to climbe up together with his businesses, and sins creep upon him onely by accidents and occasions; whereas to an idle person they come in a full body, and with open violence, and the impudence of a restlesse importunity.

Idlenesse is called *the sin of Sodom and her daughters*, and indeed is *the burial of a living man*, an idle person being so uselesse to any purposes of God and man, that he is like one that is dead, unconcerned in the changes and necessities of the world: and he onely lives to spend his time, and eat the fruits of the earth, like vermin or a wolf, when their time comes they dye and perish, and in the mean time do no good; they neither plow nor carry burdens: all that they do, either is unprofitable, or mischievous.

Idlenesse is the greatest prodigality in the world: it throwes away that, which is invaluable in respect of its present use, and irreparable when it is past, being to be recovered by no power of art or nature. (1)

The Presence of God

God is *especially present* in the hearts of his people *by his holy Spirit*: and indeed the hearts of holy men are Temples in the truth of things, and in type and shadow they are of Heaven it self. For God *reigns* in the hearts of his servants. *There is his Kingdom.* The power of grace hath *subdued* all his enemies. There is, *his power.* They *serve* him night and day and give him thanks and praise; that is, *his glory*: This is the religion and worship of God in the Temple. The temple it self is the heart of man; Christ is the High Priest, who from thence sends up the incense of prayers and joyns them to his own intercession, and presents all together to his Father; and the Holy Ghost by his dwelling there, hath also consecrated it into a Temple; and God dwels in our hearts by faith, and Christ by his Spirit, and the Spirit by his purities; so that we are also Cabinets of the Mysterious Trinity; and what is this short of Heaven it self, but as infancy is short of manhood, and letters of words? The same state of life it is, but not the same age. It is *Heaven in a Looking-glasse*, (dark, but yet true) representing the beauties of the soul, and the graces of God, and the images of his eternal glory by the reality of a special presence. (2)

Matrimonial Chastity

Concerning married persons; besides the keeping of their mutual faith, and contract with each other, these particulars are useful to be observed.

1. Although their mutual endearments are safe within the protection of marriage, yet they that have Wives or Husbands must be as though they had them not; that is, they must have an affection greater to each other than they have to any person in the world, but not greater than they have to God: but that they be ready to part with all interest in each others person rather than sin against God.

2. In their permissions and license they must be sure to observe the order of Nature, and the ends of God. *He is an ill Husband that uses his Wife as a man treats a Harlot*, having no other end but pleasure. Concerning which our best rule is, that although in this, as in eating and drinking there is an appetite to be satisfied, which cannot be done without pleasing that desire, yet since that desire and satisfaction was intended by Nature for other ends, they should never be separate from those ends, but alwayes be joyned with all or one of these ends; *with a desire of children, or to avoyd fornication, or to lighten and ease the cares and sadnesses of houshold affairs, or to endear each other*: but never with a purpose either in act or desire to separate the sensuality from these ends which hallow it. (3)

The Eucharistic Table

For as God descended and came into the tabernacle invested with a cloud, so Christ comes to meet us clothed with a mystery. He hath a house below as well as above; here is his dwelling and here are his provisions; here is his fire and here his meat; hither God sends his Son, and here his Son manifests himself. The church and the holy table of the Lord, the assemblies of saints and the devotions of his people, the word and the sacrament, the oblation of bread and wine and the offering of ourselves, the consecration and the communion, are the things of God and of Jesus Christ; and he that is employed in these is there where God loves to be, and where Christ is to be found; in the employments in which God delights, in the ministeries of his own choice, in the work of the Gospel and the methods of grace, in the economy of heaven and the dispensations of eternal happiness.

And now, that we may know where to find him, we must be sure to look after him. He hath told us where he would be, behind what pillar, and under what cloud, and covered with what veil, and conveyed by what ministry, and present in what sacrament. And we must not look for him in the highways of ambition and pride, of wealth or sensual pleasures; these things are not found in the house of his Father, neither may they come near his dwelling. But if we seek for Christ, we shall find him in the methods of virtue and the paths of God's commandments, in the houses of prayer and the offices of religion, in the persons of the poor and the retirements of an afflicted soul; we shall find him in holy reading and pious meditation, in our penitential sorrows and in the time of trouble, in pulpits and upon altars, in the word and in the sacraments: if we come hither as we ought, we are sure to find our Beloved, him whom our soul longeth after. (4)

Prayer after Baptism

O God, be Thou his father for ever, Christ his elder brother and his Lord, the church his mother; let the body of Christ be his food, the blood of Christ his drink, and the Spirit the earnest of his inheritance. Let faith be his learning, religion his employment, his whole life be spiritual, heaven the object of his hopes and the end of his labours; let him be Thy servant in the kingdom of grace, and Thy son in the kingdom of glory, through Jesus Christ our Lord. *Amen* (5)

Private Prayer

In private prayers it is permitted to every man to speak his prayers, or only to think them, which is a speaking to God. Vocal or mental prayer is all one to God, but in order to us they have their several advantages. The sacrifice of the heart, and the calves of the lips, make up a holocaust to God: but words are the arrest of the desires, and keep the spirit fixed, and, in less permissions, to wander from fancy to fancy; and mental prayer is apt to make the greater fervour, if it wander not: our office is more determined by words; but we then actually think of God, when our spirits only speak. Mental prayer, when our spirits wander, is like a watch standing still, because the spring is down; wind it up again, and it goes on regularly: but in vocal prayer, if the words run on, and the spirit wanders, the clock strikes false, the hand points not to the right hour, because something is in disorder, and the striking is nothing but noise. In mental prayer, we confess God's omniscience; in vocal prayer, we call the angels to witness. In the first, our spirits rejoice in God; in the second, the angels rejoice in us. Mental prayer is the best remedy against lightness, and indifferency of affections; but vocal prayer is the aptest instrument of communion. That is more angelical, but yet fittest for the state of separation and glory; this is but human, but it is apter for our present constitution. They have their distinct proprieties, and may be used according to several accidents, occasions, or dispositions. (6)

Special Gifts of Grace

God loving to bless one degree of grace with another, till it comes to a confirmation in grace, which is a state of salvation directly opposite to obduration; and as this is irremediable and irrecoverable, so is the other inadmissible: as God never saves a person obdurate and obstinately impenitent, so he never loses a man, whom he hath confirmed in grace; 'whom he' so 'loves, he loves unto the end;' and to others, indeed, he offers his persevering love, but they will not entertain it with a persevering duty, they will not be beloved unto the end. But I insert this caution, that every man, that is in this condition of a confirmed grace, does not always know it; but sometimes God draws aside the curtains of peace, and shows him his throne, and visits him with irradiations of glory, and sends him a little star to stand over his dwelling, and then again covers it with a cloud. It is certain, concerning some persons, that they shall never fall, and that God will not permit them to the danger or probability of it: to such it is morally impossible: but these are but few, and themselves know it not, as they know a demonstrative proposition, but as they see the sun, sometimes breaking from a cloud very brightly, but all day long giving necessary and sufficient light. (7)

Jesus Washes the Disciples' Feet

When the holy Jesus had finished his last Mosaic rite, he descends to give example of the first fruit of evangelical graces: 'he rises from supper, lays aside his garment' like a servant, and, with all the circumstances of an humble ministry, 'washes the feet of his disciples,' beginning at the first, St Peter, until he came to Judas, the traitor; that we might, in one scheme, see a rare conjunction of charity and humility, of self-denial and indifferency, represented by a person glorious and great, their Lord and Master, sad and troubled. And he chose to wash their feet rather than their head, that he might have the opportunity of a more humble posture, and a more apt signification of his charity. Thus God lays every thing aside, that he may serve his servants; heaven stoops to earth, and one abyss calls upon another, and the miseries of man, which were next to infinite, are excelled by a mercy equal to the immensity of God. (8)

Jesus Prays for His Followers

Now that the holy Jesus began to taste the bitter cup, he betook him to his great antidote, which himself, the great Physician of our souls, prescribed to all the world to cure their calamities, and to make them pass from miseries into virtue, that so they may arrive at glory; he prays to his heavenly Father, he kneels down, and not only so, but 'falls flat upon the earth,' and would, in humility and fervent adoration, have descended low as the centre; he prays with an intension great as his sorrow, and yet with a dereliction so great, and a conformity to the Divine will so ready, as if it had been the most indifferent thing in the world for him to be delivered to death, or from it: for, though his nature did decline death, as that which hath a natural horror and contradiction to the present interest of its preservation; yet when he looked upon it, as his heavenly Father had put it into the order of redemption of the world, it was that 'baptism,' which he was 'straitened, till he had accomplished.' And now there is not in the world any condition of prayer which is essential to the duty, or any circumstances of advantage to its performance, but were concentred in this one instance; humility of spirit, lowliness of deportment, importunity of desire, a fervent spirit, a lawful matter, resignation to the will of God, great love, the love of a Son to his Father; which appellative was the form of his address; perseverance; he went thrice, and prayed the same prayer; it was not long, and it was so retired as to have the advantages of a sufficient solitude and opportune recollection; for he was withdrawn from the most of his disciples: and yet not so alone as to lose the benefit of communion; for Peter and the two Boanerges were near him. Christ, in this prayer, which was the most fervent that he ever made on earth, intending to transmit to all the world a precedent of devotion to be transcribed and imitated; that we should cast all our cares, and empty them in the bosom of God, being content to receive such a portion of our trouble back again, which he assigns us for our spiritual emolument. (9)

Advice on Daily Living

Suppose every day to be a day of business; for your whole life is a race and a battle, a merchandize, and a journey: every day propound to yourself a rosary, or a chaplet of good works, to present to God at night . . .

Read not much at a time; but meditate as much as your time, and capacity, and disposition will give you leave: ever remembering, that little reading, and much thinking; little speaking, and much hearing; frequent and short prayers, and great devotion, is the best way to be wise, to be holy, to be devout . . .

Receive the blessed sacrament as often as you can: endeavour to have it once a month, besides the solemn and great festivals of the year.

Confess your sins often, hear the word of God, make religion the business of your life, your study and chiefest care; and be sure that in all things a spiritual guide take you by the hand.

Thou shalt always rejoice in the evening, if thou dost spend the day virtuously. (10)

NOTES / SOURCES

1. Jeremy Taylor 'Holy Living' (1650), in Peter Stanwood (ed.), *Jeremy Taylor: Holy Living and Holy Dying*, Oxford, 1989, pp. 19–21
2. Ibid., p. 37
3. Ibid., p. 81
4. Jeremy Taylor 'Worthy Communicant' (1660) in Heber, R. and Eden, C. (eds.) *The Whole Works of Jeremy Taylor*, Vol. III, London, 1850, pp. 6–7
5. *A Collection of Offices* (1658), in Ibid., Vol. III p. 638
6. *The Great Exemplar* (1649), in Ibid., Vol. II p. 482
7. Ibid., Vol. II pp. 554–5
8. Ibid., Vol. II pp. 628–9
9. Ibid., Vol. II pp. 661–2
10. *The Golden Grove* (1655) in Ibid., Vol. XV pp. 610, 615, 617

John Pearson   1613–1686

An ardent supporter of the Royalist cause during the Civil War, John Pearson remained in London until the Restoration. In 1650 he accepted the post of weekly preacher at St Clement's, East Cheap, London, from which sermons came the work for which he is best known, *An Exposition of The Creed* (1659). After the Restoration he became Master successively of Jesus College (1660), and of Trinity College (1662), Cambridge, Lady Margaret Professor of Divinity (1661–1672), and later Bishop of Chester (1673). His discourses are marked out by his concern to uphold the Church of England against both Roman Catholicism and Nonconformity.

The Communion of Saints

But because there is more than an outward vocation, and a charitable presumption, necessary to make a man holy; therefore we must find some other qualification which must make him really and truly such, not only by an extrinsical denomination, but by a real and internal affection. What this sanctity is, and who are capable of this title properly, we must learn out of the gospel of Christ; by which alone, ever since the church of Christ was founded, any man can become a saint. Now by the tenure of the gospel we shall find that those are truly and properly saints which are 'sanctified in Christ Jesus:' (1 Cor. i. 2:) First. In respect of their holy faith, by which they are regenerated; for 'whosoever believeth that Jesus is the Christ is born of God;' (1 John v. 1;) by which they are purged, God himself 'purifying their hearts by faith;' (Acts xv. 9;) whereby 'they are washed, sanctified, and justified in the name of the Lord Jesus,' (1 Cor. vi. 11,) 'in whom also after that they believe; they are sealed with the Holy Spirit of promise.' (Eph. i. 13) Secondly. In respect of their conversation: for 'as he which hath called them is holy,' so are 'they holy in all manner of conversation;' (1 Peter i. 15;) 'adding to their faith virtue, and to virtue knowledge, and to knowledge temperance, and to temperance patience, and to patience [godliness, and to godliness] brotherly kindness, and to brotherly kindness charity; that they may neither be barren nor unfruitful in the knowledge of our Lord Jesus Christ.' (2 Peter i. 5-8) Such persons then as are called by a holy calling, and not disobedient unto it; such as are endued with a holy faith, and purified thereby; such as are sanctified by the Holy Spirit of God, and by virtue thereof do lead a holy life, 'perfecting holiness in the fear of God;' (2 Cor. vii. 1;) such persons, I say, are really and truly saints; and being of the church of Christ, (as all such now must of necessity be,) are the proper subject of this part of the Article, 'the communion of saints,' as it is added to the former, 'the holy catholic church.'

Now as these are the saints of the church of Christ, from whence they were called the 'churches of the saints;' (1 Cor. xiv. 33;) so there was never any church of God, but there were such persons in it as were saints. We read in the Psalms of 'the congregation and the assembly of the saints;' (Psalm lxxxix. 5, 7; cxlix. 1;) and Moses assured the people of Israel, that all the saints of God were in his hand: (Deut. xxxiii. 3:) we read in the prophets of 'the saints of the Most High;' (Dan. vii. 25;) and at our Saviour's death 'the bodies of such saints which slept arose.' (Matt. xxvii. 52) Where again we may observe, that they were saints while their bodies were in the grave; as Aaron in the time of David kept the name of 'the saint of the Lord.' (Psalm cvi. 16) Such as are holy in their lives do not lose their sanctity, but improve it, at their deaths; nor can they lose the honour of that appellation, while that which gives it doth acquire perfection.

Hence grows that necessary distinction of the saints on earth, and the saints in heaven; the first belonging to the militant, the second to the triumphant, church. Of the first the prophet David speaketh expressly: 'Thou art my Lord: my goodness extendeth not to thee; but to the saints that are in the earth:' (Psalm xvi. 2, 3:) of these do we read in the Acts of the Apostles; to these did St Paul direct his Epistles. Of the second doth the Apostle make that question, 'Do ye not know that the saints shall judge the world?' (1 Cor. vi. 2) And all those which were spoken of as saints then in earth, if truly such, and departed so, are now, and shall for ever continue, saints in heaven.

NOTES / SOURCES

John Pearson *An Exposition of the Creed* (1659), London, 1854, pp. 504–5

William Thomas   1613–1689

William Thomas, one time Fellow of Jesus College, Oxford, was ejected from the living of Laugharne in 1644 but returned at the Restoration in 1660. As Chaplain to the Duke of York he attended him in his discussions with the Dutch. As Bishop of St Davids (1677) he identified himself closely with the interests of his Diocese and was known very much as a Welshman. He became Bishop of Worcester in 1683 but refused to distribute the Declaration of Indulgence (1688) among his clergy, nor would he take the Oath of Allegiance to William III and was therefore suspended in 1689.

The Inward Fruits not always Apparent

'These scoffers you tax may (by God's grace) mourn for their scoffs. Those prophane persons, who o'erflow in their cups, may o'erflow in their sorrows, and exchange a deluge of distempers for tears, their frequent oaths and imprecations, for penitent prayers and supplications. And though the outward fruit be blasted, to your eye; yet there may be secret buds and blossoms discernable to God and acceptable in Christ, notwithstanding those apparent witherings. There may be deep sighs and sobs of spirit, passionate yearnings, and pantings for Grace, where there are no manifest effects of it. Will you deny the balm of Gilead to these bleeding wounds of Souls? *The sound have no need of the physician but the sick.*'

NOTES / SOURCES

William Thomas *An Apology for the Church of England*, London, 1679, p. 165

Peter Gunning   1614–1684

A staunch Royalist who opposed the excesses of Roman Catholicism and of Puritanism, Peter Gunning continued to celebrate Prayer Book services at Exeter House in the Strand during the Commonwealth. At the Restoration in 1660 he became Lady Margaret Professor and then Regius Professor of Divinity at Cambridge. Later he was appointed Bishop of Chichester and then Ely. He took a leading part at the Savoy Conference of 1661, which attempted to enable Presbyterians to remain members of the Established Church.

Humbling Ourselves before God

For the honour of the divine holiness of God our Father, who is a God of most pure eyes, who without respect of persons will judge every man that judgeth not himself; we therefore necessarily so judge ourselves by such self-afflictions and real acknowledgments, that His not judging us may not possibly be by any thought His accepting our persons to the favouring of our sin: it is a stopping of the mouth of blasphemy in the enemies of God, when they shall see the sins of God's children so condemned, punished, and persecuted by the offenders themselves, and that in order to regain the favour of God and His sparing of them, and therefore surely those sins much more condemned by God, for if our own hearts judge us so worthy to be punished, God is greater and holier than our hearts: but because also He is most faithful in His promises of mercy, and His ways higher than man's ways, we judging ourselves, He will not judge us; we abhorring ourselves in dust and ashes, He will not abhor us.

NOTES / SOURCES

Peter Gunning *The Paschal or Lent Fast*, Oxford, 1845, p. 171

Daniel Brevint   1616–1695

Educated at the Protestant University of Samur, Daniel Brevint had his degree incorporated by Oxford University in 1638. When he was deprived of his Fellowship at Jesus College, Oxford, he retired to his native Jersey, and thereafter took up residence in France. He was ordained as an Anglican in Paris in 1651, John Cosin (q.v.) presenting him and preaching the sermon. At the Restoration, he became Canon Treasurer of Durham (1660) and later Dean of Lincoln (1682). A noted polemicist in the Protestant cause, he also published devotional works, notably *Christian Sacrament and Sacrifice* (1673), which had a strong influence on the eucharistic hymns of John and Charles Wesley (q.v.).

The Presence of Christ

This victim having been offered up both in the fulness of time and in the midst of the habitable world, which properly is Christ's great temple, and thence being carried up to heaven, which is his proper sanctuary, thence He spreads all about us salvation, as the burnt-offering did its smoke, as the golden altar did its perfumes, and as the burning candlestick its lights. And thus Christ's body and blood have every where, but especially at the holy Communion, a most true and *real presence*. When He offered himself upon earth, the vapour of his atonement went up and darkened the very sun; and by rending the great veil, it clearly shewed He had made a way into heaven. Now since He is gone up to heaven, thence He sends down on earth the graces that spring continually both from his everlasting Sacrifice, and from the continual intercessions which attend it. So that it is in vain to say, *who will go up into heaven?* since, without either ascending or descending, this sacred body of Jesus fills with atonement and blessing the remotest parts of this temple. (1)

The Lord's Table as the Place of Peace Offering

Thus this great and holy mystery extends and communicates the death of the Lord, both as *offering Himself to God*, and as *giving Himself to men*. As He offered himself to God, it enters me both into that mysterial body which is reputed as dead with Christ, and into their society, privilege, and communion, for whom He was pleased to die; it sets me among the precious stones of Aaron's ephod (Exod. xxviii.), close to the breast, and on the very shoulders of that eternal Priest, whilst

He offers up Himself and intercedes for his spiritual Israel; and by this means it conveys to me the *communion of his sufferings*, (Philip. iii. 10), whence will infallibly proceed another communion in all his graces and glories. Under the second notion, as *He offers Himself to men*, the holy Eucharist is, after the Sacrifice for sin, the true festival and Sacrifice of peace-offerings, and the *table* purposely set up to receive those mercies that are sent down from the *altar. Take and eat; this is my body which was broken for you; and this is the blood which was shed for you.* (2)

NOTES / SOURCES

1. Daniel Brevint *Christian Sacrament and Sacrifice* (1673), Oxford, 1847, pp. 37–8
2. Ibid., p. 40

Ralph Cudworth   1617–1688

Ralph Cudworth became successively Fellow of Emmanuel College, Cambridge (1639), Master of Clare Hall (1645), Regius Professor of Hebrew (1645–88), and Master of Christ's College, Cambridge (1654). He was one of the leaders of the 'Cambridge Platonists', and sought to combat both religious dogmatism and Hobbesian atheism. He was a strong influence on a whole generation of students, including Simon Patrick (q.v.). Perhaps his most public contribution to the religious–political debates of his time was the sermon he preached to the House of Commons in 1647.

The Assurance of Christ's Love

Those divine purposes, whatsoever they be are altogether unsearchable and unknowable by us, they lie wrapt up in everlasting, darknesse, and covered in a deep Abysse; who is able to fathom the bottome of them? Let us not therefore make this our first attempt towards God and Religion, to perswade our selves strongly of these everlasting Decrees: for if at our first flight we aime so high, we shall happily but scorch our wings, and be struck back with lightning, as those *Giants* of old were, that would needs attempt to invade and assault heaven. And it is indeed a most *Giganticall* Essay, to thrust our selves so boldly into the lap of heaven; it is the pranck of a *Nimrod*, of a *mighty Hunter* thus rudely to deal with God, and to force heaven and happinesse before his face whether he will or no. The way to obtain a good assurance indeed of our title to heaven, is not to clamber up to it, by a ladder of our own ungrounded perswasions; but to dig as low as hell by humility and self-denyall in our own hearts: and though this may seem to be the furthest way about; yet it is indeed the neerest, and safest way to it. We must *ascend downward, and descend upward*; if we would indeed come to heaven, or get any true perswasion of our title to it. The most gallant and triumphant confidence of a Christian, riseth safely and surely upon this low foundation, that lies deep under ground; and there stands firmely and stedfastly. When our heart is once tuned into a conformity with the word of God, when we feel our will, perfectly to concurre with his will, we shal then presently perceive a *Spirit of adoption* within our selves, teaching us to cry *Abba. Father*. We shall not then care for peeping into those hidden Records of Eternity, to see whether our names be written there in golden characters: no, we shall find a copy of Gods thoughts concerning us, written in our own breasts. There we may read the characters of his favour to us, there we may feel an inward sense of his love to us, flowing out of our hearty and unfained love to him. And we shall be more undoubtedly perswaded of it, then if any of those winged *Watchmen* above, that are privie to heavens secrets, should come and tel us; that they saw our names enrolled in those *volumes of eternity.* Whereas on the contrary; though we strive to perswade our selves never so confidently, that God from all eternity hath loved us, and elected us to life and happinesse; if we do yet in the mean time entertain any iniquity within our hearts, and willingly close with any lust; do what we can, we shall find many a cold qualme ever now and then seizing upon us at approching dangers; and when death itself shall grimly look us in the face, we shall feel our hearts even to die within us, and our spirits quite faint away, though we strive to raise them and recover them never so much, with the *Strong Waters* and *Aqua vitæ* of our own ungrounded presumptions. The least inward lust willingly continued in, will be like a *worme*, fretting the *Gourd* of our jolly confidence, and presumptuous perswasion of Gods love, and always gnawing at the root of it: and though we strive to keep it alive, and continually besprinkle it with some dews of our own; yet it will alwayes be dying and withering in our bosomes. But a good Conscience within, will be alwayes better to a Christian, then *health to his navell, and marrow to his bones*; it will be an everlasting cordiall to his heart; it will be softer to him then a bed of doune, and he may sleep securely upon it, in the midst of raging and tempestuous seas, when the winds bluster, and the waves beat round about him. A good conscience, is the best looking-glasse of heaven; in which the soul may see God's thoughts and purposes concerning it, as so many shining starres reflected to it. *Hereby we know that we know Christ, hereby we know that Christ loves us, if we keep his Commandments.*

NOTES / SOURCES

Ralph Cudworth, *A Sermon Preached before The Honourable House of Commons at Westminster*, Cambridge 1647, pp. 9–13

Richard Allestree   1619–1681

A lifelong supporter of the Stuart monarchy, Richard Allestree served in the Royalist Forces and was twice captured but released. Expelled from Oxford by the Parliament- arians in 1648, he continued to say Church of England services privately during the Commonwealth. Regius Professor of Divinity at Oxford (1663–1679) and also Provost of Eton College, he is best remembered as the author to whom *The Whole Duty of Man* (1657) is ascribed.

Necessity of Caring for the Soul

The only intent of this ensuing treatise, is to be a short and plain direction to the very meanest readers, to behave themselves so in this world, that they may be happy for ever in the next. But because it is in vain to tell men their duty till they be persuaded of the necessity of performing it, I shall, before I proceed to the particulars required of every Christian, endeavour to win them to the practice of one general duty preparatory to all the rest; and that is the consideration and care of their own souls, without which they will never think themselves much concerned in the other.

Man, we know, is made up of two parts, a body and a soul: the body only the husk or shell of the soul, a lump of flesh, subject to many diseases and pains while it lives, and at last to death itself; and then it is so far from being valued, that it is not to be endured above ground, but laid to rot in the earth. Yet to this viler part of us we perform a great deal of care; all the labour and toil we are at is to maintain that. But the more precious part, the soul, is little thought of, no care taken how it fares, but as if it were a thing that nothing concerned us, is left quite neglected, never considered by us.

This carelessness of the soul is the root of all the sin we commit, and therefore whosoever intends to set upon a Christian course, must in the first place amend that: to the doing whereof, there needs no deep learning, or extraordinary parts; the simplest man living (that is not a natural fool) hath understanding enough for it, if he will but act in this by the same rules of common reason, whereby he proceeds in his worldly business. I will therefore now briefly set down some of those motives, which use to stir up our care of any outward thing, and then apply them to the soul. (1)

Self-examination before Communion

Let this therefore be your first business; try whether you rightly understand what that covenant is which you entered into at your baptism, what be the mercies promised on God's part, and the duties on yours. And because the covenant made with each of us in baptism is only the applying to our particulars the covenant made by God in Christ with all mankind in general, you are to consider whether you understand that; if you do not, you must immediately seek for instruction in it. And till we have means of gaining better, look over what is briefly said in the entrance to this treatise concerning the second covenant, which is the foundation of that covenant which God makes with us in our baptism. And because you will there find that obedience to all God's commands is the condition required of us, and is also that which we expressly vow in our baptism, it is necessary you should likewise know what those commands of God are. Therefore if you find you are ignorant of them, never be at rest till you have got yourself instructed in them, and have gained such a measure of knowledge as may direct you to do that whole duty of man which God requires. And the giving thee this instruction is the only aim of this book, which, the more ignorant thou art, the more earnestly I shall entreat thee diligently to read. And if thou hast heretofore approached to this holy sacrament in utter ignorance of these necessary things, bewail thy sin in so doing, but presume not to come again till thou hast by gaining this necessary knowledge fitted thyself for it, which thou must hasten to do. For though no man must come to the sacrament in such ignorance, yet if he wilfully continue in it, that will be no excuse to him for keeping from this holy table. (2)

Frequent Communion

But though the obligation of every [such] single vow reach to the utmost day of our lives, yet are we often to renew it, that is, we are often to receive the Holy Sacrament, for that being the means of conveying to us so great and invaluable benefits, and it being also a command of Christ, that we should do this in remembrance of Him, we are in respect both of reason and duty to omit no fit opportunity of partaking of that holy table. I have now shewed you what that reverence is which we are to pay to God in his sacrament. (3)

A Brief Paraphrase of the Lord's Prayer

To be used as a Prayer

OUR FATHER WHICH ART IN HEAVEN

O Lord, who dwellest in the highest heavens, Thou art the author of our being, Thou hast also begotten us again unto a lively hope, and carriest towards us the tenderness and bowels of a compassionate Father. O make us to render to Thee the love and obedience of children; and that we may resemble Thee our Father in heaven (that place of true delight and purity), give us a holy disdain of all the deceitful pleasures and foul pollutions of this world, and so raise up our minds, that we may always have our conversation in heaven, from whence we look for our Saviour the Lord Jesus Christ.

1. HALLOWED BE THY NAME

Strike such an awe in our hearts, that we may humbly reverence Thee in Thy name, which is great, wonderful, and holy; and carry such a sacred respect to all things that relate to Thee and Thy worship, as may express our reverence to Thy great Majesty. Let all the people praise Thee, O God, let all the people praise Thee.

2. THY KINGDOM COME

Establish Thy throne and rule for ever in our souls by the power of Thy grace, subdue all those rebellious corruptions that exalt themselves against Thee; they are those enemies of Thine which would not Thou shouldst reign over them. O let them be brought forth and slain before Thee, and make us such faithful subjects of this Thy kingdom of grace, that we may be capable of the kingdom of glory, and then Lord Jesus come quickly.

3. THY WILL BE DONE IN EARTH, ETC

Enable us by Thy grace cheerfully to suffer Thy will in all Thy afflictions, and readily perform it in all Thy commands. Give us of that heavenly zeal to Thy service, wherewith the blessed angels of Thy presence are inspired, that we may obey Thee with the like fervour and alacrity, and that following them in their obedience, we may be joined with them to sing eternal praises in Thy kingdom, to God and to the Lamb for ever.

4. GIVE US THIS DAY OUR, ETC

Give us that continual supply of Thy grace, which may sustain and nourish our souls unto eternal life. And be Thou pleased also to provide for our bodies all those things which Thou seest fit for their support through this our earthly pilgrimage, and make us cheerfully to rest on Thee for them, first seeking Thy kingdom and the righteousness thereof, and then not doubting but all these things shall be added unto us.

5. FORGIVE US OUR TRESPASSES, ETC

Heal our souls, O Lord, for we have sinned against Thee, let Thy tender mercies abound towards us in the forgiveness of all our offences; and grant, O Lord, that we may never forfeit this pardon of Thine by denying ours to our brethren, but give us those bowels of compassion to others which we stand in so much greater need of from Thee, that we may forgive as fully and finally upon Christ's command as we desire to be forgiven, for His merits and intercession.

6. LEAD US NOT INTO TEMPTATION, ETC

O Lord, we have no strength against those multitudes of temptations that daily assault us, only our eyes are upon Thee; O be Thou pleased either to restrain them or assist us, and in Thy faithfulness suffer us not to be tempted above that we are able, but in all our temptations make us a way to escape, that we be not overcome by them, but may, when Thou shalt call us to it, resist even unto blood, striving against sin, that we being faithful unto death, Thou mayest give us the crown of life.

7. FOR THINE IS THE KINGDOM, ETC

Hear us, and graciously answer our petitions, for Thou art the good King over all the earth, whose power is infinite, and art able to do for us above all that we can ask or think, and to whom belongeth the glory of all that good Thou workest in us or for us. Therefore blessing, honour, glory, and power be unto Him that sitteth upon the throne, to our God for ever and ever. Amen. (4)

NOTES / SOURCES

1. Richard Allestree, *The Whole Duty of Man*, London, 1657, 1700, Preface, pp. 3–4
2. Ibid., pp. 63–4
3. Ibid., pp. 89–90
4. Ibid., pp. 405–8

John Evelyn   1620–1706

A noted diarist, John Evelyn travelled extensively on the Continent in the 1640s, finally returning to settle at Sayes Court, near Deptford, in 1652. With John Wilkins and Robert Boyle he proposed the formation of what became the Royal Society. An Adviser to Charles II and James II, he held a number of royal appointments and was a recognised authority on numismatics, architecture, and landscape gardening. He was a devotee of Jeremy Taylor (q.v.).

Christmas Day 1657

I went to London with my wife, to celebrate Christmas-day, Mr Gunning preaching in Exeter Chapell, on 7 Michah 2. Sermon ended, as he was giving us the Holy Sacrament, the chapell was surrounded with souldiers, and all the communicants and assembly surpriz'd and kept prisoners by them, some in the house, others carried away. It fell to my share to be confin'd to a roome in the house, where yet I was permitted to dine with the master of it, the Countesse of Dorset, Lady Hatton, and some others of quality who invited me. In the afternoone came Col. Whaly, Goffe and others, from White-hall, to examine us one by one; some they committed to the Marshall, some to prison. When I came before them they tooke my name and abode, examin'd me why, contrarie to an ordinance made that none should any longer observe the superstitious time of the Nativity (so esteem'd by them), I durst offend, and particularly be at Common Prayers, which they told me was but the masse in English, and particularly pray for Charles Steuart, for which we had no Scripture. I told them we did not pray for Cha. Stewart, but for all Christian Kings, Princes, and Governors. They replied, in so doing we praid for the K. of Spaine too, who was their enemie and a papist, with other frivolous and insnaring questions and much threatning; and finding no colour to detaine me, they dismiss'd me with much pitty of my ignorance. These were men of high flight and above ordinances, and spake spiteful things of our Lord's Nativity. As we went up to receive the Sacrament the miscreants held their muskets against us as if they would have shot us at the altar, but yet suffering us to finish the office of Communion, as perhaps not having instructions what to do in case they found us in that action. So I got home late the next day, blessed be God. (1)

Frequent Communion

There are some who think frequent Communion apt to produce too greate Familiarity, and consequently abate of the Reverence with which we should approch the dreadful Mysteries: 'Tis true, Familiarity amongst men, creates many times contempt; because the more we are acquainted with one another, the more we discover our Infirmities and defects, and that lessens our esteeme; But 'tis quite otherwise with God, whom the more we know and Contemplate, the more we Love, and the more we Love the more we admire and Revere; because he is all perfection; and therefore those who are much given to Converse with God, by Prayer, close Meditation, and frequent Communion, do usualy far exceede in Holynesse, and vertue, those who onely Contemplate his attributes at Distance, and approach him but seldom. Moses's face did not shine 'till he had been forty-dayes and nights Conversing in the Mount with God; and if their Countenances have not that Lustre here, who oft converse with *JESUS* the Son of God, upon the Crosse; their Lives and Conversation shine; and so shall theire Bodys too, Bright as those Angels who continually behold the Face of God.

   As Love then is better than Feare, nay as Love is the noblest passion, and highest felicity which the Soule is capable of in this, or the Life to come; So doubtlesse, if Love carry us to this Lover of Soules, we cannot come too often to this Holy Table (2)

The Oblation

Behold, ô Father, I offer up to thee, thy Blessed CHRIST! The Son of thy Love;
his purity, Inocency, Humilitie, perfections, and consummate goodnesse, to
satisfie for my Filthenesse, Falsenesse, pride, Defects and Imperfections:—See, ô
Lord! rather how he offers himselfe on the bloody Crosse, and now on the
unbloodie Altar! Him, ô permit thy Servant to offer also in Lieu of all the Honors,
Homages, Gratitude and Services, due to thy sovraine greatnesse from me, and all
thy Creatures: ô Monarch of both worlds, that thou shouldst humble thyselfe for
such a worm! Such an handfull of dust! (3)

NOTES / SOURCES

1. Christmas Day 1657 in *The Diary of John Evelyn*, London, n.d.
2. *A Devotionarie Book of John Evelyn of Wootton*, London, 1935, p. 12
3. Ibid., pp. 41–2

Samuel Crossman   1624?–1684

A noted seventeenth-century poet and divine, Samuel Crossman was educated at
Pembroke College, Cambridge. He was appointed to the living of Little Henny in Essex,
which he was forced to abandon (1662) for his nonconformity. He later took the Oath of
Conformity and became Prebendary (1667) and then Dean of Bristol (1683–1684). As
well as a number of homiletic poems and sermons, Crossman also published (1664)
The Young Man's Monitor ('a modest offer towards the pious and virtuous composure
of life') and *The Young Man's Meditations* (Sacred Poems) in which appeared what has
become the popular hymn 'My song is love unknown', where the second line of the last
verse was altered from 'my story' to 'No story' when first sung as a hymn in 1868.

Love Unknown

My song is love unknown;
　　My Saviour's love to me.
Love to the loveless shown,
　　That they might lovely be.
　　　O who am I
　　　　That for my sake
　　　　My Lord should take
　　　Frail flesh, and die.

He came from his bless'd throne,
　　Salvation to bestow:
But men made strange, and none
　　The long'd-for Christ would know
　　　But Oh! my Friend,
　　　　My Friend indeed,
　　　　Who at my need
　　　His life did spend.

Sometimes they strow his way,
  And his sweet praises sing:
Resounding all the day,
  Hosannah's to their King.
    Then crucify
      Is all their breath,
      And for his death
    They thirst and cry.

Why, what hath my Lord done?
  What makes this rage, and spite?
He made the lame to run,
  He gave the Blind their sight.
    Sweet injuries!
      Yet they at these
      Themselves displease,
    And 'gainst him rise.

They rise, and needs will have
  My dear Lord made away,
A Murderer they save,
  The Prince of Life they slay.
    Yet cheerful he
      To Suff'ring goes,
      That he his Foes
    From thence might free.

In life no house, no home,
  My Lord on earth might have;
In death no friendly tomb,
  But what a stranger gave.
    What may I say?
      Heav'n was his home;
      But mine the tomb
    Wherein he lay.

Here might I stay, and sing;
  My story so divine.
Never was love, dear King!
  Never was grief like thine.
    This is my friend,
      In whose sweet praise
      I all my days
    Could gladly spend. (1)

Advice on Holiness

You have more particularly two great concerns lying now upon your hand, which had need both of them be seriously thought upon, and duly provided for, before you slip any longer time. The one is, the wise ordering and improvement of this present life; which is commonly spoiled in youth, and scarcely ever recovered in riper years. The other, the religious providing for a better, which no man can be too diligent in. He that is truly faithful in either, will be in some measure conscionable in both. These both God joined together, and happy is that man who hath learned to each its due, and through a well-led life with men on earth, to pass to a better with God himself hereafter in Heaven.

It will be your wisdom to understand aright the good consistency of both these together. That so you may neither on the one hand think hardly of Religion, as that which quencheth the subordinate sweetness of life; as that which overthrows what were other ways lovely in Nature: nor yet on the other hand content yourselves with bare Nature, without the true grace of God; which is ten thousand times more worth, and better indeed than life itself . . . Be in God's name frugal of all the just comforts of this life, flight them not, waste them not, they are the dear gifts of God, the God of all our mercies, the portion that is given us outwardly under the sun. But if the Lord be willing to sanctify these and bestow yet greater than them upon us, let us not neglect, let us not despise our own advantages: but accept it with all humble thankfulness, that our water may thus be turned into wine. (2)

NOTES/SOURCES

1. Samuel Crossman, *The Young Man's Meditations*, London, 1664, pp. 10–11
2. Samuel Crossman, *The Young Man's Monitor*, London, 1664, p. 14

The Book of Common Prayer   1662

The Book of Common Prayer of 1662 resulted from the Restoration Settlement. Based largely on that of 1559, there were a number of significant additions, including the General Thanksgiving, widely regarded as the work of Edward Reynolds (1599–1676), a Presbyterian who was made Bishop of Norwich in 1661.

A General Thanksgiving

Almighty God, Father of all mercies, we thine unworthy servants do give thee most humble and hearty thanks for all thy goodness and loving-kindness to us and to all men; [*particularly to *those* who *desire* now to offer up *their* praises and thanks-givings for thy late mercies vouchsafed unto *them*.] We bless thee for our creation, preservation, and all the   *This to be said when any desire to return praise.

blessings of this life; but above all for thine inestimable love in the redemption of the world by our Lord Jesus Christ, for the means of grace, and for the hope of glory. And we beseech thee, give us that due sense of all thy mercies, that our hearts may be unfeignedly thankful, and that we shew forth thy praise, not only with our lips, but in our lives; by giving up ourselves to thy service, and by walking before thee in holiness and righteousness all our days; through Jesus Christ our Lord, to whom with thee and the Holy Ghost be all honour and glory, world without end. *Amen*

A Week's Preparation   1679

In addition to the devotional writing about the Eucharist by such authors as Jeremy Taylor and Simon Patrick (q.v.), the Restoration period saw several anonymous publications, chief among which was *A Week's Preparation towards a Worthy Receiving of the Lord's Supper*, which first appeared in 1679, and was frequently reprinted thereafter, right into the nineteenth century.

Before Communion

O My Jesus, Thou savedst me by Thy blood! In this Thy Sacrament Thou art set forth crucified, and I behold Thy wounds, from whence by the hand of faith I pluck forth these comfortable words of life, 'My Lord and my God'. My God! Mine, for Thou hast partaken of my human nature, and Thou hast made me to partake of Thy divine nature; Thou hast taken upon Thee my flesh, and Thou hast communicated unto me of Thy Spirit.

After Communion

Vouchsafe, good Lord, I humbly beseech Thee, so to work in my heart by Thy Grace and Holy Spirit that I may worthily receive these heavenly mysteries to the reviving and refreshing of my sinful soul; that I may purge out the old leaven of my corrupt and wicked nature by hearty and unfeigned repentance; that I may spiritually eat Christ's flesh, and drink His blood by a true and lively faith; that I may effectually feed upon the merits of His Incarnation, passion, resurrection, and ascension by virtue of Thy sweet and comfortable promises made unto us in the word of Thy Holy Gospel; finally, that I may be partaker of all the fruits and benefits of that most precious and perfect sacrifice which He in the body of His flesh offered up once for all uopn the cross for the redemption and salvation of mankind.

NOTES / SOURCES

A Week's Preparation towards a Worthy Receiving of the Lord's Supper (1679), London, 1855, p. 4

Simon Patrick   1625–1707

After studying at Cambridge, Patrick was ordained as a Presbyterian in 1653, but he decided to seek episcopal ordination in the following year through the influence of Herbert Thorndike (q.v.). His election as President of Queens' College, Cambridge, was overridden by a Royal Mandate: he became successively Dean of Peterborough (1679),

Bishop of Chichester (1689), and of Ely (1691). One of the founders of the Society for Promoting Christian Knowledge, he also supported the Society for the Propagation of the Gospel. He was a highly popular writer on the theological and devotional aspects of the sacraments, who combined the traditions of Hooker and Andrewes with the Platonism of Ralph Cudworth and John Smith, and was part of the 'men of latitude', subsequently (inaccurately) nicknamed 'Latitudinarian'.

Baptism and the Covenant of Grace

God receives us into a state of pardon and forgiveness. He assures us that Adam's sin shall not undo us, and that every sin of our own shall not exclude us out of heaven; but that we shall have the benefit of repentance, and an allowance to retract our follies; yea, and grace so to do if we will make use of it. He admits us into that covenant of grace, which accepts of repentance instead of innocence, and of amendment instead of an unerring obedience. This is one of the special favours of the gospel which by baptism is consigned unto us, that former iniquities shall not be remembered; and that every breach of our covenant, if there be a real change wrought in us, shall not void it, and make it null and ineffectual unto us. So in Mark i. 4, John is said to *preach the baptism of repentance for remission of sin.* And Ananias saith, *Arise, and be baptized, and wash away thy sins.* And the Greek church after baptism sings those words three times, 'Blessed is he whose iniquity is forgiven.' As those who came to the baptism of John did thereby receive a distinguishing mark and character, that they should not be destroyed in the ruin of the nation; insomuch that he saith to the Pharisees that desired baptism, *Who hath warned you to flee from the wrath to come?* so they that are baptized into Christ do thereby receive a pledge, that no sin which they stand guilty of shall bring the anger of God upon their heads if they will keep his covenant; but all shall be crossed out which they are charged with, and be like words writ in the water, that are obliterated and vanished, nowhere more to be found. (1)

The Purpose of the Sacrament

God, who is simple and removed far from all sense, considering the weakness of man's soul, and how unable he is to conceive of things spiritual purely and nakedly in themselves; and yet having a mind to be better known unto us, and to make himself more manifest than ever, was pleased in his infinite goodness to dwell in flesh, and appear here in the person of his Son, who was made like to man, to shew what God is in our nature. This Son of his, being to die and part with his life for great ends and purposes, which he would not have us to forget, was pleased to take the same course to convey to our minds spiritual notions by outward and sensible signs, and to impress on our hearts what he hath done and suffered, by a visible representation of it in bodily things, and not only by a plain description of it in the gospel. He knew very well that a picture and image of a thing doth more affect us than an historical narration; and that the more lively and express that image is, the more lively motions it makes within us. A dead corpse is but the shadow of a man, and yet we find that our souls are more assaulted and all our passions stirred by the sight of the face of a dead friend, than by all the reports that are brought us of his death. And long after his corpse is mouldered in the grave, if we see a child of his that hath his exact features, manners, and carriage, it renews a fresh remembrance in us of that person, and stirs up the images that are in our mind more powerfully than we can do ourselves by reflections upon them. (2)

The Eucharistic Memorial

We do *shew it forth* and declare it unto men, which is sufficiently clear by all that hath been said. We do publish and annunciate unto all that he is the Saviour of the world, and that he hath died for us, and purchased blessings thereby beyond the estimate and account of human thought. And further, the word καταγγέλλειν may import, that we do extol, predicate, magnify and highly lift up in our praises this great benefit, so that all may come to the knowledge of it, as far as is in our powers to procure. This commemoration the minister chiefly makes unto the people, and all the people together with him to all that are present, so that all may wonder at his love.

When our Saviour therefore saith, *Do this in remembrance of me*, the meaning is, Do this in remembrance that I dwelt in flesh, in memory of what I suffered, in memory of the infinite price of my blood which I shed for you, in memory of the victory that I have obtained by it over the enemies and tyrants of your souls; in memory of the immortal glory that I have purchased for you: celebrate this feast in memory of all these things, and when I am dead, let me alway live in your heart. Tell them one to another in a solemn manner, and declare them in the face of my church. Let all ages know these things, as long as the world shall last; that as the benefit is of infinite merit, so may the acknowledgment be an eternal memorial. Be so careful in doing this, that when I come again I may find you so doing. (3)

A Short Prayer for the Use of a Little Child

O Lord, my most loving Saviour and merciful Redeemer, who commandest that the little children should come unto thee, and didst take them up in thine arms, lay thy hands upon them, and bless them; look graciously upon me, I humbly beseech thee, and bless me, who am one of thy children, dedicated to thy service. Pity the weakness of my tender age, and prevent me betimes with thy grace. Make me seriously to remember my Creator in the days of my youth. Endue me with the fear of my God, and make me always mindful of the vow and promise that was made in my name when I was baptized; 'to forsake the devil and all his works, to believe in God and to serve him.'

Make me dutiful (as thou, O Lord Jesus, wast) unto my parents [loving to my brethren and sisters], obedient to my instructors; thankful for the good counsel of my friends, humble and reverent to my betters, and meek and gentle to all men. That as I grow in years, so I may grow in wisdom and favour with thee, and with all those who are good.

Preserve me from all dangers; let thy good angels be my keepers and defenders; and guide me by thy Holy Spirit, that the longer I live the better I may be, to the comfort of my parents, the honour and glory of my God, and my own happiness here and for ever. Amen. (4)

A Short Prayer for a Student

I look up unto thee, O Lord, *from whom cometh every good and perfect gift*, beseeching thee to direct, assist, and bless all the labours of my mind. Illuminate my understanding, O Father of lights, and lead me unto right apprehensions of all things. Endue me with that humility and soberness of mind which thou delightest to reward with more of thy gifts and graces. Bestow upon me a discerning spirit, a sound judgment, and an honest and good heart, sincerely disposed to employ all the talents which thou hast or shalt intrust me withal, to thy honour and glory, and to the good of mankind.

For which end, I beseech thee to excite my thirst after useful rather than much knowledge. And especially enrich me with the treasures of that inspired wisdom contained in thy holy Scriptures, which are able to *make me wise unto salvation*; that, growing in understanding and goodness, as I grow in years, my profiting may be apparent unto all men; and I may give a comfortable account of my time to thee, my God, at the day of the Lord Jesus. Amen. (5)

The Duty of Receiving Communion

When God's minister declares, as he is required to do, that he intends on such a day to administer the most comfortable sacrament of Christ's body and blood; and invites you to it, beseeching you to dispose yourselves religiously and devoutly for it: you must consider that it is your duty to prepare yourselves to come and partake of so great a blessing, and not to think it enough that you have been present at divine service, and heard the sermon, and then may turn your back on the table of the Lord: which is a very great disrespect to him, and forgetfulness of him, and cannot be excused so easily as men's naughty hearts incline them to believe. For though God's goodness is such, that he prefers works of mercy to your neighbours before sacrifice to himself, when one of them must be omitted, yet he doth not make the same allowance for your worldly business, (which well may be let alone till another time,) much less for your vain pleasures or recreations, which never ought to hinder or put by this or any other holy duty in the season proper for it.

Come, therefore, as oft as you are invited; and when God's minister, after sermon ended, goes up to the holy table to prepare this heavenly food for you, (that is, to consecrate bread broken and wine poured out, that it may represent the death of Christ to you, and to give it you, saying, *Take, eat and drink this in remembrance of Christ,*) do you stay in God's house, and draw near unto his table and thankfully receive it from him, for that end for which he gives it, in commemoration of Christ's death and passion upon the cross for your sake.

It is the duty of God's minister to set the bread and wine apart; to present them unto God, to break the one and pour out the other, to bless them, and to give them unto you: and then it is your duty to look upon this bread and wine, thus blessed, as representing Christ unto you; and accordingly to receive them, not as mere bread and wine, but as things deputed by Christ to be instead of his body and blood, and to communicate them to worthy receivers. (6)

The Necessity of Prayer

Upon this account, as much as any other, prayer is necessary, that we may be put into a temper of love and gratitude, and obedience unto him who is the donor of all good things; and who expects that we should acknowledge the propriety he hath in all the gifts which his bounty bestows upon us. Which we do by prayer: whereby we are constantly put in mind, in what tenure we hold all the blessings we receive from his hands; which we may not therefore use as we please, but as he allows and directs. And if we do at any time use them otherwise, and thereby give just offence to God, their owner and ours, prayer both naturally calls such offences to mind, and makes us more fearful hereafter to offend.

For no man comes to ask a benefit of another, (as Mr Hooker, if I forget not, very pertinently observes,) but, if he have given him any offence, he will then unavoidably remember it; and in the very first place cast himself down at his feet, and beg pardon, with a resolution not willingly to offend him again. Which resolution is maintained and supported by the very same thing which constrained us to make it; that is, the constant necessity we are in to ask for new benefits. For all men are naturally afraid to offend those into whose presence they must frequently come to sue for favours. This keeps them in awe, and makes them careful how they behave themselves, that their suits may not be rejected.

We are not fit then to receive, or to enjoy any thing from God, without devout prayer to him. And therefore we ought constantly to perform this duty; because otherwise we take things by stealth, and lay hold on the blessings of Heaven without asking him leave; and we ought to perform it seriously, because it will not otherwise have the forementioned effect, of making us afraid to offend him, without which our prayers are nothing worth, and can obtain nothing from him.

To end this let us consider that we do not pray that we may alter the mind of God; who is always the same, unchangeable goodness, ready to give unto those who are qualified to receive his favours; but that we may alter and change our own mind for the better, and thereby become disposed for the good things of which we are desirous. And nothing alters us so much as serious prayer, which puts a new mind into us, and for the present makes us quite another sort of creatures.

We are forgetful of God; lovers of ourselves; confident in our own strength; doaters upon this present world; too much wedded to our own will and pleasure; complainers, murmurers, envious, wavering and inconstant in our good purposes, unmindful of other men's miseries, revengeful and implacable, which are all bars to the obtaining of God's mercy. And therefore prayer is absolutely necessary to remove them; that is, to remember us of God; to keep him in remembrance, and to maintain an acquaintance with him; to fill us with love to him; to humble and abase us in our own thoughts; to draw our hearts off from this vain world, and to settle our trust in him alone; to fix our dependence on him, and subdue our wills to his; to give us a taste of spiritual pleasures; to make us thankful, contented, and well satisfied; to move our compassion towards others who stand in need of our help, as we do of the help of God; to incline us to be pitiful, and to do good and forgive; without which we confess, in our very prayers, that we cannot expect forgiveness from God. (7)

NOTES / SOURCES

1. Simon Patrick, 'Aqua Genitalis' (1658), in *The Works of Simon Patrick* Vol. I, Oxford, 1848, p. 25
2. 'Mensa Mystica' (1660) ibid., pp. 71–2
3. Ibid. pp. 99–100
4. 'The Devout Christian' (1672), in *The Works of Simon Patrick*, Vol. II, Oxford, 1848, pp. 282–3
5. Ibid. p. 329
6. 'A Book for Beginners, or An Help to Young Communicants' (1674), in *The Works of Simon Patrick* Vol. I, Oxford, 1848, p. 592
7. 'Discourse Concerning Prayer' (1686) in *The Works of Simon Patrick* Vol. IV, Oxford, 1848, pp. 651–2

Susanna Hopton   1627–1709

A devotional writer, Susanna Hopton was 'acquainted with the best Divines of the Church of England' by her husband Richard Hopton, the Welsh judge, in the hope of her return to the Church of England, which took place at the Restoration. Her extensive correspondence reveals the depth of her devotional practices, as well as the breadth of her contacts, many of whom were Nonjurors.

Christ's Sermon on the Mount. *Matt. 6*

O Blessed Jesus, having before taught us how to give Alms, and how to pray, thou hast now join'd fasting with the former Duties, and art pleased to teach us how to fast, not only by thy Example, as before, but by Precept also now; the Implication being the strongest Injunction; and therefore supposing that fast we do, and fast we must here, thou teachest how to fast, saying, *when ye fast be not as the Hypocrites*, Fasting being such a corporal Work of Humiliation, that if it be done without Hypocrisy, and in Sincerity, it ever finds thy gracious Reward and Acceptation:

I praise and magnify thy Name.

And I beseech thee, give me the Gift of discreet Abstinence, and the Integrity of true Self-denial in it, and never let me falsly pretend Inability to evade this necessary Duty, nor yet destroy so excellent a Duty by Hypocrisy. Give me therefore, I beseech thee, a cheerful Obedience unto thy Church, and a glad and willing Imitation of thee, true Self-denyal, and a full Command over my sensitive Appetite, that I may subdue my Body, and enlarge my Spirit, abate my own Provisions to give Portions to the Poor, and employ my usual time of eating, in Prayer and Meditation; that by these excellent Helps, and Wings of Devotion and Prayer, I may soar up unto thee, and enjoy divine Union with thee for evermore. *Amen.*

O blessed Jesus, thou hast told us *No Man can serve two Masters*, that we *cannot serve God and Mammon*:

I praise and magnify thy Name.

And I beseech thee, deliver me from mingling any Impiety or Prophaneness, sinister Interest, or sensual Affection with thy Service. Pardon, I beseech thee, all those sacrilegious Mixtures I have made; abusing holy things with Prophaneness, and thy Mercies and thee in all.

But I humbly and earnestly beseech thee to let it be so no more, make me to forego all the Allurements of the World to serve thee, and rather to distaste all the World, than offend thee.

O that thou wouldst please rather to take me out of the World, than suffer me to live to offend thee in any one wilful and known Sin in the World any more. *Amen.*

O blessed Jesus, who hast commanded us not to be too solicitious for the Things of this Life, but to seek first the Kingdom of Heaven and the Right-eousness thereof; since in doing so, thou hast promised that all other things shall be added thereunto:

I praise and magnify thy Name.

And I beseech thee, take away from me all Distrust in thy Power and Providence, thy Mercy and Goodness; make me first to do and perform all my Duties unto thee, and then with Care and Diligence, Industry and Conscience, perform all the Duties of my Calling, and to live in Confidence of thy Blessing, Dependence upon thy Power, and intire Resignation unto thy holy Will. *Amen.* (1)

On our Saviour's Prayer *John 17*

After all the foregoing Precepts of Holiness, and Promises of Mercy and Comforts, which thou, O blessed Jesus, didst give unto thy Disciples, and in them to all thine, what a Prayer of Zeal, Love, Care, Wisdom, Power, and Efficacy, didst thou make for thy self, for thine Apostles, Disciples, and all thine, lifting up thine Eyes to Heaven, and praying for thine own Glory, saying, *Father glorify thy Son, that thy Son also may glorify thee: As thou hast given him Power over all Flesh, that he should give eternal Life to as many as thou hast given him: And this is Life eternal to know thee, the only true God, and Jesus Christ whom thou hast sent:*

I praise and magnify thy Name.

And I beseech thee lift up mine Heart and Eyes unto thee; and thou who knowest what eternal Life is, shew a Glympse thereof unto me. For I see the Knowledge of God is eternal Life, O grant that Knowledge unto me. *Amen.*

This Knowledge is as infinite in Blessedness, as it is endless in Extent; it is a Life of Communion with God in all his Counsels, Attributes, Ways, Works, Laws and Praises; it is as sublime as it is glorious, it is as mysterious as it is joyful; for to know thee is to know our selves, before all Worlds beloved of thee. O let me melt with Admiration of thy Goodness and Glory, that I may be zealous and courageous in honour, praise, and glorify thee, for thy redeeming Love; the Mercies and Joys of which are so great, that scarce any mention is made of Paradise, because those Joys are all obscured by the surpassing Excellency of these.

O what Madness then is it to set our Affections upon the perishable things of this World, who may attain the Joys even of eternal Life by knowing thee. The Hour is come, O Jesus, wean me from the World, and secure me wholly unto thee, and give me this Life eternal to know and glorify thee. Let me know I came out from thee, and must return unto thee, that I may walk always before thee, and be always mindful of thy inhabiting Presence with me. Let it be my Meat and Drink to do thy holy Will, and my only Joy to glorify thy Name. *Amen.*

Did not I come out from thee as a Branch proceedeth from the Vine? And art not thou my Root? Do I not live, move, and have all my Being in thee? Must not then all my Life be directed to thee, and be in thee? Tho' therefore thou art above the Heavens, yet I beseech thee let me feel in my Soul (which is thine own Similitude) what Relation I have to thee, and let me live according to that noble Nature and Capacity thou hast given me, wholly to the Honour and Praise of thee. *Amen.*

O that I might honour thee as much as ever any did! O that I had the Powers and Affections of all Angels, Saints, and Men, to honour and glorify thee with them all. *Amen.*

Appear, dear Lord, to this poor Soul of mine which thou hast given me, and shew me the glorious Use and Benefit of all the Powers thou hast given me, and give me a grateful Use, and true Employments, and right Enjoyment of them. *Amen.*

O holy Father, I beseech thee for the Merits of this only begotten Son of thine, glorify all those whom he hath redeemed, assist and comfort them in their Hour of Sorrow, as thou didst comfort, and at last glorify him. And seeing all his are thine, am not I thine also? For I am his. O then take care of my Soul and Body, for both are thine: Take care of my Senses and Faculties, for they are thine: Conserve, encrease, and nourish all the good Purposes thou hast inspir'd into me, for they also are thine. *Amen.*

I am all thine, save me; my Understanding is thine, illuminate it; my Will is thine, govern it; my Memory is thine, fill it; my Life is thine, preserve it; my Estate is thine, bless it; my Friends are thine, bless them, and secure them all to thy self, for all is thine. *Amen.* (2)

Christ's Passion

His Agony and Prayer in the Garden

O Blessed Jesus, who after thou hadst ended thy glorious Sermon, and Prayer for thy Apostles, wentest forth over the Brook *Cedron* into the Mount of *Olives*, to *Gethsemane*, where was a Garden into which thou didst enter, tho' thou knewest thou shouldst be apprehended and taken there; yet so much didst thou long for our Redemption, that thou wouldst not delay thine own Sufferings any longer, but readily wentest to meet them:

I praise and magnify thy Name.

And I beseech thee make me as ready to meet and embrace Tribulation, when thou wilt have it so, as thou wert to meet Afflictions and Sufferings for me. Let the Sense of thy Love make me careful for nothing so much as that I may manifest and express my Love to thee. *Amen.* (3)

A Thanksgiving at Home after the Holy Communion

Blessed art thou, O Lord God, and blessed be thy holy Name for ever, who hast now vouchsafed to feed me with the Bread of Life, and hast given me to drink the Cup of Eternity, the holy and heavenly Mysteries of the Body and Blood of my Saviour; thereby assuring my Soul of thy Favour and Goodness towards me, for the increase of my Faith, for the Pardon of my Sins, for the obtaining of my Peace, and all other Benefits of Christ's blessed Passion.

I now must humbly beseech thee to assist me with thy heavenly Grace, that I may continue thine for ever, and be made a Temple of thy holy Spirit; and that having now Christ dwelling in me by Faith, I may accomplish the rest of my Life in Repentance and Godly Fear, in mortifying my own sinful desires, and in keeping thy holy Commandments; for which end, guide me with thy Power, enlighten me with thy Word, quicken me with thy Spirit, elevate my Senses, compose my Memory, and order my Conversation aright; for thou art able to do abundantly above what I can ask or think; by which thy great and bountiful Goodness towards me, thou wilt glorify thy Name in me, and bring me at last to thine eternal Kingdom of Glory, through him who is the King of Glory, my blessed Lord and Saviour Jesus Christ. *Amen.*

I adore thee, I bless thee, I praise and magnify thy holy Name, O my God, for this and all thy Blessings bestowed upon me in Christ Jesus my Saviour. *Amen.*

O my dearest Saviour, thou hast now entered my Soul, never let my Sins remove thee thence. Give me a clean Heart, and renew a right Spirit within me. And having thus fitted me for thy self, tarry with me, reign in me, guide and direct me, watch over me for Good, preserve me in all Trials and Temptations, and never leave me, nor forsake me, till thou shalt have brought me to thy heavenly Kingdom. *Amen.*

What shall I render unto the Lord for all that he hath done unto me, I will take the Cup of Salvation, and call upon the Name of the Lord. Praise thou the Lord, O my Soul, praise the Lord. Worthy is the Lamb that was slain, to receive Power and Riches, and Wisdom, and Strength, and Honour, and Glory, and Blessing. And oh! may All, both Angels and Men joyn together with me in one universal Hymn of Praise, saying with those in the Apocalypse; Blessing and Honour, and Glory, and Power, be to him that sitteth on the Throne, and to the Lamb for ever and ever. *Amen.* (4)

NOTES / SOURCES

1. Anonymous? *A Collection of Meditations and Devotions,* London, 1717, pp. 136–7
2. Ibid., pp. 237–9
3. Ibid., p. 241
4. Ibid., pp. 417–9

John Tillotson   1630 1694

The son of a dissenting family, John Tillotson was deprived of his Fellowship at Clare Hall, Cambridge, in 1661. A notable preacher at Lincoln's Inn and St Lawrence Jewry, London, he brought clarity and brevity as well as reason and feeling to his sermons. He attended the Savoy Conference in 1661 in support of the presbyterian side and later published the *Rule of Faith* (1666), a polemical work against Roman Catholics. In 1689 he became Dean of St Paul's and was a close companion of William III, whose daily prayers he composed. Appointed Archbishop of Canterbury in 1691, he was noted for his hostility towards the Roman Catholic Church and his evident willingness to include Protestant dissenters.

The Gift of the Spirit of Adoption

The whole force of the argument comes to this, that if we believe that earthly parents have any good inclinations toward their children, and are willing to bestow upon them the necessaries of life, we have much more reason to believe that GOD our heavenly FATHER is much more ready 'to give his HOLY SPIRIT to them that ask him;' whether we consider the quality of the giver, or the nature of the gift.

I should now have proceeded to the other particulars which I propounded; but I shall only at present make some short reflexions upon what hath already been delivered.

What a comfortable consideration is this, to be so fully assured of GOD's readiness to bestow all good things upon his children, and even his HOLY SPIRIT, if we ask it of him? and what an encouragement is here to constant and fervent prayer to GOD, who will not deny us the gift of his HOLY SPIRIT, if we heartily and earnestly beg it of him? and what an encouragement is here likewise to the resolutions and endeavours of a good life, that so powerful an assistance is so freely offer'd to us, to enable us to 'run the ways of GOD's commandments;' that GOD hath promised his HOLY SPIRIT to reside and dwell in us, to be a principle of spiritual life to us, and to enable us to all the purposes of obedience and a holy life?

And what infinite cause have we to bless GOD for the gift of his HOLY SPIRIT, and to say with St Paul, 'Blessed be GOD for his unspeakable gift.' That he hath given his HOLY SPIRIT to his church, at first in miraculous powers and gifts for the preaching of the christian religion in the world, and ever since in such degrees of assistance, as were necessary in the several ages of the church, for the preservation of the christian religion in the world; that he hath given his HOLY SPIRIT to every particular member of his church, for the sanctifying and renewing of our natures, 'to strengthen us to every good word and work, and to keep us by his mighty power through faith unto salvation?'

And this sanctifying virtue of the HOLY GHOST, enabling us to do the will of GOD, is more than any miraculous powers whatsover. So our SAVIOUR tells us, Matth. vii. 21, 22, 23. 'Not every one that saith unto me, LORD, LORD, shall enter into the kingdom of heaven:— but he that doth the will of my FATHER which is in heaven. Many will say to me in that day, LORD, LORD, have we not prophesied in thy name? and in thy name have cast out devils? and in thy name done many wonderful works? and then will I profess unto them, I never knew you: depart from me, ye that work iniquity.' Men may do wonders by the power of the HOLY GHOST, and yet be shut out of the kingdom of heaven; only they that are assisted by the SPIRIT of GOD to do the will of GOD shall be admitted into heaven.

And this is matter of greater joy and comfort to us, than to work the greatest wonders, and to have power over devils, to cast them out of the bodies of men, Luke x. 20. 'Rejoice not in this,' faith our blessed SAVIOUR, 'that the SPIRITS are made subject to you, but rejoice in this, that your names are written in heaven.' How is that the sanctifying virtue of GOD's SPIRIT is the pledge and earnest of our heavenly inheritance, and that whereby we are 'sealed to the day of redemption.' (1)

A Prayer used by King William III

A prayer for the grace and assistance of GOD'S HOLY SPIRIT,
to enable me to resolve and to do better for the future

And now, O LORD, in confidence of thy great mercy and goodness to all that are truly penitent, and sincerely resolve to do better, I most humbly implore the grace and assistance of thy HOLY SPIRIT, to enable me to become every day better, and to reform whatever has been amiss in the temper and disposition of my mind, or in any of the actions of my life. Grant me the wisdom and understanding to know my duty, and the heart and will to do it. Vouchsafe to me the continual presence and direction, the assistance and comforts of thy HOLY SPIRIT; whereby I may be disposed and enabled to do thy will with delight and chearfulness, and with patience and contentedness to submit to it in all things. Endue me, O LORD, with the true fear and love of thee, and with a prudent zeal for thy glory. Increase in me more and more the graces of charity and meekness, of truth, and justice, and fidelity; give me humility and patience, and a firmness of spirit to bear every condition with constancy and equality of mind.

Enable me, O LORD, by thy grace to govern all my appetites, and every inordinate lust and passion, by temperance and purity, and meekness of wisdom; setting thee always before me, that I may not sin against thee. Create in me a clean heart, O GOD, and renew a right spirit within me; purify my soul from all evil thoughts and inclinations, from all bad intentions and designs. Deliver me, O LORD, from pride and vanity, from immoderate self-love, and obstinate self-will, and from all malice and envy, and ill-will towards any.

Make me to love thee, as I ought, above all things; and let the interest of thy honour and glory be ever dearer to me than my own will, or reputation, or any temporal advantage whatsoever.

Subdue in me the evil spirit of wrath and revenge; and dispose my heart patiently to bear reproaches and wrongs, and to be ready not only to forgive, but to return good for evil.

Assist me, O LORD, more especially in the faithful and conscientious discharge of the duties of that high station in which thou hast placed me: And grant that I may employ all that power and authority which thou hast invested me with, for thy glory and the public good; that I may rule over men in thy fear, with justice and equity, ever studying and endeavouring the good of the people committed to my charge, and as much as in me lies the peace and prosperity, the welfare and happiness of mankind.

Confirm me, O my GOD, in all these holy Resolutions; and do thou keep it for ever in the purpose of my heart, to perform them to the utmost of my power: All which I humbly beg for thy mercies sake in JESUS CHRIST. *Amen.* (2)

NOTES / SOURCES

1. John Tillotson, Sermon on 'The Reasonableness of fearing God more than men', in *Sermons by Dr John Tillotson*, Vol. XII, London, 1757, pp. 266–8
2. 'Prayers written for King William III' in ibid., pp. 343–5

George Bull   1634–1710

After studying at Exeter College, Oxford, Bull refused to take the Oath to the
Commonwealth, and was ordained by Robert Skinner, the ejected Bishop of Oxford,
in 1655. He held a number of parish livings before and after the Restoration, became
Archdeacon of Llandaff in 1686, and Bishop of St Davids in 1795. He was a High
Churchman, whose theological stance was similar to Simon Patrick (q.v.), and whose
treatises and sermons reflect the progressive traditionalism of many of the writers of
the time.

The Blessed Virgin Mary

The blessedness of the holy Virgin is not so altogether proper to her, or
incommunicable to others, but that the meanest sincere Christian may share
with her in the better part of it. Wonderful and full of comfort are the words of
our Saviour, Luke xi. where, when a certain woman, hearing his excellent
discourse, cried out, *Blessed is the womb that bare thee, and the paps which thou
hast sucked*, ver 27, our Saviour answers, ver. 28, *Yea rather, blessed are they that
hear the word of God, and keep it.* Which is not a negation of the blessedness of his
mother, (for that would be a plain contradiction to my text,) but a correction of
the woman's mistake, who so admired the blessedness of the mother of such a
son, that she scarce thought of any other blessedness. Our Saviour therefore tells
her, *that blessed are they also, yea and chiefly, that hear the word of God, and keep it.*
And in another place our gracious Lord being told that his mother and brethren
desired to speak with him, gave this short answer, *Who is my mother? and who are
my brethren? And he stretched forth his hands towards his disciples, and said, Behold
my mother and my brethren! for whosoever shall do the will of my Father which is in
heaven, the same is my brother, and sister, and mother.* Matt. xii. 48, 49, 50. Where I
think there is a mighty emphasis in those words of our Saviour, *my Father which
is in heaven*; as if he had said, You Jews think of me as a mere man, and
understand not any other relation that I have, besides that which is according to
the flesh: but know ye that I am of a higher original, even the eternal Son of the
eternal God dwelling in heaven; and as such I own no relation but what is
spiritual, and every obedient disciple of mine is to me as a brother, or sister, or
mother. Indeed, the Virgin herself was more blessed by conceiving Christ in her
heart by faith, than by conceiving him in her womb. And in this her chiefest
blessedness the meanest Christian, that is a sincere one, may be a sharer with her.
Christ may be thus formed, nay he must be so in every one that shall be saved,
Galatians iv. 19. And if we be true Christians, though all generations do not call us
blessed, as the holy Virgin, yet together with her we shall be indeed blessed
beyond all generations, even for ever and ever.

   To God the Father, Son, and Holy Ghost, be given and ascribed all honour and
glory, all religious worship and adoration, now and for evermore. *Amen.*

NOTES / SOURCES

George Bull, 'Sermon IV: on the Low and Mean conditions of the Blessed Virgin Mary' in *The Works of
George Bull*, Vol. I, Oxford, 1846, pp. 110–12

Thomas Traherne   1637–1674

Supported through his education at Brasenose College, Oxford, by a relative, Thomas Traherne was presented to the living of Credenhill, Herefordshire, in 1657, a post which he held until his death. He appears to have made only occasional visits to the parish and in 1667 became Private Chaplain to Sir Orlando Bridgman, Lord Keeper of the Great Seal, with whom he remained until his death. Although Traherne's *Christian Ethicks* was published the year after his death, his other works, which are continually being identified, have only come to public attention in the last century. His modern reputation as a metaphysical poet stems from the publication of some of his poems after their discovery in manuscript by Bertram Dobell in 1908.

To be Holy

To be Holy is so Zealously to Desire, so vastly to Esteem, and so Earnestly to Endeavour it, that we would not for millions of Gold and Silver, Decline, nor fail, nor Mistake in a Tittle. For then we Pleas God when we are most like Him. we are like Him when our Minds are in Frame. our Minds are in Frame when our Thoughts are like his. And our Thoughts are then like his when we hav such Conceptions of all objects as God hath, and Prize all Things according to their value. For God doth Prize all Things rightly. Which is a Key that Opens into the very Thoughts of his Bosom. It seemeth Arrogance to pretend to the Knowledg of his Secret Thoughts. But how shall we hav the Mind of God, unless we Know his Thoughts? Or how shall we be led by his Divine Spirit, till we hav his Mind? His Thoughts are Hidden: but he hath revealed unto us the Hidden Things of Darkness. By his Works and by his Attributs we know His Thoughts. And by Thinking the same are Divine and Blessed. (1)

The Communion of Saints

There are a sort of Saints meet to be your Companions, in another maner. But that they lie concealed. You must therfore make your self exceeding Virtuous, that by the very Splendor of your Fame you may find them out. While the Wicked are like Heaps of Rubbish, these few Jewels lie buried in the Ruins of Mankind: and must Diligently be Digd for. You may Know them by their Lustre. and by the very Desire and Esteem they hav of you when you are virtuous. For as it is the Glory of the Sun that Darkness cannot approach it, becaus it is always encompassed with its own Beams; so it is the Priviledge of Holy Souls, that they are always secure in their own Light, which driveth away Divels and Evil Men: And is accessible by none, but Lovers of Virtue. Beginners and Desirers will give you the Opportunity of infusing your self and your Principles into them. Practicers and Growers will mingle souls and be Delightfull Companions, The Sublime and Perfect, in the Lustre of their Spirit will shew you the Image of Almighty God and the Joys of Heaven. They will Allure Protect Encourage Comfort Teach Honor and Delight you But you must be very Good, for that is the way to find them And very Patient to endure som time, and very Diligent to observ where they are. (2)

Christian Upbringing

By this let Nurses, and those Parents that desire Holy Children learn to make them Possessors of Heaven and Earth betimes. to remove silly Objects from before them, to Magnify nothing but what is Great indeed, and to talk of God to them and of His Works and Ways before they can either Speak or go. For Nothing is so Easy as to teach the Truth becaus the Nature of the Thing confirms the Doctrine. As when we say The Sun is Glorious, A Man is a Beautifull Creature, Soveraign over Beasts and Fowls and Fishes, The Stars Minister unto us, The World was made for you, etc. But to say This Hous is yours, and these Lands are another Mans and this Bauble is a Jewel and this Gugaw a fine Thing, this Rattle makes Musick etc. is deadly Barbarous and uncouth to a little Child; and makes him suspect all you say, becaus the Nature of the Thing contradicts your Words. Yet doth that Blot out all Noble and Divine Ideas, Dissettle his foundation, render him uncertain in all Things, and Divide him from GOD. To teach him those Objects are little vanities, and that tho GOD made them, by the Ministery of Man, yet Better and more Glorious Things are more to be Esteemed, is Natural and Easy. (3)

Traherne's Childhood Vision of Heaven

When I came into the Country, and saw that I had all time in my own hands, having devoted it wholy to the study of Felicitie, I knew not where to begin or End; nor what Objects to chuse, upon which most Profitably I might fix my Contemplation. I saw my self like som Traveller, that had Destined his Life to journeys, and was resolved to spend his Days in visiting Strange Places: who might wander in vain, unless his Undertakings were guided by som certain Rule; and that innumerable Millions of Objects were presented before me, unto any of which I might take my journey. fain I would hav visited them all, but that was impossible. What then I should do? Even imitat a Traveller, who becaus He cannot visit all Coasts, Wildernesses, Sandy Deserts, Seas, Hills, Springs and Mountains, chuseth the most Populous and flourishing Cities, where he might see the fairest Prospects, Wonders, and Rarities, and be entertained with greatest Courtesie: and where indeed he might most Benefit himself with Knowledg Profit and Delight: leaving the rest, even the naked and Empty Places unseen. For which caus I made it my Prayer to GOD Almighty, that He, whose Eys are open upon all Things, would guid me to the fairest and Divinest. (4)

The Nature of Holiness

The infinite love of His own goodness is the holiness of God. There are infinite pleasures and perfections in its nature that merit an infinite esteem and desire. His goodness is all beauty, and His holiness all fire and flame in pursuing it. His holiness is all beauty, and His goodness all fire and flame to enkindle it. The infinite excess of His eternal goodness is its own holiness, and the beauty of holiness is excess of goodness. For if righteousness and holiness be well distinguished, righteousness is that virtue by which God doth apprehend, affect and esteem all excellent things according to their value, and choose and do always the best and most excellent. Holiness is the love which He beareth to His own righteousness, which, being infinite, makes Him infinitely enflamed with the love of the most perfect actions, and carries Him with an infinite ardour to the performance of them. For though it be a righteous thing to esteem the righteousness of God in an infinite manner, yet there is as much difference between righteousness and the love of righteousness as between an object and the affection embracing it.

Holiness, if it be strictly defined, is that virtue in God by which He loveth the most perfect things, and infinitely delighteth in them. For by virtue of this affection He shunneth and hateth all that is profane, pursuing and delighting in all that is holy; for the object of holiness may be holy, as well as the affection. Whereupon it followeth that holiness is of two kinds; either the holiness of the affection, or the holiness of the object. They bear a relation to each other, yet are absolute perfections in themselves. For the hatred of all defects, imperfections, blemishes and errors is a glorious thing in itself, yet relates to the perfections of those objects from which it would remove those odious imperfections. The perfection of all objects when they are free from all blemishes is a glorious thing in itself too, yet is acceptable to that affection that desires to see a completeness and perfection in every object. And all is resolved into the same goodness of which we have been speaking.

For infinite goodness must needs desire with an infinite violence that all goodness should be complete and perfect; and that desire, which makes to the perfection of all goodness, must infinitely avoid every slur and miscarriage as unclean, and infinitely aim at every grace and beauty that tends to make the object infinitely perfect which it would enjoy. It cannot desire less than infinite perfection, nor less than hate all imperfection in an infinite manner. All objects are made and sanctified by the holiness of God. It is the measure and strength and perfection of goodness. (5)

The Excellency of Admiration

Its Excellency is Discernable by its Uses, by the Order of Nature wherin it Standeth, and the individual neerness wherin it is Allied unto Happiness. That I have this Faculty is my Joy and Admiration. It is Worth all the Gold in a thousand Worlds. More profitable unto me, and pleasing to others. All the Admirableness of Wonderfull Things would be lost unto me were it not for this. It giveth their valu to them, which is infusd into it. Hills of Adamant and Pearl would be but Desolat without it. Ask not why Sweetness is in the Action, it is part of the Soul. All Materials are Dross without it, Useless Dregs without Life, and life without this a Burden. It is better than Life. And Love it self without this would lose one of its graces. Admiration is an Ingredient in Happiness so Compleat, that without this it would be without the Crown of Glory: and Defectiv of its Sovereign Delight, its Excessiveness. All Extasie and Rapture in Blessedness is made of Admiration: All Ravishment in Love is made of Admiration. It is the sweetest of Things. When a Man loseth himself at the Greatness of the Good that hath betyded him: and is delightfully Blind at his own Happiness. He is as if the very Excess of Knowledg maketh him Ignorant: Amazd at the Greatness of his own felicity, and scarce knows Himself or anything els, becaus beyond all Knowledg he enjoyeth Himself and all Things els. The Soul could not be so Capable of Bliss as it now is, were it not for this. (6)

Manna

That precious Wheat which from the Earth doth rise
As Great a Miracle as Manna is,
But while his Methods he diversifies,
His Truth he more and more doth prove our Bliss:
And tho Corruption doth our Nature leaven,
Makes it apparent we are fed by Heaven.
Even Earthly Corn from Heaven comes, tho sence
Discerneth not the secret Influence
From which it Springs; even Rie is rooted there
Altho the Ear and Blade do flourish here.
But we are inconsiderat and Dead
And Blind and Deaf, unsensible as Lead:
And till the Ordinance of Nature change,
And som New Way, as Easy, but more strange,
Awakens us, that Heavenly Influence
From whence they come affecteth not the sence.
And doubtless tis as Good, as Great a Treasure,
But Common Benefits afford no Pleasure,
At least to Bruitish souls: And therfore we
This very Manna loathd at last do see.
This teacheth us how we should prize that Grain
Which by a Daily Wonder down doth rain
And yet by miracle springs from the Earth
Beneath, that for our Greater Joy and Mirth
Both Worlds might Married be, and neither prov
Abortive Tokens of their makers Love,
Nor useless be and poor, but rich in fruits,
While either to our pleasure contributes.
If Novelties delight the Mind so much,
And if Varieties alone have such
Effects; then let us not in Egypt sit
Continualy, where we the Benefit
Of all his Love in our abundance lose,
Among the Brick kilns and our Mortal foes
Let not the Stench of Onions Cloy our sent,
Let not our Lives in Bondage still be pent
Where Dirty Cares and Labors blind the Mind,
And evil Customs in vile pleasures bind.
Lets rather banish all our thoughts awhile,
And flie the Places which our souls defile:
Let not the Limits of the World confine
Our Better Part: but that we may Divine

Becom, lets go beyond the very Skies
And travail over all Eternities.
Lets sojourn in the Desert Wilderness
Of long and uncreated nothing, guess
What may the Dismall Chaos be, and view
The vacant Ages, while he nought did doe.
Those Empty Barren Spaces will appear
At last as if they all at once were here
The Silence Darkness and Deformitie
In which we nothing plainly nothing see
Will make the Univers enlightning them
Even like unto the new Jerusalem.
And while we wisely seek for Heaven there,
Twill clearly make us find our Heaven here.
And all these strange and Glorious works will be
A Sacred Mirror of the Deitie.
An Orient Gem the world will then be found,
A Diadem wherwith even God is Crownd.
The very Earth the seas the stars the skies,
Springs, Rivers, Trees, the Brightness of our Eys
All will be Manna to the Hungry Soul,
Or Living Waters in a Chrystal Bowl.
All Pleasant, all Delightfull, Angels food
To us, as unto God, Supremely Good
For he beheld them when they all were New;
And he who cannot erre, who first did view
Their Glories, having seen them, understood.
And plainly said they were exceeding Good.
O that we had but his Diviner Sence.
Then Man would be a pure Intelligence (7)

NOTES / SOURCES

1. Thomas Traherne, *Centuries, Poems and Thanksgivings*, Vol. I, Oxford, 1958, p. 7
2. Ibid., p. 44
3. Ibid., p. 117
4. Ibid., p. 141
5. Thomas Traherne, 'The Way to Blessedness' in Margaret Bottrall, ed. *Christian Ethicks*, London, 1962, pp. 99–100
6. Thomas Traherne, *Commentaries of Heaven*, Oxford, 1989, pp. 17–18
7. Thomas Traherne, *The Ceremonial Law*, PN Review 124, 1998, pp. 27–8

William Beveridge   1637–1708

Ordained both Deacon and Priest in 1661, William Beveridge was immediately appointed Vicar of Ealing. Later, as Prebendary of Canterbury, he was offered the bishopric of Bath and Wells, of which Thomas Ken (q.v.) had been deprived in 1691. Because of his own Nonjuror sympathies he declined, but later became Bishop of St Asaph (1704). A strong supporter of the Society for Promoting Christian Knowledge, he encouraged the Society to translate works into Welsh. He was a highly influential devotional writer and preacher.

The Urgency of the Time

Wherefore, all ye that desire to go to Heaven, to have Him that made you reconciled unto you, and smile upon you; or that desire to be really and truly happy, set upon the work which God sent you into the world about; put it not off any longer, and make no more vain excuses, but from this day forward let the service of God be your daily, your continual employment and pleasure; study and contrive each day how to advance His glory and interest in the world, and how you may walk more strictly, more circumspectly, more conformably to His laws than ever. But whatsoever service you perform unto Him, be sure to do it 'with a perfect heart and a willing mind.' Think not to put Him off with fancy instead of faith, or with outward performances instead of real duties: but remember that He 'searcheth the hearts, and trieth the reins of the sons of men,' and observes the inward motions of the soul, as well as the outward actions of the life: and therefore, wheresoever you are, whatsoever you do, still bethink yourselves, that He that made you still looks upon you; taking notice not only of the matter of the actions which you perform, but also of the manner of your performing them; and therefore be sure to have a special care in all your services for or unto God, that your hearts be sincere before Him, and your minds inclined to Him, that so you may 'serve Him with a perfect heart and a willing mind.'

But to conclude; whoever you are that read this discourse, I have here shewn you the 'things that belong unto your everlasting peace,' having acquainted you with the method and manner of your serving God in time, in order to your enjoyment of Him to eternity; how you are affected with what you have read, and whether you be resolved to practise it, yea, or no, it is only the Eternal God that knows. But this I know, that if you will not be persuaded to serve God, yea, and to serve Him too 'with a perfect heart and a willing mind,' you will one day wish you had, but then it will be too late. And therefore, if you will put it to the venture, go on still, and with the unprofitable servant, 'hide your talents in a napkin,' or lavish them out in the revels of sin and vanity; let thy belly be still thy god, and the world thy lord; serve thyself or Satan, instead of the Living God: 'but know that for all this God will bring thee into judgment;' after which, expect nothing else but to be overwhelmed with horror and confusion to eternity.

Whereas, on the other side, such amongst you as shall sincerely endeavour from henceforth to serve God 'with a perfect heart and a willing mind,' I dare, I do assure them in the Name of God, their 'labour shall not be in vain in the Lord:' for God suffers not His enemies to go unpunished, nor His servants unrewarded.

And therefore go on with joy and triumph in the service of so great and so good a Master, and devote yourselves wholly to His service, and employ your talents faithfully for His glory. Remember the time is but short; and Christ Himself will receive you into eternal glory, saying, 'Well done, good and faithful servants.' (1)

The Trinity

Now from hence we may learn, how necessary it is to believe in the most Blessed Trinity, the Father, the Son, and the Holy Ghost, Three Persons, One God ; seeing they all are pleased to concern themselves so much about us, and our happiness depends upon them all. Hence we may learn to confide and trust on all and every one of these Divine Persons, for all things relating to our happiness and Salvation. Hence we may learn what infinite cause we have to praise and adore God for His infinite goodness to us poor mortals upon earth, and to sing with the choir of Heaven, 'Holy, Holy, Holy is the Lord of Hosts, the whole earth is full of His glory.'

Hence we may learn how much we are obliged to serve, and love, and please God the Father, God the Son, and God the Holy Ghost, who is thus infinitely gracious, and loving, and bountiful unto us. Hence we may learn what great reason our Church hath to appoint, that at the end of every Psalm, as well as upon other occasions, we should say or sing, 'Glory be to the Father, and to the Son, and to the Holy Ghost.' Hence, lastly, we may learn, wherefore our Church concludes her daily prayers, as the Apostle doth this Epistle, with the words of my text, even because they contain in short all that we can pray for, and are in effect the same, the form which God Himself prescribed, wherewith the Priests should bless the people. 'On this wise,' saith He, 'ye shall bless the children of Israel; the Lord bless thee and keep thee: the Lord make His face shine upon thee, and be gracious unto thee: the Lord lift up His countenance upon thee, and give thee peace.' Where Jehovah, the Lord, is thrice repeated, and in the original hath in each place a several accent, to denote, as the Jews themselves acknowledge, some great mystery; which can be no other but the most Blessed Trinity, all the three Persons whereof are here called, every one, the Lord, Jehovah. The Father is placed first; but the blessings bestowed severally by each Person, are the same which are ascribed to them in my text. And when the Priest pronounced this blessing to the people (as we still do in the visitation of the sick), God promised that He Himself would accordingly bless them. And if you faithfully and devoutly receive it as ye ought, I do not question but He will do so now, upon my pronouncing in His Name the same Blessing, according to this Apostolical form in my text; 'The Grace of the Lord Jesus Christ, and the Love of God, and the Communion of the Holy Ghost, be with you all.' Amen. (2)

NOTES / SOURCES

1. William Beveridge, 'Private Thoughts upon a Christian Life', in *The Theological Works of William Beveridge*, Vol. 8, Oxford, 1846, pp. 327–9
2. 'Sermon XII: The Sacerdotal Benediction in the Name of the Trinity', in *The Theological Works of William Beveridge*, Vol. 1, Oxford, 1844, pp. 230–1

Thomas Ken   1637–1711

Thomas Ken was Rector of a number of parishes before becoming Chaplain to Princess Mary at The Hague (1679–1680). As Chaplain to Charles II, he earned his respect when he refused to receive Nell Gwyn at his house. In recognition of this boldness he was appointed Bishop of Bath and Wells in 1684. He attended Charles II at his deathbed. Refusing to make oaths of allegiance to William and Mary, he was deprived of his bishopric. Thereafter he lived as a Nonjuror, although he did not become closely involved with them. Best known for his *Manual of Prayers for Winchester Scholars* (1695), which contained a number of well-known hymns, his works were translated into French and Italian.

Ascription of Praise to the Trinity

To God the Father, who first loved us, and made us accepted in the beloved; to God the Son, who loved us, and washed us from our sins in his own blood; to God the Holy Ghost, who sheds the love of God abroad in our hearts, be all love, and all glory, for time, and for eternity. Amen. (1)

What is Lent?

For what is Lent, in its original institution, but a spiritual conflict, to subdue the flesh to the spirit, to beat down our bodies, and to bring them into subjection? What is it, but a penitential martyrdom for so many weeks together, which we suffer for our own and other sins? A devout soul, that is able duly to observe it, fastens himself to the cross on Ash Wednesday, and hangs crucified by contrition all the Lent long; that having felt in his closet, the burthen and the anguish, the nails and the thorns, and tasted the gall of his own sins, he may by his own crucifixion be better disposed to be crucified with Christ on Good Friday, and most tenderly sympathize with all the dolours, and pressures, and anguish, and torments, and desertion, infinite, unknown, and unspeakable, which God incarnate endured, when he bled upon the cross for the sins of the world; that being purified by repentance, and made conformable to Christ crucified; he may offer up a pure oblation at Easter, and feel the power and the joys, and the triumph of his Saviour's resurrection. And to encourage you to such a devotion, thus enforced with fasting, and mourning, and alms, as was this of Daniel, reflect on the wonderful success he found; for when he began his supplications, the angel Gabriel was sent to him by God, and arrived before he had ended them; and by that heavenly messenger, God then honoured him with that glorious prophecy of the seventy weeks. And the prophet Ezekiel joins Daniel with Noah and Job, as the three greatest instances of prevalence with God that ever prayed.

You have seen how Daniel served his God; and you are next to see how he served his prince, I may add, the people too; for the prince and the people have but one common interest, which is the public prosperity; and none can serve the prince well, but he does serve the people too: and Daniel served his prince and not himself; the love of God had given him an utter contempt of the world. And this made him despise Belshazzar's presents, 'Thy gifts be to thyself, and give thy rewards to another' to shew, that it was a cordial zeal for the king, and not self-interest, that inclined him to his service. This was evident in all his ministry; insomuch, that when the Median presidents and princes combined in his destruction, he had so industriously done the king's business, was so remarkably righteous a person, so faithful in the discharge of his duty, both to king and people, so beneficial to all, and offensive to none, so remote from all flattery, so courageous on just and fit occasions, in warning his great masters of their dangers, and minding them of their duty; he had so universal a benignity to all, so sincerely sought the good of Babylon, was so forward to rescue an injured innocence, as he did Susanna; so tender of men's lives, that he was never at rest till he saved all the wise men of Babylon, when the decree was gone out for their massacre; so careful of their peace and prosperity that he sat in the gate of the king to hear every man's cause, and with great patience and assiduity to do justice to all: he had behaved himself so irreproachably, that they could find 'no occasion nor fault in him concerning the kingdom; forasmuch as he was faithful neither was there any error or fault found in him'. (2)

A Morning Hymn

Awake, my soul, and with the sun,
Thy daily stage of duty run;
Shake off dull sloth, and joyful rise,
To pay thy morning sacrifice.

Thy precious time mispent, redeem,
Each present day thy last esteem;
Improve thy talent with due care,
For the great day thyself prepare.

In conversation be sincere,
Keep conscience as the noon-tide clear.
Think how all-seeing God thy ways,
And all thy secret thoughts surveys.

By influence of the light divine,
Let thy own light to others shine,
Reflect all heaven's propitious rays,
In ardent love, and cheerful praise.

'Wake, and lift up thyself my heart,
And with the angels bear thy part,
Who all night long unwearied sing,
High praise to the eternal King.

I wake, I wake, ye heavenly choir,
May your devotion me inspire,
That I like you my age may spend,
Like you may on my God attend.

May I like you on God delight,
Have all day long my God in sight,
Perform like you my Maker's will,
O may I never more do ill.

Had I your wings to heaven I'd fly,
But God shall that defect supply;
And my soul wing'd with warm desire,
Shall all day long to heaven aspire.

All praise to thee, who safe hast kept,
And hast refresh'd me whilst I slept:
Grant, Lord, when I from death shall wake,
I may of endless light partake.

I would not wake, nor rise again,
Even heaven itself I would disdain,
Wert not thou there to be enjoy'd,
And I in hymns to be employed.

Heav'n is, dear Lord, where e'er thou art,
O never then from me depart:
For to my soul, 'tis hell to be,
But for one moment void of thee.

Lord, I my vows to thee renew;
Disperse my sins as morning dew:
Guard my first springs of thought and will,
And with thyself my spirit fill.

Direct, control, suggest, this day,
All I design, or do, or say;
That all my powers with all their might,
In thy sole glory may unite.

Praise God from whom all blessings flow,
Praise him all creatures here below,
Praise him above ye heavenly host,
Praise Father, Son, and Holy Ghost. (3)

NOTES / SOURCES

1. Thomas Ken, 'Exposition of the Church's Catechism' (1685) in *The Prose Works of Thomas Ken*, London, 1838, p. 335
2. 'A Sermon preached in the King's Chapel at Whitehall' in 1685, in ibid., pp. 163–5
3. Ibid. pp. 435–7

Gilbert Burnet   1643–1715

Having travelled widely on the Continent, Gilbert Burnet became Professor of Divinity at Glasgow University at the age of twenty-six. He later settled in England and was Chaplain to the Master of the Rolls (1675–1684). He withdrew abroad on James II's accession, and in the course of his travels became an intimate of William of Orange and Mary, accompanying William to Torbay and London (1688). The following year he became Bishop of Salisbury and his episcopacy was marked by his broad theological principles.

Clarity and Application in Preaching

Things must be put in a clear Light, and brought out in as short periods, and in as plain Words as may be. The Reasons of them must be made as sensible to the People as is possible: As in Virtues and Vices, their Tendencies and Effects, their being suitable and unsuitable to our Powers, to both Souls and Bodies, to the Interests of this Life as well as the next; and the Good or Evil that they do to human Societies, Families, and Neighbourhoods, ought to be fully and frequently opened. In setting these forth, such a Measure is to be kept, that the Hearers may perceive that Things are not strained in the Way of a Declamation, into forced Characters; but that they are set out, as truly they are, without making them seem better by imaginary Perfections, or worse by an undue aggravation. For the carrying those Matters beyond the plain Observation of Mankind, makes that the Whole is looked on as a Piece of Rhetorick; the Preacher seeming to intend rather to show his Skill, in raising his Subject too high, or running it down too low, than to lay before them the native Consequences of Things; and that which, upon Reflection, they may be all able to perceive is really true. *Virtue* is so good in itself, that it needs no false Paint to make it look better; and *Vice* is so bad, that it can never look so ugly as when shewed in its own natural Colours: So that an undue *Sublime* in such Descriptions does Hurt, and can do no Good.

When the explanatory Part of the Sermon is over, the Application comes next. And here great Judgment must be used, to make it fall the heaviest, and lie the longest, upon such Particulars as may be within the Compass of the Auditory. Directions concerning a high Devotion, to a stupid, ignorant Company,—or of Generosity and Bounty, to very poor People,—against Pride and Ambition, to such as are dull and low-minded,—are ill suited, and so must have little Effect upon them: Therefore Care must be taken that the Application be useful and proper; that it make the Hearers apprehend some of their Sins and Defects, and see how to perform their Duty; that it awaken them to it, and direct them in it: And therefore the most common Sins,—such as Mens neglecting their Duty to God, in the several Branches of it,—their setting their Hearts inordinately upon the World,—their Lying in Discourse, but chiefly in Bargainings,—their Evil-speaking, and their Hatred and Malice,—ought to be very often brought in. Some one or other of these, ought to be in every Application that is made, by which they may see, that the whole Design of Religion lies against them. Such particular Sins, Swearing, Drunkenness, or Lewdness, as abound in any Place, must likewise be frequently brought in here. The Application must be clear and short, very weighty, and free of every Thing that looks like the Affectations of Wit and Eloquence; here the Preacher must be all Heart and Soul, designing the Good of his People. The whole Sermon is directed to this: Therefore, as it is fit that the chief Point which a Sermon drives at, should come often over and over, that so the Hearers may never lose sight of it, but keep it still in View; so, in the Application, the Text must be shewed to speak it; all the Parts of the Explanation must come in to enforce it: The Application must be opened in the several Views that it may have, but those must be chiefly insisted on, that are most suitable both to the Capacities and the Circumstances of the People: And in Conclusion, all ought to be summed up in a weighty Period or two; and some other signal Passages of the Scriptures relating to it may be sought for, that so the Matter may be left upon the Auditory in the solemnest Manner possible.

Thus I have led a Preacher, through the Composition of his Sermon; I will next lay before him some Particulars relating to it. The shorter Sermons are, they are generally both better heard, and better remembered. The Custom of an Hour's Length forces many Preachers to trifle away much of the Time, and to spin out their Matter, so as to hold out. So great a Length does also flat the Hearers, and tempt them to sleep; especially when, as is usual, the first Part of the Sermon is languid and heavy. In half an Hour, a Man may lay open his Matter in its full Extent, and cut off those Superfluities which come in only to lengthen the Discourse: And he may hope to keep up the Attention of his People all the while. As to the *style*, Sermons ought to be very plain; the Figures must be easy; not mean, but noble, and brought in upon Design to make the Matter better understood. The Words in a Sermon must be simple, and in common Use; not savouring of the Schools, nor above the Understanding of the People. All long *Periods*, such as carry two or three different Thoughts in them, must be avoided; for few Hearers can follow or apprehend these: Niceties of *Style* are lost before a common Auditory. But if an easy Simplicity of Style should run through the whole Composition, it should take Place most of all in the explanatory Part; for the Thing being there offered to be understood, it should be stript of all Garnishing: *Definitions* should not be offered in the Terms, or Method, that Logick directs. In short, a *Preacher* is to fancy himself, as in the Room of the most unlearned Man in his whole Parish; and therefore he must put such Parts of his Discourse as he would have all understand, in so plain a Form of Words, that it may not be beyond the meanest of them. This he will certainly study to do, if his Desire is to edify them, rather than to make them admire himself as a learned and high-spoken Man.

But in the applicatory Part, if he has a true Taste of Eloquence, and is a master at it, he is to employ it all in giving sometimes such tender Touches, as may soften, and deeper Gashes, such as may awaken his Hearers. A vain Eloquence here is very ill placed; for if that can be borne any where, it is in illustrating the Matter; but all must be grave, where one would persuade: The most natural, but the most sensible Expressions come in best here. Such an Eloquence as makes the Hearers look grave, and as it were out of Countenance, is the properest. That which makes them look lively, and as it were, smile upon one another, may be pretty; but it only tickles the Imagination, and pleases the Ear; whereas that which goes to the Heart, and wounds it, makes the Hearer rather look down, and turn his Thoughts inward upon himself. For it is certain that a Sermon, the Conclusion whereof makes the Auditory look pleased, and sets them all a talking one to another, was either not right spoken, or not right heard; it has been fine, and has probably delighted the Congregation, rather than edified it. But that Sermon that makes every one go away silent and grave, and hastening to be alone, to meditate or pray over the Matter of it in secret, has had its true Effect.

NOTES / SOURCES

Gilbert Burnet, *A Discourse of the Pastoral Care* (1692), London, 1766, pp. 195–200

Margaret Godolphin   1652–1678

Margaret Godolphin was maid of honour to the Duchess of York and to Queen Catherine. She married privately Sidney (later Earl of) Godolphin in 1675. John Evelyn's (q.v.) account of her life of piety was published in 1847.

Mrs Godolphin

Let me then first Call to Remembrance how she usualy passed the *Day*; for an Instance almost *Inimitable* in the station where she was at *Court*: I will begin with *Sonday*, 30 the *First* of the *Week*.

Were it never so Dark, Wet or Uncomfortable Weather, she rarely omitted being at the *Chapell* by Seaven a Clock-Prayers: And if a *Comunion*-day (how late-soever her Attendance on the *Queene*, and her owne extraordinary Preparation kept her up) she would be dress'd, and at her privat Devotions some houres before the Public Office began: This brings to mind, (what I could not then but smile-at) That finding one morning a *Pack-thread*, Passing thro' the *Key-hole* of her Chamber doore, and reaching to her Beds-head, opposite to that of your Ladyship's *Sisters* (if I be not mistaken) and inquiring what it Signify'd: I at last understood, it was to Awaken her Early in the Morning: The *Centinel* (whose *post* was of Course near the Entrance) being desir'd to pull it pretty hard, at such an houre, whilst the other end was tyed fast to her *Wrist*, fearing least her *Ma'd* should over-Sleepe her-selfe, or call her later than she had appointed.

But besids the Monethly *Communions*, she seldome miss'd a *Son-day* thro' the whole Yeare, where in she did not Receive the *Holy Sacrament* if she were in Towne, & tollerable Health: And I well know, she had those who gave her constant advertisement where it was Celebrated, upon more Solemn *Festivals*; besids, not seldome on the Weeke-days, Assisting at some poore Creature or other: And when sometimes being in the Country, or on a Journey (she had not those Opportunitys) She made Use of a Devout Meditation upon that Sacred *Mystery*, by Way of *Mental Comunion*: so as she was in a *Continual State of Preparation*: And ôh with what unspeakable Care & Niceness did she Use to dresse & trim her Soule against this heavenly Banket! With what flagrant Devotion at the *Altar*! I do assure your Ladyship, I have seene her receive the holy *Symbols* with Such an humble & mealting Joy in her Countenance, as seem'd to be something of *Transport* (not to say *Angelick*) some thing I cannot describe; and has her-selfe confess'd to me, to have felt in her *Soule*. Such *Influxes of heavenly joy*, as has almost caryed her into another World: I do not call them *Rapts* & *Elapses*; because she would not have Indur'd to be esteem'd above other humble *Christians*. But that she was sometimes Regâld with *Extraordinary Favours*, I have many reasons to believe: Se upon another Occasion, she Writes to me—

'*Ô my Friend*, how happy was I on *Sonday* last! By reason of this foolish Play (*of which I have already given your Ladyship* an *account*) most Imperfect were my Prayers & Preparations; and yet I don't remember, that God was ever more Gracious to me but Once before; and indeede, That Time, I had so greate a sense of my owne Unworthynesse & the Wonderful Condescention and Love of God; that I had like to have fall'n flat on my face: But *that* excepted, *This* was the most

Refreshing: *Ô Jesu* said I! how happy are We! how Blessed! that have the Lord for oure God; and *You* Blessed *Angels*, who are Present at these Assemblys, admiring this heavenly Bounty: I tell you, I was even *disolv'd* with *love to God*, and yet after all this (such wretched things we are) I was drowsy at Church; Wand'ring in my Thoughts, & forgetfull of these favours, that very-day: Thus I Acknowledge to you Gods Love to my poore Soule, and my foule Ingratitude to him; That you may pray for the Continuance of the *One*, and I trust, the *other* will in time grow lesse'.

NOTES / SOURCES

John Evelyn, *The Life of Margaret Godolphin*, Oxford, 1939, pp. 85–7

James Bonnell   1653–1699

Born to English parents living in Genoa, James Bonnell came to England where his father had been appointed Account General of Ireland in recognition of his services to Charles II whilst the latter was in exile. After his studies at St Catherine's Hall, Cambridge, he undertook the same duties (as Account General of Ireland) as his father. *The Exemplary Life and Character of James Bonnell*, by William Hamilton, is a good example of Caroline spirituality and religious practice.

James Bonnell's Character

He used to wish there were some Church in Dublin, wherein the Holy Sacrament were administered every Lord's day; 'for going about from Church to Church,' he said, 'had something of ostentation in it;' and it was with difficulty that he at last conquered this scruple. And when he went to Churches, to which he was not accustomed, he generally chose the most private place, where he might be least observed, and least disturbed; and when he was so happily placed, he always continued upon his knees, at his private devotions, till the public service began. But if he was forced to be satisfied with a more public seat, and there were company about him, he shortened his private prayers, that he might not be taken notice of; for he avoided being singular and remarkable in all his actions, much more in those of religion; in them he aimed at something greater than fame, more lasting and substantial than the vain applause of men; even those praises which are endless, and that honour which never can decay.

But his opinion of the secrecy of religious actions, and his practice too, the reader will best learn from himself, in the two following meditations; which are still farther instances of his humility, and his great watchfulness against whatever had the least tendency to vanity.

'My right hand,' says he, 'is the grace of God : my left, my spiritual friend. In acts of devotion, fasting and charity, I am to be exceeding nice, how I let one of these know what the other enables me to do. To sound a trumpet, and tell all the world what you do, is certainly a mark of a dissolute and unspiritual mind, not ambitious of heavenly rewards, nor sensible of spiritual pleasures. To reveal these only to a spiritual friend, may perhaps in some cases be necessary; but if you would be perfect, subject them only to the eyes of God; he will be your sufficient counsellor. For the advantages you may reap by revealing them to men, in any prudent instructions or encouragements, will not countervail the hazard you undergo of self-complacency, in the opinion another may have in your being devout, mortified, or charitable, and of losing your comfort; the greatest encouragement you have to persist in those charming duties, which wholly lose their sweetness, when you, in any measure, sink into flesh and blood; your comfort, I say, which wholly consists in acquitting yourself in secret, to your heavenly Father, and approving yourself to him.'

The other meditation is as follows :

'We lose,' says he, 'something of spiritual strength, (as Samson did,) by discovering secret transactions between God and our souls; for this gives our conscience a damp, since it tends to magnify ourselves, and looks like boasting of secret favours, which is a means of lessening favours among men. If what I speak of this sort tends to magnify myself, as being a favourite of God, I cannot be too jealous of myself because our hearts are deceitful, and very treacherous; and something of secret pride will be apt to steal in upon us, in such relations. If I tell of raptures and elevations vouchsafed to me in prayer; of ardent desires after the holy communion, and longings for heaven, and the like; I must be well made indeed, and strongly armed with the grace of God within me, if I do all this only for the edification of my neighbour, and to provoke him to praise God on my behalf, without any by-design to recommend myself to his esteem.'

NOTES / SOURCES

William Hamilton, *The Exemplary Life and Character of James Bonnell*, London, 1829, pp. 92–4

Nathaniel Spinckes   1654–1727

A leading Nonjuror, Nathaniel Spinckes was deprived of his office of Prebendary and Rector of St Martin's, Salisbury, because of his refusal to take an Oath of Allegiance to William and Mary (1690). George Hicks, consecrated titular bishop of Thetford by the Nonjurors, was anxious to continue the succession and consecrated Spinckes, who took no title. In the internal dispute among Nonjurors about usages in 1719, he advocated the retention of *The Book of Common Prayer* as it was, rather than a return to the first book of Edward VI. A devotional writer himself, he is also known for a collection of prayers and meditations from Lancelot Andrewes (q.v.), William Laud (q.v.), and Thomas Ken (q.v.) entitled *The True Church of England Man's Companion to the Closet* (1721), which came to be known as *Spinckes' Devotions*.

Daily Devotions

A preparatory Prayer

Prevent me, I beseech thee, O Lord, in all my doings with thy most gracious inspirations, and further me with thy continued help, that every prayer and religious duty of mine may begin always from thee, and in thee be happily ended, and more especially the service I am now entring upon; suffer not the vanities of this world to divert my thoughts from what I am about, or to distract my attention, and carry away my affections from thee. O let me not incur the guilt of drawing near to thee with my lips, while my heart is far from thee: But quicken my soul, which cleaveth to the dust; spiritualize my groveling affections, possess my heart, which opens itself to thy gracious influences, with such a strong and vigorous love toward thee, that whenever I prostrate myself before thee, my heart may be fixed and stay'd on thee, and my cold and earthly desires touch'd with an outstretched ray from thyself, till they flame up to thee in fervors answerable to my pressing wants; that I may so ask as to receive, so seek as to find, so knock that it may be opened unto me, through *Jesus Christ* my blessed Lord and Redeemer. *Amen.*

NOTES / SOURCES

Nathaniel Spinckes, *Directions concerning the Method of Daily Devotions* (1721), London, 1739, pp. 51–2

Robert Nelson   1656–1715

Under the influence of George Bull, his private tutor, Robert Nelson was a layman with Nonjuring sympathies. He spent some time on the Continent to avoid the Revolution of 1688. He eventually returned to the Church of England in 1710. He supported both the Society for Promoting Christian Knowledge and the Society for the Propagation of the Gospel and published a number of devotional works, mainly concerned with the history and meaning of the Christian Year and the Eucharist.

Saints' Days as Heavenly Birthdays

Q. *Why did they call the* Days *of their* Death *their* Birth-Days?

A. Because they looked upon those as the true Days of their Nativity, wherein they were freed from the Pains and Sorrows of a troublesome World, placed out of the reach of Sin and Temptation, delivered from this Valley of Tears, these Regions of Death and Misery; and born again unto the Joys and Happiness of an endless Life, an Inheritance incorruptible, that fadeth not away.

Q. *How ought we to observe the* Festivals *of the* Church?

A. In such a manner as may answer the Ends for which they were appointed: That God may be glorified by an humble and grateful Acknowledgment of his Mercies; and that the Salvation of our Souls may be advanced, by firmly believing the Mysteries of our Redemption; and by imitating the Example of those primitive Patterns of Piety that are set before us.

Q. *What manner of* keeping *these* Days *answers these* Ends?

A. We should constantly attend the *Publick Worship*, and partake of the Blessed *Sacrament*, if it be administred. In private we should enlarge our *Devotions*, and suffer the Affairs of the World to interrupt us as little as may be. We should particularly express our Rejoicing by *Love* and *Charity* to our poor Neighbours. If we commemorate any *Mystery* of our *Redemption*, or Article of our Faith, we ought to confirm our Belief of it, by considering all those Reasons upon which it is built; that we may be able to give a good Account of the Hope that is in us. We should from our Hearts offer to God the *Sacrifice* of *Thanksgiving*, and resolve to perform all those Duties which result from the belief of such an Article. If we commemorate any *Saint*, we should consider the Virtues for which he was most eminent, and by what Steps he arrived at so great Perfection; and then examine ourselves how far we are defective in our Duty, and earnestly beg God's Pardon for our past Failings, and his Grace to enable us to conform our Lives for the Time to come to those admirable Examples that are set before us. (1)

Candlemas

Q. *What Offerings did the blessed Virgin make?*

A. The Offerings of the Poor, a *Pair of Turtles*, or *two young Pigeons*. Such mean and low Circumstances did our blessed *Saviour* chuse when he came into the World upon the Work of our Redemption; such was his great Bounty and Kindness, that *though he was rich, yet for our sakes he became poor, that we through his Poverty might be rich.*

Q. *How was our blessed Saviour known to* Simeon *and* Anna?

A. *Simeon* being a just and devout Man, waiting for the Consolation of *Israel*, which was the Expectation of the promised *Messias*, God was pleased to reveal to him, that he should not see Death before he had seen the Lord's *Christ*; and at this very Time, when *Christ* was presented in the Temple, he was by the Guidance and Dictate of God's Spirit brought thither. And the Prophetess *Anna* constantly attending the Service of the Temple, remarkable for Mortification and Devotion, came in at the same Instant. They both gave Thanks unto the Lord, and spake of him to all that looked for Redemption in *Jerusalem*; *Simeon* in that admirable *Hymn*, which our Church hath adopted into her Offices, and with which she daily nourishes the Devotion of her Children.

Q. *What may we learn from this* Hymn *we so frequently repeat?*

A. That though we cannot see our Saviour with our bodily Eyes, as *Simeon* did, yet he being daily in the holy Scriptures presented to the Eyes of our Faith, we ought to thank God for that wonderful Salvation he hath prepared both for *Jew* and *Gentile*. That we must never think of dying in Peace, till we have embraced our Saviour with our Understandings and Affections; till we heartily believe what he revealed; and sincerely practise what he taught. That nothing will stand us in Stead in a dying Hour, and support us when all earthly Comforts forsake us, but the Remembrance of a well-spent Life, and the Performance of those Conditions upon which Salvation is promised.

Q. *What doth this great Honour bestowed upon* Simeon *and* Anna *teach us?*

A. Constantly and devoutly to attend the Ordinances of our Religion; not to neglect those Means God hath established for the building us up in his holy Faith. For if we fervently persevere, God will abundantly communicate his Grace and Favour towards us. (2)

NOTES / SOURCES

1. Robert Nelson, *A Companion for the Festivals and Fasts of the Church of England* (1704), London, 1744, pp. 8–9
2. Ibid., pp. 146–7

John Norris   1657–1711

Appointed as a Fellow of All Souls, Oxford, at the age of twenty-three, he became Rector of Bemerton, George Herbert's (q.v.) parish, from 1692 until his death. An opponent of both Whigs and Quakers, he was strongly influenced by Christian Platonism. He published devotional works, including metaphysical poems.

Hymn to Darkness

Hail, thou most sacred venerable thing!
   What Muse is worthy thee to sing?
Thee, from whose pregnant universal womb,
All things, even Light thy rival, first did come.
What dares he not attempt that sings of thee
   Thou first and greatest mystery?
Who can the secrets of thy essence tell?
Thou like the light of God art inaccessible.

Before great Love this monument did raise,
   This ample theatre of praise;
Before the folding circles of the sky
Were tuned by Him Who is all harmony;
Before the morning stars their hymn began,
   The counsel held for man;
Before the birth of either Time or Place,
Thou reign'st unquestioned monarch in the empty space.

Thy native lot thou didst to Light resign,
   But still half of the globe is thine.
Here with a quiet and yet aweful hand,
Like the best emperors thou dost command.
To thee the stars above their brightness owe,
   And mortals their repose below.
To thy protection Fear and Sorrow flee,
And those that weary are of light find rest in thee.

Though light and glory be the Almighty's throne,
   Darkness is His pavilion.
From that His radiant beauty, but from thee
He has His terror and His majesty.
Thus when He first proclaimed His sacred Law,
   And would His rebel subjects awe,
Like princes on some great solemnity
He appeared in 's robes of state and clad Himself with thee.

NOTES / SOURCES

John Norris, *A Collection of Miscellanies: consisting of Poems, Essays, Discourses and Letters, Occasionally written*, London, 1710, pp. 29–30

William Wake   1657–1737

Educated at Christ Church, Oxford, William Wake was Chaplain to the Embassy in Paris, from which he developed a keen sense of attachment to the French Church. Appointed Dean of Exeter (1703), and Bishop of Lincoln (1705), he became Archbishop of Canterbury (1716). He was involved in negotiations with French Church leaders, some of whom were committed to a 'Gallican' awareness within their tradition of the French Church, but the death of his French counterpart, Dupin, in 1719 brought the project to a close. He published a popular commentary on The Book of Common Prayer Catechism, *The Principles of the Christian Religion* (1700).

A Sermon on Christian Giving

The Opening

That They Do Good, that they be Rich in Good Works, Ready to Distribute; Willing to Communicate.   I TIMOTHY vi. 18

The Words are part of that *Charge*, which St *Paul* commanded *Timothy* to give to *Them that are Rich in this World*, v. 17. The City of *Ephesus*, like all other great and populous Cities, abounded with Many of *These*; and the *Advice* was such as if well Received, and duly Observed by them, would prove no less useful to Themselves, than advantagious to others.

There is Something in the *Riches of this World* so contrary to the *Spirit of Christianity*; so apt to take off mens Hearts and Affections from their Duty, and to run them into a thousand Vanities and Follies utterly destructive of all true Piety; that our *Saviour* seems sometimes to represent those Men as almost *Uncapable* of being *His Disciples*, who have any large Superfluity of Them. Pride, Covetousness, Sensuality, Oppression; and an innumerable Train of other irregular Lusts, and Vices, commonly follow the Possession of Them: And hard it is for any one to abound in a plentiful enjoyment of the Good things of this World, without being proportionably Poor, and Destitute, with respect to the Other. (1)

The Conclusion

Only, my Brethren, *be not weary in well doing*; but as you here plainly see the happy Fruits of this *Charity* before your Eyes, so let that induce you, beyond all other Persuasives, to go on, and abound, in it more and more. The Design is certainly Useful; 'tis Pious; 'tis Excellent. Oh! let it not fail for want of a suitable Encouragement; but as ever you hope for a Blessing from God upon your own Children, and Families, shew some regard to the Necessities of those, who cannot otherwise provide for the good Education of theirs.

And may *that God who ministreth Seed to the Sower, multiply the Seed which ye shall sow, and increase the fruits of your Righteousness!* That, if it be his Will, you may reap the Benefits of it a hundred fold now in this present time, and in the World to come may attain Life Everlasting;

Through Jesus Christ our Lord; to whom with the Father, and the Holy Ghost, be all Honour and Glory, now, and for ever. Amen (2)

NOTES / SOURCES

1. William Wake 'Sermon VII: Preached in the Parish Church of St Margaret's, Westminster, 8 January, 1709, being the day of the yearly collection for the poor children of the Grey-Coat Hospital', in *Sermons preached upon Several Occasions*, Vol. III, London, 1722, pp. 184–5
2. Ibid., p. 212

John Johnson   1662–1725

Vicar of St John's, Margate (1697), and of Cranbrook, Kent (1710), John Johnson published a number of theological works displaying his affinity with the Nonjurors. Amongst these is his treatise *The Unbloody Sacrifice and Altar Unvailed and Supported* (1714–18), in which he held that Christ was present in the eucharistic elements in power and effect rather than in actuality, and in which he argued for a doctrine of eucharistic sacrifice that was more akin to the Eastern and Western Fathers than to the controversies of the Reformation era.

The Frequency of the Eucharist

We may be convinced of the great necessity of the frequent use of the Eucharist, if we consider it as a means of covenanting, and communicating with God and each other.

By the Gospel-Covenant only, we are capable of salvation; and therefore it greatly concerns us to be well assured, that we duly lay hold on this Covenant, and renew our claims, and repair the breaches of it; and this can be done in and by the Eucharist only. Herein we do in the most perfect manner communicate with God and His Church, as has been shewed in the two foregoing Sections. Now this Communion with God and His Church does not consist in one transient action, but in the frequent and constant repeating this action. No man is reputed to be a member of a family, because he does sometimes occasionally or accidentally sit down at the same table and feast with them. Nothing but a continual taking his meals, or (to say the least) a very frequent eating with them, is sufficient to this purpose; and therefore none ought to think himself of 'the household of God,' but he who does on every opportunity eat the 'Bread of God,' together with his fellow-servants.

The Communion of Christ with His Church, and of the members of this Church with each other, is in the Scripture compared to that of a branch with the stock or tree, and of a limb with the body. Now it is certain, that, if the branch cease to partake of the juice or sap, it forthwith dies and is fit for nothing but the fire; and the limb, that does not partake of the blood and spirits which circulate in the body, becomes perfectly useless and an encumbrance. And from this we are given to understand, that our Communion with God and His Church is obstructed and annulled by any wilful neglect of the means appointed for maintenance of this communion; and of these means, I suppose, all will allow the Eucharist to be the principal. The union between Christ and His Church, and of Christians between each other, does not consist in now and then accidentally meeting together, but in a perpetual uninterrupted conjunction. It is true, some allowance must always be made for parables and similes; it cannot be expected, that men should always, night and day (in the literal sense), be employed in this or any other duty; but, certainly, for a man to pretend to be of Christ's Body, and yet not to join in that action, by which the unity of this Body is to be preserved, once a week or even once a month, is such a Communion as may rather be called a 'separation.' And if 'we are made One Body by being partakers of the One Loaf,' if 'we are made to drink into the One Spirit' by partaking of the Cup in the Eucharist, as St Paul plainly teaches us; then, certainly, those Christians have a very sad account to give of themselves, who choose for the most part or very often to turn their backs upon this Divine ordinance, and so wilfully interrupt the Communion betwixt God and their own souls, betwixt the Church of Christ and themselves. And the case is very plain; for if 'he, who feedeth on the Flesh of Christ, dwelleth in Him,' then he, who seldom or never eats It, cannot have Christ dwelling in him, but must be alienated from the Life of God. (1)

Preparation for the Eucharist

On our part, covenanting and communicating with God implies a sincere exercise of all Christian virtues and graces at present, and a resolution of continuing in the practice of them for the future. No man is fit for the Eucharist but he, who has a sincere love and charity for all men, and such a love to God as prevails over all other affections of his soul; none but he that is so humble, as not to assume any thing to himself that is above him; so content, as to use no unjust means in order to mend his condition; so patient, as not to murmur against God's Providence; so chaste and temperate, as not to have (of late at least) committed any wilful uncleanness or excess; so devout, as to be fully convinced that he owes all the spiritual and temporal blessings he enjoys to God's goodness, and that from Him alone he must expect whatever he wants, and therefore comes to the Holy Sacrament with a heart full of thanks for what he has already received, and of zeal and pious desires of those graces of which he most of all stands in need; and especially he must be so penitent, as to be truly grieved for all his known sins, and earnest in his petitions for pardon for all sins, whether known or unknown. He, who wants any of these holy dispositions, can by no means be fit for the Eucharist; because there can be no communion betwixt God and a vicious soul; for 'what fellowship hath light with darkness?' This is the fundamental article of the Christian Covenant, that 'Whoever names the Name of Christ must depart from all iniquity;' and 'Without peace and holiness no man can see the Lord:' therefore, since in the Eucharist we do profess to covenant and have communion with God, it does from thence plainly follow, that no man is a proper guest for the Lord's Table but he, who has a sincere aversion to and hatred of all sin, and a real disposition to all the virtues and graces, which the Gospel requires of us. And it was evidently the design of Christ in instituting the Eucharist, to bring all His disciples under the strictest obligation to the duties of religion; and all serious Christians are so sensible of this, that they do never presume to receive the Sacrament, until they have wrought themselves for the present into a real sorrow for all their past sins, and into a resolution of avoiding those sins, and 'walking in all the commandments and ordinances of the Lord' for the time to come. (2)

NOTES / SOURCES

1. John Johnson 'The Unbloody Sacrifice' (1714–1718), in *The Theological Works of John Johnson*, Vol. II, Oxford, 1847, pp. 190–1
2. Ibid., pp. 193–4

Thomas Wilson   1663–1755

Consecrated Bishop in 1698, Thomas Wilson remained Bishop of Sodor and Man for 57 years. His episcopacy was marked by his attempts to raise the standards of spiritual life on the Island and was also influential in the establishment of public libraries. Enjoying the freedom of the Manx Church from the English Parliament, his controversial use of episcopal authority drew him into frequent disputes with civil and ecclesiastical authorities. His *Principles and Duties of Christianity* (1707) was the first book printed in Manx, and his book of devotions, the *Sacra Privata*, has been reprinted repeatedly since.

Baptismal Vow

By Thee, O God and Father, I was created! By Thee, O Jesus, I was redeemed! By Thee, O Holy Ghost, I was sanctified! O holy, blessed, and glorious Trinity, three Persons and one God, to whom I was dedicated in Baptism, and to whom I was devoted at Confirmation, I do now renew the vows I then made of becoming Thy faithful servant unto my life's end.

I renounce the devil and all his works; the world and all that is evil in it; the lusts of the flesh, the lust of the eye, and the pride of life; resolving, by Thy grace, neither to follow, nor be led by them. I believe all the Articles of the Christian Faith; and I will, by the grace of God, keep His holy Will and Commandments all the days of my life. Amen. (1)

Virtues of an Holy Life

Fervency in devotion; frequency in prayer; aspiring after the love of God continually; striving to get above the world and the body; loving silence and solitude, as far as one's condition will permit; humble and affable to all; patient in suffering affronts and contradictions; glad of occasions of doing good even to enemies; doing the will of God, and promoting His honour to the utmost of one's power; resolving never to offend Him willingly, for any temporal *pleasure, profit,* or *loss.* These are virtues highly pleasing to God.

Dr Henry More. 'A choice receipt for those that will use it; the greatest that one friend can communicate to another, viz. every day to deny one's self in things indifferent, (consistent with health and civility to others,) and not to please one's self in any thing.'

There is no pleasure comparable to the not being captivated to any external thing whatever.

Self-denial does not consist in fasting and other mortifications only, but in an *indifference for the world,* its *profits pleasures, honours,* and its other idols.

It is a part of special prudence, never to do any thing because one has an inclination to it; but because it is one's duty, or it is reasonable; for he who follows his inclination, *because he wills*, in one thing, will do it in another.

He that will not command his thoughts and his will, will soon lose the command of his actions.

Always suspect yourself, when your inclinations are strong and importunate.

It is necessary that we deny ourselves in little and indifferent things, when reason and conscience, which is the voice of God, suggests it to us, as ever we hope to get the rule over our own will.

Say not, 'it is a trifle, and not fit to make a sacrifice of to God.' He that will not sacrifice a little affection will hardly offer a greater. It is not the thing, but the reason and manner of doing it, namely, for God's sake, and that I may accustom myself to obey His voice, that God regards, and rewards with greater degrees of grace.

Romans xv. 3. *Even Jesus Christ pleased not Himself.* As appears in the meanness of His birth, relations, form of a servant, the company He kept, His life, death, etc.

The greater your self-denial, the firmer your faith, and more acceptable to God. The sincere devotion of the rich; the alms of the poor; the humility of the great; the faith of such whose condition is desperate; the contemning the world when one can command it at pleasure; continuing instant in prayer even when we want the consolation we expected: these, and such like instances of self-denial, God will greatly reward.

They who imagine that self-denial intrenches upon our liberty, do not know that it is this only that can make us free indeed; giving us the victory over ourselves; setting us free from the bondage of our corruption; enabling us to bear afflictions, (which will come one time or other;) to foresee them without amazement; enlightening the mind, sanctifying the will, and making us to slight those baubles which others so eagerly contend for.

Mortification consists in 'such a sparing use of the creatures, as may deaden our love for them, and make us more indifferent in the enjoyment of them.' This lessens the weight of concupiscence, which carries us to evil, and so makes the grace of God 'more effectual to turn the balance of the will.'

It is the greatest mercy, that God does not consult our inclinations, in laying upon us the Cross, which is the only way to happiness. Jesus Christ crucified would have few imitators, if God did not lay it upon us, by the hands of men, and by His providence. (2)

The Preacher's Task

The design of religion being to lead men to the knowledge of God, how He is to be worshipped, appeased, honoured; and to make men holy, that they may be capable of being happy when they die; the great business of a preacher should be, to shew how the Christian religion and all its parts contribute to this end.

They that recommended eternal possessions to others, ought to shew by their lives that they are themselves verily persuaded of the vanity of all earthly pleasures, avoiding superfluities, etc. Jesus Christ preached up the contempt of the world, by contemning it Himself.

A pastor's knowledge need not extend so far as is imagined. If he knows the Scriptures, and what concerns the kingdom of God, and the way of leading souls thither, he, etc.

We must speak to the heart as well as to the understanding. While we attack the men's reason only, they will hear with patience; but when we attack the heart and its corruption, then they are uneasy.

I would rather send away a hearer smiting his breast, than please the most learned audience with a fine sermon against any vice.

The end of preaching is to turn men from sin unto God. He that has not this in his aim, etc. to convince men of the reality of a future state of happiness or misery, and how to avoid the one and gain the other, etc.

Let people feel that you are in earnest, that you believe and are deeply affected with the great truths you would recommend.

Avoid such discourses and subjects as would divert the mind without instructing it.

Never consult your own fancy in the choice of subjects, but the necessities of your flock. (3)

Holiness

O God, who hast called me to a high degree of holiness, give me a firm faith in Thy power, through our Lord Jesus Christ, that by this assistance I may get the mastery over all my sins and corruptions; that I may be redeemed from *all* iniquity; that I may be holy, as He who has called me is holy.

Jesus—Saviour.—This Name shall ever be my refuge and confidence, my strength and support, my peace and consolation. O Jesu, be my Saviour, now and at the hour of death.

We glorify Thee, O Lord, for Thy mercy towards sinners, and we beg the same for ourselves.

Possess my soul with an earnest desire of pleasing Thee, and with a fear of offending Thee.

Let me be ever ready to forgive injuries, and backward to offer any.

Give me, O Lord, faith and patience, that I may neither murmur at Thy appointments, nor be angry against the instruments of Thy justice.

Deliver me from the errors and vices of the age we live in; from infidelity, wicked principles; from profaneness, heresies, and schism.

I most heartily thank God for His perpetual care over me; for all His mercies bestowed upon me; for the blessings of nature and of grace.

Give a blessing to those means which Thou Thyself hast appointed.

Grant, O God, that I may never receive Thy grace in vain, but that I may live like one who believes and hopes for the joys of heaven. (4)

NOTES / SOURCES

1. Thomas Wilson 'A Short and Plain Instruction for the Better Understanding of the Lord's Supper' (1734), in *The Works of Thomas Wilson* Vol. IV, Oxford, 1851, p. 383
2. 'Sacra Privata', ibid., Vol. V, Oxford, 1853, pp. 152–4
3. Ibid., pp. 213–4
4. Ibid., pp. 284–5

William Nicholls   1664–1712

A Canon of Chichester (1707), William Nicholls published a number of theological works of which his *Comment on the Book of Common Prayer* (1710) was the most influential, reflecting both a considerable understanding of the Prayer Book services, and at the same time a readiness to paraphrase individual prayers in the more florid style of the time.

Paraphrase on the Prayer of St Chrysostom

All powerful God, to whose grace and favour we owe it, that we have had this opportunity of addressing ourselves unto thee, in the public service of the Church; and who has promised, in the holy Word, that *when two or three are gathered together in thy Name, thou art in the midst of them* (Mt 18:19), and that *what they agree on, shall be done for them in Heaven* (Mt 18:18), relying therefore upon thy gracious promise which thou hast been pleased to make to thy Church, we humbly put in our plea at the throne of grace, to grant all that we have prayed for, so far forth (especially as to temporal blessings) as thou in thy heavenly wisdom shalt judge expedient: desiring, however, of thy goodness, to grant us all necessary knowledge and truths of religion, whilst we live in this world, and when we shall pass to the other, that thou wouldest bestow upon us everlasting life. Amen.

I now close, my Christian brethren, this part of the service with a benediction used by St Paul, (2 Cor 13:14), committing both you and myself to the care and protection of the ever-blessed Trinity; beseeching the great God, who is three persons in one nature, that the grace obtained for us by our blessed Lord Jesus in our redemption, may absolve us: that the love of the Father, who is now reconciled to us through his blood, may justify us: and lastly, that by partaking of the communication of the Holy Ghost we may be sanctified. Amen.

NOTES / SOURCES

William Nicholls, *A Comment on the Book of Common Prayer*, London, 1710

Jonathan Swift   1667–1745

As well as being Dean of St Patrick's, Dublin (from 1713), Jonathan Swift is perhaps best known in the popular mind as a satirist. The famed author of *Gulliver's Travels* (1726), his numerous writings were almost without exception published anonymously. A staunch supporter of the Church of England, he nonetheless vented his sense of injustice at English misrule in Ireland. Following a long association with the Whigs, he eventually went over to the Tories on the issue of Dissent in 1710. A person of considerable generosity, he spent a third of his income on charities and it was only for *Gulliver's Travels* that he received any payment.

To a Young Clergyman

And upon this account it is, that among hard words, I number likewise those which are peculiar to divinity as it is a science, because I have observed several clergymen, otherwise little fond of obscure terms, yet in their sermons very liberal of those which they find in ecclesiastical writers, as if it were our duty to understand them; which I am sure it is not. And I defy the greatest divine to produce any law either of God or man, which obliges me to comprehend the meaning of *omniscience, omnipresence, ubiquity, attribute, beatific vision,* with a thousand others so frequent in pulpits, any more than that of *eccentric, idiosyncracy, entity,* and the like. I believe I may venture to insist farther, that many terms used in Holy Writ, particularly by St Paul, might with more discretion be changed into plainer speech, except when they are introduced as part of a quotation.

I am the more earnest in this matter, because it is a general complaint, and the justest in the world. For a divine has nothing to say to the wisest congregation of any parish in this kingdom, which he may not express in a manner to be understood by the meanest among them. And this assertion must be true, or else God requires from us more than we are able to perform. However, not to contend whether a logician might possibly put a case that would serve for an exception, I will appeal to any man of letters, whether at least nineteen in twenty of those perplexing words might not be changed into easy ones, such as naturally first occur to ordinary men, and probably did so at first to those very gentlemen who are so fond of the former. (1)

[. . .]

I do not find that you are anywhere directed in the canons or articles, to attempt explaining the mysteries of the Christian religion. And indeed since Providence intended there should be mysteries, I do not see how it can be agreeable to piety, orthodoxy or good sense, to go about such a work. For, to me there seems to be a manifest dilemma in the case: if you explain them, they are mysteries no longer; if you fail, you have laboured to no purpose. What I should think most reasonable and safe for you to do upon this occasion is, upon solemn days to deliver the doctrine as the Church holds it, and confirm it by Scripture. For my part, having considered the matter impartially, I can see no great reason which those gentlemen you call the freethinkers can have for their clamour against religious mysteries; since it is plain, they were not invented by the clergy, to whom they bring no profit, nor acquire any honour. For every clergyman is ready either to tell us the utmost he knows, or to confess that he does not understand them; neither is it strange that there should be mysteries in divinity as well as in the commonest operations of nature. (2)

A Prayer for Stella in her Last Sickness

Almighty and most gracious Lord God, extend, we beseech Thee, Thy pity and compassion towards this Thy languishing servant: Teach her to place her hope and confidence entirely in Thee; give her a true sense of the emptiness and vanity of all earthly things; make her truly sensible of all the infirmities of her life past, and grant to her such a true sincere repentance as is not to be repented of. Preserve her, O Lord, in a sound mind and understanding, during this Thy visitation: Keep her from both the sad extremes of presumption and despair. If Thou shalt please to restore her to her former health, give her grace to be ever mindful of that mercy, and to keep those good resolutions she now makes in her sickness, so that no length of time, nor prosperity, may entice her to forget them. Let no thought of her misfortunes distract her mind, and prevent the means towards her recovery, or disturb her in her preparations for a better life. We beseech Thee also, O Lord, of Thy infinite goodness to remember the good actions of this Thy servant; that the naked she hath clothed, the hungry she hath fed, the sick and the fatherless whom she hath relieved, may be reckoned according to Thy gracious promise, as if they had been done unto Thee. Hearken, O Lord, to the prayers offered up by the friends of this Thy servant in her behalf, and especially those now made by us unto Thee. Give Thy blessing to those endeavours used for her recovery; but take from her all violent desire, either of life or death, further than with resignation to Thy holy will. And now, O Lord, we implore Thy gracious favour towards us here met together; grant that the sense of this Thy servant's weakness may add strength to our faith, that we, considering the infirmities of our nature, and the uncertainty of life, may, by this example, be drawn to repentance before it shall please Thee to visit us in the like manner. Accept these prayers, we beseech Thee, for the sake of Thy dear Son Jesus Christ, our Lord; who, with Thee and the Holy Ghost, liveth and reigneth ever one God world without end. Amen. (3)

NOTES / SOURCES

1. Jonathan Swift 'A letter to a Young Gentleman lately enter'd into Holy Orders' (1721) in *The Prose Works of Jonathan Swift* Vol. III, London, 1909, pp. 202–3
2. Ibid., pp. 213–4
3. Jonathan Swift, 'Three Prayers used by the Dean for Mrs Johnson' (1727) in ibid., pp. 311–12

Mary Astell   1668–1731

In 1694 Mary Astell published anonymously her *Serious Proposal to Ladies* in which she proposed a scheme of religious retirement for women living in a community which was 'rather academic than monastic' and founded on the principles of the Church of England. Whilst the scheme drew considerable discussion, it aroused opposition, especially from Bishop Burnett (q.v.), and never bore fruit. She later entered into controversy with the Platonist John Norris (q.v.) of Bemerton about the pure love of God. Writing anonymously, but swiftly identified, she also published *The Christian Religion as Profess'd by a Daughter of the Church of England*, and *Occasional Communion*, (1705).

Women and Religion

A peaceable woman, indeed, will not carry it so far, she will neither question her husband's right, nor his fitness, to govern, but how? Not as an absolute Lord and Master, with an arbitrary and tyrannical sway, but as reason governs and conducts a man, by proposing what is just and fit. And the man who acts according to that wisdom he assumes, who would not have that superiority he pretends to, acknowledged just, will receive no injury by anything that has been offered here. A woman will value him the more who is so wise and good, when he discerns how much he excels the rest of his noble sex; the less he requires, the more he will merit that esteem and deference which those who are so forward to exact, seem conscious they don't deserve. (1)

If all men are born free, how is that all women are born slaves?
'Tis true, that God told Eve after the fall, that her husband should rule over her: and so it is, that he told Esau by the mouth of Isaac, his Father, that he should serve his younger brother, and should in time, and when he was strong enough to do it, break the yoke from off his neck. Now, why one text should be a command any more than the other, and not both of them be predictions only; or why the former should prove Adam's natural right to rule, and much less every man's, any more than the latter is a proof of Jacob's right to rule, and of Esau's to rebel, one is yet to learn? The text in both cases foretelling what would be; but neither of them determining what *ought* to be. (2)

The Christian Woman

If God had not intended that women should use their reason, He would not have given them any, for He does nothing in vain. If they are to use their reason, certainly it ought to be employed about the noblest objects, and in business of the greatest consequence, therefore, in religion. That our Godfathers and God-mothers answer'd for us at the font, was an act of charity in them, and will be a great benefit to us if we make a right use of it; but it will be our own condemnation if we are Christians merely upon this account, for that only can be imputed to a free agent which is done with understanding and choice. A Christian woman therefore must not be a child in understanding; she must serve God with understanding as well as with affection; must love Him with all her mind and soul, as well as with all her heart and strength; in a word, must perform a reasonable service if she means to be acceptable to her maker. (3)

Revelation and Guidance

If God had not given us sufficient light to discern between the evil and the good, nor motives strong enough to incline us to pursue the one and to avoid the other; if He had not put happiness in our own choice, but had inevitably determined us to destruction, this indeed had been a want of mercy and goodness, if not a want of justice towards His creatures. (4)

Where God has given but little light, no doubt He makes great allowances; this we may be sure of, that He is no hard master, nor requires an increase beyond the talents He has given us. But though the light shine ever so bright about us, we can have no vision unless we open our eyes. Tho' the motives are ever so strong and powerful yet they are *but* motives; they are most proper to persuade, but neither can or ought to compel. (5)

Beauty and Holiness

Every one knows, that the mind will not be kept from contemplating what it loves in the midst of crowds and business. Hence come those frequent absences, so observable in conversation; for whilst the body is confined to present company, the mind is flown to that which it delights in. If God then be the object of our desires, we shall relieve ourselves in the common uneasiness of life, by contemplating His beauty. For certainly there cannot be a higher pleasure than to think that we love and are beloved by the most amiable and best Being. Whom the more we contemplate the more we shall desire, and the more we desire the more we shall enjoy. This desire having the pre-eminence of all other desires, as in every other thing so particularly in this, that it can't be disappointed; no one who brings a sincere heart, being ever rejected by this divine lover. Whose eyes pierce the soul, as He can't be deceiv'd by an imposture, so He never mistakes or neglects the faithful affection; which too seldom finds ways to make itself understood among mortals, even by those who pretend to be the most discerning, but who give themselves up to the flatterers and deceivers, whilst they treat the plain and honest person with the utmost outrage. (6)

The Eucharist

Our blessed saviour has set us the brightest pattern of every virtue, and the best thing we can do is to form ourselves upon this most perfect example; but this is not the only thing to be remembered at His table. He did for us which no mere man, no nor the whole creation, could possibly perform, He satisfied divine justice for the sins of the whole world. And 'having made peace through the blood of His cross,' as the scripture speaks, 'reconciled all things unto the Father'; so that we have 'redemption through His blood, even the forgiveness of sins' (Col 1:14–20). And the Lord's Supper is a sacrament of our redemption by Christ's death: it is not only a badge or token of our profession, but rather a certain sure witness and effectual sign of grace and God's goodwill towards us, by the which He doth work invisibly in us, and doth not only quicken, but also strengthen and confirm our faith in him: as the Church teaches in her Articles, which our divine having subscribed, this must needs be his sense, for we may not suspect him of prevarication. She says indeed very truly, that our preparation for the Lord's table, should not be accompanied with anxieties. For as we can't well understand why people will take the liberty to do that presently after the Holy Sacrament, which they would not allow themselves two or three days before; so neither they make that a task and toil, a sort of penance which is in itself is a most delightful performance, a feast of joy and gladness. Or what can the meaning of those melancholy looks and airs that are then put on, unless it be that believing it necessary to dismiss our sins at the Lord's table, we are sad and out of humour till we think we may meet again. (7)

Soundness of Judgement

So that tho' moral and intellectual improvements may be considered apart, they can't really be separated, at least not in a Christian sense. There is a natural connection between purity of manners, and soundness of judgement: if any man will do God's will, says our Lord, he shall know the doctrine whether it be of God. For every sin, and more particularly, impurity, pride, and worldly interest, is a prejudice that shuts out the light of truth, keeps men obstinate in error, and hardens their minds against conviction. And therefore having Solomon on my side, and which is more, that Divine Spirit by which he wrote, I shall not scruple to call the sinner a fool, tho' he be ever so learned, so witty, so ingenious, or what passes with the most for the top of wisdom, so cunning and so worldly wise. For since wisdom consists in pursuing a worthy God by proper means, he whose God is to be despised and abhorr'd can't be a wise man, but is only the more foolish, by how much he is the more artful and industrious in pursuit of it. But the Christian, whatever his understanding may be in other matters, is wise in respect of his end, which is the main point of wisdom; and according to his capacity he will be wise with regard to the means of obtaining it. Indeed I heartily wish that we were all better instructed in this part of wisdom, and more diligent in the practice. (8)

NOTES / SOURCES

1. Mary Astell, *Some Reflections upon Marriage*, London, 1730, pp. 126–7
2. Ibid., pp. 150–1
3. Mary Astell, *The Christian Religion as Profess'd by a Daughter of the Church of England*, London, 1705, p. 6
4. Ibid., p. 92
5. Ibid., p. 93
6. Ibid., pp. 151–2
7. Ibid., pp. 158–9
8. Ibid., pp. 290–1

Edmund Gibson   1669–1748

After serving as Chaplain to Archbishop Tennison and Librarian at Lambeth, Gibson sided with the Archbishop in the Convocation controversy against Francis Atterbury who joined with the 'inferior clergy' against the bishops. From this he published two major works, *The Synodus Anglicana; all the constitution and proceedings of an English convocation* (1702), and later the *Codex Iuris Ecclesiastici Anglicani* (1713). He fell from political grace over his opposition to the Quakers Relief Bill (1736) by which time he had been made Bishop of Lincoln in 1716, and translated to London (1723). He was noted for his promotion of the spiritual needs of the American colonists, who at that time came under the jurisdiction of London.

Prayer

Prayer is a service that we owe to Almighty God, and he is our creator and preserver, and we his creatures, who depend upon him for the comforts and necessaries of body and soul. Which service is not only in itself most reasonable, as it is a humble acknowledgement of God's dominion and sovereignty over us: but is in many places of scripture expressly enjoin'd by Christ and his apostles, as a necessary condition, and a sure means of having our necessities suppli'd . . .

Now, the reason why God requires us to pray to him for his blessing and assistance, is not that he wants to be inform'd what our necessities are; for he understands them much better than we ourselves . . . That the great end of making prayer a religious ordinance, and of obliging Christians to ask that they may receive, is to preserve upon their minds a perpetual sense of their dependence upon God, and of their manifold obligations to him; to the end, that these daily acknowledgements of the divine pow'r and goodness, may keep up in creatures a due fear and love of their Creator, and an habitual reverence and obedience to him and his laws. (1)

A Morning Prayer

Almighty and everlasting God, in whom all things live and move and have their being, and whose mercy is over all thy works: we thy needy creatures, in a thankful sense of thy good providence over us, render thee our humblest praises for thy preservation of us from the beginning of our lives to this day. Blessed be thy holy Name for the continual protections of thy hand, by which we have been defended amidst the changes and chances of this mortal life, and kept and deliver'd from innumerable dangers, and particularly from the terrors and evil accidents of the past night. To thy watchful providence we wholly owe it, that no disturbance hath come nigh our dwelling, but that we have enjoy'd quiet and refreshing sleep, and are brought in safety to the beginning of the day. For these and all thy other mercies, our souls do bless and magnify thy glorious Name: humbly beseeching thee to accept this morning sacrifice of praise and thanksgiving for his sake, who lay down in the grave and rose again for us, thy Son our Saviour Jesus Christ. (2)

The Centrality of Worship

My brethren, the two things, which above all others, help to preserve in Christians a spirit of religion and a reverence of Almighty God, are Daily Prayer, and the frequent receiving of the Holy Sacrament. None who duly attend these two offices, can ever be unacquainted with God and his soul: and I may add, that whoever lives in the neglect of them, lives also in an habitual forgetfulness of God, his duty and the next world: or at best is luke-warm and indifferent in the concerns of religion. (3)

The Benefits of the Eucharist

So many and great are the spiritual benefits accruing to devout Christians, from the frequent receiving of the Holy Sacrament: all of which they happily forego, who live in the neglect of this Holy Ordinance; whether such neglect arise from any mistakes concerning it (which is the case of some), or for the love of their sins, and an aversion to religious exercises, which are generally the true causes why they care not to come to the Lord's Table, whatever excuses they may pretend to colour over the guilt and shame of condemning the highest ordinance of the Christian religion. They say, they want time and opportunity to prepare themselves for it: but let them only bring their hearts to a sincere resolution that they will forsake their sins and live as becomes Christians; and, as to further preparations, God requires no more, than every man's condition and circumstances in the world will conveniently allow. (4)

When the Minister is Drawing Near to Give Communion

I behold by faith my crucifi'd Lord dying for me; and as my only Saviour and Redeemer I adore and worship him. O Lord, increase and enliven my faith; and grant that in these holy mysteries I may receive the remission of my sins and the comfortable assistance of thy Holy Spirit. (5)

NOTES / SOURCES

1. Edmund Gibson, *Family Devotions*, London, 1705, pp. 7–8
2. Ibid., pp. 19–20. (Note the echoes of the Third Collect at Morning Prayer)
3. Edmund Gibson, *The Holy Sacrament Explained*, London, 1705, p. 3
4. Ibid., pp. 53–4
5. Ibid., p. 103

Joseph Addison   1672–1719

Joseph Addison distinguished himself as a classical scholar during his time as a student and then Fellow at Oxford. He was a Member of Parliament for Lostwithiel (1708) and then Malmesbury. He also held the post of Under-Secretary of State. Through his friendship with Swift (q.v.) and Steele, he contributed to *The Tatler*, *The Spectator*, and *The Guardian*. He is perhaps best known as the author of the poem, 'The spacious firmament on high', which reflects the interest of the time in creation as part of an ordered universe.

The Praise of Cheerfulness

I have always preferred chearfulness to mirth. The latter I consider as an act, the former as a habit of the mind. Mirth is short and transient, chearfulness fixed and permanent. Those are often raised into the greatest transports of mirth who are subject to the greatest depressions of melancholy: on the contrary, chearfulness, though it does not give the mind such an exquisite gladness, prevents us from falling into any depths of sorrow. Mirth is like a flash of lightning, that breaks through a gloom of clouds, and glitters for a moment; chearfulness keeps up a kind of day-light in the mind, and fills it with a steady and perpetual serenity.

Men of austere principles look upon mirth as too wanton and dissolute for a state of probation, and as filled with a certain triumph and insolence of heart, that is inconsistent with a life which is every moment obnoxious to the greatest dangers. Writers of this complexion have observed, that the sacred person who was the great pattern of perfection was never seen to laugh.

Chearfulness of mind is not liable to any of these exceptions: it is of a serious and composed nature; it does not throw the mind into a condition improper for the present state of humanity, and is very conspicuous in the characters of those who are looked upon as the greatest philosophers among the heathens, as well as among those who have been deservedly esteemed as saints and holy men among Christians.

If we consider chearfulness in three lights, with regard to ourselves, to those we converse with, and to the great Author of our being, it will not a little recommend itself on each of these accounts. The man who is possessed of this excellent frame of mind, is not only easy in his thoughts, but a perfect master of all the powers and faculties of his soul: his imagination is always clear, and his judgment undisturbed; his temper is even and unruffled, whether in action or in solitude. He comes with a relish to all those goods which nature has provided for him, tastes all the pleasures of the creation which are poured about him, and does not feel the full weight of those accidental evils which may befal him.

If we consider him in relation to the persons whom he converses with, it naturally produces love and good-will towards him. A chearful mind is not only disposed to be affable and obliging, but raises the same good humour in those who come within its influence. A man finds himself pleased, he does not know why, with the chearfulness of his companion: it is like a sudden sunshine that awakens a secret delight in the mind, without her attending to it: the heart rejoices of its own accord, and naturally flows out into friendship and benevolence towards the person who has so kindly an effect upon it. (1)

The Confirmation of Faith

The spacious firmament on high,
With all the blue ethereal sky,
And spangled heavens, a shining frame,
Their great original proclaim:
Th' unwearied sun, from day to day,
Does his Creator's power display,
And publishes to every land
The work of an almighty hand.

II

Soon as the evening shades prevail,
The moon takes up the wondrous tale,
And nightly to the listening earth
Repeats the story of her birth:
Whilst all the stars that round her burn,
And all the planets in their turn,
Confirm the tidings as they roll,
And spread the truth from pole to pole.

III

What though, in solemn silence, all
Move round the dark terrestrial ball?
What though nor real voice nor sound
Amid their radiant orbs be found?

> In reason's ear they all rejoice,
> And utter forth a glorious voice,
> For ever singing, as they shine,
> 'The hand that made us is divine.' (2)

NOTES / SOURCES

1. Joseph Addison, in Thomas Arnold (ed.), *Selections from Addison's Papers Contributed to the Spectator*, Oxford, 1900, pp. 188–9
2. Ibid., pp. 471–2

Benjamin Hoadly   1676–1711

Fellow of St Catherine Hall, Cambridge (1696–1701), Benjamin Hoadly was in succession Bishop of Bangor, Hereford, Salisbury, and Winchester. His episcopacy was marked by political theological controversy, due to his strongly Latitudinarian views. He considered that the Lord's Supper was purely commemorative, a view spelled out in his *Plain Account of the Nature and End of the Sacrament* (1735).

The Lord's Supper—our Covenant with God

We may indeed, be said to acknowledge and own our Covenant with *GOD*, through *Christ*, by the *virtual professing* Our selves to be *Christians*, implied in Our *Remembring* Him as our Lord, in this *Rite*. But the same may be said of any other, even *verbal*, Profession of our *Faith* in *Christ*; which is equally an *Acknowledgment* of the same *Covenant*. But the *Repeated Acknowledgment* of our being entered into such a *Covenant*, is by no means, nor in any proper sense, the *Renewal* of that *Covenant*. They are *Two* very different *Ideas*: and ought always to be kept so.

The *Christian Religion* is considered as a *Covenant* between *GOD* and *Us*. Under this figure, The *Covenant*, on *our* Part, is, Not that We consent to forfeit his *Favor* for ever, unless We strictly and rigorously, without any one neglect or deviation, persevere to the End of Life, in the performance of his Will: but, That We will sincerely and uniformly endeavor to perform his Will; and, if in any instance We neglect or transgress it, We will not suffer this to grow into an *Habit* of Sin, but recover Ourselves by greater Watchfulness, and actual Amendment of Life. (1)

The Lord's Supper—Renewal of the Covenant

In a word, The effectual *Re-establishment* of the *Christian Covenant* on *our* part, if it has been shaken by Our Sins, can be only compassed by that *Actual Amendment*, which is part of the *Covenant*. And therefore, as the *partaking* of the *Lord's Supper* is *not* the *Actual Amendment* of our *Lives*, but is only that *One* Instance of our *Christianity*, by which we do in effect acknowledge our Obligation to it; and by which, as by a *Mean*, We are naturally, and by the Appointment of *Christ*, led to it; Let not That *Benefit* be annexed to the *Mean*, which belongs only to the *End*, served by That *Mean*; nor those *Privileges* be given to *One Act of religious Profession*, which are constantly and plainly taught by GOD himself, to belong to the *Actual Amendment* of our *Lives*, and the sincere performance of his whole Will. And this being so, that the *Actual Amendment* of our lives is the only Security to this *Covenant*, on *our* part; it follows, that neither the *Partaking* of the *Lord's Supper*, nor Any thing else, which is not *Actual Amendment*, can be spoken of, with any propriety, under that *Character*. (2)

NOTES / SOURCES

1. Benjamin Hoadly, *A Plain Account of the Nature and End of the Sacrament of the Lord's Supper* (1735 and 1772) pp. 154–5
2. Ibid., p. 157

Daniel Waterland   1683–1740

Fellow and Master of Magdalene College, Cambridge (1713), he was appointed Chaplain to the King (1717), Chancellor to the Diocese of York (1722), Canon of Windsor (1727), and Archdeacon of Middlesex (1730). He took part in numerous theological controversies in relation to the divinity of Christ and the Trinity and concerning the Eucharist, especially in his *Review of the Doctrine of the Eucharist* (1738). On the Eucharist, he took a middle course between the Nonjurors and the strongly Latitudinarian views of Hoadly (q.v.). Waterland's intermediate position was widely adhered to.

The Eucharist a Spiritual Sacrifice

Return we but to the ancient ideas of spiritual sacrifice, and then all will be clear, just, and uniform. We need not then be vainly searching for a sacrifice (as the Romanists have been before us) among texts that speak nothing of one, from Melchizedek in Genesis down to Hebrews the thirteenth. Our proofs will be found to lie where the spiritual services lie, and where they are called sacrifices. The Eucharist contains many of them, and must therefore be a proper sacrifice, in the strength of those texts, and cannot be otherwise. Here the primitive Fathers rested that matter; and here may we rest it, us upon firm ground. Let us not presume to offer the Almighty any dead sacrifice in the Eucharist; he does not offer us empty signs: but as he conveys to us the choicest of his blessings by those signs, so by the same signs (not sacrifices) ought we to convey our choicest gifts, the Gospel services, the true sacrifices, which he has commanded. So will the federal league of amity be mutually kept up and perfected. Our sacrifices will then be magnificent, and our priesthood glorious; our altar high and heavenly, and our Eucharist a constant lesson of good life; every way fitted to draw down from above those inestimable blessings which we so justly expect from it. Let but the work or service be esteemed the sacrifice, rather than the material elements, and then there will be no pretence or colour left for absurdly supposing, that any sacrifice of ours can be expiatory, or more valuable than ourselves; or that our hopes of pardon, grace, and salvation can depend upon any sacrifice extrinsic, save only the all-sufficient sacrifice of Christ.

NOTES / SOURCES

Daniel Waterland, 'The Christian Sacrifice Explained in a Charge delivered to the Middlesex Clergy', (1738) in *A Review of the Doctrine of the Eucharist by Daniel Waterland*, 1856, Oxford, 1896, pp. 487–8

The New Week's Preparation for a Worthy Receiving of the Lord's Supper

1749

The New Week's Preparation first appeared in 1749, as a counterpoint to the (still popular) *Week's Preparation* of 1679. Theologically more moderate than its predecessor, and influenced by Daniel Waterland (q.v.), it became very popular and was reprinted right into the following century, though it never replaced *The Week's Preparation*, which continued to be published as well.

A Prayer on *Saturday Evening,* for *a Worthy Receiving of the Holy Sacrament*

I will wash my hands in innocency, O Lord, and so will I go to thine altar.
Psalm xxvi. 6.

O Crucified *Jesu!* who at thy last supper didst ordain the holy eucharist, the sacrament and bond of *christian* love, for the continual remembrance of the sacrifice of thy death; and hast commanded us to do this in remembrance of thee: let that propitiatory sacrifice of thy death, which thou didst offer upon the cross for the sins of the whole world, and particularly for my sins, be ever fresh in my remembrance.

O blessed Saviour, let that mighty salvation thy love hath wrought for us, never slip our of my mind, but especially let my remembrance of thee in the holy sacrament be always most lively and affecting. So that if I love thee truly, I shall be sure to frequent thy altar, that I may often remember all the wonderful loves of my crucified Redeemer. Yet, forasmuch as I know, O my God, that a bare remembrance of thee is not enough; fix in me such a remembrance of thee, as is suitable to the infinite love I am to remember; work in me all those holy and heavenly affections, which become the remembrance of a crucified Saviour; and do thou so dispose my heart to be thy guest at thy holy table, that I may feel all the sweet influences of love crucified, the strengthening and refreshing of my soul by thy body and blood, as my body is by the bread and wine.

O merciful *Jesu!* let that immortal food, which in the holy eucharist thou vouchsafest me, pour into my weak and languishing soul new supplies of grace, new life, new love, new vigour, and new resolutions, that I may never more faint or droop, or faulter in my duty. *Amen*, Lord *Jesus, Amen.*

NOTES / SOURCES

The New Week's Preparation for a Worthy Receiving of the Lord's Supper (1749), London, 1810, pp. 90–1

Griffith Jones 1683–1761

Griffith Jones of Llanddowror was educated at Carmarthen Grammar School, ordained priest in 1708, and founded the Welsh Circulating Schools, which taught ordinary people to read and write, in what could be described as the first adult literacy campaign. Catherine the Great sent an emissary to see how it was done.

Charity and Faith

Can it consist with our Christian profession to neglect this? An uncharitable Christian is a down-right contradiction. Of all the enjoyments of this world, of all endowments of the human mind, and of all the heaven-born graces which adorn a pious soul, the most amiable and excellent charity is the greatest.

It is charity that crowns and consummates the Christian character; which every genuine Christian aspires after, and can never be a Christian indeed without it. In brief, it is the substance of every virtue, of every duty, and of all obedience: without it, faith itself can avail no more to salvation, than infidelity. It unites the spirits of all good men in the bond of peace, and smothers all contention; softens all severe censure, and covereth a multitude of sins. It is indeed the sum of present and future bliss; and its nature, reward and joy never fail, but remains for ever, durable as eternity! In a word, it is the divine nature, and the offspring of God; and, if I may presume to advance one step farther, charity is so essential to goodness, perfection and felicity, that the want of it, if that was possible, (with awful reverence I write it) would divest the great Jehovah of his divinity; for God is love. And can we then be Christians, good or happy, without it?

NOTES / SOURCES

W. Moses Williams (ed.), Griffith Jones, *Selections from the Welch Piety*, Cardiff, 1938, pp. 70–1

Thomas Rattray 1684–1743

A Scottish Nonjuring Bishop of Brechin (1727), he helped to formulate the Scottish Church canons. His appointment aroused considerable opposition because James Edward, the Old Pretender, had not agreed to his election. He was chosen as Primus in 1739. *The Ancient Liturgy of the Church of Jerusalem* was published posthumously in 1744.

The Appeal of the Ancient Liturgies

From the (ancient) Liturgies of St *Mark*, St *Chrysostom*, and St *Basil* may be seen the wonderful Harmony and Agreement that is among them all in the following Particulars, *viz.* (after the Peoples bringing their Oblations to the Priest, and his presenting them on the Altar) in the Sursum Corda, *Lift up your Hearts*, with the Peoples Response Habemus ad Dominum, *We lift them up unto the Lord*; in the Thanksgiving introductory to the Words of Institution, and the Peoples joining with the Priest in the Ἐπινίκιον (as the *Greeks* called it) or *Seraphick Hymn*,

Holy, Holy, Holy, etc. which always made a part of it; in rehearsing the History of the Institution; in the Prayer of Oblation, or solemn Offering the Bread and Cup as the Antitypes of the Body and Blood of Christ, in Commemoration of his Death and Passion; in the Invocation for the Descent of the holy Ghost upon them, to make them that very Body and Blood (as the instituted Representatives of which they had been just before offered up) to make them, I say, by a mysterious Change, though not in their Substance, yet at least in their Qualities, that very Body and Blood in Energy and life-giving Power, by which their Consecration is fully completed: In the Intercession in Virtue of this commemorative Sacrifice, in which there was always a Commemoration of and Prayer for the Dead: In the παράθεσις or *Commendatio*, beseeching God to sanctify their Souls and Bodies, and make them worthy to communicate in these sacred Mysteries.

NOTES / SOURCES

Thomas Rattray, *The Ancient Liturgy of the Church of Jerusalem*, London, 1744, p. xi

The Scottish Liturgy   1764

The Scottish Church finally split into Presbyterians and Episcopalians in 1689 with the accession of King William III and Queen Mary II, Episcopalians refusing to accept him as monarch. Thereafter many of them supported the claims of the Stuarts to the throne, resulting in their persecution as a minority. English people living in Scotland often had their own chapels, which used the 1662 Prayer Book, but the Episcopalians started to experiment, particularly with the eucharistic liturgy. The 1764 rite represents the high water mark of this work, and the influence of Thomas Rattray (q.v.) was strong, as well as some of the small band of English Nonjurors. The eucharistic prayer is modelled for its structure on the Greek liturgies, with an oblation of the elements and an epiclesis of the Holy Spirit. The two extracts are the central part of the eucharistic prayer and the bidding for prayer after communion.

The Scottish Liturgy of 1764—the Prayer of Consecration

All glory be to thee, Almighty God, our heavenly Father, for that thou of thy tender mercy didst give thy only Son Jesus Christ to suffer death upon the cross for our redemption; who (by his own oblation of himself once offered) made a full, perfect, and sufficient sacrifice, oblation, and satisfaction, for the sins of the whole world, and did institute, and in his holy gospel command us to continue a perpetual memorial of that his precious death and sacrifice until his coming again. For, in the night that he was betrayed, (*a*) he took bread; and when he had given thanks, (*b*) he brake it, and gave it to his disciples, saying, Take, eat, (*c*) THIS IS MY BODY, which is given for you: DO this in remembrance of me. Likewise

(*a*)   *Here the Presbyter is to take the paten in his hands:*

(*b*)   *And here to break the bread:*

(*c*)   *And here to lay his hands upon all the bread.*

after supper (*d*) he took the cup; and when he had given thanks, he gave it to them, saying, Drink ye all of this, for (*e*) THIS IS MY BLOOD, of the new testament, which is shed for you and for many, for the remission of sins: DO this as oft as ye shall drink it in remembrance of me.

(*d*) *Here he is to take the cup into his hand:*

(*e*) *And here to lay his hand upon every vessel (be it chalice or flagon) in which there is any wine to be consecrated.*

Wherefore, O Lord, and heavenly Father, according to the institution of thy dearly beloved Son our Saviour Jesus Christ, we

The Oblation.

thy humble servants do celebrate and make here before thy divine majesty, with these thy holy gifts, WHICH WE NOW OFFER UNTO THEE, the memorial thy Son hath commanded us to make; having in remembrance his blessed passion, and precious death, his mighty resurrection, and glorious ascension; rendering unto thee most hearty thanks for the innumerable benefits procured unto us by the same. And we most humbly beseech thee, O merciful Father, to hear us, and of thy almighty goodness vouchsafe to bless and

The Invocation.

sanctify, with thy word and Holy Spirit, these thy gifts and creatures of bread and wine, that they may become the body and blood of thy most dearly beloved Son. And we earnestly desire thy fatherly goodness, mercifully to accept this our sacrifice of praise and thanksgiving, most humbly beseeching thee to grant, that by the merits and death of thy Son Jesus Christ, and through faith in his blood, we (and all thy whole church) may obtain remission of our sins, and all other benefits of his passion. And here we humbly offer and present unto thee, O Lord, ourselves, our souls and bodies, to be a reasonable, holy and lively sacrifice unto thee, beseeching thee, that whosoever shall be partakers of this holy Communion, may worthily receive the most precious body and blood of thy Son Jesus Christ, and be filled with thy grace and heavenly benediction, and made one body with him, that he may dwell in them, and they in him. And although we are unworthy, through our manifold sins, to offer unto thee any sacrifice; yet we beseech thee to accept this our bounden duty and service, not weighing our merits, but pardoning our offences, through Jesus our Lord: by whom, and with whom, in the unity of the Holy Ghost, all honour and glory be unto thee, O Father Almighty, world without end. *Amen.* (1)

The Bidding after Communion

Having now received the precious body and blood of Christ, let us give thanks to our Lord God, who hath graciously vouchsafed to admit us to the participation of his holy mysteries; and let us beg of him grace to perform our vows, and to persevere in our good resolutions; and that being made holy, we may obtain everlasting life, through the merits of the all-sufficient sacrifice of our Lord and Saviour Jesus Christ. (2)

NOTES / SOURCES

1. John Dowden, *An Historical Account of the Scottish Communion Office*, Edinburgh, 1884, pp. 12–15
2. Ibid., pp. 21–2

William Law   1686–1761

On the accession of George I, William Law refused the Oath of Allegiance and was deprived of his Fellowship at Emmanuel College, Cambridge. He returned to Kingscliff, Northamptonshire, the town of his birth, in order to organize schools and almshouses, leading a life of ascetic simplicity in accordance with his writings. Most well known is his *Serious Call to a Devout and Holy Life* (1728) in which he encourages the Christian to lead a life of temperance, humility, and self-denial, and to make public worship the outward expression of an inward commitment, rather than a public duty and no more. The work was influential with John Wesley and John Keble, amongst others. Later in life he was influenced by the writings of the German Protestant mystic Jacob Boehme and, whilst he remained faithful to the Church of England, this estranged many of his followers.

The Nature and Extent of Christian Devotion

Devotion is neither *private* nor *public* Prayer, but Prayers whether private or public, are particular parts or instances of Devotion. Devotion signifies a life given, or *devoted* to God.

He therefore is the devout man, who lives no longer to his own *will*, or the *way* and *spirit* of the world, but to the sole will of God, who considers God in everything, who serves God in everything, who makes all the parts of his *common* life, parts of piety, by doing everything in the name of God, and under such rules as are conformable to his Glory.

We readily acknowledge, that God alone is to be the rule and measure of our *Prayers;* that in them we are to look *wholly* unto him, and act wholly for him; that we are only to pray in *such a manner*, for *such things*, and *such ends*, as are suitable to his Glory.

Now let anyone but find out the reason, why he is to be thus strictly pious in his prayers, and he will find the same as strong a reason, to be as strictly pious in all the other parts of his life. For there is not the least shadow of a reason, why we should make God the *rule* and *measure* of our prayers; why we should then look *wholly* unto him, and pray according to his will; but what equally proves it necessary for us to look *wholly* unto God, and make him the *rule* and *measure* of all the other actions of our life. For any ways of life, any employment of our talents, whether of our *parts*, our *time*, or *money*, that is not *strictly* according to the will of God, that is not for such *ends* as are suitable to his glory, are as great *absurdities* and *failings*, as prayers that are not according to the will of God. For there is no other reason, why our prayers should be according to the will of God, why they should have nothing in them, but what is *wise*, and *holy*, and *heavenly*, there is no other reason for this, but that our lives may be of the same nature, full of the same *wisdom, holiness*, and *heavenly* tempers, that we may *live* unto God in the *same spirit* that we pray unto him. Were it not our strict duty to live by *reason*, to devote *all* the actions of our lives to God, were it not absolutely necessary to walk before him in wisdom and holiness and all heavenly conversation, doing everything in his name, and for his glory, there would be no excellency or wisdom in the most *heavenly prayers*. Nay, such prayers would be absurdities, they would be like Prayers for *wings*, when it was no part of our duty to *fly*.

As sure, therefore, as there is any wisdom in praying for the spirit of God, so sure is it, that we are to make that Spirit the rule of *all* our actions; as sure as it is our duty to look *wholly* unto God in our Prayers, so sure is it, that it is our duty to live *wholly* unto God in our lives. But we can no more be said to live unto God, unless we live unto him in all the *ordinary* actions of our life, unless he be the rule and measure of all our ways, than we can be said to pray unto God, unless our Prayers look *wholly* unto him. So that unreasonable and absurd ways of life, whether in *labour* or *diversion*, whether they consume our *time*, or our *money*, are alike unreasonable and absurd Prayers, and are as truly an offence unto God.

'Tis for want of knowing, or at least considering this, that we see such a *mixture* of Ridicule in the lives of many People. You see them strict as to some *times* and *places* of Devotion, but when the service of the *Church* is over, they are but like those who seldom or never come there. In their way of life, their manner of spending their *time* and *money*, in their *cares* and *fears*, in their *pleasures* and *indulgences*, in their labour and diversions, they are like the rest of the world. This makes the loose part of the world generally make a jest of those who are *devout*, because they see their Devotion goes no further than their *Prayers*, and that when they are over, they live no more unto God, till the time of Prayer returns again; but live by the same *humour* and *fancy*, and in as full an enjoyment of all the *follies* of life as other People. This is the reason why they are the jest and scorn of careless and worldly People; not because they are really devoted to God, but because they appear to have no other Devotion, but that of *occasional Prayers*. (1)

The Reasons why Christians Fall Short of Holiness

It may now be reasonably inquired, how it comes to pass, that the lives even of the better sort of people, are thus strangely contrary to the principles of Christianity?

But before I give a direct answer to this, I desire it may also be inquired, how it comes to pass that *swearing* is so common a vice amongst Christians? It is indeed not *yet* so common amongst *women*, as it is amongst *men*. But amongst men this sin is so common, that perhaps there are more than *two* in *three* that are guilty of it through the whole course of their lives, swearing *more* or *less*, just as it happens, some constantly, others only now and then as it were by chance. Now, I ask how comes it, that two in three of the men are guilty of so gross and profane a sin as this is? There is neither ignorance, nor human infirmity to plead for it: It is against an express commandment, and the most plain Doctrine of our blessed Saviour.

Do but now find the reason why the generality of men live in this notorious vice, and then you will have found the reason why the generality even of the better sort of people, live so contrary to Christianity.

Now the reason of common swearing is this, it is because men have not so much as the *intention to please God in all their actions*. For let a man but have so much piety as to *intend to please God in all the actions of his life, as the happiest and best thing in the world*, and then he will never swear more. It will be as impossible for him to swear, whilst he feels *this intention* within himself, as it is impossible for a man who intends to please his Prince, to go up and abuse him to his face.

It seems but a small and necessary part of piety to have such a *sincere intention* as this; and that he has no reason to look upon himself as a Disciple of Christ, who is not thus far advanced in piety. And yet it is purely for want of this degree of piety, that you see such a mixture of sin and folly in the lives even of the better sort of People. It is for want of this *intention*, that you see men who profess religion, yet live in *swearing* and *sensuality*; that you see *Clergymen* given to pride and covetousness, and worldly enjoyments. It is for want of this *intention*, that you see *women* who profess Devotion, yet living in all the folly and vanity of *dress*, wasting their time in *idleness* and *pleasures*, and in all such instances of state and equipage as their estates will reach. For let but a woman feel her heart full of *this intention*, and she will find it as impossible to *patch* or *paint*, as to curse or swear; she will no more desire to shine at *Balls* and *Assemblies*, or make a figure amongst those who are most finely dressed, than she will desire to dance upon a *Rope* to please Spectators: She will know, that the one is as far from the *wisdom* and *excellency* of the Christian Spirit, as the other.

It was this *general intention*, that made the *primitive Christians* such eminent instances of piety, that made the goodly fellowship of the *saints*, and all the glorious army of *martyrs* and *confessors*. And if you will here stop, and ask yourself, why you are not as pious as the primitive Christians were, your own heart will tell you, that it is neither through *ignorance*, nor *inability*, but purely because you never *thoroughly intended* it. You observe the same *Sunday-worship* that they did; and you are *strict* in it, because it is your full *intention* to be so. And when you as fully intend to be like them in their *ordinary common* life, when you intend to please God in *all your actions*, you will find it as possible, as to be strictly exact in the service of the Church. And when you have this *intention to please God in all your actions, as the happiest and best thing in the world*, you will find in you as great an aversion to everything that is *vain* and *impertinent* in common life, whether of business or pleasure, as you now have to anything that is *profane*. You will be as fearful of living in any foolish way, either of spending your *time*, or your *fortune*, as you are now fearful of neglecting the public Worship. (2)

Preparation for Prayer

But above all, one certain benefit from this method you will be sure of having, it will best fit and prepare you for the reception of the Holy Spirit. When you thus begin the day in the spirit of religion, renouncing sleep, because you are to renounce softness, and redeem your time; this disposition, as it puts your heart into a good state, so it will procure the assistance of the Holy Spirit; what is so planted and watered, will certainly have an increase from God. You will then speak from your heart, your soul will be awake, your prayers will refresh you like meat and drink, you will feel what you say, and begin to know what saints and holy men have meant, by fervours of devotion.

He that is thus prepared for prayer, who rises with these dispositions, is in a very different state from him, who has no rules of this kind; who rises by chance, as he happens to be weary of his bed, or is able to sleep no longer. If such a one prays only with his mouth; if his heart feels nothing of that which he says; if his prayers are only things of course; if they are a lifeless form of words, which he only repeats because they are soon said, there is nothing to be wondered at in all this; for such dispositions are the natural effects of such a state of life.

Hoping therefore, that you are now enough convinced of the necessity of rising early to your prayers, I shall proceed to lay before you a method of daily prayer.

I do not take upon me to prescribe to you the use of any *particular forms* of prayer, but only to show you the necessity of praying at such times, and in such a manner.

You will here find some helps, how to furnish yourself with such *forms* of prayer, as shall be useful to you. And if you are such a proficient in the spirit of devotion, that your heart is always ready to pray in its own language, in this case I press no necessity of borrowed forms.

For though I think a form of prayer very *necessary* and *expedient* for *public* worship, yet if anyone can find a better way of raising his heart unto God in private, than by *prepared forms* of prayer, I have nothing to object against it; my design being only to assist and direct such as stand in need of assistance.

Thus much, I believe, is certain, that the *generality* of Christians ought to use *forms* of prayer, at all the regular times of prayer. It seems right for everyone to begin with a *form* of prayer; and if in the midst of his devotions, he finds his heart ready to break forth into new and higher strains of devotion, he should leave his *form* for a while, and follow those fervours of his heart, till it again wants the assistance of his usual petitions.

This seems to be the *true liberty* of *private* devotion; it should be under the direction of some *form*; but not so tied down to it, but that it may be free to take such new expressions, as its present fervours happen to furnish it with; which sometimes are more affecting, and carry the soul more powerfully to God, than any expressions that were ever used before. (3)

Devotion

Devotion is nothing else but *right apprehensions* and *right affections* towards God.

All practices therefore that heighten and improve our true apprehensions of God, all ways of life that tend to *nourish, raise*, and fix our affections upon him, are to be reckoned so many helps and means to fill us with devotion.

As *Prayer* is the proper fuel of this holy flame, so we must use all our care and contrivance to give prayer its full power ; as by *alms, self-denial,* frequent *retirements*, and *holy readings*, composing *forms* for ourselves, or using the *best* we can get, adding *length* of time, and observing *hours* of Prayer; *changing, improving*, and *suiting* our devotions to the condition of our lives, and the state of our hearts.

Those who have most leisure, seem more especially called to a more eminent observance of these holy rules of a devout life. And they who by the necessity of their state, and not through their own choice, have but little time to employ thus, must make the best use of that little they have.

For this is the certain way of making devotion produce a devout life. (4)

Christian Perfection

All Christians are required to imitate the Life and Example of Jesus Christ

Our Religion teaches us, that as we have *borne the Image of the Earthly, so we shall bear the Image of the Heavenly*, that after our Death we shall rise to a State of Life and Happiness, like to that Life and Happiness, which our Blessed Saviour enjoys at the Right Hand of God. Since therefore it is the great End of our Religion to make us Fellow-Heirs with Christ, and Partakers of the same Happiness, it is not to be wondered at, that our Religion should require us to be like Christ in this Life, to imitate his Example, that we may enter into that State of Happiness, which he enjoys in the Kingdom of Heaven.

For how can we think that we are going to the Blessed Jesus, that we are to be hereafter as he is, unless we conform to his Spirit in this Life, and make it our great Endeavour to be what he was, when he was here. Let it therefore here be observed, that the *Nature* of our Religion teaches us this Duty in a more convincing Manner, than any particular Precepts concerning it. For the most ordinary Understanding must feel the Force and Reasonableness of this Argument. You are born to depart out of this World, to ascend to that State of Bliss, to live in such Enjoyment of God to all Eternity, as our Blessed Saviour now enjoys, you are therefore to live in the Spirit and Temper that he lived, and make yourselves first like him here, that you may be like him hereafter. So that we need not look for particular Texts of Scripture, which command us to imitate the Life of Christ, because we are taught this Duty by a Stronger and more convincing Authority; because as the End and Design of our Religion, is to make us one with Christ hereafter, Partakers of the same State of Life, so it plainly calls us to be one with him here, and to be Partakers of that same Spirit and Temper in which he lived on Earth. When it is said that we are to imitate the Life of Christ, it is not meant that we are called to the same manner of Life, or the same sort of Actions, for this cannot be, but it is certain that we are called to the same Spirit and Temper, which was the Spirit and Temper of our Blessed Saviour's Life and Actions. We are to be like him in Heart and Mind, to act by the same Rule, to look towards the same End, and to govern our Lives by the same Spirit. This is an Imitation of Jesus Christ, which is as necessary to Salvation, as it is necessary to believe in his Name. This is the sole End of all the Counsels, Commands and Doctrines of Christ, to make us like himself, to fill us with his *Spirit* and *Temper*, and make us live according to the Rule and Manner of his Life. As no Doctrines are true, but such as are according to the Doctrines of Christ, so it is equally certain, that no Life is regular or Christian, but such as is according to the Pattern and Example of the Life of Christ. For he lived as infallibly as he taught, and it is as irregular, to vary from his Example, as it is false, to dissent from his Doctrines. To live as he lived, is as certainly the one sole Way of living as we ought, as to believe as he taught, is the one sole Way of believing as we ought. I am, saith the Blessed Jesus, *The Way, the Truth, and the Life, no Man cometh unto the Father but by me.* Christians often hear these Words, and perhaps think that they have enough fulfilled them by believing in Jesus Christ. But they should consider, that when Jesus Christ saith he is the *Way*, his meaning is, that his way of Life is to be the way, in which all Christians are to live, and that it is by living after the manner of his Life, that any Man cometh unto the Father. So that the Doctrine of this Passage is this, that however we may call ourselves Christians, or Disciples of Christ, yet we cannot come unto God the Father, but by entering into that way of Life, which was the way of our Saviour's Life. And we must remember, that there is no other way besides this, nothing can possibly bring us to God, but that way of Life, which first makes us one with Christ, and teacheth us to walk as he walked. For we may as well expect to go to a Heaven where Christ is not, as to go to that where he is, without the Spirit and Temper which carried him thither. If Christians would but suffer themselves to reflect upon this Duty, their own Minds would soon convince them of the Reasonableness and Necessity of it. For who can find the least Shadow of a Reason, why he should not imitate the Life of Christ, or why Christians should think of any other Rule of Life? It would be as easy to show that Christ acted amiss, as that we need not act after his Example. And to think that these are Degrees of Holiness, which though very good in themselves, are yet not necessary for us to aspire after, is the same Absurdity as to think, that it was not necessary for our Saviour to have been so perfect himself as he was. For, give but the Reason why such Degrees of Holiness and Purity became our Saviour, and you will give as good a Reason for us to aspire after them. For as the Blessed Jesus took not on him the Nature of Angels, but the Nature of Man, as he was in all Points made like unto us, Sin only excepted, so we are sure, that there was no Spirit or Temper that was Excellent in him, that recommended him to God, but would be also Excellent in us, and recommend us to God, if we could arrive at it. (5)

Redemption is God's Mercy

But the Truth of the Matter is this; Christian Redemption is God's Mercy to all Mankind; but it could not be so, if every fallen Man, *as such*, had not some Fitness and Capacity to lay hold of it. It must have no Dependence upon Times and Places, or the Ages and several Conditions of the World, or any outward Circumstance of Life; as the First Man partook of it, so must the last; the learned Linguist, and the Blind, the Deaf and Dumb, have but one and the same common Way of finding Life in it. And he that writes large Commentaries upon the whole Bible, must be saved by *something* full as different from Book knowledge, as they were, who lived when there was neither Book nor any Alphabet in the World.

For this Salvation, which is God's *Mercy* to the fallen Soul of Man, merely as fallen, must be something that *meets* every Man; and which every Man, as fallen, has *something* that directs him to turn to it. For as the Fall of Man is the Reason of this Mercy, so the Fall must be the Guide to it; the Want must show the Thing that is wanted. And therefore the Manifestation of this one Salvation, or Mercy to Man, must have a Nature suitable, not to this or that great Reader of History, or able Critic in *Hebrew* Roots and *Greek* Phrases, but suitable to the common State and Condition of every Son of *Adam*. It must be something as grounded in human Nature, as the Fall itself is, which wants no Art to make it known; but to which the common Nature of Man is the only Guide in one Man, as well as another. Now this *something*, which is thus obvious to every Man, and which opens the Way to Christian Redemption in every Soul, is *a sense of the Vanity and Misery of this World; and a Prayer of Faith and Hope to God, to be raised to a better State.*

Now in this *Sensibility*, which every Man's own Nature leads him into, lies the Whole of Man's Salvation; here the *Mercy* of God and the *Misery* of Man are met together; here the *Fall* and the *Redemption* kiss each other. This is the Christianity which is as old as the *Fall*; which alone saved the First Man, and can alone save the last. This is it, on which hang all the Law and the Prophets, and which fulfils them both; for they have only this End, to turn Man from the Lusts of this Life, to a

Desire, and Faith, and Hope of a better. Thus does the whole of Christian Redemption, considered on the Part of Man, stand in this Degree of Nearness and Plainness to all Mankind; it is as simple and plain as the feeling our own Evil and Misery, and as natural as the Desire of being saved and delivered from it.

This is the Christianity which every Man must first be made sensible of, not from Hearsay, but as a Growth or Degree of Life within himself, before he can have any Fitness, or the least Pretence to judge or speak a Word about the further Mysteries of the Gospel. (6)

NOTES / SOURCES

1. William Law 'A Serious Call to a Devout and Holy Life' (1728), in *The Works of William Law*, Vol. IV, London, 1893, pp. 7–8
2. Ibid., pp. 15–16
3. Ibid., pp. 134–5
4. Ibid., p. 145
5. Ibid., pp. 215–217
6. Ibid., pp. 179–180

Charles Wheatly   1686–1742

A Fellow of St John's College, Oxford (1707–13), Charles Wheatly was a Lecturer at two London churches, and, from 1726 until his death, Vicar of Furneaux Pelham, St Albans. He preached one of the earliest sermons against the rise of Methodism (1739) and wrote a popular commentary on *The Book of Common Prayer*, which was first published in 1710, but whose third edition in 1720 indicated a shift towards a more High Church position, through an ever-increasing interest in the origins of the Prayer Book services.

Of the Order of the Administration of the Lord's Supper (1720)

Whatever Benefits we now enjoy, or hope hereafter to receive from Almighty God; they are all purchased by the Death, and must be obtained through the Intercession, of the Holy Jesus. We are therefore not only taught to mention his Name continually in our Prayers, but are also commanded, by visible Signs, to represent and set forth to His Heavenly Father, His all sufficient and meritorious Death and Sacrifice, as a more powerful way of interceding and obtaining the Divine Acceptance. So that what we more compendiously express in that general Conclusion of our Prayers (*through Jesus Christ our Lord*) we more fully and forcibly represent in the Celebration of the Holy Eucharist: wherein we intercede on Earth in conjunction with the great Intercession of a High Priest of Heaven, and plead in the Virtue and Merits of the same Sacrifice here, which he is continually urging for us there. And because of this mere Alliance between Praying and Communicating, we find the Eucharist was always in the purest Ages of the Church a daily part of the Common-Prayer.

NOTES / SOURCES

Charles Wheatly, *A Rational Illustration of the Book of Common Prayer*, London, 1720, p. 255

Joseph Butler   1692–1752

Although born and brought up a Presbyterian, Joseph Butler abandoned this when he went to Oriel College, Oxford, and was ordained in Salisbury (1718). His *Fifteen Sermons Preached at the Rolls Chapel* (1726) were highly influential in his own time as a leading exponent of natural theology, in defence of a Christian world view. Later through the nineteenth century he was widely studied by Anglican ordinands, amongst whom John Henry Newman acknowledged his debt. Appointed Bishop of Bristol (1736) where he encountered the hostility of John Wesley and George Whitefield, he later became Bishop of Durham (1750).

Worldly Happiness is not Enough

Take a survey of mankind: the world in general, the good and bad, almost without exception, equally are agreed, that were religion out of the case, the happiness of the present life would consist in a manner wholly in riches, honours, sensual gratifications; insomuch that one scarce hears a reflection made upon prudence, life, conduct, but upon this supposition. Yet on the contrary, that persons in the greatest affluence of fortune are no happier than such as have only a competency; that the cares and disappointments of ambition for the most part far exceed the satisfactions of it; as also the miserable intervals of intemperance and excess, and the many untimely deaths occasioned by a dissolute course of life: these things are all seen, acknowledged, by every one acknowledged; but are thought no objections against, though they expressly contradict, this universal principle, that the happiness of the present life consists in one or other of them. Whence is all this absurdity and contradiction? Is not the middle way obvious? Can anything be more manifest, than that the happiness of life consists in these possessed and enjoyed only to a certain degree; that to pursue them beyond this degree, is always attended with more inconvenience than advantage to a man's self, and often with extreme misery and unhappiness. Whence then, I say, is all this absurdity and contradiction? Is it really the result of consideration in mankind, how they may become most easy to themselves, most free from care, and enjoy the chief happiness attainable in this world? Or is it not manifestly owing either to this, that they have not cool and reasonable concern enough for themselves to consider wherein their chief happiness in the present life consists; or else, if they do consider it, that they will not act conformably to what is the result of that consideration: *i.e.* reasonable concern for themselves, or cool self-love is prevailed over by passion and appetite. So that from what appears, there is no ground to assert [that those principles in the nature of man, which most directly lead to promote the good of our fellow-creatures, are more generally or in a greater degree violated, than those, which most directly lead us to promote our own private good and happiness.]

The sum of the whole is plainly this. The nature of man considered in his single capacity, and with respect only to the present world, is adapted and leads him to attain the greatest happiness he can for himself in the present world. The nature of man considered in his public or social capacity leads him to a right behaviour in society, to that course of life which we call virtue. Men follow or obey their nature in both these capacities and respects to a certain degree, but not entirely: their actions do not come up to the whole of what their nature leads them to in either of these capacities or respects: and they often violate their nature in both. *I.e.* as they neglect the duties they owe to their fellow-creatures, to which their nature leads them ; and are injurious, to which their nature is abhorrent: so there is a manifest negligence in men of their real happiness or interest in the present world, when that interest is inconsistent with a present gratification ; for the sake of which they negligently, nay, even knowingly, are the authors and instruments of their own misery and ruin. Thus they are as often unjust to themselves as to others, and for the most part are equally so to both by the same actions. (1)

Humanity Truly Motivated by Love

That which we more strictly call piety, or the love of God, and which is an essential part of a right temper, some may perhaps imagine no way connected with benevolence: yet surely they must be connected, if there be indeed in being an object infinitely good. Human nature is so constituted, that every good affection implies the love of itself; *i.e.* becomes the object of a new affection in the same person. Thus, to be righteous, implies in it the love of righteousness; to be benevolent, the love of benevolence; to be good, the love of goodness; whether this righteousness, benevolence, or goodness, be viewed as in our own mind, or in another's: and the love of God as being perfectly good, is the love of perfect goodness contemplated in a being or person. Thus morality and religion, virtue and piety, will at last necessarily coincide, run up into one and the same point, and love will be in all senses 'the end of the commandment.'

O Almighty God, inspire us with this divine principle; kill in us all the seeds of envy and ill-will; and help us, by cultivating within ourselves the love of our neighbour, to improve in the love of Thee. Thou hast placed us in various kindreds, friendships, and relations, as the school of discipline for our affections: help us, by the due exercise of them, to improve to perfection; till all partial affection be lost in that entire universal one, and Thou, O God, shalt be all in all. (2)

NOTES / SOURCES

1. Joseph Butler 'Sermon I: Upon Human Nature' in *The Works of Bishop Butler*, Vol. I, London, 1900, pp. 36–7
2. Joseph Butler 'Sermon II: Upon Human Nature' ibid., pp. 167–8

Thomas Secker   1693–1768

Having studied as a Doctor of Medicine at the University of Leiden (1721), he graduated from Oxford and was ordained in 1723. In succession he became Bishop of Bristol (1735) and Oxford (1737), and, finally, Archbishop of Canterbury (1758). Although he was hostile to the advances made by Methodism, he nonetheless admired their piety. He was active in supporting sending bishops to American colonies. In contrast to Benjamin Hoadly, he advocated tolerance and common sense, and combined an historical perspective with an openness to the spirit of the times in his teaching and sermons.

Reason and Revelation

We must consider yet further, that reason, where it improves to the utmost, cannot discover to us all that we are to believe and do: but a large and most important part of it is to be learnt from the revelation made to us in God's holy word. And this, though perfectly well suited to purposes for which it was designed, yet being originally delivered at very distant times, to very different sorts of persons, on very different occasions; and the several articles of faith and precepts of conduct, which it prescribes, not being collected and laid down methodically in any one part of it, but dispersed with irregular beauty through the whole, as the riches of nature are through the creation; the informations of them must be in many respects needful, to prepare the more ignorant for receiving the benefits, for which they are capable from reading the scriptures. And particularly, giving them beforehand a summary and orderly view of the principal points comprehended in it, will qualify them better than any other thing to discern its true meaning, insofar as is requisite, in each part.

Nor does reason only, but experience too, show the need of timely institution in piety and virtue. For is it not visible, that principally for want of it, multitudes of unhappy creatures, in all ranks of life, set out from the first in sin, and follow it on as securely, as if it were the only way they had to take; to unspeakable mischief in the world, and utterly undo themselves, body and soul: whilst others, of no better natural dispositions, but only better taught, are harmless and useful, esteemed and honoured, go through life with comfort, and meet death with joyful hope? There are doubtless, in such numbers, exceptions on both sides; but this is undeniably the ordinary, the probable, the always to be expected course of things. (1)

'I Believe in God the Father'

'*I believe in God the Father . . .*' But then observe further, that supposing you do not disbelieve God at all, yet if you think of him, this is not, to any good purpose, believing in him at all: and if you think of him but seldom, it is believing in him but little. He, on whom we depend continually, to whom we owe duty continually, and in whose presence we continually are, ought never to be far from our thoughts: we should set him before our eyes so constantly, as to live in his fear always. Doing this need not keep us from common business; it need not keep us from innocent pleasures. But it should influence us all effectually, (and happy are we if it doth,) to conduct ourselves in everything, as persons who act under the inspection of a wise and just superior: and we may indeed forget, if we will; but shall be remembered by him: from whom we may depart, but cannot escape. In our choice it is, whether we will be the better or the worse for him. But one we must: and that beyond expression. *For God will bring any worker to judgement, with every secret thing; whether it be good, or whether it be evil* (Ecclesiastes 12: 14). (2)

NOTES / SOURCES

1. Thomas Secker 'Lectures', in *The Works of Thomas Secker* Vol. IV, London, 1804, pp. 232–3
2. Ibid., p. 272

Samuel Johnson   1696–1772

Born in the New England colony of Connecticut, Samuel Johnson was one of a group of seven prominent Congregationalist ministers who took the occasion of the commencement of the academic year at Yale College on 11 September 1722 to announce that 'they could no longer keep out of the communion of the Holy Catholic Church, and that (they) . . . were persuaded of the invalidity of Presbyterian Orders in opposition to Episcopal'. After this event, which became known as the 'dark day at Yale', Johnson along with most of the group left for England for episcopal ordination. Upon his return, he was appointed the Society for the Propagation of the Gospel's Missionary at Stratford, Connecticut. In 1754, as a recognition of the respect in which he was held, Johnson became the first President of King's College (later Columbia University), in New York City. His staunch advocacy of episcopacy establishes Johnson as the primary precursor of Samuel Seabury.

Worship

Worship consists in a most serious and solemn address to the great creator, preserver, and governor of the world; testifying from the bottom of our hearts our dependence upon Him, and submission to Him; praising Him for every thing we enjoy, praying to Him for whatsoever we want, and devoting ourselves sincerely and entirely to his service. Now all these things are abundantly provided for in our forms, as I shall show you presently: and that in the best manner, which is certainly best done by public forms, established by lawful authority, and known and agreed to by all the worshippers. For how can I worship God with the full devotion of my soul, unless I have beforehand satisfied myself with what I am to offer up? And how can a worshipping assembly jointly and with one heart and soul, and with a full assurance of faith, offer up their prayers and praises to God, unless they have properly a Common Prayer, and are beforehand all satisfied that what is to be offered is both agreeable to the will of God, and suitable to their common necessities and occasions? And how can they otherwise offer up their public devotions agreeable to Christ's express instructions, who plainly requireth, they should be agreed touching what they would ask, as a condition of their receiving it? Mat. xviii. 19. If two of you shall agree on earth, as touching any thing they shall ask, it shall be done for them of my Father which is in Heaven. If there were a number of us to ask a favor of an earthly prince or governor, we should be very careful and exact in composing our address; we should take great care that it be well ordered, and that we be all fully agreed beforehand, both in the matter and manner of our address. How much more when we are to address the great God of Heaven and earth, and that for the life, even the eternal life of our souls, how fit and necessary is it, that we should accurately compose our address, and be beforehand well agreed and satisfied, both in the matter and manner of it; so as to have nothing to do when we come to offer it, but to offer up our whole souls with it, and make it our most devout free act and deed? (1)

Set Forms of Worship

How happy are we, my brethren, who have a most excellent form prepared for us, by some of the wisest and best men that ever lived, and many of whom underwent the fire of martyrdom for what they did! I say, that we have, by them an excellent form of public devotion compiled for us, chiefly out of the Word of God, and conformed to it, in which, therefore, if we believe the Scriptures, we must be perfectly agreed and satisfied; so that when we come to worship God in public, we have nothing else to do but to prepare our hearts, and give up our whole souls, and exert the utmost force of our minds and hearts in offering it up to our Heavenly Father; and so can with one mind and one mouth, glorify God, even the Father of our Lord Jesus Christ, as St Paul requires, Rom. xv. 16 (which is scarcely possible in the extempore way) and which we plainly see to be a true method of worship, as it contains praises to God for every thing we enjoy, both temporal and spiritual and prayers for every thing we can want, either for soul or body, either for ourselves or others. Let us therefore be heartily thankful to God's good providence, that we have such an excellent method of public worship, and let us make a faithful use of it to the best purposes; in order to which, let each one have his Book, and keep it in his eye, the better to engage his attention, that avoiding all indecent gazing about, we may make it the business of our souls, in the House of God, to offer it up with the sincerest and most intense devotion . . . Our worship is a most holy worship, and tends in the best manner to promote holiness, both in our hearts and lives. And holiness becomes thy House, O Lord, for ever. Now holiness consists in being heartily devoted to God, so as to hate what he hates, and love what he loves; and in being concerned above all things to be conformed to his purity, righteousness, goodness and truth. As therefore God hates all sin and wickedness, that must be a most holy worship that testifies the utmost abhorrence of every thing sinful, wicked and impure. And as he loves all purity, righteousness, truth, goodness and mercy, that must be a most holy worship that tends to make us love and practise every thing that is pure and holy, true and righteous, kind and merciful. And as the love of God is the foundation of all religion and virtue, that must be a most holy worship that tends to inspire us with the supreme love of God, which will dispose us to do him the utmost honor, and make us like Him, and as obedient to Him as ever we are able. By these principles then let us try the worship of the Church of England. (2)

The Eucharist

As to our Communion Office . . . what is there can more conduce to make us holy in all manner of conversation, than to have each of God's holy commandments rehearsed in a most grave and solemn manner, and for all the people, after every one of them, to pray for God's mercy to pardon their offenses against it, and his grace to incline their hearts to keep it for the future, and to write all his laws in their hearts? And, as the Holy Sacrament is the most divine and heavenly institution of our religion, and the most solemn act of our worship, the design of which is, to inspire our souls with a most grateful sense of the mighty love of our blessed lord and master in dying for us, in order to destroy both the power and guilt of sin; and to seal a pardon to us upon our true repentance, and fill us with the most ardent devotion to God and our Lord Jesus, and the most affectionate charity one towards another; so the manner of our administering and receiving it in the Church is excellent beyond that of any others. For which we are prepared, by a very suitable exhortation and confession of our sins, with the declaration of our pardon and the great and precious promises whereof this Sacrament is a seal. We are then called upon to lift up our hearts to God in the most seraphic form of thanksgiving, wherein the Church militant on earth joins, and, as it were, holds communion with the holy Church triumphant which is above; the angels and archangels, and all the company of heaven; saying, Holy, Holy, Holy, Lord God Almighty; Heaven and Earth are full of Thy Glory; Glory be to thee O Lord most High. Amen. The elements are then consecrated or set apart to represent the body and blood of Christ, in the gravest and most solemn manner, with the words of our blessed Lord's institution; and in the administration the inestimable benefits of his death are expressed in the delivery of them, to each particular person, receiving them in the devoutest manner upon his knees; which is the most decent posture wherein to receive the seal of our pardon. And lastly, the whole office is concluded with devoting ourselves to God both in body and soul, in our Lord's Prayer and others, the devoutest prayers and thanksgivings, and ends with an excellent benediction; than all which, I must think nothing can be imagined more conducive to train us up in all holiness, devotion and virtue for the glories of the heavenly state. (3)

NOTES / SOURCES

1. Samuel Johnson 'Sermon on the Beauty of Holiness', (1749) in *Samuel Johnson, President of King's College—His Career and Writings*, Vol. III, New York, 1929, pp. 520–1
2. Ibid., pp. 522–3
3. Ibid., pp. 529–30

John Hume   1703–1782

Following studies at Christ Church, Oxford, he was made Prebendary of Westminster Abbey (1742) and held the living of Barn Elms in Surrey (1747). He became Bishop of Oxford and Dean of St Paul's in 1758, from where he was translated to the See of Salisbury in 1766 where he remained until his death.

Prayers Drawn up by Bishop Hume for the Duke of Newcastle (Thomas Pelham-Hollis)

O Almighty God, the Author and Preserver of my Being, to whom I owe every blessing that I have enjoyed, and on whom I depend for all my future happiness, accept the humble homage of Thy creature that lifts up his soul to Thee, not confiding in his own merit, but in Thy gracious goodness and great mercy. Thou knowest, Lord, the secrets of my heart, the weakness of my understanding and the instability of my best resolutions. O touch my heart that I may love Thee, and my understanding that I may worship Thee as I ought! Teach me to do the thing that pleaseth Thee; confirm and strengthen my weak endeavours and guide me in the way to everlasting life which Thou hast revealed and promised us through our Lord and Saviour, Jesus Christ. Amen.

A short prayer to be used Night and Morning:

Unto Thy grace and protection O Lord we commend our souls and bodies this day (or this night) and for evermore, through Jesus Christ our Lord. Amen.

A Prayer of Thanksgiving

O God the Author and Preserver of my being, in whose hands are the issues of life and death, to Thee I bow down my soul in humble adoration of Thy Supreme Goodness. Thou hast raised me up from the bed of sickness; Thou hast touched my heart that I should feel Thy mercy; Thou hast restored me to health that I should live to praise Thee. But how, O Lord, can Thy poor and dependent creature adore and thank Thee as he ought. Thy mercies surpass the utmost stretch of my powers to praise Thee. O preserve me in that sense of them which Thou hast now given me, and perfect the good work which Thou hast begun in me. Confirm and strengthen every good resolution I have formed when I was in trouble, and help me to act up to them with firmness, consistency and devotion. O suffer me no longer to fluctuate through life under the divided influence of Thee and the world. But let Thy kingdom in my heart be absolute. Let Thy will be my guide to lead me and comfort me; that I may go on from strength to strength, from loving, obeying and praising Thee on earth to that everlasting state of bliss in heaven, which Thou hast promised to all that love and seek Thee. Through the merits and mediation of Thy Son, Jesus Christ our Lord. Amen.

Devotions for the Holy Communion

Before the minister begins the service.	I lift up my soul to Thee, O God, humbly imploring Thy blessing upon me, and gracious assistance of me, for the holy action I am now about. Forgive my want of due preparation, and accept of my sincere desire to perform an acceptable service to Thee. Through Jesus Christ our Lord.
Before receiving of the Bread.	I am not worthy of the crumbs that fall from Thy Table.
After the receiving of it.	Greater love than this hath no man, that a man lay down his life for his friends.
Before receiving the Cup.	What shall I render to the Lord for all His blessings? I will receive the cup of salvation: I will bless the name of the Lord.
After the receiving of it.	Blessed be God for this unspeakable gift, His dearly beloved Son, Jesus Christ; in whom we have redemption through His blood, even the forgiveness of sins.

| After the conclusion of the whole action. | Bless the Lord, O my soul, and all that is within me, bless His holy name. Bless the Lord, O my soul, and forget not all His benefits, who forgiveth all thine iniquities and healeth all thy diseases. Who redeemeth thy life from destruction and crowneth thee with loving kindness and tender mercies; who satisfieth thy mouth with good things. Bless the Lord, O my soul. |

A Prayer to be used in Private Afterwards

I praise and magnify Thy great and glorious name, O Lord my God, for the blessed opportunity afforded to me this day of commemorating Thy infinite goodness and mercy to me and all mankind, in sending Thy only Son into the world, to take our nature upon Him, to submit to the infirmities and miseries of it, to live among us and to die for us; and to preserve the memory of this great love and goodness of Thine to us for ever in our hearts, that Thou hast been pleased to appoint the blessed Sacrament for a solemn remembrance of it. Grant O Lord that I may faithfully keep and perform that Holy Covenant which I have this day so solemnly renewed and confirmed in Thy Presence and at Thy Table. Let it be an eternal obligation upon me of perpetual love and obedience to Thee. Let nothing seem hard for me to do or grievous for me to suffer for Thy sake, who, whilst I was a sinner and an enemy to Thee, loved me at such a rate as never any man did his friend. Grant that by this Sacrament, there may be conveyed to my soul new spiritual life and strength and such a measure of Thy grace and assistance as may enable me to a greater care of my duty for the future. That I may henceforth live as becomes the redeemed of the Lord; even to Him who died for my sins and rose again for my justification and is now sat down on the right hand of the throne of God to make intercession for me; in His holy Name and words I conclude my imperfect prayers; Our Father, which art in heaven, hallowed be Thy Name; Thy kingdom come, Thy will be done on earth as it is in heaven. Give us this day our daily bread, and forgive us our trespasses as we forgive them that trespass against us. And lead us not into temptation, but deliver us from evil, for Thine is the kingdom, and the power, and the glory, for ever and ever. Amen.

NOTES / SOURCES

John Hume 'Prayers for the Duke of Newcastle', in Norman Sykes, *Church and State in England in the XVIIIth Century*, Cambridge, 1934, pp. 437–9

John Wesley   1703–1791

Brought up with his brother Charles (q.v.) at Epworth, Lincolnshire, where his father Samuel was rector, in 1726 John Wesley was elected a Fellow of Lincoln College, Oxford where he formed a 'Holy Club', nicknamed 'Methodists' after their strict rule of life. On 24 May, 1738, he underwent a conversion experience at a meeting in London. Thereafter he committed himself to a life of itinerant preaching, often outdoors, to reach the unchurched. The tensions between the Church of England and his organization of lay preachers and societies came to a head in 1784 when he ordained Thomas Coke as 'Superintendent' for the growing Methodist community in the United States. Wesley was no ordinary evangelical but a man who blended Protestant and Catholic traditions. He combined a firm belief in justification by faith with a strong sacramentalism and passionate devotion to the pursuit of perfection inherited from Catholic spirituality.

Wesley's Conversion

I think it was about five this morning that I opened my Testament on those words: 'There are given unto us exceeding great and precious promises, even that you should be partakers of the divine nature.' Just as I went out, I opened it again on those words, 'You are not far from the kingdom of God.' In the afternoon I was asked to go to St Paul's. The anthem was 'Out of the deep have I called unto you, O Lord: Lord, hear my voice.'

In the evening I went very unwillingly to a society in Aldersgate Street, where one was reading Luther's preface to the Epistle to the Romans. About a quarter before nine, while he was describing the change which God works in the heart through faith in Christ, I felt my heart strangely warmed. I felt I did trust in Christ, Christ alone, for salvation: and an assurance was given me that he had taken away my sins, even mine, and saved me from the law of sin and death.

I began to pray with all my might for those who had in a more especial manner despitefully used me and persecuted me. I then testified openly to all there, what I now first felt in my heart. But it was not long before the enemy suggested, 'This cannot be faith; for where is thy joy?' Then was I taught, that peace and victory over sin are essential to faith in the Captain of our salvation; but that, as to the transports of joy that usually attend the beginning of it, especially in those who have mourned deeply, God sometimes giveth, sometimes withholdeth them, according to the counsels of his own will.

After my return home, I was much buffeted with temptations; but cried out, and they fled away. They returned again and again. I as often lifted up my eyes, and 'he sent me help from his holy place'. And herein I found [in what] the difference between this and my former state chiefly consisted. I was striving, yea, fighting with all my might under the law, as well as under grace. But then I was sometimes, if not often, conquered; now, I was always conqueror. (1)

Sermon on Salvation by Faith

Preached at St. Mary's, Oxford, before the University, on June 11, 1738.

By grace are ye saved through faith.
Eph. ii. 8.

All the blessings which God hath bestowed upon man are of His mere grace, bounty, or favour; His free, undeserved favour; favour altogether undeserved; man having no claim to the least of His mercies. It was free grace that 'formed man of the dust of the ground, and breathed into him a living soul,' and stamped on that soul the image of God, and 'put all things under his feet.' The same free grace continues to us, at this day, life, and breath, and all things. For there is nothing we are, or have, or do, which can deserve the least thing at God's hand. 'All our works, Thou, O God, hast wrought in us.' These, therefore, are so many more instances of free mercy: and whatever righteousness may be found in man, this is also the gift of God.

2. Wherewithal then shall a sinful man atone for any the least of his sins? With his own works? No. Were they ever so many or holy, they are not his own, but God's. But indeed they are all unholy and sinful themselves, so that every one of them needs a fresh atonement. Only corrupt fruit grows on a corrupt tree. And his heart is altogether corrupt and abominable; being 'come short of the glory of God,' the glorious righteousness at first impressed on his soul, after the image of his great Creator. Therefore, having nothing, neither righteousness nor works, to plead, his mouth is utterly stopped before God.

3. If then sinful men find favour with God, it is 'grace upon grace!' If God vouchsafe still to pour fresh blessings upon us, yea, the greatest of all blessings, salvation; what can we say to these things, but, 'Thanks be unto God for His unspeakable gift!' And thus it is. Herein 'God commendeth His love toward us, in that, while we were yet sinners, Christ died' to save us. 'By grace' then 'are ye saved through faith.' Grace is the source, faith the condition, of salvation. (2)

Sermon on Catholic Spirit

And when he was departed thence, he lighted on Jehonadab the son of Rechab coming to meet him: and he saluted him, and said to him, Is thine heart right, as my heart is with thy heart? And Jehonadab answered, It is. If it be, give me thine hand.

2 *Kings* x. 15.

It is allowed even by those who do not pay this great debt, that love is due to all mankind; the royal law, 'Thou shalt love thy neighbour as thyself,' carrying its own evidence to all that hear it: and that, not according to the miserable construction put upon it by the zealots of old times, 'Thou shalt love thy neighbour,' thy relation, acquaintance, friend, 'and hate thine enemy': not so; 'I say unto you,' saith our Lord, 'Love your enemies, bless them that curse you, do good to them that hate you, and pray for them that despitefully use you, and persecute you; that ye may be the children,' may appear so to all mankind, 'of your Father which is in heaven; who maketh His sun to rise on the evil and on the good, and sendeth rain on the just and on the unjust.'

2. But it is sure, there is a peculiar love which we owe to those that love God. So David: 'All my delight is upon the saints that are in the earth, and upon such as excel in virtue.' And so a greater than he: 'A new commandment I give unto you, That ye love one another; as I have loved you, that ye also love one another. By this shall all men know that ye are My disciples, if ye have love one to another' (John xiii. 34, 35). This is that love on which the Apostle John so frequently and strongly insists: 'This,' saith he, 'is the message that ye heard from the beginning, that we should love one another' (1 John iii. 11). 'Hereby perceive we the love of God, because He laid down His life for us: and we ought,' if love should call us thereto, 'to lay down our lives for the brethren' (verse 16). And again: 'Beloved, let

us love one another: for love is of God. He that loveth not, knoweth not God; for God is love' (iv. 7, 8). 'Not that we loved God, but that He loved us, and sent His Son to be the propitiation for our sins. Beloved, if God so loved us, we ought also to love one another' (verses 10, 11).

3. All men approve of this; but do all men practise it? Daily experience shows the contrary. Where are even the Christians who 'love one another as He hath given us commandment'? How many hindrances lie in the way! The two grand, general hindrances are, first, that they cannot all think alike; and, in consequence of this, secondly, they cannot all walk alike; but in several smaller points their practice must differ in proportion to the difference of their sentiments. (3)

Sermon on Christian Perfection

1. In the first place, I shall endeavour to show, in what sense Christians are *not perfect*. And both from experience and Scripture it appears, first, that they are not perfect in knowledge. They are not so perfect in this life as to be free from ignorance. They know, it may be, in common with other men, many things relating to the present world; and they know, with regard to the world to come, the general truths which God hath revealed. They know likewise (what the natural man receiveth not; for these things are spiritually discerned) 'what manner of love' it is, wherewith 'the Father' hath loved them, 'that they should be called the sons of God.' They know the mighty working of His Spirit in their hearts; and the wisdom of His providence, directing all their paths, and causing all things to work together for their good. Yea, they know in every circumstance of life what the Lord requireth of them, and how keep a conscience void of offence both toward God and toward man.

2. But innumerable are the things which they know not. Touching the Almighty Himself, they cannot search Him out to perfection. 'Lo, these are but a part of His ways; but the thunder of His power, who can understand?' They cannot understand, I will not say, how 'there are Three that bear record in heaven, the Father, the Son, and the Holy Spirit, and these Three are One'; or how the eternal Son of God 'took upon Himself the form of a servant';—but not any one attribute, not any one circumstance, of the divine nature. Neither is it for them to know the times and seasons when God will work His great works upon the earth; no, not even those which He hath in part revealed by His servants and prophets since the world began. Much less do they know when God, having 'accomplished the number of His elect, will hasten His kingdom'; when 'the heavens shall pass away with a great noise, and the elements shall melt with fervent heat.'

3. They know not the reasons even of many of His present dispensations with the sons of men; but are constrained to rest here: Though 'clouds and darkness are round about Him, righteousness and judgement are the habitation of His seat.' Yea, often with regard to His dealings with themselves, doth their Lord say unto them, 'What I do, thou knowest not now; but thou shalt know hereafter.' And how little do they know of what is ever before them, of even the visible works of His hands!—how 'He spreadeth the north over the empty place, and hangeth the earth upon nothing'; how He unites all the parts of this vast machine by a

secret chain, which cannot be broken. So great is the ignorance, so very little the knowledge, of even the best of men!

4. No one, then, is so perfect in this life, as to be free from ignorance. Nor, secondly, from mistake; which indeed is almost an unavoidable consequence of it; seeing those who 'know but in part' are ever liable to err touching the things which they know not. It is true, the children of God do not mistake as to the things essential to salvation: they do not 'put darkness for light, or light for darkness'; neither 'seek death in the error of their life.' For they are 'taught of God'; and the way which He teaches them, the way of holiness, is so plain, that 'the wayfaring man, though a fool, need not err therein.' But in things unessential to salvation they do err, and that frequently. The best and wisest of men are frequently mistaken even with regard to facts; believing those things not to have been which really were, or those to have been done which were not. Or, suppose they are not mistaken as to the fact itself, they may be with regard to its circumstances; believing them, or many of them, to have been quite different from what, in truth, they were. And hence cannot but arise many farther mistakes. Hence they may believe either past or present actions which were or are evil, to be good; and such as were or are good, to be evil. Hence also they may judge not according to truth with regard to the characters of men; and that, not only by supposing good men to be better, or wicked men to be worse, than they are; but by believing them to have been or to be good men, who were or are very wicked; or perhaps those to have been or to be wicked men, who were or are holy and unreprovable.

5. Nay, with regard to the holy Scriptures themselves, as careful as they are to avoid it, the best of men are liable to mistake, and do mistake day by day; especially with respect to those parts thereof which less immediately relate to practice. Hence, even the children of God are not agreed as to the interpretation of many places in holy writ; nor is their difference of opinion any proof that they are not the children of God, on either side; but it is a proof that we are no more to expect any living man to be infallible, than to be omniscient.

. . . .

1. In what sense, then, are Christians perfect? This is what I shall endeavour, in the second place, to show. But it should be premised, that there are several stages in Christian life, as in natural; some of the children of God being but new-born babes, others having attained to more maturity. And accordingly St. John, in his First Epistle (ii. 12, etc.), applies himself severally to those he terms 'little children,' those he styles 'young men,' and those whom he entitles 'fathers.' 'I write unto you, little children,' saith the Apostle, 'because your sins are forgiven you': because thus far you have attained; being 'justified freely,' you 'have peace with God through Jesus Christ.' 'I write unto you, young men, because ye have overcome the wicked one': or (as he afterwards addeth), 'because ye are strong, and the word of God abideth in you.' Ye have quenched the fiery darts of the wicked one, the doubts and fears wherewith he disturbed your first peace; and the witness of God, that your sins are forgiven, now abideth in your heart. 'I write unto you, fathers, because ye have known Him that is from the beginning.' Ye have known both the Father, and the Son, and the Spirit of Christ, in your inmost

soul. Ye are 'perfect men,' being grown up to 'the measure of the stature of the fullness of Christ.'

2. It is of these chiefly I speak in the latter part of this discourse; for these only are perfect Christians. But even babes in Christ are in such a sense perfect, or born of God (an expression taken also in divers senses), as, first, not to commit sin. If any doubt of this privilege of the sons of God, the question is not to be decided by abstract reasonings, which may be drawn out into an endless length, and leave the point just as it was before. Neither is it to be determined by the experience of this or that particular person. Many may suppose they do not commit sin, when they do; but this proves nothing either way. To the law and to the testimony we appeal. 'Let God be true, and every man a liar.' By His Word will we abide, and that alone. Hereby we ought to be judged.

3. Now, the Word of God plainly declares, that even those who are justified, who are born again in the lowest sense, 'do not continue in sin'; that they cannot 'live any longer therein' (Rom. vi. 1, 2); that they are 'planted together in the likeness of the death' of Christ (verse 5); that their 'old man is crucified with Him,' the body of sin being destroyed, so that henceforth they do not serve sin; that, being dead with Christ, they are free from sin (verses 6, 7); that they are 'dead unto sin, and alive unto God' (verse 11); that 'sin hath no more dominion over them,' who are 'not under the law, but under grace'; but that these, 'being free from sin are become the servants of righteousness' (verses 14, 18).

4. The very least which can be implied in these words, is, that the persons spoken of therein, namely, all real Christians, or believers in Christ, are made free from outward sin. And the same freedom, which St. Paul here expresses in such variety of phrases, St. Peter expresses in that one (1 Pet. iv. 1, 2): 'He that hath suffered in the flesh hath ceased from sin; that he no longer should live to the desires of men, but to the will of God.' For this *ceasing from sin*, if it be interpreted in the lowest sense, as regarding only the outward behaviour, must denote the ceasing from the outward act, from any outward transgression of the law. (4)

Luke 23. 34: *Then said Jesus*—Our Lord passed most of the time on the cross in silence: yet seven sentences which he spoke thereon are recorded by the four evangelists, though no one evangelist has recorded them all. Hence it appears, that the four Gospels are as it were four parts, which, joined together, make one symphony; sometimes one of these only, sometimes two or three, sometimes all, sound together. *Father*—So he speaks both in the beginning and at the end of his sufferings on the cross. *Forgive them*—How striking is this passage! While they are actually nailing him to the cross, he seems to feel the injury they did to their own souls, more than the wounds they gave him; and, as it were, to forget his own anguish out of a concern for their own salvation.

And how eminently was his prayer heard! It procured forgiveness for all that were penitent, and a suspension of vengeance even for the impenitent. (5)

1 Corinthians 3. 9: Has not all this reasoning the same force still? Ministers are still barely instruments in God's hand, and depend as entirely as ever on his blessing, to give the increase to their labours. Without this, they are nothing: with it, their part is so small, that they hardly deserve to be mentioned. May their hearts and hands be more united; and, retaining a due sense of the honour God

doeth them in employing them, may they faithfully labour, not as for themselves, but for the great Proprietor of all, till the day come when he will reward them in full proportion to their fidelity and diligence! (6)

NOTES / SOURCES

1. There are many editions of the *Journal*. For the most recent and authoritative see *The Works of John Wesley*, Nashville, 1984–, vols. 18–24, *Journals and Diaries*, ed. W. R. Ward and R. P. Heitzenrater, 1988–. The conversion account is printed in vol. 1, pp. 249–50.
2. This sermon was first printed in London, 1738, and included in Wesley's *Sermons on Several Occasions*, London, 1746. The best modern edition is to be found in *The Works of John Wesley*, vol. I, *Sermons* I, ed. Albert C. Outler, Nashville, 1984.
3. London, 1755; reprinted in *Sermons on Several Occasions*. See *Works*, 2, *Sermons*, II, ed. Outler, 1985.
4. London, 1741; reprinted in *Sermons on Several Occasions*. See *Works*, 2, *Sermons*, II, ed. Outler, 1985.
5. *Explanatory Notes Upon the New Testament*, London, 1755. There are many later editions.
6. Ibid.

Charles Wesley   1707–1788

While at Oxford Charles Wesley drew about him a group of undergraduates noted for their strict religious observance – regular communion, prayer, Bible reading, and visiting poor people and prisoners. His brother John joined the group on his return to Oxford and, being the only ordained clergyman among them, became the acknowledged leader. They were nicknamed first the 'Holy Club' and, later, the 'Methodists'. Through his contact with Peter Bohler and the Moravian Church, Charles had a conversion experience on Whit Sunday 1738. A tireless hymn writer, he composed between 5,000 and 6,000 hymns of which some 500 are still in use. He disagreed very strongly with the Methodist movement's increasing separation from the Church of England, and in particular John's ordination of superintendents and presbyters. His eucharistic theology, expressed in his hymns, is profoundly influenced by Brevint (q.v.).

Exhorting, and Beseeching to return to God

O for a thousand tongues to sing
　My dear Redeemer's praise!
The glories of my God and King,
　The triumphs of his grace!

My gracious Master, and my God,
　Assist me to proclaim,
To spread through all the earth abroad
　The honours of thy name.

Jesus, the name that charms our fears,
　That bids our sorrows cease—
'Tis music in the sinner's ears,
　'Tis life, and health, and peace.

He breaks the power of cancelled sin,
  He sets the prisoner free;
His blood can make the foulest clean—
  His blood availed for me.

Hear him, ye deaf; his praise, ye dumb,
  Your loosened tongues employ;
Ye blind, behold your Saviour come,
  And leap, ye lame, for joy!

Look unto him, ye nations, own
  Your God, ye fallen race;
Look, and be saved through faith alone,
  Be justified by grace!

See all your sins on Jesus laid:
  The Lamb of God was slain,
His soul was once an offering made
  For every soul of man.

Awake from guilty nature's sleep,
  And Christ shall give you light,
Cast all your sins into the deep,
  And wash the Ethiop white.

With me, your chief, ye then shall know,
  Shall feel your sins forgiven;
Anticipate your heaven below,
  And own that love is heaven. (1)

Wrestling Jacob

Come, O thou Traveller unknown,
  Whom still I hold, but cannot see!
My company before is gone,
  And I am left alone with thee;
With thee all night I mean to stay,
And wrestle till the break of day.

I need not tell thee who I am,
  My misery or sin declare;
Thyself hast called me by my name,
  Look on thy hands, and read it there.
But who, I ask thee, who art thou?
Tell me thy name, and tell me now.

In vain thou strugglest to get free,
   I never will unloose my hold;
Art thou the Man that died for me?
   The secret of thy love unfold:
Wrestling, I will not let thee go
Till I thy name, thy nature know.

Wilt thou not yet to me reveal
   Thy new, unutterable name?
Tell me, I still beseech thee, tell;
   To know it now resolved I am:
Wrestling, I will not let thee go
Till I thy name, thy nature know.

What though my shrinking flesh complain
   And murmur to contend so long?
I rise superior to my pain:
   When I am weak, then I am strong;
And when my all of strength shall fail
I shall with the God-man prevail.

Yield to me now—for I am weak,
   But confident in self-despair!
Speak to my heart, in blessings speak,
   Be conquered by my instant prayer:
Speak, or thou never hence shalt move,
And tell me if thy name is LOVE.

'Tis Love! 'Tis Love! Thou diedst for me;
   I hear thy whisper in my heart.
The morning breaks, the shadows flee,
   Pure Universal Love thou art:
To me, to all, thy bowels move—
Thy nature, and thy name, is LOVE.

My prayer hath power with God; the grace
   Unspeakable I now receive;
Through faith I see thee face to face;
   I see thee face to face, and live!
In vain I have not wept and strove—
Thy nature, and thy name, is LOVE.

I know thee, Saviour, who thou art—
   Jesus, the feeble sinner's friend;
Nor wilt thou with the night depart,
   But stay, and love me to the end:
Thy mercies never shall remove,
Thy nature, and thy name, is LOVE.

The Sun of Righteousness on me
    Hath rose with healing in his wings;
Withered my nature's strength; from thee
    My soul its life and succour brings;
My help is all laid up above:
Thy nature, and thy name, is LOVE.

Contented now upon my thigh
    I halt, till life's short journey end;
All helplessness, all weakness, I
    On thee alone for strength depend;
Nor have I power from thee to move:
Thy nature, and thy name, is LOVE.

Lame as I am, I take the prey,
    Hell, earth, and sin with ease o'ercome;
I leap for joy, pursue my way,
    And as a bounding hart fly home,
Through all eternity to prove,
Thy nature, and thy name, is LOVE. (2)

Love divine

Love divine, all loves excelling,
    Joy of heaven, to earth come down,
Fix in us thy humble dwelling,
    All thy faithful mercies crown!
Jesu, thou art all compassion,
    Pure, unbounded love thou art;
Visit us with thy salvation!
    Enter every trembling heart.

Come, almighty to deliver,
    Let us all thy grace receive;
Suddenly return, and never,
    Never more thy temples leave.
Thee we would be always blessing,
    Serve thee as thy hosts above,
Pray, and praise thee without ceasing,
    Glory in thy perfect love.

Finish then thy new creation,
    Pure and spotless let us be;
Let us see thy great salvation
    Perfectly restored in thee;
Changed from glory into glory,
    Till in heaven we take our place,
Till we cast our crowns before thee,
    Lost in wonder, love, and praise. (3)

The Communion of Saints

Christ, from whom all blessings flow,
Perfecting the saints below,
Hear us, who thy nature share,
Who thy mystic body are.

Join us, in one spirit join,
Let us still receive of thine;
Still for more on thee we call,
Thee who fillest all in all!

Closer knit to thee our Head,
Nourish us, O Christ, and feed!
Let us daily growth receive,
More and more in Jesus live.

Jesus, we thy members are,
Cherish us with kindest care;
Of thy flesh and of thy bone,
Love, forever love thy own!

Move, and actuate, and guide,
Divers gifts to each divide;
Placed according to thy will,
Let us all our work fulfil.

Never from our office move,
Needful to each other prove;
Use the grace on each bestowed,
Tempered by the art of God.

Sweetly may we all agree,
Touched with softest sympathy;
Kindly for each other care,
Every member feel its share.

Wounded by the grief of one,
Now let all the members groan;
Honoured if one member is,
All partake the common bliss.

Many are we now, and one,
We who Jesus have put on;
There is neither bond nor free,
Male nor female, Lord, in thee!

Love, like death, hath all destroyed,
Rendered our distinctions void!
Names, and sects, and parties fall,
Thou, O Christ, art all in all! (4)

Two Hymns on the Lord's Supper

Blest by the Lord forever blest
   Who bought us with a Price,
And bids his ransom'd Servants feast
   On his great Sacrifice.

Thy Blood was shed upon the Cross
   To wash us white as Snow,
Broken for us thy Body was
   To feed our Souls below.

Now on the sacred Table laid
   Thy flesh becomes our Food.
Thy life is to our Souls convey'd
   In Sacramental Blood.

We eat the Offerings of our Peace,
   The hidden Manna prove,
And only live t'adore and bless
   Thine all-sufficient Love.

Jesu, my lord and God bestow
All which thy Sacrament doth shew.
   And make the real Sign
A sure effectual Means of Grace,
Then Sanctify my Heart and bless,
   And make it all like thine.

Great is thy Faithfulness and Love,
Thine Ordinance can never prove
   Of none Effect and vain,
Only do Thou my Heart prepare,
To find thy Real Presence there,
   And all thy Fullness gain. (5)

Christmas

Angels speak, let Man give Ear,
   Sent from high,
   They are nigh,
And forbid our Fear.

News they bring us of Salvation,
  Sounds of Joy
  To employ
Every Tongue and Nation.

Welcome Tidings! to retrieve us
  From our Fall,
  Born for All,
Christ is born to save us.

Born his Creatures to restore,
  Abject Earth
  Sees His Birth,
Whom the Heavens adore.

Wrapt in Swaths th'Immortal Stranger
  Man with Men
  We have seen,
Lying in a Manger. (6)

The Resurrection

By the Mystery of thy holy Incarnation; by thy holy Nativity and Circumcision; by thy Baptism, Fasting, and Temptation; by thine Agony and bloody Sweat; by thy Cross and Passion; by thy precious Death and Burial; by thy glorious Resurrection and Ascension; and by the Coming of the Holy Ghost, Good Lord, deliver us. [Prayer Book Litany].

Jesu, shew us thy Salvation,
  [In thy Strength we strive with Thee]
By thy Mystic Incarnation,
  By thy pure Nativity,
Save us Thou, our New-Creator,
  Into all our Souls impart,
Thy Divine Unsinning Nature,
  Form Thyself within our Heart.

By thy First Blood-shedding heal us;
  Cut us off from every Sin,
By thy Circumcision seal us,
  Write thy Law of Love within;
By thy Spirit circumcise us,
  Kindle in our Hearts a Flame;
By thy Baptism baptize us
  Into all thy Glorious Name.

By thy Fasting and Temptation
  Mortify our vain Desires,
Take away what Sense, or Passion,
  Appetite, or Flesh requires:

Arm us with thy Self-denial,
 Every tempted Soul defend,
Save us in the Firey Trial,
 Make us faithful to the End.

By thy Sorer Sufferings save us,
 Save us when conform'd to Thee,
By thy Miseries relieve us,
 By thy painful Agony;
When beneath thy Frown we languish,
 When we feel thine Anger's Weight,
Save us by thine unknown Anguish,
 Save us by thy Bloody Sweat.

By that highest Point of Passion,
 By thy Sufferings on the Tree,
Save us from the Indignation
 Due to all Mankind, and me
Hanging bleeding, panting, dying,
 Gasping out thy latest Breath,
By thy precious Death's Applying
 Save us from Eternal Death.

From the World of Care release us,
 By thy decent Burial save,
Crucified with Thee, O Jesus,
 Hide us in thy quiet Grave:
By thy Power divinely glorious,
 By thy Resurrection's Power
Raise us up, o'er Sin victorious,
 Raise us up to fall no more.

By the Pomp of thine Ascending,
 Live we here to Heaven restor'd
Live in Pleasures never ending,
 Share the Portion of our Lord:
Let us have our Blessed Spirits
 With the Blessed Spirits above
Sav'd with all that great Salvation,
 Perfectly renew'd in Love.

Glorious Head, triumphant Saviour,
 High enthron'd above all Height,
We have now thro' Thee found Favour,
 Righteous in thy Father's sight:
Hears He not thy prayer unceasing?
 Can He turn away thy Face?
Send us down the purchased Blessing,
 Fulness of the Gospel-Grace.

By the coming of thy Spirit
    As a mighty rushing Wind,
Save us unto all thy Merit,
    Into all thy Sinless Mind.
Let the perfect Gift be given,
    Let thy will in us be seen,
Done on earth as 'tis in Heaven:
    Lord, thy Spirit cries Amen!

The Trinity

The dispensation of the grace of God, which is given me to you-ward: how
that by Revelation He made known to me the mystery.   *Eph.* iii. 2, 3.

I neither received it of man, neither was I taught it, but by The Revelation of
Jesus Christ.   *Gal.* i. 12.

God made known the mystery,
    The gospel of his grace,
Call'd the messenger to see
    His God in Jesus' face:
God by revelation gave
    The power to preach a dying God,
Ministerial power to save
    Believers in his blood.

I receiv'd it not of man,
    Of man I was not taught;
Jesus did himself explain
    The grace for sinners bought:
Christ did to my heart reveal
    The welcome news of sin forgiven,
News of joy unspeakable,
    And peace 'twixt earth and heaven.

Every chosen instrument
    Ordain'd by the Most High,
Every minister is sent
    Of Christ to testify:
Lo, we preach his Name abroad;
    Know all the truth in us reveal'd,
Sinners by the blood of God
    Receive your pardon seal'd. (8)

To the Trinity

FATHER, in whom we live,
In whom we are, and move,
The glory, power, and praise receive
Of Thy creating love:
Let all the angel-thong
Give thanks to God on high,
While earth repeats the joyful song,
And echoes to the sky.

Incarnate Deity,
Let all the ransom'd race
Render in thanks their lives to Thee,
For Thy redeeming grace:
The grace to sinners show'd
Ye heavenly choirs proclaim,
And cry, Salvation to our God,
Salvation to the Lamb!

Spirit of Holiness,
Let all Thy saints adore
Thy sacred energy, and bless
Thine heart-renewing power:
Not angel-tongues can tell
Thy love's ecstatic height,
The glorious joy unspeakable,
The beatific sight.

Eternal triune Lord,
Let all the hosts above,
Let all the sons of men record,
And dwell upon Thy love:
When heaven and earth are fled
Before Thy glorious face,
Sing all the saints Thy love hath made.
Thine everlasting praise! (9)

Hymn for Easter-Day

'CHRIST the Lord is risen to-day,'
Sons of men and angels say!
Raise your joys and triumphs high;
Sing, ye heavens; and, earth, reply.

Love's redeeming work is done,
Fought the fight, the battle won:
Lo! our Sun's eclipse is o'er;
Lo! He sets in blood no more.

Vain the stone, the watch, the seal;
Christ has burst the gates of hell!
Death in vain forbids His rise:
Christ has open'd paradise!

Lives again our glorious King:
Where, O Death, is now thy sting?
Dying once, He all doth save:
Where thy victory, O Grave?

Soar we now, where Christ has led?
Following our exalted Head,
Made like Him, like Him we rise,
Ours the cross, the grave, the skies!

What though once we perish'd all,
Partners in our parent's fall?
Second life we all receive,
In our Heavenly *Adam* live.

Risen with Him, we upward move;
Still we seek the things above;
Still pursue, and kiss the Son
Seated on His Father's throne:

Scarce on earth a thought bestow,
Dead to all we leave below;
Heaven our aim, and loved abode,
Hid our life with Christ in God!

Hid; till Christ, our Life, appear,
Glorious in His members here:
Join'd to Him, we then shall shine
All immortal, all Divine!

Hail, the Lord of earth and heaven!
Praise to Thee by both be given:
Thee we greet triumphant now;
Hail, the Resurrection Thou!

King of glory, Soul of bliss,
Everlasting life is this,
Thee to know, Thy power to prove,
Thus to sing, and thus to love! (10)

NOTES / SOURCES

1. *The Works of Charles Wesley* Vol. VII, Oxford, 1983, pp. 79–81
2. Ibid., pp. 250–2
3. Ibid., pp. 545–7
4. Ibid., pp. 693–4

5. Charles Wesley, *Hymns on the Lord's Supper* (1745), Madison, 1995, p. 48
6. Charles Wesley, *Hymns for the Nativity of Our Lord* (1745), Madison, 1991, p. 4
7. Charles Wesley, *Hymns for our Lord's Resurrection* (1746), Madison, 1992, pp. 10–12
8. Charles Wesley, *Hymns on the Trinity* (1767), Madison, 1998, p. 32
9. Charles Wesley, *Hymns for those that seek and those that have Redemption in the Blood of Jesus Christ* (1747), pp. 254–5
10. Charles Wesley 'Hymns and Poems', in *The Practical Works of John and Charles Wesley* Vol. I, Oxford, 1868, pp. 185–6

Samuel Johnson   1709–1784

Samuel Johnson—not to be confused with the American writer of the same name—was the son of a Lichfield bookseller and studied at Pembroke College, Oxford. Greatly influenced as a young man by reading William Law's (q.v.) 'Serious Call', he became a High Churchman who took his religious duties seriously, and was markedly hostile to Nonconformist religion and tolerant of Roman Catholicism. Best known as a Lexicographer, his dictionary of the English language (two volumes) was published in 1755. A friend of Sir Joshua Reynolds (who painted his portrait on four occasions), Johnson was well known in the literary circles of his day and on occasion met with George III. So often known to history as 'Dr Johnson', he rarely styles himself as such.

Prayers and Meditations

January 1, after 3 in the morning, 1749

Almighty God, by whose will I was created, and by whose providence I have been sustained, by whose mercy I have been called to the knowledge of my REDEEMER, and by whose grace whatever I have thought or acted acceptable to Thee has been inspired and directed; grant, O LORD, that in reviewing my past life, I may recollect Thy mercies to my preservation, in whatsoever state Thou preparest for me; that in affliction I may remember how often I have been succoured; and in prosperity may know and confess from whose hand the blessing is received. Let me, O LORD, so remember my sins, that I may abolish them by true repentance, and so improve the year to which Thou hast graciously extended my life, and all the years which Thou shalt yet allow me, that I may hourly become purer in Thy sight; so that I may live in Thy fear, and die in Thy favour, and find mercy at the last day, for the sake of JESUS CHRIST. Amen. (1)

On Easter Day   April 22.

O Lord, who givest the grace of repentance, and hearest the prayers of the penitent, grant, that by true contrition, I may obtain forgiveness of all the sins committed, and of all duties neglected, in my union with the wife whom Thou hast taken from me; for the neglect of joint devotion, patient exhortation, and mild instruction. And, O LORD, who canst change evil to good, grant that the loss of my wife may so mortify all inordinate affections in me, that I may henceforth please Thee by holiness of life.

And, O LORD, so far as it may be lawful for me, I commend to Thy fatherly goodness the soul of my departed wife; beseeching Thee to grant her whatever is best in her present state, and finally to receive her to eternal happiness. All this I beg for JESUS CHRIST's sake, whose death I am now about to commemorate. To whom, etc. Amen.

This I repeated sometimes at Church. (2)

Bed-Time

Lent 2. 1768

Almightly God, who seest that I have no power of myself to help myself; keep me both outwardly in my body, and inwardly in my soul, that I may be defended from all adversities that may happen to the body, and from all evil thoughts which may assault and hurt the soul, through JESUS CHRIST our LORD. Amen.

This prayer may be said before or after the entrance into bed, as a preparative for sleep.

When I transcribed this prayer, it was my purpose to have made this book a collection. (3)

Prayer for work on the dictionary   *April 3, 1953*

O God, who hast hitherto supported me, enable me to proceed in this labour, and in the whole task of my present state; that when I shall render up, at the last day, an account of the talent committed to me, I may receive pardon, for the sake of JESUS CHRIST. Amen. (4)

NOTES / SOURCES

1. *Prayers and Meditations composed by Samuel Johnson*, London, 1785, pp. 7–8
2. Ibid., pp. 19–20
3. Ibid., p. 79
4. Ibid., a later edition, p. 14

Samuel Walker   1714–1761

Born in Devon, Samuel Walker spent most of his ministry in Cornwall where, after being appointed Rector of Truro, he came under the influence of George Conon, the Master of Truro Grammar School. His sermons focused on the key themes of evangelical theology—repentance, faith, and new birth—themes which were closely followed by the Wesleys. Particularly in 1755 and 1756, when the question of separation from the Church of England was much to the fore, John and Charles Wesley (qq.v.) corresponded and met with Samuel Walker who tried in vain to persuade them against the schism. He disapproved strongly of the influence of lay preachers on the Methodist movement.

The End of our Being

The end of our being is to honour and serve God, and our business in this life, is to become qualified for such service, i.e. to acquire such a temper and disposition of mind here, as will fit us to find our eternal happiness in honouring and serving God hereafter. This temper and disposition is in one word *love*, or such a bearing of the whole soul towards God, such a constant conviction of the understanding, such a bias in the will, such a vehemence in the affections, as will make us like and admire God, long after him, and find incomparable delight in serving, pleasing, and enjoying him. Without this temper, we are unfit for God and unhappy. Now such is our natural corrupt estate, that we have nothing like this disposition of mind within us, no knowledge of God, no desire after him, nor pleasure in him. On the contrary, we are entirely engaged in the things which the world presents to us, we eagerly desire, and are very busy and warm to obtain them. All within us is blind and obstinate self-will, self love, pride, vanity, envy, and lust; all without a horrid scene of wickedness; and when we do but make one step towards enlarging ourselves, under the power of Christ and the guidance of his Spirit, from this tyranny of sin, instantly all is alarm about us, and the world, the flesh, and the devil are in arms to contest with us the matter of our deliverance. Nor when the deformity of outward vices hath been discovered, and we renounce and abhor them, will it be a less difficult task to reform the soul, and to bring every affection and desire to a total submission to the law of love. We may stop whilst our work remains unfinished: nay when we are upon the point of attaining, and have tasted and drank deep of the heavenly gift, being made pertakers of the Holy Ghost, we may after all fall away, and suffer the deserved wrath of God in eternal misery. From this very important representation of the work we have to perform, together with the difficulties both from within and without we have to contend with, and the infinite importance it is to us we should be successful, it may be easy to discover how great reason we have to engage the divine assistance, to guard us from so many evils that threaten us, and how earnestly we must needs call upon God to interpose his almighty power with great might to succour us. The amount of the whole is, that when we are oppressed with the load of temporal or spiritual misery, when we dread the punishment of our sins, or shrink at the difficulties and dangers which beset us in our Christian course, we cannot but flee unto God for deliverance. Now, under any such a sense of misery, or dread of danger, the litany helps us to a most passionate and affecting address to Almighty God. (1)

The Holiness of God

The holiness of God will teach us not to put our trust in any thing we can do, but to have our whole dependance upon the merits of Christ for our acceptance with God. Now this matter I think comes home with a peculiar force, under the views of God's holiness. How shall we stand before this holy Lord God? Some have been more impenitent and faithless than others it is granted; but are any of us holy or have we ever been so? Which of us can say, 'I have made my heart clean, I am pure from my sin?' The question is are any of us holy? Can a pure God find no fault in us? If not, will he lay aside his holiness and accept us as we are for our own sakes? Hath Christ too died in vain, and may we come to life in our own sufficiency, when it cost so dear to glorify God's holiness, and to save our souls? Alas, the pride of man must be brought low. We must come down before the footstool of a holy God, and thankfully receive that favour at the hands of a Redeemer, which we are utterly unworthy of ourselves.

Mean time let none forget that God loveth righteousness, as much as he hateth iniquity; that he is more highly pleased with his Son our Jesus, than he can be displeased at us, and therefore that we shall but injure his holiness if we distrust his mercies in not coming under the protection of him in whom he is well pleased. Wherefore, believing souls cannot too much consider their own impurity and the perfect righteousness and obedience of Christ, to the end that both they may see more abundantly their want of this Redeemer, and may also be more confirmed in his sufficiency, with a pure and holy God on their behalf. This will both humble and embolden them in all their approaches to the divine majesty, and keep them in that temper of reverence, humility and watchfulness, which becomes our condition and our circumstances.

The holiness of God ought greatly to alarm the impenitent sinner, who seems to have no care how he may stand before this holy Lord God. 'The Lord is righteous in all his ways and holy in all his works,' saith David; he cannot depart from the holiness of his nature in his doings, nor any more cease from hating sin than from being God. And if so thou art hated of God, O sinner, and all the declarations of his abhorrence at sin are levelled at thee. Thou livest daily hated of God; his displeasure rests upon thee day and night; wherever thou art, however employed, he cannot endure thee. He hath set a mark upon thee, and his curse is hovering over thee. In very deed dost thou not think he hates thee? What otherwise canst thou think, while thou art hugging to thy breast, that only thing he abhors, and to which he can never be reconciled, unless he forget that holiness of his which is the life and glory of his divinity? And will God ever change; if not, wilt thou ever see his face, or escape his vengeance unless thou repent? Alas, my brother, he tarrieth a little moment for the sake of his beloved Son, he waits a little for thee. But how soon will he declare his hatred of sin to thee in another manner than thou hast yet known? Death is drawing near, methinks I see him creeping up to thee, he his ready to lay his cold hand upon thee. Dost thou not see him, miserable man? Dost thou not feel him shaking thy crazy body to ashes? Where is he hurrying thee away? Stay thou king of terrors: mercy thou holy God! Yet a little moment; this sinner is unready, he is not washed nor cleansed. O spare him a little, delay to execute the terrible separation of his soul from thy presence and favour for ever! Thou knowest that thus dying he must perish, perish in a destruction suitable to the jealousy of a holy God! But sinful man, should God spare thee a thousand years, thou must repent and believe the gospel, else after all he can never be reconciled to thee. O that thou wouldest be wise, that thou wouldest consider this one thing, that God is not less holy because there are many sinners in earth and hell.

The holiness of God should stir us all up to seek and improve holiness in ourselves. We are naturally without it, and without it we can never see a holy God, yet the gospel is designed to minister it unto us. The blood of Christ invites and his righteousness encourages us to it, while also his word and Spirit will teach and work it in us. And this is the end of all, that he may purify to himself a peculiar people zealous of good works. Christians, this is your business upon earth, to be conformed to the holy God. See that ye be found so doing, having the purity of God, and his hatred of sin, so manifestly revealed in the law and the gospel, continually before your eyes. Seek that this work in you a growing hatred of sin and love of the blessed God. Mortify your lusts, die to sin daily, cherish every gracious disposition in your souls, by prayer, meditation, and every means whereby ye may derive down upon you the sanctifying influences of the blessed spirit. Nor be discouraged because ye are much defiled. Go to Jesus, he will present you in his righteousness, he knoweth whereof you are made. He will stand by you, and save you, till he present you to himself without spot. Only see that you faint not, for this is your trial, it is for your life. 'Now unto him that is able to keep you from falling, and to present you faultless before the presence of his glory with exceeding joy, to the only wise God, our Saviour, be glory and majesty, dominion and power, both now and ever. Amen.' (2)

NOTES / SOURCES

1. Samuel Walker, in *The Life, Ministry and selection from the Remains of the Revd. Samuel Walker*, London, 1835, pp. 123–5
2. Samuel Walker, 'Sermon IX: The Holiness of God', ibid., pp. 424–7

Howell Harris   1714–1773

A landowner and lay preacher, and one of the Founders of Methodism, he remained a firm member of the Church. In 1757 he founded a community at Trefeca, training preachers for the Countess of Huntingdon's Connexion. He died in 1773, and is buried in his local parish Church at Talgarth.

Spiritual Conflict

'One day in prayer I felt a strong impression on my mind to give myself to God as I was, and to leave all to follow Him. But presently felt a strong opposition to it, backed with reasons, that if I would give myself to the Lord, I should lose my liberty, and would then be not my own, or in my own power; but after a great conflict for some time, I was made willing to bid adieu to all things temporal, and chose the Lord for my portion. I believe I was then effectually called to be a follower of the Lamb.'

. . . .

'June 18th. 1735, being in secret prayer, I felt suddenly my heart melting within me like wax before the fire with love to God my Saviour; and also felt not only love, peace, etc., but longing to be dissolved, and to be with Christ. Then was a cry in my inmost soul, which I was totally unacquainted with before, Abba, Father! Abba, Father! I could not help calling God my Father; I knew that I was His child, and that He loved me and heard me. My soul being filled and satiated, crying, "Tis enough, I am satisfied. Give me strength, and I will follow Thee through fire and water." I could say I was happy indeed. There was in me a well of water, springing up to everlasting life, John 4:14. The love of God was shed abroad in my heart by the Holy Ghost, Rom. 5:5.'

NOTES / SOURCES

A Brief Account of the Life of Howell Harris, Trefeca, 1791, pp. 12–13

John Berridge   1716–1793

A student and Fellow of Clare Hall, Cambridge, he became incumbent of Everton, Bedfordshire, in 1755, remaining there until his death. Following the example of the Wesleys (qq.v.) and George Whitefield, whom he met in 1758, he undertook preaching tours in nearby counties.

The Life and Conversion of John Berridge

Reverend Dear Sir,

My desire and intention, in this Letter, is to inform you what the Lord has lately done for my soul: in order to do this, it may be needful to give you a little previous information of my manner of life, from my youth up to the present time.

When I was about the age of fourteen, God was pleased to show me that I was a sinner, and that I must be born again before I could enter into his Kingdom. Accordingly I betook myself to reading, praying and watching; and was enabled hereby to make some progress in sanctification.

In this manner I went on, though not always with the same diligence, to about half a year ago. I thought myself in the right way to heaven, though as yet I was wholly out of the way; and imagining I was travelling towards Zion, though I had never yet set my face thitherwards. Indeed, God would have shown me that I was wrong, by not earning my ministry; but I paid no regard to this for a long time, imputing my want of success to the naughty hearts of my heroes, and not my own naughty doctrine.

You may ask, perhaps, What was my doctrine? Why, dear Sir, it was the doctrine that every man will naturally hold whilst he continues in an unregenerate state, viz. that we are to be justified partly by our faith, and partly by our works. This doctrine I preached for six years at a curacy, which I served from college; and though I took some extraordinary points, and pressed sanctification upon them very earnestly, yet they continued as unsanctified as before, and not one soul was brought to Christ. There was indeed a little more of the form of religion in the parish, but not a whit more of the power. At length I removed to Everton, where I have lived altogether. Here again I pressed sanctification and regeneration as vigorously as I could; but finding no success, after two years preaching in this manner, I began to be discouraged, and now some secret misgivings arose in my mind, that I was not right myself. (This happened about Christmas last). Those misgivings grew stronger, and at last very painful. Being then under great doubts, I cried unto the Lord very earnestly. The constant language in my heart was this,—'Lord, if I am right, keep me so; if I am not right, make me so. Lead me to the knowledge of the truth as it is in Jesus.' After about ten days crying unto the Lord, he was pleased to return an answer to my prayers, and in the following wonderful manner. As I was sitting in my house one morning, and musing upon a text of scripture, the following words were darted into my mind with wonderful power, and seemed indeed like a voice from heaven, viz, 'cease from thy own works.' Before I heard these words, my mind was in an unusual calm; but as soon as I heard them, my soul was in a tempest directly, and the tears flowed from my eyes like a torrent. The scales fell from my eyes immediately, and I now clearly saw the rock I had been splitting on for nearly thirty years.

Do you ask what this rock was? Why, it was some secret reliance on my own works for salvation. I had hoped to be saved partly in my own name, and partly in Christ's name; though I am told there is salvation in no other name, except in the name of Jesus Christ, (Acts 4: 12)—I had hoped to be saved partly through my own works, and partly through Christ's mercy; though I am told we are saved by grace through faith, and not works, (Ephesians 2: 7, 8)—I had hoped to make myself acceptable to God partly through my own good works, though we are told, that we are accepted through the beloved, (Ephesians 1: 6)—I had hoped to make my peace with God partly through my own obedience to his laws, though I am told, that peace is only to be had by faith, (Romans 5: 1). I had hoped to make myself a child of God by sanctification, though we are told that we are made children of God by faith in Christ Jesus, (Galatians 3: 26). I had thought that regeneration, the new birth, or new creature, consisted in sanctification, but now I know it consists in faith, (1 John 5: 1)—compare also these two passages together, (Galatians 6: 15 and Galatians 5: 6)—where you will find that the new creature is faith working by love: the Apostle adds these words, 'working by love', in order to distinguish a living faith from a dead one. I had thought that sanctification was the way to justification, but now I am assured that sanctification follows after justification: or, in other words, that we must first be justified by faith, before we can have any true sanctification by the Spirit. When we are justified, it is done freely, i.e. graciously, without any least merits of ours, and solely by the grace of God, through Jesus Christ, (Romans 3: 24–28) . . .

Dear Sir, will you attend to the following advice, it is very safe advice, be the state of your soul what it will. Pray to God to lead you into the knowledge of the truth as it is in Jesus. Beseech God to keep you in the truth, if you have received it; or if you are in error, to reveal it unto you. If you will do this heartily, and constantly, God will not suffer you to abide long in darkness, if indeed you are in darkness, (James, 1: 5).

NOTES / SOURCES

A Short Account of the Life and Conversion of the Revd John Berridge, London, 1794, pp. 5–8, 17

John Skinner   1721–1807

As well as publishing an *Ecclesiastical History of Scotland* (1788), John Skinner, an Episcopalian clergyman of Longside, Aberdeenshire, was noted principally as a songwriter. He corresponded with Robert Burns, and his *Songs and Poems* were edited and published some fifty years after his death. He was the father of the noted Bishop of Aberdeen and Primus of the Scottish Episcopal Church, also John Skinner (1744–1816).

Heavenly Worship Known on Earth

Of Solomon's own composition, we have, besides this Song, other two pieces
much to the same purpose, though written in something of a different manner.
Let these be applied to for elucidation where they can afford it, as we would apply
to Virgil's Georgics or Æneid for elucidating one of his Eclogues, or to Horace's
Satires or Epistles for the meaning of an Ode. And, if these shall not always
answer, we have, what I may literally call comtemporary, some compositions of
his royal father David, whose language and ideas we may reasonably conclude his
son and successor Solomon would readily adopt. Here, therefore, by the rules of
even modern criticism, we have some kind of auxiliary interpretation gained. But
we have more than all this; for, upon the footing of inspiration, and by the
consequent concession of God's authorship, I can call Moses also a contemporary
writer. And, when it is remembered how solemnly the Jewish people in general
were charged to read and observe the law of Moses, and how careful the good
men among them were always so to do, we may warrantably believe the wise
Solomon would be no stranger either to Moses' doctrine or to his words,
especially such words as were of importance to convey any mysterious or
emblematical meaning. The same is to be said of all the writers that came after
Solomon. They were all confined, by their employer, to the same matter, and
taught to use much the same words. So that, upon the whole, we can be at no loss
for proper assistance in searching and studying their several writings; as it would
be a singularly strange affair, if, in such a multitude of various pens, all conducted
by the same unerring hand, and principally pointed to the same grand design, we
should not meet with something in one, to clear up and remove any apparent
difficulty in another. It is certain, our blessed Saviour, and his apostles after him,
in all their argumentations, still looked back and referred to Moses and the
prophets. And though it be lamented by some, and wondered at by many, that
there are not more of their quotations and proofs, out of these writers, recorded,
which it may be thought would have made every thing plain, and silenced all
controversy, we now see, and every humble christian will admire, the gracious
intention of this procedure, both to prevent the inconvenient bulk of our
revelation code, and to awaken our curiosity, if such matters deserve our
curiosity, to the diligent observance of that general precept, 'Search the
scriptures.' The *scriptures* recommended at this time, and by the author of this
precept, were only that ancient collection I am speaking of, in which, we are
undoubtedly sure, the poem under consideration always stood as a part, and
consequently is entitled, along with the rest, to the *search*, the *investigation* here
enjoined. The enjoiner makes no distinctive exception, and gives no preferable
direction to one part of the received collection more than to another; as well
knowing that they all pointed to the same view, and all uniformly concurred,
according to their several modes, in the one gracious work of exhibiting to the
studious *searchers* the consolatory prospect of 'eternal life, by their joint testifying
of Jesus.' And, though we meet with no quotation formally adduced out of this
mysterious part of what was included in the general injunction, yet from some of
the other parts we have a sufficient number recorded, to be both a direction and a
key to us. Our Saviour from his own mouth, and his apostles in their narrations,

have applied to him many passages out of the Old Testament, which at first sight seemed to carry no such application, as every christian must have observed, and I hope observed it with delight. And, if one or two passages in a song or psalm, or prophecy, do once appear to belong, and in a peculiar manner to Him, there is neither difficulty nor impropriety in carrying the pleasing idea through the whole; as it will not be thought altogether decent, nor found very consistent, to be jumbling the transactions of this world and the mysteries of his love and wisdom together, in one continued thread of discourse. If after all there shall still remain in any or all of these sacred publications, and in this Song among the rest, any obscurity or unfathomable depth, about which, after all our attention and diligent examination, we cannot attain to full satisfaction, let us trust the discovery of such hidden beauties, as beauties we are sure they are, to that happy state, with the prospect of which the apostle thus comforted himself—'-Now we see through a glass, darkly, but then face to face; now I know in part, but then shall I know, even as also I am known.' Till which time, let us gratefully adore where we do know, and reverently admire where we do not.

NOTES / SOURCES

John Skinner, 'The Song of Solomon', in *The Theological Works of the late Revd. John Skinner*, Vol. II, Aberdeen, 1809, pp. 143–6

Christopher Smart   1722–1770

Often referred to as 'poor Kit Smart', his writings and publications ran to nearly one thousand pages and, whilst a student, he won five prizes for poetry writing at Cambridge University. Christopher Smart published a number of works in his lifetime including a prose version of *Horace* (1756), *A Song to David* (1763), a libretto for the Oratorio *Hannah* (1764) and metrical versions of *Phaedrus* and of the Psalms (1765). He was 'twice immured in a mad house'.

The Nativity of our Lord and Saviour Jesus Christ

Where is the stupendous stranger?
 Swains of Solyma, advise,
Lead me to my Master's manger
 Show me where my Saviour lies.

O most Mighty! O most Holy!
 Far beyond the seraph's thought
Art thou then so mean and lowly,
 As unheeded prophets taught?

O the magnitude of meekness!
 Worth from worth immortal sprung;
O the strength of infant weakness,
 If eternal is so young! . . .

Nature's decorations glisten
  Far above their usual trim;
Birds on box and laurel listen
  As so near the cherubs hymn.

Boreas now no longer winters
  On the desolated coast;
Oaks no more are riven in splinters
  By the whirlwind and his host.

Spinks and ouzels sing sublimely
  'We too have a saviour born';
Whiter blossoms burst untimely
  On the blest Mosaic thorn.

God all-bounteous, all creative,
  Whom no ills from good dissuade,
Is incarnate and a native
  Of the very world he made.

NOTES / SOURCES

Christopher Smart, 'The Nativity of Our Lord', in *The Poetical Works of Christopher Smart* Vol. II, Oxford, 1983, pp. 88–9

Henry Venn   1725–1797

Henry Venn was an Evangelical Divine noted for his piety. Whilst Vicar of Huddersfield (1759–1771), he wrote *The Complete Duty of Man* (1763) as a counterpoint to *The Whole Duty of Man* (1657). Although he was forced to retire through ill health, he became Vicar of Yelling, Cambridgeshire, where he influenced Charles Simeon. He is also noted because his son, John Venn (1759–1813), was a member of the Clapham Sect and a Founder of the Church Missionary Society, and his grandson, Henry Venn (1796–1873), was a long serving secretary to CMS who secured the appointment of the first African Anglican Bishop in 1864.

The Source of Christian Happiness

The first source then of happiness peculiar to the faithful in Christ Jesus, is the excellent knowledge they have attained. God the Father in all his adorable perfections, in the works he has made, and in the word he has caused to be written, in the redemption he has provided, and in the blessings he has promised:—God the Son in his original glory, and marvellous humiliation, in all the parts and most benevolent purposes of his mediation:—God the Holy Ghost in all his influences, gifts, and graces:—with the realities of the invisible, eternal world,—constitute the pleasing subjects of meditation to the true believer. Nominal christians, it is true, hear of all these subjects, perhaps profess constantly to believe in them; but they can neither find time to take any exact survey of them, nor to ponder them in their hearts; therefore 'seeing they see, and do not perceive, and hearing they hear, and do not understand.' The knowledge of the things of God, on the contrary, which real believers possess, is lively, penetrating, and of course delightful.

No one can question the pleasures of the understanding, since thousands toil for no other reward. In the eyes of all the votaries of science, the discovery of truth has the most bewitching charms, even though the truth only relates to something in this perishing world, and is without any power to produce the dispositions essential to peace of mind. Is such knowledge pleasant?—How much more then, the discovery of truths, which, besides their novelty, have a grandeur capable of engaging the whole mind, and filling it with admiration! This grandeur is no sooner apprehended than the truths of God necessarily become a source of delight. Before, they were either despised or suspected, or blindly assented to from the force of education; now they act like themselves—they inspire new resolutions, they kindle ardent desires, they excite abundant hope: in a word, by their spiritual knowledge believers are brought into a new and glorious world, where objects interesting beyond measure, and tending to their honour and exaltation, surround them.

It is indeed most worthy of observation, that the very same language which is used to denote the joyful change from night to day, is chosen by the Holy Ghost to express the change made in the minds of believers by the knowledge they are taught of God. Of them it is said, in contradistinction to their condition by nature: 'Ye were sometimes darkness, but now are ye light in the Lord.' Ephes. v. 8. 'For God, who commanded the light to shine out of darkness, hath shined in our hearts, to give us the light of the knowledge of the glory of God in the face of Jesus Christ,' 2 Cor. iv. 6.

This pleasure, which true believers enjoy from their first acquaintance with divine truths, increases as they advance. There is a very sensible progress in divine, no less than in human science: first a faint or confused view of the truths of God, then a clear perception of their matchless excellence, and various usefulness; first a dependence upon them, mixed with hesitation and fear, afterwards a full assurance of understanding and hope, a comprehending the breadth and length and height and depth of what before was very superficially known. Such a progress is inseparable from perseverance in the faith of Christ, and a diligent use of the word of God and of prayer, and it never fails to prove a spring of fresh and increasing delight.

Further: This knowledge proves in a peculiar manner pleasant to those who possess it, from the solid benefits which it constantly confers. For whilst all other subjects, which employ the minds of men, leave them after their highest attainments painfully sensible how little there is in them to satisfy their wants, to subdue their passions, to guard against various evils, or to support them, much less to profit them, when they leave the present scene:—Believers experience in their knowledge, contentment in every condition, a preservative from the force of unruly passions, a shield against the assaults of their worst enemies. By this they are inspired with a supernatural firmness of mind, by this cheered in the hour of distress, still sure to find its immense value most, when they depart out of this mortal life. (1)

Pray for Divine Knowledge

Pray therefore for divine knowledge to correct your depraved apprehensions, and to remove your grossness and unbelief of heart. Then you will perceive that christians are not more distinguished by purity of practice, than by their superior pleasures: then you will understand (contrary to the low thoughts entertained of the christian's choice, contrary to the impious prejudices abounding every where against it,) that among all the objects of sense the eye never saw any thing so grand and beautiful, the ear never heard any thing so delightful and advantageous; amongst all the branches of science, the thoughts of man did never comprehend any thing so completely adapted to bless the whole soul, 'as the things which God hath prepared for them that love him,'—even 'before the sons of men:' which things are given to them on this side the grave, as a pledge of what they shall possess in the perfection of glory to all eternity. (2)

Go No More About Miserably

Finally, receive instruction, ye decent self-justifying professors of religion. Go no more about miserably to glean some grains of satisfaction from a good opinion of yourselves, nor labour to walk in the sparks of comfort which can be kindled from the works which you perform, and the principles from which they proceed. No longer tread the tiresome round of duties as a penance enjoined of God to escape damnation, and to gain his favour. Uncomfortable, senseless service! To such serious, but grievously mistaken souls, God thus speaks in his word:—'-Wherefore do ye spend money for that which is not bread, and your labour for that which satisfieth not? Hearken diligently unto me, and eat ye that which is good, and let your soul delight itself in fatness; for I will give you the sure mercies of David,' that is, Christ. 'Behold I have given him for a witness' (of my free grace and love) 'to the people, a leader and commander to the people.' Make him the Alpha and the Omega, the first and the last, the beginning and the end of all your religion, and great will be your peace. You shall delight yourselves in the Lord, and he shall give you your heart's desire: then shall you have cause to say, with all that are called to be one body in Christ, what Moses in triumph spoke of the church of God in old time: 'What nation is there so great, who hath God so nigh unto them as the Lord our God is in all things that we call upon him for? Happy art thou, O Israel, who is like unto thee, O people saved by the Lord? (3)

For a Spirit of Prayer

Most merciful and gracious God, who hast promised to fulfil the desire of them that fear thee, and to give to every one that asketh of thee; who, for our encouragement to come boldly to the throne of grace, hast given thy Son to be a merciful and faithful High Priest; draw us, we beseech thee, by thy Holy Spirit, to the devout exercise of prayer. Convince us deeply of our guilt and weakness, of our blindness and depravity, that so with great earnestness and constancy we may cry unto thee, the God of our life and of our strength, to enable us to perform every christian duty, to fill us with all knowledge and with all goodness.

Let not our prayer be a mere service of the lips, or be offered up only to pacify conscience. May it be the hunger and thirst of our souls after thyself, and after all those spiritual blessings, without which we must perish for ever. Create and maintain in us, O God! a sensibility of the infinite worth of spiritual blessings, and a dread of spiritual evils, that we may pray always, and not faint. Let our wants be so pressing as to force us to pray. May we understand that thy ear hearkens to the most stammering tongue, and to the groaning of all that bewail their captivity to sin. And that we may never be at a loss for matter of supplication, confession, and thanksgiving, teach us to observe narrowly the various workings of our evil nature, to know our peculiar duties and temptations, and to remember the daily mercies of our God to us sinners.

And as thou knowest the great corruption of our hearts; how apt we are, from the practice of the world and the suggestions of Satan, lightly to esteem the all-important duty of prayer; O Lord, impress with power upon our hearts the example of all thy honoured and glorified saints, and the practice of thy dear Son our only Saviour in the days of his flesh. Let their assiduity and earnestness in prayer make us always ashamed and self-condemned for any backwardness we feel to the exercise of this duty. Give us an understanding to know that the prayer of faith is the only appointed means of obtaining the blessings which enrich the soul; the only instrument of preserving the connection of all the graces of the divine life; and that no higher affront can be offered to thy name than to live without prayer.

Do thou, O God, who requirest men to come before thee with such dispositions as shall ascribe to thee the honour due to thy most holy name, prepare our hearts to pray, with a determined opposition to the whole body of sin, with a steadfast purpose to cast away all our transgressions, and to have respect to all thy commandments. Convince us, O Lord, that if we regard iniquity in our heart, thou wilt not hear us; but if we call upon thee in truth, thou wilt hear us, and bless us in our deed. (4)

Attaining Divine Knowledge

To Mr. Thomas Atkinson

Huddersfield, Sept. 6, 1763.

My Dear Friend,

Blessed be the God and Father of our Lord Jesus Christ, for His great mercy in opening your eyes, and undeceiving your foolish heart, which, through its natural pride, was darkened—darkened in the midst of religious duties and the profession of Christianity! Great is the joy I feel on your account: and, as an older traveller in the same blessed path in which you are now walking, I will give you some council, praying our gracious God to command His blessing on it.

The first thing I would press upon you is, to beg of God more light. There is not a more false maxim than this, though common in almost every mouth, that 'men know enough, if they would but practise better.' God says, on the contrary, 'My people are destroyed for lack of knowledge.' And as, at first, men live in sin, easy and well pleased, because they know not what they do, so, after they are alive and awake, they do little for God, or gain little victory over sin, through the ignorance that is in them. They have no comfort, no establishment, no certainty that they are in the right path, even when they are going to God, because the eyes of their understanding are so little enlightened to discern the things that make for their peace. Do you therefore, my dear Thomas, in all your prayers, call much upon God for Divine teaching. Insist much upon the very faint, dim perception you have of the things you already know. Tell God how little you see of the evil of sin; how far you still are from feeling yourself always that corrupt, selfish creature, His word declares you indeed are. Tell the Saviour of that which was lost—what poor, low, unaffecting views you have of His work of obedience, though He was God manifest in the flesh;—how seldom you can feel your heart happy in the persuasion that your sins were purged away by Himself, and that He now sitteth at the right hand of the Father till your enemies become His footstool, though all Scripture is written to assure you and every believer that this is the very truth. Tell Him how little you know of the excellency, strength, and unconquerableness of the Divine promises. By persevering in such confessions, and asking of the Lord such illumination, you will gradually be filled with all knowledge, and be made wise unto salvation; especially if you make request, as you are always to do, for increasing light, only that you may glorify God in your life and conversation, as you are bound to do. I have one thing only to add more, which is, that you remember, if you are either impatient, or cast down under a sight of your great ignorance in spiritual things, the cause is pride and unbelief of heart: for why should we be impatient for *instant* deliverance from our ignorance, when we deserve most righteously to be left in darkness for evermore? or why should we be cast down in the view of our ignorance, when Christ promises that all who follow Him shall not *abide* in darkness, but have the light of life abiding in them?

I had purposed giving you more directions for your comfortable walking with God; but I shall reserve these for some other epistle; intending, God willing, to keep up a correspondence with you, as you really desire to know God, and be happy in Him. From your sincere and affectionate friend and servant in Christ Jesus,

H. Venn. (5)

NOTES / SOURCES

1. Henry Venn, *The Complete Duty of Man, or A system of Doctrine and Practical Christianity*, London, 1841, pp. 320–1
2. Ibid., p. 329
3. Ibid., pp. 347–8
4. Ibid., pp. 379–80
5. *The Letters of Henry Venn*, London, 1836, pp. 106–8

John Newton   1725–1807

His early years were marked by his life at sea, following the example of his father who was a shipmaster. Even after his conversion in 1748 he continued to be a slave trader, but in later years he assisted William Wilberforce (q.v.) in his campaign against slavery. Living in Liverpool (1755–1764) where he was tide surveyor, he was influenced by

George Whitefield. Despite being drawn to Nonconformist ministry, he was ordained into the Church of England, having been offered the curacy of Olney. It was here that he collaborated with William Cowper (q.v.) to publish the *Olney Hymns* (1779), one of the most influential collections of the eighteenth century.

The Influence of Faith

Faith, then, in its practical exercise, has for its object the whole word of God, and forms its estimate of all things with which the soul is at present concerned according to the standard of Scripture. Like Moses, it endures, as seeing him who is invisible. When our Lord was upon earth, and conversed with his disciples, their eyes and hearts were fixed upon him. In danger he was their defender; their guide when in perplexity; and to him they looked for the solution of all their doubts, and the supply of all their wants. He is now withdrawn from our eyes; but faith sets him still before us, for the same purposes, and, according to its degree, with the same effects, as if we actually saw him. His spiritual presence, apprehended by faith, is a restraint from evil, an encouragement to every service, and affords a present refuge and help in every time of trouble. To this is owing the delight a believer takes in ordinances, because there he meets his Lord; and to this likewise it is owing, that his religion is not confined to public occasions; but he is the same person in secret as he appears to be in the public assembly; for he worships him who sees in secret; and dares appeal to his all-seeing eye for the sincerity of his desires and intentions. By faith he is enabled to use prosperity with moderation; and knows and feels, that what the world calls good is of small value, unless it is accompanied with the presence and blessings of him whom his soul loveth. And his faith upholds him under all trials, by assuring him, that every dispensation is under the direction of his Lord; that chastisements are a token of his love; that the season, measure, and continuance of his sufferings, are appointed by infinite wisdom, and designed to work for his everlasting good; and that grace and strength shall be afforded him, according to his day. Thus, his heart being fixed, trusting in the Lord, to whom he has committed all his concerns, and knowing that his best interests are safe, he is not greatly afraid of evil tidings, but enjoys a stable peace in the midst of a changing world. For, though he cannot tell what a day may bring forth, he believes that he who has invited and enabled him to cast all his cares upon him, will suffer nothing to befall him but what shall be made subservient to his chief desires, the glory of God in the sanctification and final salvation of his soul. And if, through the weakness of his flesh, he is liable to be startled by the first impression of a sharp and sudden trial, he quickly flees to his strong refuge, remembers it is the Lord's doing, resigns himself to his will, and patiently expects a happy issue.

By the same principle of faith, a believer's conduct is regulated towards his fellow-creatures; and in the discharge of the several duties and relations of life, his great aim is to please God, and to let his light shine in the world. He believes and feels his own weakness and unworthiness, and lives upon the grace and pardoning love of his Lord. This gives him *an* habitual tenderness and gentleness of spirit. Humbled under a sense of much forgiveness to himself, he finds it easy to forgive others, if he has aught against any. A due sense of what he is in the sight of the Lord, preserves him from giving way to anger, positiveness, and resentment; he is not easily provoked, but is 'swift to hear, 'slow to speak, slow to wrath;' and if offended, easy to be entreated, and disposed, not only to yield to a reconciliation, but to seek it. As Jesus is his life, and righteousness, and strength, so he is his pattern. By faith he contemplates and studies this great exemplar of philanthropy. With a holy ambition he treads in the footsteps of his Lord and Master, and learns of him to be meek and lowly, to requite injuries with kindness, and to overcome evil with good. From the same views, by faith he derives a benevolent spirit, and, according to his sphere and ability, he endeavours to promote the welfare of all around him. The law of love being thus written in his heart, and his soul set at liberty from the low and narrow dictates of a selfish spirit, his language will be truth, and his dealings equity. His promise may be depended on, without the interposition of oath, bond, or witness; and the feelings of his own heart under the direction of an enlightened conscience, and the precepts of Scripture, prompt him 'to do unto others as he would desire they, in the like circumstances, should do unto him.' If he is a master, he is gentle and compassionate; if a servant, he is faithful and obedient; for in either relation he acts by faith, under the eye of his Master in heaven. If he is a trader, he neither dares nor wishes to take advantage either of the ignorance or the necessities of those with whom he deals. And the same principle of love influences his whole conversation. A sense of his own infirmities makes him candid to those of others: he will not readily believe reports to their prejudice, without sufficient proof; and even then, he will not repeat them, unless he is lawfully called to it. He believes that the precept, 'Speak evil of no man,' is founded upon the same authority with those which forbid committing adultery or murder; and therefore he 'keeps his tongue as with a 'bridle.' (1)

Amazing Grace

Amazing grace! how sweet the sound
  That saved a wretch like me!
I once was lost, but now am found,
  Was blind, but now I see.

'Twas grace that taught my heart to fear,
  And grace my fears relieved;
How precious did that grace appear,
  The hour I first believed!

Through many dangers, toils and snares,
  I have already come;
'Tis grace has brought me safe thus far,
  And grace will lead me home.

The Lord has promised good to me,
  His word my hope secures;
He will my Shield and Portion be,
  As long as life endures.

Yes, when this flesh and heart shall fail,
    And mortal life shall cease;
I shall possess within the veil,
    A life of joy and peace.

There, joys unseen by mortal eyes,
    Or reason's feeble ray,
In ever-blooming prospects rise,
    Unconscious of decay.

Then now, on faith's sublimest wing,
    Let ardent wishes rise,
To those bright scenes, where pleasures spring
    Immortal in the skies. (2)

The Name of Jesus

How sweet the name of Jesus sounds
    In a believer's ear!
It soothes his sorrows, heals his wounds,
    And drives away his fear.

It makes the wounded spirit whole,
    And calms the troubled breast;
'Tis manna to the hungry soul,
    And to the weary, rest.

Dear name! the rock on which I build,
    My shield and hiding-place;
My never-failing treasury, filled
    With boundless stores of grace.

By thee my prayers acceptance gain,
    Although with sin defiled;
Satan accuses me in vain,
    And I am owned a child.

Jesus, my Shepherd, Husband, Friend,
    My Prophet, Priest, and King,
My Lord, my Life, my Way, my End,
    Accept the praise I bring.

Weak is the effort of my heart,
    And cold my warmest thought;
But when I see thee as thou art,
    I'll praise thee as I ought.

Till then, I would thy love proclaim
    With every fleeting breath;
And may the music of thy name
    Refresh my soul in death! (3)

Zion, City of Our God

ISA. XXXIII. 20, 21.

Glorious things of thee are spoken,
   Zion, city of our God!
He, whose word cannot be broken,
   Formed thee for his own abode:
On the Rock of Ages founded,
   What can shake thy sure repose?
With salvation's wall surrounded,
   Thou may'st smile at all thy foes.

See, the streams of living waters,
   Springing from eternal love,
Well supply thy sons and daughters,
   And all fears of want remove:
Who can faint while such a river
   Ever flows their thirst t'assuage?
Grace, which like the Lord, the giver,
   Never fails from age to age.

Round each habitation hovering,
   See the cloud and fire appear,
For a glory and a covering,
   Showing that the Lord is near.
Thus deriving from their banner
   Light by night, and shade by day,
Safe they feed upon the manna
   Which he gives them when they pray.

Blest inhabitants of Zion,
   Washed in the Redeemer's blood!
Jesus, whom their souls rely on,
   Makes them kings and priests to God.
'Tis his love his people raises
   Over self to reign as kings,
And as priests, his solemn praises
   Each for a thank-offering brings.

Saviour, if of Zion's city
   I through grace a member am,
Let the world deride or pity,
   I will glory in thy name.
Fading is the worldling's pleasure,
   All his boasted pomp and show;
Solid joys and lasting treasure
   None but Zion's children know. (4)

Looking at the Cross

In evil long I took delight,
    Unawed by shame or fear,
Till a new object struck my sight,
    And stopped my wild career.
I saw one hanging on a tree,
    In agonies and blood,
Who fixed his languid eyes on me,
    As near his cross I stood.

Sure, never till my latest breath
    Can I forget that look;
It seemed to charge me with his death,
    Though not a word he spoke.
My conscience felt and owned the guilt,
    And plunged me in despair;
I saw my sins his blood had spilt,
    And helped to nail him there.

Alas! I knew not what I did:
    But now my tears are vain;
Where shall my trembling soul be hid?
    For I the Lord have slain.
A second look he gave, which said,
    'I freely all forgive;
This blood is for thy ransom paid,
    I die that thou mayst live.'

Thus while his death my sin displays
    In all its blackest hue;
Such is the mystery of grace,
    It seals my pardon too.
With pleasing grief and mournful joy
    My spirit now is filled,
That I should such a life destroy,
    Yet live by him I killed. (5)

NOTES / SOURCES

1. John Newton, in *The Works of The Revd. John Newton*, Vol. I, London, 1808, pp. 146–9
2. John Newton, *Olney Hymns* (1779), Chiswick, 1831, Bk.1 no. 46
3. Ibid., Bk.1 no. 57
4. Ibid., Bk.1 no. 60
5. Ibid., Bk.2 no. 57

William Jones   1726–1800

Often referred to as 'Jones of Nayland' by dint of becoming perpetual Curate of
Nayland, Suffolk (1777), like his friend George Horne (q.v.) who was his bishop for a
short time, he was a High Churchman. He is best known for *The Catholic Doctrine of the
Trinity* (1756), where he attempted to trace the doctrine of the Trinity to its scriptural
roots.

The Pleasures of Heavenly Mindedness

As the affections of man are active and restless in the nature, they must have their
objects; and if these objects are not the things above, they will be the things below;
and if these things are in their nature unsatisfactory, such an attachment can
terminate in nothing but disappointment. The wisest of mankind, who had
experienced all the heights of worldly felicity, did long ago pass sentence of
condemnation upon the things of the world, as the instruments of vanity and
vexation; yet few can find in their hearts to take his word, 'till they have made
their unsuccessful experiments, and are convinced by the issue of them. It is a
truth, which some happily discover in due time, and which all will see at last, that
to expect substantial happiness from the things of this earth, is as impertinent as
to seek the living among the dead. That no real good can be found here, is evident
from this one consideration, that whatsoever we find we cannot keep possession
of it. Suppose the things never so good in themselves, yet such are the
conditions on which we hold them, that they cannot confer upon us the
happiness we are looking for. If the cup of life were to be mixed up at the will of
the most skilful epicure, the certainty of death, and the uncertainty of the time,
are grievances which can never be excluded, and they will never fail to embitter
the whole. For our life is but a vapour, a thing of no substance, and liable to be
dissipated by the next rough blast. If a man is unmindful of this, he is in a state
of stupefactions; and stupefaction is not enjoyment: if it lies upon his mind, it
will as surely have its effect, as the sound of a passing bell, near at hand, will
spoil a concert of music.

  Besides this, the objects so eagerly sought after are but shadows and delusions;
which borrow their greatest value from the error of our imaginations. All the
things we behold at present are but the lowest works of our Almighty Creator,
and are to endure but for a limited time. The world itself, as well as they that
inhabit it, must pass away, as a garment which is worn out, and must be changed
for that which is eternal. This being the case, there is something in the soul of
men which thirst after greater things than are here to be met with. There is in
those, who do not extinguish it, an appetite, which will not be satisfied or put off
with trifles. When a man has tried the world, and found it full of labour and
vanity and disappointment, what can he think? If he thinks at all, he must
conclude, either that God made him to disappoint him, or that there are other
better objects on which he ought to set his affections: and if there are such
objects, then there is in man an appetite toward them; for where there is not
appetite, there can be no enjoyment. But earthly things, when they are abused,
have this unhappy effect that they spoil the taste of and therefore it is said, that if

any man *love the world*, the love of the Father is not in him. It is wisely represented to us in the parable, that they whose affections were engaged by worldly occupations, partook not of that heavenly feast, which was provided for them: but the *halt*, the *lame*, and the *blind*, being disengaged from the world, were ready for the enjoyment of superior pleasures. And every wise man will endeavour to keep himself in the state of disengagement: he will be thankful to God for any of those losses of disappointments, which serve to remove the mists that are before the eyes of great men, and busy men, and men of pleasure. So long as his mind hath the use of its sight, he will consider everything in this life under that relation which it bears to eternity: and this will at once lessen the value of such things as have their end as well as their beginning in this life. As often as he looks forward to eternity he will wish to secure himself a portion there; and with this view, he will attend to the methods proposed to him in divine Revelation. He will seek for such information, as shall not only improve his head but purify his heart: for the word of God cannot make us *wise unto salvation*, but as it makes us in the end partakers of it. He will consider his *actions*, as the only sure evidences of his *affections*: for all but idiots act upon such principles as they have, whether good or bad; and therefore the affections of all men are distinguished by their fruits. (1)

My House shall be called a House of Prayer

And now, my brethren, give me leave to inform you, that I have chosen this particular subject, because the season of Lent is at hand, and our case is particular. You all know it was my practice when I came first to this place, to have weekly prayers at the Church: but my congregation, which was always small, did at length fall away so, that I was discouraged from proceeding any further. This was the first accident I had ever met with of the kind since I entered into the ministry; which made it more grievous to me. However, I will not give up a good cause in despair; and that the fault may not lie upon myself, I have determined to speak my mind freely, having some encouragement to do so. You were slack in sending your children to be catechised; but when I spoke to you upon that subject in the Church, I found an immediate attention for the better; who knows, that what I shall now say may be attended with the like happy effect? At least, I am persuaded you will do me the justice to believe, that your benefit is the principle object I have in view. Therefore, let us consider the case fairly and impartially. I know the excuse you have to offer for not attending the prayers of the Church on Wednesdays and Fridays—you are *busy*, and have not *time*—and indeed, I must admit this excuse as sufficient with those whose employment or situation places them at a great distance from the Church, and whose families depend upon their daily labour: therefore I must argue the case more particularly with those who are *near the Church*. To them I answer, that the time of their attendance is *short*, not much more than half an hour twice in a week; and that this little portion of time cannot occasion any very great interruption in their affairs. Let them ask their own hearts seriously, whether they would not be prevailed upon to spare *twice* as much time, on any day in the week, upon motives of curiosity or vanity? And is the favour of God so light a matter? Will they always think, that a trifling visit, or an empty site, is rather to be sought than the pardon of their sins, and the blessing of heaven? Will they think so in the hour of death, or the day of judgement? If they dare not insist upon such excuses, then in the presence of God, why should they depend upon them now? (2)

A Letter to the Church of England

Man being composed of soul and body, all true religion has a part for both; a *sign visible*, and *spiritual grace invisible*: baptism, which as a washing with water is effectual to wash away sin, only as it is a washing with a spirit. In the sacrament of the Lord's Supper, bread is the sign; but it is the *Bread of Life* only as it is the Body of Christ, who gave it to us with this intention, that it should be *spirit* and *life* to us. If it had nothing *nutrative* why should it be expressed by *food*? But there are too many amongst us, who, professing themselves to be wise, and to see farther than others, take away from us all the inward and vital part, and leave us nothing but the husks of religion. All the rest, they say, is a deception, of which rational men see nothing. But I say, that if our religion be anything it is a communication, restored and kept up between the spirit of God and the spirit of men. If the gospel be true in its promises, something is *now* done, whereby man becomes possessed of that *eternal life* which he shall never lose: but the new scheme of formality takes all this away and renders it impossible. To talk of *life* and *spirit* to such men, is, in their estimation, to *cant*; but in ours it is to cast pearls before swine, who trample them under their feet. Spiritual things are real, though invisible. God is not seen; the soul of man is not seen; what acts upon it is not seen; therefore it is truly said of us, that we walk by *faith*, and not by *sight*; so that without faith we see nothing; we know nothing; we receive nothing; we are nothing; and the whole gospel is no better than a dream. But this *learning*, this *reason*, which, wisely admitting what it sees, loses all the benefits of Christianity. When we affirm that *spiritual* things are *real*, it may be added, that nothing else is so; the whole world, and all things therein, are but shadows of things eternal; and like a shadow shall pass away when they have answered a temporary purpose. (3)

NOTES / SOURCES

1. William Jones, 'Sermon 2: Set your affection on things above', in *The Theological, Philosophical and Miscellaneous Works of the Revd. William Jones*, Vol. V, London, 1801, pp. 21–4
2. William Jones, 'Sermon 13: My house shall be called the house of prayer' in ibid., pp. 233–5
3. William Jones, 'A letter to the Church of England' in ibid., Vol. XII, pp. 316–17

Samuel Seabury   1729–1796

Following theological studies at Yale University, Samuel Seabury was ordained in England by the Bishop of Lincoln in 1753 before returning to New Brunswick and later New York. Throughout the War of Independence he remained loyal to the British Government but following Independence his inability to take the Oath of Allegiance compelled him to seek episcopal orders from Scotland, which resulted in his consecration at Aberdeen in 1784. The first Bishop of the Episcopal Church in the USA, his abilities in both administration and liturgy have had a lasting impact on the Episcopal Church in America.

An Earnest Persuasive to Frequent Communion

The general practice in this country is to have monthly Communions, and I bless God the Holy Ordinance is so often administered. Yet when I consider its importance, both on account of the positive command of Christ and of the many and great benefits we receive from it, I cannot but regret that it does not make a part of every Sunday's solemnity. That it was the principal part of the daily worship of the primitive Christians all the early accounts inform us. And it seems probable from the Acts of the Apostles that the Christians came together in their religious meetings chiefly for its celebration. (*Acts* 2:42, 46; 20:7.) And the ancient writers generally interpret the petition in our Lord's prayer, 'Give us this day,' or day by day, 'our daily bread,' of the spiritual food in the Holy Eucharist. Why daily nourishment should not be as necessary to our souls as to our bodies no good reason can be given.

If the Holy Communion was steadily administered whenever there is an Epistle and Gospel appointed, which seems to have been the original intention—or was it on every Sunday—I cannot help thinking that it would revive the esteem and reverence Christians once had for it, and would show its good effects in their lives and conversations. I hope the time will come when this pious and Christian practice may be renewed. And whenever it shall please God to inspire the hearts of the Communicants of any congregation with a wish to have it renewed, I flatter myself they will find a ready disposition in their minister to forward their pious desire.

In the meantime, let me beseech you to make good use of the opportunities you have; and let nothing but real necessity keep you from the heavenly banquet when you have it in your power to partake of it.

May the consideration of this subject have its proper effect upon every one of you! And the God of peace be with you—'make you perfect in every good work to do His will' (*Heb.* 13:21)—keep you in the unity of His Church, and in the bond of peace and in all righteousness of life—guide you by His Spirit through this world, and receive you to glory through Jesus Christ our Lord. Amen.
All glory to God. (1)

The Eucharist

The Eucharist is not only a memorial of the passion and death of Christ for the sin of the world, but also of that offering of himself—his natural body and blood—which, under the representation of bread and wine, he made to God at the institution of the holy ordinance. In this respect it exactly fulfills its type, the ordinance of the Jewish Passover. For that was not only a memorial of the deliverance of the Israelites from the bondage of Egypt, in the night when God slew the Egyptian firstborn, but also a memorial of the original Passover in Egypt, under the protection of the blood of which put upon the posts of their doors, they remained in safety when the firstborn of the Egyptians were slain.

Hence, also, it appears that the Eucharist is a memorial made not so much before man as before the Almighty Father. For before whom should the memorial of the offering and death of Christ be made but before him to whom the offering and death of Christ was a sacrifice for sin? If the offering was made to God, as has been proved, the memorial of that offering must also be made before God or it ceases to be a proper memorial. For a memorial is a monument or sensible sign intended to bring some event to remembrance: And the Eucharist being the memorial of Christ's offering himself to God, and of his passion and death for sin, it follows that the memorial of his offering and death must be made before God, that by it their merit and efficacy may be pleaded with him, for the remission of sin and for all other benefits and blessings which his passion and death procure for us.

In this respect, too, the Eucharist fulfills its type, the Jewish Passover. The memorial made by that was a memorial made before God by the people of Israel, as appears from their being commanded to *eat it before the Lord*; for if it were eaten or celebrated before the Lord then the memorial made by it was made before the Lord.

It appears, therefore, that the Eucharist is not only a sacrament in which, under the symbols of bread and wine, according to the institution of Christ, the faithful truly and spiritually receive the body and blood of Christ, but also a true and proper sacrifice commemorative of the original sacrifice and death of Christ for our deliverance from sin and death—a memorial made before God to put him in mind; that is, to plead with him the meritorious sacrifice and death of his dear Son, for the forgiveness of our sins, for the sanctification of his church, for a happy resurrection from death, and a glorious immortality with Christ in heaven.

From this account, the Priesthood of the Christian Church evidently appears. As a Priest, Christ offered himself a sacrifice to God in the mystery of the Eucharist; that is, under the symbols of bread and wine; and he commanded his apostles to do as he had done. If his offering were a sacrifice, theirs was also. His sacrifice was original, theirs commemorative. His was meritorious through his merit who offered it; theirs drew all its merit from the relation it had to his sacrifice and appointment. His, from the excellency of its own nature, was a true and sufficient propitiation for the sins of the whole world; theirs procures remission of sins only through the reference it has to his atonement.

When Christ commanded his apostles to celebrate the Holy Eucharist in remembrance of him, he, with the command, gave them power to do so; that is, he communicated his own priesthood to them in such measure and degree as he saw necessary for his church—to qualify them to be his representatives—to offer the Christian sacrifice of bread and wine as a memorial before God the Father of his offering himself once for all; of his passion and of his death—to render the Almighty propitious to us for his sake; and as a means of obtaining, through faith in him, all the blessings and benefits of his redemption.

And, as the Laity are permitted to partake of this sacrifice—the most holy thing—the shewbread, or bread of the presence of the Christian Church—which, under the law, was not lawful for any to eat but only for the priests; so it is evident that such portion of Christ's priesthood is given to them as qualifies them to join in offering the Christian sacrifice and to partake of it with the priests of the church. And, in this sense I take it, the whole body of Christians are called a holy priesthood, a royal priesthood—are said to be made not only *kings*, to reign with Christ in glory hereafter, but *priests* unto God. (It will by no means follow from hence that private Christians have a right or power to consecrate the Eucharist:

that right or power being by the institution itself confined to the apostles and their successors, and those empowered by them—no others being present at the time but the apostles.)

From this view of the matter we may see in what sense the consecrated, or eucharistized, bread and wine are the body and blood of Christ. They are so sacramentally or by representation—changed in their qualities, not in their substance. They continue bread and wine in their nature; they become the body and blood of Christ in signification and mystery—bread and wine to our senses; the body and blood of Christ to our understanding and faith—bread and wine in themselves; the life giving body and blood of Christ in power and virtue; that is, by the appointment of Christ and through the operation of the Holy Ghost—and the faithful receive the efficacy of Christ's sacrifice and death to all spiritual intents and purposes.

There is, therefore, in this holy institution, no ground for the errors of transubstantiation, consubstantiation, or the bodily presence of Christ with which the Church of Rome, Luther, and Calvin have deceived, beguiled, and perplexed the church. The bread and wine are, in their nature, still bread and wine—They are not transubstantiated into the natural body and blood of Christ as the Papists teach—The natural body and blood of Christ are not consubstantiated with them so as to make one substance as the Lutherans teach—Nor are the natural body and blood of Christ infused into them nor hovering over them so as to be confusedly received with them as Calvin and his followers seem to teach; for they are far from being intelligible on the subject. The natural body and blood of Christ are in heaven, in glory and exaltation—We receive them not in the communion in any sense. The bread and wine are his body and blood sacramentally and by representation. And, as it is an established maxim that all who, under the law, did eat of a sacrifice with those qualifications which the sacrifice required, were partakers of its benefits; so all who, under the gospel, eat of the Christian sacrifice of bread and wine with those qualifications which the holy solemnity requires are made partakers of all the benefits and blessings of that sacrifice of his natural body and blood which Christ Jesus made, when, under the symbols of bread and wine, he offered them to God, a propitiation for the sin of the world. (2)

NOTES / SOURCES

1. Samuel Seabury, 'An Earnest Persuasive to Frequent Communion' (1789), in J. Robert Wright (ed.), *Prayer Book Spirituality*, New York, 1989, pp. 324–5
2. Samuel Seabury, 'Discourses on Several Subjects', Vol. I (1793), in J. Robert Wright (ed.), *Prayer Book Spirituality*, New York, 1989, pp. 325–8

George Horne   1730–1792

George Horne became Bishop of Norwich following an illustrious academic career when he was President of Magdalen College, Oxford (1768–90), and held a number of ecclesiastical posts. Despite opposition, he empathized with Methodist piety and refused to ban John Wesley (q.v.) from preaching in his diocese. An able preacher, his commentary on the Psalms was published in 1771; his theological position was a blend of moderate High Church tradition.

The Trinity in Unity

Many apprehend the doctrine of the Trinity to be what is called a SPECULATIVE doctrine only, that is to say, a doctrine, concerning which men may think, and conjecture, and reason, and dispute, for their amusement, but of no effect or importance in a religious life. This is a considerable mistake in judgement; and to prove that it is so, let us only ask one question, What is the doctrine of most importance to man, in his religious concerns? Undoubtedly it is that of his redemption from sin and sorrow, from death and hell, to righteousness and joy, immortality and glory. But of such redemption what account do the Scriptures give us? By whom was the gracious scheme originally concerted, and afterwards carried into execution? Was it not by the three Persons of the ever blessed and adorable Trinity?

It was not an afterthought, a new design, formed upon the transgression and fall of our first parents. That event was foreseen, and provision made accordingly. For upon the very best authority we are informed, that Christ was 'the Lamb slain from the foundation of the world;' that is (for it cannot be otherwise understood), slain in effect; in the divine purpose and counsel. It is likewise said, that 'grace was given us in Christ Jesus, before the world began.' The words intimate, that previous to the creation of the world, something had passed in our favour above; that the plan of our future redemption was then laid; that some agreement, some covenant, relative to it, had been entered into; 'grace was given us,' not in our proper persons, for as yet we were not—we had no being—but in the person of him who was afterward to become our representative, our Saviour—'in Christ Jesus.' Now the plan must have been laid, the covenant entered into, by the parties who have since been graciously pleased to concern themselves in its execution. Who these are we cannot be ignorant. It was the Son of God who took our nature upon him, and in that nature made a full and sufficient oblation, satisfaction, and atonement, for the sins of the world. It was the Father who accepted such oblation, satisfaction, and atonement; and in consequence forgave those sins. It was the Holy Spirit who came forth from the Father and the Son, through the preaching of the word and the administration of the sacraments, by his enlightening, healing, and comforting grace, to apply to the hearts of men, for all the purposes of pardon, sanctification, and salvation, the merits and benefits of that oblation, satisfaction, and atonement.

Say no more, then, that the doctrine of the Trinity is a matter of curiosity and amusement only. Our religion is founded upon it. For what is Christianity but a manifestation of the three divine Persons, as engaged in the great work of man's redemption, begun, continued, and to be ended by them, in their several relations of Father, Son, and Holy Ghost, Creator, Redeemer, and Sanctifier, three Persons, one God? If there be no Son of God, where is our redemption? If there be no Holy Spirit, where is our sanctification? Without both, where is our salvation? And if these two Persons be any thing less than divine, why are we baptized equally in the name of the Father, and of the Son, and of the Holy Ghost? Let no man, therefore, deceive you: 'This is the TRUE GOD, and eternal life.'

And while you suffer no man to deceive you, do not, I beseech you, deceive yourselves. Benefits conferred require duties to be paid. Remember what the three divine Persons have done for you, and forget not what they expect that you should do in return. For how little will it avail you to believe aright concerning the Trinity, if you live so as to displease the Trinity?—You know and believe in the true God; you do well. But let not that which is an honour to you, be any encouragement to dishonour God; the knowledge of whom can only serve to increase your condemnation, if you live in the practice of pride and malice, envy and hatred, lust and intemperance, even as the Heathen who know him not. And though it be the faith of a Christian which distinguishes him from the rest of mankind, yet that faith, to profit him, must appear in the conduct of his life; as love to a friend is best witnessed by a readiness to do him service. It is true, the service is not the love, nor of equal value with it; yet the love that refuses the service will be accounted as nothing. 'The mystery of faith' is an invaluable treasure; but the vessel that contains it must be clean and undefiled: it must be 'holden in a pure conscience;' as the manna, that glorious symbol of the word of faith preached to us by the Gospel, was confined to the tabernacle, and preserved in a vessel of gold. A mind that is conformed to this world, and given up to its pleasures, though it repeats the creed without questioning a single article of it, will be abhorred in the sight of God, as a vessel unfit for the master's use, and unworthy, because unprepared, to stand in the most holy place. It is the great excellency of faith, that it can produce such a transformation in the life and manners, as no other principle has any power to do. But many are possessed of this truth, without applying it to their own advantage. Let them, however, bear in mind, that, without holiness no man shall see the Lord:' none of the world's dross or impurity will be suffered to continue in his sight. And in this he is no hard master, reaping where he had not sown, and requiring the fruit of good works, without giving us strength and ability to bring them forth. He has provided for us the precious blood of the Lamb, and offered to us the assistance of his Holy Spirit, that we may be enabled to serve that true and living God in whom we believe. If we are purged by HIM, we shall be clean; if he washes us, we shall be whiter than snow; and when the kingdom of God shall come, and his glory shall appear, we shall be prepared to behold his face in righteousness.

The sum of the whole matter, as St Paul has wonderfully expressed it in a single verse, is this—'Through Christ we have an access by one Spirit unto the Father' To the Father, with a due sense of this great honour and privilege, as sons of God, let us therefore address ourselves for pardon and admission to our heavenly inheritance: 'O God, the Father of heaven, have mercy upon us, miserable sinners!' But as we have no deserts of our own, no works of righteousness by which to claim his favour, and are entitled only through the sufferings and satisfaction of Christ, let us beseech HIM to intercede for us, and plead his merits with the Father: 'O God the Son, Redeemer of the world, have mercy upon us miserable sinners!' And since the benefits of his merits are applied, and our pardon sealed, and ourselves enabled to render an acceptable service, only by the operations and assistances of the Holy Spirit, let us implore HIS aid also: 'O God the Holy Ghost, proceeding from the Father and the Son, have mercy upon us miserable sinners!' Yet remembering, that, how various soever the œconomy may be, salvation is the one sole undivided end and work of all; therefore to ALL let us address our earnest prayers and invocations, as to the Great Power to whom we have consecrated ourselves and services: 'O holy, blessed, and glorious Trinity, three Persons, and one God, have mercy upon us miserable sinners!'

And thou, almighty and everlasting God, who has given unto us thy servants grace by the confession of a true faith to acknowledge the glory of the eternal Trinity, and in the power of the divine Majesty to worship the Unity; we beseech thee, that thou wouldst keep us steadfast in this faith, and evermore defend us from all adversities; who livest and reignest one God world without end.

To this one God, for the means of grace vouchsafed to us in this life, and for the hopes of glory in another, be ascribed, as is most due, all honour, majesty, and dominion, all praise and adoration, both now and for ever.

NOTES / SOURCES

George Horne, 'Discourse VII: The Trinity in Unity' (sermon preached in Canterbury Cathedral, Trinity Sunday, 1786), in *The Works of the Rt. Revd. George Horne*, Vol. IV, London, 1818, pp. 93–8

William Cowper   1731–1800

A barrister in the Middle Temple, William Cowper was offered a clerkship of the House of Lords by his cousin, also William Cowper, Clerk of the Parliaments (1763). Fearing opposition to his appointment, Cowper suffered one of the bouts of mental illness which were to scar his life and relationships. Retiring to Olney, he became a lay assistant to John Newton (q.v.), the renowned Evangelical curate there. Together they published *Olney Hymns* (1779) which included some of his finest hymns, which are still sung today.

Walking with God

Genesis 5:24

Oh! for a closer walk with GOD,
  A calm and heav'nly frame;
A light to shine upon the road
  That leads me to the Lamb!

Where is the blessedness I knew
  When first I saw the LORD?
Where is the soul-refreshing view
  Of JESUS, and his word?

What peaceful hours I once enjoy'd!
  How sweet their mem'ry still!
But they have left an aching void,
  The world can never fill.

Return, O holy Dove, return,
  Sweet messenger of rest;
I hate the sins that made thee mourn,
  And drove thee from my breast.

The dearest idol I have known,
    Whate'er that idol be;
Help me to tear it from thy throne,
    And worship only thee.

So shall my walk be close with GOD,
    Calm and serene my frame;
So purer light shall mark the road
    That leads me to the Lamb. (1)

Wisdom

Proverbs 8:22–31

Ere GOD had built the mountains,
    Or rais'd the fruitful hills;
Before he fill'd the fountains
    That feed the running rills;
In me, from everlasting,
    The wonderful I AM
Found pleasures never wasting,
    And Wisdom is my name.

When, like a tent to dwell in,
    He spread the skies abroad;
And swath'd about the swelling
    Of ocean's mighty flood;
He wrought by weight and measure,
    And I was with him then;
Myself the Father's pleasure,
    And mine, the sons of men.

Thus wisdom's words discover
    Thy glory and thy grace,
Thou everlasting lover
    Of our unworthy race!
Thy gracious eye survey'd us
    Ere stars were seen above;
In wisdom thou hast made us,
    And died for us in love.

And couldst thou be delighted
    With creatures such as we!
Who when we saw thee, slighted
    And nail'd thee to a tree?
Unfathomable wonder,
    And mystery divine!
The Voice that speaks in thunder,
    Says, 'Sinner I am thine!' (2)

God Moves in a Mysterious Way

GOD moves in a mysterious way,
   His wonders to perform;
He plants his footsteps in the sea,
   And rides upon the storm.

Deep in unfathomable mines
   Of never failing skill;
He treasures up his bright designs,
   And works his sovereign will.

Ye fearful saints fresh courage take,
   The clouds ye so much dread
Are big with mercy, and shall break
   In blessings on your head.

Judge not the LORD by feeble sense,
   But trust him for his grace;
Behind a frowning providence,
   He hides a smiling face.

His purposes will ripen fast,
   Unfolding ev'ry hour;
The bud may have a bitter taste,
   But sweet will be the flow'r.

Blind unbelief is sure to err,
   And scan his work in vain;
GOD is his own interpreter,
   And he will make it plain. (3)

Joy and Peace in Believing

Sometimes a light surprizes
   The Christian while he sings;
It is the LORD who rises
   With healing in his wings:
When comforts are declining,
   He grants the soul again
A season of clear shining
   To cheer it after rain.

In holy contemplation,
   We sweetly then pursue
The theme of GOD's salvation,
   And find it ever new:

Set free from present sorrow,
  We cheerfully can say,
E'en let th' unknown to-morrow,
  Bring with it what it may.

It can bring with it nothing
  But he will bear us thro';
Who gives the lilies clothing
  Will clothe his people too:
Beneath the spreading heavens,
  No creature but is fed;
And he who feeds the ravens,
  Will give his children bread.

Though vine, nor fig-tree neither,
  Their wonted fruit should bear,
Tho' all the fields should wither,
  Nor flocks, nor herds, be there:
Yet GOD the same abiding,
  His praise shall tune my voice;
For while in him confiding,
  I cannot but rejoice. (4)

NOTES / SOURCES

1. William Cowper, *Olney Hymns* (1779), Chiswick, 1831, Bk. 1, no. 3
2. William Cowper, ibid., Bk. 1, no. 52
3. William Cowper, ibid., Bk. 3, no. 15
4. William Cowper, ibid., Bk. 3, no. 58

Samuel Horsley   1733–1806

Samuel Horsley's interest in science is reflected in his membership and later Secretaryship of the Royal Society. In succession he was Bishop of St Davids (1788), Rochester (1793), and finally of St Asaph (1802–6). Over a seven year period (1783–90) he maintained a controversy with Joseph Priestly, the Presbyterian minister and scientist, over the impeccability and infallibility of Christ. As well as religious works, he also edited Sir Isaac Newton's works.

Three Extracts from a Christmas Sermon

We are assembled this day to commemorate our Lord's nativity. It is not as the birth-day of a prophet that this day is sanctified; but as the anniversary of that great event which had been announced by the whole succession of prophets from the beginning of the world, and in which the predictions concerning the manner of the Messiah's advent received their complete and literal accomplishment. In the predictions, as well as in the corresponding event, the circumstance of the miraculous conception makes so principal a part, that we shall not easily find subjects of meditation more suited either to the season or to the times than these two points,—the importance of this doctrine as an article of the Christian faith; and the sufficiency of the evidence by which the fact is supported.

. . . .

Thus you see the necessary connexion of the miraculous conception with the other articles of the Christian faith. The incarnation of the Divine Word, so roundly asserted by St John, and so clearly implied in innumerable passages of holy writ, in any other way had been impossible, and the Redeemer's atonement inadequate and ineffectual; insomuch, that had the extraordinary manner of our Lord's generation made no part of the evangelical narrative, the opinion might have been defended as a thing clearly implied in the evangelical doctrine.

On the other hand, it were not difficult to show that the miraculous conception, once admitted, naturally brings up after it the great doctrines of the atonement and the incarnation. The miraculous conception of our Lord evidently implies some higher purpose of his coming than the mere business of a teacher. The business of a teacher might have been performed by a mere man enlightened by the prophetic spirit; for whatever instruction men have the capacity to receive, a man might have been made the instrument to convey. Had teaching therefore been the sole purpose of our Saviour's coming, a mere man might have done the whole business; and the supernatural conception had been an unnecessary miracle. He therefore who came in this miraculous way came upon some higher business, to which a mere man was unequal: He came to be made a sin-offering for us, 'that we might be made the righteousness of God in him.'

. . . .

From what hath been said, you will easily perceive that the evidence of the fact of our Lord's miraculous conception is answerable to the great importance of the doctrine; and you will esteem it an objection of little weight, that the modern advocates of the Unitarian tenets cannot otherwise give a colour to their wretched cause than by denying the inspiration of the sacred historians, that they may seem to themselves at liberty to reject their testimony. You will remember, that the doctrines of the Christian revelation were not originally delivered in a system, but interwoven, in the history of our Saviour's life. To say, therefore, that the first preachers were not inspired in the composition of the narratives in which their doctrine is conveyed, is nearly the same thing as to deny their inspiration in general. You will perhaps think it incredible, that they who were assisted by the Divine Spirit when they preached should be deserted by that Spirit when they committed what they had preached to writing. You will think it improbable, that they who were endowed with the gift of discerning spirits should be endowed with no gift of discerning the truth of facts. You will recollect one instance upon record, in which St Peter detected a falsehood by the light of inspiration; and you will perhaps be inclined to think, that it could be of no less importance to the church that the apostles and evangelists should be enabled to detect falsehoods in the history of our Saviour's life than that St Peter should he enabled to detect Ananias's lie about the sale of his estate. You will think it unlikely, that they who were led by the Spirit into all truth should be permitted to lead the whole church for many ages into error,—that they should be permitted to leave behind them, as authentic memoirs of their Master's life, narratives compiled with little judgment or selection, from the stories of the day, from facts and fictions in promiscuous circulation. The credulity which swallows these contradictions, while it strains at mysteries, is not the faith which will remove mountains. The Ebionites of antiquity, little as they were famed for penetration and discernment, managed however the affairs of the sect with more discretion than our modern Unitarians: They questioned not the inspiration of the books which they received; but they received only one book—a spurious copy of St Matthew's Gospel, curtailed of the two first chapters. You will think it no inconsiderable confirmation of the doctrine in question, that the sect which first denied it, to palliate their infidelity, found it necessary to reject three of the gospels, and to mutilate the fourth.

Not in words therefore and in form, but with hearts full of faith and gratitude, you will join in the solemn service of the day, and return thanks to God, 'who gave his only begotten Son to take our nature upon him, and, as at this time, to be born of a pure virgin.' You will always remember, that it is the great use of a sound faith, that it furnishes the most effectual motives to a good life. You will therefore not rest in the merit of a speculative faith: You will make it your constant endeavour that your lives may adorn your profession,—that 'your light may so shine before men, that they, seeing your good works, may glorify your Father which is in heaven.'

NOTES / SOURCES

1. Samuel Horsley, 'Christmas Sermon', in *Sermons by Samuel Horsley*, Vol. III, Dundee, 1812, pp. 70–1, 80–1, 86–9; note that the concluding part of the sermon echoes the Collect for Christmas Day, and the Bidding for the Offertory which would have come immediately after the Sermon

Thomas Haweis   1734–1820

Following his studies at Oxford, Thomas Haweis became Rector of Auldwinkle, Northamptonshire, from 1764 until his death some 56 years later. Amongst other works, he published the *The Communicant's Spiritual Companion or an Evangelical Preparation for the Lord's Supper* (1763), which contains some criticisms of *The Week's Preparation* (q.v.) (1679), which was still popular among many.

'That They May Adorn the Doctrine of God' (Titus 2: 10)

God is my Saviour; that he is God is my comfort, for now I know his all sufficiency—of power and love, able to save to the uttermost, and rich in mercy to all that call upon him. I am called to adorn that doctrine which bringeth us salvation, and teacheth us to deny ungodliness and wordly lusts, and to live soberly, righteously and godly in this present world; and it is my serious purpose and desire to do so. My character in the world will call for my first regard, to walk in wisdom towards those who are without; to show a blamelessness of conversation, that they who are of a contrary part may have no evil thing justly to say of me. I will labour to show all good fidelity in my dealings, to pay a conscientious regard to truth in my words, to provide things honest in the sight of all men, to be industrious in my calling, to owe no man anything, to abstain from the appearances of evil, lest I make my brother to offend. My behaviour in my family, may it ever be such as becometh godliness; I would go in and out before them as an example unto the believers. I would watch particularly against self-will and anger: I would always speak at my meals something which should be for the use of edifying. I would be constant in prayer with them day and night, that the blessing of God may be in the midst of us. I would watch over all around me with a jealous eye, and above all, over myself, that I lay no stumbling block in their way; I would instruct them to the best of my abilities in the knowledge of the Redeemer of sinners, and seek that I and my house might serve the Lord. In my particular transactions with God in secret, I will endeavour to lay bare my heart before him; I will take his holy word; I will ask for his illuminating Spirit; I will examine my own self; no bosom sin, I trust, shall find a hiding place; my burdens of sin and sorrow will I lay at the feet of my Lord. I will plead with him his promises, and leave my case in my great Advocate's hand. In this way the desire of my soul will be answered, and my Redeemer honoured.

NOTES / SOURCES

Thomas Hawers, *The Communicant's Spiritual Companion or An Evangelical Preparation of the Lord's Supper*, London, 1763, pp. 134–5

Augustus Montague Toplady   1740–1778

Educated at Westminster, and Trinity College, Dublin, Augustus Toplady is best known for his hymns, notably 'Rock of ages, cleft for me', which was published in *The Gospel Magazine* in 1775. He became involved in a forthright disagreement with John Wesley and published *The Historic Proof of the Doctrinal Calvinism of the Church of England* (1774).

God's Mindfulness

God's mindfulness of his people is not a thing of yesterday. There never was a period, when he had not our interests at heart. The mercy of the Lord is from everlasting to everlasting upon them that fear him (Ps 103:17). It is, like himself, without beginning of days or end of years. We could not fear him from everlasting, because we did not exist until very lately; but his mercy towards us was co-eternal with himself. In consequence of this, we are made to fear him in time. Filial fear is a covenant-blessing, given only to the sons and daughters of the Lord Almighty; who says, I will put my fear into their hearts (Jer 32:40). Hence, they shall not depart from him after conversion. And thus his mercy, as it was from everlasting, is to everlasting upon them that fear him. It neither began with to-day, nor shall end with tomorrow. But he, who laid the foundation of their happiness, in his only eternal purpose, shall lay on the top-stone with joy, crying, 'Grace, grace' unto it, [Zech 4:7].—That God was mindful of us for good, appears, from the decree of election whereby we were chosen in Christ, to grace and glory, before the world began. (1)

A Prayer, Living and Dying

Rock of ages, cleft for me,
   Let me hide myself in thee;
Let the water and the blood,
   From thy riven side which flowed,
Be of sin the double cure,
   Cleanse me from its guilt and power.

Not the labours of my hands
   Can fulfil thy law's demands;
Could my zeal no respite know,
   Could my tears for ever flow,
All for sin could not atone;
   Thou must save, and thou alone.

Nothing in my hand I bring,
   Simply to thy cross I cling;
Naked, come to thee for dress;
   Helpless, look to thee for grace;
Foul, I to the fountain fly,
   Wash me, Saviour, or I die.

While I draw this fleeting breath,
   When my eye-strings break in death,
When I soar to worlds unknown
   See thee on thy judgement throne;
Rock of ages, cleft for me,
   Let me hide myself in thee. (2)

Diary Extract   *3 January 1768*

Read prayers and preached, in the morning, here at Fen-Ottery, and in the afternoon, at Harpford, to a very large congregation, considering the quantity of snow that lies on the ground and the intenseness of the frost, which render it almost equally unsafe to walk or ride. I opened the ministrations of this year with that grateful acknowledgement of the apostle, 1 Cor. 15:10, 'By the grace of God I am what I am,' which was my thesis both parts of the day. My liberty, both of spirit and utterance, was very great in the afternoon. Looking at my watch, I was surprised to find that I had detained my dear people three quarters of an hour and yet, when I concluded, they seemed unwilling to rise from their seats, notwithstanding the unusual intenseness of the cold. Lord of hosts, who hast all hearts in thy hand, work in my hearers both to be, to will, and to do, of thy good pleasure!

    This dreadfully severe weather continuing, I ordered two more bushels of wheat to be distributed as follows: to—Hooper, James Blackmore, John Sandford, Elizabeth Woodrow, Grace Mitchell and Martha Ham, one peck each and to John Trimlett, two pecks. (3)

NOTES / SOURCES

1. Augustus Toplady, 'Sermon IV', in *The Works of Augustus Toplady*, Vol. III, London, 1825, p. 108
2. Ibid., Vol. VI, pp. 413–15
3. Augustus Toplady, *Rock of Ages: The Diary of an Eighteenth-Century Country Parson by A. M. Toplady* (1987) p. 12

James Woodforde   1740–1803

Following his education at Winchester College and New College, Oxford, James Woodforde served a number of curacies in Somerset, something of a new phenomenon in the eighteenth century. As Rector of Weston Longueville in Norfolk from 1774, he kept an extensive diary until his death in 1803.

1791

Mar. 20, Sunday . . . The first thing almost that I heard this Morn' was the Death of John Greaves, my Carpenter, a very inoffensive good-kind of a young Man as any in my Parish, married about 2. Years or more ago, to a Servant Maid of Mrs Lombe's, a good kind of a young Woman, and lived very happy together and daily getting up in the World. Pray God comfort her and assist her in this Day of her great distress, and may thy good Providence protect her and her Fatherless Child, and likewise give her a safe and happy deliverance of another Child with which she expects to be brought to bed almost every hour. Defend her O Lord from the small-Pox in this time of her great necessity and trouble if it be thy good pleasure. The small-Pox being almost at present in every part of the Parish by inoculation etc—Poor John Greaves was very suddenly taken of. He had been ill but a few Days, but in a very dangerous Disorder, called the Peripneumony. Mr Thorne was sent for and attended him, but I am afraid he was not sent for soon enough. I had not the most distant Idea that he was in such danger as it turned out. He was a Man well respected by all that knew him. I am sincerely sorry for him and heartily pity his poor Widow. Pray God! befriend her and support her. I read Prayers and Preached and churched a Woman this Afternoon at Weston Church. Being a poor Woman I took nothing for churching her. None from Weston House at Church to day. We had almost all Day some falling of Rain.

1796

Dec. 25, Xmas Day, Sunday. We breakfasted, dined, etc. again at home. This Day the coldest we have had yet and Frost more severe. It froze all the Day long and within Doors, the last Night intensely cold. Mr Corbould read Prayers and administered the H. Sacrament this Morning at Weston Church. He called on us as he went and also on his return from Church. He said the cold at Church was so great as to make him tremble again. We did not go, the Weather being so severe. This being Christmas Day, the following People had their Dinner at my House, Widow Case, old Thos. Atterton, Christ. Dunnell, Edwd. Howes. Robt. Downing and my Clerk, Thos. Thurston. Dinner to day, Surloin of Beef rosted, plumb Puddings and mince Pies. My Appetite this very cold Weather very bad. The Cold pierces me thro' almost on going to bed, cannot get to sleep for a long time, We however do not have our beds warmed. Gave the People that dined here to day before they went, to each of them 1 Shilling 0. 6. 0. After they had dined they had some strong Beer.

NOTES / SOURCES

James Woodforde, *The Diary of a Country Parson (1758–1802)*, March 20, 1791 and Christmas Day 1796, London, 1934

Hannah More   1745–1833

Educated at the boarding school established by her sisters in Bristol (1757), Hannah More had contact with many literary figures of the day, including David Garrick and Dr Johnson. After Garrick's death, she became acquainted with John Newton (q.v.) and William Wilberforce (q.v.). She instituted a number of Sunday Schools in the neighbourhood of Cheddar, four of which still (2000) survive. Her published works include a reply to the French Revolution, *Village Politics* (1792). In later life she moved to Barleywood (1802) to enjoy closer contact with the Clapham Sect, and wrote a number of works on morality and faith.

The Love of God

Our love to God arises out of want. God's love to us out of fulness. Our indigence draws us to that power which can relieve, and to that goodness which can bless us. His overflowing love delights to make us partakers of the bounties he graciously imparts, not only in the gifts of his Providence, but in the richer communications of his grace. We are first drawn to love him from the consideration of his mercies, from the experience of his bounties; but this consideration and this experience in a rightly-turned mind lead us to love him for his own excellences. We can only be said to love God; when we endeavour to glorify him, when we desire a participation of his nature, when we study to imitate his perfections.

We are sometimes inclined to suspect the love of God to us. We are too little suspicious of our want of love to him. Yet if we examine the case by evidence, as we should examine any common question, what real instances can we produce of our love to Him? What imaginable instance can we not produce of his love to us? If neglect, forgetfulness, ingratitude, disobedience, coldness in our affections, deadness in our duty, be evidences of our love to him, such evidences, but such only, we can abundantly allege. If life and all the countless catalogue of mercies that makes life pleasant, be proofs of his love to us, these he has given us in hand;—if life eternal, if blessedness that knows no measure and no end, be proofs of love, these he has given us in promise—to the Christian we had almost said, he has given them in possession.

When the adoring soul is gratefully expatiating on the inexhaustible instances of the love of God to us, let it never forget to rise to its most exalted pitch, to rest on its loftiest object, *His inestimable love in the redemption of the world by our Lord Jesus Christ*. This is the crowning point; this is the gift which imparts their highest value to all his other gifts. It combines whatever can render divine munificence compleat:—pardon of sin, acceptance with God, perfection and perpetuity of blessedness. Well may the Christian in the devout contemplation of this sublime mystery, which the highest of all created intelligences 'desire to look into,' exclaim in grateful rapture, 'Thou art the God that doest wonders!' A redeemed world is the triumph of infinity. Power and goodness, truth and mercy, righteousness and peace, incorporated and lost in each other!

Love is a grace of such pre-eminent distinction, that the Redeemer is emphatically designated by it. To HIM THAT LOVED US. This is such a characteristic style and title that no name is appended to it.

It must be an irksome thing to serve a master whom we do not love; a master whom we are compelled to obey, though we think his requisitions hard, and his commands unreasonable; under whose eye we know that we continually live, though his presence is not only undelightful but formidable.

Now every creature must obey God, whether he love him or not; he must act always in his sight, whether he delight in him or not; and to a heart of any feeling, to a spirit of any liberality, nothing is so grating as constrained obedience. To love God, to serve him because we love him, is therefore no less our highest happiness, than our most bounden duty. Love makes all labor light. We serve with alacrity, where we love with cordiality.

Where the heart is devoted to an object, we require not to be perpetually reminded of our obligations to obey him: they present themselves spontaneously, we fulfil them readily, I had almost said, involuntarily; we think not so much of the service as of the object. The principle which suggests the work inspires the pleasure; to neglect it would be an injury to our feelings. The performance is the gratification. The omission is not more a pain to the conscience, than a wound to the affections. The implantation of this vital root perpetuates virtuous practice, and secures internal peace. (1)

Religion is not for an Easy Life

They who take up Religion on a false ground will never adhere to it. If they adopt it merely for the peace and pleasantness it brings, they will desert it as soon as they find their adherence to it will bring them into difficulty, distress, or discredit. It seldom answers therefore to attempt making proselytes by hanging out false colours. The Christian 'endures as seeing him who is invisible.' He who adopts Religion for the sake of immediate enjoyment, will not do a virtuous action that is disagreeable to himself; nor resist a temptation that is alluring, present pleasure being his motive. There is no sure basis for virtue but the love of God in Christ Jesus, and the bright reversion for which that love is pledged. Without this, as soon as the paths of piety become rough and thorny, we shall stray into pleasanter pastures.

Religion however has her own peculiar advantages. In the transactions of all worldly affairs, there are many and great difficulties. There may be several ways out of which to chuse. Men of the first understanding are not always certain which of these ways is the best. Persons of the deepest penetration are full of doubt and perplexity; their minds are undecided how to act, left while they pursue one road, they may be neglecting another, which might better have conducted them to their proposed end.

In Religion the case is different, and in this respect, easy. As a Christian can have but one object in view, he is also certain there is but one way of attaining it. Where there is but one end it prevents all possibility of chusing wrong, where there is but one road it takes away all perplexity as to the course of pursuit. That we so often wander wide of the mark, is not from any want of plainness in the path, but from the perverseness of our will in not chusing it, from the indolence of our minds in not following it up. (2)

A Religion all Brain and no Heart is not of the Gospel

Most sincerely do we believe, that there is nothing which the better sort of this class dread more than hypocrisy. But do they not sometimes dread the imputation almost as much as the thing? And is it not to be feared that, with the dread of this odious vice being imputed to them, is a little connected the suspicion of its existence in all who go farther than themselves? Are they not too ready to accuse of want of sincerity or of soberness, every one who rises above their own level? Is not every degree of warmth in their pious affections, every expression of zeal in their conversation, every indication of strictness in their practice, construed into an implication, that so much as this zeal and strictness exceed their own, there is in them just so much error as that excess involves?

By the class of writers to which they are attached, the pious affections are branded as the stigma of enthusiasm. But a religion which is all brain, and no heart, is not the religion of the Gospel. The spirit there exhibited is as far removed from philosophical apathy, as from the intemperate language of passion. There are minds so constituted, and hearts so touched, that they cannot mediate on the incarnation of the Son of God, his voluntary descent from the glory which he had with his Father from all eternity, his dying for us men and for our salvation—with the same unmoved temper with which they acknowledge the truth of any other fact. A grateful feeling, excited by these causes, is as different from a fanatical fervor as it is from a languid acknowledgement. It is not energy, however, which is reprobated, so much as the cause of its excitement. Should the zealous Christian change the object of his admiration, should he express the same animated feeling for Socrates, which the other had expressed for his Saviour, his enthusiasm would be ascribed to his good taste, and the object would be allowed to justify the rapture.

But, is not objecting to earnestness in religion to strike out of the catalogue of virtues that quality which so eminently distinguished the Scripture worthies? Is it not denying that 'spirit of power and of love' which, it is worth observing, the Apostle makes the associate of 'a sound mind,' to deny that Christianity ought to make an impression on the heart, and if on the heart, on the feelings? These fastidious critics place, what they call the abstract truths of religion, on the same footing with abstract truths in science; they allow only the same intellectual conviction of truth, the same cool assent, in the one case, which is given to a demonstration in the other. But would not he be thought a defective orator at the bar, or in the senate, who should plead as if he did not know that men had feelings to be touched as well as understandings to be convinced; who considered the affections as the only portion of character to which he must be careful not to advert, in addressing beings who are feeling as well as intelligent? Shall a fervent rhetoric be admired in one orator, when pleading for the freedom of men, and reprobated in another, when pleading for their salvation? Shall we be enraptured with the eloquent advocate for the Agrarian law, and disgusted with the strenuous advocate for the everlasting Gospel? (3)

NOTES / SOURCES

1. Hannah More, *Practical Piety*, Vol. I, 1811, London, 1812, pp. 150–4
2. Ibid., pp. 167–9
3. Hannah More, *Christian Morals*, Vol. II, London, 1813, pp. 82–5

Thomas Scott   1747–1821

After an uncertain start in life when he was dismissed for misconduct as an apprentice surgeon at Alford, Lincolnshire, Thomas Scott succeeded John Newton (q.v.) as Curate at Olney (1781). His major publication was *Commentary on the Bible* which reached a wide audience through its weekly serialization, though he gained little financial benefit from it. He was also the first Secretary to the Church Missionary Society, founded in 1799, and influenced the young John Henry Newman (q.v.).

Growth in Grace

Not satisfied with desiring that their 'love might abound yet more and more,'—he [Paul] subjoined these words, 'in knowledge and in all judgment;' and they suggest to us a second particular, in which growth of grace very greatly consists. There may be very high affections about religion, without the communication of holy principles: surprise at extraordinary and unexpected events; sanguine hopes of advantages, which appear very great and glorious; sudden transitions from adversity to prosperity, from sorrow to joy, or from pain to pleasure; and every circumstance which excites self-complacency or strong confidence, will involve or occasion a great flow of vehement affections, in the concerns of religion as well as in those of this life. Thus the Israelites on the banks of the Red Sea, beholding their formidable enemies dead on the shore, and amazed at their own most extraordinary deliverance, 'believed the word of the Lord and sang his praise:' but this apparently good frame in a vast majority of them continued no longer than till their inclinations were thwarted; and 'they soon forgat the works of God, and would not abide in his counsel.' These affections are not of a permanent nature: and, if a man possess nothing better, 'he has no root in himself, and in time of temptation will fall away.'

   The new convert indeed experiences and manifests a similar flow of affections. The Lord, in making a Christian, does not destroy the original constitution of the human soul; and the natural passions are useful in the infancy of the Divine life to produce a proper degree of earnestness and diligence. But with them there exists a spark of heavenly love, which gathers strength whilst they are weakened, and glows more vigorously under their almost expiring ashes. As this principle acquires energy and ascendancy, it suffices to produce activity, and thus to subordinate and regulate all inferior affections: then every kind of earnestness, which did not spring from knowledge, and was not exercised in judgment and discretion, becomes unnecessary, and may abate without any detriment.

All *holy* affections spring from Divine illumination, and increase with the advancement of spiritual knowledge and genuine experience. In proportion as the Christian is enabled to discern more clearly and distinctly the nature and excellency of heavenly things; and as he experiences more fully the pleasure they are capable of affording; the more will he love and delight in them. The reasons which induce him to love the Lord, and his truths, precepts, and people, are perceived with increasing evidence; his thirst after happiness in the favour of God, his supreme valuation of redemption and salvation in Christ, his gratitude to Him, and zeal for his glory, with attachment to his cause, and devotedness to his service, appear more and more reasonable, in proportion as his mind is truly enlightened by his influences of the Holy Spirit. He also better understands why 'he who loves God should love his brother also;' and why he ought to copy the forbearance, compassion, and mercy, of which his redeeming Lord hath given him an example. As his views enlarge, he learns to pay less regard to the strong emotions of the animal spirits, which produce very pleasing but transient sensations, than to that steady and powerful affection, which influences a man to habitual self-denying obedience; and which connects with disinterested endeavours to 'do good to all men, especially to them who are of the household of faith:' and he accustoms himself to judge of the sincerity and degree of his love, not by certain fluctuations in his feelings but by its energy, in prevailing on him to renounce, venture, and endure every thing, in promoting the glory of God and the good of his redeemed people. 'For this is the love of God, that we keep his commandments: and his commandments are not grievous.' Thus the Christian may actually abound more and more in love, as connected with knowledge, when ignorant and selfish passions have subsided: the tumult of his feelings may be greatly abated, when the energy of pure and heavenly love is proportionably increased: and, as impetuous affections and vehement zeal, accompanied with pride and anger, become less and less apparent, he may manifest far more of that love, which 'suffers long and is kind, which envieth not, vaunteth not itself, is not puffed up, does not behave itself unseemly, seeketh not its own, is not easily provoked, thinketh no evil, rejoiceth not in iniquity, but rejoiceth in the truth; which beareth all things, believeth all things, hopeth all things, and endureth all things.' In short, that love, which is shown 'in deed and in truth,' may abound exceedingly, when heavenly wisdom and deep humility have made the Christian ashamed of those ostentatious appearances of love, which consist principally 'in word and in tongue,' in high professions, noisy disputings, and cheap protestations. 1 Cor. xiii. James ii. 15, 16; iii. 13–18. 1 John iii. 16–20.

NOTES / SOURCES

The Theological Works of Thomas Scott, London, 1839, pp. 120–1

Alexander Jolly   1756–1838

Educated at Marischal College, Aberdeen, Alexander Jolly became Episcopal Minister at Turriff in 1777 and later Bishop of Moray from 1798 until his death. He was made Honorary Doctor of Divinity at Washington College, Connecticut, USA, in 1826 and published a number of works, most notably *The Christian Sacrifice in the Eucharist* (1831).

The Offering and Receiving of the Christian Sacrifice

It is ever seriously and carefully to be remembered, that, although redemption by the death of Christ is absolute, including every individual of Adam's race, for 'He tasted death for every man,' and 'gave Himself a ransom for all'—yet salvation by it is conditional. He would have all men to be saved, but, in the plan of his infinite wisdom and goodness, he will not save rational and free agents, without their concurrence with that grace, which He gives, but they may receive in vain. 'He is the Author of eternal salvation'—but it is—'to all them that obey him.' (Heb. v. 9) And therefore, in obedience to Him, we must both use the *means* of His appointment, and perform the *conditions* which He has prescribed.

The great and general means of salvation, to which all the instrumental duties of holy living may be reduced, are Baptism and the blessed Eucharist.

The holy sacrament of Baptism binds upon the receivers all the conditions of salvation, included in the solemn promise or vow then made to God, obliging to repentance or renunciation of sin, firm faith, and holy obedience. Upon this initiatory sacrament, confirmation, or the laying on of hands, under which title it ranks among the first principles of our holy religion, (Heb. vi. 1, 2.) puts the seal of the Holy Ghost, who is specially the giver of the spiritual life. Of this divine life the body and blood of Christ furnish the necessary food or nourishment, for the strengthening and refreshing of our souls. 'My flesh,' said our merciful Lord, 'is meat indeed, and my blood is drink indeed;' and—'Except ye eat the flesh of the Son of man, and drink his blood, ye have no life in you.' Such are his words in that divine sermon (St John vi. 27, etc.) which anticipated the institution, with plain respect to it, as all antiquity understood it.

These means of grace are therefore indispensably necessary to salvation, wherever they may be had, according to Christ's institution, and from those duly commissioned stewards, whom he has appointed to give his family their portion of meat in due season. And, if we do at any time neglect them, when they are in our power, we can expect no favour from God; but, by disobeying his command, shall incur his displeasure.

Very strong, indeed, is our obligation to be constant communicants in the christian sacrifice. It is bound upon us by every tie of duty, love and gratitude, as well as regard to our own eternal interest—our advancement in grace and preparation for glory. Our divine Lord's command to priests and people is most express,—to the priests to celebrate, and to the people to receive. 'Do this,' he said, 'in remembrance of me,' that is, offer this for my powerfully prevailing memorial: 'Take, eat, this is my body: drink ye all of this, for this is my blood.' In vain, then, we say or pray, Lord, Lord, or hope to enter into the kingdom of heaven, if we fail to do what is his Father's will, and His own. 'Why call ye me, Lord, Lord,' he asks, 'and do not the things that I say?' (1)

The Eucharist: Vehicle of Salvation

To this purpose, for man's salvation, He has regulated the constitution, and ordered the economy of his Church through these last days, and to the end of the world. He instituted outward visible signs of inward spiritual grace, which are rendered effectual by the sanctification of His own Holy Spirit; and the authority of administering them He committed to his Apostles, to be perpetuated in succession from them to the end of time. So we clearly observe in the initiatory sacrament of baptism; the apostolic commission being part of the original institution, and therefore essential to the right and lawful administration of it. So likewise in the sacrament, which is also the sacrifice commemorative of the death of Christ, the authority of the priest, the validity of his commission, most essentially enters into the performance: all originating from and terminating in Christ's Person, who is both Priest and Sacrifice, the Giver and the Gift; who condescends to take from among men persons to represent Him, and act in His name in things pertaining to God, that they may offer to Him the gifts which He instituted for his memorial, and that He might, by their hands and prayers, convey, in the use of those means, all the benefits of His death and passion to the well-disposed receivers.

These benefits, indeed, are immense and numberless, and no heart can conceive, nor tongue express the real nature and full extent of them. They are the unspeakable gift of God: for neither eye hath seen, nor ear heard, neither have entered into the heart of man the good things which God hath prepared for them that love him, and of which He gives them the earnest and pledge in these holy mysteries, to their great and endless comfort.

But, to assist and arrange our thoughts, they may be reduced to the three exceeding great benefits already distinguished.—1. Pardon of sins. 2. Increase of grace. 3. An assuring pledge of eternal glory. Of these, certainly, we have the greatest need at all times, and therefore should at no time fail to attend that holy ordinance; by which, as the commemorative sacrifice of Christ's death, we pray and plead, and, as being also the sacrament of His body and blood, do actually receive these inestimable blessings.

1. Without pardon of our sins, we must all perish. Now, repentance, implying a thorough change of heart and life, is the condition of forgiveness, but it is of no value in the way of merit, to claim or obtain it: *that our* divine Lord Jesus Christ, God and man, purchased for us at the immense price of his own blood; and to make us sensible of our own demerit, has been pleased to appoint external means and ministry of pardon and reconciliation. He has most graciously instituted and ordained one baptism for the remission of sins, and promised to be with His Apostles and their successors, in the administration of it—He himself being the sole giver of its grace—to the end of the world. But after this birth from above, this regeneration of water and of the Holy Spirit, in baptism, sealed by confirmation, so deep was our fall in Adam, that 'the infection of nature doth remain, yea in them that are regenerated.' 'After we have received the Holy Ghost, we may depart from grace given, and fall into sin, and, by the grace of God, we may arise again, and amend our lives. And therefore, they are to be condemned, which say they can no

more sin as long as they live here, or deny the place of forgiveness to such as truly repent.' However conscious we may be, to the praise of God's grace, of our freedom from gross, presumptuous sins, yet, in many things we offend all, through ignorance, forgetfulness, frailty, and surprise—and who can tell how oft! Even from these secret faults we require to be cleansed. Repentance, prayer, and watchfulness, striving more and more against them, to subdue and lessen them, are the conditions; but it is the blood of Jesus Christ alone that cleanseth from all sin, whether small or great. And for the application of that healing remedy. He, of his great mercy, instituted the continual memorial of his most precious blood-shedding in the blessed Eucharist, and left us that cup of salvation, to which He has expressly annexed the forgiveness of sins. Every soul, therefore, that feels the corruption of nature, and laments, as offensive to the infinite holiness of God, the frailties and infirmities of our fallen state, will desire and long for that heavenly healing medicine; that, washed in the blood of that immaculate Lamb, which was slain to take away the sins of the world, it may at length be presented pure and without spot before God. Such a person will require no exhortation to take every opportunity of approaching the altar, where only we have the promise of pardon—lamenting that those opportunities in modern times are so few; and the most gracious invitation of his loving Redeemer will ever affect his heart with feelings both of sorrow and joy—sorrow for sin, and joy for salvation from the power as well as the punishment of it— 'Come unto me all ye that labour, and are heavy laden, and I will give you rest.'

2. As here we obtain pardon of our sins past, so also we receive grace to help us against them for the time to come; and find, that Christ is our strength as well as our Redeemer: for, we are assured that we can do all things required of us, through Christ that strengthens us, (Phil. iv. 13) Our natural weakness will convince us of our continual need of divine grace—that bread of life and spiritual drink which here we receive, for the strengthening and refreshing of our souls by the body and blood of Christ, as our bodies are by bread and wine. But our highest attainments in holiness, degenerate as our nature is, must fall far short of the standard of absolute rectitude. The most exalted virtue that we can reach here below is but human virtue, and must be found very deficient when weighed in the balance. Our obedience, even when carried to the utmost, through sanctification of the Spirit, requires the sprinkling of the blood of Jesus Christ to render it matter of God's choice or election, (1 Pet.i.2.) It is that only which can render us pure and clean in the sight of the infinitely holy God. And, therefore, this most holy mystery was instituted by our most merciful God and Saviour to communicate his blood and merits to us, that our imperfect doings for his sake may be accepted and *rewarded*.

3. This—reducing the numberless mercies of these heavenly mysteries to three heads—is the last and consummating blessing: consigning the faithful receiver, as the felicity is expressed by St Peter, in the above-quoted passage, 'to an inheritance incorruptible and undefiled, and that fadeth not away, reserved in heaven for you, who are kept by the power of God through faith unto salvation, ready to be revealed in the last time.' This eternal inheritance, a state of joy and glory, without end or interruption, is a gift of grace to the highest and holiest angels, who have received and do acknowledge it as such, casting down their crowns before the high throne, and giving all glory, thanks, and praise to Him

who liveth for ever and ever. But, to sinful fallen man it is a gift of mercy as well as grace, purchased for us at a dear rate, by Jesus Christ our Lord. His bitter but infinitely-meritorious cross, to Him the tree of death, is to us the tree of life, whereby paradise is opened to us again—the heavenly instead of the earthly; where, as the earnest of our future inheritance, He gives us, by the hands of his commissioned servants, the bread of life, of which He says, 'He that eateth of this bread shall live for ever:' and, 'The bread that I will give is my flesh, which I will give for the life of the world;' and which he actually gave, in the institution of the holy Eucharist, when of the bread, which He took into his all-powerful hand, he said, 'This is my body which is given for you;' and of the cup, in like manner, 'This is my blood which is shed for you.' This repast, of his unspeakable love and bounty, He left to be the food and nourishment of our souls for life eternal—'My flesh is meat indeed, and my blood is drink indeed'—supernatural meat and drink, as constantly necessary for the spiritual life of the soul as natural food is for the body. 'Whoso eateth my flesh, and drinketh my blood, hath eternal life; and I will raise him up at the last day,' (St John, vi. 54)

These wondrously high and supernatural benefits are not to be obtained by natural means, but by mysteries transcending the power of nature, which we call sacraments, ordained by Christ himself to convey his grace, and be pledges of his love, to our great and endless comfort. And, therefore, to neglect the heavenly banquet, when we are invited to it in Christ's name, is to expose ourselves to death, by refusing the bread of life. Did we once, in our naturally starving state, feel our wants, and, in consequence, begin to hunger and thirst after righteousness—so hungry and thirsty as that our souls faint within us—most ardently should we desire the bread from heaven, and the healing stream that flows from thence, thirsting after the cup of salvation, as the panting hart does for the water-brooks. This, and whatever prepares us for it, should be the subject of our most earnest prayer. (2)

NOTES / SOURCES

1. Alexander Jolly, *The Christian Sacrifice in the Eucharist*, Aberdeen, 1831, pp. 193–5
2. Ibid., pp. 199–205

Alexander Knox   1757–1831

An Irish theologian and writer, descended from the same family as the Scottish reformer and historian, John Knox. The picture portrayed of him by Bishop John Jebb (q.v.) in his *Thirty Years Correspondence* shows the extent to which he anticipated the Oxford Movement by affirming the place of the Church of England as part of a reformed Church. He gave a particular emphasis to the mystical tradition in Christianity and, through his friendship with John Wesley (q.v.), saw the importance of regular Communion. He advocated Catholic Emancipation.

The Presence of Christ in the Eucharist

The promise, therefore, of our Lord's flesh and blood to be to them meat indeed, and drink indeed, to be the spiritual and eternal life of their souls, by virtue of which he should dwell in them and they in him, and they should live by him as he lived by the Father—this promise, I say, could not, consistently with the terms in which it is expressed, be understood to mean any thing less than an inconceivable, but most real emanation from his divine person, in which there would be the same exercise of his divine power, for the animation and sustenance of the soul, as when divine virtue had gone out of him, for the healing of the body. I conceive, they could have given no other interpretation than this to our Lord's prospective assurances. In the appointment, therefore of visible symbols, to be instrumentally effective in conveying the promised blessing, they would see nothing but that, which, according to all their experience, was suitable and proportionate. They would, moreover perceive, that a two-fold communication, the flesh and blood of the Redeemer, was provided for by a two-fold medium; the lowliness of which, only the more evinced the power of the invisible agent; while, in such an operation, it would not appear unfitting, that bread, the prime nourishment of human life; and wine, the prime cherisher of human weakness, should be the material instruments of this heavenly purpose.

I do not mean to say, that such thoughts were likely to have occurred at that hour, when the sacrament of the Eucharist was first instituted. At no time were the Apostles less competent to have discovered the weighty import of our Lord's expressions. Probably, in the depth of that sorrow which had filled their hearts, they did not recollect the particular discourse, by which alone his language could have been fully explained. But afterwards, when the promise was fulfilled, that all things which they had heard should be brought to their remembrance, the connexion between the discourse at Capernaum and the eucharistic institution, would impress itself on them in all its clearness and importance; and may it not be presumed, that the more they considered the subject, the greater reason would they perceive, for acknowledging the divine goodness and wisdom, not only in the transcendent nature of the blessing thus entailed upon the church, but also in the choice of such an appropriate provision for its stated and perpetual communication.

It would be obvious to them, that if the sacrament of the Eucharist had been ordained, merely as a commemorative celebration—that is, if our Redeemer had said nothing more than 'Do this in remembrance of me,' fits its institution would rather have implied the injunction of a permanent duty, than the pledge and means of a permanent blessing. In that view, it might have afforded an occasion for the more solemn expression of christian gratitude, or, the renewal of christian obligation; but it could not be thought to give the prospect of any special spiritual benefit, beyond what might be found in an equally ardent exercise of devotion, on any other religious occasion. The ordinary grace of God might have been relied upon, for co-operation, in such an effort of the mind to think more closely on the love of their dying Lord, or to feel it more deeply; but, as it should seem, only as equal efforts would be assisted in the common acts of pious supplication. Yet still on this ground, it might not have been easy to account satisfactorily for introducing into a simple commemoration any outward or visible part. The merely natural effect of the eucharistic signs on the external senses, would hardly explain their adoption in a religion, in which rites and ceremonies were so professedly to give place to spiritual worship; and it would be still more difficult to conceive, how the eating and drinking of those visible symbols should be an essential co-ingredient, in the exercise of a purely commemorative devotion.

But in ascribing to the eucharistic symbols the instrumental effectiveness with which the significant word of their divine Master had appeared to invest them, the Apostles would see in that institution a provision for their spiritual consolation and benefit, in which all their pre-existing habits of mind were consulted, and all their mental and moral exigencies richly supplied. The nature of the eucharistic Sacrament was clearly such, as to have in it no other virtue than what flowed into it from him by whom it was instituted. The eating of bread and drinking of wine had, in itself, neither conduciveness nor any obvious congeniality, to a spiritual purpose. It could therefore only have that precise import, which our Redeemer was pleased to give to it; namely, that it was a visible method, appointed by him, of spiritually eating his flesh and spiritually drinking his blood; and that it must accordingly derive its spiritual efficacy from the concomitancy of his omnipotent power. The Eucharist, when thus regarded, would be to the disciples of our Lord, such a pledge as was given them in no other instance, of their living by his life, being strong through his strength, and growing in grace by a vital effluence from himself.

The means otherwise afforded them, of building themselves up in their most holy faith, they would, doubtless, value and improve. But in this superadded provision, there was a source of satisfaction peculiar to itself. In all other exercises of religion, the mind was to contribute its own exertions; and though subordinately, yet directly, to minister to its own benefit or comfort. In the eucharistic institution alone, human co-operation could have no share in the effect; because the medium employed could communicate influence or blessing, only through the direct operation of Almighty Power. It was not to be questioned, that in every instance in which spiritual benefit was conferred; the goodness of God was to be regarded as its supreme source. But where the rational powers of man intervened, whether those of the recipient himself, or of any human helper of his faith, the sensible advantage would seem, more or less to resemble the blessings of nature and providence, which are apparently the result of general laws. It might therefore have appeared as reasonable, as it was gracious, that for the perpetual comfort and assurance of the Church, in the highest and noblest instance in which divine blessing was to be conferred, the supreme source of that blessing should condescend to be its direct and immediate dispenser; and should prove himself to be such, by employing means of communication, which, venerable and impressive as they should become, by being made, not merely the instruments of his power, but the effectual representatives of himself, would be not only weak but fruitless, in any other hands than his own. (1)

The Eucharist a Commemorative Sacrifice

In a word, according to the Apostle, and that universal belief to which he appeals, the commemorative celebration of the Eucharist, as a devotional act, is not that which makes it peculiarly beneficial and venerable; but it is so, because in this ordinance, the aliments which Christ has appointed, become, through his designation and blessing, the direct vehicles of his own divine influences to capable receivers. Nothing short of this notion would accord with the ascribing of spiritual virtue, specially to each visible sign; and, what is still more, to each, not as becoming efficacious through *the act of receiving*, but as endued with efficacy through *the act of consecration*.

For, we must observe, it is not 'the cup of blessing which we *drink*,' nor 'the bread which we *eat*,' that are declared to be the communion of the blood, and the communion of the body of Christ; but it is said, 'the cup of blessing which we *bless*; and the bread which we *break*;' clearly indicating, that the eucharistic elements, when once solemnly sanctified according to our Lord's appointment, are to be regarded as being, in an inexplicable, but deeply awful manner the receptacles of that heavenly virtue, which his divine power qualifies them to convey. On such a subject it would be presumptuous to indulge in any hypothetic speculation. But it would be still more blameable, and at least as prejudicial, not to allow to the Apostle's words all their due import; especially as those very words contain the only direct definition of the Eucharist in the sacred writings.

If the language of St Paul could need elucidation, it might be strictly compared with the several expressions of our Lord, already adverted to; but these must, of themselves, recur; and, at once, fix the unequivocal, however mysterious import of *the communion of his body*, and *the communion of his blood*. In this accumulated light, it must be felt impossible, that the thing signified should be disproportioned to the force of the expression; and the conclusion, on the whole, must inevitably appear to be, that as our Lord had taught his followers to expect from his divine person, such influences of his body and of his blood, as should be not figurative or illusive, but substantive and vital, and as in his institution of the Eucharist, he constituted the consecrated bread and wine, the virtual representatives of his body and blood, and by consequence the effective vehicles of their influences to all capable partakers, so, what our Lord had thus declared, and thus established, is comprehensively contained, and as if solemnly countersigned, in the clear and authoritative recognition of his Apostle. (2)

The Eucharist: the Presence Chamber of a Meek King

In this view, as often as we approach the table of the Lord, we may account ourselves to have admission, in a manner beyond human conception, into the presence chamber of the King Messiah. Under the full sense of this Christian privilege, we shall not need a Bethel, a Peniel, the Jewish sanctuary, or even its Holy of Holies. In contemplating with St Paul, the mystery of the Eucharist, the Christian cannot but see, that in this sacred ordinance, especially and most eminently, 'a new and living way' is opened for him (far above what was granted even to the Jewish High Priest,) to 'enter into the holiest by the blood of Jesus.'

Is it then, too much to say, that the Eucharist, thus apprehended, makes the richest provision which we could conceive to be made by any stated means, in this lower world, for our spiritual sustenance and comfort? While as a pledge and token of divine presence and influence, its authenticity never can be impaired—its significancy, to close and sober attention, never obscured, its invisible mystery will be as wonderful, as impressive, and as inestimable, in its latest as in its earliest celebration. The communion of the Lord's blood, and the communion of the Lord's body, must have, as terms, the same profound import—as blessings, the same infinite value, yesterday, today, and for ever. Let not, therefore, the simplicity of what is visible to our bodily sight, veil from our mental eye those invisible realities, which are to us so consolatory, and in themselves so glorious. On the contrary, let us recognize the same spirit of meek majesty, which veiled its transcendent brightness in the mystery of the incarnation, as still continuing the like gracious condescension in the mystery of the Eucharist; and let us joyfully and reverently approach to do homage to our King, who in this his own peculiar institution, comes to diffuse benediction in his mystical Zion, with the same apparent lowliness, as when in conformity with the divine prediction, he entered his literal Jerusalem 'sitting upon an ass, and upon a colt, the foal of an ass.' (3)

NOTES / SOURCES

1. Alexander Knox, 'An Inquiry into the use and import of Eucharistic Symbols' (1824) in *The Remains of Alexander Knox*, Vol. II, London, 1836, pp. 31–7
2. Ibid., pp. 45–8
3. Ibid., pp. 89–91

William Wilberforce   1759–1833

A long serving member of Parliament, William Wilberforce is principally remembered for being the Parliamentary Leader of the cause of the abolition of slavery. Although he took up leadership of the cause in 1787, the Bill did not receive Royal Assent until 1807. Outside Parliament, he was influential in the foundation of the Bishopric of Calcutta (1813) and took part in the founding of the Church Missionary Society (1799) and the Bible Society (1804). His *Practical View of the Prevailing Religious System of Professed Christians* (1797) is his main theological landmark, which set out to assert the social claims of Evangelicalism. His son, Samuel, became Bishop of Oxford.

Advice to Some who Profess their Full Assent to the Fundamental Doctrines of the Gospel

In a former chapter we largely insisted on what may be termed the fundamental practical error of the bulk of professed Christians in our days; their either overlooking or misconceiving the peculiar method, which the Gospel has provided for the renovation of our corrupted nature, and for the attainment of every Christian grace.

But there are mistakes on the right hand and on the left; and our general proneness, when we are flying from one extreme to run into an opposite error, renders it necessary to superadd another admonition. The generally prevailing error of the present day indeed is that fundamental one which has been already pointed out. But while we attend, in the first place, to that, and, on the warrant both of Scripture and experience, prescribe hearty repentance and lively faith, as the only foundation of all true holiness; we must at the same time guard against a practical mistake of another kind. They who, with penitent hearts, have humbled themselves before the cross of Christ; and who, pleading his merits as their only ground of pardon and acceptance with God, have resolved henceforth, through the help of his Spirit, to bring forth the fruits of righteousness, are sometimes apt to conduct themselves as if they considered their work as now done; or at least, as if this were the whole they had to do, as often as, by falling afresh into sin, another act of repentance and faith may seem to have become necessary. There are not a few in our relaxed age, who thus satisfy themselves with what may be termed *general* Christianity; who feel *general* penitence and humiliation from a sense of their sinfulness *in general*, and *general* desires of universal holiness; but who neglect that vigilant and jealous care, with which they should labour to extirpate every *particular* corruption, by studying its nature, its root, its ramifications, and thus becoming acquainted with its secret movements, with the means whereby it gains strength, and with the most effectual methods of resisting it. In like manner, they are far from striving with persevering alacrity, for the acquisition and improvement of every Christian grace. Nor is it unusual for ministers, who preach the truths of the Gospel with fidelity, ability, and success, to be themselves also liable to the charge of dwelling altogether in their instructions on this *general* Religion: instead of tracing and laying open all the secret motions of inward corruption, and instructing their hearers how best to conduct themselves in every distinct part of the Christian warfare; how best to strive against each particular vice, and to cultivate each grace of the Christian character. Hence it is, that in too many persons, concerning the sincerity of whose general professions of Religion we should be sorry to entertain a doubt, we yet see little progress made in the regulation of their tempers, in the improvement of their time, in the reform of their plan of life, or in ability to resist the temptation to which they are particularly exposed. They will confess themselves in general terms, to be *'miserable sinners:'* this is a tenet of their creed, and they feel even proud in avowing it. They will occasionally also lament particular failings: but this confession is sometimes obviously made, in order to draw forth a compliment for the very opposite virtue : and where this is not the case, it is often not difficult to detect, under this false guise of contrition, a secret self complacency, arising from the manifestations which they have afforded of their acuteness or candour in discovering the infirmity in question, or of their frankness or humility in acknowledging it. This will scarcely seem an illiberal suspicion to any one, who either watches the workings of his own heart, or who observes that the faults confessed in these instances are very seldom those, with which the person is most clearly and strongly chargeable.

We must plainly warn these men, and the consideration is seriously pressed on their instructors also, *that they are in danger of deceiving themselves. Let them beware lest they be nominal Christians of another sort.* These persons require to be reminded, that there is no *short compendious method of holiness;* but that it must be the business of their whole lives to grow in grace, and, continually adding one virtue to another, as far as possible, 'to go on towards perfection.' 'He only that doeth righteousness is righteous.' Unless 'they bring forth the fruits of the Spirit,' they can have no sufficient evidence that they have received that 'Spirit of Christ,' 'without which they are none of his.' But where, on the whole, our unwillingness to pass an unfavourable judgment may lead us to indulge a hope, that 'the root of the matter is found in them;' yet we must at least declare to them, that, instead of adorning the doctrine of Christ, they disparage and discredit it. The world sees not their secret humiliation, nor the exercises of their closets; but it is acute in discerning practical weaknesses : and if it observe that they have the same eagerness in the pursuit of wealth or ambition, the same vain taste for ostentation and display, the same ungoverned tempers, which are found in the generality of mankind ; it will treat with contempt their pretences to superior sanctity and indifference to worldly things, and will be hardened in its prejudices against the only mode, which God has provided for our escaping the wrath to come, and obtaining eternal happiness.

Let him then, who would be indeed a Christian, watch over his ways and over his heart with unceasing circumspection. Let him endeavour to learn, both from men and books, particularly from the lives of eminent Christians, what methods have been actually found most effectual for the conquest of every particular vice, and for improvement in every branch of holiness. Thus whilst he studies his own character, and observes the most secret workings of his own mind, and of our common nature; the knowledge which he will acquire of the human heart in general, and especially of his own, will be of the highest utility, in enabling him to avoid or to guard against the occasions of evil: and it will also tend, above all things, to the growth of humility, and to the maintenance of that sobriety of spirit and tenderness of conscience, which are eminently characteristic of the true Christian. It is by this unceasing diligence, as the Apostle declares, that the servants of Christ must make their calling sure: and it is by this only that their labour will ultimately succeed: for 'so an entrance shall be ministered unto them abundantly, into the everlasting kingdom of our Lord and Saviour Jesus Christ.'

NOTES / SOURCES

William Wilberforce, *A Practical View of the Prevailing Religious System, or Professed Christianity in the Higher and Middle Classes in this Country contrasting with Real Christianity* (1797), London, 1827, pp. 290–4

Charles Simeon   1759–1836

Ordained priest in 1783, Charles Simeon became Vicar of Holy Trinity, Cambridge, a living which he held for 53 years until his death. Under the influence of Henry Venn, his ministry was Evangelical in outlook and he exercised a highly significant ministry in the University of Cambridge. A Founder of the Church Missionary Society (1799) and a keen supporter of the Bible Society, he also founded the patronage trust which bears his name.

Growth in Grace

God is my record, how greatly I long after you all in the bowels of Jesus Christ. And this I pray, that your love may abound yet more and more in knowledge and in all judgment; that ye may approve things that are excellent; that ye may be sincere and without offence till the day of Christ; being filled with the fruits of righteousness, which are by Jesus Christ, unto the glory and praise of God.

Phil. i. 8–11.

The connexion subsisting between a pastor and his flock is set forth in the Scriptures under the most endearing images. While *they* are spoken of as his beloved children, *he* is represented as the father that begat them, and as the nursing mother who cherishes them in her bosom. Even these images seem to have been too faint to depict the tender regard which St. Paul bore towards those who had been converted by his ministry. He longed for their welfare with more than human affection. He could compare his feelings with nothing so justly as with the yearning of the Saviour's bowels over a ruined world. Nor was he actuated by partial and personal attachments: his regards were universal: they extended to every member of Christ's mystical body: yea, he could appeal to God himself, that he felt the deepest interest in the prosperity of 'all,' whether more or less distinguished by worldly rank or spiritual attainments. Among the various ways in which he manifests his concern for them, he was especially mindful of prayer and intercession; and though in these benevolent exercises he was solicitous only to approve himself to God, yet he thought it proper on many accounts to inform them of the means he used for their benefit; and to declare to them the particular things which he sought for in their behalf.

From the prayer before us, we see that he desired,

Their intellectual improvement—

'Love' is absolutely essential to a Christian: without that, whatever else we may possess, we are only as sounding brass or tinkling cymbals. Love is the characteristic feature of the Deity: and in this all his children resemble him. By this mark we are made known to others as the disciples of Christ: by this we ourselves also are assured, that we have passed from death unto life. In this amiable quality the Philippians 'abounded.' But the Apostle wished them to abound in it 'yet more and more.' He was solicitous that it should display itself in a becoming manner. He prayed therefore that their 'love might yet more and more abound,'

1. In knowledge—

Knowledge is properly the foundation of love. Whatever we fix our affections upon, we love it for some real or supposed excellence that is in it. If we are unacquainted with the qualities of any person or thing, it is not possible that we should feel any real attachment to him or it. Our love to God therefore, and to his people, should be daily nurtured and strengthened by an increasing acquaintance with them. Our views of the *Divine perfections* are, at best, but very narrow and contracted. So little are we acquainted with his *providence*, that we can only faintly guess at either the reasons or issue of his dispensations. The *mysteries of redemption* are very superficially discovered by us. What we know of *Christ* is extremely partial and defective. The nature, extent, and beauties of *holiness* are very dimly seen. The privileges and blessedness of *the Lord's people* are but little understood. Wherever we turn our eyes, we are circumscribed by very narrow limits. On every side there are heights and depths, and length and breadth, that cannot be explored. To be searching into these things is our imperative duty, our exalted privilege. If 'the angels desire to look into them,' much more should we. It is by more enlarged views of them, that our love to them must be confirmed and advanced. We should therefore labour incessantly to form a just estimate of heavenly things, and to have our affections regulated by an enlightened understanding.

2. In a spiritual perception of the things known—

Merely speculative knowledge is of little avail: it is only like the light of the moon, which dissipates obscurity indeed, but communicates neither heat nor strength. The knowledge which alone will augment our love, is that which produces suitable impressions on the mind; it is that which, like the sun-beam, enlivens and invigorates our whole frame. Now there is a great difference, even amongst good men, with respect to their perception of divine truths. There is, if we may use the expression, a spiritual taste, which is acquired and heightened by exercise. As, in reference to the objects of sense, there is an exquisite 'judgment' attained by some, so that their eye, their ear, and their palate can discern excellencies or defects, where others, with less discriminating organs, perceive nothing particular; so is there, in reference to spiritual things, an exquisite sensibility in some persons, whereby their enjoyment of divine truth is wonderfully enhanced. Now this is the knowledge which we should aspire after, and in which our love should progressively abound. We should not be satisfied with that speculative knowledge which may be gained from men and books; but should seek that spiritual discernment, which nothing but the operation of the Spirit of God upon the soul can produce. Whatever be the particular objects of our regard, we should get a realizing sense of their excellency, and be duly impressed with their importance.

NOTES / SOURCES

Charles Simeon, *Horae Homileticae: or Discourses Digested into one continued Series*, Vol. XVIII, London, 1838, pp. 6–8

Sydney Smith   1771–1845

Educated at Winchester College, and New College, Oxford, he was ordained in 1794 and became a Tutor in Edinburgh. As incumbent of Foston, near York (from 1808), he gave the Assize Sermon, an extract of which is printed below. In 1831 he became a Canon Residentiary of St Paul's Cathedral. He is known for his sharp wit.

The Conclusion of a Sermon for the Assizes, York Minster, 1824

These are the Christian excellences which the members of the profession of the Law have, above all, an opportunity of cultivating: this is your tribute to the happiness of your fellow creatures, and these your preparations for eternal life. Do not lose God in the furtherance of the business of the world; remember that the Churches of Christ are more solemn, and more sacred, than your tribunals; bow not before the judges of the King, and forget the Judge of Judges, search not other men's hearts without heeding that your own hearts will be searched; the innocent in the midst of subtlety; do not carry the lawful arts of your profession beyond your profession; but when the robe of the advocate is laid aside, so live, that no man shall dare to suppose your opinions venal, or that your talents and energy may be bought for a price: do not heap scorn and contempt upon your declining years, by precipitate ardour for success in your profession; but set out with a firm determination to be unknown, rather than ill-known; and to rise honestly if you rise at all.

Let the world see that you have risen, because the natural probity of your heart beat you to truth; because the precision and extent of your legal knowledge enables you to find the right way of doing the right thing; because a thorough knowledge of legal art or legal form, is, in your hands, not an instrument of chicanery, but the plainest, easiest, and shortest way to the end of strife. Impress upon yourselves the importance of your profession, consider that some of the greatest and most important interests of the world, are committed to your care: that you are our protectors against the encroachments of power, that you are the preservers of freedom, the defenders of weakness, the unravellers of cunning, the investigators of artifice, the humblers of pride, and the scourgers of oppression:

when you are silent, the sword leaps from its scabbard, and nations are given up to the madness of internal strife.

In all the civil difficulties of life, men depend upon your exercised faculties, and your spotless integrity; and they require of you an elevation above all that is mean, and a spirit which will never yield when it is not to yield. As long as your profession retains its character for learning, the rights of mankind will be well arranged; as long as it retains its character for virtuous boldness, those rights will be well defended; as long as it preserves itself pure, and incorruptible on other occasions not connected with your profession, those talents will never be used to the public injury, which were intended, and nurtured for the public good. I hope you will weigh these observations, and apply them to the business of the ensuing week, and beyond that, in the common occupations of your profession; always bearing in your minds the emphatic words of the text, and often in the hurry of your busy, active lives, honestly, humbly, heartily exclaiming to the Son of God, 'Master, what shall I do to inherit eternal life?'

NOTES / SOURCES

Sydney Smith, 'Sermon preached in the Cathedral Church of St Peter, York', 1 August 1824, pp. 15–17

Samuel Taylor Coleridge   1772–1834

After an ill-fated attempt to join the army, Samuel Taylor Coleridge returned to his studies in Cambridge but did not take a degree. The son of an Anglican clergyman, he came into contact with the Unitarian Church, Cambridge, and considered for a while entering its ministry. Throughout his life he was influenced by contemporary religious developments but took a pragmatic view as to religion's effect. Best known for his poetry, his life was marked by his continued addiction to opium.

Prayers and Hymns   *June 1, 1830*

There are three sorts of prayer:—1. Public; 2. Domestic; 3. Solitary. Each has its peculiar uses and character. I think the church ought to publish and authorise a directory of forms for the latter two. Yet I fear the execution would be inadequate. There is a great decay of devotional unction in the numerous books of prayers put out now-a-days.

· · · ·

I exceedingly regret that our church pays so little attention to the subject of congregational singing. See how it is! In that particular part of the public worship in which, more than in all the rest, the common people might, and ought to, join,—which, by its association with music, is meant to give a fitting vent and expression to the emotions,—in that part we all sing as Jews; or, at best, as mere men, in the abstract, without a Saviour. You know my veneration for the Book of Psalms, or most of it; but with some half-dozen exceptions, the Psalms are surely not adequate vehicles of Christian thanksgiving and joy! Upon this deficiency in our service, Wesley and Whitfield seized; and you know it is the hearty congregational singing of Christian hymns which keeps the humbler Methodists together. Luther did as much for the Reformation by his hymns as by his translation of the Bible. In Germany, the hymns are known by heart by every peasant: they advise, they argue from the hymns, and every soul in the church praises God, like a Christian, with words which are natural and yet sacred to his mind. No doubt this defect in our service proceeded from the dread which the English Reformers had of being charged with introducing anything into the worship of God but the text of Scripture. (1)

Self-love in Religion

The unselfishness of self-love in the hopes and fears of religion consists;—first,—in the previous necessity of a moral energy, in order so far to subjugate the sensual, which is indeed and properly the selfish, part of our nature, as to believe in a state after death, on the grounds of the Christian religion:—secondly,—in the abstract and, as it were, unindividual nature of the idea, self, or soul, when conceived apart from our present living body and the world of the senses. In my religious meditations of hope and fear, the reflection that this course of action will purchase heaven for me, for my soul, involves a thought of and for all men who pursue the same course. In worldly blessings, such as those promised in the Old Law, each man might make up to himself his own favourite scheme of happiness. 'I will be strictly just, and observe all the laws and ceremonies of my religion, that God may grant me such a woman for my wife, or wealth and honour, with which I will purchase such and such an estate,' etc. But the reward of heaven admits no day-dreams; its hopes and its fears are too vast to endure an outline. 'I will endeavour to abstain from vice, and force myself to do such and such acts of duty, in order that I may make myself capable of that freedom of moral being, without which heaven would be no heaven to me.' Now this very thought tends to annihilate self. For what is a self not distinguished from any other self, but like an individual circle in geometry, uncoloured, and the representative of all other circles. The circle is differenced, indeed, from a triangle or square; so is a virtuous soul from a vicious soul, a soul in bliss from a soul in misery, but no wise distinguished from other souls under the same predicament. That selfishness which includes, of necessity, the selves of all my fellow-creatures, is assuredly a social and generous principle. I speak, as before observed, of the objective or reflex self;—for as to the subjective self, it is merely synonymous with consciousness, and obtains equally whether I think of me or of him;—in both cases it is I thinking.

Still, however, I freely admit that there neither is, nor can be, any such self-oblivion in these hopes and fears when practically reflected on, as often takes place in love and acts of loving kindness, and the habit of which constitutes a sweet and loving nature. And this leads me to the third, and most important reflection, namely, that the soul's infinite capacity of pain and joy, through an infinite duration, does really, on the most high-flying notions of love and justice, make my own soul and the most anxious care for the character of its future fate, an object of emphatic duty. What can be the object of human virtue but the happiness of sentient, still more of moral beings? But an infinite duration of faculties, infinite in progression, even of one soul, is so vast, so boundless an idea, that we are unable to distinguish it from the idea of the whole race of mankind. If to seek the temporal welfare of all mankind be disinterested virtue, much more must the eternal welfare of my own soul be so; for the temporal welfare of all mankind is included within a finite space and finite number, and my imagination makes it easy by sympathies and visions of outward resemblance; but myself in eternity, as the object of my contemplation, differs unimaginably from my present self. Do but try to think of yourself in eternal misery!—you will find that you are stricken with horror for it, even as for a third person; conceive it in hazard thereof, and you will feel commiseration for it, and pray for it with an anguish of sympathy very different from the outcry of an immediate self-suffering.

Blessed be God! that which makes us capable of vicious self-interestedness, capacitates us also for disinterestedness. That I am capable of preferring a smaller advantage of my own to a far greater good of another man,—this, the power of comparing the notions of 'him and me' objectively, enables me likewise to prefer—at least furnishes the condition of my preferring—a greater good of another to a lesser good of my own;—nay, a pleasure of his, or external advantage, to an equal one of my own. And thus too, that I am capable of loving my neighbour as myself, empowers me to love myself as my neighbour, not only as much, but in the same way and with the very same feeling. (2)

Reason and Understanding

The elements (the factors, as it were) of Religion are Reason and Understanding. If the composition stopped in itself, an understanding thus rationalized would lead to the admission of the *general* doctrines of natural religion, the belief of a God, and of immortality; and probably to an acquiescence in the history and ethics of the Gospel. But still it would be a speculative faith, and in the nature of a THEORY; as if the main object of religion were to solve difficulties for the satisfaction of the intellect. Now this state of mind, which alas is the state of too many among our self-entitled *rational* religionists, is a mere balance or compromise of the two powers, not that living and generative interpenetration of both which would give being to *essential* Religion—to the RELIGION, at the birth of which 'we receive the spirit of adoption, whereby we cry Abba, Father; the Spirit itself bearing witness with our spirit, that we are the children of God.' (Rom. viii. 15, 16) In RELIGION there is no abstractions. To the unity and infinity of the Divine Nature, of which it is the partaker, it adds the fullness, and to the fullness the grace and the creative overflowing. That which intuitively it at once beholds and adores, praying always, and rejoicing always—*that* doth it tend to become. In all things and in each thing—for the Almighty Goodness doth not create generalities or abide in abstractions—in each, the meanest, object it bears witness to a mystery of infinite solution. Thus 'beholding as in a glass the glory of the Lord, it is changed into the same image from glory to glory.' (2 Cor. iii. 18) For as it is born and not made, so must it *grow*. As it is the image or symbol of its great object, by the organ of this similitude, as by an eye, it seeth that same image throughout the creation; and from the same cause sympathizeth with all creation in its groans to be redeemed. 'For we know that the whole creation groaneth and travaileth in earnest expectation' (Romans viii. 20–23) of a renewal of its forfeited power, the power, namely, of retiring into that image, which is its substantial form and true life, from the vanity of Self, which then only *is* when *for itself* it hath ceased to be. Even so doth Religion finitely express the *unity* of the infinite Spirit by being a total act of the soul. And even so doth it represent his *fullness* by its depth, by its substantiality, and by an all-pervading vital warmth which—relaxing the rigid consolidating the dissolute, and giving cohesion to that which is about to sink down and fall abroad, as into the dust and *crumble* of the Grave—is a life within life, evermore organizing the soul anew.

Nor doth it express the *fullness* only of the Spirit. It likewise represents his *Overflowing* by its communicativeness, budding and blossoming forth in all earnestness of persuasion, and in all words of sound doctrine: while, like the Citron in a genial soil and climate, it bears a golden fruitage of good-works at the same time, the example waxing in contact with the exhortation, as the ripe orange beside the opening orange-flower. Yea, even his Creativeness doth it shadow out by its own powers of impregnation and production, ('being such a one as Paul the aged, and also a prisoner for Jesus Christ, who begat to a lively hope his son Onesimus in his bonds') regenerating in and through the Spirit the slaves of corruption, and fugitives from a far greater master than Philemon. The love of God, and therefore God himself who is Love, RELIGION strives to express *by* Love, and measures its growth by the increase and activity of its Love. For Christian Love is the last and divinest birth, the harmony, unity, and god-like transfiguration of all the vital, intellectual, moral, and spiritual powers. Now it manifests itself as the sparkling and ebullient spring of well-doing in gifts and in labors; and now as a silent fountain of patience and long-suffering, the fullness of which no hatred or persecution can exhaust or diminish; a more than conqueror in the persuasion, 'that neither death, nor life, nor angels, nor principalities, nor powers, nor things present, nor things to come, nor height, nor depth, nor any other creature, shall be able to separate it from the Love of God which is in Christ Jesus the Lord.' (Rom. viii. 38, 39)

From God's Love through his Son, crucified for us from the beginning of the world, Religion begins: and in Love towards God and the creatures of God it hath its end and completion. O how heavenlike it is to sit among brethren at the feet of a minister who speaks under the influence of Love and is heard under the same influence! For all abiding and spiritual knowledge, infused into a grateful and affectionate fellow-christian, is as the child of the mind that infuses it. The delight which he gives he receives; and in that bright and liberal hour the gladdened preacher can scarce gather the ripe produce of to-day without discovering and looking forward to the green fruits and embryons, the heritage and reversionary wealth of the days to come; till he bursts forth in prayer and thanksgiving—The harvest truly is plenteous, but the labourers few. O gracious Lord of the harvest, send forth labourers into thy harvest! There is no difference between the Jew and the Greek. Thou, Lord over all, art rich to all that call upon thee. But how shall they call on him in whom they have not believed? and how shall they believe in him of whom they have not heard? and how shall they hear without a preacher? and how shall they preach except they be sent? And O! how beautiful upon the mountains are the feet of him that bringeth good tidings, that publisheth peace, that bringeth glad tidings of good things, that publisheth salvation; that saith unto the captive soul, Thy God reigneth! God manifested in the flesh hath redeemed thee! O Lord of the harvest, send forth labourers into thy harvest!!

Join with me, Reader! in the fervent prayer, that we may seek within us, what we can never find elsewhere, that we may find within us what no words can put there, that one only true religion, which elevateth Knowing into Being, which is at once the Science of Being, the Being and the Life of all genuine Science. (3)

Sonnet

Sept. 20, 1796

On Receiving a Letter Informing me of the Birth of a Son

> When they did greet me father, sudden awe
>> Weigh'd down my spirit: I retired and knelt
>> Seeking the throne of grace, but inly felt
> No heavenly visitation upwards draw
> My feeble mind, nor cheering ray impart.
>> Ah me! before the Eternal Sire I brought
>> Th' unquiet silence of confused thought
> And shapeless feelings: my o'erwhelmed heart
> Trembled, and vacant tears stream'd down my face.
> And now once more, O Lord! to thee I bend,
>> Lover of souls! and groan for future grace,
> That ere my babe youth's perilous maze have trod,
>> Thy overshadowing Spirit may descend,
>> And he be born again, a child of God. (4)

My Baptismal Birth-Day

28 October 1833

> God's child in Christ adopted,—Christ my all,—
> What that earth boasts were not lost cheaply, rather
> Than forfeit that blest name, by which I call
> The Holy One, the Almighty God, my Father?—
> Father! in Christ we live, and Christ in Thee—
> Eternal Thou, and everlasting we.
> The heir of heaven, henceforth I fear not death:
> In Christ I live! in Christ I draw the breath
> Of the true life!—Let then earth, sea, and sky
> Make war against me! On my heart I show
> Their mighty master's seal. In vain they try
> To end my life, that can but end its woe.—
> Is that a death-bed where a Christian lies?—
> Yes! but not his—'tis Death itself there dies. (5)

NOTES / SOURCES

1. Samuel Taylor Coleridge, *The Table Talk and Omniana of Samuel Taylor Coleridge*, London, 1884, pp. 90–1
2. Ibid., pp. 404–5
3. Samuel Taylor Coleridge, *Lay Sermons*, Princeton, 1972, pp. 89–93
4. *The Poems of Samuel Taylor Coleridge*, Oxford, 1902, pp. 152–3
5. Ibid., pp. 490–1. He describes his 'baptism day' as his 'spiritual birthday'

John Henry Hobart   1775–1830

Deeply committed to the theological tenets of pre-Tractarian High Churchmanship, John Henry Hobart paid particular regard to the Apostolic succession of the episcopate and with it a profound understanding of Holy Orders. After serving at Trinity Church, New York City, he was elected to the episcopate in New York in 1811, at the age of 36. His episcopal ministry in New York was characterized by an extraordinary zeal for fulfilment of the high demands which he placed upon his office, in particular with regard to the practice of confirmation. His overwhelming commitment was thought a contributory factor in his death at the age of 55 during a missionary tour of the western limit of his diocese.

Participation in Worship

Let a regard for the honour of the Church, and for the glory of GOD who delights in order in his worship, awaken the zeal of every member of the Church. Let him preserve silence in the parts of the service performed by the minister; joining in them not with his voice, but with sincerity of mind and heart. Let him, however, consider it as a sacred duty to *repeat aloud* the parts in the service assigned to the people. He will thus have the satisfaction of performing his share in the important and honourable duty of worshiping GOD. Confession will be rendered more lively, supplication more animated, and praise more ardent when the people join in the service with their *voices* as well as with their *hearts*. Both minister and people thus faithfully performing the respective parts allotted to them, the service of the Church will be exhibited in all its majesty, beauty, and affecting solemnity; and the worship of the Sanctuary will ascend as acceptable incense to the LORD OF HOSTS. (1)

The Peculiar Excellences of the Liturgy

In the Liturgy of our Church there is an admirable mixture of instruction and devotion. The Lessons, the Creeds, the Commandments, the Epistles and Gospels contain the most important and impressive instruction on the doctrines and duties of religion; while the Confession, the Collects and Prayers, the Litany and Thanksgivings lead the understanding and the heart through all the sublime and affecting exercises of devotion. In this truly evangelical and excellent Liturgy the supreme Lord of the universe is invoked by the most appropriate, affecting, and sublime epithets; all the wants to which man, as a dependent and sinful being, is subject are expressed in language at once simple, concise, and comprehensive; these wants are urged by confessions the most humble, and supplications the most reverential and ardent. The all-sufficient merits of Jesus Christ, the Savior of the world, are uniformly urged as the only effectual plea, the only certain pledge of divine mercy and grace; and with the most instructive lessons from the sacred oracles and the most profound confessions and supplications is mingled the sublime chorus of praise, begun by the minister and responded with one heart and one voice from the assembled congregation. The mind, continually passing from one exercise of worship to another, and, instead of one continued and uniform prayer, sending up its wishes and aspirations in short and varied collects and supplications, is never suffered to grow languid or weary. The affections of the worshiper ever kept alive by the tender and animating fervour which breathes through the service, he worships his God and Redeemer in spirit and in truth, with reverence and awe, with lively gratitude and love; the exalted joys of devotion are poured upon his soul; he feels that it is good for him to draw near unto God, and that a day spent in his courts, is better than a thousand passed in the tents of the ungodly. (2)

NOTES / SOURCES

1. John Henry Hobart, 'A Companion to the Book of Common Prayer' (1805/1827), in J. Robert Wright (ed.), *Prayer Book Spirituality*, New York, 1989, p. 56
2. John Henry Hobart, 'A Companion for the Festivals and Fasts of the Protestant Episcopal Church' (1804), in ibid., pp. 94–5

John Jebb   1775–1833

Following studies at Trinity College, Dublin, John Jebb later became Bishop of Limerick (1822) after the publication in 1820 of his *Essay on Sacred Literature*. A friend for many years of Alexander Knox (q.v.), he is regarded as pioneer of the Oxford Movement, stressing the elements of continuity and the 'Via Media' of the Church of England. His Tract on *The Peculiar Character of the Church of England* had a formative influence on John Henry Newman's *Lectures on the Prophetical Office of the Church* (1837).

The Anglican Genius

Church of England steers a middle course. She reveres the Scripture: she respects tradition. She encourages investigation: but she checks presumption. She bows to the authority of ages: but she owns no living master upon earth. She rejects alike, the wild extravagance of unauthorized opinion, and the tame subjection of compulsory belief. Where the Scripture clearly and freely speaks, she receives its dictates as the voice of God. When Scripture is either not clear, or explicit; or when it may demand expansion and illustration, she refers her sons to an authoritative standard of interpretation; but a standard, which it is their privilege to apply for themselves. And when Scripture is altogether silent, she provides a supplemental guidance: but a guidance, neither fluctuating nor arbitrary; the same in all times, and under all circumstances; which no private interest can warp, and no temporary prejudice can lead astray. Thus, her appeal is made to past ages, against every possible error of the present. Thus, though the great mass of Christendom, and even though the vast majority of our own national church, were to depart from the purity of Christian faith and practice, yet, no well-taught member of that church need hesitate, or tremble. His path is plain. It is not, merely, his own judgment; it is not, by any means, the dictatorial mandate of an ecclesiastical director, which is to silence his scruples, and dissolve his doubts. His resort is, that concurrent, universal, and undeviating sense of pious antiquity, which he has been instructed, and should be encouraged, to embrace, to follow, and revere.

NOTES / SOURCES

John Jebb, *Sermons on Subjects chiefly practical with illustrative notes, and an appendix*, London, 1815, pp. 397–8.

John Marriott   (1780–1825)

John Marriott was private tutor to George Henry, Lord Scott (1804–1808), and an intimate of Sir Walter Scott. He became Rector of Church Lawford, Warwickshire (1807), and held curacies in Devon. A writer of hymns and poetry, he contributed to Scott's *Minstrelsy of the Scottish Bard*. This hymn to the Trinity is probably his best known work; written in 1813, it was altered slightly in 1866 for ease of singing.

A Hymn to the Trinity

Thou, Whose Eternal Word
Chaos and darkness heard,
    And took their flight;
Hear us, we humbly pray,
And where the Gospel-day
Sheds not its glorious ray,
    Let there be light!

Thou, who didst come to bring
On thy redeeming wing
    Healing and sight,
Health to the sick in mind,
Sight to the inly blind,
O now to all mankind
    Let there be light!

Spirit of truth and love,
Life-giving, holy Dove,
    Speed forth thy flight;
Move on the water's face,
Bearing the lamp of grace,
And in earth's darkest place
    Let there be light!

Blessed and holy and
Glorious Trinity,
    Wisdom, Love, Might;
Boundless as ocean's tide
Rolling in fullest pride,
Through the world far and wide
    Let there be light!

NOTES / SOURCES
John Marriott, in *Historical Companion to Hymns Ancient and Modern*, London, 1962, p. 288

Reginald Heber   1783–1826

Having won a number of prizes for English and Latin, he became Fellow of All Souls College, Oxford, in 1805. In 1815 he gave the Bampton Lectures on 'The Personality and Office of the Christian Comforter'. During his three years as Bishop of Calcutta (1823–1826), he was active in finalizing the establishment of its Bishop's College. He published a life and edited writings of Jeremy Taylor (q.v.). A firm advocate of the importance of hymnody, several of his popular compositions are still sung.

The Trinity

Holy, Holy, Holy! LORD GOD Almighty!
　　Early in the morning our song shall rise to Thee:
Holy, Holy, Holy! Merciful and Mighty!
　　GOD in Three Persons, Blessèd TRINITY!

Holy, Holy, Holy! all the Saints adore Thee,
　　Casting down their golden crowns around the glassy sea;
Cherubim and Seraphim falling down before Thee,
　　Which wert, and art, and evermore shalt be.

Holy, Holy, Holy! though the darkness hide Thee,
　　Though the eye of sinful man Thy glory may not see,
Only Thou art Holy, there is none beside Thee
　　Perfect in power, in love, and purity.

Holy, Holy, Holy! LORD GOD Almighty!
　　All Thy works shall praise Thy Name, in earth, and sky, and sea;
Holy, Holy, Holy! Merciful and Mighty!
　　GOD in Three Persons, Blessèd TRINITY! Amen. (1)

The Worship of the Incarnate Christ

Virgin-born, we bow before Thee;
Blessèd was the womb that bore Thee;
　　Mary, Mother meek and mild,
　　Blessèd was she in her Child.

Blessèd was the breast that fed Thee;
Blessèd was the hand that led Thee;
　　Blessèd was the parent's eye
　　That watch'd Thy slumbering infancy.

Blessèd she by all creation,
Who brought forth the world's salvation,
   Blessèd they—for ever blest,
   Who love Thee most and serve Thee best.

Virgin-born, we bow before Thee;
Blessèd was the womb that bore Thee;
   Mary, Mother meek and mild,
   Blessèd was she in her Child. Amen. (2)

Foreign Missions

All the ends of the earth shall see the salvation of our God.   *Isai.* lii. 10.

From Greenland's icy mountains,
   From India's coral strand,
Where Afric's sunny fountains
   Roll down their golden sand,
From many an ancient river,
   From many a palmy plain,
They call us to deliver
   Their land from error's chain.

What though the spicy breezes
   Blow soft o'er Ceylon's isle,
Though every prospect pleases
   And only man is vile,
In vain with lavish kindness
   The gifts of GOD are strown,
The heathen in his blindness
   Bows down to wood and stone.

Can we, whose souls are lighted
   With wisdom from on high,
Can we to men benighted
   The lamp of life deny?
Salvation! Oh, salvation!
   The joyful sound proclaim,
Till each remotest nation
   Has learn'd Messiah's name.

Waft, waft, ye winds, His story,
   And you, ye waters, roll,
Till, like a sea of glory,
   It spreads from pole to pole;
Till o'er our ransom'd nature
   The Lamb for sinners slain,
Redeemer, King, Creator,
   In bliss returns to reign. Amen. (3)

NOTES / SOURCES

1. Reginald Heber, in *Hymns Ancient and Modern: Historical Edition*, London, 1909, p. 426
2. Ibid., p. 322
3. Ibid., p. 663

PART 3

1830 – 2001

Introduction

FROM 1830 to the death of Archbishop Michael Ramsey in 1988, Anglicanism, in common with the rest of the world, experienced massive changes in context and in culture. At the start of this period Anglicanism still meant largely the Church of England and Ireland, whose Establishment included Wales, together with the small Episcopal Church of Scotland emerging from a period of penal laws. Following the American War of Independence the Protestant Episcopal Church of the United States was beginning to find how it could exist as an independent episcopal church, and was even looked to by John Henry Newman as a hopeful sign for the future, with an episcopal order of government free from the constraints of Establishment, though he was puzzled as to how a High Church American bishop (John Henry Hobart of New York) could combine sound doctrine with political republicanism. The appointment of Thomas Fanshawe Middleton as bishop of Calcutta (in reality all the territory of the East India Company) in 1814 had signalled a new departure for Anglicanism in India, and for the rest of the nineteenth century Anglicanism expanded in every part of the globe colonized by Britain, as well as in countries such as Korea and Japan. In the twentieth century there was an even wider spread into such places as French-speaking Africa.

In England the removal of many of the disabilities suffered by Dissenters and the abolition of Anglican religious tests for membership of Parliament and for the holding of local civic office marked a change in the old confessional state. It is not surprising that, as a consequence, questions were asked about the identity of the Church of England, questions which contributed in a particular way to the emergence of the Oxford Movement, with John Keble's Assize Sermon of 1833 and the subsequent publication of the *Tracts for the Times*. The Irish Church was disestablished in 1869, and the Welsh Church somewhat later in 1920. The Universities of Oxford and Cambridge, which for centuries had nurtured the majority of Anglican clergy, ceased to be Anglican preserves with the passing of the Universities Tests Act in 1870.

It is significant that the word 'Anglicanism' (though not the word 'Anglican') is a nineteenth-century coinage. This in itself witnesses to the nineteenth-century quest for an Anglican ecclesial identity. The French Catholic writer Felicité de Lamennais spoke of *anglicanisme* in 1817, by analogy with *gallicanisme* as a term for the Catholic Church in France, and Newman provided the first English instance of its use in 1838. It is not surprising that this growing concern with self-definition led to the development of more defined 'parties' within the Church of England and within Anglicanism more generally. These 'parties' were frequently differentiated by traditions of piety, and liturgical expression, though labelling is often difficult and it is a mistake to present these parties as having hard and fast boundaries. In particular the growing Catholic Revival throughout the nineteenth century and for the earlier part of the twentieth, was a powerful influence on Anglican worship and devotion, but there were equally significant currents stemming from the eighteenth-century Evangelical revival, some of which flowed into the Catholic revival, and some of which were strongly differentiated from it. The impact of American Revivalism through such figures as Dwight Moody and Ira D. Sankey, and from the mission preaching of French Catholicism shaped a greater involvement with revival and mission by both Evangelicals and 'Ritualists'. The Keswick Conventions began in 1875 with the aim of 'the promotion of Practical Holiness'. The Broad Church tradition comprised both those seeking a 'middle way' between Catholic and Evangelical, but also those powerfully influenced by the critical questions arising from the historical study of the Bible and from the new scientific movements. The theological tradition associated with Frederick Denison Maurice (1805–1872) is often labelled as Broad Church but owes more to Coleridge and the influence of Platonism. The Greek Fathers were significant for both this tradition and the Tractarians. Later in the nineteenth century, idealist philosophy was a significant influence on Anglican theology and to some extent devotion. Theologically an emphasis on the incarnation characterized both Anglican writing and spirituality, and the vision of *Christus consummator*, Christ the fulfiller, expressed a high doctrine of creation and may have contributed to the relative ease with which most Anglicans were able to come to terms with the evolutionary understanding of the world characteristic of much nineteenth-century philosophy and, of course, particularly in the scientific theories of Charles Darwin. In the twentieth century, following the First World War, which had a significant impact on Anglican devotion, notably in winning a wider acceptance for prayer for the departed, as well as revealing the alienation of many from the Christian faith, there was a recovery of the importance of *Christus Redemptor*, and Karl Barth's theology of revelation shaped the sharp theological understanding of thinkers like Sir Edwyn Hoskyns.

In England the Catholic Revival was marked by a development of ritual and ceremonial in worship, richer and more elaborate liturgical developments provoking conflict with Evangelicals who saw such developments as a revival of popish practices outlawed at the Reformation. A series of Ritualist prosecutions made martyrs of some Ritualist priests and may well have had the opposite effect from that intended by those who initiated such lawsuits in entrenching and encouraging more catholic forms of devotion. Those touched by the Catholic Revival were not only active in new parishes in expanding urban areas in England, but were as committed as Evangelicals to missionary work overseas, where liturgical innovation could often be pursued with a greater freedom than in England. So Catholic liturgical forms could be found in many of the great American Anglo-Catholic Churches, in places like Nashotah House in the mission field of the Midwest, and in significant parts of Africa and in some parts of Asia.

One of the consequences of the development of the Catholic movement and the ritual controversies was an increasing pressure to revise *The Book of Common Prayer*. The Episcopal Church of Scotland and the Protestant Episcopal Church in the United States already had their own prayer books, recognizably of the family of the English Prayer Book but with their own variations. The Church of Ireland and the Church in Wales were to follow suit. In England the Royal Commission on Ecclesiastical Discipline (1906) concluded that the legal restrictions on worship and ceremonial were 'too narrow for the religious life of this generation' and this led to the process of Prayer Book revision that culminated in the 1927, and then the 1928, revised Prayer Book, which failed in the end to gain the sanction of Parliament. Revisions in other parts of the Anglican Communion were not so hampered, but from the 1960s all Western churches were engaged with revisions of their forms of worship, a notable impetus coming from the liturgical reforms in the Roman Catholic Church of the Second Vatican Council, when worship in the vernacular became all but universal in the Catholic Church. The revisions of the later part of the twentieth century, the *Alternative Service Book 1980* in England and parallel revisions elsewhere, have led to an increasing use of contemporary language, and the disappearance of a single, unifying liturgical text used by all Anglicans. *Common Worship* (2000) is a further English revision, no longer published in a single book and with a much wider range of options. As the change from manuscript to printing standardized liturgy, so the information technology revolution has created liturgy shaped in a broad common pattern but no longer a common prayer whose words can be engraved on the worshipper's heart. If there is gain in being able to compile special services for special occasions, and in an ever-increasing ecumenical exchange, there is loss undoubtedly in the weakening of the memory of common prayer. The days when the Sunday collect was learned by heart have gone for ever. The 1998 Lambeth Conference witnessed to an energy of liturgical revision around the Communion, and also to a variety of cultural styles of presentation, yet the shape of the eucharistic liturgy was recognisably the same and it would be too drastic a judgement to say that common prayer as a unifying constituent of Anglicanism, and the essential foundation of growth in holiness, has evaporated.

When George Augustus Selwyn went as bishop to New Zealand, where Queen Victoria had assigned him a large part of Polynesia as well as the two islands of New Zealand itself, he realized the need for synodical forms to be developed to give Anglicanism outside of the Church of England establishment a coherent theological structure. In the twentieth century those synodical forms became the pattern of church polity in all parts of what developed as the Anglican Communion, particularly as churches in Africa and Asia achieved self-government in a way which was often parallel with independence from colonial rule by Britain. With the first Lambeth Conference in 1867, there began the series of Lambeth Conferences which have been a chief means of holding together an increasingly widespread Communion now rooted in many different cultures, and freed from domination first by the British Empire, then by English education and language. Inevitably, perhaps, many of the expressions of the quest for holiness found in the churches in Africa, Asia, and Australasia begin with the testimony of missionaries from England and elsewhere and the impact they made on the early converts. In India, where there was a need to engage with a strong, literary culture shaped by other faiths, there was a stronger tradition of written reflection on the spiritual life and it is not surprising that Indian writers have therefore a strong representation in this anthology. If there is less representation of Africa than might be expected in this final section of this anthology it is largely because until very recent times Africa unlike India has been a less literary culture.

A central concern of the Oxford Movement was the renewal of the church in holiness. The first sermon of Newman's *Parochial and Plain Sermons* bears the title 'Holiness necessary for Future Blessedness', and in his *Apologia pro vita sua* (1864) he notes how he used almost as proverbs the words of Thomas Scott, the Evangelical biblical commentator of the previous century, 'holiness before peace' and 'growth is the only evidence of life'. Newman's strong sense of providential guidance sprang from his early Evangelicalism, and is echoed in his poem *The Pillar of the Cloud* ('Lead, kindly light') which became popular and influential as a hymn. John Keble's *Christian Year* (1827), consisting of poems built on scriptural texts on the services and calendar of the Prayer Book, was concerned to shape 'a sober standard of feeling', disciplining the religious emotions, and inculcating a strongly sacramental sense of the world as God's creation, influenced both by contemporary romanticism and the theology of the Greek Fathers. Both Keble and Newman taught a doctrine of 'reserve' in relation to religious knowledge, stressing the mystery that was inseparable from revelation, and a sense of 'economy' or 'dispensation' in God's self-disclosure. A renewed interest in the doctrine of the church was coupled with a revival in eucharistic devotion. An emphasis on baptismal regeneration and the awesome character of the Christian calling to live out the baptismal life led to a new emphasis on sacramental confession as the appointed means by which Christians might be restored after serious sin to a renewed following of the life of grace. Dr Pusey was the author of a major tract on baptism, and was condemned by the University of Oxford for the high doctrine of the Eucharist expounded in his 1843 sermon, *The Holy Eucharist a Comfort to the Penitent*. Widely used as a confessor, Pusey also played a leading part in the revival of the religious life in Anglicanism. His disciple, Richard Meux Benson (1824–1915) founded the Society of St John the Evangelist (the Cowley Fathers), and, along with other members of the Society, was a notable teacher and spiritual guide. From the first appearance of the term in 1838 (when it tended to refer to the English manifestation of the Catholic Church), Anglo-Catholicism became a defining word for the heirs of the Oxford Movement. Recent study has seen the movement as in many ways a counter-cultural one, whose sacerdotalism, aesthetic attraction, social concern, and repudiation of much Victorian 'muscular Christianity' combined with other forces making for a 'party' identity. At its high water mark in England at the time of the inter-war Anglo-Catholic congresses, when it became for adherents just their conventional pattern of Anglicanism, it had also become a legitimate expression of Anglicanism.

There was cross-fertilization between Anglicans and Roman Catholics in the adaptation by Anglicans of Roman books of devotion, in the translation of many Latin hymns, in the influence of French religious orders on the rules of some of the new Anglican sisterhoods and communities, and of French mission preaching in Anglican missions and revivals, which also drew on Protestant revivalist techniques. Hymns, which apart from the *Veni Creator* in the ordination service had no place in *The Book of Common Prayer*, in the nineteenth century became a major part of Anglican devotional life. A defining moment was the publication of *Hymns Ancient and Modern* in 1861 which set the pattern for Anglican hymn books in providing hymns for the liturgical year as well as hymns of personal devotion. *The English Hymnal* (1906) continued and built on this process. In their preface the compilers noted the ecumenical character of hymnody as witnessing 'to the fact that in the worship of God Christians are drawn the closer together as they are drawn more closely to the one Lord.' 'The hymns of Christendom show more clearly than anything else that there is even now such a thing as the unity of the Spirit.' The work of John Mason Neale in translating hymns from Greek sources ensured a significant influence from the Orthodox tradition, Gerard Moultrie's *Let all mortal flesh keep silence* a paraphrase of the hymn at the Great Entrance in the Orthodox Liturgy of St James is a powerful example of this, and it has seemed right to include a few of these translations because they have become so integrally part of Anglican worship and devotion. William Bright, besides his fine eucharistic hymn, *And now, O Father, mindful of the love*, translated many Latin prayers in his *Ancient Collects* (1861), and also composed some original ones which have passed into wide Anglican usage. Eric Milner-White, Dean of King's College, Cambridge, and later York, was a master of resonant language for liturgical prayer as well as shaping the Christmas service of Nine Lessons and Carols which has through broadcasting probably become the Anglican service shared by the largest number of people.

The sermon continued for the nineteenth century to be a principle vehicle for Anglicans of all traditions for teaching about growth in Christian holiness. John Henry Newman's *Parochial and Plain Sermons*, interestingly republished with scarcely any alteration after he became a Roman Catholic, are among the classics of Christian preaching. John Keble's sermons were collected and published after his death in 1866 and, like Newman's, explore the mysteries of faith in relation to the Christian Year. Pusey is the only one of the Oxford Movement fathers who might be called ecstatic, and his sermons not only draw copiously on the Fathers and on a wide range of medieval spiritual writers, but reveal a deep awareness of God's transcendence and the transfiguring grace of the Holy Spirit. Manning's Anglican sermons show some of the same characteristics. In the twentieth century Sir Edwyn Hoskyns (1884–1937) was a powerful academic preacher, who searchingly explored the Christian life, and later still Austin Farrer (1904–1968) was a masterly writer of English prose as well as a profound theologian. R. E. C. Browne (1906–1975) in his *Ministry of the Word* (1958) explored in a penetrating way the spirituality of preaching.

The growing awareness of the practice of spiritual direction, and again perhaps Roman Catholic influence, meant that letters of spiritual guidance begin to figure more prominently in the quest for holiness, and it should not be forgotten that diaries and journals grew out of the keeping of spiritual journals. It is not surprising to find members of the new religious orders, such as R. M. Benson, William O'Brien, and the American, Shirley Hughson, among such letter writers, but Evelyn Underhill (1875–1941) stands out as a correspondent and as the author of significant retreat addresses as well as one who had reflected deeply on the meaning of worship and the nature of Christian mysticism. She has fair claim to a significant place not only among Christian women but among leading writers on the practice of prayer and the spiritual life. In more recent times Mother Mary Clare of the Sisters of the Love of God had a similarly penetrating vision, and another religious, Christopher Bryant, SSJE, produced important books integrating Jungian psychology with the Christian spiritual tradition.

It has often been remarked how close is the connection between literature and Anglican spirituality. Although not in many ways as obvious in this later period as in earlier centuries, there are still significant poets and powerful prose writers. Newman would be a master in any generation, but some of the significant writers of the twentieth century are T. S. Eliot, Charles Williams, and C. S. Lewis. In his *Four Quartets* Eliot explored in powerful symbolic language the spiritual journey with a strong sense of how the past is both elusive and appropriated, drawing on Lancelot Andrewes for the final lines of 'Little Gidding', when 'the end of all our exploring will be to arrive where we started and know the place for the first time'. Williams and Lewis were both members of the group of Oxford friends known as the 'Inklings', which included the Roman Catholic, J. R. R. Tolkien. Williams wrote powerfully in novels, poetry, plays, and essays about the Christian life as being at its heart a way of co-inherence, and Lewis proved to be one of the most doughty of Christian apologists of the twentieth century, as well as in his Narnia stories creating an imaginative world that is grounded in a theology of grace and redemption. As A. M. Allchin has commented 'this is a tradition which by its form as well as its content seems to speak of a particular perception of the link between grace and nature, faith and culture, divine and human, which has been characteristic of Anglican spirituality as a whole, and has had its influence more widely in the intellectual history of the English-speaking world'.[1] In the context of the trenches of the First World War, Geoffrey Studdert Kennedy ('Woodbine Willie', 1883–1929) expressed in passionate poetry the dilemma of believing in a God who permitted such appalling suffering, and found that only in the cross was any possible answer to be found.

---

[1] A. M. Allchin, 'Anglican Spirituality' in Stephen Sykes and John Booty (eds.), SPCK/Fortress Press, London and Philadelphia, 1988, p. 316

It is only to be expected that much of Christian writing on the way of holiness will be concerned with the practice of prayer and the ascetic discipline of personal life, but this is far from meaning that holiness is an otherworldly quality removed from seeking peace and justice and the command that we should love our neighbour. As St John reminds us, if we do not love our brother whom we have seen how can we love God whom we have not seen? To be formed in the likeness of Christ means to be formed in the likeness of his serving love. The devoted ministry of a slum priest like Charles Lowder; the concern for the kingdom of God of Frederick Denison Maurice; the protests of Stewart Headlam at the end of the nineteenth century; and a century later of the American, William Stringfellow; as well as the intellectual weight of a scholar such as R. H. Tawney and the leadership of a William Temple, combining social concern with a theology of divine order and a spirituality, particularly attracted, as many Anglicans have been, to the Gospel of John, all witness to a road to holiness leading through the world and not apart from it. When John Keble wrote in well-known lines:

> *We need not bid, for cloister'd cell,*
> *Our neighbour and our work farewell*

and reminded his readers that

> *The trivial round, the common task,*
> *Will furnish all we ought to ask;*
> *Room to deny ourselves; a road*
> *To bring us, daily, nearer God*

he underlined the fact that the way of holiness was a way of love and not something esoteric. Faithful discipleship in the place where God has placed us is one with a concern for the poor and needy, by which such discipleship needs continually to be challenged. Part of that challenge is necessarily addressed to the temptations of the religious to be absorbed in 'churchy' concerns, and a particularly powerful example of this is the address of Bishop Frank Weston of Zanzibar to the Anglo-Catholic congress of 1923 with its passionate appeal to Anglo-Catholics to find Christ not just present in the Sacrament but in the destitute and deprived.

In many parts of the world the context in which Anglicans have prayed and worshipped has been one of other faiths and not surprisingly it was the Indian subcontinent that first had to wrestle with the relation of Christian worship and devotion to Hindu and Buddhist patterns of prayer. William Hodge Mill's *Christa-sangita* (1838) is a significant early example of a combination of Christian devotion and Sanskrit poetry. Later writers like C. F. Andrews (1871–1940) together with many notable Indians, and bishops, such as Lakshman Wickreme-singhe (1927–1983) in Sri Lanka, explored both the uniqueness of Christ and the way in which Christ could be seen as fulfilling the religious aspirations of the Vedas.

During the almost two centuries represented by this final section of this anthology of Anglican writings on holiness there have been immense cultural changes, affecting in particular the Western world, and these have left their mark on Anglican writing about the Christian spiritual journey. The nineteenth-century saw the emergence of the critical study of the Bible, with its sharp questions about the evolution of the biblical text and the historicity of many of the events described in it. Such analysis could call into question the devotional use of Scripture that had been the pattern for earlier generations, but that this was not more destructive was the consequence of the combination of profound scholarship and deep devotion in scholar bishops such as Joseph Barber Lightfoot (1828–1889), Brooke Foss Westcott (1825–1901) and William Temple (1881–1944). Michael Ramsey, Archbishop of Canterbury from 1961 to 1974, was a biblical, and profoundly Trinitarian, theologian who drank deep at the wells of Orthodoxy, and it is notable that both the Trinitarian emphasis and an openness to the riches of the Eastern Christian tradition, not least through the growing appreciation of icons as aids to devotion, has continued to shape Anglican life and spirituality. Ramsey believed passionately that contemplative prayer was not just for enclosed religious, and this was undoubtedly significant when the sharp questioning of religious language provoked the theological storms of the 1960s. It is good that Bishop John Robinson, author of *Honest to God*, is represented here as well as Michael Ramsey. The emergence of a scientific world view troubled the nineteenth-century in the controversies surrounding evolution and Darwin's theory of natural selection in *The Origin of Species* (1859), yet there were also distinguished scientist priests such as Charles Raven (1865–1964), and Charles Kingsley's comment on the evolutionary controversies that whereas it was 'once thought God made all things, now we know something even more wonderful, he made all things make themselves' sums up a characteristically Anglican sympathy with new knowledge.

John Henry Newman said of the church that 'it changes always in order to remain the same'. The call to holiness is the call of Jesus Christ, yesterday, today, and for ever, but the way of holiness necessarily runs through the landscapes of particular cultures and particular traditions. The self-denying ordinance in the choice of writings from this last period, that nothing is taken from authors who are still living, inevitably means that there is less than there otherwise might be from feminist spirituality or from representatives of contemporary charismatic writing. But there are tongues of flame in plenty here and, at the end, as T. S. Eliot reminds us in echoes of Lancelot Andrewes, speaking of the Christian hope of participation in the life of God, those tongues of flame will be 'in-folded into the crowned knot of fire, and the fire and the rose are one'. Or, as St Paul said, 'God will be all in all'.

Harriet Auber 1773–1862

Born in London, Harriet Auber lived for the greater part of her life at Broxbourne and Hoddesdon in Hertfordshire. She was the author of many devotional poems including the *Spirit of the Psalms* (1829), from which a number of psalm versions were included in hymn books.

Our Blest Redeemer

Our Blest Redeemer, ere He breathed
　His tender last farewell,
A Guide, a Comforter, bequethed
　With us to dwell.

He came in semblance of a dove,
　With sheltering wings outspread,
The holy balm of peace and love
　On earth to shed.

He came in tongues of living flame
　To teach, convince, subdue,
All powerful as the wind He came
　As viewless too.

He came sweet influence to impart,
　A gracious willing Guest,
While He can find one humble heart
　Wherein to rest.

And His that gentle voice we hear,
　Soft as the breath of even,
That checks each fault, that calms each fear,
　And speaks of heaven.

And every virtue we possess,
　And every conquest won,
And every thought of holiness,
　Are His alone.

SPIRIT of purity and grace,
　Our weakness, pitying, see:
O make our hearts Thy dwelling-place,
　And worthier Thee.

NOTES / SOURCES

Harriet Auber, in *Hymns Ancient & Modern Second Edition*, London, 1875, No. 207
Verse 2 as quoted in *Companion to Hymns and Psalms*, Peterborough, 1988
Verse 3 as quoted in Julian, *A Dictionary of Hymnology*, London, 1892

Edward Bickersteth 1786–1850

Originally a solicitor by training and practice, following ordination Bickersteth served as a secretary of the Church Missionary Society from 1816–1830 when he became Vicar of Watton in Hertfordshire. An opponent of both Roman Catholicism and Tractarianism within the Church of England, he was one of the founders of the Parker Society and of the Evangelical Alliance. He published a number of devotional treatises on prayer (1818), on the Lord's Supper (1822), and on baptism (1840). After the death of Charles Simeon in 1836 he became, until his own death, a leader of the Evangelicals. A friend of Lord Shaftesbury, he was a social campaigner in the cause against children working in factories.

The Lord's Supper is a Pleading of Christ's Sacrifice

The Lord's Supper was designed to represent, commemorate, and shew forth the Lord's death as a sacrifice for sin. This is done for our own edification, as a testimony to the world and as a prevailing mode of pleading his merits before God. It has been observed that 'What we more compendiously express in that general conclusion of our prayers, *through Jesus Christ our Lord*, we more fully and forcibly represent in the celebration of the Holy Eucharist, wherein we plead the virtue and merits of the same sacrifice here, that our great High Priest is continually urging for us in heaven.'

Whenever then, Christian reader, you celebrate this ordinance, we exhort you in the expressive words of a late writer. 'Look up to the offering of Jesus Christ once for all: look to him as dying for the remission of your sins; washing them away in his precious blood, suffering that you might be saved. And while you are kneeling under his cross, touched with the utmost possible sense of God's love, who gave his only-begotten Son, and affected with sentiments of the most tender devotion to him who gave himself for you; embrace also with your good will all mankind whom he loved for his sake. Then rise up, by his grace, to the sober, continual practice of everything that is good and excellent, and praiseworthy, and conformable to such sentiments and affections, and the obligations laid on you by his infinite love.'

The observance of the Lord's Supper contains also a virtual DECLARATION OF OUR EXPECTATION OF HIS COMING AGAIN. We shew forth the Lord's death *till he come.*

By this ordinance we acknowledge that Jesus Christ will come to JUDGE THE WORLD. We shew that we believe that a solemn day is approaching, when *God shall bring every work into judgment, with every secret thing, whether it be good or evil*—that all mankind shall then be divided into two classes, and only two, the righteous and the wicked—the future inhabitants of heaven and of hell—of everlasting punishment and everlasting life. Partaking of the Lord's Supper is an implied and public avowal of this expectation. How important is this avowal! How well calculated to restrain evil, and encourage righteousness! How suited to fill us with a holy reverence of God, and a just fear of displeasing him! (1)

The Whole Service of Holy Communion is Full of Meaning

The whole of this service may be considered, as a public record, of the most solemn and important transaction that can take place on earth, between the fallen spirit of man, accepting salvation by Jesus Christ, and *the God of the spirits of all flesh*, giving the pledge of that salvation by his Ministers.

The service begins with the Lord's Prayer; well may we commence this solemn transaction with addressing God as a Father, and with petitions for the advancement of his glory, the gift of our daily bread and the forgiveness of our own sins, with a profession to forgive all others sinning against us. These petitions will all bear an edifying reference to the important duty, in which we are about to engage.

The affecting prayer that God would 'cleanse the thoughts of our hearts, by the inspiration of his Holy Spirit,' is adapted to our fallen and impure state, unable of ourselves to think any thing aright, and yet hoping for the promised aid of the Holy Spirit. To pray that we may perfectly love God, is a suitable introduction to the ten commandments, which are next brought before us, Love being the fulfilling of the law.

The compilers of our Liturgy knowing that *by the law is the knowledge of sin*, and that a penitent heart is most needful for a due reception of the Lord's Supper, have well placed, at the commencement of this service, THE TEN COMMAND-MENTS, containing a comprehensive summary of the holy law of God. We must not suppose that these precepts relate only to the outward act of sin; our Lord has shewn us that they forbid that principle, or love of sin, which leads to outward iniquity. When for instance, it is said, *Thou shalt have none other Gods but me*, it forbids our forgetfulness of God, and our love of the world; *if any man love the world, the love of the Father is not in him*. When it is said, *thou shall do no murder*, angry thoughts, and malice, and revenge are forbidden, as well as murder. When we are told, *Thou shalt not commit adultery*, impure thoughts are equally forbidden. This manifestly is the obedience which the Lord of all requires. Mat. v, 21, 22, 27, 28. Hence you observe that after every command the congregation are directed to say, 'Lord have mercy on us,' hereby, as it is said in the rubric, 'asking God mercy for their transgressions thereof for the time past.' You should enquire, therefore, whether, when you have repeated these words after each command, you really felt that you had in the sight of God broken that command, and needed his pardoning mercy. We are farther taught to add, 'and incline our hearts to keep this law.' This plainly expresses, if we repeat it in sincerity, that we are convinced that we have neither natural inclination, nor power of ourselves, to obey God's holy commands; but look up to him and depend wholly on him, to dispose and enable us to do his will; and really purpose and desire to obey his holy law. (2)

A Prayer for Parents after the Baptism of their Child

O Lord God Almighty, in pursuance of our Saviour's gracious words, suffer little children to come unto me, we have taken our child, in faith and prayer, unto thee; we beseech thee give us the full blessing which we have asked, and enable us to bring up this child day by day in thy faith, fear, and love. O make all our plans for its spiritual welfare effectual, by thine own mighty and invincible Spirit, that the old man may be daily mortified and subdued, and the new man be quickened and strengthened to thy glory, and the everlasting salvation of our beloved child, through Jesus, our Redeemer. Amen. (3)

Prayers before and after Confirmation

Almighty Father, I bless thy holy name that when I was young, I was, by the care and love of others, early consecrated to thee, and baptized in the name of Jesus. And now I desire to reap the full benefit of thine ordinance, by confirming with my own mouth what was done for me when young. Help me by thine own spirit, to believe with the heart all thy love in Christ Jesus. I praise thee, who hast called me to be a member of Christ, a child of God, and an inheritor of the kingdom of heaven. With joy of heart enable me to confess with my mouth the Lord Jesus. Let thy Holy Spirit so teach me that I may fully realize the blessings which thou hast given me in him, and yield myself, and all I am wholly and entirely to him, who has bought me with his blood. May I joyfully suffer with him here, that I may reign with him for ever hereafter; daily taking up my cross, and following my crucified Saviour. Hear me, for his great name's sake.

After Confirmation.

My Lord and my God, I am thine; keep me thine for ever; uphold my goings in thy paths to the end. Shed abroad thy love in my heart, by the Holy Ghost, more and more; and knowing and believing the love which thou hast towards me, may that love constrain me every day not to live to myself, but to him who died for me. In the hour of temptation succour me; amidst the scorn of evil men sustain my soul, that I may never deny my Lord and Saviour, but ever tread in his steps, and wear his image, and glory in him, till the day of his appearing and return, in the glory of his Father. Hear me for his sake. (4)

NOTES / SOURCES

1. Edward Bickersteth, *A Treatise on the Lord's Supper, designed as a Guide and Companion to the Holy Communion*, London, 1822, pp. 56–7
2. Ibid., pp. 158–9
3. Edward Bickersteth (ed.), *The Church Book of Private Devotions: containing a collection of the most valuable early devotions of the Reformers and their successors in the English Church*, London, 1859, p. 404
4. Ibid., pp. 405–6

Charlotte Elliott   1789–1871

Daughter of Charles Elliott of Clapham, and grand-daughter of Henry Venn of Huddersfield, she lived first in Clapham and then at Brighton. She was the author of about 150 hymns, some published in a collection by her brother, Henry Venn Elliott. In poor health for much of her life, she was influenced by the evangelical theology of Charles Malan of Geneva.

Just as I am

Just as I am, without one plea
But that Thy Blood was shed for me,
And that Thou bidd'st me come to Thee,
    O LAMB of GOD, I come.

Just as I am, though tossed about
With many a conflict, many a doubt,
Fightings within, and fears without,
    O LAMB of GOD, I come.

Just as I am, poor, wretched, blind;
Sight, riches, healing of the mind,
Yea all I need, in Thee to find,
    O LAMB of GOD, I come.

Just as I am, Thou wilt receive,
Wilt welcome, pardon, cleanse, relieve;
Because Thy promise I believe,
    O LAMB of GOD, I come.

Just as I am (Thy love unknown
Has broken every barrier down),
Now to be Thine, yea, Thine alone,
    O LAMB of GOD, I come.

Just as I am, of that free love
The breadth, length, depth and height to prove,
Here for a season, then above,
    O LAMB of GOD, I come.

NOTES / SOURCES

Charlotte Elliott, in *Hymns Ancient & Modern*, Second Edition, London, 1875, No. 255

John Keble   1792–1866

The son of a Gloucestershire parish priest, John Keble was one of the first to gain a double First at Oxford, where he became a Fellow of Oriel at the age of 19. Ordained in 1815, his collection of poems, *The Christian Year* appeared in 1827. His Assize Sermon of 1833 on 'National Apostasy' is usually regarded as the beginning of the Oxford Movement. Parish priest of Hursley near Winchester from 1836 until his death, he was a model pastor and spiritual teacher, and was revered for the beauty of his Christian character. Keble College, Oxford, was founded in his memory.

Stanzas from 'Morning'

His compassions fail not; they are new every morning.
Lamen. iii. 22, 23.

Oh! timely happy, timely wise,
Hearts that with rising morn arise!
Eyes that the beam celestial view,
Which evermore makes all things new!

New every morning is the love
Our wakening and uprising prove;
Through sleep and darkness safely brought,
Restored to life, and power, and thought.

New mercies, each returning day,
Hover around us while we pray;
New perils past, new sins forgiven,
New thoughts of God, new hopes of heaven.

If on our daily course our mind
Be set to hallow all we find,
New treasures still, of countless price,
God will provide for sacrifice.

Old friends, old scenes, will lovelier be,
As more of heaven in each we see:
Some softening gleam of love and prayer
Shall dawn on every cross and care.

As for some dear familiar strain
Untired we ask, and ask again,
Ever, in its melodious store,
Finding a spell unheard before;

Such is the bliss of souls serene,
When they have sworn, and steadfast mean,
Counting the cost, in all t'espy
Their God, in all themselves deny.

O could we learn that sacrifice,
What lights would all around us rise!
How would our hearts with wisdom talk
Along Life's dullest dreariest walk!

We need not bid, for cloister'd cell,
Our neighbour and our work farewell,

Nor strive to wind ourselves too high
For sinful man beneath the sky:

The trivial round, the common task,
Would furnish all we ought to ask;
Room to deny ourselves; a road
To bring us, daily, nearer God.

Seek we no more; content with these,
Let present Rapture, Comfort, Ease,
As Heaven shall bid them, come and go:—
The secret this of Rest below.

Only, O Lord, in Thy dear love
Fit us for perfect Rest above;
And help us, this and every day,
To live more nearly as we pray. (1)

Septuagesima Sunday

The invisible things of Him from the creation of the world are clearly seen,
being understood by the things which are made.

Romans i. 20.

There is a book, who runs may read,
    Which heavenly truth imparts,
And all the lore its scholars need,
    Pure eyes and Christian hearts.

The works of God above, below,
    Within us and around,
Are pages in that book, to show
    How God Himself is found.

The glorious sky embracing all
    Is like the Maker's love,
Wherewith encompass'd, great and small
    In peace and order move.

The Moon above, the Church below,
    A wondrous race they run,
But all their radiance, all their glow,
    Each borrows of its Sun.

The Saviour lends the light and heat
    That crowns His holy hill;

The saints, like stars, around His seat
  Perform their courses still.

The saints above are stars in Heaven—
  What are the saints on earth?
Like trees they stand whom God has given,
  Our Eden's happy birth.

Faith is their fix'd unswerving root,
  Hope their unfading flower,
Fair deeds of charity their fruit,
  The glory of their bower.

The dew of heaven is like Thy grace,
  It steals in silence down;
But where it lights, the favour'd place
  By richest fruits is known.

One Name above all glorious names
  With its ten thousand tongues
The everlasting sea proclaims,
  Echoing angelic songs.

The raging Fire, the roaring Wind,
  Thy boundless power display:
But in the gentler breeze we find
  Thy Spirit's viewless way.

Two worlds are ours: 'tis only Sin
  Forbids us to descry
The mystic heaven and earth within,
  Plain as the sea and sky.

Thou, who hast given me eyes to see
  And love this sight so fair,
Give me a heart to find out Thee,
  And read Thee every where. (2)

The Sacramental Character of the Material World

It is the principle of natural piety, 'things are such, because God made and keeps them such': the most skilful analyst, the most dextrous combiner of machinery, must come to this at last: and if he would but be content to refer to it, and realize his dependence on it, throughout, he would go far towards securing himself from the peculiar dangers of his line of study.

   But the one great and effectual safeguard against such idolizing of the material world, or rather of our own minds acting upon it, is the habit of considering it in that other point of view, to which Christian Antiquity would guide us, as earnestly as it would withdraw us from the speculations of the mere natural philosopher. I mean the way of regarding external things, either as fraught with imaginative associations, or as parabolical lessons of conduct, or as a symbolical language in which God speaks to us of a world out of sight: which three might, perhaps, be not quite inaptly entitled, the Poetical, the Moral, and the Mystical phases or aspects of this visible world.

Of these, the Poetical comes first in order, as the natural groundwork or rudiment of the other two. This is indicated by all languages, and by the conversation of uneducated persons in all countries. There is everywhere a tendency to make the things we see represent the things we do not see, to invent or remark mutual associations between them, to call the one sort by the names of the other.

The second, the Moral use of the material world, is the improvement of the poetical or imaginative use of it, for the good of human life and conduct, by considerate persons, according to the best of their own judgment, antecedent to, or apart from, all revealed information on the subject.

In like manner, the Mystical, or Christian, or Theological use of it is the reducing it to a particular set of symbols and associations, which we have reason to believe has, more or less, the authority of the great Creator Himself.

Now the first peculiarity of the Fathers' teaching on this head having been shewn to be their jealousy of the merely scientific use of the external world, the next appears to be their instinctively substituting the mystical use in its room; not a merely *poetical*, or a merely *moral*, but a *mystical*, use of things visible; according to the exposition of the word *mystical* just above given.

To state the matter somewhat differently: If we suppose Poetry in general to mean the expression of an overflowing mind, relieving itself, more or less indirectly and reservedly, of the thoughts and passions which most oppress it:—on which hypothesis each person will have a Poetry of his own, a set of associations appropriate to himself for the works of nature and other visible objects, in themselves common to him with others:—if this be so, what follows will not perhaps be thought altogether an unwarrantable conjecture; proposed, as it ought, and is wished to be, with all fear and religious reverence. May it not, then, be so, that our blessed Lord, in union and communion with all His members, is represented to us as constituting, in a certain sense, one great and manifold Person, into which, by degrees, all souls of men, who do not cast themselves away, are to be absorbed? And as it is a Scriptural and ecclesiastical way of speaking, to say, Christ suffers in our flesh, is put to shame in our sins, our members are part of Him; so may it not be affirmed that He condescends in like manner to have a Poetry of His own, a set of holy and divine associations and meanings, wherewith it is His will to invest all material things? And the authentic records of His will, in this, as in all other truths supernatural, are, of course, Holy Scripture, and the consent of ecclesiastical writers. (3)

NOTES / SOURCES

1. John Keble, *The Christian Year: Thoughts in Verse for the Sundays and Holydays throughout the Year*, London, 1827, pp. 1–4
2. Ibid pp. 72–4
3. John Keble, *On the Mysticism attributed to the Early Fathers of the Church (No. LXXXIX of* 'Tracts for the Times'), Oxford, 1868, pp. 146–7

William Hodge Mill   1792–1853

Mill was born in Middlesex, England. He studied oriental languages at Trinity College, Cambridge. Identified as a member of the High Church 'Hackney Phalanx', Mill was an SPG missionary and the first Principal of Bishop's College, Calcutta from 1820 to 1838. His Sanskrit studies led to his massive and brilliant poetic production the *Christa-sangita*, a life of Christ, drawing on the riches of Sanskrit poetics. Illness drove him back to Britain, where he became Regius Professor of Hebrew at Cambridge.

Hymn to the Birth of Jesus

(from the Sanskrit)

As the fruit whose avatara (incarnation) is praised
may he be my Saviour.
For his sake may God the Father
Look at those fallen into the well of darkness.

The Merciful gave his only beloved son
to deliver the evil ones.
O God! Listen to my cry,
not seeing my good-deeds which are undeserving.

May he come to me with a happy message of salvation
through my salutations and sincere listening.
May he shine through the Holy Spirit,
establishing his spirit in my heart through his counsel.

He who was praised at the birth of John,
may he find a purified path in me,
when the mountains and forests of selfishness,
which were hindrances for Saccidananda
have been removed.

He who was born of a Virgin in a stable,
may he not abandon those who are pure and humble.
May he who came into the world of bondage,
making himself equal here, protect me always.

He who suffered various kinds of tortures
in the midst of his followers, may he protect me.
He who is pure, may he favour me, a sinner
who is at the point of death enduring pain.

May he who obtained the seal of purification
take away lust and other impurities.
He who is called the Blessed Saviour, may he conquer
my senses by the miraculous power of his own passion.

He who appeared beforehand to the wise men of the East,
may he also remove my darkness by his rays.
May he guide my way to him.
May he accept my prayer and oblation.
May the holy one receive my simple offering
which is given by me at the feet of the holy one.
May he accept my supplication at the feet of the one
who is of jasmine-like fragrance and pure body.

Though he dwells in his house, pure,
may he lead me to his Father.
Let him lead me, leaving aside my sins,
to the heavenly abode after purifying me
by his own holiness.

Though worthy of punishment I received favour,
purified by the fruit of his birth.
I speak out to him along with the heavenly court
these praises because of my deliverance from the enemy.

Glory to God in heaven
and peace to men of goodwill on earth.
Thus the birth of Christ was sung
in all the three worlds by all creatures.

NOTES / SOURCES

William Hodge Mill, Prayers concluding the 'Hymn to the Birth of Jesus', the fourteenth Canto of
Book I of his Sanskrit poem on the life of Christ, the Christa-sangita (1838) (Anand, India, 1995) pp.
251–4

Trans. A. Amaladass SJ and R. F. Young, in *The Indian Christiad: A Concise Anthology of Didactic and
Devotional Literature in Early Church Sanskrit*

Henry Francis Lyte   1793–1847

Chiefly remembered for his hymns, of which 'Abide with me' is the most famous, Henry
Lyte was educated at Trinity College, Dublin, and served for the greater part of his
ministry at Brixham In Devon. His *Poems, chiefly religious* appeared in 1833. Other
well-known hymns by him are 'Praise, my soul, the King of heaven' and 'God of mercy,
God of grace'. The text of 'Abide with me' printed here includes one of three verses
omitted from modern hymn books.

Abide with me

Abide with me; fast falls the eventide;
The darkness deepens; Lord, with me abide;
When other helpers fail, and comforts flee,
Help of the helpless, oh abide with me.

Swift to its close ebbs out life's little day;
Earth's joys grow dim, its glories pass away;
Change and decay in all around I see;
O thou who changest not, abide with me.

Come not in terrors, as the King of kings;
But kind and good, with healing in thy wings;
Tears for all woes, a heart for every plea;
Come, friend of sinners, and abide with me.

I need thy presence every passing hour;
What but thy grace can foil the tempter's power?
Who like thyself my guide and stay can be?
Through cloud and sunshine, Lord, abide with me.

I fear no foe with thee at hand to bless;
Ills have no weight, and tears no bitterness;
Where is death's sting? where, grave, thy victory?
I triumph still, if thou abide with me.

Hold then thy cross before my closing eyes;
Shine through the gloom, and point me to the skies;
Heaven's morning breaks, and earth's vain shadows flee;
In life, in death, O Lord, abide with me.

NOTES / SOURCES

The Oxford Hymn Book No. 10, Oxford, 1908

Marianne Williams   1793–1879

Born in Yorkshire, England, Marianne Coldham was trained for a career in teaching, home care, and maternity nursing. In 1823 she travelled to New Zealand with her husband, the Revd (later Archdeacon) Henry Williams, to join the Church Missionary Society mission station at Paihia in the Bay of Islands, in northern New Zealand. In her work as teacher, nurse, confidante, and friend to the indigenous Maori people and European (*pakeha*) missionaries alike, Marianne's indomitable faith and strength of character sustained her during her husband's long periods of absence from the mission station, when she was often confronted by the hostility, fear, misunderstanding, and resentment engendered on all sides during the many conflicts which broke out between the English settlers and the local Maori people. A prolific letter writer, Marianne's correspondence and journals give a lively and detailed picture of life and conditions of this period in New Zealand's history. Her radiant faith and love won many to Christian faith and earned her the title *Mata* (our Mother) among the Maori people whom she served in the Bay of Islands and later in Pakaraka, for 56 years.

Missionary Life in New Zealand

If you visit Paihia today you will see a stone set by the Historic Places Trust to mark the spot where Henry and the mission carpenter, William Fairburn, built their first storehouse and reed hut. You can be shown, too, a lemon tree planted by Henry which, in 1967, was still producing somewhat gnarled lemons. If one looks at the picture of their hut one can see its walls of raupo reed stalks and its roof thatched with raupo leaves. It had four rooms, two for Henry and Marianne and their three children, and two for the Fairburns with their three children. Each room measured 10′ × 15′, so they must have felt very cramped for space, especially in wet weather. They lived in this hut for several years while Henry concentrated on building a schooner, a church and a school. Like most Victorian families they multiplied rapidly and by the time they moved into a roomier home the Williamses had six children. I do not know how many the Fairburns had but it is just as well that in May, 1824, they (the Fairburns) moved into a separate building made of proper timber. It is not surprising that Marianne called their hut 'The Beehive'. It certainly must have swarmed with life and activity.

Because it was built of highly-inflammable reeds they could never risk lighting a fire in it. So for years Marianne had to do all her cooking for her own family and the many Maori children who came to attend their school over an open fire with only a sailcloth to protect her from the wind and rain. It is worth remembering that before she came to New Zealand she had never had to do any cooking. She had to wait four years before she had a kitchen.

But she was so pleased and happy with her home on the September day when Henry proudly sailed her and the children down from Kerikeri to Paihia. This is how she describes it in a happy letter to her mother-in-law: 'I accompanied Henry down in his boat to our new home; the day was beautiful, the only fine day in the midst of a fortnight's storm and rain . . . The beach was crowded with natives who pulled me up while sitting in the boat with great apparent glee, exclaiming "*Te Wahine*" (the wife) and holding our their hands saying "*Tena ra koe koe*" (How do you do) and "*Homai te ringaringa*" (Give me your hand) . . . The cultivated land, on which were springing up our crops of oats and barley, extended close down to the fine flat beach . . . Within an enclosure stood our raupo hut . . . By the side stood the store and scattered about were the cart, timber carriage, goats, fowls, and horse, and near the beach were the saw-pits. Behind was a large garden, already partially green with numerous rows of peas and beans. The entrance to the house was dark, and within were two rooms with no floors, and boards nailed up where sash-lights were to be placed. Mr Fairburn and Henry laid me a boarded floor in the bedroom before night and I never rested more comfortably. On Sunday Henry opened another raupo hut for a chapel.'

A week later they had Mr. Marsden as their first visitor and he stayed a week. He brought with him Mr Kemp, the mission blacksmith from Kerikeri, and the Ngapuhi chief Hongi Hika. Where on earth did they all sleep? You may well ask. Here is Marianne's description of how she coped, and remember that this was less than a month before her fourth child was to be born.

'. . . I had just finished ironing before teatime. Henry helped me to wash the children; and overcome with fatigue I did as I have often done before—threw myself on the bed to refresh myself with a good cry, when a boat was announced and I was aroused anew to exertion to receive Mr Marsden, Mr Kemp, and the celebrated Hongi, to get out blankets, sheets, and bedding etc. It will amuse you to know how many people slept in our hut. Mr Marsden, Mr Kemp, and Hongi Hika in the sitting-room, five Maori girls in the entrance 'room', four Maori men of the boat's crew in the Fairburns' sitting room; all these in addition to the Fairburns, ourselves and the seven children (Mrs Fairburn had recently had a baby) in a rush dwelling 40ft. long and 15ft. broad.'

Of course she had to feed all those extra people too. How did she manage this? 'The meeting of Hongi Hika and our head chief, Tehoki, at tea was very entertaining. Tehoki placed a chair at the table for Hongi and sat himself on the ground beside him . . . Tehoki told us to give his friend plenty to eat and to remember that although we pakehas eat very little, "the tangata Maori eats a great deal!". My visitors ate up my whole batch of newly baked bread, which happily held out, and the boat's crew had enough also.'

Next day of course she had to bake a fresh batch of bread in her camp oven over the open fire and it was raining. Furthermore, all the sheets would have to be washed out and wrung by hand, on top of all her other chores . . .

Here are some brief extracts from Marianne's letters in June and July 1844. Her family now numbered eleven—six sons and five daughters—and she herself was fifty years old. She must often have felt weary but she was always quick to respond to a call for help. One of those who leaned heavily on her support and comfort was Mrs Busby, wife of James Busby, the Resident Magistrate. They lived in the Treaty House at Waitangi, about 2½ miles north along the Bay from Paihia. Marianne writes, (14 June, 1844): 'I sent milk and home-made biscuits to Mrs Busby's little boys to keep them quiet, prescribed treatment for Mrs Pugh's bad leg, ironed my starched things, drew a goose for Sunday, and then went across by boat to Waitangi to spend the night with Mrs Busby who is ailing. We were up and about in the night with her little girl, who is teething.'

(5 July 1844): 'I made up a bed ready for Bishop Selwyn's coming and was all over the house to put things in order, and had many Maoris in for medicine, nursing, and bandaging. The Bishop and Henry arrived wet through having walked through floods up to the middle. Hot tubs and fire and tea and soup all in turn.'

(9 July, 1844): 'I moved all my things back to my own room again (she had vacated it for the Bishop to use). I feel quite knocked up but it being the first day of Mrs. Busby's being left alone I took Catherine (13) and Caroline (12) in Hemi's sailing boat. It blew hard and I did not at all like it and the stone ballast. But it was a great comfort to see Mrs Busby looking so comfortable . . . After tea my legs were so exceedingly painful I was glad to put them up on the sofa.'

(20 August, 1844): 'The great Kawakawa canoe came down to show off . . . James Clendon (the American consul) and Henry Swan came to fetch Mrs Clendon who had been staying with me. But it was so rough that they all stayed to dine and sleep. Our party increased like a snowball and such lots of young men. It rained hard at tea—twenty "pakehas" to tea as well as all our Maori pupils to feed. We placed all the field beds on the living-room floor for the young men to sleep.' (This was when Hone Heke was attacking Kororareka, across the Bay, and cutting down the flagstaff.)

(21 August, 1844): 'Ten departures from "Williams Hotel"! A beautiful day, canoes paddling about showing off.'

(2 September, 1844): 'Mrs Busby sent word to tell me that Captain Swayne (the whaling Captain) had been killed by a whale . . . John and Hemi took me in their sailing boat up the Waikari to see poor widowed Mrs Swayne. There was more wind than agreeable for our journey. I found the widow in bed, overcome with grief, and was able to be some comfort and assistance.'

NOTES / SOURCES

Sybil Woods, *Marianne Williams: A study of life in the Bay of Islands, New Zealand 1823–1879*, New Zealand, 1977, pp. 29–33, 65–8

Allen Francis Gardiner   1794–1851

Allen Gardiner, founder of the Patagonian Missionary Society (1844), joined the Navy at age of 14 and rose to the rank of Commander. On the death of his wife in 1834 he dedicated his remaining years to God, to make Christ known in the regions where he was still unknown. This decision eventually led him to the attempt to evangelize the Yagan Indians of the channels of Tierra del Fuego. He led a party of seven men (including Richard Williams (q.v.)), who all died at Spaniard Harbour in the Beagle Channel. They set out to reach the totally uncivilized Yagan boat people, a people who were to be almost exterminated by 'white men's' diseases by the end of the century. The hostility of the Yagans, which forced Gardiner to move to a cove without fishing, and an oversight leading to a lack of gunpowder, left them dependent on promised supplies. They did not arrive and the last entry in Allen Gardiner's journal is dated 6 September 1851, by which time scurvy and starvation had probably taken the rest of the party.

Extracts from Captain Allen Gardiner's Journal

August 7, 1851, Pioneer Cavern. On this day eleven months we left England for this country, and have been graciously preserved through many dangers and troubles. The Lord in His providence has seen fit to bring us very low, and to remove many of the blessings which we have so long been partakers of; but this is in infinite wisdom, mercy and love. These seasons of affliction are all appointed, are measured and limited by a God of mercy, who doth not afflict willingly, but for our good . . .

How have I abused the manifold gifts of God. How unmindful of the daily comforts which I have so unremittingly experienced, although unworthy of the very least of them! Lord have mercy upon me, a sinner. Grant that I may be humbled under Thy mighty hand, deeply sensible of my need of chastisement; that I may not be tempted of Satan to repine, neither to despise, nor to faint, but to wait upon Thee, in the posture of a suppliant for grace to profit by this and every other dispensation of Thy providence.

I know, O Lord, that there is a deep necessity for this trial, or Thou wouldst not have sent it; and I humbly beseech Thee to vouchsafe to me the full benefit which

Thou dost design in it. Make me to see myself in the light of Thy holy word, to search and try my heart by it, and may Thy Holy Spirit work in me the grace of true contrition, and renew in me the graces of love, faith and obedience . . .

Let not this mission fail, though we should not be permitted to labour in it, but graciously raise up other labourers, who may convey the saving truths of Thy gospel to the poor blind heathen around us . . . (1)

My prayer is, that the Lord my God may be glorified in me whatever it be, by life or death, and that he will, should we fall, vouchsafe to raise up, and send forth, other labourers into this harvest, that his name may be magnified, and his kingdom enlarged, in the salvation of multitudes from among the inhabitants of this pagan land, who, by the instrumentality of his servants, may, under the divine blessing upon their labours, be translated from the power of darkness, into the glorious liberty of the children of God. (2)

But the Lord is very pitiful, and of tender compassion. He knows our frames; He appoints and measures all his afflictive dispensations, and when his set time is fully come, He will either remove us to his eternal and glorious kingdom, or supply our languishing bodies with food convenient for us. I pray that in whatsoever state, by his wise and gracious providence I may be placed, I may therewith be content, and patiently await the development of his righteous will concerning me, knowing that he doeth all things well. (3)

. . . but I am by his abounding grace kept in perfect peace, refreshed with a sense of my Saviour's love, and an assurance that all is wisely and mercifully appointed, and pray that I may receive the full blessing which it is doubtless designed to bestow. My care is all cast upon God, and I am only waiting his time and his good pleasure to dispose of me as he shall see fit. Whether I live or die, may it be in him. I commend my body and soul into his care and keeping, and earnestly pray that he will mercifully take my dear wife and children under the shadow of his wings, comfort, guide strengthen, and sanctify them wholly, that we may together, in a brighter and eternal world, praise and adore his goodness and grace, in redeeming us with his precious blood. (4)

NOTES / SOURCES

1. Phyllis Thompson, *An Unquenchable Flame. Biography of Allen Gardiner, founder of the South American Missionary Society*, London, 1983, pp. 178–9
2. Allen Francis Gardiner in George Pakenham Despard, (ed.) *Hope deferred, not lost; A narrative of missionary effort in South America*, London, 1854, p. 249
3. Ibid., p. 256
4. Ibid., pp. 257–8

Julius Charles Hare   1795–1855

A Broad Churchman, Julius Hare had one of the most substantial theological libraries in England at his rectory at Hurstmonceux, Sussex. Widely acquainted with and influenced by German theology, he published with his brother Augustus *Guesses at Truth* (1827) which was widely read. He translated (with Connop Thirlwall) Niebuhr's *History of Rome* and other German works. As Archdeacon of Lewes he was a colleague of H. E. Manning in his time as Archdeacon of Chichester.

The Threefold Work of the Comforter

Our Lord, while still speaking of the coming of the Comforter, says, *He shall glorify Me; for He shall receive of Mine, and shall show it to you.* This, we have seen, is what the Comforter does through the whole of His threefold work. In every part of it He glorifies Christ. In convincing us of sin, He convinces us of the sin of not believing in Christ. In convincing us of righteousness, he convinces us of the righteousness of Christ, of that righteousness which was made manifest in Christ's going to the Father, and which He received to bestow it on all such as should believe in Him. And lastly, in convincing us of judgement, He convinces us that the Prince of this world was judged in the life and by the death of Christ. Thus throughout Christ is glorified; and that which the Comforter shews to us relates in all its parts to the life and work of the Incarnate Son of God. In like manner all the graces which the Spirit bestows, are the graces which were manifested in the life of Christ. It is Christ's love that He shews to us and gives to us, the love through which Christ laid down His life for His Church,—and Christ's joy in His communion with His Father,—and the peace which Christ had when He had overcome the world,—and Christ's longsuffering in praying that His murderers might be forgiven,—and Christ's bounty in giving of all the treasures of heaven,—and the faithfulness of Him who is the faithful Witness, Himself the Truth,—and the gentleness with which Christ took up little children in His arms and blest them,—and Christ's meekness in never answering again,—and the temperance of Christ, who made it His meat and drink to do the will of His Father. All these graces were manifested upon earth in their heavenly perfection, when the fulness of the God-head dwelt in the Man Christ Jesus; and all these graces the Spirit of God desires to give to all who believe in Christ Jesus. All these graces He desires to give to every one of you, so that Christ may be formed in you, and that your life may be swallowed up in His life. Thus shall you too glorify Christ; and with Him you will glorify the Father. Let this be the glory which you seek, not your own vain, fleeting glory, but the glory wherewith you may glorify Christ and the Father; and this glory shall abide with you for ever.

NOTES / SOURCES

Julius Charles Hare, *The Mission of the Comforter*, London, 1850, pp. 178–9

John Gregg
1798–1878

Bishop of Cork, Cloyne, and Ross from 1862 until his death, John Gregg was responsible for the building of the new cathedral of Cork. He previously served in Dublin as incumbent of Trinity Church (1839–62) and as Archdeacon of Kildare (1857–62).

Preach Jesus

Preach Jesus, the true sacrifice for sin, offered by Himself, not any miserable substitute offered by men. Distinguish well the visible from the spiritual Church, the outward from the inward man; so shall you keep separate the shadow from the substance, the semblance from the truth. Preach Jesus the true Priest for ever, the high Priest in heaven, not the Clergy or Bishops, weak worms of the earth. 'We preach not ourselves' saith the apostle, 'but Christ Jesus the Lord.' Preach Jesus, 'the Minister of the sanctuary, and of the true tabernacle which the Lord pitched and not man.' No breathing thoughts or burning words, no tongue of angel or of flaming seraph can tell the treasures of this matchless name; Jesus the name above every name, has been preached in city and in country, in cottage and in dungeon, in caverns of the earth, on wildest hill side and on solitary shore, and wherever preached in simplicity, faith and prayer, grace has been given and power bestowed, sinners have wept and prayed and trusted, while angels sang in ecstasy and heaven has rung with joy. The poor, the miserable, the lonely and forsaken, the heirs of sorrow and the sons of shame, have been gladdened by His Gospel and cheered by His love; no music to their ears like the music of His mercy, no cordial for their heart, like the balm of His blood; no cover for their nakedness like the garment of His righteousness, and no procession for their wonder, like the going forth of Jesus their Redeemer, to conquer and to save. No structure raised by mortal hands, however stately and however costly, can satisfy their taste or come up to their desire, they look for the 'habitation of God' that Jesus is erecting of living stones, hewn out and fashioned by the Almighty's hand, growing and glittering in the sunshine of His favour, and resting secure on His everlasting strength. Already in anticipation and contemplation thereof, are they charmed with a beauty such as eye never saw, and regaled with a music such as ear never heard. (1)

Anglican Worship

How beautiful is the theory of our public worship, the sacred day, the Sabbath bell, the house of prayer, the gathering people, the mingled multitude of rich and poor and old and young together, the opening scripture; the lowly voice of supplication, wafting our wants to heaven, the humble joy, the lively thanks giving, the adoring praise, 'We praise thee, O God,' rejoicing 'in the strength of our salvation;' the holy words of inspiration, venerable with hoary years, the pause, the solemn pause to remember the poor and needy, an offering and sacrifice well pleasing to God; with praise in hymn or psalm or spiritual song poured forth in melodious accents, or with solemn chant, the man of God ascends his throne, and stands erect to teach, to preach the truth, to point to Jesus, and show the road to heaven. The character of the man, the look, the voice, the words, arrest and fix the mind, affect the heart and move and melt the soul, with thoughts that burn and breathe of heaven. The voice is still, the silent supplication rises, the prayer of faith is heard, the healthful spirit of grace descends, the dew of blessing falls; minds are solemnized, souls are kindled and humble hearts refreshed. The holy table spread, the heavenly feast, the sacrifice of praise, the 'Glory be to God on high,' the close in prayer and blessing, knowledge, peace and love; the slowly retiring multitude go on their way rejoicing, musing praise and looking thoughts of heaven. 'Truly it is good to be here, this is none other than the house of God.' (2)

NOTES / SOURCES

1. John Gregg, *A Charge to the Clergy of the United Dioceses of Cork, Cloyne, and Ross at the Ordinary Visitation, October 1867*, Dublin, 1867, pp. 12–13
2. Ibid., pp. 13–14

Walter Farquhar Hook   1798–1875

Vicar of Leeds from 1837 to 1859 and Dean of Chichester from 1859 until his death, Hook was a notable parochial reformer and High Churchman, though he latterly distanced himself from Pusey and ritualist developments. A prolific author and church historian, he was a major contributor to ecclesiastical biography with his *Lives of the Archbishops of Canterbury*.

Temptations of a Clergyman and a Soldier Compared

Leeds: December 31, 1855.

. . . The temptations of the army, as you say, are great; but are they greater than those of the clerical profession? When we think so, are we not taking the worldly rather than the revealed view of sin, thinking one class of sin more venial than another?

I have seen so much of clerical life that I have a dread of *hereditary* clergymen; of those, I mean, who simply take Orders because they have been bred in a clergyman's house. The temptations of a young clergyman are to idleness, hypocrisy, and malignity. And they are fearful temptations, creating Pharisaism. The temptation of idleness is not so great as it was. But hypocrisy is variously disguised. It lies under the question which is so often asked, is this or that clerical? A young clergyman is tempted to appear better than he is. And the controversies of the day encourage a malignant spirit, which is mistaken for Christian zeal.

In the army I do not find any great inclination to treat religion with disrespect, though the temptation is to that kind of hypocrisy which induces men to appear less religious than they really are. The great temptation is to the sins of sensuality; but is a good regiment in this respect worse than a college?

NOTES / SOURCES

Walter Farquhar Hook, in W. R. W. Stephens *The Life and letters of Walter Farquhar Hook*, London, 1880, pp. 365–6

George Washington Doane   1799–1859

Born in New Jersey, Doane was ordained by John Henry Hobart in 1821 and shared Hobart's High Churchmanship with its defence of evangelical truth and apostolic order. From 1832 he was Bishop of New Jersey. Like John Keble, whose *Christian Year* he published in an American edition, Doane was a poet as well as a churchman.

Thou art the Way: by Thee alone

Thou art the Way; by Thee alone
   From sin and death we flee:
And he who would the FATHER seek
   Must seek Him, LORD, by Thee.

Thou art the Truth; Thy Word alone
   True wisdom can impart;
Thou only canst inform the mind,
   And purify the heart.

Thou art the Life; the rending tomb
   Proclaims Thy conquering arm;
And those who put their trust in Thee
   Nor death nor hell shall harm.

Thou art the Way, the Truth, the Life,
   Grant us that Way to know,
That Truth to keep, that Life to win,
   Whose joys eternal flow.

NOTES / SOURCES

George Washington Doane, in *Hymns Ancient & Modern*, Second Edition, London, 1875, No. 199

Edward Bouverie Pusey   1800–1882

A leader of the Oxford Movement, Pusey was Regius Professor of Hebrew and a Canon of Christ Church, Oxford, from 1828 until his death. He wrote on the theology of baptism, the eucharist, and priestly absolution (this last including two controversial sermons). His *Eirenicon* (1865) urged reunion with Rome on the basis of offical teaching, discounting popular devotion. His many sermons contain ecstatic passages, which have led some to characterize him as the '*doctor mysticus*' of the Oxford Movement. He was a strong supporter of the revival of the religious life within Anglicanism.

The Incarnation, a Lesson of Humility

But what (if we may speak reverently of these mysteries), seems yet more amazing, He was content to veil even that, in Himself, wherein, so to say, God is most God, the Glory of the Divinity, His Holy Being, whereby He hateth all iniquity. He, Who is 'the Truth,' was contented to be called 'that deceiver;' they said of Him, 'Nay, but He deceiveth the people.' He hid His Holiness, so that His apostate angel shrank not from approaching Him, to tempt Him. He came in the likeness of sinful flesh, so that His fallen creature thought that He might become as himself. He veiled the very humility wherewith He humbled Himself to be obedient, so that Satan thought that He might be tempted through pride. He was content to be thought able to covet the creatures which He had made, and, like us, to prefer them to the Father; yea, and the very lowest of the creatures, which even man can despise. They called Him 'a gluttonous man, and a winebibber.' 'We know,' say they, 'that this man is a sinner.' They reproached Him for disobedience to the Father, and breaking the law which He gave. So wholly was He made like unto us, in all things, sin only excepted, that man could not discern that He, the Holy God, was not (shocking to say) unholy man.

It surpasses all thought, it amazes, it confounds, to think of God becoming man; the Infinite enshrined within the finite, the Lord of all blended with His servant, the Creator with His creature! It is a depth of mystery unsearchable. We must shrink with awe when we pronounce it Of old they fell down and worshipped, when, in our Creed, they uttered it—'God was made Man.' It was an unimaginable condescension for God to create. From Eternity, *in* Eternity, (since it had no beginning), He was Ever-blessed, Love loving Love in the Holy Spirit, Who is the Bond of Love and Unity. He was, in Himself, All-perfect. He needed nothing, changed not. And yet, in that He created, He did a new thing, and formed those who needed Him, as though *He* needed them. He formed them to serve Him Who needed them not, and He accepted their service. It was much, as Scripture saith, to 'humble Himself to behold the things which are in Heaven and earth.' But that He, Who was Perfect in Himself, should take into Himself something without Him; that He, Who is All in all, should add something to Himself; that He Who is a Spirit, should take into Himself that which was material; in a word, that God (if we realize to ourselves what that word GOD is) should take into Himself what is not GOD; one must stand speechless with awe at so amazing a mystery. How must we be amazed and scarce believe for joy, to think that that which He so took was man, ourselves, our fallen, sinful, in Him Alone unsinful, unsinning nature. (1)

Deification: the Easter Life of Christians in Christ

All which our Lord has is ours, if we are indeed His. As Man, He received Gifts, that He might give them to men. To Him, as Man, though God, 'was given all Power in Heaven and in earth,' that He might bestow on His all things in Heaven and earth; that all things, in both, might work and serve together to the good of His Elect. As Man, He received the Holy Spirit, that He might again dwell in man, clothe us with the Robe of supernatural Grace and Holiness, which we lost in Adam, and were found naked. For our sakes He sanctified Himself, that we also might be sanctified by the Truth. He sanctified His Human Nature by His Indwelling Godhead, that so He might sanctify our nature by Himself, Who is the Word of Truth. For us the Spirit of God rested upon Him with His Sevenfold Gifts, 'the Spirit of Wisdom and Understanding, the Spirit of Counsel and Might, the Spirit of Knowledge and True, Godliness, the Spirit of Holy Fear,' that through Him It might stream down upon all His members, as the holy oil which was poured upon Aaron's head 'went down to the skirts of his clothing,' hallowing, and giving a sweet savour to all his body. For us, the Spirit was 'given without measure to Him,' that from Him It might be parted to us His members, as we severally need, or are found worthy. Our's were, what in the past Holy

Season we dwelt upon, and while we dwelt upon, they became again our's—our's were His Wounds, Stripes, Bruises, His Crown of Thorns, His Bloody Sweat, 'His Tears, Groans, and Cry,' His Body and Blood, His Life and Death. 'For our transgressions was He bruised; by His Stripes are we healed.' His Bloody Sweat sanctifies the woe pronounced on man, 'in the sweat of thy brow shalt thou eat bread.' His Thorns were our sins; and thenceforth the thorns our human nature bears do but let out our festering evils, while they pierce us. He wept, that we might weep no more; but God should be 'very gracious to us at the voice of our cry.' Through His Groans are those Unutterable Groanings heard, where by 'The Spirit maketh Intercession for us, according to the Will of God.' By that Cry did He, with His Own Blessed Spirit, commend our spirits also to the Father. For us, 'though He were a Son, yet learned He obedience by the things which He suffered;' that 'being made perfect,' He might become 'the Author of Eternal Salvation to all them that obey Him.' His Shame is our glory; His Blood our ransom; His Sweat our refreshment; the Streams from His Side our Sacraments; His Wounded Side our hiding-place from our own sins, and Satan's wrath; His Death our life.

And what, then, on this 'our triumphant Holy Day,' should His Life be? What but the Sealing to us of all which He had wrought for us? What but the bursting of the bars of our prison-house, the restoration, of our lost Paradise, the opening of the Kingdom of Heaven, the earnest of our Endless Life, the binding of the strong man, and letting us, his lawful prisoners, free, the bringing in of Incorruption, the Conquest, in the Head, of the last enemy, that he may, one by one, be conquered in us too, and the death of our bodies may be the deliverance from 'this body of death,' our souls' perfected life?

Can there be more than this? There can. The text unfolds to us a yet deeper Mystery, that all this is to us 'in Christ,' 'In Christ shall all be made alive.' The Endless Life, which they shall live who are counted worthy of it, shall then not be a life such as men seem to live here where our true life is unseen, as if we were so many creatures of God's Hand, each having his existence wholly separate from his fellows, upheld in being by God, yet, as it seems, apart from God, having his own wills, affections, tastes, pursuits, passsions, love, hatred, interests, joys, sufferings. Our life then shall not be, as it seems here, and as it truly is in the ungodly, separate from God, and in the good indistinctly and imperfectly united with Him. It shall be a life 'in God.' 'In Christ shall all be made alive.' We shall live then, not only as having our souls restored to our bodies, and souls and bodies living on in the Presence of Almighty God. Great and unutterable as were this Blessedness, there is a higher yet in store,—to live on 'in Christ.' For this implies Christ's living on in us. These two are spoken of together in Holy Scripture. 'He that dwelleth in love, dwelleth in God, and God in Him,' and 'he that keepeth His commandments dwelleth in Him, and He in him;' and in the service for the Holy Communion, we pray that 'we may so eat the Flesh of Christ and drink His Blood, that we may evermore dwell in Him, and He in us.' For we can only dwell in God by His Dwelling in us. To dwell in God is not to dwell on God only. It is no mere lifting up of our affections to Him, no being enwrapt in the contemplation of Him, no going forth of ourselves to cleave to Him. All this is our seeking Him, not His taking us up; our stretching after Him, not our attaining Him; our knocking, not His Opening. To dwell in God must be by His Dwelling in us. He takes us out of our state of nature, in which we were, fallen, estranged, in a far country, out of and away from Him, and takes us up into Himself. He cometh to us, and if we will receive Him, He dwelleth in us, and maketh His Abode in us. He enlargeth our hearts by His Sanctifying Spirit which He giveth us, by the obedience which He enables us to yield, by the acts of Faith and Love which He strengthens us to do, and then dwelleth in those who are His more largely. By dwelling in us, He makes us parts of Himself, so that in the Ancient Church they could boldly say, 'He Deifieth Me;' that is, He makes me part of Him, of His Body, Who is God. (2)

Heaven the Christian's Home

This then is the great blessedness of this our citizenship, as of every other Gift of Grace or Glory, that we have it not in ourselves, but of, and in Christ. We belong to Heaven, because we belong to Him, 'members,' the Apostle says, 'of His Body, of His Flesh, and of His Bones;' His Temple, knit into One with Him, Who 'knitteth in one all things in Heaven and in earth.' All in us, which is of Heaven, is of His Spirit in us. His Holy Spirit, the Bond of the Oneness of the Father and the Son, Which encircleth all things, taketh us up into Himself. Faith makes present to us things unseen; Hope bears us beyond all time to That we hope for; and he 'who dwelleth in Love, dwelleth in God, and God in him;' yet by Faith, and Hope, and Love, we dwell in Heaven, not by any power or virtue even of these Heavenly Graces, but because they are the Effluence of His Spirit, coming forth from Him to us, and bearing us up into Himself. 'Standing on earth, thou art in Heaven, if thou lovest God; for not so as the body is uplifted, is the soul uplifted. The body, to be uplifted, changeth its place; the heart, its affection; "For unto Thee, O Lord, do I lift up my soul."'

This, again, is the very Mystery and Blessedness of the Sacraments; that by the one, Christ knit us into Himself; by the other, He descendeth to us, that He may become 'One with us, and we with Him.' This is the force of prayer, that it is a calling down of God into ourselves, a going forth of ourselves to God. A calling of God into ourselves, for our Blessed Lord says, 'Shall not your Heavenly Father give the Holy Spirit to them that ask Him?' a going forth of ourselves to God, for 'the Spirit' which He hath given us, 'maketh intercession for us.' It is not we alone who pray, if we pray aright; but He, our Lord, Who is prayed by us, Himself prayeth in us, by His Holy 'Spirit which He hath given us.' Our prayers go up unto the Throne of God, because they are His Voice in us. 'No greater gifts,' says a father, 'could God give to man, than that He should make His Word, through Whom He created all things, a Head unto them, and should conjoin them to Him as members. So that He should be Son of God, and Son of Man, One God with the Father, One Man with men; so that both when we speak in prayer to God, we do not separate from Him the Son, and when the Body of the Son prayeth, it separateth not from Itself Its Head, and He Himself, our Lord Jesus Christ, the Son of God, is the One Saviour of the body, Who both prayeth for us, and prayeth in us, and is prayed by us. He prayeth for us as our High Priest; He prayeth in us, as our Head; He is prayed by us as our God. Let us own then both our words in Him, and His Words in us.'

Where is the soul of the devout Communicant? in Heaven or on earth? Surely not on earth, which it is taught to forget, through the Holy Sweetness which streams forth upon it, and the joy which bedews it, that it is washed through its Saviour's Blood. Where is the soul of the penitent, as it poureth forth its sorrows at its Redeemer's Feet, mourns, for love of Him, that it ever offended Him, and abashed and affrighted at itself, and knowing not where to hide itself from itself, hides itself under the Hem of His Garment, yea, would bury itself in His Sacred Side. Whence issued 'the Fountain for sin and for uncleanness?' Even a heathen will tell us where. 'The soul of one who greatly loveth, is much more in the heart it loveth, than in itself.' It is the very character of pure, intense, earthly love, as the image and offspring of Divine, that it is, as it were, out of itself; the heart findeth no rest in itself; it dwelleth not in itself; it is there where it loveth: there it is at ease, there rests, for that careth; it forgetteth itself, seeketh nothing for itself, but only to be there allowed to dwell, where it loveth to be, rather than in itself. And if death, or the Will of God, sever it from that it loves, how does it seem pent within itself, a burthen to itself, unless it can anew go forth out of itself unto Him, the One Object of its being, Who made it for Himself. And shall not that be much more true of the Love of God, 'the soul is much more where it loveth, than where it liveth?' When St. Paul was caught up into Paradise, where his body was, he knew not. 'Whether in the body, I cannot tell; or whether out of the body, I cannot tell: God knoweth.' But where his spirit, where himself was, that he knew. 'Such an one was caught up into the third Heaven.' And if God have, at any time, vouchsafed unto any of us, any more fervent prayer, any longing for Himself, any desire to escape from the misery which sin brought upon us, any yearning for something which shall satisfy the soul, which things seen cannot satisfy, (because they are of earth, it is of Heaven; they from beneath, it, with its Lord, from Above; they of this world, it not of this world;) what is all, from the first gushing forth of the tears of penitence, the first restored feeling of child-like love, the first faint trembling hope that it may again call God, Father; even that unspeakable presence with his Lord, whereby St. Paul was caught up into Paradise, – what is it all but a going forth out of itself? And to Whom does it, to Whom other can it go? save to Him, Who Himself, by Bonds of His Love, draws it; by His Spirit upbears it.

And so when our hearts are most out of ourselves for joy, when we are most longing for that Ineffable Gift of Himself in His Sacrament, the Priest says, 'Lift up your hearts,' and ye answer, 'We lift them up unto the Lord;' 'lift up our hearts with our hands unto Him that dwelleth in the Heavens.' Where are they then? with us? Nay, but we have 'lift them up,' not in place, but in love; not in space, (as if God were in Heaven only, not every where, since in Him 'we live and move, and have our being,') yet in truth. They are borne out of themselves in thankful love and longing, and are more with Him they would long for, than with our bodies which for the time they inhabit. The spirit, lifted up by the Spirit, is more with the Father of Spirits than with the flesh. The 'firstfruits of the Spirit,' return unto God Who gave it, the foretaste of the Everlasting Dwelling with Him, by Whose Love it loves, and is borne to Him.

We cannot of ourselves, go forth of ourselves, any more than we can of ourselves in body leave this earth. But for this cause did our Lord come down to this earth, that He might with us ascend whither He was before, that we might through His Spirit, in spirit thither 'ascend' now, 'and with Him continually dwell,' that hereafter we might in the body also, be 'caught to meet the Lord in the air, and so for ever to be with the Lord.' But we can, at least, follow Him Who draweth us. We can, at least, not hold back, when He, as on this day, by the very Mysteries of our Faith, lifts us up above all created things, draws our eyes up and up to follow our Ascending Lord out of sight, until we lose ourselves amid the Choirs of Angels, as they sing, 'Who is the King of Glory? Even the Lord of Hosts, He is the King of Glory.' (3)

Thanksgiving

The heathen were without excuse, if they did not praise God, thank God. Nature itself crieth within us, that we owe ourselves, our very being, all that we are, and all that we have, all within us and without us, to Him Who made us, and all things for us, to use and to enjoy. And therefore nature itself crieth aloud within us, that we should love Him wholly, thank Him wholly, to Whom we owe our very being and all which maketh our being a joy to us. To Him we owe our whole mind and heart and soul and strength; therefore with our whole mind and heart and soul and strength which we owe to Him, we should praise Him. 'When shall we cease to praise Him? When we cease to have from Him, for which to praise Him. And since He always blesses us, we must evermore bless Him, and His praise be ever in our mouth.' 'What better,' says a father, 'can we have in our hearts, and utter with our mouth than thanks be to God? Nothing can be said more briefly, or heard more gladly, understood more grandly, or done more fruitfully. Whence Christians were even mocked by scoffers, because they so often said, when they met one another, 'Thanks be to God.'

And yet if such should be the thanks of mere nature, what should be the thanks of grace! If such be the thanks due that we are, that we live, that we behold heaven and earth, have mind and reason, memory and free-will, what, that we may live to God, that earth is for us, and heaven is ours, this fair earth is but a sojourning-place, where to gain heaven? What, when every thing beautiful in it, every thing which in it we love, is but a picture of some higher beauty and loveliness and love, in store for us if we love God? What, when not heaven alone or earth is ours, but the Father of heaven and earth, God Himself is ours, to be our own God, if we will, for ever and ever?

And should we the less love God for this, and praise God for all this, because they are so common, because so many besides us have them? Nay, rather, we should the more bless God, and praise God, because so many besides us have them. In that ocean of joy, which there shall be in the world to come, we shall have the more joy, because so many whom we shall love, shall have the same or greater joy. Is it not a joy to us here, with the little love which we have, to see others whom we love, have the same joy as ourselves? Does it not so increase our joy, if we deeply love, that we then begin deeply to joy, when those whom our inmost hearts love, share our joy? And there, in heaven, we shall all so deeply love, that our deepest love here will be but a shadow of the lowest love there; and we shall love all, and so shall share the joy of all there with a more inward joy than here we share the joy of those whose joy is as our own. (4)

NOTES / SOURCES

1. E. B. Pusey, *Sermons during the season from Advert to Whitsuntide*, Oxford, 1848, pp. 64–5
2. Ibid., pp. 230–3
3. Ibid., pp. 335–8
4. E. B. Pusey, *Parochial and Cathedral Sermons*, Oxford, 1882, pp. 288–9

John Henry Newman   1801–1890

An outstanding theologian and leader of the Oxford Movement until he joined the Church of Rome in 1845, John Henry Newman experienced an evangelical conversion in 1815 and then encountered the liberalism of Richard Whately and the Oriel Noetics. Influenced by John Keble and Hurrell Froude he became a leader of the Oxford Movement, contributing to *Tracts for the Times* and preaching powerful sermons at St Mary's, Oxford, where he was vicar. As a Fellow of Oriel he published works on the Arian controversy, a study of the Anglican *Via Media, Lectures on Justification* (1838) and finally *An Essay on the Development of Christian Doctrine* (1845). As a Roman Catholic he founded the Birmingham Oratory, and was made a Cardinal in 1879.

On his Ordination

Friday June 11 [1824]

As the time approaches for my ordination, thank God, I feel more and more happy. Make me Thy instrument . . . make use of me, when Thou wilt, and dash me to pieces when Thou wilt. Let me, living or dying, in fortune and misfortune, in joy and sadness, in health & Sickness, in honour and dishonour, be Thine.

Saturday June 12

Now, on returning home, how hard my heart is, how dead my faith. I seem to have an unwillingness to take the vows, a dread of so irreparable a step, a doubting whether the office is so blessed, the Christian religion so true. I am fasting today. I am licensed after the Ordination tomorrow, I believe. The salary £45 besides surplice fees.

Sunday June 13

It is over. I am thine, O Lord; I seem quite dizzy, and cannot altogether believe and understand it. At first, after the hands were laid on me, my heart shuddered within me; the words 'for ever' are so terrible. It was hardly a godly feeling which made me feel melancholy at the idea of giving up all for God. At times indeed my heart burnt within me, particularly during the singing of the Veni Creator. Yet, Lord, I ask not for comfort in comparison of sanctification . . . I feel as a man thrown suddenly into deep water.

Monday June 14

Just now, as we were on the point of beginning our prayers, I asked Francis whether he was present at the whole Ordination yesterday. He replied, Yes, except that he went out for a short time after my ordination. Of course I perceived this was for the purpose of praying for me, *me* who at the time was so hard and miserable. This thought affected me so much that I got very little way in the form of prayer, before I found a difficulty of proceeding; and when I came to read Deut. xxxiii I was obliged to give up the book to him, my tears burst out so violently. I made one more attempt to read and could not. I went on sobbing, while he read, to the end. O the evil of my heart, so vile, and so proud. How I behave to *him*! 'For ever,' words never to be recalled. I have the responsibility of souls on me to the day of my death . . . What a blessed day was yesterday. I was not sensible of it at the time—it will never come again. (1)

His Father's Death

Saturday Septr 25 [1824]

Summoned to Town by my Father's illness. What will be the end of this? What may have happened, before I open this book again!

Sunday Octr 3

That dread event has happened. Is it possible! O my Father, where art Thou? I got to Town Sunday morning. He knew me, tried to put out his hand and said 'God bless you.' Towards the evening of Monday he said his last words. He seemed in great peace of mind. He could, however, only articulate, 'God bless you, thank my God, thank my God[']—and lastly 'my dear.' Dr C. came on Wednesday, and pronounced him dying; he might live 12 hours. Towards evening we joined in prayer, commending his soul to God. Of late he had thought his end approaching. One day on the river, he told my Mother, 'I shall never see another summer.' On Thursday he looked beautiful, such calmness, sweetness, composure, and majesty were in this countenance. Can a man be a materialist who sees a dead body? I had never seen one before. (His last words to me, or all but his last, were to bid me to read to him the 33 chapter of Isaiah. 'Who hath believed' etc.)

Wednesday Octr 6

Performed the last sad duties to my dear Father. When I die, shall I be followed to the grave by my children? my Mother said the other day she hoped to live to see me married, but *I* think I shall either die within a College walls, or a Missionary in a foreign land—no matter where, so that I die in Christ. (2)

Lent at Littlemore

Littlemore 1842. Good Friday. March 25.

I have not been quite so strict this Lent as last. I have been stricter in one point, that I have eaten nothing between breakfast and tea and in not eating even fish—but I have relaxed, in having tea and butter, and hot milk, and in taking breakfast the first three days of this week, and in not using all the Offices every day till Passion (this) week.

I have done as follows.

I have abstained on week days (except St Matthias) from flesh of all kinds (exept salt fish twice) cheese, vegetables, toast, pastry, (except some times a plain pudding) fruit, sugar, milk in tea, fermented liquors (except principally in one week a glass of wine for a reason given on page opposite.) I have been much tried the earlier weeks and by an acute face ache—little tried the latter.

I have taken only two meals, breakfast 8 AM and tea 6 PM—when I have commonly taken bread, butter, eggs, and tea without milk, or hot bread and milk.

On Wednesday and Friday I have eaten nothing all day till 6 PM, sometimes drank a glass of water

On Sundays and St Matthias I dined on eggs and bacon, or cold meat, and cheese—and allowed also a glass of wine or beer, milk in tea, and toast.

I did not dine out, I did not wear gloves—I eat rhubarb commonly with my butter. I have not seen the Oxford or London (except once) Papers, (except the Record)

I did not make any alteration, as I had done the last Lents, in the Tempus Passionis. And the first three days of this I took breakfast—and yesterday and today though no breakfast (and so tomorrow. Sabbat. Sanct.) yet tea as other evenings.

I mean to end the fast as usual at 6 PM on Saturday.

I tried in Long Vac^n, and so now, not sleeping in bed, but found it [did] not succeed. I cannot get to sleep without being warm and then I am too warm. In Long Vac^n I slept always on straw mattress here. (3)

Meditation on the End of Man [1843]

The main subject of the meditation, that we are created to serve God, is rather abstract. My thoughts wandered (as I think, for a moment,) now and then. That dreadful thought about D. hurried me off. And I got troubled how God could be bearing so many of us at once; it seemed to make His Presence more unreal to me. I hardly could frame the scene at all. (Nor could I to keep it up in scarcely any that followed.)

The thoughts that struck me most were,—that God put it into my heart, when 5 or 6 years old, to ask *what* and *why* I was, yet now I am forty two, and have never answered it in *my conduct*; that if disobedience is *against nature*, I am, in the sight of Angels, like some odious *monster* which people put out of sight; that I have acted hardly ever for God's glory, that my motive in all my exertions during the last 10 years, has been the pleasure of energizing intellectually, as if my talents were given me to play a game with, (and hence I care as little about the event as one does about a game); that it is fearful to think how little I have used my gifts in God's service; that I have used them for myself. Hence that Selflove in one shape or another, e.g. vanity, desire of the good opinion of friends, etc. have been my motive; and that possibly it is *the* sovereign sin in my heart; and that therefore it will be well to make it the subject of the Particular Examen.

At the end I solemnly gave myself up to God to do what He would with me—to make me what He would—to put what He would upon me. (4)

The Pillar of the Cloud

Lead, Kindly Light, amid the encircling gloom,
    Lead Thou me on!
The night is dark, and I am far from home—
    Lead Thou me on!
Keep Thou my feet; I do not ask to see
The distant scene,—one step enough for me.

I was not ever thus, nor pray'd that Thou
    Shouldst lead me on.
I loved to choose and see my path; but now
    Lead Thou me on!
I loved the garish day, and, spite of fears,
Pride ruled my will: remember not past years.

So long Thy power hath blest me, sure it still
    Will lead me on,
O'er moor and fen, o'er crag and torrent, till
    The night is gone;
And with the morn those angel faces smile
Which I have loved long since, and lost awhile.

At Sea. June 16, 1833. (5)

Holiness Necessary for Future Blessedness

A Sermon

Holiness, without which no man shall see the Lord.
Hebrews xii. 14

In this text it has seemed good to the Holy Spirit to convey a chief truth of religion in a few words. It is this circumstance which makes it especially impressive; for the truth itself is declared in one form or other in every part of Scripture. It is told us again and again, that to make sinful creatures holy was the great end which our Lord had in view in taking upon Him our nature, and thus none but the holy will be accepted for His sake at the last day. The whole history of redemption, the covenant of mercy in all its parts and provisions, attests the necessity of holiness in order to salvation; as indeed even our natural conscience bears witness also. But in the text what is elsewhere implied in history, and enjoined by precept, is stated doctrinally, as a momentous and necessary fact, the result of some awful irreversible law in the nature of things, and the inscrutable determination of the Divine Will.

    Now some one may ask, 'Why is it that holiness is a necessary qualification for our being received into heaven? why is it that the Bible enjoins upon us so strictly to love, fear, and obey God, to be just, honest, meek, pure in heart, forgiving, heavenly-minded, self-denying, humble, and resigned? Man is confessedly weak and corrupt; *why* then is he enjoined to be so religious, so unearthly? *why* is he required (in the strong language of Scripture) to become "a new creature"? Since he is by nature what he is, would it not be an act of greater mercy in God to save him altogether without this holiness, which it is so difficult, yet (as it appears) so necessary for him to possess?'

Now we have no right to ask this question. Surely it is quite enough for a sinner to know, that a way has been opened through God's grace for his salvation, without being informed why that way, and not another way, was chosen by Divine Wisdom. Eternal life is 'the *gift* of God.' Undoubtedly He may prescribe the terms on which He will give it; and if He has determined holiness to be the way of life, it is enough; it is not for us to inquire why He has so determined.

Yet the question may be asked reverently, and with a view to enlarge our insight into our own condition and prospects; and in that case the attempt to answer it will be profitable, if it be made soberly. I proceed, therefore, to state one of the reasons, assigned in Scripture, why present holiness is necessary, as the text declares to us, for future happiness.

To be holy is, in our Church's words, to have 'the true circumcision of the Spirit;' that is, to be separate from sin, to hate the works of the world, the flesh, and the devil; to take pleasure in keeping God's commandments; to do things as He would have us do them; to live habitually as in the sight of the world to come, as if we had broken the ties of this life, and were dead already. Why cannot we be saved without possessing such a frame and temper of mind?

I answer as follows: That, even supposing a man of unholy life were suffered to enter heaven, *he would not be happy there;* so that it would be no mercy to permit him to enter.

We are apt to deceive ourselves, and to consider heaven a place like this earth; I mean, a place where every one may choose and take his *own* pleasure. We see that in this world, active men have their own enjoyments, and domestic men have theirs; men of literature of science, of political talent, have their respective pursuits and pleasures. Hence we are led to act as if it will be the same in another world. The only difference we put between this world and the next, is that *here*, (as we know well,) men are *not always sure*, but *there*, we suppose they *will be always sure*, of obtaining what they seek after. And accordingly we conclude, that *any man*, whatever his habits, tastes, or manner of life, if *once admitted* into heaven, would be happy there. Not that we altogether deny, that some preparation is necessary for the next world; but we do not estimate its real extent and importance. We think we can reconcile ourselves to God when we will; as if nothing were required in the case of men in general, but some temporary attention, more than ordinary, to our religious duties,—some strictness, during our last sickness, in the services of the Church, as men of business arrange their letters and papers on taking a journey or balancing an account. But an opinion like this, though commonly acted on, is refuted as soon as put into words. For heaven, it is plain from Scripture, is not a place where many different and discordant pursuits can be carried on at once, as is the case in this world. Here every man can do his *own* pleasure, but there he must do *God's* pleasure. It would be presumption to attempt to determine the employments of that eternal life which good men are to pass in God's presence, or to deny that that state which eye hath not seen, nor ear heard, nor mind conceived, may comprise an infinite variety of pursuits and occupations. Still so far we are distinctly told, that that future life will be spent in God's *presence*, in a sense which does not apply to our present life; so that it may be best described as an endless and uninterrupted worship of the Eternal Father, Son, and Spirit. 'They serve Him day and night in His temple, and He that sitteth on the throne shall dwell among them . . . The Lamb which is in the midst of the throne shall feed them, and shall lead them unto living fountains of waters.' Again, 'The city had no need of the sun, neither of the moon to shine in it, for the glory of God did lighten it, and the Lamb is the light thereof. And the nations of them which are saved shall walk in the light of it, and the kings of the earth do bring their glory and honour into it.' (Rev. vii. 15.17; xxi. 23, 24) These passages from St John are sufficient to remind us of many others.

Heaven then is not like this world; I will say what it is much more like,—*a church*. For in a place of public worship no language of this world is heard; there are no schemes brought forward for temporal objects, great or small; no information how to strengthen our worldly interests, extend our influence, or establish our credit. These things indeed may be right in their way, so that we do not set our hearts upon them; still (I repeat), it is certain that we hear nothing of them in a church. Here we hear solely and entirely of *God*. We praise Him, worship Him, sing to Him, thank Him, confess to Him, give ourselves up to Him, and ask His blessing. And *therefore*, a church is like heaven; viz. because both in the one and the other, there is one single sovereign subject—religion—brought before us.

Supposing, then, instead of it being said that no irreligious man could serve and attend on God in heaven (or see Him, as the text expresses it), we were told that no irreligious man could worship, or spiritually see Him in church; should we not at once perceive the meaning of the doctrine? viz. that, were a man to come hither, who had suffered his mind to grow up in its own way, as nature or chance determined, without any deliberate habitual effort after truth and purity, he would find no real pleasure here, but would soon get weary of the place; because, in this house of God, he would hear only of that one subject which he cared little or nothing about, and nothing at all of those things which excited his hopes and fears, his sympathies and energies. If then a man without religion (supposing it possible) were admitted into heaven, doubtless he would sustain a great disappointment. Before, indeed, he fancied that he could be happy there; but when he arrived there, he would find no discourse but that which he had shunned on earth, no pursuits but those he had disliked or despised, nothing which bound him to aught *else* in the universe, and made him feel at home, nothing which he could enter into and rest upon. He would perceive himself to be an isolated being, cut away by Supreme Power from those objects which were still entwined around his heart. Nay, he would be in the presence of that Supreme Power, whom he never on earth could bring himself steadily to think upon, and whom now he regarded only as the destroyer of all that was precious and dear to him. Ah! he could not *bear* the face of the Living God; the Holy God would be no object of joy to him. 'Let us alone! What have we to do with thee?' is the sole thought and desire of unclean souls, even while they acknowledge His majesty. None but the holy can look upon the Holy One; without holiness no man can endure to see the Lord.

When, then, we think to take part in the joys of heaven without holiness, we are as inconsiderate as if we supposed we could take an interest in the worship of Christians here below without possessing it in our measure. A careless, a sensual, an unbelieving mind, a mind destitute of the love and fear of God, with narrow views and earthly aims, a low standard of duty, and a benighted conscience, a mind contented with itself, and unresigned to God's will, would feel as little pleasure, at the last day, at the words, 'Enter into the joy of thy Lord,' as it does now at the words, 'Let us pray.' Nay, much less, because, while we are in a church, we may turn our thoughts to other subjects, and contrive to forget that God is looking on us; but that will not be possible in heaven.

We see, then, that holiness, or inward separation from the world, is necessary to our admission into heaven, because heaven is *not* heaven, is not a place of happiness *except* to the holy. There are bodily indispositions which affect the taste, so that the sweetest flavours become ungrateful to the palate; and indispositions which impair the sight, tinging the fair face of nature with some sickly hue. In like manner, there is a moral malady which disorders the inward sight and taste; and no man labouring under it is in a condition to enjoy what Scripture calls 'the fulness of joy in God's presence, and pleasures at His right hand for evermore.'

Nay, I will venture to say more than this;—it is fearful, but it is right to say it;—that if we wished to imagine a punishment for an unholy, reprobate soul, we perhaps could not fancy a greater than to *summon it to heaven*. Heaven would be hell to an irreligious man. We know how unhappy we are apt to feel at present, when alone in the midst of strangers, or of men of different tastes and habits from ourselves. How miserable, for example, would it be to have to live in a foreign land, among a people whose faces we never saw before, and whose language we could not learn. And this is but a faint illustration of the loneliness of a man of earthly dispositions and tastes, thrust into the society of saints and angels. How forlorn would he wander through the courts of heaven! He would find no one like himself; he would see in every direction the marks of God's holiness, and these would make him shudder. He would feel himself always in His presence. He could no longer turn his thoughts another way, as he does now, when conscience reproaches him. He would know that the Eternal Eye was ever upon him; and that Eye of holiness, which is joy and life to holy creatures, would seem to him an Eye of wrath and punishment. God cannot change His nature. Holy He must ever be. But while He is holy, no unholy soul can be happy in heaven. Fire does not inflame iron, but it inflames straw. It would cease to be fire if it did not. And so heaven itself would be fire to those, who would fain escape across the great gulf from the torments of hell. The finger of Lazarus would but increase their thirst. The very 'heaven that is over their head' will be 'brass' to them.

And now I have partly explained why it is that holiness is prescribed to us as the condition on our part for our admission into heaven. It seems to be necessary from the very nature of things. We do not see how it could be otherwise. Now then I will mention two important truths which seem to follow from what has been said.

1. If a certain character of mind, a certain state of the heart and affections, be necessary for entering heaven, our *actions* will avail for our salvation, chiefly as they tend to produce or evidence this frame of mind. Good works (as they are

called) are required, not as if they had any thing of merit in them, not as if they could of themselves turn away God's anger for our sins, or purchase heaven for us, but because they are the means, under God's grace, of strengthening and showing forth that holy principle which God implants in the heart and without which (as the text tells us) we cannot see Him. The more numerous are our acts of charity, self-denial, and forbearance, of course the more will our minds be schooled into a charitable, self-denying, and forbearing temper. The more frequent are our prayers, the more humble, patient, and religious are our daily deeds, this communion with God, these holy works, will be the means of making our hearts holy, and of preparing us for the future presence of God. Outward acts, done on principle, create inward habits. I repeat, the separate acts of obedience to the will of God, good works as they are called, are of service to us, as gradually severing us from this world of sense, and impressing our hearts with a heavenly character.

It is plain, then, what works are *not* of service to our salvation;—all those which either have no effect upon the heart to change it, or which have a bad effect. What then must be said of those who think it an easy thing to please God, and to recommend themselves to Him; who do a few scanty services, call these the walk of faith, and are satisfied with them? Such men, it is too evident, instead of being themselves profited by their acts, such as they are, of benevolence, honesty, or justice, may be (I might even say) injured by them. For these very acts, even though good in themselves, are made to foster in these persons a bad spirit, a corrupt state of heart; viz. self-love, self-conceit, self-reliance, instead of tending to turn them from this world to the Father of spirits. In like manner, the mere outward acts of coming to church, and saying prayers, which are, of course, duties imperative upon all of us, are really serviceable to those only who do them in a heavenward spirit. Because such men only use these good deeds to the improvement of the heart; whereas even the most exact outward devotion avails not a man, if it does not improve it.

2. But observe what follows from this. If holiness be not merely the doing a certain number of good actions, but is an inward character which follows, under God's grace, from doing them, how far distant from that holiness are the multitude of men! They are not yet even obedient in outward deeds, which is the first step towards possessing it. They have even to learn to practise good works, as the means of changing their hearts, which is the end. It follows at once, even though Scripture did not plainly tell us so, that no one is able to prepare himself for heaven, that is, make himself holy, in a short time;—at least we do not see how it is possible; and this, viewed merely as a deduction of the reason, is a serious thought. Yet, alas! as there are persons who think to be saved by a few scanty performances, so there are others who suppose they may be saved all at once by a sudden and easily acquired faith. Most men who are living in neglect of God, silence their consciences, when troublesome, with the promise of repenting some future day. How often are they thus led on till death surprises them! But we will suppose they *do* begin to repent when that future day comes. Nay, we will even suppose that Almighty God were to forgive them, and to admit them into His holy heaven. Well, but is nothing more requisite? are they in a fit state to *do Him service in heaven?* is not this the very point I have been so insisting on, that they are *not* in a fit state? has it not been shown that, even if admitted there without a

change of heart, they would find no pleasure in heaven? and is a change of heart wrought in a day? Which of our tastes or likings can we change at our will in a moment? Not the most superficial. Can we then at a word change the whole frame and character of our minds? Is not holiness the result of many patient, repeated efforts after obedience, gradually working on us, and first modifying and then changing our hearts? We dare not, of course, set bounds to God's mercy and power in cases of repentance late in life, even where He has revealed to us the general rule of His moral governance; yet, surely, it is our duty ever to keep steadily before us, and act upon, those general truths which His Holy Word has declared. His Holy Word in various ways warns us, that, as no one will find happiness in heaven, who is not holy, so no one can learn to be so, in a short time, and when he will. It implies it in the text, which names a qualification, which we know in matter of fact does ordinarily take time to gain. It propounds it clearly, though in figure, in the parable of the wedding garment, in which inward sanctification is made a condition distinct from our acceptance of the proffer of mercy, and not negligently to be passed over in our thoughts as if a necessary consequence of it; and in that of the ten virgins, which shows us that we must meet the bridegroom with the oil of holiness, and that it takes time to procure it. And it solemnly assures us in St Paul's Epistles, that it is possible so to presume on Divine grace, as to let slip the accepted time, and be sealed even before the end of life to a reprobate mind. (Heb. vi. 4–6; x. 26–29. Vide also 2 Pet. ii. 20. 22)

I wish to speak to you, my brethren, not as if aliens from God's mercies, but as partakers of His gracious covenant in Christ; and for this reason in especial peril, since those only can incur the sin of making void His covenant, who have the privilege of it. Yet neither on the other hand do I speak to you as wilful and obstinate sinners, exposed to the imminent risk of forfeiting, or the chance of having forfeited, your hope of heaven. But I fear there are those, who, if they dealt faithfully with their consciences, would be obliged to own that they had not made the service of God their first and great concern; that their obedience, so to call it, has been a matter of course, in which the heart has had no part; that they have acted uprightly in worldly matters chiefly for the sake of their worldly interest. I fear there are those, who, whatever be their sense of religion, still have such misgivings about themselves, as lead them to make resolve to obey God more exactly some future day, such misgivings as convict them of sin, though not enough to bring home to them its heinousness or its peril. Such men are trifling with the appointed season of mercy. To obtain the gift of holiness is the work of a *life*. No man will ever be perfect here, so sinful is our nature. Thus, in putting off the day of repentance, these men are reserving for a few chance years, when strength and vigour are gone, that WORK for which a *whole* life would not be enough. That work is great and arduous beyond expression. There is much of sin remaining even in the best of men, and 'if the righteous scarcely be saved, where shall the ungodly and the sinner appear?' (1 Pet. iv. 18) Their doom may be fixed any moment; and though this thought should not make a man despair to-day, yet it should ever make him tremble for to-morrow.

Perhaps, however, others may say:—'We know something of the power of religion—we love it in a measure—we have many right thoughts—we come to church to pray; this is a proof that we are prepared for heaven:—we are safe, and what has been said does not apply to us.' But be not you, my brethren, in the number of these. One principal test of our being true servants of God is our wishing to serve Him better; and be quite sure that a man who is contented with his own proficiency in Christian holiness, is at best in a dark state, or rather in great peril. If we are really imbued with the grace of holiness, we shall abhor sin as something base, irrational, and polluting. Many men, it is true, are contented with partial and indistinct views of religion, and mixed motives. Be you content with nothing short of perfection; exert yourselves day by day to grow in knowledge and grace; that, if so be, you may at length attain to the presence of Almighty God.

Lastly; while we thus labour to mould our hearts after the pattern of the holiness of our Heavenly Father, it is our comfort to know, what I have already implied, that we are not left to ourselves, but that the Holy Ghost is graciously present with us, and enables us to triumph over, and to change our own minds. It is a comfort and encouragement, while it is an anxious and awful thing, to know that God works in and through us. (Phil. ii. 12. 19) We are the instruments, but we are only the instruments, of our own salvation. Let no one say that I discourage him, and propose to him a task beyond his strength. All of us have the gifts of grace pledged to us from our youth up. We know this well; but we do not use our privilege. We form mean ideas of the difficulty, and in consequence never enter into the greatness of the gifts given us to meet it. Then afterwards, if perchance we gain a deeper insight into the work we have to do, we think God a hard master, who commands much from a sinful race. Narrow, indeed, is the way of life, but infinite is His love and power who is with the Church, in Christ's place, to guide us along it. (6)

NOTES / SOURCES

1. John Henry Newman, *Autobiographical Writings*, ed. Henry Tristram, London, 1956, pp. 200–1
2. Ibid., pp. 202–3
3. Ibid., pp. 220–1
4. Ibid., p. 223
5. John Henry Newman, *Verses on Various Occasions*, London, 1868, pp. 133–4
6. John Henry Newman, *Parochial and Plain Sermons*, Vol. I, London, 1875, pp. 1–14

Robert Isaac Wilberforce   1802–75

Second son of William Wilberforce and brother of Samuel, he was one of the most learned of the Tractarians. In 1841 he was appointed Archdeacon of the East Riding and was in close correspondence with H. E. Manning. He was the author of major theological studies of Baptism, the Eucharist, and the Incarnation. In 1854 he was received into the Church of Rome and died in Rome whilst preparing for the Catholic priesthood.

The Meaning of the Sacraments

Now the means whereby Christ's human nature acts upon ours is confessedly by Sacraments. In these there is a sort of external machinery, there are outward elements, there are means which our hands handle, and our lips receive, the use whereof can be subjected to man's laws, and made matter of Church regulation. And hence some persons have lost sight of the interior nature of these blessed ordinances; their secret significance, as the means whereby we are united to the Incarnate Word, has been forgotten; their real worth has not been estimated; and they have been treated as a mere outward sign, which it was as safe to despise as to reverence. What we want then is, to discern that Our Lord's humanity is the vital principle of life in all His people. This truth once appreciated, the use and importance of all those means whereby we are actually united to Him, will at once be manifest. We shall no longer look upon the ordinances of His grace as an artificial framework, which may sometimes further the spiritual action of our own minds, and sometimes impede it, but we shall recognize His nearness to us in those living means whereby He dispenses Himself; and what is outward will be kindled into reality by His inward presence. This is the true work of faith; of that eye of the soul, whereby we discover in things outward what is spiritual and unseen. Thus it is, as the Apostle expresses it, that we discern the Lord's Body.

We speak not of course of any carnal presence, nor as though outward elements, such as water, or bread, or wine, were so far changed as that they could work effects beyond nature, but we tell you of the doctrine of grace as depending on the sanctification of Our Lord's humanity, and we testify the blessedness of being united to Him, who is the Head of our renewed Being. The gifts of grace were in a degree bestowed upon the Jew, and possibly upon the Heathen. But when God became man, they were poured out in a common stream, and in more abundant measure. This was first given to Him who might claim it of right, that from Him it might be conveyed to us, who can claim it only of bounty. 'For it pleased the Father that in Him should all fulness dwell.' 'And of His fulness have all we received, and grace for grace.' (1)

The Nature of Grace

In its literal sense grace means favour. And since favour is, or ought to be, the result of desert, therefore in things earthly the term grace is rather applied to those whose character conciliates favour, than to those who entertain it. Hence does grace of body imply those external qualities which win favour. This is its common sense in the languages of classical antiquity. In Holy Scripture however the word is not limited to the graces of the body, but implies all those qualities which conciliate esteem. It was not only because he was well favoured, but by virtue of Joseph's whole character, that he found grace in the sight of his master the Egyptian. The favour or grace of man, then, depends not so much on the party which entertains, as on the party which deserves it: its source lies in the excellence of the graceful object, more than in the original stock of kindness, of which the beholder may be possessed. For though man be a free agent, so that he can choose which impulses it is his will to follow, yet they must be impulses which make part of his nature, and his nature is to favour those whose character calls forth his love. For man has no power of creating what is foreign to himself: he cannot go out of himself and render his neighbours other than they are: and therefore he cannot feel favour except towards those who either are, or are supposed to be, fit objects of his preference.

But with God it is wholly different. The favour of God has not its source in the excellence of the finite beings who attract, but in the boundless excellence of the Infinite Being who possesses it. For 'He is good and kind to the unthankful and to the evil.' Therefore only is divine grace exhaustless, because it is sovereign as the Majesty, and boundless as the Infinity of God. It has its fountain in those unsearchable stores of the divine love, which were the original cause of all existence. When this love moved forth from the inscrutable repose of its eternal existence, its will was to call into being heaven and earth. To this act nothing outward contributed by any external persuasion: 'the Lord hath made all things for Himself:' God's Will, like His Word, was the creative cause of all things. 'God said, Let there be light: and there was light.'

And so, too, when the object was to renew the souls whom He had made, it was still God's love, which was the only beginning of their recovery. For God commended His love to us, in that when we were yet sinners Christ died for us.' 'Of His own will begat He us by the Word of Life.' So that God's grace is wholly other than the grace of man: it has its root in His own nature, it is a producing cause of goodness in those whom His mercy favours. Its fountain is that unfathomable ocean of love, which is stored up in His Infinite Being. Thence it issues to bring into existence the objects which it desires. 'In all ages entering into holy souls, it maketh them to be sons of God and prophets.' It comes forth like the sun's light for the renewal of the world. Thus *creative* is that love of God which is the principle of grace. It is Himself in action, going forth through that most precious attribute of His nature, to effect the work which it is His pleasure to perform. For 'God is love, and he that dwelleth in love dwelleth in God, and God in him.' Such then is the nature of grace—God Himself working through His highest Attribute—the love of God in action. (2)

NOTES / SOURCES

1. Robert Isaac Wilberforce, *Sermons on the New Birth of Man's Nature*, London, 1850, pp. 22–3
2. Ibid., pp. 198–200

Frederick Denison Maurice   1805–1872

The son of a Unitarian minister, Maurice was educated at Trinity College, Cambridge, and subsequently at Exeter College, Oxford. Ordained in 1834, he was a professor at King's College, London, until his celebrated dismissal for denying a hell of eternal torment in 1853. A Christian Socialist, his prolific writings include *The Kingdom of Christ* (1838) and *Theological Essays* (1853). His ecumenical concerns led him to oppose church parties and to be one of the first Anglicans to study other faiths sympathetically.

Our Father which art in Heaven

Once more: the words '*In Heaven*,' as they are closely united with those which went before in meaning, so too, like them, come into collision with some of our strongest evil tendencies. The impulse of ordinary polytheists was to bring God down to earth; to make Him like themselves. Against this impulse the philosopher protested, representing the Divine Nature as wholly inactive, self-concentrated, removed from mundane interests. The Gospel justifies the truth which was implied in the error of the first; Christ, taking flesh, and dwelling among men, declares that Heaven has stooped to earth. But here a great many would stop; they would bring back Paganism through Christianity. The Son of God, they say, has become incarnate; now fleshly things are again divine, earth is overshadowed by Heaven; it is no longer sin to worship that which He has glorified. In the manger of Bethlehem they sink the Resurrection and Ascension: they will only look at one part of the great Redemption, not at the whole of it; at the condescension to our vileness, not at the deliverance from that vileness, which the Son accomplished when he sat down at the right hand of the Father. But He does not sanction this partial and grovelling view. 'After this manner,' he taught his disciples, even while he was upon earth, 'pray ye, Our Father which art in Heaven.' As if he had said, Do not think that I am come to make your thoughts of God less awful than those of Moses were, when he put his shoes off his feet and durst not behold; than Solomon's were, when he said, 'He is in Heaven and thou upon earth, therefore let thy words be few.' The revelation of the divine mystery in me is not given that you may entertain it better in your low carnal hearts, that you may mingle it more with the things which you see and handle; that each of you may have a warrant for the form of idolatry which is dear to him. This revelation is given that the mystery may be no longer one of darkness, but of perfect light: light which you will enter into more and more as your eyes are purged; but which, if it colour the mists of earth for a moment, will at last scatter them altogether.

'*Our Father*:' there lies the expression of that fixed eternal relation which Christ's birth and death have established between the littleness of the creature and the Majesty of the Creator; the one great practical answer to the philosopher who would make heaven clear by making it cold; would assert the dignity of the Divine Essence, by emptying it of its love, and reducing it into nothingness. Our Father, *which art in Heaven*: there lies the answer to all the miserable substitutes for faith, by which the invisible has been lowered to the visible; which have insulted the understanding and cheated the heart; which have made united worship impossible, because that can only be when there is One Being, eternal, immortal, invisible, to whom all may look up together, into whose presence a way is opened for all, whose presence is a refuge from the confusions, perplexities, and divisions of this world; that home which the spirits of men were ever seeking, and could not find, till He who had borne their sorrows and died their death, entered within the veil, having obtained eternal redemption for them, till He bade them sit with Him in heavenly places.

What I have said may have seemed to prove that this simple prayer is too high and too deep for creatures such as we are. Would you have it otherwise? Would you have a prayer which you can comprehend and fathom? I am sure the conscience and reason would reject such a prayer as a delusion, an evident self-contradiction. I have said nothing to show that this prayer is unsuitable to the wants and ignorance of any beggar in our streets. I have shown only, that the wisest man, who will not use it as that beggar does, who will try it by his own narrow methods and measures, will find that he has never entered into the sense of it, that he is condemning himself in the repetition of it. And if, brethren, we all know that we have been guilty of this mockery again and again, how clearly do our consciences witness, that it is after this manner, and no other, we must make our confession. What despair we should be in, if our unbelief were indeed truth, and not a lie! If the word 'Our' did *not* express the truth, that we participate in the blessings, as well as the curses, of the whole race; if the word 'Father' were a word merely, and not the expression of an eternal truth; if we might think of Him as not nigh, but afar off; in a book, not as one in whom we are living and having our being; if He were subject to the changes of earth, not for ever fixed in Heaven, whither could we turn under the overpowering sense of our own sinfulness and heartlessness? It is the full conviction that our misery has proceeded from ourselves, from our maintaining a resolute war with facts and reality, which can alone give us encouragement. For we know there is One who is willing to teach us how to pray this prayer in spirit and in truth; we know that there is One who is praying it. He who died for us and for all mankind, He who is ascended into Heaven, He, who is true and in whom is no lie, did when He was here clothed with our mortality, does now in his glorified humanity say, in the full meaning of the words, for us and for his whole family above and below, 'Our Father which art in Heaven.' (1)

Hallowed be Thy Name

We are in danger alike from the invasion of all old superstitions, and of a fanatical Atheism; for they have a common ground. All superstition, all idolatry has its root in the belief that God is made in our image, and not we in His: the most prevalent assumption of the modern as of the ancient sophist is, that man is the measure of all things; that there is nothing great or holy which is not his creation. Do not wonder, then, at any combinations you may see in our day between parties seemingly the most hostile—at any apparently sudden transitions from one camp to the other. There is no real inconsistency, no abandonment of principle. Do not let us be hasty in urging that charge or any charge. But let us be very careful in understanding the temptation of the age, because it is certainly our own. Let us not think we escape it by doing just the opposite of those who seem to us to have fallen into it; by cultivating all opinions and notions which they reject; by fearing a truth when they speak it. We may find that their practical conclusions meet us at the point which we thought the furthest from them, and that we have turned away from the very principle with which we might have strengthened ourselves, if not have done some good to them. Still less let us refuse to have our own loose and incoherent notions brought to trial, lest in losing them we should lose the eternal truths of God's Word. Depend upon it they are in the greatest peril from every insincere habit of mind we tolerate in ourselves; they will come out with a brightness we have never dreamed of when we are made simple and honest. Therefore let us pray this prayer, 'Hallowed be Thy Name,' believing that it has been answered, and being confident that it will be answered. It was answered in the old time by God's covenant; by the calling of every holy man; by the Divine law; by all the ordinances of family and national life; by every prophet and teacher whom God sent; by every witness which He bore to one people or another, in their consciences, in the discipline of their lives, through nature, through death, of His own character. It was answered by the whole life and death of the only-begotten Son, the firstborn of many brethren, the Prince of all the kings of the earth. It was answered by the gift of the Holy Spirit to abide with the Church for ever, for this end, that He might teach men of the Father and the Son. It is answered by our baptism into the holy and blessed Name, the Father, the Son, and the Holy Ghost. It is answered by confirmation and prayers, and holy communions, by individual trials, by visitations to nations, by the gift of new life to churches, by the conversion of sinners, by dying beds. It will be answered when we all yield ourselves up in deed and truth to the Spirit of God, that we like our Lord may glorify His Name upon the earth, and may accomplish the work which He has given us to do. (2)

Thy Kingdom Come

When we say, 'Thy Kingdom come,' We desire that the King of kings and Lord of lords will reign over our spirits and souls and bodies, which are His, and which He has redeemed. We pray for the extinction of all tyranny, whether lodged in particular men or in multitudes; for the exposure and destruction of corruptions inward and outward; for truth in all departments of government, art, science; for the true dignity of professions; for right dealings in the commonest transactions of trade; for blessings that shall be felt in every hovel. We pray for these things, knowing that we pray according to God's will; knowing that He will hear us. If He had not heard this prayer going up from tens of thousands in all ages, the earth would have been a den of robbers. He will so answer it, that all which He has made shall become as it was when He beheld it on the seventh day, and, lo, it was very good. (3)

The Prayer which Begins and Ends in Sacrifice and Adoration

I have desired that we should meditate upon the prayer of our childhood, in which lies, I believe, the charm against all that has assaulted us in our manhood. Within the few weeks that we have been considering it, as many events have been passing before us as might fill many centuries; it has seemed to meet them all; to be the best and fullest language, in which we can express our fears, hopes, longings, for ourselves, our nation, the world. We have not found that the wants and sorrows of Humanity were forgotten in it, because it begins from a higher ground, because it starts from a Father, because it acknowledges all the highest and lowest blessings as proceeding from Him. If we believe that this Father beholds Humanity, created, redeemed, glorified, in His beloved Son; if we believe that in that Son we may behold it and behold Him; that being members of His body we may see Christ in each and Christ in all; we cannot think less nobly of our kind than those do who shut their eyes to the facts of its corruption and misery, or who will not acknowledge that this corruption comes from our refusal to retain God in our knowledge. If we believe that the Holy Spirit, the Spirit of the Father and Son, is given to us that we may be united to each other, that we may be fitted for all knowledge and all love, we cannot have less noble anticipations of that for which man is destined than those who speak most loudly of his emancipation from all thraldom, and of his infinite capacities. But what we desire for ourselves and for our race—the greatest redemption we can dream of—is gathered up in the words, 'Thine is the glory.' Self-willing, self-seeking, self-glorying, here is the curse: no shackles remain when these are gone: nothing can be wanting when the spirit sees itself, loses itself, in Him who is Light, and in whom is no darkness at all. In these words therefore we see the ground and consummation of our prayer; they show how prayer begins and ends in Sacrifice and Adoration. They teach us how prayer, which we might fancy was derived from the wants of an imperfect suffering creature, belongs equally to the redeemed and perfected. In these the craving for independence has ceased; they are content to ask and to receive. But their desire of knowledge and love never ceases. They have awaked up after His likeness, and are satisfied with it; but the thought, 'Thine is the glory,' opens to them a vision which must become wider and brighter for ever and ever. Amen. (4)

NOTES / SOURCES

1. Frederick Denison Maurice, *The Prayer-Book and The Lord's Prayer*, London, 1880, pp. 290–3
2. Ibid., pp. 302–3
3. Ibid., p. 316
4. Ibid., pp. 398–9

Samuel Wilberforce   1805–73

The third son of William Wilberforce, Samuel Wilberforce was Bishop of Oxford from 1845 to 1869. Vigorous and eloquent he energetically campaigned for the revival of convocation, inaugurated diocesan reforms, campaigned for the appointment of missionary bishops overseas, and encouraged sisterhoods and theological colleges. Nicknamed 'Soapy Sam' for his fluency as a speaker and his links with the court, he was one of the most significant Victorian bishops.

Personality as an Awful Gift

This is the very character of the life of each one of us Christians—that we are brought under a set of divine influences by which our evil and perverted will may be thus healed and ordered. From our infancy no doubt this gracious power works upon us. From our baptism certainly God's Holy Spirit strives with us. From that period, even with the first dawning of the reason, the awful reality of a life is unfolding its eternal issues. Every day is provided with its checks and its encouragements; with its difficulties to be met, its temptations to be resisted, its opportunities to be used. Before a few, even a very few years are passed, a certain character is stamped upon us, of truth or falsehood, of self-restraint or rebellious appetite, of a reasonable obedience or of a stubborn self-will, of a will, enslaved by passion, or, calm in its enlightened supremacy. A careful eye may trace these features even in early childhood; in common they grow into deeper furrows, as every year passes by, and marks its lines upon us. And all this discipline of daily life is ordered for us by a loving Father, that there may, through it as an instrument, by the power of His heavenly grace, be formed within us the blessedness of a holy character. And in this mighty work never is He wanting to us; never, if it prosper not within us, is it that 'His arm is shortened,' or 'His ear heavy;' never does His Spirit forsake or fail those who seek Him; every day would add its healing to our will, its new line to our redeemed character, if we would not throw away the precious opportunities, and trifle with the unspeakable gift. Circumstances which seem the most unpropitious, are truly sent to us by Him, because they have in them exactly that discipline which we need, and which the presence of His Holy Spirit will enable us to find in them, if we will. All things are ordered for us with that just balance of trial and assistance which we require, as much as if there were no other being in the world to divide with us the love and the care of God through Christ. We are before Him in the singleness of that individual being which He has given to us. There is for us a sweet in every bitter, if we will draw it forth; healing in every wound, if we will seek it. Our own will, hardening itself against Him,—this; by its mysterious energy, may be our ruin; but besides this neither man nor accident, nor the might of any contrary powers, can take us from the blessed fashioning of His saving hand.

Herein lies the unspeakable worth of every life; that in it this awful question is being settled for an enduring spirit; that the will of each of us is, every day, through the multitude of our common actions, hardening itself in rebellion against the one true central will of God, or is being drawn lovingly by His grace into harmonious action with it. This is why the word of truth declares to us that every man must bear his own burden; and the practical lessons which flow from this are plain and most momentous.

1. For, first, it shews us the great importance of acting in the remembrance of this fearful condition of our lives. We are apt to let them, or, at the best, great portions of them, slip by us, as to any good purpose, because we forget this. We do not remember that it is by acting, and for the most part in the multitude of little things, in one way or another, that our will is affected; that, as there is this individuality of soul belonging to each of us, there is a character daily strengthening itself in each of us as we act; that every act has its influence on us; that the very spirit in which we perform these acts, tends, under God, to establish within us one or other set of dispositions; that if we act purely, simply, sincerely, kindly, thoughtfully; with an eye to God, remembering Christ our Saviour, trusting in His blessed Spirit; our will is being harmonised to His, and those lineaments are being marked upon us which will one day reflect the light of the heavenly glory. But that, on the other hand, if in our ordinary life we are cold and careless, or merely self-choosing, without the sense of living under a law, and being born anew; if we are serving the flesh, or the earthly mind; if in our common conduct and relation to those around us we are not sanctified by the blessed Spirit; that then, every day there is forming in us a character which cannot rejoice in God; because, from the mystery of our being, our will and His will are daily parting more utterly asunder. Here, then, is our first lesson,—the exceeding importance of action, and especially in that multitude of small things which make up our lives. The aspect of the heaven as the clouds sweep over it, leaving it now dark and heavy with vapours, and anon bright as the breath of the morning, is not fuller of variety than is the changing spirit of a man under the influence of his daily thoughts and actions.

2. From this same cause we may gather the importance of our securing times for self-examination and more serious communing with God and ourselves; that we may give a deeper and more inner tone to our lives; that we may ponder our

ways; that we may meditate on Him; that we may acquaint ourselves with Him, and know the calm peace of His hidden presence. For, unless we stay the ordinary stream of our lives in these sleeping pools and more solemn pauses, they soon run themselves shallow in the multiplicity of worldly objects, and like hasty brooks in their stony beds, even dry up under the hotness of a summer's sun. Our whole characters become thin and empty, outward and unmeaning; and we shall have surely to bear at last, as our own, the burden of a wasted life.

3. And, lastly, we may learn most surely this further lesson; the need of claiming earnestly for ourselves our own place in Christ Jesus our Lord, the new and living Man. Have we in us this fearful mystery of a separate life, of an enduring will? Is there daily growing upon us, even unawares, from our allowed thoughts and commonest actions, this settled cast of spiritual features; and are our temptations so numberless, our dangers so constant, our strength so weak? Have we an evil world without, malignant spirits ever present with us, an earthly body, and a deceitful heart; and shall we not earnestly and hourly cast ourselves on His strength who only can bear us through? Temptations we cannot fly: we must think, we must feel, we must act, we must be; and thinking, feeling, acting, being,—these all are moulding us; these are giving its type to the separate, single, hermit spirit which is lodged within us. To fly timidly from the face of every seeming temptation is only to meet with a more hidden one; to leave the world and its duties is only to find our evil selves and our present enemy stronger in the waste. We must pass through the struggle; for this end we were born; for this end we were baptised. We must become what that struggle shall make us; we must bear our own burden. We have the awful gift of life, the yet more awful gift of the new life; these must carry us on to the great end of judgment. Surely, then, we should earnestly and hourly cast our weakness on His strength who has so wonderfully made us His, and made Himself ours in the Church of the redeemed; we should wait upon Him and seek His presence in the ordinances of His Church; for how without Him shall we do otherwise than fail certainly? We should take our will to Him in prayer and supplication, that by His blessed Spirit it may be healed and strengthened; we should bring Him into all our actions; bid Him to our wedding-feast and our daily meals, that He may turn for us the water into wine; we should lean upon Him the fearfulness of our being, that, He being indeed with us, we may each one be able in the coming day of trial to bear his own burden. (1)

Prayer

What, then, is prayer? It is the conscious drawing near of the soul of a sinful, weak, ignorant, self-willed creature to its holy, loving, all-wise, and almighty Creator. It is the coming of a creature who has a will, and who knows that he has it; who knows that he cannot help willing and choosing, and that, whatever his words may say, or whatever part of him may feel, or whatever he may desire to feel, yet that he, the true creature, is governed by that will of his, and that he cannot, at last, choose what it will not;—that he may be crushed by force from without, but that by no such force can his will be altered:—it is the coming of such a creature as this to God. And it cannot, therefore, be his coming with the form of request, and the real meaning, 'Do as Thou wilt in spite of me and my prayers:' this cannot be prayer. But neither can it be the drawing near with this request, 'I know what is best for me, and therefore I ask this of Thee whether Thou wilt or not:' this, surely, were no real prayer; this were to put down the Creator from His throne, and to put our own blind and wavering fancy on it in His stead.

If, therefore, neither of these be prayer, what must it be? It must be the approach of one conscious of possessing a will, to the Supreme Will, with this true supplication: 'I have these desires; I cannot still them; and they combine together into the voice of my soul. They grow up into my will, and I cannot choose against my will. Yet I would not set it up against Thy will. Give me the good after which my soul longs; give me the true good, and not the seeming good; all good is in Thee. It is after this that I am inarticulately craving. These desires of good, Thou must satisfy them, and therefore I come to Thee. This will of mine, it is now uncertain, varying, wayward, blind, and passionate. Lord, make it like Thy will. Make it straight, firm, and right.' Now in all this there is a real prayer. This may be the prayer of one who is yet far from having secured the peace and blessedness of a will which is in true harmony with the Will of God. It may be the cry against himself of one deeply conscious of much remaining rebellion—the one true note amidst abounding discords—the reaching out of a withered arm; such an one may truly long for his own straightening, and may thus ask it sincerely of God: and in some measure there must be this character about all real prayer.

And this may be present even in the most particular supplication; even when we go to ask of God some special temporal boon; when we beg of Him the life of some child, the turning aside of some calamity, the averting of some darkness, the gift of some desired object; yet still in the soul of the true child of God there is this calming undersong; this more than a merely negative resigning itself to God; this earnest craving after a straightened, quickened will: even in the trembling of the needle, in the midst of all these desires, still his inmost soul may point to its one right aim; there may be still the one highest longing to find in God the true good, which, with such an apparent reality, seems to be now present in this or that particular object of desire.

And this is the true character of all petitions for earthly things, if they are indeed to deserve the name of prayers. They must, in their essence, be not the mere seeking for some outward good, but the seeking for it in God. It is not enough that we ask with a certain submission to His will; for, after all, that is only seeking Him for this outward object. This may be, and it often is, the beginning of true prayer—so graciously does God lure us through our wants unto Himself; but so long as it remains in this, it is not yet true prayer. We do not pray truly till our earthly wants lead us to seek Him for Himself; to go not only for the gift but for the Giver; to find in Him what cannot be in them. This is prayer indeed. And so we may see, that mere earnest supplication is often scarcely to be called prayer. For it may be nothing more than the expression of the passionate longings of an earthly heart, casting itself forth in the decent seemliness of a religious garb. So, doubtless, Saul of Tarsus had often called earnestly upon God out of the boiling surges of that impetuous self-willed spirit which ruled within him; and yet until he had learnt to say, 'Lord, what wilt Thou have me do?' he had never prayed. If this were prayer, who could pray more fervently than Baal's priests, or than many of the heathen, who at one time cry to their gods with passionate entreaties, 'cutting themselves with knives and lancets,' and then turn their prayer into threats if their supplications are not granted. But this is no true prayer: for prayer must be the reaching forth of the soul, not after other things through God, but through all other things after God. (2)

NOTES / SOURCES

1. Samuel Wilberforce, *Sermons*, London, 1844, pp. 98–106
2. Ibid., pp. 153–7

Christopher Wordsworth   1807–1885

Youngest son of Christopher Wordsworth, Master of Trinity College, Cambridge, and a nephew of William Wordsworth, the poet, Christopher Wordsworth was Bishop of Lincoln from 1869 until his death. A conservative High Churchman with a veneration for the Fathers he was a learned patristic scholar and the author of many hymns often of a typological character, published in *The Holy Year* (1862).

Confirmation Hymns

Confirmation

PART I

Sung by the whole Congregation.

FATHER of all, in Whom we live,
To Thee we praise and glory give;
Fountain of Love! Who didst by Grace
Create anew our fallen race,
Making us sons of God to be,
Adopted in Thy Son by Thee,
O may Thy Blessing on us shine,
And, Father, keep us ever Thine!

O SON of GOD, through Whom we live;
To Thee we praise and glory give;
O God made Flesh, Who hast renew'd
Man in Thine own similitude;
Baptiz'd into Thy Body, Lord,
And grafted in the Incarnate Word,
May we for ever in Thee dwell;
Be ever our Emmanuel!

O HOLY GHOST, by Whom we live;
To Thee we praise and glory give;
Thou, Blessèd Spirit, Holy Dove,
Who dost on hallow'd waters move;

By Whom in them we joinèd are
To Christ, and God's own nature share;
Brood o'er us with the shadowings
For ever of Thy golden wings!   Amen.

PART II

To be used before the Laying on of hands.

O God, in Whose all-searching eye
Thy servants stand, to ratify
The Vow Baptismal by them made
When first Thy hand was on them laid;
Bless them, O holy Father, bless
Who Thee with heart and voice confess;
May they, acknowledg'd as Thine own,
Stand evermore before Thy Throne!

O Christ, Who didst at Pentecost
Send down from heaven the Holy Ghost;
And at Samaria baptize
Those whom Thou didst evangelize;
And then on Thy baptiz'd confer
Thy best of gifts, the Comforter,
By Apostolic hands and prayer;
Be with us now, as Thou wert there.

Arm these Thy soldiers, Mighty Lord,
With shield of Faith, and Spirit's sword;
Forth to the battle may they go,
And boldly fight against the foe,
With banner of the Cross unfurl'd,
And by it overcome the World;
And so at last receive from Thee
The Palm and Crown of Victory.

Come, Ever-blessed Spirit, come,
And make Thy servants' hearts Thy home;
May each a living Temple be,
Hallow'd for ever, Lord, to Thee;
Enrich that Temple's holy shrine
With sevenfold gifts of grace divine;
With Wisdom, Light, and Knowledge bless,
Strength, Counsel, Fear, and Godliness.

O Trinity in Unity,
One Only God, and Persons Three;
In Whom, through Whom, by Whom we live,
To Thee we praise and glory give;

O grant us so to use Thy grace,
That we may see Thy glorious face,
And ever with the heavenly host
Praise Father, Son, and Holy Ghost.   AMEN.

PART III

*After the Laying on of the hands of the Bishop; to be sung
specially by those who have been confirmed.*

Our hearts and voices let us raise
To God in songs of thanks and praise;
We bless Thee for the Gift which Thou
Hast given to us Thy servants now;
Gift from Thy Love's exhaustless store,
Seal of past graces, pledge of more,
Of graces that for ever grow
As onward on our course we go.

Pilgrims in this world's wilderness,
We see Thee near, and seeing bless;
Ours are the mercies now which Christ
Grants in the Holy Eucharist;
The Manna now to us is given,
The Living Bread that comes from heaven;
The Rock for us with water flows;
Himself on us the Lord bestows.

O speed us onward to the race,
From strength to strength, from grace to grace;
So may we, by Thy Spirit blest,
Come to the Canaan of our rest,
Mounting on wings of Faith and Love
To Thy Jerusalem above;
And praise Thee everlastingly,
One only God and Persons Three.   AMEN. (1)

At Confirmation

Lord, be Thy Word my rule;
    In it may I rejoice;
Thy glory be my aim,
    Thy holy will my choice;

Thy promises my hope,
    Thy Providence my guard;
Thine arm my strong support,
    Thyself my great reward!   AMEN. (2)

NOTES / SOURCES

1. Christopher Wordsworth, *Miscellanies Literary and Religious*, Oxford, 1879, pp. 361–2
2. Ibid., p. 381

Thomas Thellusson Carter 1808–1901

T. T. Carter belonged to the second generation of the Catholic revival. As Rector of Clewer, near Windsor, he founded a House of Mercy there in 1849, and a sisterhood, the Community of St John the Baptist, in 1852. His *Treasury of Devotion* (1869) was widely used, and he played a prominent part in the Confraternity of the Blessed Sacrament, the English Church Union, and the Society of the Holy Cross. He was a strong defender of sacramental confession.

A Letter of Direction

'MY DEAR—,

'I trust your home life is peaceful, and that you are exact in the fulfilment of all duties. Any special trials should be calls for patience and loving helpfulness.

'I suppose you keep some midday prayer, renewing spiritual desires at such times. And can you give more time for reading some helpful book—half an hour in the day at least? And it would be well to make some special grace to be remembered about midday and about five o'clock—

'Readiness to help.

'Endurance.

'Self-sacrifice.

'Prayerfulness.

'Thankfulness.

'To make more than usual intercessory prayers.

'To keep certain times of reading devout subjects daily.

'To offer each night thankfulness for any special blessing, or regret for any failing in speech.

'Nothing unnecessarily against another; care of thought; keeping off unkindliness of any kind to any one.

'Regularity in duties; carefulness as to any light matter.

'The grace—such as patience, perseverance, readiness to help. Contentment with things that come unexpectedly, and such-like. God bless you.

'Yours affectionately,
'T. T. C.' (1)

The Objectivity of the Sacraments a Gift of the Spirit

'MY DEAR—,

'There have always been minds which have been influenced by purely subjective realization of God. We cannot limit the Holy Spirit's work, and such persons may be quite true and possessed with the belief of their God's work in them. But history has shown the extreme danger of such purely internal and subjective communion with God and heavenly things, and of the sad effects that may arise from such a view of religion. Some may be preternaturally guarded from such effects, while many have been seen to fall into them, self-confidence and self-conceit being the very least among such effects. God knows us better than we know ourselves, and He knows that we need an objective system of Sacraments for external use, or He would not have ordained them. Nothing can be clearer than the ordinances of Baptism, Absolution, Holy Communion, and of the necessity of membership with an organized body, and of the gifts of grace and peace being associated with such sacramental ordinances and fellowship. The same God Who by His Spirit speaks directly to the soul, gave us this system, as not only a channel of His grace, but also a witness and a guard, uniting the outward and the inward; and this undoubtedly is the Catholic order of Communion between our souls and Himself and Christian life. (2)

NOTES / SOURCES

1. T. T. Carter, in *Life and Letters of Thomas Thellusson Carter* ed. W. H. Hutchings, London, 1903, p. 185
2. Ibid., p. 313

Henry Edward Manning   1808–1892

Educated at Harrow and Balliol College, Oxford, Manning was ordained in 1832 and began his ministry as curate of Lavington in Sussex, becoming Archdeacon of Chichester in 1841. Following the Gorham Judgement, in which a secular court decided Anglican doctrine, he was received into the Church of Rome where he eventually became Cardinal Archbishop of Westminster and a notable supporter of the definition of Papal Infallibility at the First Vatican Council. His Anglican sermons are marked by the same concern for holiness and stress on the doctrine of the Holy Spirit that marked his writings and concerns as a Roman Catholic.

Short Devotions a Hindrance to Prayer

If we will but consider what the act of prayer is, we shall see that, of all the spiritual powers of the regenerate soul, it is the highest, and most nearly akin to perfection. It is no less than speaking with God, under a consciousness of His presence, with kindled desires, and a submitted will. It implies the presence and energy of faith, love, and repentance. Such as we are, such our prayers will be. It is the unfolding of ourselves in God's sight; and there must needs go before it and with it a knowledge of ourselves, founded on habitual self-examination. And for this, stated and not short seasons of silence and retirement in the presence of God are absolutely needed.

Now what is actually the state of most people? They pray twice in the day. Their prayers are, for the most part, certain fixed and ever-recurring forms of devotion; in themselves good, but necessarily general both in confession and petition. These prayers are said over with more or less of attention, desire, feeling, and emotion. They take, it may be, a quarter of an hour in the morning, and the same at night. They are often not preceded by conscious preparation, nor followed by prescribed acts of reflection. They are parentheses in the day which will not read into the context of life, but are entered and left by a sensible transition of the mind. To this, perhaps, is added, in most cases, a reading of the Bible once in the course of the day. With some there lingers still the remains of an excellent and most significant practice of reading the appointed Psalms and Lessons—a memorial of better times, and an unconscious act of unity, in spirit and intention, with those who daily pray before the altars of the Church. Now the time spent in these habits is half an hour in prayer, and perhaps the same in reading. If to this be added family prayers, a quarter of an hour in the morning, and the same at night, I believe we shall have taken no unfavourable sample of the measure of time given to their daily prayers by persons even of a serious and religious character. It cannot be doubted that such people would pass for devout persons; nor will I, which God forbid, gainsay their claim to be so esteemed. But what does it come to, after all? One hour and a half in every twenty-four. And how are the rest allotted? Nine or ten to sleep and its circumstantials, two or three hours spent over food; four or five, that is, whole mornings and whole evenings, given up to conversation, visits, amusements, and what the world calls society; the rest consumed in various employments of various degrees of nearness to, or remoteness from, the presence and thought of God. Now, assuredly, if this world were not a fallen world, if all its spontaneous daily movements were in harmony with the will of God and the state beyond the grave, there would be no harm in resting upon those movements, and in being borne along with them. But if it be indeed a world fallen from God; and if in its fairest forms it be still, at least by privation of righteousness, sinful in His sight, then to live in it as if it were not fallen cannot but estrange us from real communion with Him. An hour and a half of better thoughts in every day will not disinfect our hearts, and counterwork the perpetual and transforming action of the world in all the rest of our time. In this point, busy and toilworn people have an advantage over the more leisurely; for business and labour are a part of the fall, and have in them chastisement and humiliation. There is great danger, in cases like that which I have taken, lest such minds, though in many ways blameless and pure, should be strangers to the deeper things of God, and to the realities of compunction and devotion. (1)

Frequent Communion Demands Habitual Devotion

And one more thought we may take from this blessed mystery; I mean, with what veneration and devotion we ought to behave ourselves towards the Presence of Christ in the Sacrament of His Body and Blood.

The first truth which must force itself upon every one who has faith in this great gift of love is, the duty and blessedness of celebrating it with the greatest possible frequency. Nothing surely ought to restrain this frequency, except the awfulness of the blessed Sacrament, and the danger of unworthiness in the celebrant and the receivers. But this is a subject far too wide to enter upon by the way. Frequent communion does indeed demand a high tone of habitual devotion and of inward recollection in the pastors of the Church. And this is both their highest blessing and their strictest law of life. Happy, and full of all benediction to ourselves and to our flocks, if we could so live as to be always meet to draw near to Him. But it is not more certain that frequent communion demands high devotion, than that a belief in the Real Presence demands frequent celebration.

How can we be said to believe what we do not act upon? 'Shew me thy faith without thy works, and I will shew thee my faith by my works.' (St. James ii. 18.) Surely, if there be any thing in which 'faith without works is dead,' it is in a profession of believing Christ's Presence in the holy Sacrament while we rarely celebrate it. They who do not believe in this divine gift are consistent in approaching it once a year: but should we be consistent, if, believing, we celebrate it but three or four times a year? A living faith in this spiritual reality would make infrequent communion impossible. Where the holy Eucharist is not, the ritual of the Church is as a day when the sun goes down at noon. We should feel as if the worship of God through Christ had lost its central light. All the whole life of the regenerate is related to this great fountain of grace; all issues from it, and returns into it again. When the altar stands cold and bare, they are bid to go empty away.

But if this be the effect of such a faith upon the frequency, what must it also be upon the manner of celebrating this holy sacrament? What do mean and naked altars, often wormed and decaying; worn and paltry furniture, worthless vessels, and, worse than all, rough and reckless handling, certainly reveal? Belief of His presence, or assurance of His absence? But alas, our own sins are enough—too many and too deep that we should look on others'. With what a conscious feeling of direct and personal service done to our Master should we tend and dress that which is a shadow of His cross and of His grave; with what respect should we handle and care for even the least and poorest vessel, sacred by relation to His presence. Above all, with what a collected sense of His nearness ought we to fulfil our function in offering the memorial of His one only sacrifice, by taking, blessing, breaking the bread of life to His people! If only we could apprehend by a living faith, and realise the very truth of what we do, we should feel that after His sacramental Presence, and our standing there to serve before Him, nothing remains but the homage of the blessed in the vision of His face in heaven. (2)

Praise

'Ye shall have a song, as in the night when a holy solemnity is kept; and gladness of heart as when one goeth with a pipe to come into the mountain of the Lord, to the mighty One of Israel.' (Isaiah 30.29)

This sets vividly before us a state of heart, a temper of love and thanksgiving, a filial and almost childlike simplicity of grateful joy; and in this way it brings out, more clearly than any words, what is the full meaning of praise; from what source it springs, and in what ways it is expressed. If we are to define it in words, we may say that praise is thankful, lowly, loving worship of the goodness and majesty of God. And therefore we often find the word 'praise' joined with 'blessing' and 'thanksgiving:' but though all three are akin to each other, they are not all alike. They are steps in a gradual scale—a song of degrees. Thanksgiving runs up into blessing, and blessing ascends into praise: for praise comprehends both, and is the highest and most perfect work of all living spirits. (3)

NOTES / SOURCES

1. Henry Edward Manning, *Sermons II*, London, 1846, pp. 352–4
2. H. E. Manning. *Sermons IV*, London, 1850, pp. 206–9
3. Ibid., p. 279

William Ewart Gladstone   1809–98

British statesman, leader of the Liberal Party from 1867, and several times Prime Minister, Gladstone was a devout High Churchman, who moved from being a strong supporter of Establishment to advocating disestablishment of the Church of Ireland. A weekly communicant he was generous in almsgiving and played a significant part in the founding of many new sees in the British Empire. A wide and voracious reader he maintained a continuous interest in theological as well as political affairs.

The Christian Life of a Busy Statesman

A Letter to Henry Manning

Hawarden, Sunday, December 28, 1845.

My dear Manning,

. . . I write respecting your sermons, and in their bearing on myself . . .

You teach that daily prayers, the observance of fast and festival, and considerable application of time to private devotion and to Scripture, ought not to be omitted *e.g.*, by me: because, great as is the difficulty, the need is enhanced in the same proportion, the balance is the same.

You think, very charitably, that ordinary persons, or such who have a right general intention in respect to religion, give an hour and a half to its direct duties; and if they add attendance at both daily services, raising it to three, you consider that still a scanty allowance while some sixteen or seventeen are given to sleep, food, and recreation.

Now, I cannot deny this position with respect to the increase of the need—that you cannot overstate. But I think there are two ways in which God is wont to provide a remedy for real and lawful need—one by augmenting supply, the other by intercepting the natural and ordinary consequences of the deficiency. I am desirous really to look the question full in the face: and then I come to the conclusion that, if I were to include the daily services now in my list of daily duties, my next step ought to be resignation.

Let me describe to you what has been at former times, when *in London and in office*, the very narrow measure of my stated religious observances: on week days I cannot estimate the one family prayer together with morning and evening prayer at more than three-quarters of an hour, even if so much. Sunday is reserved, with rare exceptions, for religious employments, and it was my practice in general to receive the Holy Communion weekly. Of daily services, except a little before and after Easter, not one in a fortnight, perhaps one in a month. Different individuals have different degrees of facility in supplying the lack of regular devotion by that which is occasional, but it is hard for one to measure this resource in his own case.

I cannot well estimate, on the other hand, the amount of relaxation which used then to accrue to me. Last year I endeavoured in town to apply a rule to the distribution of my hours, and took ten for sleep, food, and recreation, understanding this last word so as to include *whatever* really refreshes mind or body or has a fair chance of doing so. Now my exigencies for sleep are great. As long as I rise feeling like a stone, I do not think there is too much, and this is the general description of my waking sense, in office and during the session, but I consider seven and a half hours the least I ought then to have, and I should be better with eight. I know the old stories about retrenching sleep, and how people have deceived themselves: with me it may be so, but I think it is not. I have never summed up my figures, but my impression is that last year, upon the average, I was under and not over the ten for the particulars named—I should say between nine and ten. But last year was a holiday year as to pressure upon mind and body, in comparison with those that preceded it. Further, people are very different as to the rate at which they expend their vigour during their work—my habit, perhaps my misfortune, is, and peculiarly with work that I dislike, to labour at the very top of my strength, so that after five or six hours of my office I was frequently in a state of great exhaustion. How can you apply the duty of saving time for prayer out of sleep and recreation to a man in these circumstances?

Again, take fasting. I had begun to form to myself some ideas upon this head; but I felt, though without a positive decision to that effect, that I could not and must not apply them if I should come again into political activity. I speak now of fasting in quantity, fasting in nutrition; as to fasting in quality, I see that the argument is even strengthened, subject only to the exception that in times of mental anxiety it becomes impossible to receive much healthy food with which a sound appetite would have no difficulty. The fact is undoubted; it is extremely hard to keep the bodily frame *up* to its work under the twofold condition of activity in office and in Parliament. I take it then that to fast in the usual sense would generally be a sin, and not a duty—I make a little exception for the time immediately preceding Easter, as then there is a short remission of Parliamentary duties.

I need not, perhaps, say more now. You see my agreement with you, and that I differ, it may be, where the pinch comes upon myself. But I speak freely, in order to give scope for opposite reasoning—in order that I may be convicted if possible, as then I hope also to be convinced.

There is the greatest difference, as I find, between simple occupation, however intense, and occupation with anxiety as its perpetual accompaniment. Serious reading and hard writing even for the same number of hours that my now imminent duties may absorb, I for one can bear without feeling that I am living too fast; but when that one element of habitual anxiety is added, Nature is spurred on beyond her own pace under an excessive burden, and vital forces waste rapidly away. I should be more suspicious of myself than I now am in the argument I have made, were it not that I have had experience of occupation in both forms, and know the gulf between them.

I ought to have added the other *sting*, of official situations combined with Parliament. It is the sad irregularity of one's life. The only fixed points are prayers and breakfast in the morning, and Sunday at the beginning of the week. It is Sunday, I am convinced, that has kept me alive and well, even to a marvel, in times of considerable labour; for I must not conceal from you, even though you may think it a sad bathos, that I have never at any time been prevented by illness from attending either Parliament or my office. The only experience I have had of the dangers from which I argue, in results, has been in weakness and exhaustion from the brain downwards; it is impossible for me to be thankful enough for the exemptions I enjoy, especially when I see far stronger constitutions—constitutions truly Herculean—breaking down around me. I hope I may be preserved from the guilt and ingratitude of indulging sensual sloth under the mask of wise and necessary precautions.

Do not trouble yourself to write at length, but revolve these matters in the casuistical chamber of the mind, and either before or when we meet give me an opinion which I trust will be frank and fearless.

There is one retrenchment I could make: it would be to take from activity outwards in matter of religion, in order to give to prayer. But I have given a misdescription. What I could economize is chiefly reading: but reading nowadays I almost always shall have to resort to—at least so it was before—by way of repose. Devotion is by far the best sedative to excitement: but, then, it requires great and sustained exertion (to speak humanly and under the supposition of the Divine grace) or else powerful external helps, or both. Those mere dregs of the natural energies which too often are all that occupation leaves are fit for little beyond *passivity*—only for reading when not severe.

Reading all this you may the more easily understand my tone sometimes about public life as a whole.

Joy to you at this blessed time and at all times!

Your affectionate friend,
W. E. Gladstone. (1)

Advice for his Eldest Son

1. Little prayers.

(1) Upon entering a church, bow the head or close the eyes, think on God, and say, either aloud *or* to yourself:

'Oh how amiable are Thy dwellings, Thou Lord of Hosts !' (Ps. lxxxiv. 1).

(2)Before reading Holy Scripture, do in like manner, and say as above:

'Thy hands have made me and fashioned me: oh, give me understanding, that I may learn Thy commandments' (Ps. cix. 73).

(3) In church, before Divine service begins:

'O Lord Jesus Christ, Shepherd of the lambs, help me so to pray, and so to hear this day in Thy holy house on earth, that at the last I may join with holy children, to praise Thee for evermore, before Thy glorious throne in heaven.'

(4) After Divine service has ended, before leaving church:

'O God, hear me in that I have prayed to Thee, and pardon me in that my mind hath gone astray from Thee, and open Thou mine eyes that I may see Thee: through Jesus Christ our Lord.'

(5) In bed, before going to sleep, you may say:

'For He shall give His angels charge over thee, to keep thee in all thy ways.

'They shall bear thee in their hands: that thou hurt not thy foot against a stone' (Ps. xci. 11, 12).

2. *Morning and Evening Prayers.*

Before morning or evening prayer, collect your thoughts: place yourself by reflection before God: and say:

'In the name of the Father, and of the Son, and of the Holy Ghost.'

Then go on as follows:

I. IN THE MORNING

Bless the Lord, O my soul, and all that is within me praise His holy name: for the mercies of the past night; for . . . all His goodness, and loving kindness, to me and to all men; but above all for our redemption in Jesus Christ.

Forgive me, O Lord, for His sake, all the sins of my past life. Make me grieve that I ever offended Thee, who hast so loved me. Grant that this day I may watch against sin, deny myself for the sake of the Lord Christ, and strive to avoid all temptation. [Here stop, and think of the kinds of temptation that you suffer most.]

Make me to live as a child of God, a member of Christ, and an heir of heaven. Make me gentle and loving to all men: lowly and obedient to my parents and elders, diligent and firm in all manner of duty, just and true and pure: that so living in this world, I may come to Thine everlasting kingdom in heaven.

Bless, O Lord, my father and mother, my grandpapa, my grandmama, my brother Stephen, my sisters Agnes and Jessy, all who are near and dear to me, all who are in need and sorrow, all the Bishops and clergy, and all Thy Holy Church throughout the world. All this I ask through Jesus Christ our only Saviour. Amen.

Our Father, which art, etc.

The grace of our Lord, etc.

II. IN THE EVENING

O almighty and tender Father, bless me before I lie down to rest. Forgive me through the precious blood of Christ whatever I have sinned this day [here stop: recollect, and confess distinctly whatever sins you have done or duties you have left undone] in thought, in word, or in deed. Enable me to serve Thee truly for the time to come, and to love Thee with all my heart.

Bless my father and mother, my brother Stephen, and sisters Agnes and Jessy, my grandpapa, my grandmama, those who teach me and attend me, and all for whom I ought to pray. And, oh, be Thou about my bed and about my path, and let Thine holy angels watch over me and keep me safe from evil in the watches of the night, through the merits of Jesus Christ our Lord. Amen.

Our Father, etc.

The grace of our Lord, etc.

3. *Counsels, 1854–1857*

(1) On no consideration whatever omit your morning or evening prayers. If any obstacle prevent them at the proper time, say them at the first moment when you are free. If from illness or otherwise you cannot say them kneeling, say them in such place and posture as you can.

(2) Remember the Psalmist's words, 'I have set God always before me': which mean by taking care not only not to break His commands, but to cherish in the

mind an abiding sense of His presence, of being near to Him, and even when in society or in bustle alone with Him.

(3) This sense of God's presence will both help and be helped by the practice of prayer by silent ejaculation, or inwardly addressing God in short sentences, though of but two or three words: although so short, their wings may be strong enough to carry upwards many a fervent desire and earnest seeking after God.

(4) So also it is good to form inwardly and to bear about with you upon the eye of your mind the image of Christ in whom we live: especially of Christ crucified, as He bled for us, and of Christ glorified, as at His Father's right hand He still offers the one everlasting sacrifice of Himself on our behalf.

(5) Let no day pass without reading some portion of the Holy Scripture. If you can, let this course of reading follow the course of the Psalms, or of some of the Lessons, according to the Prayer-Book. It is good to acquire a habit of reading the New Testament for devotion in the Greek when you can do it with ease, by which much is learned that the English translation of necessity leaves in the shade.

(6) Sunday, the day of the Resurrection, is at once the emblem, the earnest, and the joy, of the renewed life: cherish it accordingly: grudge, and as it were resent, any intrusion of worldly thoughts or conversation: except upon real necessity, strive to shut out rigorously any worldly business: always view the devotion of the day to God, not as a yoke, but as a privilege; and be assured that it and so far as this view of it shall seem overstrained, the soul is not in its health.

(7) Remember that the avoidance of sin, indispensable as it is, is the lower part of our religion: from which we should ever be striving onwards to the higher —namely, the life of Divine love, fed continually by the contemplation of God as He is revealed to us in Christ, nowhere better described in brief than by the Psalmist when he says: 'As for me, I will behold Thy presence in righteousness: and when I awake up after Thy likeness I shall be satisfied with it'—words which, like most words of Scripture, open deeper and more satisfying truths the more we humbly ponder them.

(8) Look to the Holy Communion as a great and wondrous key to unlock the things of God. In it our prayers are especially united with that sacrifice of Christ, and a new power seems to be given to them: whatever can at any time render them acceptable, there is a larger union with His people, the living and the departed—the whole family in heaven and earth,' as St. Paul says: a nearer identification with Him: and not a foretaste only, but, as it were, a taste of entry into His joy.

(9) The Christian should never forego any opportunity which may be offered him of access to that Heavenly Feast.

December 3, 1854

Prayer, if understood as the mere repetition, with consciousness of their meaning, of words of petition addressed to God, may be, as most men think it, a business requiring no great stretch or effort of mind. But, in truth, when it is such as it ought to be, it is the highest and most sustained energy of which the human mind is capable: and until we have come to know this each for ourselves, we may be assured that we have never yet prayed as we may and as we ought.

The precept, 'If any man will come after Me, let him deny himself, and take up his cross daily and follow Me,' is the perpetual and inseparable badge of a Christian. But so much are the contrivances of ease and of enjoyment multiplied nowadays, that many souls are utterly lost from want of occasions to remind them of this great precept and bring them into real contact with it. It is therefore an excellent rule to fix this, at least, that no day shall pass without some restraint put upon our natural inclination: not merely in the avoidance of sin, which is an absolute and uniform duty, but in our employments, recreations, or enjoyments —as, for example, in choosing the first according to duty and feeling, that they are not regulated by mere will and preference: in restricting the quantity of the latter: in doing some things for the pleasure or good of others, to our own inconvenience or distaste: or otherwise stinting the flesh, keeping the mind lowly, and strengthening the spirit.

Do not, because of the want of sensible fruit, grudge the time given to your prayers; and be liberal of it. As the keeping what is called good company leaves its mark on the manners of a man, so will it powerfully influence the tone of his spiritual life to have been much with God.

I add first a few words upon what are called *relative* duties—*i.e.*, your duties to others. Do to them as you would they should do to you: and construe this precept liberally. Be strictly just to them: and not only so, but where there is a real doubt decide in their favour, not in your own. Always put upon their words and actions the best construction they will bear: you will find afterwards that it was the true one in many cases where at the time it seemed to you improbable. While avoiding all outward cringing and arts of currying favour, be most careful to cherish inwardly a habit of estimating yourself both as to intellectual and especially as to moral gifts meanly in comparison with others. No two things combine together better than meekness in asserting your rights and resolute resistance against all solicitations to do wrong, with a manifest determination to be governed in your conduct by your own judgment of right and wrong, and not by theirs. Of course this does not exclude deference to authority, age, experience, or superior means of forming a right judgment: but it is rather a rule for the common intercourse of companions. You have, I do not doubt, long known that kindness and a disposition to oblige are necessary parts of the Christian law of love. And that cheerfulness in bearing what is disagreeable, though it costs an effort at first, well and soon repays it by the goodwill which it honestly earns.

As to the duties of *self*-government, I add a few words on each of these three:

(1) Self-examination.
(2) Self-observation.
(3) Self-denial.

Give heed to self-examination; use it from time to time: perhaps if used at fixed periodical times, with intervals not too long between them, it will thus be most profitable.

It will be of especial use in detecting, and after detection tracking, your besetting sin. When this is found, keep the eye close upon it, follow it up, drag it from its hiding-places, make no terms with it, never remit the pursuit; and so by the grace of God's Holy Spirit may you cast it out.

When you have both found what was your besetting sin—that is, the sin *most easily* besetting you—and have by the same grace conquered it, then take the sin which besets you *next most easily*, and deal with it in like manner.

Besides self-examination, which is an act to be done from time to time, form a habit of self-observation. This will come to be a never-sleeping censor and corrector of your actions, always holding the rule of God's law against them and detecting them when they swerve.

The divisions of money necessary in order either to the use or even the waste of it give us, without any trouble upon our own part, some sense of the relative quantities of it. But the more precious gift of our time is passing through our hands in a continuous and never-ending flow, and its parts are not separated from one another except by our own care. Without this division of it into parts we cannot tell what is little and what is much: above all, we cannot apply it in due proportion to our several duties, pursuits, and recreations. But we should deal with our *time* as we see in a shop a grocer deal with tea and sugar, or a haberdasher with stuffs and ribbons: weighing or measuring it out in proportions adjusted to that which we are to get for and by it. This is the express command of St. Paul, who bids us ἐξαγοράζεσθαι τὸν καῖρον, imperfectly rendered by our version 'to redeem the time': for it means to make merchandise of it, and to deal strictly with it, as men deal with goods by which they mean to make a profit: to pursue the same means they pursue, energy, care, watchfulness, forethought, attention to small things, in order that we, too, may make that profit the greatest possible. (2)

NOTES / SOURCES

1. D. C. Lathbury, *Correspondence on Church and Religion of William Ewart Gladstone*, London, 1910, pp. 266–70
2. Ibid., pp. 411–16

John S. B. Monsell   1811–1875

Of Irish origin, J. S. B. Monsell was successively Chancellor of the Diocese of Connor, Vicar of Egham, and Rector of St Nicholas, Guildford. Standing in the Catholic tradition, he was a popular writer of hymns and religious verse. His sister, Harriet, was Superior of the Clewer Community.

Hymns

The following Hymns were written to illustrate an idea which has long filled their author's mind, that such portions of our Divine worship should be more fervent and joyous, more expressive of real and personal love to God than they are in general found to be.

We are, alas! too distant and reserved in our praises. We sing not, as if our hearts were on fire with the flame of Divine love and joy; as we should sing to Him, and of Him, Who is Chief among ten thousand, and altogether lovely. If we loved Him as we ought to do, we could not be so cold.

Toward the removal of this dulness and formality, few things are more helpful than glowing tender Hymns; they quicken as well as convey the desires of the soul, they say for us what many are unable to say for themselves, what a lifted eye, a voiceless breathing, has often said to God for us all; and in the use of them the spirit catches their heavenly fervour, and draws nearer to Him it is adoring.

That these Hymns are altogether of such a character their author does not venture to assume. They are however the utterances of a soul conscious of most intense longings for closer communion with God; and as such they may be helpful to others, gladdening and warming spiritual life in some hearts and homes of His people.

Their name tells what they desire to express,—Love to, and Praise of God: and if they tend in any degree to make that love in others more fervent and real, that praise more joyous and bright, they have not been written in vain. (1)

Second Sunday In Advent

God of Hope! my heart's devotion
    Wholly unto Thee belongs,
Wilt Thou not forgive its frailty?
    Wilt Thou not accept its songs?
Praise to God the glorious Giver,
    Christ the Saviour of the lost,
And the Comforter for ever,
    Father, Son, and Holy Ghost !

O my God, how Thy Salvation
    Fills my soul with peace and joy,
Patience gives, and consolation
    Which the world cannot destroy:
Praise to God the glorious Giver,
    Christ the Saviour of the lost,
And the Comforter for ever,
    Father, Son, and Holy Ghost!

For that Love whose tender mercies
    Purest joys do daily bring,
I will in my life confess Thee,
    With my mouth Thy praises sing:
Praise to God the glorious Giver,
    Christ the Saviour of the lost,
And the Comforter for ever,
    Father, Son, and Holy Ghost! (2)

Fourth Sunday after Easter.

Worship the Lord in the beauty of holiness.
1 *Chron.* xvi. 29.

O Worship the Lord in the beauty of holiness!
    Bow down before Him, His glory proclaim,
With gold of obedience, and incense of lowliness,
    Kneel and adore Him, the Lord is His Name!

Low at His feet lay thy burden of carefulness,
  High on His heart He will bear it for thee,
Comfort thy sorrows, and answer thy prayerfulness,
  Guiding thy steps as may best for thee be.

Fear not to enter His courts in the slenderness
  Of the poor wealth thou wouldst reckon as thine,
Truth in its beauty, and love in its tenderness,
  These are the offerings to lay on His shrine.

These, though we bring them in trembling and fearfulness,
  He will accept for the Name that is dear;
Mornings of joy give for evenings of tearfulness,
  Trust for our trembling, and hope for our fear.

O, worship the Lord in the beauty of holiness!
  Bow down before Him, His glory proclaim,
With gold of obedience, and incense of lowliness,
  Kneel and adore Him, the Lord is His Name! (3)

NOTES / SOURCES

1. John S. B. Monsell, *Hymns of Love and Praise for the Church's Year*, London, 1866, pp. ix–x
2. Ibid., p. 8
3. Ibid., pp. 64–5

Krishna Moham Banerjea   1813–1885

Born into an orthodox Brahmin family, Banerjea was caught up in the social and intellectual ferment known as the Bengal Renaissance, himself becoming a leading player. He was baptized by the Scottish missionary, Alexander Duff, and subsequently ordained in the Anglican Church, becoming a Canon of St Paul's Cathedral and a teacher for many years at Bishop's College, Calcutta. An ardent nationalist, he opposed the missionary domination of the Church. He was also a fine Sanskrit scholar, and proposed in his writings an anticipatory role for the Vedas comparable to that of the Hebrew Scriptures.

Hinduism and a Self-Sacrificing Saviour

The fundamental principles of Christian doctrine in relation to the salvation of the world find a remarkable counterpart in the Vedic principles of primitive Hinduism in relation to the destruction of sin, and the redemption of the sinner by the efficacy of Sacrifice, itself a figure of *Prajapati*, the Lord and Saviour of the Creation, who had given himself up as an offering for that purpose . . .

. . . The meaning of *Prajapati*, an appellative variously described as *Purusha* begotten in the beginning, as *Viswakarma* the creator of all, singularly coincides with the meaning of the name and offices of the historical reality Jesus Christ, and that no other person than Jesus of Nazareth has ever appeared in the world claiming the character and position of the self-sacrificing *Prajapati*, at the same time both mortal and immortal . . .

The Christian, with the wide sympathy which incites him to invite all nations to the faith of Christ can only rejoice that the Jesus of the Gospels responds to the self-sacrificing *Prajapati* of the Vedas, and that the evangelist's chief work will be to exhibit, before his neighbours and fellow subjects, the true Ark of salvation—that true 'vessel of sacrifice by which we may escape all sin.' He will only have to exhibit, for the faith of the Hindus, the real personality of the true *Purusha* 'begotten before the worlds,' mortal and yet divine, 'whose shadow, whose death is immortality itself.'

The tolerant Hindu, on the other hand, who has in so many departments of knowledge shown his aptitude for the ready reception of truth under any garb, and from any quarter, especially where its rudiments are cognizable in the ancient systems of his own country, who can recognize in the *Principia* the perfect development of the elementary conception of *akarshana* in the *Siddhanta Siromani*, and who can look proudly on Newton carrying out the principles of *Bhaskaracharya*, cannot find any difficulty, any national humiliation, in acknowledging the historical 'Jesus' of the New Testament to correspond to the ideal *Prajapati* of the Veda, and to strengthen the corner-stone of the Vedic system, however corrupted by the impure accretions of ages, and disfigured by the rubbish of ignorance and castecraft.

It is remarkable that while the elementary articles are so much alike, there is no rival hierarchy in India to declare for the ideal of the Vedic *Prajapati*. The doctrine of a self-sacrificing Saviour, who by death overcame Death, appears to have vanished from the Sastras without a representative succession. Although we have millions of gods in the Hindu pantheon, yet we have none who proposes to be a substitute or successor of Him who offered Himself a sacrifice for the emancipation of mortals, and left the institution of sacrifice as a 'figure' of Himself. That doctrine has long become obsolete. The position of *Prajapati*, himself the priest and himself the victim, no member of that Pantheon has dared to occupy. His throne is vacant, and his crown without an owner. No one now can claim that crown and that throne in the hearts of Hindus who are true to the original teaching of the Vedas, so rightfully as the historical Jesus, who in name and character, as we have seen, closely resembles our primitive '*Prajapati*.' I have known good Christian people stand aghast at all these ideas. I do not wonder at it. Even in apostolic times, Peter was impeached for consorting with 'men uncircumcised,' and much evidence had to be adduced before the brethren could hold their peace and glorify God, saying, 'then hath God also to the Gentiles granted repentance unto life.' So long have Hindus been classed with inveterate idolaters and Gentiles, that some may well be amazed at finding germs of Christian mysteries in the Heathen Vedas. But facts cannot be denied; we cannot shut our eyes to actual realities. Instead of indulging in mere feelings of wonder, let us give glory to God, whose mercy and grace cannot be contracted within the narrow limits of our puny ideas. Nor is there any reason here for doing otherwise than extolling God for having vouchsafed so much light, more perhaps than we could have expected *a priori*, to certain Indian *Rishis*. We must remember that the distinguished man, so much honoured in the Bible, who bore the title of 'King of Righteousness,' to whom Abraham himself gave tithes, and who was an acknowledged type of Christ, was himself a Gentile.

NOTES / SOURCES

K. M. Banerjea, Extracts from a lecture delivered in Calcutta and published as *The Relation between Christianity and Hinduism* in 1881

Richard Williams   1815–1851

Richard Williams studied medicine at University College, London, and became a popular practitioner in Burslem, Staffs. A severe illness in 1846 brought overwhelming sensations of his need of Christ, and subsequent belief. In 1850 he decided to devote his whole life and services to the cause of God. He was accepted as a lay catechist to join the fatal mission to Tierra del Fuego with five other men, under Captain Allen Gardiner (q.v.).

Extracts from the Journal of Mr Richard Williams, Surgeon & Catechist

Surely the land of Fuegia is the land of darkness, the country of gloom, a scene of wild desolation, both land and climate agreed as to character, the one frowning and desolate, the other black and tempestuous. A few, and only a few, cheering smiles has the sun beamed upon us, and the cold snows upon the rough masses of Staten Island put on an unnatural appearance, and looked more and more pale under the reviving influences of the light. If such the land and such the climate, we have reason to expect the people will likewise not fall short of congruity with either. Well, and how do I bear up under these not very flattering prospects? Have I had my expectations pointed to such an agreeable picture? What shall I say? I will own the truth, I have not been ignorant of the fact, that such was the character of the country and climate, to which I was bound.

Captain Fitzroy, and especially Mr Darwin, in his journal, had made this sufficiently clear, yet I certainly had not realised in any degree the truth, from what I had learnt from them. How different is the acquaintance we get by reading, to that we acquire by personal experience of things! In our parlours at home we shiver not at the thoughts of the cold scenes we read of, but rather enjoy by contrast our present comforts. It is singular that amidst all the working of my mind in connexion with this great undertaking, that I never contemplated it in the character of one of great suffering and great trial, I was not ignorant that such it would assuredly prove itself to be, but I troubled not myself with the thought of it. I have all along felt that it was required at my hand to make the sacrifice of everything to God; but I have had some such feeling as was suggested by Abraham to his son Isaac, when he was on his way to the altar of sacrificing, with the wood on his back, 'whereon he should be offered, that though thus palpably going to the very ordeal, yet God would provide for himself a lamb for the sacrifice.' The truth is, I could in anticipation cast all my care so entirely upon the Lord, that I took no other care but to ascertain that it was his will that I should thus serve him, assured that in the hour of my need he would strengthen my heart, and be with me to sustain me. Have I then been taken unawares? No. Have I been disappointed? No. The hour has come, though I have never painted to my mind all that I should have to encounter, yet I am not any the less unprepared for the trial, because I have not to grapple with the trial in my own strength, nor to prepare myself for the encounter; but believing when the evil day did come, the Lord would assuredly be my helper, and give grace according to my day, and I was in this respect well prepared, and beforehand with my troubles. I verified this yesterday (Sunday) morning in a remarkable manner, whilst engaged in reading the 12th Romans. God's Holy Spirit engaged my soul in fervent prayer for grace to help me, I was led out in spirit to offer up my body as a living sacrifice unto God, and with my whole heart consenting, with my entire will prostrate and subjected to the will of God, that I might prove what is his good, and acceptable, and perfect will. I surrendered myself into the hand of the Lord Jesus, with so complete a trust in him, and love to him, as was delightful indeed to feel; and how shall I praise the mercy and grace, and condescending goodness of God! I felt a sensible manifestation of God to my soul, accepting my offer. My heart was broken by a sense of God's love, that streamed in upon it, and my tears and upheaving breast alone could speak my gratitude and praise. Praise, praise to the Lord. (1)

I am not disappointed, rather do I rejoice greatly, that now it seems manifestly the design of God to take me hence. I have time after time felt an inexpressible desire to be with Christ, and to-day I have been ravished with the love of Christ; should this then be the will of God, then, my beloved ones, weep not for me, let no mourning thought possess your hearts, or sigh of sadness once escape your lips; say rejoicingly, triumphantly, How good was the Lord! how greatly was he blessed of God, and he is gone to be with Jesus! where we, we, yea, you, you, you, my beloved ones—you, my mother, you, my sisters, may all of you; will, oh yes, you will shortly meet me, will you not? Hail the glorious change! My soul rejoices in the Lord, and I would not exchange my dying hopes, surrounded as now I am, with all *earthly discomforts*, for the greatest luxuries, and all the blandishments the world could possibly devise or set before me, nay, nor stop one minute hence my onward flight to God, were the whole realm of nature, and every monarch with his crown, inviting me to linger for awhile, and taste of honour, power and earthly good. No, oh no! All, all is vanity, vanity, because it is really a shadow; vanity, because it is a mere empty pageant, there is nothing real in it, a delusion; for there is no other happiness but in knowing God, and Jesus Christ whom he has sent, in knowing him as our merciful, gracious, long-suffering God; forgiving iniquity, transgression and sin—and Jesus Christ as—no words can say what Jesus Christ is when you know him; this is the new white stone, inscribed with a name which no one knows, but he to whom it is given. O Jesus, blessed Mediator, and Intercessor, into thy hands I commit my beloved ones; do thou effectually prevail in the behalf of each, so that all may receive thy Holy Spirit, and the gift of eternal life, as thy own, and the Father's everlasting glory, world without end. Amen.

Ah, I am happy day and night, hour by hour. Asleep or awake, I am happy beyond words and the poor compass of language can tell; my joys are with him, whose delights have always been with the sons of men. And my heart and spirit are in heaven with the blessed. I have felt how holy is that company, I have felt how pure is their affection, and I have washed me in the blood of the Lamb, and asked my Lord for the white garment, that I, too, may mingle with the blaze of day, and be amongst them one of the sons of light. (2)

NOTES / SOURCES

1. Richard Williams, in George Pakenham Despard, (ed.) *Hope deferred, not lost: A narrative of missionary effort in South America*, London, 1854, pp. 309–11
2. Ibid., pp. 419–21

Richard William Church   1815–1890

Sometimes described as 'the Anglican Newman', Richard Church was born in Lisbon and brought up in Florence, going up to Wadham College, Oxford, in 1833, the year of John Keble's (q.v.) Assize Sermon marking the beginning of the Oxford Movement, of which he wrote the classic history. Elected a Fellow of Oriel in 1838 he remained there until he became Rector of Whatley in Somerset in 1852. From there he was appointed as Dean of St Paul's, where he exercised a notable ministry as a preacher and teacher.

The Gift of the Holy Spirit

We celebrate to-day the greatest gift ever made to man. I am not speaking of things done for him, and without him. I am not speaking of the gift of the Father's Eternal Son to be man's Redeemer, Brother, Atonement, Pattern. But the gift of to-day was the greatest change that was ever made in what man is in himself, in his powers and spiritual endowments, in what he can himself become. There have been other great revolutions in his history; crises and epochs which made things henceforth new, in the various stages of that order by which God has been bringing back the world unto Himself. There was the Law, the long discipline of Prophecy, the Cross, the Resurrection, the Ascension. There was the opening message of the Gospel to the Gentiles, the breaking down the middle wall which had separated mankind, the transformation of the Synagogue into the Church Universal. Of course all these profuse outpourings of God's bounty have altered indefinitely our condition, our hopes, our motives. And there were, besides them, other gifts belonging to what we call the sphere of nature, put into the hands of man, which make him what he is: the homely and familiar arts which so touched the imagination of the ancient poets, and raised their wonder more than they do ours; the discoveries, the capacities, the knowledge of later times, at which even we who possess them, stand amazed.

But here is a gift of a different order. It brings with it, indeed, light; it brings with it truth. But the essential and characteristic part of it is, that it brings with it changes within us,—changes unthought of,—in the moral and spiritual nature and capacities of man. It is a gift, altering and raising the powers by which he chooses, and wills, and acts,—the affections, the heart, the character, which make him a moral being, with power to do right, to feel right, to wish and desire right. It is the gift which opens to him, in a degree unknown before, the life of holiness, the life which makes him really like God, really able to know God, to love Him, to live with Him. It is the gift which, in the language of Holy Scripture, has renewed, has created afresh, our nature as men. Christmas is the commemoration of the birthday, the new birth in time, of the Only-begotten, the second Adam, the Head of redeemed Humanity. Pentecost is the commemoration of the birthday of the new birth of Humanity itself; of the day when a new divine power came into the very inmost souls and beings of men, changing them from their old selves, filling them with new energies fresh from the very heart of God, begetting them anew from the deadness of sin, giving them, by a new birth through the Spirit, the power to become the sons of God. (1)

The Imperfections of Religious Believers

For there are temptations and mischiefs arising out of our religion itself; out of the position in which it places us, and the things which it encourages in us. Let me take two or three examples.

1. 'Who loved me,' says St Paul, 'the Son of God, who loved me, and gave Himself for me.' There are hardly more affecting words in the New Testament, and they describe what must thrill through any man's mind, who believes in the Cross of Christ, just in proportion as he grasps its meaning. A religious man feels that he, his soul, his salvation, is the centre of a great interposition of God's mercy and love. It is as if all were for him: as if there were no one else in the universe whom God so loved, for whom God had done such wonderful things, as if he were the one lost sheep whom Christ had sought and saved and died for. But it is not without reason that we are told that what should kindle his boundless devotion may be full of peril. It may touch the subtle springs of selfishness. There may be a feverish, faithless selfishness, in the anxiety to save one's soul, to be sure that all is right within, to be sure that all is safe. Or, a man may be tempted, while he realises what he has been, and is, to God, into a sense of self-importance, into a hard self-complacency. He may be, as men have been, tempted to think of himself as the favourite of heaven, allowed liberties forbidden to other men, forgiven, when others are not excused. Or again, he may be thrown inward on himself, to watch and study with unhealthy eagerness the vicissitudes of what is to him the most interesting of histories, the history of his religious experience. Watching all this, comparing himself with others, finding checks and differences, he becomes querulous, captious, censorious. It is not every one who can dare to repeat the experiment of St Augustine's confessions. Religious autobiography is not without warnings that the true and awful words—'What shall a man give in exchange for his soul?'—may be perverted into a narrow and timid care for it, worried with petty fears and scruples; a care ignoble and degrading, because without interest in God's great purposes, without a generous trust in His wisdom and mercy, without sympathy for others.

2. Again, religion must be active; and towards the evils which are in the world it is bound to be hostile and aggressive. And yet this necessity shows us too often a religion, a very sincere and honest religion, which cannot avoid the dangers which come with activity and with conflict. It sometimes seems to lose itself and its end in the energy with which it pursues its end. The zeal for a great cause, the fear of being idle and inactive, may pass insensibly but too easily into a passionate longing for immediate results and visible success: a man becomes entangled in a whirl of business arrangements, in questions of machinery and agitation, in

secular details with religious names, in keen excitement, or a love of management and contrivance, which subtly eat into the best part of a man's nature; and with the great duty of resisting evil may come other evils too natural to men, veiled, sanctioned, guaranteed as the friends and allies of religion—that host of evil things which sin against charity and truth. We cannot shut our eyes to what the history of religion shows but too clearly—that with religion may come very uncongenial elements—the habit of hasty and harsh and ungenerous judgment; the freedom given to antipathies and detraction; the heavy fault of unfairness, of having a different moral measure for our friends and our opponents. I say nothing of party spirit, dangerous as it is, because there is a great deal of thoughtless and unreal talking about it. People talk about it glibly, who are blindly led by it. When men are together under strong convictions, opponents will always call them partisans. What is wanted is, not that men should not be partisans, but that they should be just and considerate and generous partisans. I am afraid that real religion on all sides has been compatible with insolence, with violence, with flattery—with the pride of being on the right side, of being able to look down on our neighbours—with love of importance, with the temper of contempt and scorn; nay, at last, the inconsistency has ended in a gradual lowering of our religious ideal, with increasing narrowness and meanness of thought, with increasing readiness to seek our own advantage, as our due and reward for our religious zeal and service. We have seen this sometimes in others. Can we doubt that we are in danger from this ourselves?

3. Again, religion is a matter of the affections: and men may be led astray by their affections, in religion as in other things. We read the proof of it at large in the vast and double-sided history of mysticism in various ages of the Church. It shows us in endless forms the deep passion of the human soul to fulfil the 'First and Great Commandment' of the Son of God: it shows us with what beauty and glory these supreme heights of devotion, of adoration, of divine love, have been reached: it shows us also what fearful dangers encompassed the attempt—how easily the true point was passed, and then how, like an exquisite but transient flower, or a generous but too delicate wine, the perfection, which was but for a moment, vanished, and corruption set in, irresistible and hopeless. We see it in those deplorable disputes on the love of God, its measures, its motives, its reward, in which even such men as Bossuet and Fénélon hardly found their way. These are almost the most incomprehensible chapters in Christian history—strange above measure that, in desiring to know and to realise the love of God, devout souls should have gone astray: but we know it has been so, and that in times far separated and outwardly most different from one another. These are not, I suppose, our special dangers: mysticism, in its best and in its worst form, is not in much honour now, except perhaps in poetry. But our religion is not therefore safe on its emotional side. Our dangers lie another way—not in detachment from the world and effort to rise above it and above self, but in what is sentimental and fanciful and effeminate; in artificial frames of mind, combined with loose or technical views of duty; in a self-pleasing and self-indulgent devotion; in unreal words, and affectations, perhaps unconscious, and exaggerations of feeling—talking lightly because it is the fashion, in advance of what we really feel, beyond what we really think. These are formidable dangers; and they are dangers to those who yet are very serious about religion, and think that they are acting on its call. (2)

NOTES / SOURCES

R. W. Church, *Cathedral and University Sermons*, London, 1893, pp. 169–71
Ibid., pp. 284–88

Cecil Frances Alexander   1818–1895

Cecil Frances Humphreys married William Alexander, Bishop of Derry and later Archbishop of Armagh, and as Mrs Alexander became well known as the composer of hymns and poems, a number for children. Her best known hymns are 'All things bright and beautiful', 'There is a green hill far away' (written for a Sunday School class in Derry in 1848), and 'Once in Royal David's city'. She was a pioneer of the teaching of deaf and dumb children.

There is a green hill

There is a green hill far away,
　　Without a city wall,
Where the dear LORD was crucified
　　Who died to save us all.

We may not know, we cannot tell
　　What pains he had to bear,
But we believe it was for us
　　He hung and suffered there.

He died that we might be forgiven,
　　He died to make us good,
That we might go at last to heaven,
　　Saved by His precious Blood.

There was no other good enough
　　To pay the price of sin,
He only could unlock the gate
　　Of heaven, and let us in.

O, dearly, dearly has He loved,
　　And we must love Him too,
And trust in His redeeming Blood,
　　And try His works to do.

NOTES / SOURCES

Cecil Frances Alexander, in *Hymns Ancient & Modern* Second Edition, London, 1875, No. 332

John Mason Neale   1818–1866

With particular gifts as a hymn writer, Neale was responsible for English translations of many notable hymns from both the Greek and Latin traditions, as well as writing many original compositions. From 1846 until his death he was Warden of Sackville College, East Grinstead, an ancient charitable foundation, and it was at East Grinstead that he founded the religious sisterhood of the Society of St Margaret in 1855. He had a particular interest in the Eastern Church and his writings and translations of Eastern hymns helped to make Orthodox history, theology, and devotion known to Anglicans.

Adoro Te Devote [St Thomas Aquinas]

Humbly I adore Thee, hidden Deity,
Which beneath these figures art concealed from me;
Wholly in submission Thee my spirit hails,
For in contemplating Thee it wholly fails.

Taste and touch and vision in Thee are deceived:
But the hearing only may be well believed:
I believe whatever GOD's own SON averred;
Nothing can be truer than Truth's very Word.

On the Cross lay hidden but Thy Deity:
Here is also hidden Thy Humanity:
But in both believing and confessing, LORD,
Ask I what the dying thief of Thee implored.

Though Thy Wounds, like Thomas, I behold not now,
Thee my LORD confessing, and my GOD, I bow:
Give me ever stronger faith in Thee above,
Give me ever stronger hope and stronger love.

O most sweet memorial of His death and woe,
Living Bread, Which givest life to man below,
Let my spirit ever eat of Thee and live,
And the blest fruition of Thy sweetness give!

Pelican of Mercy, JESU, LORD and GOD,
Cleanse me, wretched sinner, in Thy Precious Blood:
Blood, whereof one drop for humankind outpoured
Might from all transgression have the world restored.

Jesu, Whom thus veiled, I must see below,
When shall that be given which I long for so,
That at last beholding Thy uncover'd Face,
Thou wouldst satisfy me with Thy fullest grace? (1)

The Name of Jesus

To the Name that brings Salvation
  Honour, worship, laud we pay:
That for many a generation
  Hid in GOD's foreknowledge lay;
But to every tongue and nation
  Holy Church proclaims to-day.

Name of gladness, Name of pleasure,
  By the tongue ineffable,
Name of sweetness passing measure,
  To the ear delectable,
'Tis our safeguard and our treasure,
  'Tis our help 'gainst sin and hell.

'Tis the Name for adoration,
  'Tis the Name of victory;
'Tis the Name for meditation
  In the vale of misery:
'Tis the Name for veneration
  By the Citizens on high.

'Tis the Name that whoso preaches
  Finds it music in his ear:
'Tis the Name that whoso teaches
  Finds more sweet than honey's cheer:
Who its perfect wisdom reaches
  Makes his ghostly vision clear.

'Tis the Name by right exalted
  Over every other Name:
That when we are sore assaulted
  Puts our enemies to shame:
Strength to them that else had halted,
  Eyes to blind, and feet to lame.

Jesu, we Thy Name adoring
  Long to see Thee as Thou art:
Of Thy clemency imploring
  So to write it in our heart,
That, hereafter, upward soaring,
  We with Angels may have part.   Amen. (2)

Transfiguration

Amongst His Twelve Apostles
    Christ spake the Words of Life,
And shew'd a realm of beauty
    Beyond a world of strife:
'When all My FATHER's glory
    Shall shine express'd in Me,
Then praise Him, then exalt Him,
    For magnified is He!'

Upon the Mount of Tabor
    The promise was made good;
When, baring all the Godhead,
    In light itself He stood:
And they, in awe beholding,
    The Apostolic Three,
Sang out to GOD their Saviour,
    For magnified was He!

All hours and days inclin'd there,
    And did Thee worship meet;
The sun himself adored Thee,
    And bow'd him at Thy feet:
While Moses and Elias,
    Upon the Holy Mount,
The co-eternal glory
    Of Christ our God recount.

O holy, wondrous Vision!
    But what, when this life past,
The beauty of Mount Tabor
    Shall end in Heav'n at last?
But what, when all the glory
    Of uncreated light
Shall be the promis'd guerdon
    Of them that win the fight? (3)

The Ascension and Pentecost

Ode IX

ὦ τῶν δωρεῶν

Holy gift, surpassing comprehension!
    Wond'rous mystery of each fiery tongue!
    CHRIST made good His Promise in Ascension:
    O'er the Twelve the cloven flames have hung!

Spake the LORD, or ere He left the Eleven:
  'Here in Salem wait the Gift I send:
  Till the PARACLETE come down from Heaven:
  Everlasting Guide and Guard and Friend.'

O that shame, now ended in that glory!
  Pain untold, now lost in joy unknown!
  Tell it out with praise, the whole glad story,
  Human nature at the FATHER's Throne!

Catavasia.

Declare, ye Angel Bands that dwell on high,
  How saw ye Him, the Victor, drawing nigh?
  What strange new visions burst upon your sight?
  One in the Form of Man, That claims by right
The very Throne of GOD, the unapproached Light!

Exaposteilarion.

Eternal! After Thine own will
    Thou born in time would'st be:
After the self-same counsel still
    Was Thine Epiphany:

Thou in our flesh didst yield Thy breath,
    Immortal GOD, for man:
Thou by Thy death didst conquer Death,
    Through Thine Almighty plan:
Thou, rising Victor to the sky,
    Fill'st Heav'n and earth above:
And send'st the Promise from on high,
    The SPIRIT of Thy love! (4)

NOTES / SOURCES

1. John Mason Neale, *Collected Hymns, Sequences and Carols*, London, 1914, p. 63
2. Ibid., p. 73
3. Ibid., pp. 248–9
4. Ibid., pp. 268–9

Charles Fuge Lowder   1820–1880

Charles Lowder was a notable Anglo-Catholic slum priest who had a significant ministry in East London, particularly at St Peter's, London Docks. In 1855 he founded, with others, the Society of the Holy Cross (SSC), stressing the importance for mission work of groups of celibate clergy living under a simple rule.

The Pattern of Life in an East End Clergy House

The first bell for rising was rung at 6.30; we said Prime in the oratory at 7; Matins was said at St Peter's and St Saviour's at 7.30; the celebration of the Holy Eucharist followed. After breakfast, followed by Terce, the clergy and teachers went to their respective work—some in school, some in the study or district. Sext was said at 12.45, immediately before dinner, when the household were again assembled; and on Fridays and fast days some book, such as the 'Lives of the Saints' or Ecclesiastical History, was read at table. After dinner, rest, letters, visiting, or school work, as the case might be, and then tea at 5.30 p.m. After tea, choir practice, classes, reading, or visiting again until Evensong at 8 p.m. After service the clergy were often engaged in classes, hearing confessions, or attending to special cases. Supper at 9.15, followed by Compline, when those who had, finished their work retired to their rooms. It was desired that all should be in bed at 11 p.m., when the gas was put out; but, of course, in the case of the clergy, much of whose work was late in the evening with those who could not come to them at any other time, it was impossible absolutely to observe this rule. In an active community the rules of the house must yield to the necessities of spiritual duties. (1)

The Priest as Teacher Through the Eucharist

Mr Lowder was a thorough Church of England man. He was not a Ritualist at all in the modern sense of the word, after the gushing, effeminate, sentimental manner of young shop-boys, or those who simply ape the ways of Rome. He had glorious ritual in his church because he thought the service of God could not be too magnifical. He considered that it was as much his duty as parish priest to put before the eyes of his people the pattern or the worship in Heaven, as it was his duty to preach the Gospel. He felt that he had no more right to alter the features of the heavenly worship, as represented in the earthly service, than he had to alter the faith once delivered to the saints. He understood that those features are made known to us by our Lord's command, 'Do this,' by the revelation of heavenly worship to St John, and by the testimony of the unbroken custom of the Christian Church. In a word, he believed that the Holy Eucharist is the divinely appointed act of worship which we are commanded to *do* on earth as it is done by our High Priest in heaven, pleading before God the merits of the all-sufficient sacrifice of Christ. (2)

NOTES / SOURCES

1. M. Trench, *Charles Lowder: A Biography*, London, 1882, pp. 157–8
2. Ibid., p. 284

Richard Meux Benson   1824–1915

Richard Meux Benson founded the Society of St John the Evangelist, the first religious order for men in the Church of England, in 1865. Deeply influenced by the Oxford Movement, his many writings—sermons, retreat addresses, and letters—reveal a penetrating and powerful biblically-based spirituality.

Enlarging the Heart

The Divine love enlarges the heart in proportion to the correspondence of the saint with the Sanctifier. The more we exercise God's love, the more does He strengthen us with the capacity of doing every thing in love to Himself. We grow to that which God Himself is until we lose ourselves in God. The Heart of Jesus is the Mediatorial principle in fellowship wherewith this love must be exercised. Our heart must grow to the largeness of His Love by the inspiration of His Holy Spirit. So we must attain to 'the fulness of the measure of the stature of Christ.'

Our feet tread the dust, but our heart must expand with all the love of heaven, to love all that God loves, to love God in all, to love with the love which God Himself gives, and whereby He makes us one with Himself, to love Jesus the Personal Head of the Church. Jesus Himself is the Heart whereby the Body of His Redeemed ones live in love for evermore.

The eternal Act of God in His Triune Essence is the source of that love: the triumphant endurance of the all-redeeming Passion is the measure of its created manifestation, that we may live therein as the sons of God and the members of Christ crucified on earth and enthroned at God's Right Hand for ever. (1)

Life in God

Faith delights in God's commandments and welcomes the gift of living right-eousness. It is made perfect in love rising up to the eternal relationships of the Divine love. The gift of a spiritual understanding enables us to exercise this life that we may be enabled 'to know the glory of His inheritance in the saints' (*Eph.* i. 18). For this understanding we must continually pray that it may be developed within us more and more. It is the vision of love. 'This is life eternal.' This is the knowledge which none but the loving soul can win. (2)

Daily Bread

O Lord, our Father, which art in heaven,
grant unto us thy grace,
as the children of thy kingdom,
that we labour not only for the meat which perisheth,
but for that meat which endureth unto everlasting life.
Give us the true bread from heaven,
even the flesh of thy dear Son,
for he is our spiritual food and sustenance,
without which we can have no life in us.

By participation in this bread
thy faithful people are all made one bread, one body,
in union with each other,
and with Christ the Head,
through the operation of the Holy Ghost,
consecrating the sacrament thereof,
and quickening those who partake of the sacrament.

Multiply throughout the whole world
the opportunities of grace,
making high the heap of corn in the earth,
lowly in outward form,
as being upon earth the food of the lowly,
but high above the hills of the earth,
as being given from heaven—
the food which shall raise us up at the last day—.

Quicken our desire for this food;
vainly is it given unless thou first give to love and desire it.
Give us a loving faith
frequently to approach thine altar,
profitably to partake of the divine mysteries
thereon presented to us,
habitually to cherish the gift of union with thy Son
as the strength of our daily life.

Grant unto us, as a consequence of this sacramental union,
that we may daily live by his energy;
and that, being sustained
by the word which proceedeth from thy mouth,
it may be our daily meat to do thy will.
Strengthen our spiritual life
by all those works to which thou callest us.
Help us to find in the accidents of the world
occasions of communion with thee.
As all things carry out thy will towards us,
let all things bind us to thyself;
and being thus bound in the bundle of life
with thee, our God,
let that contact nourish us
by the emanation of thy goodness.

Give us eyes to see thy wisdom
in the dispensation of all thy creatures;
and a heart to embrace thy goodness
acting towards·us in them all—
in all labour, to seek thee as our only rest—;
in all rest, to labour after thy divine contemplation;
by the hope of thee, to be stimulated;
by the faith of thee, to be invigorated;
by the love of thee, to be fed;
daily to know thy presence,
and in that knowledge to find daily nourishment
unto everlasting life. (3)

The Resurrection

The Glorified Humanity

No eye of man witnessed the Resurrection, for it was an act which human understanding could not fathom. As the act of Creation baffles the cognisance of human senses, so does the Resurrection of Jesus. It is not like the resurrection of Lazarus, coming back bound in grave-clothes to the life of earth, as if waking up from sleep. It is the beginning of a new Creation, the exaltation of man's nature to a region of spiritual power that is altogether new.

The Resurrection of Christ could not be seen by man, for it was a resurrection into a world where no human senses could follow it. There are many powers in nature to which we can have no immediate outer testimony. We know their existence by their results. So is it with the Resurrection of Jesus Christ. We experience its power because He went into a world beyond our natural gaze. He has entered upon the exercise of powers whose influence we acknowledge, and from whose control none can escape.

We are not to think merely that He lived before in the region of the natural world, and is now passed over into the spiritual world. He might have done so, using His material organism as the instrument of action while He was here, and casting it away so as to act by purely spiritual power in His new estate. He has done much more than this. He has elevated His material nature to be for evermore the instrument of spiritual action, acting not according to the limitations proper to itself, but according to the powers of the spiritual world with whose operations it is henceforth to be identified. 'It is raised,' says St. Paul, 'a spiritual body' (1 Cor. xv. 44). That which lay in the sepulchre is transformed and glorified. It is not that it shines with the light of the Divine presence within it. So it shone once at the Transfiguration. Now it has passed into the world of spirit-life, and it manifests itself in this lower world, not by subjecting itself to our natural senses, but by communicating to those to whom its manifestation is made the supernatural power of the Spirit by which alone it can be perceived, as by that power alone it can draw near.

The whole human being of our Lord Jesus was glorified by the Resurrection. There was no part of it left in the grave. All was transformed. The unction of the Divine presence filled the whole manhood, body and soul, with the renewed spiritual life which Adam's sin had forfeited, and the union with Godhead was a better, closer union than Adam could claim. Adam lost the companionship of the Holy Ghost which filled his soul with spiritual life. Jesus being consubstantially united with the Godhead can have no part of His Being withdrawn from that Divine life. Whatever belongs to Him as a Person is, and must be, under the quickening influence of His Divinity. The law of His human life could suffer no violation. His human organism could not be maimed. All that He had assumed into vital connection with Himself He glorified, for that vitality was imperishable.

His material nature was thus completely taken up into the condition of spiritual life, and exempted from those conditions which fetter the created world.

That which makes a substance to be what it is, is force or power. Created substances are formed as parts of a whole, so as to be dependent one upon the other, with mutual attraction and antagonism. The Body of Christ was taken up by the resurrection so as to act with the sovereign power of the inherent Godhead, unimpeded by any lower forces belonging to the created world.

Space is the contemporaneous manifestation of many created forces as combined and opposed. The Body of Jesus is taken into a condition of superiority to all. Nothing can oppose it. It is therefore capable of appearing in any point of space at any moment. It disturbs not those forces in the midst of which it makes itself manifest, for disturbance implies antagonism, and antagonism implies the kindred character of those substances which replace one another. The Body of Jesus consequently appears as He wills. Space has for Him no limitative power. He leaves the tomb, as afterwards He enters the Apostolic chamber, without any aperture through which to pass. He rises from the grave and shows Himself in various places, but it is without motion. Natural substances existing under the laws of space move in space by a change of relationship to the forces round about them. The Body of Jesus abides in its own glorious sovereignty, supreme over created forces. He has but to will, and instantly His Body is present to act upon the created forces round about Him in any place, without being Himself limited or opposed by any power, however solid it may seem. He Himself says, 'All power is given unto Me both in Heaven and upon earth.'

This condition of supreme power is altogether beyond our perception. We may argue up towards it, but we cannot apprehend it. We may experience its results, but we cannot know it in itself. All our knowledge is the result of experience, and until we are taken into the higher condition of life wherein Jesus is glorified we cannot know it. We never indeed can attain to know it as peers. It never can be to us an external object of observation. We can only know it as being made His members and living ourselves in Him. In proportion as the force of His Resurrection-Body moves us, we shall know the reality of the power of His resurrection. To see the Body of Christ as an external object would necessitate its becoming a co-ordinate object with the eye or the mind of the observer. If He condescends to make His presence manifest in any way to our senses, it is by the exercise of a power of adaptation within Himself. In Himself He remains superior to all created knowledge. As no man knoweth the things of a man save the spirit of a man which is in Him, even so the things of the risen Christ 'knoweth no' created being 'but the Spirit of Christ alone,' and He to whom this Spirit communicates the fellowship of the same life. (4)

NOTES / SOURCES

1. R. M. Benson SSJE, *The Way of Holiness: An exposition of Psalm CXIX Analytical and Devotional*, London, 1901, p. 74
2. Ibid., p. 232
3. *Colloquies and Prayers for Holy Communion from the writings of Richard Meux Benson*, compiled G. T. Pulley SSJE, London, 1934 pp. 11–13
4. R. M. Benson SSJE, *The Life Beyond the Grave: A Series of Meditations upon the Resurrection and Ascension of Our Lord Jesus Christ*, London, 1885 pp. 22–6

William Bright

1824–1901

A church historian, who was Regius Professor of Ecclesiastical History and a Canon of Christ Church, Oxford, from 1868 until his death, William Bright was a noted (and devoted) patristic scholar. He was a strong High Churchman who was the author of a number of hymns as well as the compiler of a notable anthology of prayers, *Ancient Collects*, together with major historical works on the early church.

And now, O Father, Mindful of the Love

And now, O FATHER, mindful of the love
    That bought us, once for all, on Calvary's Tree,
And having with us Him that pleads above,
    We here present, we here spread forth to Thee
That only Offering perfect in Thine eyes,
The one true, pure, immortal Sacrifice.

Look, FATHER, look on His Anointed Face,
    And only look on us as found in Him;
Look not on our misusings of Thy grace,
    Our prayer so languid, and our faith so dim;
For lo, between our sins and their reward
We set the Passion of Thy SON our LORD.

And then for those, our dearest and our best,
    By this prevailing Presence we appeal;
O fold them closer to Thy mercy's breast,
    O do Thine utmost for their souls' true weal;
From tainting mischief keep them white and clear
And crown Thy gifts with grace to persevere.

And so we come; O draw us to Thy feet
    Most patient Saviour, Who canst love us still;
And by this Food, so awful and so sweet,
    Deliver us from every touch of ill:
In Thine own service make us glad and free,
And grant us never more to part from Thee. (1)

Ancient Collects and Other Prayers

For the Spirit of Prayer

O Almighty God, from Whom every good prayer cometh, and Who pourest out on all who desire it the Spirit of grace and supplications; deliver us, when we draw nigh to Thee; from coldness of heart and wanderings of mind; that with stedfast thoughts and kindled affections we may worship Thee in spirit and in truth; through Jesus Christ our Lord.

Sunday Evening

O Lord, Who by triumphing over the powers of darkness, didst prepare our place in the New Jerusalem; grant us, who have this day given thanks for Thy Resurrection, to praise Thee in that City whereof Thou art the Light; where with the Father, etc.

For Guidance

O God, by Whom the meek are guided in judgement, and light riseth up in darkness for the godly; grant us, in all our doubts and uncertainties, the grace to ask what Thou wouldest have us to do; that the Spirit of wisdom may save us from all false choices, and that in Thy light we may see light, and in Thy straight path may not stumble; through Jesus Christ our Lord.

On the Example of the Blessed Virgin

O Christ our God Incarnate, Whose Virgin Mother was blessed in bearing Thee, but still more blessed in keeping Thy word; grant us, who honour the exaltation of her lowliness, to follow the example of her devotion to Thy will, Who livest, etc.

For a Friend

I pray Thee, good Lord Jesus, by the love which Thou hadst for him that lay on Thy bosom, to make me thankful for all that Thou hast given me in Thy servant N. and to bless *him* exceedingly abundantly, above all that I can ask or think. Help us to love each other in Thee and for Thee, to be one in heart through all separations, and to walk as friends in the path of Thy service; and finally unite us for ever at Thy feet, where peace and love are perfect and immortal, and Thou, with the Father, etc. (2)

NOTES / SOURCES

1. William Bright, in *Hymns Ancient & Modern* Second Edition, London, 1875, No. 322
2. William Bright, *Ancient Collects and Other Prayers*, James Parker & Co, Oxford, 1902, pp. 233–7

Nathaniel Dimock   1825–1900

A notable Evangelical theologian, Nathaniel Dimock graduated from St John's College, Oxford, in 1847. From 1848 to 1887 he held various livings in Kent and wrote significant works on sacramental theology. In 1900 he was a participant in the conference organized by Bishop Mandell Creighton on 'The discipline of the Holy Communion and its legitimate expression in ritual.'

The Meaning of the Holy Communion

It is the Flesh of Christ as given for the life of the world, as indwelt by the Divine Power, which after death would raise Him from the dead; it is the Blood of Christ as in sacrificial death poured out; it is the Blood of Atonement as such, the Blood of Redemption for souls, the Blood of the Son of God shed for the remission of sins—this it is which the faith of the sinner is to look to, and which the faith of the believer has to feed on . . .

. . . There is something unspeakably grand—yes, grand and glorious and very blessed—in the conception of the man Christ Jesus—the man who bore our griefs and carried our sorrows, now exalted to God's right hand with all power in heaven and in earth, angels and authorities and powers subject to Him, and exalted for our sake, after purging our sins; and yet with all the compassion of His humanity and all the power of His Godhead still present in His Church with the real presence of His Divinity—that Divinity still (in some very true and real and blessed sense) the Divinity of the man Christ Jesus, and inseparable from His perfect humanity, and inseparable even from His Human Body in heaven; still watching over His people—still Himself sustaining, strengthening, feeding them—as the Good Shepherd leading them beside the waters of comfort, pouring the oil and wine of His grace into their wounded hearts, and still Himself saying to each contrite soul, 'Thy sins be forgiven thee, go in peace,' that they may return to follow Him—Himself the present Shepherd and Bishop of their souls, as truly the Saviour, the Friend, the Brother of each, as if He were not also the Saviour, the Friend, the Brother of all.

NOTES / SOURCES

N. Dimock, *On Encharistic Worship in the English Church*, London, 1911, pp. 80, 111–12

Nilakantha Nehemiah Goreh SSJE   1825–1885

From an orthodox Brahmin family, Nilakantha Goreh was educated in Varanasi where he engaged in public controversy with the CMS missionary, William Smith. He was eventually baptized there in the face of fierce Hindu hostility but sustained by the Sanskrit poetry of W. H. Mill (q.v.). Ordained, he had pastoral appointments and taught at Bishop's College, Calcutta. He was increasingly attracted by the ascetic and theological ideals of the Tractarians, and in later life was a member of the Society of St John the Evangelist.

The Eucharist a Partaking in the Divine Nature

In the eucharist, we behold the Lamb of God sacrificed for us once for all on Calvary, who comes, we know not how, with His fresh wounds and with His precious Blood overflowing to drown and annihilate our sins therein, in His amazing love, to meet us, to be received by us, to dwell in us, yea, to unite us with Himself, and through Himself with the Father. He, as the Mediator between God and men, being one in nature with His Father in His Godhead having taken our flesh, and giving that very flesh to us in the Holy Eucharist, and thus uniting us with Himself even in nature through that flesh, though not personally, (we still remain distinct in person from Him) but mystically (therefore the Church is wont to call herself His mystical Body) yet really and truly, and thus through Himself unites us to the Father, yea, makes us 'partakers' as the Scripture says, 'of the Divine Nature'. O Glorious Gift! O Amazing Love! May we, the sons of India, say that the unity with God, Whom our fathers delighted to call 'Sat Chit Ananda Brahman,' after which they ardently aspired, but in a wrong sense, for in that sense a creature can never be united with the Creator, yet after which they ardently aspired, God has granted us their children to realize in the right sense? Was that aspiration and longing, though misunderstood by them, a presentiment of the future Gift? I indeed have often delighted to think so. (1)

Hinduism a preparation for Christianity

But a genuine Hindu is rather prepared to receive the teaching of Christianity . . . Providence has certainly prepared us, the Hindus, to receive Christianity, in a way in which, it seems to me, no other nation—excepting the Jews, of course— has been prepared. Most erroneous as is the teaching of such books as the *Bhagavadgita*, the *Bhagvata*, etc., yet they have taught us something of *ananyabhakti* (undivided devotedness to God), of *vairagya* (giving up the world), of *namrata* (humility), of *ksama* (forbearance), etc., which enables us to appreciate the precepts of Christianity. (2)

NOTES / SOURCES

1. Nilakantha Nehemiah Goreh SSJE, 'On Objections against the Catholic Doctrine of Eternal Punishment', 1868, in *An Introduction to Indian Christian Theology*, R. H. S. Boyd, Madras, 1969, pp. 53–4
2. N. N. Goreh SSJE, 'Proofs of the Divinity of Our Lord, stated in a letter to a Friend', 1887 [the friend was Pandita Ramabai] in Ibid., p. 55

Brook Foss Westcott   1825–1901

Educated at King Edward VI School, Birmingham, where he formed a close friendship with J. B. Lightfoot (q.v.), Westcott went to Trinity College, Cambridge, and was ordained in 1851. After a time teaching at Harrow he returned to Cambridge as Regius Professor of Divinity where he prepared with F. J. A. Hort (q.v.) a critical edition of the Greek New Testament. Westcott House, Cambridge, and the Cambridge Mission to Delhi owe their existence to his inspiration and direction. Consecrated as Bishop of Durham in 1890 he made social problems his special concern. He taught a strongly incarnational theology of *Christus Consummator*.

The Gospel of Creation

The true Protevangelium is to be found in the revelation of Creation, or in other words that the Incarnation was independent of the Fall. All our present ideas of human life necessarily involve thoughts of pain and suffering and weakness. Such thoughts however are wholly excluded from the conception of that manhood which we regard as predestined in the eternal and absolute counsel of God for union with the Word, or (to look at it from the other side) as answering to Him of whom it was, in some sense which we cannot strictly define, the image, related as a copy to the archetype. In order to gain, however imperfectly and transiently, this conception, we endeavour to present to ourselves humanity made in God's image and advancing in harmonious cooperation with His Grace towards His likeness. We look upon men and man, upon the race as well as upon the individual, as fa as we can, growing perfect as God is perfect, holy as God is holy. We follow this progress to its consummation; and then having so gained a conception of manhood, answering to what is made known of the divine idea of man, we go on to say that it is most consonant to what God has revealed to believe that it was His pleasure that humanity, so consummated in its proper development in many parts, should find its true personality by union with His Son. According to this view man's self-will by which he fell was not the occasion of the supreme manifestation of the love of God in 'the taking of manhood unto God.' That was the end of Creation from the beginning. The Fall, and here lies the greatest mystery of divine love, did not frustrate this end which it might seem to have made unattainable consistently with that truth and justice which define omnipotence.

There is no question on any side that everything of suffering and shame connected with the Incarnation was due to the Fall: there is no question that in our imagination the voluntary endurance of these by the Son of God makes His love appear greater. But indeed nothing finite can appreciably alter the love manifested in the Incarnation which is essentially infinite; and it can be fairly maintained that we are led by Scripture to regard the circumstances of the Incarnation as separable from the idea of the Incarnation, and to hold that the circumstances of the Incarnation were due to sin, while the idea of the Incarnation was due to the primal and absolute purpose of love foreshadowed in Creation, apart from sin which was contingent . . .

. . . The thought that the Incarnation, the union of man with God, and of creation in man, was part of the Divine purpose in Creation, opens unto us, as I believe, wider views of the wisdom of God than we commonly embrace, which must react upon life.

It presents to us the highest manifestation of Divine love as answering to the idea of man, and not as dependent upon that which lay outside the Father's Will.

It reveals to us how the Divine purpose is fulfilled in unexpected and unimaginable ways in spite of man's selfishness and sin.

It indicates, at least, how that unity to which many physical and historical researches point is not only to be found in a dispersive connexion of multi-tudinous parts, but is summed up finally in one life.

It helps us to feel a little more, and this is the sum of all, what the Incarnation is, what it involves, what it promises, what it enforces, what it inspires; that Fact which we strive to believe, and which is ever escaping from us; that Fact which sets before us with invincible majesty Christ's 'power to subdue all things to Himself.[1]

---

[1] Phil. iii. 21.

NOTES / SOURCES

Brooke Foss Westcott, *The Epistles of St John: The Greek Text with Notes and Essays*, London, 1883, pp. 274–5, 315

Frederick Meyrick   1827–1906

An ardent Evangelical educated at Trinity College, Oxford, Frederick Meyrick founded the Anglo-Continental Society in 1853. He helped organize the Bonn Conferences on reunion in 1874–5, publishing several anti-Roman pamphlets. His *Memories of Life at Oxford*, which also gives accounts of his European travels, provides interesting sidelights on church life and notable church figures of the nineteenth century.

The Meaning of the Holy Communion

The Holy Communion is a Remembrance, a Sacrifice, a means of Feeding, a means of Incorporation, a Pledge.

It is a Remembrance in so far as its object is to recall to the minds of Christians the love of Christ as exhibited in the sacrifice of His death; in so far as it commemorates by an outward act that Divine sacrifice; and in so far as it is a memorial of Christ and His death before man and before God.

It is a Sacrifice, inasmuch as it is an offering made to God as an act of religious worship—a *spiritual* sacrifice, as being a sacrifice of prayer and praise to God for the benefits received by the sacrifice of the death of Christ; a *material* sacrifice, in so far as the bread and wine are regarded as gifts of homage to God in acknowledgment of His creative and sustaining power; a *commemorative* sacrifice, inasmuch as it commemorates the great Sacrifice of the Cross—the words 'commemorative sacrifice' meaning, in this acceptation, a commemoration of the sacrifice. But it is not a sacrifice of Christ to His Father, whereby God is propitiated and man's sins expiated.

It is a means of Feeding upon Christ; but this feeding is not effected by the elements to be eaten being changed into Christ—an hypothesis which grew up in the ninth century among a rude and uninstructed populace, forced its way into the theology of the Western Church in the eleventh century, although opposed to the tradition of the Church, the true interpretation of Scripture, and the tenets of philosophy—an hypothesis which has led to the practices of Reservation, Procession of the Sacrament, Elevation, Adoration, Communion in one kind, Fasting Reception (imposed as of necessity), and the belief that Christ's Body is eaten by the wicked.

Nor is our Feeding on Christ effected by our eating His material Body, together with the bread and wine, which the theory of Consubstantiation.

But it is effected by the spiritual Presence of Christ, and the benefits of. His blood-shedding on the Cross being conveyed to the soul of the humble recipient qualified by faith and love towards God and man.

It is a means of Incorporation, inasmuch as by it we are more and more made part of the mystical Body of Christ, and united with its other members.

It is a Pledge, inasmuch as it serves to the humble Christian as a symbolical assurance of God's past forgiveness, and of His present favour towards him, and of a future inheritance graciously reserved for him.

Remembrance, Sacrifice, Feeding, Incorporation, Pledge. Regard any one of these ideas as an adequate expression of the doctrine of the Holy Communion, and we shall have only a partial conception of it. Combine them, and we attain as nearly to a complete notion and apprehension of it as the nature of a mystery will admit.

NOTES / SOURCES

F. Meyrick, *The Doctrine of the Church of England on the Holy Communion: Restated as a guide at the present time*, London, 1908, pp. 201–3

John Coleridge Patteson 1827–1871

Coming from a devout legal family, Patteson was educated at Eton and Balliol College, Oxford. Ordained in 1853, he was persuaded by Bishop Selwyn to assist in the work of the Melanesian Mission in 1855, and sailed for the South Pacific. Patteson toured many of the islands and learnt their languages, founding a college on Norfolk Island for the training of Melanesian boys. Consecrated in 1861 as the first Bishop of Melanesia, he was murdered on the island of Nukapu in 1871. The killing was thought to be in revenge for the kidnapping of some of the inhabitants by white men a few months earlier. His death made a great impression in England and aroused interest in missionary work and opposition to the practice of recruiting Melanesians to work as indentured labour in Fiji and Queensland.

An Example of Christian Service

This is what they did for the sick. They were not ashamed to carry the bucket of waste matter and take it to the sea, they washed out the bucket and brought it back into the sickroom. Then I thought that they were doing what the Bishop had told us in school, that we should love one another and look after each other with love, without despising anyone; we should help the weak. All this they did to those who were sick. Then I thought that it was true, if anyone taught the Law of God and the things that Jesus did and his way of life, he must follow it himself, and humble himself and be quiet and slow to speak; his conduct must be good in the sight of all men; he must speak without cursing; he must visit the sick; all this work must follow the teaching of him who teaches. But if he merely teaches but does not follow it in his life, it is no good, and his work will remain fruitless, people will not listen to his teaching or believe what he says, nor will they respect him in his work. But whoever teaches must follow his teaching himself, and people will know him by the work he does, and they will like him for his work, and will listen to him and respect him because when he teaches them he does not speak of his own accord, but speaks to them in the name of Jesus, and his teaching has power.

And this is what I saw Bishop Patteson doing at Kohimarama. When school was over some of us went into the gardens, some to the kitchen, but he went and sat in his house, reading and writing. He wrote sitting down and wrote standing up. When he had been writing standing up, he sat down again, his eyes always on his book, reading and writing. All the white men did that, but I noticed Bishop Patteson especially.

NOTES / SOURCES

George Sarawia, *They came to my island*, privately published by the Diocese of Melanesia Press, Taroaniara (nd), p. 26

H. A. Krishna Pillai   1827–1900

Krishna Pillai was born into a high-caste Hindu family, and baptized aged 31 into the vigorous Anglican community in Tirunelveli, South India. A teacher for most of his adult life in Anglican schools and colleges, his great passion and achievement was the expression of his Christian faith in Tamil poetry. Though not the earliest, he is among the best known of a group of Tamil Christian poets steeped in the lyrical devotional tradition of the region.

Tamil Devotions

Rakshanya Yatrikam I

O Sea of Love!
O Sun of Wisdom dispelling the darkness of sin!
O God who for thy humble servant's sake didst become man
    and didst give up thy life!
I knew not this truth, and was a worthless wretch.
Now is the time to make me thine.
I offer up my heart to thee, O Prince of Virtue! (1)

Rakshanya Manoharam

By birth I was a zealous worshipper of Vishnu.
For thirty years I was caught in the lure of the world and
    roamed in utter darkness.
I did dark sinful deeds and yielded to wicked longings.
Filled with disgrace, I was spiritually poor.
Thou has brought me under thy flowery feet.
Thou has given me measureless grace.
Thou hast marked me and watched over me these many years.
A man of little intelligence, I do not realise all this fully.
My sin of ingratitude has never, never left me.
Seated on God's right hand, thou art ever pleading for those
    who seek thy grace.
Thou art a cloud of mercy.
Thou alone art God of the whole world.
Thou, Lord Jesus Christ! (2)

Rakshanya Ratrikam

He, whose eyes are free from guile,
Who, to save my base, deceitful self,
Did flood me with his grace like rain;
He, the life of all terrestrial lives;
He, the clear eternal ambrosia and sweet Fruit—
'Tis He I see upon the Cross

He who matched the threefold powers
Of creation, preservation and destruction,
With Trinity of Father, Son and Holy Spirit;
The God in whom the Three are One,
And who is One in Three;
Holy One in body, speech and mind;
In form the peerless Mother of all good deeds
And all worthy to be praised—
Himself the precious Medicine for sin—
'Tis He I see upon the Cross (3)

Rakshanya Yatrikam II

Hearken to this, my son!
The mountain spring murmured in its spray;
And the birds twittered in the wood;
From these sounds mingling rose sweet music,
Like unto the song of the holy ones,
Gathered in the heavens,
With desire impelled
To witness the great wonder
Of the Lord's Resurrection.

The wood was gay
With blooms of varied hue,
Thick-clustering the tall and mighty trees
That shot up to the skies,
In serried ranks.
The flowers their pollen shed;
And sweet honey trickling thence
Mingled with the dew
Falling from heaven, pure,
And was wafted in the wind,
To reflect the radiant form
Of our Lord Divine! (4)

Rakshanya Yatrikam III

The face of Jesus lovely as the moon,
His mouth like a well-ripened scarlet fruit,
His eyes pouring forth love and grace,
his glowing body and his feet pink like the Lotus—
The desire to see all these burns within me.
Open wide the door of Heaven
Suffer me to behold him. (5)

Rakshanya Yatrikam IV

Let my heart always think of him,
Let my head always bow down to him,
Let my lips always sing his praise,
Let my hands always worship him,
Let my body always serve him with love
Jesus who is seated within my heart,
    fragrant like a flower. (6)

NOTES / SOURCES

1. A. J. Appasamy, *Tamil Christian Poet: The Life and Writings of H. A. Krishna Pillai* Vol. 1, London, 1966, p. xxiii
2. Ibid., p. 25
3. Ibid., p. 158
4. Ibid., pp. 302–8
5. Ibid., p. xxx
6. Ibid., p. xliv

Fenton John Anthony Hort   1828–1892

With J. B. Lightfoot (q.v.) and B. F. Westcott (q.v.) he formed part of a Cambridge trio of theologians who advocated a constructively critical approach to the New Testament. Together with Westcott he produced a significant edition of the Greek text of the New Testament to which he contributed a notable introduction. As parish priest of St Ippolyts, Hertfordshire, and Hulsean, and later Lady Margaret Professor at Cambridge, his theology was influenced by F. D. Maurice and Charles Kingsley and by his own knowledge of the natural sciences.

The Call to Holy Orders

To the Rev. Gerald Blunt

CAMBRIDGE, *May* 31st, 1854.

My dear Blunt—It is not very easy to answer your question fairly without seeming to beat about the bush; but I will try. I think you have rather confused the 'inward motion of the Spirit' with the 'call,' which are not exactly coincident, though they must be mostly considered together.

First observe the distinct phrase used by the Church, 'Do you *trust* that you are inwardly moved?' etc. The matter is frankly set forth as one of faith, not of sensible consciousness. The motion of the Spirit is to be inferred from its effects in and on our spirit; any other view is likely to degrade and carnalize our apprehensions of spiritual operations, not exalt them. Now I do not think it possible for one man to lay down absolutely for another what inward thoughts and aspirations are or are not trustworthy indices to a genuine motion of the Holy Ghost; but the Church's words do themselves suggest some necessary elements of them,—a direct and unmixed (I mean, clearly realizable and distinguishable) desire to be specially employed in promoting God's glory and building up His people. You will say that this is after all the duty, not specially of a clergyman, but of every Christian man. I cannot deny it, though I do not know why I should wish to deny an inference to which the Church herself so plainly leads me. Perhaps we may find it a most pregnant and significant intimation of the real nature of the priestly and the simply Christian life, and their relation to each other. The one great work of a priest is to set forth what a man is and is meant to be; if we set this fundamental truth aside, we affect a more saintly eminence than our High Priest, the Son of Man. We have therefore, I quite allow, the strongest reasons for saying that the glory of God and the building up of his brethren must be the common daily work-day aim of every man; but this may be done mediately or immediately. Plato has taught us that every craft and profession has some special human work (some particular way of glorifying God, as we should say), which must not be confused with its adjuncts and accessories. The healing of bodies is the work of a physician, so far as he is a physician,—not the supporting himself, etc. These subsidiary results must follow, not lead or even, in some sense, accompany, the primary work. And so it is with the clergyman's work. He must have a desire to set forth the glory of God simply and directly, in those forms which show it forth most nakedly. He must not only act it out but speak of it, make men know it and consciously enter into it. None of the phenomena of life are primarily his province, but the glory and the love which underlie them all. He is not simply an officer or servant of God or workman of God, but His ambassador and herald to tell men about God Himself. He must bring distinctly before men the reality of the heaven, of which the earth and all that it contains is but the symbol and vesture. And, since all human teaching is but the purging of the ear to hear God's teaching, and since the whole man, and not certain faculties only, must enter into the divine presence, the sacraments must be the centre and crown (I don't mean central *subject*) of his teaching, for there the real heights and depths of heaven are most fully revealed, and at the same time the commonest acts and things of earth are most closely and clearly connected with the highest heaven. This is, briefly, my view of a clergyman's work; and by this, I think, must the nature of the Spirit's inward motion be determined. If a man does not feel a clear paramount desire,—often interrupted and diluted and even counteracted, but still distinctly present whenever he is in his right mind,—to tell men of God and Jesus Christ whom He has sent,—in a word, to preach the Gospel, that is, announce the Good Tidings,—I very much doubt whether he has a right to 'trust that' he is 'inwardly moved by the Holy Ghost.'

But this desire may be present in a greater or less degree, and with a greater or less commixture of other thoughts. In some it is so strong that any other way of accomplishing God's glory would be irksome to them, except as a subsidiary part of their lives. But in the vast majority of cases where the desire is really present, it is not so overwhelming but that it may be subordinated to others, if circumstances should be unfavourable. I do not think that this at all necessarily implies any moral declension. A man may honestly and truly desire to preach the Gospel, and yet he may best do God's will by becoming squire, attorney, or shoemaker. It is here, I think, that the wishes of parents or other circumstances may and must have their effect. Of course I cannot shrink from considering the converse case. A man's own thoughts may have lain in another direction, and yet subsequent external circumstances may, I think, justify his taking orders, but only under certain conditions. If he cannot find in himself any of the special desires which mark God's inspiration of His own special priests and prophets, I do not think that any outward circumstances can supply the place. But it must be remembered that circumstances do not act upon us only at one crisis of our lives; they belong to our childhood and youth as well as our manhood. And therefore it may be that the genuine desire has been really latent in a man's mind for years, hidden and kept down by one set of circumstances and brought to light and consciousness by the pressure of another. In short, when we speak of a 'call,' we must take great care lest we introduce notions which may altogether distort our views of the Spirit and His operations. We must not think of ourselves as cut off from the complicated mass of events and influences around us, or forget that the same God, who holds them all in His hand, does also call us to His work, and inspire us with the desire and the strength to accomplish it. We do not honour the Spirit, but subject Him to our own private fancies, when we refuse to recognize a call in His ordering of events. I do not mean that *outward* events or things independent of ourselves entirely constitute our circumstances; our own inward history, our present inclinations, even our felt capacities, are all, I think, part of our circumstances, but in these we need more care to avoid self-delusion, and it is not often that we are justified in consulting them alone. But no circumstances can justify us in following a profession for the work of which we have *no* desire.—I say 'work,' because that seems the best word; but of course I do not mean outward employments, except in a subordinate sense; they are but the outcome and embodiment of our real inward 'work.'—The case is precisely analogous to that of ordinary morality, which requires us to be led by circumstances and not to yield to them. The eternal laws of morality are paramount over all temporal circumstances. If they were not, there could be no such thing as sin. Ordination is no exception to the general rule. The Church requires a trust that we are inwardly moved (Lord, we believe! help Thou our unbelief!) by the Holy Ghost; and that must be present, or else we become the slaves of circumstances and so fall into sin.

I have doubts whether you will think this letter a satisfactory answer to your question. But I am convinced that no answer can be a righteous and true one, which supplies a mechanical test easy of application, and exempts a man from the awful responsibility of deciding for himself alone before God.

But there are two obvious truths, which ought to be kept distinctly in mind, if duty and responsibility are not to remain in a cold and cheerless light, which is by no means divine. If it is the Spirit that moves the inward man, and the Spirit that gives the call in whatever shape it may come, it is the same Spirit that clears the eye and strengthens the heart to decide truly whether either the motion or the call do really exist. And again it is the same Spirit who fills us with Himself at ordination. The Reformers may have been quite right in denying the name 'Sacrament' to an institution belonging only to a part of mankind; but it is most truly (what the Greeks called Sacraments) a mystery and sacramental. It is God that makes us priests, and not we ourselves; and so it is not our own previous or succeeding desire to set forth His glory that enables us to do anything for Him, but only the anointing of His grace.—Ever yours affectionately,

FENTON J. A. HORT.

P.S.—One word more on a point that I forgot. You seem to speak as if a love of outdoor occupations were something like a disqualification for a clergyman. I cannot allow this. I do not think my standard is lower than the popular one, but it is certainly different. With regard to such employments in themselves, the whole of society has relinquished them to a most injurious extent; and I cannot see harm, looking especially to the future, in a clergyman's cultivating in due proportion that which I believe to be an integral part of a healthy human life; and still more with respect to the tone of mind which such employments induce and from which the love of them springs. Nothing is more wanted for the regeneration of England than a vast increase of manliness, courage, and simplicity in English clergymen. These are moral qualities; but the breezes of heaven and the use of the muscles have not a little effect in cultivating them. God knows there are temptations enough in this direction as in every other; but better be anything than an effeminate sneak. (1)

The Lessons of Life

. . . It seems as if nothing short of varied and mostly sad experience can give reality and meaning to our highest beliefs. At the beginning of life we repeat them in words with perhaps little doubting, but we do not and cannot as yet *know* their truth. Only when we have struggled through hopes unfulfilled, and efforts that seemed to end only in waste and failure, and when on the other hand we have been forced to recognize blessings springing up under our feet where we looked for only barrenness, are we able to see for ourselves that all is indeed well, because all is part of the gracious discipline by which God is ever striving to mould us to His will. Such at least has been my own experience, and I think it is that of others. And on the other hand, as far as I have been able to observe, unbroken success and satisfaction is to all except a few of unusually lofty character the worst of fates, deadening nearly all real growth, and ensuring a perpetual poverty of nature. But this belief seems to me to bring rightly with it two other beliefs which are not always recognized. *First* that, though we do well to leave our past behind us, it is not well to strive wholly to forget it; the steps and stages of our life should always be precious in our memories, partly because they belong to that which is deepest in ourselves and cannot be wholly sacrificed to the present and the future without irreparable loss; partly because they may be to us a kind of personal 'sacred history,' in which we may at all times read the purposes of God's love. *Second*, that the dearly purchased lesson of the seriousness of life ought never to make us indifferent to its fruits and flowers, which never cease to surround us if we only have an eye to see them. Sometimes it is hard work to win even endurance; yet to be content with endurance is not Christian, but Pagan. It has been said with true wisdom that God means man not only to work but to be happy in his work. Only those who have tried know how difficult it is to carry out this principle; but I believe there are few more important. Without some sunshine we can never ripen into what we are meant to be. Prudence may tell us that, since hopes and wishes have come to nothing, and enjoyment ended in pain, we shall act wisely if we hope, wish, and enjoy no longer. But this is for the most part selfish economy, not Christian sacrifice. A larger wisdom would bid us go on hoping, wishing, and enjoying in simple faith; knowing that fresh disappointments will indeed surely come sooner or later, but knowing also that it will be our own fault if both present possession and future loss do not make us richer in that which has an abiding worth. To draw ourselves closely in, and shrink from all ventures of feeling, is to cultivate spiritual death.

. . . During the last fifteen years my thoughts and pursuits have grown and expanded, but not considerably changed. Theology is now with me as it has always been, the chief subject of interest, while I have by no means abandoned the other subjects of various kinds which have occupied me at different times. To give them up would be not merely a severe privation to myself, but an injury to whatever little I may ever be able to do in Theology, for that is a study which always becomes corrupted by being pursued exclusively.

In Theology itself I am obliged to hold a peculiar position, belonging to no party, yet having important agreements and sympathies with all, and possessing valued friends in all. What I am chiefly is no doubt what Rugby and Arnold made me. In other words I have perhaps more in common with the Liberal party than with the others, through a certain amount of agreement in belief, and because in these days of suspicion and doubt I look upon freedom and a wide toleration as indispensable for the wellbeing of the Church. At the same time I feel most strongly that there can be no higher aim than to help to maintain a genuine Christian faith, and a reverence for the Bible at once hearty and intelligent. (2)

The Atonement and Sacrifice: Universal and Particular

Christian peace comes not from sin denied, or sin ignored, but sin washed away. If it was not washed effectually away once for all upon the Cross, an awakened conscience has no refuge but in futile efforts after a heathenish self-atonement. Nor can I see how, man being what he is now, the Incarnation could bring about a complete redemption unless it included a true Atonement. The Resurrection itself loses more than half its power, if spiritual death has not been conquered as well as natural death. About the manner of the Atonement, we must all feel that it lies in a region into which we can have only glimpses, and that all figures taken from things below are of necessity partial and imperfect. It is the vain attempt to bring the Divine truth down to the level of our own understandings that has created all the dark perversions of the Atonement which have justly offended sensitive consciences, and so given occasion to the denial of the truth itself.

But it does not seem to me any disparagement to the sufferings and death of the Cross to believe that they were the acting out and the manifestation of an eternal sacrifice, even as we believe that the sonship proceeding from the miraculous birth of the Virgin Mary was the acting out and manifestation of the eternal Sonship. So also the uniqueness of the great Sacrifice seems to me not to consist in its being a substitute which makes all other sacrifices useless and unmeaning, but in its giving them the power and meaning which of themselves they could not have. Christ is not merely our Priest but our High priest, or priest of priests; and this title seems to me to give reality to Christian, as it did to Jewish, priesthood; both to the universal priesthood of the Church and to the representative priesthood of the apostolic ministry, without which the idea of any priesthood vanishes into an empty metaphor. (3)

Purgatory

'Purgatory' is an ambiguous term. It is commonly understood as literally a place of purgation. Most instructed Roman Catholics would decline to insist on its being literally a place, and would prefer to say that by a natural figure a state is spoken of as if it were a place. 'Purgatory' is not a word that I should myself spontaneously adopt, because it is associated with Roman theories about the future state for which I see no foundation. But the idea of purgation, of cleansing as by fire, seems to me inseparable from what the Bible teaches us of the Divine chastisements; and, though little is directly said respecting the future state, it seems to me incredible that the Divine chastisements should in this respect change their character when this visible life is ended. Neither now nor hereafter is there reason to suppose that they act mechanically as by an irresistible natural process, irrespectively of human will and acceptance. But I do not believe that God's purposes of love can ever cease towards us in any stage of our existence, or that they can accomplish themselves by our purification and perfection without painful processes. It has been well said that the heaviest sentence which could be pronounced on a sinful man would be, 'Let him alone.' (4)

One Body, One Spirit

One Body, One Spirit. Each implies the other. In the religious life of men the Bible knows nothing of a Spirit floating, as it were, detached and unclothed. The operation of the Spirit is in the life and harmony of the parts and particles of the body in which, so to speak, it resides. And conversely a society of men deserves the name of a body in the Scriptural sense in proportion as it becomes a perfect vehicle and instrument of the Spirit.

What then is this One Body, *unum corpus*, ἕν σῶμα? It is possible that, taken in their context, these two words refer first to the local body formed of those Christians to whom the Epistle was addressed. But at least they derive their ultimate force from a reference, tacit if it be not express, to the one universal Body and the one universal Spirit of which St Paul speaks elsewhere. That body is, I need hardly say, the Universal Church made up of men in great part divided from each other by all sorts of earthly conditions, but united by the confession of the One Lord, which unfolds itself into the one faith, and is sealed and consecrated by the one baptism; appointed to be the representatives of God and His presence to mankind, the leaven which is to work till all humanity is leavened. This comprehensive society is described by the image of a body with reference to two equally vital truths; the mutual need and mutual service of the individual Christians who are its members; and the dependence of each and all for unity and life and all things on Him who is in St Paul's language the Head. 'For as the body is one,' he writes to the Corinthians (1 Cor. xii. 12 ff.), 'and hath many members, and all the members of the body, being many, are one body, so also is Christ. For in one Spirit were we all baptised into one body, whether Jews or Greeks, whether bond or free; and were all made to drink of one Spirit. For the body is not one member, but many.'

But while St Paul thus raises our thoughts to the contemplation of that universal Body which now stretches through so many centuries and among such countless races, he at the same time brings its religious import very close to us in the narrow circles of our own surroundings. 'In Christ Jesus,' he told the Ephesians, 'each several building fitly framed together groweth into a holy temple in the Lord; in whom ye also are builded together for a habitation of God in the Spirit.'

We must pause for a moment to observe that the image here is changed. We seem to hear now not of a body but of a building. But elsewhere in the Epistle the two images are carefully interwoven one with another:—'unto the building up of the body of Christ' (iv. 12): 'maketh the increase of the body unto the building up of itself in love' (iv. 16). So also by a bold paradox St Peter makes mention of 'living stones built up into a spiritual house.' The image of the body speaks to us of life, movement, growth, feeling, diversity of functions: the image of the building speaks to us of permanence, of foundation and superstructure, of the fitting and compacting of sharply individual units, but most of all of habitation; the universal body formed of Christian men, not a stone fabric built by human hands, being according to the New Testament the true dwelling place of God on earth.

But what should specially be noticed in the text which we are now considering is that the truth taught by St Paul with reference to the highest sphere is a principle of universal application for every society, great or small, which with others goes to make up the supreme society. Each several building formed by the gathering together of Christians into one society shares all the privileges of the one all-comprehending building or body. Its unity and its strength come from the invisible Lord in the heavens who holds it together: in fulfilling its own limited purpose it becomes a holy temple in the midst of which, to use the figurative language which alone is possible on such high themes, God Himself makes His abode. (5)

NOTES / SOURCES

1. Arthur Fenton Hort, *The Life and Letters of Fenton John Anthony Hort* (Vol. I), London, 1896, pp. 278–82
2. Arthur Fenton Hort, *The Life and Letters of Fenton John Anthony Hort* (Vol. II), London, 1896, pp. 62–3
3. Ibid., pp. 157–8
4. Ibid., p. 336
5. Fenton John Anthony Hort, *The Christian Ecclesia: A course of lectures on the early history and early conceptions of the ecclesia and four sermons*, London, 1897, pp. 272–5

Joseph Barber Lightfoot   1828–1889

Bishop of Durham for the last ten years of his life, Lightfoot had been a private pupil at Cambridge of B. F. Westcott (q.v.), and later, as Lady Margaret Professor, was involved in producing the New Testament text of the Revised Version of the Bible. His scholarship in his commentary on the Pauline Epistles and his work on the Apostolic Fathers was notable and enduring. His ordination addresses reveal his own high pastoral ideals.

God's Kingdom in the Midst of You

This little society of men and women; this motley group of Jews, Greeks, Syrians, immigrants from all parts of the world; mostly gathered together from the middle and lower classes of society, artisans and small shopkeepers, where they were not slaves; poor, ill-educated, struggling for a livelihood; despised, where they were not ignored, by mighty Rome in the heart of which they lived; this little society, with its trials and its sufferings and its dissensions, *is* the kingdom of God, *is* the kingdom of heaven. The Gospel message cannot mean less than this. It tells us that God has come down from heaven, that He has pitched His tabernacle in the flesh, has made His abode among men. And so henceforth His kingdom is in the midst of you, is within you. Here He holds His court; here He keeps state. Hence His glory radiates, invisible to the mere eye of flesh, but transcendently bright to the spiritual organs of faith. And just in proportion as we realise this fact, just in proportion as we recognise the kingdom as a present kingdom, just in proportion as we see our Sovereign in the midst of us, will the glory stream in upon us, in our parish, in our schools, in our studies, in our homes, cheering our hearts and enlightening our path. The sunlight of the Eternal Presence will pierce and scatter the fogs and smoke of this beclouded world, and above the ceaseless din of traffic will be heard the angel voices of the Seraphim singing 'thrice holy' to the Lord of Hosts. (1)

Against Party Spirit

'Let each esteem other better than themselves.' Try and find out what is good in the sect or the individual or the tenet, with whom or with which your controversy lies. Strive to recognise any quality in your opponent in which he is your superior. You will have no difficulty in doing this, if only you search honestly. This man, who holds what seems to you a dangerous error, is more courageous, or more persistently energetic, or more truthful and straightforward, or more self-sacrificing, or more patient, or more widely sympathetic; he is an example to you in his domestic life, or in his official work. This will be a doubly valuable discipline to you. It will mitigate and correct the promptings to party-spirit; and it will shame and stimulate you to supply the defects in your own character and conduct. And generally, even where party controversy is not involved, what a golden rule of life is this precept of the Apostle, not found here alone, 'In lowliness of mind let each esteem other better than themselves,' 'In honour preferring one another!' Nothing is more degrading to the soul of man, nothing more warping to the judgment, nothing more blinding to the eyes and withering to the heart, nothing more fatal to that joy and peace which is the promise of the Gospel, than the pessimist temper, which fastens on all the faults and ignores all the virtues and graces of others, which suspects where it does not know, which assumes that every man is worse than he appears. Nay rather, learn to seek out, learn to admire and respect, learn to reverence, in others the image of God imprinted on their souls; for there it is, if only we will set ourselves to find it. This admiration, this respect, this reverence of others, will be a very joy and comfort and refreshment to yourself. In one word, absorb into your own mind the mind of Christ Jesus. 'Let this mind be in you, which was also in Christ Jesus.' 'Let your moderation be known unto all men.' (2)

NOTES / SOURCES

1. J.B. Lightfoot, *Ordination Addresses and Counsels to Clergy*, London, 1891, pp. 208–9
2. Ibid., pp. 268–70

George Ridding

1828–1904

Headmaster of Winchester College and first Bishop of Southwell (1884–1904), he was often called the 'second founder' of Winchester College, and was responsible for the founding of the school mission at Landport, Portsmouth, later made famous by the ministry of Father Dolling (q.v.). He created a notable corporate spirit in the new diocese of Southwell.

A Litany of Remembrance Compiled for Retreats and Clergy Quiet Days

The Minister shall read this Preface following:

Seeing, brethren, that we are weak men but entrusted with a great office, and that we cannot but be liable to hinder the work entrusted to us by our infirmities of body, soul, and spirit: both those common to all men, and those especially attaching to our Office, let us pray God to save us and help us from the several weaknesses which beset us severally, that He will make us know what faults we have not known, that He will show us the harm of what we have not cared to control, that He will give us strength and wisdom to do more perfectly the work to which our lives have been consecrated,—for no less service than the Honour of God and the edifying of His Church.

Let us pray.

O Lord, open Thou our minds to see ourselves as Thou seest us, or even as others see us and we see others, and from all unwillingness to know our infirmities, *Save us and help us, we humbly beseech Thee, O Lord.*

O Lord, strengthen our infirmities, especially those which hinder our ministry beyond our control; give us nerve to overcome the shyness that fetters utterance, and ease for awkwardness of address; turn us from our sensitive consciousness of ourselves, that we may think with freedom of what is in our heart, and of the people with whom we are concerned; and from all hindrances of physical weakness,

Save us, etc.

From moral weakness of spirit, from timidity, from hesitation, from fear of men and dread of responsibility, strengthen us to courage to speak the truth as our Ministry requires, with the strength that can yet speak in love and self-control; and alike from the weakness of hasty violence and the weakness of moral cowardice,

Save us, etc.

From weakness of judgment, from the indecision that can make no choice, and the irresolution that carries no choice into act, strengthen our eye to see and our will to choose the right; and from losing opportunities and perplexing our people with uncertainties,

Save us, etc.

From infirmity of purpose, from want of earnest care and interest, from the sluggishness of indolence, and the slackness of indifference, and from all spiritual deadness of heart,

Save us, etc.

From dulness of conscience, from feeble sense of duty, from thoughtless disregard of consequences to others, from a low idea of the obligations of our Ministry, and from all half-heartedness in our Office,

Save us, etc.

From weariness in continuing struggles, from despondency in failure and disappointment, from overburdened sense of unworthiness, from morbid fancies of imaginary backslidings, raise us to a lively hope and trust in Thy presence and mercy, in the power of faith and prayer; and from all exaggerated fears and vexations,

Save us, etc.

From self-conceit and vanity and boasting, from delight in supposed success and superiority, raise us to the modesty and humility of true sense and taste and reality; and from all the harms and hindrances of offensive manners and self-assertion,

Save us, etc.

From affectation and untruth, conscious or unconscious, from pretence and acting a part which is hypocrisy, from impulsive self adaptation to the moment in unreality to please persons or make circumstances easy, strengthen us to manly simplicity to be, and be seen to be, true men; and from all false appearances,

Save us, etc.

From love of flattery, from over-ready belief in praise, from dislike of criticism and hatred of independence; from the comfort of self-deception in persuading ourselves that others think better than the truth of us,

Save us, etc.

From all love of display and sacrifice to popularity; from thought of ourselves in our ministrations, in forgetfulness of Thee in our worship, and of our people in our teaching; hold our minds in spiritual reverence, that if we sing we may sing unto the Lord, and if we preach we may preach as of a gift that God giveth not for our glory, but for the edification of His people; and in all our words and works from all self-glorification,

Save us, etc.

From pride and self-will, from desire ever to have our own way in all things, from overwhelming love of our own ideas and blindness to the value of others: from resentment against opposition and contempt for the claims of others, enlarge the generosity of our hearts and enlighten the fairness of our judgments;—and from all selfish arbitrariness of temper,

Save us, etc.

From all jealousy, whether of equals or superiors, from grudging others success, from impatience of submission and eagerness for authority: give us the spirit of brotherhood to share loyally with fellow-workers in all true proportions; —and from all insubordination to law, order, and authority,

Save us, etc.

From all hasty utterances of impatience, from the retort of irrtation and the taunt of sarcasm; from all infirmity of temper in provoking or being provoked; from love of unkind gossip, and from all idle words that may do hurt,

Save us, etc.

In all times of temptation to follow pleasure, to leave duty for amusement, to indulge in distraction and dissipation, in dishonesty and debt, to degrade our high calling and forget our holy vows, and in all times of frailty in our flesh,

Save us, etc.

In all times of ignorance and perplexity as to what is right and best to do in our Ministry, do Thou, O Lord, direct us with wisdom to judge aright; order our ways and overrule our circumstances as Thou canst in Thy good Providence; and in our mistakes and misunderstandings,

Save us, etc.

In times of doubts and questionings, when our belief is perplexed by new learning, new teaching, new thought; when our faith is strained by Creeds, by doctrines, by mysteries, beyond our understanding,—give us the faithfulness of learners and the courage of believers in Thee; give us boldness to examine and faith to trust all truth; patience and insight to master difficulties; stability to hold fast our tradition with enlightened interpretation to admit all fresh truth made known to us; and in times of trouble to grasp new knowledge really and to combine it loyally and honestly with the old; alike from stubborn rejection of new revelations, and from hasty assurance that we are wiser than our fathers,

Save us, etc

From strife and partisanship and division among the brethren, from magnifying our certainties to condemn all differences, from magnifying our Office and system for worldly interest or policy, from all arrogance in our dealings with men as Ministers of God,

Save us, etc.

Give us knowledge of ourselves, our powers and weaknesses, our spirit, our sympathy, our imagination, our knowledge, our truth; teach us by the standard of Thy Word, by the judgments of others, by examinations of ourselves; give us earnest desire to strengthen ourselves continually by study, by diligence, by prayer and meditation; and from all fancies, delusions, and prejudices of habit or temper or society,

Save us, etc.

Give us true knowledge of our people, in their differences from us and in their likenesses to us, that we may deal with their real selves, measuring their feelings by our own, but patiently considering their varied lives and thoughts and circumstances; and in all our ministrations to them, from false judgments of our own, from misplaced teaching, from misplaced trust and distrust, from misplaced giving and refusing, from misplaced praise and rebuke,

Save us, etc.

Chiefly, O Lord, we pray Thee, give us knowledge of Thee, to see Thee in all Thy works, always to feel Thy Presence near, to hear and know Thy Call. May Thy Spirit be our spirit, our words Thy Words, Thy Will our will, that in all our Ministry we may be true prophets of Thine; in all our intercourse be Thou a power of contact between us and Thy people; and in all our shortcomings and infirmities may we have sure Faith in Thee,

Save us, etc.

Finally, O Lord, we humbly beseech Thee, blot out our past transgressions, heal the evils of our past negligences and ignorances, make us amend our past mistakes and misunderstandings; uplift our hearts to new love, new energy and devotion, that we may be unburthened from the grief and shame of past faithlessness to go forth in Thy strength to persevere through success and failure, through good report and evil report, even to the end;—and in all time of our tribulation, in all time of our wealth,

Save us and help us, we humbly beseech Thee, O Lord.

NOTES / SOURCES

Lady Laura Ridding, *George Ridding: Schoolmaster and Bishop*, London, 1908, pp. 352–5

Edward White Benson   1829–1896

Edward White Benson began his ministry as a schoolmaster priest at Rugby and was then Master of Wellington College. As Chancellor of Lincoln he founded the theological college there and was subsequently the first Bishop of Truro (1877–1883) and then Archbishop of Canterbury (1883–1896). He encouraged the institutional recognition of the laity in church affairs, and by his 'Lincoln Judgement' (1890) in the case of Bishop Edward King, contributed to the ending of vexatious litigation over ritual and ceremonial.

Ave Maria

Hark! the Angel greets the Maiden,
   'Christ is born, if thou believe,
Solace of the sorrow-laden,
   Ransom of the sin of Eve.'

Lowly in her lowly dwelling,
   With a holy virgin fear,
To the glorious Angel telling
   God's high grace, she bow'd her ear.

So the Spirit came upon her;
    Moved as o'er the ancient deep;
Gave her—O the unearthly honour!
    God for her own Son to keep.

Jesu Maker, Jesu Brother,
    Lift me, gently leading on,
From the bosom of thy Mother
    To thy Cross, and then thy throne. (1)

The Spirit of Godliness

The power to worship God is a 'Gift' of God. The noble Reverence whereof Worship is the consummate expression, is one of the Seven immediate Gifts of the Holy Ghost—a Charisma.

There is great sublimity in the thought of all that is holy and true flowing forth from God through all created spirits, and back into Himself with gathered praise. It is figured, as it were, by rivers falling back into ocean, back into the home whence they first arose in unseen vapour.

But the thought comes to a climax when we think that εὐσέβεια, the very principle of Worship, is God in us moving us to God. Hence some of the highest principles we know: such as that though God *is* in all righteousness, all justice, and the like, yet it is in relation to *Worship* that God the Son, the Word, the Reason, speaks of being present Himself as a person with persons, and by that presence assuring the fulfilment of *every* petition offered by a two or three. Hence it is, because Worship is a Divine *Gift*, like other free gifts, that there are some whose natural religion does not seem to include much feeling for worship; that there are good men who, having never asked for the gift, soon grow weary of the act of devotion; that there are employments and habits of thought which nearly extinguish it; that others are favourable to it; that there are forms of religious belief, even with emotional tendencies, from which reverence, and so real Worship, are altogether absent; that there are necessarily conventions as to the expression and the intelligence of it; that accordingly the expression may be cultivated to a high degree by itself without reference to the reality of the feeling; that the beauty of either ceremonial, or of sacred rhetoric, may be in esteem without moral cultivation. These and kindred phenomena, which are well worth observation, group themselves around the fact that spiritual Reverence is a distinct, and as the world's history shows, a very powerful *Gift*. Like the other Gifts of the Spirit, you find traces and reflections of it in heathen sects and communities; you see it in Christendom moulding Society to many beautiful forms when it is lovingly welcomed; judging Society by inflicting hardness on it where it is neglected; punishing Society very literally where it is pretended, or formalised, or only acted.

The Church, therefore, treats Worship as a Duty, not as an inclination. And while she shuns both vacant and extravagant expressions of it, yet she lays stress on comely expression as well as on inner devoutness. (2)

NOTES / SOURCES

1. Edward White Benson, in *Songs of Syon: A Collection of Psalms, Hymns and Spiritual Songs for Public and Private Use*, ed. G. R. Woodward, London, 1908, No. 248 pp. 220–21
2. Edward White Benson *The Seven Gifts: Addressed to the Diocese of Canterbury in his primary visitation*, London, 1885, pp. 157–9

Edward King   1829–1910

Edward King was Bishop of Lincoln from 1885 until his death. A Tractarian High Churchman and friend of Pusey (q.v.) and Liddon (q.v.), he exercised a remarkable pastoral ministry first as Principal of Cuddesdon Theological College, then as Regius Professor of Pastoral Theology at Oxford, and finally as Bishop of Lincoln. His *Spiritual Letters* of advice and guidance, mostly to ordinands, are something of a minor classic.

Self-Examination

In the 'Purgatorio,' Canto IX, Dante speaks of the first beginning of the mount of cleansing where he saw an angel sitting upon a stone of adamant. There were three steps up which Dante had to walk before he could reach that stone.

The first stone was white marble, so white and so clear that in it he could see himself. What did he mean by that? Sincerity, knowledge of oneself, seeing what one is in oneself; that is the first step. The poem is marvellously full of ethics, teaching us things helpful for the cleansing of the soul.

And the next stone seemed to be burnt with fire and cracked all along the length and breadth of it. He had to stand upon this stone. What was the meaning of this cracked stone? Surely contrition, a broken and a contrite heart. Self-examination is to lead us to true self-knowledge, to sincerity; not to end there, but knowing oneself one should get oneself on to the second stone which seems burnt and cracked all along the length and breadth of it, contrition.

Yet there was a third stone that he had to stand on that seemed like porphyry, red like blood. What is the meaning of that stone? What but that it is red with the stream which flows from the heart, and the heart is the symbol of love. So one gets it; there is first the white stone, clear as a mirror in which he could see himself; that is sincerity, knowledge of self; not stopping there but then mounting to the second step, the stone burnt and cracked, i.e. true contrition, a broken heart; not stopping there but going beyond it to stand thirdly upon the stone, red as with blood, having a heart poured out as with the full abandon of real love. So with self-examination; it is not a mere morbid self-introspection, not a wretched slavish religious anatomy, it is not to be used morbidly or wearisomely like slaves having to give an account to a cruel, hard task-master, 'I must give an account or he will be down upon me'; that is not the spirit of it; but the first thing is the stone of white marble, to be quite clear, quite honest, asking God to show one, wishing to know oneself; then the stone of contrition; and then the stone of the fullness of love. (1)

Sloth

We may define sloth as an inordinate heaviness, and fastidious distaste for virtuous exertion.

It makes us irregular in our work; we work by fits and starts, and continually change our plans. It is the cause of delay and procrastination; we begin to do things but only do them for a short time; we become lax as to rules.

It is the great enemy to strength of will; it causes repugnance, and makes us put off duties till we are forced to do them by necessity, till we have to do them whether we like them or not; and so it takes away our freedom and independence, and the moral value of our actions. A man who is always behind hand is being driven about like a slave.

It destroys proper confidence in self—makes us timid, nervous, distrustful, makes us say, 'It is no good—I never could—it is no use trying,' and so it leads to despondency.

It makes us lose confidence in God, that He has not given us enough, and so on. It was the slothful man in the parable who called his lord a hard master.

It leads to religious lukewarmness. We don't do long what we know we do badly; going back to a duty omitted has a double difficulty—the original one of distastefulness, with its undoneness, e.g. letters left unanswered till we are *obliged* to answer them. It is a hard tyrant and forces us to duties left undone. It has much to do with wandering thoughts in prayer, which we all complain of; we should remember to attend to what we are doing at the time, and then in devotion there will be a better chance of keeping our attention there also. There should be energy and despatch in everything. Get rid of sloth and lethargy in all actions, and then there will be less wandering thoughts. Let our own aim be that of St Paul—'The prize of our high calling.' (2)

NOTES / SOURCES

1. B. W. Randolph, *Lent Readings from Bishop King*, London, 1922, pp. 19–21
2. Ibid., pp. 33–5

Henry Parry Liddon   1829–1890

An ardent disciple of Edward Pusey (q.v.), Liddon was a notable spiritual director from his time as Vice-Principal of Cuddesdon Theological College (1854–9). He stood firm for Catholic principles, and defended a strictly orthodox Christology in his 1867 Bampton Lectures, *The Divinity of our Lord*. A canon of St Paul's from 1870 until his death, his powerful preaching attracted a large following. In his later years he devoted much effort to writing the life of E. B. Pusey, which, however, had to be completed by others at his death.

Letter to One about to be Ordained

O Holy Father we implore Thy blessing upon one dear to us, who is about to enter the Ministry of Thy Church. Fill him with a deep apprehension of the awfulness of Thy Service, of the preciousness of Souls, and of the love of Our Lord Jesus Christ.

Enable him to put aside all earthly motives and to seek Thee for Thyself alone and Thy greater glory. Make all labour rest unto him which is borne for Thee, and all rest willsome, which is not in Thee. Confirm him ever more and more to the Spirit and Image of our all-holy Redeemer, that going from strength to strength he may by Thy mercy, turn many to righteousness and shine as the stars for ever and ever. Grant this O heavenly Father for J. C. sake our Mediator and Advocate. Amen.

NOTES / SOURCES

H. P. Liddon Unpublished Prayer found among letters to Reginald Porter, student at Cuddesdon, probably 1856

Gerard Moultrie   1829–1885

Son of the Rector of Rugby and educated at Rugby and Exeter College, Oxford, Moultrie was ordained and served a number of curacies and chaplaincies before becoming Vicar of Southleigh in 1869. He translated many hymns from Greek, Latin, and German and also wrote a number of his own, especially for Saints' Days and special occasions, many found in his *Cantica Sanctorum* (1880). He also translated the Latin Primer.

Let all Mortal Flesh

Let all mortal flesh keep silence, and with fear and trembling stand;
Ponder nothing earthly-minded, for with blessing in his hand,
Christ our God to earth descendeth, our full homage to demand.

King of kings, yet born of Mary, as of old on earth he stood,
Lord of lords, in human vesture—in the Body and the Blood:
He will give to all the faithful his own Self for heavenly Food.

Rank on rank the host of heaven spreads its vanguard on the way,
As the Light of light descendeth from the realms of endless day,
That the powers of hell may vanish as the darkness clears away.

At his feet the six-winged Seraph; Cherubim with sleepless eye,
Veil their faces to the Presence, as with ceaseless voice they cry,
Alleluya, Alleluya, Alleluya, Lord most high.

NOTES / SOURCES

Gerald Moultrie, in *The English Hymnal*, No. 318, London, 1906, (From the Liturgy of St James)

Charles Chapman Grafton   1830–1912

Born in Boston, Grafton was ordained in Maryland by William Whittingham, serving initially in Baltimore. Coming to England in 1864 he was one of the founding members of the Cowley Fathers (SSJE), and remained in the community until he returned to Boston in 1872. In 1889 he was consecrated as Bishop of Fond du Lac in Wisconsin, where he promoted Catholic ritual and ceremonial, and also strove for closer links with the Orthodox and the Old Catholics. He was a profound Tractarian who criticized Broad Churchmen as 'Episcopal Unitarians' and was one of the most controversial and outspoken leaders of the Catholic party in the Episcopal Church.

Prayer for Personal Transformation

O God, dearest and best, may the increase of Thy accidental glory be the chief end of my life! May Thy ever blessed making will be the law of my being and of all my actions and desires! May Thy transforming and uniting love be the permanent and imperative motive of all my actions, duties, labors, thoughts, and words! May the life of my blessed Lord be the model and mould of my own, that being melted by penitence, I may be recast and recreated in Thee! May the Holy Spirit so rule and govern my interior, all my emotions, fears, hopes, sorrows, and joys, that I may rest peacefully in Thee, and be an instrument for the conversion of others! (1)

Asceticism

The condemnation of asceticism is a frequent topic with a certain class of preachers who do not understand the Christian principle on which it is based. It differs in character from the asceticism practised in India or by the Manichæans. They would punish or destroy the flesh, in which they believe some evil principle resides. But the Christian principle is not to free the soul from the body, but as St Paul said, to bring the body under subjection. It is, moreover, practised as a loving union with Christ, for He, although He mingled in the world, was the greatest of all ascetics.

In the intensity of their love for Him the saints have sought for a share in His life. Unless love enters into the ascetic practice, it is worthless. But every act of mortification, like the abstinence from flesh meat on Fridays, little bodily mortifications, practice of any self-denial, which all good churchmen practise, should be done out of love of a crucified Lord, and be used as a means of increasing our love to Him. (2)

Christ and us in the Eucharist

Our relation to Christ is far closer and dearer than that of the Apostles when He was visible among them. They could follow Him, but did not receive Him into themselves as we do. He comes to enfold us in His own life, to communicate to us His own virtue. By an act most tender, loving, and sweet, He feeds us with His own Body and Blood, and gives us the grace of His soul, and strengthens us with His divine Nature. Here His love breaks out to us and claims us for His own. Around the altar, though unseen, are the angel choirs. They come not to receive, but by their presence to do honor to, and worship the Blessed Lord. The Eucharist is an extension to them of that night when they sang that Gloria in Excelsis over the Babe of Bethlehem. The great Memorial Sacrifice of the altar moves the Heart of God with its ever fresh offering. Here is set forth and pleaded, with the consecrated Broken Bread and outpoured Blood, the effectual Sacrifice of Calvary. Here we ask God to behold our Defender, and to look upon the face of His Anointed. Here the heavy laden, and the rejoicing souls bring their needs and petitions, and they are united to the great offering. God answers every Eucharistic sacrifice with new gifts of His protecting love. To the devout communicant this world changes its aspect as a thing of desire, and heaven becomes permanent to his illuminated vision. (3)

Inner Stillness

The power of the retreat lies largely in its solitude. The soul goes apart to the dear and only God. It rigidly shuts out the world, one's duties and one's cares. It is in solitude that Christ speaks to the soul, one cannot tell when or how. It may be by some text, or word of a conductor, or interior inspiration. As it is the still lake that reflects the heavens, so it is the still soul that is receptive of God's inspiration. (4)

Penitence and the Love of Christ

What hinders the spiritual advance of so many? 'Why is it,' said a holy man, 'that so many Christians seem to be walking up and down on a level terrace, and ever remaining where they are in the spiritual life, without advancement?' After much consideration he concluded, because they were lacking in an abiding sorrow for sin . . . I have never forgotten to pray that God would give me an abiding sorrow for sin, a fear of its little beginnings, a hatred of all that is connected with it, and a humble trust in Christ's acceptance and the cleansing of His precious Blood. But how natural it is, having experienced Christ's loving pardon and our acceptance, and possession of His peace, to think no more of the past. It should be remembered as a ground of our faith, as we realize the mercy of its great deliverance. He has plucked us as brands from the burning. He has opened His arms and gathered us into their safety, as our true City of Refuge. However great our sins may be, He knows them all, and He who knows us, forgives and loves us, and we can trust that love. (5)

Sacramental Confession

In this holy mystery Christ comes seeking us. As if we were His only care, He makes search for us as the Good Shepherd. He comes to find us in our wandering, to rescue us from the thickets wherein we have been caught, to take us up trembling and with bleeding feet, and in His own arms to bear us safely back to the Fold. He comes as the good Samaritan to save us, robbed and wounded and ready to perish. But ere He bears us to the shelter and care of the Inn He first probes and cleanses our wounds, and pours in the oil and wine, and setting us on His own beast, reconciles us to Himself. We are wanderers from Jerusalem, and Christ must come and walk beside us and light again the torch of Faith in our hearts ere He can enter in and abide with us and we discern Him in the breaking of bread. In the Holy Eucharist He invites us to be His guests at the Marriage Feast. Baptism and Absolution for our post-baptismal sins provide the wedding garment. Weekly Communions are fraught with danger if souls venture into the King's presence unprepared. In the Eucharist Jesus summons us to the Banquet of His Love, and by His loving washing of our feet He prepares us for it.

Confession is not only for the weak, the falling, the sin-stained, but for the soul as it advances in grace. It has been likened to medicine, a remedy for sickness; but it is also health-food for the convalescent. As the soul grows in love it deepens in its contrition. It feels more and more the stain of little sins. Its cry is, 'Amplius': 'Wash me more and more.' Jesus, in His tribunal of mercy, draws us with an increasing attraction. The soul advanced in piety comes to confession because Jesus loves her to come. He bought the right to forgive at the price of His own costly Passion. He loves to exercise the right and to cleanse His dear child more and more. No mother loves to adorn her infant as Jesus loves to adorn, with increasing grace and beauty, His elect. Confession and absolution have a fresh meaning to them, and they resort to the mystery as a means of increasing love. (6)

Fallen Human Nature

Our nature is not, as Luther taught, totally depraved. It is a good, though an injured, one. In every soul there shines a light from heaven. The wounded man, whom the good Samaritan succoured, was robbed and left half dead. The life was yet in him. So it is with us. Yet the extent of the weaknesses, infirmities, tendencies of our nature must be realized if we are to lay a deep foundation on which to build our spiritual life. How can we get such a vivid realization of our condition as to work in us a permanent distrust of self? Now in Holy Scripture we have a mirror of man's nature. We can look into it and see ourselves. We have not committed all the sins recorded there, but have we not in us the germs of them all? (7)

Acts of Devotion

Acts of Faith

Blessed art Thou, Wonder-worker of Creation's Mystery.
Blessed art Thou in its development in the Incarnation.
Blessed art Thou in the Sacrament of the altar.
        O Lord, I believe in Thee.

O Holy and Merciful One, the Burden-bearer of our sins,
O Thou, the Sin Victim, by whose stripes we are healed,
Blessed Jesus, whose Precious Blood cleanses from all sin,
        I rest on Thy merits and in Thy love.

All glory be to Thee, Jesus Christ, reigning at God's right hand,
All glory be to Thee, ever abiding in Thy Church,
All glory be to Thee, dwelling in the hearts and wills of Thy people,
        With heart, mind, and will I adore Thee.

Hail, most gracious Saviour, dying for us on the Cross,
Blessed art Thou, rising triumphant from the grave,
Blessed art Thou, hidden in Thy Sacramental cloud,
    until the day of Thine unveiling.
      I love Thee. May I love Thee more.

All glory be to Thee, whom the choirs of angels worship,
Blessed art Thou, whom Thy saints in glory adore,
All laud to Thee, whom Thy Church in patience serves,
      To Thee I give myself, and all I have and am.

Hail, most sweet Lord Jesus Christ, Incarnate God and Man,
Hail, our Prophet, Priest, and King, our Redeemer and Advocate,
Hail, dearest Lord, our Mediator, Saviour, and our God.
      Blessed Jesus, Thou art our All in All.

Blessed and Most Holy One, our Re-maker and Re-creator,
Blessed Life of our life and Soul of our soul,
In whom we are re-created and accepted in the Beloved—
      I look for Thy glory and rejoice in Thy Love.

Acts of Resignation

I resign myself, my body, soul, and spirit to Thy loving care and keeping, who
    loves me and whom I love.
I resign myself to suffer what in Thy good pleasure Thou shalt let befall me,
    that it may bind me more closely to Thee.
I am content to serve Thee with the abilities and means Thou givest me, and to
    be little in the sight of men.
I renounce all affection of creatures that hinders my supreme love of Thee.
I renounce government by the world's maxims, being governed by Thee.
I purpose to take up my Cross daily and follow Thee, trusting in Thy promised
    aid and deliverance in the time of trial.
I will live for Thee and in Thee, taking this life but as a probation and training
    school for heaven. (8)

Prayer

What gravitation is to the material universe, prayer is to the spiritual one. By that
we mean that it is a fundamental law. God wills to be moved by prayer, and God
governs the world. Prayer also keeps man in communion with God, and God is
the life of the soul. Our spiritual life depends upon it, as the body does upon the
air. It is a perpetual source of light and warmth and growth and joy. (9)

Transformed by Love

As love becomes the ruling principle within us, it fills our whole nature. The soul,
being emptied of self-love, attains to a heavenly calm and assured peace. As we
become one with God, God puts Himself at our disposal, for our wills are His.

Secured in the love of God, the soul passes safely through the purifying desolation which may beset it. Even here God fills it with the sweetness and light of joy and transformation, and becomes the life of its life and the soul of its soul.

O Lord, in Thy tender mercy give me an emptied heart, a heart emptied of all worldly desire, ambition, and all self-seeking and self-love.

Give me a detached heart, made free, even by Thy discipline, from all inordinate affections. May it be set on Thee as the supreme Lover and Governor of my soul.

Give me, O Blessed Lord, a humble and lowly heart like unto Thine own. Hide me, Dearest, in Thine own hiddenness and fill me with Thy peace. Give me, O Jesus, my King, my God, a resigned heart. May Thy will be done in me and by me, and may I have my joy in that Thou hast Thy will. Give me, O Lord, ever present in Thy Church and people, a recollected heart. May I guard Thine indwelling as a sacred trust. Give me the chivalry and the loyalty of a true knight of Thine. Clothe me with the heavenly armor. And grant me perseverance unto the end! (10)

NOTES / SOURCES

1. Charles C. Grafton *A Journey Godward*, New York, 1914, p. 63
2. Ibid., pp. 64–5
3. Ibid., pp. 122–3
4. Ibid., p. 131
5. Ibid., p. 135
6. Ibid., pp. 147–8
7. Ibid., p. 211
8. Ibid., pp. 228–9
9. Ibid., p. 233
10. Ibid., pp. 243–4

Christina Georgina Rossetti   1830–1894

The sister of Dante Gabriel Rossetti and closely associated with the Pre-Raphaelite Brotherhood, Christina Rossetti was a deeply Christian poet as well as the author of a number of religious books. Her best known verse is the carol 'In the bleak mid-winter'.

Sloth

Sloth does not at a first glance seem the deadliest of the seven deadly sins, yet under one aspect it can fairly be reckoned such. The others may consist with energy, and energy may always be turned to good account.

Sloth precludes energy.

Sloth may accompany a great many amiable tempers and skin-deep charms: but sloth runs no race.

And a race is the one thing set before us. We are not summoned to pose picturesquely in *tableaux vivants*, or die away gracefully like dissolving views.

We are called to run a race, and woe is us if we run it not lawfully, and with patience and with pressing toward the mark.

Sloth tends to paralyse the will. Blessed are those merciful who labour to help the self-helpless slothful, and betimes to arouse him.

It is never too early to fight against sloth in one committed to my charge—or in myself. It is never too early, but ere long it may be too late. (1)

'The love of Christ which Passeth Knowledge.'

I bore with thee long weary days and nights,
    Through many pangs of heart, through many tears;
I bore with thee, thy hardness, coldness, slights,
    For three and thirty years.

Who else had dared for thee what I have dared?
    I plunged the depth most deep from bliss above;
I not My flesh, I not My spirit spared:
    Give thou Me love for love.

For thee I thirsted in the daily drouth,
    For thee I trembled in the nightly frost:
Much sweeter thou than honey to My mouth:
    Why wilt thou still be lost?

I bore thee on My shoulders and rejoiced:
    Men only marked upon My shoulders borne
The branding cross; and shouted hungry-voiced,
    Or wagged their heads in scorn.

Thee did nails grave upon My hands, thy name
    Did thorns for frontlets stamp between Mine eyes:
I, Holy One, put on thy guilt and shame;
    I, God, Priest, Sacrifice.

A thief upon My right hand and My left;
    Six hours alone, athirst, in misery:
At length in death one smote My heart and cleft
    A hiding-place for thee.

Nailed to the racking cross, than bed of down
    More dear, whereon to stretch Myself and sleep:
So did I win a kingdom,—share My crown;
    A harvest,—come and reap. (2)

'Cried out with Tears.'

Lord, I believe, help Thou mine unbelief:
    Lord, I repent, help mine impenitence:
    Hide not Thy Face from me, nor spurn me hence,
Nor utterly despise me in my grief;

Nor say me nay, who worship with the thief
   Bemoaning my so long lost innocence:—
   Ah me! my penitence a fresh offence,
Too tardy and too tepid and too brief.
Lord, must I perish, I who look to Thee?
   Look Thou upon me, bid me live, not die;
      Say 'Come,' say not 'Depart,' tho' Thou art just:
      Yea, Lord, be mindful how out of the dust
I look to Thee while Thou dost look on me,
   Thou Face to face with me and Eye to eye.

O Lord, on Whom we gaze and dare not gaze,
   Increase our faith that gazing we may see,
   And seeing love, and loving worship Thee
Thro' all our days, our long and lengthening days.
O Lord, accessible to prayer and praise,
   Kind Lord, Companion of the two or three,
   Good Lord, be gracious to all men and me,
Lighten our darkness and amend our ways.
Call up our hearts to Thee, that where Thou art
   Our treasure and our heart may dwell at one:
   Then let the pallid moon pursue her sun,
So long as it shall please Thee, far apart,—
   Yet art Thou with us, Thou to Whom we run,
We hand in hand with Thee and heart in heart. (3)

NOTES / SOURCES

1. Christina G. Rossetti, *Time flies: A reading diary*, London, 1885, p. 40
2. *The Complete Poems of Christina Rossetti*, A Variorum Edition, Volume I, ed. R. W. Crump, Baton-Rouge, USA, 1985, pp. 66–7
3. *The Complete Poems of Christina Rossetti*, A Variorum Edition, Volume II, ed. R. W. Crump, Baton-Rouge, USA, 1985, pp. 184–5

Richard Frederick Littledale   1833–1890

Born in Dublin, Littledale had a distinguished career at Trinity College. He came to England in 1855 and was ordained the following year. He served brief curacies in Norwich and then in Soho before ill health forced his retirement from parochial work. He wrote prolifically on theological, liturgical, and historical subjects. A hymn writer himself he also translated a large number of hymns from seven different languages, of which the best known is his version of Bianco da Siena's *Discendi amor santo*, 'Come down, O Love divine.' An Anglo-Catholic apologist he completed John Mason Neale's *Commentary on the Psalms from Primitive and Medieval Writers* and was the first editor of *The Priest's Prayer Book* (1864)

Come Down, O Love Divine

Come down, O Love divine,
Seek thou this soul of mine,
And visit it with thine own ardour glowing;
O Comforter, draw near,
Within my heart appear,
And kindle it, thy holy flame bestowing.

O let it freely burn,
Till earthly passions turn
To dust and ashes in its heat consuming;
And let thy glorious light
Shine ever on my sight,
And clothe me round, the while my path illuming.

Let holy charity
Mine outward vesture be,
And lowliness become mine inner clothing;
True lowliness of heart,
Which takes the humbler part,
And o'er its own shortcomings weeps with loathing.

And so the yearning strong,
With which the soul will long,
Shall far outpass the power of human telling;
For none can guess its grace,
Till he become the place
Wherein the Holy Spirit makes his dwelling.

NOTES / SOURCES

Richard Frederick Littledale, in *English Hymnal*, London, 1906, No. 152

George Howard Wilkinson   1833–1907

A devotional teacher and writer, G. H. Wilkinson, after graduating from Oriel College, Oxford, in 1854, served as vicar of Bishop Auckland and as vicar of St Peter's, Eaton Square, London from 1870–83 where he had a notable preaching ministry. Bishop of Truro from 1883 to 1891, he was elected as Bishop of St Andrews in 1893 and became Primus of the Scottish Episcopal Church in 1904.

Being 'from Above'

In all our strivings after the development of the higher life, it is important that we begin as GOD and the Church taught us to begin, with the Creed, 'I believe in GOD the FATHER, the SON, and the HOLY GHOST.'

Of course there is a blessed benefit in self-examination, in introspection, in all that side of the Christian life about which I have so often spoken to you. But as our LORD said when He was on earth, so will it be even to the end. If we are to be subjected to the influence of the HOLY GHOST, we must begin 'from above.' No amount of struggling to bring ourselves into a condition in which we can claim the power of the HOLY SPIRIT will ever land us in anything but hopeless despair. We should start with this: that 'this is the will of GOD, even our sanctification'; I am GOD's workmanship, I have been created in CHRIST JESUS unto all good works,' which GOD, before I was born, prepared for me, and He intended that I should walk in them. That text turned a man who had merely been a believer in CHRIST and at peace with GOD, but a powerless Christian, into one who has ministered now to the spiritual life of thousands: that one thought breaking on his mind, that GOD had created him for the very object that he might be holy, that he might walk in good works, that he might abound in the fruits of the Spirit.

It is important not merely to begin but to carry on that thought. When, for example, we find our own progress very slow, when we find ourselves continually falling back, we sink into utter despondency unless we remind ourselves that GOD never changes; that it is GOD the HOLY GHOST Who is working in us; that it is GOD Who wills that we should be sanctified. (1)

The Temptation of Formalism

Now, the temptation of compounding for inward sin by correctness of outward conduct will press most heavily upon those who, without any real change of heart, have come to be considered as religious. In a time of much spiritual earnestness, at a mission, at their Confirmation, after some great sorrow, they have felt the power of GOD, and now they are regarded by their family, their friends, their clergyman, as active, earnest Churchmen or real Gospel Christians, large-hearted evangelical Churchmen, or whatever may be the phrase which expresses the approval of the society in which they live. They feel in their own consciences that all is not right with GOD. They have great doubts whether they are really religious, whether they are ready to die and appear before the judgement-seat of CHRIST. Yet they shrink from so humbling themselves as to acknowledge the false foundation on which their spiritual fabric has been raised. Their character for godliness is too precious a possession to be lightly abandoned. So, instead of falling down on their knees and praying GOD Almighty to create in them a clean heart and renew a right spirit within them, they direct all their efforts to preserving the appearance of goodness, are mere miserable counterfeits, so the process goes on very easily and very surely under the crafty guidance of the master spirit of deceit. Conscience is soothed, the still small voice is silenced, and unless the Spirit of GOD arrest their downward course they become at last like whited sepulchres—all is well on the outside; they are fair and spotless in the eye of man. Sunday school teachers, it may be, clergymen, upright men of business, respected and respectable, the backbone of their country for honesty and straight-forwardness. But within there is no love for GOD, no warmth of self-sacrifice, no sorrow for sin, no enthusiasm for their LORD, no growing religious life—only the cold chill of death, the second death—the death of the soul! (2)

NOTES / SOURCES

1. *The Heavenly Vision: A second selection of sermons preached by George Howard Wilkinson*, London, 1909, p. 156
2. *The Invisible Glory: selected sermons preached by George Howard Wilkinson*, London, 1908, pp. 66–7

Phillips Brooks   1835–1893

Bishop of Massachusetts for the last two years of his life, Phillips Brooks was probably the most considerable American preacher of his generation. Born in Boston and ordained in 1859, he was influenced by the theological work of F. D. Maurice (q.v.) and F. W. Robertson. For some twenty years from 1869 he was Rector of Holy Trinity, Boston, and is now most widely known for the carol 'O little town of Bethlehem' (1868).

Putting Ourselves in the Way of God's Overflowing Love

233 CLARENDON STREET, BOSTON, June 30, 1891.

My dear Addison,—I am sure you will not think that I dream that I have any secret to tell. I have only the testimony to bear which any friend may fully bear to his friend when he is cordially asked for it, as you have asked me.

Indeed the more I have thought it over, the less in some sense I have seemed to have to say. And yet the more sure it has seemed to me that these last years have had a peace and fulness which there did not use to be. I say it in deep reverence and humility. I do not think it is the mere quietness of advancing age. I am sure it is not indifference to anything which I used to care for. I am sure that it is a deeper knowledge and truer love of Christ.

And it seems to me impossible that this should have come in any way except by the experience of life. I find myself pitying the friends of my youth, who died when we were twenty-five years old, because whatever may be the richness of the life to which they have gone, and in which they have been living ever since, they never can know that particular manifestation of Christ which He makes to us here on earth, at each successive period of our human life. All experience comes to be but more and more of pressure of His life on ours. It cannot come by one flash of light, or one great convulsive event. It comes without haste and without rest in this perpetual living of our life with Him. And all the history, of outer or inner life, of the changes of circumstances, or the changes of thought, gets its meaning and value from this constantly growing relation to Christ.

I cannot tell you how personal this grows to me. He is here. He knows me and I know Him. It is no figure of speech. It is the reallest thing in the world. And every day makes it realler. And one wonders with delight what it will grow to as the years go on.

The ministry in which these years have been spent seems to me the fulfilment of life. It is man living the best human life with the greatest opportunities of character and service. And therefore on the ministry most closely may come the pressure of Christ. Therefore let us thank God that we are ministers.

Less and less, I think, grows the consciousness of seeking God. Greater and greater grows the certainty that He is seeking us and giving Himself to us to the complete measure of our present capacity. That is Love,—not that we loved Him, but that He loved us. I am sure that we ought to dwell far more upon God's love for us than on our love for Him. There is such a thing as putting ourselves in the way of God's overflowing love and letting it break upon us till the response of love to Him comes, not by struggle, not even by deliberation, but by necessity, as the echo comes when the sound strikes the rock. And this which must have been true wherever the soul of God and the soul of man have lived is perfectly and finally manifest in the Christhood of which it is the heart and soul. (1)

From 'O Little Town of Bethlehem'

O holy Child of Bethlehem,
Descend to us, we pray;
Cast out our sin, and enter in,
Be born in us to-day.
We hear the Christmas Angels
The great glad tidings tell:
O come to us, abide with us,
Our Lord Emmanuel.

NOTES / SOURCES

1. Alexander V. G. Allen, *Life and Letters of Phillips Brooks*, London, 1900 pp. 870–1
2. Phillips Brooks, in *English Hymnal*, London, 1906, No. 15

Edwin Hatch   1835–1889

After study at Pembroke College, Oxford, Edwin Hatch taught in Canada at Toronto and Quebec before returning to Oxford as vice-principal of St Mary Hall, Oxford (1867–1885). His Bampton Lectures of 1880 on *The Organization of the Early Christian Churches* traced the origin of the Christian episcopate to the financial administrators of Greek religious associations.

The Threefold Benediction.

Westminster Abbey, Trinity Sunday, 1888.

The grace of the Lord Jesus Christ, and the love of God, and the communion of the Holy Ghost, be with you all.

2 Cor. xiii. 14.

It is remarkable that one of the two most explicit recognitions of the three Persons of the Holy Trinity in the New Testament should be in the form of a benediction. The fact is itself a sermon. It is full of instructive lessons. It tells us, above all, that the revelation of the Trinity is a revelation not of an object of speculation, but of a living truth. It recalls us from metaphysics to life. It reminds us that in our world of effort and failure we need the varied help of God. It reveals to us that God, who in His trinity of Persons is very near to us, is near to us with a trinity of blessings.

He reveals Himself to us as a trinity of Persons: the Eternal Father, of whom we are the children; the Eternal Son, who brings back to us our lost sonship; the Eternal Spirit, by whom we and all things live, are severally close to us. And yet they are not three Gods, but one God.

It is a trinity of benedictions. The love of the Father, the grace of the Son, the fellowship of the Spirit, come each of them round us, and enfold us in the wings of blessing. And yet they are not three benedictions, but one. The love, and the grace, and the fellowship are not different and apart; but one and the same.

The Apostle begins with the grace of our Lord Jesus Christ, because that seems to be nearer to us; it is, as it were, the doorway through which we pass to the sense of the love of God. Grace means 'gift.' It was a word which seemed best to sum up that which Jesus Christ did for us. It was a short technical expression which included at once redemption and atonement, the knowledge of God, and the hope of eternal life. The world had been seeking for redemption from the power of the body which held the spirit as its slave, for some visible sign and manifestation that conquest was possible. It had been seeking for certain knowledge, for some sure stairway into the far-off heaven which pure souls saw in the infinite heights above them and which they could not reach; it had been seeking for light and for hope; for it had struggled with its pain, it had struggled with its sorrow, with the problem of its disappointment and its failure—it could not always beat the air in a fruitless battle: and there was coming over them, as the slow mist creeps over the fair landscape in an autumn afternoon, the sense of a supreme despair.

And to men came the grace, the gift which Jesus Christ brought of a Divine knowledge, of a Divine manifestation of conquest over the flesh, of a Divine hope, which was not to vanish—not a dim, but a sure and certain, faith that God was in the world, and had not left us to be the struggling but inevitable prey of passion, and darkness, and death. It was the sense of a Divine sonship.

'The grace of our Lord Jesus Christ' was also, and thereby, 'the love of God.' There are many Christian men who have been so long the slaves of the ideas which Roman law brought into Western Christianity, that the old truth seems so unfamiliar as to be almost new: 'The Father Himself loveth you.' The very significance of the word Father is lost to us. We speak of the Almighty, of Providence, as though He were not a person, but an abstraction. Many think of Him as the Supreme Judge and Supreme Ruler, and forget the infinite depths of love. He reveals Himself to us as a father; as a father He loves us. We measure His love by the love that those of us who are fathers feel, that all of us who are sons have felt. He loved us in infinitely greater degree, but in some way like the way in which we love our children. He forgives us when we go back to Him and throw our arms round about Him, as it were, and tell Him that we know we were wrong. He helps us on our way when we tend to stumble; He gives us, as it were, a Father's arm upon which to lean, and a Father's hand to guide us through the darkness. He not only loves us but He loves us all as children. The benediction is the sense of it. The love of the Father is like the sun which shines in the heaven, it shines alike upon one field and another; but upon one field is a crop of grain, upon another is a crop of useless and baleful weeds: the difference lies not in the sunshine but in the preparation of the ground. So it is with human souls. The love of the Father comes to us all, but the blessing of that love comes to us in proportion as we till the soil of our souls. It is dependent so far upon our effort; it comes not to supersede our labour but to call it forth and to bless it. He blesses us in proportion as we are ready for His blessing—in proportion as we prepare our souls to receive it. And He helps us to prepare them.

And so 'the love of God' becomes 'the fellowship of the Holy Spirit.' The eternal Father has not placed His love in some infinitely distant space, to blaze and burn like Sirius in some field of the universe which we can only see in the distance, which touches us with no warmth, which enlightens us with no knowledge, and which only reveals to us the unimaginable vastness of His power. He has not mocked us with a panorama of sunlight, and the luxuriant growths that come of sunlight, passing as it were like a vast moving spectacle before our eyes. He comes close to us; He holds communion with us; He touches us with warmth. It is the fellowship of the Holy Ghost; He enlightens us with His light; He comes close to us with the awful revelation of His infinity. And then, in close communion with us, He whispers to us with tenderness, as of a mother to her son, 'I, God, am yours; I, your God, am your Father and love you; I, your God, am your Saviour and have redeemed you; I, your God, am your Helper and can sustain you.'

Thus it is that 'the grace of our Lord Jesus Christ, and the love of God, and the communion of the Holy Ghost' are not three benedictions, but only three forms of one. The sense of the gift of a Divine Sonship, the sense of the love of a Divine Father, the sense of a Divine communion, are but the prismatic colours of one perfect light.

But I feel almost a sense of paralysis as I draw this feeble sketch of what these words mean. They are the whole Gospel; they are all that Paul preached. They are all that Paul's Master and ours revealed. They burn within me; and they burn within me because I want you also to feel their supreme, their awful benediction. What do I want, what do you want for this world and for the worlds beyond the world, but the 'grace of our Lord Jesus Christ, and the love of God, and the communion of the Holy Ghost'? If you ask me to translate all that into the language of philosophy; if you tell me that no ray of that Divine light can reach my soul until I have told you of what chemical elements it is composed, I answer, Nay. The sun was shining in the heavens, revealing to the world the infinite beauty of form and colour, for untold ages before its rays were analyzed by the prism. It was bringing forth verdure by its warmth for untold ages before it was found out that oceans of hydrogen surge upon its surface, and that its heat like its light is a mode of motion. What you and I want, what you and I have, is not the bare truth that there is a sun, but the sense of his warmth. What you and I want, and what you and I have, is not an analysis of what the idea of God means, but the sense that there is a Father who loves us, the sense that there is a God who holds communion with us.

I will ask you thus to think of the Trinity to-day. I will ask you to let the thought of God, as He is revealed to us, be with you, not as a dogma, but as an ever-present benediction. I will ask you to pray each for himself the prayer which the Apostle prayed for himself and for all the world. It is not a selfish prayer. The benediction of God is like the sunlight which must radiate back again from all those upon whom it shines. The love of the Father cannot be in our hearts without shining, it must needs shine upon our fellow-men. The grace of our Lord Jesus Christ cannot be hid. The fellowship of the Divine Spirit is a sharing in His Divine activity, in an unresting and untiring life, always moving, because motion and not rest is the essence of His nature—always moving with a blessing. There are some men who seem to think that the love of God is so personal, so private a possession, that it can be, as it were, locked up in a casket, upon which they may gaze with a selfish and exclusive adoration, but which none can see but themselves.

It was a dream of many men in old times—it is a dream of some men now—that the highest revelation of God to man was not only made to the individual soul, but also made so personally and individually that no one else could know that it had been made; and they went into the desert, or they lived in their solitary cells, that they might spend their lives in adoration, in private communion with God. Can you conceive their theory to be true, can you conceive that if this prayer of the Apostle were fully answered for every one of us it would turn us all into silent mystics; that the stir of life would be checked by the presence of the Divine benediction; that men would cease to move and would stand still for ever gazing upon the infinite Son? It cannot be: the blessing of God, if it be within us, must shine forth from us. No one can see God face to face without his own face shining. No one can have within him this supreme benediction of the love of God without moving, as the love of God is always moving, in an unresting activity.

The activity takes innumerable forms. It sometimes takes the form of the activity of knowledge. In some men the communion of the Holy Ghost is a communion of insight. They cannot rest until they know; they cannot rest when they know until they have told their fellows; and they cannot rest when they have told their fellows until they have plunged again and again into the deep seas of the unknown, and have brought up new pearls of knowledge that men may again and again be thankful. It sometimes shows itself within us in the activity of benevolence. The fellowship of the Holy Ghost is a fellowship of beneficence. It stirs men to a sense of the wants of others, and to effort to help them. The love of God shines out with the warmth of a Divine fire upon those who are sick, and those who are weak, and those who are needy, and those who are in distress. It sends men into far-off lands, burning with enthusiasm, to bring the degraded populations of our race to a higher level. It sends men into the homes of the poor that they may be helped to rise to a higher life, to a higher status, that their lives may be brightened and blest. It stirs men to move about the common society which is around them, and touch every soul that comes in contact with them with love and sympathy. It sometimes shows itself within us as the activity of moral growth.

The fellowship of the Holy Ghost is a fellowship of goodness. It never rests with being what it is: it is always striving to be better. And if it were given to me to pray for one benediction more than another, for one form of Divine fellowship more than another, I should pray for this benediction and the fellowship of spiritual growth. I should pray, if I had but one thing to pray for, not for the activity of knowledge (though I value knowledge), not for the activity of doing good, but for the activity of spiritual growth. I should pray that my light might, by the help of God, so shine before men that they might glorify our Father who is in heaven. I should pray for this because it gathers up all else into itself.

To be good is to do good. To attempt to do good without being good is to beat the air. Do you suppose that your missionaries will convert the heathen world while the Christian men and women who live surrounded by heathen society live the lives not of the Christian ideal but of heathen practice? Do you suppose that you who are fathers and mothers, for all your precepts and your kindness, your children will grow up to be what you want them if, day by day, in your common intercourse with them, with one another, with the society in which you move, you show yourselves irritable and uncharitable and censorious; if you show that your life has no loftier aim than commercial, or literary, or social success; if in ten thousand little ways there shines out from you upon them, not the pure light of the Divine benediction of charity and truth and self-control, but the baneful fires of selfishness and unreality, of an unrestrained appetite and an ungoverned tongue?

If God's benediction be upon us, if the communion of the Holy Ghost be really ours, it must shine out in ten thousand ways in our daily lives.

When we pray, therefore, this prayer for the trinity of benedictions, we are praying not a selfish prayer, but a prayer for others as well as for ourselves. It is not given to us to determine the form in which the blessing of God shall be manifested in us. He has given to everyone of us his own separate capacity, his own separate powers, and He worketh in each of us severally as He will.

But it is given to us as we think of God to think of Him as blessing us. It is given to us to pray for one another this prayer of the Apostle, that His grace, His love, His communion, may be always with us. And the special purpose of to-day's festival is not that we may once more lose ourselves in the mazes of speculation in which the Greeks of old time loved to wander, but that just for a moment or two we may pause upon our journey to drink a new draught of the well of life; that just for a moment or two we may, like Moses, gaze upon some part of the infinite glory and bow our heads in adoration of the infinite and ineffable majesty, and then come down, as it were, from the height into our common life, move among our fellow-men, baptized with the baptism of this threefold benediction: 'The grace of the Lord Jesus Christ, and the love of God, and the communion of the Holy Ghost.' (1).

Breathe on Me, Breath of God

Breathe on me, Breath of God,
Fill me with life anew,
That I may love what thou dost love,
And do what thou wouldst do.

Breathe on me, Breath of God,
Until my heart is pure,
Until with thee I will one will,
To do and to endure.

Breathe on me, Breath of God,
Blend all my soul with thine,
Until this earthly part of me
Glows with thy fire divine.

Breathe on me, Breath of God,
So shall I never die,
But live with thee the perfect life
Of thine eternity. (2)

NOTES / SOURCES

1. *Memorials of Edwin Hatch*, Edited by his brother, London, 1890, pp. 328–336
2. Edwin Hatch, in *Songs of Praise*, London, 1925, No. 210

William Porcher DuBose   1836–1918

William DuBose, reared in a devout Huguenot plantation family in South Carolina, had a 'conversion experience' at the age of eighteen which led to confirmation and aspirations of ministry. Elected chaplain and Professor of Moral Theology at the University of the South in Sewanee, Tennessee, DuBose had a wide influence as a teacher and, once the School of Theology was founded, began there his life's work as a divine and philosopher of the Christian religion. DuBose's perspectives were deeply influenced by the writings of St Paul, and his six books on theological topics form an extended commentary on the New Testament generally. All DuBose's writings combine an evangelical fervour with an Anglo-Catholic modernist perspective.

The Living Christ

Seeing, then, in Jesus Christ all that I do—the divine predestination and potentiality of my Self, as of all human selfhood; myself, not only thus purposed and promised, but in Him realized and fulfilled; the outer man in me displaced by the inner, the old by the new, the flesh by the spirit, the Adam by the Christ, nature and self in me by God—Jesus Christ is to me, not a name, nor a memory or tradition, nor an idea or sentiment, nor a personification, but a living and personal reality, presence, and power. He is God for me, to me, in me, and myself in God. Wherein else do we see God, know God, possess God than as we are in Him, and He in us? And wherein else are we so in Him and He in us, as in Jesus Christ? If God is unknowable in Himself, whether as immanent in, beneath and behind, or transcendent above all nature and all else, where does He become knowable but in His Word to us and His Spirit in us: and that is what we mean by Jesus Christ, and what He is, to and in us. If God is not a Presence, a Reality, and a Power in Him, He is so nowhere. And if we are not to worship Him there, we worship Him not at all. 'There is none other Name under heaven given among men, wherein we must be saved.' And 'in His name' means 'in Him,' and 'in Him' means 'in His death and resurrection.' (1)

Law and Grace

A man therefore does not love, is not righteous, by law. The law, as such, only calls upon his part, it does not contribute God's part, in the common act and life of love and righteousness. He has a part, and the function of the law in calling it out is a very essential one; but in doing so the uttermost reach and benefit of the law is, not to make him righteous, but to reveal to him his own personal incapability of righteousness: by the law is the knowledge of sin, and, with it, the need of God, which is the necessary condition and beginning of religion. This is wholly the mind and attitude of Jesus, told in the language of Paul. What does our Lord Himself say?—'I am not come to call the righteous, but sinners:' He knows not the righteous; they are of all men the most repellent to Him, and He to them. The types most acceptable to Him are those whose language is, 'God, be merciful to me a sinner!' and 'Father, I have sinned against heaven and before thee, and am not worthy to be called thy son.'

What then is Grace? It is simply that we are not to bring our goodness to God, but to bring it from Him. He is not our Father because we are His children; but we are His children because He is our Father. He does not love us because we love Him, but we love Him because He first loved us. In our relations with God we are to come to Him with the nothing that we are, and receive from Him the all things that He is. Rather, as our Lord teaches, God comes to us in His person, with all that He is, and makes it all ours before we have come to Him: Blessed are the poor, for before they ask, before they have known their poverty, already theirs is the kingdom of heaven. Heaven is not ours because we win it; we can win it only as it is ours and in us. (2)

Knowing the Spirit of God

As we can know the eternal and universal Sonship incarnate in Jesus Christ only in the perfection of the human sonship realized in Him—in other words, as we can know the Word or Son of God only in the man Christ Jesus, so we can know the Spirit of God only in ourselves or in our own spirit. We cannot know any spirit other than our own otherwise than through a certain oneness or identity of it with our own. There must be both an inter-penetration of the two as distinct and the identification of them as one. Hence the common demand upon men to be of one spirit. What a subject of reflection then, and of realization or actualization, is there for us in the fact of our fellowship, our participation, with the Father and the Son in the unity and identity of a common Spirit. It is in this eternal Spirit that God Himself is God and is Love. It was in this eternal Spirit that the whole creation in humanity offered itself without spot to God in the person of Jesus Christ; and in that consummate act fulfilled His relation to it through realizing its own relation with Him. It is through this eternal Spirit, which is God's and Christ's and ours, that we pass from ourselves into Christ and through Christ into God. (3)

Salvation in Christ

Salvation, however, cannot be fully understood so long as it is regarded merely as an individual concern. It is impossible to limit 'the incarnation of the Divine in Human Flesh' to the 'individual' incarnation, manifested in its historic process in the development and perfecting of the human nature and personality of Jesus from His birth at Bethlehem until He sat down with His Father on His Throne after His Ascension. For Jesus Christ, even as 'an individual,' stands in an unique and organic relation to every member of the race. No one of us, as the study of Salvation showed, can become his true self, or in Bible language 'win his own soul,' unless he surrenders it to Christ, becoming a living organ of His Will, an instrument for the manifestation of His abiding Presence by the execution of His purposes in the world. In so doing he is taken up into the incarnation of Jesus Christ. He becomes a member of His Body, and thereby in finding himself he finds also his fellow-members. He learns that he is no isolated independent unit, but part of a living whole, 'the Great Church,' membership in which is the primary fact for all who are alive to their relation to their Head—membership in any subordinate group, whether Anglican or any other, being secondary. (4)

NOTES / SOURCES

1. William Porcher DuBose, *The Reason of Life*, London, 1911, pp. 162–3
2. Ibid., pp. 270–1
3. William Porcher DuBose, *The Gospel in the Gospels*, New York, 1906, p. 287
4. J. O. F. Murray, *DuBose as a Prophet of Unity: A Series of Lectures on the DuBose Foundation delivered at the University of the South*, London, 1924, p. 9

Arthur Henry Stanton   1839–1913

Curate of St Alban's, Holborn, for fifty years from 1862, Arthur Stanton was a notable Anglo-Catholic priest and preacher. He succeeded in influencing many thousands of people including men from one of the roughest parts of London.

Christmas

Christ was born on Christmas Day, so we sing and so we say. The 25th of December will do just as well as any other date. Why not? We who live under the conditions of minutes, hours, days and months and years, we must have our dates. Let it be so. Christmas Day is the 25th of December. That is man's computation—that is not God's. The date with God is this: 'When the fulness of the time was come.' God Who lives in eternity alone can know 'the fulness of the time.' And when in the eternal wisdom of God the fulness of time came for which the ages had been waiting, then that hour struck which never can be struck again, and GOD the SON leapt out of Eternity into Time across the hills of frankincense and the mountains of myrrh, and was born amongst us—born of a woman, was wrapped in swaddling clothes and laid in a manger. (1)

The Miracle of Christian faith

If there be not God, there is no miracle. If there be no miracle, there is no God, and this is the miracle of Christ crucified. They say, 'You men teach the miracle of the Mass.' We teach the miracle of Christ that He was born of the Virgin Mary by the power of the Holy Ghost for us men and for our salvation. We teach the miracle that Christ died on Calvary for all men. For whom did Christ die ? Christ died for sinners, and that is the miracle of Calvary. We teach the miracle of the Resurrection, that in Christ all shall rise again in His glorious Resurrection. We teach the miracle of the Ascension, that He who went up into Heaven shall so come again as we have seen Him go up. Our whole faith is miracle from the beginning to the end. It is all miracle. It is the miracle of God. And the greatest of all miracles to me is this: that I can say 'He loved me and died for me.' You cannot get any greater miracle than that. And so, dear brethren, death is swallowed up in victory, the sadness is swallowed up in the gladness of God, and the agony in the peace of God, and the misery in the happiness of God. The redemption of Christ is infinite. (2)

The Blood of Christ: a Personal Saviour

Then, there are two things I want to say this morning on the Feast of All Saints.

1. Never you be ashamed of the Blood of Christ. I know it is not the popular religion of the day. They will call it mediævalism, but you know as well as possible that the whole Bible from cover to cover is incarminated, reddened, with the Blood of Christ.

Never you be ashamed of the Blood of Christ. You are Blood-bought Christians. It is the song of the redeemed, of the saints, and of all Christains on earth—redeemed by His Blood. *You* never be ashamed of it. The uniform we Christians wear is scarlet. If you are ashamed of your uniform, for goodness' sake, man, leave the service. Oh! never be ashamed of Christ! That is the song of the redeemed: 'To Him be glory and praise for ever and ever, Amen.'

2. And the second thing is this: Let us all remember that our religion is the religion of a personal Saviour. It is not a system of ethics, it is not a scheme of philosophy, it is not a conclusion of science, but it is personal love to a personal living Saviour—that is our religion! Why, you can hear the voice of Christ off the altar to-day at Mass, 'Do this in remembrance of Me.' '*You*' and '*Me*.' He 'Christ—"me"—remembrance'—'Don't you forget Me here at the Altar' our Lord says to you—'I will never forget you—don't you ever forget Me.' 'Do this in remembrance of Me.' It is a personal religion, by which we can say, 'He loved me, and gave Himself for me'—'The life which I now live in the flesh, I live by the faith of the Son of God, who loved me and gave Himself for me.' And then, in all your experiences, however deep they may be, when you enter the shadow of death, and go through the agony of the dissolution of your body—you can say: 'He loved me, and gave Himself for me.' He loved me and washed me from my sins in His Blood, to Him be glory and dominion and praise henceforth and for ever, Amen.' (3)

NOTES / SOURCES

1. *Father Stanton's Last Sermons in S. Alban's, Holborn,* ed. E. F. Russell, London, 1916, p. 16
2. Ibid., p. 295
3. Ibid., pp. 312–13

George Body   1840–1911

Canon Missioner of Durham from 1883 to 1911, George Body combined evangelical fervour with Tractarian principles and is a notable example of 'Catholic Evangelicalism'. The author of many devotional works, he ended his ministry as a lecturer in pastoral theology at King's College London.

The Joy of Christian Worship

There are two orders of worship revealed to us in the Word of GOD. The first of these is the worship of GOD in Himself,—that worship which was shown in vision to Isaiah (Isa. vi. 1–4) when he heard the glorious seraphic song since embodied in the 'Ter Sanctus' of the Church on earth; but that worship, though it has received through the clearer revelation of the Gospel an intensity of expression which it lacked before CHRIST came, is yet not the distinctive feature of the Christian Church. Where GOD is known GOD is worshipped, and we Christians worship GOD in Himself the more intelligently because He has revealed to us the mystery of His Tri-Une Nature, and we worship Him as One GOD in Trinity and Trinity in Unity. But the distinctive worship of the Christian Church is the worship of the Incarnate GOD, the Man CHRIST JESUS, Who in our nature is seated at GOD's Right Hand, and in that nature is by us to be adored. The Ascension Day marked a distinct crisis in the worship of GOD both in Heaven and on earth. Until that mysterious morning when JESUS in His assumed Humanity passed within the Veil and took His place within the true Holy of Holies, the 'Agnus Dei,' the great hymn of Christendom, had never rung through the courts of Heaven; but when the thronging Angels watched the Ascent of the Sacred Humanity of JESUS,—and saw its mysterious flight cease only when it was throned on the Right Hand of the Eternal,—a new light flashed across their intellects, a new adoration filled their spirits, a new song burst from their lips, a new worship was begun, the worship of JESUS CHRIST: 'Worthy is the Lamb that was slain to receive power, and riches, and wisdom, and strength, and honour, and glory, and blessing!' (Rev. v. 12). And as the Ascension of JESUS formed a crisis in the worship of Heaven, so was it also on earth. 'They worshipped Him,'—His very withdrawal from among them, His very elevation to the Throne of GOD, was the development of new relations between the disciples and their LORD. As long as He was on the earth the worship of Him was not the principal feature of their life; but as soon as He was withdrawn from them and seated at GOD's Right Hand in the Heavenly places, the adoration of the Lamb,—the worship of JESUS Incarnate, Crucified, Risen, Ascended, Enthroned,—the distinctive worship of the Christian Church,—began to be. And a new aspect stood revealed of that holy Eucharist which He had ordained: it was to be the earthly centre of that glorious worship wherewith, in Heaven, in Paradise, and on earth, the Ascended JESUS is ever adored.

It is important to remember that this posture of worship towards the Incarnate, this adoration of the Lamb, is both our duty and our privilege; for it meets a difficulty that is sometimes raised against the worship of the Church. That worship is a beautiful worship,—into its use all forms of beauty are brought—beauty of architecture, of painting, of music and song, of colour, of needlework,—every lovely creation of art is by the Church called into her service as expressing her love and adoration of her LORD. But to this it is objected that such worship is unfitting, because the GOD Whom we worship is pure Spirit, and they that, worship Him must worship Him in spirit and in truth. But, supposing us to accept the premiss, we must deny the application, because we believe that, even as pure Spirit, GOD is well pleased with the offering of a beautiful worship, since all beauty is His Own creation, called into being for His Own enjoyment; and the Bible tells us, 'The LORD shall rejoice in His works' (Ps. civ. 31). But we cannot accept the premiss, because ours is not the worship of One Who is pure Spirit and that alone; if we were to hold that opinion we should be denying our position as Christians and allowing ourselves to drift back into Theism. We worship GOD-made-Man, Whom we adore not only in His Divine but in His Human Nature; and all that man in the highest perfection of his nature, in his most developed state, loves and appreciates, that the One Ideal Man loves and appreciates too. Whatever faculty is in the creature must first be in the Creator, and the love of the beautiful, and the power of art to gratify that love, could not exist in man if they had not their source and spring in the Divine Nature. The beauty of nature is a joy to the Heart of GOD,—'He hath made every thing beautiful in his time' (Eccles. iii. 11),—and if He rejoices in the beautiful things which are His immediate creation, will He not take delight in those beauties of art which are also His creation through the medium of the mind of man,—when they have not only an intrinsic but also a *moral* beauty as the offering to Him of His children's adoration? Therefore it is our belief that the worship which we offer as Catholic Christians is acceptable to our Ascended King both in His Divine and in His Human Nature. (1)

NOTES / SOURCES

1. George Body, *The Activities of the Ascended Lord*, London, 1891, pp. 130–3

Handley Carr Glyn Moule   1841–1920

An Evangelical, who was the first Principal of Ridley Hall, Cambridge, Moule succeeded B. F. Westcott (q.v.) as Bishop of Durham in 1901, where he continued to promote Evangelical ideals. Among his theological and devotional writings are *Veni Creator* (1890) and studies in Philippians, Colossians, and Ephesians.

The Sacrament

The Church is silent, the white Table spread
With ordered elements, the Wine, the Bread;
The Pastor lifts the hand and speaks the word,
And lo—Thy Blood, Thy Body, dying Lord!

So Faith can see. To her illumined eyes
The Scene around puts on another guise:
The Chancel seems a Chamber; in the shade
Of evening see the Paschal board arrayed.
The mortal Pastor here no longer stands:
Christ speaks the word and spreads His hallowing Hands:
Christ breaks the Bread and pours the purple Wine,
And carries to His guests the Meal Divine.
Again the Vision melts: the Syrian sun
Sets slowly on the great last Offering done;
Yon Cross the broken Body yet sustains,
The spear-drawn Blood yon rock of Calvary stains,
And man is ransomed by Messiah's pains.
Faith scans the Deed: Faith proves the Covenant good;
And in that Sacrifice finds heavenly Food.
Soon, all too soon, from this blessed Sacrament
Back to the glare of day our feet are bent.
But we who from that Paschal Chamber come
Still in its shadows find our quiet home,
Safe in its precincts, near our Master's heart,
'Midst all the stress of travel, school and mart.
And still that Cross goes with us on our way;
We feast on that great Sacrifice all day.
The sealing symbol comes but then and there;
The Truth is ever ours and everywhere;
Faith needs but stretch her hand and lift her eyes
And ready still for us her Banquet always lies. (1)

Look for Christ in the Path

My experience (blessed be God, it says also that there is a glorious deliverance) amply illustrates to me what you say of the sorrow of alternations between fervour, and brightness in prayer, and then failure in practical things.

Let us begin by a quiet avowal to ourselves that such a life is *not* the Lord's intention: that *somehow* He is able to make us walk evenly in spite of our miserable selves.

May I offer a few simple and homely suggestions:

1. First, as to your words about the possible advantage of self-denial in this or that habit. I do not advise exactly any acts of (so to speak) *invented* or *gratuitous* self-discipline. Fasting has a true place in Christian life, but it is not for all, if I am right. I don't feel sure it is for you. But I *do* counsel the sort of self-discipline which comes straight in the way of duty, a watchful avoidance of self-indulgent habits; such as carelessness about giving trouble, slowness to take or (for others) save trouble. Study an unpretending simplicity about comforts, luxuries, dressing, etc. (I speak, of course, utterly in the dark as to your actual ways.) Such things are 'in the path of His commandments.' Look for Him in the path.

2. Then, let me say, practise the remembrance that the Lord Jesus is a Living

Person, *not* yourself; *'objective' to you*, and therefore to be addressed, consulted, appealed to, drawn upon, quite simply. Do you tell Him 'what is the matter,' quite as simply as you have told me? only, doing it at every turn, doing it (if I may say so, this is important) just *before* every turn?

A few weeks ago a sorely tried friend found that very simple suggestion a mighty help, to remember that He is just a glorified *Someone else* on whom care is cast, in the way at least of consultation.

Then, if failure does come, do you *at once* take it to the Cross for pardon (real, instant pardon: 1 John i. 9), extenuating nothing, but accepting full forgiveness? and do you take it to the Living Lord 'to manage it for you' (as an old Christian last century said) next time? Do not look too far ahead, one step at a time. Not, 'I will never do it again,' or even 'Let me never do it again,' but, 'Lord keep me *now*, and just *next time*,' and so on again.

Lastly, remember the *facts* on which faith is to rest and walk. Remember Jesus bore for you *that* sin, and *that*, and *that*, the meanest, the lowest, worst sins. And remember *your Body is the Temple of the Holy Spirit*, you have *Him on the spot*. Use Him. The Life of Faith is the Life that *uses* the Lord.

Now I commend you to Him, and the Word of His Grace. Be of good cheer. We *are* well able to overcome in Him. (2)

The Spirit of Worship

The recollection and application of the Presence will surely prove withal the inmost school of the spirit of Worship, without which true religion can never for a moment be itself. For such is the Lord, the Christ of the written Word and the revealing Spirit, that precisely with the growth of experience of His radiant proximity, with the intimacy of the soul with His love, grows its passion for adoration. The nearer to Him, in spirit and in truth, the more the happy and wondering disciple finds rest only at His feet, under His feet, awed before His unutterable betterness, His absoluteness of goodness and of glory, while yet, and only all the more, he reposes upon His Saviour's heart.

As with the man, so with the Church, the spiritual organism of true discipleship. For it also worship, adoration, the holy fear which means holy love upon its knees, is absolutely vital to its true life. Let the Church grow slack and cold in her principle and practice of adoration, and the mischief will be felt through all her faith and all her life. Let the maxim *laborare est orare* be misinterpreted, as if the mechanism and bustle of Church activities were the main thing; let the simplicity of faith and the liberty of sonship be so travestied as to allow the Bride to forget to adore as well as to embrace the Bridegroom; and experience tell us that disasters to faith itself are sure to follow. The spirit of humblest worship is vital to the Church. And this is best assured by a perpetual recollection of the Presence. A God far off may be talked about, may be an interest, may perhaps be a dread. It is the Lord very near, robed in His promises, laying His right hand upon us, who draws out all the hallowing bliss of adoration. (3)

The Power of the Eucharist

For all that it is given to be, as the divine memorial, in the soul and in the Church, of the Atoning Passion—that central fire and light of the Faith, that supreme magnet to the believing sinner's worshipping love—let the Holy Communion be always more to us than ever, always more gracious, beautiful, venerable, dear. For all that it is given to us to be, as the imperial seal of Heaven upon the whole eternal Covenant of abundant pardon and victorious holiness, for all that it is as the authentic and certifying adjunct of the Word, from which it is never to be parted, let it seem always more desirable to us, more light-giving, more life-giving, to receive in worshipping wonder the hallowed Bread and Wine, as from the hands of the blessed Christ Himself, that so the better, in the heart, by faith, we may feed on HIM. Let our conduct of the great Rite, and our use of it, be steeped in the tranquil but profound reverence of faith and love, and also in the glory of that blessed hope of which it is full. For we 'shew the Death' with a perfectly definite *terminus ad quem* in view; 'till He come.' So let us go forth from it strengthened and refreshed in our whole being, pledged anew to an unreserved surrender to our once surrendered and suffering King, and better able to recollect, to adore, and to use, everywhere and every hour, 'all the days and all day long,' in the assemblies of the Church, and in our own most solitary or most crowded time, the entire and real Presence, living, life-giving, human, divine, of our Lord Jesus Christ. (4)

The Indwelling Christ

'*That the love wherewith thou lovedst Me may be in them.*' Here is the precise and inmost aim of all the 'making known.' Supremely true to Himself, now as ever, the Lord makes all *knowledge* wholly subservient to divine *love*; and He connects Himself inseparably with all the experiences of that love in redeemed man. He cannot for a moment rest short of that goal for the souls of His disciples. It would be absolutely futile, in the estimate of Christ, that they should be only Theists, however philosophically sound, that they should be only Trinitarians, however deeply and watchfully orthodox upon the great mystery of the Triune glory. All would be vain, for all would fall fatally short of the divine purpose of revelation, if the contact of love were not set up between the human soul and 'the only true God.'

To Him (and let it therefore be also to us) there can be no *Theology* worthy of the name that does not issue in this, for the living man who really apprehends it. That great word, *Theology*, has been 'soiled' with all manner of 'ignoble use,' till it has come to cover types and fields of knowledge or enquiry which have no more to do with a knowledge of the Eternal Personal Being than arithmetic or geography may have. But in its true meaning, in the sense of 'the Science of GOD,' Theology soars to His very heart, and there, and there only, finds its rest and life. And then, what a rest, and what a life! The man who learns that science in the school of the Spirit finds not only that he ought to love God, but that God inexpressibly loves Him. And this He finds not anywise, but in 'the Son of the Father's love' (Col. i. 13). United by faith to his Saviour, and seeing his Saviour as the Beloved Son, he 'knows and believes the love of God' (1 John iv. 16), and finds it to be nothing short of the paternal tenderness of the Blessed Father, who, loving the Son immeasurably, loves unspeakably the man whom he beholds 'joined to his Lord, one spirit' (1 Cor. vi. 17). That Father's deepest love is on him, nay, it is 'in' him; it lives and moves within the soul, formative, creative, an inward light and fire.

'*And I in them.*' Thus finally and supremely does the Lord, in the act of unveiling the Father's love, embody it as it were altogether in Himself. He is eternally the Receiver, the Object, of that infinite affection. And He, so loved, is, by His Spirit, nothing less than the Inhabitant of the surrendered and believing heart (Eph. iii. 17). So deeply does He love the man that He can be content with no exterior contact, however close; He must have His personal abode in the sanctuary of the human personality itself. Into that sanctuary He carries with Him the love that was His own possession 'before the foundation of the world.' And there, from Him the Indweller, from Him in His precious immanence, it is 'shed abroad' (Rom. v. 5), it is 'poured out,' to fill and beautify the being.

So the great High Priest concludes the Intercession. It began with Himself, and with Himself it ends; He is its Alpha, and its deep Omega too. If He were less than the co-equal Son it would be tremendous. As it is, it is the music of the heaven of heavens. It speaks ultimate and self-attesting truth to the inmost human heart, as it reveals to it the love of the Father for the Son, the love of the Son for the disciple, the wonderful union of the disciple with the Son, and his possession thus, in Him, of the very love with which the Son is loved eternally.

As He then interceded, so now He intercedes, 'ever living.' To Him be glory. Amen. (5)

NOTES / SOURCES

1. J. B. Harford and F. C. MacDonald, *Handley Carr Glyn Moule, Bishop of Durham: A Biography*, London, 1922, p. 180
2. Ibid., pp. 290–1
3. Ibid., p. 357
4. Ibid., pp. 362–3
5. H. C. G. Moule, *The High Priestly Prayer: A devotional commentary on the seventeenth chapter of St John*, London, 1908, pp. 217–20

Mandell Creighton   1843–1901

A distinguished church historian, and Bishop of London from 1897 to 1901, Mandell Creighton was the author of *The History of the Papacy*. The first Dixie Professor of Ecclesiastical History at Cambridge he was consecrated Bishop of Peterborough in 1891. As a rural parish priest in Northumberland he had played a major part in organizing the new diocese of Newcastle upon Tyne (1881).

A Marriage Hymn

O Thou who gavest power to love
That we might fix our hearts on Thee,
Preparing us for joys above
By that which here on earth we see.

Thy spirit trains our souls to know
The growing purpose of Thy will,
And gives to love the power to show
That purpose growing larger still.

Larger, as love to reverent eyes
Makes manifest another soul,
And shows to life a richer prize,
A clearer course, a nobler goal.

Lord, grant Thy servants who implore
Thy blessing on the hearts they blend,
That from that union evermore
New joys may blossom to the end.

Make what is best in each combine
To purge all earthly dross away,
To strengthen, purify, refine,
To beautify each coming day.

So may they hand in hand advance
Along life's path from troubles free;
Brave to meet adverse circumstance
Because their love points up to Thee.

NOTES / SOURCES

L. Creighton, *Life and Letters of Mandell Creighton*, London, 1913, p. 513

Stewart D. Headlam   1847–1924

Educated at Eton and Cambridge, Headlam served as curate of St Matthew's, Bethnal Green, where he formed the Guild of St Matthew in 1877. A Fabian Socialist he was a member of the London County Council from 1888. A High Churchman who advocated secular education, he had been influenced by F. D. Maurice. More radical than the members of the more establishment Christian Social Union, Headlam urged redistribution of wealth and was a devotee of the theatre and ballet at a time when these were looked at askance by many clergy.

The Secular Value of the Church Catechism

I want to point out to you to-night how the Church Catechism is valuable not merely as a preparation for a life after death, a life in another world, but for this life, life in this world; a valuable piece of instruction as to what men must do in order to be good individually, and as members of families, and as citizens. Whether this is the strictly proper use of the word secular I will not now discuss, I rather think that good authorities might be quoted to prove that secular means properly that which lasts for ages; that it might almost be maintained that secular and eternal are synonymous words: however, be that as it may, I use secular to-night in its popular sense, and shall try to show you how in that sense the Church Catechism is a valuable document.

The Catechism begins by calling out the sense of individuality in the person to whom it is being taught: by making the child feel, in a very real, practical way, that he in some sense stands alone: that whatever his circumstances and antecedents may be, he is personally responsible: the child is asked, generally in the presence of many others, often under circumstances of some solemnity, What is your name? and he has to answer, not the name of the family into which he was born, but his own name: thus from the beginning in the English child there is encouraged a healthy, sturdy independence. The bonds of the family are rightly round him in all their strength, his surname has for him most sacred associations, but the owners of that name had, he is taught, recognized that there was another society vaster than their family, other relationships on which theirs were grounded: his father and mother had let him be taken from the home to the church, and there from other lips than theirs his own name was given him.

At the same time he was baptized. Of the meaning of baptism, of its tremendous secular value, we shall hear more further on, but at present we notice that the child is taught that he was made, constituted or set apart as a member of Christ, the Child of God, and an inheritor of the Kingdom of Heaven.

A member of Christ: that is, his life consists in being at one with Christ, in recognizing that he and others are (morally) united to Christ and to each other, as the limbs are to the body. The secular value of this lesson depends upon the secular value of Christ's work: I have tried to show in a little pamphlet which was the cause of this lecture that Christ—the Christ of the New Testament, not the Christ of the religious world, or the lying Christ of the French romance—was a great secular worker. I will therefore merely refer you to that lecture, reminding you that the Christ of the Gospels worked hard against disease, sin, and pre-mature death: that He was a great emancipator, that He went right against the narrow religious cant of His time, that He died rather than give up the truth: by union in character with such a one the child is taught he will have true life.

The Child of God: almost all the misery which religion has caused in the world has come from men being afraid of some unseen being whom they have imagined for themselves, or of whom they have been taught: measure then if you can the enormous secular value of this lesson that God is our Father: if there is anyone who most shortsightedly has assumed that Theology is altogether an unpractical matter, I would say that if only it were for the sake of delivering thousands from the misery caused by the thought of a God who will be cruel and unfatherly, it would be worth while, by every possible means, to encourage the conviction that God is our Father. I say boldly that almost all the evils which men now rightly attribute to religion would disappear before the teaching that men are the children of God: that you are not to dare to attribute to God that which would be bad in a father on earth.

Thirdly, the child is taught that he is 'an inheritor of the Kingdom of Heaven.' Notice if you please—and remember that there was a great controversy with the Puritans about it,—notice, it is an inheritor, not an heir: for heaven, we teach the child, is not a cloudy reward in the future for being good now, it is a kingdom to which he belongs here: we teach the child that he is here admitted into a society of which righteousness is the note, that he is to seek those things which are above, pure, noble, human things, instead of falling into foul, mean, inhuman acts and habits. If any of you will make a special study of Christ's teaching about the Kingdom of Heaven you will see how our Catechism is at one with it, and how far they are both removed from what may be called the popular religionists' and secularists' teaching about heaven.

We next come to the threefold promise of renunciation, faith, and obedience, made in the child's name; and justly made in his name, because they are not promises that he will do this or that special thing, but simply that he will live a true human life. To promise that a child shall be a teetotaler, or a clergyman, would be wrong perhaps, but to say he shall be a man and not an angel, or a beast, or a devil, is, it seems to me, reasonable. The child then is taught that *he is bound* to renounce all those acts which are so notoriously bad that we call them devilish—'the devil and all his works,'—and may be taught also that the word devil means slanderer, and that therefore he is bound to renounce all that darkens, misrepresents God to man, or men to each other; that he is bound to renounce all that is silly, empty, bad in the current opinions of the time; and that he is bound to renounce the appetites in their wrong place: he is not taught to go against the world in which he lives,—though pretty often, if he is to be worth his salt, he will have to do so; he is not taught to avoid and be callous to the beauty of the external universe, to keep out of theatres, or not to dance, or play cards; but he is taught that all that is wicked and silly in the world has no right to him. Again, he is not taught to be a Manichee, he is not taught that the appetites and desires of the body are bad things, but he is taught that it is possible for him to be injured by them if he lets them rule over him, if he does not rule over them; this seems to me to be healthy and necessary teaching, good secular instruction. (1)

The Eucharist the Sacrifice of Redemption

A sense of sin is absolutely essential for you if you would be true men and women: nothing is more fatal to progress than for men to be thoroughly satisfied with themselves, and the world around them: a divine discontent is an essentially Christian quality. We are sinners and miserable sinners: we do wrong and we suffer for it: we miss the mark at which we are aiming: we wander away from the path which we know is the right path: we utterly fail to attain to the ideal standard which has been set up for us: we do not 'think clear, feel deep, bear fruit well'; but are sadly lacking in intelligence, superficial in our silly sentiments, often outrageous, always faulty in our conduct. There is no truer word than this, that we are miserable sinners—and the sooner we face the fact the better. The cry 'Lord have mercy, Christ have mercy,' with which in all ages the offering of the Sacrifice of our Redemption has been begun, is a genuine human cry, and the more you realize that the Eternal God who is the Righteous God has come down to us men in the perfect Man, Jesus Christ—the more acute does this cry become, for your ideal standard becomes higher, and you feel the more intensely that in sinning you have wronged the Friend of Man.

But this is not all: if it were all we should fall into despair or carelessness or reckless living: and so we have to learn that notwithstanding our sins it can still be well with us: that we have a Redeemer—a Great High Priest who is always in absolution, and in whose name the priests in all the Churches are bound to act. And so most wisely the one great Christian service is called the Sacrifice of our Redemption, because by means of it the enemy that reckons up our sins, and seeks accusations against us, is trodden under foot. You see that just as it would never do to be without a sense of sin, so also it would be fatal to all true human life and progress for men to be going about with the burden of their sins upon them. Some devout men and women have made their lives a nuisance to themselves and their neighbours by doing this: they have need to remember Bishop Butler's prayer 'to be delivered from the offendiculum of scrupulousness': they have need to remember the words I have quoted from St Augustine—that it is the part of the enemy, and not of the Friend, of man to be reckoning up sins and seeking accusations: that every time the Holy Sacrifice is offered it is made clear that that enemy is trodden under foot: that the handwriting against us is blotted out. That no man or devil is powerful enough to pluck us out of our Redeemer's hand, for none can pay the price He paid to make us His—the sacrifice of His perfect life. (2)

NOTES / SOURCES

1. Stewart D. Headlam, *Priestcraft and Progress; being Sermons and Lectures*, London, 1878, pp. 98–101 [A lecture given before the Dialectical Society, London, 1876]
2. Stewart D. Headlam, *The meaning of the Mass: Five Lectures with other Sermons and Addresses*, London, 1905, pp. 10–11

Henry Scott Holland   1847–1918

Educated at Eton and Balliol College, Oxford, where he came under the influence of the idealist philosopher, T. H. Green, Scott Holland was a senior student of Christ Church, then a Canon of St Paul's from 1884 to 1910, and finally Regius Professor of Divinity at Oxford. A contributor to *Lux Mundi*, he was instrumental in establishing the Christian Social Union, and was a notable preacher.

Christ the Crown and Sum of Humanity

And Jesus Christ is the Crown and Sum of humanity, and this one thing, therefore, He does, He gives thanks for ever and for ever; He takes all our loaves, takes all the poor, scant, pitiful offerings we can bring out of our niggardly baskets, and over all He lifts up His eyes to Heaven and blesses the Name of the Lord. And the thanksgiving is mighty; it works and stirs in the heart of the Church; it warms, quickens expands, and lo! the strange, unceasing change begins. Under its working dead things live, and dumb things speak, and blind things see, and dry things soften, and every stone becomes bread, and frozen things yield, and run, and sing, like rivers among the hills, and all silent things shake themselves loose and break into vigorous life. The breath of the Lord fills His Church as He spreads His Hands abroad and offers His great Eucharist. And we, too, stand with Him. We are empowered by His intercession, we are authorized by His brotherhood; we, in Him, complete the perfect office of a redeemed mankind, and all our growth and all our force come to us out of the heart of those hours, those blessed hours, when with Angels and Archangels, and all the company of Heaven, we, too, take our place and mingle our voices in amongst the thousand times ten thousand who, as the sound of many waters, sing the new and eternal song of the Lamb, and cry to one another and say, 'Holy, holy, holy! we praise Thee; we bless Thee; we give thanks to Thee for Thy great glory!' (1)

Faith

Faith, then, is, from first to last, a spiritual act of the deepest personal will, proceeding out of that central core of the being, where the self is integral and whole, before it has sundered itself off into divided faculties. There, in that root-self, lie the germs of all that appears in the separate qualities and gifts—in feelings, in reason, in imagination, in desire; and faith, the central activity, has in it, therefore, the germs of all these several activities. It has in it that which becomes feeling, yet is not itself a feeling. It has in it that which becomes reason, yet is not itself the reason. It holds in it imaginative elements, yet is no exercise of the imagination. It is alive with that which desires, craves, loves; yet is not itself merely an appetite, a desire, a passion. In all these qualities it has its part: it shares their nature; it has kindred motions; it shows itself, sometimes through the one, and sometimes through the other, according to the varieties of human characters. In this man, it can make the feeling its main instrument and channel; in that man, it will find the intellect its chief minister; in another, it will make its presence known along the track of his innermost craving for a support in will and in love. But it will always remain something over, and beyond, any one of its distinctive media; and not one of these specialities of gift will ever, therefore, be able to account wholly for the faith which puts it to use. That is why faith must always remain beyond its realised evidences. If it finds, in some cases, its chief evidences in the region of feeling, it is nevertheless open to deadly ruin, if ever it identifies itself with these evidences, as if it could rely on them to carry it through. It may come into being by their help; but it is never genuine faith, until it can abide in self-security at those dry hours, when the evidences of positive feeling have been totally withdrawn. And as with feeling; so with reason. Faith looks to reason for its proofs: it must count on finding them; it offers for itself intellectual justifications. It may arrive at a man by this road. But it is not itself reason; it can never confuse itself with a merely intellectual process. It cannot, therefore, find, in reason, the full grounds for its ultimate convictions. Ever it retains its own inherent character, by which it is constituted an act of personal trust—an act of willing and loving self-surrender to the dominant sway of another's personality. It is always this, whether it springs up instinctively, out of the roots of our being, anticipating all after-proof, or whether it is summoned out into vitality at the close of a long and late argumentative process. No argument, no array of arguments, however long, however massive, can succeed in excusing it from that momentous effort of the inner man, which is its very essence. Let reason do its perfect work: let it heap up witness upon witness, proof upon proof. Still there will come at last the moment when the call to believe will be just the same to the complete and reasonable man as it always is to the simplest child—the call to trust Another with a confidence which reason can justify but can never create. This act, which is faith, must have in it that spirit of venture, which closes with Another's invitation, which yields to Another's call. It must still have in it and about it the character of a vital motion,—of a leap upward, which dares to count on the prompting energies felt astir within it. (2)

A Sacramental Act

A symbol remains always outside that which it signified. It may be most beautiful, helpful, expedient; it may represent the noblest spiritual truth; it may have the highest sanction, the most historic authority; associations may have endeared it and wound their fibres about it. But, still, it is separable from the reality; it is accidental; it is without actuality. And hence, do what we will, it has a chill and lifeless touch about it. Like the picture of a dear friend, it suggests so much more than it can realize; and, therefore, the years tell upon it; at first, in the full warmth of wounded love, it brings a vivid consolation; but slowly, as its inadequacy to supply his presence enforces itself, it becomes disappointing, uneventful; even something of uncomfortable weariness may creep over it. So, to endure through the long ages of Christian Covenant, we need something more than a touching picture or a noble symbol. We need something that will replenish itself ever and again with its primitive freshness; something that has inherent, and radical, and necessary vitality.

This we have and hold, if an act of the Living Will strike it through all the symbolic framework, and quicken it into a bodily organ of its own spiritual energy. Now, that which was a symbol becomes a living thing. Its verity is within it, not elsewhere. It, and its spiritual reality, are made one; are identified, are inseparable. It is possessed by an indwelling force; it is the material of an Act of GOD.

An Act! As we pass from the language of high symbolism to the language of the Sacramental Presence, we feel that we have crossed from the world of Ideas to that of Acts. Not that ideas are not real objective, actual. But, nevertheless, this objectivity of ideas, attains its fullest and richest reality in acts. And the Gospel, let us remember, is, primarily, a revelation of Divine Acts—not of Divine Ideas. It tells of an Act done by GOD on our behalf, 'not in word but in power.' And all its dispensation is a series of acts operated upon us, and in us. GOD arrives and works; and this is the whole life of grace. Our part lies solely in the effort to admit GOD to do HIS work; and the effort is Faith.

Now, it is here, through this belief in the Eucharist as an Act, that we naturally use about it language which sounds cramping, materialistic, narrow, to those who are still moving in a world of Ideas. For Acts—acts of will—do not suffer, like Ideas, from being localized, fixed, limited. On the contrary, these terms are congenial to the acts of will, as we know them. The will rejoices to embody itself in temporal external deeds. They are a sheer gain to it. They are limited of course; but what the will loses in limitation, it gains in intensity and concentration. A truthful man gains something by the opportunities given him of telling the truth. Not that his truthfulness is confined to these limited occasions; it exists, in continuity, as a quality of his permanent character; but it realizes itself in separate acts of truth. They carry it forward; they embody it; they establish it; they win for it vivid and solid actuality.

The contrast, therefore, between the universal and the local, between the inner meaning and the outer representation—a contrast so significant in the region of ideas—ceases to have any importance when we come to acts of will. A will realises itself in acts; it is its nature, its freedom to externalize itself—to fling itself out in particular moments of actuality. And the Eucharist is for us, above all things, an Act—an Act done into us by the personal Will of GOD. It is right for it therefore, to happen here and now—to take place at a distinct time, in a definite spot. We should expect this of it. Such action does not deny, or ignore the wider, more continuous, pervading action of the Will of GOD upon us. Rather, it rests upon this; it pre-supposes this. GOD has brought us within HIS embracing Presence already. We could not approach the Eucharist, unless we were within that Presence. We can only come as members of HIS Kingdom, as redeemed in HIS Love. This is taken for granted. We exist in GOD's Presence, Who is at all times and in all places. And, now, on the top of that, by the aid of that, supported and assisted by that, HE opens to us a yet nearer approach; HE puts out upon us a fresh act of will; HE enters in and sups with us; HE uses HIS persuasive Presence as the means of a new arrival. Not only are we within HIS embrace but we may take, and eat, and drink, of that which HE gives, which is HIMSELF.

To say that this narrows down the wider love by localising it seems to us like saying that a truthful man narrows down his native quality by telling a particular truth; as if his virtue lost something by being limited to a temporary act. The self-realization of himself in a definite act is sheer gain to his inner motive. It wins for it momentum—security—force. So, to our belief, the wide love of God goes forward a step; gains more secure possession; intensifies its momentum, by the opportunity of realization in a positive, and temporal, Act of Grace. It wins its advance by so narrowing itself down, by so drawing together all its vital energies into a concentrated moment of heightened intensity. High in Heaven, the tremendous action of the Eternal Sacrifice for ever proceeds; and, here on earth, that action strikes through our earthly crust in the flash of the will that makes. Here, on that altar, an Act of GOD is done; in the midst of the congregation, it is enacted. It is present among us, real, living, actual, as a flame that burns. It is spiritual; for the will is spiritual. It is objective; for a will is a positive force. There it is; and our part is to bring ourselves into contact with it. 'If we but touch, though it be but the hem of HIS garment, we shall be whole.'

All this line of thinking repeats and corroborates itself, as we recall that it is the Body and Blood—the Humanity—of the REDEEMER that is the peculiar characteristic of the Life given through the Sacrament. Here, again, we have language which entitles us to look for its arrival through a positive, objective, formal, outward material, quickened to become its active organ. We cannot be put off by the taunt that the terms are temporal and local; for these are essential to the conception of Body.

And, far from these terms representing a lapse from the wider conception of Spirit, it is the Spirit itself with which we are first endowed through Baptism and Confirmation, which, now, in the uplifting arm of its spiritual energy, encourages us to go forward, and to close with this richest, highest, and most intense act of communion, realized through the power of the risen Body. This is the very purpose for which body exists—to realize, to complete, to effect, to sum up, to actualise, to intensify the communion for which the Spirit aspires. Spirit quickens; body attains. Spirit moves; body consummates. This is the law of our humanity; and it is to our humanity that the Eucharist appeals.

Body becomes, then, not a spiritual hindrance, but a spiritual gain. The Spirit in man as we know him has not arrived at its crown—its fulness—until it has objectively realized itself through the body. In stooping to the narrower limitations, it wins for itself a fuller satisfaction—a more perfect significance—a deeper joy. (3)

NOTES / SOURCES

1. H. S. Holland, *Creed and Character: Sermons by the Rev. H. S. Holland*, London, 1887, pp. 115–6
2. H. S. Holland in *Lux Mundi: A series of studies in the Religion of the Incarnation*, Charles Gore, ed. London, 1889, pp. 51–3
3. H. S. Holland, *Scott Holland's Goodwill: A reprint of Canon Holland's Articles in 'Goodwill'*, James Adderley, ed. London, 1905, pp. 118–23

A. S. Appasamy Pillai   1848–1927

Appasamy Pillai was brought up in an orthodox Hindu family in Tirunelveli, South India. He was converted to Christianity and became an Anglican through the influence of the poet Krishna Pillai (q.v.). A lawyer by profession, and legal adviser to the maharaja, he gave this up in his early fifties to pursue evangelistic work. In the course of this, he rediscovered his Hindu heritage, particularly the Rig Veda and Advaitic Yoga, and this represented for him, now in alliance with his Christian faith, a 'promised land'.

The Mystical Christ

Twelve years ago . . . I was led to the guru who opened the way to the promised land of which I was in search. He tried to ascertain in the usual manner whether I was fit for the life of contemplation and for the ceremony of initiation. After he had satisfied himself on this point, he sought to create in me a desire to see God, and to realize the Holy Spirit and the many gifts that He alone could give. As a convinced Christian of long standing I tried on my part to persuade him to be a Christian and to receive the rite of baptism. He is a believer in Christ and said that the baptism I spoke of was merely baptism with water referred to by John in his Gospel. There was a higher baptism, i.e., baptism with fire and the Holy Spirit and he had received such baptism from the guru who had initiated him. He further said he knew the Holy Ghost and could lead me to Him. I then became anxious for the gift of the Spirit and prayed earnestly that the same might be granted to me. I was with this teacher for three months, incessantly engaged on studying the Holy Scriptures with special reference to the Spirit and discussing with him its various manifestations as reported in the Bible.

Then one night when I was alone by myself, filled with enthusiasm, I saw a blazing light in the room, filling the place with glory. This vision lasted for some minutes and I was enchanted by it. At the same time the guru, who was in an adjacent room, saw the anointing of a person, which meant to him permission to initiate me. When we met the next morning, I told him what I had seen and he found that I had obtained what we were both praying for. From that day on I called him my 'brother in the Lord' and said that spiritually our relation was that of brothers, the same as the relation of Ananias to St Paul when the former opened his eyes after a season of darkness.

Soon after this I was initiated, the ceremony consisting of his pointing out something for me to see and my seeing it. We met for the purpose in a quiet corner of nature, smiling with green grass. A smooth green lawn is said to be favourable for the reflection of the glory we are to see. In support he quoted the passages in the Bible relating to the green pastures to which the Lord leads His sheep and to John lifting up his eyes in the green plains of Jordan to see Jesus. He asked me to look at the place to which he pointed and to behold something. I, alas, could see nothing! I prayed then earnestly for some while that I should be permitted to see and pleaded the promise in the Bible! 'If ye then being evil know how to give good gifts unto your children, how much more shall your heavenly father give the Holy Spirit to them that ask him.' Then I saw some brightness upon the green fields. He said that henceforth his function was finished and the Spirit itself would lead me to penetrate into all truth and all mysteries and make me grow in power and vision. It was surprising that I did not see things exactly as he saw and described them to me.

My next experience took me a step further. It occurred one midnight after some months. There was a small lamp burning in the room. I was gazing on it intently. The light suddenly seemed to grow big and become a great blaze of light which filled the entire room. In the midst of the blaze I saw a ruddy golden figure answering to the description given in the first chapter of Revelation: 'I saw one like unto the son of man clothed with a garment to the foot and girt about with a golden girdle.' It was a dazzling and enchanting sight which was ravishing in its delight. It lasted quite a long time till I fell asleep. From the next morning on, whenever I engage in the prayer of contemplation I see the same figure. It seemed to develop and become more distinct little by little, the final form being that which I now steadily see for some years, viz., that full figure of Christ with a golden form and crown.

Then later on, I do not now remember how much later, I saw additional figures. First, the figure of the Father on the left side of Christ, with a cord connecting the two figures. The Father, however, has not any image or bodily appearance. Then a little later, on the left side of the Father was seen the Holy Spirit with a cord again connecting Him with the Father. His appearance was rather hazy and undeveloped and was not in human form. (1)

God Speaks Directly to the Soul

God speaks through the Bible, and also directly soul to soul. Men who are filled with an eager desire to see Him and wait in prayer will see Him. And Yoga, which according to some scholars means union, has been to me the type of prayer in which God has revealed Himself to me. The Yoga of the Advaita Vedantin is based on the conviction that God and the human soul are one. I practise this Yoga, though I do not maintain that God and man are entirely one. Men have a share in the Divine nature . . . They are children of God, possessing some of His qualities, though in a very small measure. With this belief, I practise Advaitic Yoga and I behold God as pure Light. He has no form; He appears to me in His primeval and original condition as Light, before the Son and the Holy Ghost came forth. When I practise another type of Yoga, resting on the belief that God and man are different, I see the Christ appear before me in His *suksma sarira* (spiritual body) of dazzling 'glory.' Vedantic friends tell me that it is idolatry to see God endowed with a form. I do not think so. I firmly believe that to satisfy the longing of men to see Him, Christ appears in His *suksma sarira* and lets them have their fill of gazing at its 'glory' and radiance. Often the prayers of Christians are mere words. But the prayer of saintly Hindus as well as of Christian mystics is meditation or contemplation as taught by Yogins. I have not given up the private devotions and family prayers which Christians generally use but add to them daily this contemplative prayer; the latter, however, is more dear to me. (2)

Christ the Supreme Guru

The inner experiences of Yoga are not always divulged. The importance to be attached to visions does not, however, lead to the inference that all Christians should see visions, and that those who do not see visions have not attained the summit of Christian experience: the gifts of the Spirit are diverse and men are summoned by God to minister in His Kingdom in diverse ways. Even men, who have what might appear to our understanding as elementary Christian gifts, are probably quite important to the Kingdom. A knowledge of the alphabet is never to be despised, for it is the first step on the road that leads gradually, stage by stage, to the highest learning.

A great many Christians do not see God, not because they cannot, but because they will not. It is the heritage of all Christians. The trouble is with themselves. They do not claim it. Just as some men can work out a knotty mathematical problem by themselves, and others need a tutor to help them, so some men attain to this deep experience by a natural capacity, stimulated by meditation, prayer and asceticism, or by persistent, almost dogged, resolution to make themselves worthy of this great gift of the Spirit, whereas others reach this experience with the help of a human guru. To both classes alike, Christ is the supreme Guru, in the first instance. The mystic rite of initiation is administered by Him, not in an explicit human ceremony, but often in an awakening of the Spirit whose movements are as mysterious as those of the wind. In thus enjoying visions and allowing ourselves to be largely influenced by them in the understanding, in the judgement, and in action, we need not, however, despise reason.

Reason is a God-given gift and should be fully exercised. When difficult problems arise, we should endeavour to reason and to come to a conclusion. Faithfully and earnestly must we seek to make clear to ourselves the issues to be decided and the considerations that can be urged on either side. But, when we reach the point where we find ourselves helpless, then we may resort to the prayer of contemplation. In contemplation, reason ceases to function, but problems solve themselves naturally: the decision we are unable to reach in the normal human way by processes of thought become quite clear to us.

It may be asked what effect the practice of Yoga has on other spiritual exercises like vocal prayer and participation in Holy Communion. The practice of ineffable communion with Christ in contemplative prayer tends to reduce to its minimum the element of petition in prayer. We are inclined to ask for less and less as we grow in the life of contemplation. While the necessity for vocal prayer more or less ceases at least as far as the individual is concerned, its necessity still remains as long as he continues to have fellowship with others in the life of prayer. If we want to unite with others in prayer, vocal prayer is almost necessary, for not many are in the habit of engaging in the corporate prayer that dispenses with words. Whenever possible, I partake of the Eucharist; on one critical occasion I took it every morning. Even though I do not now partake of the Eucharist every day, I remember the Lord's death in my morning meal. As I eat, I do so with the words of our Lord. 'This is my body which is given for you.' And as I drink, I do so with the thought: 'This is my blood of the New Testament which is shed for many.' (3)

NOTES / SOURCES

1. A. S. Appasamy Pillai, *The Use of Yoga in Prayer*, Madras, 1926
2. Quoted by his son A. J. Appasamy in *An Indian Interpretation of Christianity*, Madras, 1924
3. A. S. Appasamy Pillai, *The Use of Yoga in Prayer*, Madras, 1926

Robert William Radclyffe Dolling   1851–1902

A notable Anglo-Catholic missioner and 'slum priest', Robert Dolling, a nephew of William Alexander, Archbishop of Armagh, was influenced by Arthur Stanton of St Alban's, Holborn. In 1885 he was put in charge of St Agatha's, Landport, in Portsmouth, and had a notable ministry there for ten years. From 1898 until his death he was Vicar of St Saviour's, Poplar, in the East End of London. He had a significant influence on the development of the Roman Catholic 'modernist' George Tyrrell.

The Political Dimension of Christian Faith

I feel an interest in politics, and express that interest, first of all, because I am a Christian, and, secondly, because I am an Englishman. There was a day, you know, when in a large measure the Church of God exercised a mighty influence by speaking the truth upon political subjects. If you take, for instance, the Old Testament, you will find that in the Book of Psalms, which are, I suppose, the part of the Old Testament most read by modern Christians, the chief idea which underlies large parts of that wonderful collection is the right of the poor to be heard alike by God and man in all their needs and necessities, and to gain the redress of their wrongs. If you go farther into the Old Testament, and take the lives of God's prophets and their words, you will find that, as a rule, they were essentially political and social reformers, speaking with the authority of the voice of God, and under the influence of a power which carried them into the palaces of kings and made their voice heard throughout the land of Israel, and even penetrated into the countries which were brought in contact with their own nation. You find these inspired men of God having one single purpose, and that was to preach the God of Justice, a purpose the execution of which involved a most vigorous onslaught on every kind of oppression and on every species of wrong.

In fact, I suppose there has never been gathered together in any volume such magnificent statements of the rights of the weak and the helpless as you will find in almost every one of the writings of the prophets of the Old Testament.

Then you must remember that these are but the forerunners of Jesus Christ, that He is Himself the gatherer up of all that the psalmists sung, of all that the prophets foretold, and therefore you may expect to find in Him also the Champion of the weak and oppressed, and something more than that—the One who preached with a voice which is still sounding throughout the world the royalty of every single man, who revealed to man His Divine origin, and showed not merely God's unceasing care for humanity, but God's desire that by his own actions, by using the powers which He had given him, that man should be lifted up even to the very highest of all ideals, that there should be no altitude of virtue or intelligence that it should not be possible for man to attain to, if he were but true to the power which God had placed in his soul. Looking round on the world, Christ discovered that there were those who had, as it were, absorbed or monopolised these human rights, and rendered well-nigh impossible the development of man, and who had by that very monopoly denied to him the possibility of his attainment to the ideal which God had willed for him. Therefore the voice of Christ, whether it speaks from Galilee or whether it speaks in the courts of the temple, sounds and resounds to-day, and it shall never cease to re-echo as long as the world has Christianity existing in its midst. It bids a man not merely to be free in the sense in which human laws could give freedom—that is, to be free from the bondage or the oppression with which the cruelty of others had bound him—but to be free in a much higher and truer sense, that he may reach the stature which our Lord Himself foresaw for him when He made him in the Divine Image. And if there be in any country in which men live any custom, any privilege of others which denies to men this opportunity, the Christian, be he priest or be he layman, must never cease raising his voice until such restriction is removed, until such privilege has been abolished, and the man is able in the fulness of his Manhood to realise God's eternal Will for him. (1)

The Blessed Sacrament the Foundation of Christian Life and Ministry

I hope through all this description of social work at Landport, Winchester, Oxford, and elsewhere, you have been able to read a deeper truth than mere Socialism even at its best. The lesson which is the foundation of all work like ours is that, however earnestly you may strive to change circumstances, you must realise that change of character is the thing to be aimed at, and practically if you do not achieve this, you have hardly achieved anything at all. And I know but one method by which this change of character can be effected, the method of Jesus Christ, not merely to show to people the perfection and beauty of His character—that often-times might lead only to despair—but to enable them, by the means which He Himself has ordained, to be partakers of His very nature. To say to the poor sin-ruled creature, whom you know all his old companions, every public-house door as it swings open, will allure into the ways of sin again, 'Be like Jesus, be good,' is only making a demand that you yourself know can never be fulfilled. But to be able to say to him, 'Here is this Jesus, Who for your sake became a real man, as you are a man, Who worked in the carpenter's shop, earning, with the sweat of His brow, daily bread for Himself, His dear mother, and her husband, Who was disappointed and injured by His friends as well as by His enemies, Who was really tempted by the devil, Whose life in many respects was just like your own, Who never turned away His face from any poor wretched outcast, but spoke to them tenderly and gently words of love and hope, Who when He could do no more for you by way of example, willed to die for you: having nothing else to give, He gave His own life-blood, and in the giving of that, won for you a power of union with Himself, that though you must do your part, and be sorry for your sins, and try to be better, He will as surely do His part by letting His precious blood wash away your sin, and strengthen you to live an amended life. Here is this Jesus standing as it were between the living and the dead, so few, few living, so many, many dead, dead with a death more terrible far than the worm and corruption can effect, for they but touch the outward covering of a man, with a death which has destroyed the real life, the knowledge that God was their Father, that they had souls capable of everything that was beautiful and true. Here is Jesus, Who can give even to the clumsy vulgar body the power of doing gracious acts, of speaking true words, Who can give to the intellect the power of realising true noble ideals, and so assimilating them, that they may become a very fibre of their thoughts. In almost all our people there was this death, this living, hopeless, faithless death. Who could deliver them from the body of this death? One Who could restore to them faith in the supernatural, hope in themselves, love towards their fellow-men. No preaching can do this. I believe nothing can but the Blessed Sacrament. The compassion, which Jesus learned in the trials of His life, taught Him to realise that man, if he is to be touched, must be touched in his entirety, that an attempt to deal with him spiritually alone is bound to fail. How Christ-destroying is all that theology that tries to be wiser and more spiritual than the Christ! The Blessed Sacrament is not only the prolongation of the Incarnation in the world, but it is a means by which Jesus wills that He shall be apprehended by the multitude. And so ten and a half years ago I set before myself this as the method of my ministry. Some I know make the Blessed Sacrament the crown of their religion. I desired to make it the foundation as well. As the Incarnation is the revelation to us of God the Father, so the Divine Son wills to be known in the breaking of bread. (2)

NOTES / SOURCES

1. C. E. Osborne, *The Life of Father Dolling*, London, 1903, pp. 131–2
2. Robert R. Dolling, *Ten Years in a Portsmouth Slum*, London, 1903, pp. 198–200

Francis Paget   1851–1911

Francis Paget spent his entire ministry in Oxford, apart from a brief interlude as Vicar of Bromsgrove. A student of Christ Church, then Professor of Pastoral Theology and Dean of Christ Church (1892–1901), he was Bishop of Oxford from 1901 to 1911. A contributor to *Lux Mundi* (1889) he revised John Keble's edition of Richard Hooker. His *Spirit of Discipline* was a significant contribution to Anglican spiritual writing.

Accidie—Spiritual Depression

'The sorrow of the world.' No discipline or chastening of the soul; no grief that looks towards God, or gropes after His presence in the mystery of pain; no anguish that even through the darkness—aye, even, it may be, through the passing storms of bitterness and impatience—He can use and sanctify, for the deepening of character, the softening of strength, the growth of light and peace. No, none of these; but a sorrow that is only of this world, that hangs in the low and misty air—a wilful sorrow that men make or cherish for themselves, being, as Shakespeare says, 'as sad as night only for wantonness.' This is, surely, the inner character of 'the sorrow of the world.' This makes its essential contrast with the sorrow that could be Divine; the sorrow that Christ shared and knows and blesses; the grief with which He was acquainted. This is the sorrow that worketh death; the sorrow that the great poet of the things unseen sets close by anger. Let us try to think about it for a little while.

The sin whose final issue, in those who wholly yield their souls to it, with utter hardness and impenitence, Dante depicts in the passage which I have quoted —the sin whose expiation, in those who can be cleansed from it, he describes in the eighteenth canto of the 'Purgatorio'—was known in his day, and had been known through many centuries of human experience, by a name in frequent use and well understood. It was ranged, by writers on Christian ethics, on the same level with such sins as hatred, envy, discord; with pride, anger, and vainglory; it would be recalled in self-examination by any one who was taking pains to amend his life and cleanse his heart; it was known as prominent and cruel among a man's assailants in the spiritual combat. Through all the changeful course of history, nothing, I suppose, has changed so little as the conditions and issues of that combat. And yet now the mention of this sin may sound strange, if not unintelligible, to many of us; so that it seems at first as though it might belong essentially to those bygone days when men watched and fought and prayed so earnestly against it; and there is no one word, I think, which will perfectly express its name in modern English. But we know that the devil has no shrewder trick than to sham dead; and so I venture to believe that it may be worth while to look somewhat more closely at a temptation which seems to be now so much less feared than once it was.

I. The sin of 'acedia,' or, according to the somewhat misleading form which the word assumed in English, 'accidie,' had, before Dante's time, received many definitions; and while they agree in the main, their differences in detail show that the evil was felt to be subtle and complex. As one compares the various estimates of the sin, one can mark three main elements which help to make it what it is—elements which can be distinguished, though in experience, I think, they almost always tend to meet and mingle; they are *gloom* and *sloth* and *irritation.* The first and third of the three seem foremost in Dante's thoughts about the doom of accidie; the second comes to the front when he is thinking how the penitent may be cleansed from it in the intermediate state. Gloom and sloth—a sullen, heavy, dreary mist about the heart, chilling and darkening it, till the least thing may make it fretful and angry;—such was the misery of the 'accidiosus.' So one Father is quoted as defining the sin to be 'fastidium interni boni'—'a distaste for the soul's good;' another calls it 'a languid dejection of body and soul about the praiseworthy exercise of virtues;' and another, 'a sluggishness of the mind that cares not to set about good works, nor to keep them up.' And so, too, in later times, it was said to be 'a certain sadness which weighs down the spirit of man in such wise that there is nothing that he likes to do;' or 'a sadness of the mind which weighs upon the spirit, so that the person conceives no will towards well-doing, but rather feels it irksome.' So Chaucer also, 'Accidie or slouth maketh a man hevy, thoughtful, and wrawe. Envie and ire make bitterness in heart, which bitterness is mother of accidie, and benimeth [or taketh away] the love of all goodness: than is accidie the anguish of a trouble heart. . . . Of accidie cometh first that a man is annoyed and encumbered for to do any goodness. . . . For accidie loveth no besinesse at all.' Lastly, let me cite two writers who speak more fully of the character and signs and outcome of the sin.

The first is Cassian, who naturally has a great deal to say about it. For all the conditions of a hermit's life, the solitude, the sameness, the austerity the brooding introspection, in which he lived, made it likely and common that this should be his besetting sin; and Cassian had marked it as such during the years he spent among the solitaries of the Egyptian deserts. In that book of his 'Institutes' which he devotes to it, he defines it as a weariness or anxiety of heart, a fierce and frequent foe to those who dwell in solitude; and elsewhere he speaks of it as a sin that comes with no external occasion, and often and most bitterly harasses those who live apart from their fellow-men. There is something of humour and something of pathos in the vivid picture which he draws of the hermit who is yielding to accidie: how utterly all charm and reality fade for him out of the life that he has chosen—the life of ceaseless prayer and contemplation of the Divine Beauty; how he hates his lonely cell, and all that he has to do there; how hard, disparaging thoughts of others, who live near him, crowd into his mind; how he idles and grumbles till the dull gloom settles down over heart and mind, and all spiritual energy dies away in him.

It is a curious and truthful-seeming sketch, presenting certain traits which, across all the vast diversity of circumstance, may perhaps claim kindred with temptations such as some of us even now may know.

But of far deeper interest, of surer and wider value, is the treatment of acedia by St Thomas Aquinas. The very place which it holds in the scheme of his great work reveals at once its true character, the secret of its harmfulness, its essential antagonism to the Christian life, and the means by resisting and conquering it.—'The fruit of the Spirit,' wrote St Paul to the Galatians, 'is love, joy, peace.' And so Aquinas has been speaking of love, joy, peace, and pity, as the first effects upon the inner life of that *caritas* which is the form, the root, the mother, of all virtues. *Caritas*, that true friendship of man with God; that all-embracing gift which is the fulfilling of the Law; that 'one inward principle of life,' as it has been called, 'adequate in its fulness to meet and embrace the range of duties which externally confront it;'—*caritas*, which is in fact nothing else but 'the energy and the representative of the Spirit in our hearts,' expands and asserts itself, and makes its power to be known by its fruits of love, joy, peace, and pity in the character of man. Mark, then, how joy springs out at once as the unfailing token of the Holy Spirit's presence, the first sign that He is having His Own way with a man's heart. The joy of the Lord, the joy that is strength, the joy that no man taketh from us, the joy wherewith we joy before God, the abundant joy of faith and hope and love and praise,—this it is that gathers like a radiant, fostering, cheering air around the soul that yields itself to the grace of God, to do His holy, loving Will.—But, over against that joy, different as winter from summer, as night from day, ay, even as death from life, looms the dreary, joyless, thankless, fruitless gloom of sullenness, the sour sorrow of the world, the sin of accidie; that wanton, wilful self-distressing that numbs all love and zeal for good; that sickly, morbid weariness in which the soul abhors all manner of meat, and is even hard at death's door; that woful lovelessness in which all upward longing fails out of the heart and will—the sin that is opposed to the joy of love. So St Thomas speaks of accidie, and so he brings it near, surely, to the conscience of many men in every age.

II. Yes, let us put together in thought the traits which meet in the picture of accidie; let us think of it in its contrast with that brightness of spiritual joy which plays around some lives, and makes the nameless, winning beauty of some souls—ay, and even of some faces—and we may recognize it, perhaps, as a cloud that has sometimes lowered near our own lives; as a storm that we have seen sweeping across the sky and hiding the horizon, even though, it may be, by God's grace only the edge of it reached to us—only a few drops fell where we were. Heaviness, gloom, coldness, sullenness, distaste and desultory sloth in work and prayer, joylessness and thanklessness,—do we not know something of the threatenings, at least, of a mood in which these meet? The mood of days on which it seems as though we cannot genuinely laugh, as though we cannot get rid of a dull or acrid tone in our voice; when it seems impossible frankly to 'rejoice with them that do rejoice,' and equally impossible to go freely out in any true, unselfish sympathy with sorrow; days when, as one has said, 'everything that everybody does seem inopportune and out of good taste;' days when the things that are true and honest, just and pure, lovely and of good report, seem to have lost all loveliness and glow and charm of hue, and look as dismal as a flat country in the drizzling mist of an east wind; days when we might be cynical if we had a little more energy in us; when all enthusiasm and confidence of hope, all sense of a Divine impulse, flags out of our work; when the schemes which we have begun look stale and poor and unattractive as the scenery of an empty stage by daylight; days when there is nothing that we *like* to do—when, without anything to complain of, nothing stirs so readily in us as complaint. Oh, if we know anything at all of such a mood as this, let us be careful how we think of it, how we deal with it; for perhaps it may not be far from that 'sorrow of the world' which, in those who willingly indulge and welcome and invite its presence, 'worketh death.'

III. It occurs to one at once that this misery of accidie lies on the border-line between the physical and the spiritual life; that if there is something to be said of it as a sin, there is also something to be said of it as an ailment. It is a truth that was recognized long ago both by Cassian and by St Thomas Aquinas, who expressly discusses and dismisses this objection against regarding accidie as a sin at all.[1] Undoubtedly physical conditions of temperament and constitution, of

[1] S. Th. 2da 2^{dae}, xxxv. 1, ad 2^{dum}.

weakness, illness, harassing, weariness, overwork, may give at times to such a mood of mind and heart a strange power against us; at times the forces for resistance may seem frail and few. It is a truth which should make us endlessly charitable, endlessly forbearing and considerate and uncritical towards others; but surely it is a truth that we had better be shy of using for ourselves. It will do us no harm to over-estimate the degree in which our own gloom and sullenness are voluntary; it will do us very great harm to get into the way of exaggerating whatever there may be in them that is physical and involuntary. For the border-line over which accidie hovers is, practically, a shifting and uncertain line, and 'possunt quia posse videntur' may be true of the powers upon either side of it. We need not bring speculative questions out of their proper place to confuse the distinctness of the practical issue. We have ample warrant, by manifold evidence, by clear experience, for being sure for ourselves that the worth and happiness of life depend just on this—that in the strength which God gives, and in the eagerness of His service, the will should ever be extending the range of its dominion, ever refusing to be shut out or overborne, ever restless in defeat, ever pushing on its frontier. Surely it has been the secret of some of the highest, noblest lives that have helped the world, that men have refused to make allowances for themselves; refused to limit their aspiration and effort by the disadvantages with which they started; refused to take the easy tasks which their hindrances might seem to justify, or to draw premature boundaries for the power of their will. As there are some men to whom the things that should have been for their wealth are, indeed, an occasion of falling, so are there others to whom the things that might have been for their hindrance are an occasion of rising; 'who going through the vale of misery use it for a well, and the pools are filled with water.'—And 'they shall go from strength to strength'—in all things more than conquerors through Him Who loveth them; wresting out of the very difficulties of life a more acceptable and glorious sacrifice to lift to Him; welcoming and sanctifying the very hindrances that beset them as the conditions of that part which they, perhaps, alone can bear in the perfecting of His saints, in the edifying of the body of Christ. And in that day when every man's work shall be made manifest, it may be found, perhaps, that none have done Him better service than some of those who, all through this life, have been His ambassadors in bonds.

NOTES / SOURCES

The Spirit of Discipline: Sermons preached by Francis Paget, London, 1891, pp. 52–63

Charles Gore 1853–1932

An aristocratically connected High Churchman, Charles Gore was the first Principal of Pusey House, Oxford. Editor of and contributor to *Lux Mundi* (1889), Gore's espousal of the doctrine of *kenosis* in relation to Christ's knowledge in the incarnation disturbed many conservative theologians. A founder of the Community of the Resurrection, he was consecrated Bishop of Worcester in 1902 and was subsequently (1905) first Bishop of Birmingham and finally of Oxford (1911–1919). A forceful and prophetic character, he was a strong supporter of the Christian Social Union.

The Personal Spiritual Struggle

The ethics of Christianity are, as has appeared, social ethics, the ethics of a society organized in mutual relationships: and Christianity is concerned with the whole life of man, body as well as soul, his commerce and his politics as well as his religion. But because this requires to be made emphatic, does it follow that we are to neglect or depreciate the inward, personal, spiritual struggle? Are we to give a reduced, because we give a better balanced, importance to 'saving one's own soul,' that is preserving or recovering into its full power and supremacy one's own spiritual personality? Of course not: because social health depends on personal character. The more a good man throws himself into social, including ecclesiastical, duties the more he feels the need of character in himself and others. And the more serious a man is about his character, the more deeply he feels the attention and self-discipline that character needs. Certainly the most ascetic words of our Lord—those in which He speaks of the necessity for cutting off or plucking out hand or eye if hand or eye cause us to stumble, and warns us that we must be strong at the spiritual centre of our being, before we can be free in exterior action—are likely to come home to no one with more force than to one who would do his duty in Church or state. Christ cannot redeem the world without Himself passing through the temptation and the agony in the garden. And thus St Paul, after he has been dwelling on the fraternal and corporate character of the Christian life, comes back at the last to emphasize the personal spiritual struggle. To be a good member of the body, he says in effect, you must be in personal character a strong man, strong enough in Christ's might to win the victory in a fearful struggle.

Against what is our spiritual struggle? It is against the weakness and lawlessness of our own flesh. 'The spirit is willing, but the flesh is weak.' 'Our eye and hand and foot cause us to stumble.' Or again it is the world which is too much for us. 'We seek honour one of another and not the glory that cometh from the only God.' Quite true. But behind the manifest disorder of our nature and the insistence of worldly motives there are other less apparent forces; and these, in St Paul's mind, so overshadow the more visible and tangible ones that, in the Biblical manner of speech, he denies for the moment the reality of the latter. 'We wrestle not against flesh and blood,' not against our own flesh or a visibly corrupt public, but against an unseen spiritual host organized for evil.

It was noticed above that St Paul has no doubt at all that moral evil has its origin and spring in the dark background behind human nature—in the rebel wills of devils. It has become customary to regard belief in devils or angels as fanciful and perhaps superstitious. Now no doubt theological and popular fancy has intruded itself into the things it has not seen, and, instead of the studiously vague[1] language of St Paul, has developed a sort of geography and ethnology for spirits good and bad which is mythological and allied to superstition. But it has acted in the same way, and shown the same resentment of the discipline of ignorance, in the case of even more central spiritual realities. No doubt again the belief in the devil has sometimes become, in practical force, belief in a rival God. But this sort of Manichaeism or dualism represents a very permanent tendency in

---

[1] Col. i. 16.

the untrained religious instincts of men, which the Bible is occupied in restraining. In the Bible certainly Satan and his hosts are rebel angels and not rival Gods. Once more undoubtedly demonology has been a source of much misery and many degrading practices. But demonology represents a natural religious instinct. It is older than the Bible. And what our religion has done, where it has been true to itself, is to purge away the noxious and non-moral superstitions. St Paul is representative of true Christianity in his stern refusal to use the services of contemporary soothsaying and magic and sorcery.[1] One has only to compare the exorcisms of our Lord with contemporary Jewish exorcism to note the moral difference. And every truth has its exaggeration and its abuse. The question still remains; are there no spiritual beings but men? Is there no moral evil, but in the human heart? Our Lord gives the most emphatic negative answer. His teaching about evil (and good) spirits is unmistakable and constant. If He is an absolutely trustworthy teacher in the spiritual concerns of life, then temptation from evil spirits is a reality, and a reality to be held constantly in view. And our Lord's authority is confirmed by our own experiences. Sometimes experience irresistibly suggests to us the presence of unseen bad companions who can make vivid suggestions to our minds. Or we are impressed like St Paul with the delusive, lying character of evil, which makes the belief in a malevolent will almost inevitable. Or the continuity in evil influences, social or personal, seems to disclose to us an organized plan or 'method,'[2] a kingdom of evil.

It is then in view of unseen but personal spiritual adversaries organized against us as armies, under leaders who have at their control wide-reaching social forces of evil, and who intrude themselves into the highest spiritual regions 'the heavenly places' to which in their own nature they belong, that St Paul would have us equip ourselves for fighting in 'the armour of light.'[3]

If there is a spiritual battle, armour defensive and offensive becomes a natural metaphor which St Paul frequently uses.[4] But in his imprisonment he must have become specially habituated to the armour of Roman soldiers, and here, as it were, he makes a spiritual meditation on the pieces of the 'panoply' which were continually under his observation.

We are, then, to 'take up' or 'put on' the panoply or whole armour of God. This means more than the armour which God supplies. It is probably like 'the righteousness of God,' something which is not only a gift of God, but a gift of His own self. Our righteousness is Christ, and He is our armour. Christ, the 'stronger man,' who overthrew 'the strong man armed' in His own person,[5] and 'took away from him his panoply in which he trusted,' is to be our defence. And by no external protection; we are to clothe ourselves in His nature, to put Him on as our armour. His is the strength in which we are, like Him, to come triumphant through the hour of darkness.

Now the parts of the armour, the elements of Christ's unconquerable moral strength, what are they?

The belt which keeps all else in its place is for the Christian, truth—that is,

[1] Acts xiii. 6–12; xvi. 16–18; xix. 13–20.
[2] This is akin to St Paul's word in the Greek, Eph. iv. 14; vi. 11.   [3] Rom. xiii. 12.
[4] Rom. vi. 13; xiii. 12; 2 Cor. vi. 7; x. 4; 1 Thess. v. 8. Cf. Isa. xi. 4, 5, and Wisd. v. 19.
[5] Luke xi. 21, 22.

singleness of eye or perfect sincerity—the pure and simple desire of the light. 'Unless the vessel be clean (or *sincere*),' said the old Roman proverb, 'whatever you put into it turns sour.' A lack of sincerity at the heart of the spiritual life will destroy it all. Then the breastplate which covers vital organs is, for the Christian, righteousness—the specific righteousness of Christ, St Paul seems to imply,[1] in which in its indivisible unity he is to enwrap himself. And, as the feet of the soldier must be well shod not only for protection but also to facilitate free movement on all sorts of ground, the Christian too is to be so possessed with the good tidings of peace that he is 'prepared' to move and act under all circumstances—all hesitations, and delays, and uncertainties which hinder movement gone—his feet shod with the preparedness which belongs to those who have peace at the heart. ('How beautiful upon the mountains are the feet of him that bringeth glad tidings, that publisheth peace.') In these three funda-mental dispositions—single-mindedness, whole-hearted following of Christ, readiness such as belongs to a believer in the good tidings—lies the Christian's strength. But the armour is not yet complete.

The attacks of the enemy upon the thoughts will be frequent and fiery. A constant and rapid action of the will will be necessary to protect ourselves from evil suggestions lest they obtain a lodgement. And the method of self-protection is to look continually and deliberately out of ourselves up to Christ—to appeal to Him, to invoke His name, to draw upon His strength by acts of our will. Thus faith, continually at every fresh assault looking instinctively to Christ and drawing upon His help, is to be our shield, off which the enemy's darts will glance harmless, their hurtful fire quenched. And in thus defending ourselves we must have continually in mind that God has delivered man by a great redemption.[2] It is the sense of this great salvation, the conviction of each Christian that he is among those who have been saved and are tasting this salvation, which is to cover his head from attack like a helmet.[3] And God's word—God's specific and particular utterances, through inspired prophets and psalmists— is to equip his mouth with a sword of power; as in His temptation and on the cross, Christ 'put off from Himself the principalities and powers, and made a show of them, triumphing over them openly' by the words of Holy Scripture; as Bunyan's Christian, when 'Apollyon was fetching him his last blow, nimbly stretched out his hand and caught' for his 'sword' the word of Micah, 'when I fall I shall arise.' This is one fruit of constant meditation on the words of Holy Scripture, that they recur to our minds when we most need them. And then St Paul passes from metaphor to simple speech, and for the last weapon bids the Christians use 'always' that most powerful of all spiritual weapons for themselves and others, 'prayer and supplication' of all kinds and 'in all seasons.' But it is not to be ignorant and blind prayer; it is to be prayer 'in the spirit,' 'who helpeth our infirmities, for we know not of ourselves how to pray as we ought.' 'The things of God none knoweth, save the Spirit of God';[4] and it is to be the sort of prayer about which trouble is taken, and which is persevering; and it is to be prayer for

---

[1] By the use of the articles. Contrast Is. lix. 17 which he is quoting.   [2] Isa. lix. 17.

[3] 'Salvation' is sometimes viewed as already accomplished, i.e. in the victory of Christ: sometimes as still to be realized at 'the redemption of our bodies': so in 1 Thess. v. 8 the helmet is 'the hope of salvation' yet to be attained.

[4] Rom. viii. 26; 1 Cor. ii. 11.

others as well as for themselves, 'for all the saints.' And St Paul uses the pastor's privilege, and asks for himself the support of his converts' prayers, that he may have both power of speech and courage to proclaim the good tidings of the divine secret disclosed, for which he is already suffering as a prisoner.

Finally, be strong in the Lord, and in the strength of his might. Put on the whole armour of God, that ye may be able to stand against the wiles of the devil. For our wrestling is not against flesh and blood, but against the principalities, against the powers, against the world-rulers of this darkness, against the spiritual *hosts* of wickedness in the heavenly *places*. Wherefore take up the whole armour of God, that ye may be able to withstand in the evil day, and, having done all, to stand. Stand therefore, having girded your loins with truth, and having put on the breastplate of righteousness, and having shod your feet with the preparation of the gospel of peace; withal taking up the shield of faith, wherewith ye shall be able to quench all the fiery darts of the evil *one*. And take the helmet of salvation, and the sword of the Spirit, which is the word of God: with all prayer and supplication praying at all seasons in the Spirit, and watching thereunto in all perseverance and supplication for all the saints, and on my behalf, that utterance may be given unto me in opening my mouth, to make known with boldness the mystery of the gospel, for which I am an ambassador in chains; that in it I may speak boldly, as I ought to speak.

St Paul does not only exhort Christians to pray, but he gives them abundant examples. In this epistle there are two specimens[1] of prayer for the spiritual progress of his converts, mingled with thanksgivings and praise. We habitually pray for others that they may be delivered from temporal evils, or that they may be converted from flagrant sin or unbelief. But surely we very seldom pray rich prayers, like those of St Paul's, for others' progress in spiritual apprehension. (1)

The Desire for Holiness and the Sense of Sin

. . . to interpret Christ we have to recognise even from the beginning the reality of sin, as something which appears nowhere below in nature but first in man, the rebellion of free-wills. In other words, we have to recognise—what it is hard to see how any moralist can deny—that human nature, as we have had experience of it in history, presents in great measure a scene of moral ruin, so that Christ enters not merely to consummate an order but to restore it, not to accomplish only but to redeem. He is not only 'Christus consummator' but also 'Christus redemptor.' This idea of redemption will in its turn appear natural in proportion as it is believed, faintly or decisively, that God is good, and realized on the other hand that man is sinful. The more you contemplate from a moral point of view the condition of man, the more luminously certain it becomes that the Christian view of sin is the right one, so far as that sin as we know it now, in ourselves and in the world, is lawlessness—the violation of our true nature, not its expression, the taint in our development and not simply its necessary condition. 'Our life is a false nature,' as Byron cried, ' 'tis not in the harmony of things.' Grant this, and you find it surely credible on evidence that the goodness of God should have moved Him to redemption. Thus it comes about that our readiness to believe in the Redeemer does in fact depend upon the strength of the impression made upon our minds by the sin of the world. Whatever impulse to belief may come

---

[1] Eph. i. 15 II.; iii. 14 ff.

from intellectual or aesthetic considerations, the primary force which stimulates to belief is the desire for righteousness and the sense of sin.

And here we must not fail to remind ourselves how possible it is to weaken or even to lose this desire for holiness, and this sense of sin, through diverting our faculties into other channels. It is very well known how Darwin describes his own mind as having 'become a kind of machine for grinding general laws out of large collections of facts,' with the result of producing 'atrophy of that part of the brain on which the higher tastes depend.' What is singular about this confession is probably its honesty. But we must not hesitate to recognise that a mind thus exclusively organized for physical investigation is not a mind 'disposed,' as St Luke expresses it, for eternal life. Christ would naturally seem to such a mind an alien object. What Darwin is speaking of in his own case is the atrophy of aesthetic, rather than of moral, faculty. But a similar abnormal atrophy is possible in the case of all disused faculties and in all pursuits. For example, the pursuits of the priest and pastor may tend of themselves to disqualify the mind for physical or historical enquiry. At present, however, we are concerned to notice this only: that the atrophy of a man's *moral* faculty is a probable event in certain cases. Thus literary or classical studies, intense concentration on business, exaggerated athleticism, absorption in pleasures, higher or lower, each of these may preoccupy the whole man, stunting and overgrowing the moral faculties, making the Christ seem a remote figure, the crucifix an unmeaning and disagreeable object, the vocabulary of Christianity unnecessary and unreal. But it needs only to rekindle in a man the hunger and thirst after righteousness, in himself or in the world, in order to bring Christ near to him, and to teach him to look upon His person with different eyes. Whatever in fact reawakens in him the sense of God and eternity gives him faculties to acknowledge Christ. It may be any experience which stirs the depths of his being, possibly the death of some one with whom his life was bound up, and the sense which comes with it of the fragmentariness and incompleteness of the world. It may be also something less personal to himself. For example, suppose a man to devote himself to the bettering of social conditions: suppose him so far Christian—and it is a great way on the road—as to realize that he is his brother's keeper and must go out to bear his share of the world's burden. Such an one after a few years' work will surely be impressed with the truth that, much as can be done by improved laws, improved social adjustment, improved organization, to remedy the evils under which society groans, the heart of the matter lies in character. The obstacles to progress in every class are within rather than without; they lie in jealousy, in suspicion, in self-assertion, in lust, in dishonesty, in carelessness—in a word in sin. In sin, in the omnipresent fact of sin, there is the evil. In redemption, redemption from sin, there is the central and fundamental remedy and the thing supremely needful. More and more, behind legislator, instructor, economist, agitator, there dawns upon the horizon of the true reformer, to refresh his exhausted brain, to reinvigorate his desponding heart, the true emancipator of man, his redeemer, Jesus of Nazareth, whose remedies alone are adequate to human ills, because He gauges so profoundly, so accurately the nature and seat of man's disease, because He deals with men as individual characters, and bases the regeneration of society on the conversion and renewal of men. In a word, brethren, the Son of man will seem in the highest sense natural to you in proportion as you are human, in proportion, that is, as what you are in contact with is not merely things or laws or minds but persons, not problems merely but characters. (2)

The New Life a Corporate Life

The first characteristic of the new life dwelt upon is its corporate character, as a life lived by those who are 'members one of another,' and have therefore a common aim. In a body of people working with a common aim there may be a healthy rivalry and competition in doing good work, a manifold spirit of initiation and inventiveness, and there may be rewards of labour, proportioned not merely to needs but to these personal excellences. But what there cannot be is a competition which runs to the point of mutual destructiveness, or such accumulation of the fruits of skill and labour in a few hands as maims or starves the life of the majority. The common interest prevents this. 'The members must have the same care one of another,' so that 'when one member suffers all the members suffer with it.'[1] The life is the life of a body, and the general well-being is therefore the common interest of all the members, for the weakening or decay of one is the weakening and decay of a more or less valuable part of a connected life. This is the general principle on which the Church is based. This is the moral meaning of churchmanship. 'Ye are members one of another.'

Various specific obligations follow from this general principle.

(a) *Truthfulness and openness*; for falsehood and concealment belong to a life of separated and conflicting interests. The prophetic ideal for the restored Israel is to be realized among Christians. 'Speak ye every man truth with his neighbour: execute the judgement of truth and peace in your gates: and let none of you imagine evil in your hearts against his neighbour: and love no false oath.'[2]

(b) *Self-restraint in temper*. We must not injure one another in life and limb, or wound one another in feelings. Therefore we must watch the first beginnings of anger, as the Psalmist[3] warns us, lest they lead to sin and give the devil, i.e. the slanderer of his brethren, the inspirer of all mutual recriminations, room and scope to work in.

(c) *Labour for the purpose of mutual beneficence*. Under the old covenant God had contented Himself with forbidding stealing. Under the new covenant the prohibition of what is wrong passes into the injunction of what is right. Labour of whatever kind, labour directed to produce something good, is required of all. 'If any man will not work, neither let him eat.'[4] The idle man in fact violates the fundamental conditions of the Christian covenant as truly as if he were denying the rudiments of the Christian faith. Now the object of labouring is to acquire 'property,' which is in one sense 'private,' and in another sense is not. The labourer may have, under his own free administration, the fruits of his labour, but he is to administer his property with the motive, not only of supporting himself, but of helping his weaker and more needy brethren.

(d) *Profitable speech*. Here again the Christian is not to be content with avoiding noxious conversation. His talk is to be, not indeed 'edifying' in the narrowest sense, but such as 'builds up what is lacking' in life, or supplies a need, whether by counselling, or informing, or refreshing, or cheering; so that it may

---

[1] 1 Cor. xiii. 25, 26.   [2] Zech. viii. 16, 17.

[3] Ps. iv. 4, according to the LXX. But the English version 'Stand in awe and sin not' is probably correct.

[4] 2 Thess. iii. 10.

'give grace,'[1] that is, afford pleasure and, in the widest sense, bring a blessing to the hearers.

In all their conduct Christians are to have two masterful thoughts. (1) They are to think of the divine purpose of the Holy Ghost who has entered into the Church to 'seal' or mark it as an elect body destined for full redemption from all evil, in body and soul, at the climax of God's dealings, the last day. The Holy Ghost, with all His personal love, will be grieved if we thwart His rich purpose for the whole body by anything which is contrary to brotherhood in the thoughts of our hearts, or the words of our lips, or our outward conduct.

(2) They are to remember the divine pattern of life. God has shown His own heart to us in the free forgiveness which He has given us in Christ. Being in constant receipt of that forgiveness, we must not prove ourselves hard and unforgiving towards one another.

> Wherefore, putting away falsehood, speak ye truth each one with his neighbour: for we are members one of another. Be ye angry, and sin not: let not the sun go down upon your wrath: neither give place to the devil. Let him that stole steal no more: but rather let him labour, working with his hands the thing that is good, that he may have whereof to give to him that hath need. Let no corrupt speech proceed out of your mouth, but such as is good for edifying as the need may be, that it may give grace to them that hear. And grieve not the Holy Spirit of God, in whom ye were sealed unto the day of redemption. Let all bitterness, and wrath, and anger, and clamour, and railing, be put away from you, with all malice: and be ye kind one to another, tenderhearted, forgiving each other, even as God also in Christ forgave you.

Here, then, St Paul sketches catholicity in practice. The very idea of the Church is that of a fellowship of naturally unlike individuals, harmonized into unity by the new 'truth and grace' of God, which has been made theirs in their regenerate life. It is this endowment of the regenerate life that is to enable them to transcend, and overstep, and defeat natural incompatibilities of temper, and to be one body in Christ. The practical meaning of catholicity is brotherhood. It is love, as St Augustine says, grown as wide as the world.

Why has the world lost this sense of the moral meaning of catholic churchmanship? Why has 'ecclesiastical' come to mean something quite different to 'brotherly'? Or it is a more profitable question to ask, How shall we make it mean the same thing again? There are many who would give up the very effort after recovering the church principle, the obligation of the 'one body.' But this, as has been said, is to abandon the ultimate catholic principle of Christianity. For the very purpose of the one church for all the men of faith in Jesus, is that the necessity for belonging to one body—a necessity grounded on divine appointment—shall force together into a unity men of all sorts and different kinds; and the forces of the new life which they share in common are to overcome their natural repugnance and antipathies, and to make the forbearance and love and mutual helpfulness which corporate life requires, if not easy, at least possible for them.

This is the principle which must not be abandoned. We must assert the theological principle of the Church because it is that and that alone which can impress on men practically the obligation and possibility of a catholic brotherhood.

[1] Cf. Col. iv. 6: 'Let your speech be always with grace' or 'graciousness'; Luke iv. 22: 'gracious words'; Ps. xlv. 2: 'Grace is poured into thy lips'; Eccles. x. 12: 'The words of a wise man's mouth are gracious'; Ecclus. xxi. 16: 'Grace shall be found in the lips of the wise.'

But it is folly to assert the theological truth of churchmanship, and neglect its moral meaning. Quite recently the bishops of the Lambeth Conference have striven to impress anew the ethics of churchmanship upon the conscience of the faithful. The principle of brotherhood must act as a constant counterpoise to the instinct of competition. The principle of labour shows that the idle and selfish are 'out of place' in a Christian community. The principle of justice forces us to recognize that the true interest of each member of the body politic must be consulted. The principle of public responsibility reminds us that each one is his brother's keeper. Once more the Church has been aroused to its prophetic task of 'binding' and 'loosing' the consciences of men in regard specially to those matters which concern the corporate life and the relations of classes to one another. And we pray God that the work of our bishops may not be in vain. What we want is not more Christians, but, much rather, better Christians—that is to say, Christians who have more perception of what the moral effort required for membership in the catholic brotherhood really is.

No doubt the needed social reformation is of vast difficulty. For instance, one who contemplates our commercial relations in the world may indeed be tempted to despair of the possibility of recovering the practical application to 'business' of the law of truthfulness; and many a one who is practically engaged in commerce, in higher or lower station, finds that to act upon the law may involve something like martyrdom. But the very meaning of divine faith is that we do, in spite of all discouragements, hold that to be practicable which is the will of God; and it is nothing new in the history of Christianity if at a crisis we need 'the blood of martyrs'—or something morally equivalent to their blood—for 'a seed,' the seed of a fresh growth of Christian corporate life. No fresh start worth making is possible without personal sacrifices; and to recover anything resembling St Paul's ethical standard for Christian society we need indeed a fresh start. But the few Tractarians of sixty years ago by industry, patience and prayer effected a kind of revolution in the Church as a whole; and reformers of Christian social relations may with the same weapons—and with no other—do the like. (3)

NOTES / SOURCES

1. Charles Gore, *St Paul's Epistle to the Ephesians*, London, 1902, pp. 237–47
2. Charles Gore, *The Incarnation of the Son of God*, London, 1891, pp. 36–9
3. Charles Gore, *St Paul's Epistle to the Ephesians*, London, 1902, pp. 184–5

Thomas Alexander Lacey   1853 1931

Thomas Alexander Lacey, a Canon of Worcester Cathedral from 1918, was a strong Anglo-Catholic advocate of unity between Anglicans and Roman Catholics. He took an active part in pressing the Anglican case during the Papal Commission which examined (and condemned) Anglican orders in 1896.

Catholicity

Catholicity is not an added grace, but an inherent quality of the Christian religion. A Christian does not become Catholic; he was not baptized into anything smaller than the organic unity of the Catholic Church. But he may cease to be Catholic; he may develop flaws in his religion that will deprive him of that character; he may fall into schism. But he began well. 'Go into your infant-school,' I once heard Fr. Benson say, 'as into a community of saints.' Baptized, you were baptized into the Catholic Church, and in the Catholic Church you remain unless you are cut off. You are not Catholic because you adhere to a particularly organized community; you belong to a particularly organized community because you are a Catholic Christian. You are Catholic unless you are schismatic. What is true of you is true of others. You must acknowledge a Christian to be Catholic unless you can prove him to be schismatic. (1)

The Imperfect Realization of Holiness and Catholicity

You will not unfrequently find Catholics doing very uncatholic things; you are not therefore to deny the name of Catholic either to them or to the Church which more or less willingly tolerates them. You will find many in the Church doing unholy things, but they are not the less saints in the making, and the Church is not the less holy. Holiness and Catholicity are on the same footing, both as necessary qualities of the Church, and as qualities which are very imperfectly in evidence. The Church is One, Holy, Catholic, Apostolic. Why should you expect any one of these qualities to be more completely or more inevitably brought to fruition than the rest? In a sense all are alike inevitable, indestructible. The Church is one, for there is none other; that one Church is sanctified by the indwelling Spirit; it is indestructibly apostolic by origin and by tradition; it is of necessity Catholic in more than one of the senses which we have been considering; but the flower and fruit of all four qualities will be achieved only by those efforts of faulty fellow-workers with God, in which there is always mingled some defect of human weakness, and often some strength of human perversity. (2)

Confirmation

Confirmation is the ceremonial completion of baptism.[1] It is administered by the bishop alone, as chief pastor of the Church, in order that the admission of the baptized to the privileges of the House of God may be properly attested. It does not appear that any special gift, in addition to the gift of the new life, is conveyed by this means; the grace of confirmation is rather a strengthening of that life. The prayers used in the administration of the sacrament are our best guide to its meaning. They speak of a daily increase in the manifold gifts of grace that began with regeneration and the forgiveness of sins. These manifold gifts are evidently the powers of the new life regarded in their various manifestations, and are summarized in the seven-fold endowment of the Spirit—wisdom and under-standing, counsel and strength, knowledge, godliness, and holy fear. These are representative activities of eternal life; the bishop, confirming the baptized, prays that he may continue in the life begun, and may daily increase in the power

---

[1] This appears, in fact, to be the meaning of the word. In like manner the deacon who gave the chalice was said, in the *Ordo Romanus*, to *confirm* the people: that is to say, he completed the administration of the sacrament to them.

bestowed upon him by the Holy Ghost. The grace of confirmation, therefore, is the continuance and increase of the grace of baptism. (3)

NOTES / SOURCES

1. T. A. Lacey, *Catholicity*, London, 1914, pp. 58–9
2. Ibid., pp. 105–6
3. T. A. Lacey, *The Mysteries of Grace*, London, 1908, pp. 29–30

William Turton   1856–1938

The son of an army officer, William Turton was born in India and educated at Clifton College and the Royal Military Academy in England. He was commissioned in 1876 as a Lieutenant in the Royal Engineers. The hymn below was written for the English Church Union Anniversary Service at St Mary Magdalene's in Munster Square, London, in 1881.

O Thou, Who at Thy Eucharist Didst Pray

O Thou, who at thy Eucharist didst pray
    That all thy Church might be for ever one,
Grant us at every Eucharist to say
    With longing heart and soul, 'Thy will be done.'
Oh, may we all one Bread, one Body be,
One through this Sacrament of unity.

For all thy Church, O Lord, we intercede;
    Make thou our sad divisions soon to cease;
Draw us the nearer each to thee, we plead,
    By drawing all to thee, O Prince of Peace:
Thus may we all one Bread, one Body be,
One through this Sacrament of unity.

We pray thee too for wanderers from thy fold;
    O bring them back, good Shepherd of the sheep,
Back to the faith which saints believed of old,
    Back to the Church which still that faith doth keep:
Soon may we all one Bread, one Body be,
One through this Sacrament of unity.

So, Lord, at length when sacraments shall cease,
    May we be one with all thy Church above,
One with thy saints in one unbroken peace,
    One with thy saints in one unbounded love:
More blessèd still, in peace and love to be
One with the Trinity in Unity.

NOTES / SOURCES

New English Hymnal, Norwich, 1986, no. 302

Pandita Ramabai Sarasvati 1858–1922

Ramabai was a Brahmin in Western India. Through her father, she became a noted Sanskrit scholar, deeply versed in Hindu tradition. The influence of the Community of St Mary the Virgin at Pune, a visit to England, and a crucial correspondence with Goreh (*q.v.*) brought her to baptism. She was devoted to the welfare of Indian women, particularly to the social rehabilitation of Hindu widows, and also engaged in distinguished Bible translation work.

Hinduism and Christianity

After my visit to the Homes at Fulham, where I saw the works of mercy carried on by the Sisters of the Cross, I began to think that there was a real difference between Hinduism and Christianity. I asked the [CSMV] Sister who instructed me what it was that made the Christians care for, and reclaim the 'fallen women.' She read me the story of Christ meeting the Samaritan woman and His wonderful discourse on the nature of true worship, and explained it to me. She spoke of the infinite love of Christ for sinners. He did not despise them, but came to save them. I realized, after reading the fourth chapter of St John's Gospel, that Christ was truly the Divine Saviour He claimed to be, and no one but He could transform and uplift and downtrodden womanhood of India and of every land. (1)

At the Feet of Jesus

Some wear beads around their neck
Some place the mark of religion on the forehead
But my mind found joy
At the feet of Jesus

Some besmear their body with holy ashes
Some meditate sitting on deer-skin
But my mind found joy
At the feet of Jesus

Some worship gods and goddesses
Some go and bathe in the Holy Ganges
But my mind found joy
At the feet of Jesus

Some make penance going through the fire
I abandoned all these falsehoods
But my mind found joy
At the feet of Jesus

Oh! separation from Jesus of young and old
Means hovering over dream-land in space
But my mind found joy
At the feet of Jesus (2)

NOTES / SOURCES

1. Pandita Ramabai Sarasvati, *A Testimony*, Kedgaon, Maharashtra, 1917
2. Pandita Ramabai Sarasvati (1902), in the Hindi Hymn Book *Masihi Geet Sangrah* (no. 343) translated by S. M. Adhav in his *Pandita Ramabai*, Christian Literature Society, Madras, 1979, pp. 192–3

George Lansbury 1859–1940

Labour leader and politician, Lansbury was an East End Labour MP, whose socialism and uncompromising pacifism sprang from spiritual conviction. A non-smoker and teetotaller, he was a supporter of votes for women and a defender of conscientious objectors, as well as being a committed Anglican.

The Eucharist the Imperative of Peace

Kneeling with others at the altar of the sacraments will and can bring no real peace unless those who so kneel spend their lives as brothers and sisters, and this is quite impossible within a system of life which depends on the ability of the children of God to dispute, quarrel and fight for their daily bread.

NOTES / SOURCES

George Lansbury, *Socialism for the Poor, The End of Pauperism* (1909) in Penelope Fitzgerald, *The Knox Brothers* (Macmillan), 1978, pp. 101–2

William Ralph Inge 1860–1954

Dean of St Paul's Cathedral (1911–1934), and popularly known as 'the gloomy dean', he had strong sympathies with Platonic spirituality. His many theological and devotional writings included his 1899 Bampton Lectures, *Christian Mysticism* and 1918 Gifford Lectures, *The Philosophy of Plotinus*. A considerable stylist and provocative writer, he disliked the vulgarity of industrial competition and thought the servant problem the most pressing issue of the day.

Holiness and Righteousness

What is the difference between holiness and righteousness or moral goodness? Most lay Christians, I suppose, wish to be good, and do not exactly wish to be holy. Holiness for them means a soft kind of goodness, that sort of unworldliness which comes from ignorance of the world. Holy people, they think, constitute a sort of third sex, and they rightly believe that a good Christian man ought to remain a man and a good Christian woman a woman. They do not admire the intermediate type. This, however, is not the true idea of holiness. If we want to understand what holiness means, and has meant, in religion, we must go back to the earlier books of the Old Testament, and even to more primitive sources—and religious beliefs of barbarians—for it is one of the most rudimentary ideas of all religion. The original idea of holiness is separation; that is holy which is stamped, as it were, as belonging to God and is appropriated to Him. Holy places, things and persons, are the special property of God, or the Gods. They are set apart as sacred, and profane contact with them is fraught with danger. (1)

Prayer: A Lifting of the Soul to God, the Descent of the Spirit of God into the Soul

Prayer is the very breathing of religion, its most essential and characteristic activity.

Let us, then, ask ourselves what prayer is in itself. It is a mystical experience which is common to all religious persons, even the most unmystical. It consists of a lifting up of the soul to God—that is one side of it; and of a descent of the Spirit of God into the human soul—that is the other side of it. If either of these is absent, there is no true prayer. The Johannine Christ clearly lays down this condition for effectual prayer: 'If ye abide in me, and my words abide in you, ye shall ask what ye will and it shall be done unto you.' In true prayer, as St Paul says, 'the Spirit helpeth our infirmities'. It by no means follows that the Godward, supernatural side is always *felt*. Unconscious experience is no contradiction. But wherever there is true prayer it consists of these two elements and no others.

No narrower conception of prayer will serve. We may enumerate, with our authorities, the various particular *kinds*—petition, thanksgiving, intercession, meditation, contemplation, vocal prayer, orison or silent prayer. Possibly we may allow the mystics to teach us that the silent yearning of the soul, which is in truth a careful preparation of the channels through which the deeper consciousness is to flow; is a more perfect form of prayer than the utterance of words; but in this case to keep the balance between contemplation and action even, we must remember *laborare est orare*, and admit that *some* outward action, when performed *sacramentally*, as it were, is a real acted prayer, though the mind may not at the time be directly turned to thoughts of God. But, in any case, *petition* is neither the whole of prayer nor the main part of it. (2)

Interesting Ourselves in the Things that Really Matter

To a large extent we can and must prepare for them. In religion the *will* must never be passive. 'Ye are as holy as ye truly wish to be holy,' said Ruysbroek. Prayer is simply a *wish* uttered in God's presence. There can be no prayer without wishing. And if we pray truly, the answer is (in a manner) contained in the prayer itself. He who rises from his knees a better man, his prayer has been granted. And the way to strengthen the will and direct it in the right way, is to *interest* ourselves in the things that really matter. A man's rank in the scale of living beings is determined entirely by the objects in which he is really *interested*. I commend this as one of the most vital truths of practical philosophy. Let us take St Paul's list of the things which the Christian ought to care about, and, 'if there be any virtue, and if there be any praise, think on these things.' And let us remember that λογίζεσθε does not mean 'dream,' but 'ponder,' like rational beings, who know that well-being must consist in a ψυχῆς ἐνέργεια. And the ἐνέργεια of faith, St Paul tells us, is love. (3)

Consecration and Dedication

When an elderly man looks back upon his early life, he wants to help the young to avoid some of the mistakes which he made himself. My conscience tells me that my own worst fault as a young man was not slackness but over anxiety about my future—anxiety not so much to win success as to avoid humiliating failure, of which I was never really in much danger. This may have been partly a matter of temperament; but I know I should have been much happier if I had made just that act of self-dedication which I am pressing upon you. 'Show thou me the way that I should walk in, for I lift up my soul unto Thee. Take me with my faults and capacities, such as they are, and use me as Thou seest fit. Lo, I come to do Thy will, O God.' When that choice has been made, a man gains an inward peace and serenity which is reflected in his outward demeanour. He can enjoy the little humours of life and take its ups and downs good-naturedly, because he has come to see things in their true proportions. He is not careful and troubled about many things, because he knows that most things do not matter very much. Thus to dedicate oneself may be as necessary and salutary for those who are naturally disposed to take life too hard as for those who are naturally disposed to take it too easy.

But perhaps in substituting the word 'dedicate' for the 'consecrate' or 'sanctify' of the New Testament, I have missed something which the great high-priestly prayer of Christ was meant to teach us. I think I have missed something, and I must try to pick it up. 'For their sakes I consecrate or sanctify myself.' The words holiness and saintliness are not popular; but we must not forget that as Christians we are called to something more than active, cheerful usefulness. At the very heart of Christianity is the belief that the Holy Spirit of God, who is the glorified Christ under another form, dwells within us, 'unless we be reprobates.' And therefore, as St Paul says, 'I beseech you, by the mercies of God, that ye present your bodies a living sacrifice, holy, acceptable to God, which is your reasonable service.' Your reasonable service—$\lambda o\gamma\iota\kappa\grave{\eta}$ $\lambda\alpha\tau\rho\epsilon i\alpha$. Instead of the outward ceremonies and sacrifices of the Old Covenant, we present ourselves to God, a sacrifice, but a living sacrifice. And as nothing impure or maimed could be presented to God, we must see to it that our whole personality—spirit, soul, and body—is preserved blameless, so far as that is possible. If we grieve or quench the Spirit, that sanctifying presence will leave us. 'Ye are not your own. Ye are bought with a price. Therefore glorify God in your body and in your spirit, which are God's.' Dedication to God is a very solemn thing. 'The temple of God is holy, which temple ye are. If any man defile the temple of God, him shall God destroy.'

And this consecration is to be for the sake of others as well as for ourselves. 'For their sakes I consecrate myself.' We are helping or hindering others every day of our lives, not by what we do or say, but by what we are. There are some men in whose presence evil is ashamed. We are always the better for their company. And there are others of whom the opposite must be said. It is not necessary to show much deliberately, for concealment is impossible. Our minds are dyed the colour of our leisure thoughts, and the inner man makes the outer. Transparency of character is one of the marks of the Christian, who has nothing to hide. We may think of 1 Corinthians xiii, which a classical scholar has declared to be the finest thing written in Greek since the old Athenian masters, and enumerate, with the apostle, all the marks of Love or Charity as they show themselves in the life and conversation of the true Christian. Or we may remember that other remarkable passage where the apostle, contrary to his wont, appeals to the heathen ideals of 'virtue' and the desire of 'praise.' 'Finally, my brethren, whatsoever things are true, whatsoever things are honourable, whatsoever things are just, whatsoever things are pure, whatsoever things are lovely, whatsoever things are of good report, if there be any virtue and if there be any praise, think on these things.' It is as if he said, 'For once I appeal to you not as Christians but as gentlemen.' (4)

NOTES / SOURCES

1. William Ralph Inge, *Goodness and Truth*, London, 1958, p. 65
2. Ibid., pp. 91–2
3. W. R. Inge, *Faith and Knowledge: Sermons by W. R. Inge*, Edinburgh, 1905, pp. 170–1
4. W. R. Inge, *The Gate of Life*, London, 1935, pp. 58–61

Herbert H. Kelly SSM   1860–1950

The son of an Evangelical priest in Manchester, Herbert Kelly went up to Oxford where he gained an undistinguished degree in mathematics. Breaking with Evangelicalism through reading F. D. Maurice, he discovered the catholic tradition in Anglicanism and was ordained in 1883. Joining the Korean Missionary Brotherhood in 1890, two years later he founded the Society of the Sacred Mission (SSM) in 1892, with a determination to found a college to train for the ministry young men with no money and no special education. The society moved to Kelham in Nottinghamshire in 1903, where Kelly's vision was realized. SSM worked in Korea and Japan, Kelly himself working in Japan during the First World War. A powerful personality, he made notable contributions to training for the priesthood, ecumenism, and the theology of mission and of the religious life.

God and Religion

I am trying to write a book about God, and the place God has in our life. In the common way of talking what is concerned with God is called Religion. It will naturally be assumed that I am writing about religion, a subject on which people are always writing books. Some of us think it a very important subject, while others deny its importance. I only want to insist that God and Religion are not quite the same, although in a book about God one cannot very well help talking about religion.

Religion properly denotes all the human activity, sometimes the practices—-what man does—sometimes his feelings, sometimes his ideas or thoughts, so far as they are concerned with God. We generally use the word in its specific sense of things like church-going, prayer, or meditation, which are directly concerned with God, but anything may come into it that is done as for God's sake. In all cases, however, religion is some activity of our own.

The New Testament very seldom uses the word at all. St Paul speaks of religion twice, and twice he uses an equivalent word we might translate as 'cult', but only when speaking of heathenism or of pharisaic Judaism, never of Christianity. St James speaks of 'pure religion' as consisting in visiting the afflicted and in moral purity, without referring to its specific sense.

Religion is, by origin, a heathen word. The heathen were always talking about it, while they had very vague and uncertain ideas about God. Christianity, on the other hand, is first of all and distinctively a Gospel, a very wonderful story or message about God, about what God has done. Thence, it is a Faith, and this word means, not an acceptance of certain doctrines or beliefs, but a trust in God, and in what God has worked or effected in the way related in the story. The New Testament writers habitually speak of Christianity as a message or as a faith.

Of course, it is true that there is also a Christian religion. If we believe the Gospel, then there is a practice, a feeling, a thinking, which make up our response to that faith, but it is the peculiarity of Christianity that the religion is and remains secondary; the faith is primary. The order makes a great difference. I think it is plain, and it is most important that we should realize, that to believe in God, to look to and think about God and what God does is not the same as believing in religion, which in fact means believing in and thinking about certain practices and states of mind of our own.

In any case it is my business here to talk about what God means to us, what God means in a world, what difference faith in God would make in our lives; to show how men have tried to believe in God, how some at least have been brought to believe in God; to show how men can lose that faith, why faith is so difficult to hold even when we have reached it. As I shall try to explain, I think, so far as we today are concerned, the confusion in our minds between God and that state of our own which we call Religion is a very large part of our difficulties. Indeed, I cannot help thinking that, certainly with many people, the worship of 'Religion' has become a great stumbling-block in the way of the worship of God.

This way of talking about religion may seem strange. Whether there is any reason for it we shall see presently; anyhow if I am to talk about God, I at least ought not to start with religion, but still less ought I to start by talking of morality. If religion is our response, our way of holding ourselves towards God, morality is concerned with our conduct towards men, ourselves or others. But then I am not talking of God only as a thing apart, but of God, and his world. Our Gospel is a story about God, but it is a Gospel preached to men; it is a Gospel for human life. (1)

A Dialogue of the Soul with God

There is, as I imagine it, a Dialogue of the Soul with God, more or less common to all mankind, as it cries out of the dark to God:

'Lord, why have you made me thus?'

And there is an answer given to all—'Beloved, I made you for myself.'

'But why am I in the dark and in confusion?'

'Beloved, you are in the dark and in confusion, because you are seeking for light and wisdom in yourself. You will not find them there.'

'But why cannot I know what you are doing?'

'Because that is part of a whole universe of meaning, and you cannot know universes. You want to be a God—a Lord of the world—when you are only a little self and my child.'

'But would you have me placid and content?'

'I made you for hope, desire, effort, progress, in order that you might learn. I would have you content with nothing; for content, placidity, quietism, indifference, are the substance of death—except one content, and that is beatitude, content to be small, content to be my child.'

'Can I do nothing?'

You can do a great many things; then you will help others. And a great many things you cannot do; then others will have to help you, though you will not like it.'

'What can I do? How am I to know?'

'That I shall not tell you. You must use your own judgment, make your own mistakes, and go on trying. You will fail at a lot of things, and that you will like still less.'

'How can I find God?'

'Beloved, you cannot find me, but I have found you.'

'If I cannot find God, how can I come to love him?'

'Love is not a thing you do or come to. It comes to, overcomes, you. Realize this first, that your life is in my hands, not your own; accept it so, and where faith meets hope, love is born. Believe this first, that God so loved his world that he sent his only begotten Son into the world, that you might live through him, and that the cosmos through him should be saved.' (2)

Keep Yourself from Idols

Is God more than a vision of mine, or a dream? Can God at-one this broken life of mine? How can I see more than a vision, or think more than my own thoughts? I had heard of God, and my heart awoke, for it might mean so much. But what does God do? I do not know. I do not see how I could know, and the hope dies down. It was then the message came to me. We value St John's Epistle because it contains some remarkable passages on the essential love (the Holy Spirit) who is in God, who is God. But most of that Epistle is about the Incarnation. I gave the beginning before, and this is the end:

> We know that the Son of God is come
> And we are in him that is true,
> Even in his Son, Jesus Christ.
> This is true God, and eternal life.
>
> Little children, keep yourselves from idols.

I wonder how many stop to realize the tremendous warning in the apparent irrelevance of that last line, which is not part of the rhythm. If you would ever come to truth, that it may ever come to you, this first—you must keep yourself from the worship of your own visions, ideals, experiences. In place of our efforts to apprehend God—not, indeed, displacing them, rather glorifying them with its own light—stands this assurance of a Gospel. You may believe it or not, but there is no other:

Now is Christ risen from the dead,
And become the first-fruits
  Of them that sleep;
For as in Adam (in man) all die,
  Even so in Christ shall all be made to live. (3)

Evangelical and Catholic

'Evangelical—belonging to a Gospel.' That is the very first of Christian words. The New Testament is all about a Gospel, and that means a story, not about opinions, nor about ethical ideals, nor about doctrines, but a story of something God did, a story of how God Himself, the Son of God, came to men, died, rose, ascended, that men in Him might be reconciled to God.

'Catholic' is a Greek word. It means belonging to a whole. It does not appear in the New Testament in this shape, but the idea comes very often in many ways. Both Christ and the Apostles are always talking of 'Salvation.' Quite commonly people use the word as if it meant safety, and very often as if it meant getting to heaven. It is the same word as health, and it means being made whole (Matt. ix. 21 f.); it is used most often of the health of the mind or soul.

Salvation seems to refer to personal wholeness, but there are two other words which go with it. The first is 'Oneness.' Christ has drawn all men unto Himself, in order that all mankind should be one in Him. St John's Gospel and St Paul's letters are full of this thought.

The other word is 'Common.' Our English Bible sometimes speaks of *Communion*, sometimes of *Fellowship*, of *partaking* or *sharing*. There is one God; what He is and what He has done is the same for all of us. So St Paul speaks of the 'common' faith (Titus i. 4), and St Jude of the 'common' salvation. We may call it a Catholic Gospel because it makes a wholeness of all the broken purposes of the individual life; it is also Catholic because it is for all mankind, and in it all mankind, with all its contrary purposes, is being reconciled in one unity to God. (4)

The Catholic Spirit

The Christian or Catholic spirit, which we want to find in men and in ourselves, follows on the Christian or Catholic faith. In regard to God, we believe in the Father, the Son, and the Holy Spirit, and these three are one God. As regards men, we can follow God by Love, Faith, Hope, and these three are of one character, which we may call Humility or Self-forgetfulness. Love is the forgetting of the self because we are thinking of someone else. Faith is the forgetting, the looking away from, one's own power or wisdom, and a looking up to someone else. Hope has the promise of a reward which somehow will come to us.

We men have nothing which is really and wholly our own, except the self-will which is our foolishness. I said of pride, we cannot wholly escape it, because we cannot wholly escape the foolishness which belongs to our littleness. No, but we can confess it. So we cannot really be Catholic, because we cannot know the whole truth. No, but holding fast to what God has given us, we can be ready to learn from all, and ready to confess our own mistakes. To hold the Catholic faith is to hold something of infinite meaning. It is not at all the same as believing that we know all about it, nor even that we have wholly understood it. (5)

Sacraments

Let us consider the meaning of a Sacrament first in its general sense, which is very well given in our Catechism—'an outward and visible (or material) sign of an inward and spiritual grace.' It is obvious that these two parts are intimately concerned with the question of the material and the spiritual which we discussed before.

In this general sense, all the universe and all our life is sacramental. The stars and the cherry-blossom, the rays of light and the waterfall are all material, but they are also divine. God made them, and rejoiced in them, and had a meaning for them. The spoken word is a material sound and the written word is a material mark of a spiritual meaning, producing spiritual effects for good, in sermons or in Holy Scripture; or it may be for evil, when set on fire of hell, as St James says.

In our life, acts also are the outward expression of an inner meaning, and not less sacramental than words. We may call them signs or symbols, but let us understand these words. The material thing or act which we see is a sign of that which it is, belongs to, and comes from. We think in words, and the artist sees a vision of beauty. Our speech and his picture are signs in so far as they are that thought or vision, given in sounds or in paint, just as a kindly act is an interior kindness made actual and effective.

Words and acts, therefore, are the means by which a relation is created between ourselves and others, who will use, understand, and enter into what we have shown. We may say or do a great many things without meaning anything; then our words and acts are false; but plainly there can be no relations at all between us, whether true or false, whether friendly or hostile, if we have nothing to do with one another.

Our Church Catechism, however, speaks of the Sacraments of the Gospels as those 'given by Christ Himself.' If, then, everything is in the end a sign or sacrament of some purpose of God Who made it, the Sacraments of the Gospel were instituted to be, not only in the end, but directly and immediately, the signs of God's action. Let us consider three points.

1. The Sacraments of Christ, being first of all His acts, establish a relation between us and Christ. That relation is essentially Catholic. I only share in what He is doing for all, and by sharing I am also brought into relation with the whole family; but the relation to God always comes first, and the relation to other men is a consequence.

2. By direct and immediate, we do not of course mean that these are the only ways in which God acts. The Bible is a directly inspired book, and prophets are directly inspired people; both are the chosen signs and means of God's teaching, but they are not the only way in which He speaks. So on our side, prayer—-including all its forms—is the direct service of God, but it is not the only service we are to give. I have heard people talk as if God could not act outside the Sacraments, and as if the Bible alone was inspired, or as if prayer were the whole of religion, but I do not think they really meant it. In all cases the direct and

immediate is a sign and means of the sanctity of all the rest, as St Paul says that every created thing is sanctified by the word and prayer (1 Tim. iv. 5), and, in the highest case of all, the human nature of Christ has sanctified all mankind.

3. The whole New Testament shows us how the Gospel is set before us in two ways—in Sacraments by means of acts, in Scripture and in preaching by means of words. What are the relation between acts and words? Acts seem to us simple, for they often take longer to explain than to do, but it may take very much longer to reach the end of their consequences. God sent forth His Only Begotten Son, Who was made flesh and dwelt among us. Perhaps that took thirty-three years, but for nineteen hundred years the Holy Spirit has been bringing mankind into the faith and some comprehension of what was done. Then for us, once in a lifetime and also week by week, the Sacraments set the Gospel before us in two very simple acts, 'given unto us by Christ Himself' and so appointed. In all our life the Holy Spirit is explaining to us, and bringing us to enter into, the meaning of that Gospel through the preaching of His ministers and in many other ways.

God has given us His Gospel through preaching and in sacraments. Each has its own value, and each by itself has its own weaknesses. Acts by themselves may be close enough to heathenism, as easy by themselves as ringing a gong in a temple. So St Paul preached to the Athenians: 'Whom you worship ignorantly—without understanding what you do—Him I declare to you.' On the other hand, preaching by itself may be a mere tossing about of ideas, interesting, novel, clever; they are not the same as worship. It was a very sincere theological student who said: 'I saw for the first time that Christ called for worship, not only for discussion.'

Thought, feeling, worship are the three necessities of the Christian life. I might call them two, since feeling is a necessity of both the others. They are expressed in words and acts, preaching and sacraments. I will use no party words, but while I am fully persuaded that, except as the realization of evangelical conviction, all mere observances are fundamentally heathen, however sacramental they may call themselves, I am no less persuaded that evangelical preaching does in the end lose the sense of worship and of reality unless it is coupled with a genuine sacramental faith.

I am well aware that nobody means to separate these two elements; nobody will admit he does, and that is really our danger. There is a whole nest of controversial words—heathen, magic, superstition, idolatry, heresy. They are all somewhat mischievous, because, being offensive terms, they set others on justifying instead of examining themselves. They are mischievous also to ourselves, because they lead us to imagine that such horrible evils must be somebody else's sins, when in fact they are the common temptations from which none of us wholly escape. It is quite true that our sacramental use is constantly involving itself in idolatry and magic as we assume that our acts have value in themselves, but just the same thing is true in preaching, and in all use of words. We love listening to what sounds profound and inspiring as if the words had reality of themselves, even when we do not quite know what they mean. There are enough theological explanations, and a multitude of pious phrases, which will paint over anything we like doing without asking whether we are really acting on them. (6)

Confession

The plain fact is that this intense resentment we feel at confessing to anybody is the very essence of the whole business. Sin is selfness, self-concentration, that is, isolation. By its very essence it is the secret of the soul; more, its nature consists of secretiveness. Sin is the one thing a man has which is purely his own, and it consists in trying to have 'my own.' Confession of any kind whatever is hateful; it is breaking down that fortress of the self which is, in truth, its prison.

Try it. Look carefully and honestly at what you have actually done. Put it in plain words, and read it out loud—to the bed-post, if you like. The result will be the same; every fibre of the self cries indignantly: 'I won't. I won't. I won't.' It might seem easier to confess to the bed-post than to someone else, but that is not so. In practice you cannot, and will not, deal honestly with yourself without craving for someone who has 'power and commandment' to meet you with the assurance of absolution. In the Methodist class meeting and in the Group Movement, confession one to another has taken a real place, but, for quite ordinary people, a priest is, like a doctor, a man professionally accustomed to hearing things without being either shocked or frightened at them.

I do not think it possible to deny that under all abuses, and in the worst moral conditions, the practice of confession did keep alive and build up a sense of sin. Now I have no doubt that multitudes of devout Protestants have a most profound sense of sin and of penitence, and that their confessions to God are intensely real, but it seems to me one of the weaknesses of our modern religious fashions that we frame our ideals according to the possibilities of devout people, and that we think hardly at all about quite ordinary people. In very wide circles, the practical loss of the habit of confessing to a priest—as a quite normal thing—has led to an almost complete loss of any sense of sin. It is not because confession is too easy, but because it is too difficult. We try for self-justification, but most of us know ourselves too well to be really self-satisfied. We have not got what the Prayer Book calls 'a quiet conscience,' but we try to think we have. Then, if we will not face the trouble and humiliation of confession, we take refuge in that indifference which is so terribly common. (7)

NOTES / SOURCES

1. Herbert Kelly SSM, *The Gospel of God*, London, 1959, pp. 49–51
2. Ibid., pp. 129–30
3. Ibid., pp. 151
4. Herbert Kelly SSM, *Catholicity*, London, 1932, pp. 42–3
5. Ibid., pp. 68–9
6. Ibid., pp. 99–103
7. Ibid., pp. 152–3

Arthur Cayley Headlam   1862–1947

Bishop of Gloucester from 1923 to 1925, following a time as Regius Professor of Divinity at Oxford and earlier as Principal of King's College London, Headlam was both a critic of Church politics and a strong exponent of an ecumenical ecclesiology. An influential bishop he was characterized as a 'prolific, vigorous theological writer of enlightened conservatism'.

The Destructiveness of Anglican Exclusiveness

Up till quite lately Anglicanism has been very exclusive; it has been the religion of one race and only a section of that race. It has been exclusive on various grounds. There has been great social exclusiveness. The Church of England has been in its essence the religion of the English gentleman, and it has exhibited a good deal of the exclusiveness which characterizes us as a nation, an exclusiveness, I think, which does not arise so much from social pride as from a developed and intensified habit of mind. The Englishman does not easily mix with people of other countries and traditions because he has his own traditions so strong and perhaps we may add, on the whole, so healthy. But the fact remains that he has a character in the world for aloofness, an aloofness which has been, to a certain extent, a strength, but has also often impeded his usefulness. There has certainly been this element of aloofness in Anglicanism. We have been so satisfied with our own particular religious development that we have found it very hard to accommodate ourselves to others, or even to put forward our own point of view to those who have been brought up in different traditions.

The exclusiveness of Anglicanism has been in the next place very largely an academic exclusiveness. It has been, in a way, a marked way, the religion of men brought up in the two universities of Oxford and Cambridge, and as, until a comparatively recent time, no one was admitted a member of those universities who was not a member of the Church of England, there was no body of persons outside that charmed circle with whom the Church of England Christian could have great community of mind. The exclusiveness of our universities, from which all members of Nonconformist bodies and all Roman Catholics were shut out, certainly intensified the isolation of Anglicanism and built up a strong barrier between it and Nonconformity, on the one hand, and Roman Catholicism on the other.

And then, thirdly, there was religious exclusiveness. The fundamental maxim which underlies that was the belief which has always been very widely held that it was only through episcopacy that a valid and regular commission can be given to the clergy, and that thus only can valid sacraments be celebrated. All those who are without this commission are really unauthorized intruders wherever they may be and therefore they are not part of the Christian Church. This belief has been held with varying degrees of intensity and in somewhat different forms, but it has given its fundamental colour to the Christianity of the Church of England, and has formed a great barrier of separation between it and other Churches.

Ever since the time of the Reformation there have been these elements of exclusiveness in our Church, and a certain form of piety, a certain tradition of life and worship, certain somewhat fundamental theological doctrines have been part of our characteristics. Various circumstances, which are sometimes held to have been accidental, have combined together to separate the Church of England from the religious bodies which were organized at the time of the Reformation. The Church of England has been marked by the stress it has laid on historical continuity, on its preservation of the ideal of corporate Christianity, on exhibiting a rational, ethical, wholesome doctrine of the sacraments, on preserving the great ideal of the Catholic Church, and part of the instrument—if we may call it so—by which these great theological ideals have been preserved has been the acceptance of the historical episcopate.

A time has come when there is much stirring in the religious world; people are no longer satisfied with the divided Christianity which had almost been taken as axiomatic, and many people have pointed to the Church of England as a body singularly fitted for carrying on the work of Christian union. We are naturally and rightly proud of our Church; we believe that it presents a wholesome form of Christianity; we are ready to claim for it a mission in the world; but we have to remember that this claim is made not by ourselves only, but by others. There was no one able to survey the field of history and of modern ecclesiastical conditions with the same combination of wide historical knowledge and practical experience so well as the great Old-Catholic theologian, Dr Döllinger, and he was ready to ascribe this mission to the Church of England. Others have echoed his words, and many have turned to us at the present time. I do not think we need shrink from the office that men would put upon us; we should rise to the opportunity and be ready to do our work. But if we are to be able to do this we must remember that we must break away from our old Anglican exclusiveness. If we are going to remain insular, the Church of a class, of a sect, of a school, we can never accomplish anything. We must get rid of old barriers; we must be prepared to change our hearts and our dispositions if we are to do the work that we think lies before us. Anglo-Catholicism has preserved and created a wholesome ecclesiastical ideal, but it has combined that with a narrow exclusiveness. We cannot give that ideal to the world unless we are prepared to give up our old exclusiveness.

What does that exclusiveness mean? It means, first of all, the refusal to consider all those who do not come up exactly to our own formal traditions of ecclesiastical law, to be part of the Church—to refuse this Church because it has not episcopacy, that Church because it has not a diaconate, to say that no one who is not confirmed is a member of the Church, to deny the spiritual efficacy of the sacraments of Presbyterians or Congregationalists, to limit Christianity by our own particular presentment of it. Do we realize how absurd that must appear to those outside? You visit Scotland. There is there a Scottish Episcopal Church; it numbers sixty thousand adherents out of a population of nearly four million. It is not superior in the eloquence of its preachers or the learning of its divines or its standard of Christian piety or of missionary zeal, yet it claims to be *the* Church of Scotland. It may well be that it has preserved elements of religion and life which other portions of the Church have lost, but to make any claim of being the exclusive representation of the true Church in that country is ridiculous. So in the same way if we go to America the Protestant Episcopal Church, as it calls itself, is but a small body amongst the many great Protestant communities of that country. If we go to the mission field we find how small and unimportant and even uninspired the Anglican Mission often is compared with the Presbyterian or Congregational or those of other bodies. Clearly the rigid application of our principles is landing us in something which may seem to be an absurdity. I have no objection to those whose loyalty to their Church makes them prepared to assert that theirs is a wholesome and good representation of Christendom, and that they have preserved many elements essential for the united Christian Church of the future. I am as proud of the Church of England as anyone, but I can see no justification for its claim to possess a monopoly of true Christianity or of churchmanship in any way. We must believe that the commissions of our clergy are good, but we have no right to deny the commission of the ministers of other bodies, who may often excel us in their spiritual power, their spiritual influence, and their theological knowledge; we have no right to claim that we are the Church and they are not, when we see amongst them so many fruits of true religion. We have no right to maintain that our sacraments are true and theirs are mere barren rites when we see the life nourished on those sacraments shows such abundant sense of grace.

NOTES / SOURCES

Arthur Cayley Headlam, *The Building of the Church of Christ: University and other sermons*, London, 1928, pp. 131–5

Herbert Hensley Henson   1863–1947

Bishop successively of Hereford (1918–1920) and Durham (1920–1939), Hensley Henson had a fluent and powerful pen. He moved from an earlier High Church position to a more comprehensive and latitudinarian conception of Anglicanism and was an ardent defender of a more inclusive Establishment until parliamentary rejection of the 1928 Prayer Book converted him to the belief that Establishment was incompatible with the Church's freedom. His scepticism about the Virgin Birth and miracles provoked controversy over his consecration.

The Holy Communion Christ's Ladder to Heaven

The Holy Communion is Christ's ladder set up on the earth, whose top reaches to heaven. Thereby we ascend to God through Him, for through Him we have our access in one Spirit unto the Father. The patriarch's dream revealed what actually had been existent all the while, though he knew it not. Holy Communion protests to us the unsuspected sanctity of common life, and bids us know the nearness of God. That is the central and vitalizing reality of Sacramental Worship. All else is picture, and parable, and vesture of truth. Words, gestures, the 'creatures of Bread and Wine,' have their worth and meaning as tokens and pledges of a spiritual fact, that 'in Him we live and move and have our being,' that 'we are Christ's and Christ is God's.' Therefore on the threshold of Holy Communion the words of the Gospel come to us with direct and luminous relevance: 'Let not your heart be troubled: ye believe in God, believe also in Me.' (1)

Preparation for Death

The duty of preparing for death is as obvious as it is, by most of us, neglected; on Good Friday, when we gather round the Cross on which our Saviour dies; it is a subject which we cannot ignore. It is no doubt the case that a great change has passed over our view of death. The older religious writers give death a place in their scheme of doctrine and devotion, which certainly seems to us somewhat excessive; they deliberately brought death before their minds by a system of somewhat artificial associations, which strike us now as far-fetched and, in practice, unhelpful. Take for sufficient example one of the famous Bishop Hall's 'Self-conferences.' 'Everything that I see,' he says, 'furnishes me with fair monitions of my dissolution. If I look into my garden, there I see some flowers fading, some withered; if I look to the earth, I see that mother in whose womb I must lie; if I go to church, the graves that I must step over in my way show me what I must trust to; if I look to my table, death is in every dish, since what I feed on did once live; if I look into my glass, I cannot but see death in my face; if I go to my bed, there I meet with sleep, the image of death, and the sheets which put me in mind of my winding up; if I look into my study, what are all those books but the monuments of other dead authors? O my soul, how canst thou be unmindful of our parting, when thou art plied with so many monitors.'[1]

We shall all probably agree that there is something unnatural, and even morbid, in such a habit of mind as these words appear to indicate. The severe and, as it seems to us, mechanical doctrine of perdition, which obtained among Christians until recent times, reacted inevitably on their thought about death. 'In the place where the tree falleth, there shall it be,' was the verse often on their lips, and held to be decisive on the question whether or not beyond the grave there was opportunity of redemption. We are much more sensitive now as to the moral aspect of the doctrines we maintain, much more chary of attributing to the Absolute Equity of Almighty God methods and procedures which, to our limited perceptions of what is equitable, are repellent; and all observers agree that within the last two generations there has been an immense development of secularism among us. Life has become much more interesting to most, much more attractive to many, of our people; and they have little margin of attention for the unpalatable subject of death, and the shadowy possibilities which lie beyond. And yet, when we think soberly, there is no small risk, no slight impropriety, in this easy secularism. Sure it is that we must die, and that the hour of our death is hidden from us. Sure it is that when we die we perforce make an end of these lives which, as citizens of the world, we have received; our time is up, our campaign concluded, our part played; we must hand in whatsoever work we have wrought on the earth; we must go before the Eternal Judge such men as we have brought ourselves to be. To prepare for death is so to live that the natural progress of our lives, the natural development of ourselves, will bring us peace at the last. (2)

Christianity and Politics

'*We must obey God rather than men*' is a formula of essential Christianity: and God still speaks to us, as in the old prophetic age, most authoritatively and intelligibly from within ourselves. '*He hath showed thee, O man, what is good; and what doth the Lord require of thee, but to do justly, and to love mercy, and to walk humbly with thy God.*' This interior guidance, as it is ministered in the solitude of the individual spirit, so it is incompetent for the purposes of general direction. We are rightly suspicious of appeals to conscience in the region of public policy,

---

[1] *Works*, viii. 58.

on this very account. Whatever may be the value of intuitions to those who receive them, they are clearly of no more value to others than their own judgment allows. Political wisdom is not learned in the sanctuary or in the assemblies of the saints, but in the patient study of the past and in the school of actual experience. Hardly any lesson is more consistently taught by the chequered and various history of mankind than this: that high character is no security against political folly, and noble intentions no effectual barrier against unworthy methods. We are not, therefore, to suppose that, as Christians, we possess some distinctive insight into public affairs which others do not possess, that we can take a short cut to our political decisions, and that those decisions are morally binding on the acceptance of others. To think in that way is to think fanatically, and thinking fanatically is the condition of intemperate speech and, when opportunity comes, of intolerant action. Christianity no more commits us to a specific political doctrine, or party, or programme, than to a specific nationality or government. (3)

Faith and Dogma

The Christian Church, we must always remember, did not begin with a prescribed and indispensable theology, but with a spontaneous worship. The Christian belief about CHRIST was born of the Christian experience of His spiritual power. The Church regarded the facts of CHRIST's history as factors of religion, reading them ever in terms of that spiritual life which He was actually inspiring, and which those facts seemed to explain. Thus the theologies of the New Testament are many, and hard to combine, but the faith which lies behind them all is one and the same. Many types of mind, many varieties of training and experience, have left their impress on the thought of the Church, but the subject of that thought is always the same, and all the ways of religious thinking converge to the same point—the worship of GOD in CHRIST. It is surely important to recognize the diversity of Apostolic beliefs about our LORD, for the recognition will not only bring into just prominence the central unity of Apostolic faith, but will make it easier for us to regard without alarm or dislike the theological confusion of the modern Church. As at first, so now, men find their way into the ranks of the worshippers of JESUS CHRIST by many roads, and they offer the intellectual justification of their worship by many theories. We are 'saved by faith,' not by theology. A clear vision in the realm of doctrine is conditioned by moral fidelity. 'The pure in heart shall see GOD.' Obedience brings the recompense of knowledge. 'If any man willeth to do His will, he shall know of the doctrine whether it be of GOD, or whether I speak from Myself.'

If there be any here who have been perplexed and troubled in mind by recent controversies within the Church with respect to that Article of the Creed which the festival of Christmas might be thought most to emphasise, and who, as they gather with their brethren for the festal worship, are conscious of a new sense of unsettlement and dismay, which seems to threaten the security of the old belief, then I would affectionately entreat them to remember that the core of the faith in the Divineness of JESUS did not at the first, and need not now, consist of a dogma as to His miraculous birth. Such a dogma may or may not continue to find its place in the general belief of the Church. It can never rise into an importance which it did not originally possess. It is, perhaps, only the confusion of faith and dogma which induces so many devout Christians to speak as if the Divinity of CHRIST turned on the historical value of the birth-narratives. (4)

God acting in Church History

We utterly repudiate the notion that the history of Israel can ever become empty of significance to Christians. We take up the records of that history with the conviction that we shall be able to trace in them the Divine Purpose which found its conspicuous expression in the life of Jesus Christ. We read the literature of Israel with the veneration which belongs to sacred writings inspired of God, because we have the authority of our Lord for saying that in that literature we shall find a true revelation of the Almighty. It may be true—it evidently is true—that the Hebrew literature has experienced the same fortunes, been produced under the same limitations, as those which attach, and must attach, to all human compositions. The *treasure* of Divine Revelation *is in earthen vessels*; but that circumstance only brings into greater distinctness its essential Divineness. So the argument stands thus: Human history is the revelation of the mind of God. Hebrew history is the revelation of a Divine purpose, the supreme character of which is determined by that which was the true outcome of the history—the fact of the Incarnation. That fact is the starting-point of Church History and its key. Church History is the record of the secular work of God the Holy Ghost. Read the Book of the Acts, the earliest chapter of Christian history. It begins with the coming of the Holy Ghost on the Day of Pentecost; it continuously speaks of the Holy Ghost as directing the action of the apostles, planning the policy of the Church, inspiring not alone the hearts but also the intelligence of disciples. Indeed it has been said, not altogether inaptly, that as the Gospels give the history of God the Son in the world, so does the Book of the Acts give that of God the Holy Ghost. We Christians believe that the visible Church is the temple of God the Holy Ghost. That is the reason why we link together in the Creed the article which declares belief in the Holy Ghost with that which declares belief in the Church. 'I believe in the Holy Ghost, the Holy Catholic Church.' It is manifestly an absurd supposition that the value and interest of Church History ended with the lives of the apostles. The Holy Ghost has been as really active in the Church in the following centuries as in that first century. He is as really active in the Church to-day as then. How unreasonable, then, is the neglect of Church History which obtains among modern Christians! (5)

NOTES / SOURCES

1. H. Hensley Henson, *The Value of the Bible and Other Sermons*, London, 1904, pp. 144–5
2. Ibid., pp. 286–9
3. H. Hensley Henson, *Christ and the nation: Westminster and Other Sermons*, London, 1908, pp. 80–1
4. H. Hensley Henson, *The Creed in the pulpit*, London, 1908, pp. 21–2
5. H. Hensley Henson, *Light and Leaven: Historical social sermons to general congregations*, London, 1897, pp. 28–9

Dom Denys Prideaux OSB 1864–1934

Born in Jamaica, William Prideaux read Classics and Modern Languages at Clare College, Cambridge, before going to Cuddesdon and being ordained in 1893. In 1907 he joined the Anglican Benedictine community on Caldey Island. When the community seceded to Rome in 1913 he sought to continue the Benedictine life in the Church of England at the Abbey House, Pershore, where he was installed as the first Abbot in 1922. Four years later the community moved to Nashdom Abbey where he remained Abbot until his death in 1934. Dom Denys was a friend of Charles Gore and was influenced by the *Lux Mundi* group.

The Cross the Key to Prayer

The Cross is the only key to prayer. You will never pray well unless you take the hammer and the nails, and the spear and the thorns, and the hyssop dipped in vinegar, and go to Golgotha stripped and bare, and in physical agony as well as agony of mind and soul, re-enact the Crucifixion in your own members, making up what is behind of the sufferings of Christ. You can only plead through Lips that were once parched and cracked and stained with blood—your prayer can only be heard if it is joined to that stream of intercession that pours forth unceasingly in Heaven from One who once was 'slain.' Impassible though He be now, He is not unfeeling, and His very memories of Good Friday wing your prayers. Oh yes; the Transfiguration Light may dazzle, and the soul sigh for the sweet cool converse of God walking in the evening peace of Eden, but there is no road to Eden except through the bloodsweat of Gethsemane and Calvary's long-drawn cry in the dark night of the soul—'My God, My God, why hast Thou forsaken Me?' (1)

The 'Otherness' of the Spirit

Indeed, if 'we can hurry man, we cannot hurry God' and Knowledge. Life itself—and to Life Christ appealed—shows us the dangers of the 'strenuous,' 'effortful' Will, and of the neglect of the law of alternation between quiescence or repose and activity. Excessive effort nearly always produces the opposite of what it aims at. Force yourself, *will* yourself, to love, to be sincere, and you may become insincere in the very effort. Strain your eyes to see, and blindness may result, while over-careful calculation may bring failure; scrupulous morality develop the immoral; high aims narrow the soul to specialization, deformity and spiritual obsessions. Will and intelligence are, indeed, the foundation-stones of devotion, but the balance should be kept true between the 'technique,' and the 'spirit' of our devotional life; and spirit has an 'otherness' of its own—effortful and effortless, conscious but also 'unconscious' emotion and willing; motivations and tones, shades and *nuances*, passive and active, re-flective, adorational, and contemplative. Without these we may cut the nerve of the soul. (2)

NOTES / SOURCES

1. Dom Denys Prideaux OSB, 'Prayer and Contemplation' in *Laudate (Quarterly Review)*, Nashdom Abbey, December 1944
2. Dom Denys Prideaux OSB, 'Notes on the Devotional Life' in *Laudate (Quarterly Review)*, Nashdom Abbey, June 1929

John Neville Figgis   1866–1919

The son of a minister of 'Lady Huntingdon's Connexion' he was ordained in 1894 and joined the Community of the Resurrection at Mirfield in 1907. Influenced in his historical studies by Lord Acton, he was a strong opponent of ideas of absolute sovereignty in relation to the State, and was one of the first to see the dangers to religion of the modern omnicompetent state.

Faith the Angel of an Agony

To others faith is the bright serenity of unclouded vision; to me it is the angel of an agony, the boon of daily and hourly conflict. (1)

The Insistent Call of God

It is God we are seeking for; the other world, which alone can give reality to this, alone can invest duty with enduring meaning, can find for beneficence a certain value, for knowledge an ordered place, and flash upon the shows of earthly beauty some hint at least of the eternal loveliness. Men bid us limit our aims and hopes to this life, and turn from the dazzling mirage of the other. Our answer is that we cannot. We may try, try hard, try—as a race—for generations, for centuries; but we cannot do it. God is calling us. (2)

Give All for All

That is the shining paradox of the Christian life, and it is also the paradox of all life. You must 'give all for all.' You can never win any kind of peace or self-possession unless you have risked all to get it. Ask yourself for one moment what have been your feelings on the eve of some act involving courage, whether it has been courage physical as it is commonly called, or moral, or intellectual. You want them all. They are all one. What has happened to you? If it has really called forth courage, have you not felt something like this? 'I cannot do this. This is too much for me. I shall ruin myself if I take this risk. I cannot take the leap. It is impossible. All me will be gone if I do this, and I cling to myself.'

And then supposing the spirit has conquered and you have done this impossible thing, do not you find afterwards that you possess yourself in a sense that you never have before, that there is more of you? Is not that true of every single act that has involved courage in your life, I do not care what it is? First it seems impossible, that it means the giving of your whole self, and you cling to yourself and cannot do it, and very likely you don't. But supposing you do, supposing you get over this terror, then at the end there comes back to you a great possession of the spirit and you know you are something different from what you were before, and something more. . . .

That is the choice of us all in life. It is our choice in religion. You must take either the adventure standpoint or the insurance standpoint. Are you resolved to make the great gamble with Christ as your leader, or do you want the humdrum and philistine respectability of the man who never gets high because he never goes low? If you follow Christ He will lead you by paths that you know not. I grant it. What is He going to do with me? you may ask. Where will this great love take me? I know not. Once the passion of Christ has hold of you, and you are a sharer in the secret of the world, redemption through suffering, through love, then your course can be calculated by no astrologer and no horoscope can enable you to tell the future, for your orbit has passed beyond the ken of man and you will do more and less than you imagine. 'I cannot tell,' you may say, 'what will become of me in this great quest.' Quite so. You cannot. God may use you for a little and then ruin your health, or He may take all your goods, or He may give you work that is drudgery and unprofitable, or He may shine upon your life with success and even popularity. I cannot tell. You cannot tell. You are His, not your own, and if you give yourself away, you cannot be as though you were your sole master. (3)

NOTES / SOURCES

1. Neville Figgis CR, *The Gospel of Human Needs*, London, 1910, p. 15
2. Ibid., pp. 134–5
3. Neville Figgis CR, *Anti-Christ and Other Sermons*, London, 1913, pp. 77–8, 81–2

Shirley Carter Hughson OHC   1867–1949

Born in South Carolina, Hughson became a monk of the Order of the Holy Cross, was Prior of the order's school and, later, Superior. President of the American Church Union and the author of many devotional writings and spiritual letters, he was also the main force behind the order's work in Liberia.

Epiphany

January, 1944

My very dear Child:

I have been thinking of you on this festival which to me, and I hope to you, has always been so full of deep and beautiful mystery. . . . May the Blessed Kings pray for you in the Mystical Body of our Lord, may they impart to you something of the faith that sent them on their mysterious journey, and of the joy which they found when they knelt before the Lord of Heaven made Man. It seems to me that no one has ever adequately portrayed in words the beauty of this season. Of course, it cannot be portrayed adequately, but it has always seemed to me to be possible to do more with it than has been done. But there is, on the other hand, a great advantage in not seeking to expose the mystery, even if it could be set forth. It is something like the light; at early dawn when it is dim, it presents a mystery of earth and sky that is wholly lost when it shines in its fulness and rawness at high noon. I remember years ago driving across the desert in the west, and being impressed with the glory of the early morning and of the late afternoon, in comparison with the hardness of the noonday sun. There is a new anthology recently published called *Pause to Wonder*. The title is taken from a saying of Einstein's, which is on the title page, to the effect that the most beautiful and thrilling thing in the world is the mysterious[1], and goes on to say that the man who never feels called upon to 'pause and wonder' is as good as dead. So there is something great and full in the deep mysteries of life, which is utterly lost when life is explained. The lure of the mysterious is that which has enabled men to follow after truth, and the fact that the truth always lies beyond us would seem to be a reflection of the infinite life of God Himself who is the fulness of truth. We can never compass the infinite, although through all time and eternity we shall be penetrating more deeply into it. . . . God keep you and give you all blessing, and since no man liveth unto himself, may you be able to pass these on to others. St Paul tells us that we are to labour to have, in order that we may give to him that hath need. That is the true principle of life. Pray ever for me.

Your loving father, (1)

Prayer

Prayer in some mysterious way we cannot see, has the effect of releasing the omnipotence of God upon the world. This is what St Thomas Aquinas meant by his great definition of prayer—'Prayer is the means God wills us to use in order that we might obtain the blessings He wills to give us.' Prayer is the means by the use of which we appropriate to ourselves and gain for others the gift of God's love. This Church of ours is not lacking in activity for good, but what a woeful lack of prayer there is; and, as a consequence, how thin is the life of the Church. The human element is magnified; the divine element is neglected. The Church lacks power in the world because it fails in its work of prayer. Prayer is intercourse with God, association with Him personally and lovingly. We are eager enough to do His work, but we are slow to go to Him for the power with which to work. (2)

Little Things

We cannot too often remind ourselves that life is made up of little things, and it is not only in the little things that we are to love and serve Him, but His love for us must find its place in the little things everyone of which we can offer to Him as our service of love. And it is a great thought that nothing is little with God. Whatever He touches, whatever He inspires, whatever He accepts, He thereby places an infinite value upon it. Thus are we able to offer to Him works of infinite value in His sight, and in His kingdom. Does this not show us the dignity with which He crowns those whom He calls to His loving service? It is always a false humility to think our work for Him as being of little account, and my dear old St Augustine said, 'If you do not acknowledge yourself to be holy, you are ungrateful to God.' We cannot make any contact with Him without contacting His holiness,

---

[1] *The most beautiful thing we can witness is the mysterious. He to whom this emotion is a stranger, who can no longer pause to wonder and stand wrapt in awe, is as good as dead; his eyes are closed.*

and since that holiness is infinitely communicative, we must receive of it. It gives us a realization of the honour to which He would promote us, and at the same time teaches us real humility, a real appreciation of what we are in His blessed sight. But however short we may fall, we are still His dear children, and what can the heart desire more precious than this? (3)

Solitude and Communion

He tells us that if we are in the Body of Christ, in the Communion of Saints, there can be no such thing as solitude for we are continually, and inevitably conscious of the great company of the Blessed, with whom we are one in Christ. We need what we commonly call solitude, that is withdrawal from the company of the average man, in order to, realize that communion. Solitude is not isolation. An isolated man who has not become conscious of the ultimate objective link binding him to all other men before God, is an unawakened, immature, even a mutilated man. The world uses the word 'solitary,' but we should not use it. One whose personality is built up in God is indeed solitary amongst the common average of men, because the average man has not awakened to that deep communion, and we can never be satisfied with the shallow ties of mere interest or pleasure, and earthly things which bind most men together in a superficial and evanescent community. He who is 'in Christ,' is never solitary in the sense of being isolated from others. . . . He cannot be unalive to that ultimate, triumphant sense of unity with his brother whom he sees in the place where every man stands before God. He can have no sense of antagonism or indifference towards any human being, for though there are those who are not yet reborn, yet he sees in every man a potential child of God, a potential brother in Christ, a potential member of the same heavenly family in union with which he rejoices. Those who love solitude rejoice in it, rejoice in that condition which alone can make them conscious of the 'great multitude which no man can number of every nation and kindred and tongue which stand before the throne and before the Lamb.' (4)

NOTES / SOURCES

1. *The Spiritual Letters of Father Hughson*, London, 1953, pp. 64–5
2. Ibid., p. 70
3. Ibid., p. 110
4. Ibid., p. 231

Father Andrew SDC (Henry Ernest Hardy)   1869–1946

Born in India, the son of an army officer, Ernest Hardy was educated at Clifton College and Keble College, Oxford. This was followed by a period of residence at Oxford House, Bethnal Green, from where he went to Ely Theological College to train for ordination. Already fired by a vision of a Franciscan order, in January 1894 he took the name of Brother Andrew and with James Adderley and two others founded the Society of the Divine Compassion, soon to be based at St Philip's, Plaistow, in London's East End. With the exception of a year spent in Rhodesia in 1932, he was to be there for the whole of his ministry. A painter and a poet as well as a priest and a religious, Father Andrew was a discerning spiritual guide and teacher of prayer as is evident from his many letters.

Practice Continually the Companionship of Christ

Spiritually, we have to work out our own technique just as we do artistically. But I think these thoughts will help you. When you pray, don't really ask God for things. Ask for virtues, ask for courage, faith, patience, a right vision of our Lord, a right moral sense, a true vision of His love and a right response thereto. Talk to God about anything and everything. Try to practice continually the companionship of Christ, but don't ask for things. Ask for virtues to meet what you have to meet, but just trust about things.

In the same sort of way, don't fuss about what you do. Actions really are symptoms. As the value of a word is in the thought which it is meant to express, and which God always and alone really knows, so the value of an act is in the motive which it expresses in God's sight. Of course, the classic example is the widow's mite. God judged the mite by the motive and counted it a very great gift indeed.

Just bring your motives to God in simplicity. When motives are right, actions in God's sight are right. We all of us have very mixed motives. We can only bring them to God, and He is educating us all the while.

God bless you tenderly in His love. (1)

The Life of Each of Us is Our Prayer

Now about prayer. Don't make prayer a department of your life. It is that in your life which makes all the departments of your life part of itself. As 'the Life was the Light of men,' the whole of it, because the whole of it was His self-revealing, and the whole of it was needed for His self-revealing, so the life of each one of us is our prayer, and the whole of it is needed for our self-giving.

Don't get in bondage to Evelyn Underhill, or Mrs Grundy, or any creature, but just try to live in the power of the Blessed Spirit Who dances in the children and sings in the birds and is the Spirit of life and liberty.

I have met Evelyn Underhill, and she has made a great contribution to the Church, but sometimes she has reminded me of a strange type of person who finds a hobby in making out journeys with Bradshaw. He can tell you anywhere you want to go, with the best route and the proper connections, but when you ask him about the character of the places he can only tell you what he has heard, because he has never been there himself.

Just as the artist in me would prefer to paint you just as God has made you, so the priest in me wants you to be just that creation of God which He made, died for, and would lead to its true, separate, individual, spiritual destiny. Your prayer is just *you* praying, and that is what God wants. (2)

Darkness and Sacrifice

Remember, Moses went *up* into the thick darkness where God was. That is the way of sacrifice, the way every follower of the Crucified must go. Poetry begins with rhymes but leaves them behind. Music begins with tunes but goes on beyond. Religion begins with emotions but soars to sacrifice. Feelings about God are not God, and it is God we trust; and that we may have the honour of trusting Him completely He does us the honour of trusting us in the very Night He knew Himself when he made the great sacrifice for love of us. (3)

Prayer and Conversion

Prayer is turning from self to God. That is what conversion is, but it has got to *go on*. Prayer is not asking God for things as if He would not give, or telling Him things as if He did not know, but living *with* Him. Prayer begins in feeling and ends in sacrifice. (4)

NOTES / SOURCES

1. *The Life and Letters of Father Andrew SDC*, ed. Kathleen E. Burne, London, 1948, p. 235
2. Ibid., p. 238
3. Ibid., p. 253
4. Ibid., p. 258

Charles Freer Andrews   1871–1940

Brought up by his parents in the Catholic Apostolic Church in Birmingham, Andrews was confirmed in the Church of England, much under the influence of B. F. Westcott, shortly after graduating at Cambridge. He was ordained in 1897, and devoted his life to India from 1904 to his death, beginning with ten years as a member of the Cambridge Mission to Delhi and its Brotherhood. Thereafter, his Christianity found expression in the context of India's freedom struggle, and was marked by profound friendships with M. K. Gandhi and Rabindranath Tagore.

A Missionary's Experience[1]

The *sacramental* view of the Christian faith has become deeper and more prominent to me through my missionary experience; at the same time it has become wider and more all-embracing. To put this in another form, I now look at all human life and human history more from the central standpoint of the Incarnation. I think more of the extension of the Incarnate life in wider and wider reaches of humanity, till all is summed up in Christ himself. This is my continual and central thought, rather than starting primarily from the Death of Christ as

[2] 'This is a very early piece, Andrews's response to the question, 'Has your experience in missionary labour altered either in form or substance your impression as to what constitutes the most important and vital elements in the Christian Gospel?' This was one of the questions put to missionary correspondents in preparation for the work of Commission IV at the World Missionary Conference, Edinburgh 1910.

consequent on the Fall, and regarding the saving of individual souls from the punishment due to sin as the one great objective, and viewing all human history as one great mistake, as it were,—one great calamity with one single narrow method or remedy and reconciliation. I hope that the 'exceeding sinfulness of sin' has not become obscured to me, nor the greatness of the Sacrifice of Redemption. But the thought of the Atonement has widened and I view it now more in the light of the Incarnation than I did before. I am more attracted today by Illingworth and Moberly than by Dale, more by S Athanasius than by S Augustine. To the word 'Sacramental' which I have used above in connection with the Incarnation I should add the word 'mystical.' I find that the mystics, especially those of the Middle Ages, bring me more help in understanding Hindu thought and re-shaping my own, than books of a more formal type. The *De Imitatione* has become especially dear to me, and also the teachings of such lives as those of S Bernard, S Francis, S Theresa, Julian of Norwich, Bishop Hall. In the New Testament, the Epistle to the Ephesians and the Johannine writings have become more and more luminous and inspiring.

Again, the *Catholic* side of Christianity (I do not mean its dogma, but its ethos) appeals to me now as it did not in the past, the Daily Eucharist hallowing every act of the day and transfiguring all life and nature,—the joy of piercing through the outward, as through a veil, into the eternal (which the outward dimly expresses) and finding new visions of Christ there, in one's Christian friends and students, in one's Hindu friends and students, in human history, in literature, in art, in nature—all this, and with it the *consecration* of all these (with their own special gifts and treasures) to Christ, to make up His Completeness. That is to say, not a single narrow scheme or plan of salvation dominating my thoughts as in times past,—a salvation concerned solely and entirely with individual souls, as so many atoms or isolated units, but a redemption, a reconstruction, a consecration of all life, of society as well as the individual,—of thought, art, literature, nature,—of all that colours the soul and enriches the soul and is itself in some real sense 'soul' and 'spirit.' I am continually thinking and working towards a unity that is infinitely varied, catholic, all-embracing.

With all this comes in part a weakening (or perhaps the truer word would be a 'widening') of the dogmatic side of the faith. I have a conscious desire to stretch all dogmas to their widest limits, the Sacraments, the Church, the Incarnation itself, the Atonement. These dogmas are not confined to me within the narrow bounds that they once were; though, as I have said, I am consciously more a sacramentalist than ever, and I would add, I am more a 'churchman' than ever. For I rejoice as I never did before in the continuity of Church life, in the thought of the 'Body of the Christ,' in the saint-heritage of the past with its traditions and memories (not one of which I would wish obscured or forgotten) in the communion of saints, in the conscious, prayerful unity of living and departed. But at the same time I could not now speak of the Episcopacy as of the 'Esse' of the Church, or regard a Quaker who had conscientious scruples as to Baptism as not belonging to the 'Body of the Christ,' or consider a Presbyterian or Congregational Sacrament of Holy Communion as *ipso facto* invalid, or speak as I used to do of nonconformity as outside or half outside the covenant, etc. The world of the mission field has made me long for corporate organic unity with an intense passionate longing, but it has made me also realize that the pathway to corporate Unity is not so narrow and so exactly defined as I had imagined and that the variety within the One Body is as important as the unity.

I find the same thing happening within the more intellectual sphere of dogma. I am not so anxious, for instance, as in the past, to *define* the Divinity of our Blessed Lord though it is to me more than before the centre of thought. The Greek Theology appears to me, in its later stages, especially to have gone too far in definition, and Latin Theology still more narrowly to have defined and confined the Faith, which should have been left more wholly a matter of heart and moral apprehension than a matter of intellect and logical reasoning. I should not condemn anyone who said he did not *wish* to define his belief in the Divinity of Christ, but who could from his heart say with the Apostle Thomas 'My Lord and my God,' or with Simon Peter 'Lord, to whom else should we go? Thou hast the words of eternal life.' I should not condemn anyone who could not hold as an article of faith the Virgin Birth. I would not condemn a doubt as to the 'objectivity' of the Resurrection of Christ, if the fact of the Living Christ were granted and His Living Presence were a daily experience.

Again, I now find the *anima Christiana* in Guru Nanak, and Tulsi Das, and Kabir (according to John 1.9) in a way I never did before and I cannot use the word 'heathen' as I used to do. I seem to lay stress on the ethical following of Christ and the practice of the Christ-life, as the supreme criterion, far more than I did in earlier days and the picture of Christ in the Synoptic Gospels as He accredits and approves this person and that, not as belonging to God's chosen People, but as being humble, devout, sincere, unselfish (see such passages as Mt. 8.10, 15.28, 25.37–40; Lk. 10.33–37).

The picture now appears to me here in the Mission Field (with devout, sincere Hindus and other around me) in a way that is quite different from my previous picture.

I should add that a whole field of the New Testament has been opened out to me and the Book reads like a new Book with regard to the great critical question here in India of Racial Unity within the Church. The history of the Apostolic age, the foundation of Catholic as opposed to Judaic Christianity, the life-struggle of the Apostle Paul for racial unity and brotherhood on terms of equality and freedom,—all this has gained a new vividness and a colour and a glory which has made, as I have said, the New Testament a New Book to me. I can hardly describe the different eyes with which I now read its pages. And this root principle of Christianity now dominates my ideas of Human Society, past, present and future.

The Apocalypse has also become a new book to me in the Mission Field. I can now see in it, as I never did before, the martyr-struggle of the early Church, as it tried to keep pure from the 'mark of the Beast,' to avoid that idol-pollution and all its concomitants, undergoing social ostracism and persecution of the most cruel kind. These worst forms of persecution in India now are not as common, but one meets today, and honours as 'Confessors' those that have come out of the great tribulation and have not defiled their robes. The social ostracism which still takes place gives one even now a glowing and vivid picture of Asia Minor at the end of the 1st Century, and the Book in consequence has become an open Book.

In many ways I feel that the change which has been produced in one by my experience in the Mission Field is still proceeding. The pendulum is still swinging sometimes back to the older thoughts, sometimes forwards. I have tried to put down as unreservedly as possible the point which I now seem to have reached. (1)

The Indentured Coolie

There he crouched
Back and arms scarred, like a hunted thing,
Terror-stricken.
All within me surged towards him
While the tears rushed.
Then, a change.
Through his eyes I saw Thy glorious face—
Ah, the wonder!
Calm, unveiled in deathless beauty,
Lord of sorrow. (2)

The Burden Bearer

This is what I saw—

Simla was nearly empty, the season was over;
The Viceroy and his staff had just gone down;
Outside the Secretariat stood piles of cases
Ready to be taken down by train to New Delhi.
On Sunday morning I had started out alone
For the little Church of All Saints at Boileau Ganj,
The snows were shining white in the blue distance,
Eternal, radiant, calm.
The azure sky above, the light amid the trees,
The green earth and the laughing flowers—
Dahlias, cosmos, michaelmas daisies—
Filled with me with an overflowing joy.

   'We praise Thee, O God'—the words came to me,
   'We acknowledge Thee to be the Lord
   All the earth doth worship Thee.'

     Then—this is what I saw!

Struggling along the hill-side up above me,
In a long line, bent down beneath their loads,
Men and boys were panting, straining,
With burdens on their backs—large packing cases,
Filled with papers, files, ledgers, reports,
Cruelly weighted, carrying them down the hill
With heavy plodding steps to the railway station.

This is how I saw them:

Some were strong; they bore their cases lightly
On their broad backs; but others soon had halted
By the hill side, leaving their loads and resting.
Their hollow cheeks and coughing chests betokened
A weak heart over-strained.

One young lad I saw, with a look of pain
In his young eyes, as he struggled on,
Bending beneath his load;
And the thought came to me of the lonely Christ,
Bearing His Cross,
On the way to Golgotha.

      A solemn stillness reigned
In the quiet church. The beautiful light was streaming
Through the stained glass window, where our Lord in judgement
With a sad sorrowful face, crowned with awful justice,
Seemed to say, 'Is it nothing to you, all ye that pass by?'
'Behold and see, if there be any sorrow,
Like unto my sorrow.'

      The sacrament was ended.
The glory of His love had been remembered.
The comfortable words—'Come unto Me,
All ye that are weary and heavy-laden,
And I will give you rest'—
Had brought us joy and peace. For a brief moment,
We had been with him in Paradise,
'Lift up your hearts'—'Sursum Corda'—had been said.
'We lift them up unto the Lord,' we had replied.

      Then—again I saw them,

As I walked back—that long line of men and boys,
With their bodies bent almost double, straining, toiling,
Weary and heavy-laden, with none to give them rest,
For them no glimpse of Paradise,
No gleam of joy at God's own beautiful creation,
No rest, no joy, no peace.
But a comfortless toil, day after day—hungry, thirsty,
Ill-clad, ill-housed, ill-fed.
While His sad sorrowful face, crowned with awful justice,
Looked down on us in judgement.—'I was a stranger,' He said,
'Sick, and in prison, hungry, thirsty, naked,
In as much as ye did it not to one to these—
To one of the very least of these My brothers
Ye did it not to Me!' (3)

On Christ

It is extremely difficult for me to write dispassionately about the strongest conviction of my own life and the foundation of my own moral character, which both have been sustained throughout by one supreme faith in Christ, as my Master and my Lord. Though I have gone through many hard struggles of faith and met with many moral failures and intellectual difficulties, this foundation has not been shaken. What I have experienced has been graphically described in the Epistle to the Hebrews where the writer says that there must always come to the children of faith in their pilgrimage through the world 'shaking of those things that can be shaken in order that those things which cannot be shaken may remain.'

While struggling with sin and evil, within and without, the things which have never been shaken are those foundation beliefs in God and Immortality, which have been revealed to us in the clearest light through Christ.

Before my conversion, when I was eighteen years old, these fundamental facts of life were only held by me as hearsay things which my mother and father taught me. Apart from Christ in my inner life they meant little to me. They did not grip me. But after my conversion God and Immortality became to me not hearsay things at all but eternal verities. Since that time I have felt intuitively that they needed no proof and no argument. 'Solvitur ambulando' was the one way forward which never failed to bring me nearer to God.

When I tried to prove and argue, then trouble began. When I did not argue at all, but simply went down to the depths of my own personal experience, then faith revived. Faith actually became to me 'the substance of things hoped for, the evidence of things not seen.'

Since then, the years of my life have passed by one by one until the three score years mentioned by the Psalmist have been already exceeded. In these intervening years, the settled facts of my inner experience have given me ever greater clearness of vision and comfort of soul. Now, whatever may happen in the years to come, it is impossible for me even for a moment to think that these fundamentals can ever change. They are fixed like the stars and strong as the everlasting hills.

If this conviction that I have spoken about is called intuitive rather than rational, I shall not trouble about names. To me such a conviction represents the reason of all reasons upon which my very existence depends; and I can make no difference between the intuition which is a shining light within the soul and the reasoned expression of that intuition as it issues forth to the world.

There is one line of Robert Browning which continually comes back to my mind when I hear arguments raised in contradiction to these fundamental truths of my own inner being. In 'Abt Vogler' he writes, 'The rest may reason and welcome: 'tis we musicians know.' If God and Immortality and Christ are really truths of life, as I sincerely believe them to be, then it is surely obvious that they must come like music to harmonize our human existence, and not be merely a one-sided factor in it. Logical truths appeal to the intellect only; they make little appeal to the heart. But vital truths touch the whole of life. They are the music which harmonizes the Beauty and Truth, Truth and Beauty, making them one. The heart has its own reasons as the French writer, Pascal, has finely stated.

If someone were to tell me that Homer would pass out of human thought as a living inspiration for the poets and artists of all future ages, I should laugh at the absurdity of such a conception. For I know, without a doubt, that the music of his words will spread in wider and wider circles till it embraces all humanity. If, again, it were said to me that Beethoven would be forgotten, it would seem to me equally absurd. Rather I am certain that his greatest music will appeal to the East as well as to the West. He is one of the Universals.

Christ holds, for me, in the moral and spiritual realm of human life, the same supreme place. Every century makes it more secure. He stands out among the classics of the human race as finally and ultimately supreme in His moral perfection. As the centuries have advanced other names have been brought forward into the full light of historical research and study, and the name of Gautama the Buddha has recently risen again like a star in the East with a new prominence and illumination which is altogether deserved. Indeed this star of the first magnitude has not yet reached its full brightness. But few if any today would place the Buddha's personality above that of Christ though many would apportion to him (as I would myself) the second place in human history, as its spiritual Uplifter and Inspirer towards a better and humaner world. But, as I have said, Christ remains for all time and for all future ages the Supreme Classic of the religious history of mankind.

'Ars longa, vita brevis.' More and more we are coming to the conception of life itself as a supreme Art to be lived, both in relation to the Divine life around us and above us and within us and also in relation to our fellowmen. Here Christ is the Supreme Artist. He gives us that perfect grace and beauty in the moral life which is the counterpart and also the completion of moral truth. St John has told us in his opening chapter how 'the Word was made flesh and dwelt among us, and we beheld His glory, the glory as of the only begotten of the Father full of grace and truth.' In this organic unity of 'grace' and 'truth' in a single supreme personality lies, above all, in our modern age, the sovereign human appeal of Christ.

If, further, the question be asked on what grounds I base my faith in Christ, as finally supreme in human history, the first answer I should give is that He is supreme in my own life and thoughts. From this inner conviction I naturally deduce the thought that He must be supreme in the life of others. My own human experience is not individual but rather in its main outlook the common experience of my fellowmen which I share with them. Therefore I assume a kinship of thought about Christ's moral appeal.

Wherever I have made this assumption, I have found that experience among others justifies that which I believe to be true. But the proof at this point becomes still more convincing when I find that in every part of the world where I have gone and among every nation of men the appeal of Christ's moral character is the same. He is universal.

I would take one example of this universal appeal of Christ's own words of life to all sorts and conditions of men. The eldest brother of the poet Rabindranath Tagore was residing in retirement at Santiniketan for many years before he died. He was a Hindu and he had been a great poet in his younger days. He had a beautiful tolerance of spirit and the heart of a little child. As a philosopher his intellect was profound and his range of knowledge vast. Wrapt in silent meditation he led his innocent life at Santiniketan gently to its close. He lived in the serene atmosphere of a few great texts, which he had found by long experience to have the power of lifting his soul up to God.

With all his immense learning, he was simple and humble in spirit, and truth was ever on his lips. Each day at sunset he would wish to have me with him. At that sunset hour, he would gather up the supreme thoughts that had come to him during the day and tell me about them. During the last years of his life, he would go for these constantly to the Sermon on the Mount and dwell on its central sayings.

'They are my food and drink,' he said to me one day, 'so simple in their setting that a child can understand them and yet so profound in their inner meaning. Along with the words of the Upanishads and the Gita, they are among the few great classical things left to us in this world. What a daring saying is that of Christ, when He says, "My words shall never pass away." Yet it has proved to be altogether true. Day after day, I ponder over them.. And when I lie awake, during the sleepless hours of the night, they come back to me. I never seem to grow tired of them or to get to the end of their significance. They contain those truths that sustain a man at the last, even in the presence of death.'

The one saying of Jesus that meant most of all to him was 'Blessed are the pure in heart, for they shall see God.' This gave him a satisfaction, in its completeness, that no other word could give, and he often returned to it. One other saying which was almost equally dear to him was, 'The Kingdom of God is within you.' He would repeat this sentence to me with a touch of awe in the very tone of his voice, that added mystery to the words themselves as he used them. Especially he would love to dwell upon their inward meaning, as representing the Kingdom of the heart—the Heaven within.

With his own deep spiritual nature, he would not seldom bring out some fresh interpretation that I had never seen mentioned before. Thus his rendering would often differ from my own; but he would say to me that the depth of the words of a great Master, such as Christ, are literally unfathomable. They are like a living fountain of pure water, overflowing to satisfy the spiritual thirst of mankind. Each age goes back to them afresh in order to drink at the fountainhead. Future ages would do the same. So long as man's nature remains with its ultimate needs.

During my life in the East, the startling originality of Jesus Christ as the most revolutionary thinker whom the world has ever seen has come home to me even more than in the West. There is a true and rightful place for the calm serenity of the Buddha, as old age is reached with its ripe wisdom, but Jesus Christ died upon the Cross in the fullness of His youth. His Spirit is in our own day the one dynamic force that is able to move and to restore mankind.

The curse of convention has continually bound fast the seed of the new life in Christ, as it struggles to burst through the hard ground, and blossom and flower forth and bear fruit. The dead wrappings of the past have always tended to confine the insurgent spirit of man. Christ comes again, in His own right to set us free. (4)

NOTES / SOURCES

1. C. F. Andrews: 'A Missionary's Experience' in *The Indian Interpreter*, Poona, October 1909
2. C. F. Andrews, 'The Indentured Coolie' in *The Modern Review*, Calcutta, 1915
3. C. F. Andrews, 'The Burden Bearer' in *The C. F. Andrews Centenary Souvenir*, Calcutta, 1971
4. 'Articles and Speeches by C. F. Andrews in mss', 1930s, Chaturvedi Collection, National Archives of India, New Delhi

Frank Weston   1871–1924

Bishop of Zanzibar from 1908 until his death, Frank Weston was a convinced Anglo-Catholic. He had an outstanding ministry in Africa but caused controversy by his protest against the recognition of the sacraments of non-episcopal churches in the proposals formulated at a missionary conference at Kikuyu in Kenya in 1913. In *Serfs of Great Britain* he protested against forced labour in Africa. His social conscience was evident in his powerful speech as president to the Second Anglo-Catholic Congress a year before his death.

The Naked Christ of Calvary

We appear to forget that our essential relation with eternal love is through the Response of Love incarnate, Jesus, the 'coloured' man of Nazareth. Moreover we ignore our relation with the poor Man of Galilee, the naked Christ of Calvary. And we allow ourselves to be, almost entirely, dominated by standards of wealth and caste the world about us approves . . . Eternal love, when He takes flesh, comes as a poor, coloured Man, whereas we dislike poverty and despise colour! How then can we preach love incarnate? (1)

The African Reality of Gethsemane and Calvary

You will bear me out that Gethsemane and Calvary are most real in Africa; that Christ is brutally crucified here, crucified in the persons of Africans, by his professing followers . . . God in manhood, God on the Cross, God of the empty tomb.

Now into the glory of our Calvary breaks the voice of prelatical and priestly liberalism. And its message, what is it?

It is that Africans cannot possibly understand the Gospels, Church or sacraments until they re-interpret them in the light of modern European thought! Poor Africans: not yet among the wise of European thought. (2)

Christ in the Sacrament and in the Slum

But I say to you, and I say it with all the earnestness that I have, if you are prepared to fight for the right of adoring Jesus in His Blessed Sacrament, then, when you come out from before your tabernacles, you must walk with Christ, mystically present in you, through the streets of this country, and find the same Christ in the peoples of your cities and villages. You cannot claim to worship Jesus in the tabernacle if you do not pity Jesus in the slum. . . . It is folly, it is madness, to suppose that you can worship Jesus in the Sacrament and Jesus on the throne of glory, when you are sweating Him in the bodies and souls of His children. . . . You have your Mass, you have your altars, you have begun to get your tabernacles. Now go out into the highways and hedges, and look for Jesus in the ragged and the naked, in the oppressed and the sweated, in those who have lost hope, and in those who are struggling to make good. Look for Jesus in them;

and, when you have found Him, gird yourself with His towel of fellowship and
wash His feet in the person of His brethren.

NOTES / SOURCES

1. Frank Weston, *The Revelation of Eternal Love. Christianity Stated in Terms of Love*, London &
   Oxford, 1920, p. 157
2. Frank Weston, *The Christ and the Critics*, London & Oxford, 1919, pp. 68–9
3. H. Maynard Smith, *Frank, Bishop of Zanzibar: Life of Frank Weston, D.D. 1871–1924*, London, 1926,
   p. 302

John Macleod Campbell Crum   1872–1958

Educated at Eton and New College, Oxford, Crum served as chaplain to Bishop Paget of
Oxford, and subsequently as Rector of Farnham and then as a Canon of Canterbury. He
was the author and translator of a number of hymns, many written for the children in
the Sunday Schools of his parish or for special occasions, including *Eia, Jesu adorande*
by John Mauburn (d. 1503).

O Lord Jesus, I Adore Thee

PART 1

O Lord Jesus, I adore thee
For the bread of worth untold
Freely given in thy Communion,
   Wonderful a thousandfold,
Given to-day in loving bounty
   More than my poor heart can hold.

Make thou of my soul an orchard
   Quickened into fruitfulness;
Come, O come, life-giving Manna,
   Making glad my wilderness:
Sweeter far than any sweetness
   Tongue can taste, or words express.

PART 2

Ah, Lord Jesus, go not from me,
   Stay, ah, stay with me, my Lord;
Make me shrink from whatsoever
   Will not with thy name accord;
Act through me in every action,
   Speak through me in every word.

Would that I could keep thee always
   In mine inmost heart to be,
Thou and only thou suggesting
   Every thought and wish in me;
All my soul, with singing, offered
   For a sacrifice to thee.

NOTES / SOURCES

[Translated by J. M. C. Crum from the original by John Mauburn] No: 388, *Hymns Ancient & Modern* Revised Edition, 1950

William Braithwaite O'Brien SSJE 1874–1960

Father O'Brien was a member of the Cowley Fathers for fifty years and Superior from 1931–1949. He devoted much energy to directing women's Religious Communities and was amongst the Anglo-Catholic voices concerned about the ecclesiological consequences of the formation of the Church of South India. He was a notable spiritual director.

God in Godless Places

(1928) I am afraid it does not sound altogether like a change for the better. It must be very difficult to live in faith and love in a place such as you are in. I am afraid our institutions are terribly godless places. And yet God is there; for he is everywhere and he is there in love and power, though men by their words and acts deny him and make it very hard for others to believe this. You can live as if God were not there; but just as others in word and deed, but you will not be able to do it without a bad conscience and a great danger to your own soul, as you accept the struggle and pray for faith and love and guidance to behave as a Christian should in such a condition.

You know God acts in this world largely *through* our fellow men. If we were all doing his will as it is done in heaven this world would be all peace and love, it would be heaven; and God would be ten thousand times more manifest than he is. The suffering and the evil in life come because men do not do his will and so the world becomes more like hell than heaven and then men blame the world, but it is what we have made it, not what God intended.

And yet God goes on patiently seeking to make himself known through our words and acts of love and kindness and truth to one another. Our Lord taught us this, it was the sign of being his disciples 'that ye love one another.' So brutality and foul talk and hard selfishness deny God while love and patience and quiet strength reveal him. You may think it is little you can do, or you may in a false humility, think you are not fit to attempt to do anything, but none the less you are there to make your light shine. Where all is dark even a feeble glimmer of light goes a long way.

Just try and think God is here, God wants to show his love in this place through me; God is not indifferent to these ruined lives, they have another state before them in the life to come, their feeble brains only belong to this life, perhaps I can bring a little of God's light into their lives—it will seem very useless and at times you will be tempted to give up and yet if you persevere maybe you will be doing just the thing God is asking of you and he will bless it with results both to them and yourself such as in this life we cannot even imagine.

You may have to act severely—more so than you would wish but I cannot help thinking you may be able to find many a way to show that the patients are to you human beings with souls, needing kindness, needing something to help the self-respect which such an institution tends to kill.

(1928) Yes. I am very glad to hear you are sticking to it. It is the hard things in life that are worth doing though at the moment we don't always feel like that. Thank you for your thankoffering. I am putting it to our little fund for the children's work in our church. Few things help me more than to remember that I have not got to go on in my own strength or to depend on my own will. We have the life of Christ in us—through our baptism and our communions and just as we begin each new day on waking with minds and bodies refreshed by sleep so also we begin our spiritual life afresh too each morning. The daily renewal of his life in us is a great truth which we learn more and more to depend on as we get to know better our own weakness and changefulness. (1)

The Depression of Old Age

Old age is depressing, and our constant failures and slow progress are depressing—the weather is depressing and makes all the depressing things seem worse, but they do not separate us from God. They are meant to draw us nearer to him who *is* so near to us in order to *revive* us. You will say, But I cannot find him. Perhaps not; but he is finding you, and perhaps the fault is that you do not know where to look for him. I think you should look for him in just the things which seem to keep you from him. Take your troubles to him; speak to him as you would to me; tell out to him the hardness of your circumstances and the hardness of a selfish unloving heart and ask his help. You would not be so conscious of this unloving spirit if there was *no* love or generosity in your heart. You look to him to change your circumstances, or to take away the selfish heart and suddenly plant within you a new and unselfish heart. Well, actually he is trying to change your heart, and is working in your heart. Pray to him as one that is working in you; ask for more grace to believe in, hope in, and trust in his sure working. He has given you grace to persevere with your confessions. That means coming to him that he may *revive* your heart and encourage you to persevere. There are many like you in old age, full of self-pity; but only complaining and never turning to him for help. If God has taken away all hope in yourself and in the world around you, it is in order that at last you may learn to hope in him and in all his gracious promises.

I expect it would be good to get away from where you now live, and as the infirmities of age increase to seek some Home where you would get care and nursing. But such a life would not be an easy one for you unless you continue the effort to seek God and not yourself; *his* will, not yours. (2)

Prayer Increasingly an Act of the Will

I am not clear as to whether it was in your retreat or some time before that you found yourself led into the prayer of holding your will resolutely in a conscious realization of God or not. But, whether this was the special grace of your retreat or not, it is a quite right and normal development of prayer, which should become increasingly an act of the will rather than of intellect or emotion. Indeed a prayer which is very dry, and consequently a good deal bothered by involuntary distractions, may be a purer offering to God than one in which we are conscious of much help and refreshment, if only our wills remain steadfast in a quiet trustful waiting upon God. If we cannot persevere through these times of difficulty we certainly cannot make progress. Dom Chapman has a useful hint when he says that as some new development of prayer comes to us we must never think that now we have found a safe and satisfying way of prayer. I do not quote his exact words but I am sure there is no safe and easy stage in our prayer; no method that will work easily and without cost to ourselves. For most people the kind of prayer to which you find yourself led is like leaving the quiet cultivated lands of civilization for a desert with occasional oases which probably get more and more rare.

Once more it is the advice of Dom Chapman to come to our prayer as receiving it from God and to take with complete surrender to him whatever he gives. In regard to your questions I should say certainly persevere in the kind of prayer you used in your retreat. It should be daily except Sundays, half an hour is enough except in retreat and times when you feel urged to do more for some special reason. Of course this prayer is harder in the midst of work and worry than in times of retreat. In regard to reverting to other kinds of prayer I think it is likely that you are definitely called to another stage and I should say stick to that, but it is not *wrong* to use another form of mental prayer such as you found helpful in the past, only you will probably find that now it does not help you and only makes things worse. What one should avoid is starting to pray in this attitude of waiting upon God and then changing to something easier. If you were unwell or very tired or felt drawn to begin with a prayer on the lines of meditation there would be no harm and it might result in your passing into a simple prayer of the will; but as a rule when the change comes we find we simply cannot meditate; the effort becomes wearisome and distasteful. The pity is that so few realize this, and see that it does not mean they are losing the power to pray but only passing into a new stage of their prayer.

May I lastly say a word about reading books on prayer. You chose the right kind of books but you will not learn to pray from books but only by praying. It is the holy Spirit who teaches us to pray; a great deal of knowledge from books may even be a hindrance to actual prayer. Let God be your guide; seek *him* in your prayer, not progress to something you have read about in books. Do not worry about the 'Dark Night' in prayer or other states of prayer; seek God and his will. If you are finding special difficulties and unfamiliar experiences; if you are feeling baffled in your prayer and beginning to wonder whether you are praying at all, it is good to seek guidance from someone but otherwise do not watch your prayer anxiously any more than your health. But you should make room in your day for bible study. It is the Bible which brings to us most illumination. If you no longer meditate in your time of prayer, you need to make your bible study a kind of meditation. It has been found useful by some to take the passage they study and look out the marginal references and then write down their own reflections and afterwards compare them with a good commentary. However that may be, find that way which makes the Bible interesting to you even if it is only for a short time each day. You will get more light from this direct study of the sacred text than from any books. At the same time it is useful occasionally to read books on prayer in order to stimulate your own desire for prayer. (3)

The Chastening of God's Love

(1940) Since God *is* love he cannot but act in love. Your long continued distress of soul is the chastening of his love. It may seem to you as though you had no faith or spiritual life, but it needs only a breath of the holy Spirit to make faith and love shoot up with flames that reach to heaven.

God does not leave himself without witness though it may seem to you that you are in unrelieved darkness. You have *desire*; and no feeble desire, but one which causes a real suffering of hunger and thirst. It is inconceivable that God should himself give such desire to a soul unless he means to satisfy it. We have our Lord's own word for that. I do not doubt that God is purifying you and preparing you for a deeper union with himself—and a greater degree of joy. What does matter so much is that you should remember you are dealing with God and that the profoundest and deepest submission to his will is your part. Do not question, do not complain, except that you are quite right to write to me of all that you feel and experience. (4)

Old Age and Death

You mustn't be too much distressed because you can't experience the realization and feeling you had years ago; that happens as we grow older but we know and must believe the reality is still there and you must give up trying to live in the past and must overcome the thought that life is dreary. Thank God for all the happiness he has given you in the past and try to serve him faithfully in the present. There is so much he wants us to do.

As age advances, a lot is taken out of our life and patience tried, and very sorely tried, yet through these things have you not learned to make sacrifices to God?

How wonderful life is and death. It does seem to be the way that our life passes through different stages: childhood passes into youth, youth to maturity and on to increasing age, when life does seem to get more difficult as we get into the background as it were and everything is restricted and we have to accept more and more the lowest places, as our Lord said to St Peter, 'Another shall gird thee and carry thee whither thou wouldest not.' Our Lord in his loving providence seems to try to detach us from the things of this life and prepare us for the eternal realities of the life beyond. 'Eye hath not seen nor ear heard, neither have entered into the heart of man the things which God has prepared for them that love him.'

Both —— and myself are looking forward now rather than backward—forward to the great purposes of God and to greater revelations of his love. I am very close to eighty-two and am now one of the 'older fathers.' Thank God I have good health and still some work to do. (5)

NOTES / SOURCES

1. *A Cowley Father's letters: selected from the letters of W. B. O'Brien SSJE*, London, 1962, pp. 5–6
2. Ibid., pp. 55–6
3. Ibid., pp. 61–2
4. Ibid., p. 88
5. Ibid., pp. 147–8

Timothy Rees CR   1874–1939

Timothy Rees CR, a priest of the Community of the Resurrection, was Bishop of Llandaff from 1931 to 1939. A devotional writer and powerful preacher, he was the author of a number of hymns and retreat addresses.

Thirsting for God – A Hymn

O God of love, O Lord of life,
  Without Thy gifts I cease to be;
Yet all Thy gifts fill not my soul—
  I thirst for Thee, for Thee.

'Tis not Thy wisdom, or Thy strength,
  Thy knowledge, or Thy sanctity
I long to touch, but Thee Thyself—
  I thirst for Thee, for Thee.

Thou, God, art infinitely near,
  Thy life divine encircles me;
Yet more, still more, my soul demands—
  I thirst for Thee, for Thee.

O Thou eternal loveliness,
  What joy the sight of Thee must be!
Yet 'tis not joy I crave for, Lord—
  I thirst for Thee, for Thee.

Thou, God, hast made me for Thyself—
  Thy life to share, Thy face to see;
And deep to deep must ever call—
  I thirst for Thee, for Thee.

NOTES / SOURCES

Timothy Rees CR in *Edward Keble Talbot: His Community and His Friends*, compiled by G. P. H. Pawson CR, London, 1954, p. 93

Evelyn Underhill   1875–1941

An outstanding student of the Christian mystical tradition, Evelyn Underhill was a pioneer of the retreat movement in the Church of England, founding the House of Retreat at Pleshey near Chelmsford in 1919. Owing much to the spiritual direction of the (Roman) Catholic Modernist, Baron Friedrich von Hügel (1852–1925), she was herself a notable spiritual director.

Missa Cantata

Once in an abbey-church, the while we prayed,
   All silent at the lifting of the Host,
A little bird through some high window strayed;
      And to and fro
     Like a wee angel lost
That on a sudden finds its heaven below,
    It went the morning long
And made our Eucharist more glad with song.

It sang, it sang! and as the quiet priest
   Far off about the lighted altar moved,
The awful substance of the mystic feast
      All hushed before
     It like a thing that loved,
Yet loved in liberty, would plunge and soar
    Beneath the vault in play
And thence toss down the oblation of its lay.

The walls that went our sanctuary around
   Did as of old, to that sweet summons yield.
New scents and sounds within our gates were found,
      The cry of kine,
     The fragrance of the field,
All woodland whispers, hastened to the shrine,
    The country side was come
Eager and joyful, to its spirit's home.

Far stretched I saw the cornfield and the plough,
   The scudding cloud, the cleanly running brook,
The humble kindly turf, the tossing bough,
      That all their light
     From Love's own furnace took;
This altar, where one angel brownly bright
    Proclaimed the sylvan creed,
And sang the Benedictus of the mead.

All earth was lifted to communion then,
   All lovely life was there to meet its King;
Ah, not the little arid souls of men
      But sun and wind
     And all desirous thing
The ground of their beseeching here did find;
    All with one self same bread,
And all by one eternal priest were fed. (1)

Meditation

Meditation is a word which covers a considerable range of devotional states. It is perhaps most simply defined as thinking in the Presence of God. And since our ordinary thoughts are scattered, seldom poised for long on one point, but evoked and influenced by a multitude of external things, real meditation requires as its preliminary what aesthetic writers call recollection—a deliberate gathering of ourselves together, a retreat into our own souls. This is more easily done by a simple exercise of the imagination, a gentle turning to God, than by those ferocious efforts towards concentrating which some manuals advise, and which often end by concentrating attention on the concentration itself. I will not go further into their technical descriptions of method; which seem so difficult when we read them, and often worry people needlessly. There is no virtue in any one method, except in so far as it succeeds; and different methods succeed with different souls. For some, the slow reading of a passage in the Bible or the *Imitation* leads directly to a state of prayer: for others, a quiet dwelling on one of God's attributes is a gateway to adoration. Articulate speech is now left aside, but the ceaseless stream of inward discourse may persist, and become a secret conversation with God; while others will be led to consideration, a quiet ruminating on spiritual things. As to Three-point Meditations and so on, it is perhaps, enough if we keep in mind that every real meditation, however short, natural and artless, does involve three points: for our mind, will and feelings are all exercised in it. We think in some way of the subject of our meditation. We feel the emotion, whether of love, penitence or joy, which it suggests to us. And finally, the aim of all meditative prayer is a resolution, or a renewal of our surrender to God: and this is an act of the will. (2)

The Sacramental Principle

It is true that at bottom worship is a spiritual activity; but we are not pure spirits, and therefore we cannot expect to do it in purely spiritual ways. That is the lesson of the Incarnation. Thus liturgies, music, symbols, sacraments, devotional attitudes and acts have their rightful part to play in the worshipping life; and it is both shallow and arrogant to reject them *en masse* and assume that there is something particularly religious in leaving out the senses when we turn to God. Through such use of the senses man can receive powerful religious suggestions, and by their help can impregnate an ever wider area of his life and consciousness with the spirit of adoration. If music is something that may awaken the awed awareness of the Holy, if pictures can tell us secrets that are beyond speech, if food and water, fragrance and lights, all bear with them a memory of sacred use—then the ordinary deeds of secular life will become more and more woven into the seamless robe that veils the Glory of God. But this will not happen unless the sacramental principle—the principle of the spiritual significance of visible deeds and things—has a definite expression in our organized religious life. (3)

The Distinctive Character of Christian Mysticism

If we leave these general ideas, and consider what mysticism is and means within Christianity we see that the great Christian mystical tradition, having its roots in the New Testament and including as it does some of the greatest of the saints, has a special quality which distinguishes it from those who have responded to the attraction of God from within other faiths. We should, of course, expect this, if the claim of Christianity to be a unique revelation of God, and the claim of the Church to be a supernatural society fostering the supernatural life of the soul, are true. Christianity is the religion of the Word Incarnate, and in the great Christian mystic something which has a certain relation to the mystery of the Incarnation takes place. He becomes at his full development a creative personality, a tool of God. The promise made in the first chapters of Acts is literally fulfilled in him; his loving contemplation of the Eternal, his prayer in the Spirit, produces power.

A non-Christian mystic, such as the great Plotinus, may describe his ecstatic experience of God as a solitary flight from this world with its demands, imperfections, and confusions, and a self-loss in the peace and blessedness of eternity. The Christian mystic knows these wonderful moments too; but for him they are only wonderful moments. His experience of eternal life includes the Incarnation, with its voluntary acceptance of all the circumstances of our common situation, its ministry of healing and enlightenment, its redemptive suffering. He cannot, therefore, contract out of existence with its tensions and demands. For him union with God means self-giving to the purposes of the divine energy and love.

Here is the secret of the strange power of St Paul, St Bernard, St Francis, John Wesley, Elizabeth Fry, the Curé d'Ars, and thousands more. 'Our works,' says St Teresa, speaking for all of them, 'are the best proof that the favours we have received come from God.' Thus she and her companion, St John of the Cross, the prince of transcendentalists, labour and suffer for the reform of the religious life; Wesley takes the world for his parish; the Curé d'Ars becomes the conscience of France. 'All Friends everywhere,' said George Fox, 'keep all your meetings waiting on the Light.' That is a demand for a corporate act of mystical devotion; and we know what the lives of Friends in the world were required to be. All these endorse the saying of Ruysbroeck that the final state of the mystic is not ecstatic self-loss in the Godhead but something at once more difficult and more divine—'a widespreading love towards all in common.' Indeed this must be so, because the God with whom he is united is the Absolute Love.

That which makes Christian mysticism so rich, deep, life-giving, and beautiful is, therefore, the Christian doctrine of the nature and action of God. It is different because it is based on the Incarnation, the redemptive self-giving of the Eternal Charity. The Christian mystic tries to continue in his own life Christ's balanced life of ceaseless communion with the Father and homely service to the crowd. His love of God and thirst for God have been cleansed by long discipline from all self-interest; and the more profound his contemplation of God, the more he loves the world and tries to serve it as a tool of the divine creative love. And indeed, a spiritual life which cuts the world into two mutually exclusive halves, and tries to achieve the Infinite by ignoring the finite and its obligations, could never be satisfactory for men; who need, in proportion to their spiritual enthusiasm, a constant remembrance of Plato's warning that it is not well to exercise the soul without the body or the body without the soul.

Though mysticism be indeed the living heart of all religion, this does not mean that religion does, or can, consist of nothing but heart. The Church is a Body with head, hands, feet, flesh, and hard bones: none of them any use, it is true, if the heart does not function, but all needed for the full expression of the Christian spiritual life. This acceptance of our whole life of thought, feeling, and action, as material to be transformed and used in our life towards God, is what Baron von Hügel meant by 'inclusive mysticism.' It alone is truly Christian; because its philosophic basis is the doctrine of the Incarnation, with its continuance in the Church and Sacraments. Its opposite, exclusive mysticism, the attempt to ascend to the vision of God by turning away from His creatures by an unmitigated other-worldliness, is not Christian at all. It ends, says that same great theologian, in something which cannot be distinguished from mere Pantheism: or, on more popular levels, in sloppy claims to be in tune with the Infinite. (4)

Staying an Anglican

9 June, 1931

To Dom John Chapman

This is really an answer to the last bit of your letter, because I feel I owe you an explanation of my 'position' which must seem to you a very inconsistent one. I have been for years now a practising Anglo-Catholic . . . and solidly believe in the Catholic status of the Anglican Church, as to orders and sacraments, little as I appreciate many of the things done among us. It seems to me a respectable suburb of the city of God—but all the same, part of 'greater London.' I appreciate the superior food, etc., to be had nearer the centre of things. But the *whole* point to me is in the fact that our Lord has put me *here*, keeps on giving me more and more jobs to do for souls here, and has never given me orders to move. In fact, when I have been inclined to think of this, something has always stopped me: and if I did it, it would be purely an act of spiritual self-interest and self-will. I know what the push of God is like, and should obey it if it came—at least I trust and believe so. When . . . I put myself under Baron von Hügel's direction, five years before his death, he went into all this, and said I must never think of moving on account of my own religious preferences, comforts or advantages—but only if so decisively called by God that I felt it wrong to resist—and he was satisfied that up to date I had not received this call. Nor have I done so since. I promised him that if ever I did receive it I should obey. Under God, I owe him my whole spiritual life, and there would be much more of it than there is, if I had been more courageous and stern with myself and followed his directions more thoroughly. And it seems to me a sort of secondary evidence that God means me to be where I am, that He gave me that immense and transforming help, and yet with a quite clear light that I am to stay here and not 'down tools.' Of course I know I might get other orders at any moment, but so far that is not so. After all He has lots of terribly hungry sheep in Wimbledon, and if it is my job to try and help with them a bit it is no use saying I should rather fancy a flat in Mayfair, is it?

Please do not think this cheek. It is not meant so, but it is so much easier to write quite straight and simply. (5)

The Substance of Prayer and the Heart of the Eucharist

The graph of Christian prayer conforms very closely to the central action of the Eucharist. First the Sanctus, the type of all adoring worship 'with angels and archangels glorifying the Holy Name' and lifting heart and mind to the contemplation of Reality. Then the bread and wine, the ordinary stuff of life raised to the plane of sacrifice and freely offered that it may be blessed and transformed by the action of the Holy, made the food and salvation of the soul. And now we stand at the central point on which all this is poised: where the heavenly prayer and the earthly prayer meet. Our Father, which art in heaven . . . Thy Will be done on earth as it is in heaven. The Will: that mysterious attribute of the Living Godhead of which a little crumb is given to men, in order that it may be united in love to the Whole from which it came. Once again the priority of the Holy, the overruling interests of the Transcendent are re-affirmed as the very substance of the creature's adoring prayer. (6)

The Vision of Christ and the Demand for Dedication

Passion Sunday: March 18, 1923

Today my God and Joy I felt and knew Thee, Eternal, Unchanging, transfusing all things, and most wholly and perfectly given to us in Christ—our in-dwelling with Him a Total Surrender to Thee—Thyself in all, the one medium of our union—at Communion to find and love Thee in each soul at which Thou hast given Thyself.

To know and find Thee, actually and substantially, in all nations and races and persons—*this* nourishes love and solves the intercession problem. 'Not grace alone, nor us alone, but Thy Grace in us.' To *use* and cultivate it. I think the parable of the talents meant this. How far beyond anything one conceived the mysteries seem to stretch now.

The more vivid the vision of Christ grows and the more insistent the demand for dedication, the more one can escape by this path from the maze of self-occupation. He draws, and we run after. (7)

Anger

What is the raw stuff of anger, the reflex action of our vigorous instinctive nature? Is it not resenting and attacking what opposes it; hitting back, personal wrath, wrong and wasteful use of that energy. Given to God it can be the source of that rightfully indignant action which helps to bring the world a little nearer to the Divine pattern. When our Lord cleansed the Temple it was rightful indignation; the whole drive of His human nature for the purposes of God.

The death of personal anger does not mean mere limp acquiescence which is no virtue but second cousin to Sloth. But it means getting rid of the psychic hurricanes which always have self at their centre and which dissipate our real strength and in which we cannot be quiet with God. It means seeing that over-sensitiveness which swells up at a touch for the silly bit of egoism it really is and quietly dropping the irritability which so easily imagines a tickle that is not really there.

Now there are two main directions from which these storms of anger come to us; whether in the form of deep depressions or shallow centres of disturbance they are equally destructive of spiritual good weather. First, anger with circum-stances and second, anger with ourselves.

(1) We are angry with circumstances because they oppose our ideas, plans, rights, ideals, sense of justice and spiritual preferences, all of which are of course very imperfect and limited. We must include here those high-minded sulkings about life, resentment at God's mysterious ways (one of the peculiar sins of moderns) a hostile, exasperated attitude to existence. Also a self-occupied brooding over our own wrongs, frustrations or disappointments, health, failure, loneliness, lack of scope. This brooding anger, this sense of having a grievance, whether directed to persons or things, is like the ground swell persisting after a storm; it is not very obvious on the surface but utterly destructive of peace and quiet. Nothing quiets it but a sense of God more profound than any sense of self, sinking deeper and deeper into the Ocean of His Reality.

Now what we have to say about all this is, how we waste all this splendid material! material indwelt by God and used to train our souls. *All* the ups and downs and inequalities of the world used rightly, can train us for God. Every missed tram and crowded bus and tiresome neighbour, just as, if they are used wrongly, they can alienate us from Him. The life of business, of the home, of sport, hotel-life—all these are full of the stuff which can discipline and make supple our souls. So can external religion: Church life is sure to contain many things we do not like. Nature gets us ready for super-nature; the life of the social organism trains us to take our place in that more mysterious organism, the Body of Christ.

We must be faithful and selfless in our handling of small things, before we can be trusted with great things and enter into the Joy of the Lord. Yet we are so stupid about life, we fail to use all these rich opportunities of discipline. Instead we stiffen up and resist God's moulding action by our angry reactions! When we have massage to get the stiffness out of our joints and make them useful and supple, it often hurts; but we do not for that reason bite and scratch the masseur. Yet many souls react to the blows and rubs and pinches through which the Holy Ghost works on them, with something very like a scratch or bite, or at the very least with a dull, rigid resistance. The result is that the process hurts twice as much as it should, because we are not using the blessed power of relaxation and acceptance given by God as the right way of taking the buffets of personal life. So, one way of mortifying our general human tendency to anger, is to keep in mind the absolutely essential part played by vexations and trials in humbling and bracing our spirits, making them fit for God and therefore meeting them with gratitude and joy. I remember Friedrich von Hügel saying, 'It is only suffering, meekly accepted, willed, transfigured by the love of God and of Christ—it is only such that will purify or cure anything.' So let us use our material, every bit of it, do not waste it. There is something for us in every small prick as well as in the big blows. God uses a hypodermic syringe quite as often as a surgical knife.

(2) Anger with ourselves is a far more insidious and enduring temptation than anger with circumstance, for those trying to lead the life of prayer. 'The true lover of Christ,' says Hilton, 'is little stirred by the jangles of men.' But it is when the jangles stir in our own insides, that the situation becomes serious. And any undue preoccupation with our own state, any anxious striving or exasperation over failure, is sure to bring these jangles on. We waste a lot of energy being angry with ourselves, because our prayer, our character, our life is not what *we* think it ought to be. Because humiliating faults persist and the power of carrying out resolutions does not come, and time after time we let slip the opportunity for Christ-like action and time after time forget till too late, to bridle our tongues. Gentleness in devotion, doing steadily and faithfully what we can do and leaving the rest to God, is a great spiritual grace. And gentleness in contrition is a greater grace still, impossible without much humility. When tempted to be too intense and irritable because we seem to accomplish so little, remember 'My joy is to wait upon the Lord' and then make a little meditation on what really good waiting is like—easy, calm, apparently unhurried but never negligent. Set before your eyes the picture of a perfect waitress. She has forgotten herself in her work: she is not strung up, tense; she does not scuttle or suddenly lose her head because she has forgotten something and dash round the table the wrong way; she is not anxiously preoccupied with her own shortcomings: *those* are the kind who spill the sauce and break the vegetable dish.

Remember the wonderful opening of the 65th Psalm: '*Unto Thee stillness is praise, O God, in Zion!*' That is the literal translation. And by the word stillness, the Hebrew poets meant the quietude of the soul utterly given into God's hand. '*Only unto God is my soul's stillness*', says the writer of the 62nd Psalm. There we reach that spiritual state which does away with our tumults, purifies us from our angry, petty reactions to life; the state of surrender, of loving sacrifice. (8)

To be Refreshed by Christ's Presence

O blessed Jesu Christ, who didst bid all who carry heavy burdens to come to Thee, refresh us with Thy Presence and Thy Power. Quiet our understandings and give ease to our hearts, by bringing us close to things Infinite and Eternal. Open to us the mind of God that in His light we may see light. And crown Thy choice of us to be Thy servants by making us springs of strength and joy to all whom we serve. (9)

NOTES / SOURCES

1. Margaret Cropper, *Evelyn Underhill*, London, 1958, pp. 39–40
2. *Collected Papers of Evelyn Underhill* (ed. Lucy Menzies), London, 1946, pp. 43–4
3. Ibid., pp. 67–8
4. Ibid., pp. 114–16
5. *The Letters of Evelyn Underhill* (ed. Charles Williams), London, 1943, pp. 195–6
6. Evelyn Underhill, *Abba: Meditations based on the Lord's Prayer*, London, 1945, p. 39
7. *Fragments from an Inner Life: The Notebooks of Evelyn Underhill* (ed. Dana Greene), Harrisburg, Pennsylvania, 1993, pp. 39–40

8. Evelyn Underhill, *The Mount of Purification (With Meditations and Prayers, 1949 and Collected Papers, 1946)*, London, 1960, pp. 33–7
9. Ibid., p. 93

Edward Keble Talbot   1877–1949

The son of Bishop Edward Stuart Talbot, E. K. Talbot was educated at Winchester and Christ Church. Ordained in 1904 he joined the Community of the Resurrection in 1910 and served as Superior from 1922 to 1940. A stimulating retreat conductor, he was influenced by Von Hügel, and by Henry Scott Holland (q.v.), who was his godfather.

Growing by Stern Climbing

Most of us have found that prayer is not easy. We started and found it hard and gave up. Here again let us recognize that what we do in prayer is not an added or an occasional little activity. It has got to do with the whole of life; it is the very nerve of our life. Prayer is desire. Praying is the school of desire. Our real prayer is our most prevailing desire which, whether uttered as a prayer or not, God recognizes as such: 'Almighty God, unto whom all hearts be open, all desires known and from whom no secrets are hid' . . . these are awe-inspiring words. Prayer is something which has to do with the central energy of our life. If the desire has got to be purified, enlarged to the scale of what our little souls are capable of receiving from God, it is not an easy way. If you have known someone much greater, richer, deeper than yourself, you know what it is to desire to be with that person and then to shrink away in embarrassment. Our littleness stands out against that magnanimity; our little, narrow judgements are not sarcastically rebuked, but probed by the very act of that great mind's estimate. There will be something challenging, purifying, straining if the relation is to be maintained. Prayer is the disposition of our souls to that which is most real and supremely great.

There is an urgency in our Lord's sayings. Ask, seek, knock. These are big words as if no haphazard listlessness constituted prayer but long, long perseverance. Nobody is going to last for more than a week in perseverance unless he recognizes the vastness of it and of the knowledge of God. We shall really, seriously recognize that, if we are to grow, it is not by a slow meandering along pleasant paths, but by stern climbing, ready for all the adventures of the way, all the different climates through which we must pass. God tempers our souls to be strong, supple, serviceable, pliant weapons in his hands. Prayer is just clinging to God with one hand when the other has failed; if both have failed then, somehow, clinging on by the eyelids; like a cat which clings on to you and if you detach one claw there is always another claw and then another. (1)

Redemption

Oh! let us always remember that our Lord has redeemed us by a genuine work of moral energy from within our human nature; not by an act of transcendent power from above. (2)

NOTES / SOURCES

1. *Fr Keble Talbot CR: Retreat Addresses*, (ed. Lucy Menzies), London, 1954, pp. 44–5
2. Ibid., p. 88

Dick (Hugh Richard Lawrie) Sheppard   1880–1937

'Dick' Sheppard was vicar of St Martin-in-the-Fields, London, from 1914 to 1927 where he kept the church open day and night and linked it with the growth in broadcasting. With William Temple he inaugurated the 'Life and Liberty' movement and in his last years was an ardent supporter of pacifism. He was briefly (1929–1931) Dean of Canterbury and (1934–1935) a Canon of St Paul's.

A Vision for a Parish Church

Dick had told his people, told first the eleven people who came to his Induction on that foggy November day in 1914, into what manner of church he had seen St Martin's transfigured, when he was away in the mud in Flanders.

I stood on the west steps, and saw what this Church would be to the life of the people. There passed me, into its warm inside, hundreds and hundreds of all sorts of people, going up to the temple of their Lord, with all their difficulties, trials and sorrows. I saw it full of people, dropping in at all hours of the day and night. It was never dark, it was lighted all night and all day, and often and often tired bits of humanity swept in. And I said to them as they passed: 'Where are you going?' And they said only one thing: 'This is our home. This is where we are going to learn of the love of Jesus Christ. This is the Altar of our Lord, where all our peace lies. This is St Martin's.' It was all reverent and full of love and they never pushed me behind a pillar because I was poor. And day by day they told me the dear Lord's Supper was there on His Altar waiting to be given. They spoke to me two words only, one was the word 'home' and the other was 'love'. (1)

The Call of the Church to Christlikeness

Maybe it is time that the Churches, following the example of their Master, should die for the people; they have lived for themselves too long. I pray that my Church—which, let me frankly acknowledge, I believe to be the largest-hearted Church in Christendom and which I love dearly, not perhaps as it is but as it might be—and that every other Church should ask of itself this one straightforward question: 'If this Church to which I belong is not everywhere assisting men to be what at their best moments they desire to be, that is, followers of the standards of Christ; if it is identified with values that Jesus Christ would not approve and is not identified with Christlikeness; if Christ is not at its centre; if it is uncharitable and crippled by the spirit of exclusiveness; what should be done without delay by way of amendment and by way of sacrifice that the voice of Christ may be heard in all its original freshness, that the power of God may be known and that the attractiveness of unconscious goodness may be brought into its own?' (2)

notes / sources
1. R. E. Roberts, *H. R. L. Sheppard, Life and Letters*, London, 1942, pp. 91–2
2. Dick Sheppard, *The Impatience of a Parson*, London, 1927, pp. 88–9

Richard Henry Tawney   1880–1962

Educated at Rugby and Balliol College, Oxford, R. H. Tawney taught political economy at Glasgow and later at the London School of Economics, where he held a chair from 1931 to 1949. A member of the Fabian Society and the Independent Labour Party he wrote on social theory, education, and industrial issues from a Christian Socialist perspective, his most notable book being *Religion and the Rise of Capitalism* (1926).

A True Conservatism

All decent people are at heart conservatives, in the sense of desiring to conserve the human associations, loyalties, affections, pious bonds between man and man which express a man's personality and become at once a sheltering nest for his spirit and a kind of watch-tower from which he may see visions of a more spacious and bountiful land. . . . (1)

All the Discoveries Worth Making are as Old as the Hills

One of the things which strikes me as I grow older is the extraordinary truth and subtlety of the religious dogmas at which, as an undergraduate, I used to laugh. 'Original sin' that what goodness we have reached is a house built on piles driven into black slime and always slipping down into it unless we are building day and night. 'Grace' that wickedness in oneself is not overcome by willing: every day of one's life one learns this, and I at least forget it every day. Religious people say that one [*sic*] grace enables one to overcome sin. What seems to happen to one is this. As long as one is making an effort to overcome bad temper, one does not get on at all; at least I don't. Bad temper simply gets put on its metal [*sic*]. But if one relaxes the effort and so to speak, throws oneself flat and lets whatever power there is take possession of one and do with one what it likes, one's mind gets peaceful and smoothed out without a conscious effort. In fact 'grace' does what 'will' can't—all the discoveries worth making are as old as the hills. (2)

The Worth of the Human Being

No one has any business to expect to be paid 'what he is worth,' for what he is worth is a matter between his own soul and God. (3)

The Demands of a Christian Society

'*He hath put down the mighty from their seat, and hath exalted the humble and meek.*' A society which is fortunate enough to possess so revolutionary a basis, a society whose Founder was executed as the enemy of law and order, need not seek to soften the materialism of principalities and powers with mild doses of piety administered in an apologetic whisper. It will teach as one having authority, and will have sufficient confidence in its Faith to believe that it requires neither artificial protection nor judicious under-statement in order that such truth as there is in it may prevail. It will appeal to mankind, not because its standards are identical with those of the world, but because they are profoundly different. It will win its converts, not because membership involves no change in their manner of life, but because it involves a change so complete as to be ineffaceable. (4)

NOTES / SOURCES

1. *R. H. Tawney's Commonplace Book* (ed. J. M. Winter and D. M. Joslin), Cambridge, 1972, p. 14
2. Ibid., p. 15
3. R. H. Tawney, *The Acquisitive Society*, London, 1921, p. 221
4. Ibid., pp. 238–9

George Kennedy Allen Bell   1881–1958

Bishop of Chichester from 1929 to 1958, George Bell had previously been secretary to Archbishop Randall Davidson, whose biography he subsequently wrote, and Dean of Canterbury from 1924 to 1929. A leading figure in the ecumenical movement, he maintained a close relationship with Dietrich Bonhoeffer and the Confessing Church during the Second World War. His strong condemnation of the bombing of Dresden is thought to have prevented his being appointed to Canterbury on the death of William Temple in 1944.

The Church Founded in the Gospel of Redemption

Although it must be free always to witness to basic moral principles, both in the social and in the international order, the characteristic function of the Church is of a different kind. And therefore the characteristic expression of its solidarity with the nation is also different. The Church stands for the Cross, the gospel of redemption. It cannot, therefore, speak of any earthly war as a 'crusade,' for the one thing for which it is impossible to fight with earthly weapons is the Cross. Its supreme concern is not the victory of the national cause. It is a hard thing to say, but it is vital. Its supreme concern is the doing of the Will of God, whoever wins, and the declaring of the Mercy of God to all men and nations. The ministers, especially the leaders of the Church, have a great responsibility for making this plain. It is not only that the Church, if its clergy preach the gospel, offers a counter-balancing force of undoubted authority to the waves of national emotion, and so helps to preserve spiritual integrity. That is important. But what is still more important is the fact that the Church is the trustee of the gospel of redemption; and unless the gospel is preached, the Church is not the Church.

It is implicit in what I have written that the Church is universal. Its message is for all nations. The Church in any country fails to be the Church if it forgets that its members in one nation have a fellowship with its members in every nation. The Church also stands for a supernatural event as the centre of life. That event is the Incarnation, the Cross and the Resurrection. The Church fails to be the Church if it does not make that the centre of its teaching. It is a God-given reality. (1)

No Fugitive and Cloistered Church

One of the most monstrous offences against religion is to regard Christianity as utterly unrelated to present-day life and as something eccentric and peculiar, or to regard the Church either as a hot-house or a prison. They are its worst foes who keep Christianity apart from Science, apart from Art, or apart from all manner of social and political life. They are the enemies of the Church who place a barrier between it and music, drama, poetry, sculpture, painting, or forbid any traffic with philosophy and modern thought. A wise old writer in the Apocrypha, describing the occupation of working men in most vivid language, ends up with these words: 'They will maintain the fabric of the world, and in the handiwork of their craft is their prayer'. For my part I whole-heartedly believe that the serious exercise of a man's art is itself an act of worship, and that the offering of the very best that is in him, be it poem, picture or sculpture, nobly conceived and wrought, or whatever mighty work of the inspired imagination, is a song of praise and thanksgiving, or maybe a poem of intercession for God's creatures. It is for the Church, as I believe, to welcome the artist, to rejoice in his inspiration as springing from God, from Whom cometh every good and every perfect gift. It is for the Church also, as I believe, to welcome the man of science and to rejoice in his research, as also directed by God, the Fountain of all Wisdom. Bad art, bad science, she will reject as she will also eschew the proud or self-assertive artist and scientist; the same with bad politics and the selfish politician. The Church ought to stand for the best and highest in every branch of life—and she would do so if the best and the noblest men and women in every branch rallied around her and insisted that their cause was hers. And you will not be surprised to hear that, thinking these things so strongly, as I do, I believe that the Church should always be ready to blow a trumpet for Education, for Health, for Science, for Art, and now for a National Theatre. She should also blow a trumpet for Peace and for Justice, and, so stiff and unyielding should she be in her loyalty to the best, that she should not be afraid when need is, of denouncing authority in the wrong, and even opposing all her moral forces, in defence of her ideal and her trust, to the princes of the world.

I have wandered a little, you will say, from the point where I first made my start. But I do not think I have really gone astray. It is a Christmas Point of View. And Christmas stands for a historical event—the birth of one in whom Christians see the invisible coming into the visible. That is the heart of the Christian religion. And if the Church (as Christians believe) with all its imperfections is still the embodiment of the invisible Christ, of his courage and sacrifice and love, and the sacrament of the invisible society whose centre he is, it is right that it should itself still invade, as it were, the visible world, and the interests and activities and endeavours of earth, should be not world-fleeing but world transforming. 'I cannot praise', said John Milton, 'a fugitive and cloistered virtue, unexercised and unbreathed, that never sallies out and sees her adversary, but slinks out of the race where that immortal garland is to be run for, not without dust and heat'. Nor, least of all on Christmas Day, can I praise a fugitive and cloistered Church. (2)

NOTES / SOURCES

1. George Bell, *The Church and Humanity*, London, 1945, pp. 27–8
2. George Bell, 'Christmas Broadcast' in *The Listener*, 25 December 1929

William Temple   1881–1944

Son of Archbishop Frederick Temple, William Temple was briefly Archbishop of Canterbury from 1942 to 1944, having previously been Bishop of Manchester (1921 to 1929) and Archbishop of York (1929 to 1942). He worked through the Life and Liberty Movement for a greater autonomy for the Church of England, and was concerned to relate Christianity to social, economic, and international questions. Influenced in his early Oxford training by idealist philosophy, he developed a powerful philosophical theology and a deep biblical spirituality, exemplified by his *Readings in St John's Gospel* (1939).

Worship the Vital Way to Influence the World

This detachment to which the Church is called, but which Churchmen have seldom attained, is not a hermit-like withdrawal from the world; on the contrary it is the way by which the Church may most influence the world. For the way to spiritual power over the world lies through worship and sanctification. If the Church is to supply to Christian people the quality enabling them to convert the world, they (or at least a large proportion of them) must be Churchmen before they are citizens, recognising that their highest duty and privilege is to worship God made known in Jesus Christ, to quicken their consciences by His holiness, to feed their minds on His truth, to purify their imaginations by His beauty, to open their hearts to His love, to submit their wills to His purpose. Worship includes all those elements. Worship so understood is the activity whereby and wherein men become more fully incorporated into the Body of Christ, thus enabling the Church to become its true self and to do its true work.

Of course such worship is a continuous and lifelong enterprise. To 'go to Church' and there sit, stand, and kneel while other people say things and sing things may be better than nothing, for it is an act of witness; but it is not certain that it is better than nothing, but such a Churchgoer lowers the temperature of the whole congregation. It is not possible to worship truly while the daily life is far from God; and it is not possible to bring the daily life much nearer to God except by the best worship of which we are capable.

Thus worship is the distinctive and specially characteristic activity of the Church; but then worship includes all life and the moments spent in concentrated worship, whether 'in Church' or elsewhere, are the focussing points of the sustaining and directing energy of the worshipper's whole life.

It would strike many people as absurd to say that the cure for unemployment is to be found through worship; but it would be quite true.

If then the Christian citizen is to make his Christianity tell upon his politics, his business, his social enterprises, he must be a Churchman—consciously belonging to the worshipping fellowship and sharing its worship—before he is a citizen; he must bring the concerns of his citizenship and his business before God, and go forth to them carrying God's inspiration with him.

This is all expressed in the Eucharist. There we bring familiar forms of economic wealth, which is always the product of man's labour exercised upon God's gifts, and offer them as symbols of our earthly life. If God had not given to the seed its life and to the soil the quality to nurture it, there would be neither harvest nor bread. Equally, if man had not ploughed the soil and scattered the seed, there would be neither harvest nor bread. Bread is a product of man's labour exercised upon God's gift for the satisfaction of man's need. So is wine. These are our 'oblations' at the 'offertory'—often also accompanied by 'alms' expressing the charity which seeks to share with others the good things which God has given to us.

These representatives of all earthly 'goods' we offer to God in union with the act of Christ at the Last Supper when, in preparatory interpretation of His death, He took the bread, called it His Body, and broke it—took the wine, called it His Blood and gave it. Because we have offered our 'earthly' goods to God, He gives them back to us as heavenly goods, binding us into union with Christ in that self-offering which is His royalty, so that we give not only our goods but ourselves, and thus become strengthened as members of His Body to do His will in the various departments of our life.

The Eucharist divorced from life loses reality; life devoid of worship loses direction and power. It is the worshipping life that can transform the world.

History is full of illustrations of this truth. But it is also, even more continuously, full of the opportunities which were lost because the actual Church was not a true Church, not a Body of Christ responsive in all its members to His Spirit.

If the Church is not like that the fault is in the members, who are so imperfectly subordinated to the Head. If the Church in my country, in my parish, is not like that, it is partly because my own response to Christ and my own self-dedication are so incomplete.

When Christians in sufficient numbers are truly converted, dedicated, sanctified, they will make the several associations which they serve handmaids of the one Divine Family, and they will make their natural communities provinces in the Kingdom of God. The Christian has no need to be greatly interested in the question how far this may come to pass on earth. That it should come to pass must be our prayer and effort. But history in any case derives its meaning from a consummation beyond itself, and what is begun here may be perfected hereafter. (1)

Idolatry—Perverted Religion

We are not tempted to confess a belief in other gods under that name. But, of course, we find it most difficult to avoid this kind of idolatry in practice. We do in practice tend to put pleasure, or comfort, or wealth, or power, in a position which gives it sovereignty over some of our time and some of our energy. This is idolatry, as St Paul showed when he said that a covetous man is an idolater (Eph.

v. 5; Col. iii. 5). But though we practise it, we know that it is wrong. We know that the first place belongs to God alone, and that He alone is rightful Sovereign over every moment of our time, every fraction of our energy. And if we have any kind of religious practice, we set apart definite times for concentrated attention and devotion to God. It is precisely this which makes uniquely important the conception of God which we hold.

If we believe in God at all, what we believe about Him matters more than anything else in our composition. To believe in God falsely conceived may easily be worse than to disbelieve in Him altogether. For we tend to become like that which we worship. The good influence of a true faith and the bad influence of a false faith pervade all life; in a thousand subconscious ways faith moulds or checks both thoughts and desires. But its influence alike for good and for evil is, of course, enormously increased if there is a regular and sincere practice of devotion. For then the whole heart is opened for the God to whom worship is addressed to enter in and take possession. If the idea of God with which you fill your mind is that of a proud Being, or capricious, or vindictive, your own character will be more marked by pride or caprice or vindictiveness in proportion as your worship is genuine and deep. The great perversions of conscience recorded in history are nearly all due to religion. The old summary of Lucretius is historically well founded:

> Tantum religio potuit suadere malorum.
> To such a mass of evil could religion win assent.

Idolatry is indeed a deadly thing. False religion can be worse than atheism; scepticism is less dangerous than credulity. The atheist, who has no belief in God and no experience of religion, misses all that is best in life; but he is safe from all that is worst. Just because religion is the greatest power in the world, touching men's souls at a depth which nothing else can reach, it can, if it is perverted, do greater harm than anything else. (2)

Forgiveness

If the sins that we ought to confess depend upon our relationship to other members of the one family of God, so does our forgiveness. There seems to me to be a very surprising feature in most of the books that I have read and the sermons that I have heard on this subject. Over and over again it is said that Our Lord promises forgiveness to those who repent; there is often some discussion of the question how far His death was a necessary condition of forgiveness on the side of God; but there is almost complete agreement that the one condition required on our side is repentance. Of course there is in the Gospels an immense insistence on the need for repentance. Also there is the reference to repentance in Our Lord's teaching about our duty to forgive others. But when He is actually speaking about God's forgiveness of us it is not 'repentance' that He mentions; it is our own forgiveness of those who have injured us. Only one petition in the Lord's Prayer has any condition attached to it: it is the petition for forgiveness; and the condition attached to it is this. No doubt if by repentance we mean all that the word means in the New Testament, it will include a forgiving spirit; for to repent is to change one's outlook and to regard men and the world as God regards them.

But everyone can feel that the emphasis would be quite different if the words were 'Forgive us our trespasses, for we do truly repent of them.' This would be like saying, 'I am so sorry; and I won't do it again; do forgive me.' In other words, the plea for forgiveness would rest on an apology and a promise made to God; and that is not the basis on which Our Lord bids us rest our plea. It is to rest on our attitude, not towards God, but towards His other children. He is always ready and eager to forgive; but how can He restore us to the freedom and intimacy of the family life if there are other members of the family towards whom we refuse to be friendly?

The strongest expression of Our Lord's teaching on this subject is found in the parable of the unforgiving servant. We sometimes miss part of the meaning of that parable through our unfamiliarity with the money-terms in which the story is told. The debt owed by the first servant to the king was two and a half million pounds, so that when he said, 'Have patience with me and I will pay thee all,' he was promising what both he and the king knew that he could never perform. But the debt which the other servant owed to him was about £5, which easily might be repaid if time were allowed. So we come to God to ask forgiveness for offences for which reparation is impossible; we owe Him all our time and all our strength; even if we serve Him perfectly from now to the end of eternity, it is only our bounden duty; it makes no amends for the past. We cannot repay; yet we ask for forgiveness. And the one condition is, not that we should be full of remorse, but that we should be ready to forgive others the paltry injuries they do to us.

This is not at all difficult to understand if we keep the family relationship full in view as the true type of our relationship to God. But if we once let the analogy of the Law Courts possess our minds, all hope of a Christian notion of forgiveness is gone. That is exactly where so many theories of the Atonement have failed. They picture the sinner as prisoner in the dock, and God as the Judge on the bench. That puts the fundamental relationship utterly wrong, for the prisoner in the dock has not injured the judge, nor is he in any way concerned with the judge, except to know what the judge is going to do to him. His concern with the judge is self-centred; and our concern with God ought not to be self-centred. The judge has not been crucified to win his love; he is only an official discharging a public duty. God is our Father; He yearns over us with an unquenchable love; and when we turn to Him as penitents, it is not to ask for remission of penalty, it is to ask that we may be taken to His heart once more. (3)

Church, Christendom, Kingdom

There are three terms that we shall need, if we are to keep distinct three aspects of the subject, which are all vital, all different, and all mutually connected: the Church, Christendom, the Kingdom. It is partly through the omission of the second of these from our thinking in recent years that we have become confused. The Church is the fellowship of Christ's disciples, welded together by the operation of His Spirit within them into the organised society which is His Body. It may contain a small or a large proportion of the citizens of any country where it works. Its own distinctive activity is worship, the imparting and receiving of the Word and Sacraments, and the self-dedication of its members to His service in the world. As they thus serve Him, they leaven society; and so there grows up a whole civilization which is in greater or less degree Christian, in the sense that it is moulded by the principles of the Gospel. This takes place in many countries; and those countries form Christendom. The Church is not the nations, though the nations are within the Church. The difference between them is not in membership but in function. It is still the business of the Church to inspire; it is the business of the nations and their citizens to act on that inspiration in the various affairs of life. If we can imagine all men and women to be (1) perfectly dedicated to God through their worship, and (2) perfectly responsive to His will in their citizenship, that would be the completed Kingdom of God. The Kingdom, in its completeness, is a Christendom extended to include all mankind, utterly leavened by a Church consisting of perfectly converted members. The necessary factors in this result are: (1) the conversion of all the world to Christianity; (2) perfect self-dedication in all who are so converted; (3) absolute correspondence of life, private and public, with that self-dedication; (4) a resultant world-wide fellowship of men united in the love of God. That, and nothing less, is what we are plainly taught to pray for, in the first three petitions of the Lord's Prayer. (4)

The Fundamental Character of Worship

The fundamental business of life is always worship. At the root of all your being, your intellectual studies, the games you play, whatever it is, the impulse to do them well is and ought to be understood as being an impulse towards God, the source of all that is excellent. All life ought to be worship; and we know quite well there is no chance it will be worship unless we have times when we have worship and nothing else. No doubt when we are perfect, when fellowship with God is a constant realisation and joy, we shall not have to go backwards and forwards between times of worship and of the activities in which we show forth our loyalty to God; but we must do so now. Otherwise our interests in the world will cease for us to have any connection with God. It is our duty for a great part of the day to forget God, because if we are thinking about Him we shall not be thinking whole-heartedly about our duty in the world. Our duty to God requires that we should, for a good part of our time, be not consciously thinking about Him. That makes it absolutely necessary, if our life is to be a life of fellowship with Him, that we should have our times which are worship, pure and simple.

The test of these is whether, as a result of them, we have more love for our fellow-men. This is one of the differences between the emotional condition of real worship and the emotional condition generated by great art. They feel very much alike, but for many people at least the experience of great art creates a feeling of sensitiveness to the unsatisfying qualities of life and of our neighbours. When we have been absorbed in great music, I do not think we generally feel particularly charitable to the people we meet outside. They seem to be of a coarser fibre than that into which we have been entering. That could never be true of our worship if it has really been worship of God, not some indulgence of our own spiritual emotion, but the concentration of mind, heart and will on Him. You will be full of kindness for everybody as you go out from such worship. It is only as the world gets hold of you again that that begins to fail, and you have to come again and kindle the fire of your worship until it lasts undying.

People are always thinking that conduct is supremely important, and that because prayer helps it, therefore prayer is good. That is true as far as it goes; still truer is it to say that worship is of supreme importance and conduct tests it. Conduct tests how much of yourself was in the worship you gave to God. You get most help from religion when you have stopped thinking about your needs, even for spiritual strength, and think about God. Gaze and gaze on Him. (5)

Temple's Prayer at the End of the Oxford University Mission

O Lord Jesu Christ, Thou Word and Revelation of the Eternal Father, come, we beseech Thee, and take possession of our souls. So fill our minds with the thought and our imaginations with the picture of Thy love, that there may be in us no room for any thought or desire that is discordant with Thy holy will. Cleanse us, we pray Thee, of all that may make us deaf to Thy call or slow to obey it, Who with the Father and the Holy Ghost art one God, blessed for evermore. Amen. (6)

NOTES / SOURCES

1. William Temple, *Citizen and Churchman*, London, 1941, pp. 100–3
2. William Temple, *Personal Religion and the Life of Fellowship*, London, 1926, pp. 2–3
3. Ibid., pp. 46–7
4. Ibid., p. 72
5. William Temple, *Christian Faith and Life: Being eight addresses delivered in The University Church at Oxford, February 8th–15th, 1931*, London, 1931, pp. 18–20
6. Ibid., p. 139

Reginald Somerset Ward   1881–1962

Born in the Potteries, where his father was Vicar of St George's, Newcastle under Lyme, Reginald Somerset Ward was educated at Pembroke College, Cambridge. Ordained in 1904, he served curacies at Camberwell and Barnsbury. By the time he moved to Chiddingfold as incumbent in 1913 he was already being drawn in a deeper way to the life of prayer and to a ministry of spiritual direction and guidance. He took this up with the support of Bishop Edward Talbot of Winchester, and moved to a house in Farncombe. From there he exercised an itinerant and largely hidden ministry of spiritual guidance which had a deep significance for many Anglicans. In the service of Thanksgiving and Requiem held in Westminster Abbey after his death the Dean of Westminster spoke of him as possessing 'a cure of souls that was charismatic, and, because charismatic, was wise with the wisdom of God, discerning with the piercing of the Spirit's sword, stern with the divine judgement, and compassionate with the Redeemer's mercy'.

The Body in Prayer

What part does the body play in prayer? It seems evident that the bodily part in prayer centres around what we call 'attention.' It is probable that the rules of reverence, and the mass of religious ceremonial, have all originated in the effort of human beings to fix their attention on God. Human consciousness has been likened to a perpetually flowing stream passing betwixt banks adorned with the most varied scenery. The scenery is reflected in the stream, but, at intervals, a bright beam of sunlight shining on one spot brings a reflection in the stream of unusual brilliancy. This lighted spot is attention. Our effort is to keep the position of this more vivid consciousness fixed amid the ever-moving stream. This effort, while it originates in the will, appears to be largely the work of our flesh and blood brain. The ease or difficulty of the effort varies from hour to hour with our bodily conditions. If this explanation be translated into terms of prayer, it may be said that prayer originates in desire; but that the first step in it consists of the collection of our attention and its projection towards God. This first step is to a very large extent purely physical.

It is very suggestive to note how much of the ceremonial attached to worship has, from the earliest times, had the effect of attracting the attention of the worshippers to a central spot. The oldest adjunct to worship in the history of the world is the altar. The use of an altar is above all marked by the fact that it draws the eyes of a collection of human beings to one spot and holds them there. Further, in the evolution of religion, the figure of the priest has always emerged in witness to the fact that individual action was found to be distracting, and that there was a need to embody the action of all the individuals in one figure. The appearance of the apse and the chancel in ecclesiastical architecture may well have been a response to a deep-seated human need of concentrating attention. It is hardly surprising, in view of this, that our common experience tells us that it is much more difficult to offer private prayer in a nonconformist chapel than in a church, for in the one there is no point of concentration for the attention, and in the other there is. It is often said that people find private devotion much easier in a church where the Blessed Sacrament is reserved: very possibly this is due in part to the fact that in such a church there is a very powerful centre of attention.

It would seem from these reflections that mankind has rightly recognized the physical starting-point in prayer, and has striven to help prayer by providing assistance for the bodily part of the effort of prayer. If we judge by the analogy of our experience in the other parts of prayer, we are meant to use all such aids in order that we may learn how to train the body to accomplish always more quickly and effectively its part in prayer.

There have been two tendencies at work in organized religion, which are connected with this analysis of prayer. One of them, which is represented in its extreme form by the Quakers, is based on the fact that the activity of prayer, though it may start in the body, ends in a different sphere. This tendency has in practice aimed at eliminating the physical side of prayer as much as possible in order to reach more quickly its spiritual goal.

The second tendency, which is represented by elaborate ceremonial, has endeavoured to insure the starting-point of prayer through the bodily senses, in the belief that once prayer has started it would proceed to its natural destination. The experience of the majority of those who have been held by mankind to be most advanced in the art of prayer would seem to prove that the best way lies betwixt these two tendencies. It is less helpful to try to eliminate one part of prayer than to combine both. The wise man will recognize that while the bodily activity in prayer ranks below the inner and more spiritual activity, it has nevertheless an essential part to play in the worship of the Divine Being Who created man a dual being.

We are therefore faced by the problem of how we can best train our bodies to take their proper part in prayer. The work of the body is to secure concentration, to gather up and fix attention on God. It is to be noted that, as in every other bodily activity, habit has a large place in the accomplishment of this. The body learns to carry out any part of its work well and quickly by constant repetition. I think this is one reason why it is, in some measure, more difficult for our generation to pray than it was for those who lived in the middle ages. We make far more frequent and diverse calls on our bodies for concentration than they did, and therefore divide our energy into smaller portions. Nevertheless, repetition of effort still remains a sovereign remedy; for each repetition of an action tends to lessen the amount of initial energy required.

The first necessity in the training of the body to pray, is the rule of prayer. By this means we obtain a regular repetition of the effort of concentration. A road is cut and metalled in the brain along which energy can travel with less waste. The person who only prays occasionally has to expend most of the energy at his disposal on the initial and preparatory work of fixing his attention. Such prayers are apt to be very short, because there is no reserve of power left for the continuance of prayer.

But the regular recurrence of a time of prayer, while it is a great help, is not of itself sufficient to procure attention. Within the habit of giving time, there has to be built up a habit of using time. It is a great mistake to rush into prayer; the recognition of the fact that some portion of the allotted time must be set apart for preparation is of the first importance for those who would avoid drifting into vagueness.

The second necessity in the training of the body to pray is the provision of a point, or points, on which attention can be concentrated. By general consent, attention in prayer is to be fixed on God. But God is infinite, and the body is finite. For bodily attention a limited point is required. When the body has done its part, the soul of man, endowed with wonderful gifts, may contemplate the infinite: but the starting-point must always be finite. The exercise most fitted to form the habit of reaching out to this transition is to be found in meditation. In this the attention is concentrated on a text or a passage, and when it is fixed, the soul is allowed to go free in its search for God.

There are many different ways in which the senses are enabled to form the habit of fixing the attention. In some cases the use of an imaginary or real picture, a crucifix, or a vocal prayer, are found to attain the end in view. In the services of the Church some central prayer, or act, or object, provide a gathering point for concentration. The aim of all preparation for prayer should be the discovery of a series of centres for attention, which will in succession stimulate the physical activities in prayer.

It must be recognized that this assistance to the body, if it is carried to extremes, falls into a danger which may make it a hindrance instead of a help to prayer. Too many points of concentration simply lead to distraction. Very ornate services are apt to bewilder the brain, and a succession of symbols disperse rather than gather our thoughts. In like manner too elaborate a programme of prayer, or the use of long lists of intercessions, soon lead to the weariness of dissipated energy. There must be a great difference in individual experience, owing to the great diversity in training and gifts: for the normal individual it would seem that in any period of prayer three points of concentration are sufficient. Many would prefer less.

But these points must be chosen and studied with care. Experience and individual preference will count for much in their choice. Points of concentration get worn out with use, and new ones have to be substituted. The orientation of spiritual interest which changes from time to time must be followed. The inner experiences of the soul, or interior messages, provide, for the period following them, the ideal centre of attention. The interests of daily life or work are not usually helpful points of concentration, and should be avoided. The posture of the body and the use of devotional gestures have their place in assisting the starting of prayer, but their value is rather transitory. In all these matters, those who desire to pray will find a fitting subject for thought and consideration.

It must be evident to all who have seriously reflected on this matter, that it brings into view a difficult, and even terrible, problem. Since the body has this important part to play in prayer, what is to happen when illness or infirmity makes it impossible for the body to give its contribution? Is prayer dependent on bodily health? The answer to this question is not easy. The greater part of prayer is dependent on the soul, but the form of prayer is to a large extent dependent on the body. The pious books of my childhood always insinuated that a bed of sickness was an ideal place for prayer. That is an exploded theory. Our common experience teaches us that, although a bed of sickness can be, and often is, a place of great spiritual happiness and welfare, it is one of the worst places in the world for the practice of prayer in the form to which we are accustomed.

It is unfortunate from our point of view that the first of all our powers to suffer from bodily ill-health is concentration. It begins to fail before any physical signs of disease appear. It is usually the last of our qualities to recover. After an operation, when the doctor has declared that our body is restored to health, a further period must pass before we are capable of any sustained attention. It must also be remembered that a greater degree of concentration is usually required for prayer than would be required for reading a heavy book. This provides a rough and ready test for measuring our responsibility for attention in prayer. If during any period of prayer we could have read with profit a solid book on some subject which interested us, we may be sure that we ought to have been able to make the effort required for concentration in our prayer.

In view of these facts, it might seem that prayer during illness must be dismissed as a hopeless task. Such is not the case, because there is fortunately one form of prayer which is immune from bodily obstruction. This form is termed ejaculatory prayer. It is a prayer which consists of short sentences or ejaculations of momentary duration. It requires the very smallest amount of attention or concentration. It is particularly suitable to times of illness or worry, because pain or anxiety automatically suggest it and remind us of it. It is of great spiritual value, because it insures a very frequent recollection of God, which greatly strengths the soul. Moreover this habit of ejaculatory prayer learnt in sickness, persists afterwards in health, and so our crosses are crowned with profit.

Those who are ill will do well, if the illness is such as to prevent them from doing their daily work, to give up their rule of prayer and replace it by frequent ejaculatory prayer. As they emerge from illness the rule of prayer should be gradually replaced by taking up a small daily time of prayer, which can be increased week by week. Many people have suffered much from the fear that they had failed or sinned because they were unable to force themselves to pray during times of ill-health; but if these simple suggestions are followed, such times may prove to have benefited the life of the soul instead of hindering it.

We cannot in religion cut out one half of God's construction of mankind; we must therefore take into account in all questions of prayer the needs of the body. Nevertheless we are responsible for training the body to assist and not to hinder the spiritual life. The keystone of the Creed is the Incarnation of the Son of God, and right at the centre of Incarnation is to be found the body. It must therefore have its rightful and important place in all religion, and in our own spiritual life. (1)

Use of Time and Energy

God has placed our souls in bodies and any religion which forgets this fact degenerates into heresy. Since God enshrined souls in bodies He meant the two to work together, the body subservient to the soul but a partner with it. It is for this reason that, as bodily strength grows less, we have to replace our loss of physical energy by the skill with which we use it for God's service. When we face this question of the natural decline of energy, whether it is due to age or disease, we are confronted by two dangers, one on each side of the way.

The first danger lies in the temptation to allow things to drift, to make no plans or calculations, to go on working as we have always worked without thought for God's need of us on the morrow. I have known some people who called this faith, but it seems to me that faith is only possible where there has been effort. It is idle to pray 'Give us this day our daily bread' if we do not use also the hands and brains with which God has provided us in order that we may use His instrument, the body, for His purposes. If we do not plan how to get the best results and the best work out of the body, we tie up a precious treasure in a napkin of overwork and bury it in a useless grave. To drift into an avoidable breakdown is not faith, but a careless waste of God's substance. Every Christian who has had a warning of this danger is bound in duty to reconsider the arrangement of his life and work.

The opposite danger is to sacrifice faith to planning. It is very dangerous for a human being to think much about his ailments. We can easily exaggerate the loss of energy as we grow older, until it blots out God's life and power. To be planning for the care of the body perpetually is a short and easy way to send the soul to sleep. If the body, by its ailments, shows that planning is necessary then, with the help of prayer and the doctor's advice, make your plan and, having made it, use your faith. You have then used the powers God gave you, you have tried to learn His lesson, and you must leave the result in absolute faith in His hands.

Such are the two dangers I see, but they do not for an instant rank in importance with the guiding principle which must dominate this and every other side of our lives—the principle that we desire above all that God should possess us and use us to satisfy His love and His will. If this desire dominates our lives everything else will fall into place. At first we love a Giver, and it is very natural that much of our attention should be occupied with His gifts; but He leads us on to love One Who loves us, and then we become much more occupied with living than with gifts. To return the love of God to God is the end of religion. If this is the end of our religion, we shall both plan in order to get the best out of our bodies, and we shall trust that the best will be used to satisfy God. (2)

The Right Method of Making a Decision

1. Offer to God the choice before you, surrendering your own will, and praying earnestly that His purpose for you may be carried out in the final result.

2. Set aside a quiet period for consideration. First consider the reasons for or against the various courses as they present themselves to your mind; then consider the advice you have sought. Two kinds of advice are of special value, the advice of one with special knowledge of the technical points in the choice, and the advice of a spiritual director who has a close knowledge of your character and your difficulties.

3. After this period and further prayer, reach a decision and act upon it, with a confident faith that if it is not in God's purpose He will stop its fulfilment, and that you have done all that He requires in order that the responsibility for the result should rest with Him. (3)

Mental Prayer

1. In the first place, Mental Prayer is, above all things, the natural medium of communication with God. I am going to try and work out this point more thoroughly, for ignorance of it has deprived many lives of much comfort which they might have claimed as their due.

Why should it be so important that our prayers should be natural? The great principle which is our warrant for insisting upon it is the infinity of God's love. We, with our poor, limited humanity, cannot conceive of universal love. Our love is given in fragments, and shut up in many a prison cell, but the love of God is boundless, and it embraces all. There is no corner in all this wide world where God's love does not penetrate, no tiny hole or cranny which it does not fill. So often we fall into the mistake of thinking that God's love is confined to great things. We forget that God is infinite in His littleness as well as in His greatness.

In my own life I have known and realized God's majesty most in the tiny things of life. It is when the sky opens and God's hand is put forth to alter some trivial thing, to remove some tiny obstacle, that I have been most abased before the majesty of His love. Believe me, God's love is so infinitely close to you, so incessantly caring for you, that if it was only visible to earthly eyes we should, each of us, stand this moment in the midst of a cloud of glory.

It follows from this infinity of God's love that all the tiniest parts of our lives concern Him, and that in our communication with Him they all have their place; to leave them out is to narrow His love. We can never meet His love adequately in our prayers unless we are supremely natural, unless we talk to Him of all we are thinking or feeling at the moment.

We can only do this in Mental Prayer; that is, by a conversation with God, where we do not try to put our thoughts into very set or grammatical forms of words, but are content to think them towards God, in such disjointed phrases as may rise in our minds.

In all that I have known personally of my Lord, I have been struck by the fact of how much more natural He is than men suppose. Those who write of Him, or attempt to picture Him, never make Him natural and simple as He really is. And in the same way I have always found that I have been nearest to Him when I have been most natural myself. You may have been struck at some time, in reading the lives or words of the saints, by their audacity. Yet the saints are guilty neither of presumption nor audacity; they are simple people, who have learnt to be natural with God.

If you would reap the full benefit of Mental Prayer, you must learn to make it express yourself to God. Speak to Him in it without strain, think nothing too small or too foolish to bring before Him. Remember that His love cares not for a part but for the whole of your life.

2. In the second place, Mental Prayer is most emphatically two-sided. If this were not so the learning element which is so rich a part of prayer would be left out. It is one of the greatest defects of Vocal Prayer that there are not enough pauses in it. If we take earthly conversation as a picture of prayer, we can understand the importance of this point. We could never get to know a person on earth if all our conversation was one-sided. It is surely only when they reply, when there is an interchange of thought, that we get to know them. The same holds good in Mental Prayer, for this way of praying is like a very close sort of conversation, where all the explanations and forms which make conversation so cumbrous are left out, because both parties understand them. Thus, those engaged in this way of prayer are never alone, for two persons take part in it—the soul and God.

Why should we think that God does not talk to us? The Bible is surely full of nothing else save the talking of God to souls. Prophets, priests and just ordinary individuals like you and me are constantly talking to and hearing Him on every page of the Bible. If we are to judge by the Gospels, Christ talked far more to others than they to Him.

Now this is a matter of enormous importance to us, for it is vital that we should know God. If we do not get to know God, then what is the use of our lives, or what can they result in, save confusion and despair? Once in my life, when I was quite a small boy, I had an extraordinarily vivid dream, which remains always in my memory. I dreamed I was standing before a huge curtain, which seemed to reach up to heaven, and on the curtain were displayed all the things that ever happen, or ever would happen. And as I looked it seemed to be utter confusion, a whirling madness. Then just as I awoke, I seemed for an instant to see that there was a key by which the whole curtain would fall into place and order. It took me many years to find out that key was knowing God. I venture to describe the dream because surely it is a picture of the soul, looking out on the world and life. All seems to be confusion, and the only thing that can straighten it is to know God. Now we can know God best and most truly by listening to Him, and when we know Him all the facts of our life and of life in general fall into place and display the perfect plan of His love.

It is for this reason that I would most strongly suggest that you should make pauses in your Mental Prayer that you should have short periods of silence when you try to listen instead of speaking to Him.

And if you will persevere in this, you will find that He is indeed speaking. He does not speak in any words you can hear with your ears, or even fully understand with your mind, but by sudden illuminations, by secret intuitions and by convincing certainties. He makes His meaning and His will clear to the soul who is seeking the inner knowledge.

3. In the third place, it is a matter of experience that Mental Prayer is life-giving. The life of the soul is the most mysterious thing in the world; that there is a life in the soul it is impossible to doubt, for the evidences of its existence are plainly visible. We see somebody suddenly change their habits, their way of thought and life, and we cannot explain such a change except on the supposition that there is deep within them some strong energy, full of vigour and fire, forcing its way out into action. In those moments, when spiritual sight is clear, I seem to see the soul in the likeness of a tiny spark, encased in the crushed clinkers of self, a glimmering light, a tiny sparkle. There is something pathetic in its glimmering light. Then on a sudden it bursts into white-hot flame, transforming the crust of self, and giving forth the light which never shone on land or sea, but which has shone through many a soul. So I picture the life which enters the soul in moments of Mental Prayer. For in such moments as God wills, a very flood of vitality seems to be poured into the soul through this way of prayer. And such life-giving as this is surely of the very essence of communion, for by it God shares His life with the poor and wretched soul. We are blinded by our faithlessness to many of God's miracles, and often we pass them unnoticed, and not the least of these miracles are the cases of new life given in prayer.

I have seen many people changed and made into new persons by the life which has flowed into them in prayer. And I think you must have been conscious at times in your life when you have prayed very earnestly, that you rose from your knees possessing a new and mysterious vigour which was not there before.

Thus, then, in Mental Prayer we find the most natural outlet for desire, the most close contact for learning, and the truly vivifying channel for communion.

4. I said in my last address that each way of prayer has its dangers, and this is no exception to the rule. For in Mental Prayer the soul meets the temptation (which arises from its very personal character) of spiritual selfishness. Yet, after all, it is very easy to avoid the danger, for a right use of intercession will keep the soul from spiritual self-love. A further difficulty arises from the fact that so many souls, having naturally so little power of concentration, are apt to become vague in Mental Prayer. The soul does need bye-laws for the regulation of its activity, and this difficulty cannot be lightly swept aside, but I will leave it for the present, for it comes under a future part of the subject.

A third danger, more common than at first sight appears, lies in spiritual pride. The soul which has discovered Mental Prayer knows it has found something higher and better than Vocal Prayer, and begins too often to look down on those who are confined to the use of Vocal Prayer. For such souls is the lesson of the widow's mite. The golden piece which the rich men cast into the treasury were doubtless more beautiful than the 'two mites,' but they did not meet with as much commendation from our Lord, for He looked to the motive behind the act.

So also He sees behind every prayer the desire which inspires it, and the Mental Prayer is weighed against the Vocal Prayer in the balance of desire. No soul who has experienced the two kinds of prayer can doubt which is better fitted for communication with God, but no soul who has learned the measure by which God judges our prayers will dare to say any particular Mental Prayer is of more value than the Vocal Prayer which is offered by another.

We grow, alas! so used to phrases and ideas that they lose the beauty which belongs to them, but it seems to me that the very climax of beauty in this world is to be found in the reality of this way of prayer. Think of it! Our poor, wretched, helpless souls, rapt out of themselves for a space, and entering, in trust and confidence, into communion with God; the soul and its Creator, no longer separated, but together in converse, receiving and giving in intimate love, which needs few words, and is rather apprehended than understood. This is the way of Mental Prayer. (4)

NOTES / SOURCES

1. R. Somerset Ward, *To Jerusalem: Devotional Studies in Mystical Religion*, London, 1994, pp. 153–60
2. *Reginald Somerset Ward 1881–1962: His Life and Letters* (ed. Edmund R. Morgan), London, 1963, pp. 82–3
3. Ibid., pp. 91–2
4. Ibid., pp. 125–30

Richard Godfrey Parsons   1882–1948

Educated at Durham School and Magdalen College, Oxford, he was ordained to a Fellowship at University College, Oxford, and then served as Principal of Wells Theological College from 1911 to 1916. After a time in the parochial ministry in the north-west he was nominated by William Temple as first Bishop of Middleton in 1927 and served as Bishop of Manchester from 1932 to 1941 and Bishop of Hereford from 1941 to 1948.

We Hail Thy Presence Glorious

We hail thy Presence glorious,
    O Christ our great High Priest,
O'er sin and death victorious,
    At thy thanksgiving feast:
As thou art interceding
    For us in heaven above,
Thy Church on earth is pleading
    Thy perfect work of love.

Through thee in every nation
    Thine own their hearts upraise,
Offering one pure Oblation,
    One Sacrifice of praise:
With thee in blest communion
    The living and the dead
Are joined in closest union,
    One Body with one Head.

O Living Bread from heaven,
　　Jesu, our Saviour good,
Who thine own self hast given
　　To be our souls' true food;
For us thy body broken
　　Hung on the Cross of shame:
This Bread, its hallowed token
　　We break in thy dear name.

O stream of love unending,
　　Poured from the one true Vine,
With our weak nature blending
　　The strength of life divine;
Our thankful faith confessing
　　In thy life-blood outpoured,
We drink this Cup of blessing
　　And praise thy name, O Lord.

NOTES / SOURCES

Richard Godfrey Parsons in *Hymns Ancient & Modern*, Revised Edition, No. 403, London, 1950

Oswin Creighton CF   1883–1918

Son of Mandell Creighton, (q.v.), Bishop of London and church historian, Oswin Creighton was educated at Marlborough and Keble College, Oxford. Trained for the ministry at Farnham under B. K. Cunningham, he served in Notting Hill and then as a missionary in Canada. In 1914 he became an Army Chaplain, serving in England, Gallipoli, and France, where he was killed in 1918 visiting men in a battery position.

Human Friendship the Only Way to Touch the Heart

I sometimes feel inclined to wonder why God hides Himself so inscrutably from our experience. Or is it that the Church has taught us for so long to look for Him in the wrong places?

. . . .

Well, how are we going to fill these empty stomachs with the food that will really satisfy? The Creeds, ministry of women, Prayer Book reform, *Life and Liberty*, the whole caboodle have all gone overboard as far as we are concerned. We don't really care about any of them. 'Well, you are a beastly, destructive, negative lot.' Granted. 'You don't care about anything.' No; false, quite false. We are sick—this is my point—sick to death of *abstractions*. We are learning that it is only human beings that count, and that if the Christian religion is to prosper on earth, it can *only* be by Christians understanding and serving their fellow-men. Discussions, conferences, inquiries, etc., simply do not interest or move us. But if a soldier hears the vicar has been looking after his wife and children in his absence—if the wife hears from the chaplain when her husband has been killed—if there is any touch of human friendship and understanding, then we get near the foundation of all things, the heart of man.

NOTES / SOURCES

Letters of Oswin Creighton CF, London, 1920, pp. 202–3

Geoffrey Anketell Studdert Kennedy 1883–1929

Geoffrey Anketell Studdert Kennedy was a priest who made his reputation as a Chaplain to the Forces in the First World War, where his ministry earned him the nickname from the troops of 'Woodbine Willie'. A mission preacher and poet, he later worked with the Industrial Christian Fellowship. His popular style of writing and his experience of the horrors of the trenches led him to question the traditional doctrine of God's impassibility, and to emphasize the Divine compassion.

The Cross Set Up in Every Slum

On June 7th, 1917, I was running to our lines half mad with fright, though running in the right direction, thank God, through what had been once a wooded copse. It was being heavily shelled. As I ran I stumbled and fell over something. I stopped to see what it was. It was an undersized, underfed German boy, with a wound in his stomach and a hole in his head. I remember muttering, 'You poor little devil, what had you got to do with it? Not much great blonde Prussian about you.' Then there came light. It may have been pure imagination, but that does not mean that it was not also reality, for what is called imagination is often the road to reality. It seemed to me that the boy disappeared and in his place there lay the Christ upon His Cross, and cried. 'Inasmuch as ye have done it unto the least of these my little ones you have done it unto me.' From that moment on I never saw a battlefield as anything but a Crucifix. From that moment on I have never seen the world as anything but a Crucifix. I see the Cross set up in every slum, in every filthy overcrowded quarter, in every vulgar flaring street that speaks of luxury and waste of life. I see Him staring up at me from the pages of the newspaper that tells of a tortured, lost, bewildered world. (1)

High and Lifted Up

Seated on the throne of power with the sceptre in Thine hand,
While a host of eager angels ready for Thy Service stand.
So it was the prophet saw Thee, in his agony of prayer,
While the sound of many waters swelled in music on the air,
Swelled until it burst like thunder in a shout of perfect praise,
'Holy, Holy, Holy Father, Potentate of years and days.
Thine is the Kingdom, Thine the glory, Thine the splendour of the sun,
Thine the wisdom, Thine the honour, Thine the crown of victory won.'
So it was the prophet saw Thee, so this artist saw Thee too,
Flung his vision into colour, mystery of gold and blue.
But I stand in woe and wonder; God, my God, I cannot see,

Darkness deep and deeper darkness—all the world is dark to me.
Where is power? Where is glory? Where is any victory won?
Where is wisdom? Where is honour? Where the splendour of the sun?
God, I hate this splendid vision—all its splendour is a lie,
Splendid fools see splendid folly, splendid mirage born to die.
As imaginary waters to an agony of thirst,
As the vision of a banquet to a body hunger-cursed,
As the thought of anæsthetic to a soldier mad with pain,
While his torn and tortured body turns and twists and writhes again,
So this splendid lying vision turns within my doubting heart,
Like a bit of rusty bayonet in a torn and festering part.
Preachers give it me for comfort, and I curse them to their face,
Puny, petty-minded priestlings prate to me of power and grace;
Prate of power and boundless wisdom that takes count of little birds,
Sentimental poisoned sugar in a sickening stream of words.
Platitudinously pious far beyond all doubts and fears,
They will patter of God's mercy that can wipe away our tears.
All their speech is drowned in sobbing, and I hear the great world groan,
As I see a million mothers sitting weeping all alone,
See a host of English maidens making pictures in the fire,
While a host of broken bodies quiver still on German wire.
And I hate the God of Power on His hellish heavenly throne,
Looking down on rape and murder, hearing little children moan.
Though a million angels hail Thee King of Kings, yet cannot I.
There is nought can break the silence of my sorrow save the cry,
'Thou who rul'st this world of sinners with Thy heavy iron rod,
Was there ever any sinner who has sinned the sin of God?
Was there ever any dastard who would stand and watch a Hun
Ram his bayonet through the bowels of a baby just for fun?
Praise to God in Heaven's highest and in all the depths be praise,
Who in all His works is brutal, like a beast in all His ways.'
God, the God I love and worship, reigns in sorrow on the Tree,
Broken, bleeding, but unconquered, very God of God to me.
All that showy pomp and splendour, all that sheen of angel wings,
Was but borrowed from the baubles that surround our earthly kings.
Thought is weak and speech is weaker, and the vision that He sees
Strikes with dumbness any preacher, brings him humbly to his knees.
But the word that Thou hast spoken borrows nought from kings and thrones,
Vain to rack a royal palace for the echo of Thy tones.
In a manger, in a cottage, in an honest workman's shed,
In the homes of humble peasants, and the simple lives they led,
In the life of one an outcast and a vagabond on earth,
In the common things He valued, and proclaimed of priceless worth,
And above all in the horror of the cruel death He died,
Thou hast bid us seek Thy glory, in a criminal crucified.
And we find it—for Thy glory is the glory of Love's loss,
And Thou hast no other splendour but the splendour of the Cross.
For in Christ I see the martyrs and the beauty of their pain,

And in Him I hear the promise that my dead shall rise again.
High and lifted up, I see Him on the eternal Calvary,
And two piercèd hands are stretching east and west o'er land and sea.
On my knees I fall and worship that great Cross that shines above,
For the very God of Heaven is not Power, but Power of Love. (2)

At the Eucharist

How through this Sacrament of simple things
The great God burns His way,
I know not—He is there.
The silent air
Is pulsing with the presence of His grace,
Almost I feel a face
Bend o'er me as I kneel,
While on my ears there steal
The strains of 'Agnus Dei' softly sung.
How it calls—calls Heaven to earth,
Calls Christ to birth,
And pleads for man's Redemption
With his God.
Here star and sod
Unite to sing their Maker's praise,
While, through the windows, broken rays
Of crimson sunlight make a path
For Him to tread.
Just common bread?
The artist's colour blazing bright,
The subtle scheme of shade and light,
That thrills our souls to ecstasy,
Is bread.
The notes that wed,
And weave a wonderland of sound,
Wherein our hearts may wander round,
And reach the heart of God's red rose,
Where beauty dwells alone and grows
Sublime in solitude,
All these are bread.
Are they not born of earth and rain
Becoming tissue of man's brain,
The vehicle of every thought?
The Spirit that our God bestows,
The mystery that loves and knows,
The very soul our Saviour bought
Speaks through a body born of bread—
And wine.
The clinging vine
That climbs some crumbled wall in France,

Drinks in the Love of God,
His precious Blood,
Poured out in beams that dance
Through long-drawn summer days,
Swift golden rays of sunshine,
That are stored within the grape
Until it swells
And spills their splendour
Into wine
To fill the chalice of the Lord.
Then earth and heaven intertwine;
The Word
Takes flesh and dwells with men,
And once again
Dim eyes may see
His gentle glory shine,
The glory of humility,
Which in creation stoops to raise,
Through time's eternity of days,
Our weakness to His strength,
For neither length,
Nor breadth nor depth nor height,
Stays now the piercing of that light
Of omnipresent Love,
It runs red fire through our veins;
The Life divine,
In common wine,
Thrills through the matter of our brains,
Begetting dreams,
And gleams
Of God—swift golden speech,
And charity that burns to reach
The very depths of hell,
And lift them up to Christ,
Who has our thirsty souls sufficed,
Till they are drunk with God. (3)

NOTES / SOURCES

1. G. A. Studdert Kennedy, *The World and the Work*, Longmans, Green & Co., 1925, pp. 57–8
2. G. A. Studdert Kennedy, *The Unutterable Beauty*, Hodder and Stoughton, 1961, pp. 44–8
3. Ibid., pp. 58–60

Edwyn Clement Hoskyns   1884–1937

Ordained in 1908 and Dean of Chapel of Corpus Christi College, Cambridge (1919–1937), Hoskyns had studied on the Continent, where he became a friend of Albert Schweitzer. Standing in a broadly Catholic tradition he was critical of Liberal Protestant assumptions about the historical Jesus and was later much influenced by Barth's *Commentary on Romans* which he translated. His work (with F. N. Davey) *The Riddle of the New Testament* (1931) enjoyed a deserved popularity.

Eschatology

The word Eschatology means the expectation that the end of the world or of the present order is imminent. It is a woeful misunderstanding of the Christian religion to find in it merely an unsatisfied longing for a future catastrophe in which the world as we know it will suddenly come to an end, and a totally new order come into being. To be a Christian is, rather, the recognition that the great catastrophe lies in the past, that God has acted and is acting energetically, that righteousness has been attained by men and women and is attainable by us through the grace of God; that the divisions of sex and race and class are surmounted and overcome in the great catholic fellowship of men and women, Greek and barbarian, Jew and Gentile, bond and free; that God has ceased to be unknown and unrecognised, energetic in Heaven, but inactive in the affairs of men; rather His word 'is nigh thee in thy mouth and in thy heart', since we have 'the knowledge of the glory of God in the face of Jesus Christ'. The Ecclesia of God, the Church of Christ, stands in the world as the home of salvation, because within it God is actively at work: it is the sphere of His authority, the realm of His Spirit, the Body of His Son. Salvation from sin, from pessimism, from the sense that all things pass to inevitable destruction, from materialism, is not for us Christians to be attained by dreaming of a world beyond this world, or by believing in some imminent catastrophe, but by plunging head first into Christian faith and fellowship, believing that the Ecclesia of God is the visible expression in the world of His love and His mercy.

This is Christian language: it is lyrical, it is poetic, but it is not for that reason unreal: it is rather the song of the Christian religion, the song of experienced salvation from the corruption which surrounds us.

The greatness of St Paul lay largely in the clarity of his insight into the significance of the Christian religion, and of the little groups of converted men and women, scattered about in the great cities of the Empire: and consequently, though hardly realizing precisely what he was doing, he transferred the language hitherto used to describe what would follow the end of the world in order to describe the fruits of the Spirit actually being given by God to the faithful Christians.

For St Paul the New Age had come; it was a New Creation, and Christianity was the goal of history and the fulfilment of the promises of God. The Church was heaven upon earth, and the fulfilment of the eschatological hope, the hope, that is, that the Last Things were at hand. All the merely physical accompaniments of the traditional imagery of the End of the world tend to drop into the background, the stars do not fall from heaven, but goodness, self-discipline, charity, peace have in very truth dropped from heaven as the gifts of the mercy of God. (1)

Sin

We tend, under the influence of an evil tradition, to regard the Seven Deadly Sins as actions dependent upon an act of the will, and therefore to confine Sin to sins which are committed in direct and conscious defiance of a known and accepted moral law. This is, however, to misunderstand completely the very essence of the Christian religion. That we should so misunderstand it is not surprising, since Western moral ideas spring largely either from that moral theology which has been developed under the influence of the confessional or from that moralism which emerges from the reflections of philosophers, and in both cases a wrong action tends to be defined as culpable only when it is a wilful act. For example, a modern Roman theologian opens his series of volumes on moral theology with the following definition: 'The terms sin, transgression, iniquity, offence, and disobedience are synonymously employed by Holy Scripture to designate a wilful transgression of the Law of God, or voluntary disregard of His will.' If we omit the words 'synonymously', 'voluntary' and 'wilful', the definition might stand, but if these be included in the definition, the whole Christian conception of sin is emasculated at the outset, and a casual glance at the Seven Deadly Sins shews this at once. Avarice, which proceeds from the desire of the possession of material things, and the attachment of the heart to such things, is not a passion which springs from the conscious will: it is part of our very being as men of flesh and blood, it surges up within us. So is Anger, so is Lust, so are Pride and Envy. We do not create these things by our wills. They rise and submerge us. The conscious wilful voluntary action is the least serious element, since it does but make manifest the underlying forces which course within us.

We must rid our minds of this paralysing idea that sins are a series of forbidden actions which we can, if we will, avoid. Sin is this world, with its desires and passions, running its course till ultimately we lie dead, a corpse, the material world having won its victory and itself then passing to corruption. Death is therefore the complete and adequate symbol of sin, and Accidie or Sloth is the runner-up of death.

But we must not think of sin merely in terms of the material world. The catalogue itself forbids this. Pride, *Superbia*, majestically heads the list, followed by Envy. Here we are on another plane, far more subtle, and far more devastating. Pride is the capital sin, the sin which controls our minds and heads, not our bodies merely. Pride belongs to us when we become the centre of the Universe, when everything revolves about us and everything is judged as it affects us, when our achievements dominate our ideas. And Envy is Pride's younger sister, that sadness which occupies us when others intrude into that central position which we imagine to be ours. And Pride is atheism, just as Lust is barbarism; for Pride is not merely jealousy of other men, it is inevitably jealousy of God. (2)

Word and Revelation

Can we rescue a word, and discover a universe? Can we study a language, and awake to the Truth? Can we bury ourselves in a lexicon, and arise in the presence of God? (3)

Sin and the Remission of Sin

And so we have reached one of those paradoxes which meet us when we start to grapple with the meaning of our Faith. The Church is set in the midst of the world, in direct opposition to it. And we rightly use language which emphasises the contrast, till perhaps we are led to quote St Paul to make our meaning clear. Outside the Ecclesia of God men are dead through their trespasses and sins, wherein they walk according to the course of this world, according to the prince of the power of the air, sons of unbelief and disobedience, swayed by the lusts of the flesh and inflamed by evil imaginings, without hope and without God in the world. And on the other hand, through the love of God with which He loved us, and quickened us and raised us, and set us in the heavenly places, we are His workmanship, created for good works, fellow citizens with the saints, of the household of God, built upon the foundation of the apostles and prophets, stones fitted together to make the temple of the Lord in the midst of the world.

And yet the moment we have said this we must take it all back. In the Ecclesia of God we struggle and fight, not with the world but with our brothers and sisters in the Church. 'It hath been signified to me that there are contentions among you. Now this I mean that each one of you saith, I am of Paul; and I of Apollos; and I of Cephas; and I of Christ. Are ye not men?' Yes, we are men, and not angels. Men of flesh and blood, not merely quarrelling, but swayed by unworthy passions and desires. And St Paul can write even after his conversion, 'Not what I would that do I practise, but what I hate, that I do. For I delight in the law of God after the inward man: but I see a different law in my members, warring against the law of my mind, and bringing me into captivity under the law of sin which is in my members. O wretched man that I am!'

That is the tragic paradox. The Church separated from the world and yet not only in it, but of it.

Can you see that the word Church is a more real word than the word Christian? A Christian means a man who exhibits the spirit, and follows the precepts and example of Christ. 'To be a Christian,' wrote Dean Farrar, 'is to act as Christ acted.' Can you or I dare to arrogate to ourselves such a title? or can we even accept its application to ourselves without indignant repudiation? How rarely the word Christian occurs in the New Testament compared with the word Church! And this is significant. The word Church as we have seen suggests the people of Israel, sinful, disobedient, thoroughly unsatisfactory, and yet possessing the revealed Law of God, chosen by God to proclaim not their goodness or their righteousness but His power and His mercy. So it is with the Church. We do not claim anything for ourselves. We, as those outside, are under the judgment of God. But as men of His Ecclesia, we possess the word of God; we proclaim Christ Crucified, the power of God and the wisdom of God; we share in the worship of God in spirit and in truth. We are, or we should be, witnesses to the truth, with no real confidence in our power to explain or interpret according to the wisdom of men, with no desire to set up ourselves as models of righteousness, but confident that the revelation of God, I will not say *stands* in the Bible, in the sacraments, in the creeds and in the Christ, but occurs, acts, is energetic and effective through them.

This is what St Paul and what our Lord meant by the word Mystery. A mystery is that which reveals the secret and invisible power of the Unseen God. The structure of the world is a mystery. That does not mean it is beyond our comprehension, though of course it is: it means that it is a revelation of the power of God. The invisible things of God, His everlasting power and divinity, says St Paul, are perceived through the structure of the universe. The parables of the Lord are in this correct sense mysteries, they reveal the Kingdom of God. So too the Church is the revelation of God. But you and I are unfortunately not mysteries, at least I do not know of such an application of the word. We are the objects of the mercy of God, points to which His power is directed: not vehicles of revelation, for we obstruct it and obscure it. And so I would urge you not to assess the power of God by measuring and weighing the righteousness of those who believe, and setting it in the scales against the righteousness of those who stand outside the Ecclesia of God. Judge not that ye be not judged, and condemn not that ye be not condemned. Judgment and condemnation are the way of the Pharisee. Christianity is not anthropology; it is the revelation of the power and of the mercy of God. As the power of God is revealed in the heavens, so His mercy is displayed in the Church. And the Gospel of the Church is the Remission of Sin. (4)

The Language of the Church

Be ye not unwise, but understanding what the will of the Lord is.
Ephesians v. 17

The Church has a language: it possesses words and phrases: for example; Faith, Righteousness, Sin, Judgment, Flesh and Blood, Spirit, Death—Life, Darkness—-Light, Wrath—Love, Evil—Good, the Devil—God. Upon the fabric of human life the Church embroiders its pictures and patterns by mingling in sharp contrasts the richly coloured threads of its language: or, putting the same thing in another way, upon the rich matter of men and women and things the Church stamps the form or impress of its words. But those metaphors are inadequate, for, in fact, the Church adds nothing either to the fabric or to the matter of human life: it does not, like some cosmopolitan organisation, seek to impose its will upon others for their good or for their destruction. For the fabric of human life has the picture and pattern already embroidered on it, and the matter is already stamped with form and impress. God has already woven both fabric and picture into one indissoluble whole; He has already stamped men and things with His image; and the Church does but, like some John the Baptist, point to what the world is. The Church does not manipulate or 'propagand': it bears witness, or rather, if it does juggle with human life and 'propagand' and manipulate, it becomes an object abhorrent both to God and to men.

The language of the Church is, then, no new language. The Church does not create its words any more than it creates its worship. It uses words which are common to all languages of all epochs, just as it uses worship familiar to all peoples of all times. The Church does not require of us that we should master a new vocabulary, but that we should apprehend the meaning of the commonest words in our language; it demands that we should not, at the critical moment, turn away from the meaning of words, but that we should wrestle with them and refuse to let them go. For from these common words, from 'life' and 'death', from 'good' and 'evil', from 'judgment' and 'mercy', there peers out at us from our quite normal, ordinary life, from the world of men and of things, a secret which concerns us and from which we cannot escape.

In spite of all that is said to the contrary, the Church is the enemy of all romanticism, if by 'romanticism' is meant a flight from the rough and tumble of things as they are into some dream world of our imaginings. The Church refuses to allow us to creep into some comfortable nook or to discover some 'cosy corner'; or, if we do take refuge in some such place, the Church soon reminds us that the place we have selected has a charge of dynamite under it, which may explode at any moment. Nor does the Church point to these explosions in order to pretend that she herself is the proper refuge of men, for the dynamite under the Church is most especially explosive. The Church has always a dagger at its heart, for it cannot long escape from its own theme, the theme which it is bound to proclaim—Christ Crucified. But we must not forget that even this theme is not something imposed by the Church upon the world, it is not some peculiar truth: it is rather that by which men are enabled to see clearly the tribulation which underlies their own selected place of security, whatever it may be. Every visible 'Christ' upon which they think they can stand, every '-ism' which we so passionately proclaim, every 'Movement' which we join, every truth *we* enunciate, every scepticism of which we are so proud when we have cynically detached ourselves from all 'Movements', all the pride of our aloofness and freedom from the superstition of every church and every conventicle, all our scepticism of science, not to mention our scepticism of theology—all these positions which we occupy pass like the Gospel story from Galilee to Jerusalem, from life to death.

But, though compelled by its theme to see and to announce this movement from Galilee to Jerusalem and to see it everywhere, the Church does not thereby make nonsense of human life; the Church is not so *unwise*, not so irrational, not so lacking in understanding what the will of the Lord is. For precisely at the point where it is confronted by crucifixion it proclaims resurrection. It proclaims Christ Risen, it announces a new heaven and a new earth, it announces consolation in tribulation. It makes sense of the nonsense, for, knowing that all visible things are done in parables, it proclaims the glory and righteousness of God, and it sees His glory and His righteousness made known where our glory and our righteousness manifestly break down.

Did we say that the Church makes sense of the nonsense? No, a thousand times no. *It* does not *make* sense, as though once again it were manipulating and propaganding: it simply sees that the sense is everywhere, because it sees, beyond human sin and inadequacy which is everywhere, not a void, not nonsense, but the fulness of the glory of God.

And so, though the Church seems so often to be moving towards cynicism and scepticism and irrationalism, at the supreme point, at Jerusalem where the Lord was crucified, the whole world—please notice, the *whole world*—comes back to us in all its vigorous energy, shining with the reflected glory of the God who made it and us, and with the reflected love of the God who has redeemed both it and us.

It is therefore precisely our failure, our sin, and finally our death which prevent us from supposing that we are sufficient of ourselves, and which make room for the glory of God.

The theme of the Church—Crucifixion–Resurrection—is therefore the song which is sung, whether it be recognised or not, by the whole world of men and things in their tribulation and in their merriment. This is the Gospel of the Church; the Gospel, because it is the Gospel—of God. There is no question here of bringing men within the sphere of the Truth, for they are already there. God is not the God of the Jews only, but of the Gentiles also, of the Anti-clericals and the Communists, of all the 'Movements' which tingle with resentment against the Church. He is also the God of the superior, detached person who, like Gallio, pins his faith neither on the Church nor on its opponents.

Yet, though the Church cannot bring men within the sphere of the Truth since they are already there, it can, if it be true to the theme by which its pride is destroyed, enable men to see the Truth in which men are standing. (5)

NOTES / SOURCES

1. Edwyn Clement Hoskyns, *Cambridge Sermons*, London, 1938, pp. 27–9
2. Ibid., pp. 48–9
3. Ibid., p. 70
4. Ibid., pp. 76–9
5. Ibid., pp. 90–3

Eric Milner-White   1884–1963

Born in Southampton, the son of the owner of a department store, Eric Milner-White was educated at Harrow and King's College, Cambridge. After training for the ministry at Cuddesdon he served as a curate in South London before returning to King's as chaplain and shortly afterwards became a chaplain to the forces, receiving the DSO. Returning to Cambridge in 1918, he was made Dean of King's the following year. On Christmas Eve 1918 the first service of Nine Lessons and Carols was held, which is one of Milner-White's enduring legacies. During his thirty-three years at King's he was a member and later Superior of the Oratory of the Good Shepherd, and developed his considerable gift for composing prayers in resonant and sensitive language. He became Dean of York in 1941 and both there and at King's enhanced the great buildings in his care with aesthetic and liturgical skill.

Before Prayer

LORD, thou hast given me this space for prayer:
　　fill it with thy gifts of grace;
　　fill it with the shewings of thy truth,
　　　with holy counsels and inspirations,
　　　with the communion of peace;

Occupy it with the work of love,—
　　　　to beg thy mercies upon them I love,
　　　　upon all mine acquaintance,
　　　　upon all in need,
　　　　upon all whom thou lovest.

Overshadow me with thy Spirit,
    with the light that is THOU;
Banish distraction, inattention, coldness;
Make mine eyes to see, mine ears to hear,
    my tongue to speak, my soul to be still;
And then be merciful to my prayer,
    and to me, a sinner;
      for Christ's sake. (1)

Before Service in Church

LET me come into the church of God
    to meet the Spirit of GOD:
not to give religion an hour,
    but to live in the eternal;
not to maintain a decorous habit,
    but to bow in the holy place before the Holy One;
not to judge the words of a preacher,
    but to draw life from the Word and Truth everlasting;
not to be moved or soothed by music,
    but to sing from the heart divine praises;
not that mine eyes roam over architecture or congregation,
    but that my soul look up to the King in his beauty,
    and my heart plead the needs of thy children;
not that my thoughts escape out into the world,
    but that they be still, and know that thou art GOD.

Let me go, and go again, into the house of the Lord,
    and be glad, and give thanks, and adore
      my King and my GOD. (2)

Choice

LORD, in the choices of every day,
    grant me to choose aright
      as in thy Presence and to thy glory:
to discriminate not only between the good and the evil
    but between the good and the better,
      and to do the best.

Save me from treason to thee,
    O my Master and King,
    by disguising to myself thy demands,
    by any choice of ashes for bread,
    by any surrender to popular standards,
    by any accommodation of duty or faith to mine own ease,
    by any the least betrayal of purity.

Rather grant me the Spirit of judgement
   to choose with clear eyes
     the ways of grace,
     the eternal wisdom and the eternal will:
  not only to choose, but to pursue
   all that is true, all that is of good report,
    all that is lovely;
  and in all to exalt thy praise and honour,
   my LORD and my GOD. (3)

Lent

LORD, bless to me this Lent.

Lord, let me fast most truly and profitably,
  by feeding in prayer on thy Spirit;
   reveal me to myself
    in the light of thy holiness.

Suffer me never to think
  that I have knowledge enough to need no teaching,
   wisdom enough to need no correction,
   talents enough to need no grace,
   goodness enough to need no progress,
   humility enough to need no repentance,
   devotion enough to need no quickening,
   strength sufficient without thy Spirit;
  lest, standing still, I fall back for evermore.

Shew me the desires that should be disciplined,
  and sloths to be slain.
Shew me the omissions to be made up
  and the habits to be mended.
And behind these, weaken, humble and annihilate in me
  self-will, self-righteousness, self-satisfaction,
  self-sufficiency, self-assertion, vainglory.

May my whole effort be to return to thee;
  O make it serious and sincere
  persevering and fruitful in result,
   by the help of thy Holy Spirit
    and to thy glory,
     my Lord and my GOD. (4)

Confession

Forgive me, O Lord,
O Lord forgive me my sins,
   the sins of my youth,
   the sins of the present;
   the sins I laid upon myself in an ill pleasure,
   the sins I cast upon others in an ill example;
   the sins which are manifest to all the world,
   the sins which I have laboured to hide from mine acquaintance,
      from my own conscience,
      and even from my memory;

   my crying sins and my whispering sins,
   my ignorant sins and my wilful;
   sins against my superiors, equals, servants,
      against my lovers and benefactors,
   sins against myself, mine own body, my own soul;
   sins against thee, O almighty Father, O merciful Son,
      O blessed Spirit of GOD.

Forgive me, O Lord, forgive me all my sins;
Say to me, *Son be of good comfort*
     thy sins are forgiven thee
   in the merits of thine Anointed,
     my Saviour Jesus Christ. (5)

Thy God Thy Glory

Shew me, O GOD most holy,
   according to the measure of our mortal sight,
      THY GLORY.
Disclose the splendours of thy power, thy wisdom and thy love,
   as the rising sun breaks upon the night shadows
      and day leaps into joy.

But day is here; thy glory thou hast revealed
   already, wonderfully, if we will but see;
glory, more glorious than might or majesty
   or any magnificence of imagined heaven,
in the face of a little Child, thy Son, my Christ,
   come that men might call thee FATHER
      and be called thy sons;
   the effulgence of thy glory:

the glory of One despised and rejected of men
   dying without the gates,
who has washed us clean from our sins in his own blood
     to make us priests and kings:

the glory of the Living One, Beginning and End of all,
   the image of the invisible GOD,
   shining as the sun shines in strength,
freely imparting to us the Spirit of his glory
    that we may live and not die.

     O GOD, most glorious,
       make our life the vision of thee
        to the praise of thy glory;
       that we all as a mirror may reflect it,
       and be transformed into the same image
        from glory to glory,
         world without end. (6)

The Spirit of Life

O HOLY GHOST
    giver of light and life;
Impart to us thoughts higher than our own thoughts,
  and prayers better than our own prayers,
  and powers beyond our own powers;
that we may spend and be spent
    in the ways of love and goodness,
  after the perfect image
    of our Lord and Saviour Jesus Christ. (7)

The Lord's Supper

LORD this is thy feast,
  prepared by thy longing,
  spread at thy command,
  attended at thine invitation,
  blessed by thine own Word,
  distributed by thine own hand,
  the undying memorial of thy sacrifice
    upon the Cross,
  the full gift of thine everlasting love,
  and its perpetuation till time shall end.

LORD, this is Bread of heaven,
    Bread of life,
  that, whoso eateth, never shall hunger more.
  And this the Cup of pardon, healing, gladness,
    strength,
  that, whoso drinketh, thirsteth not again.

So may we come, O Lord, to thy Table;
  Lord Jesus, come to us. (8)

NOTES / SOURCES

1. Eric Milner-White, *My God My Glory: Aspirations, Acts and Prayers on the Desire for God*, London, 1954, p. 1
2. Ibid., p. 3
3. Ibid., p. 16
4. Ibid., p. 21
5. Ibid., p. 25
6. Ibid., p. 36
7. Ibid., p. 56
8. Ibid., p. 70

Hubert Northcott CR   1884–1967

Hubert Northcott was the son of a vicar and was educated at Rossall and Oxford. Following a curacy he joined the Community of the Resurrection and was professed in 1918. He represented the most austere strain within the Community, having originally wished to join SSJE, and created the first proper novitiate. His own prayer was much influenced by St John of the Cross and he was widely read in the history of religious life and in the traditions of spirituality. He emphasized the Eucharist primarily as sacrifice, reservation of the Sacrament for prayer and devotions, contemplation, and mortification, believing that 'moderation is not a characteristic of the Catholic religion'. As a spiritual director he was fatherly in the best sense of the word, caring deeply for his charges, yet never intruding or bullying, and always encouraging the truest and most natural growth that was appropriate. For the latter part of his life at Mirfield and for eleven years on a mission in Sekhukhuniland in the Transvaal, he gave himself deeply to the prayer of intercession.

Worship

Those obligations may be summed up in the one word 'worship'. For worship (worth-ship) is the rendering to God 'the honour due unto His Name'. 'Worship the Lord with holy worship', and that includes the offering of the whole life. St Thomas Aquinas for this reason declares religion to be a part of the virtue of Justice, the creature paying what is due from him to the Creator. Here we will use the word in its narrower sense of prayer and praise, offered directly to God. Man has a special obligation to render such worship. All creation bears the impress of God and proclaims His glory. But it does so unconsciously, by the faithfulness of each creature to the law of its being. The bird sings because that is its nature: the lily spreads forth its threefold splendours because it is made that way; in so doing they unwittingly proclaim the glory of Him who could create such wonders. Only man has the gift of reason to recognize that glory and whence it came, and the power to offer free and rational praise therefor. So he is the appointed mouthpiece of creation, to give conscious and significant expression, as it were, to the song of the bird, or the fairness of the lily, as also to the grimmer aspects, as of the tiger or the thunderstorm. The world waits for him to fulfil this duty. 'The earnest expectation of the creature waiteth for the revealing of the Sons of God.' (Rom. 8. 19) (1)

The Glory of God the End of the Liturgy

The objective of the Liturgy is primarily the glory of God—that and nothing else. In countless other ways, e.g. through his works, through his friendships, through his recreations, man may and should indirectly be serving and praising God. But here he renders immediate honour, laying aside everything else for the time, that he may voice creation's worship of the Creator. Whether he himself feels any the better while doing so, or whether he feels more devout when otherwise employed, has little or nothing to do with the matter. He takes part in that worship primarily to pay his due of praise to God—to give, so far as the creature can give anything to his Creator, that amount of time and attention solely to Him and for no other purpose. And no man can sincerely attempt that without being the better for it. This aspect of the Liturgy particularly needs emphasizing in these days. Men tend far too much to estimate things according to their present utility; what will be their effect on the individual's conduct or on society? They can see a certain value in prayer as a means to guide and strengthen action here and now. But the prayer of adoration, directed purely to God with no other object in view, seems a waste of time. In the Middle Ages men raised magnificent churches to the glory of God and many of them still stand bearing their witness. They still convey some breath of the eternal, of aspiration that seeks God for His own sake, prodigal of labour and expense, if so it may glorify Him. They are pregnant with the spirit of the Liturgy. Our tendency has been to consider the number of seats to be provided and then to reckon on how economically they can be housed. However, recently signs have appeared of a better understanding, and churches have been raised which have caught something of the true spirit, and their architects have sought to express in stone what the Liturgy expresses in its rites and ceremonies. (2)

The Joy of Meeting Those for Whom We have Prayed

Perhaps one of the joys reserved for us hereafter will be to learn what became of our intercessions, and to meet the souls they supported in time of need. And for ourselves, there will be the joy of meeting those who have prayed for us, and so of realizing from a new angle our share in the Communion of Saints. If so, we may learn then how much the Church owes, and we ourselves as members of it, to the artless prayers uttered by simple child-like souls, the value of whose intercession we should have little suspected. (3)

NOTES / SOURCES

1. Hubert Northcott CR, *The Venture of Prayer*, London, 1954, p. 53
2. Ibid., p. 54
3. Ibid., p. 143

Ernest H. Burgmann   1885–1967

Bishop Burgmann, who had been a bushman and bullock driver before he was ordained for the provincial diocese of Newcastle in Australia, had an abiding sympathy for the working man. A pragmatic Christian socialist, Ernest Burgmann was an outspoken social commentator in the troubled 1920s and 30s. In 1934 he was consecrated Bishop of Goulburn (NSW), the diocese in which the new national capital of Canberra had been planted just seven years previously. Burgmann, who was to become a prolific author during his episcopate, had also been warden of St John's Theological College, first in Armidale NSW and then in Newcastle. From 1961, after he resigned as diocesan, he was warden of another theological institution, St Mark's, Canberra.

Education and Play

Education begins in play. It continues in play, and remains possible while ever the spirit of play survives. Play is spontaneous living, and in it we enter into relations with our world and with our fellows. Play is the activity by which we explore not only our world, but our own capacities. In play we try things out. We are not really old till we can no longer play. While we can play we can retain our interest in life and our education can still go on. We were born to play. The purpose of education is to take hold of our spontaneous play activities and to bring into them a social discipline and a sense of responsibility. The art of education is to do this without reducing the energy of play, in fact, we should aim at enhancing and increasing it. We also equip the play activity with knowledge and under-standing.

For instance, the child's capacity to pretend is the scientist's ability to fashion an hypothesis, the philosopher's vision of a universal system of thought, and the saint's ground for faith. The child pretends he is the butcher or baker, the father or doctor, and by degrees he settles down to become one or more of the things he pretended to be. He eventually makes his play dream come true by dealing faithfully with the facts of life. He begins that faithful dealing in play. The form of the play can be transformed into work. The play spirit can keep the work fresh and resilient and creative to the end of his days.

The scientist says in effect, 'Let us pretend that this hypothesis is true' and then he proceeds to test it out on facts. The play spirit will keep his imagination alert and sensitive. He will be able to see all the more quickly and modify his hypotheses all the more readily if he keeps that spirit fresh.

The philosopher says more profoundly, 'Let us pretend that we are looking at all things at once from the point of view of eternity, seeing all things clearly and seeing them whole'. The play spirit will sharpen his insight, and prevent him from taking himself too seriously in this very ambitious attempt at understanding. It is the spirit of play that makes the great philosopher something of the artist also. Plato is a good story-teller.

The saint keeps the spirit of play in the most child-like form of all. He says, 'Let us pretend that God is disinterested love, and let us live it out in life'. He tests this till it becomes his character. He becomes completely convinced that he has hit upon the most important truth of all. It has the power of giving him a kind of eternal youthfulness and an indestructible freshness. Saint Francis and many others never seem to grow old. They remain delightfully teachable and un-predictable. The real saint is eternally child-like.

Age therefore is relative to the energy of the spirit of play within us. There are also degrees of quality in play. Play may degenerate into a mere business of filling in time with sensational amusements or trivial occupations. Where, however, the spirit of play remains rich and vigorous it is the energy which enables man to keep up his joyful attack on life. The passing of years need not affect this spirit very much at all. Some people remain fresh and young to a ripe old age. Some people seem to be born old and tired, and never become young at all. The educator is not so much concerned with a person's years as with his teachability. When educators are wise enough they may be able to make the young in years young in spirit also, and prevent all from dying in spirit before they die in body. This entails the transforming, not the destroying, of the spirit of play. Education should be the work of a lifetime. Whatever a man's occupation may be he should enjoy learning all his days. A lifetime is all too short for the work that education can do. The work of education is not done until every man has become something of a saint.

This spontaneous, instinctive spirit which manifests itself in play is always the raw material in education. As we grow older we should not be taught to play less, but to play more responsibly and intelligently. To kill the spirit of play is to puncture personal energy and educability. So much that goes by the name of education devitalizes the process before it begins. An adult should be, not a person who has finished his play, but a person who has grown responsible and disciplined, a person, who by his play, has accumulated much knowledge.

Such a person can then turn back and help the young to grow. Social responsibility is the mark of the real adult. A society can only grow and become creative if its members are alive to their responsibility to each other. They must feel that they are members one of another. The spirit of mutual loyalty must be strong in any community that is going to count for anything in the world.

The responsible adult should see that the comradeship born in the play of children is ripened into the loyalty that enables a man to live for his friends, for his country, for truth and righteousness, for the God of the saint.

NOTES / SOURCES

E. H. Burgmann, *The Education of an Australian* (first printed Sydney, 1944), Canberra, 1991, pp. 110–12

Charles Raven   1885–1964

Regius Professor of Divinity at Cambridge (1932–1950) and (from 1939) also Master of Christ's College, Charles Raven was both a scientist and a theologian. A strong pacifist, he was one of the sponsors of the Peace Pledge Union, and also an early advocate of the ordination of women.

Knowing God in Christ

To have known God vaguely but very really in nature and humanity, and then to discover Him translated into a human comrade, is to find awe quickened into devotion, and reverence into love. The Eternal may stir me in certain moods and certain elements of my being: only love of person for person can possess me entire. Art, reason, virtue, these appeal to particular functions: a friend, a lover, affects every fibre as my whole self goes out freely in response. If it be true that it is through relationship with others that we achieve personality, and that the quality of our friends determines our own, then the comradeship of Jesus should lift and integrate our nature as nothing else could do. And if in love we become what we love, and if Jesus be for us God, then indeed to love Him is to become in some sort divine. (1)

The Religious Basis of Pacifism

'Why then do we claim,' he writes, 'that pacifism is the inevitable corollary of our theological and religions convictions? Because for us pacifism is involved in

(a) our concept of God and of His mode of creative activity
(b) our understanding of Jesus and the method of His redemptive and atoning work
(c) our apprehension of the Holy Spirit and of the Koinonia established by Him

Put less technically these involve:

(a) a belief that in the nature of God, and therefore, in His dealings with man and in man's true way of life, love is always primary and justice derivative
(b) that in the teaching and atoning work of Jesus it is plain not only that those who take the sword perish by the sword but that the sole redemptive activity is the power of the love that gives and suffers, that is of the Cross;
(c) that worship and fellowship, the love of God and the love of men, are inseparably united; that what is wrong for the individual cannot be right for the community, that the fruit of the Spirit is love, joy, peace—a way of living of which modern warfare is a flagrant denial, and that it is only as this way of life is realised that the ministry of the Church can become creative, regenerative and inspirational.' (2)

Christianity and Science

It is because the appeal of the universe is primarily to the artist in us that art is obviously the first, and in some sense the most adequate, interpretation of it. The truth which cannot yet or by us be told in terms of the intellect is expressed, if anywhere, in music, poetry, architecture, dancing, the drama. We common folks are inarticulate, untrained in aesthetic appreciation, too self-conscious to give our impulses free play. But even so, we can recognise that in all art worthy of the name there is a touch of eternity, of a reality too large for definition, of a truth universal in its appeal, and that in the hands of a master his medium is the only appropriate means by which such eternity can be interpreted. Even those who, like myself, are infants in aesthetic equipment know beyond question that here in the handful of supreme achievements is the authentic mystery, and that translated into such terms we others can begin to conceive and to explain it. Here is the same wonder and awe, the same sense of illimitable and apprehended unity;

and the artist gives me a sacramental expression of that infinity far more exact than any intellectual formula or elaborate analysis. He, a man like myself, does for me what I cannot do for myself. He feels and fixes and transmits to me the elusive beauty by which I too am haunted. He gives me eyes and ears that I in my small way may share what he has seen and heard.

If his primary impression of Nature is that of creative art, the student will soon find that he cannot rest in the realm of feeling. Wonder leads on to interest, contemplation to enquiry, the aesthetic to the intellectual. As the child does not long remain content with cognition and comment, but at an early age satisfies its curiosity by interminable questioning, so the world around us presents an immediate stimulus to mental activity. No one can watch with any sympathy the growth of plants, the behaviour of insects, the ways of birds and beasts, the motions of the stars, without the stirring of a desire to understand, to ask first 'Why?' and then 'How?' To seek for the purpose before we know the mode is characteristic: we are mythologists before we are scientists: religion is older than physics or chemistry. But if we are to look for satisfying answers, we must reverse the order of our desires, and study the workings of Nature before we enquire its meaning, remembering always that to give an account of a thing is not to account for it.

It is no part of our purpose to discuss the stages of our enquiry, though these necessarily follow a regular sequence. We must first name and classify carrying on Adam's task and imposing what order we can upon the objects that we identify. Nomenclature and systematology have a fascination of their own, quite apart from any further knowledge. Indeed to imagine that we have explained when we have labelled and catalogued, is a failing so common to humanity that it is not surprising to find scientists occasionally, even now, succumbing to it. Like the collections which illustrate it, and the formation of which is too often the extent of an amateur scientist's achievement, it represents a necessary, but preliminary, stage. Fortunately, if it is to be done with any accuracy it inevitably leads on to morphology. Superficial study may place the bats among the birds, or the whales among the fishes; knowledge of structure will be necessary if we are to separate the swifts from the swallows or the owls from the 'Raptores.' And to study form is to discover adaptation. Take a simple instance. Cormorant and Gannet, though very closely related, are as different in habits and appearance as two water birds could be—the first a diver, pursuing its prey with the thrust of huge feet to the depths, but heavy on the wing and only flying to change its feeding-ground; the second a bird of the air, tirelessly buoyant, rarely settling on the sea, and plunging from on high with a sheer 'nose-dive' upon fish far below the surface. Dissect them and observe the structure (say) of the sternum and shoulder-girdle. Here are the same bones characteristic of the order and peculiar in the joining of the coracoid, clavicle and scapula, and in the ankylosis of the clavicle with the keel of the sternum. Yet the shape and proportion of them are moulded to suit the life of each; the Cormorant's specialised like a Grebe's, with broad surfaces for muscle-attachment to give elasticity for a rapid wing-beat, long and slender coracoids and furcula, and plates of bone stretching back over the belly; the Gannet's modified for flight, clavicle and coracoids short and stout, keel projecting, sternum narrow and raked forward, the whole suited to the bunched and powerful but inelastic fibres of the pectoral muscles that drive the long slow pinions. So morphology leads on to teleology, the study of form to that of function. Noting peculiarities of adaptation, we set ourselves to explain them, and in so doing plunge into the mid-stream of modern science. Here are problems on every side and in every department; theories to be tested; observations to be extended; deductions to be drawn. The last half-century has been lavish in its hypotheses; for explanation goes hand in hand with investigation. We have given instances enough to show their manifest attractiveness and the magnificent ingenuity of their authors. If that first heyday of speculation is, in certain spheres, and very notably in biology, passing away; if for the explanation of animal life the biochemists and bio-physicists, on the one hand, and the comparative psychologists, on the other, have the future in their keeping, there remain, in cosmogony and pure physics at one end of the scale, and in anthropology, psychology, and psychic research at the other, fields where speculation has still a wide range.

Throughout, such study is concerned with process, with the discovery of the modes of development, with the exact formulation of what are popularly called the laws of Nature, with the provision of evidence for the philosopher and the man of affairs. The scientist as such is concerned solely with knowledge, not with religion or politics—hence his title; and his motto is, 'This man decided not to live, but know.' Fortunately for himself, he is also a man, a citizen of earth and heaven, like the rest of us; but, like all specialists, he will sacrifice something of proportion and breadth, and will in most cases be disqualified thereby as a philosopher or a prophet, as the 'religions' of science have too often demonstrated. Yet in his own sphere how enormous is his contribution, controlling as he does the intellectual life of man! For science claims nothing less than to survey the whole field of human experience, to arrange and explain and interpret it intelligibly. Whatever men can know, this is material for the scientist. Religion itself, so far as it is concerned with intelligible truth, is his concern; and, indeed, in studying psychology he will deal with aesthetics and ethics as well. In this way and ideally the fields of religion and science are identical, and they themselves only differ in as much as religion is concerned not merely with knowledge, but with life. Every religious man should be a scientist; a scientist as such need not necessarily be religious, though he could only not be so as he became not a man, but a thinking-machine.

This is the first and obvious lesson of the study of Nature for the Christian—that it is by scientific methods alone that the intellectual validity of his belief can be tested. Ultimately an interpretation of it in the categories of thought may fail; life, and not logic, is the ultimate test; but it will only fail in so far as life contains certain experiences of the eternal which cannot be handled by mental processes. The nature of this exception is important: it concerns only the sphere which neither science nor religion can translate precisely into formulated doctrine. Whatever is capable of formulation will have to receive the endorse-ment of science if it is to be accepted as valid. In these days, when men still divide the supernatural from the natural, faith from reason, infallible creeds or scriptures from other hypotheses and literature, and refuse to submit the former in each case to criticism, and yet claim to argue about it and impose it, such a warning is not unnecessary. We are no longer living in the age of tabu and 'acts of God' and special providences: if God is in the universe at all, He is in it all, and is everywhere to be studied sincerely and exactly. There will be much that eludes our understanding, much on which the evidence will leave us unable to speak with confidence, much of which we shall be wise to confess ignorance. But only disaster awaits the religion which accepts such ignorance as a licence to credulity, or tries to fit God into the gaps left by scientific study.

For the most obvious lesson of such study is that the universe is a cosmos, a system of relationships intimately interdependent, a reign of law in which nothing happens by accident and there are no intrusions. It is just as much within this one order that the Spirit works in creation as in those fuller manifestations which we call the Incarnation and the Atonement. 'Science,' as Dr Inge asserts, 'will never renounce the attempt to bring everything under a single system of laws.' Scientists have seen one barrier after another broken down, one inviolable territory after another entered. The authorities which stood across their path have been driven often ignominiously into retreat; and efforts to resist which failed when the doctrine of special creations or of scriptural inerrancy were concerned are not likely to succeed in defence of the Athanasian Creed, or transubstantiation. Those of us who have come to Christianity by way of science, who are convinced that *credo quia incredible* is a counsel of despair, and who value the freedom to investigate as the peculiar glory of Anglicanism, can hardly be expected to sympathise with the pathetic and well-meant but wholly mischievous attitude which clings to 'old paths in perilous times.' We must be monists, and take the consequences. Truth will in good time prevail. If Christianity be true, we shall not have lived altogether in vain; if it be false, then at least let us discover our mistake as soon as we can. (3)

NOTES / SOURCES

1. Charles Raven, *The Wanderer's Way*, London, 1928, p. 64
2. F. W. Dillistone, *Charles Raven: Naturalist, Historian, Theologian*, London, 1975, pp. 225–6
3. Charles E. Raven, *The Creator Spirit: A Survey of Christian Doctrine in the light of Biology, Psychology and Mysticism*, The Hulsean Lectures, Cambridge, 1926–7, The Noble Lectures, Harvard, 1926, London, 1927, pp. 108–14

Gilbert Shaw   1886–1967

Barrister turned priest and East End political activist, Gilbert Shaw was among the most important spiritual directors of the 20th century. Admired by members of the Orthodox Churches and people such as T. S. Eliot, Dorothy L. Sayers, and J. H. Oldham (with whom he was a member of an important wartime think tank), Shaw was misunderstood within his own church. He was a pioneer in the study of psychic phenomena and for a long time a leading exorcist in the Church of England. In his late seventies he was enabled to play a major part in the recovery of the solitary life in the Church and the development of the contemplative life for women and men, most notably with the Sisters of the Love of God at Fairacres, Oxford.

A Last Homily – Words of Advice to the Sisters of the Love of God

THE HOLY SPIRIT will never give you stuff on a plate – you've got to work for it.
Your work is LISTENING – taking the situation you're in and holding it in courage, not being beaten down by it.
Your work is STANDING – holding things without being deflected by your own

desires or the desires of other people round you. Then things work out just through patience. How things alter we don't know, but the situation alters.

There must be dialogue in patience and charity – then something seems to turn up that wasn't there before.

We must take people as they are and where they are – not going too far ahead or too fast for them, but listening to their needs and supporting them in their following.

The Holy Spirit brings things new and old out of the treasure.

Intercessors bring the 'deaf and dumb' to Christ, that is their part.

Seek for points of unity and stand on those rather than on principles.

Have the patience that refuses to be pushed out; the patience that refuses to be disillusioned.

There must be dialogue—or there will be no development. (1)

The Service of Love

We can only know ourselves and the meaning of creation and re-creation in the light which comes from eternity, in which each one of us in the differing vocations of the Body of Christ reflects as in a mirror the splendour of the Lord, being transfigured into his likeness from splendour to splendour.

. . . .

As long as there is something in us that is not wholly reconciled to the vertical, to complete dependence, we are in sin and only the Precious Blood washes that sin away. The fire of the self-sacrificing love of Christ burns it out. We must put ourselves into the fire to be the fire. This dead weight of iron is put into the fire, it begins to glow, and at last the iron is the fire and the fire is the iron, and that is sanctity. It is to that we are called – to be wholly in the vertical.

. . . .

Christ is the vertical, the Way, Truth and Life of our ascent to worship the Father in the renewed Sonship, for he has descended to take the whole manhood into God. In every occasion and anxiety, in every relation of the conscious on the horizontal level, as well as the whole of the unconscious, he asks that we should surrender completely to him. He stands as the Servant at our door that we should open to him fully, to be wholly dependent on him in penitence, so that in the light of the cell of self-knowledge, as the Spirit burns in it, there is nothing that we would hold back, that as the bondslave of Christ we may know the intimacy of his service—'I will sup with him and he with me.'

. . . faith, penance for every bit of our holding back, praying always, which is simply being always with God, so that all things are begun, continued and ended in him.

. . . we must not be discouraged when we see what we have to throw away. Little by little, desire by desire, our conversion must be made real through the endurance of the ascent. The one necessity is faith to go on. . . . bringing the End into the present.

It is God who enlightens our understanding. Our part is to keep putting ourselves into his hands by a continual conversion. (2)

1. Gilbert Shaw, privately printed and distributed by SLG Charitable Trust Limited (n.d.).
2. *The Service of Love*, a retreat given by Gilbert Shaw to the Sisters of the Love of God, at the Convent of the Incarnation, Fairacres, Oxford, September 1963, unpublished, pp. 18, 33, 36–7, 53

Charles Walter Stanesby Williams · 1886–1945

In poetry, 'supernatural novels', and theological writings, Williams, who worked in the London publishing house of Oxford University Press, was a notable Christian apologist. Along with C. S. Lewis (q.v.) and J. R. R. Tolkien he was a member of the 'Inklings'. He was a proponent of the theology of romantic love and of the theological principles of substitution, of which the Atonement was the culminating example and co-inherence.

The Cross

There is another point of the same kind. It is often said that He was put to death by evil men. Caiaphas and Pilate and Herod are denounced. It is, of course, in some sense true that it was evil which persecuted Him. But I have myself felt that the destructiveness was more common to our experience if we hold, as we very well may, that Caiaphas and Pilate were each of them doing his best in the duty presented to them. The high priest was condemning a blasphemer. The Roman governor was attempting to maintain the peace. At the present time, for example, it is clear that one man must suffer for the people—and many more than one man, whether they consent or not. It is, no doubt, inevitable; it may be right. But we can hardly blame those earlier supporters of the same law. Humanly speaking, they were doing the best they could. They chose the least imperfect good that they could see. And their choice crucified the Good.

It is this agonizing fact which is too often present in our own experience. Certainly our sins and faults destroy the good. But our efforts after the good also destroy it. The very pursuit of goodness becomes a hunt; that which was to be our lord becomes a victim. It is necessary to behave well here? We do. What is the result? The destruction of some equal good. There is no more significant or more terrible tale in the New Testament than that which surrounded the young Incarnacy with the dying Innocents: the chastisement of His peace was upon them. At the end He paid back the debt—to God if not to them; He too perished innocently. With Him also (morally) there was nothing else to be done.

He had put Himself then to His own law, in every sense. Man (perhaps ignorantly, but none the less truly for that) executed justice upon Him. This was the world He maintained in creation? *This* was the world He maintained in creation. This was the best law, the clearest justice, man could find, and He did well to accept it. If they had known it was He, they could have done no less and no better. They crucified Him; let it be said, they did well. But then let it be said also, that the Sublimity itself had done well: adorable He might be by awful definition of His Nature, but at least He had shown Himself honourable in His choice. He accepted Job's challenge of long ago, talked with His enemy in the gate, and outside the gate suffered (as the men He made so often do) from both His friends and His enemies. Which of us has not known and has not been a Judas? He had nowhere to lay His head? And we? 'Behold my mother and my brethren.'

This then has seemed to me now for long perhaps the most flagrant significance of the Cross; it does enable us to use the word 'justice' without shame—which otherwise we could not. God therefore becomes tolerable as well as credible. Our justice condemned the innocent, but the innocent it condemned was one who was fundamentally responsible for the existence of all injustice—its existence in the mere, but necessary, sense of time, which His will created and prolonged. (1)

The Way of Exchange

The doctrine of the Christian Church has declared that the mystery of the Christian religion is a doctrine of co-inherence and substitution. The Divine Word co-inheres in God the Father (as the Father in Him and the Spirit in Both), but also He has substituted His Manhood for ours in the secrets of the Incarnation and Atonement. The principle of the Passion is that He gave His life 'for'—that is, instead of and on behalf of—ours. In that sense He lives in us and we in Him, He and we co-inhere. 'I live; yet not I but Christ liveth in me' said St Paul, and defined the web of universal power towards substitution. To love God and to love one's neighbour are but two movements of the same principle, and so are nature and grace; and the principle is the Word by whom all things were made and who gave Himself for the redemption of all things. It was precisely the breach in that original nature which the new Nature entered to fulfil. But either way it is our nature that is concerned. Our natural life begins by being borne in another; our mothers have to carry us. This is not (so far as we know) by our own will. The Christian Church demands that we shall carry out that principle everywhere by our will—with our friends and with our neighbours, whether we like our neighbours or not. (2)

The Beginning and End of the Church

The beginning of Christendom is, strictly, at a point out of time. A metaphysical trigonometry finds it among the spiritual Secrets, at the meeting of two heavenward lines, one drawn from Bethany along the Ascent of Messias, the other from Jerusalem against the Descent of the Paraclete. That measurement, the measurement of eternity in operation, of the bright cloud and the rushing wind, is, in effect, theology.

The history of Christendom is the history of an operation. It is an operation of the Holy Ghost towards Christ, under the conditions of our humanity; and it was our humanity which gave the signal, as it were, for that operation. The visible beginning of the Church is at Pentecost, but that is only a result of its actual beginning—and ending—in heaven. (3)

The Order of Co-inherence

At the beginning of life in the natural order is an act of substitution and co-inherence. A man can have no child unless his seed is received and carried by a woman; a woman can have no child unless she receives and carries the seed of a man—literally bearing the burden. It is not only a mutual act; it is a mutual act of substitution. The child itself for nine months literally co-inheres in its mother; there is no human creature that has not sprung from such a period of such an interior growth.

In that natural co-inherence the Christian Church has understood another; the about-to-be-born already co-inheres in an ancestral and contemporary guilt. It is shapen in wickedness, and in sin has its mother conceived it. The fundamental fact of itself is already opposed to the principle of the universe; it knows that good as evil, and therefore it derives and desires its own good disorderly. It has been sown in corruption, and in corruption it emerges into separate life.

It has been the habit of the Church to baptize it, as soon as it has emerged, by the formula of the Trinity-in-Unity. As it passes from the most material co-inherence it is received into the supernatural; and it is received by a deliberate act. The godparents present themselves as its substitutes; by their intentions and their belief (and they are there to present even for 'those of riper years') the new-born is granted 'that which by nature he cannot have,' he is 'incorporated' into the Church, he is made 'partaker' of death and resurrection. It is this co-inherence which, at the confirmation, he himself confesses and ratifies.

The Faith into which he is received has declared that principle to be the root and the pattern of the supernatural as of the natural world. And the Faith is the only body to have done so. It has proclaimed that this is due to the deliberate choice and operation of the Divine Word. Had he willed, he could presumably have raised for his Incarnation a body in some other way than he chose. But he preferred to shape himself within the womb, to become hereditary, to owe to humanity the flesh he divinitized by the same principle—'not by conversion of the Godhead into flesh, but by taking of the Manhood into God.' By an act of substitution he reconciled the natural world with the world of the kingdom of heaven, sensuality with substance. He restored substitution and co-inherence everywhere; up and down the ladder of that great substitution all our lesser substitutions run; within that sublime co-inherence all our lesser co-inherences inhere. And when the Christian Church desired to define the nature of the Alone, she found no other term; It mutually co-inheres by Its own nature. The triune formula by which the child is baptized is precisely the incomprehensible formula of this.

It is supernatural, but also it is natural. The dreams of nationality and communism use no other language. The denunciation of individualism means this or it means nothing. The praise of individualism must allow for this or it is mere impossible anarchy. It is experienced, at their best moments of delight, by lovers and friends. It is the manner of childbirth. It is the image everywhere of supernatural charity, and the measure of this or of the refusal of this is the cause of all the images.

The apprehension of this order, in nature and in grace, without and within Christendom, should be, now, one of our chief concerns; it might indeed be worth the foundation of an Order within the Christian Church. Such a foundation would, in one sense, mean nothing, for all that it could do is already exposed and prepared, and the Church has suffered something from its interior organizations. About this there need be little organization; it could do no more than communicate an increased awareness of that duty which is part of the very nature of the Church itself. But in our present distresses, of international and social schism, among the praises of separation here or there, the pattern might be stressed, the image affirmed. The Order of the Co-inherence would exist only for that, to meditate and practise it. The principle is one of the open secrets of the saints; we might draw the smallest step nearer sanctity if we used it. Substitutions in love, exchanges in love, are a part of it; 'oneself' and 'others' are only the specialized terms of its technique. The technique needs much discovery; the Order would have no easy labour. But, more than can be imagined, it might find that, in this present world, its labour was never more needed, its concentration never more important, its profit never perhaps more great. (4)

NOTES / SOURCES

1. Charles Williams: *The Image of the City and other Essays*, selected by Anne Ridler, London, 1958, pp. 132–3
2. Ibid., p. 129
3. Charles Williams, *The Descent of the Dove: A Short History of the Holy Spirit in the Church*, London, 1939, p. 1
4. Ibid., pp. 234–6

Thomas Stearns Eliot   1888–1956

Born in America, Eliot came to England, where he was baptized as an Anglican in 1927, at which time he declared himself to be a 'classicist in literature, royalist in politics and Anglo-Catholic in religion'. His religious quest was powerfully expressed in his poetry, notably *Ash Wednesday*, *The Journey of the Magi* and *Four Quartets*. He had a particular veneration for the seventeenth-century Anglican tradition.

Life Together

Thus your fathers were made
Fellow citizens of the saints, of the household of GOD, being built upon the foundation
Of apostles and prophets, Christ Jesus Himself the chief cornerstone.
But you, have you built well, that you now sit helpless in a ruined house?
Where many are born to idleness, to frittered lives and squalid deaths, embittered scorn in honeyless hives,
And those who would build and restore turn out the palms of their hands, or

look in vain towards foreign lands for alms to be more or the urn to be
     filled.
Your building not fitly framed together, you sit ashamed and wonder whether
     and how you may be builded together for a habitation of GOD in the Spirit, the
     Spirit which moved on the face of the waters like a lantern set on the back of a
     tortoise.
And some say: 'How can we love our neighbour? For love must be made real in
     act, as desire unites with desired; we have only our labour to give and our
     labour is not required.
We wait on corners, with nothing to bring but the songs we can sing which
     nobody wants to hear sung;
Waiting to be flung in the end, on a heap less useful than dung'.
You, have you built well, have you forgotten the cornerstone?
Talking of right relations of men, but not of relations of men to GOD.
'Our citizenship is in Heaven'; yes, but that is the model and type for your
     citizenship upon earth. . . .

What life have you if you have not life together?
There is no life that is not in community,
And no community not lived in praise of GOD.
Even the anchorite who meditates alone,
For whom the days and nights repeat the praise of GOD,
Prays for the Church, the Body of Christ incarnate.
And now you live dispersed on ribbon roads,
And no man knows or cares who is his neighbour
Unless his neighbour makes too much disturbance,
But all dash to and fro in motor cars,
Familiar with the roads and settled nowhere.
Nor does the family even move about together,
But every son would have his motor cycle,
And daughters ride away on casual pillions.

Much to cast down, much to build, much to restore;
Let the work not delay, time and the arm not waste;
Let the clay be dug from the pit, let the saw cut the stone,
Let the fire not be quenched in the forge. (1)

The Hint Half Guessed, the Gift Half Understood

Men's curiosity searches past and future
And clings to that dimension. But to apprehend
The point of intersection of the timeless
With time, is an occupation for the saint—
No occupation either, but something given
And taken, in a lifetime's death in love,
Ardour and selflessness and self-surrender.
For most of us, there is only the unattended
Moment, the moment in and out of time,

The distraction fit, lost in a shaft of sunlight,
The wild thyme unseen, or the winter lightning
Or the waterfall, or music heard so deeply
That it is not heard at all, but you are the music
While the music lasts. These are only hints and guesses,
Hints followed by guesses; and the rest
Is prayer, observance, discipline, thought and action.
The hint half guessed, the gift half understood, is Incarnation. (2)

The Dove Descending

The dove descending breaks the air
With flame of incandescent terror
Of which the tongues declare
The one discharge from sin and error.
The only hope, or else despair
   Lies in the choice of pyre or pyre—
   To be redeemed from fire by fire.

Who then devised the torment? Love.
Love is the unfamiliar Name
Behind the hands that wove
The intolerable shirt of flame
Which human power cannot remove.
   We only live, only suspire
   Consumed by either fire or fire. (3)

The End of all our Exploring

With the drawing of this Love and the voice of this Calling

We shall not cease from exploration
And the end of all our exploring
Will be to arrive where we started
And know the place for the first time.
Through the unknown, remembered gate
When the last of earth left to discover
Is that which was the beginning;
At the source of the longest river
The voice of the hidden waterfall
And the children in the apple-tree
Not known, because not looked for
But heard, half-heard, in the stillness
Between two waves of the sea.
Quick now, here, now, always—
A condition of complete simplicity
(Costing not less than everything)
And all shall be well and

All manner of thing shall be well
When the tongues of flame are in-folded
Into the crowned knot of fire
And the fire and the rose are one. (4)

Martyrdom

Interlude

'Glory to God in the highest, and on earth peace to men of good will.' *The fourteenth verse of the second chapter of the Gospel according to Saint Luke.* In the Name of the Father, and of the Son, and of the Holy Ghost. Amen.

Dear children of God, my sermon this Christmas morning will be a very short one. I wish only that you should meditate in your hearts the deep meaning and mystery of our masses of Christmas Day. For whenever Mass is said, we re-enact the Passion and Death of Our Lord; and on this Christmas Day we do this in celebration of His Birth. So that at the same moment we rejoice in His coming for the salvation of men, and offer again to God His Body and Blood in sacrifice, oblation and satisfaction for the sins of the whole world. It was in this same night that has just passed, that a multitude of the heavenly host appeared before the shepherds at Bethlehem, saying 'Glory to God in the highest, and on earth peace to men of good will'; at this same time of all the year that we celebrate at once the Birth of Our Lord and His Passion and Death upon the Cross. Beloved, as the World sees, this is to behave in a strange fashion. For who in the World will both mourn and rejoice at once and for the same reason? For either joy will be overborne by mourning, or mourning will be cast out by joy; so it is only in these our Christian mysteries that we can rejoice and mourn at once for the same reason. Now think for a moment about the meaning of this word 'peace'. Does it seem strange to you that the angels should have announced Peace, when ceaselessly the world has been stricken with War and the fear of War? Does it seem to you that the angelic voices were mistaken, and that the promise was a disappointment and a cheat?

Reflect now, how Our Lord Himself spoke of Peace. He said to His disciples, 'Peace I leave with you, my peace I give unto you.' Did He mean peace as we think of it: the kingdom of England at peace with its neighbours, the barons at peace with the King, the householder counting over his peaceful gains, the swept hearth, his best wine for a friend at the table, his wife singing to the children? Those men His disciples knew no such things: they went forth to journey afar, to suffer by land and sea, to know torture, imprisonment, disappointment, to suffer death by martyrdom. What then did He mean? If you ask that, remember then that He said also, 'Not as the world gives, give I unto you.' So then, He gave to His disciples peace, but not peace as the world gives.

Consider also one thing of which you have probably never thought. Not only do we at the feast of Christmas celebrate at once Our Lord's Birth and His Death:

but on the next day we celebrate the martyrdom of His first martyr, the blessed Stephen. Is it an accident, do you think, that the day of the first martyr follows immediately the day of the Birth of Christ? By no means. Just as we rejoice and mourn at once, in the Birth and the Passion of Our Lord; so also, in a smaller figure, we both rejoice and mourn in the death of martyrs. We mourn, for the sins of the world that has martyred them; we rejoice, that another soul is numbered among the Saints in Heaven, for the glory of God and for the salvation of men.

Beloved, we do not think of a martyr simply as a good Christian who has been killed because he is a Christian: for that would be solely to mourn. We do not think of him simply as a good Christian who has been elevated to the company of the Saints: for that would be simply to rejoice: and neither our mourning nor our rejoicing is as the world's is. A Christian martyrdom is never an accident, for Saints are not made by accident. Still less is a Christian martyrdom the effect of a man's will to become a Saint, as a man by willing and contriving may become a ruler of men. A martyrdom is always the design of God, for His love of men, to warn them and to lead them, to bring them back to His ways. It is never the design of man; for the true martyr is he who has become the instrument of God, who has lost his will in the will of God, and who no longer desires anything for himself, not even the glory of being a martyr. So thus as on earth the Church mourns and rejoices at once, in a fashion that the world cannot understand; so in Heaven the Saints are most high, having made themselves most low, and are seen, not as we see them, but in the light of the Godhead from which they draw their being.

I have spoken to you to-day, dear children of God, of the martyrs of the past, asking you to remember especially our martyr of Canterbury, the blessed Archbishop Elphege; because it is fitting, on Christ's birth day, to remember what is that Peace which He brought; and because, dear children, I do not think I shall ever preach to you again; and because it is possible that in a short time you may have yet another martyr, and that one perhaps not the last. I would have you keep in your hearts these words that I say, and think of them at another time. In the Name of the Father, and of the Son, and of the Holy Ghost. Amen. (5)

NOTES / SOURCES

1. Choruses from 'The Rock', 1934, II, *The Complete Poems and Plays of T. S. Eliot*, London, 1969, pp. 151–3
2. 'The Dry Salvages', V, 'Four Quartets', ibid., pp. 189–90
3. 'Little Gidding', IV, 'Four Quartets', ibid., p. 196
4. 'Little Gidding', V, 'Four Quartets', ibid., pp. 197–8
5. 'Murder in the Cathedral', Interlude, ibid., pp. 260–2

Edmund Robert Morgan   1888–1979

Whenever people talked of Edmund Morgan, the adjective 'saintly' soon featured in the conversation. Although his career looked privileged—Winchester, New College, Bishop's Chaplain, Archdeacon, Suffragan Bishop of Southampton, then Bishop of Truro—Morgan was an essentially humble and rather shy man. He deplored ambition in a priest and never sought the limelight. His seven books, for example, were written simply as fruits of personal reflection on a variety of themes rather than with an eye to publicity. Losing two sons in World War II, he experienced suffering in its sharpest form and a mark of his pastoral sensitivity was his communication with the bereaved. He epitomized that godliness and good learning which is the essence of episcopacy at its best.

A Bishop's Life of Prayer

Eternity was his centre. It was a world he inhabited—almost, indeed, he took it for granted. The Christian faith was nonsense unless this dimension was seen as a central truth. He often said it was through this perspective that one saw the world in its true light. A Christian approach to the problems of our age which left this out of account was bound to be superficial and partial. Many would say it is a perspective we need to recapture with some urgency.

An implication of this perspective of eternity was obviously the priority of prayer in his ministry. From this quite literally all else flowed. There is perhaps no better gift to us from this man of Godliness and good learning than his own words:

'It is to the Ascended Christ that the bishop must direct his gaze, to him he must be attached and responsible, with him that he must be clothed; for it is by the bishop's Godward life that his ministry will bear fruit and be controlled. In order to guard against overwork, to counteract the snare of activism, to curb his concern for his reputation, to overcome the temptation to love the praise of men more than the glory of God, his life must be a continual Sursum Corda; he must be ever groping, fighting, leaping Godwards. He must in fact give priority to spirituality, abiding in the certainty that God, and not merely "the things of God," is central in life, personal, ministerial and social. It is God's world, God's church, God's diocese, God's parish. From the Bishop's Godward apostolate there will flow the energy of divine love. By his self-offering in union with the Ascended Christ he will help to hold the door open for God to take possession.'

NOTES / SOURCES

A. J. and E. M. Beach, *Edmund Robert Morgan*, undated, private publication by the authors, p. 162

Sundar Singh   1889–1929?

Singh belonged to a Sikh family in the Punjab, North India. Against family opposition, he was baptized and confirmed as a young man in the diocese of Lahore. He developed an Indian form of evangelistic ministry as a wandering *sadhu*, which he pursued, interspersed with lionizing tours in the West, until his disappearance while itinerating among Himalayan villages in 1929. He taught in parables, and these, recorded in a series of small books, enshrine an influential and attractive Indian appropriation of Christian faith.

The Unique Grace of the Cross

On the way to Ilom in Nepal I passed many villages where people whole-heartedly heard the Word of God. In this territory the roads are awful. One is tired by ascents and descents and the crossing of streams. June 7, 1914, will always be in my memory—the fatigue of the journey, the extreme hunger and thirst, the heavy showers of rain and the ascent of seven miles. A terrible blast of wind threw me into a cave. O praised be the Lord; though I fell from such a height, I did not get any hurt at all. Yes! The cave became the lap of God for me, where no hurt was possible and that ascent turned into a reach of Paradise. The blast of wind turned into a wave of love and the shower of rain into a shower of grace; the hunger and thirst turned into satisfaction, the fatigue into refreshment, and the Cross into peace. The different stages of the Crucifixion of Jesus came before me in a vision, that first of all He was awake in the Garden of Gethsemane the whole night; secondly, He was hungry and thirsty; thirdly, due to lashes and the crown of thorns He was bleeding; fourthly, besides all these troubles He had to lift up the Cross Himself. For these reasons He fell When He was climbing Golgotha. My cross is nothing before Thine and, O dear Lord, by the unique love and grace of Thy Cross, I have received and will receive blessings.

I wish I could show this peace of my soul which cannot be described to those brothers of mine who are quite empty and unaware of it; but how is it possible? This is the 'hidden manna' which cannot be understood except by one who had received it (Rev. 2. 17). I can say this much from my personal experience, that the Cross lifts those who lift it. It carries them to the streams of peace in this world (which is full of pain) and it takes to heaven those who follow Christ by lifting the Cross. (1)

The Communion of Saints: an Indian Perspective

In this book I have attempted to write about some of the visions which God has given me. Had I considered my own inclinations, I would not have published the account of these visions during my lifetime; but friends, whose judgment I value, have been insistent that, as a spiritual help to others, the publication of the teaching of these visions should not be delayed. In deference to the wish of these friends this book is now presented to the public.

At Kotgarh, fourteen years ago, while I was praying my eyes were opened to the Heavenly Vision. So vividly did I see it all that I thought I must have died, and that my soul had passed into the glory of heaven; but throughout the intervening years these visions have continued to enrich my life. I cannot call them up at will, but, usually when I am praying or meditating, sometimes as often as eight or ten times in a month, my spiritual eyes are opened to see within the heavens, and, for an hour or two, I walk in the glory of the heavenly sphere with Christ Jesus, and hold converse with angels and spirits. Their answers to my questions have provided much of the material that has already been published in my books and the unutterable ecstasy of that spiritual communion makes me long for the time when I shall enter in permanently to the bliss and fellowship of the redeemed.

Some may consider that these visions are merely a form of spiritualism, but I would emphasise that there is one very essential difference. Spiritualism does presume to produce messages and signs from spirits out of the dark, but they are usually so fragmentary and unintelligible, if not actually deceptive, that they lead their followers away from, rather than to, the truth. In these visions, on other hand, I see vividly and clearly every detail of the glory of the spiritual world, and I have the uplifting experience of very real fellowship with the saints, amid the inconceivably bright and beautiful surroundings of a spiritual world made visible. It is from these angels and saints that I have received, not vague, broken and elusive messages from the unseen, but clear and rational elucidations of many of the problems that have troubled me.

This Communion of the Saints was a fact so real in the experience of the early Church that it is given a place among the necessary articles of its faith, as stated in the 'Apostles' Creed.' Once, in a vision, I asked the saints for a proof from the Bible of this communion of saints and was told that it was to be found clearly given in Zechariah 3. 7–8, where 'those that were standing by were not angels, nor "men" of flesh and blood, but saints in glory'; and God's promise, on condition of Joshua fulfilling His command, is that he will be given 'a place [access] to walk among them [saints] that stand by' and these are his 'fellows'—the spirits of men made perfect with whom he could commune.

There is repeated mention of Spirits, Saints and Angels in this book. The distinction I would make between them is that Spirits are both good and bad, who after death exist in a state intermediate between heaven and hell. Saints are those who have passed on through this stage into the higher sphere of the spiritual world, and have had special service allotted to them. Angels are those glorious beings to whom all kinds of superior service have been allotted, and among them are included many saints from other worlds, as well as from this world of ours, who all live together as one family. They serve one another in love, and, in the effulgence of God's glory, are eternally happy. The World of Spirits means that intermediate state into which Spirits enter after leaving the body. By the Spiritual World is meant all spiritual beings that progress through the stages between the darkness of the bottomless pit and the throne of the Lord in light. (2)

One Fold and One Shepherd

A German gentleman who was an interested supporter of missions asked me, 'What form of Church organization will be adopted if all India becomes Christian?' I replied: 'There is no country in the world that is wholly Christian and there never will be, and even if India ever becomes Christian, it will be only to the extent that any of the countries of the West are Christian. For as long as the world lasts, good and bad, and earnest and indifferent, will always be found. Only if all were changed in heart and life could we say that the Kingdom of heaven had come, but then the world would not be world, it would be heaven.'

About the Church: people are continually introducing changes in worship and creating new sects, but they are not satisfied with any of them. The real need is not that we should adopt new forms, but that through the Living Christ, rivers of living water should begin to flow through us. When the water of an Himalayan mountain stream reaches the plains men dig canals for it; but away among the great mountains it makes its own way past cliff, and rock, and valley, and no one digs a channel for it. So the new life at first snakes its way through the lives of individual Christians but they feel no need of organizing channels for it, but when it flows through whole communities, then they will organize channels, or churches, for it to meet their needs. At that time the man-made sects will disappear, and there will be only one Church of the Living Christ, and there shall be 'one fold and one Shepherd' (John 10. 16). (3)

NOTES / SOURCES

1. Sundar Singh, 'The Lap of God', published in *Nur Afshan*, a weekly Christian journal in Urdu, Ludhiana, Punjab, 3 July 1914
2. Sundar Singh, Preface to *Visions of the Spiritual World*, London, 1926
3. Sundar Singh, 'Christ and His Church', first published in *With and Without Christ*, Madras, 1971

Aiyadurai Jesudasen Appasamy 1891–1975

Son of A. S. Appasamy Pillai (q.v.), A. J. Appasamy was brought up in the Anglican community of Tirunelveli in South India. His doctoral research at Oxford comparing the Johannine writings with some Indian devotional writings marked the beginning of a lifetime of perceptive exploration and persuasive writing on the possibility of a Christianity rooted in India's religious heritage. He combined this from 1950 with responsibilities as Bishop in Coimbatore in the Church of South India.

Abiding in Christ

The majority of mankind cannot claim, and are perhaps incapable of, that full absorption in religion which has characterised the saints and seers of the world. Natural instincts, early training and circumstance in life make them engage in avocations and form interests which take up the greater share of their time. But all men can abide in God in the sense that underlying all their pursuits there can be a deep and strong undercurrent of devotion to God. This desire to serve God, to love Him and to carry out His will is not merely established once for ever in the soul and thereafter taken for granted. It continually impinges into our waking moments and fills all our active thought and life with a glorious radiance. This consciousness of our contact with Christ constantly emerges into the open daylight of our busy life and fills it with a new beauty.

It is not enough to suppose that we have yielded up ourselves to God, that we are doing God's work, that we are engaged in Divine tasks. Even for those who are busy with the religious calling, chosen in moments of deliberate consecration to God, it is necessary that there should be a perpetual realization of the divine Spirit which environs us. We do know that there is such an encompassing Reality by whose might we are continually strengthened; it is necessary that this knowledge should emerge from time to time into our consciousness. He who abides in Christ not merely surrenders himself to the love and all-comprehensive sweep of His gracious energy, but continues perpetually to dwell in closest relation to Him, lives in most intimate touch with Him.

Our life in God is like the water coursing in underground pipes below the surface of a great city. The water is all over the city and at all times. Wherever the need is greatest, a tap is opened and the water gushes forth pure and sparkling to do its great work of sustaining life. Our relation to God likewise is a continual fact in our life determining our character and impinging on our spirit whenever occasion demands it.

Is this what is meant by abiding in Christ? A vast world of light may be all around us but only that much light enters our house as our window permits. The experience described here is what has been most vital to me. There are others by whom life in God has been most vividly and clearly perceived in visions. The relation with God has with these souls been most keenly felt in moments of beautiful ecstasy. Yet others have felt work and service to be the best channels through which their sense of God has formed its best outlet. Brother Lawrence said that he was 'more united to God in his outward employments than when he left them for devotion in retirement.' So was the Maharishi Devendranath Tagore. In whatever particular way the experience may be mediated, the primary and all-important fact is that the soul should live in God and that God should be recognized as living in the soul. (1)

Oneness with God

While on the surface the words, 'I and the Father are one,' bear a striking and almost exact resemblance to some of the monistic utterances in the religious literature of India, they will be found on a closer scrutiny to contain an altogether different import. It would be wrong to build upon them a whole interpretation of Christianity which emphasizes the identity between God and man. Our relation to God is to be of the same pattern as the relation of Jesus to God. This was not one of identity but of fellowship. Therefore it is obvious that there can be no identity between ourselves and God. It is not by becoming aware in some vividly luminous moment of our identity with God that we can experience the joys of mystic union. Fellowship with God does not consist in such a realization of our ultimate kinship with God, a kinship which always exists though hidden by mists of illusion and which has only to be made clear to the soul by some rapturous glimpse of Reality. But it is the harmony of the individual soul with the Divine soul in thought and imagination, in purpose and will, in humble deed and adoring devotion. Oneness with God consists in the continuous orientation of the human personality towards the Divine so that floods of God's love and power keep running into man's soul. The vast energies of God inundate the soul of man from time to time, and every moment he lives in the consciousness of receiving them. From him proceed prayers, aspirations, longings and decisions which continually keep flowing into God. Thus there is a perpetual flux of life from God into man and then again from man into God. (2)

NOTES / SOURCES

1. A. J. Appasamy, *The Johannine Doctrine of Life: A Study of Christian and Indian Thought*, London, 1934, pp. 41–3
2. A. J. Appasamy, ibid., pp. 67–8

Clive Staples Lewis   1898–1963

Born in Belfast, C. S. Lewis was Tutor and Fellow in English at Magdalen College, Oxford, from 1925 to 1956 and later Professor of Medieval and Renaissance Literature at Cambridge. Returning to Christian faith, described in his spiritual autobiography *Surprised by Joy* (1955), he became a skilful and widely read Christian apologist both in his theological writing and in his imaginative 'Narnia' stories for children. With Charles Williams (q.v.) and J. R. R. Tolkien he was a member of the 'Inklings'.

Prayer

Master, they say that when I seem
    To be in speech with you,
Since you make no replies, it's all a dream
    —One talker aping two.

They are half right, but not as they
    Imagine; rather, I
Seek in myself the things I meant to say,
    And lo! the wells are dry.

Then, seeing me empty, you forsake
    The Listener's rôle, and through
My dead lips breathe and into utterance wake
    The thoughts I never knew.

And thus you neither need reply
    Nor can; thus, while we seem
Two talking, thou art One forever, and I
    No dreamer, but thy dream. (1)

No Beauty We Could Desire

Yes, you are always everywhere. But I,
Hunting in such immeasurable forests,
Could never bring the noble Hart to bay.

The scent was too perplexing for my hounds;
Nowhere sometimes, then again everywhere.
Other scents, too, seemed to them almost the same.

Therefore I turn my back on the unapproachable
Stars and horizons and all musical sounds,
Poetry itself, and the winding stair of thought.

Leaving the forests where you are pursued in vain
—Often a mere white gleam—I turn instead
To the appointed place where you pursue.

Not in Nature, not even in Man, but in one
Particular Man, with a date, so tall, weighing
So much, talking Aramaic, having learned a trade;

Not in all food, not in all bread and wine
(Not, I mean, as my littleness requires)
But this wine, this bread . . . no beauty we could desire. (2)

Footnote to all Prayers

He whom I bow to only knows to whom I bow
When I attempt the ineffable Name, murmuring *Thou*,
And dream of Pheidian fancies and embrace in heart
Symbols (I know) which cannot be the thing Thou art.
Thus always, taken at their word, all prayers blaspheme
Worshipping with frail images a folk-lore dream,
And all men in their praying, self-deceived, address
The coinage of their own unquiet thoughts, unless
Thou in magnetic mercy to Thyself divert
Our arrows, aimed unskilfully, beyond desert;
And all men are idolators, crying unheard
To a deaf idol, if Thou take them at their word.

Take not, oh Lord, our literal sense. Lord, in Thy great,
Unbroken speech our limping metaphor translate. (3)

The God Who Prays in Us

An ordinary simple Christian kneels down to say his prayers. He is trying to get in touch with God. But if he is a Christian he knows that what is prompting him to pray is also God: God, so to speak, inside him. But he also knows that all his real knowledge of God comes through Christ, the Man who was God—that Christ is standing beside him, helping him to pray, praying for him. You see what is happening. God is the thing to which he is praying—the goal he is trying to reach. God is also the thing inside him which is pushing him on—the motive power. God is also the road or bridge along which he is being pushed to that goal. So that the whole threefold life of the three-personal Being is actually going on in that ordinary little bedroom where an ordinary man is saying his prayers. The man is being caught up into the higher kind of life—what I called *Zoe* or spiritual life: he is being pulled into God, by God, while still remaining himself. (4)

Love and God

One thing, however, marriage has done for me. I can never again believe that religion is manufactured out of our unconscious, starved desires and is a substitute for sex. For those few years H. and I feasted on love; every mode of it—solemn and merry, romantic and realistic, sometimes as dramatic as a thunder-storm, sometimes as comfortable and unemphatic as putting on your soft slippers. No cranny of heart or body remained unsatisfied. If God were a substitute for love we ought to have lost all interest in Him. Who'd bother about substitutes when he has the thing itself? But that isn't what happens. We both knew we wanted something besides one another—quite a different kind of something, a quite different kind of want. (5)

Prayer and Reality

What I call 'myself' (for all practical, everyday purposes) is also a dramatic construction; memories, glimpses in the shaving-glass, and snatches of the very fallible activity called 'introspection', are the principal ingredients. Normally I call this construction 'me', and the stage set 'the real world.'

Now the moment of prayer is for me—or involves for me as its condition—the awareness, the re-awakened awareness, that this 'real world' and 'real self' are very far from being rock-bottom realities. I cannot, in the flesh, leave the stage, either to go behind the scenes or to take my seat in the pit; but I can remember that these regions exist. And I also remember that my apparent self—this clown or hero or super—under his grease-paint is a real person with an off-stage life. The dramatic person could not tread the stage unless he concealed a real person: unless the real and unknown I existed, I would not even make mistakes about the imagined me. And in prayer this real I struggles to speak, for once, from his real being, and to address, for once, not the other actors, but—what shall I call Him? The Author, for He invented us all? The Producer, for He controls all? Or the Audience, for He watches, and will judge, the performance?

The attempt is not to escape from space and time and from my creaturely situation as a subject facing objects. It is more modest: to re-awake the awareness of that situation. If that can be done, there is no need to go anywhere else. This situation itself, is, at every moment, a possible theophany. Here is the holy ground; the Bush is burning now.

Of course this attempt may be attended with almost every degree of success or failure. The prayer preceding all prayers is, 'May it be the real I who speaks. May it be the real Thou that I speak to.' Infinitely various are the levels from which we pray. Emotional intensity is in itself no proof of spiritual depth. If we pray in terror we shall pray earnestly; it only proves that terror is an earnest emotion. Only God Himself can let the bucket down to the depths in us. And, on the other side, He must constantly work as the iconoclast. Every idea of Him we form, He must in mercy shatter. The most blessed result of prayer would be to rise thinking, 'But I never knew before. I never dreamed . . .' I suppose it was at such a moment that Thomas Aquinas said of all his own theology: 'It reminds me of straw.' (6)

Joy the Serious Business of Heaven

I do *not* think that the life of Heaven bears any analogy to play or dance in respect of frivolity. I do think that while we are in this 'valley of tears', cursed with labour, hemmed round with necessities, tripped up with frustrations, doomed to perpetual plannings, puzzlings, and anxieties, certain qualities that must belong to the celestial condition have no chance to get through, can project no image of themselves, except in activities which, for us here and now, are frivolous. For surely we must suppose the life of the blessed to be an end in itself, indeed The End: to be utterly spontaneous; to be the complete reconciliation of boundless freedom with order—with the most delicately adjusted, supple, intricate, and beautiful order? How can you find any image of this in the 'serious' activities either of our natural or of our (present) spiritual life?—either in our precarious and heart-broken affections or in the Way which is always, in some degree, a *via crucis*: No, Malcolm. It is only in our 'hours-off', only in our moments of permitted festivity, that we find an analogy. Dance and game *are* frivolous, unimportant down here; for 'down here' is not their natural place. Here, they are a moment's rest from the life we were placed here to live. But in this world everything is upside down. That which, if it could be prolonged here, would be a truancy, is likest that which in a better country is the End of ends. Joy is the serious business of Heaven. (7)

Wrath and Pardon

Wrath and pardon are both, as applied to God, analogies; but they belong together to the same circle of analogy—the circle of life, and love, and deeply personal relationships. All the liberalising and 'civilising' analogies only lead us astray. Turn God's wrath into mere enlightened disapproval, and you also turn His love into mere humanitarianism. The 'consuming fire' and the 'perfect beauty' both vanish. We have, instead, a judicious headmistress or a conscientious magistrate. It comes of being high-minded. (8)

Membership of the Body

The society into which the Christian is called at baptism is not a collective but a Body. It is in fact that Body of which the family is an image on the natural level. If anyone came to it with the misconception that membership of the Church was membership in a debased modern sense—a massing together of persons as if they were pennies or counters—he would be corrected at the threshold by the discovery that the Head of this Body is so unlike the inferior members that they share no predicate with Him save by analogy. We are summoned from the outset to combine as creatures with our Creator, as mortals with immortal, as redeemed sinners with sinless Redeemer. His presence, the interaction between Him and us, must always be the overwhelmingly dominant factor in the life we are to lead within the Body; and any conception of Christian fellowship which does not mean primarily fellowship with Him is out of court. After that it seems almost trivial to trace further down the diversity of operations to the unity of the Spirit. But it is very plainly there. There are priests divided from the laity, catechumens divided from those who are in full fellowship. There is authority of husbands over wives and parents over children. There is, in forms too subtle for official embodiment, a continual interchange of complementary ministrations. We are all constantly teaching and learning, forgiving and being forgiven, representing Christ to man when we intercede, and man to Christ when others intercede for us. The sacrifice of selfish privacy which is daily demanded of us is daily repaid a hundredfold in the true growth of personality which the life of the Body encourages. Those who are members of one another become as diverse as the hand and the ear. That is why the worldlings are so monotonously alike compared with the almost fantastic variety of the saints. Obedience is the road to freedom, humility the road to pleasure, unity the road to personality. (9)

Glory and Reward

The promises of Scripture may very roughly be reduced to five heads. It is promised, firstly, that we shall be with Christ; secondly, that we shall be like Him; thirdly, with an enormous wealth of imagery, that we shall have 'glory'; fourthly, that we shall, in some sense, be fed or feasted or entertained; and, finally, that we shall have some sort of official position in the universe—ruling cities, judging angels, being pillars of God's temple. The first question I ask about these promises is: 'Why any of them except the first?' Can anything be added to the conception of being with Christ? For it must be true, as an old writer says, that he who has God and everything else has no more than he who has God only. I think the answer turns again on the nature of symbols. For though it may escape our notice at first glance, yet it is true than any conception of being with Christ which most of us can now form will be not very much less symbolical than the other promises; for it will smuggle in ideas of proximity in space and loving conversation as we now understand conversation, and it will probably concentrate on the humanity of Christ to the exclusion of His deity. And, in fact, we find that those Christians who attend solely to this first promise always do fill it up with very earthly imagery indeed—in fact, with hymeneal or erotic imagery. I am not for a moment condemning such imagery. I heartily wish I could enter into it more deeply than I do, and pray that I yet shall. But my point is that this also is only a symbol, like the reality in some respects, but unlike it in others, and therefore needs correction from the different symbols in the other promises. The variation of the promises does not mean that anything other than God will be our ultimate bliss; but because God is more than a Person, and lest we should imagine the joy of His presence too exclusively in terms of our present poor experience of personal love, with all its narrowness and strain and monotony, a dozen changing images, correcting and relieving each other, are supplied.

I turn next to the idea of glory. There is no getting away from the fact that this idea is very prominent in the New Testament and in early Christian writings. Salvation is constantly associated with palms, crowns, white robes, thrones, and splendour like the sun and stars. All this makes no immediate appeal to me at all, and in that respect I fancy I am a typical modern. Glory suggests two ideas to me, of which one seems wicked and the other ridiculous. Either glory means to me fame, or it means luminosity. As for the first, since to be famous means to be better known than other people, the desire for fame appears to me as a competitive passion and therefore of hell rather than heaven. As for the second, who wishes to become a kind of living electric light bulb?

When I began to look into this matter I was shocked to find such different Christians as Milton, Johnson and Thomas Aquinas taking heavenly glory quite frankly in the sense of fame or good report. But not fame conferred by our fellow creatures—fame with God, approval or (I might say) 'appreciation' by God. And then, when I had thought it over, I saw that this view was scriptural; nothing can eliminate from the parable the divine *accolade*, 'Well done, thou good and faithful servant.' With that, a good deal of what I had been thinking all my life fell down like a house of cards. I suddenly remembered that no one can enter heaven except as a child; and nothing is so obvious in a child—not in a conceited child, but in a good child—as its great and undisguised pleasure in being praised. Not only in a child, either, but even in a dog or a horse. Apparently what I had mistaken for humility had, all these years, prevented me from understanding what is in fact the humblest, the most childlike, the most creaturely of pleasures—nay, the specific pleasure of the inferior: the pleasure of a beast before men, a child before its father, a pupil before his teacher, a creature before its Creator. I am not forgetting how horribly this most innocent desire is parodied in our human ambitions, or how very quickly, in my own experience, the lawful pleasure of praise from those whom it was my duty to please turns into the deadly poison of self-admiration. But I thought I could detect a moment—a very, very short moment—before this happened, during which the satisfaction of having pleased those whom I rightly loved and rightly feared was pure. And that is enough to raise our thoughts to what may happen when the redeemed soul, beyond all hope and nearly beyond belief, learns at last that she has pleased Him whom she was created to please. There will be no room for vanity then. She will be free from the miserable illusion that it is her doing. With no taint of what we should now call self-approval she will most innocently rejoice in the thing that God has made her to be, and the moment which heals her old inferiority complex for ever will also drown her pride deeper than Prospero's book. Perfect humility dispenses with modesty. If God is satisfied with the work, the work may be satisfied with itself; 'it is not for her to bandy compliments with her Sovereign.' (10)

NOTES / SOURCES

1. *Poems by C. S. Lewis* (ed. Walter Hooper), London, 1964, pp. 122–3
2. Ibid., p. 124
3. Ibid., p. 129
4. C. S. Lewis, 'Mere Christianity' bk. 4, ch. 2, in *A Mind Awake: An Anthology of C. S. Lewis* (ed. Clyde S. Kilby), New York, 1968, p. 82
5. Ibid., p. 238, 'A Grief Observed' ch. 1
6. C. S. Lewis, *Letters to Malcolm: Chiefly on Prayer*, London, 1964, pp. 108–9
7. Ibid., pp. 121–2
8. Ibid., pp. 126–7
9. Ibid., pp. 35–6
10. C. S. Lewis, *The Weight of Glory and other addresses*, Michigan, USA, 1965, pp. 7–9

Dorothy Leigh Sayers   1893–1957

The daughter of an Anglican clergyman, Dorothy Sayers published a number of novels and wrote religious plays for the Canterbury Festival. Her radio dramatization of the life of Christ *The Man Born to be King* (1941–1942) caused controversy because Christ was portrayed by an actor. She published a major annotated English verse translation of Dante's *Divine Comedy*.

Sacrifice

'Sacrifice' is another word liable to misunderstanding. It is generally held to be noble and loving in proportion as its sacrificial nature is consciously felt by the person who is sacrificing himself. The direct contrary is the truth. To feel sacrifice consciously as self-sacrifice argues a failure in love. When a job is undertaken from necessity, or from a grim sense of disagreeable duty, the worker is self-consciously aware of the toils and pains he undergoes, and will say: 'I have made such and such sacrifices for this.' But when the job is a labour of love, the sacrifices will present themselves to the worker—strange as it may seem—in the guise of enjoyment. Moralists, looking on at this, will always judge that the former kind of sacrifice is more admirable than the latter, because the moralist, whatever he may pretend, has far more respect for pride than for love. The Puritan assumption that all action disagreeable to the doer is *ipso facto* more meritorious than enjoyable action is firmly rooted in this exaggerated valuation set on pride. I do not mean that there is no nobility in doing unpleasant things from a sense of duty, but only that there is more nobility in doing them gladly out of sheer love of the job. The Puritan thinks otherwise; he is inclined to say, 'Of course So-and-so works very hard and has given up a good deal for such-and-such a cause, but there's no merit in that—he enjoys it.' The merit, of course, lies precisely in the enjoyment, and the nobility of So-and-so consists in the very fact that he is the kind of person to whom the doing of that piece of work is delightful.[1]

It is because, behind the restrictions of the moral code, we instinctively recognise the greater validity of the law of nature, that we do always in our heart of hearts prefer the children of grace to the children of legality. We recognize a false ring in the demanding voice which proclaims: 'I have sacrificed the best years of my life to my profession (my family, my country, or whatever it may be), and have a right to expect some return.' The code compels us to admit the claim, but there is something in the expression of it that repels us. Conversely, however, the children of legality are shocked by the resolute refusal of the children of light to insist on this kind of claim and—still more disconcertingly— by their angry assertion of love's right to self-sacrifice. Those, for example, who obligingly inform creative artists of methods by which (with a little corrupting of their creative purpose) they could make more money, are often very excusably shocked by the fury with which they are sent about their business. Indeed, creative love has its darker aspects, and will sacrifice, not only itself, but others to its overmastering ends. Somerset Maugham, in *The Moon and Sixpence*, has given convincing expression to these dark fires of the artist's devouring passion; and the meaning of the story is lost unless we recognise that Strickland's terrible sacrifices, suffered and exacted, are the assertion of a love so tremendous that it has passed beyond even the desire of happiness. A passion of this temper does not resign itself to sacrifice, but embraces it, and sweeps the world up in the same embrace. It is not without reason that we feel a certain uneasy suspicion of that inert phrase, 'Christian resignation'; an inner voice reminds us that the Christian God is Love, and that love and resignation can find no common ground to stand on. So much the human creator can tell us, if we like to listen to him.

---

[1] So Spenser:

> For some so goodly gratious are by kind,
> That every action doth them much commend,
> And in the eyes of men great liking find,
> Which others that have greater skill in mind,
> Though they enforce themselves, cannot attaine;
> *For everything to which one is enclin'd*
> *Doth best become and greatest grace doth gaine:*
> Yet praise likewise deserve good thewes enforst with paine.
>   *Faery Queene*: VI. 11, 2

Our confusion on the subject is caused by a dissipation and eclecticism in our associations with the word 'love'. We connect it too exclusively with the sexual and material passions, whose anti-passion is possessiveness, and with indulgent affection, whose anti-passion is sentimentality. Concentrated, and freed from its anti-passions, love is the Energy of creation:

> In the juvescence of the year
> Came Christ the tiger—[1]

a disturbing thought.

NOTES / SOURCES

Dorothy L. Sayers, *The Mind of the Maker*, London, 1994, pp. 107–9

Father Algy SSF (William Strowan Amhurst Robertson)
1894–1955

Known from his schooldays as Algy, William Robertson was attracted to India. He joined Christa Seva Sangha, a brotherhood of Indians and Europeans in Poona in 1928. Invalided home, he became Vicar of St Ives where he formed a branch of CSS which (in 1937) joined Brother Douglas in Dorset to form the Society of Saint Francis. As Guardian at Hilfield, Father Algy regularized the life of the Friary. A sick man but a magnetic personality, he also inspired the growth of the Third Order and the foundation of the Order of St Clare. He was well known as a missioner, retreat conductor, and spiritual director.

Christa Seva Sengha: the Vision of an Indian Christianity

Christianity is not a product of the West. Its divine Founder lived in an Eastern land. The great churches of its glorious youth with that roll of doctors and martyrs belonged chiefly not to Europe but to Africa and the East. We must therefore desire to go to a land like India as little as possible as Westerners. We must give every encouragement to the clothing of the Catholic faith and the worship that enshrines it in Indian garments. Our vision must be that of a real Indian Church.

'Our ideal is to live in simplicity as far as possible in the Indian way. Our hope is that if we are faithful God will enable us to make some contribution to the Church in India by helping forward the naturalising of her theology and worship. You will like to know something of our life.

'You must picture a Camp in a big field of several acres with building operations going on in several parts. We have lived in tents, but when the rainy season begins in June we hope to have the Ashram at least partly built. It will be very simple and Indian in character with cells for the Brothers built round a square, and a small house in which there will be a Refectory, Library and Parlour. On the roof of this we shall have our temporary Chapel. Little by little we hope to build with our own hands a larger House of God which will be Indian in its style

---

[1] T. S. Eliot: *Gerontion.*

of architecture. In about a year's time we hope to have a hostel for Indian students where they will live in a Christian atmosphere with the Brothers who are in charge.

'Our life is modelled on the life of the old Monasteries with certain adaptations to suit India. It enshrines three features which are characteristic of Hindu teaching at its best:

Bhakti Marga which is the way of prayer and devotion.
Dnyana Marga which is the way of knowledge and sacred study.
Karma Marga which is the way of works, in which we include manual labour, and the work of spreading the love of Christ by loving service and teaching.

'Every day, very early, the morning prayers are said by the Brothers sitting on the ground under the stars. Slowly the light fills the sky. Then all go into Chapel for the Mass. After refreshment comes the hour of meditation, and until this is over the rule of silence is strictly observed. At intervals during the day the Brothers are called to prayer. A good many hours are reserved for study. In the late afternoon when it is cool, it is possible for the Brothers to go out on social service, giving lectures, taking classes, making friends with students; then at the lovely hour of sunset all gather together, and seated as in the morning under the open sky the Brothers say the evening prayers. Often the beautiful religious songs of the Marathi Christian poet, Tilak, are sung, and always at the end comes a period of silence during the brief Indian twilight. Then with the stars above them, and maybe the moon, all repair to the Refectory for supper. This like the other meals is normally silent. All sit on the ground, and no forks or knives are used. No meat is taken, and the food is simple and Indian in character. Spiritual books are read.

'Our hope is that our Ashram will be so Indian in character that many Hindus will feel at home in it, and will readily stay with us. Hospitality will always be part of our programme, and we hope soon to have accommodation for a number of guests. We hope also to undertake works of social service, and some of us may teach in schools. It has been suggested that we should visit the prison, the leper asylum and the hospitals. In this way rather than in preaching we believe that we can show forth the spirit of Jesus, our Lord.

NOTES / SOURCES

Father Denis SSF, *Father Algy*, London, 1964, pp. 83–5

Philip Nigel Warrington Strong   1899–1983

Philip Strong was born in Derbyshire and was educated at King's School, Worcester, and Selwyn College, Cambridge. He was ordained in 1922 by Hensley Henson (q.v.) and served as a curate at St Mary's, Tynedock, before becoming Vicar of Christ Church, Leeds, in 1926. In 1931 Strong went to St Ignatius, Sunderland, from where he was called in 1936 to become Bishop of New Guinea. He was Archbishop of Brisbane from 1963 to 1970 and Primate of Australia from 1966 to 1970. Brought up an evangelical, he was drawn to the Catholic expression of Anglicanism during his years at Cambridge.

A Phalanx of Divine Grace

Now I would like a heart-to-heart talk with you. As far as I know, you are all at your posts and I am very glad and thankful about this. I have from the first felt that we must endeavour to carry on our work in all circumstances no matter what the cost may ultimately be to any of us individually. God expects this of us. The Church at home, which sent us out, will surely expect it of us. The Universal Church expects it. The tradition and history of missions requires it of us. Missionaries who have been faithful to the uttermost and are now at rest are surely expecting it of us. The people whom we serve expect it of us. We could never hold up our faces again, if, for our own safety, we all forsook Him and fled when the shadows of the Passion began to gather around Him in his Spiritual Body, the Church in Papua. Our life in the future would be burdened with shame and we could not come back here and face our people again; and we would be conscious always of rejected opportunities. The history of the Church tells us that missionaries do not think of themselves in the hour of danger and crisis, but of the Master who called them to give their all, and of the people they have been trusted to serve and love to the uttermost. His watchword is none the less true today, as it was when he gave it to the first disciples—'Whosoever will save his life will lose it, and whosoever will lose his life for My sake and the Gospel's shall find it.'

No one requires us to leave. No one has required us to leave. The reports some of you have heard of orders to this effect did not emanate from official or authoritative sources. But even if anyone had required us to leave, we should then have had to obey God rather than men. We could not leave unless God, who called us, required it of us, and our spiritual instinct tells us He would never require such a thing at such an hour.

Our people need us now more than ever before in the whole history of the mission. To give but two examples:

1. *Our Native Ministry.* We have accepted a big responsibility in the eyes of all Christendom in founding a native ministry. We have given birth to it. We are responsible before God and the Church for his growth and development on sound Catholic lines. It is still but in its infancy. We cannot leave it to sink back into heathenism. We must stand by that to which we have given birth.

2. *Our Papuan Women.* Our influence is just beginning to tell with them. how would they fare if all our women missionaries left? It would take years to recover what the locusts had eaten. Our Papuan women need the influence of women missionaries today more than ever.

No, my brothers and sisters, fellow workers in Christ, whatever others may do, we cannot leave. We shall not leave. We shall stand by our trust. We shall stand by our vocation.

We do not know what it may mean to us. Many think us fools and mad. What does that matter? If we are fools, 'we are fools for Christ's sake'. I cannot foretell the future. I cannot guarantee that all will be well—that we shall all come through unscathed. One thing only I can guarantee is that if we do not forsake Christ here in Papua in His Body, the Church, He will not forsake us. He will uphold us; He will strengthen us and He will guide us and keep us through the days that lie ahead. If we all left, it would take years for the Church to recover from our betrayal of our trust. If we remain—and even if the worst came to the worst and we were all to perish in remaining—the Church will not perish, for there would have been no breach of trust in its walls, but its foundations and structure would have received added strength for the future building by our faithfulness unto death.

This, I believe, is the resolution of you all. Indeed, I have been deeply moved and cheered more than I can say by letters I have received from many of our staff this week who have been in a position to communicate with me, and I have reason to believe that others who have not had that opportunity think and feel the same way. Our staff, I believe, stands as a solid phalanx in this time of uncertainty. Their influence has already had a stabilizing effect on the community, and though harm has already been done, counsels of sanity are beginning to prevail again in the territory before the damage has become irretrievable. However, let us not judge others, but let us only follow duty as we see it. if we are a solid phalanx, let us see to it in the days to come that it is a phalanx of Divine Grace, for only so can it remain unshaken.

I know there are special circumstances which may make it imperative for one or two to go (if arrangements can be made for them to do so). For the rest of us, we have made our resolution to stay. Let us not shrink from it. Let us not go back on it. Let us trust and not be afraid.

To you all I send my blessing. The Lord be with you.

NOTES / SOURCES

The New Guinea Diaries of Philip Strong (ed. David Wetherell), Melbourne, 1981, pp. 222–3

Alexander Roper Vidler 1899–1991

A priest of the Oratory of the Good Shepherd at the beginning of his ministry, Alec Vidler served in an Anglo-Catholic parish in Birmingham. He went on to be Warden of St Deiniol's Library, Hawarden, and a Canon of Windsor. As Dean of King's College, Cambridge, he was a notable church historian, particularly of Catholic Modernism, and part of the group of Cambridge theologians who produced the collection of essays, *Soundings* in 1962.

Exiles of the Dispersion

We have for the most part ceased to be aware of another world, an eternal kingdom of heaven; we have ceased to take it seriously. All our interest has been in this world; it never entered our heads that here we are and always shall be 'exiles of the Dispersion'. Our horizons make no provision for an unseen world of mystery where all things are being made new, and where we might be even more at home than we are in this world.

But if it is true that our final home is in another world, it has got somehow or other to get back into our heads. We have to find a way of combining an awareness of, and a loyalty to, our eternal home with a zealous concern for the affairs of this world. And that will not be easy. It is like having to learn a new and very strange language—the language of the Bible in fact. Great Bible words like apostle and Messiah and the new creation, the kingdom of heaven and eternal life, and a hundred others, will have to take hold of our minds and of our imaginations and acquire a vivid meaning for us. Then we shall begin to realize that the Bible is talking about facts which have been hidden from us in the blinding haze of the twentieth century, but which are there waiting to be rediscovered; facts which may have the most extraordinary effect both upon us and other people when they are rediscovered. The time may be coming when we shall realize as we have not done yet that this world is not and cannot be our home, but that we have as a result of the work of Christ 'a better country, that is a heavenly one', and that we might already in this world be living and working as citizens of that imperishable kingdom. (1)

'Through Jesus Christ our Lord'

Christ our Head gathers together all the dim and faltering prayers of his members, our futile prayers, our sighs and groans that cannot be put into words, our numbness and our silence, and he interprets and presents them to the one God and Father of all.

That is why we regularly end our prayers with the words 'through Jesus Christ our Lord.' At the end of my personal prayers, I do not say, 'O God, that is Alec Vidler who has been speaking,' but I say 'through Jesus Christ our Lord', by which I mean that Jesus Christ my Head and the Head of the whole Church will explain to my heavenly Father what I have been trying to say and what I have failed to say, and that it is because of him, and not because of any virtue or merit in myself, that I know I shall be heard.

Likewise, with our common prayers at public worship. The minor canon, when he sings the Collects, does not end them by saying, 'O God, you have been listening to the prayers of the congregation in St George's Chapel, Windsor,' but the concluding words are nearly always 'through Jesus Christ our Lord' or words to that effect. (2)

Christianity, Liberalism and Liberality

The Spirit bloweth where it listeth, but it will be astonishing indeed if it blows a renewal of Christianity and of civilization out of Liberal divinity.

What then should we say of the prospects of 'Christian Liberalism'? Men may of course define words as they please. But I suggest that the term 'Liberalism' should be kept for the nineteenth-century phenomenon which Morley espoused and Newman attacked, but which they were sufficiently agreed in defining. Liberalism, which flowered in the nineteenth century, has run to seed in the twentieth. Much of the seed, though not, or not yet, in Britain, has produced dragon's teeth. In Britain it has left us with a confused crop of rather sickly tares and wheat. But while Liberalism, whether Christian or otherwise, can be dated and dated without compunction, this is by no means the case with the virtues, the temper and the cast of mind that I would use the epithet 'liberal' (with a small 'l') to denote, with liberality as its substantive. These qualities are much older than

Liberalism. They have their roots in classical antiquity. They are as old as a liberal education.

Here the word 'liberal' denotes not a creed or a set of philosophical assumptions or any 'ism, but a frame of mind, a quality of character, which it is easier no doubt to discern than to define. A liberal-minded man is free from narrow prejudice, generous in his judgment of others, open-minded, especially to the reception of new ideas or proposals for reform. Liberal is the opposite not of conservative, but of fanatical or bigoted or intransigent. It points to the *esprit large* and away from the *idée fixe*. The liberal temper or frame of mind is not common and perhaps is never likely to be. It can be preserved, even by those who have once possessed it, only by constant vigilance and exercise. For most men's minds and ideas tend to become set and inflexible as they grow old, indeed as they grow middle-aged—and sometimes while they are still young—and it is as rare as it is delightful to find an old man who possesses a mature wisdom and at the same time can really receive new ideas and sympathise with them, play with them and work with them. The liberal frame of mind does not appear to be more common among the adherents of Liberalism, or other 'isms that are ostensibly progressive, than among the adherents of systems that are professedly conservative. Morley acknowledged that this was so. 'The vanity and egoism of rationalistic sects', he said, 'can be as fatal to candour justice and compassion as the intolerant pride of great churches.'[1] For it is the law of systems of thought and of sets of ideas, of sects and parties, whatever their original aim, to harden and become inflexible, and so for their vitality to ebb. 'In its prime', said Whitehead, 'every system is a triumphant success; in its decay it is an obstinate nuisance.'[2] Thus every 'ism that was once a spur, becomes in the end an obstacle, to movement.

The liberal temper is not peculiarly Christian, though the Christian man, wherever he finds it, will acknowledge God as its author. Ancient Greece and China would confute any claim on the part of Christians to have a monopoly of it. It may be described as one of the natural virtues, provided that by the word 'natural' we do not intend to exclude the Holy Spirit from originating and inspiring it. It is a virture which the gospel ought to affirm and deepen and perfect. But we must admit that in some periods the conditions within and without the Church are more favourable than in others to its cultivation. In the Old Testament it is more in evidence in the Wisdom literature than in the prophets. The liberal temper is not as conspicuous in the New Testament (though we know how much people succeed in reading into that) as in the Greek Apologists or as in Clement of Alexandria and Origen. Yet without the publication of the gospel of the New Covenant the later men could not have done their own special work. It would seem that great truths have first to be boldly and provocatively proclaimed, in a raw and rugged manner, and that only afterwards comes the time for analyzing, qualifying, refining and systematizing them. It is at this latter stage that men of liberal temper can do their best work. It is then that their prospects are brightest and their accomplishments are most appreciated.

Perhaps it was the tragedy of the Reformation, which was at first another

---

[1] Morley, *Rousseau*, ii. 82.   [2] Quoted by S. A. Cook, *The 'Truth' of the Bible* (1938), p. 129.

proclamation of great truths and a release of new forces, that those who followed on and consolidated the work of the original Reformers were not men of liberal temper but (with rare exceptions like the judicious Hooker) hard and fanatical systematizers. Thus Christian theology lost its flexibility and vitality in the arid marshes of Catholic and Protestant scholasticism, and though it may have recovered its flexibility it has hardly yet renewed its vitality.

A rejuvenation of theology is not likely to be brought about by the intellectual refinement in which liberal divines excel. What is needed now is a profound and revolutionary rediscovery of theological truth, which is likely to be very *un*refined in its first manifestations. Perhaps God in the pulpit of history is about to utter, indeed has for some time been uttering, some crude words. These words are as shocking to the liberal temper as to every other. While the liberal-minded may at first be the most nonplussed, there will nevertheless, if history continues, be work ahead for them to do, and for which they can already be preparing.

There is in fact plenty to be done. All Christians ought to be opening their minds more widely and deeply to the revelation of the living God to which the Bible bears witness, and nature and history too in their own ambiguous ways. It ought at present to be the particular task of liberal divines to be getting under the skin of the Marxists and the Freudians and the linguistic philosophers, and to be treading the dark night of the intellect which awaits those who go deeply into the relativity and sociology of knowledge. For the minds to which the rediscovered gospel will have to be commended will have been shaped or confounded by such disciplines and scepticisms as these. I do not know what Christians there are yet in Britain who are on the way to being qualified to communicate with such minds.

Professor H. A. Hodges has finely said: 'In the fact of error, as in face of evil, the Christian has a choice of two types of strategy. The first is that of firm resistance, stone-walling as it might be called, meeting every move of his opponent with a steady denial, and a steady reassertion of the principles to which he is himself committed. . . . It fights the enemy to a standstill, but it does not convert him.' I interject that that is broadly speaking, the strategy of the Vatican, and its effectiveness and impressiveness should not be underestimated. 'The second type of strategy [continues Hodges] is that of comprehension, which enters into the mind of the enemy and transcends him from within. The Christian here is not the soldier of pure truth in conflict with the servant of the lie. He stands side by side with his opponent, sinner with sinner, under the judgment of God which condemns and transforms them both. He carries his opponent with him into the Presence, and shares with him both the inevitable death and the promised resurrection. To let down our barriers, to enter into the heart of the modern intellectual situation, to undergo in ourselves something of what the Christless world perpetually endures, and in the midst of the storm to invoke Him who commands the wind and the waves on behalf of those who do not know His name—this is not easy, but it is the only way of redemption. It is the way of the cross, and, indeed, there is an intellectual as well as a moral and a spiritual cross to be borne.'[1]

Finally, we may say that the perennial office of the liberal in the Church and in

[1] Essay on 'The Crisis in Philosophy' in *Reformation Old and New*, ed. F. W. Camfield (1947), p. 194.

society is to be critical and astringently so; critical of prevalent moods and popular fashions and hidden assumptions and powerful cliques, and not least of himself and his friends. He must be *impartial* in his criticism, which is to say that the formation of a liberal party in the Church is a double contradiction in terms. Liberals will always be in a minority. Their role is a subordinate, but a salutary, an antiseptic or aperient, one. While they have their own peculiar temptations to pride, yet if they do their work well they will keep the Church humble. Archbishop Whately of Dublin was a good liberal when he said that he was 'even more mortified by weak arguments in favour of his own views than by strong ones against them.'[1] And so was Principal Denney when he said that 'if one lectured for a session without leaving a deep impression of ignorance, it would be the most pitiable of all failures.'[2] So again was Dr Figgis who was once out for a walk at Cambridge with Dr Barnes, the late Bishop of Birmingham: when Barnes turned to Figgis at a certain point and said, 'The trouble with you, Figgis, is that you don't get to the bottom of things,' Figgis replied, 'Barnes, there is no bottom.'[3] And Walter Bagehot's words about Clough are a tribute to a liberal mind: 'He saw what it is considered cynical to see—the absurdities of many persons, the pomposities of many creeds, the splendid zeal with which missionaries rush on to teach what they do not know; the wonderful earnestness with which the most incomplete solutions of the universe are thrust upon us as complete and satisfying.'[4]

The liberal vocation, faithfully exercised, is not only humbling but also reconciling. It has the effect of showing that no party or school of thought or phase of orthodoxy is ever as right as its protagonists are inclined to suppose, and that men, including Christian men, have much more in common both of frailty and strength, both of falsehood and truth, than the makers of systems and sects acknowledge. But great works of construction will not be done, so far as we can see, by liberals as such, nor great decisions taken. So far it has been the Luthers and not the Erasmuses who have changed the course of history. As F. S. Oliver said in his Life of Alexander Hamilton: 'In the supreme events, it is not sufficient to be reasonably persuaded; the man who is to succeed must be unreasonably confident.'[5] But the liberal *ex officio* is *not* unreasonably confident.

That, I suppose, is why great preachers have seldom been characterized by the liberal virtues. Liberality is not what most men look for nor what they need in preaching. 'Assertions, hesitatingly expressed or qualified with modest reserve, may suit the lecture-room or the study, but they are out of place in the pulpit. An eager, heavy-laden soul crying out from his heart, "What must I do to be saved?" will listen only to a preacher who shows that he believes himself with all his energy in the answer that he gives.' Nor are liberals usually pioneers in the propagation of the gospel. P. T. Forsyth called attention to the fact that the great Protestant missions of the last hundred and fifty years, which have spread light and healing round the world, 'did not arise out of the liberal thinkers, the humanitarian philosophers of the day, who were its worst enemies, but with a few

---

[1] E. Jane Whately, *Life and Correspondence of Richard Whately* (1866), ii. 28.
[2] James Denney, *Letters to His Family and Friends*, ed. J. Moffatt, p. 74.
[3] See M. G. Tucker, *J. N. Figgis* (1950), p. 55.   [4] See W. Ward, *Ten Personal Studies* (1908), p. 91.
[5] Op. cit. (1928), p. 412

men—Carey, Marshman, Ward and the like—whose Calvinistic theology we should now consider very narrow'.

It would appear then that in the economy of the Church there is need for both types—the unreasonably confident and the astringently sceptical; both have their indispensable contribution to make to the mission and message of a church. Hitherto they have been separate and even rival types. I should like to raise the question whether they need always be so; the question is whether we shall always have to choose between Luther and Erasmus. May it not be that it is within the resources of the Holy Ghost to knit together in the same persons both apostleship and liberality—both the unshakeable conviction of the prophet and the cleansing scepticism of the wise man? Perhaps a German theological student was on the right track who was reported as having said: 'We must try to be at one and the same time *for* the Church and *against* the Church. They alone can serve her faithfully whose consciences are continually exercised as to whether they ought not, for Christ's sake, to leave her.' (3)

NOTES / SOURCES

1. Alec R. Vidler, *Windsor Sermons*, London, 1958, pp. 82–3
2. Ibid., p. 127
3. Alec R. Vidler, *Essays in Liberality*, London, 1957, pp. 21–7

Ini Kopuria   1900(?)–1945

As a native policeman, Ini Kopuria's job took him all over Guadalcanal in the Solomon Islands, but a vision of Jesus, calling him to do different work for his people, led him to a life of evangelism in which he aimed to take and live the gospel in the remotest villages and islands in Melanesia. He began a Brotherhood for Melanesians in 1925 and, with help from his bishop, prepared a Rule and made vows himself in which he dedicated his life and his land to God. Men were asked to make only a five-year commitment to service within the community and many came to join him and stayed for much longer. It quickly grew into one of the largest religious communities in the Anglican Communion and its methods of evangelism proved highly effective.

Ini Kopuria's Profession as a Member of the Melanesian Brotherhood

He began by sketching precisely the situation on Guadalcanal, detailing the heathen villages in the various districts by name, and estimating that, of the population of about 12,000, there remained three or four thousand untouched by Christian influence. Then the challenge was issued, based on the text in S. John, 'And other sheep I have . . .' This he developed on the lines that Christ did not seek only those in the fold, and it was the task of those already called, few though their numbers might be, to draw others to enter. 'The door,' he wrote, 'is open for ever and cannot be closed.' Then, thinking of the ship which plays so large a part in Church life, in Melanesia, he saw it as the means by which the sheep should be carried to the fold. Ship and Fold were the Church, entered by means of the Wharf, Baptism. And on the ship were to be found both Master and Captain, with the Holy Spirit Himself as the Engine. 'And the Engine is altogether lovely, It lasts for ever, It cannot get out of order on the passage to Heaven. The Engine lasts on, the Fire is always hot and cannot die out for It is eternal.'

On the feast of SS. Simon and Jude, 1925, standing under a large tree on this site, Ini made his profession before the Bishop, the Assistant Bishop, and one of the white priests, in words he had himself drawn up.

'In the Name of the Father, and of the Son, and of the Holy Ghost. Amen.

'Lord have mercy, Christ have mercy, Lord have mercy.

'Our Father . . .

'Trinity All Holy; from to-day until the day of my death, I promise in the Name of the Father, and of the Son, and of the Holy Ghost, and before Archangels and Angels, Spirits and Saints, and before the Bishop, John Manwaring Steward, Bishop Frederick Merivale Molyneux and the Rev Arthur Innes Hopkins, representing the Church here in Melanesia, I promise three things. I give myself and my land, together with all that is mine, to Thee. I will take no payment from the Mission for the work to which Thou sendest me. I will remain Thy celibate always till my death. Strengthen me that I may remain firm, remain peaceful, remain faithful therein all my days till death: Who livest and reignest, Three in One God, world without end. Amen.'

This act has been taken to mark the foundation of the Brotherhood and the day of the taking of the vow was chosen for the Annual Chapter. Conditions in the islands, however, postponed the actual gathering of the first Brothers and their first missionary adventure on Guadalcanal until the following Whitsuntide. The *Southern Cross*, the Mission ship, is the chief, often the only, means of communication throughout the diocese, and, at that time, she made two voyages every year. As Ini's promise was made in the concluding months of 1925, those willing to join him could only be gathered together during the first voyage of 1926, and brought to Siota when the ship returned there in May. Thus there was a pause before Ini could set out, as he planned, into the heathen bush. The time was spent in appealing for young men to join him. He went with the ship, making a personal appeal for recruits at the different islands she touched, at the same time making known his ideas in a striking contribution to *O Sala Ususur*. (1)

Memories of Ini Kopuria

There died in his own village in Maravovo in Guadalcanal on 6 June 1945 Ini Kopuria, founder of the Melanesian Brotherhood. He was, I think, one of the ablest Melanesians I have ever known. What things stood out about his character?

First I think his spirituality. Prayer was a very real thing for Ini: he was the most reverent Melanesian I have met, and that is saying a lot. God was all his thought. Second, his joyousness. He was almost always in high spirits, full of fun, full of the joy of being alive: it was good to live with him. Third, his deep understanding of the thoughts of Melanesians. At Brothers' Meetings when disputes were often hot, Ini always knew who was really in the wrong, and generally got that Brother to say so. Fourth, his common sense. He always knew what was practicable and kept discussions to that.

Reverent, joyful, sympathetic, wise, these the brothers knew him to be. He was not popular with the white staff who thought him conceited. There was a little truth in this, for he felt his own gifts, though I don't think the conceit went deep; but he was very sensitive to colour feeling. He thought it all wrong that *every* Melanesian because of his colour, should be inferior to every white man because of his colour. He felt that there was this feeling even within the Mission and the Church itself.

One of my strongest memories of Ini is of a baptism when Ini and I stood deep in the very cold water of a mountain river for several hours while streams of people came to us from the heathen side, were baptized by us and passed over to the Christian side where the bishop sat in his chair on a high grassy bank with the few already Christian around him. There the newly baptized dressed in white loin cloths, and finally a great procession, led by the cross, set off for the church—a procession so long that they were singing different hymns in different parts without realising it, or caring either, so joyful did they feel. That is just one of my many memories of Ini. What great days those were!

In the end, in the early days of the war, Ini left the Brotherhood. He asked to be released from his vows and was released by the bishop. Then came the Americans in their thousands. It was a time of great unsettlement for everyone; and for a time Ini went, as the bishop wrote, 'into a far country'. There followed soon the sickness from which he died, but not before he had come back to full communion. The last period of failure was perhaps needed for the final lesson of humility, so hard for men of great gifts. The failure did not last long. It was as though God took his hand away for a moment in order that he might hold Ini for ever.

So on 6 June this brilliant, wayward, valiant leader of men found final happiness. As for us the Brotherhood, he always held our hearts and can never be forgotten. Rest in peace. (2)

NOTES / SOURCES

1. Margaret Rycett, *Brothers: The story of the Nature Brotherhood of Melanesia*, London, 1935, pp. 17–19
2. Charles Fox in 'The Southern Cross Log', January 1946, Melanesian Mission, London, p. 5

Stephen Charles Neill   1900–1984

Born in Edinburgh, Neill was a missionary, church historian, teacher, and ecumenical theologian, who was first principal of a theological college and then Bishop of Tinnevelly in South India. For a short period (1948–1950) he served as Associate General Secretary of the World Council of Churches with responsibility for its study programme, and later was Professor of Mission and Ecumenics at the University of Hamburg (1962–1969) and Professor of Philosophy at the University of Nairobi (1970–1973). A prolific writer he was co-editor of *The History of the Ecumenical Movement 1517–1948* and author of *Anglicanism* (1958) and *A History of Christian Missions* (1982).

The Transformation of Holiness by Jesus

Jesus is the Holy One of God. The term still moves in the purely religious sphere. He is the appointed one of God, the one who has come forth from the mysterious realm in which God dwells. In the intensely solemn prayer addressed to the Holy Father, He speaks of sanctifying Himself: 'For their sakes I sanctify myself, that they also might be sanctified through the truth' (John 17. 19). Here the primary emphasis is not ethical. The phrase does not mean, 'I devote myself to living an ethically superior life, in order that they may do the same'. We encounter once again the exclusive and polemical idea of holiness: 'I commit myself wholly to that inexorable, almost implacable, holiness of God, to total surrender and obedience to it'; and, under the conditions of a sinful world, that means in effect self-surrender unto death. The sacrificial ring is present in the words; in the Old Testament 'to sanctify' and 'to sacrifice' are almost synonymous terms. What Jesus does for Himself He does also for His followers; He sets them apart for total dedication to the will of God, and for them too this must mean a willingness to be as corns of wheat that fall into the ground and die. They are to be sanctified in the truth; that means, in the idiom of the Fourth Gospel, in *reality*. The law could give only a ritual, external holiness; this is now to be replaced by ultimate reality, the total setting apart of the disciples to the will of a God who demands man's all; at this point the doctrine of this Gospel comes near to that of the Epistle to the Hebrews (see Heb. 10. 1 ff.).

This is the godward side of the holiness of Jesus. But in the seventeenth chapter of John, from which we have already quoted, the threefold relationships—the Father, the Son, the Disciples—are intricately entwined with one another. There is also a manward aspect of this holiness. This too is related to the purpose of God, whose will it is to bring all things back to that state in which once again He can look on them and see that everything that He has made is very good. This climax is expressed in the concluding verse of the chapter—'that the love wherewith thou hast loved me may be in them and I in them' (John 17. 26). The relationship between Jesus and the disciples is to be reflected in that which will subsist between them as His disciples; it is for that reason that He gives them the new commandment that they are to love one another. It is only in relationship to holiness that the nature of love in the biblical sense of the term can be understood—it is simply the translation of holiness into terms of personal relationships.

Such a relationship can never adequately be expressed in terms of rules and ethical formulae, though, as we shall later see, these may have their value even in a world which is to be under the sway of love. What is involved is a total self-commitment of one to the other, in relation to the fulfilment of a purpose of God. Such a relationship is, in point of fact, a seamless robe, a single whole which does not lend itself readily to any kind of analysis. Yet even pure light can be split up into the seven colours of the spectrum. Similarly, for convenience of understanding, it may be possible to isolate and present separately certain factors which seem to be always present in the holiness of Jesus, when this is understood in the context of His relationship to those whom He loves and serves.

The first of these elements is realism. 'He knew what was in man' (John 2. 25).

Nothing could be further from His spirit than any kind of sentimentalism, any evasion of the harsh realities of the human situation. It not rarely happens that a doctor, consulted by someone about some apparently trivial symptom, sees with dismay that the apparently trivial is in truth the outward sign of a malady that has driven its ravages far into the recesses of the human system. So Jesus, in His realism, is well aware that what ails the human race is no trifling malady. It is the whole man that is sick. Here is no case for some kindly good advice, for some general rules of ethical conduct. Nothing will avail but a total transformation, and, for the accomplishment of this, nothing less than the total resources of the everlasting God will be required.

The second quality is austerity, even sternness. He who is holy demands of His people nothing less than that they should grow into the pattern of His holiness. His Church, as He understands it, is to be a training ground for athletes, for heroes; it is we who have given it much more the appearance of a hospital for sick souls. Jesus is well aware of what it will cost a man to follow Him. If He could spare us these ruthless demands, no doubt He would. But no one can follow the Crucified who is not willing to take up and carry his own cross.

The third quality is compassion. It is noteworthy that this strong, deep word occurs in all the three greatest parables of the Lord—the Good Samaritan, the Unmerciful Servant, and the Prodigal Son. This is not a general, pitying kindliness. It is, among other things, an unemotional recognition of the help-lessness of the one towards whom the compassion is directed. And it is always a sympathy which serves as a spur to redemptive action.

Fourthly, patience is always an ingredient of this kind of holiness. Jesus demands a complete transformation of human nature, but He recognizes that time is needed for this transformation to take effect. Even the disciples are slow to understand and to follow. They still want to call down fire from heaven on their enemies (Luke 9. 54). They are still interested in the pettinesses of personal ambition. At times Jesus does gently reproach them: 'Have I been so long with you, Philip, and yet hast thou not known me?' (John 14. 9). What they are suffering from is not just natural human stupidity; it is in part the unresponsive-ness of the will, that does not wish to have all its favourite ideas and inclinations overthrown by the invading power of the love of God. But Jesus will bear with both stupidity and obstinacy; the time till the harvest comes may be long, but it will come in its appointed hour.

Finally, the holiness of Jesus is related to hope. Hope in the Bible bears no relationship to the shallow optimism which men often call by that name; it is always related to the faithfulness of God. God has created, and He has not forsaken the works of His hands. Jesus is not dismayed by all that He sees of evil and failure in the world, since His assurance is deeply founded in the faithfulness of God, and since He maintains an unalterable faith in what the almightiness of God can achieve with even the poorest of materials.

Once again we note the link between the doctrine of creation and the doctrine of holiness. What Jesus has come to do is to restore the race of men to that which in the original creation it was intended that it should be, and so to lead it forward to that final destiny in which the transitoriness of man is caught up into the eternity of God. (1)

Astonished Joy

There are only two choices before us—to be either a forgiven sinner or an unforgiven sinner; and all eternity cannot change that. What we shall be is wonderful; but it cannot be what it would have been had we never sinned. Then, with increasing knowledge, there is an ever deeper sensitiveness to our failure to make the best of the opportunities that God has given. Perhaps the actual and identifiable sins are few; but, given such opportunities as have been given us, what would Jesus have made of them? For here is the heart of it all. To move forward on the road of holiness means to know Jesus better. To Him we always return. The better we come to know Him, the more plainly we shall see how little like Him we are, how very little we have drunk of His spirit.

So it comes about that there has never yet been a saint who knew that he was a saint. If you happen ever to have told an obvious saint that he was one, you will have noted the almost agonized horror with which he repudiates the term. And yet the use of the term may have been fully justified.

Those who have been privileged to share the confidence of one who has gone far on the road that we have been discussing know well that one constant factor in his experience is surprise. He is astonished that God should ever have bothered to take note of a creature so wholly undeserving of His attention. He is astonished that such sins as he has committed could ever be forgiven—and yet he knows that they have been forgiven. He is astonished that God should be so patient with one so hopelessly wayward and ungrateful, such a silly and infuriating sheep—and yet he knows that God has not cast him off and that he is not reprobate. I am inclined to think that this astonishment will not end with our pilgrimage upon earth. I can imagine myself waking up one day in the home of the blessed, and saying to myself in astonishment, 'Now, how in the world do I come to be here?' I can also imagine myself meeting some of my friends, as I hope to do, in those blessed fields and saying to them, 'Well now, how in the world do you come to be here?' Perhaps we shall look at one another in mutual surprise.

If you ask me what I expect to be the chief characteristic of that life that will follow, when we have come to the end of the road, and sin and sorrow and conflict are no more, I think that perhaps I would be inclined to reply 'Astonishment', or to put it a little more precisely, 'Astonished joy'. (2)

NOTES / SOURCES

1. Stephen Neill, *Christian Holiness: The Carnahan Lectures for 1958*, London, 1960, pp. 21–3
2. Ibid., pp. 129–30

Dom Gregory (George Eglington Alston) Dix OSB   1901–1952

George Eglington Alston Dix was educated at Westminster School and Merton College, Oxford, entering the Benedictine Community of Nashdom in 1926 in which he was solemnly professed in 1940, taking the name Gregory. His *Shape of the Liturgy* (1945) was widely influential in the revival of liturgical studies and his brilliance, unconventionality, and good humour as a conversationalist gave him considerable influence in the Church of England.

The Dynamic Centrality of the Eucharist

At the heart of it all is the eucharistic action, a thing of an absolute simplicity—the taking, blessing, breaking and giving of bread and the taking, blessing and giving of a cup of wine and water, as these were first done with their new meaning by a young Jew before and after supper with His friends on the night before He died. Soon it was simplified still further, by leaving out the supper and combining the double grouping before and after it into a single rite. So the four-action Shape of the Liturgy was found by the end of the first century. He had told His friends to do this henceforward with the new meaning 'for the *anamnesis*' of Him, and they have done it always since.

Was ever anther command so obeyed? For century after century, spreading slowly to every continent and country and among every race on earth, this action has been done, in every conceivable human circumstance, for every conceivable human need from infancy and before it to extreme old age and after it, from the pinnacles of earthly greatness to the refuge of fugitives in the caves and dens of the earth. Men have found no better thing than this to do for kings at their crowning and for criminals going to the scaffold; for armies in triumph or for a bride and bridegroom in a little country church; for the proclamation of a dogma or for a good crop of wheat; for the wisdom of the Parliament of a mighty nation or for a sick old woman afraid to die; for a schoolboy sitting an examination or for Columbus setting out to discover America; for the famine of whole provinces or for the soul of a dead lover; in thankfulness because my father did not die of pneumonia; for a village headman much tempted to return to fetich because the yams had failed; because the Turk was at the gates of Vienna; for the repentance of Margaret; for the settlement of a strike; for a son for a barren woman; for Captain so-and-so, wounded and prisoner of war; while the lions roared in the nearby amphitheatre; on the beach at Dunkirk; while the hiss of scythes in the thick June grass came faintly through the windows of the church; tremulously, by an old monk on the fiftieth anniversary of his vows; furtively, by an exiled bishop who had hewn timber all day in a prison camp near Murmansk; gorgeously, for the canonisation of S. Joan of Arc—one could fill many pages with the reasons why men have done this, and not tell a hundredth part of them. And best of all, week by week and month by month, on a hundred thousand successive Sundays, faithfully, unfailingly, across all the parishes of christendom, the pastors have done this just to *make* the *plebs sancta Dei*—the holy common people of God.

To those who know a little of christian history probably the most moving of all the reflections it brings is not the thought of the great events and the well-remembered saints, but of those innumerable millions of entirely obscure faithful men and women, every one with his or her own individual hopes and fears and joys and sorrows and loves—and sins and temptations and prayers—once every whit as vivid and alive as mine are now. They have left no slightest trace in this world, not even a name, but have passed to God utterly forgotten by men. Yet each of them once believed and prayed as I believe and pray, and found it hard and grew slack and sinned and repented and fell again. Each of them worshipped at the eucharist, and found their thoughts wandering and tried again, and felt heavy and unresponsive and yet knew—just as really and pathetically as I do these things. There is a little ill-spelled ill-carved rustic epitaph of the fourth century from Asia Minor:—'Here sleeps the blessed Chione, who has found Jerusalem for she prayed much'. Not another word is known of Chione, some peasant woman who lived in that vanished world of christian Anatolia. But how lovely if all that should survive after sixteen centuries were that one had prayed much, so that the neighbours who saw all one's life were sure one must have found Jerusalem! What did the Sunday eucharist in her village church every week for a life-time mean to the blessed Chione—and to the millions like her then, and every year since? The sheer stupendous *quantity* of the love of God which this ever repeated action has drawn from the obscure christian multitudes through the centuries is in itself an overwhelming thought. (All that going with one to the altar every morning!)

It is because it became embedded deep down in the life of the christian peoples, colouring all the *via vitae* of the ordinary man and woman, marking its personal turning-points, marriage, sickness, death and the rest, running through it year by year with the feasts and fasts and the rhythm of the Sundays, that the eucharistic action became inextricably woven into the public history of the Western world. The thought of it is inseparable from its great turning-points also. Pope Leo doing this in the morning before he went out to daunt Attila, on the day that saw the continuity of Europe saved; and another Leo doing this three and a half centuries later when he crowned Charlemagne Roman Emperor, on the day that saw that continuity fulfilled. Or again, Alfred wandering defeated by the Danes staying his soul on this, while medieval England struggled to be born; and Charles I also, on that morning of his execution when medieval England came to its final end. Such things strike the mind with their suggestions of a certain timelessness about the eucharistic action and an independence of its setting, in keeping with the stability in an ever-changing world of the forms of the liturgy themselves. At Constantinople they 'do this' yet with the identical words and gestures that they used while the silver trumpets of the Basileus still called across the Bosphorus, in what seems to us now the strange fairy-tale land of the Byzantine empire. In this twentieth century Charles de Foucauld in his hermitage in the Sahara 'did this' with the same rite as Cuthbert twelve centuries before in his hermitage on Lindisfarne in the Northern seas. This very morning I did this with a set of texts which has not changed by more than a few syllables since Augustine used those very words at Canterbury on the third Sunday of Easter in the summer after he landed. Yet 'this' can still take hold of a man's life and work with it.

NOTES / SOURCES

Dom Gregory Dix, *The Shape of the Liturgy*, London, 1945, pp. 743–5

H. Lakdasa Jacob de Mel   1902–1976

Born in Sri Lanka (then Ceylon) Lakdasa de Mel was educated at Keble College, Oxford, and Cuddesdon, and was ordained to a short curacy at St John the Divine, Kennington, before returning to work in Sri Lanka. Consecrated as assistant Bishop of Colombo in 1945, he was the first Sri Lankan national to be raised to the episcopate. In 1950 he became the first Bishop of Kurunegala and in 1962 was elected Metropolitan of India,

Pakistan, Burma, and Ceylon, moving to be Bishop of Calcutta, before retiring in 1970. An outstanding leader in the unity schemes in North India and Pakistan, he was also concerned for the indigenization of the Church in Asia.

Worship—the Submission of all our Nature and Environment to God

Set forms of public worship are handed down from the early Scriptures, including the Psalms, and also the order of the service. In Christian experience through the ages certain forms of prayer have proved themselves. We gladly incorporate the skills and beauty from those parts of the world which sent us the Gospel, for Christianity is an international religion. An affected originality could not be permitted to throw away treasure belonging to the universal Church, but there is great scope for local initiative. Worship is not the half-apprehended imitation of others, but the submission of all our nature and environment to God, who, when we draw near to him free of barriers, can quicken our consciences by his holiness, nourish the mind with his truth, and purify the imagination with this beauty. Nevertheless, he who fears to make a mistake makes nothing. With a waiting upon the Holy Spirit, the work must go on, remembering that the early Church was incredibly daring, by baptising the national cultures into Christ. For there we find an undivided Church, conscious that man's religion had to enter into his environment and culture, taking over places, seasons and customs associated with pre-Christian religious observances, and with inspired intuition turning them to Christian profit: a site once given to idolatry could be claimed for Christian worship; the winter solstice was made the festival of our Lord's Nativity; the marriage customs of the Romans were raised to the moral requirements of Christ's teaching in the rite of Holy Matrimony. The scope of our era may not be so wide, but how differing is our approach. Imagination is needed. (1)

Indigenous Worship

We must continue to find new ways not only to give God what is his due, but also to inspire power in the worshippers whose being expands as they adore in an idiom which is congenial and uninhibited. Countries like Ceylon which have a history going back long before the Christian faith, have inherited certain ways of thinking and looking at life. Christ crowns all this. Christians should regard this as an historical preparation for Christ; and where tradition is apposite, Christianity should take it, develop it, and be alive to it. Sensitive souls discern that the Church should be increasingly indigenous, of the earth, earthy, intelligible to all at the deepest levels, and Christian truth should be expressed within the thought forms of our ancestors wherever possible. Worship in the Sinhala language is not fully Sinhala worship until all the music, dance, arts and crafts are presented to God as a combined contribution. As our people increasingly learn to worship in buildings reminiscent of their own history, with the suggestion of native arts around them, and uplifted by the chants and music which are part of their heritage, the whole texture of the country's life will be brought to the feet of God. He who accepts and blesses these gifts will commun-icate new power to face the new situations which affect daily life. A church or worship need not be primarily national so much as natural, wherein life can be fully lived within its own environment . . .

. . . Another development could be the practice of reciting our public prayers in the manner natural to people who normally use a recitative when reading prose aloud. The 'saying' of prayers and psalms is a modern Western importa-tion. Our tradition is to chant prose. (2)

A Valiant Spirit as well as a Contrite Heart

There must be more prayer for vision, without which people will perish. The call comes to clear our minds and to put first things first. And once the call of God is heard then everything else shrinks into insignificance. Prepare then for more frustration and abuse, all of which can save our souls if they are thereby turned Godwards. We have to pray for a valiant spirit as well as a contrite heart. (3)

The Gospel is not mere Information

Our own devotional lives must deepen, for we cannot play our part and give out if it is not within. Through the work of the Holy Spirit we must possess that closeness to God which means we can help others. God's concern is for the whole world, so we must show that personal relationships with him are possible. Sometimes there are difficulties in communicating the Gospel, we know that mystical things are in some sense incommunicable. The Gospel is not mere information and has to be caught not taught. (4)

Harmony not Uniformity

There are many criticisms made of the Church. We must seek to show quite clearly that the Church is an international body which at the same time takes notice of national gifts given by God so that we look enthusiastically for the glory of the nations being brought into the Kingdom of God. Our Incarnate Lord in his final command bade them make disciples of all nations. He took notice of a certain corporate personality given to people of different religions, expressing variety of temperament, language and religious inheritance; and he who has no favourites among the nations wishes all this to be an offering to him in the common household of the Holy Catholic Church. He has willed harmony, not uniformity, and this is where the Christian can bring with him the harmonising co-operation and fellowship with other races which he has learned to experience and value in the life of the Church. Our Lord calls us to go forward as the servant Church to serve people, quite regardless of race or religion. (5)

The Law of Love the Shaper of all Conduct

. . . the discontents of the present time are a God-given chance for the Church to deepen her religious life. We are being called to live more devoutly. The trouble is that our Christianity is too weak. Spiritually we need a revival. Not noisy manifestations which degrade religion and bring it down to the level of a spectacle; but that quiet deep revival of faith which enthrones the love of holiness in the heart and issues forth in purity of life and conduct. How necessary this is in a world where moral standards are slipping and over-emphasis is given to political rights rather than duties, to sex rather than self-control, and to enjoyment rather than hard work. Let us pray with faith, offering our fidelity and service to God, remaining quite calm when some people tend to get excited. In Christ a superstructural and super-national focus of unity came. Men are no longer seen primarily as white or brown, or as different nationalities, but in their filial relation to God. The religious way of putting this is, 'seeing God is all other men and in nations of men'. Christian love is shown to be God's very way of life and essence which we must share with him if this universe is to continue to be habitable by man. It is as difficult to ignore the law of gravity in physics as it is to transgress the law of love in conduct, without coming to grief. (6)

NOTES / SOURCES

1. Joan de Mel, *Lakdasa de Mel—God's servant—World citizen—Lanka's Son*, Delhi, 1980, pp. 92–3
2. Ibid., p. 93
3. Ibid., p. 96
4. Ibid., p. 97
5. Ibid., p. 102
6. Ibid., pp. 102–3

Alan Ecclestone   1904–1992

Alan Ecclestone came under the influence of the Catholic Crusade whilst still at school. He read English and History at Cambridge and taught English at Durham for three years before being ordained. He served in Carlisle Diocese, moving to Sheffield for 27 years where he became best known for the parish meeting, an attempt to broaden the focus of parish life. He was also, for fifty years, an active member of the Communist Party. After retirement he wrote a number of distinguished books, largely on spirituality, the most well-known being *Yes to God* (1975) and *A Staircase for Silence* (1977).

Prayer is not a Rockpool but an Ocean

Long-established habits do their best for us, but habits however good, can do no more than habits are devised to do, and praying wants to do more than this. Prayer seeks to break new ground. Prayer wants a world made new. Prayer tries to find its own authentic voice. The great books on prayer and meditation, the classics of the spiritual life, will help at times, and leave us glad and grateful for their wisdom. They too, however, can also leave us finding that we are not now the persons who can use or profit by their excellent advice. Their words are unexceptionably good; they might well have inspired us deeply had we not been so inert and dull and resistant to all inspiration. Our very familiarity with them as the years go by begins to mock our efforts to observe them once again. We are not the persons who once warmed to such direction. Not even the Lord's Prayer, it seems, at times can take possession of our random being and give it steadiness towards and hold on Him to whom we want to turn. We simply cannot do the thing we would. It is an old and commonplace experience, and no easier to bear for that. Charles Péguy thought that the 'Ave Maria' was our last resource. 'With that,' he said, 'you can't be lost.' But that too would be for very many still a forms of words, of words that failed them in a desperate hour.

It is not to be supposed then that any book, and certainly not this one, could solve our problem and enable us to pray as our hearts long to do. Praying is too great a venture of the spirit in Man to be delivered from its difficulties like that. A book of such a kind has not been written nor ever can be, for praying comes not as a problem to be solved but as a venture to be lived out. It is so difficult a thing because it attempts so much. In prayer, Man sets his sights upon the Infinite. What could he expect but to discover over and over again that he is lost? He launches this pleasing anxious limited being upon a sea that knows no bounds in time or space. Small wonder that he finds himself beset by fears and darkness, by the dread feeling that he has lost his way, by suspicion that no way is to be found. Or he may, of course, protest that his intentions are more modest. All that he asks or seeks to do is but to speak in friendly trustful fashion with his Father in Heaven. 'No more but so?' But prayer itself is not a rockpool but an ocean. (1)

Praying Begins with Hearing

We pray then because there is pain and love in life, because we both suffer and rejoice, because we try to find meaning in it, because we want to share this with another. No doubt a good deal of our praying is shallow and insincere, selfish and immature. What we are as persons speaks for itself in our prayers. It may be the best or the worst that speaks, but what we most deeply need to do is to learn to pray quite honestly as we are, to love and rejoice from the depths of our being. How deep are those depths? Psycho-analysis, had it done nothing else, would have done a work of immense importance here. The most shallow, trivial-minded, apparently characterless person among us carries within himself, it appears, such worlds of passion, hopes and fears, ancestral dreams and twisted purposes, that like the once solid atom, our selves now show themselves to be strange galaxies of particles and energies at work. But that we had bad dreams, we might, like Hamlet, be content with this, or even as Caliban waking might cry to dream again. We have hopes and longings and hungers that aspire to a life transformed. From out the unplumbed depths of this being there is heard at times a voice which is ours yet not ours only. Praying begins with hearing. All prayer attempts to enter those depths below the troubled chaotic self to listen and to respond to a conversation which reveals and summons and helps us to participate in an I-in-You, You-in-Me relation with the Spirit who gives it life. (2)

Silence

We need silence. We need to learn what silence is. We need the time and space which silence alone can provide to get the measure of our secret ladder, to face and not be outfaced by the multitudinous demands of life in the world today. We need to know the kind of silence that makes possible the kind of communication that Pascal hungered for which is communion, a thing not to be gained by dodging unpleasant things like Harold Skimpole nor by denouncing them as a pack of cards like Alice. The spirituality we seek must reckon with the mire and clay, the shouting and the torches, the accusations and the mockery. It needs silence to enable it to grapple with that task.

Contemplative prayer and liturgical practice have always known that this is so. Was it not when all things were silent, *dum medium silentium*, that the Word became flesh? Was not the Christ Himself silent at some moments, making known that a new beginning of things was being effected? So men, whether in the celebration of mysteries or in acts of prayer needed silence to make sense of the words they used, to make room for the unspoken. 'Silence', wrote Pierre Charles, 'is always more eloquent than speech, because it is far deeper and more complete'. Silence alone can provide for both the extremities of our need and the operation of God's grace, permit the insufficiencies of our attention to be checked and erase the blundering grossness of our insensitive observations. Yet we are far from honouring this necessity in the conduct of our lives.

There is in Kierkegaard's essay *For Self-Examination*, an insistence upon the need for silence, couched in the form of a physician's advice when called upon to prescribe for the sickness of the world: 'What dost thou think must be done? I should answer, "the first, the unconditional condition of doing anything, and therefore the first thing to be done is, procure silence, introduce silence; God's Word cannot be heard, and if, served by noisy expedients, it is to be shouted out so clamorously so as to be heard in the midst of the din, it is no longer God's Word. Procure silence".' (3)

NOTES / SOURCES

1. Alan Ecclestone, *Yes to God*, London, 1975, p. 8
2. Ibid., p. 39
3. Alan Ecclestone, *A Staircase for Silence*, London, 1977, pp. 38–9

Austin Marsden Farrer   1904–1968

The son of Baptist parents, Austin Farrer became an Anglican as an undergraduate at Oxford, where he read Classics and Theology. After a curacy in Dewsbury he returned to Oxford in 1930, and in 1935 succeeded Kenneth Kirk as chaplain of Trinity, where he served for twenty-five years, until his final eight years as Warden of Keble. A devout Tractarian in spirituality, he was a notable philosopher of religion, an imaginative student of scripture, and one of the most brilliant preachers of his generation.

Engaging with the Will of God

You will not find God in the conscience, any more than you will in any other direction, unless you go all the way there is to go, and uncover the ultimate claims which, without destroying your soul, you cannot refuse. You see these claims to lie in the true being of mankind; and when you note which that is, you see that it is what a perfect and a sovereign will is working out: in yourself, just as much as in any other man. And when you have seen this, a prayer rises in your heart, the prayer to know and to feel and to love the work that God is working, so that you may be spared the misery of frustrating it.

What your conscience is up against in people is God's will for them, God's love of them; and God's will, God's love are not abstractions, they are God Himself. We talk of a clash of personalities, a direct encounter, when there is a battle of wills between any two of us. And yet my will is not me. It may be a freak of accursed obstinacy which sets me at issue with you; and once the heat of the battle is over, I may be at a loss to conceive how I could be such a fool as to fight it. Or if it is, by a miracle my better nature, say my championship of a friend, with which you clash; then alas, how far from true it is that such occasional sallies of generous feeling are just me, or representative of me. But God—God has no caprices, He does not vary or repent; His will is just His being, His life, His love, His mind, coming to bear on the point at which we clash with Him.

To take it a stage further: you may, if you like, imagine a man whose deeds are all consistent, always generous. But it will still remain that his several actions are distinct events, each divided from another. To-day's decision is a new birth, it is no mere continuation of yesterday's. No man, however wise, however good, can decide upon to-day's action, until he sees what the day may bring. But God's action is all one piece; He meets no surprises, He makes no extemporisations, for He sees from the beginning to the end. His will most tranquilly unfolds in an all-embracing care, infinite in detail and single in scope. What touches us, when God's will touches us, is not one of God's actions, but that action which is God. No wonder, then, if conscience quivers at the touch; and feeling her opposition to what she encounters, acknowledges the violation of a sanctity. There is none holy but God alone; and there are only two ways, in any act or thought, of our being related to His holy life. Either we live in Him, or we cut across Him.

Whose teaching do you think is this? Who said, that what calls to us from the being of our fellows is the majesty of God? He who took a child, and set him in the midst of His disciples, and when He had taken him in His arms, declared: 'Whosoever receiveth one such in My name, receiveth Me; and he that receiveth Me, receiveth Him that sent Me.' Whom that we may everlastingly receive and not forego, we implore the grace of threefold sovereignty, of Father, Son and Holy Ghost. (1)

Biblical Inspiration and the Rendering of Scripture

If God inspires St Paul to speak, how are we to strain out St Paul, so as to be left with the pure word of God? . . . How are we to draw the line between the Apostle's oddities and the word of God?

It would save us a lot of trouble if we could find a cut-and-dried answer to that question; but cut-and-dried answers to spiritual questions are always false, and in the special matter of understanding God's word Christ rules such answers out. 'He that hath an ear to hear, let him hear', said he. We cannot hear the voice of God in Christ's words, let alone in St Paul's or Isaiah's, unless we have an ear attuned. After we have done our best to understand the words by the aid of mere honest scholarship, there is still something to be done, and that is the most important thing of all: to use our spiritual ears. If we do not believe that the same God who moved St Paul can move us to understand what he moved St Paul to say, then (once again) it isn't much use our bothering about St Paul's writings. 'God is his own interpreter, and he will make it plain.'

'God is his own interpreter.' Does that mean that each of us is to take any given text to signify just what we happen to feel about it at the moment of reading? Certainly not. God is his own interpreter, but he does not interpret himself only by speaking in the single reader's mind, he interprets himself by speaking in the Church, the whole organized body of Christian minds; we are not alone, we have the mind of Christendom, the Catholic Faith, to guide us. God is his own interpreter in another way, too: he gives us one text by which to interpret another. The God who spoke in St Paul spoke also in St John, he who inspired one page of St John also inspired the next page, and the one will cast light upon the other. And above all lights, most clear and most brilliant, is the light of Christ.

People used to talk about the *verbal* inspiration of Scripture, that is, the inspiration of the actual words. In one sense that is absolutely right, but in another sense it is misleading. Verbal inspiration is a misleading expression, if it means that every word is guaranteed to be free from human error or bias, so that (for example) St Luke's dates, St John's history, and St Paul's astronomy are absolutely beyond criticism. That is not so: St Paul's astronomy is (as astronomy) no good to us at all. St Luke appears to have made one or two slips in dating, and St John was often content with a very broad or general historical effect, and concentrated more on what things meant than just the way they happened. It does not matter. God can and does teach us the things necessary to our salvation in spite of these human imperfections in the texts.

But in another sense *verbal inspiration* is a proper expression; indeed it stands for the very thing we need to think about most. It is not true that every word is guaranteed, but it is true that the inspiration is to be found in the very words and nowhere else. What God inspired St Paul to do was to use the very words he used; just as, when God inspires you to do a good action, the action itself is what God inspires. He doesn't put some sort of vague blue-print for action into the back of your head, and leave you to carry it out according to your own ability. He inspires the action, and if we want to see God's spirit expressed in the lives of his true servants, we don't look for it in any general ideas, policies, or attitudes they may have, but in the particular things they do. Every detail counts; the tone of the voice, the gesture of the hand can make the difference between social hypocrisy and Christian kindness. So too it is in the detail of expression, in the living words of divine Scripture that we hear the voice of the divine Spirit, not in any general (and therefore dead) ideas. We are listening to the voice of God, not reading a text book of theology; we must attend, therefore, to the homely phrases, the soaring poetry, the figures of speech, the changes of mood; for these are the alphabet of the divine utterance.

I take up the Bible and I read. Here are a million or so printed words, in which divine gold and human clay are mixed, and I have to take the gold and leave the clay. Is there clay everywhere mixed with the gold, does no part of the text speak with a simple and absolute authority? Indeed it does in some part, for some part of it is the voice and recorded action of Christ, and in Christ the divine does not need to be sorted from the human, the two are run into one, for here is God in human nature by personal presence. Christ is the golden heart of Scripture. Indeed, if he were not there, the rest would not concern me. Why do I read St

Paul? Because he sets Christ forth. Why do I read the Old Testament? Because it is the spiritual inheritance Christ received, it is what he filled his mind with, it is the soil in which his thought grew, it is the alphabet in which he spelled, it is the body of doctrine which he took over and transformed. So whenever I am reading the Old Testament I am asking, 'What does this mean when it is transformed in Christ?' and whenever I am reading the New Testament I am asking, 'How does this set Christ forth to us?'

There is no part of the Bible which is not inspired, because there is no part that does not either illuminate, or receive light from, the figure of Christ. But obviously not all parts are equally important, and some of them are more the concern of theologians than of laymen. Begin from the most important parts; read the Gospels and Epistles, read Genesis, Exodus, Deuteronomy, Psalms, and Isaiah, and when you are full of those, spread your net wider.

People will always ask why God gives us his truth in such a mixed form; just as they will always ask why God made the world such a mixed affair. And those who are looking for excuses to live without God will say that, until God speaks more clear, they cannot be bothered to listen; but people who care about God will listen to him here, because this is where he can be heard and because it's a matter of life and death. What is the Bible like? Like a letter which a soldier wrote to his wife about the disposition of his affairs and the care of his children in case he should chance to be killed. And the next day he was shot, and died, and the letter was torn and stained with his blood. Her friends said to the woman: The letter is of no binding force; it is not a legal will, and it is so injured by the accidents of the writer's death you cannot even prove what it means. But she said: I know the man, and I am satisfied I can see what he means. And I shall do it because it is what he wanted me to do, and because he died next day. (2)

The Narrow Gulf

The world spreads round me in circles. The first circle is feeling, which reaches as far as the boundaries of my body. The second circle is sight, which slides out along the lines of light as far as sun, moon and stars. The third circle is thought, which, building on the evidence of instruments, extends into a world of stars beyond the stars I see. My knowledge fans outwards from my body to the bodies which make my environment, and so out and out to bodies beyond these, until my environment includes the universe of stars. My habit is to plot the position of everything I take for real somewhere in the unending field of bodies. If I said of something that it was outside the bodily field I could only mean that it was in the outer part of it, beyond any bodies my thought had previously reached.

Where then, in all my spreading world is Jesus Christ, the man risen and glorified? When clouds received him from our sight, into what height, what distance did he go? However far away I place him, I gain nothing by it: he fits no better beyond Orion than behind the nearest trees. His risen being is no part of our interlocked system of bodily force, whether far or near. He is nowhere in this world. He is not outside it, either, for it hasn't got an outside where he could be. Where is he, then?

It is useless to start from me, and to fan out and out, looking for Jesus Christ: I must start from Jesus Christ, and fan out from there until I reach myself. Jesus is the heart and centre of heaven, just as each of us is the heart and centre of our own world. He is assured of his own world as each of us is assured of ours—through his own living existence: he knows he is there, and as the action of his life is more intense and wakeful than ours, he has less temptation than the best employed of us ever to take existence from a dream. His life is even less locked than ours is within his own breast. Radiating through lines of heavenly sympathy, his soul knows what is next to him, blessed saints whose society forms the very place of his existence; and so out and out, without failure or weakening of sight, his eyes embrace a universe of spirits, as many as the stars we see. Without thinning or flattening of sound he may converse with the distant as with the near, and receive back voices in answer to his voice, expressing each in its unique and personal colour the glory and the love of God.

At first it may seem that we have two answers, spreading on independent planes and nowhere touching at a single point. Christ's universe of spirit, and ours of physical force. Yet thinking further we perceive that it cannot be so. For while it is indeed impossible to place heaven in the world, it is impossible not to place the world in heaven. If Christ's knowledge is spiritual, as ours is physical, then he knows us, for we are spirits too, spirits in fleshly bodies; and if he knows our spirits, he knows what our spirits know, including their bodily knowledge. He hears us speak from within our throats; he thinks our thoughts as fast as we can form them. But he feels in our fingers too, and looks through our eyes; he lives out along the lines of our vision, and our sun, moon and stars are his. By sheer love, heaven grafts the world into itself, and roots our universe in its own heart.

Jesus Christ, living Son of the living God, clothed in our nature, I cannot place you in my world, but neither can I escape from yours. I cannot reach you by many steps, but I can reach you by one, the single step of faith which lands me in the heart of heaven. If ever I am to end with you, it is from you I must begin. Thou God seest me; and if ever I am to see across the gulf from me to you, it will be by starting with you, and seeing myself through your holy and compassionate eyes. (3)

Prayer not as Colloquy but Diaphanous Thought

I should now like to ask how important it is deemed to be that the philosopher's experience should fall into the form of an inward colloquy, with one part of his thought addressing another as though with the voice of God. I have a special and personal interest in challenging the colloquy-form, because of an obstacle I remember encountering in my own adolescence. I had myself (this at least is the impression I retain) been reared in a personalism which might satisfy the most ardent of Dr Buber's disciples. I thought of myself as set over against deity as one man faces another across a table, except that God was invisible and indefinitely great. And I hoped that he would signify his presence to me by way of colloquy; but neither out of the scripture I read nor in the prayers I tried to make did any mental voice address me. I believe at that time anything would have satisfied me, but nothing came: no 'other' stood beside me, no shadow of presence fell upon me. I owe my liberation from this *impasse*, as far as I can remember, to reading Spinoza's Ethics. Those phrases which now strike me as so flat and sinister, so ultimately atheistic, *Deus sive Natura* (God, or call it Nature), *Deus, quantenus consideratur ut constituens essentiam humanae mentis* (God, in so far as he is regarded as constituting the being of the human mind)—these phrases were to me light and liberation, not because I was or desired to be a pantheist, but because I could not find the wished-for colloquy with God.

Undoubtedly I misunderstood Spinoza, in somewhat the same fashion as (to quote a high example) St Augustine misunderstood Plotinus, turning him to Christian uses. Here, anyhow, is what I took from Spinozism. I would no longer attempt, with the psalmist, 'to set God before my face'. I would see him as the underlying cause of my thinking, especially of those thoughts in which I tried to think of him. I would dare to hope that sometimes my thought would become diaphanous, so that there should be some perception of the divine cause shining through the created effect, as a deep pool, settling into a clear tranquillity, permits us to see the spring in the bottom of it from which its waters rise. I would dare to hope that through a second cause the First Cause might be felt, when the second cause in question was itself a spirit, made in the image of the divine Spirit, and perpetually welling up out of his creative act.

Such things, I say, I dared to hope for, and I will not say that my hope was in any way remarkably fulfilled, but I will say that by so viewing my attempted work of prayer, I was rid of the frustration which had baffled me before. (4)

NOTES / SOURCES

1. Austin Farrer, *God and the Universe: A course of sermons preached in the chapel of Pusey House, Oxford*, London, 1960, pp. 36–7
2. Austin Farrer, *Interpretation and Belief*, London, 1976, pp. 11–13
3. Austin Farrer, *Words for Life* (ed. Charles Conti and Leslie Houlden), London, 1993, pp. 32–4
4. Austin Farrer, *The Bampton Lectures: The Glass of Vision*, Dacre Press, London, 1948, pp. 7–8

Arthur Michael Ramsey 1904–1988

Archbishop of Canterbury from 1961 to 1974, and before that Bishop of Durham and Archbishop of York, Michael Ramsey was a theologian in the Catholic tradition influenced by the biblical theology movement. With a deep concern for Christian unity, he also took a prominent part in the public debates of his time, but was above all concerned to commend the importance of contemplative prayer to all Christians.

A Retreat with Michael Ramsey

He was valued as a conductor of retreats; not surprisingly. About the silences of a retreat he was humane, for when he conducted a retreat at Cuddesdon he introduced silent croquet into the programme.

We have a portrait of him by someone who attended a retreat which he gave at the retreat house at Pleshey in Essex. He sat in front of the altar of the little chapel with his prayer book and notes on a little stool, but never referred to them. He could quote not just a sentence but long passages from memory—the hymn 'O Strength and Stay', the hazel-nut of the Lady Julian of Norwich, a passage from St Irenaeus out of the second century. The only sign of age was an increased waddle in the gait. He talked on the transfiguration, one of his favourite themes. He occasionally used Greek words to add to a point, but always explained them. It was a biblical, very biblical, indeed evangelical exegesis of the gospel texts. Once he said '*gooder*' and hastily corrected to '*better*' showing that he had not intended the word. Suddenly he would break into poetry—St Peter making shelters on the mountain to make them stay and not melt away like mists on the mountain-side—but the line was thrown away, he had no consciousness that it was poetry, there was no sense of rhetoric nor of anything artificial. He would use an occasional startling phrase. The only non-biblical phrase which he used was 'the night of sense—I believe that this phrase of the spiritual writers conveys much truth'. Some of the utterances were memorable—'There are *people* who make God near. This is the marvellous thing that one human being can do to another.' He conveyed a sense of glory; of closeness to God; and an unearthly sort of comfort from that. When he said a thing was *tremendous* or *exciting* the hearers realized that it was indeed tremendous and exciting. They did not subtract from these words of conventional overstatement.

He thought for himself all the time. He had a closeness of meditation on the passion; almost line by line. He loved the symbolism of St John's gospel. An address on the washing of the feet in St John was full of humour, wreathed in smiles, punctuated with chuckles, radiant with happiness. The address had a total simplicity of idea and construction, yet the simplicity was somehow elaborated without being elaborate. He dwelt on the text with affection, almost with glee. He never hesitated or said 'Er'. He never needed to go back in a sentence to correct the grammar. All flowed in perfect construction of sentences. He once said 'between he and us' and he once used the non-existent verb *ultimatize* to mean, making the State into the end of life.

The addresses were shot through with smiles and amusement without the least detraction from reverence or the least lowering of tone. The amusement relieved the high language and made it sound still higher. The retreat addresses were quite short; probably less than fifteen minutes each. No one could fail to be lifted towards the rest of their soul in God. The last address was on heaven, and was perfect eloquence for the highest of themes—and without notes. He bubbled with ecstasy over the beatific vision. He had so real a sense of the joining with angels and archangels here and now in worship. He ended movingly, 'Thank you so much for letting me join you. Alleluia, Amen.'

Going into breakfast someone smiled at him. He looked at him sourly. He celebrated the holy communion, Rite A, with a profound quiet, and without emphases. He could be heard humming the tune of the hymn when it was played over (this hum was celebrated, it led some people to nickname him Winnie-the-Pooh) and he sang all the verses of the hymn though he had no book in front of him. In the confessional he was affectionate, humane, and wise—accepting an attrait but adding to it with a delicacy and sureness of touch.

Such is the portrait of Ramsey conducting a retreat. A retreat is a time when the personality of the conductor is very exposed to his hearers. All this was at the centre of his personality.

If he sat down at a meal he could make no effort to start a conversation with his neighbour if that neighbour was an adult and unknown to him—if the neighbour was a student it could be different. If he were placed next to another shy person at a meal, the two would sit side by side in silence throughout the meal and the hostess or host would wonder desperately what to do about the situation. There was a rumour that when he was at York the general officer commanding the army in the north came to pay a courtesy call and the conversation came to a total halt. Some people regarded small talk as courtesy and thought that anyone unable to discuss whether it will rain tomorrow was guilty of not making an effort needed by society. Such people were apt to think him inconsiderate or even rude. They did not realise that he did not regard words as an essential means of communicating between human beings.

These silences were more awkward with women than men. Women would sit next to him at a meal and come away afterwards with no sense of rapport whatever. The exception to this rule was widows when their husbands had just died and they needed comfort. He would say nothing or almost nothing, but he would seize her hand and shake it again and again and again, with an inarticulate passing into her of the sincerity and warmth of his fellow-feeling and his pity. (1)

A Church for Ministry in the World

It is good to recall the story of the great Anglican divine Richard Hooker when he lay dying. They asked him what he was thinking about, and he replied 'the number of angels and the excellence of their order, joying that it was so in heaven and would that it might be so on earth'. Our concerns as Christians, and no less as priests, is with a divine order embracing heaven and earth, and with its reflection in every part of human affairs. That is the true context of our witness within the social scene. Our otherworldly calling tells us of the goal and helps us not to lose heart or lose patience as we witness to justice and brotherhood and human dignity in the community where we are.

If these are some broad principles to guide us, what counsels have I in particular for you who are to be priests at a time when these questions press themselves urgently and even violently upon us? I claim no oracular authority, but I speak from an experience of public affairs which has been fairly stormy, and I know how hard it is to be sure whether one is saying too much or too little, or being too timid or too rash. From my own tangle of experience I will dare to give you this advice.

1. Be aware of the new and powerful trends in the world which bear upon the Church and its mission. A country or a town or a village may feel itself to be peaceful and secure, and upheavals of one kind or another can be very near. I have, for instance, seen our sister Anglican Church in the United States in one decade feel utterly secure in its prosperity and in the apparent impregnability of the 'American way of life', and in the next decade convulsed by the onset of violent social upheavals. Notice also the new role which the race problem is assuming in many parts of the world. To my generation with its old-fashioned liberalism the race problem meant getting white people and black people to be kind to one another. To your generation the race problem often means the seething unrest of black people who will tolerate white domination no longer, and who ask why if it was right for us white people in Europe to fight for liberation from Hitler it is wrong for them to fight for liberation from their oppressors. It is in such a world that you will be ministering, and one part of it

has repercussions upon another. And even when a particular problem or tragedy does not seem immediately to come your way remember your fellow Christians for whom it does, and see your ministry as a part of the Church's witness in every place.

2. Take your share in the task of Christian people to study together and form right judgements based on knowledge and Christian insight. I am thinking of such issues as industrial relations, the third world in its relation to our world, war and violence, obscenity and censorship, race relations. It may often be for you as priests to rouse the laity to think responsibly about these questions, but when they are aroused you will find that they have knowledge which you have not and you will be learning from them in a partnership of Christian concern. That is how the mind of the Church is to be formed.

3. Help your congregation to be a caring congregation, active in its service of some human need or distress. But always let the caring for human need be linked with the caring for God himself and the winning of lives to him. Never let your leadership in social causes weaken your pastoral ministry to your own people. There is a world of difference between the priest who compensates for pastoral failure with his own people by an embittered advocacy of public causes and the priest whose power of public prophecy is drawn from the hard school of personal pastoral experience.

4. Amidst the vast scene of the world's problems and tragedies you may feel that your own ministry seems so small, so insignificant, so concerned with the trivial. What a tiny difference it can make to the world that you should run a youth club, or preach to a few people in a church, or visit families with seemingly small result. But consider: the glory of Christianity is its claim that small things really matter and that the small company, the very few, the one man, the one woman, the one child are of infinite worth to God. Let that be your inspiration. Consider our Lord himself. Amidst a vast world with its vast empires and vast events and tragedies our Lord devoted himself to a small country, to small things and to individual men and women, often giving hours of time to the very few or to the one man or woman. In a country where there were movements and causes which excited the allegiance of many—the Pharisees, the Zealots, the Essenes, and others—our Lord gives many hours to one woman of Samaria, one Nicodemus, one Martha, one Mary, one Lazarus, one Simon Peter, for the infinite worth of the one is the key to the Christian understanding of the many.

It is to a ministry like that of our Lord himself that you are called. The Gospel you preach affects the salvation of the world, and you may help your people to influence the world's problems. But you will never be nearer to Christ than in caring for the one man, the one woman, the one child. His authority will be given to you as you do this, and his joy will be yours as well. (2)

Rest, See, Love, Praise—

Christian prayer and Christian life are properly inseparable. As the Sonship of Jesus on earth was a relation to the Father in words, in wordless converse and in the obedience of a life and death, so the adopted sonship of the Christians has its facets of word and silence and act. The Sonship of Jesus was to the Father's glory, and in the serving of that glory he consecrated himself on the world's behalf. So too the Christians know the worship of God to be first of all, and know also that this worship is an idolatrous perversion unless it is reflected in compassion towards the world. 'As the soul is in the body so are the Christians in the world.'

Within the worship of the Christians are acts of wonder at the beauty of God in the created world and his transcending holiness beyond it; and acts of gratitude for his costly redemption of mankind in Jesus. It is a worship in which sometimes the mind and the imagination dwell upon God's beauty and goodness, and sometimes mind and imagination enter the darkness as the unimaginable love of God is poured into the soul. It is a worship whereby the pain of the world is held upon the heart in God's presence, and the desires of men are turned towards the desire of God as we pray in the name of Jesus.

This book has recalled some of the phases in a continuing story. There is the inarticulate yearning towards God found in the human race before and behind the more conscious yearning of the world's religions. There is Israel's worship of its King and Father who is also the world's creator. There is the *Abba* prayer of Jesus in life and in death, and his teaching of the disciples to 'pray like this', to utter their desires and frame them to the divine will. There is the fuller revelation of the Father in the death and resurrection of Jesus, evoking the prayer of St Paul and many others. There is the summary through the veil in the Epistle to the Hebrews with an other-worldliness which gives reality to the present life. There are the mount and the plain which are the scenes of the Lord's exodus. Through the centuries the story continues.

It has been the Christian conviction that the goal of heaven is anticipated in the present life. The Holy Spirit is the first fruits of the heavenly harvest, the first instalment of the heavenly treasure, and the Christians in the apostolic age believed their life in Christ to be an anticipation of the goal which was to come. Both the life in Christ in St Paul and the eternal life here and now in St John tell of this. Indeed the words 'your life is hid with Christ in God' suggest that heaven is not only the goal towards which we journey but a treasure locked in our hearts and one day to be made visible to our eyes (Colossians 3. 1–2).

Here the Christian Eucharist speaks. In the Eucharist, with the Risen Jesus present as our food, we are worshipping with the saints and angels in heaven. But the Risen Jesus who is the heart of the heavenly worship is also a Jesus who was crucified, and we share in heaven's worship only as sharing also in the Jesus who suffers in the world around us, reminding us to meet him there and to serve him in those who suffer. Indeed in the Eucharist we are summoned by two voices, which are really one voice: 'Come, the heavenly banquet is here. Join with me and my mother and my friends in the heavenly supper.' 'Come, I am here in this world in those who suffer. Come to me, come with me, and serve me in them.'

But how may we think of heaven? Christianity has known many pictures of heaven from the Apocalypse of John onwards. But here let some words of St Augustine be recalled, for they are words which not only tell of heaven but are also powerfully suggestive of heaven's present anticipations. In his work *The City of God* St Augustine told of heaven thus. 'We shall rest and we shall see, we shall see and we shall love, we shall love and we shall praise, in the end which is no end.'

Rest: we shall be freed from the busy and fussy activity in which we get in our own light and expose ourselves to our self-centredness. Resting, we shall find that we **see** in a new way, without the old hindrances. We shall see our neighbours as what they really are, creatures and children of God in whom is the divine image, and that image will become newly visible to us. We shall see ourselves too as God's infinitesimally small creatures: and we shall begin to see God himself in his beauty. Seeing, we shall **love**, for how shall we not love God in his beauty and how shall we not love all our neighbours in whom the image of God is now visible to us? **Praise** will be the last word, for all is of God and none is of our own achievement, and we shall know the depth of gratitude and adoration. St Augustine adds 'in the end which is no end'. It will be the end, for here is perfection and nothing can be more final. It will be no end, for within the resting, seeing, loving and praising there is an inexhaustible adventure of new and ceaseless discovery. Such is the heaven for which we were created.

Resting, seeing, loving and praising: these words describe not only the goal of heaven but the message of Christianity in the world. The world has lost the way of resting, seeing, loving, praising. Swept along in ceaseless activity the world does not pause to consider. With no resting and no considering the power to see is lost: to see where we are going, to see the larger perspectives, to see beyond the group or the nation or the race, to see human beings as they really are with the image of God in them. Where seeing is dim, love becomes faint; and praise is lost for we praise only when first we have seen and loved. Man loses the praise of his creator which is the end of his existence and the source of his resting, seeing and loving.

If the words 'rest, see, love, praise' tell both of heaven and of the true life of man on earth, they tell no less of the Church's renewal at this and at any time. It has been all too possible in the life of the Church for rest to mean a complacently tranquil piety; for seeing to be the seeing of tradition without contemporary awareness, or the seeing of some contemporary enthusiasms without the perspective of history; for loving to be within the circle of the likeable; for praising to be a kind of aesthetic enjoyment. The renewal of the Church will mean, indeed there are signs that it does already mean, a rest which is exposed to the darkness and light of contemplation, a seeing of both the heavenly perspective and the distresses of the world, a loving which passes into costly service, and a praising which is from the depth of the soul.

While however renewal seems to demand the recovery of the unities of understanding which this book has tried to describe, it can never be a tidy pattern which we can know and plan. Our wisdom as well as our folly faces the darkness of Calvary and the light of Easter. Jesus suffered outside the gate, and he summons us to go out to him bearing his reproach. (3)

Fearfully and Wonderfully Made

Our Christian creed begins with the great affirmation that God is the creator of the world. To say that God created the world and that all existence depends upon Him often conveys little to peoples' minds when it is made as a prose propositional statement. Indeed, God's creation of the world and the dependence of all existence upon Him may be conveyed through poetic imagination. This is how the poetic spirit of the Lady Julian of Norwich expressed it in one of her Revelations of the Lord:

He showed me a little thing the size of a hazel nut in the palm of my hand, and it was as round as a ball. I looked with the eye of my understanding and thought 'What might this little thing be?' and it was answered 'This is all that is made.' And I marvelled how it might last for methought that it might have fallen to nought for very littleness, and it was answered 'It lasts and ever shall last for that God loves it.' So I understood that all thing hath the being by the love of God.

And there is perhaps conveyed to us that all existence is like the little hazel nut in the palm of the hand of the Creator. It is thus that we understand the word God, infinite, eternal, and all existence finite, creaturely, dependent. Pray that we may recover a little of this realisation that God is all and we are as nothing. Yet, in this little hazel nut of a universe in the palm of the hand of the Creator, there is man; man created in God's own image after God's own likeness. The line of distinction between Creator and creature can never be blurred. Yet for all that unblurrable line of distinction, there is in man a real affinity to his Maker. That affinity makes possible the closest conceivable fellowship between man and his Creator, and it was for this fellowship with his Creator that man was made, for God so loves man. But there is fellowship and fellowship, and the fellowship with God for which man is made is indeed described in Holy Scripture in terms of friendship; God is the Friend of man; man is to be the friend of God, but it is a friendship shot through with awe, dependence, the realisation of creatureliness.

This relation of friendship blended with awe and dependence is described in one of the unique, really unparaphraseable biblical words, glory, glorify. When man glorifies God he reflects God's character like a mirror reflecting the light, but while he reflects God's character like the light, becoming in the end through God's goodness as like God as it is possible for him to become, the more he reflects God's character like a mirror, the more he becomes like God, the deeper his realisation of his utter dependence. So glorify, while meaning reflecting and resembling, means no less praising, ascribing worth, realising more and more deeply the awe and dependence. Thus man glorifies God, and glorifying God is what is seen, again and again, in those men and women who are called saints. They may become wonderfully godlike, yet the more godlike they become the more are they humble, knowing that nothing is from themselves, but all is from God upon Whose unmerited goodness they depend utterly, the friendship which is blended with awe and dependence.

Now man's glorifying of God is not in a vacuum. It is done in the midst of the world of nature, the world which God also created. What is man's true relation to the world of which he is a part? The classic account of this is in Psalm 8. Man is given by the Creator a certain power over the created world. He is allowed in a measure to rule it, to control it, to use it and to exploit it, but he does this under God's ultimate sovereignty and as itself in subjection to that sovereignty.

O Lord our Governor, how excellent is Thy Name in all the world.

It is under the excellent name of God's government, that man is allowed to govern. The Psalmist depicts it as governing the fields, the cattle, and the fish in the sea. A modern paraphrase, invoking immensely greater knowledge of the world, sees man as governing by his use of the sciences many of the world's forces and increasing his government over it. But man is sent to govern the world and in a measure to control its forces in humble dependence upon the Creator in mutual unselfish service, not exploiting and distorting the world of nature, but using it with reverence as it, too, is of God's making and reflects God's Glory; and doing all not for the aggrandisement of a group against a group, an individual against other individuals, or a nation over other nations, but doing it all in mutual humble self-giving service for the glory of God the Creator and in recognition that every man, woman and child has a destiny with God beyond the world of nature altogether. (4)

Transfiguration

Transfiguration is one of the true and legitimate descriptions of the Gospel entrusted to us and of the Christian life which we are called to be living and leading others in the living of. There is a striking passage in Toynbee's work on the interpretation of history, in which Toynbee describes the various attitudes possible in what he calls a declining and frustrated civilisation. Toynbee says that the possible attitudes are these. The first he calls archaism, and by that he means an attempt to put the clock back and to reconstruct some state of affairs which had previously existed. Another attitude he calls futurism, and by that he means to despair of the existing world order and to try to force our way forward to some totally new order unrelated to it, so unrelated to it, that it can only be brought about by violence. The third attitude he calls detachment, but as there is a kind of detachment quite different from what he means, he would have done better to have called it escapism, for by this attitude, he means despairing of the world order and retreating from it into a kind of zone of spirituality apart from the world and its troubles. Rejecting these three attitudes as unsatisfactory, archaism, futurism and detachment, Toynbee says that the true attitude that makes sense is transfiguration, and he describes transfiguration thus: 'To accept the situation just as it is and to carry it into a larger context which makes sense of it and gives the power to grapple with it.' And that is striking language for one who is writing not as a theologian, but as a historical analyst and commentator. What exactly he meant, thought he meant, may be rather hard to grasp, but I think the words have immense suggestiveness for us Christians. Transfiguration is to accept the situation as it is, and to carry it into some larger context which makes some sense of it and gives the power to grapple with it. That larger context is Jesus crucified and risen, and we are called, again and again, to be lifting human situations into that context and finding that in that context new and exciting things begin to happen to the situations, and to us who are confronting them.

Recall just a few ways in which this Gospel of transfiguration is for us a great reality. Suffering is transfigured. That is something that every priest has the joy of seeing, again and again, in the lives of people he meets. People who suffer greatly, and yet through their nearness to Christ, something different happens. They suffer still, but yet there is a sympathy, a gentleness, a sweetness, a power of love, a power of prayer that makes all the difference to them and to those who know them. Suffering transfigured. Situations transfigured. We find ourselves up against something that completely baffles us in any kind of rational terms. We are completely perplexed, and we cannot, as it were, get through the situation, or get round the situation, or retreat from the situation. But see it in the larger context of Jesus crucified and risen, and while it goes on being the painful situation that it was before, somehow it is in a different light, and a different light comes to us, and it was wrong for us to be making hasty judgements about it before we took it into the context of Jesus crucified and risen. Then human lives are transfigured. That is what we have all seen happening in human lives, where by God's grace the mingled experiences of sorrow and joy bring about a transforming, the growth in grace, the growth in Christlikeness is a reality.

But what about the transforming of our own lives? Our prayers, our reception of the sacraments, our Christian hope, so much of the language that we use, implies our faith that we ourselves can be transformed, and are being transformed by the power of Christ. Is it really happening? It is never apparent to ourselves that it is happening and again and again it may seem to ourselves that nothing is really happening as regards any growth in Christlikeness in us. But if we did perceive ourselves growing Christlike, we could be quite sure that our own perception would be wrong, because we are not the judges of our own states, and furthermore, any kind of selfconscious awareness of spiritual progress is a contradiction in terms. Rather it is for us, putting ourselves in Christ's hands, to be forgetting ourselves altogether, but entrusting ourselves into Christ's hands, we know by faith that the power of Christ can and does work in us, and we can leave it at that, by faith, and not by sight. This is summed up by Saint Paul. I finish with just a glance at Saint Paul. It is at the end of II Corinthians 3; Saint Paul describes how the Apostles gaze at the Glory of Christ as reflected in a mirror and while gazing at the Glory of Christ as in a mirror, they are themselves being transformed into Christ's own likeness, from glory to glory by the power of the Spirit Who is Lord. (5)

Mysticism and Contemplation

Mysticism in the proper sense is an intense realisation of God within the self and the self embraced within God in vivid nearness. It is a phenomenon known in a number of religions, and in those religions very similar language is used in describing the experience. There is deep darkness, the darkness of not knowing; and there is light with flashes in which the self knows the unknowable terribly near and knows itself as never before. Now through the centuries Christian teaching has emphasized that the significant thing is not just the mystic experience in itself but its place and its context within the whole life of a Christian. The experience is given by God sometimes to one who seeks God in a life of humility and charity, turned towards the righteousness as well as the beauty of God. And the effect of the experience of mystic union, sometimes described as 'passive contemplation', is not to cause the person to long to have the experience again but to long to serve God and to do his will. Those who have had mystic experience will not want to tell everyone about it: they will have a longing to serve God in daily life, for in his *will* is our peace.

Mystic experience is given to some. But contemplation is for all Christians. Allow me a word about that prayer which is indeed for all of us. The prayer of Jesus our high priest is classically described in the sentence 'he ever lives to make intercession for us'. Now the Greek word which is here, and elsewhere, translated 'intercede' does not mean to speak or to plead or to make requests or petitions: it means to *meet* someone, to *be with* someone in relation to or on behalf of others.

Jesus is with the Father, for us. And our own prayer means essentially our being with God, putting ourselves in his presence, being hungry and thirsty for him, wanting him, letting heart and mind and will move towards him; with the needs of our world on our heart. It is a rhythmic movement of our personality into the eternity and peace of God and no less into the turmoil of the world for whose sake as for ours we are seeking God. If that is the heart of prayer, then the contemplative part of it will be large. And a Church which starves itself and its members in the contemplative life deserves whatever spiritual leanness it may experience. (6)

NOTES / SOURCES

1. Owen Chadwick, *Michael Ramsey: A Life*, Oxford, 1990, pp. 357–8
2. Michael Ramsey, *The Christian Priest Today*, London, 1972, pp. 40–2
3. Michael Ramsey, *Be Still and Know: A Study in the Life of Prayer*, London, 1982, pp. 120–4
4. Michael Ramsey, *Retreat Addresses given to the Oratory of the Good Shepherd*, Clewer, 1972, pp. 6–7
5. Ibid., pp. 22–3
6. Michael Ramsey, *Canterbury Pilgrim*, London, 1974, pp. 59–60

Max Warren   1904–1977

Max Warren was born in Ireland of Irish missionary parents and spent his early years in India. He read history and then theology at Cambridge, and after ordination went with the Church Missionary Society (CMS) to Nigeria, but had to return home having contracted tuberculosis. Vicar of Holy Trinity, Cambridge, from 1936 to 1942, his major ministry was as General Secretary of the CMS from 1942 to 1963. His monthly *CMS Newsletter* in which he wrote perceptively on many issues of the day was widely read and influential. A key adviser to Archbishop Geoffrey Fisher, from 1963 to 1973 he was Canon and Sub-Dean of Westminster Abbey.

The Theology of Intercession

Now to the serious business of commenting on your own reflections. First then to consider your thoughts on 'Intercession' as expressed in your letter of August 24 which reached us just before we flew off to S. Africa. . . .

Intercession has a three-pointed base or you might say three inextricably united elements which comprise its basis.

(1) The quite deliberate involvement of oneself in affection and concern with the other person(s). The number, I think, is of secondary importance in getting the pattern clear. This involvement means that the person(s) is (are) part of the fabric of one's living and thinking. I don't mean conscious thinking, but something much deeper. One is involved in this way when some sudden event or experience *automatically* sends one's mind racing back to that person or persons. They, those for whom we intercede are there 'within' us, and their presence 'surfaces' naturally where a stimulus is given by event or experience. . . .

Theologically speaking this is an inescapable inference from the doctrine of the Body of Christ (Paul) and that of the enhypostatic union (John cf. 17. 20–23). . . .

(2) Then (not a 'then' of *time* but of the argument!) there is the articulation

of one's awareness of the presence of the person(s) when one is in the act of intercession. Here, of course, there is an element of the time-factor which is indispensable. One must have a discipline—a rule of which, irrespective of whether the person(s) is immediately on the surface of consciousness, one does bring them there!

Now here I'm sure there is a great variety of practice and properly so. There is the 'arrow prayer'—'God bless so and so'—not to be despised if point (1) has been taken seriously. The 'time factor' in life is such that only an 'arrow prayer' may be possible at that disciplined moment of remembrance. But the arrow will come from a bow at full stretch (which is a good analogy for point (1)!)

It was a great help to me once when a wise man said that in his very busy life he made a practice of 'lifting his friends up by name unto the "river of the love of God"'. He didn't ask anything for them at that moment. He just remembered them and God together. . . .

(3) The *third* point of the base co-incident with the other two, almost one might say the 'procession' from (1) and (2) is the deliberate acceptance of *obligation* to the person(s) for whom one is praying. This can mean a thousand things e.g. writing a letter to them, sending them a paper or a book, talking to someone else about them, doing something they've asked you to do, or perhaps writing to someone who will be glad of news of them etc., etc., etc.

Now it seems to me that if that base is firmly made then upon it one can build these occasional acts of intercession which are the spontaneous response to some incident, to an individuals request 'pray for me on such and such a day'. And on the base one can build up one's own prayers of intercession within the Liturgical frameworks of worship e.g. In the Abbey one remembers each day one diocese of the Anglican Communion, its bishop (by name), and its clergy and people. . . .

NOTES / SOURCES

Max Warren to his son-in-law, Roger Hooker, during his service in India, 19 October 1965, in Graham Kings, *Christianity Connected: Hindus, Muslims and the World in the Letters of Max Warren and Roger Hooker* (Boekencentrum, Zoetermeer), pp. 192–3

Christopher Rex Bryant SSJE 1905–1985

Christopher Bryant became a priest member of the Society of St John the Evangelist in 1935 at Oxford. In 1955 he became Superior of the Society's House in Westminster. He soon became widely known as a conductor of retreats and schools of prayer, and many people looked to him for spiritual direction. In the last ten years of his life he blossomed as the writer of five books on the psychology of the spiritual life.

Wholeness and *Metanoia*

My belief is that the whole of man's life is lived whether consciously or unconsciously in the presence of God. This is true of all, believers and atheists, religious and irreligious alike. No one, I believe, is without the unseen, fostering, influence of God pressing him towards his self-realisation in whatever way however unlikely, this can best be achieved. But I believe that it is an advantage beyond price for a person to be able to realise this Presence and consciously respond to it, to be able to rely on a Wisdom and Strength greater than his own and to try to follow the direction in which divine Wisdom guides and divine Strength enables. Earlier I spoke of the probability that many who do not profess belief in God do nevertheless rely on him and follow his guidance under some other name, or perhaps without any name at all. It would also seem that there are those who do profess to believe in God but do not consciously either seek his guidance or rely on his grace. All the same, despite the loose ends and general untidiness, the imponderables and the unexplainables, that characterize human life it is an immense blessing for a person to realize his life as resting in the hand of God, of One who with unsleeping care is pressing him to grow to his full human stature, to grow into one who can relate to him as a son to a Father. This is journey's end as I see it: to have reached, by whatever strange vicissitudes a lasting relationship to the Creator of all that is. We could never hope to reach this end if God had not set himself to lead us there. We could not find our way without immense help from God all through life, given through innumerable agencies, events and circumstances. Nor can we reach life's goal unless we want it and freely choose it.

I have described the goal of life as a deep and lasting relationship to God. But this relationship cannot be understood apart from two other relationships which are bound up with it, with other people and with ourselves. Indeed the relationship to God, to other people and to ourselves forms a trinity in unity. Each relationship requires and depends upon the others, so that if one is defective the others will be defective too. It is through other people's love that God's love is first mediated to us. To attempt to be open to God and closed to our fellows is to drive uphill with all our brakes on. But equally important is it for me to come to terms with the whole of myself. My own personality to begin with is an unplumbed mystery as much to myself as to others. It may indeed be so totally unknown that I may not have an inkling that there is anything to know. I should then be like a man who all unknowingly carries about in his hand luggage a poisonous snake or a bomb that explodes on impact. We come bit by bit through the processes of growing up and establishing ourselves in our social world to know ourselves better. The task of exploring the unknown continent of our total personality is best done in middle life or later. Introspection can be a danger for those who are not fairly firmly established in social relationships. Like the youth Narcissus in the Greek myth who fell in love with his own beauty a person may become so interested in his own depths that he has no energy available for forming friendships or for the other tasks of life. Further we grow in self-awareness not only by introspection but by tackling the jobs that lie to hand, by measuring our strength and skill against taxing work and difficult people. In middle and later life after the heat of the struggle to succeed is over and such measure of success as we have attained has lost all its novelty and most of its charm, then especially we are ready to devote energy to the task of gaining deeper self-awareness. Until we know ourselves we cannot really possess ourselves. And until we possess ourselves and have the inner peace that comes from self-possession we shall find it impossible to relate to other people except either by trying to possess and dominate them or by letting them possess or dominate us.

The human journey rightly understood is a movement of *metanoia*. Repentance, the usual translation of this Greek word, is an unsatisfactory one, because it too much suggests self-blame and the acknowledgment of sin, instead of hope which is its essential characteristic. The word means literally change of mind or change of attitude; and though self-blame and the realisation of guilt may prepare the way for *metanoia* it is hope that brings about the change of heart and mind which effects a new orientation in a person's life. In the story of the prodigal son it was hope that set the young man on the journey home, though it was his state of spiritual destitution and wretchedness that brought him to the point of *metanoia*. If we are right in seeing with John Hick the perfection of man not as something from which we have fallen in primeval times but as something to be striven for, a goal to be achieved in the future, then hope rather than self-blame or sorrow for sin is all the more plainly the primary incentive in the human journey. The hope that will enable effective *metanoia* includes the hope of becoming more and more completely what in essence we are, of living our own truth to the full; but it includes also the hope of cooperating with our fellows in building a society favourable to growth in humanity; it will include the hope of a city where men will live at peace with men, where the natural environment will be cared for and not recklessly exploited, where men will have learnt to live together as a family because they worship a common Father and Creator.

To insist on hope as the mainspring of *metanoia* does not as we have seen ignore the fact of human evil, of man's perversity and blindness, his arrogance, cruelty and sloth and his timid refusal to respond to the summons to change. But psychology makes for a merciful view of human sin, and without condoning wrong-doing makes it possible to feel compassion for the sinner and to hope that divine mercy will heal and forgive him as we pray that our sin may be forgiven and healed.

NOTES / SOURCES

Christopher Bryant SSJE, *The River Within: The Search for God in Depth*, London, 1978, pp. 141–4

Herbert Arthur Hodges 1905–1976

Born in Sheffield to a Methodist family, Herbert Hodges read Greats at Balliol College, Oxford, during which time he became an Anglican, largely through the influence of Austin Farrer (q.v.). He became a Tutor at New College, Oxford, and went on to become Lecturer and later Professor of Philosophy at Reading University. He represented the Church of England at the first World Council of Churches Assembly in 1948. Author of numerous works on philosophy, theology, and Welsh hymnody, notably *The Pattern of Atonement* (1955), he worked for ecumenical causes all his life and had a special interest in Eastern Orthodoxy and Welsh nonconformity.

The Self-Disclosure of God

What is it that the Father has told us through the Son? What is it that the Son has said to us in the Father's name?

First of all, He has given us a summons to perfection, combined with a staggering notion of what that perfection may mean. This is the true significance of the famous Sermon on the Mount. It is not merely a fine collection of discourses put together by a skilful biographer to give us a notion of the speaker's style. It is the Second Moses ascending His mountain and proclaiming His Law. And as the Old Testament Law was summed up in the demand for holiness, so this new one is summed up in the phrase—is it a command or an invitation or a promise?—*you shall be perfect as your Father in heaven is perfect.*

But secondly, along with this He gives us a declaration of readiness to accept here and now, from each one of us, what we have to give, however far we may fall short of understanding His summons or the full meaning of His commands and promises. If, in the light of what we do understand, we with free generosity and true sincerity offer Him what we now have it in us to offer, that He will accept. So He accepts the homage of pagans and of recently converted publicans and of a crucified brigand. We cannot suppose that these people were either deep in theological insight or far advanced in the spiritual and moral life. But they did recognize in Him the accents of lordship, and they did offer Him freely and sincerely the homage which they saw He deserved and which they had it in them to give. This is the most that any of us can do, and this He accepts. It is very little in comparison with His precepts and His invitation, but it is a beginning. If we let Him have His way with us, He will make it more.

Thirdly, He gives us a declaration of free forgiveness for our past ignoring of His summons and our present inadequacy in understanding and answering it. I said free forgiveness, and so it is in a manner; it is free in that we could never make any beginning of earning it, and can only receive it from Him as a gift. But in another sense it is not free, for there is a condition attached, and it is a condition which may well give us pause. It is that as we wish to be forgiven, so we shall forgive. After telling us the story of the Ungenerous Slave, and how in the end he was handed over to the torturers until he should pay his impossible debt, He goes on: *So will My heavenly Father do to you unless you forgive one another from your hearts.*

All this is much, yet it is not all. Beyond all this He has shown us, in His Passion and Triumph, God's own participation in our life and in our struggle. God Himself in Christ's person has participated, not, indeed, in our sin, but in bear-ing the consequences of that sin and in fighting the battle to deliver us from it—fulfilling His own law, exemplifying His own perfection, sealing our acceptance, strengthening us in our loyalty and our devotion to Him. And as the Passion and the Triumph which He enacted are God's own participation in our life, so we in return are called to participate in His Passion and in His Triumph, and to share the very life of God. The two chief sacraments which He has founded both proclaim and effect this. In Baptism we are initiated into the death and resurrection of Christ, that we may die to what we are of ourselves and rise to a new life in Him. In the Eucharist we plead His death in the symbols of the broken body and the shed blood, and are fed with the life of Him who was dead and is alive for evermore. It is a food, as St Gregory of Nyssa says, which transforms the eater into its own likeness. So the death and the life energize in us, and we are drawn into the offering and the acceptance to suffer and reign with him. (1)

Justification by Faith

The doctrine of justification by faith . . . was never meant as a piece of scientific analysis, a contribution towards a systematic theology. It is an attempt, and a brilliantly successful one, to lay bare the central nerve of the Old Testament, the central principle of God's dealings with Israel and with all mankind; it is written in a strongly polemical spirit. The dialectical edge of the phrase 'by faith' lies in its negative implication, 'not by works'. The heart of the meaning is that our deliverance from the consequences of sin and from sin itself is God's work and not our own, a gift to us and not our achievement. God alone is the Saviour, and to Him alone glory is due; from the beginning to the end man is dependent upon Him. In an adult human being who has been properly instructed, that dependence should be conscious and should take the form of Abrahamic faith, and it is an important moment in a man's growth towards spiritual maturity when he awakens to the significance of the Epistle to the Romans. Protestant tradition is fully justified in emphasising this as it does. But this is merely one stage, and not the first stage, in the normal path of the soul's development under favourable conditions. It is not an absolute and inflexible requirement before a man can become a member of Christ. God bestows grace where He will; He has declared His will to bestow it in the sacraments. It has long seemed to me, and I think history confirms it, that the Reformation principle of the sovereign grace of God is set forth and embodied in Catholic teaching and practice not less truly, and a good deal less abstractly, than in the Reformation doctrines themselves. (2)

NOTES / SOURCES

1. H. A. Hodges, in *God and the Universe: A course of sermons preached in the Chapel of Pusey House, Oxford*, London, 1960, pp. 51–3
2. H. A. Hodges, *The Pattern of Atonement*, London, 1955, pp. 100–1

Dom Augustine (David Freestone) Morris OSB   1905–1997

Educated at Christ's Hospital, David Morris joined the Anglican Benedictine community at Abbey House, Pershore, in 1923. He moved with the community to Nashdom Abbey in 1926 and to Elmore Abbey in 1987. Dom Augustine became the third Abbot of the Community from 1948 to 1974. A great raconteur with a gift for friendship, his publications include *Straight Course to God* (1949) and *Oblated—Life with St Benedict* (1992).

The Cross and the Crown

There is some strange stupidity in human nature which is always trying to limit God's action and reduce the number of ways by which we may approach him. This stupidity takes the greatest variety of forms and the tendency manifests itself in many fields. We must not, we are told, pray to our Lady and the saints, for that is derogatory to God; we must not fear hell or hope for heaven because that is selfish; we must not give rein to our emotions in the spiritual life because that is childish and sentimental; we must not give way to natural affection because that is dangerous; we must not enjoy doing our duty because then it is easy, and nothing is ever any good unless it is hard and grim. There are many, many more such limitations. What a lot of nonsense this is! Would it not be a great deal better to behave as children in our Father's house, and accept gratefully whatever he gives us? Let us pray to our Lady and the saints, for they are links with him and will help us to love him more; let us indeed fear hell and hope for heaven (has not our Lord commanded it?); let us make use, if we can, of our emotions, even though we must keep them under discipline, using them to build up our will; let us give ourselves to others in natural affection, so long as we never allow its claims to cause us to deviate from the love of God; let us whenever possible be happy and joyful in the exercise of our duty, whatever that duty may be. Every various channel of approach to God should be used. Let us go to him by suffering and by joy: by health and by sickness: by success and by frustration: by fasting and by food: by sacrament of the Church and by beauty of nature: by art, by literature and by music: by business and by recreation: by social service and by divine worship: by direct prayer to God and by invoking the aid of saints and angels as well: by denial of self and by spending of self. For the true purpose of all these things and of all else that life involves is to be links binding us to God, channels by which he approaches us and by which we may attain to him. As the spiritual life progresses, all our activities will be unified and integrated: they will all mean one thing—the love of God. Our wandering footsteps wander no more, for they are set on the straight course which leads to God. Life is reduced to simplicity, for to live is to love.

Our Lord summons us to follow him in self-denial and the cross. 'Let him deny himself, and take up his cross and follow me.' If we follow, where will he lead? He will lead us through life's sorrows and joys, sharing them with us in love and endurance. He will lead us up to and through the ultimate mortification of death: there also he will be with us and in us, so that our death becomes one with his, a sacrifice well pleasing to the Father, a moment of indescribable blessing, however horrible its outward semblance. He will lead us through death to life immortal, to reign with him in his kingdom. Having shared his cross, we shall share also his crown. The engine of suffering may still have its work to do if purgatory must receive us for a season to purify us, burn out of us the remnants of the selfish self, the image of sin, and prepare us for the expression of the fullest love of which we are capable. But the hour will come when its work is done, and then that other engine, joy, will spring into action as never before, with full stroke pulsating, generating a love all but infinite. Upon earth, often enough, to love is to suffer. In heaven to love is to enjoy: for love is joy and joy is love. To see God, to know him even as we are known, is to taste joy in its source and essence. His outpouring of love upon us in heaven calls forth at once love unfathomable and joy unimaginable.

'If we suffer with him, we shall also reign with him.' Not only in the life to come, but even in this life shall these words be fulfilled. 'Nay, in all these things we are more than conquerors through him that loved us' (Rom. 8. 37). The soul that loves God is greater than a Napoleon at the height of his power. I make no doubt that there is to-day in a wretched hovel in a Russian village some haggard poverty-stricken old woman kneeling furtively before the ikon on the wall in piteous and almost despairing prayer. Compared with that poor ignorant peasant woman, the greatest of dictators is a mere nonentity. He, and all that he stands for, will pass: she, and all that she stands for, will abide. For in the one there is, only too often, enmity towards God: in the other, at least some spark of love. For the least act of love towards God is greater than all power, all science, all earthly renown, as much greater than they, as they in turn are greater than stocks and stones. It belongs to a new and higher sphere of being; it reaches out from the merely temporal and stretches up to the eternal. Worth while then any labour, any suffering, though it be for a lifetime, if by that endurance we may from one single soul produce one single spark of divine love. Labour and suffering will pass: but that act of love abides in eternity. For that love is the meaning of all human life.

NOTES / SOURCES

Dom Augustine Morris OSB, *Straight Course to God*, Nashdom Abbey, 1949, pp. 118–20

Eric Symes Abbott   1906–1983

Educated at Nottingham High School and Jesus College, Cambridge, Eric Abbott was Chaplain and then Dean at King's College London, during which time he created a postgraduate college at Warminster for the immediate pre-ordination training of King's ordinands. After a brief time (1956–1960) as Warden of Keble College, Oxford, he was appointed Dean of Westminster Abbey in 1959, retiring in 1974. The inscription on the stone marking his burial place in Westminster Abbey reads 'Friend and Counsellor of many, he loved the Church of England striving to make this House of Kings a place of pilgrimage and prayer for all peoples. Pastor Pastorum'.

Asking for Christ's Forgiveness

It does seem that people
come to themselves when
they are able to repent and
certainly when they are forgiven.
Love when it is true longs
to forgive. Forgiveness does not
mean forgetting; it means
remembering the past in a new way.
When we ask for Christ's forgiveness,
the effect is that in so far as
the past is remembered again,
it will have lost its power to hurt us
and make us afraid. (1)

Ministers of Acceptance

We are all persons in the making
and in a real sense we are
making and re-making one another.

But how often personal relationships
are marred by hasty, partial or
over-severe judgments.
We must help one another,
not judge one another, and
we must leave the final judgment
to the Divine Patience.
One of the greatest promises
in the New Testament is that
we are accepted in the Beloved.
Let us try to be the ministers
of acceptance. (2)

Spaces of Silence

Whatever we may say about particular
times and methods of prayer,
this much is essential, that each day
should have some dedicated silence in it.
This is the gift of our time to God.
We are to put ourselves at God's disposal
in the quietness. The prayer
will be dispersed throughout our day,
throughout our activity, but there will be
some dedicated spaces of silence. (3)

Compassion learnt through Suffering

As we all suffer in degrees more or less,
what we become in and through the
suffering is vital. Shall we become more
full of love and acceptance,
of compassion with other sufferers,
 even more full of a certain kind
of peace and joy? Or shall we become
narrower, more self-enclosed,
more self-pitying? (4)

The Need to be set Free from our Hostilities

How can I love my neighbour as myself
when I need him as my enemy—
when I see in him the self I fear to own
and cannot love?

How can there be peace on earth
while our hostilities are our most
cherished possessions—

defining our identity, confirming
our innocence? (5)

The Uniqueness of Particular Lives

When we come to the end, let us
commend our spirits to God
our Creator and redeemer in faith,
believing that he who raised
Jesus from the dead will be able
to take what we have done
for him, whether explicitly or
implicitly, and will gather
it into his Kingdom,
to be in that Kingdom that
particular enrichment of the
Kingdom's glory which our
particular life had to contribute.
For there is something
which only you can bring
into the Kingdom of God. (6)

NOTES / SOURCES

1. *Invitations to Prayer: Selections from the Writings of Eric Symes Abbott, Dean of Westminster, 1959–1974*, Cincinatti, USA, 1989, p. 23
2. Ibid., p. 27
3. Ibid., p. 37
4. Ibid., p. 59
5. Ibid., p. 83
6. Ibid., p. 87

R. E. Charles Browne   1906–1975

Son of a Church of Ireland rector in Belfast, Charles Browne graduated from Trinity College, Dublin. He was ordained in 1929 and served in Belfast and as chaplain of St Columba's, Rathfarnham. From 1949 until 1959 he ministered in Manchester. In *The Ministry of the Word* he revealed a profound interest in the nature of religious language and his writings show an emphasis on the transcendence and glory of God.

The Eucharist and the Universe

Neither death, nor life, nor angels, nor principalities, nor things present, nor things to come, nor powers, nor height, nor depth, nor anything else in all creation will be able to separate us from the love of God in Christ Jesus our Lord.   *Romans* 8. 38–39

Every act of creation is an act of revelation. To reveal is not the mere presentation of a spectacle. To accept what is revealed is no mechanical or chance happening with fleeting consequences cancelled out by subsequent experiences. To see what is revealed means that your gait of thought is changed and the pattern of your feelings altered, the whole of life is reorientated.

We cannot think about an object any way we like. The form of our thinking is dictated to us by the nature of the object we regard. Man is meant to extend the kind of control he exercises over his body so that this kind of control embraces more and more of the whole physical world of which man is a part. In studying an object a union is established in which an exact division between student and object is seen to be impossible. To turn St Paul's words positively: death, life, angels, principalities, things present, things to come, height, depth, and all other creatures can lead us into the love of God which is in Christ Jesus our Lord.

Love always must have active expression. Love of God is actively expressed through love of his things: in our loving his things he draws us into union with him. To love his things is not to be confused with haphazard attention to what immediately attracts us. To love his things is an enduring, imaginative, intelligent and humble attention, which, of course, includes use of his things according to their nature. There is a way of regarding the cornfield that sways and sighs in the autumn breeze. There is a way of regarding the unconsecrated bread and wine upon the altar. There is also a way of regarding the consecrated bread and wine upon the altar which leads us into an awareness of the great mysteries of birth and life and death, of redemption and time and sin. There in the scrap of broken bread is dimly seen the triumph over death and life and principalities and powers, things present and things to come. It is a triumph that is not equivalent to total destruction. He did not come down from Heaven to unmake but to remake, to restore what sin has broken so that we are gathered up as fragments into the unity of men and angels where time and eternity, earth and Heaven lose their distinction in him who is our beginning and our end.

> Our Saviour Jesus Christ . . . in the same night that he was betrayed, took break, and when he had given thanks, he brake it and gave it to his disciples . . . Likewise after supper, he took the cup, and when he had given thanks he gave it to them . . .   *Book of Common Prayer*

To reflect on the Eucharist is to reflect on the mysteries of God and man, of creation and redemption; it is to reflect on our life in time and space and on our deliverance from the bondage of time and space by the same power which frees us from the prison of sin and death.

To reflect on the Eucharist is to see again the hands that moved in the lamplight. It is to sense again the stillness of the lamplit room, the stillness that was not merely absence of sound and movement. His voice broke the silence. He took the loaf into his hands; at that moment for the disciples there was nothing to be heard but the sound of his voice, nothing to be seen but the movement of his hands as he broke the flat Jewish loaf. The movement of his hands in the lamplight became for them, as for us, a lasting image which the whole pageantry of the mind's imagery does not obscure. It is the image in which countless images have their origin and their interpretation.

He took bread and broke it. Physically speaking, he performed an act of cosmic importance. Physicists tell us that every physical act sets in motion a complexity of happenings which go on reverberating long after the initial act has been performed. Every movement affects the whole pattern of energy within the universe. He took bread and broke it; physically speaking, he performed an act of cosmic importance, he performed an act which physically speaking had the timelessness characteristic of all acts. Physically speaking, an act is only to be described by postulating a complexity of causes and a complexity of results. Physicists are tentative in putting down either the causes or results, for the causes of a great many physical happenings are either obscure or apparently non-existent. The breaking of bread, at any time, by any person, physically speaking is more than we understand.

What of the agent who uses and sets in motion physical forces outside his knowledge or control? To speak of the agent in physical terms is to deal with the fact that no neat boundary between a man and the universe can fairly be made. You need air to breathe, you need the light to see by and to be seen, you need water to drink, food to eat and the earth to walk on. A man's body is his medium of expression, his means of communication. A man's body is so joined to the universe that he needs the whole universe to express himself and to be himself. A man is immanent in every expression of himself and at the same time there is a part of himself which he knows he can never express to any fellow-creature. His expressions of himself are so characteristic of him and yet so inadequate, so fragmentary. To express ourselves, to communicate with our fellows, we need the whole universe, we use the universe as if it were an extension of our body. At this present moment we owe our very being to physical happenings whose date is antique, whose force is operative now. To break bread at your own table with your friends is to perform physical acts of deep mystery and of far reaching consequences. The whole dynamic pattern of the universe's energy is affected, the effects will reverberate so long as the life of the universe continues. There is a timelessness about all acts which bewilders us till we overcome our rigid distinction between past, present and future. We are redeemed from time, from living on the edge of a double dread: the fear of what has been done and the fear of what is to come while we are enclosed in the prison of the present, regretting and waiting anxiously. To be redeemed is to be saved from both the past and the future and brought into the eternal present, for all time is one in God. In him, here and now, we are made strong to bear the burden of finiteness; in our faith we are reconciled to the puzzling knowledge given us by physicists; more than that, we know that to rejoice in such knowledge is to touch the hem of his garment.

To touch the hem of his garment is never enough and can never be as satisfying as to sit at his table, his known and invited guests. No matter how ill at ease we may be there, we know that it is where we should be rather than anonymously and timidly plucking the hem of his garment. It is right that he should be known in the laboratory, it is right that we should share, as far as we can, the exultation of physicists in the increase of our common human knowledge. We rejoice in the mysteries of the unconsecrated bread; at the Eucharist we specially rejoice in that it reminds us that the moments of time do not separate us from the deeds of God. We are as near to him who broke the bread on Maundy Thursday night as were

Peter and James and John, and Thomas who had such difficulties. All are one in God, all times are one time in God.

'Nature has no outline, but imagination has.' Physically, we tend to divide the indivisible, we tend to isolate the units of creation and treat as separate what God made in unity. We tend to isolate the human body from the rest of matter, and, to use contemporary language, we tend to treat the human body as an autonomous centre of energy whereas it is a centre within a universal system. 'Nature has no outline, but imagination has.' When we use outlines we must be careful to describe a totality embracing each singular.

Psychically speaking, we tend to isolate the individual and treat him as a separate entity who breaches a gulf between himself and his fellows by an act of will or an act of love; the breaching is described in different ways. Psychically speaking we are, to use a metaphor, busy hotels rather than quiet detatched villas. All sorts of people throng our premises and there is no closing time; even in sleep the doors are open for all who come and go. In spite of our togetherness each one of us is a unique individual who does not develop his uniqueness in isolation but in community. The mystery is mutely described in the Eucharist by the fact that one loaf is used but a piece is broken off from it for each individual. Man is made in the image of God; not individual man, but mankind—that is, mankind is a diversity in unity and a unity in diversity. Each man is public, inclusive, yet different from his fellows, unique. The claim of the individual to be selective, exclusive, private, aloof, is one way of talking about the sin that is the root of all sins—the sin of attempting to be a god, controlling one's own destiny; but no man could control his own destiny unless he also controlled the whole physical universe and whole world of men. The petition that asks 'Make an exception in my case, or in our case' needs to be carefully examined, just as the attitude that God will always take care of the universal at the expense of the individual proclaims the inability of God to be God, for God's care of the individual and the universal arouses no question of conflicting interests in his mind, the cause of the universal and the individual are identical.

We are not isolated and our uniqueness is not shattered by lack of private psychic life. All men meet in each man, yet every man is a unique centre of being, capable of maintaining his uniqueness if he is prepared to receive as well as to give. To reflect on the Eucharist is to see again the company of men in the lamp-lit room, it is not any meal on any occasion—there are stirrings of glory and stirrings of danger. The disciples are shortly to learn that without him they cannot bear one another; one of them finds that he cannot bear himself without his Master. In the shadow of the sacrifice of Christ we see the suicide of Judas. We see the poor distracted man shedding his own blood to atone for his own sins in contrast to the One who shed his Blood to redeem all men from the unbearable-ness of life without him in whom all creatures consist. There were stirrings of glory and stirrings of danger in the Upper Room. So there are at every Eucharist; the eucharistic food is the food for pilgrims. Our pilgrimage takes us into realms of life where we cannot always find words or images to describe what we see. Our pilgrimage takes us into realms of life where we see that both desires for visible security, tangible realities and a desperate clinging to what we understand are sinful. We know the point where we must abandon attempts at self-made security if we are to go on. Our pilgrimage brings us to fuller awareness that we are to think and pray and work as men whose most insignificant acts have consequences too wide to be measured by time or confined within the boundaries of a particular locality or of a particular group of people.

When the celebrant takes and blesses and breaks the bread, he is setting in motion a complexity of movements which go on and on affecting the whole existence of men and things until all comes to rest in the strange peace of God. Each communicant, of course, in co-operation with the celebrant, has his or her essential place in the cosmic, timeless acts. 'I am Alpha and Omega, saith the Lord, the beginning and the end.' Each Eucharist reminds us of our journey from God to God, and the eucharistic food is more than a remembrance that God sustains us throughout our journey; the eucharistic food is our sustenance. We can only talk about the mysteries of life by adding analogy to analogy, in God 'we live and move and have our being.' By the use of such language as this we do not deny the reality of this transitory world: bread and wine are frail creatures of time; our days are gone like a shadow, the time of our years is swifter than thought; but through our use of things impermanent God vouchsafes to us the permanent. Bread and wine, frail creatures of time, when blessed become the doors to timelessness. The Eucharist is the moment in and out of time.

I would end by making a soliloquy. The celebrant is one of the company who live in and out of time. His unworthiness is never the test of value of the Eucharist. His unworthiness can be a cloud between the people and God; a translucent cloud, but nevertheless a cloud. Sometimes the priest's unholiness is expressed in the minute blasphemy of littleness, of living in a small world bounded by parochial and domestic walls. Our pilgrimage lies across trackless stretches of barren land, where no water is and where no bird sings . . . across the distance the horizon calls; our plans for security—personal, domestic, parochial or diocesan—are then like scraps of paper whirled in the wind. Holiness is a matter of both size and order. The size and order of the celebrant's life is to be expressed in his voice, his movements and his silences in the sanctuary. Elsewhere it is to be seen in his compassion and in his firmness; in a gaiety devoid of frivolity; in a seriousness that is never grim; in hope that is quite distinct from secular optimism; in faith without sentimentality; in charity without dissimulation.

Let me conclude this soliloquy with words that are not mine:

> A holy priest makes a fervent people;
> A fervent priest, a pious people;
> A pious priest, a decent people;
> A decent priest, a godless people. (1)

The Theology of Prayer

1. Faith and Knowledge

The great human questions—what am I? What am I to do? Am I my brother's keeper? Is he mine? Does it matter what I do?—drive us to despair or prayer.

Now we know in part, but fragmentary knowledge is real knowledge.

We walk by faith, not by sight. For St Paul the opposite of faith is not doubt but sight. That is, we walk by faith and knowledge but depend more on faith than on knowledge. Faith and knowledge grow up together and nourish one another.

Every time I say: 'I believe in God' I make an affirmation that I am a being capable of making an act of faith.

Theology is not a subject to be studied but a discipline which entails the maintenance of a special way of thinking, speaking and acting. Bishop Westcott held that theology is only pure when it is applied. In other words, we do not theologise about theology but we think theologically about all men and all things.

Theology normally begins in prayer, continues in thought and ends in prayer.

Theology shows that individuals and things cannot be understood in isolation but must be looked at in their context.

Prayer cannot be considered apart from the individual, the church and the world.

No scientist would be ready to give a literal description of the universe. No theologian should be ready to describe exactly what happens when a man prays. To give a literal description we would need to know all about the world of men and how God deals with it.

2. The World and the Church

What am I doing when I am praying? It is well not to be too curious. No man can think and pray at the same time and do both well.

What we do when we are not praying shapes what we do when we pray. What we do when we are praying shapes what we do when we are not praying. Theology safeguards these facts with its emphasis on man's responsibility for his actions.

Individuals, the world and the church live and move and have their being in God.

I do not believe in God because I believe in the world; I believe in the world because I believe in God who loves the world. I do not believe in God because I believe in the church; I believe in the church because I believe in God. I believe in the world and the church because I am sure that in them God provides the situation in which a man may be a man.

When I pray for the church and the world I find that I am praying for myself, and when I pray for myself I find I am praying for the world and the church.

'Those whom God hath joined together let no man put asunder.' The individual, the world and the church are one in God.

In God all things have their origin; he is to be thought of as the maker of words, bread, wine and prayers—all our operations are co-operations with him, and though the help we give him is fragmentary we know that fragmentary help is real help.

3. General Reflections

The theology of prayer does not tell me exactly what I am doing when I pray but tells me how to think of what I am doing when I pray.

Prayer is stillness, quietness, movement, sometimes depending on a form of words or a single word, or a mood which is more easily recognised than described. Prayer is a creative activity because it gives a person power and peace and vision. While prayer begins by paying attention to some particular thing or person it may end in starting a process beyond human control.

A conversation can turn into prayer in the form of a dialogue.

In public worship, worshippers are ministers of grace to one another. A man needs both solitude and society if he is to live fully. The one who is too solitary becomes distorted; the one who is too social is in danger of becoming busy and empty.

Both public and private worship are hard, and few there be who bear the hardship.

Prayer may be called: a relationship that includes all relationships; a longing for the experience that includes all experiences; a realisation that the knower, the known and the knowing are one; an adventure that takes me into mysterious parts of my being. Prayer may be called an expansion of my self-awareness which is another way of describing the feeling of having found God in myself and myself in him.

We must never be worried if we pray badly; it is better to pray badly than not to pray at all.

We must learn not to measure spiritual happenings by the clock. A person's most important experience may all be over in the flash of a second but the afterglow remains.

Our prayers will often disturb us, as through them we see more clearly the obligations consequent upon our relations with other people.

We find life rushed, noisy, never free from movement. If we are to remain spiritually alive we need determination and skill to train ourselves to be flexible, that is, to turn from work to prayer and back again without the work suffering from lack of concentration or the prayer becoming mechanical. It is not that the Christian is to leave people and the world to pray and be holy; he is to be holy wherever he is in the noise and disturbance of modern conditions.

Often prayer disturbs us by revealing to us that Christians are called not to goodness but to greatness.

4. Summary

Jesus said: 'When you pray, go into your room and shut the door and pray to your Father who is in secret; and your Father who sees in secret will reward you'.

God became man without ceasing to be God that men might be godly without ceasing to be men. (2)

Preaching Doctrine

Eloquence is the art of putting into words that which is extremely difficult to put into words. It is the minister of the Word's vocation to be eloquent in this sense. That eloquence cannot be without the adventure of holding doctrine in such a way that one is always in danger of losing one's grip of it. Our religion rests on the foundation of theism which can only be made real to the mind by continual meditation on the doctrine of creation, which puts one in danger of pantheism and a denial of the necessity of the Incarnation. It is only by reflection on the creative activity of God that the full glory of the Incarnation can be seen, for when every creative act is recognized as an act of revelation then it can be seen how the one act that is the revelation of revelations illuminates and is illuminated by all other acts of God. It is only by thinking emphatically about the humanity of our Lord that one can realise his divinity, while it is only by concentrated reflection on his divinity that the reality of his manhood is apprehended. In other words, meditation on his being must always be concerned both with his earthly ministry and his eternal sovereignty, because meditation is not part of a process that ends in a finished conclusion, it is the prelude to adoration of the mystery that is God. All theology begins in adoration and ends in adoration, but it can only end in adoration if emotion, imagination, intelligence are not stifled but used by the preacher in the pursuit of his calling, which may be described as an attempt to master words sufficiently to expound the truth which in mastering men frees them from the errors born in sin and from the errors that give birth to sins. And at this point one is led to remember that it is only by considering the power of God's grace that one begins to understand the nature of the human effort required in individual man's salvation; it is only by seriously considering the nature of this human effort that one begins to know the ceaseless activity of God in which all human action has its beginning. It is by devotion to Christ in the Blessed Sacrament that one discovers most fully that where the Word is not spoken the bread will not be broken. It is only through diligent attention to the necessity for the spoken word that the essential nature of the sacraments is realised—where the bread is not broken soon the Word will not be spoken. The importance of the ministry is most clearly seen when one is at the point of denying it; the significance of the Church's corporate life can best be seen at the point where one is about to deny it in emphasizing the value of the individual; the value of each individual is most clearly seen when one is about to deny it in affirming the value of the corporate. A truth is often capable of being most clearly seen when it is about to be denied.

The minister of the Word does his clearest thinking on the edges of error, he is most orthodox when on the point of coming to heretical conclusions. In a sense thinking means submitting to the movement of the mind, not blindly or mechanically but maintaining a remote control over the movement. This remote control is maintained by the Christian through constant reflection on the limits of his creatureliness in the light of his doctrine. The image for thinking is not movement within a square marked by firm thick lines but rather that of movement in a space bounded by distant but discernible boundaries. Doctrine is not held by suppression of thoughts that challenge its truth but by their proper development. Thoughts are not isolated happenings, nor are they like things that can be picked up and thrown away. Each thought is a movement within the movement of the whole mind, and enriches the mind as long as the movement of the mind remains under the remote control of the thinker. The mind is never static: it is always active, often in turmoil, sometimes almost stagnant but never motionless, and no Christian doctrine indicates that a man can completely master his mind by his own efforts; each can understand what these lines signify:

> I said to my soul, be still, and wait without hope
> For hope would be hope for the wrong thing: wait without love
> For love would be love of the wrong thing; there is yet faith

But the faith and the love and the hope are all in the waiting.
Wait without thought, for you are not ready for thought:
So the darkness shall be the light, and the stillness the dancing.[1]

The stillness is not made by immobility but by the rhythmic movements of a mind that waits in the dark: the waiting becomes the dance and the darkness the light. Ultimately doctrine can only be held by the movement of the whole mind in prayer, where prayer is understood as a habitual state with characteristic activities. The man of prayer, like every creative worker, holds all his powers in tension till he is 'ready for thought'. This is the poise, the active stillness of the creative mind, which no one can maintain indefinitely; from time to time the poise is lost, the stillness is gone and chaos reigns. Again and again order and law must be established, poise recovered and stillness remade. All speech that moves men was minted when some man's mind was poised and still.

To expound doctrine is not to teach a system of thought and then demonstrate that no experience can disturb it. It is not that doctrine is supremely important and that life proves its importance; it is that life is supremely important and doctrine illuminates it. The minister of the Word is called to be an expert in living rather than an expert in doctrine. At the command of the Lord he studies doctrine, he teaches it that people may have life and that they may have it more abundantly. As this chapter is showing, the way doctrine is held shapes the way it is expounded and the way it is held is determined by what a man thinks about its nature and content. Christian doctrine does not provide the answer to every question but the way to begin answering; doctrine does not tell a man what to think but how to think. Revelation is not a huge gift which makes man's work unnecessary and takes away from him all need of initiative. We are given sufficient knowledge to make the life of faith possible, but to live faithfully does not mean that one is given all knowledge, but rather the ability to live the full human life, being reconciled to and rejoicing in the reality of partial human knowledge. 'He that endures to the end shall be saved': he will have to endure finiteness, he will have to bear the burdens of perplexity and bewilderment, but a man can be steadied for this by all that doctrine shows him about his own nature. He has to be helped to keep in his mind that he is a creature, limited in knowledge and power, that he is a being made in the image of God and capable of relationship with him, that he is a sinner in constant need of forgiveness. These three facts must be kept before his mind at the same time, while he considers the implications of the threefold commandment that is at the centre of our religion, namely, 'Thou shalt love the Lord thy God with all thy heart, with all thy mind and with all thy soul and with all thy strength . . . thou shalt love thy neighbour as thyself.' That is, love God, love your neighbour, love yourself. To love yourself is to think the highest thoughts about yourself, to realise your value as a unique individual and your ability to bring new things into being. The revelation of human greatness is painful when seen in individual terms, it shows the enormity of wasting life on trivialities and the hideousness of the corruption of creative ability which we call sin. The potential goodness of man must be emphasized in such a way that he sees his sinfulness without thinking that he is to regard himself as being unredeemable. There can be no formula for this; the way to attempt it lies both in the minister of the Word's belief about the nature

[1] T. S. Eliot, *Four Quartets*, Faber & Faber, 1944, p. 19.

of doctrine and its content and in his understanding of and relationship with the individuals and groups among whom he moves. No one lectures abstractly on doctrine; one talks it to people who are fellow human beings if not also fellow church members; always there is a common tie which makes conversation possible and has much to do with its form. Relationships are living, changing things which make it impossible for any minister of the Word to depend on a few invariable forms for his use in saying what he has to say. The mental and psychic atmosphere of the day decides the pattern of his secret reflections about doctrine. The more compassionate a pastor is, the more he is in danger of speaking heretically, but that danger is inevitable if he is to discover a way of making himself clear to the men and women of his generation with that degree of clarity which his subject permits. But who can be entirely coherent about the whole of life? That is the size of the preacher's subject, but he can hope that doctrinal integrity will sharpen the edges of his intelligibility sufficiently for it to cut through the traffic that blocks the minds of so many who listen.

Perhaps the most significant consideration of doctrine for the minister of the Word is that which is concerned with all that the doctrine of creation implies. This has a direct effect on his whole conception of preaching and it also enables him to speak in the pulpit and out of the pulpit in the ways that are most expedient for this generation. To take the first point: belief in preaching, or indeed in meaningful conversation, has doctrinal roots or else it has no roots. To go on believing in the value of human speech and the possibility of communication can only be justified by what one believes about the nature of reality. More than that, human speech is not fully appreciated till it is recognized as a part of creation just as much as landscapes and shifting clouds. That is, no poem or sermon comes into being without the divine initiation. A poem or sermon is made in much the same way as bread is made. Bread ultimately consists of the energy of the sun, the sustenance given by rain and soil and the mysterious energy of life within the seeds sown by men. The loaf on the table is there because God ceaselessly provides all the raw materials necessary including the psychic energy which enables men to work and co-operate with one another. The making of bread is a significant human action which we proclaim every time we reverently place the common bread on the altar; this common unconsecrated bread is only less wonderful than the consecrated bread. Before the altar we are reminded that man does not live by bread alone. He needs the things that are made by human speech which are nourishment for his mind. Music and the visual arts have their place in life, but whenever speech is absent or deficient the human spirit dwindles and the human mind is bewildered and becomes brutal. The utterances of men are possible because God ceaselessly brings into being the raw materials necessary for their making: we can neither contemplate fulness of human life nor the possibility of our religion bringing that fulness to perfection without the arts, and in particular without the art of ordered speech. (3)

Listening to a Sermon

Listening to a sermon is like attending to a work of art. To attend to a work of art is not to share an identical experience with the person who made it. If you were to talk to him about your experience of it he would be surprised at the significance you saw in his work and he would be amazed at the intentions you imputed to him. The poet gives his poem a title as the merest guide to those who pay attention, but not in an attempt to arrange that all who pay heed may see and feel only what he wishes them to see and feel. To examine a work of art is always to examine yourself; to know a work of art is to know yourself, though, paradoxically, it is only possible to know a work of art if you know yourself. Knowing is here used not so much in the sense of acquiring factual knowledge as in the sense of acquaintanceship. To be acquainted with yourself is to be at ease with yourself in recognizing the manifold movements of thoughts and wishes within you and to be ready to extend the area of consciousness through the experiences that make this extension possible. Attention to a work of art is one of the experiences which extends self-awareness; the height of this attention comes where there is the intimacy of acquaintanceship which T. S. Eliot describes in speaking of

> '. . . music heard so deeply
> That it is not heard at all, but you are the music
> While the music lasts.'

In the case of preaching, preacher, congregation and sermon are one while the preaching lasts, and in their unity the divine power moves, affecting them in ways that can be neither commanded nor foretold. (4)

Word and Sacrament

> We who must die demand a miracle.
> How could the Eternal do a temporal act,
> The Infinite become a finite fact?
> Nothing can save us that is possible:
> We who must die demand a miracle.[1]

The miracle takes place whenever the Word is spoken and the bread is broken, for these are cosmic timeless acts affecting the entire physical universe and changing the whole of humanity. When these things are done the smallest church becomes an everywhere and an hour becomes a timeless moment. The Word resounds in the words spoken, it is the meaning of the meaning of what is said, it is the power of the release men know when great and terrible truths are spoken, it is the strength of minds delivered from the narrowness of time, it is the mirror in which men see themselves and are saved from the trivialities and folly of their sins. The bread that is broken is the bread of truth and the bread of life, it is the food of the full-grown, 'whosoever eateth of this bread shall never hunger'. Here is no magic but the miracle by which those who must die shall live; this is the temporal act of the Eternal, this is the Infinite becoming a finite fact, this is the moment of full human consciousness—a moment unlike all other moments, a moment when we express our connectedness with all things and all men in God 'in whom we live and move and have our being'. Commonplace words are taken and transformed through the speaking and the listening, common bread is taken and transformed through the blessing, the breaking and the sharing of it. Through the Word

[1] W. H. Auden, 'For the Time Being' from *Collected Longer Poems*, Faber & Faber, 1968.

spoken and the bread broken the many are given power to be one through the intensification of the individuality of each and the sharpening of the identity of each; a scrap of bread broken from one loaf is given to each, the Word spoken is directly addressed to each and yet belongs to all, for all belong to it.

We do not say that the ministry of the Word is more important than the ministry of the sacrament or that the ministry of the sacrament is more important than the ministry of the Word. The two ministries are complementary, rather, two expressions of one ministry. Whenever the minister of the Word prepares to preach he is to remember that he is also the priest at the altar; whenever the priest prepares himself to celebrate the eucharist he must remember that he is also the minister of the Word. His preparation for both consists in all that is entailed in his habitual reverence for common words and common bread. Our use of them is a participation in God's creative work: we take and transform what he forms, so discovering the wonder of human speech and the marvels of human manufacture. In the processes of manufacture man is changed by what he changes. We grow in mind, we grow in understanding of one another, we grow in realisation of the powers in the universe which are outside human control. Creative work can be a sort of worship; it can also be a blasphemy: bread can be blessed on the altar or it can be reserved in the market for those who are rich enough to buy it; it can be used as a bribe or a weapon.

Words are created things just as loaves are; the making of them is similar. They are not made without the divine work or without the work of man. Before there can be the perfect order of speech there is the ceaseless human labour in the making of words; there are times when new words are to be brought into language, there are times when technical words have to be brought into common usage, there are times when words, once good, must be replaced because they have become defaced in use. Words are not static things that men make and use like bricks. Words are made in the image of those who make them and use them, showing the marks of human creativity and restlessness, of human nobility and depravity. Words can be used to bless and to curse, to flatter, to intimidate or to manifest the truth through the beauty of rhythm and the pattern of meaning. Words are nurture for the mind just as bread is for the body, and both have their origin in God without whom no thing or word is made and used. God supplies the raw materials out of which words are made, but the transformation of the raw materials is the work of man's imagination, memory, intelligence and determination; the psychic energy by which all mental effort is made is sustained by the ceaseless activity of God 'in whom we live and move and have our being'.

> The Lord who created must wish us to create
> And employ our creation again in His service
> Which is already His service in creating.[1]

In the pulpit and at the altar the minister of the Word takes created things, words and bread, and in their use performs deeds he never fully understands. To take part in the Church's liturgical activity through sermon and eucharist is a participation in events that cannot be defined but only incompletely described. Physical descriptions can be made: a physicist would say that every

[1] T. S. Eliot, 'Choruses from "The Rock"' from *Collected Poems 1909–1962*, Faber & Faber, 1963.

word spoken sets in motion a minute change in the physical universe which has endless physical ramifications; he would say the same about the breaking of bread in the eucharistic action. A psychologist would make a description in psychic terms; he would say that the very fact of people gathering in one place would cause psychic changes in all of them through the interplay of suggestions consciously and unconsciously given and received. He would go on to explain that what was said alters both the speaker and those who listen in a variety of ways not to be uncovered by a rational analysis of the utterance. He would draw attention to the effect of the spoken words on the whole of humanity through the speaker and listeners. Whenever one man speaks to another, both of them affect all other lives in varying degrees through their corporate act. A psychological description of the eucharist, while drawing attention to certain truths about it, would be equally inadequate; every kind of scientific description would have many limitations. The nature of sermon and eucharist can only be tentatively described; no description could presume to delineate the divine operation in each, which operation cannot be seen within simple terms of discernible cause and effect. In sermon and sacrament we are given what we are too ignorant to desire and unworthy to deserve. Here is not magic but miracle, the Eternal doing a temporal act, the Infinite becoming a finite fact, without ceasing to be eternal or ceasing to be infinite. That is, God acting in time without ceasing to be God in order that men may be godly without ceasing to be men. The Gospel discloses the mystery that this can be, and we are left to wonder and adore, bearing in faith the fragmentariness of our knowledge but rejoicing in its reality.

We are not to live in a closed esoteric circle, we are to be ready to encourage and answer whatever questions men may ask us about the way of life which has its origin and power in sacrament, sermon and Scriptures. Our answers will be as fragmentary as our knowledge and our language ambiguous but used with the precision that is born of faith, nurtured in humility and matured by constant reflection on the truths of revelation. For ministers of the Word this means frequent remembrance of the cosmic timeless acts they are given to perform when the Word resounds in their words, when with frail human hands they break the bread of life in the name of him who is the way, the truth and the life, without whom nothing is made that is made. (5)

NOTES / SOURCES

1. R. E. C. Browne, *Love of the World: Meditations* (ed. Ian Corbett), Worthing, West Sussex, 1986, pp. 96–101
2. Ibid., pp. 117–19
3. R. E. C. Browne, *The Ministry of the Word*, London, 1958, pp. 45–50
4. Ibid., p. 75
5. Ibid., pp. 124–7

Mother Mary Clare SLG 1906–1988

Mother Mary Clare, the daughter of Charles Henry Sampson, a Fellow of Brasenose College, Oxford, entered the Sisters of the Love of God, an enclosed, contemplative sisterhood at Fairacres, Oxford, in 1941, and served as Reverend Mother from 1954 to

1973. Influenced by the Carmelite tradition of spirituality and the guidance of Cowley Fathers such as Father Lucius Cary, and Father Gilbert Shaw (q.v.), she exercised a notable ministry of spiritual guidance both within and outside her community.

Prayer the Gateway to the Vision of God

Prayer is the gateway to the vision of God for which we were created. It is the means for free and conscious intercourse between the creature and his creator, and it expresses the union between the two. It is the art of spiritual living, and it will be incomplete if it includes only the presence of God without the necessary complement of the presence of man. It is an entirely false dichotomy which distinguishes between prayer as a purely Godward or personal activity on the one hand, and on the other as a compassionate involvement with the world's pain, insecurity and frustration which would seem to make prayer in the old, traditional sense of the word irrelevant. When we pray, we are being united with Jesus Christ in his own redemptive action; we are being drawn into the great cosmic battle against evil, which is to bring into the here and now of our daily lives the fruits of Christ's victorious passion. (1)

Prayer and Conversion of Life

The first lesson we have to learn about prayer is that it is God's activity in us, and not a self-activated process of our own. The Desert Fathers, those great masters of the spiritual life, knew all about the essential condition of learning to pray. They called it 'purity of heart', without which there could be no true *metanoia* or conversion. We can pray only if our hearts are truly pure in the sense of Jesus' teaching in the Sermon on the Mount, where the pure in heart shall see God. Prayer and daily life are individable. We must learn to pray as we are, and accept ourselves as we are, and not as the ideal people we would like to imagine ourselves to be. We must grow to understand ourselves and accept that it is at the time when our natural passions are most active, and our minds most distracted, that we can grow to a knowledge of ourselves as real persons. That is the point of tension at which we must offer ourselves to God in prayer.

At the beginning of our learning to pray, therefore, we must relate prayer to conversion of life. Prayer, which is the fruit of true conversion, is an activity, an adventure, and sometimes a dangerous one, since there are occasions when it brings neither peace nor comfort, but challenge, conflict and new responsibility. This is why so many old ways of praying, and books about prayer, seem to have let us down. Too often when we used them we were hoping to get something for ourselves from prayer, perhaps security or a growing sensible realisation and knowledge of God. To seek such things in prayer is a mistake. The essential heart of prayer is the throwing away of ourselves in self-oblation to God, so that he can do with us what he wills. Any form of prayer which does not incite a costing giving in love soon becomes sterile, dry and a formal duty. (2)

Contemplation

When we first enter upon the way of silence, the mere lack of noise may be more disturbing than the continuous noise of the radio or the roaring of jet planes overhead, for in the exterior silence we find inner noise cutting across the attention we desire to give to God. This need not cause very much worry, but when we become aware of it, we should return gently to the still centre of our being where God is at work imperceptibly but surely.

Silence is the doorway into the need of the world, the condition of the prayer which arises out from the heart of the universe, because it expresses the love of Christ, crucified and risen for the world. Such profound prayer, however, is not concerned only with the world as a whole, but also with the most mundane details of our ordinary, everyday lives. Prayer is not a part-time occupation, and there can no more be part-time contemplatives than part-time Christians. Without the contemplative dimension in our lives, we cannot be fully human. This contemplative dimension is the fruit of our willingness to meet the discipline of learning to wait in silence and stillness, as well as the boredom and loneliness and sometimes the apparent emptiness which confront us in the waiting. Contemplation and action are both necessary to basic stability. There is a need to take regular times of quiet in order to be disciplined in the generous giving of self in our activity.

Interior peace is the fruit of Christ's overcoming and of the Holy Spirit's outpouring. This peace is the ground of Christian contemplation. T. S. Eliot's quest 'to apprehend the point of intersection of the timeless with time' is not a vague anticipation of the confrontation with God which will come to us all at the moment of death. Contemplation, in the Christian sense, is a living in the *now* of daily life in preparation for that moment of truth; it is a living in the realisation of God's love and his claim upon us. Indeed, any experience of the reality of God rests upon the belief that we are able to love him because his love has created and redeemed us. For the Christian, the end of man is union with God in love, and we are meant to know something of that love in this present life. We are able to know it by prayer and contemplation and in loving relationship one with another in God. As St Paul tells us, we can know only in part, but we could know so much more than we do if we could face the cost of what a life lived in union with Christ demands; if we could open ourselves to the power of the Holy Spirit to enlarge and deepen those latent powers and potentialities that our human spirit possesses. After all, the Christian life is directed to a goal beyond all human expectation, a goal which can be attained only by strength far beyond our unaided human capacity. Therefore, contemplation is a gift to be received, to be prepared for, rather than something we can train ourselves to do. 'The Holy Spirit whom the Father will send in my name will teach you everything and will call to mind all that I have told you,' said Jesus. And St Paul said, 'Bear fruit in active goodness of every kind, and grow in the knowledge of God so that Christ may present us before himself as dedicated men.' Christian contemplation is incarnational, not a negative journey inwards, but the growth of unity of life and prayer, an increase in the knowledge of God shown forth by the wholeness of consecrated life. (3)

Listening Silence

Though speech is the most obvious means of communication we have, it is silence and listening which do more than anything to unite us with God and with each other. It is not our activity which blocks the lines of communication between ourselves and God, and between ourselves and those around us, but our egoism. Listening silence can be a means of purification. Only a listening silence can lead to a stilling of the mind, a cessation of the chatter surging up from the unconscious. The cleansing of memory is that aspect of purgation which makes space for the work of listening, which is our part in the dialogue of prayer with God. There is no point in trying to beat the mind into a shape of concentration: that is an effort of will very different from waiting on the power of God to draw all our faculties into unity. It is the uprising of love in the heart, the desire to belong utterly to God that cleanses us, and during this process it is for God to deal with the stirrings of our natural being. It is only when a soul is wholly given to Christ to be formed in charity that there is a complete quieting of self. Only in the willingness to listen in silence can God's will be heard. (4)

NOTES / SOURCES

1. Mother Mary Clare SLG, *Encountering the Depths* (ed. Ralph Townsend), London, 1981, p. 1
2. Ibid., pp. 4–5
3. Ibid., pp. 24–5
4. Ibid., p. 38

Emani Sambayya   1907–1972

A Brahmin convert from South India, Sambayya had university degrees from Calcutta, Serampore, and Union Seminary, New York. He was ordained after further studies at Westcott House, Cambridge, and after a short curacy in Bombay, spent most of the next thirty years in Calcutta, chiefly at Bishop's College, where he was successively a lecturer, Bursar, and, for the last ten years of his working life, Principal.

The Genius of the Anglican Communion: an Indian Perspective

For nineteen years I was brought up in the best traditions of Brahminism. In my twentieth year I accepted Jesus Christ as my personal Saviour, and was baptized by a Methodist minister. The greatest joy of those early years was the fellowship with the Living Christ. For about ten years after my baptism I lived a life detached from the Church. Sometimes it seemed as if the S.C.M., which I was serving in those days, had taken the place of Church in my life. This was, no doubt, due to my inability to appreciate the corporate nature of the Christian religion. In 1937, when I became aware of the call to the sacred Ministry, I was uncertain as to the particular branch of the Church in which I should serve as a minister. I was unable to understand why there should be so many Churches when they seemed very much alike. There was one Church, however, which attracted me since my college days; that was the Anglican Church. The Anglican worship, based on *The Book of Common Prayer*, makes an irresistible appeal to me. However, the opposition of the Anglican priest towards Intercommunion used to cause me deep indignation. The men who, through the holiness of Christ, helped me to discover my vocation to the sacred Ministry, happened to be Anglicans. I feel that it is neither by a happy accident nor by my choice that I became a priest in the Anglican Communion. It is through obedience to a definite call that I am what I am.

The genius and the enduring character of Anglicanism are seen in its worship, which is based on *The Book of Common Prayer*. To one coming from Brahminism, with its denial of reality to the world and to the individual, worship in the Anglican Communion is a most moving and uplifting experience. The recital of the Creed at every service opens up a new world for me. As I recite the Creed I find that I have a new centre of life in the household of God. The Creeds proclaim the great things which God has done for me . . . Far from being unreal, my life here and now is full of meaning to me because it is precious in the sight of God. This new truth gradually grows on me as I worship with the Church . . . Though I am thrilled at the discovery of a new centre of life in the Church, Anglican worship does not leave any chance either for developing or indulging in what is called 'individualism in religion.' It is often remarked that an Indian Christian lacks church sense, and that he is an individualist in religion. This is largely true; and the alarming lack of church sense in an Indian Christian is partly due to his Hindu heritage, and partly to the faulty instruction in so many of our churches. However that may be, the Prayer Book services leave me in no doubt that I am always worshipping with the Church. It is impossible to miss the 'we' and 'us' throughout its services. Thus in the Christian faith I not only find a new centre of life, but also I am incorporated into a vast worshipping community, partly visible, and partly invisible . . .

Now I want to say how, as an Anglican, I have come to learn that the Christian life is a call to live a supernatural life. In the days when I was preparing for baptism a very interesting proposition was presented to me by my friends and relations: 'What is the point of your joining the Christian community when you can easily remain in your own home and live a Christian life there?' After the same fashion I used to argue with myself before I became a priest, 'Let me first practise in my own life what I intend to preach from the pulpit.' It was only some time after my ordination that I was able to realise the fallacy of these two arguments. *The Book of Common Prayer* makes it abundantly clear that the supernatural life to which I am called in my baptism is possible only as I live my life in the Church, and that the Church is constantly helping me to grow in holiness. The call to a total dedication of life proceeds from the liturgical life of the Church. This seems to be the note on which the Offices of *The Book of Common Prayer* end. The daily growth in the life of prayer and conformity to the Person of Christ are not the lonely experiences of a Christian living in isolation. Such a life is lived 'in Christ,' and the whole Church is ready to foster growth and holiness with its pastoral priesthood, the sacramental system, the Church calendar, and the ministry of the Word.

NOTES / SOURCES

E. Sambayya, 'The Genius of the Anglican Communion' in E. R. Morgan and Roger Lloyd (eds.) *The Mission of the Anglican Communion*, London, 1948, pp. 18, 19, 23

Frank Woods   1907–1992

Sir Frank Woods, Archbishop of Melbourne from 1957 to 1977, was one of Australia's most beloved church leaders. An English suffragan bishop at the time of his election, sight unseen, to Melbourne, he came of a long line of distinguished English churchmen of the Evangelical tradition. Though he remained quintessentially English to the end, he came to love his adopted homeland passionately, and chose to stay in Melbourne after his retirement. His churchmanship had broadened considerably during his 20-year episcopate in Melbourne, a time when the diocese itself took on a strong appreciation of Anglican diversity. Woods was a great champion of ecumenism, and was deeply saddened at the end of his life that his high hopes of union with the Roman Catholic Church seemed doomed.

The Demand of Christ

'Which of you, intending to build a tower, sitteth not down first, and counteth the cost, whether he have sufficient to finish it? . . . Or what king, going to make war against another king, sitteth not down first, and consulteth whether he be able with ten thousand to meet him that cometh against him with twenty thousand?' (Luke 14. 28–31) These verses are set by Luke in the context of a discourse on the cost of personal discipleship. They are introduced by the demand that those who would be disciples must bear the cross, and they are concluded by a similar demand: 'So likewise, whosoever he be of you that forsaketh not all that he hath, he cannot be my disciple' (Luke 14. 33).

Here is a demand not that we count the cost but that we accept it. It is an appeal for complete personal dedication regardless of the cost. Just because I am going on to apply these parables in a different sense, I want to begin by making the same appeal. Planning, giving of money, weighing our resources, diocesan and parochial organisation, questions of man-power, the provision of churches and schools, of halls and clubs, yes, and estimating the power of the enemy, all these must come into the picture when we weigh up the resources that God has given us, but they will count for nothing unless there be first the Fellowship of the Holy Spirit, the company of committed people, if you prefer it, of surrendered or converted people, who have accepted the challenge of Our Lord to a total discipleship.

The word you use to describe it does not matter: conversion, commitment, surrender, rebirth—they all mean the same. What matters is the personal devotion to a personal Lord, a devotion which will no doubt find expression in active Christian service, but which is itself not activity but a deep quality of heart and soul, a hidden inward spirit, itself a gift of God, which St Paul calls faith, and which is nurtured by the staple food of prayer and sacrament and scripture.

Of this essential condition we all, I as well as you, need constantly to be reminded, and not least when we are gathered as we are this day, with ceremony and in strength, for an enthronement service. Unless the King of Kings and the Lord of Lords is enthroned in our hearts this service means nothing—and worse than nothing because it would be a lying parable. I dare to re-dedicate myself, and I beg of you all to rededicate yourselves here and now to this work of the enthronement of Christ Jesus in the hearts of His people. The strength of the Church at any time in its history has been in depth rather than breadth, in its dedicated few rather than in its many adherents. Our Lord's call to take up the cross is incomprehensible to any who think of the Christian faith merely as a moral guide to action. It is that, but it only becomes that when it is something far more than that. In such a civilisation as ours, where Christian standards of conduct are accepted with lip service, and where centuries of Christian teaching have moulded the frame-work of our society, it is all too easy to forget that the whole could be swept away in a few generations were it not for the hard core of converted men and women who know that the most important moments of the day are those spent on their knees; that they are sinners needing Christ's atonement; that they are poor and hungry, needing the food of eternal life. These are they who are in the world and yet not of it; who, having had a foretaste of the End for which God made them, long for that fullness which comes only from Him who filleth all in all. (1)

The Church and the Challenge of the Contemporary World

Here then is the question: you are not only called to personal devotion: you are called to a stupendous task, to be the Body of Christ in society, in the nation and in the world; to be, if you prefer St Peter's language, 'a royal priesthood, an holy nation, a peculiar people' (1 Peter 2. 9). What resources has the Lord who calls you put at your disposal?

Before we try to answer this question we may as well take stock of the situation and look the facts in the face. Some of them are ugly.

The first is that we can no longer hold the belief that the christianisation of the world will advance inexorably and inevitably 'till the earth shall be filled with the glory of God as the waters cover the sea'. The plain fact is that Christian countries can be dechristianised. 1,000 years ago Islam reduced the Christian civilisation of the Mediterranean basin to a heap of rubble. Today, in what our grandfathers had hoped would be the great Christian century, the Church's advance is actively opposed by the rulers of more than half the entire population of the globe. Doors which were open to the evangelist are now shut. Industrial materialism has caused the proletarian masses of what was once Christian Europe to lose contact with the Church and to become themselves objects of evangelism. Furthermore the birth rate is outstripping the conversion rate. There are more non-Christians in the world today than there were 50 years ago and the Christian percentage of the huge populations of India and the Far East is actually smaller than it was. Also, most sinister of all, the thought-forms of the rising generation, even in so-called Christian countries, are such as to make the great Christian concepts unintelligible. Such words as salvation, atonement, miracle, sacrament, grace, redemption, sacrifice—these words need explanation to our generation as if they came from an alien culture. The very foundation of knowledge is called in question by the prevailing school of modern philosophy. Theology, once the queen of sciences, is held to be intellectually barely respectable, and the knowledge of God declared to be guessing in the dark.

There is another fact of which we in Australia need to take note. The west has lost the moral leadership of the world. In the eyes of the seething millions of India and the East, yes, and of Africa, too, Christianity is not a message of peace and goodwill: it is synonymous with a civilization which has resorted to war twice in 50 years, war more devastating and terrible than any before in all history. Furthermore, in this same Europe, unspeakable atrocities, far outstripping in enormity and cruelty the fabulous atrocities of ancient Rome or modern savage have been committed by a nation which might well have claimed to be intellectually the most advanced in the world. No wonder the East no longer looks to the West for leadership, and in so far as the Christian faith is labelled as a Western importation the East will put up every resistance to it. We in Australia who are a Western outpost in an Eastern world are bound to observe these hard facts when we seek to commend the Gospel to our neighbours.

What shall we say then to these things? We shall say, first of all, that if God has cut away from under our feet every ground of confidence, Blessed be God! If in our day He has shown us how morally bankrupt is a godless civilization, Blessed be God! If He has taught us that it does not befit His glory to be attached to any merely national culture, Blessed be God! If He is teaching us that two thousand years have not been enough for us to be given more than a very small part of the riches of Christ, that we have hardly begun to know what Catholicity means, that the good things which He hath prepared for them that love Him can as yet be only dimly discerned, that our Western minds, unaided by the insights of Russian and Eastern faith can only apprehend the dim outlines of the glorious truth, then I say again, Blessed be God! He is forcing us out of ourselves, away from our self-reliance, onto Himself, onto prayer, miracle, revelation and inspiration, onto incarnation and resurrection. God veils the sun and plunges us into darkness only that we may learn to stretch out our hands to Him and to Him alone.

We shall say, secondly, that the tool which God has made to deal with this situation is His Church. We are members of it and cannot stand back and survey it, much less judge it, except we judge ourselves. But if we know the vastness of the task and our own impotence to deal with it, then we may ask for and expect to receive the guidance and blessing of the Holy Spirit, and be able to perceive at least that part of the truth which God sees fit to tell us. To our day it has been given to rediscover the Church, in the New Testament, in history and as part of the very Gospel itself. To three aspects of the Church I would draw your attention: to the pastoral ministry of its clergy, to the royal priesthood of its laity, and to its newly won catholicity. (2)

Become like Children

The words of Scripture I would ask you to consider with me this Christmas morning are these: 'The disciples came to Jesus saying, "Who is the greatest in the kingdom of heaven?" And calling a little child to him, he put him in the midst of them and said, "Truly I say to you, unless you turn and become like children, you will never enter the kingdom of heaven" ' (Matthew 18. 1–3). That is a hard saying for all of us sophisticated grown-ups. Our Lord said very much the same thing to Nicodemus, the much respected city councillor of Jerusalem, and he pooh-poohed the idea. 'How can a man be born again when he is old?' (Matthew 3. 4) he scornfully replied. And yet there is no doubt at all that you need a bit of childlike spirit really to enjoy Christmas as it ought to be enjoyed; and not only need it—you find yourself possessing it. Thank goodness, grown-ups don't find it as hard as all that to join hands round the tree and sing with their three-year-old

> Away in a manger, no crib for his bed
> the little Lord Jesus laid down his sweet head.
> The stars in the bright sky looked down where he lay,
> the little Lord Jesus asleep on the hay.

No, it isn't mercifully so difficult as some people seem to imagine to become at least a little, and for a short time, like children. Indeed we all enjoy letting ourselves go at times and being a little ridiculous. No doubt God made us like that so that we should be able to enjoy the deepest secrets of His love. The fact is that there is something supremely ridiculous about the whole of the Christian faith. That is why it is easier and more suitable to sing about it than to talk about it.

> He came down to earth from heaven,
> who is God and Lord of all;
> and his shelter was a stable
> and his cradle was a stall;
> with the poor and meek and lowly
> lived on earth our Saviour holy.

Of course it's ridiculous that the King of Kings and the Lord of Lords should have such a home; and not ridiculous only; the Moslem would tell you that the very idea is blasphemous. To allow yourself to imagine that the Almighty Creator of the universe could so demean himself—why, the thought is preposterous. And yet the carols pile it on:

> Our God, heaven cannot hold him nor earth sustain;
> heaven and earth shall flee away when he comes to reign:
> in the bleak midwinter, a stable place sufficed
> the Lord God almighty, Jesus Christ.
>
> Enough for him whom cherubim worship night and day
> a breastful of milk and a mangerful of hay;
> enough for him, whom angels fall down before,
> the ox and ass and camel which adore.

And if this sort of thing is shocking to the Moslem, it is equally shocking to the Hindu and the Buddhist, but for a different reason. To them God is not a personal being at all and here are we Christians not only calling God by the name of Jesus, a man, a great man and a prophet, but suggesting that:

> the great Creator makes
> himself a house of clay.
> A robe of virgin flesh he takes
> which he will wear for ay.

Do you get that? Let me repeat it: 'which he will wear for ay.' This God whom we worship is so intensely personal that he has kept the humanity which he took upon him and has taken it back with him to heaven. Nothing could be more personal than that. Children are notoriously personal. They don't think in abstract but in concrete terms. If you are to begin to understand the Christian faith you must be sufficiently like a child to think of God not as First Cause nor as

Universal Essence not as the All pervading Something but as the personal God: deeply mysterious indeed (none of us here has more than begun to understand the mystery of the Godhead) but was there ever anything more mysterious than a person?

> Hark, hark! the wise eternal Word
> like a weak infant cries
> in form of servant is the Lord
> and God in cradle lies.

God in cradle lies. It could not be put more starkly. The children don't find it impossible and if you and I accept it, then, thank God, we have been given a little of what Jesus called becoming like children. (3)

NOTES / SOURCES

1. Frank Woods, *Sermons and Addresses: Forward in Depth*, Melbourne, 1987, pp. 32–3
2. Ibid., pp. 34–6
3. Ibid., pp. 78–80

Frederick Donald Coggan   1909–2000

Educated at Merchant Taylors School and St John's College, Cambridge (where he read Oriental Languages), Donald Coggan was formed in the Evangelical tradition. Ordained in 1934 to St Mary's, Islington, three years later he took up a teaching post at Wycliffe College, Toronto. He returned to England in 1944 on his appointment as Principal of the London College of Divinity and from there was consecrated as Bishop of Bradford in 1956. Appointed Archbishop of York in 1961, he moved to Canterbury as successor to Archbishop Michael Ramsey in 1974, retiring in 1980. Possessing a special gift of biblical exposition, he was a clear and appreciated teacher both in office and in retirement.

Mary

If Matthew, in his stories of the infancy of Jesus, focuses his attention on the person of Joseph (Matthew 1. 18–25), Luke concentrates on the person of Mary. He is expert in telling a story. He is a doctor with a deep sensitivity. With great delicacy he looks at the conception and birth of Jesus as it were through the eyes of Mary, and enters into the troubled wonder with which she greeted the fact of her pregnancy. The angel seeks to reassure her—'Greetings, most favoured one! The Lord is with you.' But Mary is troubled—what does that greeting mean? 'Do not be afraid, Mary, for God has been gracious to you.' The bewilderment persists—'How can this be? I am still a virgin.' Then, deep within her comes the conviction that she is not alone—'The Holy Spirit will come upon you, and the power of the Most High will overshadow you . . . God's promises can never fail' (Luke 1. 35–37). It was like the calm which comes after a storm has blown itself out. Mary's reply is the more powerful for its superb simplicity: 'I am the Lord's servant; may it be as you have said.'

'The Lord's servant.' Here is Mary as the Servant-Mother. Hold on to that reply and ponder it. For it may be that it gives us a clue—the clue?—to the meaning of her son's life and death. The Servant-Mother was about to bear him who, above all others, was to be the servant of the Lord.

Who knows the influence of a mother on her unborn child? Here is a world of mystery which is still not wholly understood. But is it not possible that something of the concept of dedicated servanthood which was at the very heart of this young pregnant woman 'got through' to the child as yet unborn, and became an integral part in the shaping of his manhood and his ministry? There may be more in this than has been generally recognised.

Be that as it may, of this was may be certain. Mary saw, with a God-given clarity, at the moment of her greatest crisis, that servanthood lies at the very centre of the meaning of life as God intends it to be lived. Servanthood, obedience, in the great crises of life and in the little decisions of everyday, Mary saw as things of first importance. And so she doubtless taught the little boy on her lap, at her knee, through all his formative years. What greater prayer could she offer for her son than that he might grow up to be a servant of the Lord—possibly (did she glimpse it as she pondered on these things in her heart?) he might be even *the* servant of the Lord.

One of the greatest gifts that a mother can give to her children is not only to pray for them but, from their earliest years, to teach them to pray. We may be sure that Mary's little boy was not very old when he began to pray the prayer which his mother used when first she knew she was pregnant: 'I am the Lord's servant; may it be to me as you have said', or, to put it more simply and shortly, 'Your will be done'. As the boy grew older, she taught him what it meant to think of God as king, to see life lived under his kingship as the only life worth living. She taught him to pray: 'Your kingdom come'. Out of her own experience of life and prayer, she learned to pray. Out of that same experience she taught her son to pray: 'Your kingdom come, your will be done', and to do so, not grudgingly but exultingly.

It is not stretching our imagination too far to suggest that we owe to Mary those two basic clauses which come at the beginning of her son's prayer—'Your kingdom come, your will be done.'

What a debt we owe her! (1)

Paul at his Prayers

Paul the *activist*? Yes, intrepid traveller, eager to reach the world for Christ: 'I must see Rome' (Acts 19. 21) and perhaps Spain? Paul the *controversialist*? Yes, arguing at Athens, rebuking in Galatia, organising at Corinth. Paul the *sufferer*? Yes, beaten with rods, imprisoned, shipwrecked, martyred. But Paul the *man of prayer*? That is not so obvious. We must look carefully at Paul at his prayers.

There are enough prayers strewn across his letters to give us material to work with. That in itself is suggestive. Prayer and letter-writing go hand in hand. Perhaps Paul is setting us an example at this point. Perhaps he is saying: 'Letter-writing is a ministry. If, somehow, it can be intertwined with prayer, it can be a powerful ministry.' If our hearing apparatus is tuned in carefully, we might overhear him as he prays. 'Hush, hush, whisper who dares? Paul the apostle is saying his prayers'—to misquote A. A. Milne.

Prayer was no new thing to Paul when he became a Christian. As a Jewish boy with a devout Jewish background, he came of a praying people. Any nation that can produce the Book of Psalms or the drama of Job has something to teach the world about intercourse with God. But prayer was given a new dimension and a new intimacy when Saul of Tarsus became Paul the apostle. That moment when, at his baptism and entry into the church at Damascus, he came up out of the water and into the resurrection-life, he shouted with his fellow baptisands, 'Abba! Father!' Before that, he had watched Stephen in the bloody moments of his martyrdom, and had heard him praying 'Lord Jesus, receive my spirit' (Acts 7. 59) and at the very moment of death, 'Lord, do not hold this sin against them' (Acts 7. 60).

There is a delightful phrase in Paul's letters which tells us much about the man himself, about his pastoral care of people and churches, and about the interplay of letter-writing and prayer. Writing to the Romans (Romans 1. 9), to the Ephesians and others in his circular letter (Ephesians 1. 16), to the Thessalonians (1 Thessalonians 1. 2), and to the slave-owner Philemon (Philemon 4), he says that he '*mentions*' them in his prayers. It is as if he paused in his dictation or in his writing, and mentioned one here or a group there, the image of whose faces had just flashed onto the screen of his mind. He paused. It hardly took a moment. Just the mention of a name—sometimes it was literally no more than that. The Holy Spirit, working in the man at prayer, would interpret that name in the heart of the Father. Sometimes the writing stopped for quite a while while Paul held up the one mentioned, into the warmth of the Father's love, but often it was just a mention, no more. It was an arrow prayer. Letters written in that spirit get things done.

Jesus warns us about 'babbling on' in our prayers as if the more we pray, the more likely we are to be heard (Matthew 6. 7). Sometimes, of course, Paul's prayers are long, but often a name, or a few syllables, will say it all: 'Abba!'; 'Maranatha—Come, Lord!' (1 Corinthians 16. 22). And there is a repetition which is *not* 'vain', as the Church was soon to learn: 'Lord, have mercy; Christ, have mercy; Lord have mercy,' and the Jesus prayer which has blessed so many when they have learned to use it: 'Lord Jesus Christ, Son of the living God, have mercy on me, a sinner.' It is not the quantity, but the reality that matters. Paul liked to end his letters with a prayerful greeting: 'The grace of our Lord Jesus Christ be with you, my friends' (Galatians 6. 18). Or, in its fuller 'trinitarian' form: 'The grace of the Lord Jesus Christ, and the love of God, and the fellowship of the Holy Spirit, be with you all' (2 Corinthians 12. 14). There is enough in that short prayer to feed the soul and enrich the spirit for a long time. Consider the ordering of their clauses. 'The grace of the Lord Jesus' comes first. This reflects the order of Paul's experience. Saul had prayed as a boy and as a young man, and those prayers had surely been accepted, but when God had put him on his back and made him look up (his old pride shattered, his emptiness all he had to offer), it was the overwhelming *grace* of the Lord Jesus that broke him and remade him. He could never be the same again. Through the grace of his Lord Jesus Christ he saw into the heart of God, and it was all love—love for him in his plight, love for the world in its need, love to the uttermost. Grace, love and fellowship—that bond which had united the original band of disciples, so different from one another socially and politically, into a body which cohered, which held together in spite of the strains. That fellowship was the nucleus of the Christian Church.

If we wanted to find three words to sum up not only the experience of Paul but the essence of his message to the world, we could not do better than grace, love and fellowship, the key words of what has become the second-best-known prayer of the Christian Church: 'The grace of the Lord Jesus Christ, and the love of God, and the fellowship of the Holy Spirit, be with you all.' (2)

NOTES / SOURCES

1. Donald Coggan, *The Servant-Son: Jesus Then and Now*, London, 1995, pp. 3, 4
2. Donald Coggan, *Meet Paul*, London, 1998, pp. 73–5

Donald Mackenzie MacKinnon   1913–1994

Educated at Winchester and New College, Oxford, Donald MacKinnon was born in Oban and spent a significant proportion of his life as Professor of Moral Philosophy at Aberdeen. In 1960 he moved to Cambridge as Norris-Hulse Professor of Divinity, a chair he held for eighteen years. A devout High Anglican Donald MacKinnon was a man of considerable erudition and a passionate concern to press the ethical demands of Christian faith against the temptations and compromises of the Establishment, famously saying that there was a direct line from Caiaphas to Lambeth.

The Forgiveness of Sins

Now it is obvious that you cannot believe in the forgiveness of sins if there are really no sins to forgive. The Christian Church from its beginning has called upon men to seek God's forgiveness with the confession of sin upon their lips and in their hearts. But as in the understanding of forgiveness, so in the understanding of sin and guilt we have been led astray by the judicial analogy, and have confused the religious fact of sin with the legal definition of crime. Offences against society are only so many external symptoms of that sickness of soul which is the universal human condition. We are all sinners, not because we have committed this or that detectable transgression of a moral law, but because in the great phrase of St Paul we have fallen short of the glory of God. When the Apostle told his converts to fulfil the law of Christ by bearing one another's burdens, he was not thinking of the common obligation to lend a helping hand to those who are in difficulties. The burden of which he spoke was the burden of sin, and the bearing to which he called us was the acknowledgement by each of us of his share in the sins of the world. The famous exclamation of John Bradford at the sight of convicted criminals on the way to execution—'There, but for the grace of God . . .'—is questionably Christian if what the grace of God is thought to have done is no more than to preserve John Bradford from committing similar crime and suffering similar penalty. The grace of God we all need is the grace of forgiveness, which we can only receive when we understand our need of it as the need of the whole family of mankind—the family to whose life and destiny we belong, for good and ill. As others have put it, 'We are all in the human predicament together'; and it is the denial of our common humanity to thank God that we are not as other men are—whether that be unjust and extortionate even as this publican, or priggish and respectable even as this Pharisee.

NOTES / SOURCES

D. M. MacKinnon, *God, Sex and War*, London, 1963, pp. 124–5

Ronald Stuart Thomas   1913–2000

Born in Cardiff and raised in Anglesey, R. S. Thomas was educated at Holyhead, University College, Bangor, and St Michael's College, Llandaff. Ordained in 1936 he served first at Chirk in the Welsh marches, and subsequently at Manafon, Montgomery-shire, Eglwysfach in Cardiganshire, and finally at Aberdaron in the Lleyn Peninsula. Although passionately concerned for Welsh culture, and an ardent Welsh nationalist, his spare and sharp poetry was written in English. In many ways the outstanding religious poet of the latter part of the twentieth century, the stern moral passion of Thomas's poetry wrestles with the apparent absence of God and yet speaks convincingly of the elusive moments of revelation when the hidden God makes himself known.

Via Negativa

Why no! I never thought other than
That God is that great absence
In our lives, the empty silence
Within, the place where we go
Seeking, not in hope to
Arrive or find. He keeps the interstices
In our knowledge, the darkness
Between stars. His are the echoes
We follow, the footprints he has just
Left. We put our hands in
His side hoping to find
It warm. We look at people
And places as though he had looked
At them, too; but miss the reflection. (1)

Poste Restante

I want you to know how it was,
whether the Cross grinds into dust
under men's wheels or shines brightly
as a monument to a new era.

There was a church and one man
served it, and few worshipped
there in the raw light on the hill
in winter, moving among the stones

fallen about them like the ruins
of a culture they were too weak
to replace, too poor themselves
to do anything but wait
for the ending of a life
they had not asked for.
                                    The priest would come
and pull on the hoarse bell nobody
heard, and enter that place
of darkness, sour with the mould
of the years. And the spider would run
from the chalice, and the wine lie
there for a time, cold and unwanted
by all but he, while the candles
guttered as the wind picked
at the roof. And he would see
over that bare meal his face
staring at him from the cracked glass
of the window, with the lips moving
like those of an inhabitant of
a world beyond this.
                                    And so back
to the damp vestry to the book
where he would scratch his name and the date
he could hardly remember, Sunday
by Sunday, while the place sank
to its knees and the earth turned
from season to season like the wheel
of a great foundry to produce
you, friend, who will know what happened. (2)

The Bright Field

I have seen the sun break through
to illuminate a small field
for a while, and gone my way
and forgotten it. But that was the pearl
of great price, the one field that had
the treasure in it. I realise now
that I must give all that I have
to possess it. Life is not hurrying
on to a receding future, nor hankering after
an imagined past. It is the turning
aside like Moses to the miracle
of the lit bush, to a brightness
that seemed as transitory as your youth
once, but is the eternity that awaits you. (3)

Crucifixion

God's fool, God's jester
capering at his right hand
in torment, proving the fallacy
of the impassible, reminding
him of omnipotence's limits.

I have seen the figure
on our human tree, burned
into it by thought's lightning
and it writhed as I looked.

A god has no alternative
but himself. With what crown
plurality but with thorns?
Whose is the mirthless laughter
at the beloved irony
at his side? The universe over,
omniscience warns, the crosses
are being erected from such
material as is available
to remorse. What are the stars
but time's fires going out
before ever the crucified
can be taken down?
                      Today
there is only this one option
before me. Remembering,
as one goes out into space,
on the way to the sun,
how dark it will grow,
I stare up into the darkness
of his countenance, knowing it
a reflection of the three days and nights
at the back of love's looking-
glass even a god must spend.
Not the empty tomb
but the uninhabited
cross. Look long enough
and you will see the arms
put on leaves. Not a crown
of thorns, but a crown of flowers
haloing it, with a bird singing
as though perched on paradise's threshold.

We have over-furnished
our faith. Our churches
are as limousines in the procession
towards heaven. But the verities
remain: a de-nuclearised
cross, uncontaminated
by our coinage; the chalice's
ichor; and one crumb of bread
on the tongue for the bird-like
intelligence to be made tame by.

He atones not with blood
but with the transfusions
that are the substitute of its loss.

Under the arc-lamps
we suffer the kisses
of the infected needle,

satisfied to be the saviour
not of the world, not
of the species, but of the one

anonymous member
of the gambling party
at the foot of the cross.

Silent, Lord,
as you would have us be,
lips closed, eyes swerving aside
towards the equation:
$x + y^2 = y + x^2$?
It does not balance.
What has algebra to do
with a garden? Either
they preceded it or came
late. The snake's fangs
must have been aimed
at a calculable angle
against a possible refusal
of the apple of knowledge.
Was there a mathematics
before matter to which
you were committed? Or is it
man's mind is to blame,
spinning questions out of itself
in the infinite regress?
It is we gave the stars names,

yet already the Zodiac
was in place—prophesying,
reminding? The Plough
and Orion's Sword eternally
in contradiction. We close
our eyes when we pray
lest the curtain of tears
should come down on a cross
being used for the first time to prove
the correctness of a negation.

They set up their decoy
in the Hebrew sunlight. What
for? Did they expect
death to come sooner
to disprove his claim
to be God's son? Who
can shoot down God?
Darkness arrived at
midday, the shadow
of whose wing? The blood
ticked from the cross, but it was not
their time it kept. It was no
time at all, but the accompaniment
to a face staring,
as over twenty centuries
it has stared, from unfathomable
darkness into unfathomable light. (4)

Bleak Liturgies

Shall we revise the language?
And in revising the language
will we alter the doctrine?

Do we seek to plug the hole
in faith with faith's substitute
grammar? And are we to be saved

by translation? As one by one
the witnesses died off
they commended their metaphors

to our notice. For two thousand
years the simplistic recipients
of the message pointed towards

the reductionist solution. We devise
an idiom more compatible with
the furniture departments of our churches.

> Instead of the altar
> the pulpit. Instead
> of the bread the fraction
> of the language. And God
> a shadow of himself
> on a blank wall. Their prayers
> are a passing of hands
> over their brows as though
> in an effort to wipe sin
> off. Their buildings
> are in praise of concrete
> and macadam. Frowning
> upon divorce, they divorce
> art and religion.
> Ah, if one flower
> had been allowed to grow
> between the wall
> and the railings as sacrament
> of renewal. Instead
> two cypresses ail
> there, emaciated as the bodies
> of the thieves upon Calvary
> but with no Saviour between them.

> 'Alms. Alms. By Christ's
> blood I conjure you.

> a penny.' On saints'
> days the cross and

> shackles were the jewellery
> of the rich. As God

> aged, kings laundered their feet
> in the tears of the poor.

'Come,' life said
leading me on a journey
as long as that
of the wise men to the cradle,

where, in place of the child
it had brought forth,
there lay grinning the lubricated
changeling of the machine.

Where to turn? To whom
to appeal? The prayer probes
have been launched and silence
closes behind them. The Amens
are rents in the worn fabric
of meaning. Are we
our own answer? Is
to grow up to destroy
childhood's painting of one
who was nothing but vocabulary's
shadow? Where do the stone
faces come from but from
trying to meet the sky's
empty stare? The sermon
was too long. These thoughts
flew in and out of windows
He had not bothered to look through.

    The missionaries arrive now
    by fast jet. Salvation accelerates
    with the times. It is a race between
    Jesus and Lenin to become
    high-priest at the administering
    of the chrism. Science analyses
    the real presence. Crosses
    are mass-produced to be worn
    on punk chests. Theology
    connives at politics' removal
    of one word from Article
    three seven. The hierarchy in keeping
    its head has no heart for the baptism
    of love and lust's Siamese twins.

The gaps in belief are filled
with ceremonies and processions.
The organ's whirlwind follows
upon the still, small voice

of conviction, and he is not
in it. Our marriage
was contracted in front
of a green altar in technology's

childhood, and light entered
through the plain glass of
the wood's window as quietly
as a shepherd moving among his flock.

Faith can remove mountains,
        So can cordite. But faith
heals. So does valium's
        loosening of the taut nerves.

Three days the Electoral
        College waited for the Holy
Spirit to come to terms
        with the media's prediction.

Too cynical. Quantum mechanics
        restores freedom to the cowed
mind that, winking at matter,
        causes it to wink back.

        What Lent is the machine
        subjected to? It neither fasts
        nor prays. And the one cross
        of its Good Fridays is the change

        over of its gears. Its Easter
        is every day when, from the darkness
        of man's mind, it comes forth
        in a new form, but untouchable as ever.

Must the Church also
        suffer a mutation?
The communicants' jeans,
        the whiskered faces with

their imitation of Christ?
        Re-editing the scriptures
we come on a verse suggesting
        that we be gay, so gay we are.

His defences are in depth, then?
Behind the molecules are the electrons,
behind those the leptons and quarks.

And when the computers that are our spies
have opened to us from inside
he is not there; the walls fall apart

and there are only the distances
stretching away. We have captured position
after position, and his white flag

is a star receding from us
at light's speed. Is there another way
of engaging? There are those who,

thinking of him in the small hours
as eavesdropping their hearts
and challenging him to come forth,

have found, as the day dawned,
his body hanging upon the crossed tree
of man, as though he were man, too. (5)

NOTES / SOURCES

1. Ronald Stuart Thomas, *H'm*, London, 1972, p. 16
2. Ronald Stuart Thomas, *Laboratories of the Spirit*, London, 1975, pp. 13–4
3. Ibid., p. 60
4. Ronald Stuart Thomas, *Counterpoint*, Newcastle upon Tyne, 1990, pp. 35–40
5. Ronald Stuart Thomas, *Mass for Hard Times*, Newcastle upon Tyne, 1992, pp. 59–63

John Vernon Taylor   1914–2001

John Taylor was born in 1914. He studied English History at Trinity College, Cambridge and then Theology at Oxford, being ordained in 1938. After curacies in London and St Helens he went to work for the Church Missionary Society in 1945 serving in Uganda which gave him a great love for Africa, and Uganda in particular. He became General Secretary of the CMS in 1963, serving until he was consecrated as Bishop of Winchester in 1975. A creative theologian of immense imagination, his book *The Primal Vision* drew on his understanding of African culture and Christianity. *The Go Between God* was an original exploration of the doctrine of the Holy Spirit and in *Enough is Enough* he sounded a Christian warning against consumerism and its consequences.

Christ Foreshadowed

The historic Christ, the Logos fully revealed, comes as a story that must be told and an image reflected in other human lives—but he does not come as a stranger. He has been there all along, but his footprints were not on the most frequented paths and he is recognized as a face seen in half-forgotten dreams like that of the Suffering Messiah foreshadowed in the Old Testament but neglected in the on-going tradition of Judaism. He comes to his own in the other faiths in another way also, in that he, the Logos incarnate once for all in Jesus of Nazareth, matches the need and fulfils the promise of each traditional world-view as though he had emerged from within it with no less relevance than he did within Judaism. We who stand outside the other traditions may only guess how this may be . . . (1)

. . . To call the timeless Logos 'Christ' is to fasten upon him, as we should, the historical identity which he took upon himself in his incarnation. His universality was not diminished by that identification, rather was his eternal likeness revealed in sharper focus. (2)

A Prayer of Daily Dedication

Lord Jesus Christ,
alive and at large in the world,
help me to follow and find you there today,
in the places where I work,
> meet people,
> spend money
> and make plans.
Take me as a disciple of your Kingdom,
to see through your eyes,
and hear the questions you are asking,
to welcome all men with your trust and truth,
and to change the things that contradict God's love,
by the power of the cross
and the freedom of your spirit.   Amen. (3)

Two Poems Inspired by Rublev's Icon of the Holy Trinity (Genesis 18: 1–19)

Siesta

Must it be I, then, the wanderer Abraham,
Acclaimed for faith in an impossible promise,
who sits now at ease in the shade of the tree
named at the start as the place to make good the blessing?
How shall an immigrant possess the land,
or an inbred sterile clan people it?
Yet miracle it is to sit in the tent door in the heat
of the day and the day's discord.
But why this intrusion of a chosen people,
branded by covenant, tangled with God
from all creation as his partner and mirror-image?
Better the simple universal witness
of the visible world to every soul alike,
whereby we learn to live in the two Realities
of Him who is and all that is becoming,
of the Changeless and the ever-changing,
of the Stillness and the Activity.

Love's Self-Opening

Love in its fullness loomed, love
loomed at the tent door in its truth,
not the sole unique truth

reserved for the incomparable God,
but for a love consisting of communion.
I, Abraham, looked for a single
flower; but it has blossomed into a
multiple head, made for sharing.
Love's ultimate reality, gazing at the Son
proclaims 'I AM'.
And He, as love's delight,
says 'look and see'.
Their mutuality precedes creation
being Eternal, and offers the only space
in which it can exist.
So the cup of suffering at which they gaze
is the price already paid
for the world's pardon. 'The Lamb
slain before the foundation
of the world.' (4)

Prayer for the Blessing of a Parish Priest

Almight God, our heavenly Father, fill the heart of your servant *N* . . . with eager love in caring for your people; joy in affirming all that is good in this community; courage in challenging all that is mean and destructive; and unceasing thankfulness in celebrating your Holy Mysteries among them. Give him vision for his preaching, faithfulness for his teaching, diligence for his visiting, sympathy for his counselling, compassion in declaring your pardon for the penitent, and the peace that passes understanding for his daily walk with Christ, in whose name we pray. Amen. (5)

The Gospel of Life

There is a frightening amount of deadness around in our Western societies these days. It has not always been so. In other periods there has been abundant vigour, and the pre-dominant malaise was of a different sort—ingrained enmity between families and tribes at one time; avarice and heartless exploitation at another. For there is a variety of deadly sins, just as there is a variety of plagues, and, like the several plagues, they do not offer the luxury of choosing which we will have, but now one, now another, falls upon the whole community, infecting the atmosphere that we all breathe. Of those so-called deadly sins, the more virulent epidemics of the human sprit, the one that has gripped our society in this century is, without question, *accidie*, the sleeping sickness, which is not so much sloth as we understand it, as apathy, lack of response, the total antithesis of that aliveness and awareness which is my theme in this book. And if there is salvation as the Christian gospel claims, it has to come to us as the remedy for this particular scourge and bring the half-dead to life. But first we must get the diagnosis right.

This inner lifelessness is induced by fear. People shrink from the pain of being fully awake. The child who is so intensely alive to the wonder of each shell and pebble quickly discovers that he cannot tunnel that vision so as to be aware of the beautiful and happy things alone. Eyes that remain open to the glory of the world must see its ugliness as well. The exchange between living beings on which life depends must include bad things as well as good. Those who respond to the 'otherness' of other people and, in Shakespeare's phrase, take upon themselves the mystery of things, will respond with the same sensitivity to other people's mess and muddle and take upon themselves their pain and anger. Buddhists preserve the tradition that Prince Sakyamuni was guarded by his royal parents from all contact with poverty, disease and death and even from the knowledge of their existence. When the inevitable happened, and in one day he encountered all three, the discovery was devastating. Thenceforth he set himself to liberate his mind from every vestige of evasion and illusion and so attained to Buddhahood or Enlightenment.

It does involve great pain and takes enormous courage to remain fully exposed and receptive towards the reality of the world around, towards the reality of the human beings we know, towards the reality of our own selves, towards the ultimate reality beyond and within all this. It also, incidentally, brings upon us a great deal of trouble and effort, since an ability to respond makes us take responsibility, and a readiness to answer makes us answerable. Consequently, and understandably, our growing up is usually a process of closing up. We actually choose to be less alive in order to be less bothered. So in the sense the word *accidie* does mean a deadly kind of laziness or sloth. Awareness makes demands, awareness hurts, so we begin to grow a protective shell and become a little blind, a little deaf, a little dead. That is what characterized the Priest and the Levite in the parable of Jesus about the traveller who fell among thieves. They passed by without apparently noticing the victim at the side of the road. Over the years those professionally religious men had trained themselves *not* to notice. The next one to come down the road, however, had kept his awareness painfully, responsibly alive. That is what turns a stranger into a neighbour. The chorus of women of Canterbury in T. S. Eliot's *Murder in the Cathedral* speaks for all of us who are plagued by apathy, including many who are still young.

> We do not wish anything to happen.
> Seven years we have lived quietly,
> Succeeded in avoiding notice,
> Living and partly living.
> There have been oppression and luxury,
> There have been poverty and licence,
> There has been minor injustice.
> Yet we have gone on living,
> Living and partly living.

Quietly avoiding notice, and quietly avoiding having to take notice, is a recipe for making an irresponsible community in which nobody matters because nobody cares. So we invest all our expectations of a warm, living relationship in a partnership of a man and a woman. They start with an intense awareness and openness towards each other, but they find that the demands of that awareness and the embarrassment of that openness are too much for the immature and unresolved parts of themselves to sustain. So they learn to become a little more blind and deaf and dumb until communication breaks down, usually long before any serious unfaithfulness has taken place. The death of a marriage, which is now a legally recognized condition, is only another tragic casualty of that epidemic lifelessness, induced by fear, which is plaguing us at so many levels of experience.

The same deadness as afflicts our personal life also grips the institutions of power and decision-making, sapping the political will. Energies are channelled into the conflict of parties and ideologies rather than the business of getting things done. The violent posturing, the awful jargon of denigration, the masquerade of debate and conference long after decisions have been taken by quite different people—these are like the reflexes of something that has already died, while 'the common people' are everywhere paralysed by their frustration over the ineffectiveness of it all in the face of our global needs and fears. Things have grown worse rather than better since Eliot wrote in 1925, at a time when, in his own words, he had 'gone dead';

> We are the hollow men
> We are the stuffed men
> Leaning together
> Headpiece filled with straw. Alas!
> Our dried voices, when
> We whisper together
> Are quiet and meaningless
> As wind in dry grass.

This widespread malaise has much in common with pathological depression. The sufferers from that mental sickness feel they are only half alive, drained of energy and hope. The tragic multiplication of these sufferers in our day may be related to the more general lifelessness that I am talking about, but their deadness and despair is compounded by a sense of worthlessness and self-punishment generated from the unbearable ambiguity of a childhood hatred towards someone who was also loved, usually a parent. The skills of a doctor and a psychoanalyst are necessary to the restoration of such people to fullness of life, and if ever I have been called upon to help one of them it has always been in collaboration with those other practitioners. What I am concerned with in this chapter is the more general drift towards an unwitting choice of deadness rather than aliveness, and that is a *spiritual* sickness. It is described—diagnosed, you might say—in a vivid series of phrases in the New Testament Letter to the Ephesians. 'They live in the emptiness of their minds, their wits darkened, being estranged from the life which is in God through the incomprehension that is in them through the stony hardness of their hearts. They are those who have ceased to feel' (4, 17–19).

Those who choose to grow the protective shell because it is safer and more comfortable that way are not for the most part aware of their deadness, since awareness is the faculty they have anaesthetized. Something is missing, however, and they try in various ways to whip up the lost exhilaration and fend off the encroaching boredom. There are many sorts of experience that momentarily reproduce a sense of vivid life and that dissolving of boundaries by which one becomes part of the unity of things. Drugs will do this for you while they last but they let you down into a more horrible lifelessness each time. A flaming row can bring one dramatically to life for a while, and so can many other 'performances'; which is what drives the raconteur to dominate the dinner table. Yet even while the squabble or the long story is in full spate the speaker's eyes betray the knowledge that in another moment he is going to feel deflated again. Others use sex as a way of capturing the sense of aliveness and the disappearance of boundaries, but unless it leads steadily into a fuller commitment, it becomes an increasingly self-absorbed search for an illusory coming to life which cannot add any meaning to the rest of life, as genuine experiences of awareness do.

These sad simulations of life by those who shrink from the cost of being really alive lay claim to a virility they do not actually possess. They masquerade as something full-blooded or even reckless, and this is a lie that has taken in the moralists of all periods. The fact is that addiction and promiscuity and violence are all manifestations of emptiness and what they confer is boredom.

> Those who have crossed
> With direct eyes, to death's other Kingdom
> Remember us—if at all—not as lost
> Violent souls, but only
> As the hollow men
> The stuffed men . . .

There are other more respectable ways by which those who are partly living simulate an aliveness and a real identity, and because they are more socially acceptable they are more deceptive and deadly. The oldest delusion of all is that life consists of achievement. The consumer society is built upon that lie. When a man or a woman has been badly put down or treated as a nobody the commonest antidote is a spending spree. Like addicts, people crave for more possessions or higher attainments or new experiences to offset the emptiness and lack of selfhood. They sacrifice their children to the same craving, projecting upon them the hunger of their ambitions. Often they end by losing whatever real self they once had under a pile of achievements or of failures. Jesus Christ asked: 'What will it profit people, what will anyone make on the deal, if they gain the whole world and lose their own selves? What can be given to buy back life, aliveness?' (Mark 8. 36, 37).

There is a typically religious version of this delusion of gaining life through achievement, namely, gaining life through rectitude. We Christians have talked rather a lot about keeping the rules. We have argued, reasonably enough on the face of it, that because the momentary boost of drugs or sex or violent rage or a new acquisition or a fresh attainment is no substitute for being really alive, then real life is to be gained by refraining from all those things and a lot besides. Of course we also recognized that good behaviour included a great many positive activities and attitudes and that those were even more important. Nevertheless we have tended to identify aliveness with what we call 'living a good life'. But this whole position collapses every time we meet the contrast between the two kinds of family which I drew earlier in this chapter – the well-mannered socially-acceptable family in which one can never quite be oneself and the uncouth, irregular lot who exude warmth and reality. Then it becomes glaringly obvious that keeping the rules cannot be a substitute for that life which the Lord God sets before us and urges us to choose. (6)

Made Alive by the Living God

To think of God in himself is, strictly, beyond the power of human thought. He is not a being that speculation might conceive. He is not even the supreme being. He is 'Being' itself. Yet we are given clues and they confirm the truth that God in himself, Being itself, consists of what we have called 'exchange'. The name I AM, which the Jews regarded as so directly expressing God's being that they would never pronounce it, carries in Hebrew a dynamic sense: not merely 'I am' in a static state of being, but 'I am present', or 'I am for', as though even that ultimate Awareness consisted of interflow.

Now this was not the line of argument that led the early church eventually to formulate its doctrine of the Trinity. Yet that Christian understanding of the nature of God in himself does aptly endorse the idea that 'exchange' lies at the very heart of the being of God, the living God. One can say this without suggesting that there are three distinct centres of knowing, 'three gods', in the One Deity; for even in the inadequate analogy of our individual self-consciousness we can discern a dynamic dialogue between our sense perceptions, our thoughts about them and our eveluation of them, so that it is precisely when we are aware of holding a conversation within ourselves that we are most whole and most alive. This precious insight of Christian thought affirms that Being itself is an eternal giving and receiving. The same is said more simply in the words, 'God is love'—not 'God is a loving God,' nor 'God is every ready to love,' but 'God *in himself* is love.'

Something of this truth is discovered by those who persevere in their prayers beyond the level of asking for things to the point where prayer is commuion with God or simply being in his presence. They tell of becoming aware of being 'prayed through', as though they themselves were only the instument, the telephone wire, for the flow of communication of God with God, the interchange of the eternal love and joy. This is surely what St Paul was describing when he wrote about the Holy Spirit standing in for us to augment our weak ignorant prayer (Rom. 8. 26–27). This experience of those who have gone some way into prayer 'fits' remarkably with those more momentary but unforgettable encounters with the reality of God which so many people have occasionally experienced even when they were wholly out of touch with any religious practice or belief. I referred to a few such accounts in my opening chapter. Transient and highly individual these intimations of God's presence certainly are, yet they convey to the one who receives them a sense of being caught up into an immense pervading joy of giving and receiving that embraces and unifies all things.

Life, of which this dynamic, living God is the source, is relationship. The deadness, which is our sin against life, comes from our refusal of exchange, our shutting off of self so as neither to give nor receive. Being brought to life is the renewal of relationship with this living God and, in him, with all creatures.

It follows, then, that the life of the fully alive cannot be sustained in isolation or privacy, but must express itself in community. This does not mean clubs and cliques or general *bonhomie*. It means being open, whenever the opportunity is afforded, for those exchanges whereby the aliveness and freedom of the one flows to the other, or the pain and darkness of the other is shared and taken upon the one.

That was the kind of interrelationship that was held up as the ideal for the ancient Hebrews as the people of that living God. They never completely fulfilled the ideal pattern, and even the regulations in which the ideal was presented reflected the incomplete perceptions of those times, as any attempt to set down God's way for a human community is bound to do. Nevertheless we can see in the details of their social laws the dream of 'Shalom', a community that was meant to reflect the exchange of care and respect between all creatures. The poor, the unfortunates, the aliens were to be remembered and room made for them in the scheme of things. When they reaped their harvests they were not to retrace their steps to gather what had been dropped or left uncut in the corners of the cornfields. Others would be glad of that. When vines or olive trees were picked they were not to be gone over a second time. If anyone came on a wild fowl sitting on eggs they must not take both bird and eggs for their larder. It was a principle of live and let live, of fitting oneself into the pattern of the whole; it pursued the ideals of ecology before that word was invented. And this was to be the way of it because that is what it means to be alive. These were the people who had said they had chosen life rather than death. They were the people who worshipped the living God. Then let them be alive, alive to the reality of others and of all creatures, aware of the whole for which they were to be answerable to that God.

The same pattern of mutuality and exchange was set before the communities of the first Christians as the *milieu* in which alone their aliveness in Christ was to be lived out. They were in no position then to change the great structures of the Roman empire or model society on their new-found vision of aliveness to one another in Christ. Most of them came from the polyglot slave population. Yet within their own gatherings they were called to come alive to one another's reality in a new way. Instead of the universal covetousness, the 'more-and-more' sickness, they were to cultivate the strange new virtue called *epieikēs*, 'fitting in'. 'Let your fitting into the whole be patent to everyone,' wrote St Paul to the Philippians. Their awareness of one another in Christ must mean that for them there were no more distinctions and separations of Jews and Gentiles, or of slaves and free, or of men and women. Rich and poor were to become mutually aware and caring in a new way. There were to be no double standards on that score any more. But beyond these specific changes of attitude, they were called to a mutuality in depth—confiding in one another, forgiving one another, bearing one another's burdens, building one another up. That word rings like a theme song through the pages of the New Testament. It is the word which sums up the exchange of self with self which burns in the being of the living God and should burn in the reflected aliveness of God's people. (7)

NOTES / SOURCES

1. Letter from John Taylor to Canon Graham Kings, 27 July 1997 in *The Church Mission Society and World Christianity, 1799–1999*, eds. Kevin Ward and Brian Stanley, Kurzon and Eerdmans, 2000, p. 309
2. Ibid., p. 311
3. Prayer of Daily Dedication, which was used at Bishop John Taylor's Enthronement Service in 1975

4. From a Service of Thanksgiving for the life of John Vernon Taylor held on Satuday 7 April, 2001. p. 4
5. Written by Bishop John Taylor for the Winchester Diocesan Service of Institution.
6. John V. Taylor, *A Matter of Life and Death*, London, 1986, pp. 20–7
7. Ibid., pp. 72–5

Henry Robert McAdoo   1916–1988

Henry McAdoo was born in Cork in 1916, and after a distinguished education at Trinity College, Dublin was ordained in the Church of Ireland in 1939. His literary output, achieved against a background of pastoral work, was considerable: it included *The Structure of Caroline Moral Theology* (1949), *The Spirit of Anglicanism* (1965), and *The Eucharistic Theology of Jeremy Taylor Today* (1989). In 1962 he was consecrated Bishop of Ossory, Ferns and Leighlin, from where he moved to Dublin as Archbishop from 1977 to 1985. His deep reading of historical theology made him an ideal choice as the first Anglican Co-Chairman of the Anglican-Roman Catholic International Commission (ARCIC) from 1969 to 1981.

Scripture, Tradition and Reason, Now and the Future

Anglicanism's vocation of responsibility to others and to itself involves maintaining its threefold dialectic as a necessary ecumenical methodology and for the following reasons. In the first place, it is our insurance against a blindfold Christianity with earplugs. At the moment, and in more than one Church, a confident Christianity can be undermined by either or both of two trends. There is a fundamentalism of Scripture, a literalist interpretation of that which is seen by all as normative for the Church. There is also a fundamentalism of tradition which sees it much as a fly-in-amber rather than the living Church interpreting 'the faith once for all delivered' in the idiom and the life-setting of each generation. . . .

. . . The affirmation of the continuing identity of Anglicanism is no crude assertion of denominationalism but the modest insistence that the Church which has brought us to *where we are* as Anglicans has a vocation of responsibility in the company with other traditions to help to bring us all as fellow-Christians to *where we should be* in the unity for which Christ prayed. We have been listening to voices from our past and who can say that they are not evoking clear echoes and resonances in our present?

NOTES / SOURCES

H. R. McAdoo, *Anglican Heritage: Theology and Spirituality*, Norwich, 1991, pp. 103, 107

John Arthur Thomas Robinson   1919–1983

John Robinson came from a clerical family in which his father and two of his uncles were theologians. After theological studies at Cambridge he served for a time in the parochial ministry and then taught at Wells Theological College and at Clare College, Cambridge, before being consecrated as Bishop of Woolwich in 1959. Primarily a New

Testament scholar, the publication of *Honest to God* (1963) (in which, drawing on the writings of Tillich, Bultmann, and Bonhoeffer, he sought to reinterpret traditional Christian concepts) led to considerable theological debate, not least because the author was a bishop. In 1969 he returned to Cambridge where he served as Dean of Trinity College until his death from cancer in 1983.

'God' is News

Some years ago Mr Gaitskell proposed revising the famous Clause Four of the Labour Party's constitution (on nationalization).

Those who opposed him dubbed it all 'theology'—theoretical statements about things that make no practical difference. Such is the name that 'theology' has gained. But suddenly that image seems to have changed.

Up till now the Press took notice of clergymen only if they spoke on morals or politics. What they said on God and the Gospel was ignored. Archbishop William Temple constantly complained of this. But now 'God' is news!

My book seems to have touched people at a point where truth really matters to them. And of that I am glad—even if it has meant some pain. For God is to be found at the point where things really do matter to us.

What drove me to write my book was that this is simply not true for most people. What matters to them most in life seems to have nothing to do with 'God'; and God has no connection with what really concerns them day by day.

At best he seems to come in only at the edges of life. He is out there somewhere as a sort of long-stop—at death, or to turn to in tragedy (either to pray or to blame).

The traditional imagery of God simply succeeds, I believe, in making him remote for millions of men today.

What I want to do is not to deny God in any sense, but to put him back into the middle of life—where Jesus showed us he belongs.

For the Christian God is not remote. He is involved; he is implicated. If Jesus Christ means anything, he means that God belongs to this world.

So let's start not from a heavenly Being, whose very existence many would doubt. Let's start from what actually is most real to people in everyday life—and find God there.

What is most real to you? What matters most for you? Is it money, and what money can buy?

I doubt it, deep down. For you know that you 'can't take it with you'. And seldom does it bring real happiness.

Is it love? That's a good deal nearer, because it has to do with persons not things.

But what is love? Sex? Sex is a marvellous part of it. But sex by itself can leave people deeply unsatisfied. Remember Marilyn Monroe?

We all need, more than anything else, to love and be loved. That's what the psychologists tell us. But by that they mean we need to be *accepted* as persons, as whole persons for our own sake. And this is what true love does. It accepts people, without any strings, simply for what they are. It gives them worth. It 'makes their lives'.

That is precisely what we see Jesus doing in the Gospels, making and re-making men's lives, bringing meaning back to them.

In him we see love at work, in a way that the world has never seen before or since.

And that's why the New Testament sees God at work in him—for God is love. In the Cross that love comes out to the uttermost. 'There's love for you!' says Calvary.

And in the Resurrection we see that not even death was able to destroy its power to transform and heal. Love still came out top.

The Christian is the man who believes in *that* love as the last word for his life.

It is quite simply for him the ultimate reality: it is God.

The universe, like a human being, is not built merely to a mathematical formula. It's only love that gives you the deepest clue to it.

'It's love that makes the world go round.' That's what all Christians have always said. But so often they have *pictured* it in a way that makes it difficult for modern man to see it.

They have spoken as though what makes the world go round were an old man in the sky, a supernatural Person.

Of course, they don't take that literally. It helps only to make God easier to *imagine*. But it can also hinder.

Perhaps a comparison will show what I mean. The ancient Greeks thought of the earth being upheld on the shoulders of a superman called Atlas. That was their way of saying that it doesn't support itself in space.

We also know that it doesn't. For us it is held in orbit by the sun's gravitational pull.

The ancient myth was saying something true. But such language today would not convey the truth to modern man. It would be much more likely to conceal it.

So with Christian truth. The reality is that in Jesus we see the clue to all life. To say that he was the Son of a supernatural Being sent to earth from heaven may help to bring this home.

But for others it may take it out of their world altogether—so that the events of Christmas and Holy Week seem to belong to a religious fairy story. If the traditional way of putting it makes Christ real for you—the most real thing in the world—well and good. I don't want to destroy anyone's imagery of God. I wrote my book for those who have increasingly come to feel that it makes him unreal and remote.

I tried simply to be honest about what God means to me—in the second half of the twentieth century. The hundreds of letters I have received, particularly from the younger generation, inside the Church and out of it, have convinced me that I may have rung a bell for others too. For that I can only be humbly thankful.

For I want God to be as real for our modern secular, scientific world as he ever was for the 'ages of faith'. (1)

The Christian Walks by Trust not Sight

A Christian has nothing to fear but the truth. For it alone could show that his movement is not of God (Acts 5. 38 f.). But he also has nothing to fear in the truth. For to him the truth *is* Christ (John 14. 6). It is large—larger than the world—and shall prevail. It is also a living, and a growing, reality. And therefore he is free, or should be free, to follow the truth *wherever* it leads. He has no advance information or inbuilt assurance precisely where it will lead. I know that I have been led through the study of the New Testament to conclusions, both negative and positive, that I did not expect. For instance, just what underlies the birth narratives, what were the relations between the movements of John the Baptist and Jesus, how and in what way did Jesus's own understanding of his role become modified by events, how did he think of the future, did he expect to return, what is most likely to have happened at his trial and resurrection, what is the relative priority for the portrait of Jesus of our different sources, especially of the Fourth Gospel, what pattern and time-scale of early church development emerges from the dating of our documents?—on these and many other things my own mind has changed and will doubtless continue to change. And my picture will not be quite the same as anyone else's—more radical at some points, more conservative at others. There is nothing fixed or final: our knowledge and our questions are constantly expanding and shifting. And who knows what new evidence may not suddenly be dug up? Yet out of all this my trust in the primary documents of the Christian faith has been strengthened rather than shaken. The scholarship does not give me the faith; but it increases my confidence that my faith is not misplaced. Yet it provides no copper-bottomed guarantee. For the Christian walks always in this life by trust and not by sight. And he is content to close his *Te Deum*, his most confident affirmation of faith, with the prayer of vulnerability: 'O Lord, in thee have I *trusted*: let me never be confounded.' (2)

The Centre of Everything

For me the ultimate context in which life is lived is that of an I–Thou relationship with the Eternal Thou. That relationship is the umbilical cord of all that one is and all that one does. It seems to me that Jesus lived in the Abba, Father relationship, and that is the ground and basis of all one's being and of all the other relationships that one enters into. Each of these 'others' is a way through which this other relationship comes, both in grace and demand. One tries—inadequately—to respond to it, but if one is pressed back, then it seems to me that this is the final reality of life, in which and for which one is made. It is not something that begins and ends with what we call time, but it is the framework in which all things of space and time belong and are created and have their being. It is defined in Christ in terms of the love of God and fellowship and grace. It is the centre of everything and it is the context in which one tries to face everything else. (3)

Learning from Cancer

When I was last preaching here it was Trinity Sunday, and I knew I was going into Addenbrooke's the next day for an operation, which turned out to reveal an inoperable cancer. But I was determined not to give in and that I was going to keep my commitment to preach here tonight, if only to 'christen' this pulpit lectern that I wanted to bequeath as a belated thank-offering for what nearly 15 years in this place has meant to me. So I thought I would use this opportunity to reflect with you on something of what these past months have taught me at greater depth.

Two years ago I found myself having to speak at the funeral of a 16-year-old girl who died in our Yorkshire dale. I said stumblingly that God was to be found in the cancer as much as in the sunset. That I firmly believed, but it was an intellectual statement. Now I have had to ask if I can say it of myself, which is a much greater test.

When I said it from the pulpit, I gather it produced quite a shock-wave. I guess this was for two reasons.

1. Because I had mentioned the word openly in public—and even among Christians it is (or it was: for much has happened in the short time since) the great unmentionable. 'Human kind,' said Eliot, 'cannot bear very much reality.' It is difficult for me to comprehend that there are people who just do not want to know whether they have got cancer. But above all, there is a conspiracy of silence ostensibly to protect others. We think they cannot face it, though in my experience they usually know deep down; and obviously it is critical how they can face other realities, and above all how they are told and who tells them (and of course whether they really need to know). But what we are much more likely to be doing is mutually protecting ourselves—and also that goes often (though less and less) for doctors. For we dare not face it in ourselves or talk about it at the levels of reality that we might open up.

But Christians above all are those who should be able to bear reality and show others how to bear it. Or what are we to say about the Cross, the central reality of our faith? From the beginning Ruth and I were determined to know the whole truth, which after all was first of all our truth and not someone else's. And my doctors have been marvellously open, telling us as they knew everything they knew, which they are the first to say is but the tip of the iceberg. And incidentally they say how much easier it makes it for them if they know this is what the patient wants. Moreover they are fully aware in a place like Cambridge University that too many people know too much (or have access to such knowledge) for them to get away with fudging anything! So from the beginning we were in the picture as it was confirmed.

That does not make it any less of a stunning shock, and the walk from the specialist's consulting room to our car seemed a very long one. But knowing is all-important to how one handles it. For as the recent TV programme 'Mind Over Cancer' has shown, the attitude one brings to it can be quite vital—though it is important not to give the impression that *all* depends on this, or that if you die it is because your attitude is wrong, any more than to suggest, as some Christians do, that if you are not cured it is because you have not enough faith. That just induces guilt. But it is equally important to say that 'cancer' need not mean death, nor to suggest that there is nothing you can do about it. In fact there are already numerous cancers that are not necessarily fatal. There are as many sorts of it as there are of 'flu or heart disease. To lump cancer together as a summary death-sentence is as unscientific as it is self-fulfilling. Whether we die of it or of something else is partly up to us. But all of us have to die of something; and by the end of the century, thanks to the elimination of so many other things, the great majority of us will die, in roughly equal proportions, either of cardio-vascular diseases, which still lead as killers but by preventive medicine are already dropping, or of cancer. And of course progress is constantly being made here too, though again there is unlikely to be a simple 'cure' for cancer any more than for the common cold.

2. The shock-wave was also no doubt due to my saying that *God* was in the cancer. As I made absolutely clear at the time, by this I did not mean that God was in it by intending or sending it. That would make him a very devil. Yet people are always seeing these things in terms of his deliberate purpose or the failure of it. Why does he *allow* it? they say, and they get angry with God. Or rather, they project their anger on to God. And to let the anger come out is no bad thing. For so often diseases of strain and depression are caused by suppressed anger and hatred of other people or of oneself. So it is healthy that it should come out—and God can take it.

The other question people ask in such circumstances is 'Why me?' (often with the implication, 'Why does he pick on me?') or 'What have I done to deserve it?' And this, deep down, is another good question to have out. 'Why have I got this? What is there in me that has brought it about?' To which the answer is for the most part, as in so much in this field, 'I don't know.' Certainly it is in my case. But the searching, probing and often uncomfortable questions it raises are very relevant, and can be an essential part of the healing. Sometimes there are direct environmental factors (such as smoking or asbestos or radiation) which we can recognise and, if we have the will, personal or social, do something about it—like diet in heart-disease or anxiety in duodenal ulcers. But usually it goes deeper and points inwards. The evidence mounts up that resentments, guilts, unresolved conflicts, unfinished agenda of all sorts, snarl up our lives, and find physical outlet. We do not love ourselves enough: we cannot or will not face ourselves, or accept ourselves. The appearance of a cancer or of anything else is a great opportunity, which we should be prepared to use. The Psalmists of old knew this secret, and recognized God in it. 'O Lord, thou hast searched me out, and known me . . . Try me, O God, and seek the ground of my heart; prove me, and examine my thoughts. Look well if there be any way of wickedness in me.' 'So teach us to number our days, that we may apply our hearts unto wisdom.' 'I will thank the Lord for giving me warning' (and pain is a beneficent warning. One of the features of my sort of cancer is that one usually gets no warning till it is too late). For God is to be found in the cancer as in everything else. If he is not, then he is not the God of the Psalmist who said, 'If I go down to hell, thou art there also', let alone of the Christian who knows God most deeply in the Cross. And I have discovered this experience to be one full of grace and truth. I cannot say how grateful I am for all the love and kindness and goodness it has disclosed, which I am sure were always there but which it has taken this to bring home. Above all I would say it is relationships, both within the family and outside, which it has deepened and opened up. It has provided an opportunity for this and for my being made aware of it which might otherwise never have occurred. It has been a time of giving and receiving grace upon grace.

People sometimes say of a coronary, 'What a wonderful way to go', and as a process of dying for the individual concerned it must be preferable to much else. But it usually gives you no warning, no chance of making up your account. Still less does it allow loved ones to prepare. And preparing for death is increasingly recognized as a vital part of the process of grieving, of bearing reality, and of being restored to wholeness of body, mind and soul, both as individuals and as families.

But how does one prepare for death, whether of other people or of oneself? It is something we seldom talk about these days. Obviously there is the elementary duty (urged in the Prayer Book) of making one's will and other dispositions, which is no more of a morbid occupation than taking out life-insurance. And there is the deeper level of seeking to round off one's account, of ordering one's priorities and what one wants to do in the time available. And notice such as this gives concentrates the mind wonderfully and makes one realise how much of one's time one wastes or kills. When I was told that I had six months, or perhaps nine, to live, the first reaction was naturally of shock—though I also felt liberated, because, as in limited-over cricket, at least one knew the target one had to beat (and this target was but an informed guess from the experience and resources of the medical profession, by which I had no intention of being confined). But my second reaction was: 'But six months is a long time. One can do a lot in that. How am I going to use it?'

The initial response is to give up doing things—and it certainly sifts out the inessentials. My reaction was to go through the diary cancelling engagements. But I soon realised that this was purely negative; and I remembered the remark of Geoffrey Lampe, recently Regius Professor of Divinity here at Cambridge, who showed us how anyone should die of cancer: 'I can't die: my diary is far too full.'

In fact 'preparing for death' is not the other-worldly pious exercise stamped upon our minds by Victorian sentimentality, turning away from the things of earth for the things of 'heaven'. Rather, for the Christian it is preparing for 'eternal life', which means real living, more abundant life, which is begun, continued, though not ended, *now*. And this means it is about quality of life not quantity. How long it goes on here is purely secondary. So preparing for eternity means learning to live, not just concentrating on keeping alive. It means living it *up*, becoming *more* concerned with contributing to and enjoying what matters most—giving the most to life and getting the most from it, while it is on offer. So that is why, among other things, we went to Florence, where we had never been before, and to Switzerland to stay with friends we had to disappoint earlier because I entered hospital instead. I am giving myself too, in the limited working day I have before I tire, to all sorts of writing I want to finish. And if one goes for quality of life this may be the best way to extend its quantity. Seek first the kingdom of heaven—and who knows what shall be added? Pursue the wholeness of body, mind and spirit, and physical cure may, though not necessarily will, be a bonus.

'Your Life in Their Hands' is the title of another TV documentary on doctors. At one level this is true, the level of physical survival (thought it certainly is not the whole truth even of that). And my experience of the medical profession through all of this has been wholly positive. They have been superb in their skills and judgment and sensitivity—really listening rather than acting as gods who know the answers and treating you as the 'patient', the person simply on the receiving end. For the bigger men they are, and the more they know, the more they admit they don't know. Most of my month in hospital was spent simply in replumbing the stomach and getting it working again, and for this two operations proved necessary. In fact the cancer specialist did not arrive on the scene till towards the end, for there was nothing up to then that he could do. But when he did, he said: 'I know basically what your situation is; but before I say anything I want to hear how *you* feel about it.' How many professionals (and that includes not only doctors but lawyers and parsons) start like that? From the beginning I felt I was being asked to take my share of responsibility for my own health. And this was a point that came strongly through another series of BBC programmes this spring (and how fortunate we are compared with the TV of any other country I know!): 'A Gentle Way with Cancer?'. This was on the Bristol Cancer Help Centre, which is revealing and meeting an enormous need, and whose new building Prince Charles courageously opened the other day in the teeth of quite a bit of medical criticism. For this is alternative medicine, not opposing the profession and its techniques, but seeking to supplement them, at the dietary, psychological and spiritual levels (and the last level did not really come through the 'Mind Over Cancer' programme. Yet spirit over cancer is every bit as important). And at all points it is important to see these as complementary. For there are many approaches—orthodox and non-orthodox medicine, unexplained gifts of healing (which are no more necessarily connected with religion than are psychic powers) and prayer and faith-healing. I am convinced that one must be prepared, critically and siftingly (for one must test the spirits at every level), to start at all ends at once and I have been receiving the laying-on-of-hands from someone in whose approach I have great trust, which for me is a large part of faith (and I have deliberately not taken up others). In fact in everything I am a great both/and rather than either/or man. In the pursuit of truth I cannot believe that a one-eyed approach is ever sufficient. In the pursuit of peace I believe in both multilateralism and unilateralism. And in the pursuit of health this is even more obvious. For health *means* wholeness. It is concerned not simply with cure but with healing of the whole person in all his or her relationships. Hence the high-point of the Communion service, the gift of the bread of life and the cup of salvation, has traditionally been accompanied by the words, 'Preserve thy *body and soul* unto everlasting life', and it has ended with invoking 'the peace (the *shalom* or wholeness) of God which passes all understanding'.

Healing cannot be confined to any, or indeed every, level of human understanding or expectation. This is why too it shows up those twin deceivers pessimism and optimism as so shallow. In the course of nature, cancer-sufferers swing from one to the other more than most, as good days and bad days, remissions and recurrences, follow each other. But the Christian takes his stand not on optimism but on hope. This is based not on rosy prognosis (from the human point of view mine is bleak) but, as St Paul says, on suffering. For this, he says, trains us to endure, and endurance brings proof that we have stood the test, and this proof is the ground of hope—in the God who can bring resurrection out and through the other side of death. That is why he also says that though we carry death with us in our bodies (all of us) we never cease to be confident. His prayer is that 'always the greatness of Christ will shine out clearly in my person, whether through my life or through my death. For to me life is Christ, and death gain; but what if my living on in the body may serve some good purpose? Which then am I to choose? I cannot tell. I am torn two ways: what I should like'—he says more confidently than most of us could—'is to depart and be with Christ, that is better by far; but for your sake there is greater need for me to stay on in the body'. According to my chronology he lived nearly ten years after writing those words:

others would say it was shorter. But how little does it matter. He had passed beyond time and its calculations. He had risen with Christ. (4)

NOTES / SOURCES

1. John A. T. Robinson in Eric James, *A Life of Bishop John A. T. Robinson: Scholar, Pastor, Prophet*, London, 1987, pp. 116–18
2. Ibid., p. 239
3. Ibid., p. 303
4. Ibid., pp. 304–9

Gwen Harwood   1920–1995

The noted Australian poet Gwen Harwood (née Foster) was born in Brisbane, where she enjoyed a happy childhood in a comfortable middle-class family. She did not begin publishing poetry seriously until she was in her late thirties. By then she was married with four children and living in Hobart, Tasmania. Her first volume of poetry was published in 1963. She had initially hoped for a career in music, and was, before her marriage, a church organist. She had also, briefly, tested her vocation with an Anglican order in Toowong, Queensland.

Revival Rally

A delirium of shapes rising and falling:
bodies shake with salvation, arms fling wild
in appeal to the ceiling of the Gospel Hall.
A cripple throws her crutch away, revealing
a nightmare leg. A mother lifts her child,
which howls in terror at the preacher's blessing.
The wicked pianist leaps up, confessing
well-rehearsed sins; sits down; integrates all

the abundant noise with luscious harmonies.
Women who wear their makeup with the pathos
of peasant art settle their cardigans.
Their throats are hoarse, bare light bulbs sting their eyes.
They sing in hot, stale air, lapping the bathos
of a sodden hymn. Old adjectives, old rhymes
fondle their tongues. Amen. The cripple climbs
sweating after her crutch. The pianist fans

a shower of tiny insects from the keys.
The miracle of tongues has been withdrawn.
Let there be silence then. It shall inherit
the suburbs, from Eve's unblemished belly raise
a better race. Lights out. Time to shut down.
Outside, a superb nocturne: street by street
the city lifts its lamps, as if to greet
heaven with luminous gestures of the spirit. (1)

Death Has No Features of His Own

Death has no features of his own.
He'll take a young eye bathed in brightness
and the raging cheekbones of a raddled queen.
Misery's cured by his appalling taste.
His house is without issue. He appears
garlanded with lovebirds, hearts and flowers.
Anything, everything.
                              He'll wear my face and yours.
Not as we were, thank God. As we shall be
when we let go of the world, late ripe fruit falling.
What we are is beyond him utterly. (2)

NOTES / SOURCES

1. Gwen Harwood in *Anthology of Australian Religious Poetry*, selected by Les A. Murray, Victoria, Australia, 1986, pp. 10–11
2. Ibid., p. 116

Robert Alexander Kennedy Runcie   1921–2000

Born in Liverpool, Robert Runcie served in the Scots Guards during the Second World War and won an M.C. in 1945. After reading Classics at Brasenose College, Oxford, and training for ordination at Westcott House, Cambridge, he was successively curate in Gosforth, Newcastle upon Tyne, on the staff of Westcott House, Dean of Trinity Hall, Cambridge, and Principal of Cuddesdon Theological College. In 1970, he became Bishop of St Albans, and was Archbishop of Canterbury from 1980 to 1991. He was a widely respected lecturer and preacher whose wartime experience and classical formation, combined with a love of evolving tradition, made him speak out on controversial social issues.

Christ and Culture

I am encouraged by those clergy and congregations who make imaginative use of these folk festivals. On many a council estate it is the Mothering Sunday family service which is one of the best attended of the year. It is *not* Mothering Sunday and its ecclesiastical appeal which has created this. It is the commercial Mother's Day. Yes, it has sentimentalised notions of family life and motherhood, but the sheer fact that people want to put these into a religious context means that the folk festival can be fed with the resources of the Christian gospel. Christ is in culture, as well as against it. And of course you could illustrate that from customs surrounding marriage, or elsewhere from the radical way in which Indian Jesuits have developed a strategy for Christianizing Hinduism.

My point is not that we should lose the significance and distinctiveness of the Christian calendar, but rejoice at the 'rumours of God' which are stirred in the spirit of all people at these various times during the year. We do well to remind ourselves that Christmas was originally a pagan winter festival taken over by the

Church fairly late. We do well also to remind ourselves that through the feasting of that time of year numerous other ventures have arisen which presumably we would see as running with the tide of Christian teaching. I think of the extraordinary scene of the first Christmas Day during the First World War when Germans and British played football together between the trenches. I think more recently of the establishment of Crisis at Christmas—supported by politicians as much as churchmen. And there is much to rejoice at when we see society giving thanks for creation in the gifts of the harvest and expressing gratitude for motherhood and nurture within families. Our task is to 'church' these sentiments, not to belittle them.

But folk customs are one thing, philosophies and dogmas are another. Some attitudes have become so commonplace in our culture that we fail to see how much they conflict with Christ and the values of the Kingdom. Let us take just two examples: the notion of individual autonomy and the ascendancy of economic factors in moral decision making.

What is wrong with individual autonomy? Don't we all want to be free, to be responsible for our actions, to determine things for ourselves? A Christian can say at best to this, 'up to a point'. For, though we have free will, we are *not* free agents. We are accountable—to God and to each other. Christianity is a corporate religion, rooted in life within a community and our Christian character is revealed in our love of justice and love of others. The autonomous individual is on his or her own. We are not. We live by the grace of God, and in God we live, move and have our being. So a Christian is always likely to challenge a prevailing spirit of individual autonomy. It is a spurious freedom which neglects the demands of God. Remember those words of Alexander Solzhenitsyn when he diagnosed so accurately the sickness of Western society, 'Why have all these troubles come upon us? Because we have forgotten God.'

Perhaps we see more easily what is wrong with economic factors in moral decision making. In contemporary society, if a value or conviction is deemed 'uneconomic' it is too often regarded as worthless. Until recently this characterised our attitude to the environment. It was treated as a free resource. Since it had no economic price-tag, little else mattered. Aesthetic, moral, social, ecological and religious reasons for respecting the environment counted for little. And the growing change in attitude now may have more to do with the discovery of economic implications than perhaps we recognize.

Schumacher makes this point passionately in one of his books:

In the current vocabulary of condemnation there are few words as final or conclusive as 'uneconomic' . . . call a thing immoral or ugly, soul destroying or a degradation of man, a peril to the peace of the world or to the well-being of future generations; as long as you have not shown it to be 'uneconomic' you have not really questioned its right to exist, grow and prosper.

Is Christ against this element of culture? Certainly concepts like stewardship challenge it fundamentally because they contain a sense of accountability to the Creator. And it is accountability to God that contemporary Western culture finds hard to swallow. Yet our vision of the Kingdom must help us sense that God has given us a rich creation, that we live in a universe soaked in non-economic values, one in which beauty, truth and communal responsibility go alongside our stewardship of the earth's resources.

notes / sources
Adrian Hastings, *Robert Runcie*, London, 1991, pp. 3–4

Edmund John   1922–1975

Edmund John was born into a Christian family at Muheza in Tanzania. His brother, John Sepeku, later became the first Archbishop of the Church of the province of Tanzania. After a career in education and Radio Tanzania, Edmund had a vision which resulted in him starting to minister in the streets of Dar es Salaam and the beer halls. His ministry grew to include other areas of Tanzania often including miraculous healings and exorcisms. His pattern of Thursday meetings, revival groups, and visits is continued by the *Nyumba kwa Nyumba* (House to House) group now led by Cyprian Sallu.

Healing Ministry

Guidance for prayer groups in fasting and praying for the sick

1. It is desirable that the leader be a pastor wherever possible.
2. In order that the group receive the power of the Holy Spirit and have much blessing in its efforts, it must keep the following conditions:
   (a) Beginning with the pastor himself, the leader of the group and every member in the group must repent of all his sins to the Lord Jesus before climbing into his bed at night and before prayers.
   (b) He should not drink alcohol, or smoke cigarettes or tobacco.
   (c) He should pray every day, morning and evening.
   (d) Beginning with the pastor, the leader of the group and every member of the group must fast on the day of intercessions for the sick, as well as the sick people themselves and their helpers. Even the sick who are far away should fast on the day of intercessions.
   (e) The sick people must be given conditions to observe, that is, to pray, to fast, and to repent of their sins.
3. It is good for the pastor who leads the group (rather than the members of the group) to testify on Sundays in the congregation about the blessings and results of their prayers.
4. The day to pray for the sick must be observed with reverence and arranged carefully, for it is a very great worship occasion.
   (a) This service should not be held carelessly but done in good order according to the word of God.
   (b) It would be best that it should be held in a church or house which has been prepared for the purpose.
   These guidelines are those that are being used to this day in praying for the sick.

The duties of a counsellor

1. All the sick people are to be given these conditions:
   (a) To repent of the sins which are the origin of evil, difficulties, and troubles in the world. To repent secretly of these, not before other people.

(b) To accept Christ as the healer and to remove charms and anything else in which a man trusts as a talisman for his life. Let his defender be the Lord Jesus.

(c) Continue in prayer morning and evening, meanwhile give up ills such as drunkenness, smoking, and such like.

(d) On the day of arrival at the church, fasting is obligatory. Don't eat anything and continue to pray for forgiveness and place yourself under the protection of Christ.

Note carefully:

To take hospital medicine is not a bad thing. We do not want to engage in controversy with doctors. The ministry of healing the sick is something which hospital medicines cannot do, but they help to relieve pain. If sick people are patients in hospital they ought not to attend the healing service until they have obtained the doctor's permission to do so or have been discharged from the hospital.

2. Let the counsellors look out for the most needy. They will not be able to help everybody; there will be two thousand or so sick people every day.

3. Muslims and other unbelievers must be counselled to accept the Lord Jesus. But let us give them the freedom to choose for themselves. The counsellors will be able to obtain a book to help the sick in their first days of following Jesus, but this is for those whom they consider will be benefited by it. Also we must not forget that everyone should be given the Gospel of St Mark and the special leaflet *The healer is Jesus Christ.* The counsellors may not receive any money at all for the books and no gifts or such like, even on behalf of the church.

4. There will be those who are healed and those who are not healed. Let us not forget to comfort those who are not healed. Some of them need further explanation that we are sinners and need the salvation of Jesus. Let others know that healing is the will of God. Don't let the sick become discouraged. Let all of them observe the conditions and continue to pray alone or with other Christians and to read the Bible. Jesus tells everyone who is healed, 'See, you are made whole, sin no more lest a worse thing befall you' (John 5. 14 and Matthew 12. 43–46).

5. Counsellors are asked to give help if needed before the ministry begins.

NOTES / SOURCES

Joseph A. Namata, *Edmund John, Man of God: A Healing Ministry*, Kambata, A.C.T., 1986 (Translated from *Edmund John mtu wa Mungu*, Tanzania), pp. 39, 54–5

William Hubert Vanstone   1923–1999

Born in a Lancashire vicarage in a working-class parish, William Vanstone served in the RAF before taking a double First at Balliol College, Oxford, and then training for the ministry at Westcott House, Cambridge. After further study at the General Theological Seminary in New York, Vanstone was ordained in 1950. Described in one obituary as 'a 20th-century John Keble', Vanstone steadfastly refused all offers of academic posts, preferring to devote his life to pastoral ministry, serving 21 years in a Lancashire parish until a heart attack in 1975 persuaded him to accept the post of Canon Residentiary at

Chester Cathedral. His three books *Love's Endeavour, Love's Expense* (1977), *The Stature of Waiting* (1982), and *Fare Well in Christ* (1997) clearly demonstrated his frequent assertion that Christianity is not a system but a way of life.

The Recognition of the Love of God

So it is that the love of God, in waiting upon the response of recognition, waits upon its own celebration. It waits upon the response in which its own nature and quality is understood: and this response must not be interpreted as a mere 'state of mind', an impression stamped upon passive material by love's own will. It is not so that greatness in creativity is recognised or understood. The understanding of it is itself a form of creativity—an attempt to articulate, an activity of struggle between the richness of content and the discipline of form, the coming-to-be of that which was not there before. Recognition of the love of God involves, as it were, the forging of an offering: the offering is the coming-to-be of understanding: only where this understanding has come to be has love conveyed its richest blessing and completed its work in triumph. Where understanding is possible but absent, or where it is confused and inarticulate, love's work is incomplete and its issue tragic.

Thus we may say that the creativity of God is dependent, for the completion and triumph of its work, upon the emergence of a responsive creativity—the creativity of recognition. Recognition is to be understood neither as a single psychological event nor as a state of mind brought about by such an event. It is to be understood as creativity directly and explicitly responsive to the creativity of God. We may say that the response of recognition *celebrates* the love of God. The final triumph of the love of God is the celebration of His love within that universe which has received that love.

That by which, or in which, the love of God is celebrated may be called 'the Church'. The Church occupies the enclave of recognition within the area of freedom: it is all within the area of freedom which would not be if the love of God were not recognised as love: it is all that is done to articulate awareness of the Creator's love. So defined, the Church is much wider than any recognised ecclesiastical structure, and wider than the sum of all such structures. For it must include the simplest action which is done out of awareness of God's love and the most private meditation which seeks, in unspoken words, to articulate that awareness. But, on the other hand, the Church, even when so defined, is not wholly without structure and without form. For the Church is, or consists of, creative activity: and creative activity, however simple or flexible in form, is never without form. Even in the silence of private meditation there is the endeavour to give shape to awareness, to fix its transience or order its abundance by the discipline of form: and every action, even of the simplest kind, is itself the form in which the vagueness of intention is crystallised into creation. Therefore the Church, so far from being without structure or form, is the sum of all the structures and forms within which men express their recognition of the love of God: and always the being of the Church involves the elements of search and struggle, the dynamic and dialectical encounter between content and form, which is the fundamental characteristic of all creative activity. The Church, however broadly defined, is never pure spontaneity and never free from the discipline of form. Old forms may be abandoned and new forms sought, but so long as the Church is responsive creativity it can never pass beyond the need for form nor escape from the demands of form. In the Church, as in all creative activity, the demands of form, when first encountered, must appear as restriction: only when they are met are they discovered to be liberation. (1)

The Church the Offering of Love

Man in the Church is aware of himself as being under a degree of discipline. His aspiration is not to express *himself* but to express responsive love. Therefore he may not use whatever form or symbol comes most naturally to himself and is least demanding upon himself. He must use a form or symbol whose achievement makes upon him some degree of demand and involves him in some kind of cost. Within the Church, he must surrender something of his own freedom and spontaneity: he must bring his life within a form which is not entirely natural to him and not specifically adapted to his own particular temperament and needs. He must see the form of the Church as, in some degree, alien to himself, as that to which he must bring himself to conform. His sense that the Church is alien to him must be overcome not by the changing of the Church but by the changing of himself.

The Church presents itself to man as an institution with a history. It is something which the present inherits from the past, and of which the form is already given. To repudiate form simply because it is no longer 'natural' would be to refuse that surrender of one's own freedom and spontaneity which is involved in authentic love. But, on the other hand, the form of the Church is itself the product of history, and has been determined, at least in part, by the attitudes and presuppositions of other ages. It may be that a form which disciplines the response of one age distorts or destroys the response of another: that a form has come to have such associations that it can no longer express what man would say, but only distort or destroy it. The need then arises for reform. But the reform of the Church is a matter of extreme delicacy and difficulty. For the search is not for the form which will most easily contain the spontaneity of the present age, but for a form which will impose upon that spontaneity a degree of discipline. The task is not simply to bring the spontaneity of the present age within the Church: it is to form that spontaneity into the costly offering of love. Reform of the Church requires more than sociological insight into contemporary trends and attitudes: it requires also the artist's understanding and the lover's experience of the costly discipline of love.

Within the form of the Church, inherited or re-formed, man aspires to present an offering of love—an offering fashioned by discipline out of freedom. This offering is brought into being. It is something that actually is. It belongs to the same level of concrete actuality as the stones and trees and stars in which the creativity of God is expressed and completed. As the creativity of the artist is nothing until, through struggle and discipline, it discovers itself in the emergence of a work of art, so the responsive creativity of man to the love of God is nothing until it discovers itself in the emergence of the concrete actuality of the Church. The Church is not 'the cause which the Church serves' or 'the spirit in which the Church lives': the Church is the service of that cause and the actualisation of that spirit in words spoken, in bodies in a certain place or posture, in feet walking up a certain hill: in stone placed upon stone to build a Church, in wood carved into the fashion of a Cross: in music composed or practised, played or sung: in the doing of certain things upon a particular day and the giving up of certain things during a particular season: in the fashioning, out of time and care and skill, of something beautiful, and in the maintaining, out of time and care and labour, of the beauty of it: in the gathering and training of others so that they may contribute to and continue and enlarge the offering: in the going out to others so that they may share the offering: in the struggle of brain and pen to find expression and interpretation for the love of God: in the event of worship which celebrates the love of God: in hands stretched out for the receiving of Bread and in lips raised for the touch of Wine. Here, at this level of concrete actuality is the response of recognition to the love of God: here is the work of art, the offering of love, which is the Church.

The understanding of the Church as offering throws fresh light on some of those duties of Churchmanship which are felt rather than understood, and which are performed with diligence but not explained with clarity. It throws light, for example, on that attachment to the Church building itself which obstructs many proposals for reform and reorganisation of the Church. The obstructive fact is that the building is felt to be neither a necessity nor a facility but an offering. Love has been expended upon it and expressed in the care of it. In that love and care the building has been offered to God. That the building is little used, and in that sense unnecessary, is irrelevant. That a similar building stands at no great distance away is also irrelevant. The presentation of such facts as if they were decisive is often, and understandably, resented. Attachment to a Church building is by no means to be dismissed as sentimentality: it may well contain a profound, though possibly inarticulate, understanding of what that building is. In the last analysis, the only justification for the destruction of an offering is that it may become the basis or material of a richer, more lasting or more appropriate offering. This must be the principle which distinguishes the reorganisation of the Church from its destruction. (2)

NOTES / SOURCES

1. William Hubert Vanstone, *Love's Endeavour, Love's Expense: The Response of Being to the Love of God*, London, 1977, pp. 96–8
2. Ibid., pp. 107–9

Lakshman Wickremesinghe 1927–1983

Lakshman Wickremesinghe was from a high-caste landowning Sinhalese family. He studied at the University of Ceylon, and subsequently at Keble College, Oxford, and Ely Theological College, followed by ordination and a curacy in Poplar, London. He was Bishop of Kurunagala in Sri Lanka from 1962 until his early death in 1983, which left the churches in Asia bereft of one of their finest leaders. A distinguished contemporary described him as 'churchman, mystic, evangelist, human rights activist and reconciler, prophet, pastor, and theologian'.

The Worship of the Servant Lord

We Christians in Asia are caught in an ecclesio-ideological conflict between triumphalist disciples of a triumphalist Lord and servant disciples of a servant Lord; whereas the biblical insights rightly understood point to a Lord who exercises that kind of authority over others and achieves that kind of success in the world from those qualities of character which He indicated as belonging to a servant or child. There is divine wisdom in this symbolism that reminds us of the different kind of divine wisdom which humbled the triumphalist sage Markandeya in his encounter with the Supreme Lord. We Christians in Asia need to encounter afresh our only Lord so that His divine wisdom may humble us for performing service and exercising power in His name. This also was the prayer of the group of early disciples in Jerusalem in their vulnerable situation in relation to the authorities.

What are the implications then for the established church in opting to be disciples of Christ Jesus as the servant Lord? First, there are implications in the sphere of worship. The image of the Lord we worship must be that of a servant whose royalty is in His service rather than of a king whose royalty is in his majesty. There are three indigenous symbols for the Lord Jesus I see every day; two are in the Cathedral in which I take services, and one is in the house in which I live. They are creations of Buddhists working in collaboration with Christians. One is of Christ with wounds, reigning from the cross as prophet, priest and king. The second is of Christ naked on the cross, but with the poise of the dancer whose rhythmic dancebeat of love on the cross has overcome the poisonous virus of evil. The third is of an ordinary man emerging from the background of the cross with the five blood-stained wounds, standing in the midst of ordinary people to serve them. It is this third figure, of Christ as the servant Lord, that inspires me most, and is the figure that has special relevance for Christians in Asia today.

The figures or images of Jesus that dominate our imagination also shape our worship and mould our actions. In our painting and sculpture, our hymns and prayers, the image of Jesus as the servant Lord needs to be given greater prominence. Likewise, we need to make our places of worship much more places where service is rendered to others: and make places where service is rendered to others in everyday life also places of worship. Our rites and ceremonies, our forms of worship must through shared silence and shared actions and gestures, especially in small groups, convey the mystery and majesty of the lowliness of the servant Lord, rather than of the pomp and panoply of a reigning monarch. Serving food to each other, washing each other's feet in a natural way, rather than as a 'stunt,' in the context of shared worship, can convey the presence of the Lord among us as One who serves. This kind of stress on the servant Lord need not be the sole preserve of small groups of Christians outside the mainstream of the established church. The way that the late Subhir Biswas made use of St Paul's Cathedral in Calcutta through worship and service to convey Jesus as the servant Lord is an outstanding example. He showed in concrete terms what it meant to come down the ladder in lowliness, and to break down the barriers erected by society through outreaching and caring service; and he laid down his life as a result. But others can follow his example in their own way, within the congregation to which they belong. (1)

Anglican Worship in Asian Context

In our Cathedral in Kurunegala, the altar is given a very prominent place in the sanctuary as one of the major foci in the building. Behind it is a colossal figure of Jesus Christ sculptured on the east wall, like the colossal figure of the Buddha in ancient Lankatilaka. The figure is draped in the stole of a priest with arms stretched on the cross, with a crown on his head, the garment of a prophet, and the marks of the crucifixion discernible on hands, feet, and side. The all-encompassing compassion gathers up all mankind within the created order to offer the total sacrifice (of himself) as representative high-priest, to reconcile man in creation to God. It is not the nails but loving compassion that fixes him to the cross; and the crown is the symbol of exaltation of a suprahuman figure. When one looks at the altar and the supra-human high-priest on the cross, one recognises the innovation in the socio-cultural context. There is the fulfilment of the image of the 'yagna-purusha,' the primal-man, sacrificed on the altar to reconcile creation with God as depicted in Hindu scripture; and there is the fulfilment of the prophet-martyr-satyagrahi (self-sacrifice in suffering love) image which Gandhi forged in the modern Hindu tradition of activist spirituality. The marks of the crucifixion present in the supra-human and crowned figure are a symbol of the divinised Jesus subsumed within the cosmic Christ in the role of the high-priest of creation-redemption. Suffering remains, but it is absorbed into the abiding serenity conveyed by the face of the colossal Jesus Christ. Here is both innovation and continuity with biblical perspective.

When we hold high festival in this Cathedral we bring the symbols of creation and of redemption in procession to the altar as a sign of the oblation of the people of God to be taken into the oblation of the eternal high-priest, as we celebrate the Eucharist. We offer flowers, lights, incense, the sound of drumming, the melody of singing and the stylised movement of dancing, along with other offerings. Things offered depend on the specific occasion, but are from the socio-cultural environment. Alongside the sanctuary are both painting and sculpture to depict St Mary and St Thomas (patron saint of India) along with the angels, to signify the unseen dimension of the worship of the total church. The ritual is interpreted by the accompanying word and also by the interspaced silence, as the hearing of the word and the absorbing of the silence give depth to the imaginative impact of the rites. Here is innovation again, as we fulfil both the contemplative silence and the liturgical ritual which uses the senses, the body and the imagination, as witnessed in the ceremonies of Hinduism and Buddhism. But there is some continuity with biblical religion at least in its 'Catholic' aspect. (2)

Christians and Buddhist Devotion: Mutual Respect and Appropriate Boundaries

The other example relates to the visit of the Archbishop of Canterbury to the Temple of the Tooth, the central sanctuary of the Sinhala Buddhism. It has ceremonies which include both ritual acts and the chanting of scriptural texts to signify the meaning of these acts. It contains images of the Buddha, and also his tooth which is venerated as a supreme relic, and is encased in a reliquary in an inner shrine. There is no worship in Buddhism except among the superstitious. The relic, the sculpture and painting are visual aids; the placing of good before the reliquary is a manual aid, and the chanting of texts an auditory aid for the act of anamnesis. The aim is to remember the Buddha as if he were alive and present in the midst of life. Gratitude and renewed resolution to follow his path are linked. There is a numinous atmosphere, since the Buddha is viewed as the supreme example of history of the realised transcendental goal of human life. The closest parallel in Christianity would be the ceremonies, including ritual acts and chanting along with the use of incense, in a numinous atmosphere, before the reserved sacrament on the altar. All these are aids for the act of anamnesis, so that Jesus Christ, the supreme revelation of the transcendent Father, becomes alive and present in the midst of believers. Thanksgiving and inspired commitment to imitate the exalted Lord are linked to this anamnesis.

I took the Archbishop to visit this Buddhist sanctuary at the invitation of the custodian chief monk (who was his equivalent in status among the monks of Sri Lanka). We made certain gestures. We removed our footwear as is the custom. For us it was an act of reverence to Gautama the Buddha as a religious leader of spiritual insight and moral stature, whose relic was a continuing symbol of his historic personality and acknowledged saintliness. Even Clement, when referring to the barbarian philosophers, says that 'Some too of the Indians obey the precepts of the Buddha, whom on account of his exceptional holiness, they have raised to divine honours' (Stromateis 1. 15). Following some of the early Fathers like Clement, Origen, Augustine, and Niceta, we viewed Gautama as one of the 'just persons being made perfect' who belonged to the company of those who will be included within the heavenly Jerusalem. In that sense, his shrine was a sign and vehicle to us of the God whom we worshipped, who indwelt the saintly Gautama, whatever his erroneous views; and so we paid him due reverence. We also permitted the monks to chant blessings upon us, which they wished to do out of respect and goodwill to an international religious leader. However, we did not place our folded hands in front of our breasts with bowed heads as the Buddhists among us did, because we did not accept the interpretation of this blessing in the texts they chanted. We received the blessing as from God whose presence we acknowledged there; and the Archbishop wished them God's blessing in that very place where we were received officially. Like the Samaritans who offered sacrifices through their rites and ceremonies in Mount Gerazim, the monks and the Buddhist laity sharing in these rites and ceremonies in Kandy did not know the real significance of what they were doing. We knew before Whom these cultic acts were being performed, and we conveyed this understanding by our presence and the gestures we made and did not make.

We were asked whether we would place a tray of flowers before the relic; we declined. We might have done so, and not followed it by another act of holding our folded hands above our bowed heads, as Buddhists do, following Eastern tradition. The first act would have been a mere act of reverence before a saintly person's statue. The second act, which implies supreme veneration to the highest realisation on earth of the Transcendent, we could not do under any circumstances. But we abstained from the first ritual act to avoid misunderstanding and offence. Christians in Sri Lanka also offer flowers as a ritual act, as is done before the altar in our Cathedral and elsewhere. We do this to offer thanks and adoration to the Creator, whose unfading beauty is the source of the finite beauty of the flowers we offer. But when Buddhists offer flowers before the relic with accompanying manual act, they say, 'As these flowers fade, so fade I; such is the transience of life.' This ritual act of placing a tray of flowers as an offering has different meanings for Christians and Buddhists. Thus, to do so in the inner shrine room before the relic would have caused confusion among many. The simple Christian would have thought that the Archbishop was doing something idolatrous; the simple Buddhist would have thought that the Archbishop was acting out of insincere motives. St Paul's admonition about not offending the weaker brother and sister seemed the advice that the Archbishop and I, as Christian leaders, had to follow. That is why we abstained. But we did not consider that the ceremonies performed at this sanctuary were being offered simply to demons, or that the sanctuary itself was simply the abode of demons. Those who performed these ceremonies did not do something intentionally maleficent, nor were they subject to maleficent influences afterwards. We recognised that whatever good was done there was acceptable to God as we know Him in Jesus Christ, and whose Presence is everywhere in degrees of hiddenness. What was erroneous or done with an evil intention or deluded mind was due to the deception of the evil one. So, we acted according to our understanding of what was and what was not idolatry. Seeing what Clement said about the Buddha, I do not know how else he would have acted in the circumstances. (3)

NOTES / SOURCES

1. Lakshman Wickremesinghe, *Living in Christ with People*, D. T. Niles Memorial Lecture, Christian Conference of Asia Assembly, Bangalore, 1981*
2. Lakshman Wickremesinghe, *Ecclesiological Issues Emerging from Asian Manifestations of the Life, Worship and Witness of the Church*, a paper for the Christian Conference of Asia Theological Commission, Kandy, Sri Lanka, August 1982*
3. Lakshman Wickremesinghe, *Christianity Moving Eastwards*, a talk given at the House of Saints Gregory and Macrina, Oxford, 20 May 1983*
* Reprinted in the CTC *Bulletin* (Christian Conference of Asia, Singapore) Vol. 5, Nos. 1–2, April–August 1984

William Stringfellow 1929–1985

William Stringfellow was born during the Depression, the son of a knitter in the hosiery industry, who was frequently unemployed. He played an active part in student youth movements, and then qualified as a lawyer. His passion for social justice led to work as a street lawyer in Harlem, New York, and to a concern with biblical politics. He wrestled with the theology of power and the politics of spirituality (the title of his last book).

The Folly of Religion

See to it that no one makes a prey of you by philosophy and empty deceit, according to human tradition, according to the elemental spirits of the universe, and not according to Christ.

Colossians 2. 8

Personally, I find no cause to be interested in mere religion. It can be a certain diversion, I admit, to speculate and argue about religious ideas and practices, but I am no longer in college, and my law practice does not often permit the luxury of hypothetical and speculative matters. It appears to me more urgent and more necessary to deal with history, that is, with actual life as it has preceded the present time, and with the actual life of the present time. So I do not bother, as far as I am aware, with dabbling in religion. And if, as it may in my own lifetime turn out, Protestantism—like Zen, or 'religious science,' or the other sects—is or becomes only an institution of religion devoted to its own maintenance and a practice of religion for its own sake, then I am just not superstitious enough to remain a Protestant.

But when, now and then, I turn to and listen to the Bible, or when, now and then, I hear the Word of God exposed in preaching, or when, now and then, I see the gospel represented in the Holy Communion and I thereupon become a participant in and witness of the real life that is given to the world, or when, now and then, I meet some Christian, or when, now and then, I discern and encounter the presence of God's Word in the ordinary affairs of everyday existence in the world—on these occasions, in these circumstances, I am reminded, if sometimes ruefully, that the gospel is no mere religion in *any* essential respect.

For in any of these circumstances, on any of these occasions, what is emphatic and lucid and—best of all—*true* is that this gospel of Jesus Christ ends all religious speculation; demolishes all merely religious ceremonies and sacrifices appeasing unknown gods; destroys every exclusiveness that religion attaches to itself in God's name; attests that the presence of God is not remote, distant, and probably out-of-reach—but here, now, and with us in this world, already. This gospel means that the very life of God is evident in this world, in this life, because Jesus Christ once participated in the common human life in the history of our world.

The Christian faith is distinguished, diametrically, from mere religion in that religion begins with the proposition that some god exists; Christianity, meanwhile, is rejoicing in God's manifest presence among us. Religion describes human beings, mind you, usually sincere and honorable and intelligent ones, searching for God or, more characteristically, searching for some substitute for God—that is, some idea of what God may be like—or would be like—and then worshipping that idea and surrounding that substitution with dogma and discipline. But the gospel tells when and how and why and where God has sought us and found us and offered to take us into God's life. Religion is the attempt to satisfy the curiosity of human beings in this world about God; Jesus Christ is the answer to the human curiosity in this world about what it means to be truly human in this world that God created. Religion is fulfilled, always, in one of two ways: either (1) in consecrating some object or power or ideology or person—or, in earlier days, some commodity or natural phenomenon or animal or any thing—as a god and as, hopefully, *the god* or (2) in projecting god beyond history, into the unknown and the unknowable, enthroned, perhaps, before this life or in some afterlife but never in *this* life, out of this world, oblivious of the present existence and grandly indifferent to it, abstract, irrelevant, impotent, indifferent—a ridiculous god, in fact, no god at all.

So, just personally, religion does not particularly intrigue me, though the gospel does. Religion does not address my practical, everyday, working life, but the gospel does. I do not care—I do not mean to be impudent, but I, for one, do not care—if God lives somewhere and someplace else. But I care a lot when I hear—in the Bible, or in the church, or in the presence of a Christian, or in the ordinary happenings of my own life—that God is with us now, anyway and already, and even, thank God, before we call upon God. I care a lot, in other words, when I hear the news of Jesus Christ, because it is a different news than I receive when I encounter the various religions.

Part of the difference is, obviously, the news that God (even) cares for me (even). All those smaller gods—the gods of the various religions—are indifferent to that. What they care about, what idols are concerned with—is whether they are worshipped, is whether their own existence is verified and lauded. But Christ speaks very differently. Indeed, Christ embodies the difference between religion and the gospel. Christ bespeaks the care of God for everything to do with actual life, with life as it is lived by anybody and everybody day in and day out. Christ bespeaks *my* life: in all its detail and mistake and humor and fatigue and surprise and contradiction and freedom and ambiguity and quiet and wonder and sin and peace and vanity and variety and lust and triumph and defeat and rest and love and all the rest that it is from time to time; and, cheer up, with *your* life, just as much, in as full intimacy, touching your whole biography, abiding every secret, *with you*, whoever, wherever you are, any time, any place. Christ bespeaks the destinies of nations, and all the lesser principalities and powers, the corporations and universities and unions and utilities and the whole frighteningly complex constellation of authorities that assert themselves in the day-to-day life of the world.

In short, religion supposes that God is yet to be discovered; Christianity knows that God has already come among us. Religious speculation suspects there is God, somewhere, sometime; the gospel reports God's presence and action in this world even in those circumstances of which we are unaware. Religion suppresses the truth because the truth obviates religion.

The religious suppose that only the religious know about God or care about God, and that God cares only for the religious. Characteristically, religion is precious and possessive toward God and institutes and conducts itself as if God really needs religion, as if God's existence depends upon the recognition of religion. Religion considers that God is a secret disclosed only in the discipline and practice of religion. But all this is most offensive to the Word of God. The best news of God is that God is no secret. The news of God embodied in Jesus Christ is that God is openly and notoriously active in the world. In this news the Christian church is constituted; it is this news that the Christian church exists to spread. Where the church, however, asserts that God is hidden in or behind creed or ceremony—even those that are decent and that God gladly receives and blesses—or where God is thought to be confined to the sanctuary, then in such events the Christian church, forsaking the good news of God's presence in history, becomes a vulgar imitation of mere religion. The church, where faithful to the news, is not the place where people come to seek God; on the contrary, the church is just the place where human beings gather to declare that God takes the initiative in seeking them. The church, unlike any religion, exists to present to the world and to celebrate in the world, and on behalf of the world, God's presence and power and utterance and action in the ongoing life of the world. (1)

Money

Idolatry, whatever its object, represents the enshrinement of any other person or thing in the very place of God. Idolatry embraces some person or thing, instead of God, as the source and rationalization of the moral significance of this life in the world for, at least, the idolater, though not, necessarily, for anybody else at all. Thus human beings, as idolaters, have from time to time worshipped stones and snakes and suns and fire and thunder, their own dreams and hallucinations, images of themselves and of their progenitors; they have had all the Caesars, ancient and modern, as idols; others have fancied sex as a god; for many, race is an idol; some worship science, some idolize superstition. Within that pantheon, money is a most conspicuous idol.

The idolatry of money means that the moral worth of a person is judged in terms of the amount of money possessed or controlled. The acquisition and accumulation of money in itself is considered evidence of virtue. It does not so much matter how money is acquired—by work or invention, through inheritance or marriage, by luck or theft—the main thing is to get some. The corollary of this doctrine, of course, is that those without money are morally inferior—weak, or indolent, or otherwise less worthy as human beings. Where money is an idol, to be poor is a sin.

This is an obscene idea of justification, directly in contradiction with the Bible. In the gospel none are saved by any works of their own, least of all by the mere acquisition of money. In fact, the New Testament is redundant in citing the possession of riches as an impediment to salvation when money is regarded idolatrously. At the same time, the notion of justification by acquisition of money is empirically absurd, for it oversimplifies the relationship of the prosperous and the poor and overlooks the dependence of the rich upon the poor for their wealth. In this world human beings live at each other's expense, and the affluence of the few is proximately related to, and supported by, the poverty of the many.

This interdependence of rich and poor is something Americans are tempted to overlook, since so many Americans are in fact prosperous, but it is true today as it was in earlier times: the vast multitudes of people on the face of the earth are consigned to poverty for their whole lives, without any serious prospect whatever of changing their conditions. Their hardships in great measure make possible the comfort of those who are not poor; their poverty maintains the luxury of others; their deprivation purchases the abundance most Americans take for granted.

That leaves prosperous Americans with frightful questions to ask and confront, even in customs or circumstances that are regarded as trivial or straightforward or settled. Where, for instance, do the profits that enable great corporations to make large contributions to universities and churches and charity come from? Do they come from the servitude of Latin American peasants working plantations on seventy-two-hour weekly shifts for gross annual incomes of less than a hundred dollars? Do they depend upon the availability of black child labor in South Africa and Rhodesia? Are such private beneficences in fact the real earnings of some of the poor of the world?

To affirm that we live in this world at each other's expense is a confession of the truth of the Fall rather than an assertion of economic doctrine or a precise empirical statement. It is not that there is in every transaction a direct one-for-one cause and effect relationship, either individually or institutionally, between the lot of the poor and the circumstances of those who are not poor. It is not that the wealthy are wicked or that the fact of malice is implicit in affluence. It is, rather, theologically speaking, that all human and institutional relationships are profoundly distorted and so entangled that no person or principality in this world is innocent of involvement in the existence of all other persons and all institutions . . .

The idolatry of money has its most grotesque form as a doctrine of immortality. Money, is, then, not only evidence of the present moral worth of a person but also the way in which a life gains moral worth after death. If someone leaves a substantial estate, death is cheated of victory for a while, if not ultimately defeated, because the money left will sustain the memory of the person and of the fortune. The poor just die and are at once forgotten. It is supposed important to amass money not for its use in life but as a monument in death. Money thus becomes the measure of a person's moral excellence while alive and the means to purchase a certain survival of death. Money makes people not only moral but immortal; that is the most profound and popular idolatry of money.

To the Christian conscience, all ideas of immortality—along with all notions of self-justification including that of the mere acquisition of money or other property—are anathema. The gospel of Jesus Christ is not concerned with immortality but with the resurrection from death; not with the survival of death either in some 'afterlife' or in the memorialization of life after death. The gospel is, instead, distinguished by the transcendence of the power of death here and now within the precincts of life in this world. The gospel discerns and exposes *all* forms of idolatry as the worship of death, and, thus, the gospel recognizes and publicizes the idolatry of money or property in any form as both false and futile. False because where money is an idol—that is, where money is thought to impute great or even ultimate moral significance to the one who holds it—it pre-empts the place of God; futile because money, and everything whatsoever that money can buy or build or do, along with those who lust after or gain money, dies. Where money is beheld as an idol, in truth the idol that is secreted in such worship is death. The gospel is about resurrection and it is that which unmasks the fraudulent association of all promissory doctrines of immortality with idolatry in one or another fashion. The gospel, in other words, has to do with the readily available power of God's grace to emancipate human beings in this life from all idols of death, even money—and even in America.

It is the freedom from idolatry of money that Christ offers the rich young man in the parable. Remember, it is not that money is inherently evil or that the possession of money as such is sin. The issue for the Christian (and ultimately, for everyone) is whether a person trusts money more than God and comes to rely on money rather than on grace for the assurance of moral significance, both as an individual and in relationship with the whole of humanity.

As a Christian I am aware—with more intimate knowledge and, therefore, with even greater anguish than those outside the church—that the churches in American society nowadays are so much in the position of that rich young man in the parable that they are rarely in a position to preach to prosperous Americans, much less to the needy. Even where the churches are not engaged in deliberate idolatry of money, the overwhelming share of the resources in money and other property inherited by and given to the trust of the churches ends up being utilized just for the upkeep of the ecclesiastical establishment. Appeals are still being made that to give money to the churches is equivalent to giving money to God. Of course anyone, who cares to, or who is free to do so, can see through such a claim: it is just a modern—albeit less candid, yet more vulgar—sale of indulgences, an abuse against which there is a venerable history of protest beginning with Jesus himself when he evicted the money-changers from the temple.

Freedom from idolatry of money, for a Christian, means that money becomes useful only as a sacrament—as a sign of the restoration of life wrought in this world by Christ. The sacramental use of money has little to do with supporting the church after the manner of contributing to conventional charities and even less with the self-styled stewardship that solicits funds mainly for the maintenance of ecclesiastical salaries and the housekeeping of churchly properties. The church and the church's mission do not represent another charity to be subsidized as a necessary or convenient benevolence, or as a moral obligation, or in order to reassure the prosperous that they are either generous or righteous. Appeals for church support as charity or for maintenance commonly end up abetting the idolatry of money.

Such idolatry is regularly dramatized in the offertory, where it is regarded as 'the collection' and as an intermission in the worship of the people of the congregation. Actually, the offertory is integral to the sacramental existence of the church, a way of representing the oblation of the totality of life to God. No more fitting symbol of the involvement of Christians in the everyday life of the world could be imagined, in American society at least, than money, for nearly every relationship in personal and public life is characterized by the obtaining or spending or exchange of money. If then, in worship, human beings offer themselves and all of their decisions, actions, and words to God, it is well that they use money as the witness to that offering. Money is, thus, used sacramentally within the church and not contributed as to some charity or given because the church, as such, has any need of money.

The sacramental use of money in the formal and gathered worship of the church is authenticated—as are all other churchly sacramental practices—in the sacramental use of money in the common life of the world.

No end of ways exist in which money can be so appropriated and spent, but, whatever the concrete circumstances, the consistent mark of such a commitment of money is a person's freedom from idolatry of money. That includes not simply freedom from an undue affection for money but, much more than that, freedom from moral dependence upon the pursuit, acquisition, or accumulation of money for the sake of justifying oneself or one's conduct or actions or opinions, either to oneself or to anybody else. It means the freedom to have money, to use money, to spend money without worshipping money, and thus it means the freedom to do without money, if need be, or, having some, to give it away to anyone who seems to need money to maintain life a while longer.

The charity of Christians, in other words, in the use of money sacramentally—in both the liturgy and in the world—has no serious similarity to conventional charity but is always a specific dramatization of the members of the Body of Christ losing their life in order that the world be given life. For members of the church, therefore, it always implies a particular confession that their money is not their own because their lives are not their own but, by the example of God's own love, belong to the world.

That one's own life belongs to the world, that one's money and possessions, talents and time, influence and wealth, all belong to the whole world is, I trust, why the saints are habitués of poverty and ministers to the outcasts, friends of the humiliated and, commonly, unpopular themselves. Contrary to many legends, the saints are not spooky figures, morally superior, abstentious, pietistic. They are seldom even remembered, much less haloed. In truth, all human beings are called to be saints, but that just means called to be fully human, to be perfect—that is, whole, mature, fulfilled. The saints are simply those men and women who relish the event of life as a gift and who realise that the only way to honour such a gift is to give it away. (2)

NOTES / SOURCES

1. *A Keeper of the Word: Selected Writings of William Stringfellow* (ed. Bill Wylie Kellermann), Grand Rapids, Michigan, USA, 1994, pp. 119–22
2. Ibid., pp. 245–250

David Watson   1933–1984

Born into a non-churchgoing family, David Watson studied at Cambridge where he was deeply affected by a sermon on Trinity Sunday 1955 given by Cyril Bowles, Principal of Ridley Hall Theological College, on the need for ordinands. As a curate at the Round Church, Cambridge, he experienced a 'second blessing', the awareness of the powerful presence of the Holy Spirit. His ministry in York, first at St Cuthbert's (1965) and then at St Michael-le-Belfrey (1973) were marked out by his preaching ministry and innovative worship influenced by the charismatic movement. Whilst Watson feared the 'respectable objectivism end' of traditional worship, he nonetheless saw the danger of the individualistic piety characteristic of some charismatic worship.

Praise

True worship must always be first and foremost God-ward in its direction, even though the expression of worship, certainly in terms of serving and giving, may bring much blessing to other people. But when we are taken up with worship, and when we are unashamed of the fact that we are in love with God and in love with one another, that can be very powerful indeed. The world today is starved of love, suffocated with words, bereft of joy, and lacking in peace. Therefore, 'a praising community preaches to answer questions raised by its praise'. (1)

The Gift of Tongues

Then there came more fuel for the fire of opposition. After some months of prayer, David began to experience the gift of tongues. Of all the spiritual gifts, this was the most inexplicable and unacceptable to other Christians. David writes in *You Are My God*:

In our Western Christianity we have become so cautious about subjective experiences because of their obvious dangers that we tend to rule them out altogether. However, no one can read the New Testament without seeing that it is shot through with specific and often dramatic experiences of the Spirit. It is because of the comparative absence of these that the Church today stands in such desperate need of renewal.

If the spiritual gifts seem to threaten the orderly practice of biblical Christianity, so particularly did the suppression of the mind in moments of prayer when the voice spoke to God in a language which the speaker could not understand. To the non-charismatic Christian, it was so supernatural that it was weird. It could even be satanic. It was doubly suspect because the Pentecostals taught that tongues was the mark of baptism in the Spirit. Thus, it seemed, an unscriptural, divisive and elitist teaching was compounded by an unnatural and irrational activity which masqueraded as prayer. It was totally unnecessary too, for why could one not speak to the Father in a language one understood?

In *You Are My God*, David gives a simple and almost simplistic account of how he discovered tongues for himself:

I asked God to give me a language in the Spirit through which I could worship and praise him. I began to praise him in English, and then let my mind relax while my spirit went on praising with the first syllables that came to my tongue. They could be any syllables; there was nothing special or mystical about them. After some thirty seconds I stopped: 'David, you are just making this up!' I said to myself.

After a short argument with himself he began again and 'went on making these noises for about thirty minutes or more'. He had done again what he had done when he was converted, when he was filled with the Spirit, and on countless other unrecorded occasions during his life. He had taken God at his word, risking himself on the assumption that it was a trustworthy word, and acted. For David, that was what faith really meant; it was the fundamental principle of Christianity. (2)

Battling with Depression

The depth of our relationships with Christ depends on the degree to which we are willing to share our lives openly with one another, and such openness brings pain as well as joy. For example, sometimes I battle with depression. I never know all the reasons for this 'dark pit', as it seems to me. Some of it may be hurt pride. Sometimes it is obviously exhaustion, physical, mental, emotional, and spiritual. At times, when I am tired and strained, I can get angry over an incident that may be quite trivial in itself; and then I get angry with myself for getting angry. As I suppress both forms of anger, depression is the result.

I am then even more difficult to live with than usual. I do not want people to get too near to me, but I hope very much that they will not go too far away either. (3)

Facing Death

If God doesn't heal me, I think there's a mystery about it that one just doesn't understand. I think that God does have a purpose in our lives, and it is not measured by the length of our life . . . Actually, there is nothing more glorious than to be with Christ for ever, free from pain, suffering, and tears, and all the problems and injustices of this world. I genuinely am at a place now where I really want to be in heaven. The sooner the better! But I am willing to be on this earth with all its struggles, battles and problems, if he wants me here.

There will be times when we are actually angry with God; or utterly depressed or totally disillusioned because God appears to be doing nothing . . . But working through those moments of lostness ('the dark nights of the soul' as the mystics called them) so our relationship with God can deepen. If I only praise him when the sun is shining my faith is shallow.

The main thing that I worry about concerning death is my wife and children. It is very painful when I go away for a month and leave them behind. If I go away knowing that I am not going to return to see them this side of heaven, that for me is the most painful thing to come to terms with. Therefore, as an act of the will, I have had to put everything 'on an open palm' before God.

I've said, 'Lord, here's my wife, my children, my possessions, my ambitions, my all. You can take them.' The only place for peace and security for me in my heart is when I have all that on an open palm. Jesus said, 'If you lose your life you'll find it, but if you hold on to your life you're likely to lose it.' (4)

NOTES / SOURCES

1. Teddy Saunders and Hugh Sansom, *David Watson: A Biography*, London, 1992, p. 163
2. Ibid., pp. 78–9
3. Ibid., p. 195
4. Ibid , pp. 229–30

Roger Hardham Hooker   1934–1999

Hooker was one of the boldest and most profound missionary explorers of the Sanskritic Hindu tradition in the twentieth century. After education and training for the ministry at St Edmund's Hall and Wycliffe Hall, Oxford, he was a CMS missionary in North India for thirteen years, teaching theology at Bareilly and studying at the Sanskrit University at Varanasi. Returning to Britain, his ministry and that of Pat, his wife, among the Asian community settled in inner-city Birmingham was a recognized and respected model for such work in the Church of England.

An Approach to other Faiths: Hinduism

There must have been 60 or 70 people there, sitting on the floor in that Hindu house in Bareilly in North India. The *satsang* consisted largely of a series of spontaneous addresses on the 'Ramcharitamanasa' of Tulsi Das. I discovered that this was a weekly function, and so I have been going there ever since. What I am now going to describe is the regular weekly pattern which is rather different from that first occasion.

The group, which to begin with usually consists only of members of the household, starts with an act of worship. This is the same each week. They then chant 50 lines of the 'Ramcharitamanasa.' This is divided into five sections of 10 lines each. These are normally expounded by a *pundit*. If he has not arrived then one of the company reads a modern Hindi translation of the passage. This is followed by about 15 minutes of *kirtan* singing, after which the group chants five couplets of the 'Gita'. These are invariably expounded by a *shastri* who usually arrives later than the *pundit*. Finally there is a closing act of worship, and after a little conversation everyone goes home.

The *satsangis* chant only the 'Ramcharitamanasa' and the 'Gita' and when they have finished they start again. Recently they have finished their fourth reading of the Tulsi Das since they started the *satsang* 15 years ago. These two books are obviously very important to them, though now we shall be thinking mainly about the first. In order to understand them and to meet them at a deep level we have to try to understand what this book means to them. Why does it fascinate them, hold them, thrill them? As a tentative answer to that question let me describe my own thoughts and impressions as I have sat and listened from that first night two-and-a-half years ago until now.

Whenever we meet anything new we instinctively try to relate it to what we already know. Thus a Hindu attending a service of Holy Communion for the first time thinks that what the communicants are given is *prasad*, for *prasad* is what a visitor to a Hindu temple is ordinarily given. So as I began to listen to the story of Rama I found myself comparing it to the New Testament. Again and again I found myself thinking 'How like the New Testament' or 'How like Jesus!' (Whether or not such a comparison is legitimate is a large question with which however, I am not concerned at present. I am simply describing what I found myself instinctively doing.)

. . . .

Thus, such passages in this book beloved of Hindus send one's mind racing back to the Bible. At the same time there is something rather impressive about the people who attend the *satsang*; they are all deeply devoted to Rama, they come with a deep seriousness of purpose, yet at the same time there is a joy and a gaiety in the atmosphere which is both genuine and infectious.

Now what are we as Christians to make of such a book and of such people? Are they just deluded heathen, blindly groping in the dark? Is what they do at their *satsang* useless or even evil and wrong? I do not believe for one moment that it is. Indeed I would go further and say this: the God and Father of our Lord Jesus Christ is present and at work in that little group of people. To many of my fellow-

Christians that would seem perfectly obvious. Others are still surprised or even shocked at such a suggestion. What convinces me at any rate that it is true is a prayer which many Christians use every day: it begins with the words:

'O God, from whom all holy desires, all good counsels and all just works do proceed . . .' In more modern language the meaning of those words is simply this: all goodness in the lives of men comes from God. He alone is the source of all that is true and lovely and of good report, wherever it may be found. There is much in the words of Tulsi Das, and much that I see on the faces of those devotees, which I can describe only in those terms. I am therefore compelled to believe that that goodness comes from God. It cannot come from any other source. That means that when I climb on my bicycle at 7.45 on a Thursday evening and pedal off on the now familiar route to the *satsang*, I do not, as it were, leave God behind me in the Christian compound where I live; I go to meet him 'outside the camp' in that Hindu household. So I cannot treat either these Hindus or what they believe with scorn or contempt, but only with reverence and seriousness. When I take off my shoes to sit down with them, I am not just fitting in with their customs, I am performing a most Christian act, for I am coming into the presence of God.

NOTES / SOURCES

R. H. Hooker, *Uncharted Journey*, London, 1973, pp. 10–13

David Penman   1936–1989

New Zealand-born David Penman was a dynamic activist within the Australian Anglican Church during the brief five years he was Archbishop of Melbourne. Formerly a missionary in Pakistan and the Middle East, Penman had become an assistant bishop in Melbourne in 1982. Elected Archbishop in 1984, he wasted no time in championing the causes, at all levels, of multiculturalism and the ordination of women. He was well known and liked at all levels of the Australian community. Many mourned his premature death from a heart attack.

Christ across Cultures

1. *The universal Lordship and uniqueness of Christ*

I take up this theme partly because that, as we realise who Jesus is and allow our friends and neighbours to teach us, we may discover in his absolute sovereignty and authority the relativity of all cultural forms within which we try to say who he is. Possibly only in such a context shall we understand and accept the cultural plurality of those Orthodox, Catholic, and Protestant traditions around us, let alone the situation that we encounter among those of other faiths.

Let me begin with some affirmations.

The uniqueness of Jesus lies not so much in his conquering power and might but in his love and service. This is especially expressed in his suffering death. Jesus Christ is a *unique Lord* because he has identified himself forever with suffering humanity, standing in solidarity with men and women at their times of greatest need, poverty and oppression. He is a *unique Lord* because he has revealed God's righteousness in history by taking upon himself the unrighteousness of the world and offered through his own body a way of forgiveness. He is a *unique Lord* because he turned the most awful scandal into the Christian message of Easter.

There is a widespread and unfortunate tendency of Christians of every persuasion to find the language and the affirmations of universality and uniqueness difficult and even embarrassing. In my 20 years of seeking to relate to those of other faiths I would have to say that the difficulty and embarrassment is seldom if ever the concern of my friends of other faiths but rather that of my Christian brothers and sisters, who in the name of reasonableness and tolerance diminish the centrality of Jesus, and those historic claims made by him and about him throughout the ages.

For me, I am—in Pascal's famous phrase—willing to wager my life on the faith that Jesus is the ultimate source, and the final authority. To use the language of the New Testament, for me, 'Jesus is Lord', which implies a claim regarding the entire public life of mankind and the whole created world. But even more, I need to say that I make this confession only because I have been laid hold of by Another, and commissioned to do so. It is not primarily or essentially my decision. By ways which are mysterious to me, which I can only faintly trace, I have been taken over by Christ and brought to a place where I must make this confession. This is what it means to talk about the missio dei. The way and the task is not ours, but God's.

If it is true, both in Christian missionary history, and here today that in Jesus God has disclosed the shape and content of his coming kingdom, and it if it true that in Jesus we find the summation and fulfilment of all religions, *then* it must follow that the religions (including Christianity) can mediate God's presence and purpose in history only insofar as they are signs and instruments of God's coming kingdom. Puerto Rican scholar Orlando Costas suggests that this can occur under at least the following three conditions:

First, the religions may be signs and instruments of God's kingdom if they can accept the scandal of the cross of Jesus amid the human crosses of the world. Since the poor, the powerless, and the oppressed (those whose historical destiny has been marked by the crosses of exploitation, injustice and oppression) have been given a privileged place in the kingdom, it follows that no religious structure can be an adequate sign of its reality if it is not identified with the dispossessed in their misery and suffering. To be able to be such a sign, however, religious structures need to accept the representative par excellence of the poor and the oppressed: the crucified Jesus. He is the standard and measuring stick for the identification with the disenfranchised. If the scandal of his cross is not accepted, neither will the scandal of human crosses be accepted. By the same token, when the latter are *really* accepted, the cross of Jesus ceases to be a scandal and is accepted as a sign of justice, freedom and hope.

Second, religions may be signs and instruments of God's kingdom if they lead their adherents to come 'outside' the enclosed circle of their 'religious' interests to the battlefields of life and join the crucified Lord in the struggle for the liberation of the poor and oppressed of the world. Since the kingdom of God is an eschatological reality, only those religious structures that are open and committed to its future can be instrumentalities of its fulfilment. Likewise, inasmuch as the locus of God's kingdom lies in the emergence of a new world characterised by justice, freedom and peace, it follows that a religious structure can serve the kingdom if it is working *against* injustice, alienation, and war and *for* a new righteous, fraternal, and peaceful world community.

Third, the religions may be signs and instruments of God's kingdom if they are anticipating it in their inner life. This means that their inner structure must be a paradigm of justice, freedom, and hope. Conversely, it implies that they forfeit their mediating role if they allow injustice to take place in their midst, if they alienate their adherents from the struggles of history, if they do not promote social peace, and if they close the horizon of hope.[1]

The challenge to the Christian Church and to members of other faiths, if this perspective is to be conceded, is not to an ecumenical or inter-religious accommodation, but rather to 'truth-seeking' that for the Christian begins with a *confession*. I agree with Lesslie Newbigin when he says that the integrity and fruitfulness of any interfaith dialogue depends in the first place upon the extent to which the different participants take serious the full reality of their own faiths as the starting point in the search for truth, and as a basis to understand the totality of experience.

This brings me to my second concern.

2. *The transformation of culture*

It is easier for me to approach this part of my topic by several reflections of places and people.

Very early in my time in Pakistan I became painfully aware of what some scholars called 'the Latin/Victorian captivity' of the Church. Buildings were directly transplanted from the missionary culture. The prayerbook was 1662 with customs and habits predictable and traditional. We sang hymns that glorified the empire and spoke of sullen darkness in lands far away. There was no doubt in anyone's mind who was intended! In the city of Peshawar some thoughtful and creative Christians realised that if Christ was to be born into their society, and to become a turning point of their culture, then there was an urgent need for buildings to reflect appropriate aspects of local architecture. The church they built had several minarets, a pulpit like a niche in the wall, and water basins for ritual ablutions. They discarded the pews and wherever possible took on that which was already owned within the community. There were some habits and customs that defied transformation. While others, to use the language of the anthropologists received functional substitutes. The struggle was real and the price very high.

In the desert of Sind, the various missionary societies pursued a policy of 'extractionism'. Each convert was expected to conform to the patterns and habits of the foreign Church organisation. Some American Christian anthropologists suggested that the whole point of incarnational theology was to suggest that the Christ was to become flesh again and again within the context of the local people. Furthermore they recommended that their liturgy should be in the local language with music adapted from the instruments and traditions of the tribe. Sadly, strong opposition came from the traditional Church leaders, with cries that such separate development would lead to 'apartheid'.

[1] G. H. Anderson and T. F. Stransky (eds.): *Christ's Lordship and Religious Pluralism*, Orbit Books, pp. 152 and 153, 1981 (an article by Orlando Costas).

For many years I have been able to witness a marvellously practical development of my theme. The Maori people of New Zealand longed for a worshipping context that allowed the use of their own ancient language and the presence of traditional art and symbols. The discussions and debates took many years, but the result was the formation of the Bishopric of Aotearoa. It was agreed that the Maori Bishop would be a bishop in his own right caring for his people wherever they were found in New Zealand, but also an assistant to each Diocesan, who issued him the appropriate formal licence. The arrangement has had its 'moments', but is now an accepted part of the life of the New Zealand Church. Archbishop Paul Reeves (himself a Maori) has told me of the problems he has had in convincing Church leaders in some other parts of the world of the positive aspects of this development.

The rapid development in many societies of the 'house church' model is just another expression of this principle. All of this relates back to where I began. If Christ is confessed as the unique Lord of all of life, then he will fill all of life with his presence and transforming power. He will take that which is good and commission it for a fuller service. Conversely, there will be, with every culture, that which cannot be carried forward and must needs be replaced. When this occurs it is crucial that a vacuum is avoided, and that some suitable cultural substitute is found, thus presenting the community with God's *yes*, rather than his *no*.

In his paper on a Theology of Multiculturalism, Dr John Gaden takes on this theme very helpfully, and after defining a number of theories concerning Christ and culture, goes on to say:

If religions, and Christianity in particular, rightly find expression within a variety of cultures, the question arises of the cultural captivity of Anglicanism in a multi-cultural Australian society. Anglicans not at home in patriarchal Anglo-Celtic Churches are already forming or joining separate congregations—Aboriginal, Chinese, Sri Lankan, Persian, Feminist, Youth, Gay—and this trend must surely increase, requiring special ministries. This is not apartheid, since fellowship and communion continue within the one body, but the co-existence of separate cultural congregations provides security for their members to grow in a Christian context which is not alien to them. At the same time other congregations need to recognise the cultural diversity existing between their members and make provision for it in worship, teaching, pastoral care and government. We will be aided in this by a growing exposure to the multi-cultural nature of the Anglican Communion and by the developing recognition that all religious expressions are culturally conditioned, including the Anglo-Celtic.[1]

Our Western bifurcation, or separation of the sacred from the secular, combined with a pietistic hostility towards the possibility of cultural diversity, being within the purposes of God[2] has not helped us to see the radical potential that the Gospel brings to every situation. This leads to a confining of the kingdom lifestyle, with its eschatological implications, to the tiny sub-culture of the local church. Turning to Christ is not always seen as a turning to culture, where the new

[1] John R. Gaden: *From Every Nation, Tribe, People and Language—a Theology of Multiculturalism*, a paper prepared for the Commission and this Conference.
[2] David J. Penman: *Multiculturalism: A Christian Perspective*, The Beanland Lecture at the Footscray Institute of Technology, 1984.

believer rediscovers his human origins and identity, and a turning to the world in acceptance of the mission on which he is then sent. In this dimension, to be in Christ is to take on the world, and not to leave it. To be in Christ, is to discover the fuller and unrealised meaning of culture. To be in Christ, is to be a sign of the kingdom of God, and of the Lordship of Jesus over and within all of life.

Newbigin has been for long one of my gurus. He has the final word:

The mystery of the Gospel is not entrusted to the Church to be buried in the ground. It is entrusted to the Church in order to be risked in the change and interchange of the spiritual commerce of humanity. It belongs not to the Church but to the one who is both head of the Church and head of the cosmos. It is within his power and grace to bring to its full completion that long-hidden purpose, the secret of which has been entrusted to the Church in order that it may become the open manifestation of the truth to all the nations.[1]

NOTES / SOURCES

A Garden of Many Colours: The report of the Archbishop's Commission on multicultural ministry and mission presented to the Synod of the Anglican Diocese of Melbourne, March 1985 by Archbishop David Penman, pp. 157–61

John Gaden 1938–1990

Dr John Gaden, the English-born son of Church Army officers, came to Australia with his parents at the age of 13. Following outstanding academic results in both theology and classics, he was ordained for the rural New South Wales diocese of Bathurst. After completing his doctorate at General Seminary, New York, he returned to a life of teaching in Australia, ultimately in theological colleges. After a period as Director of Trinity Theological School, Melbourne, he was appointed Warden of St Barnabas' College, Adelaide, the position he held at the time of his untimely death from a heart attack in 1990. During the brief time he was at St Barnabas', he was at the centre of ongoing controversy about the ordination of women, which he championed passionately. His ten-year membership of the General Synod Doctrine Commission sparked some of his finest theological writing.

Seven Reactions to God's Wrath

1. For many the first reaction is one of anger and resentment. 'You rotten bastard'; 'Go to hell'; 'I hate you'; and it may also be expressed in some act of physical violence. While both angry words and angry deeds may be directed at fellow human beings, seen as the causes of wrath, or the nearest pillory post, often deep down the anger is directed at God.
2. For others, there will be a guilty reaction: 'I must have done something wrong and God is punishing me', and so the search for some fault in oneself begins. An unexpiated sin is unearthed, rightly or wrongly, to be viewed as the cause of this wrath.

[1] Lesslie Newbigin, *The Open Secret—Sketches for a Missionary Theology*, SPCK, London, 1978, p. 214.

3. Still others till protest their innocence: 'I haven't done anything wrong. I've always led a good life. Why has this happened to me?' So God will be charged with injustice and lack of love.

4. Some may find it impossible to cry out at all, either in anger or in protest. Instead, a silent numbness possesses them and they refuse to talk about it, but what is going on underneath no one can tell. It may be shock, passive resignation, or repressed anger and grief.

5. A different reaction is the simple cry for mercy: 'God help us'; 'I can't go on'; 'I can't stand this any more'. Tears and pleas for help are the order of the day, addressed to friends and neighbours, but ultimately to God.

6. Again, some may react by immediately fighting the situation, battling to overcome what has trapped them, using a mixture of means, but perhaps never pausing to reflect on what it is all about.

7. The opposite reaction to this is escapism into a fantasy world of drugs, black magic and the occult, or into mindless hedonism. 'Let us create a world where *we* pull the shots that matter.' (1)

The Cost of Intercession

Intercession is a way in which we share with Jesus in bearing God's anger at the sin and evil in the world, so that like Moses we stand in the breach on behalf of the world (cf. Ps. 106. 23). It is a way in which we share God's anguish over the world and it is a way in which we enter the fight against the evil powers.

Beware of trivialising intercession, for whoever would intercede must pass through the Cross of God's angered love. Since the Cross is an eschatological reality, anticipating the end, our intercessions have about them the expectation that this experience of anger will not last forever, even though it may seem to be so. Cranmer's instinct about the Litany and the Confession as places to speak of God's anger and wrath was right. (2)

Sacraments of Anger

The sacraments may be understood as sacraments of anger, for they all arise out of the paschal mystery of Christ's death and resurrection. The initiation complex of baptism, confirmation, and eucharist plunge us into Jesus' baptism of blood and fire, to drink the cup of God's wrath and to be filled with the Spirit of God's passionate love (Mark 10. 38f, 1. 7f). To celebrate these sacraments seriously is to take on the anguish of love; to abuse them is to bring judgment on ourselves (cf. 1 Cor. 11. 27–32).

Penance, or the sacrament of reconciliation, deals with anger in terms of our personal relationships with God and others, as anointing of the sick does with our suffering the more impersonal consequences of evil. Marriage has been called by one writer, 'the savage sacrament', for marriage produces more anger than any other relationship, but it also provides a context in which it may be processed creatively. This only leaves ordination and there are plenty of angry and frustrated clergy around, which has more to do with the state of the church perhaps than ordination *per se*. However, we may see ordination at one level as setting aside people to become the scapegoats and nagging goads for the community, bearers of our anger and God's, for Christ's sake in the power of the Spirit. (3)

The Experience of the Easter Mystery

Darkness and Light

Night. All is dark. I can see no sense in things. Thousands are dying of starvation, thousands drowned in floods for no reason. Nations promise one thing and do another. Our leaders mislead us. I feel repressed, restricted. All is dark. The darkness is outside; it is inside, too. In myself I see darkness, failures. I hurt those whom I love. I shout and scream at them. Is there any light?

Look! A light, but it is so faint. And there's another, and another. All through the world, and the history of humankind, I see lights. Where does this light come from? Is it a reflection? This man's life, this hero, his life stands out like a light. Or this woman, she reflects a bright spot in the gloom. This man, this woman, Gandhi, Martin Luther King, Mother Teresa, Desmond Tutu, that mother who gives herself to her family, all these and many more, appear to shine with a light that is not their own. As I look now, I can see *the* light behind them, brighter than the rest, which all the others reflect. This Light shines in the darkness, and is not put out. This Light is the life of all human beings. I turn to the Light, the Light of the world. 'Give me your light: let me reflect your light. Light of the world, Light of Christ, shine through my life too. Bright Sun, let me shine with your light, as the full moon now shines in the dark sky.'

Baptism

What is it that obscures the light in me? My failures. Knowing what I should do, the love I should have for people, I just can't rise to it. Other forces seem to tie me down. The darkness is outside and in. But I hate evil. I am against repression, the restrictions that destroy people's lives. I renounce the powers of darkness. I stand looking at the dark, and turn away to face the Light.

The Voice asks, 'What do you believe? On what do you stand against the dark?' In springtime, I have seen a daffodil unfold, the pale yellow petals burst from their green sheaths. At the tips of branches I have seen buds, pregnant with life, ready to spring forth. I put my hand to my heart and listen to the dull, pulsating beat driving the blood of life through me. I am alive, I have life. Again, I've looked up and seen a bird drifting in the wind, or at evening sat and watched the sun, a huge red ball, go down upon the sea. So I affirm, this world is good. Despite all the darkness of evil, I belong here. My life is a gracious gift, given me to live. I will be baptised in the name of the Father, Creator of heaven and earth.

But there is more than the living, physical world of beauty. I take my stand on love, the depths of love that forgives and accepts me, love that gives itself for others, love that is stronger than death, the love that I see around me in children, women and men, but most clearly in Jesus. I will be baptised in the name of the Son, Jesus Christ our Lord.

As well as love, I believe in a creative spirit, the enthusiasm of the young with their hopes and dreams, the creativity of artists, writers, musicians, poets. There is a spirit, too, which ties together those with a common purpose, families, groups, the spirit of unity, the spirit of humanity. I will be baptised in the Name of the Holy Spirit.

Yet it is not I alone making this stand. I stand with others, all those who have had this same faith and vision, all those who are here with me now. Alone, my voice is small and weak: with ten, twenty, a hundred, thousands more added, it is strong. Together we will shout down the walls that imprison us and all people.

Now I am washed clean. I have stepped out of the bath. I smell with the perfume of fragrant oil. White clothes, clean and fresh, cover me. The dawn is breaking outside, and the first fingers of light spread across the sky. I feel new, made whole. My life has meaning. The darkness has been washed away. I have seen the darkness of death, the gloom of despair. I have stood on the brink of the void of nothingness, but I am alive. Nothing can terrify me now, neither death nor prison, neither earthquake nor sin. I am Christ's and Christ is mine. Nothing can separate me from his life and love. His Spirit is with us, refreshing, comforting, insistently urging us to live.

The Eucharist

Together we move on to the Eucharist, the Great Thanksgiving for the life, death and resurrection of Jesus. We have passed from death to life. Christ our Passover is sacrificed for us; let us keep the feast. Christ is our life. Taste and see how gracious the Lord is. We feed, and are made strong in Him. Christ is our peace, who makes us one. We receive the Bread and the Wine, and feel his touch. We touch each other and know we are together in Christ. Is not this the Bread of God? Illumined by his Light, strengthened by his Life, in touch with one another, we go our ways to love and serve the world, God's world, material for God's kingdom.

'The mystery of your dispensation, O Christ our God, has been fulfilled so far as in us lies. We have made the memorial of your death, we have seen the type of your resurrection, we have been filled with your eternal life, of which, we pray, make us more worthy hereafter. And now, in the power of your holy and life-giving spirit, let us depart in peace. Amen.' (4)

NOTES / SOURCES

1. John Gaden, *A Vision of Wholeness* (ed. Duncan Reid), Sydney, 1994, p. 58
2. Ibid., p. 60
3. Ibid., pp. 60–1
4. Ibid., pp. 281–3

The Alternative Service Book 1980

Father of all, we give you thanks and praise, that
when we were still far off you met us in your Son
and brought us home. Dying and living, he
declared your love, gave us grace, and opened
the gate of glory. May we who share Christ's
body live his risen life; we who drink his cup
bring life to others; we whom the Spirit lights
give light to the world. Keep us firm in the hope
you have set before us, so we and all your
children shall be free, and the whole earth live to
praise your name; through Christ our Lord.
Amen.

NOTES / SOURCES

Post Communion Prayer from *The Alternative Service Book 1980*, Oxford, 1980, p. 144

General Index

Note: Where the same surname is shared by more than one writer; the Christian name is also given. In the case of Samuel Johnson, (Am.) or (Br.) is added to distinguish.

Index of Names

Butler, Joseph (1692–1752) xvi, 189, 193, 279–80, 506
Butler, Josephine xx
Byron, George Gordon, 6th Baron 523

Carter, Thomas Thelluson (1808–1901) 424–5
Cary, Lucius 694
Cassian, John 517, 518
Chamier, Daniel 160
Chapman, Dom John 565
Charles, Pierre 658
Chaucer, Geoffrey 157
Chrysostom see John Chrysostom, St
Church, Richard William (1815–1890) 440–2
Cicero, Marcus Tullius 39
Clarke, Samuel 191
Clement of Alexandria, St 71, 643, 740, 741
Coggan, Frederick Donald (1909–2000) xxiv, 702–705, 761
Coke, Thomas 287
Coleridge, S. T. (1772–1834) 188, 193, 200, 356–60, 370
Conon, George 304
Cosin, John 188, 211
Costas, Orlando 752–3
Coverdale, Myles (1488–1568) 20–8
Cowper, William (1731–1800) 190, 191, 317, 330–3
Cranmer, Thomas (1489–1556) xi-xii, xiii, 6, 10, 13, 28–33, 38, 52, 756
Creighton, Mandell (1843–1901) 454, 502–3, 594
Creighton, Oswin, CF (1883–1918) 594–5
Crossman, Samuel (1624?–1684) 191, 218–20
Crum, John Macleod Campbell (1872–1958) 562
Cudworth, Ralph (1617–1688) 212–13, 222
Cunningham, B. K. 594
Curé d'Ars (Jean-Baptiste Marie Vianney) 570
Cyprian, St 166

Dale, Robert William 554
Dante Alighieri 475, 516, 636
Darwin, Charles 370, 376, 438, 524
Davey, F. N. 599
Davidson, Randall Thomas 578
Davies, Sir John (1569–1626) 98, 101–3
Davies, Richard (1501?–1581) 53–6
Day, John (1522–1584) 5, 129–130
Day, Richard (1552–?1607) 6, 130
De Mel, H. Lakdasa Jacob (1902–1976) 653–656
De Sales, Francis 192
Denney, James 645
Dimock, Nathaniel (1825–1900) 454–5
Dix, Dom Gregory, OSB (George Eglington Alston) (1901–1952) xviii, xxi, 651–3
Doane, George Washington (1799–1859) 395–6
Dolling, Robert William Radclyffe (1851–1902) 470, 513–15
Donne, John (1572–1631) 8, 9, 12, 141–50, 166

DuBose, William Porcher (1836–1918) 493–5
Duff, Alexander 436
Duns Scotus 37 n.2

Ecclestone, Alan (1904–1992) 656–8
Elias Cretensis 151
Eliot, Thomas Stearns (1888–1956) xx, 374, 376, 621–5, 761
  and Charles Browne 688–9, 691, 692
  influence of 638 n.1, 726
  influences on 141, 374, 616
  and John V. Taylor 717–19
  and time 622–3, 695
Elliott, Charles 380
Elliott, Charlotte (1789–1871) 380–1
Elliott, Henry Venn 380
Erasmus, Desiderius 20, 47
Eusebius of Caesarea 11, 151
Evelyn, John (1620–1706) 185, 189–90, 216–18, 245–6

Farrar, Frederick William 601
Farrer, Austin Marsden (1904–1968) xviii, 373–4, 658–63, 675
Fénelon, François de Salignac de la Mothe 442
Ferrar, Nicholas (1592–1637) 10, 12, 163–6, 169
Field, Richard (1561–1616) 8, 133–6
Figgis, John Neville (1866–1919) xvii, 548–9, 645
Fisher, Geoffrey 672
Forbes, William (1585–1634) 8, 159–61
Forsyth, P. T. 645–6
Fox, George 570
Foxe, John, Book of Martyrs 11–12
Francis of Assisi, St 554, 570, 611
Froude, Hurrell 402
Fry, Elizabeth 570

Gaden, John R. (1938–1990) 754, 755–8
Gardiner, Allen Francis (1794–1851) 391–2, 438
Gascoigne, George (1552–1577) 98, 99
Gibson, Edmund (1669–1748) 187, 190, 262–4
Gladstone, William Ewart (1809–1898) xx, 428–34
Godolphin, Margaret (1652–1678) 190, 245–6
Gore, Charles (1853–1932) xvii, 519–27, 547
Goreh, Nilakantha Nehemiah, SSJE (1825–1885) 455–6, 530
Grafton, Charles Chapman (1830–1912) 477–82
Green, T. H. 506
Gregg, John (1798–1878) 393–4
Gregory of Nazianzus 12, 118, 152
Gregory of Nyssa, St 676, 760
Greville, Fulke (1554–1628) xx, 9, 97–8
Gunning, Peter (1614–1684) 210–11, 217

Hale, Sir Matthew (1609–1676) 189, 199
Hall, Joseph 544, 554

Index of Biblical References

Printed and bound by CPI Group (UK) Ltd, Croydon, CR0 4YY